Constitutional Law

CONSTITUTIONAL LAW: CASES IN CONTEXT

VOLUME II
CIVIL RIGHTS AND CIVIL LIBERTIES

James C. Foster
Oregon State University

Susan M. Leeson
Oregon Court of Appeals

PRENTICE HALL, UPPER SADDLE RIVER, NEW JERSEY 07458

Library of Congress Cataloging-in-Publication Data

FOSTER, JAMES C. (JAMES CARL)
    Constitutional law: cases in context/James C. Foster, Susan M.
Leeson
      p. cm.
    Leeson's name appears first on the earlier edition.
    Includes bibliographical references and index.
    Contents: v. 2. Civil rights and civil liberties.
    ISBN 0-13-568759-4 (v. 2)
    1. Constitutional law—United States—Cases. I. Leeson, Susan M.
II. Title.
    KF4549.F675 1998
    342.73'00264—dc21   97-27675
                                            CIP

Editorial director: Charlyce Jones Owen
Editor-in-chief: Nancy Roberts
Assistant editor: Nicole Signoretti
Marketing manager: Christopher DeJohn
Editorial/production supervision
   and electronic page makeup: Kari Callaghan Mazzola
Interior design and electronic art creation: John P. Mazzola
Cover director: Jayne Conte
Cover designer: Bruce Kenselaar
Buyer: Bob Anderson

This book was set in 10/12 Cheltenham Book by Big Sky Composition
and was printed and bound by Courier Companies, Inc.
The cover was printed by Phoenix Color Corp.

Printed in the United States of America
10 9 8 7 6 5 4 3 2 1

ISBN 0-13-568759-4

Prentice-Hall International (UK) Limited,London
Prentice-Hall of Australia Pty. Limited, Sydney
Prentice-Hall Canada Inc., Toronto
Prentice-Hall Hispanoamericana, S.A., Mexico
Prentice-Hall of India Private Limited, New Delhi
Prentice-Hall of Japan, Inc., Tokyo
Pearson Education Asia Pte. Ltd., Singapore
Editora Prentice-Hall do Brasil, Ltda., Rio de Janeiro

In memory of Alpheus Thomas Mason

CONTENTS

HISTORICAL ERA CONTENTS

A FOURTH ERA? (1972–PRESENT)—PRAGMATIC CONSERVATISM

PREFACE

We undertook writing this text knowing well that the field of constitutional law is crowded with texts—casebooks and noncasebooks alike. Our starting premise is that the study of doctrine—divorced from history, politics, and the workings of the legal system—leaves students with an abstract, incomplete understanding of the Supreme Court as one of the three coordinate branches of the national government. Shorn of the social and institutional contexts within which it operates, the Court and the constitutional decisions it hands down cannot be understood adequately. We also know from experience that students quickly forget abstract doctrine and often recall little about their study of constitutional law except the discipline of reading and briefing cases. Notwithstanding those concerns, we believe that Supreme Court opinions are an invaluable primary source of information about the third branch and its role in the American political system. Because we are committed to the study of constitutional law in a liberal arts setting, we have sought to give greater depth and dimension to Supreme Court opinions by placing them in their historical, political, and legal contexts.

In *Constitutional Law: Cases in Context*, we present landmark decisions of the Supreme Court of the United States in subject matter categories that reflect doctrinal evolution. Nevertheless, our approach to each of these doctrinally organized cases remains contextual: Every case excerpted in this text is presented in terms of the circumstances giving rise to the controversy, the constitutional arguments of the parties to that controversy, the doctrines, rules, and policy choices the Court announces in resolving that controversy, and the salient consequences resulting from the judicial outcome of that controversy. Thus, while this book arranges Supreme Court decisions doctrinally, it treats them historically. We also offer an Alternative Table of Contents by Historical Era for those who prefer to study and teach constitutional law chronologically. As is characteristic of two-volume constitutional law texts, the first volume focuses on federal government powers and federalism, while the second focuses on protections against governmental powers.

Several features distinguish this text from others, including the *Setting* and *Highlights of Supreme Court Arguments* sections, extensive excerpts of opinions, and *Questions* and *Comments* following each case that are designed not only to promote greater understanding of the opinions, but also to stimulate reflection and thoughtful class discussion. Because our goal in preparing these materials is to encourage further study, we also offer *Suggestions for Further Reading* at the end of each section.

The *Setting* that precedes each case provides a richer factual statement and insight into the parties and their controversy than typically appears in the opinions themselves. The *Setting* also explains the primary social and political forces that gave rise to the litigation. In addition, the *Setting* traces the evolution of a case from the time it was filed to its appearance on the Supreme Court's docket, explaining the reasoning of lower court judges along the way and demonstrating the legal climate of opinion in which the case arrived at the Supreme Court. It is our hope that the *Setting* will facilitate better understanding of cases and constitutional issues and that it will provoke students to learn more about the historical and political contexts in which the cases arose and were decided.

Supreme Court doctrine does not simply emerge from the minds of the justices. Rules are shaped by the adversary contest between the parties at every stage of the litigation process. In the section entitled *Highlights of Supreme Court Arguments*, we summarize the legal theories offered to the justices by each of the parties. Contained in those theories is the rule of law that each side hopes the Court will adopt. Sometimes the Court endorses one or more of those theories in fashioning a rule. On other occasions, the opinion suggests that the parties' arguments, while essential, were not determinative. As additional backdrop for each case, we identify the organizations (and, occasionally, the individuals) that submitted *amicus curiae* briefs in support of each side. We hope that students will want to know more about what motivates the organizations that join in the adversary competition to shape the Constitution, and will undertake research into how at least some of those organizations came into being, how they are funded, and how they work.

Excerpts of the Supreme Court's opinions tend to be more lengthy in this text than in other casebooks. This reflects our commitment to having students grapple with original sources rather than merely being told what the Court decided. In reading the excerpts, students are exposed to the ideas, thought processes, language, and debates among the justices that contribute to the development of constitutional doctrine. They also learn firsthand that there are few if any doctrines in constitutional law that are so well-established as to be beyond debate.

The *Questions* and *Comments* that follow each opinion serve a variety of functions. *Comments* provide additional information about a case or the parties to it, immediate political or legal consequences, and related and subsequent Supreme Court decisions. *Questions* are designed to facilitate better understanding of the case, its relationship to other cases and issues, and the dynamics of the interaction among the justices. *Questions* also are devised to stimulate thought about the extent to which the Court's opinion resolved or exacerbated the controversy presented to it. Often the *Questions* reflect the differences in perspective of the authors, both of whom have taught constitutional law for many years and one of whom is now a state appellate court judge. We hope that the *Comments* and *Questions* will provide additional incentive to students to inquire into the political and social reactions to the Court's decisions, for rarely, if ever, is the Supreme Court's opinion the last word on an issue.

ANNUAL SUPPLEMENTS AND WEB SITE

Beginning with the 1997–98 Term, we will provide annual, free supplements to faculty who adopt *Constitutional Law: Cases in Context*. The supplements will follow the same format as the text. Links to supplementary Supreme Court decisions will be available on Prentice Hall's web site, http://www.prenhall.com. We anticipate revising the text every four years. Questions should be referred to your local Prentice Hall sales representative.

ACKNOWLEDGMENTS

We have accumulated many debts in writing *Constitutional Law: Cases in Context*, which we gratefully acknowledge here.

Richard Breen, Willamette College of Law librarian, and his reference staff have continued to go to extraordinary lengths to provide us with access to microfiche records and briefs of cases as well as to make available the other resources in the law library. The library staff at the Supreme Court of the United States has graciously welcomed back a former judicial fellow to use original sources and found her a place to work, even when the library was closed for recarpeting. Supreme Court Deputy Clerk Frank Lorson provided statistics for the Court's 1995 Term, which appear in chart form in Chapter 1.

Oregon State University graduate Donna Shaw worked closely with Professor Foster on this book, providing research assistance and intelligent, thoughtful, and enthusiastic feedback. Oregon Deputy Public Defender Andy Simrin offered Judge Leeson constructive feedback on Chapter 8. Attorney Peter Garttan has been more help than he realizes or would admit.

Various professional colleagues provided numerous forms of support, encouragement, and suggestions during the period this book was being prepared: Henry Abraham, Audrey Bach, Donald Balmer, John Brigham, Vicki Collins, Donald Crowley, Steve DeLancey, Ilona DeRemer, Susan Dwyer-Schick, James Elkins, Donna Erickson, Leo Flynn, Howard Gillman, Edward Goldberg, Sheldon Goldman, Joel Grossman, Sandra Guy, William Haltom, Barbara Hayler, William Husband, Sam Jacobson, Patricia Lindsey, Carolyn Nestor Long, Michael McCann, Bob Noll, Don Reisman, Robert Sahr, Stuart Scheingold, Brent Steel, and Kenneth Wagner. We remain grateful for their ongoing efforts. Judge Leeson's colleagues at the Oregon Court of Appeals have provided insight and suggestions for approaches to particular cases.

The text has also had the benefit of critical reading by these reviewers selected by Prentice Hall: Carolyn Nestor Long, *Washington State University*; Bette Novit Evans, *Creighton University*; Ronald Kahn, *Oberlin College*; Jerome O'Callaghan, *SUNY Cortland*; Donald G. Balmer, *Lewis and Clark College*; William Haltom, *University of Puget Sound*; and Mary Thornberry, *Davidson College*. Although anonymous to us at the time, we appreciate the interest they took in this project and the efforts they put into refining it. This book is better for their suggestions.

Similarly, this book has benefited significantly from the various editorial and production assistance rendered by Prentice Hall personnel. At the outset, we want to thank Michael Bickerstaff for his interest in this text and his support for it. Assistant Editors, Jennie Katsaros, and later, Nicole Signoretti, professionally shepherded the book through the drafting, reviewing, and revising process. A special, heartfelt thanks goes to Kari Callaghan Mazzola of Big Sky Composition for her expertise, creative suggestions, and cheerful cooperation.

Support staff at Oregon State University—Karen Thayer, Political Science Office Coordinator, and Shannona Miller, Political Science Office Specialist— teamed to provide essential support. Their imaginative composition, tireless revision, and quick turnaround time facilitated this project.

Finally, we both thank our long-suffering spouses. From Professor Foster, as always, to Laurel Lynn Ramsey for your love, your perseverance, and for schooling me in practical romance. From Judge Leeson, as always, to Richard Samuel Hall Jr., whose love of mathematics and logic spills over into the study of history and constitutional law at the most convenient times.

J. C. F.
Corvallis, Oregon

S. M. L.
Salem, Oregon

CONSTITUTIONAL LAW

CHAPTER 1

UNDERSTANDING THE SUPREME COURT

In the 1830s, Frenchman Alexis de Tocqueville observed that "Scarcely any political question arises in the United States that is not resolved, sooner or later, into a judicial question."[1] This book expands on that theme. It examines landmark controversies in American politics that were resolved, sooner or later, into questions of constitutional law argued before the Supreme Court of the United States. Each case arose out of discrete social and political circumstances. Most were litigated in state or federal courts and worked their way to the Supreme Court, where advocates urged that Court to adopt their particular theory or theories of the Constitution. Resolution of each of the cases by the Supreme Court required the justices to interpret one or more provisions of the Constitution of the United States. The Court's decisions have furthered the development of constitutional doctrine and have had significant social and political consequences as well. The Court's decisions continue to give life and meaning to the Constitution, a relatively short document that was adopted in 1789 and amended only twenty-seven times since then.[2]

THE SUPREME COURT'S DEFINING POWER: JUDICIAL REVIEW

In interpreting the Constitution since 1803, the Supreme Court has exercised the power of judicial review, a power it claimed for itself in the famous case of *Marbury v. Madison*, 1 Cranch 137 (1803). Judicial review is the power of the Supreme Court to determine the constitutionality of acts of Congress, the executive, a state, or even a provision of a state constitution under the Constitution of the United States. In short, it is the power to declare what the Constitution means.[3]

---

[1] Alexis de Tocqueville, *Democracy in America*, ed. Phillips Bradley, 2 vols. (New York, NY: Vintage, 1945), I: 290.

[2] Refer to the Constitution of the United States reproduced at the end of this book as Appendix A. See also Sanford Levinson, ed., *Responding to Imperfection: The Theory and Practice of Constitutional Amendment* (Princeton, NJ: Princeton University Press, 1995); and David E. Kyvig, *Explicit and Authentic Acts: Amending the U.S. Constitution, 1776–1995* (Lawrence, KS: University of Kansas Press, 1996).

[3] See Henry J. Abraham, *The Judicial Process*, 6th ed. (New York, NY: Oxford University Press, 1993), pp. 270–288. *The Constitution of the United States: Analysis and Interpretation*, ed. Johnny H. Killian (Washington, D.C.: U.S. Government Printing Office, 1987), pp. 1883–2113, lists the congressional and state statutes the Supreme Court has reviewed and held unconstitutional through 1982.

Although the Supreme Court has exercised the power of judicial review at least since 1803 and its authority to do so is almost universally accepted, there has always been controversy over the propriety of the Court's exercise of judicial review in particular cases and circumstances.[4] This book examines cases that demonstrate dramatically the constitutional and political consequences of the exercise of judicial review. Those cases have involved controversies that range from early disagreements over whether Congress has the authority to charter a national bank, to issues such as the legality of slavery, school segregation, abortion, and the rights of the criminally accused.

Alexander Hamilton described the paradox of judicial review in *Federalist* No. 78: it is *essential* and it is *fragile*. Judicial review is essential, Hamilton reasoned, because some "department of the proposed government" must enforce constitutional limitations:

> Limitations ... can be preserved in practice no other way than through the medium of courts of justice, whose duty it must be to declare all acts contrary to the manifest tenor of the Constitution void. Without this, all the reservations of particular rights or privileges would amount to nothing.

Judicial review is fragile because:

> Whoever attentively considers the different departments of power must perceive that, in a government in which they are separated from each other, the judiciary, from the nature of its functions, will always be the least dangerous to the political rights of the Constitution; because it will be least in a capacity to annoy or injure them. The executive not only dispenses the honors but holds the sword of the community. The legislature not only commands the purse but prescribes the rules by which the duties and rights of every citizen are to be regulated. The judiciary, on the contrary, has no influence over either the sword or the purse; no direction either of the strength or of the wealth of the society, and can take no active resolution whatever.

Hamilton concluded that courts "may truly be said to have neither force nor will but merely judgment; and must ultimately depend upon the aid of the executive arm even for the efficacy of its judgments."[5]

In the process of examining the cases that follow, readers are invited to debate with Hamilton whether judicial review is essential to the American form of government. Even if judicial review is not essential, Hamilton was correct that it is fragile. Readers are also invited to understand that the legiti-

---

[4] The first time the Supreme Court actually reviewed a statute it did so without explicitly claiming the power of judicial review. In *Hylton v. United States*, 3 Dallas 171 (1796), the Court upheld the constitutionality of the 1794 federal Carriage Tax Act. Because it upheld this act of Congress, the Court did not have to call attention to the fact that it had tacitly exercised the power of judicial review.

[5] Clinton Rossiter, ed., *The Federalist Papers* (New York, NY: Mentor, 1961), pp. 466, 465.

macy of the power of judicial review is contingent on the justices' ability to write persuasively, on the willingness of other branches of government to enforce the Court's decisions, and on the perception of the American public that the Court's decisions are authoritative.[6]

One question that arises repeatedly throughout this book is whether judicial review has been exercised wisely, consistently, or legitimately in a particular case or series of cases dealing with the same subject. A recurring theme is that, to be authoritative, the Court's opinions not only must resolve the legal controversies posed by the parties, but its interpretation of the Constitution must respond persuasively to ongoing tensions involving the relationship of the Court to Congress and the executive branch (separation of powers), to the relationship between the states and the national government (federalism), and to the political realities of the times in which the decisions are written. An important lesson from this book is that many, if not all, of the fundamental constitutional questions that were left unresolved by the Constitutional Convention remain unresolved, notwithstanding a civil war and more than two centuries of the Supreme Court's exercise of judicial review.

PERSPECTIVES ON CONSTITUTIONAL INTERPRETATION

Reduced to its simplest terms, a lawsuit involves application of the law to facts.[7] At trial, parties to a lawsuit seek to persuade the trier of fact (judge or jury) that their version of the facts is correct. The judge then applies the law to the facts and enters judgment accordingly. Appellate litigation before the Supreme Court involves debates only about the correct rule of law to apply to the facts that have been found at trial.[8] In each of the cases in this book, the Supreme Court's determination of the rule of law applicable to the facts has required an interpretation of one or more provisions of the Constitution.

Constitutional interpretation is an intricate, difficult task. That is so, in part, because there is significant disagreement in this country about what constitutional interpretation entails.[9] This book views constitutional interpreta-

---

[6] The extent and limits of the Supreme Court's power of judicial review has been much debated. See, for example, Robert A. Dahl, "Decision Making in a Democracy: The Supreme Court as a National Policy Maker," 6 *Journal of Politics* (1957): 279; David Adamany, "Legitimacy, Realigning Elections, and the Supreme Court," 73 *Wisconsin Law Review* (1973): 790; Richard Funston, "The Supreme Court and Critical Elections," 69 *American Political Science Review* (1975): 793; Jonathan D. Casper, "The Supreme Court and National Policy Making," 70 *American Political Science Review* (1976): 50; and Roger Handberg and Harold F. Hill Jr., "Court Curbing, Court Reversals, and Judicial Review: The Supreme Court versus Congress," 14 *Law and Society Review* (1980): 309.

[7] See the Appendix to this chapter for a brief overview of the litigation process.

[8] One small exception to this rule is that the Supreme Court sits as a fact-finding body in the rare cases when it exercises original jurisdiction, spelled out in Article III of the Constitution.

[9] John H. Garvey and T. Alexander Aleinikoff, eds., *Modern Constitutional Theory: A Reader*, 3rd ed. (St. Paul, MN: West, 1994), pt. II.

tion as a creative act, constrained by rules of law. Supreme Court Justice Oliver Wendell Holmes, for example, contended:

> [W]hen we are dealing with words that also are a constituent act, like the Constitution of the United States, we must realize that they have called into life a being the development of which could not have been foreseen completely by the most gifted of its begetters....[10]

In Justice Holmes's view, the men who drafted the Constitution in Philadelphia in the summer of 1787 were "begetters" of words that are also "constituent acts"; that is, those who interpret constitutional words actively make the Constitution meaningful. Consequently, the meaning of the Constitution is not fixed. It is not a collection of axiomatic formulas that dictate the results in particular cases. From this perspective, the Constitution provides an adaptable framework for analyzing legal issues and relationships between and among the branches of government and levels of government.

Chief Justice John Marshall provided additional insight into the complexities of constitutional interpretation when he wrote:

> A constitution['s] ... nature ... requires, that only its great outlines should be marked, its important objects designated, and the minor ingredients which compose those objects be deduced from the nature of the objects themselves....[11]

From Marshall's perspective, constitutional interpretation involves a process of deducing from general principles answers to specific questions. Those answers are never self-evident from the words of the document.

Justice Thurgood Marshall provided yet another perspective on the difficulties of constitutional interpretation. In a speech commemorating the bicentennial of the Constitution in 1987, Justice Marshall observed:

> The men who gathered in Philadelphia in 1787 could not have ... imagined, nor would they have accepted, that the document they were drafting would one day be construed by a Supreme Court to which had been appointed a woman and the descendent of an African slave. "We the People" no longer enslave, but the credit does not belong to the framers. It belongs to those who refused to acquiesce in outdated notions of "liberty," "justice," and "equality," and who strived to better them.[12]

---

[10] *Missouri v. Holland*, 25 U.S. 416 (1920). Compare William Rehnquist's view, distinguishing Holmes's understanding "with which scarcely anyone would disagree," from the view taken by many lawyers that "nonelected members of the federal judiciary may address themselves to a social problem simply because other branches of government have failed or refused to do so" (Mark W. Cannon and David M. O'Brien, eds., *Views from the Bench* [Chatham, NJ: Chatham House, 1985], pp. 127, 128). Chief Justice Rehnquist quotes favorably Holmes's *Missouri v. Holland* view of the Constitution in his *The Supreme Court: How It Was, How It Is* (New York, NY: Morrow, 1987), p. 315.

[11] *McCulloch v. Maryland*, 4 Wheaton 316 (1819).

[12] Speech delivered at the Annual Seminar of the San Francisco Patent and Trademark Law Association, May 6, 1987. Reprinted in 101 *Harvard Law Review* (1987): 1, 5.

From Justice Marshall's perspective, the Constitution of 1787 was an incomplete document. Consequently, one aspect of constitutional interpretation entails construing the document in a way that fosters the justice, general welfare, and liberty to which the Constitution aspires.[13]

Despite the differences among these three justices' perspectives, they have in common the understanding that the Constitution is essentially adjustable and that judicial interpretation is a creative act.[14]

THE CONSTITUTION AS A RESPONSIVE DOCUMENT

The history of the Constitutional Convention reveals that the drafters anticipated and even intended that the Constitution be a responsive document. One reason is that on virtually every issue they faced between May and September 1787, the drafters resolved their disagreements through compromise. Embedded in the Constitution, those compromises have been the source of continuous debate and litigation.

The Great Compromise, for example, provided a solution to the disagreement over how the states should be represented in Congress: as geographic entities or by population. Under the compromise, population was accepted as the basis for representation in the House of Representatives, while each state was seen as a single geographic entity and was guaranteed equal representation in the Senate. Whether people or places should be represented in legislatures has remained a controversial subject, although the focus of the debate has shifted from Congress to state legislatures and units of local government. The Supreme Court's so-called Reapportionment Revolution of the 1960s is an example of the ongoing debate over principles of representation that was never finally resolved at the Constitutional Convention. (See Chapter 6 of this volume.)

Another compromise at the Constitutional Convention allowed the delegates to move past impasse over the question of whether Congress or the states would have responsibility for regulating of commerce. At its core, that debate raised the question of whether sovereignty—ultimate governing authority—would reside with the U.S. government or remain with the states. That impasse was resolved by including among Congress's enumerated powers in Article I, Section 8, the power to regulate commerce "among the several states," while leaving regulation of commerce off the list of powers prohibited to the states in Article I, Section 10. The compromise regarding the regulation

---

[13] See the Preamble to the Constitution in Appendix A to this volume.

[14] The first dictionary definition of *constitution* is the act or process of setting up, of establishing, of beginning. Chief Justice Marshall and Justices Holmes and Marshall agree that the Supreme Court's interpretation of the Constitution involves acts of creating meaning. As the late political philosopher Hannah Arendt observed, "Political institutions, no matter how well or how badly designed, depend for their continued existence upon acting [human beings]; their conservation is achieved by the same means that brought them into being" (Hannah Arendt, *Between Past and Future: Eight Exercises in Political Thought* [New York, NY: Viking Press], p. 153).

of commerce left unresolved the specific relationship between Congress's commerce power and the states' inherent powers to regulate, commonly known as the police powers, reserved to the states in the Tenth Amendment. It also left to another day the task of drawing lines between *inter*state and *intra*state commerce. Debate over the limits on Congress's power to regulate commerce—to say nothing of defining commerce—has occupied the Supreme Court's attention ever since, arising out of cases involving a wide range of facts. As it did at the Constitutional Convention, the debate over regulating commerce inevitably rekindles the debate over sovereignty. (See especially Chapter 3, Volume I.)

Yet another important compromise at the Constitutional Convention that allowed the delegates to move past impasse concerned slavery. The Three-Fifths Compromise involved counting "other Persons" (a euphemism for slaves) as three-fifths of "free persons" for purposes of apportioning representatives in the House of Representatives, thereby assuring the South substantial representation in the House. Other slavery compromises included giving Congress the power to prohibit the migration or importation of slaves but postponing its authority to exercise that power until at least the year 1808.[15]

The Constitution contains other significant compromises. Coupled with the ambiguous terms in which many Constitutional provisions were written, and the inherent ambiguities of language itself, those compromises have ensured that the Supreme Court has always had before it cases and controversies capable of transforming the constitutional landscape. As the late constitutional historian and scholar Alpheus Mason put it, the Supreme Court is America's "ongoing Constitutional Convention."[16]

Understanding the Supreme Court Historically

Although the cases in this text are organized by subject matter, the material introducing each case provides a glimpse into the historical contexts out of which the cases emerged. This approach blends an historical perspective on

---

[15] William M. Wiecek counts "no less [sic] than ten clauses in the Constitution that directly or indirectly accommodated the peculiar institution" (*The Sources of Antislavery Constitutionalism in America* [Ithaca, NY: Cornell University Press, 1977], pp. 62–63).

[16] This was the theme of Professor Mason's 1979 National Endowment for the Humanities Summer Seminar at Princeton University.

The late Robert G. McCloskey observed in his history of the Supreme Court: "If the framers had tried to settle all 'constitutional' questions that confronted them; if they had even assumed the more modest task of specifically circumscribing the judicial power; if the doctrine of legislative supremacy had been a little more firmly intrenched in 1789; if judges like Marshall had been a little more inclined toward abnegation and a little less inclined toward politics, the uncertainties would be very different, the tale would be of another order. But then the country it was told about would not be the historical United States" (*The American Supreme Court* [Chicago, IL: University of Chicago Press, 1960], pp. 24–25). See also Robert G. McCloskey, *The American Supreme Court*, 2nd ed., revised by Sanford Levinson (Chicago, IL: University of Chicago Press, 1994). Compare Laurence H. Tribe and Michael C. Dorf, *On Reading the Constitution* (Cambridge, MA: Harvard University Press, 1991).

the cases with the contemporary academic preference for analyzing the work of the Supreme Court in terms of the development of constitutional doctrine. However, the Court may also be understood as an institution whose work reflects three distinct eras and an emerging fourth era. Each era is marked by particular constitutional concerns and distinctive patterns of interpretation. An understanding of those eras provides helpful perspective when examining the Court's responses to particular categories of constitutional controversies.[17]

THE FIRST ERA (1793–1876)—DEFINING AMERICAN GOVERNMENT

In the first era, the Court was concerned primarily with issues of federalism. Federalism is the term that describes a form of government in which the states and the central government share governing powers and responsibilities. The term also describes the ongoing debate over the balance of power between the two levels of government.

The Supreme Court's assertion of the power of judicial review in 1803 ensured that it would play an important role in defining the powers delegated to the national government by the Constitution and those reserved to the states under the Tenth Amendment. Early decisions, frequently written by Chief Justice John Marshall, held that a strong national government is consistent with the constitutional principle of limited government. Those decisions declared that the national government has extensive powers to regulate and promote interstate commerce and that the judiciary is responsible for protecting the rights of private property owners against incursions by both national and state legislatures.

Contrary to the fears of states' rights advocates, the Court during this era, particularly under the leadership of Chief Justice Roger Brooke Taney, left undisturbed many of the important prerogatives that the states had enjoyed since the Revolution. Significantly, the Court declared that the Bill of Rights imposes limits only on the national government, not on the states.

Near the end of this era, the Civil War and the Thirteenth, Fourteenth, and Fifteenth Amendments purged the Constitution of the scourge of slavery, but they did not resolve the question of whether sovereignty lies with the national government or with the states. In 1869, the Supreme Court merely restated the ambiguity that has been present in the constitutional system since its beginning, when the Court declared that "The Constitution, in all its provisions, looks to an indestructible Union, composed of indestructible States."[18] The Court's early interpretations of the Civil War Amendments, however, severely crippled the national government's attempts to address the deep social and political problems left in the wake of slavery.

---

[17] A Table of Contents that reflects the historical eras described below is provided at the beginning of this book for those who prefer to study constitutional law historically.

[18] *Texas v. White*, 7 Wallace 700 (1896).

THE SECOND ERA (1877–1940)—GOVERNMENT AND ECONOMY

The Supreme Court's second era was concerned primarily with interpreting the Constitution in light of the nation's rapidly changing economy. The Court played a major role in determining the social as well as economic consequences of the industrial revolution by scrutinizing many state and federal regulatory statutes and by striking down important pieces of regulatory legislation. The Court defined the Due Process Clause of the Fourteenth Amendment in substantive, economic terms, declaring that due process guarantees "liberty of contract" and that the government may not intervene on behalf of labor to equalize the bargaining power between owners and workers.

The Court's opinions regarding economic regulation during this era clung tenaciously to James Madison's notion that government must remain a "neutral" umpire between competing economic interests, above and outside the competition between economic interests like capitalists and laborers. The Court's economic doctrine—commonly called economic substantive due process—and its view that government is constitutionally prohibited from ordering private market relationships, had the consequence of advancing the interests of private property owners and business enterprises during this era.

By contrast, the Court during this period construed the Civil War Amendments as giving Congress virtually no remedial powers to ameliorate the racial, social and political legacies of slavery. Racial unrest and the nation's first communist "Red Scare" after World War I failed to jar the fundamentally conservative Supreme Court. Near the end of this era, the nation sank into a deep, worldwide economic depression that called into question the viability of both capitalism and America's constitutional government.

In 1937, the Court's approach to economic regulation took a dramatic turn. In the face of threats by President Franklin Roosevelt to "pack" the Court with justices willing to declare constitutional his far-reaching social and economic reform programs designed to pull the country out of the Great Depression, the Court abruptly abandoned its constitutional opposition to government regulation of market relations. It declared: "Liberty under the Constitution is ... necessarily subject to the restraints of due process, and regulation which is reasonable in relation to its subject and is adopted in the interests of the community is due process."[19] The Court began validating economic regulatory legislation at both the national and state levels.

THE THIRD ERA (1941–1971)—CIVIL RIGHTS AND CIVIL LIBERTIES

In the third era, the justices shifted their focus from scrutinizing government regulation of the economy to protecting civil rights and civil liberties. The Due Process Clause of the Fourteenth Amendment, once a vehicle for voiding economic regulation, became a vehicle for extending many of the provisions of the

---

[19] *West Coast Hotel v. Parrish*, 300 U.S. 379 (1937).

Bill of Rights against state governments. Racial and ethnic minorities and other disenfranchised groups, such as criminal defendants, increasingly turned to the courts to achieve results denied to them in the partisan political sphere. During Chief Justice Earl Warren's leadership of the Court, these groups were frequently rewarded for their efforts. The Fourteenth Amendment's Equal Protection Clause, along with the Due Process Clause, became the engine of a judicial revolution in rights that ranged from school desegregation and reapportionment to privacy rights and the protection of the criminally accused. Hallmarks of this era were the Court's views that "at the very least," the Equal Protection Clause "demands that racial classifications ... be subjected to the 'most rigid scrutiny,'" and that "[n]othing can destroy a government more quickly than its failure to observe its own laws...."[20]

To advocates of states' rights, this third era in the Court's history appeared to sound the death knell of federalism as a balance between state and federal prerogatives. Following the Supreme Court's lead, Americans increasingly looked to the national government for solutions to social problems and frequently preferred litigation over legislative lobbying to establish rights and prerogatives.

A FOURTH ERA? (1972–PRESENT)—PRAGMATIC CONSERVATISM

Although proximity makes problematic an assessment of the Court's most recent history, there are indications that the past quarter century has been transitional. Republican Presidents Nixon, Reagan, and Bush appointed ten justices to the Court between 1969 and 1991, and President Clinton has appointed two justices since 1993. Although the Republican appointees have derailed the activist civil liberties and civil rights agenda of the Warren Court, they have not destroyed it.

In general terms, the Court's present conservatism is not of the activist variety advocated by the presidents who appointed most of today's justices. Instead, it is a pragmatic conservatism that is at once a reaction to the previous Warren Court policy agenda and a hybrid of it. While the heady days of skirmishes at the judicial frontiers over expanding equal protection and criminal due process are gone, the justices exhibit a quasi-libertarian concern to protect civil and, recently, property rights. The contemporary Court has also revitalized its traditional role of policing separation of powers and has resurrected a concern for states' rights in the federal system. This is not a revolutionary court of either the political left or right. One observer contends that the Court reflects the deep fissures dividing the society of which it is a part: "These are finger-to-the-wind days for the Justices."[21]

---

[20] The quotations are from *Loving v. Virginia*, 388 U.S. 1 (1967), and *Mapp v. Ohio*, 367 U.S. 643 (1961), respectively.

[21] Jeffrey Toobin, "Chicken Supreme: The Rehnquist Court Is Political in Every Way" *The New Yorker*, August 14, 1995, p. 82 (reviewing James F. Simon, *The Center Holds: The Power Struggle inside the Rehnquist Court* [New York, NY: Simon & Schuster, 1995]).

Understanding the Supreme Court Politically

The Supreme Court has always operated at the intersection of law and politics.[22] It is at once a court of law that resolves disputes on a case-by-case basis by applying rules and precedents to specific facts, and a branch of the U.S. government that makes public policy. The consequence is that when the Supreme Court exercises its power of judicial review to resolve a constitutional question, it shapes American politics by using legal rules, rights, principles, and precedents to fashion policy.

An example from the 1995 Term is *Romer v. Evans*, 517 U.S. 1146 (1996). (See Chapter 7 of this volume.) The Court held, by a 6–3 vote, that a Colorado statewide initiative—a provision of the Colorado Constitution known as "Amendment 2" that precluded all legislative, executive, or judicial action at any level of state or local government to protect persons based on their "homosexual, lesbian or bisexual orientation, conduct, practices or relationships"—violates the Equal Protection Clause of the Fourteenth Amendment. As a legal matter, the Court ruled that Amendment 2 classified persons based on their status, a form of classification the Equal Protection Clause does not permit. "We must conclude," wrote Justice Anthony Kennedy, "that Amendment 2 classifies homosexuals not to further a proper legislative end but to make them unequal to everyone else. This Colorado cannot do. A State cannot so deem a class of persons a stranger to its laws." The Court's holding in *Romer v. Evans* unquestionably has affected public policy in the area of gay and lesbian rights.

The importance of the Supreme Court as a coordinate branch of government cannot be overstated, because it means that rarely, if ever, are the Court's decisions on a controversial topic final. As constitutional scholars Louis Fisher and Neal Devins put it:

> The process is not linear, with the courts issuing the final word. The process is circular, turning back on itself again and again until society is satisfied with the outcome.[23]

The cases in this text demonstrate that point time and again.

Early in its history, for example, the Court was asked to declare the extent of Congress's power to regulate interstate commerce under Article I,

---

[22] See the essays collected in Martin Shapiro, *Law and Politics in the Supreme Court: New Approaches to Political Jurisprudence* (New York, NY: Free Press, 1964), esp. Chapter 1. Political scientist Mark A. Graber makes a similar point about the Court and politics: "[T]he Supreme Court is the one place in American politics where there is still some space between electorates and governing officials[.]... The issue is ... not whether [the Justices] are ... disinterested Platonic philosophers ... but what their place actually is in the web of American politics, and whether that place is desirable." Mark A. Graber [mgraber@bss2.umd.edu]. "REPLY: The Supreme Court's New Term." In *LAWCOURTS*. [lawcourts-l@usc.edu]. 4 November 1996.

[23] Louis Fisher and Neal Devins, *Political Dynamics of Constitutional Law*, 2nd ed. (St. Paul, MN: West, 1996), p. 9.

Section 8, Clause 3. Its decisions declared that Congress has broad, though not exclusive, regulatory powers. Those decisions generated intense political reactions in the states, including threats of secession. During the Great Depression of the 1930s, the Court's Commerce Clause jurisprudence again fomented a political firestorm, leading President Franklin Roosevelt to attempt to "pack" the Court with justices who would read the Commerce Clause and other constitutional provisions to legitimate his far-reaching social and economic legislation. Even in the 1990s, the Court's Commerce Clause decisions are marked by sharp divisions among the justices and are the source of intense political debate about whether the national government or the states should have the power to make particular governing decisions.[24] Despite the power of judicial review, the Court's Commerce Clause decisions have never been the final word on the meaning of that constitutional provision and the balance of power between the national government and the states. (See especially Chapter 3, Volume I.)

Abortion politics in the wake of *Roe v. Wade*, 410 U.S. 113 (1973), provides another illustration of the circular, coordinate policymaking process to which Fisher and Devins refer.[25] (See Chapter 7 of this volume.) When *Roe* came to the Court, most state statutes prohibited nontherapeutic abortions. Those laws dated back to the late nineteenth and early twentieth centuries and reflected the lobbying efforts of organizations like the American Medical Association. More than forty interest groups and some 350 individuals signed sixteen joint *amicus curiae* briefs supporting one side or the other in the legal controversy in *Roe*, in which the Court was asked to declare unconstitutional a Texas statute that banned abortions.

The Supreme Court's 7–2 decision in *Roe* invalidated the Texas statute but it did nothing to end the abortion controversy. Instead, the decision mobilized abortion opponents. By 1989, changes in the Supreme Court's personnel fueled speculation that *Roe* might be overruled. Two of the majority votes in *Roe*—Justices Powell and Stewart—had been replaced by Justices Kennedy and O'Connor, both appointed by antiabortion President Ronald Reagan. Following Chief Justice Burger's retirement, Reagan elevated Justice Rehnquist, who had dissented in *Roe*, to chief justice, and appointed Justice Scalia to the vacant seat. In *Webster v. Reproductive Health Services*, 492 U.S. 490 (1989), the Court by a 5–4 vote dashed the hopes of antiabortion forces that *Roe* would be overruled, but the *Webster* decision did send a signal that the Court would approve more restrictive regulation of the abortion practice than it had previously. (See Chapter 7 of this volume.)

---

[24] See *United States v. Lopez*, 514 U.S. 549 (1995), excerpted in Chapter 3, Volume I.

[25] Compare the case study on *Roe v. Wade* in Charles A. Johnson and Bradley C. Canon, *Judicial Policies: Implementation and Impact* (Washington, D.C.: Congressional Quarterly, 1984), pp. 4–14. See also Neal Devins, *Shaping Constitutional Values: Elected Government, the Supreme Court, and the Abortion Debate* (Baltimore, MD: The Johns Hopkins University Press, 1996); and Gerald N. Rosenberg, *The Hollow Hope: Can Courts Bring about Social Change?* (Chicago, IL: University of Chicago Press, 1991).

Clearly, the Supreme Court's exercise of its power of judicial review in *Roe v. Wade* did not resolve the abortion controversy.[26] Rather, *Roe* helped to make abortion a national issue, whereas, before *Roe,* abortion politics and law had played out primarily in the states. Like the Court's decisions regarding Congress's power to regulate interstate commerce, *Roe* illustrates the way in which Supreme Court justices engage in a "continuing colloquy with the political institutions and with society at large."[27] "Judges," observed Ruth Bader Ginsburg in 1992, the year before she was appointed to the Supreme Court, "play an interdependent part in our democracy. They do not alone shape legal doctrine but ... they participate in a dialogue with other organs of government, and with the people as well."[28]

Stories illustrating the circular, coordinate nature of Supreme Court policymaking can be told about every case in this book.[29] Each of the Court's landmark constitutional decisions has emerged out of a hotly contested political environment and has involved constitutional issues about which lower courts have been in disagreement. Although each decision has yielded a rule of constitutional law that has contributed to the evolution of legal doctrine, none has put an end to the political controversy that spawned the litigation. Consequently, it is fair to ask—do Supreme Court decisions matter?[30]

The realistic answer to that question is—it depends. Compliance with a particular judicial decision depends on how the decision is perceived by various groups in American society.[31] According to political scientists Charles A. Johnson and Bradley C. Canon, perception is shaped along four dimensions: (1) a person's attitude toward the specific policy announced in the Supreme Court's decision; (2) a person's attitude toward the Court; (3) a person's perception of the practical consequences of the decision; and (4) a person's per-

---

[26] See Robert Blank and Janna C. Merrick, *Human Reproduction, Emerging Technologies, and Conflicting Rights* (Washington, D.C.: Congressional Quarterly, 1995).

[27] Alexander Bickel, *The Least Dangerous Branch: The Supreme Court at the Bar of Politics* (Indianapolis, IN: Bobbs-Merrill, 1962), p. 240.

[28] Ruth Bader Ginsburg, "Speaking in a Judicial Voice," 67 *New York University Law Review* (1992): 1198. See Richard Funston, *A Vital National Seminar: The Supreme Court in American Political Life* (Palo Alto, CA: Mayfield, 1978).

[29] Many outstanding case studies of Supreme Court decisions already have been published. Among them are Gordon E. Baker, *The Reapportionment Revolution: Representation, Political Power, and the Supreme Court* (New York, NY: Random House, 1966); Fred W. Friendly, *Minnesota Rag: The Dramatic Story of the Landmark Supreme Court Case That Gave Meaning to Freedom of the Press* (New York, NY: Vintage, 1982); Richard Kluger, *Simple Justice* (New York, NY: Vintage, 1977); Anthony Lewis, *Gideon's Trumpet* (New York, NY: Vintage, 1964); C. Peter Magrath, *Yazoo: The Case of Fletcher v. Peck* (New York, NY: Norton, 1967); John T. Noonan, *The Antelope* (Berkeley, CA: University of California Press, 1977). Tracing the political and social consequences of any of the cases in this book is an excellent source of topics for student research papers.

[30] See Lauren Bowen, "Do Court Decisions Matter?" in *Contemplating Courts*, ed. Lee Epstein (Washington, D.C.: Congressional Quarterly, 1995), pp. 376–389.

[31] Stuart A. Scheingold refers to this process of perception as the "compliance calculation," in his *The Politics of Rights: Lawyers, Public Policy, and Political Change* (New Haven, CT: Yale University Press, 1974), pp. 123–130. Compare Michael W. McCann, *Rights at Work: Pay Equity Reform and the Politics of Legal Mobilization* (Chicago, IL: University of Chicago Press, 1994); and John Brigham, *The Constitution of Interest: Beyond the Politics of Rights* (New York, NY: New York University Press, 1996).

ception of how the decision will affect his or her role in society. Johnson and Canon write: "Behavioral responses ... are often linked to acceptance decisions. Persons who do not accept a judicial policy are likely to engage in behavior designed to defeat the policy or minimize its impact.... Those who accept a policy are likely to be more faithful or even enthusiastic in interpreting, implementing, and consuming it."[32] In most landmark Supreme Court decisions, the relevant population extends well beyond the immediate parties to the case. At the federal level, lower courts, Congress, the president, and one or more administrative agencies all make compliance calculations. Fifty state executives and state legislatures, and multiple state courts also must decide how to respond to the Court's decisions. Local law enforcement officials, school board members, bar associations and legal academics, and interest groups are also among salient populations whose responses can affect whether Supreme Court decisions meet with compliance.

As a policymaking body, observes political scientist Lawrence Baum, the Supreme Court "is neither all-powerful nor insignificant." He concludes:

> [T]he Court is perhaps most important in creating conditions for action by others. Its decisions put issues on the national agenda so that other policy makers and the general public consider them. The Court is not highly effective at enforcing rights, but it often legitimates efforts to achieve them and thus provides the impetus for people to take legal and political action. Its decisions affect the positions of interest groups and social movements, strengthening some and weakening others.[33]

THE SUPREME COURT IN THE AMERICAN JUDICIAL SYSTEM

As noted previously, the Supreme Court is not merely a coordinate branch of the national government. It also operates within a federal system. However, this was not always the case. The Articles of Confederation did not provide for a judicial branch as such, only for a mechanism to hear disputes between and among states. Each of the state governments had a judicial branch, however, so the proposal at the Constitutional Convention for a national judiciary to

---

[32] Johnson and Canon, *Judicial Policies*, pp. 23–24. Johnson and Canon identify four particularly important "populations" (groups): the interpreting population, the implementing population, the consumer population, and the secondary population. Ibid., pp. 15–22, 24.

See also Rosenberg, *The Hollow Hope*; Bradley C. Canon, "Courts and Policy: Compliance, Implementation, and Impact," in *The American Courts: A Critical Assessment*, ed. John B. Gates (Washington, D.C.: Congressional Quarterly, 1991); Sheldon Ekland-Olson and Steve J. Martin, "Organizational Compliance with Court-Ordered Reform," in *The Law & Society Reader*, ed. Richard L. Abel (New York, NY: New York University Press, 1995); Robert A. Carp and Ronald Stidham, *Judicial Process in America*, 3rd ed. (Washington, D.C.: Congressional Quarterly, 1996), Chapter 11; Stewart Macaulay, Lawrence M. Friedman, and John Stookey, eds., *Law & Society: Readings on the Social Study of Law* (New York, NY: Norton, 1995), Chapter 4; Sheldon Goldman and Austin Sarat, eds., *American Court Systems: Readings in Judicial Process and Behavior*, 2nd ed. (New York, NY: Longman, 1989), Chapters 13 and 14; and Stephen L. Wasby, *The Impact of the United States Supreme Court* (Homewood, IL: Dorsey, 1970).

[33] Lawrence Baum, *The Supreme Court*, 5th ed. (Washington, D.C.: Congressional Quarterly, 1995), p. 272, and "Courts and Policy Innovation," in Gates, *The American Courts*. Stuart A. Scheingold calls the process Baum describes the "politics of rights." See Scheingold, *The Politics of Rights*; and Lawrence Baum, *The Puzzle of Judicial Behavior* (Ann Arbor, MI: University of Michigan Press, 1997).

consist of at least one "supreme tribunal" created little stir. The delegates also agreed easily to the proposition that judges should hold their offices during good behavior. With no debate at all, the delegates voted to extend the national judicial power to cases in equity as well as law.[34] Giving the national judiciary power to dispense both legal and equitable remedies significantly consolidated the judicial function at the national level.[35]

Debate at the convention was more divisive over the method for appointing federal judges, however. By a split vote, the delegates finally agreed to nomination by the president and confirmation by the Senate. Following extensive debate, the delegates rejected a proposal for a Council of Revision consisting of the president and a "convenient number of the national judiciary" that would have examined all acts of Congress before those acts went into effect. The delegates also debated, but rejected, a proposal for a joint judicial-executive veto of congressional legislation. Instead, the delegates gave Congress power to establish "inferior courts" and to determine the size and internal organization of the Supreme Court.

In the Judiciary Act of 1789, Congress created thirteen federal district courts that were to meet in four sessions annually, and three circuit courts, to hold court twice a year in each district within the circuit. The jurisdiction of the district courts was quite narrow; most of their work consisted of admiralty cases. The circuit courts had some appellate jurisdiction over the district courts, but primarily they were trial courts for cases involving suits between citizens of different states (known as diversity of citizenship cases). Few routes of appeal existed for litigants who were dissatisfied with circuit court judgments. The Supreme Court's appellate caseload during its formative years consisted primarily of cases appealed from decisions of state courts.

Circuit courts were initially staffed by two Supreme Court justices and one district court judge. In 1793, Congress reduced the circuit-riding burden on Supreme Court justices somewhat by requiring only one justice to sit each year as a circuit judge in each district.

The federal judicial structure created by the Judiciary Act of 1789 remained essentially intact until 1891, when Congress established a set of intermediate federal courts of appeal, now known as the U.S. Courts of Appeals. Figure 1.1 gives an overview of the U.S. judicial system as it looks today.

The Supreme Court sits at the top of a complex system of federal and state courts over which it exercises appellate jurisdiction. It also sits as a trial

---

[34] In England, and in the states, separate tribunals administered legal and equitable remedies. Courts of law resolved cases involving statutes or the common law, granting monetary damages to parties who prevailed in civil litigation and imposing fines and prison terms on defendants convicted of crimes. Courts of equity administered "remedial justice." They determined the appropriate relief in situations where rules of law were incomplete or inadequate. Equitable remedies included ordering specific conduct on the part of the litigants after the suit, and issuing temporary and permanent injunctions to compel or prohibit certain actions.

[35] Peter Charles Hoffer provides an historical account of equity in Anglo-American jurisprudence and shows the Supreme Court's use of equitable principles in twentieth century civil rights and affirmative action cases in *The Law's Conscience* (Chapel Hill, NC: University of North Carolina Press, 1990).

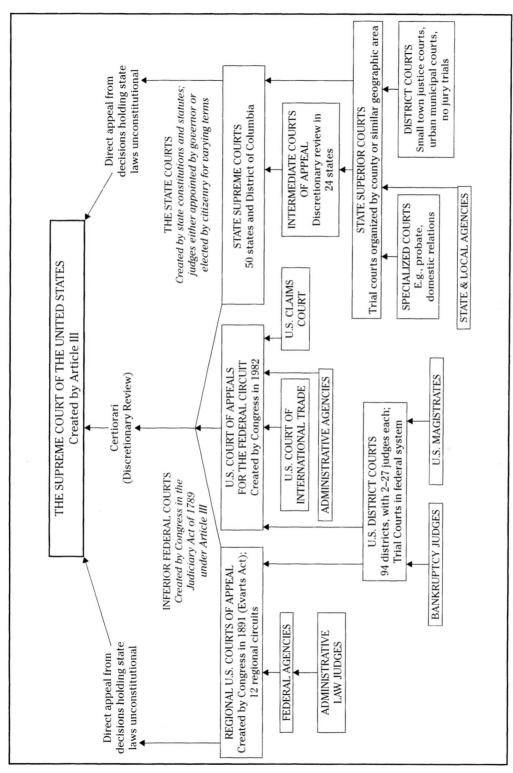

FIGURE 1.1 THE AMERICAN DUAL COURT SYSTEM

court in an extremely small number of cases, outlined in Article III, which comprise its original jurisdiction. The Supreme Court becomes involved in only a tiny fraction of the cases filed in American courts each year. Not many cases filed raise constitutional questions; not many cases that do raise constitutional questions work their way to the Supreme Court.

As Figure 1.1 also shows, the judicial system comprises both federal and state courts. State court systems have existed since the Revolution. Their organization originally reflected their English heritage. Congress's power to create "inferior" federal courts stirred political controversy among the states because of the fear that federal courts would rob state courts of their jurisdiction. Subject to the limitations in the Constitution of the United States, their own state constitutions and state law, state courts have general authority to try and decide a vast range of cases, including criminal prosecutions, personal injury cases, marital disputes, probate of estates, and land and commercial transactions. Federal courts, by comparison, are courts of limited jurisdiction. They are authorized to decide only those cases and controversies over which the Constitution of the United States or acts of Congress made pursuant to the Constitution give them jurisdiction.[36] Figure 1.2 shows boundaries of the twelve regional federal circuit courts of appeal. Those courts hear appeals from the U.S. district courts located within their boundaries.[37]

AUTHORITY OF THE SUPREME COURT

JURISDICTION

The authority of a court to try and decide a case is called jurisdiction.[38] It is of two kinds, personal and subject matter. A court does not have jurisdiction to hear a case unless it has the authority to compel the participation of the

---

[36] The distinctions between the jurisdiction of state and federal courts are set out by Fannie Klein in *Federal and State Court Systems—A Guide* (Cambridge, MA: Ballinger Publishing Co., 1977), p. 1.

[37] The Court of Appeals for the Federal Circuit is the exception to the rule of regional courts of appeal. It is a jurisdictional instead of a geographical appeals court. Created in 1982 through a merger of the U.S. Court of Claims and the U.S. Court of Customs and Patents, it hears appeals in cases from the U.S. Court of Federal Claims, the U.S. Court of International Trade, the U.S. Court of Veterans Appeals, the International Trade Commission, the Board of Contract Appeals, the Patent and Trademark Office, and the Merit Systems Protection Board. The Court of Appeals for the Federal Circuit also hears appeals from certain decisions of the secretaries of the Department of Agriculture and the Department of Commerce, cases arising from district courts involving patents, and minor claims against the federal government.

The regional courts of appeal frequently interpret federal law differently, creating what are known as "intercircuit conflicts." The Supreme Court will often await intercircuit conflicts on an issue before accepting a case for review. That way, the justices have the benefit of the reasoning of federal appellate judges in various parts of the country on an issue.

[38] Students interested in exploring details of the Court's jurisdiction, issues of justiciability, and aspects of practices and procedures before the Supreme Court are referred to Robert L. Stern, Eugene Gressman, Stephen M. Shapiro, and Kenneth S. Geller, *Supreme Court Practice*, 7th ed. (Washington, D.C.: Bureau of National Affairs, 1993). The authors note in their preface that the goal of the book is to "set forth in a single volume to the extent possible everything that a lawyer would want to know as to how to prosecute or defend a case in the Supreme Court." Also see Susan Low Bloch and Thomas G. Krattenmaker, eds., *Supreme Court Politics: The Institution and Its Procedures* (St. Paul, MN: West, 1994).

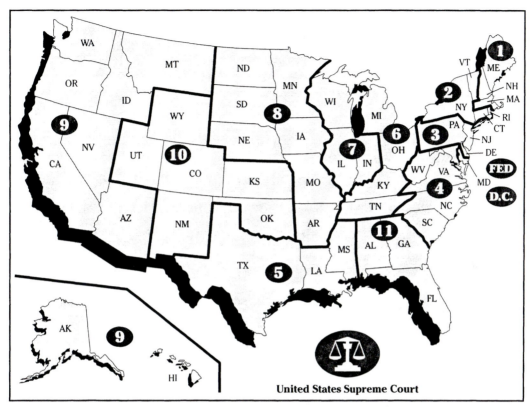

FIGURE 1.2   TWELVE REGIONAL FEDERAL CIRCUIT COURTS OF APPEAL *(Source: Map courtesy of Edward Bennett Williams Law Library, Georgetown University Law Center.)*

parties (personal jurisdiction) and the authority to render a binding decision on the issues (subject matter jurisdiction). As noted previously, state courts have traditionally been recognized as courts of general jurisdiction. They are assumed to have the authority to resolve all cases and controversies submitted to them by their own residents. Federal courts, by contrast, are courts of limited jurisdiction. They may exercise judicial power only if authority has been conferred by the Constitution or by federal statute. A party who files a case in federal court must prove that the court has jurisdiction through reference to the constitutional or federal statutory provision conferring the right to litigate in a federal court. Failure to prove federal jurisdiction results in automatic dismissal of the case, no matter how compelling the issues.

The Supreme Court exercises jurisdiction over two categories of cases. Article III of the Constitution gives it original jurisdiction over "cases affecting Ambassadors, other public Ministers and Consuls, and those in which a State shall be a Party." The Court's jurisdiction over these cases may be exclusive or concurrent with other federal or state courts. Only a few cases have ever been brought involving foreign diplomats. Disputes between states over land, boundaries, and water and mineral rights have provided the bulk of the Court's work in this realm, although these cases are rare and have comprised only a small fraction of the Court's overall caseload. When the justices hear cases in the exercise of their original jurisdiction they sit as a trial court, making findings of fact as well as conclusions of law.

The Supreme Court has appellate, or review, jurisdiction in all other cases, subject to regulations and exceptions made by Congress. Congress has considered limiting the Court's appellate jurisdiction many times over the years. During the past two decades, legislation has been introduced to curb the Court's appellate jurisdiction in four controversial areas in particular: abortion, prayer in public schools, school busing, and the rights of criminal defendants.[39] Until recently, however, the typical pattern of congressional action has been to provide litigants with more rather than fewer opportunities to request appellate review, while at the same time giving the Supreme Court more discretion over the appellate cases it will hear. The Judiciary Act of 1925, for example, replaced review as a matter of right from state and circuit courts of appeal with discretionary review by writ of certiorari.[40] The 1925 legislation did not eliminate a range of direct appeals provided by Congress, such as in cases where a federal court had invalidated a state statute or when a state court declared federal legislation unconstitutional. Beginning in 1948, however, Congress began to eliminate opportunities for nondiscretionary appeals. Following passage of the 1988 Act to Improve the Administration of

---

[39] According to attorney Ronald L. Goldfarb, as of November 1996, there were 194 resolutions for constitutional amendments pending in the House of Representatives and 55 pending in the Senate. Among these resolutions were proposed amendments designed to reverse several Supreme Court opinions, including decisions on abortion and term limits. "The 11,000th Amendment: What's Wrong with the Rush to Revise the Constitution," *Washington Post*, Sunday, November 17, 1996, C4.

The legitimacy of congressional curbs on the Court's jurisdiction is discussed by Henry M. Hart Jr., "The Power of Congress to Limit the Jurisdiction of the Federal Courts: An Exercise in Dialectic," 66 *Harvard Law Review* (1953): 1362; Leonard Ratner, "Congressional Power over the Appellate Jurisdiction of the Supreme Court," 109 *University of Pennsylvania Law Review* (1960): 157; Leonard Ratner, "Majoritarian Constraints on Judicial Review: Congressional Control of Supreme Court Jurisdiction," 27 *Villanova Law Review* (1982): 929; and Charles E. Rice, "The Constitutional Basis for the Proposals in Congress Today," 65 *Judicature* (1981): 190.

See also C. Herman Pritchett, *Congress versus the Supreme Court* (Minneapolis, MN: University of Minnesota Press, 1961); Walter F. Murphy, *Congress and the Court: A Case Study in the American Political Process* (Chicago, IL: University of Chicago Press, 1962); Stuart S. Nagel, "Court-Curbing Periods in American History," 18 *Vanderbilt Law Review* (1965): 925; Raoul Berger, *Congress v. The Supreme Court* (Cambridge, MA: Harvard University Press, 1969); John R. Schmidhauser and Larry L. Berg, *The Supreme Court and Congress: Conflict and Interaction, 1945–1968* (New York, NY: Free Press, 1972); Handberg and Hill, "Court Curbing, Court Reversals, and Judicial Review: The Supreme Court versus Congress"; Louis Fisher, *Constitutional Dialogues: Interpretation as Political Process* (Princeton, NJ: Princeton University Press, 1988); William N. Eskridge Jr., "Overriding Supreme Court Statutory Interpretation Decisions," 101 *Yale Law Journal* (1991): 331; Abner Mikva and Jeff Bleich, "When Congress Overrides the Court," 79 *California Law Review* (1991): 729; and Linda Greenhouse, "How Congress Curtailed the Courts' Jurisdiction," *New York Times*, October 27, 1996, E5.

[40] The certiorari process is explained on pp. 23–24.

Justice, almost all rights of direct appeal were eliminated.[41] Today, the certiorari process gives the Court almost complete discretion over the cases it will hear in the exercise of its appellate jurisdiction. Figure 1.3 shows the sources of Supreme Court cases docketed during the 1995 October Term.

In recent years, the Court has denied review (or the parties have withdrawn requests for review) in over 90 percent of the cases for which review has been sought. As a result, the Supreme Court hears and decides only a very small proportion of the total number of cases filed each year. The number of cases the Court hears and decides has been declining in recent years. During its 1980 Term, for example, the Court granted review in 232 (10.4 percent) of 2,256 cases on the Appellate Docket, and 27 (1.3 percent) of 2,017 cases on the Miscellaneous Docket.[42] In the 1989 Term, the numbers diminished to 171 (8.4 percent) of the 2,028 cases on its Appellate Docket and in 32 (1.1 percent) of the 2,878 cases on its Miscellaneous Docket. By its 1994 Term, the Court granted review in merely 83 (3.9 percent) of the 2,151 cases on its Appellate Docket, and only 10 (.02 percent) of the 4,979 cases on its Miscellaneous Docket. For the Supreme Court's 1995 Term, the figures are 92 (4.4 percent) of the 2,099 cases on its Appellate Docket, and 13 (.03 percent) of the 4,507 cases on its Miscellaneous Docket.[43]

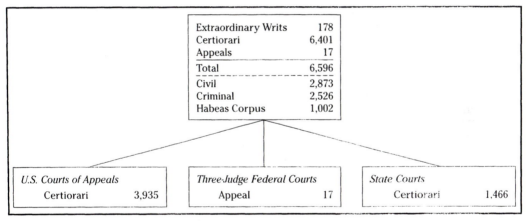

Extraordinary Writs	178
Certiorari	6,401
Appeals	17
Total	6,596
Civil	2,873
Criminal	2,526
Habeas Corpus	1,002

U.S. Courts of Appeals		Three-Judge Federal Courts		State Courts	
Certiorari	3,935	Appeal	17	Certiorari	1,466

FIGURE 1.3 CASES DOCKETED OCTOBER TERM 1995 (*Source: Clerk's Office, Supreme Court of the United States.*)

---

[41] Exceptions to the elimination of the right to appeal include appeals in reapportionment cases, suits under the Civil Rights and Voting Rights Acts, antitrust laws, and the Presidential Election Campaign Fund Act.

[42] The Appellate Docket consists of all cases for which the parties pay counsel and relevant filing fees. The Miscellaneous Docket includes cases filed in *forma pauperis* ("as a pauper," that is, permission to sue without paying any court costs).

[43] 104 *Harvard Law Review* (1990): Table I, p. 367; 104 *Harvard Law Review* (1990): Table II, p. 363; 109 *Harvard Law Review* (1995): Table II, pp. 344–345; 110 *Harvard Law Review* (1996): Table II, p. 371. Annually, the first issue (November) of each volume of the *Harvard Law Review* contains a section called "The Statistics." This section contains tables reporting, for instance, the actions of individual justices, voting alignments, unanimity, 5–4 decisions, final disposition of cases, disposition of cases reviewed on writ of certiorari, and subject matter of dispositions with full opinions.

JUSTICIABILITY

In addition to defining the Supreme Court's jurisdiction, Article III of the Constitution specifies that the Court has power over "cases and controversies." Article III provides no definition of those terms, however. Over the past two hundred years, the "case" and "controversy" requirement has evolved into a broad threshold doctrine known as justiciability. Justiciability refers to the propriety of examining a dispute in a judicial forum. While the doctrine has many dimensions, the five most important for purposes of understanding Supreme Court litigation are summarized below.[44] They are among the factors that the justices consider when deciding whether to hear a case.

1. No Advisory Opinions   As a matter of policy, courts will not issue an advisory opinion in advance of an actual case or controversy between identifiable parties. This policy was established in 1793 when George Washington directed his secretary of state, Thomas Jefferson, to write a letter to the first chief justice of the United States, John Jay, asking the Supreme Court to advise the president on twenty-nine hypothetical questions of international law and neutrality. Jay declined, saying to do so would violate the separation of powers.

The Court's refusal to issue advisory opinions was reinforced in 1911, when it refused to hear a case brought by parties in order to obtain an opinion on the constitutionality of Congressional statutes enacted in 1902 and 1907 that affected Indian lands. The statutes altered the original distribution of Cherokee tribal property and had the practical effect of reducing the amount of lands and funds to which certain Indians are entitled. This redistribution of property raised constitutional questions, which one of the statutes authorized the parties to take to the Supreme Court of the United States. Justice Day wrote that this authorization required the Court "to give opinions in the nature of advice concerning legislative action—a function never conferred upon it by the Constitution...." *Muskrat v. United States*, 219 U.S. 346 (1911).

2. No "Political Questions"   In order to protect the judiciary from becoming embroiled in partisan politics and to protect their integrity as an independent, coequal branch of government, American courts declared early in their history that they would not hear cases that raise so-called political questions.[45] If a court believes a case raises issues that are properly decided by the legislative and/or executive branches at the state or federal level, it will declare the case nonjusticiable, citing the doctrine against deciding political

---

[44] For a complete analysis of the justiciability doctrine, see the latest edition of Charles Alan Wright et al, *Federal Practice and Procedure* (*Manual for Complex Litigation*) (St. Paul, MN: West Publishing).

[45] The Court formally announced the "political question" doctrine in *Luther v. Borden*, 7 Howard 1 (1849). However, Chief Justice John Marshall wrote in *Marbury v. Madison*, 1 Cranch 137 (1803), that "The province of the court is, solely, to decide on the rights of individuals, not to inquire how the executive, or executive officers, perform duties in which they have a discretion. Questions, in their nature political ... can never be made in this court."

questions. A modern example of the Supreme Court's use of the doctrine is *Gilligan v. Morgan*, 413 U.S. 1 (1973). The Court held that questions involving the training and discipline of National Guard troops are nonjusticiable because the constitutional responsibility for organizing, arming, and disciplining the military is committed to Congress and the executive branch.

The line between a "political" and "legal" question is usually very hard to draw. Declaring that a case is nonjusticiable on the grounds that it raises a political question is frequently synonymous with deciding the issue: It effectively gives judicial sanction to a resolution by a nonjudicial body. The Supreme Court's use of the political question doctrine thus provides insight into the justices' views of the kinds of issues that they believe merit judicial resolution, which in turn is an insight into the justices' view of the proper role of the courts in our political system.

3. Parties Must Have Standing to Sue   In order to be involved in a lawsuit, parties must have definite and concrete interests in the litigation and must have adverse legal interests. With rare exceptions, third parties cannot assert the rights of others. Failure to satisfy any of the elements of the standing rule can result in dismissal of the action. An environmental dispute provides an example. In 1972, the Court rejected the Sierra Club's challenge to a proposed recreational development. The Sierra Club claimed to represent the interests of the scenery, natural and historical objects, and wildlife of the Mineral King Valley in California. The Court rejected the challenge, ruling that the Sierra Club alleged no facts showing itself or its members adversely affected by the development. The Court dismissed the case on the grounds that the Sierra Club lacked standing to sue.[46]

Like the political question doctrine, the justices exercise the standing rule with considerable flexibility. Their explanation of why a party does or does not have standing to sue provides additional perspective on their understanding of the proper exercise of judicial power. (See Chapter 2, Volume I.)

4. No Adjudication of Cases That Are Not "Ripe" or Are Moot   The concepts of ripeness and mootness refer to the time when it is appropriate for judicial resolution of an issue. If a case is dismissed for lack of ripeness, it means that the justices believe a decision would be premature for some reason. Most often, cases are dismissed for lack of ripeness because other avenues of redress, including legislative and administrative proceedings, are available, are in progress, or are pending. In cases invoking the Supreme Court's equitable jurisdiction, the justices will dismiss for lack of ripeness if they conclude that the threatened injury is too "speculative" to warrant their intervention.

An example of the Court's refusal to decide cases that it believes are not ripe for adjudication is *United Public Workers v. Mitchell*, 330 U.S. 75 (1946). In

---

[46] *Sierra Club v. Morton*, 405 U.S. 727 (1972).

that case, federal employees sought an injunction against enforcement of the federal Hatch Act, which prohibits certain federal employees from engaging in political activities. The employees sought the injunction on the ground that the First, Fifth, Ninth, and Tenth Amendments to the Constitution entitled them to engage in certain political activities. The Court refused to decide the case, claiming that the issues it posed were too speculative for judicial resolution. "A hypothetical threat is not enough," wrote Justice Reed. "It would not accord with judicial responsibility to adjudge ... between the freedom of the individual and the requirements of public order except when definite rights appear upon the one side and definite prejudicial interferences on the other."

Conversely, cases must be "live" throughout the adjudicatory process. If circumstances terminate the adverseness of the parties to a controversy before their case reaches the Supreme Court, the Court's jurisdiction ceases and the case is deemed "moot." A case can be moot if a party drops out of the litigation or if the parties decide to settle their dispute at any time during the process.

A lawsuit filed in 1971 by a white male, Marco DeFunis, that challenged the University of Washington Law School's affirmative action plan as reverse discrimination, demonstrates the mootness doctrine. By the time DeFunis's case reached the Supreme Court in 1974, he was enrolled as a student in the law school on order of a state superior court and was assured of graduation. The Supreme Court refused to rule on the constitutionality of the law school's affirmative action program because DeFunis no longer was an injured party.[47]

Like the other doctrines discussed in this section, the Court does not apply the mootness doctrine rigidly. In deciding the constitutionality of the Texas abortion statute in *Roe v. Wade*, 410 U.S. 113 (1973), for example, the Court rejected the threshold argument that the birth of the plaintiff's baby rendered the case moot. Justice Harry Blackmun noted that if mootness standards were applied strictly, it would never be possible for a woman to challenge such statutes because the normal course of litigation is much longer than the normal course of a pregnancy.

5. A Case Will Not Be Resolved on Constitutional Grounds If It Can Be Resolved on Other Grounds   A final example of judicial self-restraint is the self-imposed rule that courts will avoid construing the Constitution if there are other grounds on which to decide a case. Hence, where possible, courts will resolve cases under the terms of a state or federal statute or in accordance with common law precedents if they can do so. Constitutional resolution of a case is avoided if possible. The theory behind this rule is that courts should not prematurely foreclose debate on issues by resolving them

---

[47] *DeFunis v. Odegaard*, 416 U.S. 312 (1974). Similarly, the Court dismissed as moot two constitutional challenges to the congressional joint resolution extending the ratification period for the proposed Equal Rights Amendment. The cases arrived at the Court after the extended time period had elapsed without the requisite number of states ratifying. *National Organization for Women v. Idaho* and *Carmen v. Idaho*, 459 U.S. 809 (1982).

on constitutional grounds. In practice, however, as noted earlier, resolving an issue on constitutional grounds may actually expand and intensify debate.

These examples demonstrate that justiciability rules are not cast in concrete. Rather, they are gatekeeping norms that the Court uses in deciding whether to accept cases for resolution in order to manage its work load and to conserve its authority.[48] On occasion the Supreme Court has stretched the rules in order to hear a case. On other occasions it has strictly invoked the rules to avoid deciding a case that from the perspective of the parties or public policy would benefit from resolution. Exercising the gatekeeping function is never automatic. It always involves discretion.[49]

SUPREME COURT REVIEW

The procedures for having a case reviewed by the Supreme Court of the United States have varied over the years. Today, almost 99 percent of the Court's appellate docket is created by petitions for writs of certiorari. Under this process, a party seeking Supreme Court review requests the Court by petition (in the form of a legal brief) to issue a writ directing the lower court to send the record of the case to the Supreme Court for review. Usually the opposing party submits a petition explaining why the Court should not issue the writ. Occasionally, the parties will submit a joint petition requesting the Court to issue a writ of certiorari.

By custom, a writ of certiorari is issued when four of the nine justices vote to issue it. Under the pressure of increasing case loads, this custom, known as the "rule of four," has applied to an increasingly smaller number of

---

[48] In his concurring opinion to *Ashwander v. T.V.A.*, 297 U.S. 288 (1936), Justice Louis Brandeis thought it important to summarize the following seven rules developed by the Supreme Court "for its own governance" to avoid "passing upon a large part of all the constitutional questions pressed upon it for decision":

1. The Court will not pass upon the constitutionality of legislation in a friendly, nonadversary proceeding.
2. The Court will not anticipate a question of constitutional law in advance of the necessity of deciding it.
3. The Court will not formulate a rule of constitutional law broader than is required by the precise facts to which it is to be applied.
4. The Court will not pass upon a constitutional question although properly presented by the record, if there is also present some other ground upon which the case may be disposed of.
5. The Court will not pass upon the validity of a statute upon the complaint of one who fails to show that he is injured by its operation.
6. The Court will not pass upon the constitutionality of a statute at the instance of one who has availed himself of its benefits.
7. When the validity of an act of the Congress is drawn in question, and even if a serious doubt of constitutionality is raised, it is a cardinal principle that this Court will first ascertain whether a construction of the statute is fairly possible by which the question may be avoided.

Compare Henry J. Abraham's discussion of "The Sixteen Great Maxims of Judicial Self Restraint," *The Judicial Process*, pp. 348–370.

[49] Some view the Court's justiciability rules as contributing to its institutional conservatism. See M. Glenn Abernathy and Barbara A. Perry, *Civil Liberties under the Constitution*, 6th ed. (Columbia, SC: University of South Carolina Press, 1993).

cases, currently around 2 percent. Most often review is granted by a majority vote and unanimity on case selection is remarkably high.[50]

On average, about one case per term reaches the Court through certification. Under this procedure, if a federal court of appeals is unclear about a question of law, and hence is unable to decide a case, it may certify the legal question to the Supreme Court. The Court has discretion over whether to accept a case on certification and in recent years has shown little inclination to do so. If the Supreme Court refuses to accept a case on certification, the lower court must decide the legal question and enter a judgment. A dissatisfied party may then seek Supreme Court review.

Parties may petition the Court to issue other writs that require review of a case before the writ is issued or denied. An example is the writ of mandamus, through which a party petitions the Court to order a judge or other government official to perform a legally mandated duty. The Court must determine the nature of the duty before issuing or declining to issue such a writ. The Supreme Court issues writs of mandamus infrequently. As noted earlier, the 1988 Act to Improve the Administration of Justice gave the Supreme Court virtually complete discretion over deciding which cases to accept for review.

SUPREME COURT REVIEW PROCESS

In recent years, the Court has been asked to review between four thousand and five thousand cases during its annual eight- or nine-month term (the first Monday in October through late June or early July). All requests for review are analyzed by the office of the Clerk of the Court. If the requests satisfy the procedural requirements spelled out in the Court's rules, they are assigned docket numbers. Filings are screened by the justices or, more often, by their law clerks.[51] Since 1972, the justices have combined resources in a "cert pool," where their clerks share responsibility for winnowing the few cases to be heard from the vast majority that are rejected. Currently, all the justices except John Paul Stevens participate in the "cert pool." The decision whether to accept or deny review of cases is made by the justices in closed conference. The Court has recently reduced the number of certiorari cases discussed at conference through a device called Special List I, or "the discuss list." Before conference, the chief justice circulates a list of certiorari cases that he deems worthy of discussion. Other justices add to the list if they choose. According to the late Justice William Brennan, only about 30 percent of the docketed cases appear on the discuss list, and most of those eventually are denied review.[52]

If a case is accepted for Supreme Court review, it is normally processed

---

[50] David M. O'Brien, *Storm Center: The Supreme Court in American Politics*, 4th ed. (New York, NY: Norton, 1996), pp. 234–236.

[51] Law clerks are typically high-ranking recent graduates of the nation's prestigious law schools who have had previous experience as clerks for state or federal judges.

[52] William Brennan, "The National Court of Appeals: Another Dissent," 40 *University of Chicago Law Review* (1973): 473, 479.

through several distinct steps on the way to a decision. The process is as follows:[53]

1. Submission of Briefs The first step is for legal counsel to submit written briefs. Today, the appellant (the losing party below) has forty-five days to file a brief on the merits after being notified by the Clerk of the Court that its case has been accepted. The respondent (the winning party below) then has thirty days to file a brief that responds to the appellant's brief and seeks to persuade the Supreme Court to affirm the decision of the most recent court to rule on the case. The briefs summarize the facts, describe the rulings of the lower court(s), and identify and argue the legal points and constitutional theories that each side wishes the Court to consider. In true adversary fashion, the appellant is permitted to submit a reply brief that refutes the points made in the respondent's brief.

In order to get a broader perspective on a case, the Court can approve requests from various groups to submit *amicus curiae* or "friend of the Court" briefs. Parties *amici* can include individuals, organizations, and governmental units that have an interest in the outcome of the case but that are not parties. In the past three decades, the *amicus* brief has become a vehicle by means of which diverse interest groups lobby the Court to adopt a particular rule of law.[54]

The briefing process is carefully governed by Court rules. If a brief is particularly well-written or organized, it might be used by a justice to structure an opinion in the case.

2. Oral Argument Oral argument takes place several weeks after the justices have received the briefs and records of a case and have had an opportunity to read them and conduct preliminary legal research. The justices hear arguments four days a week during each Term. Under current Supreme Court

---

[53] On occasion, the Court has issued a decision in a case at the time it decides to review it, suggesting that the justices do not believe completion of all steps is essential in every case. See *Spain v. Rushen*, 464 U.S. 114 (1983), for an example of the majority deciding without benefit of argument that error committed at the trial level was "harmless."

[54] See Samuel Krislov, "The *Amicus Curiae* Brief: From Friendship to Advocacy," 72 *Yale Law Journal* (1963): 694; Nathan Hakman, "Lobbying the Supreme Court: An Appraisal of Political Science 'Folklore,'" 35 *Fordham Law Review* (1966): 15; Lucius Barker, "Third Parties in Litigation: A Systematic View of the Judicial Function," 29 *Journal of Politics* (1967): 41; Karen Orren, "Standing to Sue: Interest Group Conflict in Federal Courts," 70 *American Political Science Review* (1976): 723; Karen O'Connor and Lee Epstein, "Research Note: *Amicus Curiae* Participation in U.S. Supreme Court Litigation: An Appraisal of Hakman's 'Folklore,'" 16 *Law and Society Review* (1982): 701; Karen O'Connor and Lee Epstein, "The Rise of Conservative Interest Group Litigation, 45 *Journal of Politics* (1983): 479; Robert C. Bradley and Paul Gardiner, "Underdogs, Upperdogs, and the Use of the *Amicus* Brief: Trends and Explanations," 10 *Justice Systems Journal* (1985): 78; Stephen L. Wasby, "The Multi-Faceted Elephant: Litigator Perspectives on Planned Litigation," 15 *Capital University Law Review* (1986): 143; Gregory A. Caldeira and Donald J. McCrone, "Of Time and Judicial Activism: A Study of the U.S. Supreme Court, 1800–1973," in *Supreme Court Activism and Restraint*, ed. Stephen C. Halpern and Charles M. Lamb (Lexington, MA: Lexington Books, 1988); Gregory A. Caldeira, "*Amici* before the Supreme Court: Who Participates, When, and How Much?" *Journal of Politics* (1990); Lee Epstein, "Courts and Interests Groups," in *The American Courts: A Critical Assessment*, ed. John B. Gates and Charles A. Johnson (Washington, D.C.: Congressional Quarterly, 1991); and Kevin T. McGuire, "*Amici Curiae* and Strategies for Gaining Access to the Supreme Court," 47 *Political Research Quarterly* (1994): 821.

rules, each side has thirty minutes for oral argument, unless the Court grants a written request for an extension of time. Occasionally the Court permits more than one attorney to argue a case, or allows counsel for parties *amicus* to argue.

Before the Court's docket became so crowded, much more time was allowed for oral argument. In the early days of the Court, for example, argument could go on for days. By the mid-1800s, the time had been shortened to two hours per side; later, to one hour per side. The current rule governing the length of oral argument has been in effect since 1970. Since 1993, the Clerk of the Court has been sending attorneys a booklet containing advice on how to prepare for and make oral arguments.

Oral arguments range from dull expositions by counsel of the points in their briefs to heated exchanges between counsel and the bench or even between justices. Justices can and do interrupt arguments at any time with questions and counter-arguments. Oral argument allows the justices, as well as legal counsel, to test and debate constitutional theories. Reporters who cover the Court and legal scholars who seek to predict how the justices will decide a case listen to oral arguments carefully for clues about the justices' views and probable votes. Predicting outcomes based on questions posed or comments made during oral argument is as problematic as it is fascinating.[55] Expression of an opinion or point of view during oral argument is not necessarily an indication of how a particular justice or group of justices will vote.

Students of the judicial process and justices themselves disagree about the importance of oral argument.[56] Primarily, oral argument provides the jus-

---

[55] Anyone interested in participating in this parlor game can study the verbatim transcripts of oral arguments in especially significant cases printed in the *New York Times*. Access to the *New York Times* on the Internet is available at [http://www.nytimes.com/].

[56] Elder Witt, *Congressional Quarterly Guide to the U.S. Supreme Court*, 2nd ed. (Washington, D.C.: Congressional Quarterly, 1990), p. 739.

Journalists Joan Biskupic and Linda Greenhouse fueled the debate over the importance of oral argument. Biskupic wrote an article about the highly competitive, often arrogant, elite "Supreme Court bar." In her article, Biskupic recounts an episode when Matt Coles, director of the American Civil Liberties Union's Lesbian and Gay Rights Project, unsuccessfully tried to persuade Jean Dubofsky, who had argued as plaintiff's attorney against Colorado Amendment 2 in state court—*Evans v. Romer*, 854 P2d 1270 (Colo. 1993); *Evans v. Romer*, 882 P2d 1335 (Colo. 1994)—to relinquish the case to a law professor "who had helped on the case and had more experience before the justices." Dubofsky's performance at oral argument met with "mixed reviews" from Supreme Court bar critics. However, "[i]n the end," noted Biskupic, "she won—showing that the quality of the oral argument, while scrutinized by the media, lawyers and justices themselves, does not determine the outcome of the case." "Legal Elite Vie for Court Time in Pursuit of Supreme Challenge," *Washington Post*, December 2, 1996, A19. Biskupic does not report that Jean Dubofsky served on the Colorado Supreme Court from 1979 until 1987.

Linda Greenhouse apparently takes a different view of the importance of oral argument in a recent article about *Glickman v. Wileman Bros.*, 117 S.Ct. 2130 (1997), No. 95-1184, a First Amendment case in which a group of California fruit growers challenged a government-required advertising program. Greenhouse observed that the growers' attorney bungled his oral argument time: "Thomas Compagne ... failed to exploit the numerous openings the government's argument had made for him. Instead, he resisted the justices' numerous invitations to present a coherent First Amendment theory and kept returning to the details of the fruit business, ignoring warnings that he was turning his constitutional challenge into a mundane administrative-law case in which the court had little reason to be interested." "High Court Hears Case about Commercial Speech." [http://www.nytimes.com/]. 3 December 1996.

tices an opportunity to question counsel about legal theories contained in the briefs and to raise points that individual justices deem important and that may not have been addressed in the briefs.

Occasionally, the Court will order reargument in a case. Usually such an order requires the parties to submit new briefs and to appear at another oral argument. Reargument will be ordered if members of the Court conclude that important points of law were not argued adequately or that other issues need to be addressed by counsel before the Court issues an opinion. Reargument tends to be ordered when the Court considers the case to be of especially great magnitude from the perspective of public policy. School desegregation, reapportionment, and abortion are modern examples of cases raising issues for which the justices have required reargument.

3. Conference on the Merits Following oral argument, a case is declared "submitted." This means that the case is ready for discussion among the justices at their conference, for a tentative vote on the outcome, and for the assignment of the case to a justice to draft an opinion.

Supreme Court conferences are one of the last vestiges of complete secrecy in American government. Since the mid-1950s, conferences have occurred on Friday. Although there are two large conference rooms in the Supreme Court building, the justices meet in a smaller, more private room adjacent to the chief justice's chambers. No one is allowed in the conference room except the justices, and no one knows exactly what occurs during the gatherings. Tradition has it that before taking their seats to discuss cases that have been submitted, the justices shake hands with one another to symbolize the collegial nature of their decision-making process. The chief justice presides at the conference.

Conventional wisdom among students of the Court was that discussion and voting at conference proceed in two stages. According to this account, the chief justice is the first to express an opinion about a case, with other justices speaking in order of seniority. Following discussion, the justices vote on the case in reverse order of seniority.[57] However, recent scholarship and remarks by Chief Justice William Rehnquist call this version into question.[58] It is now believed that the justices discuss and vote in a single process conducted in descending order of seniority after the chief justice. Conference discussions are more in the nature of "straw polls," revealing initial positions rather than final outcomes. These exchanges begin a process of bargaining, negotiating, and maneuvering that continues through the opinion-writing stage.

---

[57] Congressional Quarterly, *Guide to the U.S. Supreme Court* (Washington D.C.: Congressional Quarterly, 1979), p. 739.

[58] Robert C. Bradley, "What Is Actually Happening behind the Closed Doors?" 6 *Law, Courts, and Judicial Process Section Newsletter*, Washington, D.C.: American Political Science Association (Summer 1989): 1–2. Chief Justice Rehnquist made his remarks on "This Honorable Court," 2 pts., Public Broadcasting System, Washington, D.C., WETA, 1987, pt. 2. Compare Rehnquist, *The Supreme Court*, pp. 289–290.

A majority vote of the nine justices is required to decide a case. A tie vote, if only eight or six justices participate, has the effect of leaving the lower court's decision in force. A majority vote is also required in order for a case to have precedential value. On occasion, a majority of the justices will agree on the result in a case but will fail to agree on the reasoning leading to that outcome.[59] A plurality decision is one that commands a majority of votes on the result but lacks majority agreement on the particular reasoning supporting that result. Such opinions have been on the increase in recent years.[60] A justice who agrees with the outcome but who disagrees about the reasons supporting it, usually files a concurring opinion that explains the grounds on which he or she would decide the case. None of the opinions in a plurality decision has value as precedent. Lawyers and judges nonetheless cite plurality opinions in an attempt to build majority support for an opinion in a subsequent case. Plurality opinions can frustrate lower courts, which are required to apply Supreme Court doctrine, because they send ambiguous and sometimes conflicting signals. They are also signals to lawyers to relitigate an issue if they desire a clear rule of law and doctrinal development in an area.

4. Opinion Drafting and Circulating   Traditionally, a chief justice who votes with the majority determines which justice will write the opinion.[61] If the chief justice votes with the minority, the most senior associate justice voting with the majority makes the assignment. Opinion drafting can be a long, tedious process, particularly if the justices voting in the majority disagree with one another about the reasoning that supports their position. Because every justice's chambers is run like a private law firm, with highly controlled access, not much is known about the process of opinion writing or the role of law clerks.[62] Recent scholarship, however, appears to confirm what has long been suspected: the drafting process can be highly con-

---

[59] A famous example is *Youngstown Sheet and Tube Co. v. Sawyer*, 343 U.S. 579 (1952). While holding unconstitutional President Truman's seizure of steel mills during the Korean War, 6–3, all six justices voting to overrule Truman's action wrote opinions. Over time, the consensus among students of the Court is that Justice Jackson's concurring opinion in *Youngstown*, not Justice Black's opinion for the Court, is the most constitutionally influential.

[60] William Reynolds, *Judicial Process in a Nutshell* (St. Paul, MN: West Publishing Co., 1980), pp. 27–31. Cf. the letters from Chief Justice Rehnquist and Professor Henry J. Abraham published in 7 *Law, Courts, and Judicial Process Section Newsletter*, Washington D.C.: American Political Science Association (Fall 1989): 8–9.

[61] Bob Woodward and Scott Armstrong report that Chief Justice Warren Burger deviated from this practice on several occasions, most notably in the 1973 abortion cases *Doe v. Bolton*, 410 U.S. 179 (1973) and *Roe v. Wade*, 410 U.S. 113 (1973). See *The Brethren* (New York, NY: Simon & Schuster, 1979), pp. 170–189, 417–438.

[62] See Woodward and Armstrong, *The Brethren*; and Jennifer Conlin, "Decisions, Decisions: Supreme Court Clerks Share Heady Secrets, Midnight Oil, and a Year of Hidden Power," *The Washingtonian* (June 1990), p. 65. Compare John Bilyeu Oakley and Robert S. Thompson, *Law Clerks and the Judicial Process: Perceptions of the Qualities and Functions of Law Clerks in American Courts* (Berkeley, CA: University of California Press, 1980).

tentious, sometimes involving emotional exchanges among two or more of the justices.[63]

When the justice assigned to write the opinion has a draft ready for circulation, it is sent to other justices for discussion. Sometimes it is necessary to rewrite certain sections of an opinion or to change language in an opinion in order to retain votes for the proposed majority opinion. If a justice decides to switch sides after a draft opinion has been circulated, the entire writing process may have to begin again.

As much as members of the Court may strive for consensus, any justice has the prerogative to write a concurring or dissenting opinion. Concurring opinions explain the reasons for joining the majority but give other grounds for arriving at that conclusion. Dissenting opinions explain disagreement with the majority view and frequently state the minority view of what the law should be.

Before John Marshall became chief justice in 1801, the Supreme Court followed the English practice of issuing opinions *seriatim*; that is, each justice wrote an individual opinion about the case. Chief Justice Marshall thought that it was important for the Court to speak as an institution, with one voice. During his chief justiceship, very few of the Court's decisions contained dissenting or concurring opinions. Over the years, however, both dissenting and concurring have become Court traditions. Some justices, like Oliver Wendell Holmes Jr., have gone down in history as "great dissenters," whose minority views at the time eventually became the Court's majority position on an issue. Justice Stephen J. Field's dissents on the issue of property rights in *The Slaughter-House Cases*, 16 Wallace 36 (1873), and *Munn v. Illinois*, 94 U.S. 113 (1877),

---

[63] For example, see Bernard Schwartz, *The Unpublished Opinions of the Warren Court* (New York, NY: Oxford University Press, 1985), esp. Chapter 8, pp. 240–303.

Justice Oliver Wendell Holmes, reflecting on the High Bench to which he had been appointed eleven years previously, mused in a 1913 speech: "We are very quiet there, but it is the quiet of a storm center, as we all know." Holmes's characterization of the Supreme Court's precincts as "quiet" is an idealization that runs counter to both the findings of scholars and to news reports about current hard feelings among the justices. Compare Chief Justice William Howard Taft's metaphor: "The Supreme Court, a stormy petrel in the politics of the country." Also compare Justice Anthony Kennedy's recent observation: "[A]fter one of these cases is decided, the five in the majority ... don't have a lot of smiles and handshakes and high fives. There's a *quietness*. There's stillness, as you recognize, no matter which case, which position prevails, that there are long-term consequences that are the result of our verdict." Jeffrey Rosen, "Annals of Law: The Agonizer," *The New Yorker*, November 11, 1996, p. 89.

See also C. Herman Pritchett, "Divisions of Opinion among Justices of the U.S. Supreme Court," 35 *American Political Science Review* (1941): 890; Walter F. Murphy, *Elements of Judicial Strategy* (Chicago, IL: University of Chicago Press, 1964); Thomas G. Walker, Lee Epstein, and William J. Dixon, "On the Mysterious Decline of Consensual Norms in the United States Supreme Court," 50 *Journal of Politics* (1988): 361; and Howard Ball, *Hugo L. Black: Cold Steel Warrior* (New York, NY: Oxford University Press, 1996). Compare Phillip J. Cooper, *Battles on the Bench: Conflict inside the Supreme Court* (Lawrence, KS: University Press of Kansas, 1995).

On the well-known contemporary hard feelings between Justice Antonin Scalia and Justice Sandra O'Connor, see Donald Baer, "Now the Court of Less Resort," *U.S. News and World Report*, July 17, 1989; David Garrow, "The Rehnquist Years," *New York Times Magazine*, October 6, 1996, pp. 68–69; and Joan Biskupic, "Nothing Subtle about Scalia, the Combative Conservative." [http://www.washingtonpost.com]. 27 February 1997.

became the majority position in *Chicago, Milwaukee and St. Paul Railroad Company v. Minnesota*, 134 U.S. 418 (1890), less than twenty years later. (See Chapter 6, Volume I.) A more contemporary example is Justice William Rehnquist's prediction in his dissent in *Garcia v. San Antonio Metropolitan Transit Authority*, 469 U.S. 528 (1985), that the Court's view of states' rights relative to the power of the national government would soon change. Only ten years later, a triumphant Chief Justice Rehnquist, in *United States v. Lopez*, 514 U.S. 549 (1995), declared unconstitutional a federal statute on the ground that it usurped the states' police powers. (See Chapter 5, Volume I.)

Whether the presence of dissenting and concurring opinions undermines public and legal respect for the Supreme Court as an institution continues to be debated. Dissenting and concurring opinions deserve to be studied as carefully as majority opinions, however, because they often signal shifting coalitions on the bench, suggest alternative litigation strategies, or indicate the need to litigate again narrow questions of law to undermine or solidify a particular doctrine.

Like all American appellate courts, the Supreme Court is a "multimember, multi-issue body."[64] This means that the justices' decision-making process is collegial, even if not always congenial.[65] Political scientists have formulated several different approaches to explain the group interactions that produce judicial opinions.[66]

Small-group analysis focuses on the way in which interpersonal give-and-take shapes judicial opinions. Adherents to this methodology posit that appellate decisions can be explained by the way that judges seek to maximize their influence over decisions by employing, consciously or unconsciously, three interrelated strategies: persuasion on the merits; bargaining; and threatening sanctions such as withdrawing a vote, willingness to dissent or, in extreme instances, going public. The chief justice can be a particularly important player in this small-group decision-making process if that person has the intellectual skill, the appropriate personality, and the will to exert influence and become *primus inter pares* (first among equals).[67]

Other students of the Court argue that although small-group process clearly plays a role in shaping judicial outcomes, other methodologies provide more instructive explanations of appellate judges' collegial behavior. One of these approaches is attitude theory. Attitude theorists posit that appellate

---

[64] This is Sanford Levinson's description. Levinson, Sanford. [slevinson@mail.law.utexas.edu]. "REPLY: Court Bashing." In *LAWCOURTS*. [lawcourts-l@usc.edu]. 5 November 1996.

[65] See O'Brien, *Storm Center*, Chapters 4 and 5.

[66] This discussion of approaches to studying collegial decision making is derived from Carp and Stidham, *Judicial Process in America*, pp. 342–364. See also the exchange between professor Howard Gillman and professors Lee Epstein and Jack Knight on "The New Institutionalism" in 7, 8 *Law and Courts* (Winter 1996–97/Spring 1997): 6, 4; and Cornell W. Clayton and David A. May, "The Supreme Court, the Political System, and a New Institutionalism," paper delivered at the annual meeting of the Pacific Northwest Political Science Association, Coeur D'Alene, ID, October 18, 1997.

[67] See David J. Danelski, "The Influence of the Chief Justice in the Decisional Process," in *Courts, Judges, and Politics: An Introduction to the Judicial Process*, 4th ed., ed. Walter F. Murphy and C. Herman Pritchett (New York, NY: Random House, 1986).

judges view cases in broadly socioeconomic terms and decide them according to their personal values and attitudes. From this perspective, judges with similar attitudes join together in voting coalitions, termed blocs. Attitude theorists study the content of appellate judges' opinions to learn the values that shape them. Based on these content analyses, attitude theorists identify the level of cohesiveness among bloc members and assign mean indices of "interagreement" among judges making up the bloc. Cohesiveness and interagreement can run along political, social, and economic lines. For instance, Glendon Schubert analyzed Supreme Court voting blocs in terms of political liberals who support civil rights and liberties and political conservatives who support law enforcement.[68]

Fact-pattern analysis is another social science methodology for studying appellate judicial behavior. According to fact-pattern analysts, the particular circumstances of each case are the best explanatory variables of any given judicial outcome. "Facts" include more than the details of the specific dispute. The gender and race of the parties, their social status, and whether their attorneys are appointed or privately retained all figure in the eventual result. Key factors are weighted employing sophisticated mathematical equations that are machine processed to determine how different facts combine to affect judicial opinions.[69]

None of these methodologies completely explains appellate court decisions or decision making, and none of their practitioners claim that they do. Scholars in recent years have conceded that models representing a *combination* of various approaches "provide much greater explanatory power than any of them taken alone."[70] Supreme Court decisions, it appears, are shaped by "multiple forces" and "the intertwining of these forces."[71]

5. *Announcement of Decisions* The Court's announcement of opinions on Decision Day is one of its most dramatic and public functions. Decision Day can occur whenever a case has been decided, or it can await the end of the Court's Term, when many decisions are issued at once. When opinions in controversial cases are expected, Decision Day can take on a circus-like atmosphere as reporters, curious onlookers, and antagonistic groups jostle to learn what the Court has decided.

In the Court's early days, justices sometimes read their entire opinions to the waiting press and public on Decision Day. Today, members of the press receive printed copies of opinions contemporaneously with the justices' announcement. The justice who drafted the opinion is called on by the chief

---

[68] Glendon Schubert, *Judicial Policy Making* (Glenview, IL: Scott, Foresman, 1974).

[69] Fred Cort, "Quantitative Analysis of Fact-Patterns in Cases and Their Impact on Judicial Decisions," in *American Court Systems*, ed. Goldman and Austin Sarat, p. 351.

[70] Carp and Stidham, *Judicial Process in America*, p. 365. See, for example, Tracey E. George and Lee Epstein, "On the Nature of Supreme Court Decision Making," 86 *American Political Science Review* (1992): 323.

[71] Baum, *The Supreme Court*, p. 183.

justice to announce the result. Rarely does a justice read an entire majority opinion from the bench. Occasionally, however, in a controversial case, a dissenting justice will make a "bench speech" explaining why, in his or her view, the case has been decided incorrectly. Perhaps the most famous outburst from the bench was delivered by Justice James C. McReynolds as he read his dissent from one of the Gold Clause Cases in 1935.[72] Justice McReynolds opposed the Court's upholding of Congress's decision to end the gold standard as the measure of the value of the American currency. During his bench speech he exclaimed, "This is Nero at his worst. The Constitution is gone!" Thirty-six years later, Justice William Brennan dissented from a 1971 decision holding that some foreign-born American citizens could lose their citizenship if they violated a residency requirement enacted by Congress in 1952. In his bench speech, Justice Brennan read from his opinion: "Since the Court this Term has already downgraded citizens receiving public welfare, and citizens having the misfortune to be illegitimate, I suppose today's decision downgrading citizens born outside the United States should have been expected."[73]

CASELOAD OF THE SUPREME COURT

The work of the Supreme Court in the eighteenth century has been described as "leisurely," although the workload of the individual justices was heavier because of their responsibilities to serve on circuit courts as well as on the Supreme Court. Before 1801, only eighty-seven appellate cases appeared on the Court's docket.[74] When Chief Justice John Marshall took office that year, a mere fifty-six cases had been decided by the Court in its entire history.[75]

The Court's workload increased as the country changed, however. Factors including quickening commercial activity, mechanical innovations such as the steam engine, population growth, and the addition of new territories during the first half of the nineteenth century resulted in a steady increase in the number of cases coming to the Supreme Court. The Civil War and the rapid industrial expansion that followed caused sharp increases in the Court's docket later in the century. By the 1870s, the Court was encountering backlogs.[76] Congress sought to eliminate the congestion in 1891 by creating the intermediate circuit courts of appeal described earlier. The impact on the Supreme Court's caseload was dramatic but short-lived.[77] Conflicts between labor and management, governmental efforts to regulate the circumstances

---

[72] *Norman v. Baltimore & Ohio Railroad Company*, 294 U.S. 240 (1935).

[73] *Rogers v. Bellei*, 401 U.S. 815 (1971). For more examples, see Abraham, *The Judicial Process*, pp. 220–223.

[74] Julius Goebel Jr., *History of the Supreme Court of the United States, Vol. 1: Antecedents and Beginnings* (New York, NY: Macmillan, 1971), pp. 662–665.

[75] John P. Frank, *Cases and Materials on Constitutional Law* (Chicago, IL: Callaghan & Co., 1952), p. 29.

[76] O'Brien, *Storm Center*, pp. 179–184.

[77] William Howard Taft, "The Jurisdiction of the Supreme Court under the Act of February 13, 1925," 35 *Yale Law Journal* (1925): 1.

and conditions of industrial production, and World War I sent the Court's docket skyrocketing again, leaving the justices with such a backlog that cases not advanced out of their filing order could not be heard for more than a year after filing.[78] The Judiciary Act of 1925, which gave the Court discretion over whether to issue writs of certiorari, was one remedy. Virtual elimination of mandatory appeals was another.

In response to social movements organized since World War II on behalf of groups including blacks, women, welfare recipients, and the environment, Congress has enacted numerous laws that create rights and make them enforceable in federal courts.[79] The Supreme Court's docket has reflected the dramatic increase in federal litigation that followed. The Court has responded to its caseload increases in a variety of ways, including the "cert pool" discussed earlier, hiring more administrative staff, automating many procedures, and adopting rules that limit the length of briefs and the amount of time allocated to each side for oral arguments. Nonetheless, as noted previously in the chapter, the Court still must process between four thousand and five thousand applications for review each year. Currently, also as noted above, the Court grants full review in fewer than one hundred cases each year.[80]

SUGGESTIONS FOR STUDYING SUPREME COURT DECISIONS

The Supreme Court's opinions are the point of departure for understanding constitutional law. Of course, as suggested throughout this chapter, those decisions must be understood in their historical, political, and institutional contexts. There are three steps to understanding Supreme Court opinions: finding them, reading them, and analyzing them.

FINDING SUPREME COURT DECISIONS

Reports of Supreme Court Decisions Alexander Dallas, a Philadelphia lawyer, began publishing the decisions of the Supreme Court of Pennsylvania in the 1790s and began including Supreme Court decisions in 1793.[81] He argued several cases before the Court and used his reports to advertise his availability as an advocate.[82] In 1800, William Cranch, a judge on the District of Columbia circuit court, began publishing a set of reports that contained only Supreme Court decisions. He found the venture unprofitable.[83] In 1817, Chief

---

[78] Ibid., p. 2.

[79] Cass R. Sunstein, *After the Rights Revolution: Reconceiving the Regulatory State* (Cambridge, MA: Harvard University Press, 1990).

[80] See the figures on review granted discussed on p. 19.

[81] G. Edward White, *The History of the Supreme Court of the United States, Vol. 3: The Marshall Court and Cultural Change* (New York, NY: Macmillan, 1988), p. 385.

[82] Carl Swisher, *History of the Supreme Court of the United States, Vol. 5: The Taney Period* (New York, NY: Macmillan, 1974), p. 293.

[83] White, *The Marshall Court and Cultural Change*, p. 387.

Justice John Marshall lent his support to a bill that had been introduced in Congress a year before to hire the reporters of decisions as government employees and to require that they publish each year's decisions promptly.[84] With Marshall's support, the bill passed.

Beginning in 1789, reports of Supreme Court decisions were cited according to the name of the reporter: Alexander *Dallas* (1789–1800); William *Cranch* (1801–1815); Henry *Wheaton* (1816–1827); Richard *Peters* Jr. (1828–1842); Benjamin *Howard* (1843–1860); Jeremiah *Black* (1861–1862); John *Wallace* (1863–1874); and William *Otto* (1875 and 1882). Since 1875, the official reports of Supreme Court decisions have been by volume number (counting Alexander Dallas's first report as number one). The volume number is followed by the designation, "U.S.," the page number on which the opinion appears, and the year of the decision. The official citation for *United States v. Carolene Products Co.,* for example, is 304 U.S. 144 (1938). That means that the report of the decision is found in volume 304 of the *United States Reports,* beginning at page 144, and was decided in 1938.

Supreme Court decisions are also published in two commercial reporters, the *Lawyers' Edition* of the United States Supreme Court Reports published by the Lawyers' Cooperative Publishing Company, and the *Supreme Court Reporter,* published by the West Publishing Company. The *Lawyers' Edition* includes notes and annotations that assist attorneys with legal research. Cases in the *Lawyers' Edition* are cited by volume, the designation "L.Ed.," the page number on which the opinion appears, and the year the decision was rendered. In the *Lawyers' Edition, United States v. Carolene Products Co.* is reported as 82 L.Ed. 1234 (1938). The *Supreme Court Reporter* follows a similar format. Cases in that system are reported by volume, the designation "S.Ct.," the page number on which the opinion appears, and the year of the decision. *United States v. Carolene Products Co.* appears in the *Supreme Court Reporter* as 58 S.Ct. 778 (1938). Both the *Lawyers' Edition* and the *Supreme Court Reporter* provide cross-references to the United States Reports.

Supreme Court Decisions on the Internet   Supreme Court decisions are also available on the Internet. Following are directions to some useful Internet sites:

1. Cornell University's Legal Information Institute (LII) search page: [http://fatty.law.cornell.edu/]

   This archive service provides decisions from May 1990 to the present. From the LII site, it is possible to link to:

   a. the LII archive of 325 Selected Historic Decisions

   b. the FedWorld/FLITE archive of decisions from 1937–75

---

[84] William Crosskey, *Politics and the Constitution,* vol. 2 (Chicago, IL: University of Chicago Press, 1952), Appendix G, pp. 1243–1245.

c. "Oyez, Oyez, Oyez," [http://oyez.at.nwu.edu/oyez.html], which provides access to audio files of Supreme Court oral arguments (Access to these arguments requires RealAudio software.)

2. The LII Supreme Court Justices page: [http://www.law.cornell.edu/supct/justices/fullcourt.html]

   This service provides access to brief biographies of present Supreme Court justices, as well as the major opinions, concurrences, and dissents that each has written.

3. *USA Today* search vehicle: [http://167.8.29.8/plweb-cgi/ixacct.pl]

   Select "News" category, type "Supreme Court" in the search field, click on "Search," then click on "Supreme Court Index." This service provides news articles about the Supreme Court and copies of its most recent decisions.

4. "CourtTV" Library page: [http://www.courttv.com/library/supreme/]

   This service provides recent Supreme Court opinions and brief biographies of current justices. (The "CourtTV" home page is: [http://www.courttv.com])

Supreme Court opinions are also available on CD-ROM:

1. Law Office Information Systems (LOIS), currently contains *U.S. Reports* of eight to nine thousand (1949 to present) Supreme Court decisions.

2. HoweData contains all three hundred thousand of the Supreme Court's decisions on a single disk.

3. In addition to the *Supreme Court Reporter*, West Publishing offers all three hundred thousand Supreme Court decisions on multiple CD-ROM disks plus West and Lawyers' annotations and hard copies of advance sheets (opinions before they are bound and indexed in reporters).

Readers are encouraged to supplement their understanding of the Supreme Court by using any of the above sources to locate and read unedited decisions in addition to the cases in this text.

READING SUPREME COURT DECISIONS

At first glance, a Supreme Court opinion is an intimidating piece of writing. The prose is often dense and interspersed with obscure Latin phrases. Seemingly important statements are frequently interrupted by citations to other opinions. Older opinions pose a particular challenge. Writing styles in the nineteenth and early twentieth centuries were very different from today's straightforward approach, sometimes making it difficult to understand exactly what a justice meant. Although the going may be difficult at the outset, the effort of reading, dissecting, and understanding a Supreme Court opinion is richly rewarding. No one else's summary of an opinion can substitute for the understanding that comes from grappling with the original source.

An appellate opinion usually contains the following elements. First is a statement of the facts. Second is an explanation of the decisions of lower courts as the case worked its way to the Supreme Court. Third is a description of the legal issue or issues raised by the facts. Fourth is an explication of the law, which is an explanation of the constitutional provision or provisions at issue and why the Court construes that provision or provisions as it does. It is in this portion of an opinion that one usually finds the rule of law that contributes to the evolution of constitutional doctrine in a particular area. Fifth is an application of the law to the facts of the case, which explains the Court's holding. Finally, if necessary, the opinion responds to concurring or dissenting opinions in an effort to persuade the reader that the majority's approach is correct. It is common for these elements to appear in the order described. Sometimes, however, a justice will vary the order.

Concurring and dissenting opinions follow much the same format. However, it is not uncommon for concurrences and dissents to contain facts that the majority has ignored or discounted and that, in the author's view, are critical to the legal issues or should affect the outcome. Concurring and dissenting opinions invariably contain a statement of the rule of law that the justices adhering to that view believe the Court should have adopted. In addition, it is not uncommon for concurring and dissenting opinions to explain what those justices believe will be the mischievous consequences of the majority opinion.[85]

In this book, the facts and decisions by lower courts are provided in the *Setting*. The goal is to provide a more complete factual statement and more historical context than is usually provided in the opinion. The information in each *Setting* is derived from the briefs submitted by the parties to the Court and from contemporary and historical sources. Each *Setting* section also describes the history of the case from the time it was filed until it appeared before the Supreme Court.

The first step in reading a Supreme Court opinion is to thoroughly understand the facts and parties, why the parties were involved in the litigation, and what result and rule of law each hoped the Supreme Court would declare. The next step is to read and *reread* the Court's opinion. The purpose of the first reading is to get a general understanding of what the Court did and why, and whether there are concurring and dissenting opinions attacking the majority. The second reading requires a more detailed analysis of the elements of the opinion described above. It is useful during the second reading to consult the glossary of legal terms at the end of this text. The first two readings of an opinion are prelude to the third step, which is reducing the case to a short synopsis called a brief.

BRIEFING AND ANALYZING SUPREME COURT DECISIONS

A brief of an opinion is a decidedly different product than a legal brief submitted to the Supreme Court by the parties. The purpose of an opinion brief is to dissect a decision into its component parts. The process of preparing an opin-

---

[85] See Ruggero J. Aldisert, *Opinion Writing* (St. Paul, MN: West Publishing, 1990). Although meant to be a guide to judges about how to write opinions, it also provides insights to readers of judicial opinions.

ion brief helps to guarantee that the reader understands the Court's decision. Briefs subsequently provide a thumbnail sketch of doctrinal development in a particular subject field and should contain the following elements:

1. Name and case citation
2. Succinct summary of the facts
3. Statement of the constitutional question or questions before the Court
4. Legal holding or holdings; i.e., how the Court answered the legal question or questions
5. The rule of law announced in the majority opinion and which justice wrote it
6. A short summary of the reasoning that led to the holding and rule
7. A summary of the concurring and dissenting opinions, if any, and which justices wrote them
8. A short evaluation of the opinion:

   Does the opinion answer all the questions posed or does it leave some unanswered?

   Is the reasoning persuasive?

   Are there hidden assumptions in the opinion?

   Does the opinion encourage more litigation on the subject?

   What are the broader implications of the opinion in terms of political, social, or economic considerations?

The goal of a brief is to be just that—brief. With practice, briefs become relatively straightforward to prepare and are invaluable in helping to develop the critical reading and analytical skills required in the study of constitutional law.

Appendix: Litigation Stages on the Way to the Supreme Court

Unless a case falls into that very small category qualifying for the Supreme Court's original jurisdiction, it must pass through several stages at the state or federal level before reaching the Supreme Court. The vast majority of cases filed each year do not survive all the steps and hence do not reach the Supreme Court. If a case raises a constitutional question, in general terms the following steps would be involved on the way to Supreme Court review.[86] These steps reflect the fact that the American system of justice is adversary in nature, which has been described as a "fight theory" rather than a "truth theory" system of justice.[87]

---

[86] A more detailed description of this process is found in Susan M. Leeson and Bryan M. Johnston, *Ending It: Dispute Resolution in America* (Cincinnati, OH: Anderson Publishing Co., 1988), Chapter 2.

[87] Jerome Frank, *Courts on Trial* (New York, NY: Atheneum, 1969).

PRETRIAL ACTIVITY

This step involves a range of activities, including the filing of the case in the proper court, submission and resolution of any pretrial motions, determination of whether a judge or jury will serve as fact finder, and discovery, which is the process by which each side learns the factual basis of the opposing side's claims. The overwhelming number of cases filed in state and federal courts are resolved at the pretrial stage. Many are dismissed because of defects in the pleadings. Others are abandoned when parties discover they lack the proof required to prevail at trial. The vast majority of cases (both civil and criminal) are settled through negotiation. A settlement is binding and nonappealable. If the parties agree, even a case that raises constitutional issues can be settled through negotiation, but the resulting settlement establishes no precedent.

TRIAL

The function of a trial is to decide which side has presented legally sufficient evidence to allow it to prevail. A trial is the prototype of the adversary process. Each side presents its strongest evidence and witnesses to persuade the fact finder that it should prevail. Each also seeks to discredit the other side's evidence and its witnesses. The plaintiff in a civil case or the state in a criminal case always has the initial burden of coming forth with evidence to prove why the status quo should change.

A trial is a highly controlled process, governed by strict rules of evidence and procedure. Rarely do parties represent themselves at trial; the services of a legally trained advocate are usually sought because even minor, unintentional errors can be fatal to the case. Parties whose case involves constitutional questions must raise them at the trial level in order to preserve the right to litigate them on appeal and before the Supreme Court. It is rare that a trial judge will be willing to apply a new constitutional rule. Most trial judges understand their role as limited to applying existing constitutional rules.

Some cases enter the judicial system through administrative agency hearings. Typically, administrative hearings deal with statutory rather than constitutional issues, but questions of agency procedures can raise constitutional questions. Routes of appeal exist from agency judgments in both state and federal court systems. Section 702 of the federal Administrative Procedure Act specifically guarantees the right of judicial review of decisions of federal administrative agencies. Most state administrative procedure acts contain similar guarantees.

APPELLATE REVIEW

All court systems in the United States provide one level of appeal to parties who lose at trial, assuming they choose to pursue the appeal. On appeal, the loser at the trial level (known as the petitioner or appellant) seeks to have the appellate court overturn the decision of the trial court. The winner at trial (known as the respondent or appellee) defends the judgment below.

The appellate process differs dramatically from the trial process: there are no witnesses, testimony, or juries. Federal appellate judges typically sit in panels of three, where they review the written submissions, called briefs, prepared by each party's attorney. Briefs outline the factual or legal errors that are alleged to have occurred at trial and argue the appropriate legal remedy. After they have reviewed the briefs and the trial record, the judges hold oral argument. Each side is given a specified amount of time to argue its case and to respond to questions from the judges. After oral argument the case is deemed submitted for decision and no additional information about the case is permitted. Although they differ from trial proceedings, appellate proceedings remain adversarial in nature. The parties continue to disagree about the legal significance of the facts that were established at trial.

Appellate judges apply various standards of review when scrutinizing cases. These standards of review determine the level of inspection the judges give to the trial record. If a case raises factual questions, for example, appellate judges tend to defer to trial court determinations and require the appellant to show that the trial court committed clear error. If a case raises a question of law, on the other hand, as is always true in constitutional litigation, appellate courts review for errors of law or in some instances apply a *de novo* standard of review, which allows the appellate court to review the entire record of the trial and the correctness of the legal determinations made during trial. Appellate judges typically issue written opinions explaining the standard of review they apply in a case, their judgment affirming or reversing the trial court, and the reasons for their holding or holdings.

Most state court systems provide for a second appeal, but give the state's highest appellate court (commonly, but not always, called the state supreme court) substantial discretion over which cases they will hear. Only the party that lost at the first level of appeal may pursue the second level of appeal in state courts.

CHAPTER 2

FREEDOM OF RELIGION

ESTABLISHMENT OF RELIGION

Engel v. Vitale
370 U.S. 421 (1962)

SETTING

The Act of Supremacy of 1534 made the episcopal and liturgical Church of England the official or "established" church of the realm and made the English monarch the supreme head of that church. Catholics, other Protestant sects, and nonbelievers soon assumed the stance of nonconformists or dissenters against the Church of England. Religious dissent was not tolerated, however. Under the Test Act of 1673, for example, religious nonconformists and Catholics were banned from civil and military office. Thousands fled their homeland in the name of religious liberty and came to the New World. Ironically, for many of the religious refugees, freedom from the Church of England meant freedom to practice their own faith. To ensure their ability to do so, many American colonists adopted official or "established" churches as part of their colonial governing structures. Only four of the original thirteen colonies—Delaware, Pennsylvania, Rhode Island, and New Jersey—did not establish a state religion. For many years before the American Revolution, intolerance and persecution of religious nonconformists was the norm in Congregational New England, Dutch Reformed New Netherlands, Catholic Massachusetts, and Anglican Virginia, just as it had been in England. Notably, only the states of Rhode Island and Maryland embraced religious diversity.

During the 1640s and 1650s, a debate between colonial clergymen John Cotton and Roger Williams exemplified the disagreement among Americans about the proper relationship between church and state. Cotton defended the establishment of the Congregational Church in New England on the ground that an official state religion was necessary to protect against corruption in worship. Williams, who had founded religiously free colonies in Rhode Island, argued that the "Garden of the Church" needed to remain separate from the "Wilderness of the World" so that the wilderness would not engulf the garden. During the Revolutionary period, Williams' views gained ascendency. In 1776,

Virginia adopted religious tolerance as part of its Declaration of Rights. Pennsylvania guaranteed all faiths the right to worship publicly. Massachusetts followed Pennsylvania's lead in 1780.

By the time of the Constitutional Convention, it was unthinkable to most Americans that the United States would have an established religion. In 1789, James Madison's original proposal for a Bill of Rights included the following provision:

> The civil rights of none shall be abridged on account of religious belief or worship, nor shall any national religion be established, nor shall the full and equal rights of conscience be in any manner, or on any pretext, infringed.

By the time the First Amendment had cleared a conference committee of the House and Senate, the religion clauses read: "Congress shall make no law respecting an establishment of religion, or prohibiting the free exercise thereof."

The Constitution thus contains two clauses relating to religion—the Establishment Clause and the Free Exercise Clause. As Justice Felix Frankfurter observed, "any attempt to formulate a bright-line distinction" between establishment and free exercise is "bound to founder" because the two terms reflect "largely overlapping areas of concern." *McGowan v. Maryland*, 366 U.S. 420 (1961) (Frankfurter, J., concurring). Nonetheless, litigation over the two clauses has proceeded on different tracks. In Establishment Clause litigation, the debate has consistently focused on how literally the words "establishment of religion" should be construed. Clearly, the Clause prohibits designation of a national church. But what does the prohibition against the establishment of religion require in the context of issues like prayer in public schools, state aid to religious institutions, and public displays of religious symbols like creches and menorahs?

In 1802, President Thomas Jefferson framed the debate over the meaning of the Establishment Clause when he wrote a letter to a group of Baptists in Danbury, Connecticut, declaring that the purpose of the First Amendment was to erect a "wall of separation between Church and State." While many Americans agreed with Jefferson—and still do—many others have taken exception to Jefferson's "wall of separation" metaphor. Another view of the First Amendment is that, although it prohibits the establishment of a national religion, it was not intended to denigrate the important role that religion plays in American life or to prevent government from accommodating religion. From this perspective, the First Amendment permits the accommodation of religion and the narrow focus of constitutional interpretation should be how much accommodation is permissible. In its simplest terms, constitutional litigation over the Establishment Clause has been an effort to have the Supreme Court declare how high the wall of separation between church and state should be in the context of state and federal statutes that attempt to accommodate religion.

Historians offer a variety of reasons for the fact that the Supreme Court was able to avoid Establishment Clause litigation until well into the twentieth century. For whatever reason, it was not until 1947, in *Everson v. Board of Education*, 330 U.S. 1, that the Court declared that the Establishment and Free

Exercise Clauses of the First Amendment are applicable against the states via the Due Process Clause of the Fourteenth Amendment. Significantly, the *Everson* Court rejected an absolutist interpretation of the Establishment Clause and held instead that the Establishment Clause requires only that government be neutral in its relations with religious and nonreligious groups.

Confident that *Everson* was a signal that nondenominational prayer in public schools was consistent with the Court's requirement of governmental neutrality toward religion, the New York State Board of Regents composed and recommended that at the beginning of every school day, New York school children should recite the following prayer:

> Almighty God, we acknowledge our dependence upon Thee, and we beg Thy blessings upon us, our parents, our teachers and our country.

Ten parents, including Steven I. Engel, whose children attended the Union Free School District, Number Nine, in New Hyde Park, New York, filed suit in the Supreme Court of New York (that state's trial court), seeking a declaration that the compelled recitation of the Regents' Prayer violated the Establishment Clause. William J. Vitale, Chairman of the Board of Education, was named as the defendant. The supreme court held that the prayer did not violate the Establishment Clause. The Appellate Division and the Court of Appeals of New York affirmed, but declared that no pupil could be compelled to join in it if the student or the student's parents objected. The Supreme Court of the United States granted Engel's petition for a writ of certiorari.

HIGHLIGHTS OF SUPREME COURT ARGUMENTS

BRIEF FOR ENGEL

♦ The Regents' Prayer is sectarian and denominational because it includes a declaration of belief in the existence of God. It also reflects a belief in a set form of worship and belief in the practice of asking God's blessing on behalf of the worshiper. The word "religion" in the First Amendment means neither more nor less than a single religious belief, such as the belief in the existence of God.

♦ The Regents' Prayer is not part of any national "tradition" or "heritage." It was composed by laypersons who are officials, acting in their official capacity.

♦ Our forefathers made a complete division between religious and civil authority. Two great drives are constantly in motion to bridge that division: introducing religious education and observances into public schools, and obtaining public funds to aid and support private religious schools. The First Amendment prohibits both.

♦ The statement of belief of the Board of Regents makes it clear that the purpose and intended effect of the prayer is to recommend prayer in public schools. Making prayer a daily procedure in the public schools promotes belief in God. Under the Constitution, taxpayers are not to be required to subsidize the teaching or practice of religion.

AMICUS CURIAE BRIEFS SUPPORTING ENGEL

American Ethical Union; American Jewish Committee and Anti-Defamation League of B'Nai B'rith; Synagogue Council of America; National Community Relations Advisory Council.

BRIEF FOR VITALE

♦ The intent of the First Amendment was to prohibit the establishment of a state religion. The amendment was not intended to prohibit the growth and development of a religious state. The Constitution merely puts denominational religion in its proper place outside of public aid or support.

♦ Recognition of Almighty God in public prayer is an integral part of our national heritage. A few seconds of voluntary prayer in the schools, with an acknowledgment of dependence on Almighty God, is consistent with our heritage of securing the blessings of freedom that are recognized in both the federal and state constitutions as having emanated from Almighty God. Voluntarily recited, the prayer represents a reasonable method of developing an appreciation and understanding of the basic principles of our national heritage.

♦ The drafters of the First Amendment did not envision or intend the idea of a wall of separation of church and state with government hostile to religion. Such hostility would be at war with our national tradition.

AMICUS CURIAE BRIEF SUPPORTING VITALE

Board of Regents of the University of the State of New York; joint brief of the attorneys general of Arkansas, Florida, Georgia, Idaho, Indiana, Kansas, Louisiana, Maryland, Mississippi, New Hampshire, New Jersey, New Mexico, North Dakota, Rhode Island, South Carolina, South Dakota, and Texas.

SUPREME COURT DECISION: 6–1

(Frankfurter and White, J.J., did not participate.)

BLACK, J.

... [W]e think that the constitutional prohibition against laws respecting an establishment of religion must at least mean that in this country it is no part of the business of government to compose official prayers for any group of the American people to recite as a part of a religious program carried on by government.

It is a matter of history that this very practice of establishing governmentally composed prayers for religious services was one of the reasons which caused many of our early colonists to leave England and seek religious freedom in America....

It is an unfortunate fact of history that when some of the very groups which had most strenuously opposed the established Church of England found themselves sufficiently in control of colonial governments in this country to write their own prayers into law, they passed laws making their own religion the official religion of their respective colonies. Indeed, as late as the time of the Revolutionary War, there were established churches in at least eight of the thirteen former colonies and established religions in at least four of the other five. But the successful Revolution against English political domination was shortly followed by intense opposition to the practice of establishing religion by law....

By the time of the adoption of the Constitution, our history shows that there was a widespread awareness among many Americans of the dangers of a union of Church and State. These people knew, some of them from bitter personal experience, that one of the greatest dangers to the freedom of the individual to worship in his own way lay in the Government's placing its official stamp of approval upon one particular kind of prayer or one particular form of religious services. They knew the anguish, hardship and bitter strife that could come when zealous religious groups struggled with one another to obtain the Government's stamp of approval from each King, Queen, or Protector that came to temporary power. The Constitution was intended to avert a part of this danger by leaving the government of this country in the hands of the people rather than in the hands of any monarch. But this safeguard was not enough. Our Founders were no more willing to let the content of their prayers and their privilege of praying whenever they pleased be influenced by the ballot box than they were to let these vital matters of personal conscience depend upon the succession of monarchs. The First Amendment was added to the Constitution to stand as a guarantee that neither the power nor the prestige of the Federal Government would be used to control, support or influence the kinds of prayer the American people can say—that the people's religions must not be subjected to the pressures of government for change each time a new political adminis-

tration is elected to office. Under that Amendment's prohibition against governmental establishment of religion, as reinforced by the provisions of the Fourteenth Amendment, government in this country, be it state or federal, is without power to prescribe by law any particular form of prayer which is to be used as an official prayer in carrying on any program of governmentally sponsored religious activity.

There can be no doubt that New York's state prayer program officially establishes the religious beliefs embodied in the Regents' prayer.... Neither the fact that the prayer may be denominationally neutral nor the fact that its observance on the part of the students is voluntary can serve to free it from the limitations of the Establishment Clause, as it might from the Free Exercise Clause, of the First Amendment, both of which are operative against the States by virtue of the Fourteenth Amendment. Although these two clauses may in certain instances overlap, they forbid two quite different kinds of governmental encroachment upon religious freedom. The Establishment Clause, unlike the Free Exercise Clause, does not depend upon any showing of direct governmental compulsion and is violated by the enactment of laws which establish an official religion whether those laws operate directly to coerce nonobserving individuals or not. This is not to say, of course, that laws officially prescribing a particular form of religious worship do not involve coercion of such individuals. When the power, prestige and financial support of government is placed behind a particular religious belief, the indirect coercive pressure upon religious minorities to conform to the prevailing officially approved religion is plain. But the purposes underlying the Establishment Clause go much further than that. Its first and most immediate purpose rested on the belief that a union of government and religion tends to destroy government and to degrade religion.... The Establishment Clause thus stands as an expression of principle on the part of the Founders of our Constitution that religion is too personal, too sacred, too holy, to permit its "unhallowed perversion" by a civil magistrate. Another purpose of the Establishment Clause rested upon an awareness of the historical fact that governmentally established religions and religious persecutions go hand in hand.... It was in large part to get completely away from ... systematic religious persecution that the Founders brought into being our Nation, our Constitution, and our Bill of Rights with its prohibition against any governmental establishment of religion. The New York laws officially prescribing the Regents' prayer are inconsistent both with the purposes of the Establishment Clause and with the Establishment Clause itself.

It has been argued that to apply the Constitution in such a way as to prohibit state laws respecting an establishment of religious services in public schools is to indicate a hostility toward religion or toward prayer. Nothing, of course, could be more wrong.... [T]he First Amendment, which tried to put an end to governmental control of religion and of prayer, was not written to destroy either.... [I]t was written to quiet well-justified fears ... that governments of the past had shackled men's tongues to make them speak only the religious thoughts that government wanted them to speak and to pray only to the God that government wanted them to pray to. It is neither sacrilegious nor antireligious to say that each separate government in this country should stay out of the business of writing or sanctioning official

prayers and leave that purely religious function to the people themselves and to those the people choose to look to for religious guidance.

It is true that New York's establishment of its Regents' prayer as an officially approved religious doctrine of that State does not amount to a total establishment of one particular religious sect to the exclusion of all others—that, indeed, the governmental endorsement of that prayer seems relatively insignificant when compared to the governmental encroachments upon religion which were commonplace 200 years ago. To those who may subscribe to the view that because the Regents' official prayer is so brief and general there can be no danger to religious freedom in its governmental establishment, however, it may be appropriate to say in the words of James Madison, the author of the First Amendment:

> [I]t is proper to take alarm at the first experiment on our liberties.... Who does not see that the same authority which can establish Christianity, in exclusion of all other Religions, may establish with the same ease any particular sect of Christians, in exclusion of all other Sects? That the same authority which can force a citizen to contribute three pence only of his property for the support of any one establishment, may force him to conform to any other establishment in all cases whatsoever?

The judgment of the Court of Appeals of New York is reversed and the cause remanded for further proceedings not inconsistent with this opinion.

Reversed and remanded.

DOUGLAS, J., CONCURRING

... The question presented by this case ... is whether New York oversteps the bounds when it finances a religious exercise....

In New York the teacher who leads in prayer is on the public payroll; and the time she takes seems minuscule as compared with the salaries appropriated by state legislatures and Congress for chaplains to conduct prayers in the legislative halls. Only a bare fraction of the teacher's time is given to reciting this short 22-word prayer, about the same amount of time that our Crier spends announcing the opening of our sessions and offering a prayer for this Court. Yet for me the principle is the same, no matter how briefly the prayer is said, for in each of the instances given the person praying is a public official on the public payroll, performing a religious exercise in a governmental institution....

Mr. Justice Rutledge stated in [his *Everson v. Board of Education*, 330 U.S. 1 (1947)] dissent what I think is durable First Amendment philosophy:

> Public money devoted to payment of religious costs, educational or other, brings the quest for more. It brings too the struggle of sect against sect for the larger share or for any. Here one by numbers alone will benefit most, there another. That is precisely the history of societies which have had an established religion and dissident groups. It is the very thing Jefferson and Madison experienced and sought to guard against, whether in its blunt or in its more screened forms....

STEWART, J., DISSENTING

... With all respect, I think the Court has misapplied a great constitutional principle. I cannot see how an "official religion" is established by letting those who want to say a prayer say it. On the contrary, I think that to deny the wish of these school children to join in reciting this prayer is to deny them the opportunity of sharing in the spiritual heritage of our Nation....

At the opening of each day's Session of this Court we stand, while one of our officials invokes the protection of God. Since the days of John Marshall our Crier has said, "God save the United States and this Honorable Court." Both the Senate and the House of Representatives open their daily Sessions with prayer. Each of our Presidents, from George Washington to John F. Kennedy, has upon assuming his Office asked the protection and help of God....

I do not believe that this Court, or the Congress, or the President has by the actions and practices I have mentioned established an "official religion" in violation of the Constitution. And I do not believe the State of New York has done so in this case. What each has done has been to recognize and to follow the deeply entrenched and highly cherished spiritual traditions of our Nation—traditions which come down to us from those who almost two hundred years ago avowed their "firm Reliance on the Protection of divine Providence" when they proclaimed the freedom and independence of this brave new world....

I dissent.

COMMENT

Bernard Schwartz reports that:

> The decision in the school prayer case [*Engel*] was met by a storm of protest. The mail attacking it was the largest in the Court's history. Warren himself later wrote, "I vividly remember one bold newspaper headline, 'Court outlaws God.' Many religious leaders in this same spirit condemned the Court." Church leaders, according to the *New York Times*, expressed

"shock and regret." "The decision," proclaimed Cardinal McIntyre in Los Angeles, "is positively shocking and scandalizing to one of American blood and principles." "It is like taking a star and stripe off the flag," complained a Methodist bishop in Georgia. Billy Graham announced that he was "shocked and disappointed." "Followed to its logical conclusion," declared the well-known preacher, "prayers cannot be said in Congress, chaplains will be taken from the armed forces, and the President will not place his hand on the Bible when he takes the oath of office." (Bernard Schwartz, *Super Chief: Earl Warren and His Supreme Court—A Judicial Biography* [New York, NY: New York University Press, 1983], p. 441)

QUESTIONS

1. In light of the Court's declaration about neutrality in *Everson*, on what ground did the majority in *Engel* find constitutional fault with the Board of Regents' nondenominational prayer? What principle of church-state relations informed the dissent in *Engel*? How do the majority and dissenting opinions in *Engel* respond to the debate about whether there should be a wall of separation between church and state and how high it should be?

2. As noted in the *Comment*, critics excoriated the *Engel* decision as being antireligious. Many religious groups had the same concern about the absence of any mention of Christianity in the Constitution. In a letter, written at the end of 1789, to concerned Presbyterians of Massachusetts and New Hampshire, George Washington said:

   > And here, I am persuaded, you will permit me to observe, that *the path of true piety is so plain, as to require but little political direction.*
   >   *To this consideration we ought to ascribe the absence of any regulation respecting religion from the Magna Charta of our country.* To the guidance of the ministers of the Gospel, this important object is, perhaps, more properly committed. It will be your care to instruct the ignorant and to reclaim the devious; And in the progress of morality and science, to which our Government will give every furtherance, we may confidently expect the advancement of true religion, and the completion of our happiness. (Quoted in Anson Phelps Stokes, *Church and State in the United States*, vol. I [New York, NY: Harper, 1950], p. 537; emphasis in original)

   Is *Engel* consistent with Washington's views? What factors might explain why Washington's views have not prevailed in public opinion?

3. Following *Engel*, many members of Congress introduced constitutional amendments to overturn the decision and allow prayer in public schools. During House Judiciary Committee hearings held in 1964, representatives of many organized religions—including the American Baptist Convention, the American Jewish Congress, the American Lutheran Church, the Episcopal Church, the National Council of Churches of Christ, the Synagogue Council of America, and the United Presbyterian Church—testified against such amendments. What might motivate such religious groups to oppose prayer in public schools?

4. A year after *Engel*, political opposition to the Court's decision showed no signs of abating. Nonetheless, in *Abington Township School District v. Schempp*, 374 U.S. 203 (1963), decided with *Murray v. Curlett*, the Court by an 8–1 vote struck down laws that required Bible verses to be read in the public schools or allowed use of the Lord's Prayer in opening exercises in public schools. The majority opinion described at length the importance of religion in American life, but explained that under the principles announced in *Engel v. Vitale*, Bible reading and school prayer violate the Establishment Clause. Critics of *Abington* charged that it showed the Court's hostility—not neutrality—toward religion. In 1980, in *Stone v. Graham*, 449 U.S. 39, the Court struck down a Kentucky statute that required a copy of the Ten Commandments to be posted on the walls of each public school classroom. Chief Justice Burger and Justices Rehnquist, Blackmun, and Stewart dissented.

In light of the political firestorm unleashed by *Engel*, were the Court's decisions in *Abington* and *Murray* examples of judicial independence or judicial arrogance? What factors might account for four dissents in *Stone*?

ESTABLISHMENT OF RELIGION

Lemon v. Kurtzman
403 U.S. 602 (1971)

SETTING

Constitutional scholars generally agree that protecting religious liberty was the ultimate goal of the First Amendment's Establishment Clause. Consensus breaks down, however, over the question of whether the clause was intended to separate religion from government altogether. Public aid to religious schools is one policy area where this issue has been fought out. The contentious history of direct government aid to the established Anglican Church in England rendered government grants to religion suspect in this country.

The Supreme Court first addressed the government assistance question when it weighed the validity of public aid to sectarian schools in *Everson v. Board of Education*, 330 U.S. 1, in 1947. In *Everson*, the Court upheld a New Jersey statute that authorized the expenditure of public funds to bus children to religious schools. The Court's opinion gave the impression that government could aid sectarian schools without violating the Establishment Clause; the only question was *how* that aid could be given.

For almost twenty years after *Everson*, governmental aid to parochial schools was relatively noncontroversial. Attention focused instead on issues like school prayer and Bible reading in public schools. During the 1960s, however, at least four factors contributed to making government aid to religious schools a topic of political and legal interest.

First, a financial crisis endangered the nation's schools. Mushrooming enrollments and increasing educational expenses rendered all school funding, public and private, increasingly problematic. In states with large parochial school enrollments many officials supported state governmental support (sometimes called "parochiaid") because they realized parochial school closings would put even greater fiscal pressures on public schools. With the support of President Nixon and many members of Congress, several states, including New York, Pennsylvania, and Ohio, adopted "purchase of service" statutes authorizing direct aid to parochial schools. These statutes provided teacher salary subsidies, tuition reimbursements, and tuition tax credits.

The growing vitality of religious education in the United States was the second factor contributing to the revival of debates about government aid to religious schools. Increasing numbers of parents turned to private education for their children as a way of reinforcing the moral and religious values they believed were being undermined by the social and cultural turmoil of the 1960s. As taxpayers obliged to support public schools, these parents turned to state legislatures with demands to use a portion of their tax dollars to subsidize their children's private education.

The third factor that rekindled controversy over governmental aid to parochial schools was the push toward private education, both secular and religious. Declining test scores in important areas like reading, mathematics, science, and history led many to question American elementary and secondary public educational standards. Not all critics of public education committed themselves to reforming public schools. Instead, some critics lobbied for the right of parents as "consumers" to choose private or parochial education for their children. To facilitate parental choice, some lobbied for the state to provide assistance to non-public schools, tax credits to parents, or direct aid to children.

Fourth, in 1965 the Supreme Court held constitutional a New York law that required local school boards to "loan" (in practice, such loans were permanent) textbooks on secular subjects to all nonprofit private schools in their districts. *Board of Education of Central School District No. 1 v. Allen*, 392 U.S. 236 (1968). Justice White's opinion in *Allen* encouraged those who advocated greater governmental support of the nation's many church-sponsored schools. Justice White's opinion also furthered the *Everson* approach of accommodating—that is, facilitating reasonable relations between—church and state. White summarized the two tests the Supreme Court had devised for determining the constitutionality of state aid:

> [W]hat are the purpose and primary effect of the enactment? If either is the advancement or inhibition of religion then the enactment exceeds the scope of legislative power as circumscribed by the Constitution.

In 1970, Chief Justice Warren Burger added a third prong to *Allen*'s "purpose and effect" tests. In *Walz v. Tax Commission*, 397 U.S. 664, the Court held that public aid to churches must also avoid excessive government entanglement with religion. Applying all three tests, Chief Justice Burger concluded that a New York statute granting property tax exemptions to church-owned land used only for religious purposes did not violate the Establishment Clause.

The following year, the Court consolidated the *Allen* and *Walz* tests to resolve a challenge to a law authorizing direct aid to parochial schools. The Pennsylvania Nonpublic Elementary and Secondary Education Act of 1968 authorized the State Superintendent of Public Instruction to contract for the purchase of secular educational services from nonpublic schools in Pennsylvania. "Secular" services were defined as courses in mathematics, modern foreign languages, physical science, and physical education. The superintendent was required to approve the textbooks and materials used in courses taught by parochial school teachers, and no payment was to be made for a course containing any subject matter expressing religious beliefs. The act provided that all revenues up to $10 million and half of all proceeds over $10 million, derived from state harness and horse racing, were to be used to finance operations under the act. In December 1968, Superintendent of Public Instruction David Kurtzman issued rules and regulations to implement the act.

In June 1969, Alton Lemon, whose child attended a public school in Pennsylvania, filed suit in the U.S. District Court for the Eastern District of Pennsylvania, naming Superintendent Kurtzman, State Treasurer Grace Sloan, and seven of the nonpublic schools due to receive monies from the state as defendants. The suit claimed that the legislation violated the Establishment and Free Exercise Clauses of the First Amendment and the Equal Protection Clause of the Fourteenth Amendment. Lemon requested that a three-judge panel be convened to declare the Pennsylvania law unconstitutional and that it enjoin Kurtzman from approving payment of any funds to the seven nonpublic schools. Lemon was joined in the suit by two other individual plaintiffs and five "institutional" plaintiffs: the Pennsylvania State Education Association, the Pennsylvania Conference of the National Association for the Advancement of Colored People, the American Civil Liberties Union of Pennsylvania, the Pennsylvania Council of Churches, the Pennsylvania Jewish Community Relations Conference, and Americans United for Separation of Church and State.

A divided three-judge district court panel dismissed the complaint, finding the act constitutional on its face, with adequate safeguards to prevent the establishment of religion. The court also ruled that the plaintiffs failed to state a cause of action on the Free Exercise claim. Lemon and the other plaintiffs appealed to the Supreme Court of the United States.

The case was consolidated with two cases from Rhode Island (*Earley v. Di Censo* and *Robinson v. Di Censo*) challenging that state's 1969 Salary Supplement Act. The Salary Supplement Act provided a 15 percent salary supplement to teachers in nonpublic schools at which the average per-pupil expenditure on secular education was below the average in public schools.

HIGHLIGHTS OF SUPREME COURT ARGUMENTS

BRIEF FOR LEMON

◆ Legislation must have a secular purpose and primary effect that neither advances nor inhibits religion. The primary purpose behind Pennsylvania's purchase of secular educational services is to help meet the financial needs of religious schools in the state. The effect of the act is to give particular assistance to Catholic schools.

◆ Government may not employ religious means to serve secular interests, however legitimate they may be, without demonstrating that nonreligious means will not suffice.

◆ The act creates an impermissible interdependence between religious institutions and the state: Religious schools take on a portion of the duty mandated in the Pennsylvania constitution to maintain a public school system, and the state in turn supports the parochial system. Such interdependence threatens the independence of each.

◆ The act violates the Fourteenth Amendment because it authorizes payment of tax funds to parochial schools that discriminate on the basis of race or religion in admissions and employment policies.

AMICUS CURIAE BRIEFS SUPPORTING LEMON

The American Association of School Administrators; United Americans for Public Schools; American Jewish Committee; Protestants and Other Americans United for Separation of Church and State; Center for Law and Education at Harvard University; and the Connecticut State Conference of Branches of the National Association for the Advancement of Colored People.

BRIEF FOR KURTZMAN

◆ None of the plaintiffs has standing to sue because no party alleges the requisite "personal stake in the outcome of the controversy." The Fourteenth Amendment challenge asks the Court to strike down the act because it might be administered in an unconstitutional manner sometime in the future.

◆ The Pennsylvania act does not subsidize parochial schools in providing for the purchase of limited secular educational services. The legislative history of the act demonstrates that its purpose is to benefit public schools in Pennsylvania. According to Supreme Court precedent, the First Amendment is not violated if parochial schools receive an incidental benefit from legislation the purpose of which is secular.

◆ The statute does not violate the First Amendment because it improves the quality of secular education for all recipients in the state. None of the parochial schools receives payment until after the secular educational services have been delivered.

◆ The statute does not violate the Free Exercise Clause because it does not operate against anyone in the practice of their religion.

AMICUS CURIAE BRIEFS SUPPORTING KURTZMAN

United States; The attorney general of Ohio; City of Philadelphia; the School District of Philadelphia; the cities Pittsburgh, Erie, and Scranton, Pennsylvania; the National Catholic Educational Association; the National Association of Independent Schools, Inc.; the Pennsylvania State AFL-CIO; Long Island Conference of Religious Elementary and Secondary School Administrators; the National Jewish Commission on Law and Public Affairs; Citizens for Educational Freedom; Polish American Congress, Inc.; and twelve individuals.

SUPREME COURT DECISION: 7–1

(Marshall, J., did not participate.)

BURGER, C.J.

… The language of the Religion Clauses of the First Amendment is at best opaque, particularly when compared with the other portions of the Amendment…. In the absence of precisely stated constitutional prohibitions, we must draw lines with reference to the three main evils against which the Establishment Clause was intended to afford protection: "sponsorship, financial support, and active involvement of the sovereign in religious activity."

Every analysis in this area must begin with consideration of the cumulative criteria developed by the Court over many years. Three such tests may be gleaned from our cases. First, the statute must have a secular legislative purpose; second, its principal or primary effect must be one that neither advances nor inhibits religion; finally, the statute must not foster "an excessive entanglement with religion."

Inquiry into the legislative purposes of the Pennsylvania and Rhode Island statutes affords no basis for a conclusion that the legislative intent was to advance religion. On the contrary, the statutes themselves clearly state that they are intended to enhance the quality of the secular education in all schools covered by the compulsory attendance laws. There is no reason to believe the legislatures meant anything else. A State always has a legitimate concern for maintaining minimum standards in all schools it allows to operate….

The two legislatures, however, have also recognized that church-related elementary and secondary schools have a significant religious mission and that a substantial portion of their activities is religiously oriented. They have therefore sought to create statutory restrictions designed to guarantee the separation between secular and religious educational functions and to ensure that State financial aid supports only the former. All these provisions are precautions taken in candid recognition that these programs approached, even if they did not intrude upon, the forbidden areas under the Religion Clauses. We need not decide whether these legislative precautions restrict the principal or primary effect of the programs to the point where they do not offend the Religion Clauses, for we conclude that the cumulative impact of the entire relationship arising under the statutes in each State involves excessive entanglement between government and religion….

Our prior holdings do not call for total separation between church and state; total separation is not possible in an absolute sense. Some relationship between government and religious organizations is inevitable. Fire inspections, building and zoning regulations, and state requirements under compulsory school-attendance laws are examples of necessary and permissible contacts.... Judicial caveats against entanglement must recognize that the line of separation, far from being a "wall," is a blurred, indistinct, and variable barrier depending on all the circumstances of a particular relationship....

In order to determine whether the government entanglement with religion is excessive, we must examine the character and purposes of the institutions that are benefited, the nature of the aid that the State provides, and the resulting relationship between the government and the religious authority.... Here we find that both statutes foster an impermissible degree of entanglement....

The Pennsylvania statute ... provides state aid to church-related schools for teachers' salaries.... [T]he very restrictions and surveillance necessary to ensure that teachers play a strictly nonideological role give rise to entanglements between church and state. The Pennsylvania statute, like that of Rhode Island, fosters this kind of relationship. Reimbursement is not only limited to courses offered in the public schools and materials approved by state officials, but the statute excludes "any subject matter expressing religious worship of any sect." In addition, schools seeking reimbursement must maintain accounting procedures that require the State to establish the cost of the secular as distinguished from the religious instruction.

The Pennsylvania statute, moreover, has the further defect of providing state financial aid directly to the church-related school....

A broader base of entanglement of yet a different character is presented by the divi-

sive political potential of these state programs. In a community where such a large number of pupils are served by church-related schools, it can be assumed that state assistance will entail considerable political activity. Partisans of parochial schools, understandably concerned with rising costs and sincerely dedicated to both the religious and secular educational missions of their schools, will inevitably champion this cause and promote political action to achieve their goals. Those who oppose state aid, whether for constitutional, religious, or fiscal reasons, will inevitably respond and employ all of the usual political campaign techniques to prevail....

Ordinarily political debate and division, however vigorous or even partisan, are normal and healthy manifestations of our democratic system of government, but political division along religious lines was one of the principal evils against which the First Amendment was intended to protect....

The potential for political divisiveness related to religious belief and practice is aggravated in these two statutory programs by the need for continuing annual appropriations and the likelihood of larger and larger demands as costs and populations grow....

[N]othing we have said can be construed to disparage the role of church-related elementary and secondary schools in our national life. Their contribution has been and is enormous.... The merit and benefits of these schools, however, are not the issue before us in these cases. The sole question is whether state aid to these schools can be squared with the dictates of the Religion Clauses....

The Constitution decrees that religion must be a private matter for the individual, the family, and the institutions of private choice, and that while some involvement and entanglement are inevitable, lines must be drawn....

The judgment of the Pennsylvania District Court ... is reversed, and the case is remanded for further proceedings consistent with this opinion.

DOUGLAS AND BLACK, J.J., CONCURRING

... [W]e have gradually edged into a situation where vast amounts of public funds are supplied each year to sectarian schools.... Sectarian instruction, in which, of course, a State may not indulge, can take place in a course on Shakespeare or in one on mathematics. No matter what the curriculum offers, the question is, what is *taught?* We deal not with evil teachers but with zealous ones who may use any opportunity to indoctrinate a class.

It is well known that everything taught in most parochial schools is taught with the ultimate goal of religious education....

In my view the taxpayers' forced contribution to the parochial schools in the present cases violates the First Amendment.

BRENNAN, J., CONCURRING

... The common ingredient of the three prongs of the test set forth at the outset of this opinion is whether the statutes involve government in the "essentially religious activities" of religious institutions. My analysis of the operation, purposes, and effects of these statutes leads me inescapably to the conclusion that they do impermissibly involve the States ... with the "essentially religious activities" of sectarian educational institutions. More specifically, ... I think each government uses "essentially religious means to

serve governmental ends, where secular means would suffice." This Nation long ago committed itself to primary reliance upon publicly supported public education to serve its important goals in secular education. Our religious diversity gave strong impetus to that commitment....

I, therefore, agree that the two state statutes that focus primarily on providing public funds to sectarian schools are unconstitutional....

WHITE, J., DISSENTING

... I cannot hold that the First Amendment forbids an agreement between the school and the State that the state funds would be used only to teach secular subjects.

I do agree, however, that the complaint [in the Pennsylvania case] should not have been dismissed for failure to state a cause of action. Although it did not specifically allege that the schools involved mixed religious teaching with secular subjects, the complaint did allege that the schools were operated to fulfill religious purposes and one of the legal theories stated in the complaint was that the Pennsylvania Act "finances and participates in the blending of sectarian and secular instruction." At trial under this complaint, evidence showing such a blend in a course supported by state funds would appear to be admissible and, if credited, would establish financing of religious instruction by the State. Hence, I would reverse the judgment of the District Court and remand the case for trial, thereby holding the Pennsylvania legislation valid on its face but leaving open the question of its validity as applied to the particular facts of this case....

COMMENTS

1. On the same day the Court decided *Lemon*, it ruled by a 5–4 vote that federal construction grants to four church-related colleges and universities in Connecticut (for construction of two library buildings, a

science building, a music, drama, and arts building, and a language laboratory) did not violate the Establishment Clause of the First Amendment. *Tilton v. Richardson*, 403 U.S. 672 (1971). The majority distinguished *Tilton* from *Lemon* on three grounds. First, there was less danger that religion would permeate the area of secular education since religious indoctrination was not a substantial purpose of the church-related colleges; second, the facilities were religiously neutral and hence required less governmental surveillance; and third, the government aid was a one-time, single-purpose construction grant with only minimal need for inspection.

2. Following the Supreme Court's decision in *Lemon*, the district court enjoined all payments under the program for services rendered after the decision, but permitted Pennsylvania to reimburse the schools for services rendered before June 28, 1971, the date of the decision. Lemon and the other plaintiffs in the first case challenged the district court's order. In a 5–3 decision (Justice Marshall again not participating), the Supreme Court affirmed the district court. *Lemon v. Kurtzman*, 411 U.S. 192 (1973). The Supreme Court held that the parochial schools had relied in good faith on the state statute and that they could not have anticipated the first *Lemon* holding. Therefore, the district court did not abuse its discretion in permitting the payments. Justices Douglas, Brennan, and Stewart in dissent claimed that the issue of the retroactivity of the decisions in *Lemon I* went "to the very core of the integrity of the judicial process.... The happenstance of litigation is no criterion for dispensing these unconstitutional subsidies."

3. On August 27, 1971, the Pennsylvania state legislature adopted a new parochial school aid law entitled, "Parent Reimbursement Act for Nonpublic Education." That act provided funds to reimburse parents for a portion of tuition expenses incurred in sending their children to nonpublic schools. In *Sloan v. Lemon*, 413 U.S. 825 (1973), the Supreme Court, by a 6–3 vote, declared the 1971 law unconstitutional because "at bottom its intended consequence is to preserve and support religion-oriented institutions."

QUESTIONS

1. What theory of the relationship between church and state does the *Lemon* test reflect? Is it accurate to characterize the test as an attempt to reconcile the "wall of separation" and "accommodationist" theories of the Establishment Clause? If so, is the test workable?

2. Does the *Lemon* test require courts to engage in exhaustive factual findings in order to resolve Establishment Clause cases? If so, might it not easily become what historian Melvin Urofsky calls a "signpost often pointed in different directions" based on judicial fact finding (Melvin I. Urofsky, *A March of Liberty* [New York, NY: Knopf, 1988], p.

924)? Could a legislature misrepresent the purpose of a statute merely to survive analysis under the *Lemon* test?

3. Barbara A. Perry and M. Glenn Abernathy identify three arguments offered in defense of state aid to parochial education: "(1) as a matter of public policy, the government should promote a strong private school sector in order to encourage diversity of training and educational choice; (2) from the standpoint of equity, those who support both private and public schools, but who do not use or burden the public school system, should receive governmental assistance to at least some extent; and (3) in order to protect against the potentially substantial costs of increased public school enrollment occasioned by large-scale failures of financially beset private schools, some governmental assistance should be provided" (*Civil Liberties under the Constitution*, 6th ed. [Columbia, SC: University of South Carolina Press, 1993], p. 179).

Are these arguments completely at odds with *Lemon*?

COMMENT

The following cases are examples of the Court's serpentine application of *Lemon* between 1973 and 1992 when it decided *Lee v. Weisman*, 505 U.S. 577 (1992), the next excerpted case.

Case: *Levitt v. Committee for Public Education*, 413 U.S. 472 (1973)
Vote: 8–1
Decision: New York's per-pupil allotments to reimburse nonpublic schools for expenses associated with administering tests, maintaining pupil enrollment and health records, and preparing various other reports to the state, has the impermissible effect of aiding religion and therefore violates the second prong of the *Lemon* test. No means are available to assure that internally prepared tests are free of religious instruction and avoid inculcating students in the religious precepts of the sponsoring church.

Case: *Committee for Public Education v. Nyquist*, 413 U.S. 756 (1973)
Vote: 6–3
Decision: New York's education and tax laws providing grants to nonpublic schools for maintenance and repairs of facilities and providing tuition reimbursements and income tax benefits to parents of children attending nonpublic schools have the effect of aiding religion in violation of the second prong of the *Lemon* test. The maintenance and repair provisions have the effect of subsidizing and advancing the religious mission of sectarian schools. Tuition reimbursements provide financial support for nonpublic schools. Income tax benefits to parents of children attending nonpublic schools impermissibly advance the sectarian activities of religious schools.

Case: *Meek v. Pittenger*, 421 U.S. 349 (1975)
Vote: 6–3
Decision: A Pennsylvania law allowing "auxiliary services" (including testing, counseling, psychological services, speech and hearing therapy, and

services for exceptional, remedial, or disadvantaged students) to nonpublic elementary and secondary schools in the state meeting the compulsory attendance requirements is an impermissible aid to religion under the second prong of the *Lemon* test. However, the loan of textbooks acceptable for use in the public schools is constitutional because it merely extends to all children the benefits of a general program to lend books free of charge. The financial beneficiaries of the loans are parents and children, not schools.

Case: *Wolman v. Walter*, 433 U.S. 229 (1977)

Vote: 5–4

Decision: An Ohio statute authorizing the state to provide nonpublic school pupils with books, standardized testing and scoring, diagnostic services, and therapeutic and remedial services does not impermissibly advance religion. Funding of field trips whose timing and frequency are controlled by the nonpublic schools, however, is an impermissible direct aid to sectarian education. The close supervision of nonpublic school teachers necessary to ensure secular use of field trip funds would involve excessive entanglement.

Case: *Committee for Public Education and Religious Liberty v. Regan*, 444 U.S. 646 (1980)

Vote: 5–4

Decision: A New York statute directing payment to nonpublic schools of the costs incurred in complying with state-mandated requirements such as testing, reporting, and record keeping does not violate the Establishment Clause. An auditing procedure guarantees that only costs of providing secular services are reimbursed out of state funds, distinguishing this statute from the one found unconstitutional in *Levitt v. Committee for Public Education*.

Case: *Stone v. Graham*, 449 U.S. 39 (1980)

Vote: 5–4

Decision: A Kentucky statute requiring that a copy of the Ten Commandments, purchased with private funds, be posted on the wall of every public school classroom throughout the state, violates the Establishment Clause. The statute has no secular purpose and is plainly religious in nature.

Case: *Larson v. Valente*, 456 U.S. 228 (1982)

Vote: 5–4

Decision: A Minnesota statute regulating charitable solicitations that excepts some, but not all, religions from its registration and reporting requirements violates the second prong of the *Lemon* test. The provision excepting religious groups that solicit more than 50 percent of their contributions from members "clearly grants denominational preferences of the sort consistently and firmly deprecated in our precedents." The law also is invalid under the excessive entanglement prong of the *Lemon* test. For the first time, the Court applied strict scrutiny in an Establishment Clause case, holding that the law was not "closely fitted to further the interest that it assertedly serves."

Case: *Mueller v. Allen*, 463 U.S. 388 (1982)

Vote: 5–4

Decision: A Minnesota statute allowing state taxpayers to deduct from their state income taxes expenses incurred in providing tuition, textbooks, and transportation for children attending nonpublic elementary or secondary schools satisfies all three prongs of the *Lemon* test. The fact that state officials must determine whether particular textbooks qualify for the tax deduction is an insufficient basis for finding impermissible entanglement.

Case: *Lynch v. Donnelly*, 465 U.S. 104 (1984)

Vote: 5–4

Decision: A Pawtucket, Rhode Island, Christmas display, owned by a nonprofit organization and erected annually on public land, which includes a nativity scene along with a Santa Claus house, a Christmas tree, and a banner reading "Seasons Greetings," does not violate the Establishment Clause. The Establishment Clause mandates accommodation with religion, not simply tolerance of it, and *Lemon* represents a more hospitable balance between church and state than the Jeffersonian metaphor of a wall of separation.

Case: *Wallace v. Jaffree*, 472 U.S. 38 (1985)

Vote: 6–3

Decision: An Alabama statute authorizing a period of silence "for meditation or voluntary prayer" was motivated by the sole purpose of expressing the state's endorsement of prayer activities. Therefore, the statute is unconstitutional under the first prong of the *Lemon* test.

Case: *Grand Rapids School District v. Ball*, 473 U.S. 373 (1985)

Vote: 5–4

Decision: School district programs offering classes to nonpublic school students at public expense, in classrooms located in and leased from the nonpublic schools, and taught by nonpublic school teachers, have the primary effect of advancing religion generally and therefore violate the Establishment Clause.

Case: *Aguilar v. Felton*, 473 U.S. 402 (1985)

Vote: 5–4

Decision: A New York City program similar in many respects to that challenged in *Ball* contains critical elements of entanglement proscribed in *Lemon* and *Meek v. Pittenger*. The New York City program contains a pervasive system for monitoring any religious content in the remedial education offered at parochial schools. It thereby further entangles the state excessively in religion, in violation of the Establishment Clause.

Case: *Witters v. Washington Department of Services for the Blind*, 474 U.S. 481 (1986)

Vote: 9–0

Decision: State rehabilitation aid payments to a blind student for education at a Christian college to become a pastor, missionary, or youth director does not advance religion in a manner inconsistent with the Establishment Clause. The rehabilitation aid is provided directly to the student who transmits it to the educational institution of choice.

Case: *Edwards v. Aguillard*, 482 U.S. 578 (1987)

Vote: 7–2

Decision: A Louisiana statute that requires public school teachers who teach evolution to give equal time to teaching "creation-science" has the impermissible purpose of advancing religion and therefore violates the first prong of the *Lemon* test.

Case: *Bowen v. Kendrick*, 487 U.S. 589 (1988)

Vote: 5–4

Decision: The Adolescent Family Life Act authorizing federal grants to private, charitable, and religious groups that undertake educational, counseling, and care programs related to teenage pregnancy, does not violate the Establishment Clause. The statute has a valid secular purpose and, although its purpose coincides with religious values, the effect of advocating religion is incidental and remote. There is no excessive entanglement with religion because grantees under the program are not pervasively sectarian in the same sense as parochial schools.

ESTABLISHMENT OF RELIGION

Lee v. Weisman
505 U.S. 577 (1992)

SETTING

As the summary of cases following *Lemon v. Kurtzman* demonstrate, the three-pronged Establishment Clause test announced in 1971 has proved controversial and difficult to apply consistently or predictably. By the 1991 Term, three associate justices (White, O'Connor, and Scalia) plus Chief Justice Rehnquist had registered various degrees of discontent with the *Lemon* test. The Court also had three new members (Kennedy, Souter, and Thomas) who many observers assumed would voice their own objections. A challenge to the Providence, Rhode Island, devotional practice of permitting invocations and benedictions at junior and senior high school graduations gave the Court an opportunity to reconsider its Establishment Clause jurisprudence and the *Lemon* test.

The Providence, Rhode Island, School Committee and the superintendent of schools sponsored graduation ceremonies in the public junior high and high schools. Their practice was to permit, but not require, school principals to include religious invocations and benedictions in those ceremonies. Between 1985 and 1989, four of five high schools and two of six middle schools elected to have invocations and benedictions as part of their graduation ceremonies. The devotional expressions were written or delivered by members of the local clergy. Participating clergy were given guidelines for the ceremonies prepared by the National Conference of Christians and Jews. The guidelines stressed that invocations and benedictions should be nondenominational. Attendance at graduation ceremonies was voluntary.

Deborah Weisman was graduated from Nathan Bishop Middle School, a public junior high school in Providence, in June 1989. Teachers at the school recommended to Principal Robert E. Lee that Rabbi Leslie Gutterman of the Temple Beth El of Providence be invited to deliver the invocation and benediction at the school's graduation ceremony.

Four days before the ceremony, Deborah's father, Daniel Weisman, sought a temporary restraining order from the U.S. District Court for the District of Rhode Island to prevent inclusion of invocations and benedictions at the graduation ceremonies of the city's public junior high and high schools. Weisman claimed that the prayers violated the Establishment Clause of the First Amendment. Claiming lack of time to adequately consider the request, the court refused to issue the order.

Deborah and her family attended the graduation ceremony nonetheless. Rabbi Gutterman gave the following invocation:

> God of the Free, Hope of the Brave:
> For the legacy of America where diversity is celebrated and the rights of minorities are protected, we thank You. May these young men and women grow up to enrich it.
> For the liberty of America, we thank You. May these new graduates grow up to guard it.
> For the political process of America in which all its citizens may participate, for its court system where all can seek justice, we thank You. May those we honor this morning always turn to it in trust.
> For the destiny of America we thank You. May the graduates of Nathan Bishop Middle School so live that they might help to share it.
> May our aspirations for our country and for these young people, who are hope for the future, be richly fulfilled. Amen.

Rabbi Gutterman's benediction similarly invoked the name of God and ended with the word, "Amen."

In July 1989, Daniel Weisman returned to the U.S. District Court seeking a permanent injunction against Principal Lee and other school officials to prevent religious invocations and benedictions in future graduation ceremonies at the Providence public junior high and high schools. The district court granted the injunction. The court characterized both the invocation and benediction as "examples of elegant simplicity, thoughtful content, and sincere citizenship." The court, nonetheless, held that both the invocation and the benediction violated the second prong of the *Lemon* test. According to the court, the practice impermissibly advanced religion "by creating an identification of school with a deity," because the school committee effectively "endorsed religion in general by authorizing an appeal to a deity in public school graduation ceremonies." The court emphasized that Rabbi Gutterman's invocation and benediction were unconstitutional solely because they made reference to a deity. Had he confined himself to a secular inspirational message, said the court, "the Establishment Clause would not be implicated." Lee appealed.

A panel of the Court of Appeals for the First Circuit affirmed by a 2–1 vote. The Supreme Court of the United States granted Lee's petition for a writ of certiorari.

HIGHLIGHTS OF SUPREME COURT ARGUMENTS

BRIEF FOR LEE

◆ The graduation prayers at issue in this case did not violate the Establishment Clause because they did not involve government coercion of religious conformity. Governmental coercion is what philosophers like John Locke and revolutionary leaders like Thomas Jefferson and James Madison sought to avoid. They distinguished between government coercion relating to religion and government expression or persuasion concerning religion.

◆ The drafters of the First Amendment did not conceive that constitutional protection against government establishments of religion would forbid the expression of religious opinions by government or its officials. As this Court has recognized, the nation's tradition of official ceremonial expressions of religious beliefs dates back to its inception.

◆ Speech alone cannot amount to the kind of governmental coercion of religious choice that implicates Establishment Clause. Further, attendance at the Nathan Bishop Middle School's graduation ceremony was entirely voluntary. Desire to attend commencement exercises does not amount to government compulsion to attend the event. Those who were present were not required to participate in any religious ceremony or activity.

◆ *Lemon* does not call for total separation between church and state. The courts below failed to employ the broader analysis mandated by this Court for application of the *Lemon* standards. The extremely limited role of religion in graduation exercises in the form of the kind of invocation and benediction involved at the Nathan Bishop Middle School does not constitute a government endorsement of religion as understood in this Court's cases.

AMICUS CURIAE BRIEFS SUPPORTING LEE

United States; The Rutherford Institute; Concerned Women for America and Free Speech Advocates; Board of Education of Alpine (Utah) School District; joint brief of Specialty Research Associates, Inc. and Free Congress Research and Education Foundation; National Jewish Commission on Law and Public Affairs; National School Boards Association; Institute in Basic Life Principles, and State of Delaware.

BRIEF FOR WEISMAN

◆ This Court has repeatedly rejected the argument that there can be no "establishment" of religion in the absence of coercion. All parties have stipulated that this is a case about prayer; this Court has consistently described prayer as an inherently religious activity.

◆ By incorporating a prayer into a major public school ceremony, the school committee violated all three prongs of the *Lemon* test. The unavoidable message to children is that school officials support and encourage participation in a religious exercise.

◆ This case is about school prayer, not the use of prayer during presidential inaugurations, congressional sessions, and proclamations of national days of thanksgiving. The Court has consistently recognized that the introduction of religion into public schools raises special and severe problems under the Establishment Clause.

AMICUS CURIAE BRIEFS SUPPORTING WEISMAN

Americans for Religious Liberty; National Education Association; National PTA and National Association of Elementary School Principals; American Civil Liberties Union of Utah; joint brief of the American Jewish Congress, Baptist Joint Committee on Public Affairs, American Jewish Committee, National Council of Churches of Christ in the U.S.A., Anti-Defamation League of B'Nai B'rith, General Conference of the Seventh-Day Adventists, People for the American Way, National Jewish Community Relations Advisory Council, New York Committee on Public Education and Religious Liberty, and James E. Andrews (Clerk of the General Assembly of the Presbyterian Church U.S.A.).

SUPREME COURT DECISION: 5–4

KENNEDY, J.

... The question before us is whether including clerical members who offer prayers as part of the official school graduation ceremony is consistent with the Religion Clauses of the First Amendment, provisions the Fourteenth Amendment makes applicable with full force to the States and their school districts....

We can decide the case without reconsidering the general constitutional framework by which public schools' efforts to accommodate religion are measured. Thus we do not accept the invitation of petitioners and *amicus* the United States to reconsider our decision in *Lemon v. Kurtzman.* The government involvement with religious activity in this case is pervasive, to the point of creating a state-sponsored and state-directed religious exercise in a public school. Conducting this formal religious observance conflicts with settled rules pertaining to prayer exercises for students, and that suffices to determine the question before us.

The principle that government may accommodate the free exercise of religion does not supersede the fundamental limitations imposed by the Establishment Clause. It is beyond dispute that, at a minimum, the Constitution guarantees that government may not coerce anyone to support or participate in religion or its exercise, or otherwise act in a way which "establishes a [state] religion or religious faith, or tends to do so." *Lynch v. Donnelly,* 465 U.S. 668 (1984) at 678. The State's involvement in the school prayers challenged today violates these central principles.

That involvement is as troubling as it is undenied. A school official, the principal, decided that an invocation and a benediction should be given; this is a choice attributable to the State, and from a constitutional perspective it is as if a state statute decreed that prayers must occur. The principal chose the religious participant, here a rabbi, and that choice is also attributable to the State. The reason for the choice of a rabbi is not disclosed by the record, but the potential for divisiveness over the choice of a particular member of the clergy to conduct the ceremony is apparent.

Divisiveness, of course, can attend any state decision respecting religions, and neither its existence nor its potential necessarily invalidates the State's attempts to accommodate religion in all cases. The potential for divisiveness is of particular relevance here though, because it centers around an overt religious exercise in a secondary school environment where ... subtle coercive pressures exist and where the student had no real alternative which would have allowed her to avoid the fact or appearance of participation.

The State's role did not end with the decision to include a prayer and with the choice of clergyman. Principal Lee provided Rabbi Gutterman with a copy of the "Guidelines for Civic Occasions," and advised him that his prayers should be nonsectarian. Through these means the principal directed and controlled the content of the prayer. Even if the only sanction for ignoring the instructions were that the rabbi would not be invited back, we think no religious representative who valued his or her continued reputation and effectiveness in the community would incur the State's displeasure in this regard. It is a cornerstone principle of our Establishment Clause jurisprudence that "it is no part of the business of government to compose official prayers for any group of the American people to recite as a part of a religious program carried on by government," and that is what the school officials attempted to do....

The First Amendment's Religion Clauses mean that religious beliefs and religious expression are too precious to be either proscribed or prescribed by the State. The design of the Constitution is that preservation and transmission of religious beliefs and worship is a responsibility and a choice committed to the private sphere, which itself is promised to pursue that mission. It must not be forgotten then, that while concern must be given to define the protection granted to an objector or a dissenting nonbeliever, these same Clauses exist to protect religion from government interference....

The degree of school involvement here made it clear that the graduation prayers bore the imprint of the State and thus put school-age children who objected in an untenable position. We turn our attention now to consider the position of the students, both those who desired the prayer and she who did not....

What to most believers may seem nothing more than a reasonable request that the nonbeliever respect their religious practices, in a school context may appear to the nonbeliever or dissenter to be an attempt to employ the machinery of the State to enforce a religious orthodoxy.

We need not look beyond the circumstances of this case to see the phenomenon at work. The undeniable fact is that the school district's supervision and control of a high school graduation ceremony places public pressure, as well as peer pressure, on attending students to stand as a group or, at least, maintain respectful silence during the Invocation and Benediction. This pressure, though subtle and indirect, can be as real as any overt compulsion. Of course, in our culture standing or remaining silent can signify adherence to a view or simple respect for the views of others. And no doubt some persons who have no desire to join a prayer have little objection to standing as a sign of respect for those who do. But for the dissenter of high school age, who has a reasonable perception that she is being forced by the State to pray in a manner her conscience will not allow, the injury is no less real. There can be no doubt that for many, if not most, of the students at the graduation, the act of standing or remaining silent was an expression of participation in the Rabbi's prayer. That was the very point of the religious exercise. It is of little comfort to a dissenter, then, to be told that for her the act of standing or remaining in silence signifies mere respect, rather than participation. What matters is that, given our social conventions, a reasonable dissenter in this milieu could believe that the group exercise signified her own participation or approval of it.

Finding no violation under these circumstances would place objectors in the dilemma of participating, with all that implies, or protesting. We do not address whether that choice is acceptable if the affected citizens are mature adults, but we think the State may not, consistent with the Establishment Clause, place primary and secondary school children in this position. Research in psychology supports the common assumption that adolescents are often susceptible to pressure from their peers toward conformity, and that the influence is strongest in matters of social convention. To recognize that the choice imposed by the State constitutes an unacceptable constraint only acknowledges that the government may no more use social pressure to enforce orthodoxy than it may use more direct means....

There was a stipulation in the District Court that attendance at graduation and promotional ceremonies is voluntary. Petitioners and the United States, as *amicus*, made this a center point of the case, arguing that the option of not attending the graduation excuses any inducement or coercion in the ceremony itself. The argument lacks all persuasion. Law reaches past formalism. And to say a teenage student has a real choice not to attend her high school graduation is formalistic in the extreme.... Everyone knows that in our society and in our culture high school graduation is one of life's most significant occasions. A school rule which excuses attendance is beside the point. Attendance may not be required by official decree, yet it is apparent that a student is not free to absent herself from the graduation exercise in any real sense of the term "voluntary," for absence would require forfeiture of those intangible benefits which have motivated the student through youth and all her high school years. Graduation is a time for family and those closest to the student to celebrate success and express mutual wishes of gratitude and respect, all to the end of impressing upon the young person the role that it is his or her right and duty to assume in the community and all of its diverse parts....

The Government's argument gives insufficient recognition to the real conflict of conscience faced by the young student. The essence of the Government's position is that with regard to a civic, social occasion of this importance it is the objector, not the majority, who must take unilateral and private action to avoid compromising religious scruples, here by electing to miss the graduation exercise. This turns conventional First Amendment analysis on its head. It is a tenet of the First Amendment that the State cannot require one of its citizens to forfeit his or her rights and benefits as the price of resisting conformance to state-sponsored religious practice....

We do not hold that every state action implicating religion is invalid if one or a few citizens find it offensive. People may take offense at all manners of religious as well as nonreligious messages, but offense alone does not in every case show a violation. We know too that sometimes to endure social isolation or even anger may be the price of conscience or nonconformity. But, by any reading of our cases, the conformity required of the student in this case was too high an exaction to withstand the test of the Establishment Clause....

Our society would be less than true to its heritage if it lacked abiding concern for the values of its young people, and we acknowledge the profound belief of adherents to many faiths that there must be a place in the student's life for precepts of a morality higher than the law we today enforce. We express no hostility to those aspirations, nor would our oath permit us to do so. A relentless and all-pervasive attempt to exclude religion from every aspect of public life could itself become inconsistent with the Constitution.... We recognize that, at graduation time and throughout the course of the educational process, there will be instances when religious values, religious practices, and religious persons will have some interaction with the public schools and their students. But these matters, often questions of accommodation of religion, are not before us....

For the reasons we have stated, the judgment of the Court of Appeals is
Affirmed.

BLACKMUN, STEVENS, AND O'CONNOR, J.J., CONCURRING

Nearly half a century of review and refinement of Establishment Clause jurisprudence has distilled one clear understanding: Government may neither promote nor affiliate itself with any religious doctrine or organization, nor may it obtrude itself in the internal affairs of any religious institution....

I join the Court's opinion today because I find nothing in it inconsistent with the essential precepts of the Establishment Clause developed in our precedents. The Court holds that the graduation prayer is unconstitutional because the State "in effect required participation in a religious exercise." Although our precedents make clear that proof of government coercion is not necessary to prove an Establishment Clause violation, it is sufficient. Government pressure to participate in a religious activity is an obvious indication that the government is endorsing or promoting religion.

But it is not enough that the government restrain from compelling religious practices; it must not engage in them either. The Court repeatedly has recognized that a violation of the Establishment Clause is not predicated on coercion....

I remain convinced that our jurisprudence is not misguided....

SOUTER, STEVENS, AND O'CONNOR, J.J., CONCURRING

I join the whole of the Court's opinion, and fully agree that prayers at public school graduation ceremonies indirectly coerce religious observance. I write separately nonetheless on two issues of Establishment Clause analysis that underlie my independent resolution of this case: whether the Clause applies to governmental practices that do not favor one religion or denomination over others, and whether state coercion of religious conformity, over and above state endorsement of religious exercise or belief, is a necessary element of an Establishment Clause violation....

Forty-five years ago, this Court announced a basic principle of constitutional law from which it has not strayed: the Establishment Clause forbids not only state practices that "aid one religion ... or prefer one religion over another," but also those that "aid all religions." *Everson v.*

Board of Education of Ewing, 330 U.S. 1 (1947). Today we reaffirm that principle, holding that the Establishment Clause forbids state-sponsored prayers in public school settings no matter now nondenominational the prayers may be. In barring the State from sponsoring generically Theistic prayers where it could not sponsor sectarian ones, we hold true to a line of precedent from which there is no adequate historical [cause] to depart....

Some have challenged [decisional] precedent by reading the Establishment Clause to permit "non-preferential" state promotion of religion. The challengers argue that, as originally understood by the Framers, "[t]he Establishment Clause did not require government neutrality between religion and irreligion nor did it prohibit the Federal Government from providing nondiscriminatory aid to religion." *Wallace v. Jaffree* [472 U.S. 38 (1985)]. While a case has been made for this position, it is not so convincing as to warrant reconsideration of our settled law; indeed, I find in the history of the Clause's textual development a more powerful argument supporting the Court's jurisprudence following *Everson*....

While these considerations are, for me, sufficient to reject the nonpreferentialist position, one further concern animates my judgment. In many contexts, including this one, nonpreferentialism requires some distinction between "sectarian" religious practice and those that would be, by some measure, ecumenical enough to pass Establishment Clause muster. Simply by requiring the enquiry, nonpreferentialists invite the courts to engage in comparative theology. I can hardly imagine a subject less amenable to the competence of the federal judiciary, or more deliberately to be avoided where possible....

Our precedents may not always have drawn perfectly straight lines. They simply cannot, however, support the position that a showing of coercion is necessary to a successful Establishment Clause claim....

Petitioners argue from the political setting in which the Establishment Clause was framed, and from the Framers' own political practices following ratification, that government may constitutionally endorse religion so long as it does not coerce religious conformity. The setting and the practices warrant canvassing, but while they yield some evidence for petitioners' argument, they do not reveal the degree of consensus in early constitutional thought that would raise a threat to *stare decisis* by challenging the presumption that the Establishment Clause adds something to the Free Exercise Clause that follows it....

While the Establishment Clause's concept of neutrality is not self-revealing, our recent cases have invested it with specific content: the state may not favor or endorse either religion generally over nonreligion or one religion over others. This principle against favoritism and endorsement has become the foundation of Establishment Clause jurisprudence, ensuring that religious belief is irrelevant to every citizen's standing in the political community. Our aspiration to religious liberty, embodied in the First Amendment, permits no other standard.

That government must remain neutral in matters of religion does not foreclose it from ever taking religion into account. The State may "accommodate" the free exercise of religion by relieving people from generally applicable rules that interfere with their religious callings....

Whatever else may define the scope of accommodation permissible under the Establishment Clause, one requirement is clear: accommodation must lift a discernible burden on the free exercise of religion. Concern for the position of religious individuals in the modern regulatory state cannot justify official solicitude for a religious practice unburdened by general rules; such gratuitous largesse would effectively favor religion over disbelief. By these lights one easily sees that, in sponsoring the graduation prayers at issue here, the State has crossed the line from permissible accommodation to unconstitutional establishment....

SCALIA, WHITE, AND THOMAS, J.J., AND REHNQUIST, C.J., DISSENTING

... [T]oday's opinion ... is conspicuously bereft of any reference to history. In holding that the Establishment Clause prohibits invocations and benedictions at a public-school graduation ceremonies, the Court—with nary a mention that it is doing so—lays waste a tradition that is as old as public-school graduation ceremonies themselves, and that is a component of an even more longstanding American tradition of nonsectarian prayer to God at public celebrations generally. As its instrument of destruction, the bulldozer of its social engineering, the Court invents a boundless, and boundlessly manipulable, test of psychological coercion....

The history and tradition of our Nation are replete with public ceremonies featuring prayers of thanksgiving and petition. Illustrations of this point have been amply provided in our prior opinions....

From our Nation's origin, prayer has been a prominent part of governmental ceremonies and proclamations....

In addition to this general tradition of prayer at public ceremonies, there exists a more specific tradition of invocations and benedictions at public-school graduation exercises....

The Court presumably would separate graduation invocations and benedictions from other instances of public "preservation and transmission of religious beliefs" on the ground that they involve "psychological coercion." I find it a sufficient embarrassment that our Establishment Clause jurisprudence regarding holiday displays has come to "requir[e] scrutiny more commonly associated with interior decorators than with the judiciary." *American Jewish Congress v. Chicago*, 827 F.2d 120 (CA 7 1987) (Easterbrook, J. dissenting.) But interior decorating is a rockhard science compared to psychology practiced by amateurs. A few citations of "[r]esearch in psychology" that have no particular bearing upon the precise issue here, cannot disguise the fact that the Court has gone beyond the realm where judges know what they are doing. The Court's argument that state officials have "coerced" students to take part in the invocation and benediction at graduation ceremonies is, not to put too fine a point on it, incoherent.

The Court identifies two "dominant facts" that it says dictate its ruling that invocations and benedictions at public-school graduation ceremonies violate the Establishment Clause. Neither of them is in any relevant sense true.

The Court declares that students' "attendance and participation in the [invocation and benediction] are in a fair and real sense obligatory." But what exactly is this "fair and real sense"?...

The opinion manifests that the Court has not given careful consideration to its test of psychological coercion....

The other "dominant fac[t]" identified by the Court is that "[s]tate officials direct the performance of a formal religious exercise" at school graduation ceremonies.... All the record shows is that principals of the Providence public schools, acting within their delegated authority, have invited clergy to deliver invocations and benedictions at graduations; and that Principal Lee invited Rabbi Gutterman, provided him a two-page flier, prepared by the National Conference of Christians and Jews, giving general advice on inclusive prayer for civic occasions, and advised him that his prayers at graduation should be nonsectarian. How these facts can fairly be transformed into the charges that Principal Lee "directed and controlled the content of [Rabbi Gutterman's] prayer," that school officials "monitor prayer," and attempted to "'compose official prayers,'" and that the "government involvement with religious activity in this case is pervasive," is difficult to fathom....

These distortions of the record are, of course, not harmless error: without them the Court's solemn assertion that the school officials could reasonably be perceived to be "enforc[ing] a religious orthodoxy," would ring as hollow as it ought.

The deeper flaw in the Court's opinion does not lie in its wrong answer to the question whether there was state-induced "peer-pressure" coercion; it lies, rather, in the Court's making violation of the Establishment Clause hinge on such a precious question. The coercion that was a hallmark of historical establishments of religion was coercion of religious orthodoxy and of financial support *by force of law and threat of penalty*....

[W]hile I have no quarrel with the Court's general proposition that the Establishment Clause "guarantees that government may not coerce anyone to support or participate in religion or its exercise," ... I see no warrant for expanding the concept of coercion beyond acts backed by threat of penalty—a brand of coercion that, happily, is readily discernible to those of us who have made a

career of reading the disciples of Blackstone rather than of Freud....

Our religion-clause jurisprudence has become bedeviled (so to speak) by reliance on formulaic abstractions that are not derived from, but positively conflict with, our long-accepted constitutional traditions. Foremost among these has been the so-called *Lemon* test, which has received well-earned criticism from many members of this Court. The Court today demonstrates the irrelevance of *Lemon* by essentially ignoring it, and the interment of that case may be the one happy byproduct of the Court's otherwise lamentable decision. Unfortunately, however, the Court has replaced *Lemon* with its psycho-coercion test, which suffers the double disability of having no roots whatever in our people's historic practice, and being as infinitely expandable as the reasons for psychotherapy itself. Another happy aspect of the case is that it is only a jurisprudential disaster and not a practical one. Given the odd basis for the Court's decision, however, invocations and benedictions will be able to be given at public-school graduations next June, as they have for the past century and a half, so long as school authorities make clear that anyone who abstains from screaming in protest does not necessarily participate in the prayers. All that is seemingly needed is an announcement, or perhaps a written insertion at the beginning of the graduation Program, to the effect that, while all are asked to rise for the invocation and benediction, none is compelled to join in them, nor will be assumed, by rising, to have done so. That obvious fact recited, the graduates and their parents may proceed to thank God, as Americans have always done, for the blessings He has generally bestowed on them and on their country....

QUESTIONS

1. What principles of Establishment Clause jurisprudence guide the majority and dissenting opinions in *Weisman*? Can the two positions be reconciled?

2. Is Justice Scalia correct that the *Weisman* decision demonstrates "the irrelevance of *Lemon*" and that its "interment" may be one of the byproducts of *Weisman*?

3. *Legal Times* reporter Tony Mauro claimed that the outcome in *Weisman* was evident following oral argument, despite prior predictions that the Court would overrule *Lemon*. He wrote that Charles Cooper, counsel for the Providence School Board, erred in asking the justices to replace *Lemon* with a "coercion" test, under which a religious practice in public life would only be struck down when it was coercive. That argument prompted Justice Scalia to tell Cooper during oral argument that a coercion test alone "simply doesn't comport with our traditions." Said Mauro, "Suddenly the *Lemon* test, and the whole range of the Court's church-state jurisprudence, which has been criticized by the majority of the justices, became like the despised uncle on his death bed who still must be spoken of with respect. Cooper had spoken ill of the dying and the Court was offended" ("A Step Back from Redoing Religion Law," *Legal Times*, November 11, 1991, p. 1, col. 1).

   Does Mauro's account make the content and tone of Justice Scalia's dissent in *Weisman* puzzling? What does his account suggest about the future of *Lemon*?

4. Rabbi Gutterman responded to the *Weisman* decision by saying: "There is general agreement among Americans that we need to teach good values, like honesty, compassion and kindness, to make us better citizens, but there is confusion over how this is to be done" (*New York Times*, June 25, 1992, C21).

   New York University professor Ruti Teitel argues that the U.S. government's interest in *Weisman* was not merely to revise the Supreme Court's Establishment Clause jurisprudence: "The debate in the entire church-state area is the future of American values and who will control the values. That's why so many of these cases involve education. That's why [*Weisman*] is important" (quoted in Marcia Coyle, "Not Just a Prayer," *National Law Journal*, November 11, 1991, pp. 1, 26, col. 1).

   What is the broader political significance of *Weisman*? In the context of pluralistic American society, is teaching "good values" as simple and noncontroversial as teaching honesty, compassion, and kindness?

COMMENT

One year after *Weisman*, a high school principal in Mississippi, Bishop Knox, was fired by the school superintendent for allowing students to read a prayer over the school's loudspeaker. Knox argued that he was justified in giving his permission because the students had voted 490–96 to allow school prayer. Following a series of protests and rallies against Knox's firing, the superintendent relented and reinstated him ("Principal in a School Prayer Dispute is Reinstated," *New York Times*, December 17, 1993, A14).

ESTABLISHMENT OF RELIGION

Board of Education of Kiryas Joel Village School District v. Grumet
512 U.S. 687 (1994)

SETTING

Creation of special school districts to accommodate religion has also proved to be a divisive issue for the Supreme Court's Establishment Clause jurisprudence. Referred to as "religious gerrymandering," the practice entails drawing public school district lines to reflect the needs of religious sects. A challenge by two officers of the New York State School Boards Association against a special school district created to accommodate Satmar Hasidim in the Village of Kiryas Joel (located about forty miles northwest of New York City) gave the Supreme Court yet another opportunity to revisit the *Lemon* test.

The Satmar Hasidim are members of an Orthodox Jewish sect representing one of the dynastic rabbinical courts that developed originally in the eighteenth century in eastern and central Europe. The sect of Hasidic Jews takes its name, Satmar, from the town near the Hungarian and Romanian border where it was formed. The Satmar Hasidim emigrated to the United States and settled in the Williamsburg section of Brooklyn, New York, following the Holocaust. They are devoutly religious, believing in a literal interpretation of the teachings of the Torah. They adhere strictly to the Talmud (the book of Jewish law and tradition) in all aspects of everyday life. Yiddish, rather than English, is commonly spoken. Satmar Hasidim are recognizable by their distinctive dress: Men, for example, wear beards and dress in dark suits, and wear long black coats and brimmed hats. Strict separation of men and women, except within the confines of the immediate family, is required to avoid "impure thoughts." Satmar Hasidim strive to avoid popular culture by excluding television, radio, and English language publications. Satmar Hasidim also subscribe to a hierarchical social order, at the top of which is the sect's religious leader, known as the Rebbe. The Rebbe exercises authority over all aspects of the life of members of his sect, from marriage to employment to medical treatment. Satmar families average ten children, in allegiance to the biblical edict to "be fruitful and multiply."

Population growth among the Satmar Hasidim during the 1970s caused them to establish outlying settlements in New York State. One of those was the Village of Kiryas Joel, named after the sect's founder, Grand Rabbi Joel

Teitelbaum. It was carved out of the Town of Monroe in March 1977. Each settlement is led by a Rov, or "town rabbi," appointed by the Rebbe. The Rov of the Village of Kiryas Joel is the Rebbe's son, Aaron Teitelbaum. The 1994 population was approximately 8,500.

In general, Satmar Hasidim educate their children in private boys' and girls' religious schools rather than in secular public schools. Most boys are educated at the United Talmudic Academy, receive a thorough grounding in the Torah, and have limited exposure to secular subjects. Girls are prepared for their roles as wives and mothers via the curriculum at Bais Rochel. The exception to the general rule of private education is for children who, due to mental or physical disabilities, are permitted to attend public school classes for the learning disabled. These children also receive counseling and physical therapy services.

For several years, public school special education and related services were made available to Satmar Hasidim children in annexes to their private schools. In 1985, however, the Supreme Court ruled that public school teachers could not work at private schools. *Aguilar v. Felton*, 473 U.S. 402 (1985). Following that decision, the Satmar Hasidim declined to accept such services in the regular classes of the public schools. They had several reservations to that plan: the cultural disruption of transporting the children out of the sheltered environment of the village, the psychological harm Satmar children would suffer from being thrust into a strange environment, the difficulties created by language and dress differences, and the lack of bilingual, bicultural programs specially adapted to meet the social, psychological, and cultural needs of Satmar children. The Monroe-Woodbury school district refused to provide services for disabled Satmar Hasidim children at any site other than regular public schools.

In 1989, the New York Legislature responded to the impasse by creating the Kiryas Joel Village School District with boundaries coterminous with the existing Village of Kiryas Joel. The purpose of the legislation was only to provide special education and related services to the approximately two hundred handicapped students residing in the village. The district had its own tax base and state aid entitlements. The creation of the district had the consequence of removing a portion of tax base of the Monroe-Woodbury district. But the new district also removed a costly educational component from that district's budget and the transportation expenses associated with it.

In an approval memorandum accompanying his signing of the legislation, Governor Mario Cuomo stated:

> I believe that this bill is a good faith effort to solve this unique problem. And, as noted above, I am advised it is facially constitutional. Of course this new school district must take pains to avoid conduct that violates the separation of church and state because then a constitutional problem would arise in the application of this law. The village officials acknowledge this responsibility. I believe they will be true to their commitment.

The village school that was constructed under the supervision of the seven-member board of education began offering services in 1990. It is separate and apart from the religious schools in the community. Instructional and noninstructional staff were selected in accordance with applicable civil service rules and regulations. It follows a secular academic calendar. Unlike the village's private Hasidic schools, instruction is coeducational, and female teachers instruct male students. English is the primary language, although bilingual and bicultural secular programs were offered.

Approximately six months before the new district began its operations, the New York State School Boards Association through officers Louis Grumet and Albert Hawk filed an action in the Supreme Court of Albany County against the New York Education Department and various state officials claiming that the legislation creating the district was facially invalid under the Establishment Clause of the Constitution of the United States and the New York Constitution. The Supreme Court of Albany County ruled that the legislation violated all three prongs of *Lemon v. Kurtzman* and was therefore facially unconstitutional under both the federal and state constitutions. The Appellate Division affirmed.

The New York Court of Appeals, the state's highest court, also affirmed. It held that the statute creating the Kiryas Joel Village School District violated the Establishment Clause because the statute effected a symbolic union of church and state that was "sufficiently likely to be perceived by the Satmarer Hasidim as an endorsement of their religious choices, or by nonadherents as a disapproval of their religious choices." It therefore struck down the statute on the ground that it had the effect of advancing religion, in violation of the second prong of the *Lemon* test. The two dissenting judges characterized the legislation as not only constitutional, but a "Solomon-like" solution. The Supreme Court of the United States granted the Kiryas Joel school district's petition for a writ of certiorari.

HIGHLIGHTS OF SUPREME COURT ARGUMENTS

BRIEF FOR BOARD OF EDUCATION OF KIRYAS JOEL VILLAGE SCHOOL DISTRICT

◆ In a facial challenge to a statute, such as here, courts should not presume that actual Establishment Clause violations will occur.

◆ The statute creating the district authorizes and provides for only secular services. Neither does the law support or finance a church or other religious institution. It provides secular services to people who happen to be religious.

◆ The statute satisfies all three prongs of the *Lemon* test. It has a valid secular purpose, does not have the effect of advancing religion, and does not foster excessive entanglements between government and religion.

◆ The statute is a valid accommodation of religion because it ameliorates a burden that results from the free exercise of religion.

◆ If the Court finds that any of the "prongs" of *Lemon* are violated by the statute, the court should overrule *Lemon*.

AMICUS CURIAE BRIEFS SUPPORTING BOARD OF EDUCATION OF KIRYAS JOEL VILLAGE SCHOOL DISTRICT

Joint brief of the Christian Legal Society, the National Association of Evangelicals, Southern Center for Law and Ethics, and the Family Research Council; Institute for Religion and Polity; National Jewish Commission on Law and Public Affairs; joint brief of the American Center for Law and Justice and the Catholic League for Religious and Civil Rights, Archdiocese of New York, Rutherford Institute, U.S. Catholic Conference, and Southern Baptist Convention Christian Life Commission; joint brief of National Jewish Commission on Law and Public Affairs, Amit Women, Agudath Harabonim of the United States and Canada, Emunah of America, National Council of Young Israel, Rabbinical Alliance of America, Rabbinical Council of America, and Torah Umesorah; Knights of Columbus; Agudath Israel of America.

BRIEF FOR BOARD OF EDUCATION OF MONROE-WOODBURY CENTRAL SCHOOL DISTRICT

◆ The statute creates a secular school district within the boundaries of the existing Village of Kiryas Joel for the purpose of providing secular special education programs and services to disabled Satmar students. The statute passes the three-pronged test of *Lemon.*

◆ It is questionable whether *Lemon* represents the current view of a majority of the justices of this Court with respect to the analysis of potential Establishment Clause violations.

◆ If the Court determines that the statute is inconsistent with *Lemon* and cannot be sustained as a permissible legislative accommodation to alleviate a burden on the Satmar Hasidim's Free Exercise rights, *Lemon* should be overruled.

◆ The statute creating the district is a valid accommodation of religion that does not advance the religious interests of the Satmar Hasidim. No benefits flow directly to the religious schools or institutions within the incorporated village.

BRIEF FOR LOUIS GRUMET AND ALBERT HAWK

◆ The statute creating the Kiryas Joel Village School District confers on an exclusive religious community the extraordinary benefit of a separate public school district to enable that community to receive public educational services in an environment that conforms to that community's religious beliefs and traditions. It thereby violates fundamental Establishment Clause principles that prohibit sponsorship, financial support, and active involvement of the sovereign in religious activity.

◆ The statute undeniably violates the second prong of the *Lemon* test because it has the primary effect of advancing religion. It fosters the religious goal of religious and cultural separation of the Satmar. The statute also violates the other two prongs of the *Lemon* test because it has no secular purpose and fosters an excessive entanglement with religion.

◆ Even if this court overrules *Lemon,* the statute is still unconstitutional because it is not a valid accommodation of religion under any Establishment Clause standard.

AMICUS CURIAE BRIEFS SUPPORTING GRUMET AND HAWK

Joint brief of the American Jewish Congress, People for the American Way, General Conference of Seventh-Day Adventists, and the Union of American Hebrew Congregations; joint brief of the National Council of Churches of Christ in the United States and James Andrews, Stated Clerk of the General Assembly of the Presbyterian Church; Committee for the Well-Being of Kiryas Joel; joint brief of the National Coalition for Public Education and Religious Liberty and the National Education Association; Council for Religious Freedom; National School Boards Association; joint brief of the New York State United Teachers, American Federation of Teachers, and AFL-CIO; Council on Religious Freedom; General Council on Finance and Administration of the United Methodist Church; New York Committee for Public Education and Religious Liberty.

SUPREME COURT DECISION: 4–2–3

SOUTER, J.

... The question is whether the Act creating the separate school district violates the Establishment Clause of the First Amendment, binding on the States through the Fourteenth Amendment. Because this unusual act is tantamount to an allocation of political power on a religious criterion and neither presupposes nor requires governmental impartiality toward religion, we hold that it violates the prohibition against establishment.

... "A proper respect for both the Free Exercise and the Establishment Clauses compels the State to pursue a course of 'neutrality' toward religion," *Committee for Public Education & Religious Liberty v. Nyquist*, 413 U.S. 756 (1973), favoring neither one religion over others nor religious adherents collectively over nonadherents.... Chapter 748, the statue creating the Kiryas Joel Village School District, departs from this constitutional command by delegating the State's discretionary authority over public schools to a group defined by its character as a religious community, in a legal and historical content that gives no assurance that governmental power has been or will be exercised neutrally.

... The Establishment Clause problem presented by Chapter 748 is ... that a State may not delegate its civic authority to a group chosen according to a religious criterion. Authority over public schools belongs to the State, ... and cannot be delegated to a local school district defined by the State in order to grant political control to a religious group....

It is undisputed that those who negotiated the village boundaries when applying the general village incorporation statute drew them so as to exclude all but Satmars, and that the New York Legislature was well aware that the village remained exclusively Satmar in 1989 when it adopted Chapter 748.... The significance of this fact to the state legislature is indicated by the further fact that carving out the village school district ran counter to customary districting practices in the State. Indeed, the trend in New York is not toward dividing school districts but toward consolidating them....

The origin of the district in a special act of the legislature, rather than the State's general laws governing school district reorganization, is likewise anomalous.... Thus the Kiryas Joel Village School District is exceptional to the point of singularity, as the only district coming to our notice that the legislature carved from a single existing district to serve local residents....

We therefore find the legislature's Act to be substantially equivalent to defining a political subdivision and hence the qualification for its franchise by a religious test, resulting in a purposeful and forbidden "fusion of governmental and religious functions." *Larkin v. Grendel's Den*, 459 U.S. 116 (1982)....

The fundamental source of constitutional concern here is that the legislature itself may fail to exercise governmental authority in a religiously neutral way. The anomalously case-specific nature of the legislature's exercise of state authority in creating this district for a religious community leaves the Court without any direct way to review such state action for the purpose of safeguarding a principle at the heart of the Establishment Clause, that government should not prefer one religion to another, or religion to irreligion.... Because the religious community of Kiryas Joel did not receive its new governmental authority simply as one of many communities eligible for equal treatment under a general law, we have no assurance that the next similarly situated group seeking a school district of its own will receive one....

The general principle that civil power must be exercised in a manner neutral to religion is ... well grounded in our case law, as we have frequently relied explicitly on the general availability of any benefit provided religious groups or individuals in turning aside Establishment Clause challenges.... Here the benefit flows only to a single sect, but aiding this single, small religious group causes no less a constitutional problem than would follow from aiding a sect with more members or religion as a whole, ... and we are forced to conclude that the State of New York has violated the Establishment Clause.

In finding that Chapter 748 violates the requirement of governmental neutrality by extending the benefit of a special franchise, we do not deny that the Constitution allows the state to accommodate religious needs by alleviating special burdens. Our cases leave no doubt that in commanding neutrality the Religion Clauses do not require the government to be oblivious to impositions that legitimate exercises of state power may place on religious belief and practice....

But accommodation is not a principle without limits, and what petitioners seek is an adjustment to the Satmars' religiously grounded preferences that our cases do not countenance.... Petitioners' proposed accommodation singles out a particular religious sect for special treatment, and whatever the limits of permissible legislative accommodations may be, ... it is clear that neutrality as among religions must be honored....

Our job, of course, would be easier if the dissent's position had prevailed with the Framers and with this Court over the years. An Establishment Clause diminished to the dimensions acceptable to Justice Scalia could be enforced by a few simple rules, and our docket would never see cases requiring the application of a principle like neutrality toward religion as well as among religious sects. But that would be as blind to history as to precedent, and the difference between Justice Scalia and the Court accordingly turns on the Court's recognition that the Establishment Clause does comprehend such a principle and obligates courts to exercise the judgment necessary to apply it....

Affirmed.

BLACKMUN, J., CONCURRING [OMITTED]

STEVENS, BLACKMUN, AND GINSBURG, J.J., CONCURRING

... By creating a school district that is specifically intended to shield children from contact with others who have "different ways," the State provided official support to cement the attachment of young adherents to a particular faith. It is telling, in this regard, that two-thirds of the school's full-time students are Hasidic handicapped children from outside the village; the Kiryas Joel school thus serves a population far wider than the village— one defined less by geography than by religion....

Affirmative state action in aid of segregation of this character is unlike the even-handed distribution of a public benefit or service, a "release time" program for public school students involving no public benefit or service, a "release time" program for public school students involving no public premises or funds, or a decision to grant an exemption from a burdensome general rule. It is, I believe, fairly characterized as establishing, rather than merely accommodating religion....

O'CONNOR, J., CONCURRING IN PART AND CONCURRING IN THE JUDGMENT

The question at the heart of this case is: What may the government do, consistently with the Establishment Clause, to accommodate people's religious beliefs?...

The Satmars' next need for accommodation arose in the mid-1980s. Satmar education is pervasively religious, and is provided through entirely private schooling. But though the Satmars could afford to educate most of their children, educating the handicapped is a difficult and expensive business. Moreover, it is a business that the government generally funds, with tax moneys that come from the Satmars as well as from everyone else. In 1984, therefore, the Monroe-Woodbury Central School District began providing handicapped education services to the Satmar children at an annex to the Satmar religious school. The curriculum and the environment of the services were entirely

secular. They were the same sort of services available to handicapped students at secular public and private schools throughout the country.

In 1985, however, we held that publicly funded classes on religious school premises violate the Establishment Clause. *School Dist. of Grand Rapids v. Ball*, 473 U.S. 373; *Aguilar v. Felton*, 473 U.S. 402. Based on these decisions, the Monroe-Woodbury Central School District stopped providing services at the Kiryas Joel site, and required the Satmar children to attend public schools outside the village. This, however, was not a satisfactory arrangement for the Satmars, in part because the Satmar children had a hard time dealing with immersion in the non-Satmar world....

In response to these difficulties came the third accommodation. In 1989 the New York Legislature passed a statute to create a special school district covering only the village of Kiryas Joel....

The ... situations outlined above shed light on an important aspect of accommodation under the First Amendment: Religious needs can be accommodated through laws that are neutral with regard to religion....

That the government is acting to accommodate religion should generally not change this analysis. What makes accommodation permissible, even praiseworthy, is not that the government is making life easier for some particular religious group as such. Rather, it is that the government is accommodating a deeply held belief. Accommodations may thus justify treating those who share this belief differently from those who do not; but they do not justify discriminations based on sect....

I join ... the Court's [holding] because I think this law, rather than being a general accommodation, singles out a particular religious group for favorable treatment. The Court's analysis of the history of this law and of the surrounding statutory scheme persuades me of this....

On its face, this statute benefits one group—the residents of Kiryas Joel. Because this benefit was given to this group based on its religion, it seems proper to treat it as a legislatively drawn religious classification....

Our invalidation of this statute in no way means that the Satmars' needs cannot be accommodated. There is nothing improper about a legislative intention to accommodate a religious group, so long as it is implemented through generally applicable legislation....

I also think there is one other accommodation that would be entirely permissible: the 1984 scheme, which was discontinued because of our decision in *Aguilar*. The Religion Clauses prohibit the government from favoring religion, but they provide no warrant for discriminating against religion. All handicapped children are entitled by law to government-funded special education.... If the government provides this education on-site at public schools and at nonsectarian private schools, it is only fair that it provide it on-site at sectarian schools as well.

I thought this to be true in *Aguilar* ... and I still believe it today.... The court should, in a proper case, be prepared to reconsider *Aguilar*, in order to bring our Establishment Clause jurisprudence back to what I think is the proper track—government impartiality, not animosity, towards religion.

One aspect of the Court's opinion in this case is worth noting: ... The Court's opinion does not focus on the Establishment Clause test we set forth in *Lemon v. Kurtzman*....

As the Court's opinion today shows, the slide away from *Lemon*'s unitary approach is well under way. A return to *Lemon*, even if possible, would likely be futile, regardless of where one stands on the substantive Establishment Clause questions. I think a less unitary approach provides a better structure for analysis. If each test covers a narrower and more homogeneous area, the tests may be more precise and therefore easier to apply. There may be more opportunity to pay attention to the specific nuances of each area. There might also be, I hope, more consensus on each of the narrow tests than there has been on a broad test. And abandoning the *Lemon* framework need not mean abandoning some of the insights that the test reflected, nor the insights of the cases that applied it....

KENNEDY, J., CONCURRING IN THE JUDGMENT

... I agree with the Court insofar as it invalidates the school district for being drawn along religious lines. As the plurality observes, the New York Legislature knew that everyone within the village was Satmar when it drew the school district along the village lines, and it determined who was to be included in the district by imposing, in effect, a religious test. There is no serious question that the legislature configured the school district, with purpose and precision, along a religious line. This explicit religious gerrymandering violates the First Amendment Establishment Clause....

The decisions in *Grand Rapids* and *Aguilar* may have been erroneous. In light of the case before us, and in the interest of sound elaboration of constitutional doctrine, it may be necessary for us to reconsider them at a later date. A neutral aid scheme, available to religious and nonreligious alike, is the preferable way to address problems such as the Satmar handicapped children have suffered.... But for *Grand Rapids* and *Aguilar*, the Satmars would have had no need to seek special accommodations or their own school district. Our decisions led them to choose that unfortunate course, with the deficiencies I have described.

One misjudgment is no excuse, however, for compounding it with another. We must confront this case as it comes before us, without bending rules to free the Satmars from a predicament into which we put them. The Establishment Clause forbids the government to draw political boundaries on the basis of religious faith. For this reason, I concur in the judgment of the Court.

SCALIA AND THOMAS, J.J., AND REHNQUIST, C.J., DISSENTING

The Court today finds that the Powers That Be, up in Albany, have conspired to effect an establishment of the Satmar Hasidim. I do not know who would be more surprised at this discovery: the Founders of our Nation or Grand Rebbe Joel Teitelbaum, founder of the Satmar.... I, however, am not surprised. Once this Court has abandoned text and history as guides, nothing prevents it from calling religious toleration the establishment of religion.

Unlike most of our Establishment Clause cases involving education [this case involves] ... no public funding, however slight or indirect, to private religious schools. [It does] not involve private schools at all. The school under scrutiny is a public school specifically designed to provide a public secular education to handicapped students.... In sum, [this case involves] only public aid to a school that is public as can be. The only thing distinctive about the school is that all the students share the same religion.

None of our cases has ever suggested that there is anything wrong with that....

Justice Souter's position boils down to the quite novel proposition that any group of citizens (say, the residents of Kiryas Joel) can be invested with political power, but not if they all belong to the same religion. Of course such *disfavoring* of religion is positively antagonistic to the purposes of the Religion Clauses, and we have rejected it before....

Since the obvious presence of a neutral, secular basis renders the asserted preferential effect of this law inadequate to invalidate it, Justice Souter is required to come forward with direct evidence that religious preference was the objective. His case could scarcely be weaker. It consists, briefly, of this: The People of New York created the Kiryas Joel Village School District in order to further the Satmar religion, rather than for any proper secular purpose, because (1) they created the district in an extraordinary manner—by special Act of the legislature, rather than under the State's general laws governing school-district reorganization; (2) the creation of the district ran counter to a State trend towards consolidation of school districts; and (3) the District includes only adherents of the Satmar religion. On this indictment, no jury would convict....

[A]ll that the first point proves ... is that New York regarded Kiryas Joel as a special case, requiring special measures. I should think it *obvious* that it did, and obvious that it *should have*....

Justice Souter's case against the statute comes down to nothing more, therefore, than ... the fact that all the residents of the Kiryas Joel Village School District are Satmars. But all its residents also wear unusual dress, have unusual civic customs, and have not much to do with people who are culturally different from them.... On what basis does Justice Souter conclude that it is the theological distinctiveness rather than the cultural distinctiveness that was the basis for New York State's decision? The normal assumption would be that it was the latter, since it was not theology but dress, language, and cultural alienation that posed the educational problem for the children. Justice Souter not only does not adopt the logical assumption, he does not even give the New York Legislature the benefit of the doubt....

[E]ven if Chapter 748 were intended to create a special arrangement for the Satmars *because of* their religion (not including ... any conferral of governmental power upon a religious entity), it would be a permissible accommodation....

This Court has also long acknowledged the permissibility of legislative accommodation....

In today's opinion, however, the Court seems uncomfortable with this aspect of our constitutional tradition. Although it acknowledges the concept of accommodation, it quickly points out that it is "not a principle without limits," and then gives reasons why the present case exceeds those limits, reasons which simply do not hold water. "[W]e have never hinted," the Court says, "that an otherwise unconstitutional delegation of political power to a religious group could be saved as a religious accommodation." Putting aside the circularity inherent in referring to a delegation as "otherwise unconstitutional" when its constitutionality turns on whether there is an accommodation, if this statement is true, it is only because we have never hinted that delegation of political power to citizens who share a particular religion could be unconstitutional....

The second and last reason the Court finds accommodation impermissible is, astoundingly, the mere risk that the State will not offer accommodation to a similar group in the future, and that neutrality will therefore not be preserved....

The Court's demand for "up front" assurances of a neutral system is at war with both traditional accommodation doctrine and the judicial role....

The Court's decision today is astounding....

QUESTIONS

1. *Lemon v. Kurtzman* figured prominently in all the briefs submitted to the Supreme Court in *Grumet*. Yet Justice Souter and the plurality ignored *Lemon* in their opinions. What standard does Justice Souter appear to substitute in concluding that the New York statute violates the Establishment Clause? Based on the various *Grumet* opinions, what was the status of *Lemon* as of the October 1993 Term?

2. Creation of the school district also created unusual factionalism among residents of the Village of Kiryas Joel. During the election to establish the first board of education for the district, Joseph Waldman, the only candidate to run without the endorsement of the Rov, was expelled from the village's main congregation and his children were expelled from the village's religious schools after he refused to renounce his candidacy. The *amicus curiae* brief from the Committee for the Well-Being of Kiryas Joel on behalf of Grumet and

Hawk represented over five hundred members of the Satmar community of the village who supported Waldman and the decision of the New York Court of Appeals.

While asserting its belief in preserving the authority of religious leadership in its community, Committee for the Well-Being of Kiryas Joel members argued that they opposed "the authority of Rabbis and unelected leaders who keep themselves above the Torah, who disrespect their own religious Jewish laws, and who abuse the power of their leadership to enhance their own agenda and political interests in a brutal manner." They urged the Supreme Court to strike down the New York statute creating the special school district on the ground that, on its face and as applied, the statute had the primary effect of endorsing religion and creating an excessive entanglement between government and religion.

If differences of opinion over the appropriate relationship between church and state divide even members of the same religious community, do principled constitutional grounds exist for resolving such deep-seated disagreements?

3. Justices O'Connor and Kennedy argued in *Grumet* that the Court's rulings in *Grand Rapids School District v. Ball*, 473 U.S. 373 (1985), and *Aguilar v. Felton*, 473 U.S. 402 (1985), were erroneous. Justice Kennedy noted: "But for *Grand Rapids* and *Aguilar*, the Satmars would have had no need to seek special accommodations or their own school district. Our decisions led them to choose that unfortunate course[.]" Yet both joined the Court's holding. Is compounding the consequences of bad law an inevitable consequence of *stare decisis*?

4. Immediately after *Grumet* was announced, and following up on arguments Justices O'Connor and Kennedy made in their respective concurrences, members of the New York State Legislature set about trying to draft a new "neutral" statute in order to accommodate the needs of the Satmar community without violating the Constitution. If you were a member of the New York Legislature, how would you proceed to achieve this goal? What guidance would the Court's opinion in *Grumet* provide you?

COMMENT

The revised act that the New York legislature eventually adopted and that was signed into law by Governor Cuomo permitted a municipality to create its own school district if it were situated wholly within a single existing school district and (1) the school-age children in the new district numbered at least two thousand but did not constitute more than 60 percent of the school-age children in the existing district; (2) at least two thousand school-age children remained in the existing school district; (3) the per pupil wealth of the new school district was at least equal to the statewide average; and (4) succession of the new district would not reduce the per pupil wealth of the old district by more than 10 percent. The village of Kiryas Joel met all of these "neutral criteria" (William W. Van Alstyne, *First Amendment: Cases and Materials*, 2nd ed. [Westbury, NY: Foundation Press, 1995], p. 946).

ESTABLISHMENT OF RELIGION

Allegheny County v. Greater Pittsburgh American Civil Liberties Union
492 U.S. 573 (1989)

SETTING

Displaying various symbols of the season during Christmas and Chanukah is a cherished American tradition. Throughout the country, people decorate their homes to commemorate their Christian or Jewish faith as well as to celebrate the secular aspects of these winter holidays. Many municipalities and other governmental jurisdictions also mount displays. Public displays of religious symbols, however, raise a variety of Establishment Clause questions.

The Supreme Court first addressed such questions in *Lynch v. Donnelly*, 465 U.S. 668 (1984). That case involved a city-owned Christmas display in Pawtucket, Rhode Island, that included a manger scene (creche). A divided Court rejected an Establishment Clause challenge to the display brought because of the Christian symbolism of the creche. Chief Justice Burger wrote for the 5–4 majority: "When viewed in the proper context of the Christmas Holiday season, it is apparent that, on this record, there is insufficient evidence to establish that the inclusion of the creche is a purposeful or surreptitious effort to express some kind of subtle governmental advocacy of a particular religious message."

Justice O'Connor wrote separately in *Lynch* "to suggest a clarification of our Establishment Clause doctrine," specifically the *Lemon* test. Justice O'Connor's criticism of *Lemon* was that "[i]t has never been entirely clear ... how the three parts of the test relate to the principles enshrined in the Establishment Clause."

Two years after *Lynch*, the Greater Pittsburgh Chapter of the American Civil Liberties Union (ACLU) initiated litigation seeking to clarify the doctrinal confusion evidenced in *Lynch*. The litigation focused on two recurring displays. The first was a creche. Donated by the Holy Name Society, a Roman Catholic group, the creche was enclosed in a fence and placed on the Allegheny County Courthouse Grand Staircase. A sign was affixed to the creche indicating the donor. Over the manger was a banner proclaiming "Gloria in Excelsis Deo," meaning Glory to God in the Highest. The creche was surrounded by red and white poinsettias and evergreen trees decorated with red bows and Christmas wreaths. The second display was an eighteen-foot menorah owned by Chabad, a local Jewish group. The City of Pittsburgh stored the menorah and annually placed it next to the city's forty-five-foot decorated Christmas tree located outside the City-County Building. After the ACLU wrote to complain about the menorah display, the city placed at the base of the tree a sign bearing the Pittsburgh mayor's name and a proclamation of the City's "salute to liberty": "During this Holiday Season, the City of Pittsburgh Salutes Liberty. Let these festive lights remind us that we are the keepers of the flame of liberty and our legacy of freedom. Richard S. Caliguiri, Mayor."

In November, 1986, the ACLU sent a letter to the Allegheny County Board of Commissioners requesting removal of the nativity scene. In their written response, the county commissioners disavowed any intent to endorse a particular religion, saying that the nativity display, along with other symbols of the season, was simply to express the wish of "Good Will to All Men." The following month, the ACLU filed suit in the U.S. District Court for the Western District of Pennsylvania, seeking to enjoin permanently the county and city from presenting these two displays because they violated the Establishment Clause. The district court permitted Chabad to intervene in support of Pittsburgh, and Malik Tunador, a Moslem Turk, to intervene in support of the ACLU. After a hearing, the court denied relief, citing *Lynch v. Donnelly*. The Court of Appeals reversed, distinguishing *Lynch v. Donnelly*, and citing *Lemon v. Kurtzman*. Allegheny County, Pittsburgh, and Chabad petitioned for a writ of certiorari.

HIGHLIGHTS OF SUPREME COURT ARGUMENTS

BRIEF FOR ALLEGHENY COUNTY

♦ *Lynch v. Donnelly* is dispositive of the issue of whether a municipal display of a nativity scene is constitutional. The *Lynch* holding cannot be distinguished on the basis of a different physical context or location.

♦ Allegheny County's Christmas display satisfies both the *Lemon* tests and the *Lynch* endorsement of religion test.

AMICUS CURIAE BRIEF SUPPORTING ALLEGHENY COUNTY

United States.

BRIEF FOR CHABAD

♦ Pittsburgh's display of the menorah is constitutional under both the majority and dissenting opinions in *Lynch v. Donnelly*.

♦ Under *Larson v. Valente*, 456 U.S. 228 (1982), Pittsburgh may not constitutionally exclude from its display symbols of religious minorities.

BRIEF FOR PITTSBURGH

♦ The Establishment Clause does not forbid government acknowledgment of our religious heritage.

◆ Application of the *Lemon* test, as interpreted in *Lynch v. Donnelly*, demonstrates that inclusion of a menorah in the city's Christmas display was not violative of the Establishment Clause.

AMICUS CURIAE BRIEF SUPPORTING PITTSBURGH

National Jewish Commission on Law and Public Affairs.

BRIEF FOR TUNADOR

◆ Displays of religious symbols in the Allegheny County Courthouse and the Pittsburgh City-County Building violate the Establishment Clause. The Court of Appeals' location-oriented analysis is mandated by the Establishment Clause.

◆ The Court of Appeals correctly distinguished *Lynch v. Donnelly*. Unlike the present case, in *Lynch* there existed no public manifestation of the government's sponsorship of the religious display.

BRIEF FOR THE AMERICAN CIVIL LIBERTIES UNION

◆ The *Lynch* majority correctly emphasized that the "effect" of a religious display inevitably turns on its context.

◆ The arguments Pittsburgh and Allegheny County advance in support of their respective public religious displays are inconsistent. Pittsburgh urges approval of the menorah display under *Lynch*, resting its arguments on a reference to context that the county rejects as constitutionally irrelevant to displaying the creche.

◆ The county and city displays violate the endorsement criteria articulated by Justice O'Connor in her *Lynch* concurrence.

◆ The religious displays in this case cannot be justified as an historical exception to the Establishment Clause or as a permissible accommodation of religion.

AMICUS CURIAE BRIEFS SUPPORTING THE AMERICAN CIVIL LIBERTIES UNION

American Jewish Committee; the National Council of the Churches of Christ in the U.S.A.; the Union of American Hebrew Congregations; the Council on Religious Freedom and Americans United for Separation of Church and State; joint brief of American Jewish Congress and National Jewish Community Relations Advisory Council.

SUPREME COURT DECISION: 5–4/6–3

BLACKMUN, J.

... In *Lemon v. Kurtzman*, the Court sought to refine [the] principles [governing relations between church and state] by focusing on three "tests" for determining whether a government practice violates the Establishment Clause. Under the *Lemon* analysis, a statute or practice which touches upon religion, if it is to be permissible under the Establishment Clause, must have a secular purpose; it must neither advance nor inhibit religion in its principal or primary effect; and it must not foster an excessive entanglement with religion. This trilogy of tests has been applied regularly in the Court's later Establishment Clause cases.

Our subsequent decisions further have refined the definition of governmental action that unconstitutionally advances religion. In recent years, we have paid particularly close attention to whether the challenged governmental practice either has the purpose or effect of "endorsing" religion, a concern that has long had a place in our Establishment Clause jurisprudence....

Whether the key word is "endorsement," "favoritism," or "promotion," the essential principle remains the same. The Establishment Clause, at the very least, prohibits government from appearing to take a position on questions of religious belief or from "making adherence to a religion relevant in any way to a person's standing in the political community." *Lynch v. Donnelly*, 465 U.S. [668 (1984)] (O'Connor, J., concurring).

[D]espite divergence at the bottom line, the five Justices in concurrence and dissent in *Lynch* agreed upon the relevant constitutional principles: the government's use of religious symbolism is unconstitutional if it has the effect of endorsing religious beliefs, and the effect of the government's use of religious symbolism depends upon its context. These general principles are sound, and have been adopted by the Court in subsequent cases.... Accordingly, our present task is to determine whether the display of the creche and the menorah, in their respective "particular physical settings," has the effect of endorsing or disapproving religious beliefs.

We turn first to the county's creche display....

Under the Court's holding in *Lynch*, the effect of a creche display turns on its setting. Here, unlike in *Lynch*, nothing in the

context of the display detracts from the creche's religious message....

Nor does the fact that the creche was the setting for the county's annual Christmas-carol program diminish its religious meaning....

Thus, by permitting the "display of the creche in this particular physical setting," *Lynch*, the county sends an unmistakable message that it supports and promotes the Christian praise to God that is the creche's religious message.

The fact that the creche bears a sign disclosing its ownership by a Roman Catholic organization does not alter this conclusion. On the contrary, the sign simply demonstrates that the government is endorsing the religious message of that organization, rather than communicating a message of its own....

[T]he claim that prohibiting government from celebrating Christmas as a religious holiday discriminates against Christians in favor of nonadherents must fail. Celebrating Christmas as a religious, as opposed to a secular, holiday, necessarily entails professing, proclaiming, or believing that Jesus of Nazareth, born in a manger in Bethlehem, is the Christ, the Messiah. If the government celebrates Christmas as a religious holiday (for example, by issuing an official proclamation saying: "We rejoice in the glory of Christ's birth!"), it means that the government really is declaring Jesus to be the Messiah, a specifically Christian belief. In contrast, confining the government's own celebration of Christmas to the holiday's secular aspects does not favor the religious beliefs of non-Christians over those of Christians. Rather, it simply permits the government to acknowledge the holiday without expressing an allegiance to Christian beliefs, an allegiance that would truly favor Christians over non-Christians....

The display of the Chanukah menorah in front of the City-County Building may well present a closer constitutional question. The menorah, one must recognize, is a religious symbol: it serves to commemorate the miracle of the oil as described in the Talmud. But the menorah's message is not exclusively religious. The menorah is the primary visual symbol for a holiday that, like Christmas, has both religious and secular dimensions.

Moreover, the menorah here stands next to a Christmas tree and a sign saluting liberty. While no challenge has been made here to the display of the tree and the sign, their presence is obviously relevant in determining the effect of the menorah's display. The necessary result of placing a menorah next to a Christmas tree is to create an "overall holiday setting" that represents both Christmas and Chanukah—two holidays, not one....

[T]he relevant question for Establishment Clause purposes is whether the combined display of the tree, the sign, and the menorah has the effect of endorsing both Christian and Jewish faiths, or rather simply recognizes that both Christmas and Chanukah are part of the same winter-holiday season, which has attained a secular status in our society. Of the two interpretations of this particular display, the latter seems far more plausible and is also in line with *Lynch*....

The judgment of the Court of Appeals is affirmed in part and reversed in part, and the cases are remanded for further proceedings.

It is so ordered.

O'CONNOR, BRENNAN, AND STEVENS, J.J., CONCURRING IN PART AND CONCURRING IN THE JUDGMENT

... The constitutionality of the two displays at issue in these cases turns on how we interpret and apply the holding in *Lynch v. Donnelly*....

[I]n my view, the central issue in *Lynch* was whether the city of Pawtucket had endorsed Christianity by displaying a creche as part of a larger exhibit of traditional secular symbols of the Christmas holiday season....

I agree that the creche displayed on the Grand Staircase of the Allegheny County Courthouse, the seat of county government, conveys a message to nonadherents of Christianity that they are not full members of the political community, and a corresponding message to Christians that they are favored members of the political community....

To require a showing of coercion, even indirect coercion, as an essential element of an Establishment Clause violation would make the Free Exercise Clause a redundancy....

I continue to believe that the endorsement test asks the right question about governmental practices challenged on Establishment Clause grounds, including challenged practices involving the display of religious symbols.... I also remain convinced that the endorsement test is capable of consistent application....

[T]he question here is whether Pittsburgh's holiday display conveys a message of endorsement of Judaism, when the menorah is the only religious symbol in the combined display and when the opinion acknowledges that the tree cannot reasonably be understood to convey an endorsement of Christianity. One need not characterize Chanukah as a "secular" holiday or strain to argue that the menorah has a "secular" dimension, in order to conclude that the city of Pittsburgh's combined display does not convey a message of endorsement of Judaism or of religion in general....

BRENNAN, MARSHALL, AND STEVENS, J.J., CONCURRING IN PART AND DISSENTING IN PART

... I ... agree with the Court that Allegheny County's display of a creche at the county courthouse signals an endorsement of the Christian faith in violation of the Establishment Clause[.]... I cannot agree, however, that the city's display of a 45-foot Christmas tree and an 18-foot Chanukah menorah at the entrance to the building housing the mayor's office shows no favoritism towards Christianity, Judaism, or both. Indeed, I should have thought that the answer as to the first display supplied the answer to the second....

[T]he decision as to the menorah rests on three premises: the Christmas tree is a secular symbol; Chanukah is a holiday with secular dimensions, symbolized by the menorah; and the government may promote pluralism by sponsoring or condoning displays having strong religious associations on its property. None of these is sound....

[The] attempt to take the "Christmas" out of the Christmas tree is unconvincing. That the tree may, without controversy, be deemed a secular symbol if found alone, does not mean that it will be so seen when combined with other symbols or objects....

The second premise on which today's decision rests is the notion that Chanukah is a partly secular holiday, for which the menorah can serve as a secular symbol. It is no surprise and no anomaly that Chanukah has historical and societal roots that range beyond the purely religious. I would venture that most, if not all, major religious holidays have beginnings and enjoy histories studded with figures, events, and practices that are not strictly religious. It does not seem to me that the mere fact that Chanukah shares this kind of background makes it a secular holiday in any meaningful sense. The menorah is indisputably a religious symbol, used ritually in a celebration that has deep religious significance. That, in my view, is all that need be said....

Nor do I discern the theory under which the government is permitted to appropriate particular holidays and religious objects to its own use in celebrating "pluralism." The message of the sign announcing a "Salute to Liberty" is not religious, but patriotic; the government's use of religion to promote its own cause is undoubtedly offensive to those whose religious beliefs are not bound up with their attitude toward the Nation....

STEVENS, BRENNAN, AND MARSHALL, J.J., CONCURRING IN PART AND DISSENTING IN PART

... In my opinion the Establishment Clause should be construed to create a strong presumption against the display of religious symbols on public property. There is always a risk that such symbols will offend nonmembers of the faith being advertised as well as adherents who consider the particular advertisement disrespectful....

KENNEDY, WHITE, AND SCALIA, J.J., AND REHNQUIST, C.J., CONCURRING IN THE JUDGMENT IN PART AND DISSENTING IN PART

The majority holds that the County of Allegheny violated the Establishment Clause by displaying a creche in the county courthouse, because the "principal or primary effect" of the display is to advance religion within the meaning of *Lemon v. Kurtzman*. This view of the Establishment Clause reflects an unjustified hostility toward religion, a hostility inconsistent with our history and our precedents, and I dissent from this holding. The creche display is constitutional, and, for the same reasons, the display of a menorah by the city of Pittsburgh is permissible as well. On this latter point, I concur in the result[.]...

In keeping with the usual fashion of recent years, the majority applies the *Lemon* test to judge the constitutionality of the holiday displays here in question. I am content for present purposes to remain within the *Lemon* framework, but do not wish to be seen as advocating, let alone adopting, that test as our primary guide in this difficult area.... Substantial revision of our Establishment Clause doctrine may be in order; but it is unnecessary to undertake that task today, for even the *Lemon* test, when applied with proper sensitivity to our traditions and our case law, supports the conclusion that both the creche and the menorah are permissible displays in the context of the holiday season....

Noncoercive government action within the realm of flexible accommodation or passive acknowledgment of existing symbols does not violate the Establishment Clause unless it benefits religion in a way more direct and more substantial than practices that are accepted in our national heritage.

These principles are not difficult to apply to the facts of the cases before us. In permitting the displays on government property of the menorah and the creche, the city and county sought to do no more than "celebrate the season," and to acknowledge, along with many of their citizens, the historical background and the religious, as well as secular, nature of the Chanukah and Christmas holidays. This interest falls well within the tradition of government accommodation and acknowledgment of religion that has marked our history from the beginning....

If *Lynch* is still good law—and until today it was—the judgment below cannot stand....

Even if *Lynch* did not control, I would not commit this Court to the test applied by the majority today....

If the endorsement test, applied without artificial exceptions for historical practice, reached results consistent with history, my objections to it would have less force. But, as I understand that test, the touchstone of an Establishment Clause violation is whether nonadherents would be made to feel like "outsiders" by government recognition or accommodation of religion. Few of our traditional practices recognizing the part religion plays in our society can withstand scrutiny under a faithful application of this formula....

Either the endorsement test must invalidate scores of traditional practices recognizing the place religion holds in our culture, or it must be twisted and stretched to avoid inconsistency with practices we know to have been permitted in the past, while condemning similar practices with no greater endorsement effect simply by reason of their lack of historical antecedent. Neither result is acceptable....

The result the Court reaches in these cases is perhaps the clearest illustration of the unwisdom of the endorsement test.... If there be such a person as the "reasonable observer," I am quite certain that he or she will take away a salient message from our holding in these cases: the Supreme Court of the United States has concluded that the First Amendment creates classes of religions based on the relative numbers of their adherents. Those religions enjoying the largest following must be consigned to the status of least-favored faiths so as to avoid any possible risk of offending members of minority religions. I would be the first to admit that many questions arising under the Establishment Clause do not admit of easy answers, but whatever the Clause requires, it is not the result reached by the Court today....

QUESTIONS

1. How did deepening divisions among the justices over the *Lemon* test shape the arguments that the parties made in *Allegheny County*? In light of the parties' arguments, and the *Allegheny County* opinions, has Justice O'Connor's concurring opinion in *Lynch v. Donnelly*, in effect, eclipsed the *Lemon* test?

2. Summarize the positions of the justices in *Allegheny County*. Does it appear that one or more viewpoints are pivotal in resolving the Court's struggle over whether to abandon *Lemon* and what Establishment Clause test to substitute for *Lemon*?

ESTABLISHMENT OF RELIGION

Lamb's Chapel v. Center Moriches Union Free School District
508 U.S. 384 (1993)

SETTING

The Supreme Court's imbroglios over devotional practices, governmental aid to parochial schools, and public displays of religious symbols analyzed earlier in this section, demonstrate some of the tensions in Establishment Clause jurisprudence. Another issue that has divided the justices is the use of public school facilities during nonschool hours. Debate over who is entitled to use such facilities implicates free speech as well as Establishment Clause considerations. In these cases, governmental neutrality has been the only touchstone.

In *Widmar v. Vincent*, 454 U.S. 263 (1981), for example, the Court invalidated a University of Missouri policy under which campus facilities were generally available to registered student groups, but not to groups meeting "for purposes of religious worship or religious teaching." The Court held that the university's policy was content-based, and that the constitutional presumption against such content-based restrictions on free speech required equal access for all student organizations. The *Widmar* rationale was threefold: (1) the university had established itself as an "open forum"; (2) an open forum policy does not violate the Establishment Clause; and (3) any interest the university might have in creating more separation between church and state than is required under Establishment Clause jurisprudence is not a sufficiently compelling interest and is limited by the Free Exercise Clause and the Free Speech Clause.

Following *Widmar*, Congress enacted the Equal Access Act of 1984 to extend the *Widmar* rationale to secondary school facilities. Under that act, any school receiving federal financial assistance that allows nonacademic groups to meet in its facilities during nonschool hours has created a "limited open forum" and the school cannot deny access to members of any group on the basis of the religious, philosophic, or political content of their speech.

In a divided opinion, the Court upheld the Equal Access Act in *Westside Community Schools v. Mergens*, 496 U.S. 226 (1990). Justice O'Connor's plurality opinion, joined by Chief Justice Rehnquist and Justices White and Blackmun, held that the "equal access principle" neither endorsed nor disapproved of religion. The Court distinguished between "*governmental* speech endorsing religion, which the Establishment Clause forbids, and *private* speech endorsing religion, which the Free Speech and Free Exercise Clauses protect."

Mergens left unanswered questions about whether the Court's relaxed review of religious uses of school facilities would extend even to the elementary level. That question arose in a case testing the validity of Section 414 of the New York Education Law that disallowed the use of school facilities for religious purposes.

Section 414 of New York Education Law authorizes local school districts to regulate the uses of school property for nonschool purposes. The regulation permits holding "social, civil and recreational meetings and entertainments, and other uses pertaining to the welfare of the community; but such meetings, entertainment and uses shall be non-exclusive and open to the general public." The list of permitted uses does not include meetings for religious purposes.

Pursuant to Section 414, the Center Moriches Union Free School District adopted rules for the use of school property when not in use for school purposes. The District's rules allow only two of the ten uses authorized by Section 414: social, civic, or recreational uses (Rule 10); and use by political organizations if secured in compliance with Section 414 (Rule 8). Consistent with Section 414, Center Moriches also provides that school premises "shall not be used by any group for religious purposes" (Rule 7). Between 1987 and 1990, groups ranging from the Manorville Humane Society and Holiday Beach Property Owners Association, to Brownie Troop #1338, and Southern Harmonize Gospel Singers received permission to conduct activities in school facilities of Center Moriches.

In December 1988 and October 1989, John Steigerwald, pastor of Lamb's Chapel, an Evangelical Christian Church, applied to use school facilities to show a six-part film series entitled *Turn Your Heart Toward Home*. The series features Reverend James Dobson, a licensed psychologist, prominent religious leader, and founder of the Family Research Council. Dr. Dobson is also president of Focus on the Family. The film series features Dobson and his wife, Shirley Dobson, author of a book on family traditions. The series addresses a variety of issues facing contemporary American families, and stresses family values "from a Christian perspective." In November 1989, Alice Schoener, business manager and district clerk of Center Moriches, rejected Pastor

Steigerwald's application, stating, "This film does appear to be church related and therefore your request must be refused." She assured Pastor Steigerwald that Lamb's Chapel would be eligible to use Center Moriches facilities as long as their activities did not have "religious purposes."

In February 1990, Lamb's Chapel filed suit in the U.S. District Court for the Eastern District of New York. Lamb's Chapel requested an injunction requiring Center Moriches to permit the church to use school facilities to show the Dobson film series and forbidding Center Moriches from discriminating against religious groups "because of the religious content ... of their speech." Lamb's Chapel also sought a declaration that Center Moriches had created an "open forum," and had engaged in unconstitutional content discrimination against Lamb's Chapel. The church alleged the school's discrimination violated the Free Speech, Free Assembly, and Free Exercise Clauses as well as the Establishment and Equal Protection Clauses.

The district court denied the motion for a preliminary injunction and subsequently granted summary judgment for Center Moriches. The U.S. Court of Appeals for the Second Circuit affirmed. The appeals court held that Center Moriches school facilities fall within the subcategory of a "limited public forum," a classification that allows it to "impose a blanket exclusion on certain types of speech" so long as it does not "selectively deny access" among expressive activities of a "certain genre." The court of appeals also found that none of the prior uses allowed by Center Moriches "were for religious purposes."

Lamb's Chapel petitioned the Supreme Court of the United States for a writ of certiorari.

HIGHLIGHTS OF SUPREME COURT ARGUMENTS

BRIEF FOR LAMB'S CHAPEL

◆ Center Moriches denied Lamb's Chapel's request to use school facilities in order to show a film series that was open to the public solely because the film series contained a religious perspective. This censorship of religious speech of private actors violates the First Amendment's right to free speech. It is a fundamental proposition of constitutional law that a governmental body may not suppress or exclude the speech of private parties for the sole reason that the speech contains a religious perspective.

◆ A governmental entity creates a "designated public forum" when it opens its facilities to general use by the public or some segment of the public. Content-based exclusions of speech from such fora are unconstitutional unless narrowly drawn to further a compelling governmental interest.

◆ Center Moriches has opened its facilities to a broad range of outside users, thereby creating a designated public forum. It is content-based censorship to forbid users from engaging in religious speech. Such censorship triggers strict judicial scrutiny. The state has shown no compelling interest supporting its policy of censorship.

◆ By targeting private religious speech for censorship from facilities made available to the general public, Center Moriches has violated the Establishment Clause. Government denial of equal access for religious speech demonstrates hostility toward religion.

AMICUS CURIAE BRIEFS SUPPORTING LAMB'S CHAPEL

Christian Legal Society; U.S. Catholic Conference; Baptist Joint Committee on Public Affairs; Family Research Council; Catholic League for Religious and Civil Rights; National Association of Evangelicals; Christian Life Commission of the Southern Baptist Convention; Home School Legal Defense Association; Lutheran Church-Missouri Synod; United States; American Civil Liberties Union; Americans United for Separation of Church and State; New York Civil Liberties Union; People for the American Way; Union of American Hebrew Congregations; American Federation of Labor and Congress of Industrial Organizations; Concerned Women for America and Free Congress Foundation; Rutherford Institute.

BRIEF FOR CENTER MORICHES UNION FREE SCHOOL DISTRICT

◆ The New York statute and Center Moriches regulations rationally limit access to public school facilities and are supported by sound public policy. If particular religious or political groups are allowed access to a public school building it is reasonable to expect problems to arise.

◆ This case requires careful consideration of public policy in light of the various interests at stake. School districts should not be required to open their doors to all speech, regardless of purpose and intent. Such a rule would require granting applications to the Neo-Nazi Party, the Ku Klux Klan, militant Muslim groups, partisan political rallies, and flea markets. Given the policy problems that could arise, an unlimited access policy is not required by the First Amendment.

◆ The unlimited access Lamb's Chapel argues for would violate the First Amendment's prohibition against state establishment of religion. It would have the primary effect of providing financial aid to religious institutions and would unnecessarily entangle government with religion, in violation of *Lemon v. Kurtzman.*

◆ The statutes and regulations at issue in this case do not demonstrate hostility toward religion and therefore do not offend the Establishment Clause. Lamb's Chapel remains free to engage in their religious activities and beliefs. It is merely required to do so in facilities other than public schools.

BRIEF FOR STATE OF NEW YORK

◆ New York has never opened its schools to indiscriminate use by the public when school is not in session. It has provided each of its more than seven hundred districts with limited discretion to determine whether to allow their local schools to be used for any of the particular purposes set forth in Education Law Section 414. The statutory uses a school district may permit do not include religious use. The absence of religious use from the list of authorized purposes neither discriminates against nor signals hostility toward religion.

◆ The Establishment Clause does not require New York to extend its limited school fora to religious uses. School districts do not become "entangled" with religion by determining which proposed uses meet the criteria of Section 414.

AMICUS CURIAE BRIEFS SUPPORTING CENTER MORICHES

New York State School Boards Association; National School Boards Association; Anti-Defamation League; Committee for Public Education and Religious Liberty.

SUPREME COURT DECISION: 9–0

WHITE, J.

... There is no question that the District, like the private owner of property, may legally preserve the property under its control for the use to which it is dedicated. It is also common ground that the District need not have permitted after-hours use of its property for any of the uses permitted by [Section] 414 of the state education law. The District, however, did open its property for 2 of the 10 uses permitted by [Section] 414....

With respect to public property that is not a designated public forum open for indiscriminate public use for communicative purposes, we have said that "[c]ontrol over access to a nonpublic forum can be based on subject matter and speaker identity so long as the distinctions drawn are reasonable in light of the purpose served by the forum and are viewpoint neutral." *Perry Education Assn.* [*v. Perry Local Educators' Assn.*, 460 U.S. 37 (1983)]. The Court of Appeals appeared to recognize that the total ban on using District property for religious purposes could survive First Amendment challenge only if excluding this category of speech was reasonable and viewpoint neutral. The court's conclusion in this case was that Rule 7 met this test. We cannot agree with this holding, for Rule 7

was unconstitutionally applied in this case.

The Court of Appeals thought that the application of Rule 7 in this case was viewpoint neutral because it had been and would be applied in the same way to all uses of school property for religious purposes. That all religions and all uses for religious purposes are treated alike under Rule 7, however, does not answer the critical question whether it discriminates on the basis of viewpoint to permit school property to be used for the presentation of all views about family issues and child-rearing except those dealing with the subject matter from a religious standpoint....

The District, as a respondent, would save its judgment below on the ground that to permit its property to be used for religious purposes would be an establishment of religion forbidden by the First Amendment. This Court suggested in *Widmar v. Vincent* that the interest of the State in avoiding an Establishment Clause violation "may be [a] compelling" one justifying an abridgment of free speech otherwise protected by the First Amendment; but the Court went on to hold that permitting use of University property for religious purposes under the open access policy involved there would not be incompatible with the Court's Establishment Clause cases.

We have no more trouble than did the *Widmar* Court in disposing of the claimed defense on the ground that the posited fears of an Establishment Clause violation are unfounded. The showing of this film would not have been during school hours, would not have been sponsored by the school, and would have been open to the public not just to church members. The District property had repeatedly been used by a wide variety of private organizations. Under these circumstances, as in *Widmar*, there would have been no realistic danger that the community would think that the District was endorsing religion or any particular creed, and any benefit to religion or to the Church would have been no more than incidental. As in *Widmar*, permitting District property to be used to exhibit the film involved in this case would not have been an establishment of religion under the three-part test articulated in *Lemon v. Kurtzman*. The challenged governmental action has a secular purpose, does not have the principal or primary effect of advancing or inhibiting religion, and does not foster an excessive entanglement with religion....[1]

Reversed.

KENNEDY, J., CONCURRING IN PART AND CONCURRING IN THE JUDGMENT

Given the issues presented as well as the apparent unanimity of our conclusion that this overt, viewpoint-based discrimination contradicts the Speech Clause of the First Amendment and that there has been no substantial showing of a potential

---

[1] While we are somewhat diverted by Justice Scalia's evening at the cinema, we return to the reality that there is a proper way to inter an established decision, and *Lemon*, however frightening it might be to some, has not been overruled....

Establishment Clause violation, I agree with Justice Scalia that the Court's citation of *Lemon v. Kurtzman* is unsettling and unnecessary. The same can be said of the Court's use of the phrase "endorsing religion," which ... cannot suffice as a rule of decision consistent with our precedents and our traditions in this part of our jurisprudence....

SCALIA, J., WITH WHOM THÓMAS, J., JOINS CONCURRING IN THE JUDGMENT

I join the Court's conclusion that the District's refusal to allow use of school facilities for petitioners' film viewing, while generally opening the schools for community activities, violates petitioners' First Amendment free-speech rights to the extent it compelled the District's denial. I also agree with the Court that allowing Lamb's Chapel to use school facilities poses "no realistic danger" of a violation of the Establishment Clause, but I cannot accept most of its reasoning in this regard. The Court explains that the showing of petitioners' film on school property after school hours would not cause the community to "think that the District was endorsing religion or any particular creed," and further notes that access to school property would not violate the three-part test articulated in *Lemon v. Kurtzman*.

As to the Court's invocation of the *Lemon* test: Like some ghoul in a late-night horror movie that repeatedly sits up in its grave and shuffles abroad, after being repeatedly killed and buried, *Lemon* stalks our Establishment Clause jurisprudence once again, frightening the little children and school attorneys of Center Moriches Union Free School District. Its most recent burial, only last Term, was, to be sure, not fully six-feet under; our decision in *Lee v. Weisman* conspicuously avoided using the supposed "test" but also declined the invitation to repudiate it. Over the years, however, no fewer than five of the currently sitting Justices have, in their own opinions, personally driven pencils through the creature's heart (the author of today's opinion repeatedly), and a sixth has joined an opinion doing so.

The secret of the *Lemon* test's survival, I think, is that it is so easy to kill. It is there to scare us (and our audience) when we wish it to do so, but we command it to return to the tomb at will....

For my part, I agree with the long list of constitutional law scholars who have criticized *Lemon* and bemoaned the strange Establishment Clause geometry of crooked lines and wavering shapes its intermittent use has produced. I will decline to apply *Lemon*—whether it validates or invalidates the government action in question—and therefore cannot join the opinion of the Court today.

I cannot join for yet another reason: the Court's statement that the proposed use of the school's facilities is constitutional because (among other things) it would not signal endorsement of religion in general. What a strange notion, that a Constitution which *itself* gives "religion in general" preferential treatment (I refer to the Free Exercise Clause) forbids endorsement of religion in general....

For the reasons given by the Court, I agree that the Free Speech Clause of the First Amendment forbids what respondents have done here. As for the asserted Establishment Clause justification, I would hold, simply and clearly, that giving Lamb's Chapel nondiscriminatory access to school facilities cannot violate that provision because it does not signify state or local embrace of a particular religious sect.

QUESTIONS

1. What explains the Court's unanimity in *Lamb's Chapel* given the divisiveness of other Establishment Clause cases?

2. Is the alliance of parties *amici* in *Lamb's Chapel* surprising? Identify the constitutional concerns in this case that allied such otherwise politically disparate groups as the Christian Legal Society, Americans United for the Separation of Church and State, the ACLU, the AFL-CIO, Concerned Women for America, and Free Congress Foundation in support of the church.

3. The justices' continued dissatisfaction with *Lemon v. Kurtzman* is apparent in *Lamb's Chapel*. They continue to express their dissatisfaction via intramural exchanges targeting one another. Of what significance is the exchange between Justices White, Kennedy, and Scalia over applying *Lemon* to *Lamb's Chapel*?

4. How might state or school district officials tailor school use regulations in the wake of *Lamb's Chapel*? Does the result in *Lamb's Chapel* create a dilemma for public school officials whereby they either open facilities to all groups and risk public hostility over some uses, or close facilities to all groups and risk public resentment due to inefficient and unresponsive use of government property?

COMMENT

The same term that it decided *Lamb's Chapel*, the Court also declined to reexamine the *Lemon* test in *Zobrest v. Catalina Foothills School District*, 509 U.S. 1 (1993). Decided by a 5–4 vote, the Court in *Zobrest* held that the Establishment Clause does not bar a public school district from using government funds to provide a sign-language interpreter to a hearing disabled child enrolled in a parochial school in order to facilitate that student's education. The Court reasoned that government programs that benefit a broad class of citizens, and that are defined without reference to religion, are not easily challenged under the Establishment Clause.

ESTABLISHMENT OF RELIGION

Rosenberger v. Rector and Visitors of the University of Virginia
515 U.S. 819 (1995)

SETTING

The Supreme Court's already troubled Establishment Clause jurisprudence encounters ever greater difficulties when Establishment Clause issues also implicate other First Amendment values such as free exercise of religion and free speech. Two cases in the Court's 1994 Term demonstrated those difficulties.

The first case involved an application by the Ohio Ku Klux Klan to place a cross in the Capitol Square in Columbus, Ohio, from December 4 to December 24, as part of that community's holiday display. The local board authorized to approve displays denied the application on the ground that placing a cross on the public square would violate the Establishment Clause. The Ku Klux Klan responded that denial of its application violated its members' rights to speak and to freely exercise their religion. In *Capitol Square Review and Advisory Board v. Pinette*, 515 U.S. 753 (1995), the Court decided that the Klan should be allowed to display the cross. Although seven justices agreed with the result, they were badly fragmented in their reasoning. Justices Scalia, Chief Justice Rehnquist, and Justices O'Connor, Kennedy, Souter, Thomas, and Breyer declared that private religious speech is protected under the First Amendment. They also agreed that, although compliance with the Establishment Clause is a state interest sufficiently compelling to justify content-based restrictions on speech, allowing the Klan to display the cross does not violate the Establishment Clause. Justice Scalia, Chief Justice Rehnquist, and Justices Kennedy and Thomas also contended that even in a public forum, religious expression does not violate the Establishment Clause if the expression is purely private and occurs in a public forum that is open to all. Justice Thomas con-

cluded that the Klan has a primarily nonreligious purpose in displaying the
cross. Justices O'Connor, Souter, and Breyer expressed the view that there is
no realistic danger that a reasonable person observing the Klan's cross would
think that the state was endorsing religion or any particular creed.

The second case decided in the 1994 Term demonstrated even more
clearly the difficulties the Court encounters when Establishment Clause, Free
Exercise Clause, and Free Speech and Press issues overlap.

In 1990, the University of Virginia supported a wide variety of student
organizations, activities, and publications through its Student Activities Fund
(SAF). The SAF was financed by a mandatory student activities fee of $14 per
student per semester. The Rector and Visitors of the University exercised control over the operation of the SAF, which they delegated to the Student Council,
an elected student body organization. The council allocated funds in accordance with the University of Virginia Student Activity Fee Funding Guidelines
established by the Rector and Visitors. Those guidelines require that for a student group to be eligible to submit bills from its outside contractors for payment, it must become a "Contracted Independent Organization" (CIO). No
direct payments are made to CIOs.

University guidelines prohibited funding for religious activities, payment
of honoraria or similar fees, social entertaining or related expenses, philanthropic contributions, political activities, or activities that would jeopardize the
university's tax exempt status. A "religious activity" was defined as any activity
that "primarily promotes or manifests a particular belie[f] in or about a deity or
an ultimate reality." During the 1990–91 school year, 118 student groups
received SAF support, including some 15 organizations defined by the guidelines as "student news, information, opinion, entertainment, or academic communications media groups."

Ronald Rosenberger, an undergraduate student, joined with other students in 1990 to form Wide Awake Productions. Wide Awake Productions
intended to publish a magazine designed to facilitate discussion and tolerance
of Christian viewpoints. The group was not affiliated with any religious institution or organization. Wide Awake Productions applied for and acquired CIO status despite the university guideline denying CIO status to religious activities. By
June 1992, the group had published three issues of the magazine entitled *Wide
Awake: A Christian Perspective on the University of Virginia*. The magazine was
distributed free of charge to about 5,000 students on campus. In January 1991,
the organization submitted an application for funding from the SAF in the
amount of $5,862 to cover publication costs. The student council denied the
request, on the ground that Wide Awake Productions "is a religious activity."
Wide Awake Productions exhausted all avenues of appeal within the university,
but the denial was upheld.

Rosenberger filed suit in U.S. District Court for the Western District of
Virginia on behalf of Wide Awake Productions challenging the denial of funding.
The suit claimed that the university's categorical denial of the otherwise eligi-
ble student publication on the basis of religious perspective violated students'

rights to freedom of speech and press, free exercise of religion, and equal protection of the law. The suit sought declaratory and injunctive relief prohibiting the university from denying funding on the basis of the content or viewpoint of the publication. The university moved for summary judgment on the ground that the university was prohibited by the Establishment Clause from funding Wide Awake Productions.

The district court granted the university's motion for summary judgment, holding that the denial of SAF support was not impermissible content or viewpoint discrimination. The district court did not rule on the Establishment Clause question. Although the Court of Appeals for the Fourth Circuit ruled that the denial of funding did impose a burden on the free speech rights of Wide Awake Productions, it affirmed. The court of appeals reasoned that the burden was justified by the university's compelling state interest in avoiding a violation of the Establishment Clause. The court further explained that the "entanglement" prong of the *Lemon* test was "most plainly implicated by this case."

The Supreme Court granted Rosenberger's petition for a writ of certiorari.

HIGHLIGHTS OF SUPREME COURT ARGUMENTS

BRIEF FOR ROSENBERGER

◆ Wide Awake Productions has satisfied all the requirements for funding eligibility from the University of Virginia. The only "problem" with its application is that the publication is rooted in the Christian religious faith of its editors.

◆ This case poses a straightforward question: Is the religious perspective of a student publication a lawful ground for excluding it from benefits otherwise available to organizations of its type?

◆ The university's denial of Wide Awake Productions' application for funding discriminates on the basis of the content of speech. This Court has made clear as recently as 1992 in *R.A.V. v. City of St. Paul*, 505 U.S. 377 (1992) that content-based discrimination against speech is "presumptively invalid." Such discrimination can be justified only on the basis of a compelling governmental purpose. The university's exclusion of organizations that engage in "religious activities" is essentially identical to the defendant's exclusion of organizations with "religious purposes" in *Lamb's Chapel v. Center Moriches School District*, which this Court unanimously held to be an impermissible viewpoint discrimination.

◆ The nondiscriminatory funding of a broad range of publications and activities, without regard to their religious, anti-religious or non-religious point of view does not violate the Establishment Clause. The Fourth Circuit's decision creates a conflict between the Establishment and Speech and Press Clauses and a conflict with the Free Exercise Clause. It strips religious speakers of the constitutional protection afforded to secular perspectives and points of view. This Court repeatedly has held that the mere receipt of government funds does not convert a private decision into state action. In this case, no one could argue that the university is responsible for the content of Wide Awake Productions.

AMICUS CURIAE BRIEFS SUPPORTING ROSENBERGER

American Center for Law and Justice; Catholic League for Religious and Civil Rights; joint brief of the Christian Legal Society, Christian Life Commission of the Southern Baptist Convention, Family Research Council, Home School Legal Defense Association, and National Association of Evangelicals; Intercollegiate Studies Institute; Governor George Allen, Commonwealth of Virginia.

BRIEF FOR UNIVERSITY OF VIRGINIA

◆ This case is not about religion. It is about the ability of public education to set priorities for the use of public funds. The University of Virginia's decision to fund only those activities closely related to the educational purpose of the university is right and necessary.

◆ In the expenditure of public funds, decisions based on the content of speech are familiar, necessary, and entirely legitimate. Any number of groups—including Young Democrats or Young Republicans—could have been denied funding on the ground that their activities were not related to the educational purposes of the University of Virginia.

◆ The Student Activity Fee Funding Guidelines are reasonable. They do not reflect an ideologically driven attempt to suppress a particular point of view. They do not aim specifically at religion or penalize any religious activity.

◆ *Lamb's Chapel* is inapposite because it dealt with access to facilities, not funding of speech. Here, the question is not whether the university will withhold a benefit that is costless to provide, but whether it will incur a cost to provide the benefit. The distinction between access and funding was recognized by this Court in *Widmar v. Vincent*, 454 U.S. 263 (1981).

◆ Student activity fees constitute a nonpublic forum. This Court has held that in the nonpublic forum, content-based rules are allowed "as long as the regulation on speech is reasonable and not an attempt to suppress expression merely because public officials oppose the speaker's view." *Perry Education Association v. Perry Local Educators' Association*, 460 U.S. 37 (1983). Both the district court and court of appeals found that the administration of the funding guidelines do not reveal any effort to suppress a particular point of view.

AMICUS CURIAE BRIEFS SUPPORTING THE UNIVERSITY OF VIRGINIA

Joint brief of Americans United for Separation of Church and State and American Jewish Committee and Anti-Defamation League; joint brief of the American Civil Liberties Union (ACLU) and ACLU of Virginia; Pacific Legal Foundation; joint brief of the Baptist Joint Committee on Public Affairs, National Council of Churches of Christ in the United States, American Jewish Congress, Union of American Hebrew Congregations, Hadassah, the Women's Zionist Organization of America, Inc., People for the American Way, and National Coalition for Public Education and Religious Liberty; Council on Religious Freedom; National School Boards Association.

AMICUS CURIAE BRIEF SUPPORTING NEITHER PARTY

Student Press Law Center.

SUPREME COURT DECISION: 5–4

KENNEDY, J.

... It is axiomatic that the government may not regulate speech based on its substantive content or the message it conveys.... Other principles follow from this precept. In the realm of private speech or expression, government regulation may not favor one speaker over another.... Discrimination against speech because of its message is presumed to be unconstitutional.... These rules informed our determination that the government offends the First Amendment when it imposes financial burdens on certain speakers based on the content of their expression.... When the government targets not subject matter but particular views taken by speakers on a subject, the violation of the First Amendment is all the more blatant. Viewpoint discrimination is thus an egregious form of content discrimination. The government must abstain from regulating speech when the specific motivating ideology or the opinion or perspective of the speaker is the rationale for the restriction....

Once it has opened a limited forum, ... the State must respect the lawful boundaries it has itself set. The State may not exclude speech where its distinction is not "reasonable in light of the purpose served by the forum," *Cornelius* [*v. NAACP Legal Defense & Education Fund, Inc.*], 473 U.S. 788 (1985), ... nor may it discriminate against speech on the basis of its viewpoint....

The [SAF] is a forum more in a metaphysical than in a spatial or geographic sense, but the same principles are applicable....

The University's denial of Wide Awake Production's request for third-party payments in the present case is based upon viewpoint discrimination not unlike the discrimination the school district relied upon in *Lamb's Chapel* and that we found invalid....

We [have] recognized that when the government appropriates public funds to promote a particular policy of its own it is entitled to say what it wishes. When the government disburses public funds to private entities to convey a governmental message, it may take legitimate and appropriate steps to ensure that its message is neither garbled nor distorted by the grantee.

It does not follow, however, ... that viewpoint-based restrictions are proper when the University does not itself speak or subsidize transmittal of a message it favors but instead expends funds to encourage a diversity of views from private speakers. A holding that the University may not discriminate based on the viewpoint of private persons whose speech it facilitates does not restrict the University's own speech, which is controlled by different principles....

Vital First Amendment speech principles are at stake here. The first danger to liberty lies in granting the State the power to examine publications to determine whether or not they are based on some ultimate idea and if so for the State to classify them. The second, and corollary, danger is to speech from the chilling of individual thought and expression. That danger is especially real in the University setting, where the State acts against a background and tradition of thought and experiment that is at the center of our intellectual and philosophic tradition....

The Guideline invoked by the University to deny third-party contractor payments on behalf of WAP effects a sweeping restriction on student thought and student inquiry in the context of University sponsored publications. The prohibition on funding on behalf of publications that "primarily promot[e] or manifes[t] a particular belie[f] in or about a deity or an ultimate reality," in its ordinary and commonsense meaning, has a vast potential reach....

Based on the principles we have discussed, we hold that the regulation invoked to deny SAF support, both in its terms and in its application to these petitioners, is a denial of their right of free speech guaranteed by the First Amendment. It remains to be considered whether the violation following from the University's action is excused by the necessity of complying with the Constitution's prohibition against state establishment of religion....

A central lesson of our decisions is that a significant factor in upholding governmental programs in the face of Establishment Clause attack is their neutrality towards religion.... More than once have we rejected the position that the Establishment Clause even justifies, much less requires, a refusal to extend free speech rights to religious speakers who participate in broad-reaching government programs neutral in design....

The governmental program here is neutral toward religion. There is no suggestion that the University created it to advance religion or adopted some ingenious device with the purpose of aiding a religious cause. The object of the SAF is to open a forum for speech and to support various student enterprises, including the publication of newspapers, in recognition of the diversity and creativity of student life....

Government neutrality is apparent in the State's over-all scheme in a further meaningful respect. The program respects the critical difference "between government speech endorsing religion, which the Establishment Clause forbids, and private speech endorsing religion, which the Free Speech and Free Exercise Clauses protect." [*Board of Education of Westside Community Schools (District 66) v.*] *Mergens* [496 U.S. 226 (1990)]. In this case, "the government has not willfully fostered or encouraged" any mistaken impression that the student newspapers speak for the University. *Capitol Square Review and Advisory Board v. Pinette.* The University has taken pains to disassociate itself from the private speech involved in this case. The Court of Appeals' apparent concern that *Wide Awake*'s religious orientation would be attributed to the University is not a plausible fear, and there is no real likelihood that the speech in question is being either endorsed or coerced by the State....

It does not violate the Establishment Clause for a public university to grant access to its facilities on a religion-neutral basis to a wide spectrum of student groups, including groups which use meeting rooms for sectarian activities, accompanied by some devotional exercises.... This is so even where the upkeep, maintenance, and repair of the facilities attributed to those uses is paid from a student activities fund to which students are required to contribute. The government usually acts by spending money. Even the provision of a meeting room ... involved governmental expenditure, if only in the form of electricity and heating or cooling costs. The error made by the Court of Appeals, as well as by the dissent, lies in focusing on the money that is undoubtedly expended by the government, rather than on the nature of the benefit received by the recipient.... [I]t follows that a public university may maintain its own computer facility and give student groups access to that facility, including the use of the printers, on a religion neutral, say first-come-first-served, basis....

The viewpoint discrimination inherent in the University's regulation required public officials to scan and interpret student publications to discern their underlying philosophic assumptions respecting religious theory and belief. That course of action was a denial of the right of free speech and would risk fostering a pervasive bias or hostility to religion, which could undermine the very neutrality the Establishment Clause requires. There is no Establishment Clause violation in the University's honoring its duties under the Free Speech Clause.

The judgment of the Court of Appeals must be, and is, reversed.

It is so ordered.

O'CONNOR, J., CONCURRING

... This case lies at the intersection of the principle of government neutrality and the prohibition on state funding of religious activities....

When two bedrock principles so conflict, understandably neither can provide the definitive answer. Reliance on categorical platitudes is unavailing. Resolution instead depends on the hard task of judging-sifting through the details and determining whether the challenged program offends the Establishment Clause. Such judgment requires courts to draw lines, sometimes quite fine, based on the particular facts of each case....

So it is in this case. The nature of the dispute does not admit of categorical answers, nor should any be inferred from the Court's decision today.... Instead, certain considerations specific to the program at issue lead me to conclude that by providing the same assistance to *Wide Awake* that it does to other publications, the University would not be endorsing the magazine's religious perspective.

First, the student organizations, at the University's insistence, remain strictly independent of the University.... Any reader of *Wide Awake* would be on notice of the publication's independence from the University....

Second, financial assistance is distributed in a manner that ensures its use only for permissible purposes.... This feature also makes this case analogous to a school providing equal access to a generally available printing press (or other physical facilities), and unlike a block grant to religious organizations.

Third, assistance is provided to the religious publication in a context that makes improbable any perception of government endorsement of the religious message. *Wide Awake* does not exist in a vacuum. It competes with 15 other magazines and newspapers for advertising and readership. The widely divergent viewpoints of these many purveyors of opinion, all supported on an equal basis by the University, significantly diminishes the danger that the message of any one publication is perceived as endorsed by the University.... This is not the harder case where religious speech threatens to dominate the forum....

Finally, although the question is not presented here, I note the possibility that the student fee is susceptible to a Free Speech Clause challenge by an objecting student that she should not be compelled to pay for speech with which she disagrees.... While the Court does not resolve the question here, ... the existence of such an opt-out possibility not available to citizens generally, ... provides a potential basis for distinguishing proceeds of the student fees in this case from proceeds of the general assessments in support of religion that lie at the core of the prohibition against religious funding....

The Court's decision today therefore neither trumpets the supremacy of the neutrality principle nor signals the demise of the funding prohibition in Establishment Clause jurisprudence....

Subject to these comments, I join the opinion of the Court.

THOMAS, J., CONCURRING

... I write separately to express my disagreement with the historical analysis put forward by the dissent. Although the dissent starts down the right path in consulting the original meaning of the Establishment Clause, its misleading application of history yields a principle that is inconsistent with our Nation's long tradition of allowing religious adherents to participate on equal terms in neutral government programs....

Though our Establishment Clause jurisprudence is in hopeless disarray, this case provides an opportunity to reaffirm one basic principle that has enjoyed an uncharacteristic degree of consensus: The Clause does not compel the exclusion of religious groups from government benefits programs that are generally available to a broad class of participants....

SOUTER, STEVENS, GINSBURG, AND BREYER, J.J., DISSENTING

The Court today, for the first time, approves direct funding of core religious activities by an arm of the State....

Using public funds for the direct subsidization of preaching the word is categorically forbidden under the Establishment Clause, and if the Clause was meant to accomplish nothing else, it was meant to bar this use of public money. Evidence on the subject antedates even the Bill of Rights itself, as may be seen in the writings of Madison, whose authority on questions about the meaning of the Establishment Clause is well settled....

"Although Establishment Clause jurisprudence is characterized by few absolutes, the Clause does absolutely prohibit government-financed ... indoctrination into the beliefs of a particular religious faith." *School* [*District of Grand Rapids*] *v. Ball*, 473 U. S. [373 (1985)]....

Given the dispositive effect of the Establishment Clause's bar to funding the magazine, there should be no need to decide whether in the absence of this bar the University would violate the Free Speech Clause by limiting funding as it has done.... But the Court's speech analysis may have independent application, and its flaws should not pass unremarked....

[T]he prohibition on viewpoint discrimination serves that important purpose of the Free Speech Clause, which is to bar the government from skewing public debate. Other things being equal, viewpoint discrimination occurs when government allows one message while prohibiting the messages of those who can reasonably be expected to respond.... It is precisely this element of taking sides in a public debate that identifies viewpoint discrimination and makes it the most pernicious of all distinctions based on content. Thus, if government assists those espousing one point of view, neutrality requires it to assist those espousing opposing points of view, as well.

There is no viewpoint discrimination in the University's application of its Guidelines to deny funding to *Wide Awake*. Under those Guidelines, a "religious activit[y]," which is not eligible for funding is "an activity which primarily promotes or manifests a particular belief(s) in or about a deity or an ultimate reality." It is clear that this is the basis on which *Wide Awake* Productions was denied funding....

If the Guidelines were written or applied so as to limit only such Christian advocacy and no other evangelical efforts that might compete with it, the discrimination would be based on viewpoint. But that is not what the regulation authorizes; it applies to Muslim and Jewish and Buddhist advocacy as well as to Christian. And since it limits funding to activities promoting or manifesting a particular belief not only "in" but "about" a deity or ultimate reality, it applies to agnostics and atheists as well as it does to deists and theists....

To put the point another way, the Court's decision equating a categorical exclusion of both sides of the religious debate with viewpoint discrimination suggests the Court has concluded that primarily religious and antireligious speech, grouped together, always provides an opposing (and not merely a related) viewpoint to any speech about any secular topic. Thus, the Court's reasoning requires a university that funds private publications about any primarily nonreligious topic also to fund publications primarily espousing adherence to or rejection of religion. But a university's decision to fund a magazine about racism, and not to fund publications aimed at urging repentance before God does not skew the debate either about racism or the desirability of religious conversion. The Court's contrary holding amounts to a significant reformulation of our viewpoint discrimination precedents and will significantly expand access to limited-access forums....

Since I cannot see the future I cannot tell whether today's decision portends much more than making a shambles out of student activity fees in public colleges. Still, my apprehension is whetted by Chief Justice Burger's warning in *Lemon v. Kurtzman*: "in constitutional adjudication some steps, which when taken were thought to approach 'the verge,' have become the platform for yet further steps. A certain momentum develops in constitutional theory and it can be a 'downhill thrust' easily set in motion but difficult to retard or stop."

I respectfully dissent.

QUESTIONS

1. The American Center for Law and Justice argued in its *amicus* brief that the *Lemon* test has produced confusion, not neutrality, and that *Lemon* and its "confusing progeny" should be overruled. What is the status of *Lemon* after *Rosenberger*?

2. One of the *amicus* briefs in support of Rosenberger against the University of Virginia came from Virginia Governor George Allen. Governor Allen argued that "It is of great concern that the University of Virginia, an institution founded by Thomas Jefferson, has been shown to have a policy of funding student publications that discriminates against students wishing to espouse religious viewpoints and that may have the practical effect of suppressing such views." He contended that the funding guidelines created "Alice-in-Wonderland distinctions" that resulted in "entanglements of the worst sort" and that such entanglement "cannot be what Mr. Jefferson had in mind when

he wrote the Virginia Statute for Religious Freedom or when he founded the University of Virginia." Is it curious that the principal executive officer of the Commonwealth of Virginia would adopt this view?

3. Assess and evaluate the Court's Establishment Clause jurisprudence as of the end of the 1994 Term. Should the Court clearly overrule *Lemon*? Is there any way out of the morass of the Court's Establishment Clause jurisprudence?

COMMENT

In March 1997, Oklahoma representative Ernest Istook Jr. introduced a "religious freedom" amendment to the Constitution in the U.S. House of Representatives. The proposed amendment had one hundred sixteen House sponsors. The proposed amendment reads:

> To secure the people's right to acknowledge God: The right to pray or acknowledge religious belief, heritage or tradition on public property, including public schools, shall not be infringed. The government shall not compel joining in prayer, initiate or compose school prayers, discriminate against or deny a benefit on account of religion.

Istook said the proposed amendment was "the only way" to end the hostility toward religious expression and symbols in American life fostered by thirty years of adverse Supreme Court rulings. New York representative Jerrold Nadler, an amendment opponent, replied: "How can people who call themselves conservatives, people who don't trust government to regulate the railroads or deadly weapons, trust the government to meddle in the religious education of our children?"

ESTABLISHMENT OF RELIGION

Agostini v. Felton
117 S.Ct. 1997 (1997)

SETTING

In 1965, Congress enacted Title I of the Elementary and Secondary Education Act, which was part of President Lyndon Johnson's "Great Society" domestic program. According to a Senate report, Title I was intended to "bring better education to millions of disadvantaged youth who need it most" by authorizing the secretary of Health, Education and Welfare (now the Department of Education) to provide financial assistance to local educational agencies that serve low-income families. Children attending both public and private schools are eligible for Title I remedial services if they meet the statutory standards of economic and educational disadvantage and are progressing at below-normal grade levels. Most Title I money is used to improve mathematics and reading scores. During its first thirty years, Title I was the federal government's largest and most important commitment to elementary and secondary education.

A year after the enactment of Title I, the Board of Education of the City of New York began to provide Title I services to students on the premises of the schools that recipient students usually attended, which meant that personnel hired to provide Title I services taught in private as well as in public schools. The services included remedial reading, reading skills, remedial mathematics, English as a second language, and guidance. In order to avoid accusations that Title I monies were being used to advance religion, the school board monitored the content of the instructional materials offered through the federally funded classes.

In 1978, Betty-Louise Felton and five other taxpayers filed suit in the U.S. District Court for the Eastern District of New York against the Secretary of the U.S. Department of Education, the Chancellor of the Board of Education of the City of New York, and the Board of Education of the City of New York. The plaintiffs asked the court to declare that having public employees provide Title I services in religious schools violates the Establishment Clause of the First Amendment, notwithstanding the board's monitoring of the curricula. Yolanda Aguilar represented the defendants. In *Aguilar v. Felton*, 473 U.S. 402 (1985), the Supreme Court agreed. It held that government monitoring of Title I personnel to assure that they do not inject religion into remedial classes taught in church-related schools "inevitably results in the excessive entanglement of church and state" and therefore violates the Establishment Clause. Justices Rehnquist and O'Connor joined Justice White and Chief Justice Burger in dissent.

In a companion case to *Aguilar—Grand Rapids School District v. Ball*, 473 U.S. 373 (1985)—the Court by the same 5–4 majority struck down a Michigan program that provided instruction in music, art, and physical education to students in religious schools. The defect in that program, said the majority, was that it "in effect subsidized the religious functions of the parochial schools by taking over a substantial portion of their responsibility for teaching secular subjects."

For approximately a dozen year after *Aguilar*, the City of New York School Board, like other school boards throughout the country, sought alternative methods for delivering Title I services to eligible children attending church-related schools. Some districts required parochial students to attend public school classrooms in order to receive the services. Others, like the City of New York, provided the services in buses equipped as classrooms that were parked near—but not on—private school premises. Still others provided the services by computer. The alternatives proved to be expensive: The City of New York School Board estimated that it spent more than $15 million per year just complying with the Supreme Court's holding in *Aguilar*. The district also believed that the alternative methods of delivering Title I services were educationally inferior.

Changes in Supreme Court personnel after 1985 resulted in a shift from the 5–4 majority by which *Aguilar* was decided. Within the decade, Chief Justice Rehnquist and Justices O'Connor, Kennedy, Scalia, and Thomas had called for *Aguilar* to be overruled.

Responding to the statements of individual justices regarding *Aguilar*, in late 1995 the Chancellor of the Board of Education of the City of New York and a group of parents of children eligible to receive Title I services—led by Rachel Agostini—filed separate motions under Rule 60(b) of the Federal Rules of Civil Procedure for relief from the judgment in *Aguilar*. That rule provides, in part:

> On motion and upon such terms as are just, the court may relieve a party or a party's legal representative from a final judgment, order, or proceeding for the following reasons: ... (5) ... it is no longer equitable that the judgment should have prospective application; or (6) any other reason justifying relief from the operation of the judgment.

The Rule 60(b) motions noted that five justices had called for the overruling of *Aguilar* and argued that decisions since *Aguilar* had been inconsistent with it.

The district court acknowledged that "it is at least unusual, if not extraordinary, that the losing parties to a Supreme Court case can point to such promising indicia that they would win the case now." Nonetheless, that court denied the motion on the ground that a lower court could not properly anticipate the overruling of *Aguilar*. The U.S. Court of Appeals for the Second Circuit affirmed. The Supreme Court of the United States granted Agostini's petition for a writ of certiorari.

HIGHLIGHTS OF SUPREME COURT ARGUMENTS

BRIEF FOR CHANCELLOR AND BOARD OF EDUCATION OF CITY OF NEW YORK

◆ Rule 60(b) is an appropriate vehicle for the relief sought in this case. Application of the rule in *Aguilar v. Felton* is no longer equitable because the rule is not supported by a majority of the Supreme Court.

◆ *Aguilar* should be overruled so that special education services may be provided to students on the premises of the sectarian schools attended by eligible students.

◆ *Aguilar* is inconsistent with the guiding principle of neutrality that has been expressed in cases like *Rosenberger v. Rector and Visitors of the University of Virginia*.

◆ Assuming that the *Lemon v. Kurtzman* test remains valid, an on-site Title I program is legal under that test. In light of the case law since *Aguilar*, there is no excessive entanglement with religion by offering Title I programs on site.

BRIEF FOR AGOSTINI

◆ In *Board of Education of Kiryas Joel Village School District v. Grumet*, a majority of this Court invited reconsideration of *Aguilar*. In Justice O'Connor's words, the Court should be prepared to reconsider *Aguilar* in order "to bring our Establishment Clause jurisprudence back to what I think is the proper track—government impartiality, not animosity, towards religion." The district court declared that there could not be a more appropriate case for reconsidering *Aguilar* than this one.

◆ *Aguilar* has disrupted the administration of Title I and has created confusion in an important area of constitutional law.

◆ *Aguilar* is inconsistent with decisions since 1985. The Court's present focus is on neutrality and no one disputes that Title I funds are used neutrally to provide services to deserving children.

◆ *Aguilar* rests on an extreme application of a repudiated notion of excessive entanglement under *Lemon*. Although the three-part *Lemon* test has not been formally repudiated by the Court as a whole, it appears to have been abandoned in favor of the unified neutrality test.

◆ If it does not repudiate *Lemon*, the Court should eliminate the entanglement prong as a formal Establishment Clause test.

◆ *Aguilar* has had a disruptive effect on Title I, which is the federal government's principal commitment to elementary and secondary education. The most profound effects have been felt by economically and educationally disadvantaged school children. Post-*Aguilar* Title I delivery methods are vastly more expensive to deliver, the result being that fewer Title I dollars are available for actual instruction to public and private school students alike.

AMICUS CURIAE BRIEFS SUPPORTING THE CHANCELLOR AND NEW YORK CITY SCHOOL BOARD AND AGOSTINI

United States; joint brief of Sarah Peter, Joan Peter, Aaron Westendorp, Krista Westendorp, and Douglas Westendorp (children with physical and cognitive disabilities who live in Minnesota); Jewish Commission on Law and Public Affairs; Knights of Columbus; U.S. Senator Robert F. Bennett; Becket Fund for Religious Liberty; joint brief of the Christian Legal Society, Association of Christian Schools International, Catholic League for Religious and Civil Rights, Christian Life Commission of the Southern Baptist Convention, Family Research Council, Focus on the Family, Lutheran Church-Missouri Synod, National Association of Evangelicals, and Southern Center for Law and Ethics; U.S. Catholic Conference; Pacific Legal Foundation.

BRIEF FOR FELTON

◆ A motion under Federal Rule of Civil Procedure 60(b) cannot be used as a vehicle to grant the relief requested in this case. There has been no change in the law that would warrant relief from the judgment entered in *Aguilar v. Felton*. Reliance on Rule 60(b) would be unprecedented and would compromise the institutional integrity of the Court. Alleged changes in factual conditions and law are no basis for invoking Rule 60(b).

◆ If the Court wishes to reconsider *Aguilar*—which it should not—it should at least remand the case to the district court to hold a plenary hearing to resolve questions of fact about issues raised by allowing Title I services to be reinstituted on the premises of religious schools of New York City.

◆ If the Court does address the merits, excessive entanglement is not the only ground on which to adhere to *Aguilar*. It should not be forgotten that in *Aguilar*, 99.76 percent of the Title I monies being administered by the City of New York went to students enrolled in religious schools (principally Catholic and Hebrew).

◆ Provision of remedial education services inside religious school buildings violates the Establishment Clause for three reasons: first, such a program creates a symbolic union of church and state in education. Second, the program subsidizes the religious functions of the religious schools. Third, there is no sure way to prevent public employees on religious school grounds from supporting the religious mission of the private schools. References to "neutrality" do not dispose of these problems.

◆ If *Aguilar* is overruled, Title I personnel will become the adjuncts of the religious schools in which they provide services.

AMICUS CURIAE BRIEFS SUPPORTING FELTON

Joint brief of the American Jewish Congress, the American Federation of Teachers, American Jewish Committee, Anti-Defamation League, Baptist Joint Committee on Public Affairs, Central Conference of American Rabbis, National Education Association, National Jewish Community Relations Advisory Council, People for the American Way, and the Union of American Hebrew Congregations; joint brief of Americans United for Separation of Church and State, the American Civil Liberties Union, and New York Civil Liberties Union; joint brief of Council on Religious Freedom, Americans for Religious Liberty, and several individuals who are parties in related litigation; New York County Lawyers Association Committee on Supreme Court of the United States.

AMICUS CURIAE BRIEF FOR NEITHER SIDE

Joint brief of the Institute for Justice, the Center for Education Reform, Parents for School Choice, and Hope for Cleveland's Children (requesting the Court to be aware of principles that would make it possible to establish the constitutionality of state-sponsored school choice).

SUPREME COURT DECISION: 5–4

O'CONNOR, J.

... [P]etitioners' ability to satisfy the prerequisites of Rule 60(b)(5) hinges on whether our later Establishment Clause cases have so undermined *Aguilar* that it is no longer good law....

Our ... recent cases have undermined the assumptions upon which [*Grand Rapids School District v.*] *Ball* and *Aguilar* relied....

First, we have abandoned the presumption erected in ... *Ball* that the placement of public employees on parochial school grounds inevitably results in the impermissible effect of state-sponsored indoctrination or constitutes a symbolic union between government and religion.... *Zobrest* [*v. Catalina Foothills School Dist.*, 509 U.S. 1 (1993)] ... expressly rejected the notion—relied on in *Ball* and *Aguilar*—that, solely because of her presence on private school property, a public employee will be presumed to inculcate religion in the students. *Zobrest* also implicitly repudiated another assumption on which *Ball* and *Aguilar* turned: that the presence of a public employee on private school property creates an impermissible "symbolic link" between government and religion....

Second, we have departed from the rule relied on in *Ball* that all government aid that directly aids the educational function of religious schools is invalid....

[U]nder current law, the Shared Time program in *Ball* and New York City's Title I program in *Aguilar* will not, as a matter of law, be deemed to have the effect of advancing religion through indoctrination. Indeed, each of the premises upon which we relied in *Ball* to reach a contrary conclusion is no longer valid. First, there is no reason to presume that, simply because she enters a parochial school classroom, a full-time public employee such as a Title I teacher will depart from her assigned duties and instructions and embark on religious indoctrination[.]...

Zobrest also repudiates *Ball*'s assumption that the presence of Title I teachers in parochial school classrooms will, without more, create the impression of a "symbolic union" between church and state....

Nor under current law can we conclude that a program placing full-time public employees on parochial campuses to provide Title I instruction would impermissibly finance religious indoctrination....

What is most fatal to the argument that New York City's Title I program directly subsidizes religion is that it applies with equal force when those services are provided off-campus, and *Aguilar* implied that providing the services off-campus is entirely consistent with the Establishment Clause.... [W]e find no logical basis upon which to conclude that Title I services are an impermissible subsidy of religion when offered on-campus, but not when offered off-campus. Accordingly, contrary to our conclusion in *Aguilar*, placing full-time employees on parochial school campuses does not as a matter of law have the impermissible effect of advancing religion through indoctrination....

[W]here the aid is allocated on the basis of neutral, secular criteria that neither favor nor disfavor religion, and is made available to both religious and secular beneficiaries on a nondiscriminatory basis[,] ... the aid is less likely to have the effect of advancing religion....

[I]t is clear that Title I services are allocated on the basis of criteria that neither favor nor disfavor religion.... The services are available to all children who meet the Act's eligibility requirements, no matter what their religious beliefs or where they go to school. The Board's program does not, therefore, give aid recipients any incentive to modify their religious beliefs or practices in order to obtain those services.

We turn now to *Aguilar*'s conclusion that New York City's Title I program resulted in an excessive entanglement between church and state....

Not all entanglements ... have the effect of advancing or inhibiting religion. Interaction between church and state is inevitable ... and we have always tolerated some level of involvement between the two. Entanglement must be "excessive" before it runs afoul of the Establishment Clause....

The pre-*Aguilar* Title I program does not result in an "excessive" entanglement that advances or inhibits religion.... [T]he Court's finding of "excessive" entanglement in *Aguilar* rested on three grounds: (i) the program would require "pervasive monitoring by public authorities" to ensure that Title I employees did not inculcate religion; (ii) the program required "administrative cooperation" between the Board and parochial schools; and (iii) the program might increase the dangers of "political divisiveness." Under our current understanding of the Establishment Clause, the last two considerations are insufficient by themselves to create an "excessive" entanglement. They are present no matter where Title I services are offered, and no court has held that Title I services cannot be offered off-campus.... Further, the assumption underlying the first consideration has been undermined. In *Aguilar*, the Court presumed that full-time public employees on parochial school grounds would be tempted to inculcate religion, despite the ethical standards they were required to uphold. Because of this risk *pervasive* monitoring would be required. But after *Zobrest* we no longer presume that public employees will inculcate religion simply because they happen to be in a sectarian environment. Since we have abandoned the assumption that properly instructed public employees will fail to discharge their duties faithfully, we must also discard the assumption that *pervasive* monitoring of Title I teachers is required....

We therefore hold that a federally funded program providing supplemental, remedial instruction to disadvantaged children on a neutral basis is not invalid under the Establishment Clause when such instruction is given on the premises of sectarian schools by government employees pursuant to a program containing safeguards such as those present here. The same considerations that justify this holding require us to conclude that this carefully constrained program also cannot reasonably be viewed as an endorsement of religion.... Accordingly, we must acknowledge that *Aguilar*, as well as the portion of *Ball* addressing Grand Rapids' Shared Time program, are no longer good law....

For these reasons, we reverse the judgment of the Court of Appeals and remand to the District Court with instructions to vacate its September 26, 1985, order.

It is so ordered.

SOUTER, STEVENS, GINSBURG, AND BREYER, J.J., DISSENTING

The [majority's] result ... repudiate[s] the very reasonable line drawn in *Aguilar* and [*Grand Rapids School District v.*] *Ball*, and ... authorize[s] direct state aid to religious institutions on an unparalleled scale, in violation of the Establishment Clause's central prohibition against religious subsidies by the government....

What ... was significant in *Aguilar* and *Ball* about the placement of state-paid teachers into the physical and social settings of the religious schools was ... that the schemes in issue assumed a teaching responsibility indistinguishable from the responsibility of the schools themselves. The obligation of primary and secondary schools to teach reading necessarily extends to teaching those who are having a hard time at it, and the same is true of math. Calling some classes remedial does not distinguish their subjects from the schools' basic subjects, however inadequately the schools may have been addressing them.

What was true of the Title I scheme as struck down in *Aguilar* will be just as true when New York reverts to the old practices with the Court's approval after today....

[I]f a line is to be drawn short of barring all state aid to religious schools for teaching standard subjects, the *Aguilar-Ball* line was a sensible one capable of principled adherence. It is no less sound, and no less necessary, today....

[N]othing since *Ball* and *Aguilar* and before this case has eroded the distinction between direct and substantial and indirect and incidental. That principled line is being breached only here and now....

GINSBURG, STEVENS, SOUTER, AND BREYER, J.J., DISSENTING

... This Court's Rules do not countenance the rehearing here granted. For good reason, a proper application of those rules and the Federal Rules of Civil Procedure would lead us to defer reconsideration of *Aguilar* until we are presented with the issue in another case....

The majority acknowledges that there has been no significant change in factual conditions. The majority also recognizes that *Aguilar* had not been overruled, but remained the governing Establishment Clause law, until this very day. Because *Aguilar* had not been overruled at the time the District Court acted, the law the District Court was bound to respect had not changed. The District Court therefore did not abuse its discretion in denying petitioners' Rule 60(b) motion....

Despite the problematic use of Rule 60(b), the Court "see[s] no reason to wait for a 'better vehicle.'...

Unlike the majority, I find just cause to await the arrival of ... another case in which our review appropriately may be sought, before deciding whether *Aguilar* should remain the law of the land. That cause lies in the maintenance of integrity in the interpretation of procedural rules, [and] preservation of the responsive, non-agenda-setting character of this Court[.]...

QUESTIONS

1. Agostini argued that:

   > *Aguilar* was the high-water mark of a flood that has since receded. In no case since *Aguilar* itself has the Court struck down a program or practice on entanglement grounds. It is apparent that the entanglement prong of *Lemon*, upon which *Aguilar* was based, has lost its vitality.

   How did the Court respond to that argument in *Agostini*? What is the status of *Lemon* in light of *Agostini*?

2. Felton argued that use of Rule 60(b) as a vehicle for reconsidering *Aguilar* would "compromise the institutional integrity" of the Court because it would signal that the individual views of justices expressed in legal dicta in opinions may constitute a "significant change in law" and would lead to "head-counting" and speculation as a ground for relief from final judgments. The brief of the American Jewish Congress argued that granting Agostini's Rule 60(b) motion would "foster the hope that such reversals can be achieved, aggravating the political tensions that too often surround the work of this Court." The brief also noted that the Court's decision in *Aguilar* was by a 5–4 vote, a

close margin that occurs only in cases that "excite the greatest public controversy."

In dissent, Justice Ginsburg urged the Court to wait for another, more appropriate, case to test its *Aguilar* precedent, in part because waiting would preserve "the responsive, non-agenda-setting character of this Court[.]"

Does use of the Rule 60(b) undermine or bolster the independence and neutrality of the Supreme Court in the American political system? What other cases might the Court be asked to reconsider using that procedure? Does use of the Rule 60(b) procedure in *Agostini* portend greater judicial activism?

3. The *Washington Post* criticized *Agostini* editorially as legitimating the kind of "church-state connection that infringes the rights of dissenters and nonbelievers, and at the same time threatens the independence of the church" ("Church and State: A Moving Line," *Washington Post*, June 24, 1997, A14). Is *Agostini* a triumph for accommodationists? Does the decision symbolize the collapse of whatever "wall of separation" may have existed between church and state? Are church-state relations now a matter of political expediency?

SUGGESTIONS FOR FURTHER READING

Brown, Ernest J., "*Quis Custodiet Ipsos Custodes?*—The School Prayer Cases," *The Supreme Court Review* (Chicago, IL: University of Chicago Press, 1963).

Carter, Lief, *An Introduction to Constitutional Interpretation: Cases in Law and Religion* (New York, NY: Longman, 1991).

Carter, Stephen, "Evolutionism, Creationism, and Treating Religion as a Hobby," *Duke Law Journal* (1987): 977.

_____, *The Culture of Disbelief: How American Law and Politics Trivialize Religious Devotion* (New York, NY: Basic Books, 1993).

Comment. "Constitutional Law—*American Civil Liberties Union v. City of Birmingham*: Establishment Clause Scrutiny of a Nativity Scene," 62 *Notre Dame Law Review* (1986): 114.

Cord, Robert L., *Separation of Church and State: Historical Fact and Current Fiction* (New York, NY: Lambeth, 1982).

Curry, Thomas J., *The First Freedoms: Church and State in America to the Passage of the First Amendment* (New York, NY: Oxford University Press, 1986).

Dolbeare, Kenneth M., and Phillip E. Hammond, *The School Prayer Decisions: From Court Policy to Local Practice* (Chicago, IL: University of Chicago Press, 1971).

Eldredge, Niles, *The Monkey Business: A Scientist Looks at Creationism* (New York, NY: Washington Square Press, 1982).

Gedicks, Frederick Mark, *The Rhetoric of Church and State* (Durham, NC: Duke University Press, 1995).

Giannella, Donald A., "*Lemon* and *Tilton*: The Bitter and the Sweet of Church-State Entanglement," *The Supreme Court Review* (Chicago, IL: University of Chicago Press, 1971).

Goldberg, Steven, "The Constitutional Status of American Science," *University of Illinois Law Forum* (1979): 1.

Greene, Abner S., "The Political Balance of the Religion Clauses," 102 *Yale Law Journal* (1993): 1611.

Howe, Mark De Wolfe, *The Garden and the Wilderness: Religion and Government in American Constitutional History* (Chicago, IL: University of Chicago Press, 1965).

Hutcheson, Richard G., Jr., *God in the White House: How Religion Has Changed the Modern Presidency* (New York, NY: Collier Macmillan, 1989).

Irons, Peter, *The Courage of Their Convictions: Sixteen Americans Who Fought Their Way to the Supreme Court* (New York, NY: Penguin, 1990), Chapters 9, 15.

Katz, Wilbur G., *Religion and American Constitutions* (Evanston, IL: Northwestern University Press, 1964).

Keynes, Edward, and Randall K. Miller, *The Court vs. Congress: Prayer, Busing and Abortion* (Durham, NC: Duke University Press, 1989).

Kobylka, Joseph F., "Leadership in the Supreme Court: Chief Justice Burger and Establishment Clause Litigation," 42 *Western Political Science Quarterly* (1989): 545.

Kurland, Philip B., "The Regents' Prayer Case: 'Full of Sound and Fury, Signifying ...'," *The Supreme Court Review* (Chicago, IL: University of Chicago Press, 1962).

Larson, Edward J., *Trial and Error: The American Controversy over Creation and Evolution* (New York, NY: Oxford University Press, 1985).

Levy, Leonard W., *The Establishment Clause: Religion and the First Amendment* (New York, NY: Macmillan, 1986).

Malbin, Michael, *Religion and Politics: The Intentions of the Authors of the First Amendment* (Washington, D.C.: American Enterprise Institute, 1978).

McConnell, Michael, "Religious Freedom at a Crossroads," 59 *University of Chicago Law Review* (1992): 115.

Morgan, Richard E., "The Establishment Clause and Sectarian Schools: A Final Installment?" *The Supreme Court Review* (Chicago, IL: University of Chicago Press, 1973).

Muir, William K., Jr., *Prayer in the Public Schools: Law and Attitude Change* (Chicago, IL: University of Chicago Press, 1967).

Note, "Freedom of Religion and Science Instruction in Public Schools," 87 *Yale Law Journal* (1978): 515.

Note, "*Lynch v. Donnelly*: Breaking Down the Barriers to Religious Displays," 71 *Cornell Law Review* (1985): 185.

Oaks, Dallin, ed., *The Wall between Church and State* (Chicago, IL: University of Chicago Press, 1963).

Parish, Daniel, "Private Religious Displays in Public Fora," 61 *University of Chicago Law Review* (1994): 253.

Pfeffer, Leo, "Freedom and/or Separation," 64 *Minnesota Law Review* (1980): 561.

_____, *Religion, State, and the Burger Court* (Buffalo, NY: Prometheus Books, 1984).

Sherry, Suzanna, "*Lee v. Weisman*: Paradox Redux," *The Supreme Court Review* (Chicago, IL: University of Chicago Press, 1992).

Sorauf, Frank J., *The Wall of Separation* (Princeton, NJ: Princeton University Press, 1976).

Story, Joseph, *Commentaries on the Constitution of the United States*, 3 vols. (Boston, MA: Hilliard, Gray & Company, 1833), vol. II.

Sutherland, Arthur E., Jr., "Establishment According to *Engel*," 76 *Harvard Law Review* (1962): 35.

Sutton, Wendell B., "*Lynch v. Donnelly*: A New Standard Is Needed to Adjudicate Municipal Displays of Religious Symbols," 38 *Oklahoma Law Review* (1985): 535.

Symposium, "Legislative Motivation," 15 *San Diego Law Review* (1978): 925.

Van Alstyne, William W., "Constitutional Separation of Church and State: The Quest for a Coherent Position," 57 *American Political Science Review* (1963): 865.

Will, George, "Good Grief, Scalia!" *Washington Post*, June 25, 1987, A17.

Wills, Garry, *Under God* (New York, NY: Simon and Schuster, 1990).

Zarrow, Joshua D., "Of Crosses and Creches: The Establishment Clause and Publicly Sponsored Displays of Religious Symbols," 35 *American Law Review* (1986): 477.

Zessar, Bruce M., "Government Participation in Holiday Religious Displays: Improving on *Lynch* and *Allegheny*," 41 *DePaul Law Review* (1991): 101.

FREE EXERCISE OF RELIGION

Reynolds v. United States
98 U.S. 145 (1878)

SETTING

In *Walz v. Tax Commission*, 397 U.S. 664 (1970), the Supreme Court observed that the purpose of the First Amendment's religion clauses was "to state an objective, not to write a statute." The clear objective of the Free Exercise

Clause, of course, is to prohibit governmental regulation of religious beliefs. Freedom to believe is absolute. However, religious beliefs often dictate certain conduct on the part of adherents and freedom to act is not absolute. The Free Exercise Clause does not prevent government from regulating or even forbidding certain conduct. The Court's first effort to describe the constitutional limitations on governmental regulations affecting the free exercise of religion occurred in the nineteenth century.

Polygamy, a marriage in which one spouse of either sex may have more than one mate at the same time, was a tenet of the Church of Jesus Christ of Latter Day Saints (Mormons). Until recognized by the Mormons in the nineteenth century, polygamy was almost exclusively a feature of Asian and African cultures. English common law never recognized the validity of polygamy. Under the Statute of [King] James I (Chapter 11), for example, conviction for practicing polygamy in England or Wales carried with it the death penalty.

Mormons believed that Joseph Smith, the church's founder and prophet, received a revelation from God in 1831 telling him that male members of the church should practice polygamy and that failure to do so would result in damnation in the life to come. After that time, Mormons practiced polygamy but did so privately, under strict regulation by the church. It was not until 1852, several years after Mormons had migrated from Ohio to the territory that became Utah, that their leader, Brigham Young, permitted the practice to become public. Polygamy remained strictly controlled by the church.

After their arrival in Utah, Mormons created the State of Deseret and sought admission into the union. Their application was rejected. Instead, Congress created the Utah Territory in 1850. Territorial status meant that the Mormon Church came within the reach of federal law.

For a variety of reasons, polygamy in the pre-Civil War era became viewed as the "twin relic" of slavery and a symbol of barbarism. In 1860, Representative Justin Morrill of Vermont introduced an antipolygamy bill into the House of Representatives. It became law in 1862 when signed by President Abraham Lincoln. It provided, in part:

> Every person having a husband or wife living, who marries another, whether married or single, in a Territory, or other place over which the United States have jurisdiction, is guilty of bigamy, and shall be punished by a fine of not more than five hundred dollars, and by imprisonment for a term not more than five years[.]...

In addition, Congress annulled all Deseret and Utah laws "which establish, support, maintain, shield, or countenance polygamy."

The Civil War and Reconstruction hampered enforcement of Morrill's antipolygamy law. By the 1870s, however, President Grant had set his sights on eliminating polygamy. At his recommendation, Congress in 1874 passed the Poland Act to facilitate enforcement of the antipolygamy Morrill Act. In the fall of 1874, Mormon leaders and federal officials agreed informally to test the validity of the Morrill Act.

George Reynolds, secretary to Brigham Young, was chosen for this test case. He was indicted on October 30, 1875, in the District Court for the Territory of Utah. The indictment stated that he married Amelia Jane Schofield in 1874, being then already married to Mary Ann Tuddenham, whom he had wed in 1865. Reynolds pleaded in abatement to the indictment, objecting that he was indicted by a grand jury containing only fifteen members when federal law required grand juries to consist of not fewer than sixteen persons. Utah territorial law, by contrast, provided that grand juries consist of "fifteen eligible men." The court overruled Reynolds's plea in abatement, stating that the territorial court must proceed in accordance with territorial law, not in accordance with the practice of U.S. courts. The case then proceeded to trial. Reynolds testified against himself, was quickly convicted, and was sentenced to a year in jail and fined. He appealed the conviction to the Supreme Court of the Territory of Utah, which reversed. The court ignored Reynolds's claim that the Morrill Act violated the Free Exercise Clause of the First Amendment, and instead ruled that the grand jury that had indicted Reynolds had been improperly constituted.

Reynolds was retried in December 1875. The second trial proceeded less as a friendly test case and more as a hostile prosecution. Reynolds again objected to the composition of the grand jury. He also objected to the trial court's decision to allow two jurors to remain on the jury panel despite statements they made during *voir dire* that, based on what they had read in newspapers, they believed Reynolds to be guilty. The trial court overruled those objections. The trial court also refused to give a jury instruction requested by Reynolds, namely, if the jury found that Reynolds was married in pursuance of and conformity with what he believed to be a religious duty, then the jury should return a verdict of not guilty. Instead, the trial court instructed the jury that if it found that Reynolds, already having a wife, deliberately married a second time, acting under a religious belief did not excuse him, and that the law in such cases implied criminal intent.

The jury returned a guilty verdict and Reynolds was sentenced to five years in prison at hard labor. He appealed to the Supreme Court of the Territory of Utah for a second time. That court affirmed, making no mention of Reynolds's religious liberty claim. The Supreme Court of the United States granted Reynolds's petition for a writ of error.

HIGHLIGHTS OF SUPREME COURT ARGUMENTS

BRIEF FOR REYNOLDS

◆ The trial court erred in allowing a grand jury composed of fewer that sixteen men to indict Reynolds.

◆ It was error for the trial court to allow jurors to remain on the jury when they stated during *voir dire* that they had already made up their minds in the case. Reynolds was denied the right to a fair and impartial trial.

◆ It was error for the trial court to allow the district attorney to ask several jurors if they were living in polygamy, and then to dismiss them from jury service when they answered in the affirmative.

◆ The trial court erred in refusing to instruct the jury that if they found that Reynolds was married in conformity with his religious duty their verdict should be "Not guilty."

◆ Bigamy is not prohibited by the general moral code. There is no command against it in the Decalogue (Ten Commandments). Consequently, Congress lacked the right to make having more than one husband or wife a criminal offense.

BRIEF FOR THE UNITED STATES

◆ The trial court did not err in following Territorial law in determining the appropriate size of the grand jury.

◆ Although two jurors stated that they had formed an opinion in the case, it is not clear from the record which party was harmed and which party benefited from the opinions. Therefore, it was not error to allow the jurors to remain on the panel.

◆ It was not error to allow jurors to be questioned about whether they were living in polygamy.

SUPREME COURT DECISION: 9–0

WAITE, C.J.

... The inquiry is not as to the power of Congress to prescribe criminal laws for the Territories, but as to the guilt of one who knowingly violates a law which has been properly enacted, if he entertains a religious belief that the law is wrong.

Congress cannot pass a law for the government of the Territories which shall prohibit the free exercise of religion. The first amendment to the Constitution expressly forbids such legislation. Religious freedom is guaranteed everywhere throughout the United States, so far as congressional interference is concerned. The question to be determined is, whether the law now under consideration comes within this prohibition.

The word "religion" is not defined in the Constitution. We must go elsewhere, therefore, to ascertain its meaning, and nowhere more appropriately, we think, than to the history of the times in the midst of which the provision was adopted. The precise point of the inquiry is, what is the religious freedom which has been guaranteed.

Before the adoption of the Constitution, attempts were made in some of the colonies and States to legislate not only in respect to the establishment of religion, but in respect to its doctrines and precepts as well. The people were taxed, against their will, for the support of religion, and sometimes for the support of particular sects to whose tenets they could not and did not subscribe. Punishments were prescribed for a failure to attend upon public worship, and sometimes for entertaining heretical opinions. The controversy upon this general subject was animated in many of the States, but seemed at last to culminate in Virginia. In 1784, the House of Delegates of that State having under consideration "a bill establishing provision for teachers of the Christian religion," postponed it until the next session, and directed that the bill should be published and distributed, and that the people be requested "to signify their opinion respecting the adoption of such a bill at the next session of assembly."

This brought out a determined opposition. Amongst others, Mr. Madison prepared a "Memorial and Remonstrance," which was widely circulated and signed, and in which he demonstrated "that religion, or the duty we owe the Creator," was not within the cognizance of civil government. At the next session the proposed bill was not only defeated, but another, "for establishing religious freedom," drafted by Mr. Jefferson, was passed. In the preamble of this act religious freedom is defined; and after a recital "that to suffer the civil magistrate to intrude his powers into the field of opinion, and to restrain the profession or propagation of principles on supposition of their ill tendency, is a dangerous fallacy which at once destroys all religious liberty," it is declared "that it is time enough for the rightful purposes of civil government for its officers to interfere when principles break out into overt acts against peace and good order." In these two sentences is found the true distinction between what properly belongs to the church and what to the State.

In a little more than a year after the passage of this statute the convention met which prepared the Constitution of the United States. Of this convention Mr. Jefferson was not a member, he being then absent as minister to France. As soon as he saw the draft of the Constitution proposed for adoption, he, in a letter to a friend, expressed his disappointment at the absence of an express declaration insuring the freedom of religion, but was willing to accept it as it was, trusting that the good sense and honest intentions of the people would bring about the neces-

sary alterations. Five of the States, while adopting the Constitution, proposed amendments. Three—New Hampshire, New York, and Virginia—included in one form or another a declaration of religious freedom in the changes they desired to have made, as did also North Carolina, where the convention at first declined to ratify the Constitution until the proposed amendments were acted upon. Accordingly, at the first session of the first Congress the amendment now under consideration was proposed with others by Mr. Madison. It met the views of the advocates of religious freedom, and was adopted. Mr. Jefferson afterwards, in reply to an address to him by a committee of the Danbury Baptist Association, took occasion to say: "Believing with you that religion is a matter which lies solely between man and his God; that he owes account to none other for his faith or his worship; that the legislative powers of the government reach actions only, and not opinions,—I contemplate with sovereign reverence that act of the whole American people which declared that their legislature should 'make no law respecting an establishment of religion or prohibiting the free exercise thereof,' thus building a wall of separation between church and State. Adhering to this expression of the supreme will of the nation in behalf of the rights of conscience, I shall see with sincere satisfaction the progress of those sentiments which tend to restore man to all his natural rights, convinced he has no natural right in opposition to his social duties." Coming as this does from an acknowledged leader of the advocates of the measure, it may be accepted almost as an authoritative declaration of the scope and effect of the amendment thus secured. Congress was deprived of all legislative power over mere opinion, but was left free to reach actions which were in violation of social duties or subversive of good order.

Polygamy has always been odious among the northern and western nations of Europe, and, until the establishment of the Mormon Church, was almost exclusively a feature of the life of Asiatic and of African people....

[I]t is impossible to believe that the constitutional guaranty of religious freedom was intended to prohibit legislation in respect to this most important feature of social life. Marriage, while from its very nature a sacred obligation, is nevertheless, in most civilized nations, a civil contract, and usually regulated by law. Upon it society may be said to be built, and out of its fruits spring social relations and social obligations and duties, with which government is necessarily required to deal....

In our opinion, the statute immediately under consideration is within the legislative power of Congress. It is constitutional and valid as prescribing a rule of action for all those residing in the Territories, and in places over which the United States have exclusive control. This being so, the only question which remains is, whether those who make polygamy a part of their religion are excepted from the operation of the statute. If they are, then those who do not make polygamy a part of their religious belief may be found guilty and punished, while those who do, must be acquitted and go free. This would be introducing a new element into criminal law. Laws are made for the government of actions, and while they cannot interfere with mere religious belief and opinions, they may with practices....

So here, as a law of the organization of society under the exclusive dominion of the United States, it is provided that plural marriages shall not be allowed. Can a man excuse his practices to the contrary because of his religious belief? To permit this would be to make the professed doctrines of religious belief superior to the law of the land, and in effect to permit every citizen to become a law unto himself. Government could exist only in name under such circumstances....

Upon a careful consideration of the whole case, we are satisfied that no error was committed by the court below.

Judgment affirmed.

FIELD, J., CONCURRING [OMITTED]

QUESTIONS

1. The U.S. brief in *Reynolds* was only two-and-a-half pages long and consisted of terse responses to the points raised by Reynolds. The brief made no reference to the Free Exercise Clause or the significance of the religious challenge posed by Reynolds's case. The Supreme Court's opinion, by contrast, was replete with history, theory, and theology to justify its reading of the Free Exercise Clause. Does this suggest that the federal government perceived the case less as an adversary confrontation than a foregone conclusion?

2. *Reynolds* was the Court's first pronouncement on the meaning of the Free Exercise Clause. Identify the rule announced in *Reynolds*. Is it consistent with the plain meaning of the Free Exercise Clause? What problems, if any, do you foresee in the application of the *Reynolds* rule?

In *McDaniel v. Paty*, 435 U.S. 618 (1978), Justice Brennan offered a different distinction than the belief/conduct dichotomy. He distinguished between a law that "establishes a religious classification ... which I believe is absolutely prohibited" and a law that "does not interfere with free exercise because it does not directly prohibit religious activity." Is this distinction more workable than the one formulated in *Reynolds*?

3. Did the Court in *Reynolds* adequately explain why it concluded that Mormon practices were incompatible with social values? Are there parallels between the social response to polygamous marriages in the late nineteenth century and the contemporary debate over same-sex marriages?

4. In *Davis v. Beason*, 113 U.S. 333 (1890), the Court again attempted to distinguish between protected belief and unprotected conduct. *Beason* also involved the Mormon Church, this time in the context of an Idaho territorial statute that denied voting rights to bigamists, polygamists, and advocates of plural marriages. The Court declared:

> It was never intended or supposed that the [First] Amendment could be evoked as a protection against legislation for the punishment of acts inimical to the peace, good order and morals of society. With man's relation to his Maker and the obligations he may think they impose, and the manner in which an expression shall be made by him of his belief on those subjects, no interference can be permitted provided always the laws of society designed to secure its peace and prosperity, and the morals of its people, are not interfered with. However free the exercise of religion may be, it must be subordinate to the criminal laws of the country, passed with reference to actions regarded by general consent as properly the subjects of punitive legislation.

Is *Beason* a logical extension of *Reynolds*? What are the implications of a distinction between protected belief and unprotected conduct for the free *exercise* of religion?

COMMENTS

1. George Reynolds petitioned the Supreme Court of the United States for rehearing. In his petition he noted that the district court had sentenced him to a term of imprisonment at hard labor, but that the federal statute under which he was indicted and convicted provided only for punishment of imprisonment. Because Reynolds had not assigned (raised) the issue as error in his appeal, the Court was not required to consider it. Nonetheless, the Court addressed the matter and remanded the case with orders to set aside the sentence insofar as it required Reynolds's imprisonment to be at hard labor.

Reynolds was sent to the Nebraska State Prison, where he remained for approximately one month. He was returned to Utah to serve the remainder of his term. Reynolds's supporters subsequently sought executive clemency on the ground that the case was a test case and that it was unjust to force Reynolds to serve his full sentence. President Hayes ignored the request, which was supported by a petition bearing the signatures of thirty-two thousand people.

2. The Mormon Church abandoned the teaching and practice of polygamy in 1890. However, individual Mormons continued the practice. As late as 1946, the Supreme Court upheld the conviction of a Mormon for crossing state lines while vacationing with multiple wives. The government prosecuted the Mormon under the 1910 Mann ("White Slavery") Act that outlawed transporting women across state lines for "immoral" purposes. *Cleveland v. United States*, 329 U.S. 14.

FREE EXERCISE OF RELIGION

Cantwell v. Connecticut
310 U.S. 296 (1940)

SETTING

Reynolds and *Beason* dealt with federal laws affecting the free exercise of religion. The validity of state laws affecting free exercise was not litigated until the 1930s. When cases eventually came before the Court, they frequently involved another American religious minority, Jehovah's Witnesses. This sect was founded in 1872 by Charles Taze Russell, a Pittsburgh businessman. Russell broke his ties with the Congregational Church over the issue of the Second Coming of Christ. He believed the Adventist doctrine that Christ's return was imminent and would trigger Armageddon, at which time believers would be saved and the unreligious would be damned. Russell incorporated the Watch Tower Bible and Tract Society in 1884. First known as "Russellites," Jehovah's Witnesses eventually became the sect's familiar name after Isaiah 43:10, "Ye are my Witnesses, saith Jehovah." They regularly organize proselytizing Watchtower Campaigns to spread Jehovah's Word. It is customary for Jehovah's Witnesses to conduct a door-to-door ministry by carrying a bag of books, pamphlets, portable phonographs, and sets of records to private homes. Witnesses give residents an opportunity to hear the playing of a record and to purchase or receive one or more of their books and pamphlets.

Confronted with litigation resulting from such proselytizing—"witnessing"—efforts, the Court initially was reluctant to implicate the Free Exercise Clause. In the first Jehovah's Witness case, *Lovell v. Griffin*, 303 U.S. 444 (1938), the Court overturned a municipal ordinance that prohibited the distribution of leaflets without a permit. The ordinance had been applied to Jehovah's Witnesses handing out religious circulars. The Court ruled that the ordinance imposed an unconstitutional prior restraint on freedom of the press. In 1939, the Court extended *Lovell* to strike down, on free press grounds, several ordinances that prohibited door-to-door solicitation or distribution of written materials without permission of local law enforcement officials. *Schneider v. Irvington*, 308 U.S. 147.

One year after *Schneider*, the Court turned its attention to legislative abridgment of the right to free exercise of religion. Newton Cantwell and his sons, Jesse (aged sixteen) and Russell (aged eighteen), were ordained ministers of Jehovah's Witnesses, representing the Watch Tower Bible and Tract Society. On Palm Sunday in April 1938, the Cantwells were preaching on Cassius Street in New Haven, Connecticut, a densely populated area where approximately 90 percent of the residents were Roman Catholic. One of the records the Cantwells offered to play was entitled "Enemies," which included an attack on the Catholic religion, characterizing it as the "Whore of Babylon." Jesse Cantwell approached two Catholic men and received permission to play the record. The two men became incensed by the content of the record. They told Jesse to be on his way, and he left their presence.

The Cantwells were later arrested and charged with violating a Connecticut statute entitled "Unlawful solicitation for philanthropic purposes." Enacted in 1917, the statute prohibited the solicitation of money for religious, charitable, or philanthropic causes without having a certificate (revocable at any time) issued by the secretary of public welfare. The Cantwells were also accused of inciting a breach of the peace. They demurred to all of the charges against them.

Following a bench trial, the judge of the Connecticut Court of Common Pleas convicted the Cantwells on charges of inciting a breach of the peace and violating the state statute requiring a certificate in order to solicit. The judge fined them each $5.00 on each of the counts. Newton Cantwell was also assessed the costs of the trial.

The Cantwells appealed their convictions to the Supreme Court of Errors. That court set aside the convictions of Russell and Newton Cantwell on the charge of inciting a breach of the peace, but sustained the conviction of Jesse Cantwell on that charge. It sustained the convictions of all three on the charge of violating the state statute requiring a certificate before soliciting. The Cantwells appealed to the Supreme Court of the United States and also petitioned for a writ of certiorari.

HIGHLIGHTS OF SUPREME COURT ARGUMENTS

BRIEF FOR CANTWELLS

◆ The Connecticut statute requiring the Cantwells to procure a certificate before engaging in their door-to-door ministry violates the Due Process Clause of the Fourteenth Amendment, because it abridges their freedom to worship God according to their consciences.

♦ In several cases the Court has recognized that the religious liberty protected by the First Amendment against invasion by the United States is protected by the Fourteenth Amendment against invasion by the states.

♦ The Cantwells violated no laws of morality or property in their door-to-door ministry, because their demeanor was peaceful and quiet.

♦ The Connecticut statute also violates the rights of free speech and free press protected against state invasion by the Fourteenth Amendment.

♦ Jesse Cantwell did not incite a breach of the peace when he played the "Enemies" record for two Catholics he stopped in the street. They invited him to play the record, which they found highly offensive to their religious beliefs. Cantwell left peacefully when they told him that he had better get off the street before something happened to him.

BRIEF FOR CONNECTICUT

♦ The purpose of the solicitation statute is to protect the public from the perpetration of fraud by solicitors under the guise of religion, charity, or philanthropy. The statute's passage was well within the state's police powers. The court's duty is to sustain the statute unless its invalidity is demonstrated beyond reasonable doubt.

♦ The statute in no way attempts to restrict the Cantwells' mode of worship or to restrict their teachings or doctrine.

♦ The statutory offense committed by the Cantwells was soliciting funds without a certificate. The statute does not prohibit them from distributing books or pamphlets and hence does not violate the First Amendment, made applicable to the states by the Fourteenth.

♦ Jesse Cantwell's conviction on breach of the peace charges should be upheld. His conduct made two Catholics he encountered want to hit him. His conduct was well within the common law definition of breach of the peace. Actual provocation and the specific intent to provoke are not required elements for conviction of breach of the peace.

SUPREME COURT DECISION: 9–0

ROBERTS, J.

... First. We hold that the statute, as construed and applied to the appellants, deprives them of their liberty without due process of law in contravention of the Fourteenth Amendment. The fundamental concept of liberty embodied in that Amendment embraces the liberties guaranteed by the First Amendment. The First Amendment declares that Congress shall make no law respecting an establishment of religion or prohibiting the free exercise thereof. The Fourteenth Amendment has rendered the legislatures of the states as incompetent as Congress to enact such laws. The constitutional inhibition of legislation on the subject of religion has a double aspect. On the one hand, it forestalls compulsion by law of the acceptance of any creed or the practice of any form of worship. Freedom of conscience and freedom to adhere to such religious organization or form of worship as the individual may choose cannot be restricted by law. On the other hand, it safeguards the free exercise of the chosen form of religion. Thus the Amendment embraces two concepts—freedom to believe and freedom to act. The first is absolute but, in the nature of things, the second cannot be. Conduct remains subject to regulation for the protection of society. The freedom to act must have appropriate definition to preserve the enforcement of that protection. In every case the power to regulate must be so exercised as not, in attaining a permissible end, unduly to infringe the protected freedom. No one would contest the proposition that a state may not, by statute, wholly deny the right to preach or to disseminate religious views. Plainly such a previous and absolute restraint would violate the terms of the guarantee. It is equally clear that a state may by general and nondiscriminatory legislation regulate the times, the places, and the manner of soliciting upon its streets, and of holding meetings thereon; and may in other respects safeguard the peace, good order, and comfort of the community, without unconstitutionally invading the liberties protected by the Fourteenth Amendment. The appellants are right in their insistence that the Act in question is not such a regulation. If a certificate is procured, solicitation is permitted without restraint but, in the absence of a certificate, solicitation is altogether prohibited....

The general regulation, in the public interest, of solicitation, which does not involve any religious test and does not unreasonably obstruct or delay the collection of funds, is not open to any constitutional objection, even though the collection be for a religious purpose. Such regulation would not constitute a prohibited previous restraint on the free exercise of religion or interpose an inadmissible obstacle to its exercise.

It will be noted, however, that the Act requires an application to the secretary of the public welfare council of the State; that he is empowered to determine whether the cause is a religious one, and that the issue of a certificate depends upon his affirmative action. If he finds that the cause is not that of religion, to solicit for it becomes a crime. He is not to issue a certificate as a matter of course. His decision to issue or refuse it involves appraisal of facts, the exercise of judgment, and the formation of an opinion. He is authorized to withhold his approval if he determines that the cause is not a religious one. Such a censorship of religion as the means of determining its right to survive is a denial of liberty protected by the First Amendment and included in the liberty which is within the protection of the Fourteenth....

Nothing we have said is intended even remotely to imply that, under the cloak of religion, persons may, with impunity, commit frauds upon the public. Certainly penal laws are available to punish such conduct. Even the exercise of religion may be at some slight inconvenience in order that the state may protect its citizens from injury. Without doubt a state may protect its citizens from fraudulent solicitation by requiring a stranger in the community, before permitting him publicly to solicit funds for any purpose, to establish his identity and his authority to act for the cause which he purports to represent. The state is likewise free to regulate the time and manner of solicitation generally, in the interest of public safety, peace, comfort, or convenience. But to condition the solicitation of aid for the perpetuation of religious views or systems upon a license, the grant of which rests in the exercise of a determination by state authority as to what is a religious cause, is to lay a forbidden burden upon the exercise of liberty protected by the Constitution.

Second. We hold that, in the circumstances disclosed, the conviction of Jesse Cantwell on the fifth count must be set aside. Decision as to the lawfulness of the conviction demands the weighing of two conflicting interests. The fundamental law declares the interest of the United States that the free exercise of religion be not prohibited and that freedom to communicate information and opinion be not abridged. The state of Connecticut has an obvious interest in the preservation and protection of peace and good order within her borders. We must determine whether the alleged protection of the State's interest, means to which end would, in the absence of limitation by the federal Constitution, lie wholly within the State's discretion, has been pressed, in this instance, to a point where it has come into fatal collision with the overriding interest protected by the federal compact....

The offense known as breach of the peace embraces a great variety of conduct destroying or menacing public order and tranquility. It includes not only violent acts but acts and words likely to produce violence in others. No one would have the hardihood to suggest that the principle of freedom of speech sanctions incitement to riot or that religious liberty connotes the privilege to exhort others to physical attack upon those belonging to another sect. When clear and present danger of riot, disorder, interference with traffic upon the public streets, or other immediate threat to public safety, peace, or order, appears, the power of the state to prevent or punish is obvious. Equally obvious is it that a state may not unduly

suppress free communication of views, religious or other, under the guise of conserving desirable conditions. Here we have a situation analogous to a conviction under a statute sweeping in a great variety of conduct under a general and indefinite characterization, and leaving to the executive and judicial branches too wide a discretion in its application.

Having these considerations in mind, we note that Jesse Cantwell, on April 26, 1938, was upon a public street, where he had a right to be, and where he had a right peacefully to impart his views to others. There is no showing that his deportment was noisy, truculent, overbearing or offensive. He requested of two pedestrians permission to play to them a phonograph record. The permission was granted. It is not claimed that he intended to insult or affront the hearers by playing the record. It is plain that he wished only to interest them in his propaganda. The sound of the phonograph is not shown to have disturbed residents of the street, to have drawn a crowd, or to have impeded traffic. Thus far he had invaded no right or interest of the public or of the men accosted.

The record played by Cantwell embodies a general attack on all organized religious systems as instruments of Satan and injurious to man; it then singles out the Roman Catholic Church for strictures couched in terms which naturally would offend not only persons of that persuasion, but all others who respect the honestly held religious faith of their fellows. The hearers were in fact highly offended. One of them said he felt like hitting Cantwell and the other that he was tempted to throw Cantwell off the street. The one who testified he felt like hitting Cantwell said, in answer to the question "Did you do anything else or have any other reaction?" "No, sir, because he said he would take the victrola and he went." The other witness testified that he told Cantwell he had better get off the street before something happened to him and that was the end of the matter as Cantwell picked up his books and walked up the street....

We find in the instant case no assault or threatening of bodily harm, no truculent bearing, no intentional discourtesy, no personal abuse. On the contrary, we find only an effort to persuade a willing listener to buy a book or to contribute money in the interest of what Cantwell, however misguided others may think him, conceived to be true religion.

In the realm of religious faith, and in that of political belief, sharp differences arise. In both fields the tenets of one man may seem the rankest error to his neighbor. To persuade others to his own point of view, the pleader, as we know, at times, resorts to exaggeration, to vilification of men who have been, or are, prominent in church or state, and even to false statement. But the people of this nation have ordained in the light of history, that, in spite of the probability of excesses and abuses, these liberties are, in the long view, essential to enlightened opinion and right conduct on the part of the citizens of a democracy.

The essential characteristic of these liberties is, that under their shield many types of life, character, opinion and belief can develop unmolested and unobstructed. Nowhere is this shield more necessary than in our own country for a people composed of many races and of many creeds. There are limits to the exercise of these liberties. The danger in these times from the coercive activities of those who in the delusion of racial or religious conceit would incite violence and breaches of the peace in order to deprive others of their equal right to the exercise of their liberties, is emphasized by events familiar to all. These and other transgressions of those limits the states appropriately may punish....

The judgment affirming the convictions on the third and fifth counts is reversed and the cause is remanded for further proceedings not inconsistent with this opinion. So ordered.

Reversed and remanded.

QUESTIONS

1. To what extent is the belief/conduct distinction that the Court drew in *Reynolds* different from that drawn in *Cantwell?*

2. *Cantwell* clearly does not sanction an unregulated right to practice one's religion on the public streets. Was it significant to the outcome in this case that the Cantwells' actions did not result in violence? Where should the line between constitutionally protected and unprotected religious acts be drawn?

3. *Cantwell* was the third in a long series of cases before the Supreme Court involving the Jehovah's Witnesses. As noted in the *Setting* on p. 121, the first two, *Lovell v. Griffin*, 303 U.S. 444 (1938), and *Schneider v. Irvington*, 308 U.S. 147 (1939), were decided in favor of the Witnesses on free speech and free press grounds. Might *Cantwell* also have been resolved on these grounds? What constitutional theory would have led to such a resolution?

COMMENT

Between *Cantwell* and *West Virginia Board of Education v. Barnette*, 319 U.S. 624 (1943), the Jehovah's Witnesses brought four more Free Exercise cases:

Case: *Minersville District v. Gobitis*, 310 U.S. 586 (1940)

Vote: 8–1

Decision: A Pennsylvania school board requirement that all children recite the pledge of allegiance daily does not violate the First Amendment. Even though pledging allegiance is objectionable to members of the Jehovah's Witness faith, who believe that such deference to the flag is forbidden by the Bible and that the Bible, as word of God, is the supreme authority, Witnesses must recite the pledge. Religious convictions do not relieve individuals from obeying otherwise valid general laws that do not promote or restrict religious beliefs.

Case: *Cox v. New Hampshire*, 312 U.S. 569 (1941)

Vote: 9–0

Decision: A precisely drawn and applied statute requiring parade permits does not violate the First Amendment. Such statutes are intended to determine the time, place, and manner of parades in order to minimize public disruption and disorder. Conviction of Jehovah's Witnesses for parading without a permit upheld.

Case: *Jones v. Opelika*, 316 U.S. 584 (1942)

Vote: 5–4

Decision: A statute imposing peddler's fees on Jehovah's Witnesses selling religious publications door to door is constitutional. Justices Douglas, Black, and Murphy, who joined the majority in *Gobitis*, dissented in *Jones*. Arguing that the *Jones* decision was a logical extension of *Gobitis*, they wrote, "Since we joined the opinion in the *Gobitis* case, we think this is an appropriate occasion to state that we now believe that it was ... wrongly decided."

Case: *Murdock v. Pennsylvania*, 319 U.S. 105 (1943)

Vote: 5–4

Decision: A city ordinance requiring licenses for all persons taking orders for or delivering goods door to door and imposing a daily tax of $1.50 on such selling is unconstitutional when applied to Jehovah's Witnesses who go from house to house soliciting new members and selling religious literature. "A state may not impose a charge for the enjoyment of a right granted by the Constitution." *Jones v. Opelika* overruled.

FREE EXERCISE OF RELIGION

West Virginia State Board of Education v. Barnette
319 U.S. 624 (1943)

SETTING

As explained in the summary of cases following *Cantwell*, the Court in *Minersville School District v. Gobitis*, 310 U.S. 586 (1940), held that children could be expelled from public school for refusing to salute the flag and recite the pledge of allegiance even though doing so violated the children's religious beliefs as Jehovah's Witnesses. When *Gobitis*—commonly referred to as the First Flag Salute Case—was decided, Europe was fully engaged in World War II and matters of loyalty and patriotism assumed heightened importance in the United States. Justice Frankfurter declared that the question of *Gobitis* was:

> When does the constitutional guarantee compel exemption from doing what society thinks necessary for the promotion of some great common end, or from a penalty for conduct which appears dangerous to the general good?

Frankfurter answered: "National unity is the basis of natural security." The legislature has "the right to select appropriate means for its attainment...."

Although Justices Black, Douglas, and Murphy voted with the *Minersville* majority, they harbored serious misgivings about the ruling. Their reservations deepened as they read press reports of escalating violence against Jehovah's Witnesses. Such violence included police brutality, arson attacks against Kingdom Halls, their meeting places, and, in one Nebraska episode, a vigilante beating and castration of a Witness. The justices were also aware of the overwhelmingly critical journalistic and scholarly evaluations of *Gobitis*. In an extraordinary move, these three justices used another Jehovah's Witness case as a vehicle to admit the error of their previous views. Two years later in *Jones v. Opelika*, 316 U.S. 584 (1942), they lamented in dissent the majority's refusal to exempt Jehovah's Witnesses from a law requiring peddlers to obtain a license: "This is but another step in the direction ... [*Gobitis*] took against the same religious minority and is a logical extension of the principles upon which that case rested. Since we joined the opinion in the *Gobitis* case, we think it is appropriate to state that we now believe that it was also wrongly decided."

The opportunity for the Court to reconsider *Gobitis* came in another flag salute case, commonly known as the Second Flag Salute Case. By the time it reached the Supreme Court, Justice Rutledge had replaced Justice Byrnes, who had joined the *Gobitis* majority.

Pursuant to a West Virginia law that prescribed civic instruction "for the purpose of teaching, fostering and perpetuating the ideas, principles and spirit of Americanism," the West Virginia Board of Education adopted a rule mandating daily "salute to the Flag of the United States." The board declared that refusing to salute was "an act of insubordination." Walter Barnette, a Jehovah's Witness, challenged the rule. He requested that the board of education allow Jehovah's Witness children to recite the following words:

> I have pledged my unqualified allegiance and devotion to Jehovah, the Almighty God, and to His Kingdom, for which Jesus commands all Christians to pray.
>
> I respect the flag of the United States and acknowledge it as a symbol of freedom and justice to all.
>
> I pledge allegiance and obedience to all the laws of the United States that are consistent with God's law, as set forth in the Bible.

When the Board refused, Barnette filed suit in the U.S. District Court for the Southern District of West Virginia seeking to enjoin enforcement of the flag salute rule. A three-judge district court panel granted the injunction. The West Virginia Board of Education appealed to the Supreme Court of the United States.

HIGHLIGHTS OF SUPREME COURT ARGUMENTS

BRIEF FOR WEST VIRGINIA STATE BOARD OF EDUCATION

◆ The constitutional questions raised in this case were answered in *Minersville School District v. Gobitis.*

AMICUS CURIAE BRIEF SUPPORTING THE WEST VIRGINIA STATE BOARD OF EDUCATION

American Legion.

BRIEF FOR BARNETTE

◆ The compulsory flag salute regulation, enforced by expulsion, abridges freedom of speech, freedom to worship, and freedom to direct the spiritual education and welfare of Jehovah's Witness children. *Gobitis* should be overruled.

◆ Freedom of worship cannot be limited unless and until it is shown that granting the children here their liberty of conscience will cause a clear, and present, and immediate danger that the government will be overthrown by force and violence, or that the educational process will be destroyed and impaired. The facts of this case eliminate any such possibility.

◆ The compulsory flag salute regulation denies Barnette's right to have his children attend the free public schools by requiring participation in an act contrary to the guarantees of the Due Process and Equal Protection Clauses of the Fourteenth Amendment.

AMICUS CURIAE BRIEFS SUPPORTING WALTER BARNETTE

American Civil Liberties Union; American Bar Association.

SUPREME COURT DECISION: 6–3

JACKSON, J.

... This case calls upon us to reconsider a precedent decision, as the Court throughout its history often has been required to do....

The *Gobitis* decision ... assumed, as did the argument in that case and in this, that power exists in the State to impose the flag salute discipline upon school children in general. The Court only examined and rejected a claim based on religious beliefs of immunity from an unquestioned general rule. The question which underlies the flag salute controversy is whether

such a ceremony so touching matters of opinion and political attitude may be imposed upon the individual by official authority under powers committed to any political organization under our Constitution. We examine rather than assume existence of this power and, against this broader definition of issues in this case, re-examine specific grounds assigned for the *Gobitis* decision.

1. It was said that the flag-salute controversy confronted the Court with the problem which Lincoln cast in memorable

dilemma: "Must a government of necessity be too strong for the liberties of its people, or too weak to maintain its own existence?" and that the answer must be in favor of strength. *Minersville School District v. Gobitis....*

Government of limited power need not be anemic government. Assurance that rights are secure tends to diminish fear and jealousy of strong government, and by making us feel safe to live under it makes for its better support. Without promise of a limiting Bill of Rights it is doubtful if our Constitution could have mustered enough strength to enable its ratification. To enforce those rights today is not to choose weak government over strong government. It is only to adhere as a means of strength to individual freedom of mind in preference to officially disciplined uniformity for which history indicates a disappointing and disastrous end....

2. It was also considered in the *Gobitis* case that functions of educational officers in states, counties and school districts were such that to interfere with their authority "would in effect make us the school board for the country."

The Fourteenth Amendment, as now applied to the States, protects the citizen against the State itself and all of its creatures—Boards of Education not excepted. These have, of course, important, delicate, and highly discretionary functions, but none that they may not perform within the limits of the Bill of Rights. That they are educating the young for citizenship is reason for scrupulous protection of Constitutional freedoms of the individual, if we are not to strangle the free mind at its source and teach youth to discount important principles of our government as mere platitudes....

3. The *Gobitis* opinion reasoned that

this is a field "where courts possess no marked and certainly no controlling competence," that it is committed to the legislatures as well as the courts to guard cherished liberties and that it is constitutionally appropriate to "fight out the wise use of legislative authority in the forum of public opinion and before legislative assemblies rather than to transfer such a contest to the judicial arena," since all the "effective means of inducing political changes are left free."

The very purpose of a Bill of Rights was to withdraw certain subjects from the vicissitudes of political controversy, to place them beyond the reach of majorities and officials and to establish them as legal principles to be applied by the courts. One's right to life, liberty, and property, to free speech, a free press, freedom of worship and assembly, and other fundamental rights may not be submitted to vote; they depend on the outcome of no elections....

4. Lastly, and this is the very heart of the *Gobitis* opinion, it reasons that "National unity is the basis of national security," that the authorities have "the right to select appropriate means for its attainment," and hence reaches the conclusion that such compulsory measures toward "national unity" are constitutional. Upon the verity of this assumption depends our answer in this case.

National unity as an end which officials may foster by persuasion and example is not in question. The problem is whether under our Constitution compulsion as here employed is a permissible means for its achievement....

It seems trite but necessary to say that the First Amendment to our Constitution was designed to avoid these ends by avoiding these beginnings. There is no mysticism in the American concept of the State or of the nature or origin of its authority. We set up government by consent of the governed, and the Bill of Rights denies those in power any legal opportunity to coerce that consent. Authority here is to be controlled by public opinion, not public opinion by authority.

The case is made difficult not because the principles of its decision are obscure but because the flag involved is our own. Nevertheless, we apply the limitations of the Constitution with no fear that freedom to be intellectually and spiritually diverse or even contrary will disintegrate the social organization. To believe that patriotism will not flourish if patriotic ceremonies are voluntary and spontaneous instead of a compulsory routine is to make an unflattering estimate of the appeal of our institutions to free minds. We can have intellectual individualism and the rich cultural diversities that we owe to exceptional minds only at the price of occasional eccentricity and abnormal attitudes. When they are so harmless to others or to the State as those we deal with here, the price is not too great. But freedom to differ is not limited to things that do not matter much. That would be a mere shadow of freedom. The test of its substance is the right to differ as to things that touch the heart of the existing order.

If there is any fixed star in our constitutional constellation, it is that no official, high or petty, can prescribe what shall be orthodox in politics, nationalism, religion, or other matters of opinion or force citizens to confess by word or act their faith therein. If there are any circumstances which permit an exception, they do not now occur to us.

We think the action of the local authorities in compelling the flag salute and pledge transcends constitutional limitations on their power and invades the sphere of intellect and spirit which it is

the purpose of the First Amendment to our Constitution to reserve from all official control.

The decision of this Court in *Minersville School District v. Gobitis* and the holdings of those few *per curiam* decisions which preceded and foreshadowed it are overruled, and the judgment enjoining enforcement of the West Virginia Regulation is affirmed.

Affirmed.

BLACK AND DOUGLAS, J.J., CONCURRING

We are substantially in agreement with the opinion just read, but since we originally joined with the Court in the *Gobitis* case, it is appropriate that we make a brief statement of reasons for our change of view.

Reluctance to make the Federal Constitution a rigid bar against state regulation of conduct thought inimical to the public welfare was the controlling influence which moved us to consent to the *Gobitis* decision. Long reflection convinced us that although the principle is sound, its application in the particular case was wrong. *Jones v. Opelika*, 316 U.S. 584 (1942). We believe that the statute before us fails to accord full scope to the freedom of religion secured to the appellees by the First and Fourteenth Amendments....

Neither our domestic tranquillity in peace nor our martial effort in war depend on compelling little children to participate in a ceremony which ends in nothing for them but a fear of spiritual condemnation. If, as we think, their fears are groundless, time and reason are the proper antidotes for their errors. The ceremonial, when enforced against conscientious objectors, more likely to defeat than to serve its high purpose, is a handy implement for disguised religious persecution. As such, it is inconsistent with our Constitution's plan and purpose.

MURPHY, J., CONCURRING [OMITTED]

ROBERTS AND REED, J.J., DISSENTING [OMITTED]

FRANKFURTER, J., DISSENTING

One who belongs to the most vilified and persecuted minority in history is not likely to be insensible to the freedoms guaranteed by our Constitution. Were my purely personal attitude relevant I should wholeheartedly associate myself with the general libertarian views in the Court's opinion, representing as they do the thought and action of a lifetime. But as judges we are neither Jew nor Gentile, neither Catholic nor agnostic. We owe equal attachment to the Constitution and are equally bound by our judicial obligations whether we derive our citizenship from the earliest or the latest immigrants to these shores. As a member of this Court I am not justified in writing my private notions of policy into the Constitution, no matter how deeply I may cherish them or how mischievous I may deem their disregard. The duty of a judge who must decide which of two claims before the Court shall prevail, that of a State to enact and enforce laws within its general competence or that of an individual to refuse obedience because of the demands of his conscience, is not that of the ordinary person. It can never be emphasized too much that one's own opinion about the wisdom or evil of a law should be excluded altogether when one is doing one's duty on the bench. The only opinion of our own even looking in that direction that is material is our opinion whether legislators could in reason have enacted such a law. In the light of all the circumstances, including the history of this question in this Court, it would require more daring than I possess to deny that reasonable legislators could have taken the action which is before us for review. Most unwillingly, therefore, I must differ from my brethren with regard to legislation like this....

Under our constitutional system the legislature is charged solely with civil concerns of society. If the avowed or intrinsic legislative purpose is either to promote or to discourage some religious community or creed, it is clearly within the constitutional restrictions imposed on legislatures and cannot stand. But it by no means follows that legislative power is wanting whenever a general non-discriminatory civil regulation in fact touches conscientious scruples or religious beliefs of an individual or a group. Regard for such scruples or beliefs undoubtedly presents one of the most reasonable claims for the exertion of legislative accommodation. It is, of course, beyond our power to rewrite the state's requirement, by providing exemptions for those who do not wish to participate in the flag salute or by making some other accommodations to meet their scruples. That wisdom might suggest the making of such accommodations and that school administration would not find it too difficult to make them and yet maintain the ceremony for those not refusing to conform, is outside our province to suggest. Tact, respect, and generosity toward variant views will always commend themselves to those charged with the duties of legislation so as to achieve a maximum of good will and to require a minimum of unwilling submission to a general law. But the real question is, who is to make such accommodations, the courts or the legislature?

This is no dry, technical matter. It cuts deep into one's conception of the democratic process—it concerns no less the practical differences between the means for making these accommodations that are open to courts and to legislatures. A court can only strike down. It can only say "This or that law is void." It cannot modify or qualify, it cannot make exceptions to a general requirement. And it strikes down not merely for a day. At least the finding of unconstitutionality ought not to have ephemeral significance unless the Constitution is to be reduced to the fugitive importance of mere legislation....

An act compelling profession of allegiance to a religion, no matter how subtly or tenuously promoted, is bad. But an act promoting good citizenship and national allegiance is within the domain of governmental authority and is therefore to be judged by the same considerations of power and of constitutionality as those involved in the many claims of immunity from civil obedience because of religious scruples....

The subjection of dissidents to the general requirement of saluting the flag, as a measure conducive to the training of children in good citizenship, is very far from being the first instance of exacting obedience to general laws that have offended deep religious scruples....

That which three years ago had seemed to five successive Courts to lie within permissible areas of legislation is now outlawed by the deciding shift of opinion of two Justices. What reason is there to believe that they or their successors may not have another view a few years hence? Is that which was deemed to be of so fundamental a nature as to be written into the Constitution to endure for all times to be the sport of shifting winds of doctrine? Of course, judicial opinions, even as to questions of constitutionality, are not immutable. As has been true in the past, the Court will from time to time reverse its position. But I believe that never before these Jehovah's Witnesses cases (except for minor deviations subsequently retraced) has this Court overruled decisions so as to restrict the powers of democratic government. Always heretofore, it has withdrawn narrow views of legislative authority so as to authorize what formerly it had denied....

QUESTIONS

1. On what basis did the Court in *Barnette* overrule *Gobitis*? Is its rationale for disregarding *stare decisis* persuasive?

2. Counsel for Barnette concluded his brief in *Barnette* with the assertion that "The compulsory flag salute is not one of the demands of Caesar which can be lawfully and reasonably required of Jehovah's Witnesses." Did the *Barnette* majority appear to agree with that assertion? If so, did the opinion identify which "demands of Caesar" might lawfully and reasonably be required of religious minorities under the First Amendment? If not, what kinds of issues are left to be litigated?

3. What constitutional principles underpin Justice Frankfurter's dissent in *Barnette*? Do those principles provide any basis for constitutional accommodation of religious minorities?

4. *Cantwell v. Connecticut* and *Barnette* both raised free speech as well

as free exercise issues under the First Amendment. Do the opinions suggest that there are principled distinctions between those rights or are they merely overlapping liberties?

COMMENT

Between 1940 and the mid-1990s, Jehovah's Witnesses brought fifty cases to the Supreme Court, winning most. Below are some prominent examples:

Case: *Martin v. City of Struthers*, 319 U.S. 141 (1943)
Vote: 6–3
Decision: A municipal ordinance making it illegal for any person distributing handbills, circulars, or other advertising to ring the doorbell, sound the door knocker, or otherwise summon the inhabitants of the residence to the door, violates the First Amendment. Jehovah's Witness defendant's rights to free speech and press have broad scope.

Case: *Marsh v. Alabama*, 326 U.S. 501 (1946)
Vote: 5–3 (Jackson, J., did not participate.)
Decision: A statute making it a crime to remain on the premises of another after being warned not to do so violates the First and Fourteenth Amendments when applied to Jehovah's Witnesses distributing literature in a company-owned town. In balancing constitutional rights of property owners against those of the people to enjoy freedom of press and religion, the latter occupy a preferred position.

Case: *Niemotko v. Maryland*, 340 U.S. 268 (1951)
Vote: 9–0
Decision: Where there was no threat of disorder, violence, or riots, the arrest of Jehovah's Witnesses for holding Bible talks in a public park without a permit violates their rights of free speech and religion under the First Amendment.

Case: *Fowler v. Rhode Island*, 345 U.S. 67 (1953)
Vote: 9–0
Decision: A Pawtucket, Rhode Island, statute forbidding any person to address any political or religious meeting in a public park violates the First and Fourteenth Amendments as applied to Jehovah's Witnesses.

Case: *Wooley v. Maynard*, 430 U.S. 705 (1977)
Vote: 7–2
Decision: Requiring members of Jehovah's Witness faith to display motor vehicle license plates embossed with the state motto, "Live Free or Die," violates the First and Fourteenth Amendments. The state's interest in promoting appreciation of history, individualism, and state pride is not sufficient to outweigh an individual's First Amendment right to avoid becoming the courier of the state's ideological message.

FREE EXERCISE OF RELIGION

Sherbert v. Verner
374 U.S. 398 (1963)

SETTING

Some laws affect both religion clauses of the First Amendment. For example, laws that require business establishments to close on Sundays—known as Sunday Closing Laws—appear to accommodate the religious beliefs of those whose Sabbath is Sunday. On the other hand, Sunday Closing Laws restrict the religious practices of others, thus calling into question their validity under the Establishment Clause. The Supreme Court first addressed the dilemma of Sunday Closing Laws in 1961. The first case, *McGowan v. Maryland*, 366 U.S. 420, involved the criminal prosecution of employees of a large discount department store who violated the state's Sunday Closing Law. Because the employees alleged only an economic injury from the law, the Supreme Court refused to address their contention that the statute violated the Free Exercise Clause. The Court rejected their Establishment Clause challenge, concluding that even though Sunday Closing Laws originally were motivated by religious forces, they now are justified on secular grounds and hence bear "no relationship to establishment of religion as those words are used in the Constitution of the United States."

In the second case decided in 1961, *Braunfeld v. Brown*, 366 U.S. 599, the justices could not avoid the Free Exercise issue. *Braunfeld* involved Jewish merchants whose clothing and home furnishings stores in Philadelphia, Pennsylvania, had traditionally been closed on Saturday in observance of their Sabbath, but were open on Sunday. The merchants sought to enjoin enforcement of a Pennsylvania Sunday Closing Law enacted in 1959. In a sharply divided opinion, the justices held that the Free Exercise Clause did not mandate an exemption from the law, even though its effect was that those who observe a Saturday Sabbath were required to be closed for business two days a week instead of one. According to the majority, Pennsylvania's law did not make the practice of any religion unlawful, it merely made the practice more expensive. Chief Justice Warren wrote:

> [I]f the State regulates conduct by enacting a general law within its power, the purpose and effect of which is to advance the State's secular goals, the statute is valid despite its indirect burden of religious observances unless the State may accomplish its purpose by means which do not impose such a burden.

The justices revisited the issue of religious exemptions from secular legislation two years later in a case from South Carolina. The Seventh-Day Adventist faith recognizes a Saturday Sabbath. When Adell H. Sherbert became a Seventh-Day Adventist in 1957, she worked Monday through Friday at the Beaumont plant of the Spartan Mills in Spartanburg, South Carolina. In 1959, her employer expanded her work schedule to six days, requiring her to work on Saturdays. Sherbert refused to work on her Sabbath and subsequently was fired. The South Carolina Employment Security Commission denied Sherbert's application for unemployment compensation benefits, stating that she refused to work on Saturdays because of her Seventh-Day Adventist beliefs and hence was unwilling to accept "available suitable work when offered." Because Sherbert was "not available for work" on Saturday, she was not entitled to unemployment benefits under the South Carolina Unemployment Law.

Sherbert filed suit in the Court of Common Pleas for Spartanburg County against Commissioner Charlie Verner and the other members of the Employment Security Commission, claiming that the state unemployment statute violated her right to free exercise of religion. That court affirmed the commission and the South Carolina Supreme Court affirmed. Sherbert petitioned the Supreme Court of the United States for a writ of certiorari.

HIGHLIGHTS OF SUPREME COURT ARGUMENTS

BRIEF FOR SHERBERT

◆ Under the First Amendment, the freedom of religious belief is absolute and cannot be invaded by federal or state legislation. The South Carolina Unemployment Compensation Law is unconstitutional because it is applied in a way that is biased against non-Sunday Sabbatarians.

◆ The requirement that an applicant for unemployment benefits be available for work on the applicant's Sabbath in effect prohibits the free exercise of religion. The requirement cannot be justified by any state interest.

◆ The requirement that Saturday Sabbatarians be available for work on Saturdays while Sunday Sabbatarians are not required to be available for work on Sundays is arbitrary and discriminatory in violation of the Equal Protection and Due Process Clauses of the Fourteenth Amendment.

AMICUS CURIAE BRIEFS SUPPORTING SHERBERT

Joint brief of the American Jewish Committee, Anti-Defamation League of B'Nai B'rith, and the American Civil Liberties Union; joint brief of the Synagogue Council of America, American Jewish Congress, Jewish Labor Committee, and Jewish War Veterans of the U.S.A.

BRIEF FOR VERNER

◆ Sherbert has failed to show that the "available for work" eligibility standard prohibits or interferes with her free exercise of religion. Ineligibility for benefits is not coercion to work on a Sabbath because no person has an absolute right to unemployment benefits.

◆ This case is controlled by *Braunfeld v. Brown*. The law merely imposes an indirect financial burden on non-Sunday Sabbatarians. That burden is not aimed at nor does it impede freedom of religion.

♦ A legislature is entitled to make reasonable classifications for the purpose of legislation. The traditional Equal Protection test is whether a state has made an invidious discrimination, such as selecting a particular race or nationality for oppressive treatment. The unemployment statute advances the state's secular goal of promoting stable employment.

♦ Mere disagreement with application of the available-for-work standard does not rise to the level of a constitutional due process objection. Sherbert does not take issue with the valid secular goal of the unemployment statute.

SUPREME COURT DECISION: 7–2

BRENNAN, J.

... It [is] apparent that appellant's declared ineligibility for unemployment benefits derives solely from the practice of her religion, [and] the pressure upon her to forego that practice is unmistakable. The ruling [of the South Carolina Supreme Court] forces her to choose between following the precepts of her religion and forfeiting benefits, on the one hand, and abandoning one of the precepts of her religion in order to accept work, on the other hand. Governmental imposition of such a choice puts the same kind of burden upon the free exercise of religion as would a fine imposed against appellant for her Saturday worship.

Nor may the South Carolina court's construction of the statute be saved from constitutional infirmity on the ground that unemployment compensation benefits are not appellant's "right" but merely a "privilege." It is too late in the day to doubt that the liberties of religion and expression may be infringed by the denial of or placing of conditions upon a benefit or privilege....

We must next consider whether some compelling state interest enforced in the eligibility provisions of the South Carolina statute justifies the substantial infringement of appellant's First Amendment right. It is basic that no showing merely of a rational relationship to some colorable state interest would suffice; in this highly sensitive constitutional area, "(o)nly the gravest abuses, endangering paramount interest, give occasion for permissible limitation," *Thomas v. Collins*, 323 U.S. 516 [(1945)]. No such abuse or danger has been advanced in the present case....

In holding as we do, plainly we are not fostering the "establishment" of the Seventh-day Adventist religion in South Carolina, for the extension of unemployment benefits to Sabbatarians in common with Sunday worshippers reflects nothing more than the governmental obligation of neutrality in the face of religious differences, and does not represent that involvement of religious with secular institutions which it is the object of the Establishment Clause to forestall....

The judgment of the South Carolina Supreme Court is reversed and the case is remanded for further proceedings not inconsistent with this opinion. It is so ordered.

Reversed and remanded.

DOUGLAS, J., CONCURRING [OMITTED]

STEWART, J., CONCURRING IN THE RESULT

Although fully agreeing with the result which the Court reaches in this case, I cannot join the Court's opinion. This case presents a double-barreled dilemma, which in all candor I think the Court's opinion has not succeeded in papering over. The dilemma ought to be resolved....

I am convinced that no liberty is more essential to the continued vitality of the free society which our Constitution guarantees than is the religious liberty protected by the Free Exercise Clause explicit in the First Amendment and imbedded in the Fourteenth. And I regret that on occasion ... the Court has shown what has seemed to me a distressing insensitivity to the appropriate demands of this constitutional guarantee. By contrast I think that the Court's approach to the Establishment Clause has on occasion ... been not only insensitive, but positively wooden, and that the Court has accorded to the Establishment Clause a meaning which neither the words, the history, nor the intention of the authors of that specific constitutional provision even remotely suggests.

But my views as to the correctness of the Court's decisions in these cases are beside the point here. The point is that the decisions are on the books. And the result is that there are many situations where legitimate claims under the Free Exercise Clause will run into head-on collision with the Court's insensitive and sterile construction of the Establishment Clause. The controversy now before us is clearly such a case.

Because the appellant refuses to accept available jobs which would require her to work on Saturdays, South Carolina has declined to pay unemployment compensation benefits to her. Her refusal to work on Saturdays is based on the tenets of her religious faith. The Court says that South Carolina cannot under these circumstances declare her to be not

"available for work" within the meaning of its statute because to do so would violate her constitutional right to the free exercise of her religion.

Yet what this Court has said about the Establishment Clause must inevitably lead to a diametrically opposite result. If the appellant's refusal to work on Saturdays were based on indolence, or on a compulsive desire to watch the Saturday television programs, no one would say that South Carolina could not hold that she was not "available for work" within the meaning of its statute. That being so, the Establishment Clause as construed by this Court not only permits but affirmatively requires South Carolina equally to deny the appellant's claim for unemployment compensation when her refusal to work on Saturdays is based upon her religious creed....

To require South Carolina to so administer its laws as to pay public money to the appellant under the circumstances of this case is thus clearly to require the State to violate the Establishment Clause as construed by this Court. This poses no problem for me, because I think the Court's mechanistic concept of the Establishment Clause is historically unsound and constitutionally wrong....

My second difference with the Court's opinion is that I cannot agree that today's decision can stand consistently with *Braunfeld v. Brown*....

I think the *Braunfeld* case was wrongly decided and should be overruled....

HARLAN AND WHITE, J.J., DISSENTING

Today's decision is disturbing both in its rejection of existing precedent and in its implications for the future....

What the Court is holding is that if the State chooses to condition unemployment compensation on the applicant's availability for work, it is constitutionally compelled to carve out an exception— and to provide benefits—for those whose unavailability is due to their religious convictions....

The meaning of today's holding ... is that the State must furnish unemployment benefits to one who is unavailable for work if the unavailability stems from the exercise of religious convictions. The State, in other words, must single out for financial assistance those whose behavior is religiously motivated, even though it denies such assistance to others whose identical behavior (in this case, inability to work on Saturdays) is not religiously motivated....

Those situations in which the Constitution may require special treatment on account of religion are, in my view, few and far between[.] Such compulsion in the present case is particularly inappropriate in light of the indirect, remote, and insubstantial effect of the decision below on the exercise of appellant's religion and in light of the direct financial assistance to religion that today's decision requires.

For these reasons I respectfully dissent from the opinion and judgment of the Court.

QUESTIONS

1. Can *Sherbert* be reconciled with *Braunfeld v. Brown*? If it cannot, should the Court have overruled *Braunfeld*? In *Barnette*, the Court was criticized for overruling *Gobitis* after only three years. Might that criticism have encouraged the Court to distinguish the seemingly inconsistent *Braunfeld*?

2. Following *Sherbert*, what test will the Court employ in determining whether a statute impermissibly infringes on the right to free exercise of religion? If the *Sherbert* test had been applied in *Reynolds v. United States* (pp. 114–121), would the result in that case have been the same or different?

3. In the early 1960s, at least thirty-five of the fifty states did not require Seventh-Day observers to forfeit unemployment benefits if they refused to accept Saturday employment. Does the fact that a majority of the states had demonstrated that they could accommodate Saturday Sabbatarians appear to be a factor in the majority's decision in *Sherbert*?

4. Also in 1963, the Court vacated the judgment of a Minnesota court that had held a woman in contempt for refusing to serve on a jury because of her religious objections. *In re Jenison*, 375 U.S. 14. Eight years later, the Court refused to confer conscientious objector status on a Catholic who was convinced for religious reasons that the Vietnam War was "unjust," but who was not a complete pacifist as required by the federal Selective Service law for draft exemption. *Gillette v. United States*, 401 U.S. 437 (1971). What principle or principles, if any, explain the different outcomes in the two cases?

FREE EXERCISE OF RELIGION

Wisconsin v. Yoder
406 U.S. 205 (1972)

SETTING

As Justice Stewart's concurrence in *Sherbert v. Verner* made clear, the Court's decision in that case challenged the vitality of *Braunfeld v. Brown*, 366 U.S. 599 (1961), but did not overrule *Braunfeld*. Litigation continued to determine whether *Sherbert* was merely an aberration or reflected the Court's new approach to Free Exercise questions. A 1972 case involving Wisconsin's compulsory school attendance law provided the opportunity for clarification.

Compulsory education laws have existed in America since colonial times because an effective democracy depends on an educated public. As Thomas Jefferson put it, the people themselves are the only "safe depositories" of governing power but "to render even them safe, their minds must be improved to a certain degree...." By 1970, every state except Mississippi and South Carolina had compulsory education laws. Wisconsin's law required parents to send their children to public or private schools until the age of sixteen. That law conflicted with the Old Order Amish religion. Old Order Amish believe that the New Testament requires them to live austere lives in separate communities and to shun such modern devices as electricity, automobiles, and television. Old Order Amish dress modestly and object to having their children attend school beyond the eighth grade. They agree that children must learn basic reading, writing, and elementary mathematics, but contend that high schools expose them inappropriately to competition, sports, and the pressures to conform at crucial periods of their lives.

In 1968, Jonas Yoder, Wallace Miller, and Adin Yutzy, the fathers of three Old Order Amish and Conservative Amish Mennonite school children, withdrew their children from the New Glarus, Wisconsin, school district after they completed the eighth grade. Kenneth J. Glewen, the school district's administrator and truant officer, filed a complaint against those three parents in the Green County Court, where they were convicted and fined five dollars each. Although the trial court found that the compulsory school attendance law interfered with the sincere religious beliefs of Yoder and the other parents, it held that the law was a "reasonable and constitutional" exercise of governmental power. The Wisconsin Circuit Court affirmed, but the Wisconsin Supreme Court reversed. It held that, under *Sherbert v. Verner*, the school district had not shown that the state's interest in establishing and maintaining an educational system overrode the free exercise rights of the Amish.

The State of Wisconsin petitioned the Supreme Court of the United States for a writ of certiorari.

HIGHLIGHTS OF SUPREME COURT ARGUMENTS

BRIEF FOR WISCONSIN

◆ The Supreme Court of Wisconsin has overlooked the facts that this Court has recognized that children have a substantive right to an education and that the state has a right to compel attendance at a public or private school. The historical development of this nation's educational system demonstrates the compelling interest the nation has in its creation and maintenance.

◆ The Wisconsin Supreme Court misapplied *Sherbert v. Verner*. That case did not involve the rights of children to education, nor the state's compelling interest in compulsory school attendance laws.

◆ The exemption from compulsory school attendance laws granted by the Wisconsin Supreme Court is not secular in purpose, evenhanded in application, or neutral in primary impact. The effect of that court's decision is to foster excessive entanglement of religion and government.

◆ It is the province of the legislature, not the courts, to determine whether and when exemptions to compulsory school attendance laws are to be granted.

BRIEF FOR YODER

◆ Under *Sherbert v. Verner*, state regulations that burden the free exercise of religion must be justified by a compelling state interest in the regulation of a subject that is within the state's constitutional power to regulate. No state interest in standardizing children justifies the free exercise rights jeopardized by Wisconsin's compulsory school attendance law.

◆ There is no question in this case about the sincerity of the religious beliefs of the Amish.

◆ The Wisconsin law directly violates Amish religious freedom by placing criminal sanctions on the enjoyment of religious liberty, parental nurture, individual choice of religion, vocation, communal association, teaching and learning, and privacy.

◆ If the Amish, a religious minority, are required to await legislative action to implement their constitutional rights, they never will enjoy those rights. It is the province and duty of the courts to grant exemptions from compulsory education laws.

AMICUS CURIAE BRIEFS SUPPORTING YODER ET AL.

General Conference of Seventh-Day Adventists; Mennonite Central Committee; National Council of the Churches of Christ in the United States of America; National Jewish Commission on Law and Public Affairs; Synagogue Council of America and its constituents (Central Conference of American Rabbis, the Rabbinical Assembly of America, the Rabbinical Council of America, the Union of American Hebrew Congregations, the Union of Orthodox Jewish Congregations of America, the United Synagogue of America); American Jewish Congress.

SUPREME COURT DECISION: *7–0 ON RESULT*

(Powell and Rehnquist, J.J., did not participate.)

BURGER, C.J.

... There is no doubt as to the power of a State, having a high responsibility for education of its citizens, to impose reasonable regulations for the control and duration of basic education. See, e.g., *Pierce v. Society of Sisters*, 268 U.S. 510 (1925)[.]... [A] State's interest in universal education, however highly we rank it, is not totally free from a balancing process when it impinges on fundamental rights and interests, such as those specifically protected by the Free Exercise Clause of the First Amendment[.]...

It follows that in order for Wisconsin to compel school attendance beyond the eighth grade against a claim that such attendance interferes with the practice of a legitimate religious belief, it must appear either that the State does not deny the free exercise of religious belief by its requirement, or that there is a state interest of sufficient magnitude to override the interest claiming protection under the Free Exercise Clause....

A way of life, however virtuous and admirable, may not be interposed as a barrier to reasonable state regulation of education if it is based on purely secular considerations; to have the protection of the Religion Clauses, the claims must be rooted in religious belief. Although a determination of what is a "religious" belief or practice entitled to constitutional protection may present a most delicate question, the very concept of ordered liberty precludes allowing every person to make his own standards on matters of conduct in which society as a whole has important interests....

[T]he record in this case abundantly supports the claim that the traditional way of life of the Amish is not merely a matter of personal preference, but one of deep religious conviction, shared by an organized group, and intimately related to daily living....

As the society around the Amish has become more populous, urban, industrialized, and complex, particularly in this century, government regulation of human affairs has correspondingly become more detailed and pervasive. The Amish mode of life has thus come into conflict increasingly with requirements of contemporary society exerting a hydraulic insistence on conformity to majoritarian standards. So long as compulsory education laws were confined to eight grades of elementary basic education imparted in a nearby rural schoolhouse, with a large proportion of students of the Amish faith, the Old Order Amish had little basis to fear that school attendance would expose their children to the worldly influence they reject. But modern compulsory secondary education in rural areas is now largely carried on in a consolidated school, often remote from the student's home and alien to his daily home life.... The conclusion is inescapable that secondary schooling, by exposing Amish children to worldly influences in terms of attitudes, goals, and values contrary to beliefs, and by substantially interfering with the religious development of the Amish child and his integration into the way of life of the Amish faith community at the crucial adolescent stage of development, contravenes the basic religious tenets and practice of the Amish faith, both as to the parent and the child....

[T]his case [cannot] be disposed of on the grounds that Wisconsin's requirement for school attendance to age 16 applies uniformly to all citizens of the State and does not, on its face, discriminate against religions or a particular religion, or that it is motivated by legitimate secular concerns. A regulation neutral on its face may, in its application, nonetheless offend the constitutional requirement for governmental neutrality if it unduly burdens the free exercise of religion. *Sherbert v. Verner*....

We turn, then, to the State's broader contention that its interest in its system of compulsory education is so compelling that even the established religious practices of the Amish must give way. Where fundamental claims of religious freedom are at stake, however, we cannot accept such a sweeping claim; despite its admitted validity in the generality of cases, we must searchingly examine the interests that the State seeks to promote by its requirement for compulsory education to age 16, and the impediment to those objectives that would flow from recognizing the claimed Amish exemption....

The State advances two primary arguments in support of its system of compulsory education. It notes, as Thomas Jefferson pointed out early in our history, that some degree of education is necessary to prepare citizens to participate effectively and intelligently in our open political system if we are to preserve freedom and independence. Further, education prepares individuals to be self-reliant and self-sufficient participants in society. We accept these propositions.

However, the evidence adduced by the Amish in this case is persuasively to the effect that an additional one or two years of formal high school for Amish children in place of their long-established program of informal vocational education would do little to serve those interests.... It is one thing to say that compulsory education for a year or two beyond the eighth grade may be necessary when its goal is the preparation of the child for life in modern society as the majority live, but it is quite another if the goal of education be viewed as the preparation of the child for life in the separated agrarian community that is the keystone of the Amish faith....

Insofar as the State's claim rests on the view that a brief additional period of formal education is imperative to enable the Amish to participate effectively and intelligently in our democratic process, it must fall. The Amish alternative to formal secondary school education has enabled them to function effectively in their day-to-day life under self-imposed limitations on relations with the world, and to survive and prosper in contemporary society as a separate, sharply identifiable and highly self-sufficient community for more than 200 years in this country. In itself this is strong evidence that they are capable of fulfilling the social and political responsibilities of citizenship without compelled attendance beyond the eighth grade at the price of jeopardizing their free exercise of religious belief....

Contrary to the suggestion of the dissenting opinion of Mr. Justice Douglas, our holding today in no degree depends on the assertion of the religious interest of the child as contrasted with that of the parents. It is the parents who are subject to prosecution here for failing to cause their children to attend school, and it is their right of free exercise, not that of their children, that must determine Wisconsin's power to impose criminal penalties on the parent. The dissent argues that a child who expresses a desire to attend public high school in conflict with the wishes of his parents should not be prevented from doing so. There is no reason for the Court to consider that point since it is not an issue in the case. The children are not parties to this litigation....

Affirmed.

STEWART AND BRENNAN, J.J., CONCURRING [OMITTED]

WHITE, BRENNAN, AND STEWART, J.J., CONCURRING

... This would be a very different case for me if respondents' claim were that their religion forbade their children from attending any school at any time and from complying in any way with the educational standards set by the State. Since the Amish children are permitted to acquire the basic tools of literacy to survive in modern society by attending grades one through eight and since the deviation from the State's compulsory-education law is relatively slight, I conclude that respondents' claim must prevail[.]...

The importance of the state interest asserted here cannot be denigrated, however[.]...

DOUGLAS, J., DISSENTING IN PART

I agree with the Court that the religious scruples of the Amish are opposed to the education of their children beyond the grade schools, yet I disagree with the Court's conclusion that the matter is within the dispensation of parents alone. The Court's analysis assumes that the only interests at stake in the case are those of the Amish parents on the one hand, and those of the State on the other. The difficulty with this approach is that, despite the Court's claim, the parents are seeking to vindicate not only their own free exercise claims, but also those of their high-school-age children....

This issue has never been squarely presented before today. Our opinions are full of talk about the power of the parents over the child's education.... Recent cases, however, have clearly held that the children themselves have constitutionally protectible interests.

These children are "persons" within the meaning of the Bill of Rights....

It is the future of the student, not the future of the parents, that is imperiled by today's decision. If a parent keeps his child out of school beyond the grade school, then the child will be forever barred from entry into the new and amazing world of diversity that we have today. The child may decide that that is the preferred course, or he may rebel. It is the student's judgment, not his parents', that is essential if we are to give full meaning to what we have said about the Bill of Rights and of the right of students to be masters of their own destiny. If he is harnessed to the Amish way of life by those in authority over him and if his education is truncated, his entire life may be stunted and deformed. The child, therefore, should be given an opportunity to be heard before the State gives the exemption which we honor today....

QUESTIONS

1. Does *Yoder* merely reaffirm *Sherbert v. Verner* or does the judicial process of balancing interests broaden *Sherbert*? After *Yoder*, what is the status of *Braunfeld v. Brown*? Has it been further restricted or overruled?

2. The *amicus* brief submitted by the Synagogue Council of America and the American Jewish Congress noted:

> The number of [those whose religious convictions do not permit public school attendance beyond elementary school] is so small as to be of insignificant effect: a few Old Order Amish, a few Hasidic Jews (who like the Amish, maintain a strong commitment to traditional customs and practices), perhaps a few others. All in all they cannot amount to more than a fraction of one percent of the population, certainly far less than the number of Jews, Seventh Day Adventists and other Sabbatarians whose right to exemption from the requirement of accepting work was upheld in *Sherbert.*

When deciding constitutional questions, of what pertinence, if any, is the number of persons affected?

3. The Court's accommodation of the Amish created a classification based on religion that legitimated Wisconsin treating this religious group differently than others under its compulsory school attendance statute. Does such an accommodation violate the norm of neutrality essential to equal protection of the law, or does the norm of neutrality require such an accommodation?

4. In *Cruz v. Belo*, 405 U.S. 319 (1972), the Court held that, under the Free Exercise Clause, the state cannot deny Buddhist prison inmates the right to hold religious ceremonies if Catholic, Protestant, and Jewish prisoners are allowed to hold religious rites. Fifteen years later, the Court ruled that prison officials can deny Islamic prisoners the right to attend Jumu'ah, the midday Friday Moslem services, for security reasons. *O'Lone v. Shabazz*, 482 U.S. 342 (1987). Can these two decisions be reconciled?

COMMENTS

Yoder confirmed the vitality of the rule announced in *Sherbert* and added a balancing test: If a statute directly or indirectly burdens the free exercise of religion, the statute must be justified by a compelling government interest. For more than twenty years after *Yoder*, Free Exercise litigation focused on the applicability of the *Sherbert/Yoder* standard. The following cases indicate how the Court applied that standard in specific instances for over twenty-five years:

Case: *Thomas v. Review Board*, 450 U.S. 707 (1981)

Vote: 8–1

Decision: Indiana may not deny unemployment compensation benefits to a Jehovah's Witness who quit his job in the armament industry because of his religious beliefs. The denial burdens the free exercise of religion and the state has not demonstrated that it has a compelling interest in forcing the employee to choose between his religious beliefs and access to public benefits.

Case: *Heffron v. International Society for Krishna Consciousness*, 452 U.S. 460 (1981)

Vote: 5–4

Decision: A state may require a religious organization that desires to distribute and sell religious literature at a state fair to conduct those activities only at an assigned location at the fairgrounds. The restriction does not exclude on the basis of religion or viewpoint and reflects a sufficient government interest in avoiding congestion and maintaining the orderly movement of crowds at the state fair.

Case: *United States v. Lee*, 455 U.S. 252 (1982)

Vote: 9–0

Decision: A self-employed farmer and carpenter, who is a member of the Old Order Amish religion, cannot claim a religious exemption from the payment of social security taxes for his employees merely because his religion prohibits the acceptance of social security benefits. Accommodating religion in this circumstance radically and impermissibly restricts the operating latitude of the legislature because of the broad public interest in maintaining a sound tax system.

Case: *Bob Jones University v. United States*, 461 U.S. 574 (1983)

Vote: 8–1

Decision: The government has a compelling interest in eradicating racial discrimination in education. Consequently, removing tax-exempt status from private religious schools that discriminate on the basis of race does not violate the Religion Clauses of the First Amendment.

Case: *Tony and Susan Alamo Foundation v. Secretary of Labor*, 471 U.S. 290 (1985)

Vote: 9–0

Decision: A nonprofit religious foundation that derives its income largely from the operation of commercial businesses staffed by "associates"—most of whom were drug addicts, derelicts, or criminals before their involvement with the foundation—is an "enterprise" within the meaning of the Fair Labor Standards Act (FLSA) and is therefore subject to the minimum wage, overtime, and recordkeeping provisions of the FLSA. There is no merit to the claim that the recordkeeping provisions of the FLSA burden the associates' rights to free exercise of religion, because the FLSA does not require associates to receive wages instead of benefits like food, clothing, and shelter.

Case: *Goldman v. Weinberger*, 475 U.S. 503 (1986)

Vote: 5–4

Decision: An Air Force regulation that generally prohibits members from wearing headgear while indoors burdens the free exercise of religion of an Orthodox Jew by preventing him from wearing the yarmulke required by his religious beliefs. However, in evaluating military restrictions on religiously motivated conduct, courts must give great deference to the judgment of military authorities. The Free Exercise Clause does not require the Air Force to accommodate the wearing of yarmulkes if such practices would detract from the uniformity sought by reasonable and evenhanded dress regulations.

Case: *Lyng v. Northwest Indian Cemetery Protective Association*, 485 U.S. 439 (1988)

Vote: 5–3 (Kennedy, J., did not participate.)

Decision: The Free Exercise Clause does not prohibit the U.S. Forest Service from permitting timber harvesting and road construction in an area of the national forest used by the members of three Indian tribes—the Yorok, Karok, and Tolowa—for religious rituals. The incidental effects of government programs, which may make it more difficult to practice certain religions but have no tendency to coerce individuals into acting contrary to their religious beliefs, do not require government to offer a compelling justification for its otherwise lawful actions.

FREE EXERCISE OF RELIGION

Employment Division, Dept. of Human Resources of Oregon v. Smith
494 U.S. 872 (1990)

SETTING

Use of small amounts of peyote in religious observances is a central element in the religious practices of the Native American Church. Membership in the church, estimated at approximately three hundred thousand, is drawn from a variety of Native American tribes in the western portion of the United States. The sacramental use of peyote by church members occurs at meetings in which members give thanks for past good fortune and seek guidance for future conduct. Members also view peyote as a protector and carry it with them in beaded pouches. The church forbids the use of peyote for nonreligious purposes.

The principal ingredient of peyote is mescaline. When taken internally in sufficient quantities, peyote produces a hallucinogenic effect. Legal opposition to peyote and its use in the United States began near the turn of the century. In 1897, the U.S. government attempted to proscribe the use of peyote by prohibiting the sale of intoxicants to Indians living on reservations. Native Americans responded that they could not be arrested or prosecuted for possessing peyote under laws forbidding the sale of intoxicants to Indians because peyote was not on the list of prohibited intoxicants. The government sought to enforce its policy through intimidation, but with limited success. Several states also enacted legislation making possession or use of peyote a crime.

State courts entered the controversy surrounding the religious use of peyote in the 1920s. Members of the Native American Church claimed that statutes prohibiting its use in their religious ceremonies violated the Free Exercise Clause of the First Amendment. In 1926, the Montana Supreme Court rejected that claim, ruling that the Free Exercise Clause does not justify practices inconsistent with the good order, peace, or safety of the state. *State v. Big Sheep*, 75 Mont. 219 (1926). In 1964, by contrast, the California Supreme Court upheld the religious use of peyote, so long as a defendant's belief in peyotism was honest and in good faith. *People v. Woody*, 61 Cal. 2d 716 (1964).

The Supreme Court of the United States was drawn into the peyote controversy during its 1989 Term. In the state of Oregon, where the case originated, peyote was classified as a dangerous Schedule I drug, similar to heroin and LSD. Possession or use of peyote was a felony punishable by up to ten years imprisonment.

Alfred Smith, a Native American, and Galen Black, a European-American, were members of the Native American Church. They were employed as drug and alcohol counselors by the Council on Alcohol and Drug Abuse Prevention and Treatment (ADAPT) in Cascadia, Oregon. A private, nonprofit organization, ADAPT hired only counselors who themselves had prior records of drug and alcohol abuse. It required its counselors to abstain from the use of alcohol and nonprescription drugs.

Smith began working for ADAPT in August 1982. Black joined the staff the next month. On September 10, 1983, Black attended a weekend Tepee ceremony of the Native American Church at which he ingested a small amount of peyote as a sacrament. He did not ingest enough to produce a hallucinogenic effect. On September 19, after his employers discovered that he had ingested peyote at the ceremony, Black was suspended from his job at ADAPT. He was discharged on October 3 when he refused to resign or undergo treatment for misconduct connected with work. The Oregon Employment Division denied Black's application for unemployment compensation, stating that use of peyote was misconduct connected with work and that employees fired for work-related misconduct do not qualify for unemployment benefits.

Smith ingested a small quantity of peyote at a weekend Tepee ceremony on March 4, 1984. He attended the ceremony as an expression of religious solidarity with Black after Black's discharge and denial of unemployment benefits. Like Black, Smith was discharged by ADAPT. The state again refused to pay unemployment benefits. Smith and Black did not challenge their discharges by ADAPT but appealed the Employment Division's denial of unemployment benefits to the Oregon Court of Appeals. They argued that since their use of peyote was for religious purposes, they were entitled to unemployment benefits.

The court of appeals reversed the Employment Division's decision to deny benefits. The state appealed to the Oregon Supreme Court. That court held that under the test in *Sherbert*, the denial of unemployment benefits significantly burdened Smith and Black's religious freedom and that the state's interest in denying benefits was no greater than it had been in *Sherbert*. The state of Oregon petitioned the Supreme Court of the United States for a writ of certiorari.

In *Employment Division, Dept. of Human Resources of Oregon v. Smith et al.* (*Smith* I), 485 U.S. 660 (1988), the Supreme Court held by a vote of 5–3 (Kennedy, J., did not participate) that if Oregon law prohibited the religious use of peyote, and if the prohibition was consistent with the Constitution of the United States, there was no federal right to engage in the religious use of peyote in that state. The Court remanded the case to the Oregon Supreme Court to resolve the question of whether the religiously motivated use of peyote was illegal under Oregon law.

On remand, the Oregon Supreme Court held that Oregon's criminal prohibitions against the use of illegal drugs extended to the ingestion of peyote for religious purposes. It then held that the Oregon law violated the protection the First Amendment extends to good faith religious peyote use by Native American Church members. The state of Oregon again petitioned the Supreme Court for a writ of certiorari.

HIGHLIGHTS OF SUPREME COURT ARGUMENTS

BRIEF FOR OREGON

◆ This case presents the straight forward question whether Oregon's criminal law prohibiting peyote possession is unconstitutional as applied to Native American Church members who ingest peyote for religious reasons. Answering this question requires a decision whether, and under what circumstances, the Free Exercise Clause protects religious drug use from the reach of generally applicable and religiously neutral drug regulations.

◆ The Oregon Supreme Court rested its holding on the grounds that Congress has determined Native American Church peyote use is constitutionally protected. Congress is not the final arbiter of the meaning of the First Amendment.

◆ In *Cantwell v. Connecticut*, the Court established the principle that, while the Constitution broadly protects religious opinions and beliefs, religious conduct must give way to regulations that serve public interests of a compelling importance. There is no dispute that government has a compelling interest in prohibiting the use of dangerous drugs, or that peyote is a powerful and dangerous hallucinogen.

◆ The Free Exercise Clause requires government to "accommodate" religious practices only if it can do so without compromising its own interest. This Court has never found room for "accommodating" religion by making religion-by-religion exemptions from neutral laws of general applicability when those laws directly served health, safety or public order interests.

◆ If the government were required to "accommodate" the religious use of peyote the result would be impermissible intrusion into religious practices in order to monitor the use.

◆ The Establishment Clause does not permit the government to crack the door open in such a way as to permit one government-favored religion to pass through while denying passage to all others. If the Constitution is interpreted to protect religious drug use, it will have to be construed to "accommodate" religious practices in work places, in government programs, and in other public and private settings as well.

BRIEF FOR SMITH

◆ Oregon's interest in protecting the fiscal integrity of its unemployment fund is not sufficient to infringe on sincere religious practices. The state supreme court decided as a matter of state law that the state's interest in proscribing drug use is irrelevant to its unemployment practice.

◆ Under the rule in *Wisconsin v. Yoder*, the state must show a compelling interest for denying unemployment benefits. The state concedes that Smith and Black have a sincere belief in the practice of their religion. In all previous cases decided by this Court where unemployment benefits have been denied because of religious beliefs and activities, the Court has ruled that the denial placed an unconstitutional burden on the free exercise of religion.

◆ Oregon's interest in proscribing dangerous drugs is not affected by exempting the religious use of peyote by the Native American Church. The strictly controlled use of peyote by church members does not sanction or promote illegal drugs, nor does it sanction or promote drug use outside of a narrowly religious context.

◆ There is no danger that upholding an exemption for the religious use of peyote from state law proscriptions of dangerous drugs will lead to a flood of other Free Exercise claims. Other states' experiences show that strict regulations and controls on peyote use by the Native American Church have prevented law enforcement problems.

AMICUS CURIAE BRIEFS SUPPORTING SMITH

Joint brief of the American Jewish Congress, American Civil Liberties Union, Association on American Indian Affairs; joint brief of seven Native American church organizations.

SUPREME COURT DECISION: 6–3

SCALIA, J.

This case requires us to decide whether the Free Exercise Clause of the First Amendment permits the State of Oregon to include religiously inspired peyote use within the reach of its general criminal prohibition on the use of that drug, and thus permits the State to deny unemployment benefits to persons dismissed from their jobs because of such religiously inspired use....

Respondents urge us to hold, quite simply, that when otherwise prohibitable conduct is accompanied by religious convictions, not only the convictions but the conduct itself must be free from governmental regulation. We have never held that, and decline to do so now. There being no contention that Oregon's drug law represents an attempt to regulate religious beliefs, the communication of religious beliefs, or the raising of one's children in those beliefs, the rule to which we have adhered ever since *Reynolds [v. United States]* plainly controls....

Respondents argue that even though exemption from generally applicable criminal laws need not automatically be extended to religiously motivated actors, at least the claim for a religious exemption must be evaluated under the balancing test set forth in *Sherbert v. Verner*. Under the *Sherbert* test, governmental actions that substantially burden a religious practice must be justified by a compelling governmental interest....

The "compelling government interest" requirement seems benign, because it is familiar from other fields. But using it as the standard that must be met before the government may accord different treatment on the basis of race, or before the government may regulate the content of speech, is not remotely comparable to using it for the purpose asserted here....

If the "compelling interest" test is to be applied at all ... it must be applied across the board, to all actions thought to be religiously commanded. Moreover, if "compelling interest" really means what it says (and watering it down here would subvert its rigor in the other fields where it is applied), many laws will not meet the test. Any society adopting such a system would be courting anarchy, but that danger increased in direct proportion to the society's diversity of religious beliefs, and its determination to coerce or suppress none of them. Precisely because "we are a cosmopolitan nation made up of people of almost every conceivable religious preference" [*Braunfeld v. Brown*, 366 U.S. 599 (1961)], and precisely because we value and protect that religious divergence, we cannot afford the luxury of deeming *presumptively invalid*, as applied to the religious objector, every regulation of conduct that does not protect an interest of the highest order. The rule respondents favor would open the prospect of constitutionally required religious exemptions from civic obligations of almost every conceivable kind—ranging from compulsory military service ... to the payment of taxes ... to health and safety regulation such as manslaughter and child neglect laws ... compulsory vaccination laws ... drug laws ... and traffic laws ... to social welfare legislation such as minimum wage laws ... child labor laws ... animal cruelty laws, see, e.g., *Church of the Lukumi Babalu Aye Inc. v. City of Hialeah*, 723 F.Supp. 1467 (SD Fla. 1989) ... environmental protection laws ... and laws providing for equality of opportunity for the races[.]... The First Amendment's protection of religious liberty does not require this.

Values that are protected against government interference though enshrinement in the Bill of Rights are not thereby banished from the political process. Just as a society that believes in the negative protection accorded to the press by the First Amendment is likely to enact laws that affirmatively foster the dissemination of the printed word, so also a society that believes in the negative protection accorded to religious belief can be expected to be solicitous of that value in its legislation as well. It is therefore not surprising that a number of States have made an exception to their drug laws for sacramental peyote use. But to say that a nondiscriminatory religious-practice exemption is permitted, or even that it is desirable, is not to say that it is constitutionally required, and that the appropriate occasions for its creation can be discerned by the courts. It may fairly be said that leaving accommodation to the political process will place at a relative disadvantage those religious practices that are not widely engaged in; but that unavoidable consequence of democratic government must be preferred to a system in which each conscience is a law unto itself or in which judges weigh the social importance of all laws against the centrality of all religious beliefs.

Because respondents' ingestion of peyote was prohibited under Oregon law, and because that prohibition is constitutional, Oregon may, consistent with the Free Exercise Clause, deny respondents unemployment compensation when their dismissal results from use of the drug. The decision of the Oregon Supreme Court is accordingly reversed.

O'CONNOR, BRENNAN, MARSHALL, AND BLACKMUN, J.J., CONCURRING IN PART

Although I agree with the result the Court reaches in this case, I cannot join its opinion. In my view, today's holding dramatically departs from well-settled First Amendment jurisprudence, appears unnecessary to resolve the question presented, and is incompatible with our Nation's fundamental commitment to individual religious liberty....

The Court today gives no convincing reason to depart from settled First Amendment jurisprudence. There is nothing talismanic about neutral laws of general applicability or general criminal prohibitions, for laws neutral toward religion can coerce a person to violate his religious conscience or intrude upon his religious duties just as effectively as laws aimed at religion. Although the Court suggests that the compelling interest test, as applied to generally applicable laws, would result in a "constitutional anomaly," the First Amendment unequivocally makes freedom of religion, like freedom from race discrimination and freedom of speech, a "constitutional nor[m]," not an "anomaly." Nor would application of our established free exercise doctrine to this case necessarily be incompatible with our equal protection cases. We have in any event recognized that the Free Exercise Clause protects values distinct from those protected by the Equal Protection Clause. As the language

of the Clause itself makes clear, an individual's free exercise of religion is a preferred constitutional activity. A law that makes criminal such an activity therefore triggers constitutional concern—and heightened judicial scrutiny—even if it does not target the particular religious conduct at issue. Our free speech cases similarly recognize that neutral regulations that affect free speech values are subject to a balancing, rather than categorical, approach. The Court's parade of horribles not only fails as a reason for discarding the compelling interest test, it instead demonstrates just the opposite: that courts have been quite capable of applying our free exercise jurisprudence to strike sensible balances between religious liberty and competing state interests.

Finally, the Court today suggests that the disfavoring of minority religions is an "unavoidable consequence" under our system of government and that accommodation of such religions must be left to the political process. In my view, however, the First Amendment was enacted precisely to protect the rights of those whose religious practices are not shared by the majority and may be viewed with hostility. The history of our free exercise doctrine amply demonstrates the harsh impact majoritarian rule has had on unpopular or emerging religious groups such as the Jehovah's Witnesses and the Amish....

The Court's holding today not only misreads settled First Amendment precedent; it appears to be unnecessary to this case. I would reach the same applying our established free exercise jurisprudence....

BLACKMUN, BRENNAN, AND MARSHALL, J.J., DISSENTING

... [A] distorted view of our precedents leads the majority to conclude that strict scrutiny of a state law burdening the free exercise of religion is a "luxury" that a well-ordered society cannot afford, and that the repression of minority religions is an "unavoidable consequence of democratic government." I do not believe the Founders thought their dearly bought freedom from religious persecution a "luxury," but an essential element of liberty— and they could not have thought religious intolerance "unavoidable," for they drafted the Religion Clauses precisely in order to avoid that intolerance....

I conclude that Oregon's interest in enforcing its drug laws against religious use of peyote is not sufficiently compelling to outweigh respondents' right to the free exercise of their religion....

I dissent.

QUESTIONS

1. Summarize the effect of *Smith* on Free Exercise jurisprudence. Is it accurate to say that *Smith* rejects the *Sherbert* "compelling interest" standard and the *Yoder* balancing test, and returns the Court to the less stringent test employed in *Reynolds*? Does it make any difference after *Smith* whether the Free Exercise claim is raised in a criminal or civil context?

2. Does *Smith* mark a return to *Braunfeld v. Brown*? What is the status of *Sherbert*?

3. The Executive Director of ADAPT testified at a hearing that the agency would have taken the same action against Smith and Black if they had "consumed wine at a Catholic ceremony." If *Smith* had involved the religious use of alcohol instead of peyote, would the Court have viewed the case differently? What, if any, significance might attach to the facts that possession and use of alcohol are widely accepted in American society and that few Americans practice Smith and Black's religion, while many Americans are Catholics and Episcopalians?

COMMENT

In light of twenty-five years of Free Exercise Clause jurisprudence guided by *Sherbert* and *Yoder*, the decision in *Smith* was both surprising and controversial. Three years later, the Court granted certiorari in *Church of the Lukumi Babalu Aye, Inc. v. City of Hialeah*, 508 U.S. 520 (1993). That case involved the Santeria religion, which is a fusion of traditional African religion with elements of Roman Catholicism. Santeria includes animal sacrifices as a principal form of devotion. Conventional wisdom was that the Court's purpose in granting certiorari in *Lukumi Babalu Aye* was to revisit *Smith*. Conventional wisdom proved wrong. Although badly fragmented in their reasoning, the justices agreed 9–0 that city ordinances that banned the ritual sacrifice of animals were unconstitutional. Seven justices agreed that the ordinances were not of general applicability and were not drawn narrowly to achieve a compelling government interest and hence violated the Free Exercise Clause. Two justices concluded that the ordinances impermissibly targeted the Santeria religion. Perhaps because of its unique facts, *Lukumi Babalu Aye* proved not to be an appropriate case for reconsidering *Smith* or clarifying the status of *Sherbert* and *Yoder* in the wake of *Smith*.

FREE EXERCISE OF RELIGION

City of Boerne v. Flores
117 S.Ct. 2157 (1997)

SETTING

The Court's decision in *Employment Division, Dept. of Human Resources of Oregon v. Smith* created huge legal and political shock waves, both because of the new Free Exercise rule Justice Scalia announced and because none of the parties in *Smith* had asked the Court to reconsider its quarter century of Free Exercise jurisprudence. A group of over one hundred law professors petitioned the justices to rehear the case. Their petition was denied. *Employment Division, Dept. of Human Resources of Oregon v. Smith*, 496 U.S. 913 (1990). Legislators responded critically and quickly to *Smith*. Oregon, for example, adopted a religious use exception to its law prohibiting the use of peyote. Or. Rev. Stat. 475.992 (1993). House Judiciary Chair Jack Brooks declared that "The Supreme Court's [*Smith*] decision ... transformed a most hallowed liberty into a mundane concept with little more status than a fishing license—thus subjecting religious freedom to the whims of Government officials." Congressional response took the form of the Religious Freedom Restoration Act of 1994 (RFRA), enacted on the authority of Congress's enforcement powers under Section 5 of the Fourteenth Amendment.

RFRA passed unanimously in the House of Representatives. It cleared the Senate by a vote of 97–3 and enjoyed the support of the Clinton administration. According to RFRA:

> Government shall not burden a person's exercise of religion even if the burden results from a rule of general applicability [unless] it demonstrates that application of the burden ... (1) furthers a compelling governmental interest, and (2) is the least restrictive means of furthering that compelling governmental interest.

RFRA, in short, incorporated the tests announced in *Sherbert* and *Yoder* into federal statute.

Soon after its enactment, P. F. Flores, the archbishop of San Antonio, Texas, invoked RFRA in an effort to shield St. Peter Catholic Church in Boerne, Texas, from the reach of a historic preservation ordinance that constrained the parish from demolishing a church building that no longer met its needs.

St. Peter Catholic Church, built in 1923, is an example of mission revival architecture reminiscent of the original Spanish missions in South Texas. The church is located on a hill in Boerne, making it a highly visible reminder of the city's history. In 1985, the city council of Boerne created a landmark commission that began to explore creation of a historic district for the city. Public hearings were held in 1990 to determine the boundaries of the district. In 1991, the city council enacted a historic landmark preservation ordinance—91-05—to "protect, enhance, and perpetuate selected historic landmarks." St. Peter Church was included in the district.

On December 14, 1993, Flores requested a building permit to demolish and expand St. Peter Church. The building, which can accommodate only 230 worshippers at a time, had become far too small to seat the close to 2,170 parishioners who wished to attend Mass on Sunday morning. The landmark commission objected to the request because of the structure's historical importance to the community. Gregory Davis, the city's building inspector, denied the permit. Flores appealed to the Boerne City Council, which upheld the denial. The city and Flores were unable to reach agreement on alternative alterations to the building. Flores then filed suit in the U.S. District Court for the Western District of Texas, claiming that Ordinance 91-05 violated the RFRA. The United States intervened on behalf of Flores.

The district court declared that RFRA was unconstitutional on its face because it infringed on the "long-settled authority of the courts" by attempting to overturn the Supreme Court's decision in *Employment Division, Dept. of Human Resources of Oregon v. Smith*. The U.S. Court of Appeals for the Fifth Circuit reversed. It ruled that RFRA "may be regarded" as an enactment to enforce the Fourteenth Amendment, which incorporates the First Amendment, and that RFRA was a legitimate exercise of Congressional authority under Section 5 of the Fourteenth Amendment to defend minority religions from laws that burden the free exercise of religion. The Fifth Circuit also held that, because governments may accommodate religion more than the Free Exercise Clause requires, Congress has the power to force all governments to accommodate all religious conduct that is substantially burdened by a generally applicable law.

The Supreme Court of the United States granted the City of Boerne's petition for a writ of certiorari.

HIGHLIGHTS OF SUPREME COURT ARGUMENTS

BRIEF FOR CITY OF BOERNE

◆ RFRA is an undisguised attempt by Congress to take over this Court's core constitutional function and to reverse this Court's statement of the meaning of the Free Exercise Clause announced in *Smith*. Since *Marbury v. Madison*, 1 Cranch 137 (1803), it has been recognized that it is the "province and duty of the judicial department to say what the law is."

◆ With enactment of RFRA, Congress has overstepped the bounds of its legitimate constitutional powers and made real the fear of "legislative usurpation" that animated the Founders' decision to institute a government of limited powers. In essence, with RFRA Congress is instructing the Supreme Court how to interpret the Free Exercise Clause.

◆ RFRA's "least restrictive means test" transforms *Smith's* presumption of validity for neutral, generally applicable laws into a standard that will ultimately lead to striking down almost any statute on the ground that the Court could think of another less restrictive way to write it.

◆ RFRA is not a legitimate exercise of Congress's power under Section 5 of the Fourteenth Amendment. That section does not give Congress the authority to preempt this Court's declared standard of review regarding a clause of the Constitution. RFRA was designed to fill in a perceived gap in free exercise protection left open by *Smith*, not to enforce rights guaranteed by the Constitution.

◆ It is true that the Voting Rights Act cases interpreted Congress's Section 5 remedial powers broadly. However, those cases reflect the Court's deference to Congress's superior fact-finding capacity while employing the standard of review articulated by the Court. RFRA, by contrast, treats Section 5 as a warrant to enforce ends not guaranteed by the Constitution. Congress engaged in no meaningful fact-finding that would support the need for a legislative remedy in the free exercise arena.

◆ RFRA violates the Establishment Clause, which is specifically directed to Congress to prevent the union of Congress with organized religions.

◆ RFRA violates *Lemon v. Kurtzman* because it has neither a secular purpose nor a secular effect. The act fails the entanglement prong by forcing every government to become expert on every religion.

AMICUS CURIAE ARGUMENTS SUPPORTING CITY OF BOERNE

National Trust for Historic Preservation; joint brief of Children's Health Care Is a Legal Duty, Inc., and American Professional Society on the Abuse of Children; Center for the Community Interest; Clarendon Foundation; joint brief of the San Antonio Conservation Society, Municipal Art Society, and National Alliance of Preservation Commissions; joint brief of States of Ohio, Arizona, Colorado, Delaware, Florida, Hawaii, Idaho, Mississippi, Nevada, New Hampshire, North Carolina, Oklahoma, and Pennsylvania, and the territories of American Samoa, Guam, and the Virgin Islands.

BRIEF FOR FLORES

◆ The only question in this case is whether RFRA is facially unconstitutional. A congressional act is entitled to a presumption of constitutionality and may be struck down only when there is no room for reasonable doubt about its constitutionality. The Congressional Research Service, various constitutional scholars, and the judiciary committees of both houses of Congress concluded that Congress had ample power to enact RFRA. Because RFRA represents the considered constitutional judgment of a coequal branch of government, the burden is on the city to show that it is not constitutional.

◆ RFRA is parallel to several of the most familiar of Congress's enforcement powers under Section 5 of the Fourteenth Amendment. Although the Constitution does not require heightened scrutiny of practices with disproportionate racial impact, Congress, through the Voting Rights Act, has entirely banned voting practices that produce discriminatory results and the Court has not objected. Even the city concedes that this Court has permitted Congress to enact prophylactic legislation that bans actions not forbidden by the Constitution for the purpose of enforcing constitutional guarantees.

◆ Congress created a substantial record of its reasons for believing that RFRA is necessary to enforce religious liberty. Specifically, it found that generally applicable laws burden religion and can be used for that purpose, litigation over governmental motives is not a reliable means of protecting religious liberty, and specific exemptions in individual laws are not a reliable means of protecting religious liberty.

◆ Most of the Court's case law on Section 5 involves laws to enforce the Equal Protection Clause. It makes no difference that this case involves a law to enforce the religious liberty component of the Due Process Clause, a right that has been incorporated from the First Amendment. Section 5 authorizes Congress to protect rights incorporated into the Fourteenth Amendment and Congress may provide greater protection for constitutional rights than this Court would provide on its own.

◆ RFRA expressly disclaims any intention to overturn the results of particular past cases or to dictate results in particular future cases. The act in no way reopens final judgments in any cases. Occasional congressional references to the effect that RFRA would overturn *Smith* were simply verbal shorthand for creation of a statutory standard that would lead to different results in future cases.

◆ The city's claim that RFRA violates the Establishment Clause is frivolous. RFRA does not require government to subsidize or benefit religion, or make religion better off than it would be if government had done nothing. The law requires only that religious conduct sometimes be left unregulated.

BRIEF FOR THE UNITED STATES

◆ Section 5 vests Congress with independent and broad authority to protect against, not just remedy, violations of the Fourteenth Amendment's guarantees. The political background against which the Civil War Amendments were adopted explains their framers' desire to carve out an independent role for Congress in securing Fourteenth Amendment liberties.

◆ If RFRA is declared unconstitutional, *Katzenbach v. Morgan*, 384 U.S. 641 (1966), must be overruled. That case recognized that Congress has independent authority to identify and invalidate specific governmental practices when it determines as a factual matter that they violate Section 1 of the Fourteenth Amendment under the standards announced by this Court. *Morgan* reflects a correct understanding of Congress's remedial powers.

◆ The fact that, in the course of passing RFRA, members of Congress criticized *Smith* has no bearing on the separation of powers. Congress's authority to legislate does not depend on its agreement with Supreme Court decisions.

AMICUS CURIAE BRIEFS SUPPORTING FLORES AND THE UNITED STATES

The Rutherford Institute; National Right to Work Legal Defense Foundation, Inc.; National Jewish Commission on Law and Public Affairs; Becket Fund for Religious Liberty; joint brief of the United States Catholic Conference, the Evangelical Lutheran Church in America, the Orthodox Church in America, and the Evangelical Covenant Church; American Bar Association; joint brief of the Minnesota Family Council, Illinois Family Institute, Indiana Family Institute, Massachusetts Family Institute, New Jersey Family Policy Council, North Carolina Family Policy Council, Oklahoma Family Policy Council, Oregon Center for Family Policy, Palmetto Family Council, Pennsylvania Family Institute, Rocky Mountain Family Council, Rocky Mountain Family Legal Foundation and Northstar Legal Center; NAACP Legal Defense and Education Fund, Inc.; joint brief of ten U.S. senators and fifteen members of the House of Representatives; joint brief of members of the Virginia House of Delegates and Virginia Senate; joint brief of the Prison Fellowship Ministries and the Aleph Institute; Knights of Columbus; joint brief of seven U.S. senators and two members of the House of Representatives; Church of Jesus Christ of Latter Day Saints; joint brief of the States of Maryland, Connecticut, Massachusetts, and New York; Coalition for the Free Exercise of Religion; American Center for Law and Justice; Defenders of Property Rights; State of Texas; Commonwealth of Virginia; Coalition for the Free Exercise of Religion.

AMICUS CURIAE BRIEFS SUPPORTING NEITHER PARTY

Thurston Greene, author of *The Language of the Constitution, a Sourcebook and Guide to the Ideas, Terms, and Vocabulary Used by the Framers of the United States Constitution* (New York, NY: Greenwood Press, 1991) (urging a distinction between "religion" and "conscience").

SUPREME COURT DECISION: 6–3

KENNEDY, J.

... [This] case calls into question the authority of Congress to enact RFRA. We conclude the statute exceeds Congress' power....

Under our Constitution, the Federal Government is one of enumerated powers. *McCulloch v. Maryland*, 4 Wheat[on] 316 (1819).... The judicial authority to determine the constitutionality of laws, in cases and controversies, is based on the premise that the "powers of the legislature are defined and limited; and that those limits may not be mistaken, or for-

gotten, the constitution is written." *Marbury v. Madison*, 1 Cranch 137 (1803).

Congress relied on its Fourteenth Amendment enforcement power in enacting the most far reaching and substantial of RFRA's provisions, those which impose its requirements on the States....

All must acknowledge that § 5 is "a positive grant of legislative power" to Congress, *Katzenbach v. Morgan*, 384 U.S. 641 (1966)....

Congress' power under § 5, however, extends only to "enforc[ing]" the provisions of the Fourteenth Amendment. The Court has described this power as "remedial," *South Carolina v. Katzenbach* [383 U.S. 301, 308 (1966)]. The design of the Amendment and the text of § 5 are inconsistent with the suggestion that Congress has the power to decree the substance of the Fourteenth Amendment's restrictions on the States. Legislation which alters the meaning of the Free Exercise Clause cannot be said to be enforcing the Clause. Congress does not enforce a constitutional right by changing what the right is. It has been given the power "to enforce," not the power to determine what constitutes a constitutional violation....

While the line between measures that remedy or prevent unconstitutional actions and measures that make a substantive change in the governing law is not easy to discern, and Congress must have wide latitude in determining where it lies, the distinction exists and must be observed. There must be a congruence and proportionality between the injury to be prevented or remedied and the means adopted to that end....

There is language in our opinion in *Katzenbach v. Morgan*, 384 U.S. 641 (1966), which could be interpreted as acknowledging a power in Congress to enact legislation that expands the rights contained in § 1 of the Fourteenth Amendment. This is not a necessary interpretation, however, or even the best one. In *Morgan*, the Court considered the constitutionality of § 4(e) of the Voting Rights Act of 1965, which provided that no person who had successfully completed the sixth primary grade in a public school in, or a private school accredited by, the Commonwealth of Puerto Rico in which the language of instruction was other than English could be denied

the right to vote because of an inability to read or write English. New York's Constitution, on the other hand, required voters to be able to read and write English. The Court provided two related rationales for its conclusion that § 4(e) could "be viewed as a measure to secure for the Puerto Rican community residing in New York nondiscriminatory treatment by government." Under the first rationale, Congress could prohibit New York from denying the right to vote to large segments of its Puerto Rican community, in order to give Puerto Ricans "enhanced political power" that would be "helpful in gaining nondiscriminatory treatment in public services for the entire Puerto Rican community." Section 4(e) thus could be justified as a remedial measure to deal with "discrimination in governmental services." The second rationale, an alternative holding, did not address discrimination in the provision of public services but "discrimination in establishing voter qualifications." The Court perceived a factual basis on which Congress could have concluded that New York's literacy requirement "constituted an invidious discrimination in violation of the Equal Protection Clause."...

If Congress could define its own powers by altering the Fourteenth Amendment's meaning, no longer would the Constitution be "superior paramount law, unchangeable by ordinary means." It would be "on a level with ordinary legislative acts, and, like other acts, ... alterable when the legislature shall please to alter it." *Marbury v. Madison.* Under this approach, it is difficult to conceive of a principle that would limit congressional power.... Shifting legislative majorities could change the Constitution and effectively circumvent the difficult and detailed amendment process contained in Article V.

We now turn to consider whether RFRA can be considered enforcement legislation under § 5 of the Fourteenth Amendment....

While preventive rules are sometimes appropriate remedial measures, there must be a congruence between the means used and the ends to be achieved. The appropriateness of remedial measures must be considered in light of the evil presented.... Strong measures appropriate to address one harm may be an unwarranted response to another, lesser one....

RFRA cannot be considered remedial, preventive legislation, if those terms are to have any meaning. RFRA is so out of proportion to a supposed remedial or preventive object that it cannot be understood as responsive to, or designed to prevent, unconstitutional behavior. It appears, instead, to attempt a substantive change in constitutional protections....

Sweeping coverage ensures [RFRA's] intrusion at every level of government, displacing laws and prohibiting official actions of almost every description and regardless of subject matter.... RFRA has no termination date or termination mechanism. Any law is subject to challenge at any time by any individual who alleges a substantial burden on his or her free exercise of religion....

The stringent test RFRA demands of state laws reflects a lack of proportionality or congruence between the means adopted and the legitimate end to be achieved. If an objector can show a substantial burden on his free exercise, the State must demonstrate a compelling governmental interest and show that the law is the least restrictive means of furthering its interest. Claims that a law substan-

tially burdens someone's exercise of religion will often be difficult to contest.... Laws valid under *Smith* would fall under RFRA without regard to whether they had the object of stifling or punishing free exercise. We make these observations not to reargue the position of the majority in *Smith* but to illustrate the substantive alteration of its holding attempted by RFRA. Even assuming RFRA would be interpreted in effect to mandate some lesser test, say one equivalent to intermediate scrutiny, the statute nevertheless would require searching judicial scrutiny of state law with the attendant likelihood of invalidation. This is a considerable congressional intrusion into the States' traditional prerogatives and general authority to regulate for the health and welfare of their citizens....

Our national experience teaches that the Constitution is preserved best when each part of the government respects both the Constitution and the proper actions and determinations of the other branches. When the Court has interpreted the Constitution, it has acted within the province of the Judicial Branch, which embraces the duty to say what the law is. *Marbury v. Madison.* When the political branches of the Government act against the background of a judicial interpretation of the Constitution already issued, it must be understood that in later cases and controversies the Court will treat its precedents with the respect due them under settled principles, including *stare decisis,* and contrary expectations must be disappointed. RFRA was designed to control cases and controversies, such as the one before us; but as the provisions of the federal statute here invoked are beyond congressional authority, it is this Court's precedent, not RFRA, which must control....

Broad as the power of Congress is under the Enforcement Clause of the Fourteenth Amendment, RFRA contradicts vital principles necessary to maintain separation of powers and the federal balance. The judgment of the Court of Appeals sustaining the Act's constitutionality is reversed.

It is so ordered.

STEVENS, J., CONCURRING

In my opinion, RFRA is a "law respecting an establishment of religion" that violates the First Amendment to the Constitution.

If the historic landmark on the hill in Boerne happened to be a museum or an art gallery owned by an atheist, it would not be eligible for an exemption from the city ordinances that forbid an enlargement of the structure. Because the landmark is owned by the Catholic Church, it is claimed that RFRA gives its owner a federal statutory entitlement to an exemption from a generally applicable, neutral civil law. Whether the Church would actually prevail under the statute or not, the statute has provided the Church with a legal weapon that no atheist or agnostic can obtain. This governmental preference for religion, as opposed to irreligion, is forbidden by the First Amendment....

SCALIA AND STEVENS, J.J., CONCURRING IN PART

I write to respond briefly to the claim of Justice O'Connor's dissent that historical materials support a result contrary to the one reached in *Employment Div., Dept. of Human Resources of Ore. v. Smith*, 494 U.S. 872 (1990)....

The issue presented by *Smith* is, quite simply, whether the people, through their elected representatives, or rather this Court, shall control the outcome of those concrete cases.... The historical evidence put forward by the dissent does nothing to undermine the conclusion we reached in *Smith*: It shall be the people.

O'CONNOR AND BREYER, J.J., DISSENTING

... The Court's analysis of whether RFRA is a constitutional exercise of Congress' § 5 power ... is premised on the assumption that *Smith* correctly interprets the Free Exercise Clause. This is an assumption that I do not accept. I continue to believe that *Smith* adopted an improper standard for deciding free exercise claims.... [T]he Clause is best understood as an affirmative guarantee of the right to participate in religious practices and conduct without impermissible governmental interference, even when such conduct conflicts with a neutral, generally applicable law. Before *Smith*, our free exercise cases were generally in keeping with this idea: where a law substantially burdened religiously motivated conduct—regardless whether it was specifically targeted at religion or applied generally—we required government to justify that law with a compelling state interest and to use means narrowly tailored to achieve that interest....

The Court's rejection of this principle in *Smith* is supported neither by precedent nor ... by history....

[E]arly leaders accorded religious exercise a special constitutional status. The right to free exercise was a substantive guarantee of individual liberty, no less important than the right to free speech or the right to just compensation for the taking of property....

[A]ll agreed that government interference in religious practice was not to be lightly countenanced.... [A]ll shared the conviction that "true religion and good morals are the only solid foundation of public liberty and happiness.'"... To give meaning to these ideas—particularly in a society characterized by religious pluralism and pervasive regulation—there will be times when the Constitution requires government to accommodate the needs of those citizens whose religious practices conflict with generally applicable law....

Although it may provide a bright line, the rule the Court declared in *Smith* does not faithfully serve the purpose of the Constitution. Accordingly, I believe that it is essential for the Court to reconsider its holding in *Smith*—and to do so in this very case. I would therefore direct the parties to brief this issue and set the case for reargument.

I respectfully dissent from the Court's disposition of this case.

BREYER, J., DISSENTING

I agree with Justice O'Connor that the Court should direct the parties to brief the question whether *Employment Div., Dept. of Human Resources of Ore. v. Smith* was correctly decided, and set this case for reargument. I do not, however, find it necessary to consider the question whether, assuming *Smith* is correct, § 5 of the Fourteenth Amendment would authorize Congress to enact the legislation before us....

SOUTER, J., DISSENTING

... I have serious doubts about the precedential value of the *Smith* rule and its entitlement to adherence. These doubts are intensified today by the historical arguments going to the original understanding of the Free Exercise Clause presented in Justice O'Connor's opinion[.]... But without briefing and argument on the merits of that rule (which this Court has never had in any case, including *Smith* itself) ... I am not now prepared to join Justice O'Connor in rejecting it or the majority in assuming it to be correct. In order to provide full adversarial consideration, this case should be set down for reargument permitting plenary reexamination of the issue.... I would therefore dismiss the writ of certiorari as improvidently granted, and I accordingly dissent from the Court's disposition of this case.

QUESTIONS

1. Identify the extent to which the Court's decision in *Boerne* reflects the Court's concerns over the relationship between legislative and judicial power, federalism, and religious liberty in the United States. Is one of those concerns more prevalent than the other?

2. Leaders of "mainline religions" expressed dissatisfaction with *Boerne*, pointing to several examples of recent legal victories that would have been defeats without the benefit of RFRA: Jehovah's Witnesses in California successfully sued over having to take a loyalty oath as a condition of employment with the state; an Amish group in Wisconsin escaped fines for refusing to post bright orange safety triangles on their horse-drawn buggies, which they believe are too "worldly"; a Presbyterian church in the District of Columbia won the right to operate a soup kitchen for the homeless after city zoning officials objected; and a Native American prison guard in New York successfully sued after he was suspended for refusing, for religious reasons, to cut his hair.

These religious leaders also cited defeats suffered in the three years between the Supreme Court's decision in *Smith* and enactment of RFRA, including: Hmong families in Rhode Island failed to stave off autopsies of dead relatives even though they believe such a procedure destroys the possibility of everlasting life; and Catholic teaching hospitals in Maryland lost accreditation because they refused to perform abortions ("Supreme Court Rules Religious Freedom Restoration Act Is Unconstitutional" [http://www.nytimes.com/], June 25, 1997).

Are these examples evidence of the need for some sort of protection for religious activities in addition to that afforded by the Supreme Court in its interpretation of the Free Exercise Clause of the First Amendment? If so, what recourse is available in the wake of *Boerne*? Does the coalition of religious groups that joined Flores as *amici* in *Boerne* suggest that mainstream religions perceive that they need additional protection just as much as minority sects do?

3. Summarize the state of Free Exercise jurisprudence as of the 1996 Term. What legal and political events are likely to follow?

SUGGESTIONS FOR FURTHER READING

Ahlstrom, Sydney E., *A Religious History of the American People* (New Haven, CT: Yale University Press, 1972).

Anderson, David L., "Tax-exempt Private Schools which Discriminate on the Basis of Race: A Proposed Revenue Procedure," 55 *Notre Dame Lawyer* (1980): 356.

Barron, Jerome A., "Sunday in North America," 79 *Harvard Law Review* (1965): 42.

Bittker, Boris I., "Churches, Taxes and the Constitution," 78 *Yale Law Journal* (1969): 1285.

Butts, Freeman, and Lawrence A. Cremin, *A History of Education in American Culture* (New York, NY: Henry Holt & Company, 1953).

Choper, Jesse H., "The Religion Clauses of the First Amendment: Reconciling the Conflict," 41 *University of Pittsburgh Law Review* (1980): 673.

———, "The Rise and Decline of the Constitutional Protection of Religious Liberty," 70 *Nebraska Law Review* (1991): 651.

Clymer, Adam, "Congress Moves to Ease Curb on Religious Acts," *New York Times*, May 10, 1993, A9.

Conkle, Daniel O., "The Religious Freedom Restoration Act: The Constitutional Significance of an Unconstitutional Statute," 56 *Montana Law Review* (1995): 39.

Danzig, Richard, "How Questions Begot Answers in Felix Frankfurter's First Flag Salute Opinion," *The Supreme Court Review* (Chicago, IL: University of Chicago Press, 1977).

————, "Justice Frankfurter's Opinions in the Flag Salute Cases: Blending Logic and Psychologic in Constitutional Decisionmaking," 36 *Stanford Law Review* (1984): 675.

Davis, Ray Jay, "The Polygamous Prelude," 6 *American Journal of Legal History* (1962): 1.

Eisgruber, Christopher L., and Lawrence C. Sager, "Why the Religious Freedom Restoration Act is Unconstitutional," 69 *New York University Law Review* (1994): 437.

Epstein, Richard, "The Supreme Court, 1987 Term—Foreword: Unconstitutional Conditions, State Power, and the Limits of Consent," 102 *Harvard Law Review* (1988): 4.

Erickson, Donald A., "The Plain People vs. The Common Schools," *Saturday Review*, November 19, 1966, p. 87.

Firmage, Edwin Brown, and Richard Collin Mangrum, *Zion in the Courts: A Legal History of the Church of Jesus Christ of Latter-Day Saints, 1830–1900* (Urbana, IL: University of Illinois Press, 1988).

Freed, Mayer, and Daniel Polsby, "Race, Religion, and Public Policy: *Bob Jones University v. United States*," *The Supreme Court Review* (Chicago, IL: University of Chicago Press, 1983).

Freeman, Louise F., "Able to Work and Available to Work," 55 *Yale Law Journal* (1945): 123.

Garraty, John A., ed., *Quarrels That Have Shaped the Constitution*, rev. ed. (New York, NY: Harper & Row, 1987), Chapter 17.

Giannella, Donald A., "Religious Liberty, Non-Establishment, and Doctrinal Development: Part I, The Religious Liberty Guarantees," 80 *Harvard Law Review* (1967): 1381.

High, Stanley, "Armageddon, Inc.," *The Saturday Evening Post*, September 14, 1940.

Hill, Marvin S., and James B. Allen, eds., *Mormonism and American Culture* (New York, NY: Harper & Row, 1972).

Holmes, John Haynes, "The Case of Jehovah's Witnesses," *The Christian Century*, July 17, 1940.

Hostetler, John A., *Amish Society*, 4th. ed. (Baltimore, MD: The Johns Hopkins University Press, 1993).

Irons, Peter, *The Courage of Their Convictions: Sixteen Americans Who Fought Their Way to the Supreme Court* (New York, NY: Penguin, 1990), Chapter 1.

"Jehovah's Witnesses, Who Refuse to Salute the Flag," *Life*, August 12, 1940.

Kannar, George, "The Constitutional Catechism of Antonin Scalia," 99 *Yale Law Journal* (1990): 1297.

Karst, Kenneth, "Religious Freedom and Equal Citizenship: Reflections on *Lukumi*," 69 *Tulane Law Review* (1994): 335.

Kauper, Paul G., *Religion and the Constitution* (Baton Rouge, LA: Louisiana University Press, 1964).

Laycock, Douglas, "Tax Exemptions for Racially Discriminatory Schools," 60 *Texas Law Review* (1982): 259.

_____, "A Survey of Religious Liberty in the United States," 47 *Ohio State Law Journal* (1986): 409.

_____, "The Remnants of Free Exercise," *The Supreme Court Review* (Chicago, IL: University of Chicago Press, 1990).

_____, "Free Exercise and the Religious Freedom Restoration Act," 62 *Fordham Law Review* (1994): 883.

Linford, Orma, "The Mormons and the Law: The Polygamy Cases, Part I" 9 *Utah Law Review* (1964): 308.

Littell, Franklin H., "Sectarian Protestantism and the Pursuit of Wisdom," in *Public Control of Nonpublic Schools*, ed. Donald A. Erickson (Chicago, IL: University of Chicago Press, 1969).

Lund, Candida, "Religion and Commerce," in *The Third Branch of Government*, ed. C. Herman Pritchett and Alan F. Westin (New York, NY: Harcourt, Brace & World, 1963).

Lupu, Ira C., "Reconstructing the Establishment Clause: The Case against the Discretionary Accommodation of Religion," 140 *University of Pennsylvania Law Review* (1991): 555.

Manwaring, David R., *Render Unto Caesar: The Flag Salute Controversy* (Chicago, IL: University of Chicago Press, 1962).

Marshall, William P., "In Defense of *Smith* and Free Exercise Revisionism," 598 *University of Chicago Law Review* (1991): 308.

McConnell, Michael, "Accommodation of Religion," *The Supreme Court Review* (Chicago, IL: University of Chicago Press, 1985).

_____, "The Origins and Historical Understanding of Free Exercise of Religion," 103 *Harvard Law Review* (1990): 1409.

_____, "Free Exercise Revisionism and the *Smith* Decision," 57 *University of Chicago Law Review* (1990): 1109.

Michelman, Frank, "Foreword: Traces of Self-Government," 100 *Harvard Law Review* (1986): 4.

Note, "The Right Not to Be Modern Men: Amish and Compulsory Education," 53 *Virginia Law Review* (1967): 925.

Note, "The First Amendment Overbreadth Doctrine," 83 *Harvard Law Review* (1970): 844.

Pepper, Stephen, "*Reynolds, Yoder*, and Beyond: Alternatives for the Free Exercise Clause," *Utah Law Review* (1981): 309.

Pfeffer, Leo, *Church, State and Freedom*, rev. ed. (Boston, MA: Beacon Press, 1967).

_____, *God, Caesar and the Constitution* (Boston, MA: Beacon Press, 1975).

Roberts, Bernard, "The Common Law Sovereignty of Religious Lawfinders and the Free Exercise Clause," 101 *Yale Law Journal* (1991): 211.

Rosen, Lawrence, "Continuing the Conversation: Creationism, the Religion Clauses and the Politics of Culture," *The Supreme Court Review* (Chicago. IL: University of Chicago Press, 1988).

Rotnem, Victor W., and F. G. Folsom Jr., "Recent Limitations upon Religious Liberty," 36 *American Political Science Review* (1942): 1053.

Simon, Karla W., "The Tax-Exempt Status of Racially Discriminatory Religious Schools," 36 *Tax Law Review* (1981): 477.

Smith, Kathleen, "Religion and Liberal Democracy," 59 *University of Chicago Law Review* (1992): 195.

Southworth, H. Rutledge, "Jehovah's 50,000 Witnesses," *The Nation*, August 10, 1940.

Stephan, Paul B., III, "*Bob Jones University v. United States*: Public Policy in Search of Tax Policy," *The Supreme Court Review* (Chicago, IL: University of Chicago Press, 1983).

Stone, Geoffrey R., "Content Regulation and the First Amendment," 25 *William & Mary Law Review* (1983): 189.

Thrower, Randolph W., "Tax-Exempt Status of Private Schools," 35 *Tax Lawyer* (1982): 701.

Waite, Edward F., "The Debt of Constitutional Law to Jehovah's Witnesses," 28 *Minnesota Law Review* (1944): 213.

Walker, Charles R., "Fifth Column Jitters," *McCall's*, November 1940.

CHAPTER 3

⟫●⟪

FREEDOM OF SPEECH

*DEFINING PROTECTED SPEECH DURING WAR
AND NATIONAL EMERGENCY*

Schenck v. United States
249 U.S. 47 (1919)

SETTING

Despite the absolute language of the Free Speech Clause—"Congress shall make no law ... abridging the freedom of speech..."—the First Amendment's protection of speech has never been unconditional. Just seven years after the First Amendment was ratified, Congress abridged freedom of speech when it passed the Alien Act, the Alien Enemies Act, and the Sedition Act of 1798. Prosecutions under the Sedition Act ignited a firestorm of political controversy that led to the election of Thomas Jefferson in 1800. The Sedition Act of 1798 expired without being tested before the Supreme Court. For the next 120 years, the Supreme Court had no occasion to directly interpret the language of the Free Speech Clause. During this period, however, two social realities had become clear about the Bill of Rights when government is in crisis.

First, civil rights do not disappear entirely during national emergencies. Addressing a civil rights issue that had arisen during the Civil War, the Court in 1866 held:

> The Constitution of the United States is a law for rulers and people, equally in war and in peace, and covers with the shield of its protection all classes of men, at all times, and under all circumstances. No doctrine, involving more pernicious consequences, was ever invented by the wit of man than that any of its provisions can be suspended during any of the great exigencies of government. Such a doctrine leads directly to anarchy or despotism.... *Ex parte Milligan*, 4 Wallace 2.

Second, the practical extent of free speech protection is nevertheless limited during times of crisis. Governmental practices during the Civil War, such as President Lincoln's suspension of the *writ of habeas corpus*, made it clear that civil liberties in a time of emergency are not necessarily as secure as during peace. It was not until the tumultuous context of World War I, the Bolshevik

Revolution in Russia, and a domestic Red Scare, that the specific question about limitations on free speech under the First Amendment came before the Court.

Although reelected at the end of 1916 in part on a platform that proclaimed "He Kept Us Out of War!" President Woodrow Wilson asked Congress to declare war against the German Empire on April 2, 1917. The following month, on May 17, 1917, Congress passed a draft law. On June 15, 1917, Congress enacted the Espionage Act, which it amended the following year with language that was referred to as "the Sedition Act." The amended Espionage Act was passed because military officials and some members of the public, alarmed by dramatic reports of Bolshevik revolution in Russia and fearful of domestic insurgency, insisted on a government crackdown. The act made it a felony to "incite mutiny or insubordination in the ranks of the armed forces," to "disrupt or discourage recruiting or enlistment service, or utter, print, or publish disloyal, profane, scurrilous, or abusive language about the form of government, the Constitution, soldiers and sailors, flag, or uniform of the armed services, or by word or act support or favor the cause of the German Empire or its allies in the present war, or by word or act oppose the cause of the United States."

Pursuant to the amended Espionage Act, the federal government undertook a dragnet against people suspected of undermining the war effort. Many thousands were indicted in 1919 and 1920. Attorney General A. Mitchell Palmer reported that, during those two years, 1,956 cases were commenced and 877 convictions were obtained. Among these cases was the indictment of Charles T. Schenck, general secretary and member of the Executive Committee of the Socialist Party.

In August 1917, the Executive Committee of the Socialist Party voted to print a message on the reverse side of an existing antidraft circular. The heading on the existing side of the circular was: "Assert Your Rights." In part it read:

> The Socialist Party says that any individual or officers of the law intrusted with the administration of conscription regulations violate the provision of the United States Constitution, the supreme law of the land, when they refuse to recognize your rights to assert your opposition to the draft....
>
> If you do not assert and support your rights, you are helping to "deny or disparage rights" which it is the solemn duty of all citizens and residents of the United States to retain.
>
> In lending tacit or silent consent to the conscription law, in neglecting to assert your rights, you are (whether unknowingly or not) helping to condone and support a most infamous and insidious conspiracy to abridge and destroy the sacred and cherished rights of a free people. You are a citizen; not a subject! You delegate your power to the officers of the law to be used for your good and welfare, not against you....

The other side of the circular was entitled, "Long Live the Constitution of the United States. Wake up, America Your Liberties Are In Danger." In part it read:

> A conscript is little better than a convict. He is deprived of his liberty and of his right to think and act as a freeman. A conscripted citizen is forced to surrender his right as a citizen and become a subject. He is forced into involun-

tary servitude. He is deprived of the protection given him by the Constitution of the United States. He is deprived of all freedom of conscience in being forced to kill against his will....

Conscription laws belong to a bygone age. Even the people of Germany, long suffering under the yoke of militarism, are beginning to demand the abolition of conscription. Do you think it has a place in the United States? Do you want to see unlimited power handed over to Wall Street's chosen few in America? If you do not, join the Socialist Party in its campaign for the repeal of the conscription act.

Fifteen thousand copies of the circular were printed by the printing shop of the newspaper, *Jewish World*. Readers were urged to go to the Socialist Party Headquarters in Philadelphia to sign a petition to repeal the "Conscription" (Selective Service) Act.

After publishing the circulars and distributing them via the U.S. mail, Schenck was indicted for three counts: (1) of conspiracy under § 4, Title I of the Espionage Act of June 15, 1917, to violate the provisions of § 3, to cause or attempt to cause insubordination, disloyalty, mutiny, or refusal of duty in the military or naval forces of the United States, or to obstruct the recruiting or enlistment service of the United States, to the injury of the service or of the United States (punishable by a fine of not more than $10,000, or imprisonment for not more than twenty years, or both); (2) of conspiracy to commit an offense against the United States—that is, the use of the mails for the transmission of matter banned by § 2, Title XII, of the act, from the mails; and (3) illegal use of the mails for the transmission of such matter.

At trial in the U.S. District Court for the Eastern District of Pennsylvania, a number of newspaper clippings, containing lists of names and addresses said to be those of persons drafted into the army, were introduced as evidence. These materials had been seized during a search of the headquarters of the Socialist Party conducted prior to Schenck's indictment. The following Socialist Party Executive Committee minutes had been seized and were also introduced as evidence: "8/13/17 (1) M. and S. The 15,000 leaflets be written to be printed on the leaflet now in use to be mailed to men who have passed exemption boards, also distribution"; (2) "M. and S. Secretary gets bids on price of leaflets"; 8/20/17 (3) "'General Secretary's report,' Obtained new leaflet from printer and started work addressing envelopes and folding and enclosing same"; (4) "'Unfinished business,' M. and S. That Comrade Schenck be authorized to spend $125 for sending leaflets through the mail. Carried." Schenck was convicted on all three counts. His counsel brought the case to the Supreme Court on a writ of error.

HIGHLIGHTS OF SUPREME COURT ARGUMENTS

BRIEF FOR SCHENCK

◆ The Espionage Act imposes punishment only after publication, which means that it falls within the rule announced by Blackstone. However, severe punishment for sedition will stop political discussion as effectively as prepublication censorship. Consequently, the act violates the First Amendment.

◆ If it is criminal to say that the draft law is wrong, then it is criminal to say that any law is wrong. Must we return to conditions that prevailed under George III and be punished for criticizing our government?

◆ Schenck is not a criminal in the ordinary sense of the word. This case involves a political question that will not be put down in spite of what the laws may say or what the laws may be.

BRIEF FOR THE UNITED STATES

◆ Any claim that Schenck was engaged in legitimate political agitation for the repeal of the draft law is negated by the fact that he chose as the recipients of his circulars young men who had already been drafted. His unlawful purpose is further shown by the text of the circulars, which is an attack on the constitutionality of the draft law and is full of bitter language against conscription.

◆ This Court has already settled the question of whether the United States has a constitutional right to prohibit a person from attempting during war to induce violations of a statute providing for military service. Consequently, the First Amendment claims raised by Schenck are frivolous.

SUPREME COURT DECISION: 9–0

HOLMES, J.

… [T]he document would not have been sent unless it had been intended to have some effect, and we do not see what effect it could be expected to have upon persons subject to the draft except to influence them to obstruct the carrying of it out....

But it is said, suppose that that was the tendency of this circular, it is protected by the First Amendment to the Constitution.... We admit that in many places and in ordinary times the defendants in saying all that was said in the circular would have been within their constitutional rights. But the character of every act depends upon the circumstances in which it is done. The most stringent protection of free speech would not protect a man in falsely shouting fire in a theatre and causing a panic. It does not even protect a man from an injunction against uttering words that may have all the effect of force. The question in every case is whether the words used are used in such circumstances and are of such a nature as to create a clear and present danger that they will bring about the substantive evils that Congress has a right to prevent. It is a question of proximity and degree. When a nation is at war many things that might be said in time of peace are such a hindrance to its effort that their utterance will not be endured so long as men fight and that no Court could regard them as protected by any constitutional right. It seems to be admitted that if an actual obstruction of the recruiting service were proved, liability for words that produced that effect might be enforced. The statute of 1917 in section 4 punishes conspiracies to obstruct as well as actual obstruction. If the act (speaking, or circulating a paper,) its tendency and the intent with which it is done are the same, we perceive no ground for saying that success alone warrants making the act a crime....

Questions

1. What core ideas are embedded in the "clear and present danger" doctrine?

2. Should the *Schenck* Court, interpreting the First Amendment in the context of that case, have adopted a literal reading of the Amendment's words? Should the Court have focused on the content of the Socialist Party circulars, especially whether they might endanger government? Or should it have employed another approach altogether?

3. Law professor Laurence H. Tribe writes:

   > [E]xpression has special value only in the context of "dialogue."... Starting with this proposition, it is reasonable to distinguish between contexts in which talk leaves room for reply and those in which talk triggers action or causes harm without the time or opportunity for response. It is not plausible to uphold the right to use words as projectiles where no exchange of views is involved. (*American Constitutional Law*, 2nd ed. [Mineola, NY: Foundation Press, 1988], p. 837)

   If the Supreme Court had used Tribe's formulation in *Schenck*, would the result have been the same?

DEFINING PROTECTED SPEECH DURING WAR AND NATIONAL EMERGENCY

Gitlow v. New York
268 U.S. 652 (1925)

Setting

America experienced four turbulent decades between 1880 and 1920. Economic depressions in the 1880s and 1890s created widespread support for national legislation to limit immigration and increase deportation of aliens with the goal of ensuring jobs for Americans. Many Americans during this period also began to fear aliens as dangerous radicals who carried "infectious" ideas and movements subversive of white, Anglo-Saxon, Protestant values. The image of alien as synonymous with radical reached a fevered pitch in September 1901, when anarchist Leon Franz Czolgosz assassinated President William McKinley while McKinley was speaking at the Pan-American Exposition in Buffalo, New York. In 1902, the New York legislature passed the first state anti-sedition law. The statute made it a felony to advocate "criminal anarchy" by word of mouth or in writing. It defined criminal anarchy as "the doctrine that organized government should be overthrown by force or violence, or by assassination of the executive head or of any of the executive officials of government, or by any unlawful means." The statute also made it a crime to join any organization that taught or advocated the doctrine.

The constitutionality of the New York statute was not tested before the Supreme Court in the years immediately following its passage because most prosecutions for sedition, like that of Charles Schenck, occurred under the 1917 federal Espionage Act. In a series of decisions after *Schenck*, however, the Supreme Court debated the First Amendment standard to be applied to political speech during times of national emergency.

In *Frohwerk v. United States*, 249 U.S. 204 (1919), and *Debs v. United States*, 249 U.S. 211 (1919), the Court unanimously upheld convictions under the amended Espionage Act for political speech that appeared to contain messages similar to the circular for which Schenck had been convicted. The Court's doctrinal unanimity in *Frohwerk* and *Debs* about the applicability of the "clear and present danger" test dissolved in a series of three other appeals from convictions under the Espionage Act.

In the first, *Abrams v. United States*, 250 U.S. 616 (1919), seven justices voted to uphold the convictions of Jacob Abrams and four other Russian-born immigrants for writing, publishing, and distributing two pamphlets attacking the U.S. government for sending troops to Russia. Justice Clarke's majority opinion was based on a test involving the subversive tendency of the published materials. Justice Holmes rejected the majority's test and, joined by Justice Brandeis, argued that the Court had mischaracterized the clear and present danger doctrine.

In the second, a majority of six justices moved even more explicitly away from Holmes's clear and present danger doctrine. *Schaefer v. United States*, 251 U.S. 466 (1920). Justice McKenna's opinion upheld the convictions of three of five officers of the German-language newspapers, *Philadelphia Tageblatt* and the *Philadelphia Sonntagsblatt*, on the ground that "The tendency of the articles and their efficacy were enough for offense." Holmes and Brandeis again dissented.

In the third, *Pierce v. United States*, 252 U.S. 239 (1920), once more over Brandeis's and Holmes's dissents, seven justices voted to uphold the convictions of those associated with distributing a pamphlet entitled, "The Price We Pay." Justice Pitney's majority opinion held that whether the words printed in the pamphlet "would in fact produce as a proximate result a material interference with the recruitment or enlistment service" was a factual question for the jury to decide, considering all of the circumstances.

The divisions among the justices that *Abrams*, *Schaefer*, and *Pierce* revealed over the correct First Amendment standard to apply to political speech during war time provided the backdrop to constitutional challenges to prosecutions arising under state laws targeting war protestors believed to be engaged in seditious activities. *Gitlow v. New York* was the first case to test the constitutionality of New York's 1902 state anti-sedition law.

Benjamin Gitlow was a member of the Left Wing section of the Socialist Party. The section was organized in June 1919 at a conference in New York City in opposition to the party's policy of "moderate Socialism." During the conference, the section adopted statements entitled the "Left Wing Manifesto," "Communist Program," and "Program of the Left Wing." At Gitlow's instruction, the statements were published the following month in the first issue of the *Revolutionary Age*, the official newspaper of the Left Wing section. Gitlow was on the board of managers of the paper and was also its business manager. He directed the mailing of sixteen thousand copies of the *Revolutionary Age* containing the statements adopted at the June conference.

Following publication of the newspaper, Gitlow and three others were indicted in the Supreme Court of New York (a state trial court) for the statutory crime of criminal anarchy. The indictment was in two counts. The first charged that Gitlow had advocated, advised, and taught the duty, necessity, and propriety of overthrowing and overturning organized government by force, violence, and unlawful means by virtue of writing "The Left Wing Manifesto." The second count charged Gitlow with printing, publishing, and knowingly circulating and distributing the *Revolutionary Age*, containing the "Left Wing Manifesto," which advocated, advised, and taught the doctrine that organized government should be overthrown by force, violence, and unlawful means.

Gitlow was tried separately and was convicted of criminal anarchy following a jury trial. He was sentenced to state prison for not less than five years and not more than ten. Gitlow appealed his conviction to the Appellate Division of the Supreme Court of New York, First Department, and then to the Court of Appeals of the State of New York. Both affirmed his conviction. Gitlow petitioned the Supreme Court for a writ of error.

HIGHLIGHTS OF SUPREME COURT ARGUMENTS

BRIEF FOR GITLOW

◆ The liberty protected by the Fourteenth Amendment includes the liberty of speech and of the press against state action. The rights of free speech and press must have equal standing and protection.

◆ Although liberty of expression is not absolute, it may be restrained only in circumstances where its exercise bears a causal relation to some substantive evil—consummated, attempted, or likely. The New York Criminal Anarchy Law takes no account of circumstances. It punishes the mere utterance—"advocacy"—whether or not such utterance is reasonably calculated to persuade persons to do the acts condemned, or to any unlawful conduct whatever, and whether or not a causal connection between the utterance and a substantive evil can be deduced from surrounding circumstances.

◆ The New York statute rests on the same principle as the federal Sedition Act of 1798. The principle on which the Sedition Act was based was subsequently condemned on constitutional grounds by all departments of government.

◆ The state's claim that the Criminal Anarchy Law is a valid exercise of its police power cannot survive if it goes further in restricting constitutional rights than the public need requires. The Court has repeatedly held that the desirable aim of maintaining public peace cannot be accomplished by laws or ordinances that deny rights created or protected by the Constitution of the United States.

FIRST BRIEF FOR NEW YORK

◆ Gitlow was not tried for heresy. He was tried and convicted because he advocated the doctrine that organized government should be overthrown by force or violence or by some unlawful means.

◆ A state has the power to make it a crime to abuse the right of free speech. The New York statute is a valid exercise of that power. The New York constitution, which recognizes the right of every citizen to freely speak, write, and publish his sentiments on all subjects, also provides that the individual is "responsible for the abuse of that right."

◆ The New York Criminal Anarchy Statute does not violate the Due Process Clause of the Fourteenth Amendment. It reflects a proper exercise by the government of the state of New York to preserve itself. If organized government is to endure, it must have the right to protect itself against any form of extraparliamentary attack upon its existence. Punishment under the statute is imposed for an act, not for a belief.

◆ Whether the statute is wise and expedient is a matter for the legislature to determine. That question cannot be considered on appeal.

BRIEF FOR THE STATE OF NEW YORK ON REARGUMENT

◆ Freedom of speech and press is subject to control by penal statutes. The First Amendment does not, by virtue of the adoption of the Fourteenth, curtail the rights of states to limit freedom of speech and press. Similar legislation in other states has been held constitutional.

◆ The New York statute is a valid exercise of the police power. Reduced to its simplest terms, the statute forbids the advocacy of murder and treason. The state has a right to pass laws prohibiting doctrines, the necessary result of which has been and is violence and disorder.

SUPREME COURT DECISION: 7–2

SANFORD, J.

... The sole contention here is, essentially, that as there was no evidence of any concrete result flowing from the publication of the Manifesto or of circumstances showing the likelihood of such result, the statute as construed and applied by the trial court penalizes the mere utterance, as such, of "doctrine" having no quality of incitement, without regard either to the circumstances of its utterance or to the likelihood of unlawful sequences; and that, as the exercise of the right of free expression with relation to government is only punishable "in circumstances involving likelihood of substantive evil," the statute contravenes the due process clause of the Fourteenth Amendment....

For present purposes we may and do assume that freedom of speech and of the press—which are protected by the First Amendment from abridgment by Congress—are among the fundamental personal rights and "liberties" protected by the due process clause of the Fourteenth Amendment from impairment by the States....

It is a fundamental principle, long established, that the freedom of speech and of the press which is secured by the Constitution, does not confer an absolute right to speak or publish, without responsibility, whatever one may choose, or an unrestricted and unbridled license that gives immunity for every possible use of language and prevents the punishment of those who abuse this freedom.... Reasonably limited ... this freedom is an inestimable privilege in a free government; without such limitation, it might become the scourge of the republic.

That a State in the exercise of its police power may punish those who abuse this freedom by utterances inimical to the public welfare, tending to corrupt public morals, incite to crime, or disturb the public peace, is not open to question....

That utterances inciting to the overthrow of organized government by unlawful means, present a sufficient danger of substantive evil to bring their punishment within the range of legislative discretion, is clear. Such utterances, by their very nature, involve danger to the public peace and to the security of the State. They threaten breaches of the peace and ultimate revolution. And the immediate danger is none the less real and substantial, because the effect of a given utterance cannot be accurately foreseen. The State cannot reasonably be required to measure the danger from every such utterance in the nice balance of a jeweler's scale. A sin-gle revolutionary spark may kindle a fire that, smouldering for a time, may burst into a sweeping and destructive conflagration. It cannot be said that the State is acting arbitrarily or unreasonably when in the exercise of its judgment as to the measures necessary to protect the public peace and safety, it seeks to extinguish the spark without waiting until it has enkindled the flame or blazed into the conflagration. It cannot reasonably be required to defer the adoption of measures for its own peace and safety until the revolutionary utterances lead to actual disturbances of the public peace or imminent and immediate danger of its own destruction; but it may, in the exercise of its judgment, suppress the threatened danger in its incipiency....

We cannot hold that the present statute is an arbitrary or unreasonable exercise of the police power of the State unwarrantably infringing the freedom of speech or press; and we must and do sustain its constitutionality....

[T]he general statement in the *Schenck Case* that the "question in every case is whether the words used are used in such circumstances and are of such a nature as to create a clear and present danger that they will bring about the substantive evils,"—upon which great reliance is placed in the defendant's argument ... has no application to [cases] like the present, where the legislative body itself has previously determined the danger of substantive evil arising from utterances of a specified character....

Affirmed.

HOLMES AND BRANDEIS, J.J., DISSENTING

... I [am] of opinion that this judgment should be reversed.... I think that the criterion sanctioned by the full Court in *Schenck v. United States* applies:

The question in every case is whether the words used are used in such circumstances and are of such a nature as to create a clear and present danger that they will bring about the substantive evils that [the State] has a right to prevent....

If what I think the correct test is applied it is manifest that there was no present danger of an attempt to overthrow the government by force on the part of the admittedly small minority who shared the defendant's views. It is said that this manifesto was more than a theory, that it was an incitement. Every idea is an incitement. It offers itself for belief and if believed it is acted on unless some other belief outweighs it or some failure of energy stifles the movement at its birth. The only difference between the expression of an opinion and an incitement in the narrower sense is the speaker's enthusiasm for the result. Eloquence may set fire to reason.

But whatever may be thought of the redundant discourse before us it had no chance of starting a present conflagration. If in the long run the beliefs expressed in proletarian dictatorship are destined to be accepted by the dominant forces of the community, the only meaning of free speech is that they should be given their chance and have their way.

If the publication of this document had been laid as an attempt to induce an uprising against government at once and not at some indefinite time in the future it would have presented a different question. The object would have been one with which the law might deal, subject to the doubt whether there was any danger that the publication could produce any result, or in other words, whether it was not futile and too remote from possible consequences. But the indictment alleges the publication and nothing more.

QUESTIONS

1. Justice Holmes, author of the clear and present danger test adopted in *Schenck*, dissented in *Gitlow*, on the ground that the majority failed to apply the proper test. Did Justice Sanford fail to apply the clear and present danger test in *Gitlow*, or did he disagree with Justice Holmes about the meaning of the *Schenck* test? How does the *Gitlow* test differ from the clear and present danger test?

2. Justice Sanford wrote, "We may and do assume that freedom of speech and of the press—which are protected by the 1st Amendment from abridgment by Congress—are among the fundamental personal rights and 'liberties' protected by the Due Process Clause of the Fourteenth Amendment by impairment by the states." What is the constitutional significance of this statement? Does it mean that the First Amendment is a limitation on the states as well as the national government?

   Gitlow inaugurated a heated debate on the Court and in the states about the extent to which different elements of the Bill of Rights should be held to be limitations on the states. After *Gitlow*, what analytical framework should the Court use for deciding whether a specific provision of the Bill of Rights should be "incorporated" by the Fourteenth Amendment as a limitation on the states?

3. By the time *Gitlow* was decided, the "Red Scare" had abated in the United States. In response, New York Governor Alfred E. Smith pardoned Gitlow and the three others convicted of violating the New York statute anti-sedition law. They served only three years of their prison terms. Did the change in public opinion, as well as Governor Smith's pardon, undermine the Court's decision or any of its reasoning in *Gitlow*?

DEFINING PROTECTED SPEECH DURING WAR AND NATIONAL EMERGENCY

Whitney v. California
274 U.S. 357 (1927)

SETTING

Two years after deciding *Gitlow v. New York*, the justices heard another appeal from a conviction under a state sedition law. The first section of California's Criminal Syndicalism Act of 1919 defined "criminal syndicalism." The second section declared that: "Any person who: ... [o]rganizes or assists in organizing, or is or knowingly becomes a member of, any organization, society, group or assemblage of persons organized or assembled to advocate, teach or aid and abet criminal syndicalism; ... is guilty of a felony punishable by imprisonment."

On November 9, 1919, Charlotte Anita Whitney, the niece of the late Supreme Court Justice Stephen J. Field, attended a convention held in Oakland for the purpose of organizing a branch of the Communist Labor Party of California (CLPC). After taking out a temporary membership in the national Communist Labor Party, Whitney attended the convention as a delegate and took an active part in its proceedings. She was elected a member of the Credentials Committee, and, as its chairman, made a report to the convention.

Whitney was also appointed a member of the Resolutions Committee, and as such signed the following resolution about political action:

> The [CLPC] fully recognizes the value of political action as a means of spreading communist propaganda; it insists that in proportion to the development of the economic strength of the working class, it, the working class, must also develop its political power. The [CLPC] proclaims and insists that the capture of political power, locally or nationally by the revolutionary working class can be of tremendous assistance to the workers in their struggle of emancipation. Therefore, we again urge the workers who are possessed of the right of franchise to cast their votes for the party which represents their immediate and final interest—the [CLPC]—at all elections, being

> fully convinced of the utter futility of obtaining any real measure of justice or freedom under officials elected by parties owned and controlled by the capitalist class.

This resolution was defeated by the convention as a whole. Instead, the delegates adopted a resolution saying that the CLPC "affiliated with" the Communist Labor Party of America, and subscribed to its Program, Platform, and Constitution, and "through this affiliation" be "joined with the Communist International of Moscow."

After the delegates voted, Whitney remained in the convention until it adjourned. She later attended, as an alternate member, one or two meetings of the State CLPC Executive Committee in San Jose and San Francisco. Whitney was arrested and charged on a five-count information filed on December 30, 1919, under the Criminal Syndicalism Law of California. She was charged with having organized, or become, or been a member of some unnamed party or assemblage. At the time of her indictment, Whitney was a noted philanthropist in her sixties. Her case was tried before the Superior Court of Alameda County. The prosecution argued that Whitney's mere presence at the CLPC organizing convention was proof of conspiracy to organize a group of persons assembled to advocate, teach, or aid and abet criminal syndicalism. Whitney stated at trial that she was then a member of the Communist Labor Party. She also testified that it was not her intention that the CLPC should be an instrument of terrorism or violence, and that it was not her purpose or that of the Convention to violate any known law.

Whitney was found guilty of one count under § 2 of the Criminal Syndicalism Law of California and sentenced to prison. The California District Court of Appeal affirmed. The California Supreme Court denied her petition for review. Whitney then filed a *writ of error* in the Supreme Court of the United States. The Court dismissed the writ for want of jurisdiction. *Whitney v. California*, 269 U.S. 530 (1925). Whitney's petition for a rehearing was granted and her case was reargued both as to jurisdiction and the merits.

HIGHLIGHTS OF SUPREME COURT ARGUMENTS

BRIEF FOR WHITNEY

◆ The information indicting Whitney named no group or party but merely charged organization, assembly, and membership in the general language of the statute. She was not apprised of the charge against her, a denial of due process of law.

◆ The crime of membership, organization, or assemblage in the California Criminal Syndicalism Law has been recognized by the Supreme Court of California as a crime of conspiracy. The trial court submitted the case to the jury and the District Court of Appeal of the State of California sustained the conviction on the theory that intent to conspire could be conclusively presumed from the mere fact of presence. Application of that presumption deprived Whitney of due process of law.

◆ The statute provides no definite test of criminality. A defendant could not know at the time of joining an organization still in its formative stage whether the action of other persons would or would not give the organization a character which the statute would condemn. Thus the statute is vague and works a denial of due process.

◆ The statute, which attaches penal consequences to attendance at a meeting for the purpose of addressing that meeting, imposes a prior restraint on freedom of speech.

◆ By aiming its penalties at advocates of "change in industrial ownership or control," Section 2, Subdivision 4, of the California Criminal Syndicalism Law discriminates between differing political and economic opinions and thus denies the equal protection of the laws.

BRIEF FOR CALIFORNIA

◆ The statute is not void for vagueness. A penal statute is sufficiently certain, although it may use general terms, if the offense is so defined as to convey to a person of ordinary intelligence an adequate description of the evil to be prohibited.

◆ The equal protection of the laws is secured where the laws operate on all alike, and do not subject the individual to an arbitrary exercise of the powers of government. Manifestly, this statute applies to all persons who do the things denounced by it. It is not limited in its language or effect to employees, but includes employers; it is not confined to laborers, but includes capitalists as well; it make no distinction between the poor "wobbly" and the rich communist.

◆ If, as has been established, this statute is constitutional, it does not become invalid by reason of the fact that any indictment or pleading under it might happen to be deficient. Therefore, it would appear that that portion of Whitney's argument that is devoted to a criticism of the sufficiency of the information is outside the question before the Court.

SUPREME COURT DECISION: 9–0

SANFORD, J.

... That the freedom of speech which is secured by the Constitution does not confer an absolute right to speak, without responsibility, whatever one may choose, or an unrestricted and unbridled license giving immunity for every possible use of language and preventing the punishment of those who abuse this freedom; and that a State in the exercise of its police power may punish those who abuse this freedom by utterances inimical to the public welfare, tending to incite to crime, disturb the public peace, or endanger the foundations of organized government and threaten its overthrow by unlawful means, is not open to question. *Gitlow v. New York.*

By enacting the provisions of the Syndicalism Act the State has declared, through its legislative body, that to knowingly be or become a member of or assist in organizing an association to advocate, teach or aid and abet the commission of crimes or unlawful acts of force, violence or terrorism as a means of accomplishing industrial or political changes, involves such danger to the public peace and the security of the State, that these acts should be penalized in the exercise of its police power. That determination must be given great weight....

The essence of the offense denounced by the Act is the combining with others in an association for the accomplishment of the desired ends through the advocacy and use of criminal and unlawful methods. It partakes of the nature of a criminal conspiracy.... That such united and joint action involves even greater danger to the public peace and security than the isolated utterances and acts of individuals is clear. We cannot hold that, as here applied, the Act is an unreasonable or arbitrary exercise of the police power of the State, unwarrantably infringing any right of free speech, assembly or association, or that those persons are protected from punishment by the due process clause who abuse such rights by joining and furthering an organization thus menacing the peace and welfare of the State.

We find no repugnancy in the Syndicalism Act as applied in this case[.]...

The order dismissing the writ of error will be vacated and set aside, and the judgment of the Court of Appeal

Affirmed.

BRANDEIS AND HOLMES, J.J., CONCURRING

... The right of free speech, the right to teach and the right of assembly are, of course, fundamental rights.... These may not be denied or abridged. But, although the rights of free speech and assembly are fundamental, they are not in their nature absolute. Their exercise is subject to restriction, if the particular restriction proposed is required in order to protect the state from destruction or from serious injury, political, economic or moral. That the necessity which is essential to a valid restriction does not exist unless speech would produce, or is intended to produce, a clear and imminent danger of some substantive evil which the state constitutionally may seek to prevent has been settled. See *Schenck v. United States....*

This court has not yet fixed the standard by which to determine when a danger shall be deemed clear; how remote the danger may be and yet be deemed present; and what degree of evil shall be deemed sufficiently substantial to justify resort to abridgment of free speech and assembly as the means of protection. To reach sound conclusions on these matters, we must bear in mind why a state is, ordinarily, denied the power to prohibit dissemination of social, economic and political doctrine which a vast majority of its citizens believes to be false and fraught with evil consequence....

Fear of serious injury cannot alone justify suppression of free speech and assembly. Men feared witches and burnt women. It is the function of speech to free men from the bondage of irrational fears. To justify suppression of free speech there must be reasonable ground to fear that serious evil will result if free speech is practiced. There must be reasonable ground to believe that the danger apprehended is imminent. There must be reasonable ground to believe that the evil to be prevented is a serious one. Every denunciation of existing law tends in some measure to increase the probability that there will be violation of it.

Condonation of a breach enhances the probability. Expressions of approval add to the probability. Propagation of the criminal state of mind by teaching syndicalism increases it. Advocacy of lawbreaking heightens it still further. But even advocacy of violation, however reprehensible morally, is not a justification for denying free speech where the advocacy falls short of incitement and there is nothing to indicate that the advocacy would be immediately acted on. The wide difference between advocacy and incitement, between preparation and attempt, between assembling and conspiracy, must be borne in mind. In order to support a finding of clear and present danger it must be shown either that immediate serious violence was to be expected or was advocated, or that the past conduct furnished reason to believe that such advocacy was then contemplated....

Moreover, even imminent danger cannot justify resort to prohibition of these functions essential to effective democracy, unless the evil apprehended is relatively serious. Prohibition of free speech and assembly is a measure so stringent that it would be inappropriate as the means for averting a relatively trivial harm to society. A police measure may be unconstitutional merely because the remedy, although effective as means of protection, is unduly harsh or oppressive. Thus, a state might, in the exercise of its police power, make any trespass upon the land of another a crime, regardless of the results or of the intent or purpose of the trespasser. It might, also, punish an attempt, a conspiracy, or an incitement to commit the trespass. But it is hardly conceivable that this court would hold constitutional a statute which punished as a felony the mere voluntary assembly with a society formed to teach that pedestri-

ans had the moral right to cross uninclosed, unposted, waste lands and to advocate their doing so, even if there was imminent danger that advocacy would lead to a trespass. The fact that speech is likely to result in some violence or in destruction of property is not enough to justify its suppression. There must be the probability of serious injury to the State. Among free men, the deterrents ordinarily to be applied to prevent crime are education and punishment for violations of the law, not abridgment of the rights of free speech and assembly....

Whether in 1919, when Miss Whitney did the things complained of, there was in California such clear and present danger of serious evil, might have been made the important issue in the case. She might have required that the issue be determined either by the court or the jury. She claimed below that the statute as applied to her violated the federal Constitution; but she did not claim that it was void because there was no clear and present danger of serious evil, nor did she request that the existence of these conditions of a valid measure thus restricting the rights of free speech and assembly be passed upon by the court of a jury. On the other hand, there was evidence on which the court or jury might have found that such danger existed. I am unable to assent to the suggestion in the opinion of the court that assembling with a political party, formed to advocate the desirability of a proletarian revolution by mass action at some date necessarily far in the future, is not a right within the protection of the Fourteenth Amendment. In the present case, however, there was other testimony which tended to establish the existence of a conspiracy, on the part of members of the International Workers of the World, to commit present serious crimes, and likewise to show that such a conspiracy would be furthered by the activity of the society of which Miss Whitney was a member. Under these circumstances the judgment of the State court cannot be disturbed....

QUESTIONS

1. The late political scientist C. Herman Pritchett noted: "It was not until *Whitney* that clear and present danger was definitely set forth as a basis on which courts, and indeed, all Americans, could 'challenge a law abridging free speech and assembly by showing that there was no emergency justifying it'" (*Constitutional Civil Liberties* [Englewood Cliffs, NJ: Prentice Hall, 1984], p. 23). It is Justice Brandeis's concurring opinion, not the majority view, that marks this development. What elements in Brandeis's concurrence transformed Holmes's aphorism into a constitutional standard?

2. Justice Brandeis argued that "no danger flowing from speech can be deemed clear and present, unless the incidence of the evil apprehended is so imminent that it may befall before there is opportunity for full discussion. If there be time to expose through discussion the falsehood and fallacies, to avert the evil by the processes of education, the remedy to be applied is more speech, not enforced silence." Are there certain types of expression, for example pornography or hate speech, that cannot be "averted" by "more speech"? Are there certain groups, such as religious or racial minorities, whose members might experience "enforced silence" because of their social circumstances?

3. Between 1919, when it was first announced in *Schenck*, and 1927, the clear and present danger test did not prevent a single dissident from being jailed for his or her statements. Why would civil libertarians applaud the doctrine if in practice it had no utility?

DEFINING PROTECTED SPEECH DURING WAR AND NATIONAL EMERGENCY

Dennis v. United States
341 U.S. 494 (1951)

SETTING

Various pieces of legislation restricting so-called "subversive" speech, enacted during America's undeclared naval war with France in 1798, during the Civil War in the 1860s, World War I after 1914, and the "Red Scare" of the 1920s, was succeeded by another set of statutes, targeting "subversives," during the Cold War. In the late 1930s, congressional conservatism and unsettling events in

Stalin's Soviet Union, Hitler's Germany, Mussolini's Italy, and Imperial Japan fed domestic paranoia about communists, radicals, fascists, "crackpots," and "internationalists" infiltrating the federal government. In 1938, the House of Representatives created a temporary committee chaired by Representative Martin Dies to investigate "un-American" activities. The next year, in the Hatch Act, Congress prohibited federal employees from joining organizations that advocated the overthrow of government. In March 1940, reacting to the Russo-German nonaggression pact of August 23, 1939, Congress reenacted the Espionage Act of 1917, with increased penalties for peacetime violations. In June, Congress adopted the Alien Registration Act, commonly known as the Smith Act. The first peacetime federal sedition act since the Sedition Act of 1798, passage of the Smith Act apparently was as much a consequence of congressional reluctance to vote against legislation directed at the Communist Party as a deliberate determination that it was necessary to take steps to protect the government from internal subversion.

The Smith Act proscribed advocacy of the overthrow by force and violence of the government of the United States. Section 2 made it unlawful to advocate through any means the propriety of overthrowing or destroying any government in the United States by force or violence. Section 2 also made it unlawful for anyone to organize, or affiliate with, any organization or assembly of persons knowing that their intent was to advocate violent overthrow of the government. Section 3 made it unlawful to attempt to commit, or to conspire to commit, any of the acts prohibited by the statute. The Smith Act was invoked only twice in the first eight years of its existence. Nonetheless, political concern over communist subversion remained high.

In 1945, the House of Representatives created a permanent House Committee on Un-American Activities (commonly referred to as the House Un-American Activities Committee or HUAC). It replaced the Dies Committee that expired in 1944. When Republicans took control of the House in 1947, HUAC, under the leadership of Representative J. Parnell Thomas, initiated an investigation into communists and "communist-sympathizers" in the federal government who, he claimed, were part of a conspiracy to overthrow the American government. Highly publicized internal security inquiries into the film industry and the State Department were launched in 1947 and 1948. In order to stave off criticism that the Truman administration was "soft on communism," Attorney General Tom Clark then began prosecuting under the Smith Act.

In 1945, the Federal Bureau of Investigation had begun compiling a dossier on the American Communist Party. A 1948 prosecution involved Eugene Dennis (also known as Francis X. Waldron Jr.), and eleven other members of the National Board of the Communist Party. They were charged under a single indictment in a U.S. District Court for the Southern District of New York for conspiring unlawfully to teach and advocate the duty and necessity of overthrowing and destroying the government of the United States by force and violence, and to organize the Communist Party for that purpose. The indictment did not allege the commission of any overt act.

Dennis and all but one of the other board members of the Communist Party were ordered to be tried together. (The trial of one defendant was severed because of his illness.) The defendants moved to dismiss the indictment on the ground that the Smith Act was unconstitutional. Their motion was denied, as was their motion to dismiss the indictment following the government's case and again at the close of their nine-month trial. All eleven defendants were convicted by a jury. All but one of the defendants were sentenced to five years in prison and fined $10,000 each. The other was sentenced to three years in prison and fined $10,000.

Dennis and his codefendants appealed their convictions to the U.S. Court of Appeals for the Second Circuit, which affirmed. Dennis and ten of the other defendants petitioned the Supreme Court of the United States for a writ of certiorari.

HIGHLIGHTS OF SUPREME COURT ARGUMENTS

BRIEF FOR DENNIS

◆ The Smith Act is unconstitutional because of its wide sweep and the vague character of its prohibitions. The act's vagueness violates both the First Amendment and the Due Process Clause of the Fifth Amendment. The conduct made criminal by Section 3 of the act is primarily mental in composition, which is especially vague. The Smith Act became law with virtually no public debate, in an atmosphere of anti-alien hysteria and war psychology that pervaded both houses of Congress. The bill's primary sponsor concedes that it is of "dubious constitutionality."

◆ The lower courts erred in applying the statute because they misconstrued the clear and present danger test of *Schenck v. United States*. Under that test, the only speech that can be proscribed is that which creates a clear and present danger that would bring about the substantive evils Congress had a right to prevent. No evidence was produced at trial that the activities of the board were on the verge of bringing about the violent overthrow of the U.S. government. Clear and present danger does not mean "clear and probable," as the lower courts held.

◆ The board members' convictions are contrary to the First Amendment. The Smith Act makes it a crime to teach and advocate certain ideas and theories wholly without regard to circumstances. In *Schenck* and cases since, the Court has ruled that the advocacy of ideas as such, or the exercise of the rights of press, speech, and assembly cannot be made criminal. The lower courts made the gravity of the evil the touchstone of constitutionality, contrary to established case law.

◆ While the lower courts' decisions might be justified by *Gitlow v. New York*, *Gitlow* is no longer good law. Although never expressly overruled, the case has been abandoned by the Court as a guide to the scope of legislative power over civil rights.

BRIEF FOR THE UNITED STATES

◆ The history of the Communist Party demonstrates that the Smith Act is a valid exercise of Congress's power to preserve democratic government. It was passed to meet the obvious dangers that the modern totalitarian movements of communism and fascism present to the free society of the United States. In this case the act was applied to the American leaders of that worldwide totalitarian movement. Events between 1940 and 1948 vindicated Congress's passage of the act. Congress and the president could reasonably conclude that the Communist Party of the United States endangered the security of the United States.

◆ The federal government possesses an inherent power to protect itself from overthrow or destruction by force or violence. The Smith Act was an exercise of that inherent power.

◆ The only substantial question in this case is whether the Smith Act violates the First Amendment. The Communist Party employs the strategy of not using tactics of violence until conditions are ripe for victory. If the First Amendment is a bar to government action until that point, the threat of violent overthrow of constitutional government could not be dealt with effectively.

◆ Teaching and advocacy can be prohibited without violating the First Amendment as long as a jury finds a specific intent and purpose to bring about such overthrow. *Gitlow v. New York* and cases since demonstrate that utterances advocating the violent overthrow of the government are not protected by the First Amendment and can be punished as crimes.

◆ The Smith Act is not unconstitutionally vague, because it explicitly informs those subject to it of the conduct that makes them liable for criminal penalties. Nothing in the statute prohibits even the most fundamental changes in America's way of life by constitutional means. Dennis and the other board members remain free to bring about their economic reforms through constitutional processes.

SUPREME COURT DECISION: 6–2

(Clark, J., did not participate.)

VINSON, C.J.

... In this case we are squarely presented with the application of the "clear and present danger" test, and must decide what that phrase imports.... Overthrow of the Government by force and violence is certainly a substantial enough interest for the Government to limit speech. Indeed, this is the ultimate value of any society, for if a society cannot protect its very structure from armed internal attack, it must follow that no subordinate value can be protected. If, then, this interest may be protected, the literal problem which is presented is what has been meant by the use of the phrase "clear and present danger" of the utterances bringing about the evil within the power of Congress to punish.

Obviously, the words cannot mean that before the Government may act, it must wait until the *putsch* is about to be executed, the plans have been laid and the signal is awaited. If Government is aware that a group aiming at its overthrow is attempting to indoctrinate its members and to commit them to a course whereby they will strike when the leaders feel the circumstances permit, action by the Government is required. The argument that there is no need for Government to concern itself, for Government is strong, it possesses ample powers to put down a rebellion, it may defeat the revolution with ease needs no answer. For that is not the question. Certainly an attempt to overthrow the Government by force, even though doomed from the outset because of inadequate numbers or power of the revolutionists, is a sufficient evil for Congress to prevent. The damage which such attempts create both physically and politically to a nation makes it impossible to measure the validity in terms of the probability of success, or the immediacy of a successful attempt. In the instant case the trial judge charged the jury that they could not convict unless they found that petitioners intended to overthrow the Government "as speedily as circumstances would permit." This does not mean, and could not properly mean, that they would not strike until there was certainty of success. What was meant was that the revolutionists would strike when they thought the time was ripe. We must therefore reject the contention that success or probability of success is the criterion....

The situation with which Justice Holmes and Brandeis were concerned [dissenting] in *Gitlow* was a comparatively isolated event, bearing little relation in their minds to any substantial threat to the safety of the community.... They were not confronted with any situation comparable to the instant one—the development of an apparatus designed and dedicated to the overthrow of the Government, in the context of world crisis after crisis.

Chief Judge Learned Hand, writing for the majority below, interpreted the [clear and present danger] phrase as follows: "In each case (courts) must ask whether the gravity of the 'evil,' discounted by its improbability, justifies such invasion of free speech as is necessary to avoid the danger." We adopt this statement of the rule....

Likewise, we are in accord with the court below, which affirmed the trial court's finding that the requisite danger existed. The mere fact that from the period 1945 to 1948 petitioners' activities did not result in an attempt to overthrow the Government by force and violence is of course no answer to the fact that there was a group that was ready to make the attempt. The formation by petitioners of such a highly organized conspiracy, with rigidly disciplined members subject to call when the leaders, these petitioners, felt that the time had come for action, coupled with the inflammable nature of world conditions, similar uprisings in other countries, and the touch-and-go nature of our relations with countries with whom petitioners were in the very least ideologically attuned, convince us that their convictions were justified on this score. And this analysis disposes of the contention that a conspiracy to advocate, as distinguished from the advocacy itself, cannot be constitutionally restrained, because it comprises only the preparation. It is the existence of the conspiracy which creates the danger. If the ingredients of the reaction are present, we cannot bind the Government to wait until the catalyst is added....

We hold that Sections 2 (a)(1), 2 (a)(3) and 3 of the Smith Act do not inherently, or as construed or applied in the instant case, violate the First Amendment and other provisions of the Bill of Rights, or the First and Fifth Amendments because of indefiniteness. Petitioners intended to overthrow the Government of the United States as speedily as the circumstances would permit. Their conspiracy to organize the Communist Party and to teach and advocate the overthrow of the Government of the United States by force and violence created a "clear and present danger" of an attempt to overthrow the Government by force and violence. They were properly and constitutionally convicted for violation of the Smith Act. The judgments of conviction are

Affirmed.

FRANKFURTER, J., CONCURRING

... Congress has determined that the danger created by advocacy of overthrow justifies the ensuring restriction on freedom of speech. The determination was made after due deliberation, and the seriousness of the congressional purpose is attested by the volume of legislation passed to effectuate the same ends....

To make validity of legislation depend on judicial reading of events still in the womb of time—a forecast, that is, of the outcome of forces at best appreciated only with knowledge of the topmost secrets of nations—is to charge the judiciary with duties beyond its equipment....

JACKSON, J.J., CONCURRING

... The authors of the clear and present danger test never applied it to a case like this, nor would I. If applied as it is proposed here, it means that the Communist plotting is protected during its period of incubation; its preliminary stages of organization and preparation are immune from the law; the Government can move only after imminent action is manifest, when it would, of course, be too late.

The highest degree of constitutional protection is due to the individual acting without conspiracy. But even an individual cannot claim that the Constitution protects him in advocating or teaching overthrow of government by force or violence....

The Constitution does not make conspiracy a civil right. The Court has never before done so and I think it should not do so now....

BLACK, J., DISSENTING

... At the outset I want to emphasize what the crime involved in this case is, and what it is not. These petitioners were not charged with an attempt to overthrow the Government. They were not charged with overt acts of any kind designed to overthrow the Government. They were not even charged with saying anything or writing anything designed to overthrow the Government. The charge was that they agreed to assemble and to talk and publish certain ideas at a later date: The indictment is that they conspired to organize the Communist Party and to use speech or newspapers and other publications in the future to teach and advocate the forcible overthrow of the Government. No matter how it is worded, this is a virulent form of prior censorship of speech and press, which I believe the First Amendment forbids. I would hold Section 3 of the Smith Act authorizing this prior restraint unconstitutional on its face and as applied....

So long as this Court exercises the power of judicial review of legislation, I cannot agree that the First Amendment permits us to sustain laws suppressing freedom of speech and press on the basis of Congress' or our own notions of mere "reasonableness." Such a doctrine waters down the First Amendment so that it amounts to little more than an admonition

to Congress. The Amendment as so construed is not likely to protect any but
those "safe" or orthodox views which
rarely need its protection....

Public opinion being what it now is, few
will protest the conviction of these
Communist petitioners. There is hope,
however, that in calmer times, when present pressures, passions and fears sub-
side, this or some later Court will restore
the First Amendment liberties to the high
preferred place where they belong in a
free society.

DOUGLAS, J., DISSENTING

... The nature of Communism as a force
on the world scene would, of course, be
relevant to the issue of clear and present
danger of petitioners' advocacy within the
United States. But the primary consideration is the strength and tactical position of
petitioners and their converts in this
country. On that there is no evidence in
the record. If we are to take judicial notice
of the threat of Communists within the
nation, it should not be difficult to conclude that *as a political party* they are of
little consequence. Communists in this

country have never made a respectable or
serious showing in any election. I would
doubt that there is a village, let alone a
city or county or state, which the
Communists could carry. Communism in
the world scene is no bogeyman; but
Communism as a political faction or party
in this country plainly is. Communism has
been so thoroughly exposed in this country that it has been crippled as a political
force. Free speech has destroyed it as an
effective political party.... The country is
not in despair; the people know Soviet
Communism; the doctrine of Soviet revolution is exposed in all of its ugliness and
the American people want none of it.

How it can be said that there is a clear
and present danger that this advocacy will
succeed is, therefore, a mystery....

Free speech—the glory of our system of
government—should not be sacrificed on
anything less than plain and objective
proof of danger that the evil advocated is
imminent. On this record no one can say
that petitioners and their converts are in
such a strategic position as to have even
the slightest chance of achieving their
aims....

QUESTIONS

1. How does Chief Justice Vinson's "sliding scale" approach to the clear
   and present danger doctrine in *Dennis* differ from the clear and present danger doctrine in *Schenck*?
2. Political scientist Martin Shapiro argues that "In *Dennis v. United States*
   the clear and present danger test was converted overtly into a clear
   and *probable* danger test.... The probable danger test held that if the
   anticipated evil were serious enough the imminence requirement [of
   the danger test] might be greatly relaxed" (*Encyclopedia of the
   American Constitution*, vol. I [New York, NY: Macmillan, 1986], p. 299).
   Michal R. Belknap refers to the *Dennis* test as the Court's "grave and
   probable danger rule" ("*Dennis v. United States*" in *The Oxford
   Companion to the Supreme Court of the United States*, ed. Kermit L. Hall
   [New York, NY: Oxford University Press, 1992], p. 226). The late Robert
   G. McCloskey observed: "Whatever name is chosen, the point is that

the judicial inquiry becomes by [the *Dennis*] formulation as broad and as conjectural as the legislative process itself" (*The Modern Supreme Court* [Cambridge, MA: Harvard University Press, 1972], p. 81). Are these assessments of the Court's rule in *Dennis* correct?

3. In a Special Term called in the summer of 1953, the Court, again over the dissents of Justices Black and Douglas, lifted the stay of execution for Julius and Ethel Rosenberg. *Rosenberg v. United States*, 346 U.S. 273 (1953.) The Rosenbergs had been convicted under the Espionage Act of 1917 for passing atomic secrets to the Soviet Union in wartime. They were electrocuted on June 19, 1953. Three days later, Justice Frankfurter belatedly dissented. He wrote, in part, "Only by sturdy self-examination and self-criticism can the necessary habits for detached and wise judgment be established and fortified so as to become effective when the judicial process is again subjected to stress and strain" (quoted in C. Herman Pritchett, *Civil Liberties and the Vinson Court* [Chicago, IL: University of Chicago Press, 1954], pp. 9–10).

To what sorts of "stress and strain" might the cold war, or any situation of national emergency—perceived or real—subject the Supreme Court? What does Justice Frankfurter's statement imply about interactions between the Court and the society of which it is a part?

COMMENT

After *Dennis*, federal authorities initiated Smith Act prosecutions against more than 120 individuals. Most defendants held second-tier leadership positions in the American Communist Party. By the time the Court handed down *Yates v. United States*, 354 U.S. 298 (1957) (described below), the government had obtained convictions in most of those prosecutions. The following summaries indicate how the Supreme Court responded to efforts to regulate and punish Communist Party activities in cases decided between *Dennis* in 1951 and *Brandenburg v. Ohio*, 395 U.S. 444 (1969), the next excerpted case.

Case: *Yates v. United States*, 354 U.S. 298 (1957)

Vote: 6–1 (Brennan and Whittaker, J.J., did not participate.)

Decision: The Smith Act does not prohibit advocating or teaching the need for the forcible overthrow of the government as an abstract principle, divorced from any effort to instigate action toward that end. The act prohibits "advocacy of action," not "advocacy in the realm of ideas." Convictions of fourteen leaders of the Communist Party in California for advocacy and organizing persons to advocate and teach the necessity and duty of overthrowing the government of the United States with force and violence reversed.

Case: *Communist Party v. Subversive Activities Control Board*, 367 U.S. 1 (1961)

Vote: 5–4

Decision: The requirement that the Communist Party of the United States register with the Subversive Activities Control Board is not unconstitutional. In concluding that the Party is "substantially directed, dominated, or controlled" by the Soviet Union, neither the board nor the lower courts erred in finding that the Party fell within the registration requirements of the Subversive Activities Control Act of 1950. The threat to national security posed by the Party outweighs any imposition on individual liberties caused by the act.

Case: *Scales v. United States*, 367 U.S. 203 (1961)

Vote: 6–3

Decision: The Membership Clause of the Smith Act, making it a felony to become or hold membership in any organization that advocates the overthrow of the United States by force and violence, does not violate the Fifth Amendment by imputing guilt to an individual merely on the basis of his associations and sympathies. A jury finding that the Party advocates the violent overthrow of the government as soon as circumstances are propitious is grounds for upholding convictions for membership in the Communist Party.

Case: *Noto v. United States*, 367 U.S. 290 (1961)

Vote: 9–0

Decision: It is present advocacy, not an intent to advocate in the future or a conspiracy to advocate in the future, that is an element of the crime under the Membership Clause of the Smith Act. Conviction for violation of Membership Clause of Smith Act reversed because of lack of evidence proving that the Communist Party presently advocates the forcible overthrow of the government, not merely as an abstract doctrine, but by use of language reasonably and ordinarily calculated to incite persons to action, immediately or in the future.

Case: *United States v. Brown*, 381 U.S. 437 (1965)

Vote: 5–4

Decision: The Labor-Management Reporting and Disclosure Act of 1959, which makes it a crime for one who belongs to the Communist Party, or who has been a member within the last five years, to serve as a member of the executive board of a labor organization, is an unconstitutional bill of attainder. Conviction of a twenty-five-year member of the Communist Party for serving on the executive board of Local 10 of the International Longshoreman's and Warehousemen's Union reversed.

Case: *Albertson v. Subversive Activities Control Board*, 382 U.S. 70 (1965)

Vote: 9–0

Decision: Failure of the Communist Party of the United States to register with the Subversive Activities Control Board following the Court's decision in *Communist Party v. Control Board* is justified by Fifth Amendment's Self-Incrimination Clause. Filing the registration form would be incriminatory because the admission of Party membership required by the form might be used as an investigatory lead or as evidence in a criminal prosecution.

Case: *United States v. Robel*, 389 U.S. 258 (1967)

Vote: 7–2

Decision: Section 5(a)(1)(D) of the Subversive Activities Control Act, making it a crime for any member of a communist-action organization required to register under the act to engage in any employment in any defense facility, is constitutionally overbroad. The section abridges the right of association protected by the First Amendment. The fact that the act was passed pursuant to Congress's "war power" to further the national defense cannot remove constitutional limitations safeguarding essential liberties.

DEFINING PROTECTED SPEECH DURING WAR AND NATIONAL EMERGENCY

Brandenburg v. Ohio
395 U.S. 444 (1969)

SETTING

Between 1917 and 1920, twenty states and two territories enacted criminal syndicalism laws. Ohio was one of those states. Its law went into effect in 1919. The statute made it a crime to "advocate ... the duty, necessity, or propriety of crime, sabotage, violence, or unlawful methods of terrorism as a means of accomplishing industrial or political reform." It also made it a crime to "voluntarily assemble with any society, group, or assemblage of persons formed to teach or advocate the doctrines of criminal syndicalism." During the 1960s, states began using their criminal syndicalism statutes to prosecute both civil rights activists and Vietnam War protesters. In 1964, the Ohio statute was invoked against the Ku Klux Klan. The Klan originated after the Civil War as a white supremacist organization opposed to Reconstruction. It declined in power in the 1920s, but experienced a resurgence in membership and activity in the 1960s in reaction to civil rights activism.

Clarence Brandenburg, a leader of the Ku Klux Klan, telephoned an announcer-reporter on the staff of a Cincinnati, Ohio, television station and invited him to come to a KKK rally at a farm in Hamilton County. The reporter attended and made videotapes of the meeting. Only the KKK members and the news reporter were present. One tape showed twelve hooded figures, some carrying firearms, gathered around a large wooden cross, which they burned. Most of the audio portion of the tape was inaudible, but portions that could be heard contained language including, "A dirty nigger," "Send the Jews back to Israel," "Save America," "Bury the niggers," "Freedom for the whites," and "Nigger will have to fight for every inch he gets from now on." Brandenburg, dressed in KKK regalia, delivered the following speech:

> This is an organizers' meeting. We have had quite a few members here today which are—we have hundreds, hundreds of members throughout the State of Ohio. I can quote from a newspaper clipping from the Columbus, Ohio, *Dispatch*, five weeks ago Sunday morning. The Klan has more members in the State of Ohio than does any other organization. We're not a revengent [sic] organization, but if our President, our Congress, our Supreme Court, continues to suppress the white, Caucasian race, it's possible that there might have to be some revengeance [sic] taken.

> We are marching on Congress July the Fourth, four hundred thousand strong. From there we are dividing into two groups, one group to march on St. Augustine, Florida, the other group to march into Mississippi. Thank you.

Another tape showed six hooded KKK members, one of them Brandenburg, who repeated a similar speech. Neither tape showed Brandenburg carrying a weapon. Portions of the tapes were shown on the local television station and on a national network.

Based on the material contained in them, Brandenburg was arrested for violating the state's criminal syndicalism act. He was indicted in September 1964, but was not tried until November 28, 1966, because of various motions, depositions, and continuances. At his trial in the Court of Common Pleas of Hamilton County, the state introduced into evidence the videotape and a pistol, rifle, shotgun, ammunition, and Bible, as well as the red hood that Brandenburg had worn. The state presented no other evidence. The defense introduced no testimony but submitted depositions and other evidence from KKK officials about the fraternal nature of the Klan and its organizational prohibition against violence. James R. Veable, an attorney and Imperial Wizard of the National Knights of the KKK stated in a deposition:

> We do not tolerate [violence]. That is, when I say that, the Imperial officers or officers of the States, even in the Klaverens, violence gets all of us in trouble, and if we want to accomplish anything, we can't afford to violate the law. I have told all of our Klan groups as well as those belonging to the National Association [for the Advancement of White People] that we couldn't use any type of violence, we had to obey the laws, whether it was good or bad, if we could unify, use the ballot box, we could accomplish this race war as you might call it.

At the conclusion of the trial, the jury was instructed that "you must find beyond a reasonable doubt ... [that] the defendant did unlawfully, voluntarily, assemble with a group of assemblage of persons formed to advocate criminal syndicalism."

Brandenburg was convicted, sentenced to one to ten years in prison, and fined $1,000. The trial court denied his motion for a new trial. The Ohio Court of Appeals for the First Appellate District affirmed without opinion, because the judge who was assigned to write the opinion for the court died before completing it. The Ohio Supreme Court dismissed Brandenburg's appeal on the ground that "no substantial constitutional question exists herein." Brandenburg appealed to the Supreme Court of the United States.

HIGHLIGHTS OF SUPREME COURT ARGUMENTS

BRIEF FOR BRANDENBURG

◆ The Ohio criminal syndicalism act is unconstitutional on its face and as construed, because it imposes criminal sanctions on the exercise of expression and assembly in violation of the First and Fourteenth Amendments.

◆ The words of the statute and the trial court's interpretation of it prohibit mere advocacy and fail to draw the necessary constitutional distinction between advocacy of abstract doctrine and advocacy directed at promoting unlawful action.

◆ A state may not punish speech and assembly unless there is a clear and present danger that the prohibited activities will bring about a punishable substantive evil. Section 2923.13 explicitly prohibits speaking, writing, and publishing, thereby directly infringing on First Amendment rights.

◆ Even if the statute is constitutional, the state failed to meet its burden of showing advocacy, assembly, and organization to propagate criminal syndicalism.

BRIEF FOR OHIO

◆ The guarantee of free speech does not include the right to persuade others to violate the law.

◆ The First Amendment does not give immunity to every possible use of language. This is not a case of teaching abstract doctrine. This is a case of hooded men with guns and weapons gathering together and being worked up to a pitch to take specific action at a specific time.

◆ It is the duty of this Court to liberally construe the Ohio statute to save it from constitutional infirmities.

◆ It would take an extreme stretch of the imagination for someone to believe, based on the facts presented to the jury and the extreme racial violence that marks this period in our history, that, at the time Brandenburg and his associates were speaking and marching around a burned cross, they were merely discussing and speaking intellectually, rather than committing overt acts of terrorism.

AMICUS CURIAE BRIEF SUPPORTING OHIO

Ohio Attorney General Paul Brown.

SUPREME COURT DECISION

(per curiam)

… In 1927, this Court sustained the constitutionality of California's Criminal Syndicalism Act the text of which is quite similar to that of the laws of Ohio. *Whitney v. California*.… But Whitney has been thoroughly discredited by later decisions.… These later decisions have fashioned the principle that the constitutional guarantees of free speech and free press do not permit a State to forbid or proscribe advocacy of the use of force or of law violation except where such advocacy is directed to inciting or producing imminent lawless action and is likely to incite or produce such action.… A statute which fails to draw this distinction impermissibly intrudes upon the freedoms guaranteed by the First and Fourteenth Amendments. It sweeps within its condemnation speech which our Constitution has immunized from governmental control.…

Measured by this test, Ohio's Criminal Syndicalism Act cannot be sustained. The Act punishes persons who "advocate or teach the duty, necessity, or propriety" of violence "as a means of accomplishing industrial or political reform"; or who publish or circulate or display any book or paper containing such advocacy; or who "justify" the commission of violent acts "with intent to exemplify, spread or advocate the propriety of the doctrines of criminal syndicalism"; or who "voluntarily assemble" with a group formed "to teach or advocate the doctrines of criminal syndicalism." Neither the indictment nor the trial judge's instructions to the jury in any way refined the statute's bald definition of the crime in terms of mere advocacy not distinguished from incitement to imminent lawless action.

Accordingly, we are here confronted with a statute which, by its own words and as applied, purports to punish mere advocacy and to forbid, on pain of criminal punishment, assembly with others merely to advocate the described type of action. Such a statute falls within the condemnation of the First and Fourteenth Amendments. The contrary teaching of *Whitney v. California* cannot be supported, and that decision is therefore overruled.

BLACK, J., CONCURRING

I agree with the views expressed by Mr. Justice Douglas in his concurring opinion in this case that the "clear and present danger" doctrine should have no place in the interpretation of the First Amendment. I join the Court's opinion, which, as I understand it, simply cites *Dennis v. United States* but does not indicate any agreement on the Court's part with the "clear and present danger" doctrine on which *Dennis* purported to rely.

DOUGLAS, J., CONCURRING

While I join the opinion of the Court, I desire to enter a caveat.

The "clear and present danger" test was adumbrated by Mr. Justice Holmes in a case arising during World War I—a war "declared" by the Congress, not by the Chief Executive.... Though I doubt if the "clear and present danger" test is congenial to the First Amendment in time of a declared war, I am certain it is not reconcilable with the First Amendment in days of peace. The Court quite properly overrules *Whitney v. California*, which involved advocacy of ideas which the majority of the Court deemed unsound and dangerous....

I see no place in the regime of the First Amendment for any "clear and present danger" test, whether strict and tight as some would make it, or free-wheeling as the Court in *Dennis* rephrased it.

When one reads the opinions closely and sees when and how the "clear and present danger" test has been applied, great misgivings are aroused. First, the threats were often loud but always puny and made serious only by judges so wedded to the status quo that critical analysis made them nervous. Second, the test was so twisted and perverted in *Dennis* as to make the trial of those teachers of Marxism an all-out political trial which was part and parcel of the cold war that has eroded substantial parts of the First Amendment.

Action is often a method of expression and within the protection of the First Amendment....

The example usually given by those who would punish speech is the case of one who falsely shouts fire in a crowded theatre. This is, however, a classic case where speech is brigaded with action. They are indeed inseparable and a prosecution can be launched for the overt acts actually caused. Apart from rare instances of that kind, speech is, I think, immune

from prosecution.... The quality of advocacy turns on the depth of the conviction;

and government has no power to invade
that sanctuary of belief and conscience.

QUESTIONS

1. Restate the test announced in *Brandenburg*. Does it afford more protection to free speech than the *Schenck* clear and present danger test?
   Why did Justice Douglas find it necessary to write a concurrence dis-
   avowing the clear and present danger test? Does his concurrence suggest that, in his view, a majority of the Court still considered the test
   viable?
2. On what basis did the Court in *Brandenburg* overrule *Whitney*? Did the
   per curiam opinion sufficiently explain the reasons for overruling its
   longstanding precedent?
3. Is it surprising that the Court would select a case involving the Ku
   Klux Klan to expand its understanding of free speech? Under what set
   of facts could Brandenburg's conviction have been upheld under the
   Court's new test?

COMMENTS

1. Law professor Gerald Gunther reports: "The phenomenon of a major
   constitutional decision appearing as a *per curiam*, unsigned opinion
   is extremely rare. There are reports that this opinion was originally
   drafted by Justice Fortas, who resigned just before the decision was
   rendered, and that the justices paid relatively little attention to the
   opinion because this was thought to be an easy case" (*Constitutional
   Law*, 12th ed. [Westbury, NY: Foundation Press, 1991], p. 1061 fn).
2. The two cases summarized below were decided, like *Brandenburg*,
   during the Vietnam War. They indicate the Court's approach to dissident speech in the late 1960s.

   Case: *Bond v. Floyd*, 385 U.S. 116 (1966)
   Vote: 9–0
   Decision: Exclusion of a duly elected Member of the Georgia House
   of Representatives, because of his statements, and statements to
   which he subscribed, criticizing the policies of the federal government in Vietnam and operation of the Selective Service laws, violates
   the First Amendment. Article VI of the Constitution of the United
   States did not authorize members of the State of Georgia to test the
   sincerity with which Julian Bond can swear to uphold the
   Constitution. Such a power could be utilized to restrict the right of
   legislators to dissent from national or state policy or that of a majority of their colleagues under the guise of judging their loyalty.

   Case: *Watts v. United States*, 394 U.S. 705 (1969)
   Vote: 5–4

Decision: A statute that makes criminal a form of pure speech must be interpreted with the commands of the First Amendment in mind. What is a threat must be distinguished from what is constitutionally protected speech. Petitioner's statement that he would refuse induction into the armed forces, that "if they ever make me carry a rifle the first man I want in my sights is L[yndon] B. J[ohnson]" and "They are not going to make me kill my black brothers" were political hyperbole and not a knowing, willful threat within the meaning of a 1917 federal statute prohibiting threats against the life of the president of the United States.

Suggestions for Further Reading

Baker, C. Edwin, "Scope of the First Amendment Freedom of Speech," 25 *University of California Los Angeles Law Review* (1978): 964.

Belknap, Michal R., *Cold War Political Justice: The Smith Act, the Communist Party and American Civil Liberties* (Westport, CT: Greenwood Press, 1977).

Blanchard, Margaret A., "Filling in the Void: Speech and Press in State Courts Prior to *Gitlow*," in *The First Amendment Reconsidered: New Perspectives on the Meaning of Freedom of Speech and Press*, ed. Bill F. Chamberlin and Charlene J. Brown (New York, NY: Longman, 1982).

Blasi, Vincent, "The Pathological Perspective and the First Amendment," 85 *Columbia Law Review* (1985): 449.

_____, "The First Amendment and the Ideal of Civic Courage: The Brandeis Opinion in *Whitney v. California*," 29 *William & Mary Law Review* (1988): 653.

Bogen, David, "The Free Speech Metamorphosis of Mr. Justice Holmes," 11 *Hofstra Law Review* (1982): 97.

Bork, Robert H., "Neutral Principles and Some First Amendment Problems," 47 *Indiana Law Journal* (1971): 1.

Brennan, William, "The Supreme Court and the Meiklejohn Interpretation of the First Amendment," 79 *Harvard Law Review* (1965): 1.

Cahn, Edmond, "Justice Black and First Amendment 'Absolutes': A Public Interview," 37 *New York University Law Review* (1962): 549.

Chaffee, Zechariah, Jr., "Freedom of Speech in Wartime," 32 *Harvard Law Review* (1919): 932.

_____, *Free Speech in the United States* (Cambridge, MA: Harvard University Press, 1941).

_____, Book Review, 62 *Harvard Law Review* (1949): 891.

Cohen, Jeremy, *Congress Shall Make No Law: Oliver Wendell Holmes, the First Amendment, and Judicial Decision Making* (Ames, IA: Iowa State University Press, 1989).

Dowell, Eldridge F., *A History of Criminal Syndicalism Laws in the United States* (Baltimore, MD: Johns Hopkins University Press, 1939).

Emerson, Thomas I., *Toward a General Theory of the First Amendment* (New York, NY: Random House, 1967).

_____, *The System of Freedom of Expression* (New York, NY: Random House, 1970).

Fishbein, Leslie, *Rebels in Bohemia: The Radicals of The Masses, 1911–1917* (Chapel Hill, NC: University of North Carolina Press, 1982).

Graber, Mark A., *Transforming Free Speech: The Ambiguous Legacy of Civil Libertarianism* (Berkeley, CA: University of California Press, 1991).

Gunther, Gerald, "Learned Hand and the Origins of Modern First Amendment Doctrine: Some Fragments of History," 27 *Stanford Law Review* (1975): 719.

Henkin, Louis, "Foreword: On Drawing Lines," 82 *Harvard Law Review* (1968): 63.

Kairys, David, "Freedom of Speech," in *The Politics of Law: A Progressive Critique*, ed. David Kairys, 2nd ed. (New York, NY: Knopf, 1990).

Kalven, Harry, Jr., "Uninhibited, Robust, and Wide-Open, A Note on Free Speech and the Warren Court," 67 *Michigan Law Review* (1968): 289.

_____, "Professor Ernst Freund and *Debs v. United States*," 40 *University of Chicago Law Review* (1973): 235.

_____, *A Worthy Tradition: Freedom of Speech in America* (New York, NY: Harper & Row, 1988).

Laswell, Harold D., *National Security and Individual Freedom* (New York, NY: McGraw-Hill, 1950).

Levy, Leonard W., *Freedom of Speech and Press in Early American History: Legacy of Suppression* (New York, NY: Harper & Row, 1963).

Linde, Hans A., "Clear and Present Danger Reexamined: Dissonance in the Brandenburg Concerto," 22 *Stanford Law Review* (1970): 1163.

Lynd, Staughton, "*Brandenburg v. Ohio*: A Speech Test for All Seasons?" 43 *University of Chicago Law Review* (1975): 151.

Martin, Charles H., *The Angelo Herndon Case and Southern Justice* (Baton Rouge, LA: Louisiana State University Press, 1976).

Meiklejohn, Alexander, *Freedom of Speech and Its Relation to Self-Government* (New York, NY: Harper, 1948).

_____, "The First Amendment Is an Absolute," *The Supreme Court Review* (Chicago, IL: University of Chicago Press, 1961).

Mendelson, Wallace, "Clear and Present Danger—From *Schenck* to *Dennis*," 52 *Columbia Law Review* (1952): 313.

_____, "On the Meaning of the First Amendment: Absolutes in the Balance," 50 *California Law Review* (1962): 821.

Murphy, Paul L., *The Meaning of Freedom of Speech: First Amendment Freedoms from Wilson to FDR* (Westport, CT: Greenwood, 1972).

Note, "The National Security Interest and Civil Liberties," 85 *Harvard Law Review* (1972): 1130.

Nye, Russel B., *Fettered Freedom: Civil Liberties and the Slavery Controversy, 1830–1860,* rev. ed. (East Lansing, MI: Michigan State University Press, 1964).

Polenberg, Richard, *Fighting Faiths: The* Abrams *Case, the Supreme Court, and Free Speech* (New York, NY: Penguin, 1989).

Rabban, David M., "The First Amendment in Its Forgotten Years," 90 *Yale Law Journal* (1981): 514.

———, "The Emergence of Modern First Amendment Doctrine," 50 *University of Chicago Law Review* (1983): 1205.

Radosh, Ronald, and Joyce Milton, *The Rosenberg File: A Search for Truth* (New York, NY: Holt, Reinhart and Winston, 1983).

Ragan, Fred, "Justice Oliver Wendell Holmes, Jr., Zechariah Chafee, Jr. and the Clear and Present Danger Test for Free Speech: The First Year, 1919," 58 *Journal of American History* (1971): 24.

Randall, James G., *Constitutional Problems under Lincoln,* rev. ed. (Glouster, MA: Peter Smith, 1963).

Rogat, Yosal, and James M. O'Fallon, "Mr. Justice Holmes: A Dissenting Opinion—The Free Speech Cases," 36 *Stanford Law Review* (1984): 1349.

Schauer, Frederick F., *Free Speech: A Philosophical Enquiry* (Cambridge, MA: Cambridge University Press, 1982).

———, "Must Speech Be Special?" 78 *Northwestern University Law Review* (1983): 1284.

———, "The Second-Best First Amendment," 31 *William & Mary Law Review* (1989): 1.

Schneir, Walter, *Invitation to an Inquest* (Garden City, NY: Doubleday, 1965).

Shiffrin, Steven H., *The First Amendment, Democracy and Romance* (Cambridge, MA: Harvard University Press, 1990).

Smith, James Morton, *Freedom's Fetters: The Alien and Sedition Laws and American Civil Liberties* (Ithaca, NY: Cornell University Press, 1956).

Strong, Frank, "Fifty Years of 'Clear and Present Danger': From *Schenck* to *Brandenburg*—and Beyond," *The Supreme Court Review* (Chicago, IL: University of Chicago Press, 1969).

Sudoplatov, Pavel A., Anatoli P. Sudoplatov, Jerrold Schecter, and Leona Schecter, *Special Tasks: The Memoirs of an Unwanted Witness, a Soviet Spymaster* (Boston, MA: Little, Brown, 1994).

Sunstein, Cass R., *Democracy and the Problem of Free Speech* (New York, NY: Basic Books, 1993).

Taylor, Telford, *Grand Inquest* (New York, NY: Simon & Schuster, 1955).

Van Alstyne, William W., "A Graphic Review of the Free Speech Clause," 70 *California Law Review* (1982): 107.

———, *Interpretations of the First Amendment* (Durham, NC: Duke University Press, 1984).

FIGHTING WORDS AND HATE SPEECH

Chaplinsky v. New Hampshire
315 U.S. 568 (1942)

SETTING

In the late 1930s, the Jehovah's Witnesses (see pp. 127–134) were a visible and unpopular religious group. During the 1935 Jehovah's Witness annual convention, the group's leader, Joseph F. Rutherford, denounced compulsory flag-salute laws, saying that Witnesses "do not 'Heil Hitler' nor any other creature." At the time, the conventional method for saluting the American flag was to raise the right arm in a position virtually identical to the raised palm of the Nazi salute. In October, 1935, two Jehovah's Witness children, Lillian and William Gobitis, refused to participate in the compulsory flag salute at their Minersville, Pennsylvania school. The following month they were expelled for their "act of insubordination." When the Gobitis children's father, Walter, sued the Minersville School Board, the publicity was widespread and largely hostile to the Jehovah's Witnesses' refusal to engage in this patriotic ritual.

While the Gobitis's flag-salute case wound its way through the federal courts on its way to the Supreme Court, some New Hampshire Jehovah's Witnesses, among them Walter Chaplinsky, became embroiled in another controversy. On Saturday April 6, 1940, Chaplinsky was witnessing on a street corner in Rochester, New Hampshire, distributing "Watchtower," "Consolation," and other Jehovah's Witnesses biblical periodicals, when an angry mob formed around him on the sidewalk. The mob, numbering fifty or sixty people, objected to Chaplinsky's work and threatened him with violence if he did not stop. As the tension level increased, a Rochester city marshal named Bowering waded into the crowd accompanied by a man named Bowman. Bowman physically assaulted Chaplinsky, grabbing him by the throat with his left hand and striking him with his right fist. Wrenching himself free of Bowman's grasp, Chaplinsky turned to Bowering and said, "Marshal, I want you to arrest this man." Bowering replied, "I will if I feel like it." Thereafter, Bowering and Bowman left the mob and walked away. Chaplinsky returned to his witnessing work.

In a few minutes, Chaplinsky saw Bowman hurrying down the street toward the mob, carrying a staff and American flag in his hand. As he rushed at Chaplinsky, Bowman lowered the staff, lunged, and attempted to impale Chaplinsky with it. Chaplinsky evaded the attack but, as he did so, Bowman pushed him into an automobile parked at the curb. Bowman walked to the corner, handed his flag to another man, and advanced again on Chaplinsky saying: "You son of a bitch. Will you salute the flag?"

Bowering, who had returned to the scene with an Officer Lapierre, picked

Chaplinsky off the ground and began shoving him roughly down the street in the direction of the Rochester City Hall. Chaplinsky turned to Bowering and asked, "Will you please arrest the ones who started this fight?" Bowering replied, "Shut up, you damn bastard, and come along." In reply, Chaplinsky retorted, "You are a damn Fascist and racketeer." As Chaplinsky entered city hall, a man approached him, identified himself as Deputy Sheriff Ralph Dunlap and said, "You son of a bitch, we ought to have left you to that crowd there and have them kill you." Thereupon, Marshal Bowering exclaimed to Chaplinsky, "You unpatriotic dog, I am going to arrest you on account you called me a God-damned Fascist."

Chaplinsky was placed under arrest. He was charged with violating Section 2 of the Public Laws of New Hampshire:

> No person shall address any offensive, derisive, or annoying word to any other person who is lawfully in the street or other public place, nor call him by any offensive or derisive name, nor make any noise or exclamation in his presence and hearing with intent to deride, annoy, or offend him or prevent him from pursuing his lawful business or occupation.

The complaint charged, "with force and arms ... [Chaplinsky] did unlawfully repeat ... 'You are a God damned racketeer' and 'a damned Fascist and the whole government of Rochester are Fascists or agents of Fascists' the same being offensive, derisive and annoying words and names."

At trial in Rochester Municipal Court, all of the state's witnesses testified that Chaplinsky had called Bowering a "God-damn racketeer" and a "damn Fascist." Chaplinsky was convicted of violating Section 2 of the Public Laws of New Hampshire. He appealed to the New Hampshire Superior Court, which accorded him a *de novo* trial before a jury. He was again found guilty and the conviction was affirmed by the New Hampshire Supreme Court. He appealed to the Supreme Court of the United States.

HIGHLIGHTS OF SUPREME COURT ARGUMENTS

BRIEF FOR CHAPLINSKY

◆ The undisputed evidence is that Chaplinsky, immediately before his unlawful arrest and during the time he was unlawfully assaulted, was engaged in exercising his right to freedom of worship and his rights of free press in distributing "Watchtower" and "Consolation" magazines. The mob that gathered around him placed an American flag in front of him and commanded that he salute it. When he refused, he was assaulted and beaten. Chaplinsky had every reason to expect police protection and the right to criticize local officials by the use of any language he desired as long as he did not incite others to use violence against the local government and overthrow it.

◆ The construction placed on the statute by the New Hampshire Supreme Court permits conviction for the exercise of the right of free speech even where there is no clear and present danger of violence or threatened violence or breach of the peace.

◆ The statute violates Due Process because it is vague and indefinite and permits a dragnet. No person of ordinary intelligence can safely discern from the statute just what is permissible speech or words. Almost anything that is said can be taken to be derisive under the statute, depending on the susceptibilities of the hearer.

◆ Evidence as to provocation is admissible as a defense to the offense charged. If the words spoken are truthful, it is a complete justification and defense to the offense charged. The New Hampshire Supreme Court erred in holding that truth is not a defense and that evidence of provocation is not a defense.

◆ Upholding the conviction in this case would mean the end of free speech and constitutional liberty in the United States. The real motive for Chaplinsky's arrest was the fact that he chose to obey Almighty God and preach the Gospel in spite of mob violence, following exactly in the footsteps of Jesus Christ's faithful apostle Paul and God's faithful prophet Jeremiah.

BRIEF FOR NEW HAMPSHIRE

◆ The New Hampshire statute may be divided into two parts. One prohibits words and names addressed to another in a public place. The other treats as an offense noises or exclamations made with intent to deride, offend, or annoy. Chaplinsky was convicted for violating the first part of the statute, the purpose of which is to preserve the public peace. Chaplinsky spoke words that were profane, vituperative, and illegal. The New Hampshire Supreme Court's construction of the statute is binding on this Court because the state's highest court is the final authority on state law.

◆ The test of criminality under the statute is what persons of common intelligence would understand to be words likely to cause an average addressee to fight. Where the meaning of a statute may be derived from common experience, the statute is not vague or overbroad.

◆ The New Hampshire statute does not violate the right to free speech. All free speech questions require a balance between the individual and social interests such as the public order. Since even nonabusive language does not enjoy absolute constitutional immunity, abusive language is entitled to even less protection because it always produces a clear and present danger of producing a public disturbance.

◆ While it is of great importance for the survival of democratic institutions that civil liberties be preserved, it is equally essential for the assurance of such civil liberties that those democratic institutions themselves be maintained in an atmosphere of public order and peace. New Hampshire's power to condemn name-calling in the public streets should be made to prevail over Chaplinsky's interest in calling a city marshal a "God damned racketeer and a damned Fascist."

SUPREME COURT DECISION: 9–0

MURPHY, J.

... Allowing the broadest scope to the language and purpose of the Fourteenth Amendment, it is well understood that the right of free speech is not absolute at all times and under all circumstances. There are certain well-defined and narrowly limited classes of speech, the prevention and punishment of which has never been thought to raise any Constitutional problem. These include the lewd and obscene, the profane, the libelous, and the insulting or "fighting" words—those which by their very utterance inflict injury or tend to incite an immediate breach of the peace. It has been well observed that such utterances are no essential part of any exposition of ideas, and are of such slight social value as a step to truth that any benefit that may be derived from them is clearly outweighed by the social interest in order and morality....

On the authority of its earlier decisions, the state court declared that the statute's purpose was to preserve the public peace, no words being "forbidden except such as have a direct tendency to cause acts of violence by the person to whom, individually, the remark is addressed." It was further said: "The word 'offensive' is not to be defined in terms of what a particular addressee thinks.... The test is what men of common intelligence would understand would be words likely to cause an average addressee to fight.... The English language has a number of words and expressions which by general consent are 'fighting words' when said without a disarming smile.... Such words, as ordinary men know, are likely to cause a fight. So are threatening, profane or obscene revilings. Derisive and annoying words can be taken as coming within the purview of the statute as heretofore interpreted only when they have this characteristic of plainly tending to excite the addressee to a breach of the peace.... The statute, as construed, does no more than prohibit the face-to-face words plainly likely to cause a breach of the peace by the addressee, words whose speaking constitute a breach of the peace by the speaker—including 'classical fighting words,' words in current use less 'classical' but equally likely to cause violence, and other disorderly words, including profanity, obscenity and threats."

We are unable to say that the limited scope of the statute as thus construed contravenes the constitutional right of free expression. It is a statute narrowly drawn and limited to define and punish specific conduct lying within the domain of state power, the use in a public place of words likely to cause a breach of the peace....

Nor can we say that the application of the statute to the facts disclosed by the record substantially or unreasonably impinges upon the privilege of free speech. Argument is unnecessary to demonstrate that the appellations "damn racketeer" and "damn Fascist" are epithets likely to provoke the average person to retaliation, and thereby cause a breach of the peace.

The refusal of the state court to admit evidence of provocation and evidence bearing on the truth or falsity of the utterances is open to no Constitutional objection. Whether the facts sought to be proved by such evidence constitute a defense to the charge or may be shown in mitigation are questions for the state court to determine. Our function is fulfilled by a determination that the challenged statute, on its face and as applied, does not contravene the Fourteenth Amendment.

Affirmed.

QUESTIONS

1. Should the circumstances surrounding Chaplinsky's arrest, as well as the general social context within which Jehovah's Witnesses were persecuted and attacked for not saluting the flag, have affected the Court's opinion in *Chaplinsky*? Was it correct for the justices to decline to take into consideration those circumstances in their *Chaplinsky* opinion, merely citing the lower court's holding "that neither provocation nor the truth of the utterance would constitute a defense to the charge"?

2. What language in Justice Murphy's opinion illustrates the "two-tier" approach he took to defining speech protected, and unprotected, under the First Amendment? Should speech lacking "social value" not be protected speech? If so, what defines "social value"?

3. The attorney general of New Hampshire argued:

   > The words of the appellant were offensive, derisive and annoying within the meaning of the statute. Racketeers are considered persons of anti-social behavior, violators of the law, exploiters, promoters of white slavery, defrauders and what not. Fascists are looked upon in the Nation as persons who achieve their ends by terrorism and resort to might. Both expressions are well calculated to cause a breach of peace especially when addressed to an officer in the performance of his duties. Such language can hardly be considered "in any proper sense communication of information or opinion and safeguarded by the constitution" to quote Mr. Justice Roberts in the *Cantwell* case.

   What standards does the Court provide in *Chaplinsky* for deciding whether words are "offensive, derisive, and annoying within the meaning of the statute" or are "communication of information or opinion" and "safeguarded by the constitution"?

4. Law professor Martin Redish contends that Chaplinsky's abusive statements may have served "as a means to vent his frustration at a system he deemed—whether rightly or wrongly—to be oppressive[.]" "Is it not a mark of individuality," Redish asks, "to be able to cry out at a society viewed as crushing the individual? Under this analysis, the so-called 'fighting words' represent a significant means of self-realization, whether or not they can be considered a means of attaining some elusive truth" ("The Value of Free Speech," 130 *University of Pennsylvania Law Review* (1982): 591). Is Redish correct?

COMMENT

Although the "fighting words" doctrine continues to be cited, since *Chaplinsky* the Court has not upheld a single conviction based on that doctrine. The cases summarized below indicate the erosion of the *Chaplinsky* doctrine.

Case: *Terminiello v. Chicago*, 337 U.S. 1 (1949)

Vote: 5–4

Decision: A breach of the peace conviction cannot stand, because, in its jury instructions, the trial court construed an Illinois statute to permit conviction for speech that stirred people to anger, invited public dispute, or brought about a condition of unrest. Such a reading invades the province of speech protected by the First Amendment. "Speech is often provocative and challenging. It may strike at prejudices and preconceptions and have profound unsettling effects as it presses for acceptance of an idea. That is why freedom of speech, though not absolute (*Chaplinsky v. New Hampshire*) is nevertheless protected against censorship or punishment, unless shown likely to produce a clear and present danger of a serious evil that rises far above public inconvenience, annoyance, or unrest."

Case: *Street v. New York*, 394 U.S. 576 (1969)

Vote: 5–4

Decision: Words spoken by petitioner, a black man, after learning of the racially motivated shooting of black University of Mississippi student James Meredith, are protected speech. His statement: "We don't need no damn flag," uttered after he set fire to an American flag, is not so inherently inflammatory as to come within that small class of "fighting words" that are "likely to provoke the average person to retaliation, and thereby cause a breach of the peace." *Chaplinsky v. New Hampshire.*

Case: *Cohen v. California*, 403 U.S. 15 (1971)

Vote: 6–3

Decision: Under the First and Fourteenth Amendments, states may not declare that the simple display of a single four-letter expletive is a criminal breach of the peace. Walking through the corridor of a municipal courthouse wearing a jacket bearing the words "Fuck the Draft" does not amount to "fighting words," "those personally abusive epithets which, when addressed to the ordinary citizen, are, as a matter of common knowledge, inherently likely to provoke violent reaction." *Chaplinsky v. New Hampshire.*

Case: *Gooding v. Wilson*, 405 U.S. 518 (1972)

Vote: 5–2 (Powell and Rehnquist, J.J., did not participate.)

Decision: A Georgia breach of the peace statute that had not been narrowed by that state's courts to "fighting words" is unconstitutional on its face as vague and overbroad under the First and Fourteenth Amendments. "Our decisions since *Chaplinsky* have continued to recognize state power conditionally to punish 'fighting' words under carefully drawn statutes not also susceptible of application to protected expression.... We affirm that proposition today.... Georgia appellate decisions have construed [the statute] to apply to utterances that, although within [the definitions of 'opprobrious' and 'abusive,'] are not 'fighting' words as *Chaplinsky* defines them ... words 'which by their very utterance ... tend to incite an immediate breach of the peace.'"

FIGHTING WORDS AND HATE SPEECH

R.A.V. v. St. Paul, Minnesota
505 U.S. 377 (1992)

SETTING

During the 1980s and 1990s, cities and states across the United States experienced escalating violence against people of color, homosexuals, Jews, and women. Hate groups like Neo-Nazi Skinheads and youth gangs sprang up around the country, perpetrating acts of violence and intimidation. In 1989, Congress responded with the Federal Religious Vandalism Act, followed in 1990 by the Federal Hate Crime Statistics Act. By 1991, more than half the states had adopted laws, commonly termed "hate-crime" legislation, seeking to deter and punish acts motivated by racial, ethnic, religious, gender, or homophobic bias.

Hate-crime laws were criticized by some groups as efforts to coerce "politically correct" behavior and speech. Some constitutional scholars worried whether the laws violated the First Amendment's guarantee of free speech. The concern that laws defining "hate crimes" might suffer constitutional defects, however, was not viewed as an automatic death knell. One reason was that in *Chaplinsky v. New Hampshire* the Court noted that the First Amendment "is not absolute at all times and under all circumstances."

A second reason potential First Amendment problems did not deter supporters of hate-crime laws was the Court's decision in *Brandenburg v. Ohio*. In that case, recall, the Court struck down Ohio's Criminal Syndicalism Act, which made it illegal to advocate violence, crime, sabotage, and terrorism to accomplish industrial or political reform. The Court declared that "[T]he constitutional guarantees of free speech and free press do not permit a State to forbid or proscribe advocacy of the use of force or of law violation *except where such advocacy is directed to inciting or producing imminent lawless action and is likely to incite or produce such action*." (Emphasis added)

To some analysts, hate-crime laws fell clearly within the purview of *Chaplinsky* and/or *Brandenburg* because the acts outlawed in the statutes fell within the "fighting words" exception or were aimed at inciting "imminent lawless action" through acts like cross burning or displays of swastikas. The opportunity to test how the Supreme Court would analyze the constitutional issues associated with hate-crime laws came during the 1991 Term of the Supreme Court in a case arising in St. Paul, Minnesota.

In 1982, the St. Paul city council enacted the "Bias-Motivated Crime Ordinance." It amended the ordinance in 1989 and 1990. The 1990 amendments brought sexual bias within the purview of the ordinance, while the 1989 amendments included Section 292.02, relating to bias-motivated disorderly conduct. That section said:

Whoever places on public or private property a symbol, object, appellation, characterization or graffiti, including, but not limited to, a burning cross or Nazi swastika, which one knows or has reasonable grounds to know arouses anger, alarm or resentment in others on the basis of race, color, creed, religion or gender commits disorderly conduct and shall be guilty of a misdemeanor.

The ordinance was invoked by prosecutors for the first time in the case of seventeen-year-old Robert A. Viktora, a high school dropout with ties to the Skinheads, a neo-Nazi group.

On the night of June 21, 1990, Viktora was at the home of eighteen-year-old Arthur Miller III in east St. Paul, along with four other friends. Viktora had been staying at the Miller home and was doing some painting. Miller lived across the street from Russ and Laura Jones and their five young children. The African-American Jones family had moved to the neighborhood three months earlier to escape drug and crime problems in the inner city. They were the only black family living in the neighborhood.

During the evening, Viktora and the others had been drinking and talking about causing some "Skinhead trouble" and "burning some niggers." Sometime between 1:00 and 3:00 A.M., they made a wooden cross out of dowels from the legs of a broken chair. They wrapped the cross in paint rags Viktora had been using, entered the Joneses' fenced front yard, and stood the cross in it. They then doused the cross with paint thinner, set it ablaze, ran to hide in the Miller home, and began producing more crosses. The Joneses heard noise in their front yard and looked out a window to see the burning cross. They called the police.

When police officers arrived at the Jones home, Viktora and the others were across the street inside the Miller home. After police left, they reemerged, placed a second cross on the boulevard across the street from the Jones residence and lit it. While it was burning, they made their way to an apartment complex a few blocks away, in which several black families lived, and lit a third cross in a parking lot across from it. The group then went back to Miller's house, where everyone but Viktora left before Miller's father came home. The following day, Viktora bragged to two different people about his involvement in the cross burnings.

On June 25, Minnesota officials filed a petition in Juvenile Court for Ramsey County charging Viktora with fourth-degree assault and bias-motivated assault in violation of Section 292.02. On July 5, 1990, the charge was reduced to bias-motivated disorderly conduct under Section 292.02. Because it was a juvenile proceeding, Viktora's initials, R. A. V., were used instead of his full name. Before his trial, Viktora's lawyer moved to dismiss the charge of bias-motivated disorderly conduct on the ground that the broad and sweeping language of Section 292.02 could not be sustained under the First Amendment. The district court granted the motion. The county appealed the order dismissing the case to the Minnesota Court of Appeals, as well as to the Minnesota Supreme Court, requesting accelerated review.

The Minnesota Supreme Court granted accelerated review, reversed the trial court, and remanded the case for trial. Although acknowledging that the ordinance "should have been more carefully drafted," the court held that it could be interpreted so as to reach "only those expressions of hatred and resorts to bias-motivated personal abuse that the First Amendment does not protect." The Minnesota court then construed the ordinance's prohibition of expression that "arouses anger, alarm or resentment in others ..." to reach only such conduct that also amounts to fighting words or incitement to imminent lawless action. In its unanimous opinion the state high court stated:

> Burning a cross in the yard of an African American family's home is deplorable conduct that the City of St. Paul may without question prohibit. The burning cross is itself an unmistakable symbol of violence and hatred based on virulent notions of racial supremacy. It is the responsibility, even the obligation, of diverse communities to confront such notions in whatever form they appear.

Viktora petitioned the Supreme Court of the United States for a writ of certiorari.

HIGHLIGHTS OF SUPREME COURT ARGUMENTS

BRIEF FOR VIKTORA

◆ The primary effect of the St. Paul ordinance is to restrict protected expression in an overbroad manner. The likelihood of impermissible application of the ordinance is great, having a chilling effect on conduct. The ordinance is applicable to all areas of the city, thereby enjoining expression in traditional public forums and designated public forums, as well as on citizens' private property and the private property of another without consent. The latter category is already prohibited by existing penal laws without regard to the content of the expression.

◆ When any overly broad law attempts to regulate expression on the basis of its content, it is subject to strict constitutional scrutiny. The government must demonstrate a compelling state interest and show that the law was narrowly tailored to achieve that legitimate goal.

◆ From the beginning of this case the government has conceded that the expressive conduct proscribed by the ordinance possesses sufficient communicative elements to fall within the parameters of the First Amendment. The ordinance regulates both symbolic conduct ("symbol, object, appellation") and written expression ("characterization or graffiti"). By including specific symbols—Nazi swastika and burning crosses—the ordinance not only regulates the content of a message but is a censorial statute directed at particular groups and viewpoints. It attempts impermissibly to protect and shield its audience.

◆ The St. Paul ordinance should be scrutinized under the same analysis as the Court used in *Schaumburg v. Citizens for a Better Environment*, 444 U.S. 620 (1980): "Broad prophylactic rules in the area of free expression are suspect. Precision of regulation is the touchstone."

◆ The triggering language of the St. Paul ordinance—"arouses anger, alarm or resentment"—could be used to describe the feelings of any audience when ridiculed outrageously, politically criticized in an undignified manner, or exposed to other forms of personally offensive expression.

◆ It would appear that the real interest advanced by the ordinance is increasing social tolerance by prohibiting intolerant expressions regarding race, color, creed, religion, and gender. While the government may have an interest in increasing understanding among its citizens, it may not promote this interest by regulating individual expression and opinion. Assuming there is some legitimate state interest that would permit the prohibition of speech and expression that "arouses anger, alarm or resentment in others," the St. Paul ordinance was not narrowly tailored to achieve that goal.

◆ The St. Paul ordinance is not susceptible to a limiting construction. Any attempt to limit it to "fighting words" or "imminent lawless action" would not cure its constitutional infirmities. It has no core of easily identifiable and constitutionally proscribable conduct that falls outside the protection of the First Amendment.

◆ This Court should not create any new exceptions to the First Amendment protection of free speech. Any expansion of narrowly recognized exceptions to the First Amendment would further diffuse the nearly indistinguishable line between permissible and proscribable expression. Further restrictions might curtail some offensive expression but only at the cost of chilling a great deal of protected speech.

AMICUS CURIAE BRIEFS SUPPORTING VIKTORA

Center for Individual Rights; American Publishers and Freedom to Read Foundation; joint brief of American Civil Liberties Union, Minnesota Civil Liberties Union, and American Jewish Congress; Patriot's Defense Foundation, Inc.

BRIEF FOR ST. PAUL

◆ The St. Paul ordinance, as construed and limited by the Minnesota Supreme Court, is neither overly broad in its reach nor impermissibly vague in what it forbids. It is an enactment proscribing fighting words, true threats, and conduct directed to inciting or producing imminent lawless action. A person prohibited from cross burning still has all other means of expression available to express his views about African Americans or any other minority group.

◆ The Minnesota Supreme Court's interpretation of the St. Paul ordinance was consistent with numerous prior decisions of that court construing identical or very similar language in state or municipal enactments.

◆ As in *Chaplinsky*, the ordinance in this case has been narrowed and clarified carefully to define what conduct is proscribed and what is not.

◆ The St. Paul ordinance has no more danger of unequal enforcement than any other enactment. The *scienter* requirement helps to assure regularity and predictability in its enforcement.

◆ The St. Paul ordinance should not be subjected to strict scrutiny because it is content-neutral in the sense that its purpose is to protect victims from carefully defined harms, rather than to impact protected speech or forbid it based on its expressive content.

◆ Even if the ordinance is assumed to be content-based, the state has a compelling interest in its existence: protecting victims from violation of their basic human rights to self-esteem and security as members of groups historically subject to discrimination. The ordinance is narrowly drawn to achieve these goals.

◆ The St. Paul ordinance may also be validly enforced as conduct directed to inciting or producing imminent lawless action and likely to incite or produce such action. Cross burning, by nature and history, is intimidating to anyone targeted. The only issue is whether the threat is clear and present. To an African American family, the meaning of a burning cross on one's lawn is not remotely ambiguous.

AMICUS CURIAE BRIEFS SUPPORTING ST. PAUL

Joint brief of the States of Minnesota, Alabama, Arizona, Connecticut, Idaho, Illinois, Kansas, Maryland, Massachusetts, Michigan, New Jersey, Ohio, Oklahoma, South Carolina, Tennessee, Virginia, and Utah; Criminal Justice Legal Foundation; National Black Women's Health Project; Anti-Defamation League of B'nai B'rith; joint brief of Asian American Legal Defense and Education Fund, Asian Law Caucus, Asian Pacific American Legal Center, and National Asian Pacific American Bar Association; joint brief of League of Minnesota Cities, City of Minneapolis, and City of St. Paul; People for the American Way; joint brief of Center for Democratic Renewal, Center for Constitutional Rights, National Conference of Black Lawyers, National Council of La Raza, International Union, United Automobile, Aerospace and Agricultural Implement Workers of America—UAW, Young Women's Christian Association of the U.S.A., National Organization of Black Law Enforcement Executives, National Lawyers Guild, United Church of Christ, Commission for Racial Justice, National Institute Against Prejudice and Violence, Greater Boston Civil Rights Coalition, and National Coalition of Black Lesbians and Gays.

SUPREME COURT DECISION

(9–0 on judgment, 5–4 on rationale)

SCALIA, J.

... The First Amendment generally prevents government from proscribing speech, or even expressive conduct, because of disapproval of the ideas expressed. Content-based regulations are presumptively invalid. From 1791 to the present, however, our society, like other free but civilized societies, has permitted restrictions upon the content of speech in a few limited areas, which are "of such slight social value as a step to truth that any benefit that may be derived from them is clearly outweighed by the social interest in order and morality." *Chaplinsky....*

Our cases surely do not establish the proposition that the First Amendment imposes no obstacle whatsoever to regulation of particular instances of such proscribable expression, so that the government "may regulate [them] freely."...

Applying these principles to the St. Paul ordinance, we conclude that, even as narrowly construed by the Minnesota Supreme Court, the ordinance is facially unconstitutional. Although the phrase in the ordinance, "arouses anger, alarm, or resentment in others," has been limited by the Minnesota Supreme Court's construction to reach only those symbols or displays that amount to "fighting words," the remaining, unmodified terms make clear that the ordinance applies only to "fighting words" that insult, or provoke violence, "on the basis of race, color, creed, religion or gender." Displays containing abusive invective, no matter how vicious or severe, are permissible unless they are addressed to one of the specified disfavored topics. Those who wish to use "fighting words" in connection with other ideas—to express hostility, for example, on the basis of political affiliation, union membership, or homosexuality—are not covered. The First Amendment does not permit St. Paul to impose special prohibitions on those speakers who express views on disfavored subjects.

In its practical operation, moreover, the ordinance goes even beyond mere content discrimination. Displays containing some words—odious racial epithets, for example—would be prohibited to proponents of all views. But "fighting words" that do not themselves invoke race, color, creed, religion, or gender—aspersions

upon a person's mother, for example—would seemingly be usable *ad libitum* in the placards of those arguing *in favor* of racial, color, etc. tolerance and equality, but could not be used by that speaker's opponents. One could hold up a sign saying, for example, that all "anti-Catholic bigots" are misbegotten; but not that all "papists" are, for that would insult and provoke violence "on the basis of religion." St. Paul has no such authority to license one side of a debate to fight freestyle, while requiring the other to follow Marquis of Queensbury Rules. [The rules governing boxing, named after the person who formulated them, Sir John Sholto Douglas, 8th Marquis of Queensbury.]

What we have here, it must be emphasized, is not a prohibition of fighting words that are directed at certain persons or groups (which would be *facially* valid if it met the requirements of the Equal Protection Clause); but rather, a prohibition of fighting words that contain (as the Minnesota Supreme Court repeatedly emphasized) messages of "bias-motivated" hatred and in particular, as applied to this case, messages "based on virulent notions of racial supremacy." One must wholeheartedly agree with the Minnesota Supreme Court that "[i]t is the responsibility, even the obligation, of diverse communities to confront such notions in whatever form they appear," but the manner of that confrontation cannot consist of selective limitations upon speech. St. Paul's brief asserts that a general "fighting words" law would not meet the city's need because only a content-specific measure can communicate to minority groups that the "group hatred" aspect of such speech "is not condoned by the majority." The point of the First Amendment is that majority preference must be expressed in some fashion other than silencing speech on the basis of its content....

The dispositive question in this case ... is whether content discrimination is reasonably necessary to achieve St. Paul's compelling interests; it plainly is not. An ordinance not limited to the favored topics, for example, would have precisely the same beneficial effect. In fact the only interest distinctively served by the content limitation is that of displaying the city council's special hostility towards the particular biases thus singled out. That is precisely what the First Amendment forbids. The politicians of St. Paul are entitled to express that hostility—but not through the means of imposing unique limitations upon speakers who (however benightedly) disagree....

WHITE, BLACKMUN, AND O'CONNOR, J.J., CONCURRING IN THE JUDGMENT, WITH STEVENS, J., JOINING IN PART

... [I]n the present case, the majority casts aside long-established First Amendment doctrine without the benefit of briefing and adopts an untried theory. This is hardly a judicious way of proceeding, and the Court's reasoning in reaching its result is transparently wrong.

This Court's decisions have plainly stated that expression falling within certain limited categories so lacks the values the First Amendment was designed to protect that the Constitution affords no protection to that expression....

We have not departed from this principle, emphasizing repeatedly that, "within the confines of [these] given classification[s], the evil to be restricted so overwhelmingly outweighs the expressive interests, if any, at stake that no process of case-by-case adjudication is required." [*New York v.*] *Ferber* [, 458 U.S. 747

(1982)]. This categorical approach has provided a principled and narrowly focused means for distinguishing between expression that the government may regulate freely and that which it may regulate on the basis of content only upon a showing of compelling need.

Today, however, the Court announces that earlier Courts did not mean their repeated statement that certain categories of expression are "not within the area of constitutionally protected speech." The present Court submits that such clear statements "must be taken in context" and are not "literally true."

To the contrary, those statements meant precisely what they said: The categorical approach is a firmly entrenched part of our First Amendment jurisprudence....

As I see it, the Court's theory does not work and will do nothing more than confuse the law. Its selection of this case to rewrite First Amendment law is particularly inexplicable, because the whole problem could have been avoided by deciding this case under settled First Amendment principles.

Although I disagree with the Court's analysis, I do agree with its conclusion: The St. Paul ordinance is unconstitutional. However, I would decide the case on overbreadth grounds....

BLACKMUN, J., CONCURRING

... I fear the Court has been distracted from its proper mission by the temptation to decide the issue over "politically correct" speech and "cultural diversity," neither of which is presented here. If this is the meaning of today's opinion, it is perhaps even more regrettable....

I concur in the judgment, however, because I agree ... that this particular ordinance reaches beyond fighting words to speech protected by the First Amendment.

STEVENS, J., CONCURRING IN THE JUDGMENT, WITH WHITE AND BLACKMUN, J.J., JOINING IN PART

... [W]hile I agree that the St. Paul ordinance is unconstitutionally overbroad for the reasons stated in Justice White's opinion, I write separately to suggest how the allure of absolute principles has skewed the analysis of both the majority and concurring opinions....

Drawing on broadly worded *dicta*, the Court establishes a near-absolute ban on content-based regulations of expression and holds that the First Amendment prohibits the regulation of fighting words by subject matter. Thus, while the Court rejects the "all-or-nothing-at-all" nature of the categorical approach, it promptly embraces an absolutism of its own: within a particular "proscribable" category of expression, the Court holds, a government must either proscribe *all* speech or no speech at all. This aspect of the Court's ruling fundamentally misunderstands the role and constitutional status of content-based regulations on speech, conflicts with the very nature of First Amendment jurisprudence, and disrupts well-settled principles of First Amendment law....

The St. Paul ordinance (as construed by the Court) regulates expressive activity that is wholly proscribable and does so not on the basis of viewpoint, but rather in recognition of the different harms caused by such activity. Taken together, these several considerations persuade me that the St. Paul ordinance is not an unconstitutional content-based regulation of speech. Thus, were the ordinance not overbroad, I would vote to uphold it.

QUESTIONS

1. Summarize the majority rule announced in *R.A.V.* Why did Justice Scalia's approach provoke such controversy on the Court, leading concurring justices to call it "folly" and "fantastical"? Is Justice Scalia's rule a triumph for the First Amendment, or might it ultimately undermine free speech by perhaps setting the stage for statutes banning all speech?

2. Identify the consensus regarding overbreadth expressed in the various opinions in *R.A.V.* How does Justice Scalia's opinion depart from that consensus?

3. Is Justice Blackmun correct that Justice Scalia's purpose in *R.A.V.* may have been to decide the controversy over "politically correct" speech and "cultural diversity"? Could the *R.A.V.* decision plausibly have that effect?

4. According to the Carnegie Foundation for the Advancement of Technology, in 1990 over sixty percent of colleges and universities it surveyed had developed or were developing written policies on bigotry, racial harassment, or sexual harassment on campus. Eleven percent of the remaining schools were working to establish similar restrictions on written, spoken, and symbolic speech (*A Special Report: Campus Life in Search of Community* [Princeton, NJ: Princeton

University Press, 1990]). If you were counsel to a college or university considering adopting regulations to counter "hate speech," how would you advise that such regulations be drafted to survive under the rule announced in *R.A.V.*? (You might find it instructive to consult Scott Jaschik, "Campus 'Hate Speech' Codes in Doubt after High Court Rejects a City Ordinance," *The Chronicle of Higher Education*, July 1, 1992, A19.)

COMMENT

Law professor Catharine MacKinnon was counsel of record for the *amicus* brief submitted on behalf of the National Black Women's Health Project in support of the St. Paul ordinance. Her brief argued that the state's compelling interest in eradicating discrimination justified any impact that application of the ordinance might have on the expressive freedoms of perpetrators of symbolic acts of bigotry.

In 1983 MacKinnon helped draft ordinances in Minneapolis and Indianapolis defining pornography as a discriminatory practice against women. Her arguments in favor of withdrawing constitutional protection from pornography and hate speech suggest that the First Amendment stands in the way of America being a society that recognizes the dignity and equality of groups traditionally denied such standing. Only the Indianapolis ordinance was enacted into law. It was overturned in *American Booksellers Association, Inc. v. Hudnut*, 771 F.2d 323 (7th Cir. 1985), and summarily affirmed, 475 U.S. 1001 (1986).

FIGHTING WORDS AND HATE SPEECH

Wisconsin v. Mitchell
508 U.S. 476 (1993)

SETTING

The Court's 1990 ruling in *R.A.V. v. St. Paul, Minnesota* raised more questions than it answered about the ability of policymakers to criminalize hate- and bias-motivated acts under the First Amendment. The 9–0 vote on the invalidity of the Minnesota statute called into question the hate-crime statutes that many state legislatures had adopted throughout the 1980s. Most of those statutes were patterned after a 1981 model drafted by the Anti-Defamation League of B'nai B'rith (ADL). The ADL approach bifurcates the judgment process in trials where bigotry is alleged. Once a jury has found an accused guilty of a crime— assault, for example—that same panel arrives at a separate judgment about whether the crime was motivated by hate or bias and, thus, is subject to a heightened penalty. If the jury finds hate or bias motivation, the convicted person's sentence is "enhanced." By 1993, twenty-seven states and the District of Columbia had such laws on their books.

Wisconsin v. Mitchell provided the Court with the chance to clarify its position with regard to these hate-crime statutes modeled on the ADL proposal. The case arose from an assault committed by a group of young black males against a fourteen-year-old white boy.

On the evening of October 7, 1989, a group of young black men and boys was gathered at the Renault apartment complex in Kenosha, Wisconsin, discussing a scene from the movie, *Mississippi Burning,* in which a young white man beat a young black boy who was praying. Nineteen-year-old Todd Mitchell joined the group about forty-five minutes after the conversation began. Several members of the group subsequently went outdoors, still talking about the movie. Mitchell asked, "Do you all feel hyped up to move on some white people?"

Soon thereafter, a fourteen-year-old white boy, Gregory Reddick, walked toward the apartment complex on the other side of the street. He said nothing to the group. As Reddick walked by, Mitchell asked his friends, "You all want to fuck somebody up? There goes a white boy; go get him." Mitchell counted to three, and pointed in Reddick's direction. Eight or ten of the black males ran across the street, knocked Reddick down, beat him severely, and stole his "British Knights" tennis shoes. Reddick was left unconscious. He suffered extensive injuries, and remained in a coma for four days.

Mitchell was charged with the felonies of aggravated battery and theft as a party to the crime. At trial it was established that, although Mitchell was not one of the group that actually attacked Reddick, he instigated the assault. Following his conviction by a jury in Kenosha County on lesser counts of battery and theft, the prosecuting attorney alleged and proved that Mitchell was subject to an enhanced sentence for the battery under Wisconsin's 1987 penalty enhancement statute for crimes directed at persons because of "race, religion, color, disability, sexual orientation, national origin or ancestry." The jury found that the state failed to meet its burden under the penalty enhancement provision regarding punishment for the theft conviction. However, the finding that Mitchell intentionally had selected Reddick as his victim because of Reddick's race subjected Mitchell to a possible additional five-year sentence beyond the two-year minimum sentence for felony battery. The trial judge imposed a four-year prison sentence for the aggravated battery, over Mitchell's objection that the penalty enhancement statute was unconstitutional.

Mitchell appealed the sentence to the Wisconsin Court of Appeals. He claimed that the penalty enhancement statute was vague and overbroad, in violation of the First Amendment, and that it violated his equal protection rights. The court of appeals rejected his vagueness argument and found that he had waived his equal protection claim. Mitchell appealed to the Wisconsin Supreme Court. It held the penalty enhancer statute "facially invalid" under the First Amendment because it "punished what the legislature has deemed to be offensive thought," and that it "violates the First Amendment indirectly by chilling free speech." The majority opinion relied heavily on *R.A.V. v. St. Paul*, particularly Justice Scalia's statement that "the only interest distinctively served by the content limitation is that of displaying the city council's special hostility towards the particular biases thus singled out. That is precisely what the First Amendment forbids." The Wisconsin Supreme Court did not address Mitchell's vagueness or equal protection claims.

The Attorney General of Wisconsin petitioned the Supreme Court of the United States for a writ of certiorari.

HIGHLIGHTS OF SUPREME COURT ARGUMENTS

BRIEF FOR WISCONSIN

◆ The Wisconsin penalty enhancement statute does not violate the First Amendment because it does not authorize punishment of any protected activity and does not chill free speech. The law is aimed at conduct that is also an act of discrimination. It authorizes an increased penalty only when the fact-finder determines that a crime has been committed, and that the offender selected the victim because of the victim's characteristics, such as race. Governments may treat two otherwise identical actors differently if the conduct of one was motivated by a desire to discriminate on the basis of a particular status.

◆ A statute that defines and sanctions discrimination is not facially invalid under the First Amendment merely because discriminatory acts reflect on the violator's beliefs. The state agrees that it may not prohibit the expression of an idea merely because it finds the idea offensive or disagreeable. However, a state may prohibit and punish discriminatory conduct that is unrelated to the suppression of speech or the punishment of beliefs.

◆ The penalty enhancement statute identifies a subset of crimes that have a dual nature: They are crimes and they are acts of discrimination. There is nothing novel about looking to the motive of a criminal offender when determining crime severity and the appropriate sanction.

◆ *R.A.V. v. St. Paul* does not govern this case. The St. Paul ordinance proscribed expression based on its content, while the Wisconsin statute does not on its face, or in effect, proscribe expression, beliefs, or thought.

◆ This statute does not punish offenders for utterances they make during their crimes. It is not plausible that people will alter their habits based on the possibility of being charged with a crime involving discrimination.

AMICUS CURIAE BRIEFS SUPPORTING WISCONSIN

United States; 31 states; American Civil Liberties Union; Anti-Defamation League; American Jewish Congress; People for the American Way; Center for Constitutional Rights; Center for Women Policy Studies; Fraternal Order of Police; Human Rights Campaign Fund; International Association of Chiefs of Police; National Council of Jewish Women; National Gay and Lesbian Task

Force; National Institute Against Prejudice and Violence; National Jewish Community Relations Advisory Council; National Organization of Black Law Enforcement Executives; Police Executive Research Forum; Southern Poverty Law Center; Union of American Hebrew Congregations; Jewish Advocacy Center; Crown Heights Coalition; NAACP Legal Defense and Education Fund, Inc.; American Jewish Committee; Chicago Lawyers' Committee for Civil Rights Under Law, Inc.; Criminal Justice Legal Foundation; National Asian Pacific American Legal Consortium; California Association of Human Rights Organizations; Center for Democratic Renewal; Community United Against Violence; Human Rights/Fair Housing Commission of Sacramento; International Association of Official Human Rights Agencies; Los Angeles County Human Relations Committee; National Association of Human Rights Workers; National Victim Center New York City Gay and Lesbian Anti-Violence Project; North Carolinians Against Racist and Religious Violence; Santa Clara County Human Relations Commission; 35 members of Congress; Appellate Committee of California District Attorneys Association; Lawyers' Committee for Civil Rights of San Francisco Bay Area; National Conference of State Legislatures; U.S. Conference of Mayors; National Governors' Association; International City/County Management Association; National Association of Counties; Council of State Governments; National Institute of Municipal Law Officers; National League of Cities; Cities of Atlanta, Baltimore, Boston, Chicago, Cleveland, Los Angeles, New York, Philadelphia, and San Francisco; Lawyers' Committee for Civil Rights Under Law.

BRIEF FOR MITCHELL

◆ Government cannot constitutionally increase penalties for criminal offenses solely because the defendant was motivated by bigoted thoughts and ideas of which government disapproves.

◆ The Wisconsin statute punishes conduct more severely because of the exercise of First Amendment rights. Bias elements in crimes may be used as evidence of neutral sentencing factors, but bias itself may not be considered an element of an offense. It is not narrowly tailored to achieve the state's legitimate goals. It chills speech and association protected by the First Amendment because proof of the bias motive rely virtually exclusively on a defendant's speech and association.

◆ This Court has held in *R.A.V. v. St. Paul* that the state's interest in regulating bias-motivated conduct cannot support regulation that draws distinctions on the basis of content and viewpoint.

◆ Civil antidiscrimination laws are readily distinguishable from the criminal enhancement statute. Those laws target discriminatory acts, while this law targets only motive.

◆ The Wisconsin penalty enhancement statute violates the Equal Protection Clause of the Fourteenth Amendment because it treats persons committing the same offenses differently, solely on the basis of their fundamental right to free thought and opinion.

AMICUS CURIAE BRIEFS SUPPORTING MITCHELL

Wisconsin Freedom of Information Council; California Attorneys for Criminal Justice; Center for Individual Rights; Seven criminal defense lawyers; Ohio Public Defender; Reason Foundation; Wisconsin Inter-Racial and Inter-Faith Coalition for Freedom of Thought; American Civil Liberties Union of Ohio; Wisconsin Association of Criminal Defense Lawyers.

SUPREME COURT DECISION: 9–0

REHNQUIST, C.J.

... We granted certiorari because of the importance of the question presented and the existence of a conflict of authority among state high courts on the constitutionality of statutes similar to Wisconsin's penalty-enhancement provision. We reverse....

Traditionally, sentencing judges have considered a wide variety of factors in addition to evidence bearing on guilt in determining what sentence to impose on a convicted defendant. The defendant's motive for committing the offense is one important factor. Thus, in many States the commission of a murder, or other capital offense, for pecuniary gain is a separate aggravating circumstance under the capital-sentencing statute.

But it is equally true that a defendant's abstract beliefs, however obnoxious to most people, may not be taken into consideration by a sentencing judge....

Mitchell argues that the Wisconsin penalty-enhancement statute is invalid because it punishes the defendant's discriminatory motive, or reason, for acting. But motive plays the same role under the Wisconsin statute as it does under federal and state antidiscrimination laws, which we have previously upheld against constitutional challenge....

Nothing in our decision last Term in *R.A.V.* compels a different result here.... Whereas the ordinance struck down in *R.A.V.* was explicitly directed at expression (*i.e.*, "speech" or "messages") the statute in this case is aimed at conduct unprotected by the First Amendment.

Moreover, the Wisconsin statute singles out for enhancement bias-inspired conduct because this conduct is thought to inflict greater individual and societal harm.... The State's desire to redress these perceived harms provides an adequate explanation for its penalty-enhancement provision over and above mere disagreement with offenders' beliefs or biases....

Finally, there remains to be considered Mitchell's argument that the Wisconsin statute is unconstitutionally overbroad because of its "chilling effect" on free speech....

The sort of chill envisioned here is far more attenuated and unlikely than that contemplated in traditional "overbreadth" cases. We must conjure up a vision of a Wisconsin citizen suppressing his unpopular bigoted opinions for fear that if he later commits an offense covered by the statute, these opinions will be offered at trial to establish that he selected his victim on account of the victim's protected status, thus qualifying him for penalty-enhancement. To stay within the realm of rationality, we must surely put to one side minor misdemeanor offenses covered by the statute, such as negligent operation of a motor vehicle, for it is difficult, if not impossible, to conceive of a situation where such offenses would be racially motivated. We are left, then with the prospect of a citizen suppressing his bigoted beliefs for fear that evidence of such beliefs will be introduced against him at trial if he commits a more serious offense against person or property. This is simply too speculative a hypothesis to support Mitchell's overbreadth claim.

The First Amendment, moreover, does not prohibit the evidentiary use of speech to establish the elements of a crime or to prove motive or intent. Evidence of a defendant's previous declarations or statements is commonly admitted in criminal trials subject to evidentiary rules dealing with relevancy, reliability, and the like....

For the foregoing reasons, we hold that Mitchell's First Amendment rights were not violated by the application of the Wisconsin penalty-enhancement provision in sentencing him. The judgment of the Supreme Court of Wisconsin is therefore reversed, and the case is remanded for further proceedings not inconsistent with this opinion.

It is so ordered.

QUESTIONS

1. What test did the Court employ in *Mitchell* to uphold the Wisconsin sentencing enhancement statute?

2. *Wisconsin v. Mitchell* pitted the national American Civil Liberties Union against one of its state affiliates. In separate *amicus* briefs, the American Civil Liberties Union supported Wisconsin while the American Civil Liberties Union of Ohio supported Mitchell. Identify the point or points of constitutional principle in this case that could divide an organization committed to the protection of individual liberties.

3. Did *Wisconsin v. Mitchell* clarify the confusion created by *R.A.V. v. St. Paul*? Identify challenges state and local officials face as they draft statutes and ordinances with both *R.A.V.* and *Mitchell* on the books. While thinking about these challenges, consider this question posed by law professor William W. Van Alstyne:

   > May *Mitchell* ... be less easy than it would seem? It is true that the defendant is not punished on account of what he says—whether to, or about, the person he assaults (and whether in scurrilous rather than nonscurrilous terms), but is it true that he is not being punished for his beliefs (or, if he is, that it is not a matter of any first amendment concern)? (*First Amendment: Cases and Materials*, 2nd ed. [Westbury, NY: Foundation Press, 1995])

4. Brian Levin, legal affairs director for the Center for the Study of Ethnic and Racial Violence, contended that "hate crimes, while rarely detected or prosecuted today, were 'very deterrable' if laws like the one the Court upheld ... were used effectively by prosecutors..." (*New York Times*, June 12, 1993, A8). Bob Purvis, legal director for the National Institute against Prejudice and Violence, noted, "Throughout

the country we find great inconsistencies. There are really only a handful of jurisdictions that have shown any real commitment" (Ibid).

In light of these comments, of what practical consequence is *Wisconsin v. Mitchell* likely to be in reducing crimes motivated by hate? Levin added that public awareness of laws like Wisconsin's might enhance their effectiveness in deterring hate crimes. Is Levin right?

COMMENT

Following *Wisconsin v. Mitchell*, Congress adopted the Violent Crime Control and Law Enforcement Act on September 13, 1994. One section of that law directs the U.S. Sentencing Commission to enhance the severity of sentences for hate crimes by adding time.

SUGGESTIONS FOR FURTHER READING

Amar, Akhil Reed, "The Case of the Missing Amendments: *R.A.V. v. City of St. Paul*," 106 *Harvard Law Review* (1992): 124.

Cleary, Edward J., *Beyond the Burning Cross: A Landmark Case of Race, Censorship, and the First Amendment* (New York, NY: Vintage, 1994).

Delgado, Richard, "Words That Wound: A Tort Action for Racial Insults, Epithets, and Name-Calling," 17 *Harvard Civil Rights-Civil Liberties Review* (1982).

_____, "Campus Antiracism Rules: Constitutional Narratives in Collision," 85 *Northwestern University Law Review* (1991): 343.

Delgado, Richard, and Jean Stefancic, *Must We Defend Nazis? Hate Speech, Pornography, and the New First Amendment* (New York, NY: New York University Press, 1997).

Fleisher, Marc, "Down the Passage Which We Should Not Take: The Folly of Hate Crime Legislation," 2 *Journal of Law and Policy* (1994): 1.

Fiss, Owen, *The Irony of Free Speech* (Cambridge, MA: Harvard University Press, 1996).

Gard, Stephen W., "Fighting Words as Free Speech," 58 *Washington University Law Quarterly* (1980): 531.

Grannis, Eric J., "Fighting Words and Fighting Freestyle: The Constitutionality of Penalty Enhancement for Bias Crimes," 94 *Columbia Law Review* (1993): 178.

Greenawalt, Kent, *Fighting Words: Individuals, Communities, and Liberties of Speech* (Princeton, NJ: Princeton University Press, 1995).

Grey, Thomas, "Civil Rights vs. Civil Liberties: The Case of Discriminatory Verbal Harassment," 8 *Social Philosophy and Policy* (1991): 81.

Gunther, Gerald, "Good Speech, Bad Speech—Should Universities Restrict

Expression that Is Racist or Otherwise Denigrating? No." 24 *Stanford Law Review* (1990): 7.

Heumann, Milton, and Thomas W. Church, eds. *Hate Speech on Campus: Cases, Case Studies, and Commentary* (Boston, MA: Northeastern University Press, 1997).

Lawrence, Charles, III, "If He Hollers Let Him Go: On Regulating Racist Speech on Campus," *Duke Law Review* (1990): 431.

MacKinnon, Catharine A., *Only Words* (Cambridge, MA: Harvard University Press, 1993).

Matsuda, Mari, "Public Response to Racist Speech: Considering the Victim's Story," 87 *Michigan Law Review* (1989): 2320.

Sedler, Robert, "Doe v. University of Michigan and Campus Bans on 'Racist Speech': The View from Within," 37 *Wayne Law Review* (1991): 1325.

Shiffrin, Steven H., "Racist Speech, Outsider Jurisprudence and the Meaning of America," 80 *Cornell Law Review* (1994): 43.

Walker, Samuel, *Hate Speech: The History of an American Controversy* (Lincoln, NE: University of Nebraska Press, 1994).

Wolfson, Nicholas, *Hate Speech, Sex Speech, Free Speech* (Westport, CT: Praeger Publishers, 1997).

SYMBOLIC SPEECH

United States v. O'Brien
391 U.S. 367 (1968)

SETTING

Another category the Supreme Court has created to analyze First Amendment questions is "symbolic speech." Although the label is a misleading, somewhat redundant, classification because every speech act—verbal and nonverbal—involves symbolism, the Supreme Court created the constitutional concept of symbolic speech in 1931. In *Stromberg v. California*, 283 U.S. 359, the Supreme Court invalidated a California law that made it a felony to display "a red flag, banner or badge or any flag, badge, banner, or device of any color or form whatever in any public place or in any meeting place or public assembly, or from or on any house, building or window as a sign, symbol or emblem of opposition to organized government or as an invitation or stimulus to anarchistic action or as an aid to propaganda that is of a seditious character." Chief Justice Hughes wrote:

> ... [W]ith respect to the display of the flag "as a sign, symbol or emblem of opposition to organized government" ... [t]he maintenance of the opportunity for free political discussion to the end that government may be responsive to the will of the people and that changes may be obtained by lawful

means, an opportunity essential to the security of the Republic, is a fundamental principle of our constitutional system

Thirty years after *Stromberg*, in *Brown v. Louisiana*, 383 U.S. 131 (1966),
Chief Justice Warren wrote that First Amendment rights "are not confined to
verbal expression...." The same year that *Brown v. Louisiana* was handed down,
the domestic debate over the war in Vietnam generated another case involving
symbolic speech.

American involvement in Vietnam had evolved over two decades. In the
late 1940s, following the Japanese withdrawal from Indo-China after World War
II, Communist guerilla fighters known as the Vietminh began waging war against
French occupiers in the jungles of the region. By 1953 they had overrun much
of the northern half of Vietnam. Fearing a communist takeover of Southeast
Asia, President Harry Truman sent a military mission to Saigon and increased
military aid to the French in Vietnam. The French were defeated and withdrew
from Vietnam in 1954, but the American presence grew stronger. By the fall of
1963, President John Kennedy had committed some sixteen thousand military
"advisers" to train South Vietnamese troops.

American military engagements in Vietnam increased dramatically during
the presidential administration of Lyndon Johnson, spurred by attacks from
Barry Goldwater during the 1964 presidential campaign that the United States'
"no win" policy in Vietnam would assure a communist victory. In August 1964,
Congress passed the Gulf of Tonkin Resolution, authorizing the president to
"take all necessary measures to repel any armed attack against the forces of the
United States and to prevent further aggression." Within just a few years, and
contrary to his 1964 campaign promise, Johnson had committed more than half
a million ground troops in Southeast Asia and had authorized extensive bombing of North Vietnam.

American involvement in the Vietnam War reached a pivotal point in 1965.
Sustained American bombing of North Vietnam began at the end of February.
The first American combat troops arrived on March 8 when marines landed to
defend Danang air base. By early July, eighteen combat battalions were sta-
tioned in the country, and President Johnson authorized an additional forty-
four battalions at the end of that month. American troop strength reached
200,000 by December. These escalations in American involvement in Vietnam
caused the nation to be torn with dissent. As American casualties mounted,
domestic concern over the costs of American involvement in that war began to
grow. Nonetheless, public support remained strong for continuing the
American commitment to South Vietnam, its ally, in the fight against communist
North Vietnam.

On a March morning in 1966, David Paul O'Brien and three other Vietnam
draft protestors burned small white cards (assumed to be their draft cards) on
the steps of the South Boston Courthouse. A sizable crowd, which included several Federal Bureau of Investigation (FBI) agents and representatives of the
news media, witnessed the event. Immediately after the burnings, members of
the crowd began attacking O'Brien and his companions. FBI agents ushered

O'Brien into the courthouse. He was arrested and charged with "willfully and knowingly" mutilating, destroying, and changing by burning his "Registration Certificate."

O'Brien was tried and convicted in the U.S. District Court for the District of Massachusetts for violating 50 U.S.C. App. § 462(b)(3), a 1965 amendment to the Universal Military Training and Service Act of 1948. The 1965 amendment, adopted in the midst of rising opposition to the Vietnam War, defined as an offense an act by any person "who forges, alters, knowingly mutilates, or in any manner changes any such certificate...." Rejecting O'Brien's argument that the 1965 amendment violated the First Amendment because it was enacted to abridge free speech, and because it served no legitimate legislative purpose, the district court concluded that it was not competent to examine the motives of Congress and that the amendment was a reasonable exercise of the congressional power to raise armies.

The First Circuit Court of Appeals reversed, holding that the 1965 amendment was "directed at public as distinguished from private destruction" and, hence, unconstitutionally abridged freedom of speech. Nevertheless, the appeals court found O'Brien's conduct punishable under a different section of the Universal Military Training and Service Act, 50 U.S.C. App. § 462(b)(6), which made it a crime to violate the Selective Service System regulation that registrants keep their registration certificate in their "personal possession at all times." The Supreme Court granted O'Brien's and the U.S. cross-petitions for writs of certiorari.

HIGHLIGHTS OF SUPREME COURT ARGUMENTS

BRIEF FOR THE UNITED STATES

◆ The 1965 amendment to the Universal Military Service and Training Act has at most an incidental and remote impact on First Amendment guarantees. It represents a reasonable exercise of Congress's power to facilitate the proper functioning of the Selective Service System.

◆ Even if the statute is unconstitutional, the court of appeals did not err in affirming O'Brien's conviction for nonpossession. When the jury convicted O'Brien of knowing destruction, it necessarily found all of the facts that it would have had to find under a charge of knowing failure to possess a draft card.

BRIEF FOR O'BRIEN

◆ The 1965 amendment to the Universal Military Training and Service Act is an unconstitutional abridgment of freedom of speech guaranteed by the First Amendment, because the legislative history unequivocally reveals a deliberate congressional intent to suppress freedom of speech.

◆ The statute seeks to punish a peaceful act of symbolic speech, conducted under circumstances which fall well within the limits of the clear and present danger test, and which, under a balancing test, compel a determination that the free speech consideration outweighs all countervailing considerations.

◆ Since the statute does not serve any rational legislative purpose, it is an unconstitutional deprivation of individual liberty contrary to the guarantee of substantive due process in the Fifth Amendment.

AMICUS CURIAE BRIEF SUPPORTING NEITHER PARTY

Joint brief of William Sloane Coffin Jr., Michael Ferber, Mitchell Goodman, Marcus Raskin, and Benjamin Spock.

SUPREME COURT DECISION: *7–1*

(Marshall, J., did not participate.)

WARREN, C.J.

... O'Brien first argues that the 1965 Amendment is unconstitutional as applied to him because his act of burning his registration certificate was protected "symbolic speech" within the First Amendment. His argument is that the freedom of expression which the First Amendment guarantees includes all modes of "communication of ideas by conduct," and that his conduct is within this definition because he did it in "demonstration against the war and against the draft."

We cannot accept the view that an apparently limitless variety of conduct can be labeled "speech" whenever the person engaging in the conduct intends thereby to express an idea. However, even on the assumption that the alleged communicative element in O'Brien's conduct is sufficient to bring into play the First Amendment, it does not necessarily follow that the destruction of a registration certificate is constitutionally protected activity. This Court has held that when "speech" and "nonspeech" elements are combined in the same course of conduct, a sufficiently important governmental interest in regulating the nonspeech element can justify incidental limi-

tations on First Amendment freedoms. To characterize the quality of the governmental interest which must appear, the Court has employed a variety of descriptive terms: compelling; substantial; subordinating; paramount; cogent; strong. Whatever imprecision inheres in these terms, we think it clear that a government regulation is sufficiently justified if it is within the constitutional power of the Government; if it furthers an important or substantial governmental interest; if the governmental interest is unrelated to the suppression of free expression; and if the incidental restriction on alleged First Amendment freedoms is no greater than is essential to the furtherance of that interest. We find that the 1965 Amendment to § 462(b)(3) of the Universal Military Training and Service Act meets all of these requirements, and consequently that O'Brien can be constitutionally convicted for violating it.

The constitutional power of Congress to raise and support armies and to make all laws necessary and proper to that end is broad and sweeping.... Pursuant to this power, Congress may establish a system of registration for individuals liable for training and service, and may require such individuals within reason to cooperate in the registration system. The issuance of certificates indicating the registration and eligibility classification of individuals is a legitimate and substantial administrative aid in the functioning of this system. And legislation to insure the continuing availability of issued certificates serves a legitimate and substantial purpose in the system's administration.

O'Brien's argument to the contrary is necessarily premised upon his unrealistic characterization of Selective Service certificates. He essentially adopts the position that such certificates are so many pieces of paper designed to notify registrants of their registration or classification, to be retained or tossed in the wastebasket according to the convenience or taste of the registrant. Once the registrant has received notification, according to this view, there is no reason for him to retain the certificates. O'Brien notes that most of the information on a registration certificate serves no notification purpose at all; the registrant hardly needs to be told his address and physical characteristics. We agree that the registration certificate contains much information of which the registrant needs no notification. This circumstance, however, does not lead to the conclusion that the certificate serves no purpose, but that, like the classification certificate, it serves purposes in addition to initial notification....

The many functions performed by Selective Service certificates establish beyond doubt that Congress has a legitimate and substantial interest in preventing their wanton and unrestrained destruction and assuring their continuing availability by punishing people who knowingly and wilfully destroy or mutilate them....

We think it apparent that the continu-ing availability to each registrant of his Selective Service certificates substantially furthers the smooth and proper functioning of the system that Congress has established to raise armies. We think it also apparent that the Nation has a vital interest in having a system for raising armies that functions with maximum efficiency and is capable of easily and quickly responding to continually changing circumstances. For these reasons, the Government has a substantial interest in assuring the continuing availability of issued Selective Service certificates.

It is equally clear that the 1965 Amendment specifically protects this substantial governmental interest. We perceive no alternative means that would more precisely and narrowly assure the continuing availability of issued Selective Service certificates than a law which prohibits their wilful mutilation or destruction....

O'Brien finally argues that the 1965 Amendment is unconstitutional as enacted because what he calls the "purpose" of Congress was "to suppress freedom of speech." We reject this argument because under settled principles the purpose of Congress, as O'Brien uses that term, is not a basis for declaring this legislation unconstitutional.

It is a familiar principle of constitutional law that this Court will not strike down an otherwise constitutional statute on the basis of an alleged illicit legislative motive....

Inquiries into congressional motives or purposes are a hazardous matter. When the issue is simply the interpretation of legislation, the Court will look to statements by legislators for guidance as to the purpose of the legislature, because the benefit to sound decision-making in this circumstance is thought sufficient to risk the possibility of misreading Congress' purpose. It is entirely a different matter when we are asked to void a statute that is, under well-settled criteria, constitutional on its face, on the basis of what fewer than a handful of Congressmen said about it. What motivates one legislator to make a speech about a statute is not necessarily what motivates scores of others to enact it, and the stakes are sufficiently high for us to eschew guesswork. We decline to void essentially on the ground that it is unwise legislation which Congress had the undoubted power to enact and which could be reenacted in its exact form if the same or another legislator made a "wiser" speech about it.

HARLAN, J., CONCURRING [OMITTED]

DOUGLAS, J., DISSENTING

The Court states that the constitutional power of Congress to raise and support armies is "broad and sweeping" and that Congress' power "to classify and conscript manpower for military service is "beyond question." This is undoubtedly true in times when, by declaration of Congress, the Nation is in a state of war. The underlying and basic problem in this case, however, is whether conscription is permissible in the absence of a declaration of war. That question has not been briefed nor was it presented in oral argument; but it is, I submit, a question upon which the litigants and the country are entitled to a ruling.... It is time that we made a ruling. This case should be put down for reargument and heard[.]...

COMMENT

Bernard Schwartz sheds light on the opinion-drafting process in *O'Brien*:

> Warren's draft opinion tried to avoid handling the case in traditional First Amendment terms. It was based upon classification of conduct in verbal and nonverbal categories. O'Brien's act was considered a nonverbal communicative act outside the amendment's protection. According to the draft, "an act unrelated to the employment of language or other inherently expressive symbols is not speech within the First Amendment if as a matter of fact the act has an immediate harmful impact not completely apart from any impact arising by virtue of the claimed communication itself."
>
> ... [P]articularly Harlan and Brennan were disturbed. Harlan circulated a concurrence criticizing the Chief's approach.... Brennan wanted Warren to recognize that the conduct involved did fall within First Amendment protection, but that the interest in regulating it was compelling.
>
> ... The revised draft [opinion] embodied much of the approach that Brennan had suggested. It recognized that the communicative element in O'Brien's conduct brought the First Amendment into play. But it found that the government had a *substantial* interest (not the *compelling* interest Brennan had urged was necessary) in assuring the continuing availability of draft cards which justified the law prohibiting their destruction. (*Super Chief: Earl Warren and His Supreme Court—A Judicial Biography* [New York, NY: New York University Press, 1983], pp. 684–685)

QUESTIONS

1. On what basis does Chief Justice Warren in *O'Brien* draw the line separating protected "speech" from unprotected expressive conduct?

2. Law professor John Hart Ely describes the First Amendment analysis employed in *O'Brien* as involving three elements: a government regulation is justified "(1) if it furthers an important or substantial governmental interest; (2) if the governmental interest is unrelated to the suppression of free expression; and (3) if the incidental restriction on alleged First Amendment freedoms is no greater than is essential to the furtherance of that interest" ("Flag Desecration: A Case Study in the Roles of Categorization and Balancing in First Amendment Analysis," 88 *Harvard Law Review* [1975]: 1482).

   Does the *O'Brien* opinion indicate that the justices subscribe to Ely's analytical framework?

3. At trial, David O'Brien offered the jury this explanation for his actions:

   > I am a pacifist and as such I cannot kill, and I would not cooperate.
   >
   > I later began to feel that there is necessity, not only to personally not kill, but to try to urge others to take this action, to urge other people to refuse to cooperate with murder.
   >
   > So I decided to publicly burn my draft card, hopefully so that other people would reevaluate their positions with Selective Service, with the armed forces, and reevaluate their place in the culture of today, to hopefully consider my position.
   >
   > And I don't contest the fact that I did burn my draft card, because I did.
   >
   > It is something that I felt I had to do, because I think we are basically living in a culture today, a society that is basically violent, it is basically a plagued society, plagued not only by wars, but by the basic inability on the part of people to look at other people as human beings, the inability to feel that we can live and love one another, and I think we can.
   >
   > So in a sense I think we are all on trial today. We all have to decide one way or the other what we want to do, whether we are going to accept death or whether we will fight to sustain life.

   What part should the speaker's motivations play in analyzing whether speech—verbal or symbolic—is entitled to constitutional protection? What about hate speech? Fighting words?

4. At the time they submitted their *amicus* brief, William Sloane Coffin Jr., Michael Ferber, Mitchell Goodman, Marcus Raskin, and Benjamin Spock were defendants under federal indictment for criminal conspiracy. All were antiwar activists opposed to American involvement in the Vietnam War. They had been charged, among other things, with conspiring to counsel persons to commit acts allegedly in violation of the selective service laws. Their brief contended that: "It would be regrettable ... if this Court, in the course of deciding the *O'Brien* case, were to foreclose future judicial consideration on a fully developed factual record of the many complex questions of governmental regulation of speech arising in the case of the *amici curiae*."

   What aspects of the *O'Brien* case might have caused these five defendants to worry about prospects for their own defense? What does the concern they articulated reveal about the ways in which people who are politically allied on some issues find themselves strategically at odds in litigation?

SYMBOLIC SPEECH

Tinker v. Des Moines Independent Community School District
393 U.S. 503 (1969)

SETTING

The Vietnam War caused a deep rift among Americans of all ages and social classes. Antiwar protests took many forms and were not limited to large public demonstrations. On December 16, 1965, for example, Mary Beth Tinker wore a black armband to her eighth-grade class at Warren Harding Junior High School in Des Moines, Iowa. She wore it to mourn those who were dying in Vietnam. That same day, Chris Eckhardt, a Tinker family friend, wore a black armband to Des Moines' Roosevelt High School. Both Tinker and Eckhardt were suspended for defying the school district's rule against wearing armbands. The next day, three more students, including Tinker's brother, John, were suspended for wearing a black armband to class at Des Moines' North High School.

The suspensions were based on a regulation adopted by the Des Moines Independent Community School District on December 14, in response to a rumor that several students intended to wear black armbands to school to protest the Vietnam War. The regulation prohibited the wearing of armbands on all school property. School board president Ora Niffenegger defended the "disciplinary measure" as necessary to prevent "disturbance" of the educational program.

Although no commotion or disturbance occurred when the Tinkers and Eckhardt wore their armbands to school, their actions and their consequent suspensions caused a deep rift in the Des Moines community. Local press coverage reflected the residents' conflicting opinions and feelings. The *Des Moines Register* printed its account of the armband controversy in a column adjoining a story about the Vietnam combat death of nineteen-year-old paratrooper Pvt. James Flagg, who had graduated from North High School. The *Register* reported that Roosevelt High senior Ross Peterson wore black clothing to school and was slugged in the mouth during lunch break. Another story contained suspended student Bruce Clark's claim that Donald Prior, the Roosevelt High football coach, had called the students who wore armbands "Communists" and that coach Prior had encouraged students in gym class to shout "Beat the Viet Cong!" as they did jumping-jacks. "They are proving their Americanism," Coach Prior said. "They are on the side of President Johnson." The *Register*'s own opinion was made clear by an editorial cartoon picturing an American soldier stabbed in the back with a knife. The knife was labeled "Viet Cong Propaganda."

On December 21, two hundred people jammed a meeting of the Des Moines School Board. A spirited two-hour public debate ensued during which both sides of the armband controversy aired their opinions. After unsuccessfully attempting to postpone any action on the issue, the School Board voted 4–3 to continue its policy prohibiting the wearing of armbands.

The following March, the Iowa Civil Liberties Union filed a complaint in U.S. District Court for the Southern District of Iowa on behalf of the Tinkers and Eckhardt. The suit sought to enjoin the Des Moines Independent Community School District from disciplining or suspending the young protesters and from interfering with their exercise of free speech.

Following an evidentiary hearing, the district court dismissed the complaint. It held that the school board's concern for "the disciplined atmosphere of the classroom" was paramount and that, because "reactions and comments from other students as a result of the armbands would be likely to disturb the disciplined atmosphere required for any classroom," the prohibition on armbands was reasonable. The court expressly declined to follow the holding of the Fifth Circuit Court of Appeals in a similar case that wearing of symbols like armbands cannot be prohibited unless it "materially and substantially interferes with the requirements of appropriate discipline in the operation of the school." *Burnside v. Byars*, 363 F.2d 744 (1966). The U.S. Court of Appeals for the Eighth Circuit, sitting *en banc*, was evenly divided, thereby affirming the district court's dismissal without opinion. The Supreme Court granted the Tinkers' and Eckhardt's petition for a writ of certiorari.

Highlights of Supreme Court Arguments

BRIEF FOR TINKERS AND ECKHARDT

◆ The First Amendment protects the free speech rights of public school students in their schools and classrooms. The Court has decided a series of cases holding that the constitutional rights of students are protected against infringement by state and school authorities. In the most recent case, *In Re Gault*, 387 U.S. 1 (1967), the Court observed that the "Bill of Rights is [not] for adults alone."

◆ The school district's prohibition against the wearing of armbands is an unconstitutional prior restraint on free speech. The prohibition was adopted in anticipation of the wearing of armbands, which is a form of expression that is dignified, peaceful, not intended to disrupt, and which is not significantly different from other types of expression that have been permitted by school officials. In the past, school officials have allowed the wearing of religious symbols, political buttons, and the Iron Cross, a symbol associated with Hitler's Third Reich.

◆ The school district's prohibition against armbands has the direct effect of suppressing free speech; the suppression is not an incidental limit on free speech while furthering an otherwise valid state interest. Since political insignia have been allowed on school property before, and since there is no evidence that the wearing of armbands would cause a disturbance, the prohibition singled out these students' political protest, an act that cuts into the core of what the First Amendment was designed to protect: the expression of unpopular views.

◆ Even if other students had reacted with hostility to the armbands, it would have been the responsibility of school officials to discipline them, rather than to deny Tinkers and Eckhardt the right to express themselves.

AMICUS CURIAE BRIEF SUPPORTING TINKERS AND ECKHARDT

The U.S. National Student Association.

BRIEF FOR DES MOINES INDEPENDENT SCHOOL DISTRICT

◆ School officials have a duty to maintain a scholarly, disciplined atmosphere in the classroom, a duty that requires wide discretion. Except for the prompt action by school administrators, the situation in Des Moines might well have developed into the type of disruptive demonstration that has erupted throughout the United States during the past few years.

◆ This case is governed by *Adderley v. State of Florida*, 385 U.S. 39 (1966), in which the Court rejected the argument that protesters have the right to demonstrate on courthouse and jailhouse lawns. In that case, the Court held that people do not have a right to protest "whenever and however and wherever they please." The Constitution does not forbid a state from controlling the use of its own property for lawful, nondiscriminatory purposes, which is what occurred in the Des Moines situation.

◆ The state has no duty under the Constitution to have its facilities used as a stage for the expression of dissident ideas. No matter what the rights of the students or parents (who in this case are professional protesters), they should not be permitted to infiltrate the schools with demonstrations and disrupt the scholarly discipline that is necessary to a school room.

◆ The school district's prohibition on armbands is reasonably calculated to promote discipline in the schools. On several occasions this Court has held that it is not for courts to consider whether a rule is expedient or wise as long as it is a reasonable exercise of the discretion of school authorities. The armband policy was affirmed by the school board following a hearing and investigations based on the board's judgment about the disturbances that could arise if armbands were worn.

SUPREME COURT DECISION: 7–2

FORTAS, J.

... First Amendment rights, applied in light of the special characteristics of the school environment, are available to teachers and students. It can hardly be argued that either students or teachers shed their constitutional rights to freedom of speech or expression at the schoolhouse gate....

On the other hand, the Court has repeatedly emphasized the need for affirming the comprehensive authority of the States and of school officials, consistent with fundamental constitutional safeguards, to prescribe and control conduct in the schools.... Our problem lies in the area where students in the exercise of First Amendment rights collide with the rules of the school authorities.

The problem posed by the present case does not relate to regulation of the length of skirts or the type of clothing, to hair style, or deportment.... It does not concern aggressive, disruptive action or even group demonstrations. Our problem involves direct, primary First Amendment rights akin to "pure speech."

The school officials banned and sought to punish petitioners for a silent, passive expression of opinion, unaccompanied by any disorder or disturbance on the part of petitioners. There is here no evidence whatever of petitioners' interference, actual or nascent, with the schools' work or of collision with the rights of other students to be secure and to be let alone. Accordingly, this case does not concern speech or action that intrudes upon the work of the schools or the rights of other students....

The District Court concluded that the action of the school authorities was reasonable because it was based upon their fear of a disturbance from the wearing of the armbands. But, in our system, undifferentiated fear or apprehension of disturbance is not enough to overcome the right to freedom of expression. Any departure from absolute regimentation may cause trouble. Any variation from the majority's opinion may inspire fear. Any word spoken, in class, in the lunchroom, or on the campus, that deviates from the views of another person may start an argument or cause a disturbance. But our Constitution says we must take this risk ... and our history says that it is this sort of hazardous freedom—this kind of openness—that is the basis of our national strength and of the independence and vigor of Americans who grow up and live in this relatively permissive, often disputatious, society.

In order for the State in the person of school officials to justify prohibition of a particular expression of opinion, it must be able to show that its action was caused by something more than a mere desire to avoid the discomfort and unpleasantness that always accompany an unpopular viewpoint....

In the present case, the District Court made no such finding, and our independent examination of the record fails to yield evidence that the school authorities had reason to anticipate that the wearing of the armbands would substantially interfere with the work of the school or impinge upon the rights of other students. Even an official memorandum prepared after the suspension that listed the reasons for the ban on wearing the armbands made no reference to the anticipation of such disruption.

On the contrary, the action of the school authorities appears to have been based upon an urgent wish to avoid the controversy which might result from the expression, even by the silent symbol of armbands, of opposition to this Nation's part in the conflagration in Vietnam. It is revealing, in this respect, that the meeting at which the school principals decided to issue the contested regulation was called in response to a student's statement to the journalism teacher in one of the schools that he wanted to write an article on Vietnam and have it published in the school paper. (The student was dissuaded.)

It is also relevant that the school authorities did not purport to prohibit the wearing of all symbols of political or controversial significance. The record shows that students in some of the schools wore buttons relating to national political campaigns, and some even wore the Iron Cross, traditionally a symbol of Nazism. The order prohibiting the wearing of armbands did not extend to these. Instead, a particular symbol—black armbands worn to exhibit opposition to this Nation's involvement in Vietnam—was singled out for prohibition. Clearly, the prohibition of expression of one particular opinion, at least without evidence that it is necessary to avoid material and substantial interference with schoolwork or discipline, is not constitutionally permissible.

In our system, state-operated schools may not be enclaves of totalitarianism. School officials do not possess absolute authority over their students. Students in school as well as out of school are "persons" under our Constitution. They are possessed of fundamental rights which the State must respect, just as they themselves must respect their obligations to the State. In our system, students may not be regarded as closed-circuit recipients of only that which the State chooses to communicate. They may not be confined to the expression of those sentiments that are officially approved. In the absence of a specific showing of constitutionally valid reasons to regulate their speech, students are entitled to freedom of expression of their views....

The principle of these cases is not confined to the supervised and ordained discussion which takes place in the classroom. The principal use to which the schools are dedicated is to accommodate students during prescribed hours for the purpose of certain types of activities. Among those activities is personal intercommunication among the students. This is not only an inevitable part of the process of attending school; it is also an important part of the educational process. A student's rights, therefore, do not embrace merely the classroom hours. When he is in the cafeteria, or on the playing field, or on the campus during the authorized hours, he may express his opinions, even on controversial subjects like the conflict in Vietnam[.]... But conduct by the student, in class or out of it, which for any reason—whether it stems from time, place, or type of behavior—materially disrupts classwork or involves substantial disorder or invasion of the rights of others is, of course, not immunized by the constitutional guarantee of freedom of speech....

Reversed and remanded.

STEWART, J., CONCURRING

Although I agree with much of what is said in the Court's opinion, and with its judgment in this case, I cannot share the Court's uncritical assumption that, school discipline aside, the First Amendment rights of children are co-extensive with those of adults....

WHITE, J., CONCURRING [OMITTED]

BLACK, J., DISSENTING

The Court's holding in this case ushers in what I deem to be an entirely new era in which the power to control pupils by the elected "officials of state supported public schools ..." in the United States is in ultimate effect transferred to the Supreme Court....

Assuming that the Court is correct in holding that the conduct of wearing arm bands for the purpose of conveying political ideas is protected by the First Amendment the crucial remaining questions are whether students and teachers may use the schools at their whim as a platform for the exercise of free speech—"symbolic" or "pure"—and whether the courts will allocate to themselves the function of deciding how the pupils' school day will be spent. While I have always believed that under the First and Fourteenth Amendments neither the State nor the Federal Government has any authority to regulate or censor the content of speech, I have never believed that any person has a right to give speeches or engage in demonstrations where he pleases and when he pleases....

The original idea of schools, which I do not believe is yet abandoned as worthless or out of date, was that children had not yet reached the point of experience and wisdom which enabled them to teach all of their elders. It may be that the Nation has outworn the old-fashioned slogan that "children are to be seen not heard," but one may, I hope, be permitted to harbor the thought that taxpayers send children to school on the premise that at their age they need to learn, not teach....

One does not need to be a prophet or the son of a prophet to know that after the Court's holding today some students in Iowa schools and indeed in all schools will be ready, able, and willing to defy their teachers on practically all orders. This is the more unfortunate for the schools since groups of students all over the land are already running loose, conducting break-ins, sit-ins, lie-ins, and smash-ins.... Students engaged in such activities are apparently confident that they know far more about how to operate public school systems than do their parents, teachers, and elected school officials. It is no answer to say that the particular students here have not yet reached such high points in their demands to attend classes in order to exercise their political pressures. Turned loose with lawsuits for damages and injunctions against their teachers as they are here, it is nothing but wishful thinking to imagine that young, immature students will not soon believe it is their right to control the schools rather than the right of the States that collect the taxes to hire the teachers for the benefit of the pupils. This case, therefore, wholly without constitutional reasons in my judgment, subjects all the public schools in the country to the whims and caprices of their loudest-mouthed, but maybe not their brightest, students. I, for one, am not fully persuaded that school pupils are wise enough, even with this Court's expert help from Washington, to run the 23,390 public school systems in our 50 States. I wish, therefore, wholly to disclaim any purpose on my part to hold that the Federal Constitution compels the teachers, parents, and elected school officials to surrender control of the American public school system to public school students. I dissent.

HARLAN, J., DISSENTING [OMITTED]

QUESTIONS

1. Apparently, the Tinker and Eckhardt children benefited judicially from the fact that no violence or school disruption attended their wearing of black armbands. Should the Court's ruling have been influenced by the absence of disruptions? More generally, should the protection of fundamental rights be contingent on the conditions surrounding their exercise?

2. In his *Tinker* concurrence, Justice Stewart wrote that he did not agree that the First Amendment rights of children are coextensive with those of adults. Which First Amendment rights do adults and children share, and which do they not? On what basis should any particular First Amendment right be assigned to one population category or the other?

3. Can Justice Black's reasoning in his bristling *Tinker* dissent be reconciled with his well-known view that the First Amendment's protection of speech should be read as an absolute bar against regulation? Political scientist Glendon Schubert ventured the opinion that Black's later views could be explained in terms of "a socio-psychological explanation of cultural [obsolescence] and ... a biological explanation of psychophysiological senescence [aging]," and that Black might have been "the only one of the justices who had reacted, rightly or wrongly, to the real world of the sixties" (quoted in Gerald T. Dunne, *Hugo Black and the Judicial Revolution* [New York, NY: Simon & Schuster, 1977], p. 419).

   Which of Schubert's explanations, if either, is convincing? Might there be principled, doctrinal reasons for Justice Black's refusal to extend First Amendment protection to school children wearing black armbands?

4. In *Tinker*, the Court recognized wearing armbands as a form of "symbolic speech." Arguing against the distinction between symbolic speech and "pure" speech in constitutional doctrine, law professor Melville B. Nimmer observed:

   > [I]n one sense all speech is symbolic. At this moment the reader is observing black markings on paper which curl and point in various directions. We call such markings letters, and in groups they are referred to as words. What is being said in this sentence is meaningful only because the reader recognizes these markings as symbols for particular ideas. The same is true for oral speech which is simply the use of symbolic sounds. Outside the science fiction realm of mind-to-mind telepathic communication, all communications necessarily involve the use of symbols. (*Encyclopedia of the American Constitution*, 4 vols. [New York, NY: Macmillan, 1986], 4: 1843)

   Even if Professor Nimmer's understanding of speech is correct, is not the distinction between "pure speech" and "symbolic speech" valid in a constitutional context? If the distinction is valid, how should the limits of symbolic speech be defined?

COMMENT

The Court has dealt with several other aspects of symbolic protest speech since *Tinker*. The following summaries illustrate the Court's approach. Three of these decisions—*Smith v. Goguen*, 415 U.S. 566 (1973), *Spence v. Washington*, 418 U.S. 405 (1974), and *Texas v. Johnson*, 491 U.S. 397 (1989)—are flag desecration cases and pertain to *United States v. Eichman*, 496 U.S. 310 (1990), the next case excerpted.

Case: *Schacht v. United States*, 398 U.S. 58 (1970)
Vote: 9–0
Decision: Conviction of an actor dressed in an army uniform during an antiwar production for unauthorized wearing of such attire violates the First Amendment. A federal statute permitting an actor portraying a member of the armed forces to wear a uniform "if the portrayal does not tend to discredit that armed force" denies the constitutional right of the actor to attack the armed forces in a theatrical production as part of an antiwar demonstration.

Case: *Smith v. Goguen*, 415 U.S. 566 (1973)
Vote: 6–3
Decision: The Massachusetts flag misuse statute is vague and overly broad in attaching criminal liability to one who "treats contemptuously" the American flag. Wearing a small cloth version of the flag on the seat of blue jeans is not punishable under the statute because the wearer had inadequate notice or warning of what action constituted a violation.

Case: *Spence v. Washington*, 418 U.S. 405 (1974)
Vote: 6–3
Decision: Hanging an American flag out the window upside down with a peace symbol made of removable black tape attached to it is the expression of an idea through activity. The antiwar message was peaceful, direct, likely to be understood, and within the contours of the First Amendment.

Case: *Clark v. Committee for Creative Non-Violence*, 468 U.S. 288 (1984)
Vote: 7–2
Decision: A National Park Service regulation prohibiting camping in certain national parks is a reasonable regulation of expression. Denial of permit to sleep in Lafayette Park in Washington, D.C., to demonstrate the plight of the homeless in America is not a violation of an organization's First Amendment rights. Reasonable time, place, and manner restrictions on the exercise of the First Amendment are valid.

Case: *Boos v. Barry*, 485 U.S. 312 (1988)
Vote: 6–2 (Kennedy, J., did not participate.)
Decision: A District of Columbia provision prohibiting display of signs that tend to bring foreign governments into "public odium" or "public disrepute," within five hundred feet of embassies, is a con-

tent-based restriction on political speech not narrowly tailored to serve a compelling state interest and thus violates the First Amendment.

Case: *Texas v. Johnson*, 491 U.S. 397 (1989)

Vote: 5–4

Decision: Conviction for intentionally desecrating an American flag, defined in the statute as a "venerated object," during the 1984 Republican National Convention, violates the First Amendment. The conduct prosecuted was protected expression and the state's interest in preserving the flag as a symbol of nationhood and national unity does not survive the most exacting scrutiny. "If there is a bedrock principle underlying the First Amendment, it is that the Government may not prohibit the expression of an idea simply because society finds the idea itself offensive or disagreeable."

SYMBOLIC SPEECH

United States v. Eichman
496 U.S. 310 (1990)

SETTING

The American flag is at once a potent and malleable symbol of patriotism. For many, "Old Glory" stands for unquestioning loyalty to country and it must be protected. For others, the American flag represents a means of communicating principled opposition and it may be modified, defiled, or even destroyed. For still others, American flags are catchy designs that can be employed in advertising. Over the years, this mixture of veneration, resistance, and commerce has proven highly conducive to controversy.

Around the turn of the nineteenth century, fear of immigrants, opposition to unions and socialist ideas, and general anxiety about disorder in a society undergoing fundamental changes fueled a highly successful American flag protection movement. Between 1890 and 1943, nine flag desecration bills were adopted by either the House of Representatives or the Senate but, before 1968, Congress had enacted only legislation that established without sanction a protocol or set of norms suggested as appropriate treatment and forms of respect for the flag of the United States. Until 1968, statutes criminalizing certain forms of hostile treatment of the American flag—with the exception of federal legislation relating to the District of Columbia—were the handiwork of state legislatures. Between 1897 and 1905, thirty-one states, and the New Mexico and Arizona Territories, adopted laws banning flag desecration.

In 1907 the Supreme Court of the United States upheld a Nebraska statute against a challenge that the desecration ban deprived two brewers of the liberty of using their property without due process of law. Nicholas V. Halter and

Harry V. Hayward had been convicted of having "printed and painted a representation of the flag of the United States" on labels of their "Stars and Stripes" beer. "Such a use," wrote Justice Harlan. "tends to degrade and cheapen the flag in the estimation of the people, as well as to defeat the object of maintaining it as an emblem of national power and national honor." *Halter v. Nebraska,* 205 U.S. 34 (1907).

Eighty-two years after *Halter,* the Supreme Court touched off a political furor with its sharply divided ruling in another flag desecration case, *Texas v. Johnson,* 491 U.S. 397 (1989). Five justices voted to reverse Gregory Johnson's conviction for "desecration of a venerated object," which resulted from his burning a flag during a political demonstration outside the 1984 Republican National Convention in Dallas, Texas. Writing for the Court, Justice Brennan invoked the standard formulated in *United States v. O'Brien,* but concluded: "If there is a bedrock principle underlying the First Amendment, it is that the government may not prohibit the expression of an idea simply because society finds the idea itself offensive or disagreeable." Chief Justice Rehnquist and Justices White, O'Connor, and Stevens dissented.

The Court's *Johnson* decision immediately ignited controversy. The Senate passed a resolution, 97–3, expressing "profound disappointment" with *Johnson.* The House followed suit, voting 411–15 its "profound concern" with the decision, then remaining in session all night to hear speeches attacking flag burners. President Bush proposed a constitutional amendment banning flag burning within a week of the Court's decision being announced. Over 170 House members and 43 Senators immediately signed on as cosponsors. For a time after June 21, when *Johnson* was announced, it appeared as though the movement for a constitutional amendment banning flag burning was a juggernaut incapable of being stopped. Toward October, however, the movement stalled, partly because both Houses of Congress had overwhelmingly passed the Flag Protection Act of 1989 (FPA). The House Judiciary Committee Report on the FPA specified:

> The bill responds to [the *Texas v. Johnson*] decision ... by amending the current Federal flag statute to make it content-neutral: that is, the amended statute focuses exclusively on the conduct of the actor, irrespective of any expressive message he or she might be intending to convey. The bill serves the national interest in protecting the physical integrity of all American flags in all circumstances. This interest is "unrelated to the suppression of free expression." *United States v. O'Brien.*

The FPA passed 380–38 in the House of Representatives, 91–9 in the Senate. President Bush allowed the bill to become law without signing it. He expressed "serious doubts that [the legislation] can withstand Supreme Court review," and made clear his position "that a constitutional amendment is the only way to ensure that our flag is protected from desecration." One FPA provision criminalized the conduct of anyone who "knowingly mutilates, defaces, physically defiles, burns, maintains on the floor or ground, or tramples upon" a U.S. flag, except conduct related to the disposal of a "worn or soiled" flag. Another provision mandated expedited Supreme Court review following any ruling on the FPA by a federal district court.

On October 30, a rally was held to protest the FPA. To test its provisions, Shawn D. Eichman, David Gerald Blalock, and Scott W. Tyler each set an American flag on fire. The protesters distributed a leaflet reading:

> The battle lines are drawn. On one side stands the government and all those in favor of compulsory patriotism and enforced rever[e]nce to the flag. On the other side are all those opposed to this. And to all the oppressed we have this to say also. This flag means one thing to the powers that be and something else to all of us. Ever[y]thing bad this system has done and continues to do to people all over this world has been done under this flag. No law, no amendment will change it, cover it up, or stiffle [sic] that truth. So to you we say, Express yourself! Burn this flag, It's quick, it's easy, it may not be the law, but it's the right thing to do.

Eichman was arrested and charged with violating the FPA. His motion to dismiss was granted by the U.S. District Court for the District of Columbia. In a case stemming from a similar demonstration in Seattle, Washington, on October 28, *United States v. Haggerty*, a motion to dismiss was granted by the U.S. District Court for the Western District of Washington. The federal government appealed both decisions to the Supreme Court, which noted probable jurisdiction and consolidated the two cases.

HIGHLIGHTS OF SUPREME COURT ARGUMENTS

BRIEF FOR UNITED STATES

◆ Longstanding precedents provide that the First Amendment does not apply where (1) the speech or expressive conduct is narrowly and precisely defined; (2) the value of the expression to the speaker is outweighed by its demonstrable destructive effect on society as a whole; and (3) the speaker has suitable alternative means to express whatever protected expression may be part of the intended message. Those constraining principles apply to the burning of the flag of the United States because flag burning is an assault on the nation's unique symbol and an assault on the most deeply shared experiences of the American people.

◆ The United States does not dispute that the flag burning in this case constitutes expressive conduct or that the FPA was enacted to prohibit that narrow category of "symbolic speech." The Court should expand the categories of expressive conduct that are not entitled to First Amendment protection. Flag burning, like obscene materials, defamatory statements, and a variety of other expressive conduct, presents substantial evils incompatible with the purpose for which government was instituted.

◆ *Texas v. Johnson*, 491 U.S. 397 (1989), involved a state law. This case concerns the Flag Protection Act of 1989, a federal statute enacted in response to *Johnson*. This Court has long acknowledged the customary deference due to acts of Congress. This Court has not had an occasion to address the

Congressional determination to protect the physical integrity of the American flag that led to enactment of the FPA. To the extent that the Court in *Johnson* held that flag burning is a form of expressive conduct meriting full First Amendment protection, that decision should be reconsidered.

◆ The FPA ensures that only unprotected expression will be prosecuted. There is no danger that a person will be prosecuted under the statute for what the person says about the flag.

AMICUS CURIAE BRIEFS SUPPORTING THE UNITED STATES

Senator Joseph Biden; New York Governor Mario M. Cuomo; Speaker and Leadership Group of the U.S. House of Representatives; U.S. Senate.

BRIEF FOR EICHMAN

◆ The only reason Congress identified for enacting the FPA was to preserve the flag's symbolic value, which is the precise interest this Court found insufficient in *Texas v. Johnson*, 491 U.S. 397 (1989). The FPA is an express legislative effort to redeem the Flag Desecration Act of 1968 from the kind of judicial scrutiny that the Court in *Johnson* declared it would apply.

◆ The U.S. flag was born of a desecration in which George Washington defaced a British flag in 1776 by ordering thirteen red and white stripes sewn on it. The question in this case is whether the U.S. government may incarcerate its citizens for engaging in similar politically expressive flag desecration. The answer in *Johnson* was no, and should remain no.

◆ The flag is not a physical object, but an infinitely reproducible symbol. The only conceivable interest for protecting the flag's "physical integrity" is to preserve its symbolic value. This Court has already held that that interest cannot justify punishing flagburning as a criminal act.

◆ The FPA cannot be upheld as a restriction on the "manner" of expression, because it is content-and-viewpoint-based by singling out a particular politically charged symbol for protection.

◆ The United States asks the Court to rule that flag burning is unprotected expression because the government finds it an offensive and unimportant form of expression. The First Amendment is needed precisely for expression that offends the government.

◆ In addition to being content-and-viewpoint-based, the FPA is unconstitutionally vague and overbroad. It is impossible to discern which "flags" are covered by the FPA's proscriptions, or when a flag becomes sufficiently "worn or soiled" to be open to desecration. The law forbids virtually all flag conduct associated with dissent.

AMICUS CURIAE BRIEFS SUPPORTING EICHMAN

American Bar Association; joint brief of the American Civil Liberties Union (ACLU), ACLU of the National Capital Area, ACLU of Washington, and the American Jewish Congress; National Association for the Advancement of Colored People; joint brief of People for the American Way, the American

Society of Newspaper Editors, the Freedom to Read Foundation, the Radio-Television News Directors Association, the Society of Professional Journalists, and the Volunteer Lawyers for the Arts.

SUPREME COURT DECISION: 5–4

BRENNAN, J.

... The Government concedes in these cases, as it must, that appellees' flag burning constituted expressive conduct, but invites us to reconsider our rejection in *Johnson* of the claim that flag burning as a mode of expression, like obscenity or "fighting words," does not enjoy the full protection of the First Amendment. Cf. *Chaplinsky v. New Hampshire*. This we decline to do. The only remaining question is whether the Flag Protection Act is sufficiently distinct from the Texas statute that it may constitutionally be applied to proscribe appellees' expressive conduct.

The Government contends that the Flag Protection Act is constitutional because, unlike the statute addressed in *Johnson*, the Act does not target expressive conduct on the basis of the content of its message. The Government asserts an interest in "protect[ing] the physical integrity of the flag under all circumstances" in order to safeguard the flag's identity "as the unique and unalloyed symbol of the Nation." The Act proscribes conduct (other than disposal) that damages or mistreats a flag, without regard to the actor's motive, his intended message, or the likely effects of his conduct on onlookers. By contrast, the Texas statute expressly prohibited only those acts of physical flag desecration "that the actor knows will seriously offend" onlookers, and the former federal statute prohibited only those acts of desecration that "cas[t] contempt upon" the flag.

Although the Flag Protection Act contains no explicit content-based limitation on the scope of prohibited conduct, it is nevertheless clear that the Government's asserted interest is "related 'to the suppression of free expression,'" and concerned with the content of such expression. The Government's interest in protecting the "physical integrity" of a privately owned flag rests upon a perceived need to preserve the flag's status as a symbol of our Nation and certain national ideals. But the mere destruction or disfigurement of a particular physical manifestation of the symbol, without more, does not diminish or otherwise affect the symbol itself in any way. For example, the secret destruction of a flag in one's own basement would not threaten the flag's recognized meaning. Rather, the Government's desire to preserve the flag as a symbol for certain national ideals is implicated "only when a person's treatment of the flag communicates [a] message" to others that is inconsistent with those ideals.

Moreover, the precise language of the Act's prohibitions confirms Congress' interest in the communicative impact of flag destruction. The Act criminalizes the conduct of anyone who "knowingly mutilates, defaces, physically defiles, burns, maintains on the floor or ground, or tramples upon any flag." Each of the specified terms—with the possible exception of "burns"—unmistakably connotes disrespectful treatment of the flag and suggests a focus on those acts likely to damage the flag's symbolic value. And the explicit exemption in Sec. 700(a)(2) for disposal of "worn or soiled" flags protects certain acts traditionally associated with patriotic respect for the flag.

As we explained in *Johnson*: "[I]f we were to hold that a State may forbid flag burning wherever it is likely to endanger the flag's symbolic role, but allow it wherever burning a flag promotes that role—as where, for example, a person ceremoniously burns a dirty flag—we would be ... permitting a State to 'prescribe what shall be orthodox' by saying that one may burn the flag to convey one's attitude toward it and its referents only if one does not endanger the flag's representation of nationhood and national unity." Although Congress cast the Flag Protection Act of 1989 in somewhat broader terms than the Texas statute at issue in *Johnson*, the Act still suffers from the same fundamental flaw: It suppresses expression out of concern for its likely communicative impact.... The Act therefore must be subjected to "the most exacting scrutiny," *Boos* [*v. Barry,* 485 U.S. 312 (1988)], and for reasons stated in *Johnson* the Government's interest cannot justify its infringement on First Amendment rights. We decline the Government's invitation to reassess this conclusion in light of Congress' recent recognition of a purported "national consensus" favoring a prohibition on flag burning. Brief for United States. Even assuming such a consensus exists, any suggestion that the Government's interest in suppressing speech becomes more weighty as popular opposition to that speech grows is foreign to the First Amendment....

Government may create national symbols, promote them, and encourage their respectful treatment. But the Flag Protection Act of 1989 goes well beyond this by criminally proscribing expressive conduct because of its likely communicative impact.

We are aware that desecration of the flag is deeply offensive to many. But the same might be said, for example, of virulent ethnic and religious epithets, ... vulgar repudiations of the draft, ... and scurrilous caricatures.... "If there is a bedrock principle underlying the First Amendment, it is that the Government may not prohibit the expression of an idea simply because society finds the idea itself offensive or disagreeable." *Johnson*. Punishing desecration of the flag dilutes the very freedom that makes this emblem so revered, and worth revering. The judgments of the District Courts are

Affirmed.

STEVENS, WHITE, AND O'CONNOR, J.J., AND REHNQUIST, C.J., DISSENTING

The Court's opinion ends where proper analysis of the issue should begin. Of course "the Government may not prohibit the expression of an idea simply because society finds the idea itself offensive or disagreeable." None of us disagrees with that proposition. But it is equally well settled that certain methods of expression may be prohibited if (a) the prohibition is supported by a legitimate societal interest that is unrelated to suppression of the ideas the speaker desires to express; (b) the prohibition does not entail any interference with the speaker's freedom to express those ideas by other means; and (c) the interest in allowing the speaker complete freedom of choice among alternative methods of expression is less important than the societal interest supporting the prohibition....

The first question the Court should consider is whether the interest in preserving the value of that symbol is unrelated to suppression of the ideas that flag burners are trying to express. In my judgment the answer depends, at least in part, on what those ideas are. A flag burner might intend various messages....

The idea expressed by a particular act of flag burning is necessarily dependent on the temporal and political context in which it occurs....

The Government's legitimate interest in preserving the symbolic value of the flag is, however, essentially the same regardless of which of many different ideas may have motivated a particular act of flag burning.... [T]he flag uniquely symbolizes the ideas of liberty, equality, and tolerance—ideas that Americans have passionately defended and debated throughout our history. The flag embodies the spirit of our national commitment to those ideals. The message thereby transmitted does not take a stand upon our disagreements, except to say that those disagreements are best regarded as competing interpretations of shared ideals. It does not judge particular policies, except to say that they command respect when they are enlightened by the spirit of liberty and equality. To the world, the flag is our promise that we will continue to strive for these ideals. To us, the flag is a reminder both that the struggle for liberty and equality is unceasing, and that our obligation of tolerance and respect for all of our fellow citizens encompasses those who disagree with us—indeed, even those whose ideas are disagreeable or offensive.

Thus, the Government may—indeed, it should—protect the symbolic value of the flag without regard to the specific content of the flag burners' speech. The prosecution in these cases does not depend upon the object of the defendants' protest. It is, moreover, equally clear that the prohibition does not entail any interference with the speaker's freedom to express his or her ideas by other means. It may well be true that other means of expression may be less effective in drawing attention to those ideas, but that is not itself a sufficient reason for immunizing flag burning....

Burning a flag is not, of course, equivalent to burning a public building. Assuming that the protester is burning his own flag, it causes no physical harm to other persons or to their property. The impact is purely symbolic, and it is apparent that some thoughtful persons believe that impact, far from depreciating the value of the symbol, will actually enhance its meaning. I most respectfully disagree. Indeed, what makes these cases particularly difficult for me is what I regard as the damage to the symbol that has already occurred as a result of this Court's decision to place its stamp of approval on the act of flag burning. A formerly dramatic expression of protest is now rather commonplace. In today's marketplace of ideas, the public burning of a Vietnam draft card is probably less provocative than lighting a cigarette. Tomorrow flag burning may produce a similar reaction. There is surely a direct relationship between the communicative value of the act of flag burning and the symbolic value of the object being burned.

The symbolic value of the American flag is not the same today as it was yesterday. Events during the last three decades have altered the country's image in the eyes of numerous Americans, and some now have difficulty understanding the message that the flag conveyed to their parents and grandparents—whether born abroad and naturalized or native born. Moreover, the integrity of the symbol has been compromised by those leaders who seem to advocate compulsory worship of the flag even by individuals whom it offends, or who seem to manipulate the symbol of national purpose into a pretext for partisan disputes about meaner ends. And, as I have suggested, the residual value of the symbol after this Court's decision in *Texas v. Johnson* is surely not the same as it was a year ago.

Given all these considerations, plus the fact that the Court today is really doing nothing more than reconfirming what it has already decided, it might be appropri-ate to defer to the judgment of the major-ity and merely apply the doctrine of *stare decisis* to the cases at hand. That action, however, would not honestly reflect my considered judgment concerning the rela-tive importance of the conflicting interests that are at stake. I remain persuaded that the considerations identified in my opin-ion in *Texas v. Johnson* are of controlling importance in these cases as well.

Accordingly, I respectfully dissent.

QUESTIONS

1. Eichman's counsel argued that the Flag Protection Act of 1989 "is unconstitutional on its face, because it is impermissibly content-based[.]... It is content-based because it singles out for protection one symbol, with a particular content, among all symbols. It is there-fore analytically indistinguishable from a statute prohibiting burning of the Democratic Party flag or copies of *The Federalist Papers*."

   Does Justice Brennan's majority opinion in *Eichman* appear to agree with this reasoning? If not, what principle underlies the major-ity opinion?

2. New York Governor Mario M. Cuomo argued in his *amicus* brief sup-porting the United States that the Flag Protection Act of 1989 cured the specific constitutional defects identified in *Texas v. Johnson*, and satisfies the *O'Brien* test. (Cuomo had submitted to the New York leg-islature a Governor's Program Bill substantially identical to the Flag Protection Act, which the legislature refused to consider unless the Flag Protection Act was sustained.) In what ways are the *Eichman* dissent and Governor Cuomo's argument similar?

3. If the Court had upheld the constitutionality of the 1989 Flag Protection Act, which, if any, of the following actions would have been punishable under its provisions?

   > Someone makes good pictures of U.S. flags, one- or two-sided, on paper or cloth[,] by color photography, color photocopy, or com-puter with ink-jet printer[,] and then publicly tramples and burns the pictures.
   >
   > An iconoclast uses small cloth pictures of the flag as handker-chiefs and distributes large ones as blankets to New York's home-less.
   >
   > A protestor projects a picture of a flag onto a white wall and then hurls mud or paint onto the image.
   >
   > A protestor wall-mounts a large flag behind cellophane, then paints or smears obscenities on the transparent covering.

A computer-animation programmer creates a realistic video of what seems to be a flag burning to charred shreds.

An artist uses a thousand tiny flags as minute elements in an obscene picture. (Ken Knowlton and Barbara Bean Knowlton, "When Is a Flag Desecrated?" *Harpers*, December 1989, p. 19)

4. Over the years, the Court has recognized a variety of categories of expression as being beyond the pale of First Amendment protection, including child pornography, speech promoting illegal activity, defamation, speech likely to incite violence, obscenity, and fighting words. Identify the qualities, if any, that are common to those categories for purposes of understanding First Amendment jurisprudence.

COMMENTS

1. The *Eichman* decision generated renewed efforts to pass a constitutional amendment criminalizing flag burning. The proposal read: "The Congress and the States shall have power to prohibit the physical desecration of the flag of the United States." On June 21, 1990, the proposal fell thirty-four votes short of obtaining the two-thirds vote in the House of Representatives required by Article V. Four days later the Senate conducted a symbolic vote where the proposal fell nine votes short. The proposal was revived in 1995 when the House of Representatives voted to support it, 312–120. It died in the Senate on December 12, 1995, by a vote of 63–36.

2. A flag controversy of a different sort rages in several southern states. *New York Times* reporter Kevin Sack describes battles over displaying publicly the "Stars and Bars," the Confederate battle flag. Sack quotes University of Mississippi historian Charles Reagan Wilson as saying that these impassioned debates are about the following:

> issues of identity and world view and ethnicity. Are we one people or two? [To cut white Southerners'] tie with the[ir] symbols, with the[ir] genealogy, is for them a kind of cultural death.... It's about who has the power, really. (Kevin Sack. "South's Symbols Split Races and Cultures" [http://www.nytimes.com/], February 8, 1997)

SUGGESTIONS FOR FURTHER READING

Alfange, Dean, Jr., "Free Speech and Symbolic Conduct: The Draft-Card Burning Case," *The Supreme Court Review* (Chicago, IL: University of Chicago Press, 1968).

Clark, John A., and Kevin T. McGuire, "Congress, the Supreme Court and the Flag," 49 *Political Research Quarterly* (1996): 771.

Denvir, John, "Justice Brennan, Justice Rehnquist and Free Speech," 80 *Northwestern University Law Review* (1985): 285.

Ely, John Hart, "Flag Desecration: A Case Study in the Roles of Categorization and Balancing in First Amendment Analysis," 88 *Harvard Law Review* (1975): 1482.

Goldstein, Robert Justin, *"Saving Old Glory": The History of the American Flag Desecration Controversy* (Boulder, CO: Westview, 1995).

———, ed., *Desecrating the American Flag: Key Documents of the Controversy from the Civil War to 1995* (Syracuse, NY: Syracuse University Press, 1997).

Greenawalt, Kent, "O'er the Land of the Free: Flagburning as Speech," 37 *University of California Los Angeles Law Review* (1990): 925.

Irons, Peter, *The Courage of Their Convictions: Sixteen Americans Who Fought Their Way to the Supreme Court* (New York, NY: Penguin), Chapter 10.

Michelman, Frank, "Saving Old Glory: On Constitutional Iconography," 42 *Stanford Law Review* (1990): 1337.

Prosser, Richard, "Desecration of the American Flag," 3 *Independent Legal Forum* (1969): 159.

Rosenblatt, Albert M., "Flag Desecration Statutes: History and Analysis," *Washington University Law Quarterly* (1972): 193.

Stone, Geoffrey, "Flag Burning and the Constitution," 75 *Iowa Law Review* (1989): 111.

Taylor, Neil R., III, "The Protection of Flag Burning as Symbolic Speech and the Congressional Attempt to Overturn the Decision," 58 *University of Cincinnati Law Review* (1990): 1477.

Tiefer, Charles, "The Flag-Burning Controversy of 1989–90: Congress' Valid Role in Constitutional Dialogue," 29 *Harvard Journal on Legislation* (1992): 357.

Tribe, Laurence H., "Give Old Glory a Break: Protect It—and Ideas," *New York Times*, July 3, 1989, p. 18.

Tuchman, Barbara W., *The First Salute* (New York, NY: Knopf, 1988).

Tushnet, Mark, "The Flag-Burning Episode: An Essay on the Constitution," 61 *University of Colorado Law Review* (1990:) 39.

CONTROVERSIES INVOLVING VARIETIES OF POLITICAL SPEECH

Lloyd Corporation, Ltd. v. Tanner
407 U.S. 551 (1972)

SETTING

Despite the First Amendment's absolute language—"Congress shall make *no* law ... abridging the freedom of speech ..." (emphasis added), the Supreme Court has never interpreted that constitutional guarantee in unconditional terms. To begin with, as explained in the previous sections, not all forms of expression qualify for constitutional protection. Even protected speech is subject to limitation by competing constitutional guarantees such as property rights, because, when two constitutionally protected social values come into conflict, one must trump the other. For example, although the First Amendment protects certain forms of expression against government limitations—including speech in public fora such as streets or town squares—there is no constitutional right to speak on private property because of constitutional guarantees of property rights. When private property has some of the characteristics of public use, however, it is not so easy to draw the lines between property and speech rights.

Company-owned towns such as Chickasaw, Alabama, demonstrate the problem. A suburb of Mobile, in 1945 Chickasaw was wholly owned by the Gulf Shipbuilding Corporation. Grace Marsh, a Jehovah's Witness, stood on the sidewalk near the Chickasaw post office and distributed religious literature. In the stores, the Gulf Shipbuilding Corporation had posted a notice reading: "This Is Private Property, and Without Written Permission, No Street, or House Vendor, Agent or Solicitation of Any Kind Will Be Permitted." Marsh was warned that she could not distribute the literature without a permit, and she was told that no permit would be issued to her. When she was asked to leave the sidewalk and Chickasaw she declined and was arrested. Marsh challenged her conviction on First Amendment grounds and the Supreme Court agreed with her. Justice Black wrote for the six-vote majority:

> Whether a corporation or a municipality owns or possesses the town the public in either case has an identical interest in the functioning of the community in such manner that the channels of communication remain free.... The managers appointed by the corporation cannot curtail the liberty of press and religion of these people consistently with the purposes of the Constitutional guarantees, and a state statute, as the one here involved, which enforces such action by criminally punishing those who attempt to distribute religious literature clearly violates the First and Fourteenth Amendments to the Constitution. *Marsh v. Alabama*, 326 U.S. 501 (1946).

Twenty-two years after deciding *Marsh*, the Court again heard a controversy over picketing on private property. The property in question was the Logan Valley Mall, located near Altoona, Pennsylvania. Logan Valley Mall successfully obtained an injunction prohibiting the Amalgamated Food Employees Union from picketing anywhere on Mall property. When the union appealed, the Supreme Court, again 6–3, sided with it. Justice Marshall wrote:

> We see no reason why access to a business district in a company town for the purpose of exercising First Amendment rights should be constitutionally required, while access for the same purpose to property functioning as a business district should be limited simply because the property surrounding the "business district" is not under the same ownership. Here the roadways provided for vehicular movement within the mall and the sidewalks leading from building to building are the functional equivalents of the streets and sidewalks of a normal municipal business district. The shopping center

premises are open to the public to the same extent as the commercial center of a normal town. *Amalgamated Food Employees Union Local 590 v. Logan Valley Plaza*, 391 U.S. 308 (1968).

Four years later, the Court agreed to hear a First Amendment case that raised the question of whether owners of the Lloyd Center, a private shopping mall in Portland, Oregon, could ban leafleting unrelated to tenant businesses. The Lloyd Center is a private shopping center the development of which was made possible by the city of Portland vacating public streets and sidewalks on what was formerly twenty-eight city blocks. Like *O'Brien* and *Tinker*, the case arose out of social divisions over the Vietnam War. Opposition to the Vietnam war was intense, particularly among young people and college students. Campus protests, marches, sit-in demonstrations, and draft resistance were commonplace during the late 1960s. Not all protests were confined to college campuses.

In November 1968, Donald Tanner, Betsy Wheeler, and Susan Roberts were part of a group who distributed anti-Vietnam War leaflets promoting what they called "National Draft Card Turn-in Day" to passersby at various points along the malls and walkways of the Lloyd Center, a privately owned, fifty-acre shopping mall in Portland, Oregon. At the time, the mall contained more than sixty commercial businesses, as well as professional offices and a skating rink. The Lloyd Corporation intended the center to be open to the general public. Nevertheless, Lloyd Corporation policy prohibited distribution of noncommercial literature in any portion of the Lloyd Center intended for use by the general public.

Uniformed guards employed by the corporation ordered Tanner and the others to stop distributing leaflets in the center, even though the distribution was peaceful and did not interfere with public use of the mall. When they refused to leave, the guards threatened to have them arrested and prosecuted for criminal trespass. To avoid arrest, they obeyed the order.

Tanner, Wheeler, and Roberts subsequently filed suit against Lloyd Corporation in the U.S. District Court for the District of Oregon to enjoin it from interfering with the peaceful and orderly distribution of noncommercial literature in the areas of the Lloyd Center open to the general public. Their suit asked the court to extend *Marsh v. Alabama*, 326 U.S. 501 (1946), and *Amalgamated Food Employees Union v. Logan Valley Plaza*, 391 U.S. 308 (1968). Tanner, Wheeler, and Roberts asked the court to build on *Marsh* and *Logan Valley* and hold that the owner of a private shopping center cannot prohibit handbilling unrelated to the business of the center.

Following a nonjury trial, the district court granted the injunction, holding that Tanner and the others had a right to distribute noncommercial handbills in a peaceful and orderly manner in the malls and walkways of the Lloyd Center when it was open to the general public. The Ninth Circuit Court of Appeals affirmed. It held that a shopping center open to the public for the transaction of business is the "functional equivalent of a public business district" and thus subject to the same exercise of First Amendment rights as municipal property.

Lloyd Corporation petitioned the Supreme Court of the United States for a writ of certiorari.

HIGHLIGHTS OF SUPREME COURT ARGUMENTS

BRIEF FOR LLOYD CORPORATION

◆ This case is important because *Logan Valley* did not decide whether a private shopping center owner can prohibit handbilling that is unrelated to the business of the center and that could be accomplished by using public streets and sidewalks. The First Amendment does not compel an affirmative response. By opening its property to the public for shopping purposes, a private property owner in no way subjects itself to a duty to provide a public forum for the discussion of every public issue.

◆ The Lloyd Corporation has a significant interest in protecting the normal business operation of the mall against noncommercial handbills. Handbilling could result in loss of business and customer goodwill, and create costs in terms of litter collection. Handbilling also competes for the time and attention of people who have been attracted to the Lloyd Center at the corporation's substantial expense. Forcing the corporation to open its property for handbilling is therefore inconsistent with the constitutional protection against confiscation of private property.

◆ Public streets and sidewalks are available for noncommercial handbilling. While circulating antiwar leaflets in the Lloyd Center was convenient for Tanner and the others, they had not demonstrated any necessity for doing so. Such necessity was shown in *Logan Valley*.

AMICUS CURIAE BRIEFS SUPPORTING LLOYD CORPORATION

The American Retail Federation and the Homart Development Company.

BRIEF FOR TANNER, WHEELER, AND ROBERTSON

◆ If Tanner and the others had distributed the leaflets on a city sidewalk in an orderly and peaceful fashion, the government could not have prohibited them or imposed prior restraints on them. If First Amendment rights cannot be exercised on the "functional equivalents" of public streets and sidewalks in privately owned shopping malls, free speech and press will be restricted in direct proportion to the growth of such malls and their replacement of public business districts. The rationale of *Marsh* applies equally to this case.

◆ The fact that leaflets could have been distributed elsewhere cannot justify the complete prohibition of political expression on walkways in private shopping centers that are open to the public. Tanner and the others could not have distributed the leaflets to comparable numbers of people in a similar period of time in any other part of Portland.

AMICUS CURIAE BRIEF SUPPORTING TANNER, WHEELER, AND ROBINSON

The People's Lobby, Inc.

SUPREME COURT DECISION: 5–4

POWELL, J.

... The handbilling by respondents in the malls of Lloyd Center had no relation to any purpose for which the center was built and being used. It is nevertheless argued by respondents that since the Center is open to the public the private owner cannot enforce a restriction against handbilling on the premises. The thrust of this argument is considerably broader than the rationale of *Logan Valley*. It requires no relationship, direct or indirect, between the purpose of the expressive activity and the business of the shopping center. The message sought to be conveyed by respondents was directed to all members of the public, not solely to patrons of Lloyd Center or of any of its operations. Respondents could have distributed these handbills on any public street, on any public sidewalk, in any public park, or in any public building in the city of Portland....

It is noteworthy that respondent's argument based on the Center being "open to the public" would apply in varying degrees to most retail stores and service establishments across the country. They are all open to the public in the sense that customers and potential customers are invited and encouraged to enter. In terms of being open to the public, there are differences only of degree—not of principle—between a free standing store and one located in a shopping center, between a small store and a large one, between a single store with small malls and open areas designed to attract customers and Lloyd Center with its elaborate malls and interior landscaping.

A further fact, distinguishing the present case from *Logan Valley*, is that the Union picketers in that case would have been deprived of all reasonable opportunity to convey their message to patrons ... had they been denied access to the shopping center. The situation at Lloyd Center was notably different. The central building complex was surrounded by public sidewalks.... All persons who enter or leave the private areas within the complex must cross public streets and sidewalks, either on foot or in automobiles. When moving to and from the privately owned parking lots, automobiles are required by law to come to a complete stop. Handbills may be distributed conveniently to pedestrians, and also to occupants of automobiles, from these public sidewalks and streets. Indeed, respondents moved to these public areas and continued distribution of their handbills after being requested to leave the interior malls. It would be an unwarranted infringement of property rights to require them to yield to the exercise of First Amendment rights under circumstances where adequate alternative avenues of communication exist. Such an accommodation would diminish property rights without significantly enhancing the asserted right of free speech. In ordering this accommodation the courts below erred in their interpretation of this Court's decision in *Marsh* and *Logan Valley*.

The basic issue in this case is whether respondents, in the exercise of asserted First Amendment rights, may distribute handbills on Lloyd's private property contrary to its wishes and contrary to a policy enforced against *all* handbilling. In addressing this issue, it must be remembered that the First and Fourteenth Amendments safeguard the rights of free speech and assembly by limitations on *state* action, not on action by the owner of private property and nondiscriminatorily for private purposes only....

[T]his court has never held that a trespasser or an uninvited guest may exercise general rights of free speech on property privately owned and used nondiscriminatorily for private purposes only....

[Private] property [does not] lose its private character merely because the public is generally invited to use it for designated purposes.... We do say that the Fifth and Fourteenth Amendment rights of private property owners, as well as the First Amendment rights of all citizens, must be respected and protected. The Framers of the Constitution certainly did not think these fundamental rights of a free society are incompatible with each other. There may be situations where accommodations between them, and the drawing of lines to assure due protection of both, are not easy. But on the facts presented in this case, the answer is clear.

We hold that there has been no such dedication of Lloyd's privately owned and operated shopping center to public use as to entitle respondents to exercise therein the asserted First Amendment rights. Accordingly, we reverse the judgment and remand the case to the Court of Appeals with directions to vacate the injunction.

It is so ordered.

Judgment reversed and case remanded.

MARSHALL, DOUGLAS, BRENNAN, AND STEWART, J.J., DISSENTING

... [T]he Lloyd Center is an integral part of the Portland community. From its inception, the city viewed it as a "business district" of the city and depended on it to supply much needed employment opportunities. To insure the success of the Center, the city carefully integrated it into the pattern of streets already established and planned future development of streets around the Center. It is plain, therefore, that Lloyd Center is the equivalent of a public "business district" within the meaning of *Marsh* and *Logan Valley*. In fact, the Lloyd Center is much more analogous to the company town in *Marsh* than was the Logan Valley Plaza....

The District Court observed that Lloyd Center invites schools to hold football rallies, presidential candidates to give speeches, and service organizations to hold Veteran's Day ceremonies on its premises. The court also observed that the Center permits the Salvation Army, the Volunteers of America, and the American Legion to solicit funds in the Mall. Thus, the court concluded that the Center was already open to First Amendment activities, and that respondents could not constitutionally be excluded from leafletting solely because Lloyd Center was not enamored of the form or substance of their speech. The Court of Appeals affirmed, taking the position that it was not extending either *Logan Valley* or *Marsh*. In other words, the District Court found that Lloyd Center had deliberately chosen to open its private property to a broad range of expression and that having done so it could not constitutionally exclude respondents, and the Court of Appeals affirmed this finding....

If the property of Lloyd Center is generally open to First Amendment activity, respondents cannot be excluded....

We must remember that it is a balance that we are striking—a balance between the freedom to speak, a freedom that is given a preferred place in our hierarchy of values, and the freedom of a private property-owner to control his property. When the competing interests are fairly weighted, the balance can only be struck in favor of speech....

[O]ne may suspect from reading the opinion of the Court that it is *Logan Valley* itself that the Court finds bothersome. The vote in *Logan Valley* was 6–3, and that decision is only four years old. But, I am aware that the composition of this Court has radically changed in four years.

The fact remains that *Logan Valley* is binding unless and until it is overruled. There is no valid distinction between that case and this one, and, therefore, the results in both cases should be the same....

When there are no effective means of communication, free speech is a mere shibboleth. I believe that the First Amendment requires it to be a reality. Accordingly, I would affirm the decision of the Court of Appeals.

QUESTIONS

1. Restate the *Lloyd Corporation* rule. What criteria should be used to define the differences between strictly private property and property that takes on the characteristics of a public forum?

   In thinking about this question, in addition to reading *Marsh* and *Logan Valley*, consider the Court's discussion of a "limited public forum" in *Perry Education Association v. Perry Local Educators' Association*, 460 U.S. 37 (1983), where the majority held that a provision of a collective bargaining agreement between a school district and teachers' exclusive bargaining representative that granted the bargaining representative exclusive access to teacher mailboxes at school and an interschool mail system, to the exclusion of a rival union, does not violate the First Amendment. Can a valid comparison be made between limited access to teachers' school mailboxes and limited access to shopping malls?

2. What bearing, if any, should the following facts have had on the *Lloyd Corporation* decision: The malls and walkways within the center were open to the public at all times. The corporation's rule against noncommercial handbilling did not prohibit solicitation of funds by the Salvation Army or Volunteers of America, sales of "Buddy Poppies" by the American Legion, displays by the Boy Scouts of America, or distribution of information about the Portland Zoo, Rose Festival, or a religious shrine known as "The Grotto." The skating rink and an auditorium in the mall were used regularly for public meetings.

3. Identify the conflicting constitutional rights at issue in *Lloyd Corporation*. Did the Court seek to "balance" those rights, or did it assume that one right is more important than the other?

4. Justice Marshall said, "The fact remains that *Logan Valley* is binding

unless and until it is overruled." In effect, does *Lloyd Corporation* overrule *Logan Valley*?

5. In *PruneYard Shopping Center v. Robins*, 447 U.S. 74 (1980), the Court held, 9–0, that the reasoning in *Lloyd Corporation* does not limit a state's authority to exercise its police power to adopt in its own constitution individual liberties more expansive than those conferred by the federal Constitution. It ruled that solicitation in a privately owned shopping center for signatures on a petition opposing a UN resolution was protected by a provision of the California constitution. Three state courts—Colorado, *Bock v. Westminster Mall Co.*, 819 P.2d (1991); New Jersey, *State v. Schmid*, 423 A.2d 615 (1980); Pennsylvania, *Commonwealth v. Tate*, 432 A.2d 1382 (1981); and Washington, *Alderwood Assoc. v. Washington Environmental Council*, 635 P.2d 108 (1981)—have also found in favor of free speech on private property based on independent state constitutional grounds.

Should states have authority under their own constitutions to grant broader First Amendment rights in privately owned shopping centers than the Court recognized in *Lloyd Corporation*? Is national uniformity preferable on First Amendment issues?

COMMENT

The "speech/property" problem has come before the Court in other contexts since *Lloyd Corporation*.

Case: *Hudgens v. National Labor Relations Board*, 424 U.S. 507 (1976)

Vote: 6–2 (Stevens, J., did not participate.)

Decision: Striking workers have no right under the First Amendment to enter a privately owned shopping center for the purpose of picketing their employer's business. The rights and liabilities of striking workers are determined entirely by the National Labor Relations Act. *Logan Valley* overruled.

Case: *Pacific Gas and Electric v. Public Utilities Commissioner*, 475 U.S. 1 (1986)

Vote: 5–3 (Blackmun, J., did not participate.)

Decision: An order by the California Public Utilities Commission requiring Pacific Gas and Electric Company to allow a consumer group to use extra space in the company's billing statements four times a year to raise funds and communicate its message on rates violates the company's rights under the First Amendment. (A plurality opinion contends that the order impermissibly burdens the company by forcing it to associate with the views of other speakers and is not a content neutral regulation of the time, place, or manner of expression. One justice contends the order's redefinition of a property right in the extra space in the billing envelope burdens the speech of one party in order to enhance the speech of another, in violation of the First Amendment.)

CONTROVERSIES INVOLVING VARIETIES OF POLITICAL SPEECH

Buckley v. Valeo
424 U.S. 1 (1976)

SETTING

Private money fuels American public life. As Jesse H. Unruh, the late Speaker of the California State Assembly put it: "Money is the mother's milk of politics." Federal campaign practices in the United States went largely unregulated throughout the nineteenth century. Early congressional election regulations passed in the wake of the Fifteenth Amendment, such as the 1870 Enforcement Act (which made it an offense to register falsely, bribe voters, or interfere with election officials), were aimed less at abolishing corrupt campaign practices than at implementing the right of blacks to vote.

Until the turn of the century, campaign finances were as freewheeling as the electoral contests of which they were an integral part. Steel and railroad trusts bribed politicians and, in some cases, entire state legislatures. The cozy relationships between robber barons and public officials in this era led humorist Mark Twain to describe the U.S. Congress as "the only truly criminal class in America."

Scandals surrounding the activities of Mark Hanna, the Ohio mining magnate who managed Republican Party finances and William McKinley's 1896 presidential election, provoked calls for campaign financing reform in the early 1900s. President Theodore Roosevelt told Congress in 1905: "The need for collecting large campaign funds would vanish if Congress provided an appropriation for the proper and legitimate expenses of each of the great national parties." Congress responded with the Tillman Act in 1907. It prohibited corporations and national banks from making money contributions to candidates for federal office. The Federal Corrupt Practices Act (FCPA) of 1910 and 1911 limited the amount that congressional candidates could contribute to their own nominating and general election campaigns, and mandated the filing of reports detailing certain campaign contributions. None of this legislation imposed significant sanctions, however, and it was generally ignored. The Supreme Court declared the FCPA invalid, insofar as it applied to primary elections and nominating conventions. *Newberry v. United States*, 256 U.S. 232 (1921). (*Newberry* was overruled in 1941, when the Court held that Congress has the authority to regulate primary as well as general elections for federal office. *United States v. Classic*, 313 U.S. 299.)

The Teapot Dome oil lease scandal, which rocked Warren G. Harding's administration, renewed the calls for campaign reform. (The scandal took its name from Teapot Dome, Wyoming, the location of one of the two naval oil reserves that Attorney General Harry Daugherty secretly leased to private oil companies in return for $400,000.) In 1925, Congress revised the FCPA in light of *Newberry*. It continued the Tillman Act prohibitions on contributions and additionally required campaign committees seeking to influence the election of presidential electors in two or more states to file contribution and spending reports that would be available to the public. Even though the Supreme Court upheld the 1925 FCPA reporting requirements in *Burroughs v. United States*, 290 U.S. 534 (1934), the FCPA was as toothless and easily evaded as its predecessor. No one in Congress was ever prosecuted for violating the FCPA.

Campaign finance reform lay largely dormant for decades. Several factors, including enlargement of the electorate, development of modern communication media, and rising costs of television campaigns, spurred Congress to pass a bill in 1970 that limited the amount that could be spent for television and radio advertising. President Richard M. Nixon vetoed the act, agreeing with broadcasters that it discriminated against them. The following year, Congress began drafting a more comprehensive bill, the Federal Elections Campaign Act (FECA). It required all federal candidates to disclose the sources of their campaign funds, limited the amount that candidates (or their families) could spend on their own campaigns, capped the amount that candidates could spend on political advertising, and required that television and radio stations charge their lowest rates for political advertising in the periods immediately preceding primary and general elections. Congress delayed final passage of the act until 1972 so that members of Congress and presidential candidates could raise more money for the campaign season that presidential election year.

Disclosures during the 1972 campaign of secret corporate funds being maintained to finance the Nixon campaign and others, as well as the revelation that the Committee for the Re-Election of the President had raised upwards of $17 million dollars from only 124 contributors giving more than $50,000 each, and that over $1.7 million of the $17 million had been received from people who subsequently received ambassadorial posts, led Congress to amend the FECA in 1974. The goal was to reduce skyrocketing election costs and eliminate the allegedly corrupting reliance of candidates on private financing. The amended FECA contained the following provisions: (a) individual political contributions were limited to $1,000 to any single candidate per election, with an overall annual limitation of $25,000 by any contributor; independent expenditures by individuals and groups "relative to a clearly identified candidate" were limited to $1,000 a year; campaign spending by candidates for various federal offices and spending for national conventions by political parties were subject to prescribed limits; (b) contributions and expenditures above certain threshold levels had to be reported and publicly disclosed; (c) a system for public funding of presidential campaign activities was established by Subtitle H of the Internal Revenue Code; and (d) a Federal Election Commission was established to administer and enforce the legislation.

In January 1975, the day after the 1974 FECA amendments became effective, U.S. Senator James Buckley, presidential candidate Eugene McCarthy, Representative William Steiger, political activist Stewart Mott, and eight organizations, including the New York Civil Liberties Union and *Human Events*, a conservative publication, filed suit in the U.S. District Court for the District of Columbia seeking a declaration that major provisions of the FECA were unconstitutional. The suit also sought an injunction against their enforcement. The defendants were Secretary of the Senate Francis Valeo, Clerk of the House of Representatives W. Pat Jennings, in their official capacities and as *ex officio* members of the Federal Election Commission, the commission itself, the attorney general of the United States, and the comptroller general of the United States. The plaintiffs requested a three-judge court to hear the case and to certify the constitutional questions to the Court of Appeals for the D.C. Circuit.

The district court denied the motion for a three-judge panel, but certified the case to the court of appeals. That court allowed several additional groups and individuals to intervene, then remanded the case to the district court to identify the constitutional issues in the complaint, take necessary evidence, make findings of fact, and then to certify constitutional questions to the court of appeals.

The three-judge panel convened on remand entered a memorandum order, adopted extensive findings of fact, and recertified the augmented record to the court of appeals. The court of appeals found one reporting section of the FECA unconstitutionally vague and overbroad, but upheld the other substantive provisions of the act regarding contributions, expenditures, disclosure, and the provisions for public funding of the three stages of the presidential selection process. It also sustained the constitutionality of the Federal Election Commission. In that court's view, contributions and expenditures for political purposes are so infected with "non-speech elements" that regulation is permissible, and that "a clear and compelling interest" in preserving the integrity of the electoral process justifies the regulations contained in the FECA. Buckley and the others appealed to the Supreme Court of the United States.

HIGHLIGHTS OF SUPREME COURT ARGUMENTS

BRIEF FOR BUCKLEY

◆ The expenditure or contribution of money for political purposes is protected by the First Amendment's guarantee of free speech. Regulations on political speech must be directly and precisely aimed at control of conduct with minimal speech elements, while intruding as little as possible on the exercise of associational rights and freedom of speech. The FECA fails to meet these criteria. Congress could have achieved its goal of eliminating corruption through more effective means that are less intrusive on the First Amendment.

◆ The FECA's limitations on campaign expenditures by candidates, parties, and committees are unconstitutional *per se* as direct abridgements on the rights of speech and association. Political speech will go unheard unless distributed widely. Limiting the expenditure of money, therefore, limits speech itself.

◆ The limitation on expenditures in presidential campaigns is tantamount to controlling the strategy of presidential campaigns and thus what a presidential candidate is trying to communicate to the party and the public. The government's purposes in imposing the restrictions are not compelling, given these extensive First Amendment infringements.

◆ The limitation on independent expenditures by the FECA is another abridgement of free speech. This restriction limits virtually all public debate and political activity to candidates' campaigns, party committees, and the institutional press. Congress justified the $1,000 limit on independent expenditures as preserving to everyone "*some* right of political expression." Such a rationale is not sufficient in light of First Amendment rights.

◆ Wholesale limits on individual contributions violate both the First Amendment and the Due Process Clause of the Fifth Amendment. Equality of political communication is not a goal that can be pursued in the law without great peril. Limiting financial contributions to candidates magnifies other inequalities, and discriminates against candidates without family wealth. The problem of corruption underlying the limitation could be addressed through properly drafted disclosure provisions.

◆ Funding campaign activities by direct payment to candidates or parties is unconstitutional because it reduces the amount of influence that citizens have over their representatives and neuters the political process by eliminating an important means by which voters can express intensely held views on public issues.

◆ The FECA's disclosure requirements for contributions to candidates for federal office is unconstitutionally overbroad and intrusive on associational privacy interests. Campaign contributions are a very sensitive matter to many individuals. Disclosure requirements need to be very narrowly drawn.

◆ The method of appointing members of the Federal Election Commission is unconstitutional because the power should rest exclusively with the president, rather than with the House, Senate, and president.

BRIEF FOR VALEO

◆ Buckley and the others have not proven that the mere existence of the FECA produced the injuries they claimed. They are in effect asking for an advisory opinion about the statute, which courts do not give.

◆ The FECA is appropriate legislation to safeguard federal elections from the improper use of money. The statute puts no limits on the content or quality of speech. The effects on speech of limiting campaign contributions and expenditures are merely incidental and justified by the need to curb the undue influence of a wealthy few on candidate positions and government actions. The need to regulate contributions and expenditures is the same constitutional motivation for the apportionment and voting rights cases—to equalize as far as practicable the relative ability of all voters to affect electoral choices.

◆ The $1,000 contribution limit to a single candidate has not been shown to discriminate against any class of which Buckley or the others are members, nor has it been shown to be unreasonable. The relatively few persons who contribute more than $1,000 to a candidate have disproportionate influence over the conduct of political campaigns and the actions of public officials after their election.

◆ Campaign disclosure requirements have been on the statute books since 1910 and have not been shown to "chill" political contributions. The reporting provisions are reasonably related to the public's First Amendment right to know and the need to enforce the remainder of the legislation.

BRIEF FOR THE FEDERAL ELECTION COMMISSION

◆ Buckley and the other plaintiffs lack standing to challenge the composition and authority of the commission on the grounds that they violate the president's appointment prerogatives. The president must make that claim himself.

◆ The appointments provision of Article II, Section 2, does not preclude Congress from exercising appointive power when the functions of the appointees are dominantly related to the performance of congressional responsibilities. Under the statute, the commission would act as Congress's delegate in performing congressional tasks. Therefore, Congress's role in making four of the six appointments to the commission on a bipartisan basis does not violate separation of powers theory.

AMICUS CURIAE BRIEFS SUPPORTING THE FEDERAL ELECTION COMMISSION

Attorney General Edward Levi; California Fair Political Practices Commission; Senator Lee Metcalf; the Socialist Labor Party; the Los Angeles County Central Committee of the Peace and Freedom Party; the Committee for Democratic Election Laws; and Senator Hugh Scott.

SUPREME COURT DECISION

(*per curiam*; Stevens, J., did not participate.)

These appeals present constitutional challenges to the key provisions of the Federal Election Campaign Act of 1971 (Act), and related provisions of the Internal Revenue Code of 1954, all as amended in 1974....

I. Contribution and Expenditure Limitations A. GENERAL PRINCIPLES The Act's contribution and expenditure limitations operate in an area of the most fundamental First Amendment activities. Discussion of public issues and debate on the qualifications of candidates are integral to the operation of the system of government established by our Constitution.

The First Amendment affords the broadest protection to such political expression in order "to assure [the] unfettered interchange of ideas for the bringing about of political and social changes desired by the people." *Roth v. United States*, 354 U.S. 476 (1957)....

The First Amendment protects political association as well as political expression....

It is with these principles in mind that we consider the primary contentions of the parties with respect to the Act's limitations upon the giving and spending of money in political campaigns. Those conflicting contentions could not more sharply define the basic issues before us. Appellees contend that what the Act regulates is conduct, and that its effect on speech and association is incidental at most. Appellants respond that contributions and expenditures are at the very core of political speech, and that the Act's limitations thus constitute restraints on First Amendment liberty that are both gross and direct....

A restriction on the amount of money a person or group can spend on political communication during a campaign necessarily reduces the quantity of expression by restricting the number of issues discussed, the depth of their exploration, and the size of the audience reached. This is because virtually every means of communicating ideas in today's mass society requires the expenditure of money. The distribution of the humblest handbill or leaflet entails printing, paper, and circulation costs. Speeches and rallies generally necessitate hiring a hall and publicizing the event. The electorate's increasing dependence on television, radio, and other mass media for news and information has made these expensive modes of communication indispensable instruments of effective political speech.

The expenditure limitations contained in the Act represent substantial rather than merely theoretical restraints on the quantity and diversity of political speech....

By contrast with a limitation upon expenditures for political expression, a limitation upon the amount that any one person or group may contribute to a candidate or political committee entails only a marginal restriction upon the contributor's ability to engage in free communication.... A limitation on the amount of money a person may give to a candidate

or campaign organization thus involves little direct restraint on his political communication, for it permits the symbolic expression of support evidenced by a contribution but does not in any way infringe the contributor's freedom to discuss candidates and issues....

In sum, although the Act's contribution and expenditure limitations both implicate fundamental First Amendment interests, its expenditure ceilings impose significantly more severe restrictions on protected freedoms of political expression and association than do its limitations on financial contributions.

B. CONTRIBUTION LIMITATIONS *1. The $1,000 Limitation on Contributions by Individuals and Groups to Candidates and Authorized Campaign Committees[.]...* It is unnecessary to look beyond the Act's primary purpose—to limit the actuality and appearance of corruption resulting from large individual financial contributions—in order to find a constitutionally sufficient justification for the $1,000 contribution limitation. Under a system of private financing of elections, a candidate lacking immense personal or family wealth must depend on financial contributions from others to provide the resources necessary to conduct a successful campaign. The increasing importance of the communications media and sophisticated mass-mailing and polling operations to effective campaigning make the raising of large sums of money an ever more essential ingredient of an effective candidacy. To the extent that large contributions are given to secure a political *quid pro quo* from current and potential office holders, the integrity of our system of representative democracy is undermined. Although the scope of such pernicious practices can never be reliably ascertained, the deeply disturbing examples surfacing after the 1972 election demonstrate that the problem is not an illusory one.

Of almost equal concern as the danger of actual *quid pro quo* arrangements is the impact of the appearance of corruption stemming from public awareness of the opportunities for abuse inherent in a regime of large individual financial contributions....

The Act's $1,000 contribution limitation focuses precisely on the problem of large campaign contributions—the narrow aspect of political association where the actuality and potential for corruption have been identified—while leaving persons free to engage in independent political expression, to associate actively through volunteering their services, and to assist to a limited but nonetheless substantial extent in supporting candidates and committees with financial resources. Significantly, the Act's contribution limitations in themselves do not undermine to any material degree the potential for robust and effective discussion of candidates and campaign issues by individual citizens, associations, the institutional press, candidates, and political parties.

We find that, under the rigorous standard of review established by our prior decisions, the weighty interests served by restricting the size of financial contributions to political candidates are sufficient to justify the limited effect upon First Amendment freedoms caused by the $1,000 contribution ceiling....

[The $5,000 limitation on contributions by political committees, limitations on volunteers' incidental expenses, and the $25,000 limitation on total contributions during any calendar year were upheld by the Court using similar reasoning.]...

C. EXPENDITURE LIMITATIONS　The Act's expenditure ceilings impose direct and substantial restraints on the quantity of political speech.... It is clear that a primary effect of these expenditure limitations is to restrict the quantity of campaign speech by individuals, groups, and candidates. The restrictions, while neutral as to the ideas expressed, limit political expression "at the core of our electoral process and of the First Amendment freedoms." *Williams v. Rhodes*, 393 U.S. 23 (1968).

1. The $1,000 Limitation on Expenditures "Relative to a Clearly Identified Candidate"　Section 608(e)(1) provides that "[n]o person may make any expenditure ... relative to a clearly identified candidate during a calendar year which, when added to all other expenditures made by such person during the year advocating the election or defeat of such candidate, exceeds $1,000." The plain effect of §608(e)(1) is to prohibit all individuals, who are neither candidates nor owners of institutional press facilities, and all groups, except political parties and campaign organizations, from voicing their views "relative to a clearly identified candidate" through means that entail aggregate expenditures of more than $1,000 during a calendar year. The provision, for example, would make it a federal criminal offense for a person or association to place a single one-quarter page advertisement "relative to a clearly identified candidate" in a major metropolitan newspaper....

We find that the governmental interest in preventing corruption is inadequate to justify §608(e)(1)'s ceiling on independent expenditures. First, assuming, *arguendo*, that large independent expenditures pose the same dangers of actual or apparent *quid pro quo* arrangements as do large contributions, §608(e)(1) does not provide an answer that sufficiently relates to the elimination of those dangers. Unlike the contribution limitations' total ban on the giving of large amounts of money to candidates, §608(e)(1) prevents only some large expenditures. So long as persons and groups eschew expenditures that in express terms advocate the election or defeat of a clearly identified candidate, they are free to spend as much as they want to promote the candidate and his views....

Second, quite apart from the shortcomings of §608(e)(1) in preventing any abuses generated by large independent expenditures, the independent advocacy restricted by the provision does not presently appear to pose dangers of real or apparent corruption comparable to those identified with large campaign contributions.... Unlike contributions, such independent expenditures may well provide little assistance to the candidate's campaign and indeed may prove counterproductive. The absence of prearrangement and coordination of an expenditure with the candidate or his agent not only undermines the value of the expenditure to the candidate, but also alleviates the danger that expenditures will be given as a *quid pro quo* for improper commitments from the candidate. Rather than preventing circumvention of the contribution limitations, §608(e)(1) severely restricts all independent advocacy despite its substantially diminished potential for abuse.

While the independent expenditure ceiling thus fails to serve any substantial governmental interest in stemming the reality or appearance of corruption in the electoral process, it heavily burdens core First Amendment expression.... Advocacy of the election or defeat of candidates for federal office is no less entitled to protection under the First Amendment than the discussion of political policy generally or advocacy of the passage or defeat of legislation.

It is argued, however, that the ancillary governmental interest in equalizing the relative ability of individuals and groups to influence the outcome of elections serves to justify the limitation on express advocacy of the election or defeat of candidates imposed by §608(e)(1)'s expenditure ceiling. But the concept that government may restrict the speech of some elements of our society in order to enhance the relative voice of others is wholly foreign to the First Amendment, which was designed "to secure 'the widest possible dissemination of information from diverse and antagonistic sources,'" and "'to assure unfettered interchange of ideas for the bringing about of political and social changes desired by the people.'" *New York Times Co. v. Sullivan*, 376 U.S. 254 (1964). The First Amendment's protection against governmental abridgment of free expression cannot properly be made to depend on a person's financial ability to engage in public discussion....

For the reasons stated, we conclude that §608(e)(1)'s independent expenditure limitation is unconstitutional under the First Amendment.

2. Limitation on Expenditures by Candidates from Personal or Family Resources The Act also sets limits on expenditures by a candidate "from his personal funds, or the personal funds of his immediate family, in connection with his campaigns during any calendar year." §608(a)(1). These ceilings vary from $50,000 for presidential or vice presidential candidates to $35,000 for senatorial candidates, and $25,000 for most candidates for the House of Representatives.

The ceiling on personal expenditures by candidates on their own behalf, like the limitations on independent expenditures contained in §608(e)(1), imposes a substantial restraint on the ability of persons to engage in protected First Amendment expression. The candidate, no less than any other person, has a First Amendment right to engage in the discussion of public issues and vigorously and tirelessly to advocate his own election and the election of other candidates....

The primary governmental interest served by the Act—the prevention of actual and apparent corruption of the political process—does not support the limitation on the candidate's expenditure of his own personal funds....

The ancillary interest in equalizing the relative financial resources of candidates competing for elective office, therefore, provides the sole relevant rationale for §608(a)'s expenditure ceiling. That interest is clearly not sufficient to justify the provision's infringement of fundamental First Amendment rights.... We therefore hold that §608(a)'s restriction on a candidate's personal expenditures is unconstitutional.

3. Limitations on Campaign Expenditures Section 608(c) places limitations on overall campaign expenditures by candidates seeking nomination for election and election to federal office. Presidential candidates may spend $10,000,000 in seeking nomination for office and an additional $20,000,000 in the general election campaign. The ceiling on senatorial campaigns is pegged to the size of the voting-age population of the State with minimum dollar amounts applicable to campaigns in States with small popula-

tions.... The Act imposes blanket $70,000 limitations on both primary campaigns and general election campaigns for the House of Representatives with the exception that the senatorial ceiling applies to campaigns in States entitled to only one Representative. These ceilings are to be adjusted upwards at the beginning of each calendar year by the average percentage rise in the consumer price index for the 12 preceding months.

No governmental interest that has been suggested is sufficient to justify the restriction on the quantity of political expression imposed by §608(c)'s campaign expenditure limitations. The major evil associated with rapidly increasing campaign expenditures is the danger of candidate dependence on large contributions. The interest in alleviating the corrupting influence of large contributions is served by the Act's contribution limitations and disclosure provisions rather than by §608(c)'s campaign expenditure ceilings....

The campaign expenditure ceilings appear to be designed primarily to serve the governmental interests in reducing the allegedly skyrocketing costs of political campaigns.... In any event, the mere growth in the cost of federal election campaigns in and of itself provides no basis for governmental restrictions on the quantity of campaign spending and the resulting limitation on the scope of federal campaigns. The First Amendment denies government the power to determine that spending to promote one's political views is wasteful, excessive, or unwise. In the free society ordained by our Constitution it is not the government, but the people—individually as citizens and candidates and collectively as associations and political committees—who must retain control over the quantity and range of debate on public issues in a political campaign.

For these reasons we hold that §608(c) is constitutionally invalid.

In sum, the provisions of the Act that impose a $1,000 limitation on contributions to a single candidate, a $5,000 limitation on contributions by a political committee to a single candidate, and a $25,000 limitation on total contributions by an individual during any calendar year, are constitutionally valid. These limitations, along with the disclosure provisions, constitute the Act's primary weapons against the reality or appearance of improper influence stemming from the dependence of candidates on large campaign contributions. The contribution ceilings thus serve the basic governmental interest in safeguarding the integrity of the electoral process without directly impinging upon the rights of individual citizens and candidates to engage in political debate and discussion. By contrast, the First Amendment requires the invalidation of the Act's independent expenditure ceiling, its limitation on a candidate's expenditures from his own personal funds, and its ceilings on overall campaign expenditures. These provisions place substantial and direct restrictions on the ability of candidates, citizens, and associations to engage in protected political expression, restrictions that the First Amendment cannot tolerate.

II. Reporting and Disclosure Requirements ... We find no constitutional infirmities in the recordkeeping reporting, and disclosure provisions of the Act.

III. Public Financing of Presidential Election Campaigns ... [The public financing of presidential election campaigns was upheld by the Court.]

Conclusion In summary, we sustain the individual contribution limits, the disclosure and reporting provisions, and the public financing scheme. We conclude, however, that the limitations on campaign expenditures, on independent expenditures by individuals and groups, and on expenditures by a candidate from his personal funds are constitutionally infirm. Finally, we hold that most of the powers conferred by the Act upon the Federal Election Commission can be exercised only by "Officers of the United States," appointed in conformity with Art. II, §2, cl[ause] 2, of the Constitution, and therefore cannot be exercised by the Commission as presently constituted....

BURGER, C.J., CONCURRING IN PART AND DISSENTING IN PART

... I dissent from those parts of the Court's holding sustaining the statutory provisions (a) for disclosure of small contributions, (b) for limitations on contributions, and (c) for public financing of Presidential campaigns. In my view, the Act's disclosure scheme is impermissibly broad and violative of the First Amendment as it relates to reporting contributions in excess of $10 and $100. The contribution limitations infringe on First Amendment liberties and suffer from the same infirmities that the Court correctly sees in the expenditure ceilings. The system for public financing of Presidential campaigns is, in my judgment, an impermissible intrusion by the Government into the traditionally private political process.

More broadly, the Court's result does violence to the intent of Congress in this comprehensive scheme of campaign finance. By dissecting the Act bit by bit, and casting off vital parts, the Court fails to recognize that the whole of this Act is greater than the sum of its parts. Congress intended to regulate all aspects of federal campaign finances, but what remains after today's holding leaves no more than a shadow of what Congress contemplated. I question whether the residue leaves a workable program....

WHITE, J., CONCURRING IN PART AND DISSENTING IN PART

... The disclosure requirements and the limitations on contributions and expenditures are challenged as invalid abridgments of the right of free speech protected by the First Amendment. I would reject these challenges. I agree with the Court's conclusion and much of its opinion with respect to sustaining the disclosure provisions. I am also in agreement with the Court's judgment upholding the limitations on contributions. I dissent, however, from the Court's view that the expenditure limitations ... violate the First Amendment.

Concededly, neither the limitations on contributions nor those on expenditures directly or indirectly purport to control the content of political speech by candidates or by their supporters or detractors. What the Act regulates is giving and spending money, acts that have First Amendment significance not because they are themselves communicative with respect to the qualifications of the candidate, but because money may be used to defray the expenses of speaking or otherwise communicating about the merits or demerits of federal candidates for election. The act of giving money to political candidates, however, may have illegal or other undesirable consequences: it may be used to secure the express or tacit understanding that the giver will enjoy political favor if the candidate is elected. Both Congress and this Court's cases have recognized this as a mortal danger against

which effective preventive and curative steps must be taken....

MARSHALL, J., CONCURRING IN PART AND DISSENTING IN PART

... The Court invalidates [the FECA section that limits the amount a candidate may spend from his personal funds, or family funds under his control, in connection with his campaigns during any calendar year] as violative of the candidate's First Amendment rights. "(T)he First Amendment," the Court explains, "simply cannot tolerate [that section's] restriction upon the freedom of a candidate to speak without legislative limit on behalf of his own candidacy." I disagree....

One of the points on which all Members of the Court agree is that money is essential for effective communication in a political campaign. It would appear to follow that the candidate with a substantial personal fortune at his disposal is off to a significant "headstart." Of course, the less wealthy candidate can potentially overcome the disparity in resources through contributions from others. But ability to generate contributions may itself depend upon a showing of a financial base for the campaign or some demonstration of pre-existing support, which in turn is facilitated by expenditures of substantial personal sums. Thus the wealthy candidate's immediate access to a substantial personal fortune may give him an initial advantage that his less wealthy opponent can never overcome. And even if the advantage can be overcome, the perception that personal wealth wins elections may not only discourage potential candidates without significant personal wealth from entering the political arena, but also undermine public confidence in the integrity of the electoral process....

BLACKMUN, J., CONCURRING IN PART AND DISSENTING IN PART

I am not persuaded that the Court makes, or indeed is able to make, a principled constitutional distinction between the contribution limitations, on the one hand, and the expenditure limitations on the other, that are involved here. I therefore ... dissent....

REHNQUIST, J., CONCURRING IN PART AND DISSENTING IN PART

... I ... join in all of the Court's opinion except [that part] which sustains, against appellants' First and Fifth Amendment challenges, the disparities found in the congressional plan for financing general Presidential elections between the two major parties, on the one hand, and minor parties and candidacies on the other.

While I am not sure that I agree with the Court's comment that "public financing is generally less restrictive of access to the electoral process than the ballot-access regulations dealt with in prior cases," in any case that is not, under my view, an adequate answer to appellants' claim....

Congress in this legislation ... has enshrined the Republican and Democratic Parties in a permanently preferred position, and has established requirements for funding minor-party and independent candidates to which the two major parties are not subject. Congress would undoubtedly be justified in treating the Presidential candidates of the two major parties differently from minor-party or independent Presidential candidates, in view of the long demonstrated public support of the former. But because of the First Amendment overtones of the appellants' Fifth Amendment equal protection claim something more than a merely rational basis for the difference in treatment must be shown, as the Court apparently recognizes. I find it impossible to subscribe to the Court's reasoning that because no third party has posed a credible threat to the two major parties in Presidential elections since 1860, Congress may by law attempt to assure that this pattern will endure forever....

QUESTIONS

1. How persuasive, for constitutional purposes, is the Court's distinction between limitations on campaign expenditures, which it rejected, and limitations on campaign contributions, which it approved? Does it make sense to link unlimited campaign expenditures with the integrity of the electoral process; or does asking the question this way prefigure an answer by assuming that spending money is equivalent to free speech? Is the Court correct that "the concept that government may restrict the speech of some elements of our society in order to enhance the relative voice of others is wholly foreign to the First Amendment"?

2. Throughout the nineteenth century, being a member of Congress was not regarded as a career and members often served only one term. From 1863 to 1969 the turnover rate declined as the proportion of first-term members in the House of Representatives fell from 58 percent to 8 percent. The figure rose slightly to around 16 percent in

1981. At present, the typical representative has served in the House for just under five terms. Since 1946, more than 90 percent of incumbent representatives seeking reelection have been returned to office. In this same period, 75 percent of incumbent senators seeking reelection have been returned. In 1948 the margin of victory in most elections where an incumbent representative was running was close, with the victor getting less than 55 percent of the vote. By 1970 winners in over three-fourths of such contests received 60 percent or more of the vote. Political scientists refer to this last phenomenon as the decline of marginal districts.

After *Buckley*, what incentives exist for sitting members of Congress to reform existing campaign finance practices?

3. Law professors Norman Dorsen and Joel Gora argue that the Burger Court protected First Amendment values "mainly when they have coincided with property interests; conversely, free expression has received diminished protection when First Amendment claims have appeared to clash with property interests" (Vincent Blasi, ed., *The Burger Court: The Counter-Revolution That Wasn't* [New Haven, CT: Yale University Press, 1983], p. 31). Do the Court's decisions in *Buckley* and *Lloyd Corporation* substantiate that contention?

4. *Buckley* sustained the legality of public financing of federal electoral campaigns as well as the legality of requiring candidates who accept public money for their campaigns to agree to spending caps, and to commit to not raising private funds. Is this approach to campaign funding a viable alternative to the present system?

COMMENT

Following *Buckley*, the Court has been asked to consider the constitutionality of other aspects of federal, state, and local campaign finance regulations. The following case summaries illustrate the Court's responses, which are not entirely consistent:

Case: *First National Bank of Boston v. Bellotti*, 435 U.S. 765 (1978)
Vote: 5–4
Decision: A Massachusetts total ban on money contributions by business corporations trying to influence the outcome of a referendum violates the First Amendment.

Case: *California Medical Association v. Federal Election Commission*, 453 U.S. 182 (1981)
Vote: 5–4
Decision: A $5,000 per year limit on contributions that an individual or unincorporated association can contribute to a political action committee does not violate the First Amendment.

Case: *Citizens against Rent Control/Coalition for Fair Housing v. City of Berkeley, CA* 454 U.S. 290 (1981)

Vote: 8–1

Decision: A city ordinance limiting to $250 the amount a citizen can contribute to a group taking a position on a ballot measure violates the First Amendment.

Case: *Common Cause v. Schmitt*, 455 U.S. 129 (1982)

Vote: 4–4 (*per curiam*; O'Connor, J., did not participate.)

Decision: Under the First Amendment, political action committees and other independent groups have a right to spend unlimited amounts in presidential campaigns, and governments may not limit campaign contributions by individuals to organizations formed to support or oppose referendum and other ballot measures. (The Supreme Court split 4–4, thereby affirming the D.C. District Court.)

Case: *Brown v. Socialist Workers '74 Campaign Committee*, 459 U.S. 87 (1982)

Vote: 6–3

Decision: An Ohio statute requiring every candidate for political office to report the names and addresses of campaign contributors and the recipients of campaign expenditures, as applied to the Socialist Worker Party, violates the First Amendment. That Amendment prohibits a state from compelling disclosures by a minor party that has historically been the object of harassment and reprisals by government officials and private parties.

Case: *Federal Election Commission v. National Right to Work Committee*, 459 U.S. 197 (1982)

Vote: 9–0

Decision: A Federal Election Campaign Act (FECA) prohibition on corporate and labor union contributions or expenditures in federal elections, except from "separate segregated funds" solicited from "members" of the corporation does not impermissibly interfere with First Amendment associational rights. The National Right to Work Committee, a corporation without capital stock, violated this FECA provision when it solicited contributions from persons insufficiently attached to the corporation to qualify as members.

Case: *Federal Election Commission v. National Conservative Political Action Committee, Democratic Party of the United States v. National Conservative Political Action Committee*, 470 U.S. 480 (1985)

Vote: 7–2

Decision: The $1,000 limit imposed by the Federal Election Campaign Act amendments on independent expenditures by Political Action Committees in presidential campaigns violates the First Amendment.

Case: *Federal Election Commission v. Massachusetts Citizens for Life, Inc.*, 479 U.S. 238 (1986)

Vote: 5–4

Decision: A Federal Election Commission regulation prohibiting political expenditures by nonprofit advocacy groups that take a position on issues such as abortion violates the First Amendment. These groups may take out advertisements urging voters to support or reject specific candidates.

Case: *Meyer v. Grant*, 486 U.S. 414 (1988)

Vote: 9–0

Decision: A Colorado statute prohibiting the collection of signatures supporting a proposed constitutional amendment ballot measure by paid petition circulators violates the First Amendment.

Case: *Austin v. Michigan Chamber of Commerce*, 494 U.S. 652 (1990)
Vote: 6–3
Decision: A Michigan statute prohibiting corporations from using corporate treasury funds for independent expenditures to support or oppose candidates in state election is constitutional.

CONTROVERSIES INVOLVING VARIETIES OF POLITICAL SPEECH

City of Ladue v. Gilleo
512 U.S. 43 (1994)

SETTING

Cases like *Lloyd Corporation v. Tanner* have addressed the issue of access to private property in order to exercise free speech. A related issue is the extent of a landowner's rights to engage in expressive conduct on his or her own private property. For instance, does the First Amendment guarantee a landowner the right to erect a billboard despite regulatory laws to the contrary? As early as 1917, the Court upheld municipal zoning ordinances, regulating the height and location of billboards, as valid exercises of the police power. *Cusack v. Chicago*, 242 U.S. 526. However, in the initial First Amendment challenge to billboard regulations, the Court overturned a statute banning all commercial and noncommercial billboards in the interests of "traffic safety and the appearance of the city." *Metromedia, Inc. v. San Diego*, 453 U.S. 490 (1981). The justices were badly divided; nevertheless, their five opinions seemed more deferential to regulations of commercial speech than to noncommercial speech.

Ten years after *Metromedia*, questions remaining about the constitutional status of laws seeking to regulate signs were addressed in a case arising out of a protest against the Persian Gulf War. That conflict lasted over a month in early 1991. On January 12, 1991, Congress passed a resolution authorizing the president to use "all means necessary" to force Iraq from Kuwait after January 15, the withdrawal deadline set by the UN Security Council. After a thirty-eight day bombing campaign against Iraqi targets, a ground attack began. One hundred hours later, on February 27, 1991, a cease fire was announced. Debates and divisions over the war echoed throughout the country.

The city of Ladue, Missouri, a suburb of St. Louis, is a residential community of approximately nine thousand population and 8.5 square miles that traces its history to settlements in the early nineteenth century. The city has adhered strictly to its original 1936 comprehensive plan, which called for large lot sizes and low building densities, and large areas of plant materials, woods, streams, and open areas. The plan was prepared by a famous city planner, Harland Bartholomew, who helped to restore the historic colonial city of Williamsburg, Virginia. Many of the city's historic buildings have been preserved. In the 1940s, Ladue established an Architectural Review Board to preserve its aesthetic and visual harmony by carefully regulating all architectural changes. It also organized a Civic Improvement Committee to foster and encourage the beautification and aesthetic improvement of all public and semi-public areas. That committee has operated continuously ever since. The consequence is a city of unusual charm and aesthetic ambience.

Since incorporation of the city in 1936, Ladue has also maintained strict sign regulations. What came to be known as "Old Chapter 35" prohibited all signs in Ladue except those expressly authorized by ordinance. Permitted signs included municipal signs, subdivision identification signs, road signs, signs on homes stating the name and profession of an occupant, real estate signs, signs for churches and schools, and a variety of commercial signs. Old Chapter 35 also permitted the city council to grant variances "where there are practical difficulties or unnecessary hardships, or where the public interest will be best served by permitting such variation."

Margaret Gilleo resided on Willow Hill Lane, in the Willow Hill subdivision of Ladue. The street is privately owned and maintained by the trustees of the subdivision and governed by a trust indenture containing restrictions on the use of one's real estate. Willow Hill has been characterized as "country-like, charming and private." In December 1990, Gilleo was deeply concerned over the prospect of a United States war with Iraq. A St. Louis area group was distributing lawn signs to raise public awareness of the issue and to encourage people to contact their elected representatives in Washington, D.C., Gilleo obtained a 24-by-36-inch sign and placed it in the front yard of her home. The text of the sign read, "Say No to War in the Persian Gulf, Call Congress Now." Shortly after she posted her sign she was informed by Ladue police that such signs were prohibited in the city.

Gilleo asked the Ladue City Council for a variance to permit her to maintain her sign. The council voted unanimously to deny the variance request, apparently in part because of the "controversial" nature of her sign.

On December 20, 1990, Gilleo filed a complaint against Ladue in U.S. District Court for the Eastern District of Missouri seeking an injunction against enforcement of the sign ordinance on the ground that it violated the First Amendment. On January 7, 1991, the district court ruled that Ladue's sign ordinance, on its face, violated the First Amendment and entered a preliminary injunction.

Fourteen days later, on January 21, 1991, Ladue repealed Old Chapter 35 and adopted a replacement ordinance. New Chapter 35 was virtually identical to the old chapter in terms of its preferential treatment of commercial speech over noncommercial speech. The principal change was a lengthy preamble captioned, "Declaration of Findings, Policies, Interests and Purposes," that declared that the sign restrictions were necessary "to protect and preserve the City of Ladue's interests in privacy, aesthetics, safety and property values."

On January 28, 1991, Gilleo filed an amended complaint challenging the constitutionality of New Chapter 35 on essentially the same basis as Old Chapter 35. By the time the city filed its counterclaim seeking a declaratory judgment that New Chapter 35 is valid, Gilleo's sign had been stolen from her front yard and she was displaying an 8 ½-by-11-inch sign inside a second-floor window of her home that stated, "For Peace in the Gulf."

Both parties moved for summary judgment. The district court granted Gilleo's motion and denied Ladue's. It ruled that the sign ordinance was facially unconstitutional and permanently enjoined its enforcement. The U.S. Court of Appeals for the Eighth Circuit affirmed, declaring New Chapter 35 to be a content-based regulation of speech that "favors commercial speech over noncommercial speech, and ... favors certain types of noncommercial speech over others." It held that the ordinance must withstand strict scrutiny to survive; that is, that it must be narrowly drawn to serve a compelling state interest. The City of Ladue, through its mayor and other officials, petitioned the Supreme Court of the United States for a writ of certiorari.

HIGHLIGHTS OF SUPREME COURT ARGUMENTS

BRIEF FOR CITY OF LADUE

◆ The uncontested record is that the City of Ladue has made a comprehensive commitment to aesthetics throughout its history.

◆ The City of Ladue's sign ordinance satisfies the test under which this Court traditionally reviews reasonable regulations of the time, place, and manner of speech on public and private property. That test is appropriate because Ladue's sign ordinance involves the regulation of signs, not a total ban on signs.

◆ This Court has held that aesthetics, privacy, safety, and the maintenance of real estate values are significant governmental interests that cities may protect. The Court should uphold the Ladue sign ordinance because it is based on a content-neutral aesthetic justification.

◆ The *Metromedia* plurality conflicts with the more recent decision in *City of Cincinnati v. Discovery Network, Inc.*, 507 U.S. 410 (1993), in which this Court invalidated an ordinance that banned from city streets sixty-two news racks that distributed commercial publications but allowed thousands of other news racks to remain. The Court declared that the ordinance "attaches more importance to the distinction between commercial and noncommercial speech than our cases warrant and seriously underestimates the value of commercial speech." Ladue's sign ordinance is not based on an erroneous constitutional distinction between commercial and noncommercial speech.

◆ Ladue has the right to regulate private property to prevent the nuisance of visual blight. That authority is rooted in the police power. Ladue's sign ordinance, designed to prevent visual blight that harms its natural landscapes and aesthetic ambience, stands on the same authority as state laws prohibiting individuals from creating nuisances on their private property.

◆ Even if Ladue's sign ordinance is deemed to regulate the content of speech, it satisfies the compelling state interest test because it permits as much speech as possible while also protecting Ladue's residents from the evils of sign proliferation.

AMICUS CURIAE BRIEFS SUPPORTING LADUE

Joint brief of the National Institute of Municipal Law Officers, International City/County Management Association, U.S. Conference of Mayors, National League of Cities, and National Association of Counties; joint brief of the States of Hawaii, Indiana, Maryland, New Hampshire, New Jersey, Pennsylvania, and Vermont.

BRIEF FOR GILLEO

◆ Gilleo's sign constituted virtually pure speech, which is at the core of the First Amendment, and concerned an issue of war and peace. It was located on private property, in such a manner as to be visible to passersby on the street. Streets are traditional public forums for the exercise of First Amendment rights.

◆ Ladue's sign ordinance is a particularly odious restraint on speech because it is content-based. It bans certain signs because of their subject matter, while allowing others. As a content-based restriction against free expression, Ladue's ordinance is subject to, and fails, strict scrutiny.

◆ Ladue's ordinance inverts the constitutional principles that noncommercial speech enjoys greater First Amendment protection than commercial speech.

◆ Ladue's effort to justify the sign ordinance as a time, place, and manner regulation is unavailing. The ordinance burdens more speech than is necessary to serve Ladue's asserted interest in aesthetics. The ordinance is not content neutral, is not narrowly tailored, and does not leave open alternative avenues for communication.

AMICUS CURIAE BRIEFS SUPPORTING GILLEO

United States; joint brief of American Advertising Federation, American Association of Advertising Agencies, Magazine Publishers of America, and the Media Institute, joint brief of People for the American Way and the American Jewish Congress, Washington Legal Foundation; Association of National Advertisers, Inc.

SUPREME COURT DECISION: *9–0*

STEVENS, J.

... The question presented is whether the ordinance [at issue] violates a Ladue resident's right to free speech....

While signs are a form of expression protected by the Free Speech Clause, they pose distinctive problems that are subject to municipalities' police powers. Unlike oral speech, signs take up space and may obstruct views, distract motorists, displace alternative uses for land, and pose other problems that legitimately call for regulation. It is common ground that governments may regulate the physical characteristics of signs—just as they can, within reasonable bounds and absent censorial purpose, regulate audible expression in its capacity as noise.... However, because regulation of a medium inevitably affects communication itself, it is not surprising that we have had occasion to review the constitutionality of municipal ordinances prohibiting the display of certain outdoor signs....

[Our] decisions identify two analytically distinct grounds for challenging the constitutionality of a municipal ordinance regulating the display of signs. One is that the measure in effect restricts too little speech because its exemptions discriminate on the basis of the signs' messages.... Alternatively, such provisions are subject to attack on the ground that they simply prohibit too much protected speech.... The City of Ladue contends, first, that the Court of Appeals' reliance on the former rationale was misplaced because the City's regulatory purposes are content-neutral, and second, that those purposes justify the comprehensiveness of the sign prohibition. A comment on the former contention will help explain why we ultimately base our decision on a rejection of the latter.

While surprising at first glance, the notion that a regulation of speech may be impermissibly underinclusive is firmly grounded in basic First Amendment principles. Thus, an exemption from an otherwise permissible regulation of speech may represent a governmental "attempt to give one side of a debatable public question an advantage in expressing its views to the people." *First National Bank of Boston v. Belloti*, 435 U.S. 765 (1978). Alternatively, through the combined

operation of a general speech restriction and its exemptions, the government might seek to select the "permissible subjects for public debate" and thereby to "control ... the search for political truth." *Consolidated Edison Co. of N.Y. v. Public Service Commission of N.Y.*, 447 U.S. 530 (1980)....

Even if we assume the validity of [the city's] arguments, the exemptions in Ladue's ordinance nevertheless shed light on the separate question of whether the ordinance prohibits too much speech.

Exemptions from an otherwise legitimate regulation of a medium of speech may be noteworthy for a reason quite apart from the risks of viewpoint and content discrimination: they may diminish the credibility of the government's rationale for restricting speech in the first place.... In this case, at the very least, the exemptions from Ladue's ordinance demonstrate that Ladue has concluded that the interest in allowing certain messages to be conveyed by means of residential signs outweighs the City's aesthetic interest in eliminating outdoor signs. Ladue has not imposed a flat ban on signs because it has determined that at least some of them are too vital to be banned.

Under the Court of Appeals' content discrimination rationale, the City might theoretically remove the defects in its ordinance by simply repealing all of the exemptions. If, however, the ordinance is also vulnerable because it prohibits too much speech, that solution would not save it. Moreover, if the prohibitions in Ladue's ordinance are impermissible, resting our decision on its exemptions would afford scant relief for respondent Gilleo. She is primarily concerned not with the scope of the exemptions available in other locations, such as commercial areas and on church property. She asserts a constitutional right to display an antiwar sign at her own home. Therefore, we first ask whether Ladue may properly prohibit Gilleo from displaying her sign, and then, only if necessary, consider the separate question whether it was improper for the City simultaneously to permit certain other signs. In examining the propriety of Ladue's near total prohibition of residential signs, we will assume, *arguendo*, the validity of the City's submission that the various exemptions are free of impermissible content of viewpoint discrimination....

Ladue has almost completely foreclosed a venerable means of communication that is both unique and important. It has totally foreclosed that medium to political, religious, or personal messages. Signs that react to a local happening or express a view on a controversial issue both reflect and animate change in the life of a community. Often placed on lawns or in windows, residential signs play an important part in political campaigns, during which they are displayed to signal the resident's support for particular candidates, parties, or causes. They may not afford the same opportunities for conveying complex ideas as do other media, but residential signs have long been an important and distinct medium of expression.

Our prior decisions have voiced particular concern with laws that foreclose an entire medium of expression....

Ladue contends, however, that its ordinance is a mere regulation of the "time, place, or manner" of speech because residents remain free to convey their desired messages by other means, such as handheld signs, "letters, handbills, flyers, telephone calls, newspaper advertisements, bumper stickers, speeches, and neighborhood or community meetings." However, even regulations that do not foreclose an entire medium of expression, but merely shift the time, place, or manner of its use, must "leave open ample alternative channels for communication." *Clark v. Community for Creative Non-Violence*, 468 U.S. 288 (1984). In this case, we are not persuaded that adequate substitutes exist for the important medium of speech that Ladue has closed off.

Displaying a sign from one's own residence often carries a message quite distinct from placing the same sign someplace else, or conveying the same text or picture by other means. Precisely because of their location such signs provide information about the identity of the "speaker."...

Residential signs are an unusually cheap and convenient form of communication. Especially for persons of modest means or limited mobility, a yard or window sign may have no practical substitute.... Even for the affluent, the added costs in money or time of taking out a newspaper advertisement, handing out leaflets on the street, or standing in front of one's house with a handheld sign may make the difference between participating and not participating in some public debate. Furthermore, a person who puts up a sign at her residence often intends to reach *neighbors*, an audience that could not be reached nearly as well by other means.

A special respect for individual liberty in the home has long been part of our culture and our law, ... that principle has special resonance when the government seeks to constrain a person's ability to *speak* there. Most Americans would be understandably dismayed, given that tradition, to learn that it was illegal to display from their window an 8- by 11-inch sign expressing their political views. Whereas the government's need to mediate among various competing uses, including expressive ones, for public streets and facilities is constant and unavoidable, ... its need to regulate temperate speech from the home is surely much less pressing....

Accordingly, the judgment of the Court of Appeals is

Affirmed.

O'CONNOR, J., CONCURRING

It is unusual for us, when faced with a regulation that on its face draws content distinctions, to "assume, *arguendo*, the validity of the City's submission that the various exemptions are free of impermissible content or viewpoint discrimination." With rare exceptions, content discrimination in regulations of the speech of private citizens on private property in a traditional public forum is presumptively impermissible, and this presumption is a very strong one.... The normal inquiry that our doctrine dictates is, first, to determine whether a regulation is content-based or content-neutral, and then, based on the answer to that question, to apply the proper level of scrutiny....

I would have preferred to apply our normal analytical structure in this case, which may well have required us to examine this law with the scrutiny appropriate to content-based regulations.

QUESTIONS

1. On what ground did the Court invalidate the City of Ladue's ordinance in *Ladue*? In what way does the majority "depart" from its "normal analytical structure?"

2. The *amicus curiae* brief on behalf of the various advertising organizations was submitted to the Court "to ensure that the right to disseminate, and the public's right to receive, truthful commercial speech about lawful products and services is protected." What principle, if any, unites Gilleo's interest with the interests of the commercial *amici*?

3. In the wake of the Court's decision in *Ladue*, how might members of a city council who wish to maintain the aesthetic qualities of their community proceed? Must they repeal their sign ordinance, or is it possible to draft an ordinance that would promote the city's goals while being consistent with free speech rights?

4. Gilleo initially displayed a 24-by-36-inch sign on her front yard and then, after that sign was stolen, she displayed an 8½-by-11-inch sign in a second-story window. Suppose that she had erected a 24-by-36-*foot* sign on her property. Or suppose that, instead of reading "Say No to War in the Persian Gulf, Call Congress Now," her original yard sign had contained expletives aimed at the president. Or suppose that Gilleo had erected flood lights to illuminate her original sign 24 hours a day. Would the First Amendment protect these forms of expression?

CONTROVERSIES INVOLVING VARIETIES OF POLITICAL SPEECH

McIntyre v. Ohio Elections Commission
514 U.S. 334 (1995)

SETTING

Anonymous speech raises another First Amendment controversy. Pseudonymous authorship has been the vehicle for political propaganda and dissident speech throughout American history. As the Supreme Court observed in *Talley v. California*, 362 U.S. 60 (1960), "Anonymous pamphlets, leaflets, brochures and even books have played an important role in the progress of mankind." In the United States, anonymous and pseudonymous pamphleteering was especially common during the Revolutionary War and the debates concerning ratification of the Constitution. Works now known as *The Federalist* and *Anti-Federalist*, penned using pseudonyms, form an integral and honored part of our political culture. As late as during the cold war, George Kennan's article in *Foreign Affairs* advocating the foreign policy of containment of Soviet expansionism appeared under the pen name of "X."

Over the years, however, states have become increasingly concerned over the accuracy of what is said and written during political campaigns. Ohio Revised Code Section 3599.09(A), for example, requires that the name and address of a person or organization that is responsible for distributing any publication aimed at influencing an election or defeating a candidate or ballot issue appear on the literature distributed by that person or organization. The purpose of the law is to make it possible to hold writers accountable for the truth of what they print.

On the evening of April 27, 1988, Margaret McIntyre, her son, and his girlfriend distributed leaflets at the Blendon Middle School in Westerville, Ohio, opposing passage of a school tax levy that was to be voted on in a referendum during the following week. They chose that location because the school was the site of a regularly scheduled school meeting at which the superintendent of schools was to address the merits of the levy. McIntyre handed out leaflets in the doorway of the meeting room, while her son and his girlfriend put them under automobile windshield wipers in the parking lot. The leaflets called the levy a "WASTE of tax payers['] dollars" and urged a "no" vote. Some of the leaflets identified Margaret McIntyre as the author. Others merely purported to express the views of "Concerned Parents and Taxpayers." J. Michael Hayfield, assistant superintendent of elementary education for the schools, informed McIntyre that her leaflets violated Section 3599.09 because they did not contain her name and address.

The next night, McIntyre again distributed the leaflets at a meeting at the Walnut Springs Middle School, where she was again informed that the leaflets did not conform to campaign regulations because they did not contain her name and address.

The school tax levy was defeated twice, and then passed in a November 1988 election. On April 6, 1989, several months after the tax increase was approved and almost a year after McIntyre had distributed leaflets at the two Westerville middle schools, McIntyre received a letter from the Ohio Elections Commission stating that a complaint had been filed by Hayfield for distributing leaflets without including her name and address. The charges initially were dismissed for want of prosecution, but were reinstated at Hayfield's request.

McIntyre represented herself at the administrative hearing before the Ohio Elections Commission. She denied any intent to violate the law, stating that "The ones I passed out, to the best of my knowledge, all of them had my name on them, all of them. I wouldn't have passed it out without my name on it." The commission fined her $100. McIntyre appealed to the Franklin County Court of Common Pleas, which reversed. Because the commission had made no factual findings, the sole issue was whether the statutory ban on anonymous campaign literature was constitutional. The Court of Common Pleas held that the statute was unconstitutional as applied. A divided Court of Appeals of Ohio for the Tenth Appellate District reversed the Court of Common Pleas and reinstated the fine. The Ohio Supreme Court, also by a divided vote, affirmed the appellate court. It analyzed McIntyre's claim under the test for evaluating the constitutionality of election laws: weighing the burden that the challenged legislation places on First Amendment rights against the legitimate interests of the state in regulating the subject matter. It concluded that Section 3599.09 is constitutional on its face and as applied to McIntyre because it placed only a modest burden on her First Amendment rights, while the state's interest in deterring fraud, misleading advertising, and libel was important to the electoral process.

The Supreme Court granted McIntyre's writ for a petition of certiorari. While the case was pending, McIntyre died and the executor of her estate, Joseph McIntyre, was substituted as the petitioner over the objection of the Ohio attorney general.

Highlights of Supreme Court Arguments

BRIEF FOR MCINTYRE

◆ This case is controlled by *Talley v. California*, 362 U.S. 60 (1960), which held that a flat ban on anonymous leafleting is unconstitutional because it deters the speech of those who fear retaliation and thereby restricts freedom of expression. This Court has repeatedly held that the First Amendment protects anonymous speech.

◆ The Ohio statute must be measured by the compelling state interest test because it is a regulation of the fundamental right to speech and press. The Ohio Supreme Court erred in concluding that the relaxed standard of review applicable to ballot access and voting regulations was applicable to this case.

Ohio has not shown a compelling state interest and has not narrowly tailored the law; the statute is not confined to intentionally false and fraudulent statements and extends to communications about referendum issues that cannot be labeled. The statute is unconstitutional on its face.

◆ The Ohio statute is unconstitutional as applied to McIntyre because she engaged in core political speech about a public issue.

AMICUS CURIAE BRIEF SUPPORTING MCINTYRE

California Political Attorneys Association.

ARGUMENT FOR OHIO ELECTIONS COMMISSION

◆ Under the test set forth in *Anderson v. Celebrezze*, 460 U.S. 780 (1983), a court is to weigh the burden of the challenged legislation against the legitimate interests of the state in regulating the electoral process. The Ohio Supreme Court properly applied that test.

◆ *Talley* is inapposite because it did not involve an election law and hence did not require application of the balancing test of *Anderson*.

◆ States are entitled to protect the integrity of the electoral process, even when First Amendment rights are implicated, as long as any action does not discriminate against the viewpoint expressed in a political message.

◆ The Ohio statute could survive strict scrutiny because of the state's compelling interest in combating election fraud.

◆ The statute at issue in this case is similar to statutes found in many other states. It is a viewpoint neutral regulation.

AMICUS CURIAE BRIEFS SUPPORTING OHIO ELECTIONS COMMISSION

Joint brief of the States of Tennessee, Alabama, Alaska, Arkansas, Colorado, Delaware, Florida, Idaho, Illinois, Indiana, Kentucky, Louisiana, Michigan, Minnesota, Mississippi, Montana, Nevada, New Hampshire, New Jersey, North Carolina, North Dakota, Oklahoma, South Carolina, South Dakota, Vermont, Virginia, West Virginia, Wisconsin, and Wyoming; joint brief of the Council of State Governments, National Conference of State Legislatures, National Association of Counties, International City/County Management Association, U.S. Conference of Mayors, and National League of Cities.

SUPREME COURT DECISION: 7–2

STEVENS, J.

... [A]n author's decision to remain anonymous, like other decisions concerning omissions or additions to the content of a publication, is an aspect of the freedom of speech protected by the First Amendment....

We must ... decide whether and to

what extent the First Amendment's protection of anonymity encompasses documents intended to influence the electoral process....

The "ordinary litigation" test does not apply here. Unlike the statutory provisions challenged in *Storer* [*v. Brown*, 415

U.S. 724 (1974)], and *Anderson* [*v. Celebrezze*, 460 U.S. 780 (1983)], 3599.09(A) of the Ohio Code does not control the mechanics of the electoral process. It is a regulation of pure speech. Moreover, even though this provision applies evenhandedly to advocates of differing view-points, it is a direct regulation of the content of speech. Every written document covered by the statute must contain "the name and residence or business address of the chairman, treasurer, or secretary of the organization issuing the same, or the person who issues, makes, or is responsible therefor." Furthermore, the category of covered documents is defined by their content—only those publications containing speech designed to influence the voters in an election need bear the required markings. Consequently, we are not faced with an ordinary election restriction; this case "involves a limitation on political expression subject to exacting scrutiny." *Meyer v. Grant*, 486 U.S. 414 (1988).

Indeed, as we have explained on many prior occasions, the category of speech regulated by the Ohio statute occupies the core of the protection afforded by the First Amendment....

Of course, core political speech need not center on a candidate for office. The principles enunciated in *Buckley* [*v. Valeo*] extend equally to issue-based elections such as the school-tax referendum that Mrs. McIntyre sought to influence through her handbills.... Indeed, the speech in which Mrs. McIntyre engaged—handing out leaflets in the advocacy of a politically controversial viewpoint—is the essence of First Amendment expression.... That this advocacy occurred in the heat of a controversial referendum vote only strengthens the protection afforded to Mrs. McIntyre's expression: urgent, important, and effective speech can be no less protected than impotent speech, lest the right to speak be relegated to those instances when it is least needed.... No form of speech is entitled to greater constitutional protection than Mrs. McIntyre's.

When a law burdens core political speech, we apply "exacting scrutiny," and we uphold the restriction only if it is narrowly tailored to serve an overriding state interest.... Our precedents thus make abundantly clear that the Ohio Supreme Court applied a significantly more lenient standard than is appropriate in a case of this kind....

Nevertheless, the State argues that even under the strictest standard of review, the disclosure requirement in 3599.09(A) is justified by two important and legitimate state interests. Ohio judges its interest in preventing fraudulent and libelous statements and its interest in providing the electorate with relevant information to be sufficiently compelling to justify the anonymous speech ban. These two interests necessarily overlap to some extent, but it is useful to discuss them separately.

Insofar as the interest in informing the electorate means nothing more than the provision of additional information that may either buttress or undermine the argument in a document, we think the identity of the speaker is no different from other components of the document's content that the author is free to include or exclude. We have already held that the State may not compel a newspaper that prints editorials critical of a particular candidate to provide space for a reply by the candidate. *Miami Herald Publishing Co. v. Tornillo*, 418 U.S. 241 (1974). The simple interest in providing voters with additional relevant information does not justify a state requirement that a writer make statements or disclosures she would otherwise omit. Moreover, in the case of a handbill written by a private citizen who is not known to the recipient, the name and address of the author adds little, if anything, to the reader's ability to evaluate the document's message. Thus, Ohio's informational interest is plainly insufficient to support the constitutionality of its disclosure requirement....

As this case demonstrates, the prohibition [of anonymous leaflets] encompasses documents that are not even arguably false or misleading. It applies not only to the activities of candidates and their organized supporters, but also to individuals acting independently and using only their own modest resources. It applies not only to elections of public officers, but also to ballot issues that present neither a substantial risk of libel nor any potential appearance of corrupt advantage. It applies not only to leaflets distributed on the eve of an election, when the opportunity for reply is limited, but also to those distributed months in advance. It applies no matter what the character or strength of the author's interest in anonymity. Moreover, as this case also demonstrates, the absence of the author's name on a document does not necessarily protect either that person or a distributor of a forbidden document from being held responsible for compliance with the election code. Nor has the State explained why it can more easily enforce the direct bans on disseminating false documents against anonymous authors and distributors than against wrongdoers who might use false names and addresses in an attempt to avoid detection. We recognize that a State's enforcement interest might justify a more limited identification requirement, but Ohio has shown scant cause for inhibiting the leafletting at issue here....

Under our Constitution, anonymous pamphleteering is not a pernicious, fraudulent practice, but an honorable tradition of advocacy and of dissent. Anonymity is a shield from the tyranny of the majority.... It thus exemplifies the purpose behind the Bill of Rights, and of the First Amendment in particular: to protect unpopular individuals from retaliation—and their ideas from suppression—at the hand of an intolerant society. The right to remain anonymous may be abused when it shields fraudulent conduct. But political speech by its nature will sometimes have unpalatable consequences, and, in general, our society accords greater weight to the value of free speech than to the dangers of its misuse.... Ohio has not shown that its interest in preventing the misuse of anonymous election-related speech justifies a prohibition of all uses of that speech. The State may, and does, punish fraud directly. But it cannot seek to punish fraud indirectly by indiscriminately outlawing a category of speech, based on its content, with no necessary relationship to the danger sought to be prevented. One would be hard pressed to think of a better example of the pitfalls of Ohio's blunderbuss approach than the facts of the case before us.

The judgment of the Ohio Supreme Court is reversed.

It is so ordered.

GINSBURG, J., CONCURRING [OMITTED]

THOMAS, J., CONCURRING

... [Historical] evidence leads me to agree with the majority's result, but not its reasoning. The majority fails to seek the original understanding of the First Amendment[.]...

While, like Justice Scalia, I am loath to overturn a century of practice shared by almost all of the States, I believe the historical evidence from the framing outweighs recent tradition.... Because the majority has adopted an analysis that is largely unconnected to the Constitution's text and history, I concur only in the judgment.

SCALIA, J., AND REHNQUIST, C.J., DISSENTING

... The question posed by the present case is not the easiest sort to answer for those who adhere to the Court's (and the society's) traditional view that the Constitution bears its original meaning and is unchanging....

Anonymous electioneering was not prohibited by law in 1791 or in 1868. In fact, it was widely practiced at the earlier date, an understandable legacy of the revolutionary era in which political dissent could produce governmental reprisal....

But to prove that anonymous electioneering was used frequently is not to establish that it is a constitutional right. Quite obviously, not every restriction upon expression that did not exist in 1791 or in 1868 is *ipso facto* unconstitutional....

Evidence that anonymous electioneering was regarded as a constitutional right is sparse, and as far as I am aware evidence that it was *generally* regarded as such is nonexistent....

A governmental practice that has become general throughout the United States, and particularly one that has the validation of long, accepted usage, bears a strong presumption of constitutionality. And that is what we have before us here....

Three basic questions must be answered to decide this case. Two of them are readily answered by our precedents; the third is readily answered by common sense and by a decent regard for the practical judgment of those more familiar with elections than we are. The first question is whether protection of the election process justifies limitations upon speech that cannot constitutionally be imposed generally.... Our cases plainly answer that question in the affirmative—indeed, they suggest that no justification for regulation is more compelling than protection of the electoral process....

The second question relevant to our decision is whether a "right to anonymity" is such a prominent value in our constitutional system that even protection of the electoral process cannot be purchased at its expense. The answer, again, is clear: no. Several of our cases have held that in peculiar circumstances the compelled disclosure of a person's identity would unconstitutionally deter the exercise of First Amendment associational rights.... But those cases did not acknowledge any general right to anonymity, or even any right on the part of all citizens to ignore the particular laws under challenge. Rather, they recognized a right to an *exemption* from otherwise valid disclosure requirements on the part of someone who could show a "reasonable probability" that the compelled disclosure would result in "threats, harassment, or reprisals from either Government officials or private parties." This last quotation is from *Buckley v. Valeo*, which prescribed the safety-valve of a similar exemption in upholding the disclosure requirements of the Federal Election Campaign Act.... Anonymity can still be enjoyed by those who require it, without utterly destroying useful disclosure laws....

The third and last question relevant to our decision is whether the prohibition of anonymous campaigning is effective in protecting and enhancing democratic elections. In answering this question no, the Justices of the majority set their own views—on a practical matter that bears closely upon the real-life experience of elected politicians and not upon that of unelected judges—up against the views of 49 (and perhaps all 50,) ... state legislatures and the federal Congress. We might also add to the list on the other side the legislatures of foreign democracies: Australia, Canada, and England, for example, all have prohibitions upon anonymous campaigning.... How is it, one must wonder, that all of these elected legislators, from around the country and around the world, could not see what six Justices of this Court see so clearly that they are willing to require the entire Nation to act upon it: that requiring identification of the source of campaign literature does not improve the quality of the campaign?...

[T]he usefulness of a signing requirement lies not only in promoting observance of the law against campaign falsehoods (though that alone is enough to sustain it). It lies also in promoting a civil and dignified level of campaign debate—which the State has no power to command, but ample power to encourage by such undemanding measures as a signature requirement. Observers of the past few national elections have expressed concern about the increase of character assassination—"mudslinging" is the colloquial term—engaged in by political candidates and their supporters to the detriment of the democratic process. Not all of this, in fact not much of it, consists of actionable untruth; most is innuendo, or demeaning characterization, or mere disclosure of items of personal life that have no bearing upon suitability for office. Imagine how much all of this would increase if it could be done anonymously. The principal impediment against it is the reluctance of most individuals and organizations to be publicly associated with uncharitable and uncivil expression. Consider, moreover, the increased potential for "dirty tricks." It is not unheard-of for campaign operatives to circulate material over the name of their opponents or their opponents' supporters (a violation of election laws) in order to attract or alienate certain interest groups.... How much easier—and sanction-free!—it would be to circulate anonymous material (for example, a really tasteless, though not actionably false, attack upon one's own candidate) with the hope and expectation that it will be attributed to, and held against, the other side....

I respectfully dissent.

QUESTIONS

1. Does the *McIntyre* ruling call into question the holding in *Buckley v. Valeo* that compelled disclosure in the context of campaign contributions and expenditures is constitutional?

2. What is the proper constitutional standard for reviewing laws like Ohio's disclosure law—rational basis, strict scrutiny, a balancing test, or some other standard? Of what value is Justice Thomas's view that the majority opinion is flawed "because it deviates from our settled approach to interpreting the Constitution and because it superimposes its modern theories concerning expression upon the constitutional text"?

3. The *amicus curiae* brief submitted on behalf of McIntyre was written

by attorneys who practice campaign, elections, and political law. It contended that its members had experienced the "unduly burdensome effect on political expression, especially political expression of those least sophisticated in exercising their First Amendment rights." Should it be the concern of the Supreme Court *whose* speech rights are burdened by a law like Ohio's? Is there any evidence of such concern in the majority or concurring opinions in *McIntyre?*

4. Justice Scalia began his dissent with this observation: "At a time when both political branches of Government and both political parties reflect a popular desire to leave more decisionmaking authority to the States, today's decision moves in the opposite direction, adding to the legacy of inflexible central mandates (irrevocable even by Congress) imposed by this Court's constitutional jurisprudence." Is the majority opinion in *McIntyre* out-of-step with present-day trends in American politics?

5. Public opinion polls indicate that many voters do not make up their minds until they enter the voting booth. Election day advocacy apparently has a major impact on the choices of reluctant or undecided voters. Should that polling information influence the Court's constitutional reasoning, one way or another, about whether anonymous pamphleteering or advertising is protected?

SUGGESTIONS FOR FURTHER READING

Alexander, Herbert E., *Financing Politics: Money, Elections, and Political Reform* (Washington, D.C.: Congressional Quarterly, 1984).

BeVier, Lillian R., "Money and Politics: A Perspective on the First Amendment and Campaign Finance Reform," 73 *California Law Review* (1985): 1045.

Blum, Jeff, "The Divisible First Amendment: A Critical Functionalist Approach to Freedom of Speech and Electoral Campaign Spending," 58 *New York University Law Review* (1983): 1273.

Brandeis, Louis D., *Other People's Money and How the Bankers Use It* (Washington, D.C.: National Home Library, 1933).

Brennan, William J., Jr., "State Constitutions and the Protection of Individual Rights," 90 *Harvard Law Review* (1977): 489.

———, "The Bill of Rights and the States: The Revival of State Constitutions as Guardians of Individual Rights," 61 *New York University Law Review* (1986): 535.

Carter, Stephen L., "Technology, Democracy, and the Manipulation of Consent," 93 *Yale Law Journal* (1984): 581.

Drew, Elizabeth, *Politics and Money: The New Road to Corruption* (New York, NY: Macmillan, 1983).

———, *Whatever It Takes: The Real Struggle for Political Power in America* (New York, NY: Viking, 1997).

Edsall, Thomas Byrne, *Power and Money: Writing About Politics, 1971–1987* (New York, NY: W. W. Norton, 1988).

Fiss, Owen, "Free Speech and Social Structure," 71 *Iowa Law Review* (1986): 1405.

Forrester, Ray, "The New Constitutional Right to Buy Elections," 69 *American Bar Association Journal* (August 1983): 1078.

Jackson, Brooks, *Honest Graft: Big Money and the American Political Process* (Washington, D.C.: Farragut Publishing, 1990).

Kiley, Thomas R., "PACing the Burger Court: The Corporate Right to Speak and the Public Right to Hear after *First National Bank of Boston v. Bellotti*," 22 *Arizona Law Review* (1980): 427.

Malbin, Michael J., ed., *Money and Politics in the United States: Financing Elections in the 1980s* (Washington, D.C.: American Enterprise Institute, 1984).

Mutch, Robert E., *Campaigns, Congress and Courts: The Making of Federal Campaign Finance Law* (New York, NY: Praeger, 1988).

Nicholson, Marlene A., "Campaign Financing and Equal Protection," 26 *Stanford Law Review* (1974): 815.

———, "*Buckley v. Valeo*," *Wisconsin Law Review* (1977): 323.

O'Kelley, Charles, "The Constitutional Rights of Corporations Revisited," 67 *Georgia Law Review* (1979): 1347.

Patton, William, and Randall Bartlett, "Corporate 'Persons' and Freedom of Speech: The Political Impact of Legal Mythology," 1981 *Wisconsin Law Review* (1981): 494.

Polsby, Daniel D., "*Buckley v. Valeo*: The Special Nature of Political Speech," *The Supreme Court Review* (Chicago, IL: University of Chicago Press, 1976).

Sabato, Larry, *PAC Power: Inside the World of Political Action Committees* (New York, NY: W. W. Norton, 1984).

Sorauf, Frank J., "Caught in the Political Thicket: The Supreme Court and Campaign Finance," 3 *Constitutional Commentary* (1986): 97.

———, *Inside Campaign Finance: Myths and Realities* (New Haven, CT: Yale University Press, 1992).

Schauer, Frederick, "*Hudgens v. N.L.R.B.* and the Problem of State Action in First Amendment Adjudication," 61 *Minnesota Law Review* (1977): 433.

———, "The Aim and the Target in Free Speech Methodology," 83 *Northwestern University Law Review* (1988): 562.

Stone, Geoffrey R., and William P. Marshall, "*Brown v. Socialist Workers*: Inequality as a Command of the First Amendment," *The Supreme Court Review* (Chicago, IL: University of Chicago Press, 1983).

Sunstein, Cass R., *Democracy and the Problem of Free Speech* (New York, NY: The Free Press, 1993).

Symposium: "Campaign Reform," 10 *Hastings Law Quarterly* (1983): 463.

Symposium: "The Emergence of State Constitutional Law," 63 *Texas Law Review* (1985): 959.

Symposium: "The Supreme Court's Meandering Path in Campaign Finance Regulation," 3 *University of Virginia Journal of Law and Politics* (1987): 509.

Tushnet, Mark V., "Corporations and Free Speech," in *The Politics of Law: A Progressive Critique*, ed. David Kairys (New York, NY: Pantheon, 1982).

Van Alstyne, William W., "The Recrudescence of Property Rights as the Foremost Principle of Civil Liberties," 43 *Law & Contemporary Problems* (1980): 66.

Wright, J. Skelly, "Politics and the Constitution: Is Money Speech?" 85 *Yale Law Journal* (1976): 1001.

_____, "Money and the Pollution of Politics: Is the First Amendment an Obstacle to Political Equality?" 82 *Columbia Law Review* (1982): 609.

COMMERCIAL SPEECH

Virginia State Board of Pharmacy v. Virginia Citizens Consumer Council
425 U.S. 748 (1976)

SETTING

Commercial speech is another example of speech that the Court has not always considered worthy of First Amendment protection. In 1939, for example, the Court noted in *dictum* that: "[w]e are not to be taken as holding that commercial solicitation and canvassing may not be subjected to such regulation as the ordinance [concerned in this case] requires." *Schneider v. Irvington*, 308 U.S. 147. Three years later, in *Valentine v. Chrestensen*, 316 U.S. 52 (1942), the Court explicitly declared, "... the Constitution imposes no ... restraint on government as respects purely commercial advertising. Whether, and to what extent, one may promote or pursue a gainful occupation in the streets, to what extent such activity shall be adjudged a derogation of the public right of user, are matters for legislative judgment." In reaching that conclusion, the unanimous *Valentine* court rejected Chrestensen's argument that, "in truth, he was engaged in the dissemination of matter proper for public information, none the less so because there was inextricably attached to the medium of such dissemination commercial advertising matter."

The first breach in the Court's wall of opposition to including commercial speech under the First Amendment came in a 1964 case arising out of the Civil Rights Movement. The *New York Times* had been sued for libel as the result of running an advertisement placed by a group of sixty-four supporters of the Reverend Martin Luther King Jr., who had been arrested in Montgomery, Alabama. The ad contained erroneous information. Holding that the *New York Times* advertisement was protected by the First Amendment, the Court said: "The publication here was not a 'commercial' advertisement in the sense in which the word was used in *Chrestensen*. It communicated information, expressed opinion, recited grievances, protested claimed abuses, and sought financial support on behalf of a movement whose existence and objectives are matters of the highest public interest and concern." *New York Times v. Sullivan*, 376 U.S. 254 (1964). (See pp. 361–370.) Eleven years later, the Court applied the *New York Times* analysis to a Virginia newspaper's ad concerning the availability of abortions in New York. The seven-vote majority cited *New York Times v. Sullivan* favorably and noted: "The fact that [*Chrestensen*] had the effect of banning a particular handbill does not mean that [it] is authority for the proposition that all statutes regulating commercial advertising are immune from constitutional challenge. The case obviously does not support any sweeping proposition that advertising is unprotected *per se*." *Bigelow v. Virginia*, 421 U.S. 809 (1975).

The next challenge to a ban on commercial speech came one year later. Virginia law provided that a pharmacist licensed in Virginia is guilty of unprofessional conduct if the pharmacist "publishes, advertises or promotes, directly or indirectly, in any manner whatsoever, any amount, price, fee, premium, discount, rebate or credit terms ... for drugs which may be dispensed only by prescription." That ban on advertising prescription drug prices was enforced by the Virginia State Board of Pharmacy (VSBP), a regulatory body governing licensing and practices of pharmacists that was authorized to discipline pharmacists who disseminate drug price information in violation of the statutory prohibition. Discipline could include the suspension or revocation of a pharmacist's license to practice.

The advertising ban was challenged by the Virginia Citizens Consumer Council, Inc. (VCCC), a nonprofit, nonpartisan, volunteer organization incorporated in Virginia, with a membership of approximately 150,000, many of whom used prescription drugs. The VCCC sought a declaration that the advertising ban violated the First and Fourteenth Amendments and an injunction against its enforcement.

A three-judge panel of the U.S. District Court for the Eastern District of Virginia declared the statute void and enjoined its enforcement. In the district court's view, the holding in *Valentine v. Chrestensen* that "purely commercial advertising" is not constitutionally protected had been tempered by later decisions of the Supreme Court of the United States, to the extent that First Amendment interests in the free flow of price information could be found to outweigh the countervailing interests of the state. The district court further found that the dangers of abuse and deception were not present when the advertised commodity was prescribed by a physician and dispensed by a licensed pharmacist. The VSBP appealed to the Supreme Court of the United States.

HIGHLIGHTS OF SUPREME COURT ARGUMENTS

BRIEF FOR VIRGINIA BOARD OF PHARMACY

◆ Dispensing prescription drugs affects the public health, safety, and welfare. Prohibiting the commercial dissemination of drugs does not violate any First Amendment rights of consumers, because the state may classify and regulate pharmacy as a professional practice. Prohibiting price advertising is a valid part of the states' rights to regulate a health profession.

◆ If this Court recognizes a First Amendment "right to know" in the field of commercial advertising, it will return the judiciary to the vintage of decisions wherein legislation was struck down if judges deemed it unwise.

◆ Recognizing a "right to know" would put states in the position of having to justify their internal and commercial affairs by a compelling interest standard.

BRIEF FOR VIRGINIA CITIZENS CONSUMER COUNCIL

◆ In *Bigelow v. Virginia*, 421 U.S. 809 (1975), this Court held unconstitutional a Virginia statute that prohibited the publication or advertising of information relating to abortion services, because the statute violated the First Amendment rights of the publisher and interfered with the public's interest in having the information. The incidental commercial context in which drug price advertising occurs does not eliminate the protection offered by the First Amendment.

◆ The First Amendment is intended to foster communication, and communication requires both the dissemination and receipt of information. The right to receive information is therefore protected by the First Amendment, as this Court has recognized.

◆ The only issue in this case is how to balance the right of citizens to receive drug price information against the state's asserted interest in preventing the dissemination of drug price information. Before those interests are weighed, the state must show, first, that it has compelling interest in achieving a legitimate end through the statute and, second, that the statute is drawn as narrowly as possible to achieve that end.

◆ This Court has never held that the compelling state interest test is any less applicable merely because protected speech occurs in a commercial context.

AMICUS CURIAE BRIEFS SUPPORTING VIRGINIA CITIZENS CONSUMER COUNCIL

Association of National Advertisers, Inc.; Osco Drug, Inc.

SUPREME COURT DECISION: 7–1

(Stevens, J., did not participate.)

BLACKMUN, J.

... Last Term, in *Bigelow v. Virginia*, 421 U.S. 809 (1975), the notion of unprotected "commercial speech" all but passed from the scene. We reversed a conviction for violation of a Virginia statute that made the circulation of any publication to encourage or promote the processing of an abortion in Virginia a misdemeanor....

Some fragment of hope for the continuing validity of a "commercial speech" exception arguably might have persisted because of the subject matter of the advertisement in *Bigelow*.... [T]he advertisement related to activity with which, at least in some respects, the State could not interfere....

Here, in contrast, the question whether there is a First Amendment exception for "commercial speech" is squarely before us. Our pharmacist does not wish to editorialize on any subject, cultural, philosophical, or political. He does not wish to report any particularly newsworthy fact, or to make generalized observations even about commercial matters. The "idea" he wishes to communicate is simply this: "I will sell you the X prescription drug at the Y price." Our question, then, is whether this communication is wholly outside the protection of the First Amendment....

If there is a kind of commercial speech that lacks all First Amendment protection, therefore, it must be distinguished by its content. Yet the speech whose content deprives it of protection cannot simply be speech on a commercial subject. No one would contend that our pharmacist may be prevented from being heard on the subject of whether, in general, pharmaceutical prices should be regulated, or their advertisement forbidden. Nor can it be dispositive that a commercial advertisement is noneditorial, and merely reports a fact. Purely factual matters of public interest may claim protection....

Our question is whether speech which does "no more than propose a commercial transaction," *Pittsburgh Press Co. v. Human Relations Comm'n*, 413 U.S. [376

(1973)] is so removed from any "exposition of ideas," *Chaplinsky v. New Hampshire*, and from "'truth, science, morality, and arts in general, in its diffusion of liberal sentiments on the administration of Government,'" *Roth v. United States*, 354 U.S. 476 (1957), that it lacks all protection. Our answer is that it is not....

As to the particular consumer's interest in the free flow of commercial information, that interest may be as keen, if not keener by far, than his interest in the day's most urgent political debate....

Generalizing, society also may have a strong interest in the free flow of commercial information. Even an individual advertisement, though entirely "commercial," may be of general public interest....

Moreover, there is another consideration that suggests that no line between publicly "interesting" or "important" commercial advertising and the opposite kind could ever be drawn. Advertising, however tasteless and excessive it sometimes may seem, is nonetheless dissemination of information as to who is producing and selling what product, for what reason, and at what price. So long as we preserve a predominantly free enterprise economy, the allocation of our resources in large measure will be made through numerous private economic decisions. It is a matter of public interest that those decisions, in the aggregate, be intelligent and well informed. To this end, the free flow of commercial information is indispensable.... And if it is indispensable to the proper allocation of resources in a free enterprise system, it is also indispensable to the formation of intelligent opinions as to how that system ought to be regulated or altered. Therefore, even if the First Amendment were thought to be primarily an instrument to enlighten public decisionmaking in a democracy, we could not say that the free flow of information does not serve that goal.

Arrayed against these substantial individual and societal interests are a number of justifications for the advertising ban. These have to do principally with maintaining a high degree of professionalism on the part of licensed pharmacists....

Price advertising, it is argued, will place in jeopardy the pharmacist's expertise and, with it, the customer's health. It is claimed that the aggressive price competition that will result from unlimited advertising will make it impossible for the pharmacist to supply professional services in the compounding, handling, and dispensing of prescription drugs....

[H]igh professional standards, to a substantial extent, are guaranteed by the close regulation to which pharmacists in Virginia are subject. And this case concerns the retail sale by the pharmacist more than it does his professional standards. Surely, any pharmacist guilty of professional dereliction that actually endangers his customer will promptly lose his license. At the same time, we cannot discount the Board's justifications entirely....

The challenge now made, however, is based on the First Amendment. This casts the Board's justifications in a different light, for on close inspection it is seen that the State's protectiveness of its citizens rests in large measure on the advantages of their being kept in ignorance....

It appears to be feared that if the pharmacist who wishes to provide low cost, and assertedly low quality, services is permitted to advertise, he will be taken up on his offer by too many unwitting customers. They will choose the low-cost, low-quality service and drive the "professional" pharmacist out of business. They will respond only to costly and excessive

advertising, and end up paying the price. They will go from one pharmacist to another, following the discount, and destroy the pharmacist-customer relationship. They will lose respect for the profession because it advertises. All this is not in their best interests, and all this can be avoided if they are not permitted to know who is charging what.

There is, of course, an alternative to this highly paternalistic approach. That alternative is to assume that this information is not in itself harmful, that people will perceive their own best interests if only they are well enough informed, and that the best means to that end is to open the channels of communication rather than to close them. If they are truly open, nothing prevents the "professional" pharmacist from marketing his own assertedly superior product, and contrasting it with that of the low-cost, high-volume prescription drug retailer. But the choice among these alternative approaches is not ours to make or the Virginia General Assembly's. It is precisely this kind of choice, between the dangers of suppressing information, and the dangers of its misuse if it is freely available, that the First Amendment makes for us. Virginia is free to require whatever professional standards it wishes of its pharmacists; it may subsidize them or protect them from competition in other ways.... But it may not do so by keeping the public in ignorance of the entirely lawful terms that competing pharmacists are offering. In this sense, the justifications Virginia has offered for suppressing the flow of prescription drug price information, far from persuading us that the flow is not protected by the First Amendment, have reinforced our view that it is. We so hold.

In concluding that commercial speech,

like other varieties, is protected, we of course do not hold that it can never be regulated in any way. Some forms of commercial speech regulation are surely permissible....

The judgment of the District Court is affirmed.

Affirmed.

BURGER, C.J., CONCURRING [OMITTED]

STEWART, J., CONCURRING

... [S]ince it is a cardinal principle of the First Amendment that "government has no power to restrict expression because of its message, its ideas, its subject matter, or its content," the Court's decision calls into immediate question the constitutional legitimacy of every state and federal law regulating false or deceptive advertising. I write separately to explain why I think today's decision does not preclude such governmental regulation....

The Court's determination that commercial advertising of the kind at issue here is not "wholly outside the protection of" the First Amendment indicates by its very phrasing that there are important differences between commercial price and product advertising, on the one hand, and ideological communication on the other. Ideological expression, be it oral, literary, pictorial, or theatrical, is integrally related to the exposition of thought that may shape our concepts of the whole universe of man. Although such expression may convey factual information relevant to social and individual decisionmaking, it is protected by the Constitution, whether or not it contains factual representations and even if it includes inaccurate assertions of fact. Indeed, disregard of the "truth" may be employed to give force to the underlying idea expressed by the speaker....

Commercial price and product advertising differs markedly from ideological expression because it is confined to the promotion of specific goods or services. The First Amendment protects the advertisement because of the "information of potential interest and value" conveyed, *Bigelow v. Virginia* [421 U.S. 809 (1975)], rather than because of any direct contribution to the interchange of ideas. Since the factual claims contained in commercial price or product advertisements relate to tangible goods or services, they may be tested empirically and corrected to reflect the truth without in any manner jeopardizing the free dissemination of thought. Indeed, the elimination of false and deceptive claims serves to promote the one facet of commercial price and product advertising that warrants First Amendment protection—its contribution to the flow of accurate and reliable information relevant to public and private decisionmaking.

REHNQUIST, J., DISSENTING

The logical consequences of the Court's decision in this case, a decision which elevates commercial intercourse between a seller hawking his wares and a buyer seeking to strike a bargain to the same plane as has been previously reserved for the free marketplace of ideas, are far reaching indeed. Under the Court's opinion the way will be open not only for dissemination of price information but for active promotion of prescription drugs, liquor, cigarettes, and other products the use of which it has previously been thought desirable to discourage. Now, however, such promotion is protected by the First Amendment so long as it is not misleading or does not promote an illegal product or enterprise. In coming to this conclusion, the Court has overruled a legislative determination that such advertising should not be allowed and has done so on behalf of a consumer group which is not directly disadvantaged by the statute in question. This effort to reach a result which the Court obviously considers desirable is a troublesome one, for two reasons. It extends standing to raise First Amendment claims beyond the previous decisions of this Court. It also extends the protection of that Amendment to purely commercial endeavors which its most vigorous champions on this Court had thought to be beyond its pale....

The issue is rather whether appellee consumers may override the legislative determination that pharmacists should not advertise even though the pharmacists themselves do not object. In deciding that they may do so, the Court necessarily adopts a rule which cannot be limited merely to dissemination of price alone, and which cannot possibly be confined to pharmacists but must likewise extend to lawyers, doctors, and all other professions....

The Court concedes that legislatures may prohibit false and misleading advertisements, and may likewise prohibit advertisements seeking to induce transactions which are themselves illegal. In the final footnote the opinion tosses a bone to the traditionalists in the legal and medical professions by suggesting that because they sell services rather than drugs the holding of this case is not automatically applicable to advertising in those professions. But if the sole limitation on permissible state proscription of advertising is that it may not be false or misleading, surely the difference between pharmacists' advertising and lawyers' and doctors' advertising can be only one

of degree and not of kind. I cannot distinguish between the public's right to know the price of drugs and its right to know the price of title searches or physical examinations or other professional services for which standardized fees are charged....

There are undoubted difficulties with an effort to draw a bright line between "commercial speech" on the one hand and "protected speech" on the other, and the Court does better to face up to these difficulties than to attempt to hide them under labels. In this case, however, the Court has unfortunately substituted for the wavering line previously thought to exist between commercial speech and protected speech a no more satisfactory line of its own—that between "truthful" commercial speech, on the one hand, and that which is "false and misleading" on the other. The difficulty with this line is not that it wavers, but on the contrary that it is simply too Procrustean to take into account the congeries of factors which I believe could, quite consistently with the First and Fourteenth Amendments, properly influence a legislative decision with respect to commercial advertising....

Here the rights of the appellees seem to me to be marginal at best. There is no ideological content to the information which they seek and it is freely available to them—they may even publish it if they so desire. The only persons directly affected by this statute are not parties to this lawsuit. On the other hand, the societal interest against the promotion of drug use for every ill, real or imaginary, seems to me extremely strong. I do not believe that the First Amendment mandates the Court's "open door policy" toward such commercial advertising.

QUESTIONS

1. On what basis does the Court conclude in *Virginia Board* that commercial speech is protected under the First Amendment? What guidelines does the Court provide regarding regulation of commercial speech?

2. During oral argument the following colloquy took place between Alan B. Morrison, representing the Virginia Citizens Consumer Council, and an unidentified justice:

    > THE COURT: The point I am driving at is, how come the pharmacists are not involved [in the instant case]?
    >
    > MR. MORRISON: The pharm—I'm sorry, Your Honor. Why aren't they plaintiffs?
    >
    > THE COURT: Yes.
    >
    > MR. MORRISON: Well, the pharmacists had a try at this in 1969 in [*Patterson Drug Company v. Kingery*, 305 F.Supp. 821 (W.D. Va. 1969)]. They didn't win that case.
    >
    > THE COURT: I see. I see.
    >
    > MR. MORRISON: These are consumers and we thought that we could do a little better.
    >
    > THE COURT: So far you have.

    In pressing for First Amendment protection of commercial speech, why did consumers fare better than pharmacists apparently would have in *Virginia Board?* Are the interests of consumers and businesses always as similar as the alliance in this case implies?

3. In his dissent in *Virginia Board*, Justice Rehnquist identified a "list of horribles" that he predicted would follow from the opinion. Is Justice Rehnquist right that those consequences follow from *Virginia Board?* If Rehnquist is correct, on what basis can distinctions between speech for profit and other sorts of expressive conduct be drawn for purposes of determining First Amendment protection?

4. Is there any doctrinal relationship between the Court's view that "money is speech," in *Buckley v. Valeo*, and the Court's decision in *Virginia Board?*

COMMENT

Between *Virginia Board* and *Central Hudson Gas & Electric v. Public Service Commission*, 447 U.S. 557 (1980), the commercial speech case that follows, the Court continued to scrutinize various regulations of advertising in light of the First Amendment. The following cases illustrate the decisional trends.

Case: *Linmark Associates, Inc. v. Willingboro Township*, 431 U.S. 85 (1977)
Vote: 9–0

Decision: A township ordinance prohibiting the posting of real estate "For Sale" and "Sold" signs, for the purpose of stemming what the township perceived as the flight of white homeowners from a racially integrated community, violates the First Amendment. The ordinance cannot be sustained on the ground that it restricts only one method of communication while leaving ample alternative communication channels open. The ordinance is not genuinely concerned with the place (front lawns) or the manner (signs) of the speech, but rather proscribes particular types of signs based on their content. Despite the importance of achieving the asserted goal of promoting stable, integrated housing, the ordinance cannot be upheld on the ground that it promotes an important governmental objective, since it does not appear that the ordinance was needed to achieve that objective and, in any event, the First Amendment disables the township from achieving that objective by restricting the free flow of truthful commercial information.

Case: *Carey v. Population Services International*, 431 U.S. 678 (1977)
Vote: 7–2
Decision: A New York statute that prohibits distribution of contraceptives to anyone under the age of 16 by anyone other than licensed pharmacists and bans advertising and display of contraceptives is unconstitutional. Regulations imposing a burden on a decision as fundamental as whether to bear or beget a child may be justified only by compelling state interest and must be narrowly drawn to express only those interests. The prohibition of distribution of nonmedical contraceptives to persons over the age of 16 except through licensed pharmacists burdens individuals' right to use contraceptives if they so desire and serves no compelling state interest. The prohibition on any advertisement or display of contraceptives that seeks to suppress completely any information about the availability and price of contraceptives cannot be justified on the ground that advertisements of contraceptive products would offend and embarrass those exposed to them and that permitting them would legitimize sexual activity by young people. These are not justifications validating suppression of expression protected by the First Amendment.

Case: *Bates v. State Bar of Arizona*, 433 U.S. 350 (1977)
Vote: 5–4
Decision: Advertising of prices for routine legal services is protected by the First Amendment. Overbreadth challenges to such commercial speech lack justification because such challenges apply weakly, if at all, in the ordinary commercial context.

Case: *In re Primus*, 436 U.S. 412 (1978)
Vote: 8–1
Decision: Solicitation of prospective litigants by nonprofit organizations that engage in litigation as a form of political expression and political association constitutes expressive and associational conduct that is entitled to First Amendment protection and government may regulate it only with narrow specificity. The action of a practicing lawyer, who was also a cooperating lawyer with the South Carolina affiliate of the American Civil Liberties Union, in advising a gathering of women with respect to their legal rights and in subsequently writing a letter to one of the women advising her of free legal assistance from the nonprofit organization with respect to an action for damages, is not subject to disciplinary action under the First Amendment.

Case: *Ohralik v. Ohio State Bar Association*, 436 U.S. 447 (1978)

Vote: 9–0

Decision: States do not lose the capacity to regulate commercial activity deemed harmful to the public merely because speech was a component of the activity. A lawyer's procurement of remunerative employment is only marginally affected with First Amendment concerns. The Ohio State Bar, authorized by the state, could constitutionally discipline a lawyer for soliciting clients in person for pecuniary gain ("ambulance chasing") under circumstances likely to pose dangers that the state has a right to prevent.

Case: *Friedman v. Rogers*, 440 U.S. 1 (1979)

Vote: 7–2

Decision: A prohibition against practicing optometry under a trade name is a permissible state regulation that furthers the goal of protecting the public from demonstrated deceptive and misleading use of optometrical trade names. A Texas statute prohibiting practice of optometry under a trade name does not violate the First Amendment protection of commercial speech.

Case: *Consolidated Edison Co. of New York, Inc. v. Public Service Commission of New York*, 447 U.S. 530 (1980)

Vote: 7–2

Decision: A New York Public Service Commission order prohibiting the inclusion by public utility companies in monthly bills of inserts discussing controversial issues of public policy directly infringes the freedom of speech protected by the First and Fourteenth Amendments. The commission's suppression of bill inserts that discuss controversial issues of public policy is neither a valid time, place, or manner restriction, nor a permissible subject-matter regulation. Neither is it a narrowly drawn prohibition justified by a compelling state interest.

COMMERCIAL SPEECH

Central Hudson Gas & Electric Corporation v. Public Service Commission of New York
447 US 557 (1980)

SETTING

The Arab-Israeli conflict of 1973 led the United States to place an embargo on the import of Arab oil in October of that year. By December, the Public Service Commission of the State of New York found that the state's electric utility system did not have sufficient fuel stocks or sources of supply to continue furnishing all customer demands for the 1973–74 winter. It therefore ordered a statewide voltage reduction and, on December 5, issued an order banning promotional advertising by electric utility companies. The ban provided that: "All electric corporations are hereby prohibited from promoting the use of electricity through the use of advertising...."

The voltage reduction order was rescinded in March 1974 after the oil embargo ended and the commission discovered that in fact the state had "substantial inventories" of fuel. However, the advertising ban remained in effect. The advertising ban was extended in orders issued by the commission on February 25 and July 14, 1977, on the ground that the increased use of electrical energy that would inevitably result if advertising were allowed "would aggravate the nation's already unacceptably high level of dependence on foreign sources of supply and would, in addition, frustrate rather than encourage conservation efforts." The 1977 orders left intact prohibitions against promotional advertising aimed at stimulating the purchase of utility services. However, it permitted "informational" advertising designed to encourage "shifts of consumption from peak demand times to periods of low electricity demand."

The 1977 orders were controversial, in part because they continued promotional advertising bans even though there was no evidence of fuel shortages in 1977 and in part because of the Supreme Court's decision in *Virginia State Board of Pharmacy* only a year earlier. Public utilities affected by the advertising ban sought unsuccessfully to persuade the commission to rescind its orders.

On November 10, 1977, Central Hudson Gas and Electric Corporation, one of the affected utilities, filed suit in the Supreme Court of Albany County, New York, for a declaration that the commission's promotional advertising ban violated the First and Fourteenth Amendments. That court affirmed the validity of the orders. It took judicial notice of "the present energy crisis" and reasoned that the ban on promotional advertising "advances a significant public interest" sufficient to justify the incursion on First Amendment values. The Appellate Division, Third Department, affirmed. It offered three reasons why the promotional advertising ban served a compelling state interest: (1) increased use of electricity resulting from advertising would cause spiraling price increases, because present rates did not cover the marginal cost of new capacity; (2) advertising gives "misleading signals" that energy conservation was unnecessary; and (3) additional usage would "increase the level of dependence on foreign sources of fuel oil."

The New York Court of Appeals affirmed the Appellate Division. It denied Central Hudson's motion for reargument and Central Hudson appealed to the Supreme Court of the United States.

Highlights of Supreme Court Arguments

BRIEF FOR CENTRAL HUDSON

◆ The commission's ban is unconstitutional under *Virginia Board of Pharmacy* and its progeny. This Court has expressed increasing concern for the rights of the recipients of information.

◆ Even though Central Hudson has a franchised monopoly on the distribution of electrical energy in its service area, it has no monopoly on the uses to which that energy is put. Its First Amendment rights are not diminished by its status as a regulated public utility.

◆ The advertising in question in this case does more than propose commercial transactions; it conveys information of value to the energy consumer and is entitled to substantial First Amendment protection.

◆ The commission's advertising ban is both vague and overbroad. It is vague because the term "promotional advertising" is susceptible to a variety of interpretations. It is overbroad because it prohibits advertising of electrical uses that conserve oil.

◆ The advertising ban also violates the Equal Protection Clause of the Fourteenth Amendment, because it treats dealers in home heating oil differently than electric utility companies. The classification is irrational, because the oil sold by those dealers constitutes over three-fourths of all residential heating energy in Central Hudson's service area.

AMICUS CURIAE BRIEFS SUPPORTING CENTRAL HUDSON

Edison Electric Institute; Long Island Lighting Company; joint brief of Mid-Atlantic Legal Foundation and Donald Powers (a Central Hudson customer); Mobil Corporation.

BRIEF FOR PUBLIC SERVICE COMMISSION

◆ This Court has always acknowledged differences between commercial speech and other kinds of speech. In the commercial speech arena, the interests purported to be served when free speech rights are abridged must be weighed against the rights of the speaker and the public to give and receive information.

◆ This case involves the speech of a highly regulated public utility, which has a monopoly on the provision of electrical service. The commission expressly found that promoting electric usage is contrary to the state and national policy of conserving energy. This case does not involve issues of commercial speech in the competitive marketplace.

◆ Central Hudson's Equal Protection challenge, although couched in overbreadth and vagueness terms, is nothing more than a challenge to the wisdom of banning promotional advertising.

◆ The ban does not deprive electric utilities of equal protection in relation to oil heat dealers, which admittedly are unaffected by the ban. The state is not required to regulate all promoters of energy at once, but may move gradually toward that goal.

Supreme Court Decision: 8–1

POWELL, J.

This case presents the question whether a regulation of the Public Service Commission of the State of New York violates the First and Fourteenth Amendments because it completely bans promotional advertising by an electrical utility....

The First Amendment's concern for commercial speech is based on the informational function of advertising....

Consequently, there can be no constitutional objection to the suppression of commercial messages that do not accurately inform the public about lawful activity....

If the communication is neither misleading nor related to unlawful activity, the government's power is more circumscribed. The State must assert a substantial interest to be achieved by restrictions on commercial speech. Moreover, the regulatory technique must be in proportion to that interest. The limitation on expression must be designed carefully to achieve the State's goal. Compliance with this requirement may be measured by two criteria. First, the restriction must directly advance the state interest involved; the regulation may not be sustained if it provides only ineffective or remote support for the government's purpose. Second, if the governmental interest could be served as well by a more limited restriction on commercial speech, the excessive restrictions cannot survive.

Under the first criterion, the Court has declined to uphold regulations that only indirectly advance the state interest involved....

The second criterion recognizes that the First Amendment mandates that speech restrictions be "narrowly drawn." *In re Primus*, 436 U.S. 412 (1978). The regulatory technique may extend only as far as the interest it serves.... In commercial speech cases, then, a four-part analysis has developed. At the outset, we must determine whether the expression is protected by the First Amendment. For commercial speech to come within that provision, it at least must concern lawful activity and not be misleading. Next, we ask whether the asserted governmental interest is substantial. If both inquiries yield positive answers, we must determine whether the regulation directly advances the governmental interest asserted, and whether it is not more extensive than is necessary to serve that interest.

We now apply this four-step analysis for commercial speech to the Commission's arguments in support of its ban on promotional advertising.

The Commission does not claim that the expression at issue either is inaccurate or relates to unlawful activity. Yet the New York Court of Appeals questioned whether Central Hudson's advertising is protected commercial speech. Because appellant holds a monopoly over the sale of electricity in its service area, the state court suggested that the Commission's order restricts no commercial speech of any worth. The court stated that advertising in a "noncompetitive market" could not improve the decisionmaking of consumers. The court saw no constitutional problem with barring commercial speech that it viewed as conveying little useful information.

This reasoning falls short of establishing that appellant's advertising is not commercial speech protected by the First Amendment. Monopoly over the supply of a product provides no protection from competition with substitutes for that product....

Even in monopoly markets, the suppression of advertising reduces the information available for consumer decisions and thereby defeats the purpose of the First Amendment....

The Commission offers two state interests as justifications for the ban on promotional advertising. The first concerns energy conservation. Any increase in demand for electricity—during peak or off-peak periods—means greater consumption of energy. The Commission argues, and the New York court agreed, that the State's interest in conserving energy is sufficient to support suppression of advertising designed to increase consumption of electricity. In view of our country's dependence on energy resources beyond our control, no one can doubt the importance of energy conservation. Plainly, therefore, the state interest asserted is substantial.

The Commission also argues that promotional advertising will aggravate inequities caused by the failure to base the utilities' rates on marginal cost. The utilities argued to the Commission that if they could promote the use of electricity in periods of low demand, they would improve their utilization of generating capacity. The Commission responded that promotion of off-peak consumption also would increase consumption during peak periods. If peak demand were to rise, the absence of marginal cost rates would mean that the rates charged for the additional power would not reflect the true costs of expanding production. Instead, the extra costs would be borne by all consumers through higher overall rates. Without promotional advertising, the Commission stated, this inequitable turn of events would be less likely to occur. The choice among rate structures involves difficult and important questions of economic supply and distributional fairness. The State's concern that rates be fair and efficient represents a clear and substantial governmental interest.

Next, we focus on the relationship between the State's interests and the advertising ban. Under this criterion, the Commission's laudable concern over the equity and efficiency of appellant's rates does not provide a constitutionally adequate reason for restricting protected speech. The link between the advertising

prohibition and appellant's rate structure is, at most, tenuous. The impact of promotional advertising on the equity of appellant's rates is highly speculative. Advertising to increase off-peak usage would have to increase peak usage, while other factors that directly affect the fairness and efficiency of appellant's rates remained constant. Such conditional and remote eventualities simply cannot justify silencing appellant's promotional advertising.

In contrast, the State's interest in energy conservation is directly advanced by the Commission order at issue here. There is an immediate connection between advertising and demand for electricity. Central Hudson would not contest the advertising ban unless it believed that promotion would increase its sales. Thus, we find a direct link between the state interest in conservation and the Commission's order.

We come finally to the critical inquiry in this case: whether the Commission's complete suppression of speech ordinarily protected by the First Amendment is no more extensive than necessary to further the State's interest in energy conservation. The Commission's order reaches all promotional advertising, regardless of the impact of the touted service on overall energy use. But the energy conservation rationale, as important as it is, cannot justify suppressing information about electric devices or services that would cause no net increase in total energy use. In addition, no showing has been made that a more limited restriction on the content of promotional advertising would not serve adequately the State's interests.

Appellant insists that but for the ban, it would advertise products and services that use energy efficiently. These include the "heat pump," which both parties acknowledge to be a major improvement in electric heating, and the use of electric heat as a "backup" to solar and other heat sources. Although the Commission has questioned the efficiency of electric heating before this Court, neither the Commission's Policy Statement nor its order denying rehearing made findings on this issue. In the absence of authoritative findings to the contrary, we must credit as within the realm of possibility the claim that electric heat can be an efficient alternative in some circumstances.

The Commission's order prevents appellant from promoting electric services that would reduce energy use by diverting demand from less efficient sources, or that would consume roughly the same amount of energy as do alternative sources. In neither situation would the utility's advertising endanger conservation or mislead the public. To the extent that the Commission's order suppresses speech that in no way impairs the State's interest in energy conservation, the Commission's order violates the First and Fourteenth Amendments and must be invalidated....

The Commission also has not demonstrated that its interest in conservation cannot be protected adequately by more limited regulation of appellant's commercial expression. To further its policy of conservation, the Commission could attempt to restrict the format and content of Central Hudson's advertising. It might, for example, require that the advertisements include information about the relative efficiency and expense of the offered service, both under current conditions and for the foreseeable future.... In the absence of a showing that more limited speech regulation would be ineffective, we cannot approve the complete suppression of Central Hudson's advertising....

Accordingly, the judgment of the New York Court of Appeals is
Reversed.

BRENNAN, J., CONCURRING IN THE JUDGMENT [OMITTED]

BLACKMUN AND BRENNAN, J.J., CONCURRING IN THE JUDGMENT

... I concur only in the Court's judgment ... because I believe the test now evolved and applied by the Court is not consistent with our prior cases and does not provide adequate protection for truthful, nonmisleading, noncoercive commercial speech....

I agree with the Court that ... intermediate scrutiny is appropriate for a restraint on commercial speech designed to protect consumers from misleading or coercive speech, or a regulation related to the time, place, or manner of commercial speech. I do not agree, however, that the Court's four-part test is the proper one to be applied when a State seeks to suppress information about a product in order to manipulate a private economic decision that the State cannot or has not regulated or outlawed directly....

If the First Amendment guarantee means anything, it means that, absent clear and present danger, government has no power to restrict expression because of the effect its message is likely to have on the public....

STEVENS AND BRENNAN, J.J., CONCURRING IN THE JUDGMENT

... I concur in the result because I do not consider this to be a "commercial speech" case. Accordingly, I see no need to decide whether the Court's four-part analysis adequately protects commercial speech—as properly defined—in the face of a blanket ban of the sort involved in this case.

REHNQUIST, J., DISSENTING

... The Court's analysis in my view is wrong in several respects. Initially, I disagree with the Court's conclusion that the speech of a state-created monopoly, which is the subject of a comprehensive regulatory scheme, is entitled to protection under the First Amendment. I also think that the Court errs here in failing to recognize that the state law is most accurately viewed as an economic regulation and that the speech involved (if it falls within the scope of the First Amendment at all) occupies a significantly more subordinate position in the hierarchy of First Amendment values than the Court gives it today. Finally, the Court in reaching its decision improperly substitutes its own judgment for that of the State in deciding how a proper ban on promotional advertising should be drafted. With regard to this latter point, the Court adopts as its final part of a four-part test a "no more extensive than necessary" analysis that will unduly impair a state legislature's ability to adopt legislation reasonably designed to promote interests that have always been rightly thought to be of great importance to the State....

This Court has previously recognized that although commercial speech may be entitled to First Amendment protection, that protection is not as extensive as that accorded to the advocacy of ideas....

The Court's decision today fails to give due deference to this subordinate position of commercial speech. The Court in so doing returns to the bygone era of *Lochner v. New York*, 198 U.S. 45 (1905), in which it was common practice for this Court to strike down economic regulations adopted by a State based on the Court's own notions of the most appropriate means for the State to implement its considered policies.

I had thought by now it had become well established that a State has broad discretion in imposing economic regulations....

The Court today holds not only that commercial speech is entitled to First Amendment protection, but also that when it is protected a State may not regulate it unless its reason for doing so amounts to a "substantial" governmental interest, its regulation "directly advances" that interest, and its manner of regulation is "not more extensive than necessary" to serve the interest. The test adopted by the Court thus elevates the protection accorded commercial speech that falls within the scope of the First Amendment to a level that is virtually indistinguishable from that of noncommercial speech.... New York's order here is in my view more akin to an economic regulation to which virtually complete deference should be accorded by this Court....

I remain of the view that the Court unlocked a Pandora's Box when it "elevated" commercial speech to the level of traditional political speech by according it First Amendment protection in *Virginia Pharmacy Board v. Virginia Citizens Consumer Council*. The line between "commercial speech," and the kind of speech that those who drafted the First Amendment had in mind, may not be a technically or intellectually easy one to draw, but it surely produced far fewer problems than has the development of judicial doctrine in this area since *Virginia Board*. For in the world of political advocacy and its marketplace of ideas, there is no such thing as a "fraudulent" idea: there may be useless proposals, totally unworkable schemes, as well as very sound proposals that will receive the imprimatur of the "marketplace of ideas" through our majoritarian system of election and representative government. The free flow of information is important in this context not because it will lead to the discovery of any objective "truth," but because it is essential to our system of self-government....

For the foregoing reasons, I would affirm the judgment of the New York Court of Appeals.

QUESTIONS

1. Does *Central Hudson* merely reaffirm *Virginia Board of Pharmacy* or does the case mark a doctrinal shift away from *Virginia Board*? What language in the opinion supports your conclusion?

2. Is it accurate to characterize the commission's ban on certain public utilities' advertising as a return to the *Gitlow* "bad tendency" test for free speech? If so, does the Court's opinion in *Central Hudson* reflect a continued rejection of that test?

3. Central Hudson argued in its brief to the Court that "[a]lthough the energy crisis (and specifically dependence on foreign oil supplies) is a national problem, no other state imposes such a prohibition, and the pertinent federal legislation affirmatively recognizes the legitimacy of promoting the use of electrical energy." Does it appear from Justice Powell's opinion that these facts influenced his thinking about the issues in *Central Hudson*?

4. The Public Service Commission argued in its brief:

   > Despite Central Hudson's glowing generalities concerning the sanctity of free speech, this case must be viewed on its own facts. The company is simply attempting to have this Court extend its prior decisions providing a measure of protection for commercial speech to the case where a regulated utility desires to promote the use of electric energy in the face of a finding by the Commission that promotion is detrimental to the public interest."

   Did the Court's opinion in *Central Hudson* have the effect the company desired? Or did the Court's "four-step analysis for commercial speech" stop short of that goal? On what set of facts might the Public Service Commission have prevailed in light of the test used in *Central Hudson*?

COMMENT

Between *Central Hudson* and *44 Liquormart, Inc. v. Rhode Island*, 116 S.Ct. 1495 (1996), the commercial speech case excerpted next, the Court often revisited this aspect of First Amendment doctrine. The following summaries indicate the major doctrines.

Case: *Metromedia, Inc. v. City of San Diego*, 453 U.S. 490 (1981)
Vote: 6–3

Decision: A municipal ordinance that permits onsite advertising but bans other commercial and noncommercial advertising on fixed-structure signs infringes on free speech rights. Four justices found the ordinance unconstitutional on its face because it controlled the communicative aspects of billboards. Two justices concluded that in practical effect the ordinance constitutes a total ban on the use of billboards to communicate to the public messages of general applicability without a showing of a sufficient governmental interest in doing so.

Case: *In re R.M.J.*, 455 U.S. 191 (1982)

Vote: 9–0

Decision: The provisions of a Missouri Supreme Court rule regulating lawyer advertising, which prohibit a lawyer from identifying the jurisdictions in which the lawyer is licensed to practice and prohibit the mailing of cards announcing the opening of an office except to "lawyers, clients, former clients, personal friends and relatives," violate the First Amendment, where there is no showing that the advertising was misleading or that supervising the mailings and handbills would be more difficult than banning them.

Case: *Village of Hoffman Estates v. The Flipside, Hoffman Estates, Inc.*, 455 U.S. 489 (1982)

Vote: 9–0

Decision: A village ordinance licensing and regulating the sale of items displayed "with" or "within proximity of" "literature encouraging illegal use of cannabis or illegal drugs" does not violate First Amendment rights of a retailer who sold smoking accessories. The ordinance does not restrict speech as such, but simply regulates commercial marketing of items that might be used for an illicit purpose. The ordinance's restriction on the manner of marketing does not appreciably limit the retailer's communication of information, except to the extent that it was directed at commercial activity promoting or encouraging illegal drug use.

Case: *Bolger v. Youngs Drug Products Corp.*, 463 U.S. 60 (1983)

Vote: 9–0

Decision: A federal statute that prohibits unsolicited mailing of contraceptive advertisements is an unconstitutional restriction on commercial speech. Advertising for contraceptives not only implicates "substantial individual and societal interests" in the free flow of commercial information, but also relates to activity that is protected from unwarranted governmental interference. Neither of the interests asserted by the Government—that the statute shields recipients of mail from materials that they are likely to find offensive and aids parents' efforts to control the manner in which their children become informed about birth control—is sufficient to justify the sweeping prohibition on the mailing of unsolicited contraceptive advertisements.

Case: *Zauderer v. Office of Disciplinary Counsel of Supreme Court of Ohio*, 471 U.S. 626 (1985)

Vote: 7–2

Decision: An attorney may not be disciplined for soliciting legal business through printed advertising that contains truthful and nondeceptive information and advice regarding the legal rights of potential clients. The requirement that an attorney advertising availability on a contingent-fee basis disclose that clients will have to pay costs, even if their lawsuits are unsuccessful, is proper if the advertisement makes no mention or distinction between "legal fees" and "costs."

Case: *Posadas de Puerto Rico Associates v. Tourism Company of Puerto Rico,* 478 U.S. 328 (1986)

Vote: 5–4

Decision: Puerto Rico's 1948 Games of Chance Act, which prohibits gambling rooms from advertising or offering their facilities to the Puerto Rican public, does not facially violate the First Amendment. The act passes muster under *Central Hudson,* first, because Puerto Rico has a substantial interest in restricting advertisement to reduce the demand for casino gambling; second, because the restrictions on this commercial speech directly advance the government's interest; and, third, because the restrictions are no more extensive than necessary to advance the government's interest. Government may ban the advertising of any activity that it may ban outright.

Case: *Board of Trustees of State University of New York v. Fox,* 492 U.S. 469 (1989)

Vote: 6–3

Decision: A resolution of the State University of New York (SUNY) that prohibits private commercial enterprises from operating in SUNY facilities, as applied by campus police to bar American Future Systems, Inc. (AFS) from demonstrating and selling its housewares at a party hosted in a student dormitory, does not violate the First Amendment. Although *Central Hudson* and other decisions have occasionally contained statements suggesting that government restrictions on commercial speech must constitute the least restrictive means of achieving the governmental interests asserted, those decisions require only a reasonable "fit" between the government's ends and the means chosen to accomplish those ends.

Case: *City of Cincinnati v. Discovery Network, Inc.,* 507 U.S. 410 (1993)

Vote: 6–3

Decision: A city's selective and categorical ban on the distribution, via newsrack, of "commercial handbills" is not consistent with the dictates of the First Amendment. Cincinnati has not met its burden of establishing a "reasonable fit" between its legitimate interests in safety and esthetics and the means it has chosen to serve those interests. Because the city's regulation of newsracks is predicated on the difference in content between ordinary newspapers and commercial speech, it is not content neutral and cannot qualify as a valid time, place, or manner restriction on protected speech.

Case: *Edenfield v. Fane,* 507 U.S. 761 (1993)

Vote: 8–1

Decision: A Florida Board of Accountancy rule prohibiting Certified Public Accountants (CPAs) from engaging in "direct, in-person, uninvited solicitation" to obtain new clients violates the First and Fourteenth Amendments. Even under the intermediate *Central Hudson* standard of review, Florida's ban cannot be sustained as applied to Fane's proposed speech. The Board has failed to demonstrate that the ban advances its interests—protecting consumers from fraud or overreaching by CPAs, maintaining CPA independence, and ensuring against conflicts of interest—in any direct and material way.

Case: *United States v. Edge Broadcasting Co.*, 509 U.S. 418 (1993)

Vote: 7–2

Decision: Federal lottery legislation that, among other things, generally prohibits the broadcast of any lottery advertisements but allows broadcasters to advertise state-run lotteries on stations licensed in a state that conducts such lotteries is constitutional. Lower courts erred in concluding that the restriction, under the four-factor test for commercial speech set forth in *Central Hudson* as applied to Edge Broadcasting, did not directly advance the asserted governmental interest of assisting states in their efforts to control this form of gambling.

Case: *Rubin v. Coors Brewing Co.*, 514 U.S. 476 (1995)

Vote: 9–0

Decision: The section of the Federal Alcohol Administration Act (FAAA) prohibiting beer labels from displaying alcohol content violates the First Amendment's protection of commercial speech. The FAAA fails *Central Hudson*'s requirement that the measure directly advance the asserted government interest. The labeling ban cannot be said to advance the governmental interest in suppressing competitive wars among brewers over product strength because other provisions of the same act directly undermine and counteract its effects. The challenged section is also more extensive than necessary, since available alternatives to the labeling ban would prove less intrusive to the First Amendment's protections for commercial speech.

Case: *Florida Bar v. Went for It, Inc.*, 515 U.S. 618 (1995)

Vote: 5–4

Decision: Florida Bar rules prohibiting personal injury lawyers from sending targeted direct-mail solicitations to victims and their relatives for thirty days following an accident or disaster do not violate the First and Fourteenth Amendments. The Florida Bar's ban withstands *Central Hudson* scrutiny. First, the Bar has substantial interest both in protecting the privacy and tranquility of personal injury victims and their loved ones against invasive, unsolicited contact by lawyers and in preventing the erosion of confidence in the profession that such repeated invasions have engendered. Second, the harms targeted by the ban are quite real. Third, the ban's scope is reasonably well tailored to its stated objectives.

COMMERCIAL SPEECH

44 Liquormart, Inc. v. Rhode Island
116 S.Ct. 1495 (1996)

SETTING

As noted above, in *Rubin v. Coors Brewing Co.*, 514 U.S. 476 (1995), the Court applied the *Central Hudson* test in a case challenging the constitutionality of a provision in the Federal Alcohol Administration Act that outlawed displaying the alcohol content of beer on beer labels. The Court struck down the prohibition on the ground that the prohibition failed the *Central Hudson* test because it was not shown to advance the government's interest in a direct and material way. *Coors Brewing*, however, left open the question of how a *state* regulation of commercial speech would fare under the *Central Hudson* test. That challenge arose in the context of a ban on price advertising of alcoholic beverages by the state of Rhode Island.

Virtually every state legislature, exercising its police powers, has adopted some form of restriction on alcoholic beverages. In 1956, the Rhode Island legislature adopted two statutes aimed at the "promotion of temperance and for the reasonable control of the traffic in alcoholic beverages" and reducing the availability of alcoholic beverages to persons of limited incomes who might abuse them. An integral part of the regulatory scheme contained in those statutes was a prohibition on the advertising of the price of alcoholic beverages by Rhode Island media and by liquor license holders. The ban prohibited advertising "in any manner whatsoever of the price of any malt beverage, cordials, wine or distilled liquor offered for sale in this state...." The legislation delegated enforcement of the statute to the Rhode Island Liquor Control administrator. The administrator, in turn, adopted a regulation that prohibited sights "visible from the exterior" of a retail alcohol outlet, but permitted price tags to be placed on or near the alcoholic merchandise.

In 1985, the Rhode Island Supreme Court upheld the constitutionality of the statutes, holding that they served the state's substantial interest in promoting temperance. *S&S Liquor Mart, Inc. v. Pastore*, 497 A. 2d 729 (1985). That court held that the Twenty-First Amendment, adopted in 1933 to end national prohibition contained in the Eighteenth Amendment, gave the regulations an added presumption of validity. Section 2 of the Twenty-first Amendment provides that, "The transportation or importation into any State, Territory, or possession of the United States for delivery or use therein of intoxicating liquors, in violation of the laws thereof, is hereby prohibited."

44 Liquor Mart, Inc., is a Rhode Island corporation located in Johnston, Rhode Island. It is a licensed retail alcohol dealer. People's Super Liquor Stores, Inc., a Massachusetts corporation, is a retail dealer of alcoholic beverages in New Bedford and Fairhaven, Massachusetts. In December 1991, 44 Liquor Mart took out an advertisement in the *Providence Journal-Bulletin* in Rhode Island. The ad displayed bottles of named brand liquors as well as peanuts, chips, alcohol mixers, and cigarettes. The ad stated the prices of non-alcohol products but not any of the alcohol products. Rather, the terms "WOW" and "SALE"—highlighted in burst form—appeared next to pictures of bottles.

On December 17, 1991, in response to complaints from competitors, Rhode Island Liquor Control Administrator Kate F. Racine held a hearing to determine whether 44 Liquor Mart had violated liquor control regulations that prohibit off-premises advertising of alcohol beverage prices. At the conclusion of the hearing, Racine determined that 44 Liquor Mart had violated the regulations, fined it $400, and ordered that the advertisement no longer appear. 44

Liquor Mart did not appeal to the Liquor Control Hearing Board, although it was entitled to do so. Instead, on February 28, 1992, it filed suit against Racine in U.S. District Court for the District of Rhode Island attacking the constitutionality of the Rhode Island statute. It was joined as plaintiff by Peoples Super Liquor. On several occasions, Peoples had sought to place its advertisements in Rhode Island newspapers and in other media outlets. It wished to include price information in the ads, but newspapers refused to accept the advertising because of the Rhode Island statute. The complaint contained several allegations including commerce and antitrust violations, but before trial all counts were dismissed except the first, which alleged that the statute violated the right of 44 Liquor Mart and Peoples Super Liquor to engage in free speech that would enhance their lawful, legitimate businesses and commercial interests and that such speech would not mislead the public. The Rhode Island Liquor Stores Association, which represents small liquor retailers, was permitted to intervene as a defendant.

Before trial, the parties agreed to a statement of facts, including a stipulation that 44 Liquor Mart and Peoples Super Liquor would each realize an economic benefit of more than $100,000 per year if the price advertising ban were lifted, that the proposed speech did not concern an illegal activity and presumably would not be false or misleading, and that the State of Rhode Island had a substantial interest in regulating the sale of alcoholic beverages. The case went to trial on the issue of whether the price advertising ban promoted temperance in the state. An economist for the state claimed that the advertising ban did in fact have a direct effect on consumption of alcohol. An expert witness for 44 Liquor Mart and Peoples claimed that there were at least twelve different conclusions that could be reached about the impact of advertising on the consumption of alcohol.

After a trial on the merits, the district court found that, under the test of *Central Hudson*, Rhode Island had failed to carry its burden of proof to show a direct correlation between the price advertising ban and reduced consumption of alcohol. It also found that the price advertising ban was more extensive than necessary to serve the state's asserted interest. The Court of Appeals for the First Circuit affirmed as to out-of-state retailers but reversed as to Rhode Island retailers. On rehearing, it reversed the decision of the district court in its entirety. It ruled that there was "inherent merit" in the state's argument about the relationship between competitive price advertising and the sale of alcoholic beverages, and that the advertising ban would have the effect of decreasing sales, which in turn would contribute to the state's interest in reducing alcohol consumption. The court of appeals agreed with the Rhode Island Supreme Court that the Twenty-first Amendment gives the statutes an added presumption of validity.

The Supreme Court granted 44 Liquor Mart and People's petition for a writ of certiorari. The Court limited review to the following question: "Whether Rhode Island may, consistent with the First Amendment, prohibit truthful, nonmisleading price advertising regarding alcoholic beverages."

HIGHLIGHTS OF SUPREME COURT ARGUMENTS

BRIEF FOR 44 LIQUOR MART AND PEOPLES

◆ Truthful, nonmisleading price advertising has been entitled to First Amendment protection since at least 1976, when this Court ruled in *Virginia State Board of Pharmacy v. Virginia Citizens Consumer Council, Inc.* that such advertising is "indispensable" to the preservation of the free enterprise economy.

◆ Rhode Island cannot show that its price advertising ban has any effect on abusive alcohol consumption. Consequently, the ban fails the third prong of the *Central Hudson* test.

◆ Rhode Island's ban on advertising the price at which retailers sell alcoholic beverages is more extensive than necessary to serve its asserted interest in reducing abuse of alcoholic beverages.

◆ The court of appeals misallocated the burden of proof in this case. This Court should clearly establish that the Twenty-first Amendment does not diminish the force of the First Amendment.

AMICUS CURIAE BRIEFS SUPPORTING 44 LIQUOR MART

Joint brief of the Association of National Advertisers, Inc., the National Association of Broadcasters, and the American Association of Advertising Agencies; joint brief of American Advertising Federation, American Association of Advertising Agencies, Magazine Publishers of America, and Direct Marketing Association; joint brief of the American Civil Liberties Union and the ACLU of Rhode Island; joint brief of the Association of National Advertisers, Inc., the National Association of Broadcasters, and the American Association of Advertising Agencies; joint brief of the Beer Institute, the Distilled Spirits Council of the United States, Inc., and the Wine Institute; joint brief of Newspaper Association of America, A. H. Belo Corporation, Advance Publications, Inc., the Copley Press, Inc., Cox Newspapers, Inc., Donrey Media Group, Dow Jones & Company, Inc., the Hearst Corporation, the New York Times Company, Providence Journal Company, Thomson Newspaper Holdings, Inc., and Tribune Company; joint brief of Washington Legal Foundation and Allied Educational Foundation.

BRIEF FOR RHODE ISLAND LIQUOR STORES ASSOCIATION

◆ The Twenty-first Amendment vests broad authority in the individual states to regulate alcoholic beverages.

◆ Even within the category of commercial speech, there is a hierarchy of more and less protected areas of speech. States have more leeway where vice is concerned. Just as there are two levels of First Amendment speech protection, with commercial speech being subordinate to noncommercial speech, there are two levels of commercial speech protection—vice regulation and professional regulation. They are afforded different levels of First Amendment protection.

◆ Rhode Island's statutes banning price advertising of alcoholic beverages are no more extensive than necessary to serve the state's interest in promoting temperance.

◆ Elimination of the advertising ban would force small liquor retailers to participate in the advertising arena, in competition with large retail chains.

BRIEF FOR RHODE ISLAND

◆ The record clearly establishes that the price advertising ban has a direct effect on the state's interest in promoting temperance and that there is a "reasonable fit" between the promotion of temperance and the ban.

◆ There is evidence in the record that if the price advertising ban were lifted, the price of alcoholic beverages in Rhode Island would go down, which would lead to increased consumption.

◆ With or without the Twenty-first Amendment, the state proved at trial that the price advertising ban directly and materially advances the state's interest in promoting temperance and controlling the traffic in alcoholic beverages, and that it is no more extensive than necessary.

AMICUS CURIAE BRIEFS SUPPORTING RHODE ISLAND LIQUOR STORES ASSOCIATION AND RHODE ISLAND

Malt Beverage Distributors Association of Pennsylvania; joint brief of Council of State Governments, National Governors' Association, National Association of Counties, International City/County Management Association, National League of Cities, U.S. Conference of Mayors, and National Conference of State Legislatures.

SUPREME COURT DECISION

(9–0 on judgment, 3–4–2 on rationale)

STEVENS, J.

... In *Central Hudson Gas & Elec. Corp. v. Public Serv. Comm'n of N.Y.*, we took stock of our developing commercial speech jurisprudence. In that case, we considered a regulation "completely" banning all promotional advertising by electric utilities. Our decision acknowledged the special features of commercial speech but identified the serious First Amendment concerns that attend blanket advertising prohibitions that do not protect consumers from commercial harms....

[T]he [*Central Hudson*] majority explained that although the special nature of commercial speech may require less than strict review of its regulation, special concerns arise from "regulations that entirely suppress commercial speech in order to pursue a nonspeech-related policy." In those circumstances, "a ban on speech could screen from public view the underlying governmental policy." As a result, the Court concluded that "special care" should attend the review of such blanket bans, and it pointedly remarked that "in recent years this Court has not approved a blanket ban on commercial speech unless the speech itself was flawed in some way, either because it was deceptive or related to unlawful activity."

As our review of the case law reveals, Rhode Island errs in concluding that all commercial speech regulations are subject to a similar form of constitutional review simply because they target a similar category of expression. The mere fact that messages propose commercial transactions does not in and of itself dictate the constitutional analysis that should apply to decisions to suppress them....

When a State regulates commercial messages to protect consumers from misleading, deceptive, or aggressive sales practices, or requires the disclosure of beneficial consumer information, the purpose of its regulation is consistent with the reasons for according constitutional protection to commercial speech and therefore justifies less than strict review. However, when a State entirely prohibits the dissemination of truthful, nonmisleading commercial messages for reasons unrelated to the preservation of a fair bargaining process, there is far less reason to depart from the rigorous review that the First Amendment generally demands....

In this case, there is no question that Rhode Island's price advertising ban constitutes a blanket prohibition against truthful, nonmisleading speech about a lawful product. There is also no question that the ban serves an end unrelated to consumer protection. Accordingly, we must review the price advertising ban with "special care," *Central Hudson*, mindful that speech prohibitions of this type rarely survive constitutional review.

The State argues that the price advertising prohibition should nevertheless be upheld because it directly advances the State's substantial interest in promoting temperance, and because it is no more extensive than necessary.... Although there is some confusion as to what Rhode Island means by temperance, we assume that the State asserts an interest in reducing alcohol consumption.

In evaluating the ban's effectiveness in advancing the State's interest, we note that a commercial speech regulation "may not be sustained if it provides only ineffective or remote support for the government's purpose." *Central Hudson*. For that reason, the State bears the burden of showing not merely that its regulation will advance its interest, but also that it will do so "to a material degree." *Edenfield [v. Fane*, 507 U.S. 761 (1993)] ... The need for the State to make such a showing is particularly great given the drastic nature of its chosen means—the wholesale suppression of truthful, nonmisleading information. Accordingly, we must determine whether the State has shown that the price advertising ban will significantly reduce alcohol consumption.

We can agree that common sense supports the conclusion that a prohibition against price advertising, like a collusive agreement among competitors to refrain from such advertising, will tend to mitigate competition and maintain prices at a higher level than would prevail in a completely free market. Despite the absence of proof on the point, we can even agree with the State's contention that it is reasonable to assume that demand, and hence consumption throughout the market, is somewhat lower whenever a higher, noncompetitive price level prevails. However, without any findings of fact, or indeed any evidentiary support whatsoever, we cannot agree with the assertion that the price advertising ban will significantly advance the State's interest in promoting temperance....

The State also cannot satisfy the requirement that its restriction on speech be no more extensive than necessary. It is perfectly obvious that alternative forms of regulation that would not involve any restriction on speech would be more likely to achieve the State's goal of promoting temperance....

As a result, even under the less than strict standard that generally applies in commercial speech cases, the State has failed to establish a "reasonable fit" between its abridgment of speech and its temperance goal....

The State responds by arguing that it merely exercised appropriate "legislative judgment" in determining that a price advertising ban would best promote temperance.... Rhode Island first argues that, because expert opinions as to the effectiveness of the price advertising ban "go both ways," the Court of Appeals correctly concluded that the ban constituted a "reasonable choice" by the legislature. The State next contends that precedent requires us to give particular deference to that legislative choice because the State could, if it chose, ban the sale of alcoholic beverages outright.... Finally, the State argues that deference is appropriate because alcoholic beverages are so-called "vice" products....

The State's first argument fails to justify the speech prohibition at issue....

[W]e conclude that a state legislature does not have the broad discretion to suppress truthful, nonmisleading information for paternalistic purposes[.]... As we explained in *Virginia Pharmacy Bd.*, "[i]t is precisely this kind of choice, between the dangers of suppressing information, and the dangers of its misuse if it is freely available, that the First Amendment makes for us."

We also cannot accept the State's second contention, which is premised entirely on the "greater-includes-the-lesser" reasoning endorsed toward the end of the majority's opinion in *Posadas* [*de Puerto*

Rico Association v. Tourism Company, 478 U.S. 328 (1986)]. There, the majority stated that "the greater power to completely ban casino gambling necessarily includes the lesser power to ban advertising of casino gambling."...

Further consideration persuades us that the "greater-includes-the-lesser" argument should be rejected [because] ... it is inconsistent with both logic and well-settled doctrine....

Finally, we find unpersuasive the State's contention that ... the price advertising ban should be upheld because it targets commercial speech that pertains to a "vice" activity....

Almost any product that poses some threat to public health or public morals might reasonably be characterized by a state legislature as relating to "vice activity." Such characterization, however, is anomalous when applied to products such as alcoholic beverages, lottery tickets, or playing cards, that may be lawfully purchased on the open market. The recognition of such an exception would also have the unfortunate consequence of either allowing state legislatures to justify censorship by the simple expedient of placing the "vice" label on selected lawful activities, or requiring the federal courts to establish a federal common law of vice....

Because Rhode Island has failed to carry its heavy burden of justifying its complete ban on price advertising, we conclude that R. I. Gen. Laws Section(s) 3-8-7 and 3-8-8.1, as well as Regulation 32 of the Rhode Island Liquor Control Administration, abridge speech in violation of the First Amendment as made applicable to the States by the Due Process Clause of the Fourteenth Amendment. The judgment of the Court of Appeals is therefore reversed.

It is so ordered.

**SCALIA, J., CONCURRING IN PART AND
CONCURRING IN THE JUDGMENT**

I share Justice Thomas's discomfort with
the *Central Hudson* test, which seems to
me to have nothing more than policy intuition to support it. I also share Justice
Stevens' aversion towards paternalistic
governmental policies that prevent men
and women from hearing facts that might
not be good for them....

**THOMAS, J., CONCURRING IN PART AND
CONCURRING IN THE JUDGMENT**

In cases such as this, in which the government's asserted interest is to keep legal
users of a product or service ignorant in
order to manipulate their choices in the
marketplace, the balancing test adopted in
Central Hudson should not be applied, in
my view. Rather, such an "interest" is *per
se* illegitimate and can no more justify regulation of "commercial" speech than it can
justify regulation of "noncommercial"
speech....

I do not join the principal opinion's
application of the *Central Hudson* balancing test because I do not believe that such
a test should be applied to a restriction of
"commercial" speech, at least when, as
here, the asserted interest is one that is to
be achieved through keeping would-be
recipients of the speech in the dark.
Application of the advancement-of-state-
interest prong of *Central Hudson* makes little sense to me in such circumstances....

Although the Court took a sudden turn
away from *Virginia Pharmacy Bd.* in *Central
Hudson*, it has never explained why manip-
ulating the choices of consumers by keeping them ignorant is more legitimate when
the ignorance is maintained through suppression of "commercial" speech than
when the same ignorance is maintained
through suppression of "noncommercial"
speech. The courts, including this Court,

have found the *Central Hudson* "test" to be,
as a general matter, very difficult to apply
with any uniformity. This may result in
part from the inherently nondeterminative
nature of a case-by-case balancing "test"
unaccompanied by any categorical rules,
and the consequent likelihood that individual judicial preferences will govern application of the test. Moreover, the second
prong of *Central Hudson*, as applied to the
facts of that case and to those here, apparently requires judges to delineate those
situations in which citizens cannot be
trusted with information, and invites
judges to decide whether they themselves
think that consumption of a product is
harmful enough that it should be discouraged. In my view, the *Central Hudson* test
asks the courts to weigh incommensu-
rables the value of knowledge versus the
value of ignorance—and to apply contradictory premises—that informed adults
are the best judges of their own interests,
and that they are not. Rather than continuing to apply a test that makes no sense to
me when the asserted state interest is of
the type involved here, I would return to
the reasoning and holding of *Virginia
Pharmacy Bd.* Under that decision, these
restrictions fall.

**O'CONNOR, SOUTER, AND BREYER, J.J.,
AND REHNQUIST, C.J., CONCURRING
IN THE JUDGMENT**

... I agree with the Court that Rhode
Island's price-advertising ban is invalid. I
would resolve this case more narrowly,
however, by applying our established
Central Hudson test to determine whether
this commercial-speech regulation survives First Amendment scrutiny....

Both parties agree that the first two
prongs of the *Central Hudson* test are met.
Even if we assume *arguendo* that Rhode
Island's regulation also satisfies the

requirement that it directly advance the governmental interest, Rhode Island's regulation fails the final prong; that is, its ban is more extensive than necessary to serve the State's interest....

The fit between Rhode Island's method and this particular goal is not reasonable. If the target is simply higher prices generally to discourage consumption, the regulation imposes too great, and unnecessary, a prohibition on speech in order to achieve it. The State has other methods at its disposal—methods that would more directly accomplish this stated goal without intruding on sellers' ability to provide truthful, nonmisleading information to customers....

Because Rhode Island's regulation fails even the less stringent standard set out in *Central Hudson*, nothing here requires adoption of a new analysis for the evaluation of commercial speech regulation. The principal opinion acknowledges that "even under the less than strict standard that generally applies in commercial speech cases, the State has failed to establish a reasonable fit between its abridgement of speech and its temperance goal." Because we need go no further, I would not here undertake the question whether the test we have employed since *Central Hudson* should be displaced....

QUESTIONS

1. Does *44 Liquor Mart* stand for the proposition that truthful commercial messages about lawful products and services are entitled to a full measure of constitutional protection? If not, would that be a superior rule?

2. The Rhode Island Liquor Stores Association argued that "There is a larger issue than Rhode Island's two statutes lurking in the wings of this case. The broader question is to what extent government, federal, state, or local, is able to legislate to protect the health, safety, and welfare of its citizens from rampant advertising of *harmful* products or activities." (Emphasis in original.) What impact, if any, does the Court's opinion in *44 Liquor Mart*, have on that "broader question?" For example, does it deprive a state of the power to ban the advertising of tobacco products? The State of Nevada has legalized prostitution under certain restrictions. Does *44 Liquor Mart* have implications for whether the Nevada legislature can prohibit the advertising of prostitution?

3. Media scholar Patrick M. Garry has characterized the Court's approach to commercial speech as "utilitarian":

    In looking at the content of speech and its contribution to the marketplace of ideas, the Court has demonstrated its willingness to protect only such speech that furthered the social interest in the free flow of information. Thus, under the commercial speech doctrine, audience interests [have] taken priority over speaker's interests. ("Commercial Speech," in *The Oxford Companion to the Supreme Court of the United States*, ed. Kermit L. Hall [New York, NY: Oxford University Press, 1992], p. 169)

    Is there merit to Garry's analysis?

SUGGESTIONS FOR FURTHER READING

Baker, C. Edwin, "Commercial Speech: A Problem in the Theory of Freedom," 62 *Iowa Law Review* (1976): 1.

Barrett, Edward L., Jr., "The Uncharted Area—Commercial Speech and the First Amendment," 13 *University of California Davis Law Review* (1980): 175.

Brudney, Victor, "Business Corporations and Stockholders' Rights under the First Amendment," 91 *Yale Law Journal* (1981): 235.

Collins, Ronald, and David Skover, "The First Amendment in an Age of Paratroopers," 68 *Texas Law Review* (1990): 1087.

_____, "Commerce and Communication," 71 *Texas Law Review* (1993): 697.

Comment, "First Amendment Protection for Commercial Advertising: The New Constitutional Doctrine," 44 *University of Chicago Law Review* (1976): 205.

"Developments—Deceptive Advertising," 80 *Harvard Law Review* (1967): 1005.

Farber, Daniel, "Commercial Speech and First Amendment Theory," 74 *Northwestern University Law Review* (1979): 372.

Goldman, Roger L., "A Doctrine of Worthier Speech: *Young v. American Mini Theaters, Inc.*," 21 *St. Louis University Law Journal* (1977): 281.

Jackson, Thomas H., and John Calvin Jeffries, "Commercial Speech: Economic Due Process and the First Amendment," 65 *Virginia Law Review* (1979): 1.

Kozinski, Alex, and Henry Banner, "Who's Afraid of Commercial Speech?" 76 *Virginia Law Review* (1990): 627.

Kurland, Philip B., "*Posadas de Puerto Rico v. Tourism Company of Puerto Rico*: 'Twas Passing Strange; 'Twas Pitiful, 'Twas Wondrous Pitiful," *The Supreme Court Review* (Chicago, IL: University of Chicago Press, 1986).

Lively, Donald, "The Supreme Court and Commercial Speech: New Words with an Old Message," 72 *Minnesota Law Review* (1987): 289.

Note, "Freedom of Expression in a Commercial Context," 78 *Harvard Law Review* (1965): 1191.

Redish, Martin, "The First Amendment in the Marketplace: Commercial Speech and the Values of Free Expression," 39 *George Washington Law Review* (1971): 429.

Schauer, Frederick, "Commercial Speech and the Architecture of the First Amendment," 56 *University of Cincinnati Law Review* (1988): 1181.

Schiro, Richard, "Commercial Speech: The Demise of a Chimera," *The Supreme Court Review* (Chicago, IL: University of Chicago Press, 1976).

Shiffrin, Steven H., "The First Amendment and Economic Regulation: Away from the General Theory of the First Amendment," 78 *Northwestern University Law Review* (1983): 1212.

SPEECH AND EMERGING TECHNOLOGIES

Denver Area Educational Telecommunications Consortium, Inc. v. Federal Communications Commission
116 S.Ct. 2374 (1996)

SETTING

Cable access television channels were first created in the 1960s, when cable operators began to receive franchises from local governments. In the early years, in order to provide the public with maximally diverse programs, those governments generally required cable operators to set aside some portion of their channel capacity for the public. In 1972, the Federal Communications Commission (FCC) adopted mandatory access rules that gave cable operators five years to offer access to the public on a first-come, nondiscriminatory basis, with the operators having no control over program content. In 1976, the FCC revised its access rules, extending them to more cable systems.

In 1984, Congress enacted the Cable Communication Policy Act, "to assure that cable communications provide ... the widest possible diversity of information sources and services to the public." The act required cable operators to set aside channels for leased access programming. Under the act, the operators were forbidden from censoring programming on the leased access channels and on the public, educational, and government access channels (known as PEGs). The act also required cable operators to provide their subscribers with "lockboxes" so that subscribers could block any cable channel during selected periods. Finally, the 1984 act shielded cable operators from all liability under federal, state, or local obscenity laws for programs carried on leased access or PEG channels.

In 1992, Congress revisited the question of cable programming on leased access and PEG channels, in response to complaints that the 1984 act had played an unfortunate, albeit unintended, role in the propagation of indecent broadcasting on cable systems. Leased access channels, members of Congress were told, were being used to display "sex shows and X-rated previews of hard-core homosexual films" and aired "ads for phone lines letting listeners eavesdrop on acts of incest." Critics also claimed that some public, educational, and governmental channels were being used "to basically solicit prostitution through easily discernible shams such as escort services [and] fantasy parties, where live participants, through two-way conversation through the telephone ... [solicit] illegal activities." Some members of Congress expressed concern that "early and sustained exposure" to indecent material on television could cause "significant physical, psychological and social damage" to children. The Cable Television Consumer Protection and Competition Act was enacted to address these concerns.

Section 10 of the act, proposed by Senator Jesse Helms, was entitled "Children's Protection from Indecent Programming on Leased Access Channels." The goal of Section 10 was "to put an end to the kind of things going on" on access channels. Section 10, unlike other provisions of the 1992 legislation, was offered as a floor amendment in the Senate, and thus was not the subject of congressional hearings or findings and was never sent to a committee.

Section 10 contained four interlocking parts: Section 10(a) authorized cable operators to ban from leased access channels what they "reasonably believe describes or depicts sexual or excretory activities or organs in a patently offensive manner as measured by contemporary community standards."

Section 10(b) required the FCC to prescribe rules requiring cable operators that have not voluntarily prohibited programming under Section 10(a) to segregate all "indecent" leased access programming on channels that must remain blocked until a subscriber requests access in writing. It also required programmers to identify for cable operators any of their programs that "would be indecent as defined by Commission regulations."

Section 10(c) applied to PEG access channels and authorized cable operators to ban "any programming which contains obscene material, sexually explicit conduct, or material soliciting or promoting unlawful conduct."

Section 10(d) eliminated the statutory immunity granted to cable operators by the 1984 legislation for access programming that "involves obscene materials."

Following adoption of the 1992 act, the FCC issued a notice of proposed rule making to implement the provisions of Section 10 and requested comments. One of the cable programmers to respond was the Denver Area Educational Telecommunications Consortium, Inc., commonly known as The 90's Channel. It is a nonprofit cable programmer in Colorado that operates a leased access cable service which, in 1993, reached approximately five hundred thousand basic cable subscribers to cable systems owned by Tele-Communications, Inc., in Arizona, California, Connecticut, Colorado, Maryland, and Michigan. Its programming focuses on documentaries and political, environmental, labor, and special topics. The 90's Channel does not carry pornographic programs, but some of its programming—dealing with topics such as censorship, gay rights, feminism, prostitution, and AIDS—does include discussion of sexuality and the description or depiction of sexual activity. For example, it has televised programs seeking to demystify gynecology and to teach women how to perform their own pelvic exams, a program on controversies surrounding a Robert Mappelthorpe art exhibit, and an annual Japanese fertility festival. The 90's Channel and the American Civil Liberties Union (ACLU) informed the FCC that, in their view, Section 10 violated the First Amendment. Specifically, they expressed concern over the meaning of the term, "indecent programming," contending that it was overbroad and would sweep away a wide variety of socially useful programming, including many of the programs on The 90's Channel.

Despite the concerns expressed by The 90's Channel, the ACLU and other local cable authorities, the FCC adopted regulations to implement Sections 10(a) and 10(b) that defined "indecent" programming almost identically to the language used in Section 10(a). The regulations authorized a cable operator to adopt and enforce a policy of banning leased access programming that it "reasonably believes" contains indecency, and, if the operator did not voluntarily adopt and enforce such a policy, required it to block all leased access programming that falls within the FCC's definition of "indecency."

The FCC subsequently adopted regulations to implement Section 10(c), relating to PEG access channels. Those regulations authorized cable operators to prohibit obscene material, indecent material, and material soliciting or promoting unlawful conduct. The regulations also authorized cable operators to require a PEG access programmer "to certify that its programming does not contain any of the materials" subject to prohibition under Section 10(c).

The 90's Channel and the ACLU petitioned the Court of Appeals for the District of Columbia for review of the FCC regulations. Their petitions were consolidated with others, including a petition from the Alliance for Community Media. The FCC and the United States were named as respondents. The court stayed implementation of the regulations pending review.

At oral argument before the D.C. Circuit, the government conceded that if Sections 10(a) and 10(c) were interpreted to involve state action, they would violate the First Amendment to the Constitution of the United States. A three-judge panel invalidated Sections 10(a) and 10(c), on the ground that permitting cable operators to ban indecent leased access and PEG programming constituted "state action." It remanded the issue of the constitutionality of Section 10(b)'s segregation and blocking scheme to the FCC for further consideration in light of its invalidation of Sections 10(a) and 10(c).

The D.C. Circuit vacated the panel opinion and ruled that it need not reach the First Amendment challenge, because the statute and implementing regulations merely authorized—rather than commanded—private parties to ban the targeted speech and because those private acts could not be attributed to the government. The court also ruled that Section 10(b) was the least restrictive means to serve the government's compelling interest in shielding minors from indecent speech and that Section 10 as a whole was not impermissibly vague. Finally, it ruled that any effect that Section 10(d)'s removal of immunity for carrying obscene programming might have on an operator's programming decision did not support attribution of the operator's decision to ban indecent programming to the government.

The Supreme Court granted writs of certiorari from The 90's Channel and the ACLU, and consolidated the case with a challenge brought by the Alliance for Community Media.

HIGHLIGHTS OF SUPREME COURT ARGUMENTS

BRIEF FOR THE 90'S CHANNEL AND ACLU

◆ It is well established that cable programmers engage in and transmit speech and that they are entitled to the protection of the speech and press provisions of the First Amendment. Their speech is no less protected when it touches on sex. Section 10 and its implementing regulations are laws regulating speech and discriminate on the basis of content and speaker identity.

◆ The issue in this case is whether Section 10 violates the Constitution, not whether particular censorship decisions of cable operators would be state action.

◆ Sections 10(a) and 10(b) establish a comprehensive scheme to censor "indecency" on leased access channels with private cable operators and the FCC playing interlocking roles: the FCC defines indecency, resolves disputes over its application, and prescribes blocking and segregation requirements, while the cable operators determine what programming falls within their "reasonable belief" of indecency and decide whether to ban or block such programming. That joint enterprise between government and private actors is subject to constitutional scrutiny.

◆ Section 10 unconstitutionally authorizes and requires censorship under vague standards and lacks essential procedural safeguards. Vague laws pose an unacceptable risk of self-censorship. The definition of "indecent" in Section 10 is substantially more vague than the three-part test upheld in *Miller v. California*, 413 U.S. 15 (1973).

◆ Section 10(b) is impermissibly overinclusive, because its restrictions on speech do not advance the government's goals. It imposes far greater burdens on speech than are necessary given available alternatives that are far less oppressive.

AMICUS CURIAE BRIEFS SUPPORTING THE 90'S CHANNEL AND ACLU

Association of American Publishers, Inc.; joint brief of American Booksellers Foundation for Free Expression, Council for Periodical Distributors Associations, Freedom to Read Foundation, Interactive Digital Software Association, International Periodical Distributors Association, Magazine Publishers of America, Inc., Motion Picture Association of America, National Association of College Stores, Inc., National Association of Recording Merchandisers, Periodical and Book Association of America, Inc., Publishers Marketing Association, Recording Industry Association of America, Inc., and Video Software Dealers Association.

BRIEF FOR FCC AND UNITED STATES

◆ The action of private cable operators in choosing whether to prohibit indecent programming on access channels on their own systems is not properly attributable to the federal government. Neither the act nor the regulations constitutes governmental censorship. Rather, they grant permission to private actors to make a choice regarding whether to transmit indecent material over their cable channels.

◆ Sections 10(a) and 10(c) are not restrictions on the right of the public to engage in free expression. They merely permit private participants in the marketplace of ideas to avoid serving as conduits for the speech of other private participants in the same marketplace. Where a challenged regulation directed at restoring editorial freedom does not restrict the overall ability of the public to engage in free expression, the regulation should be upheld so long as it is reasonable and viewpoint-neutral.

◆ The segregation and blocking scheme required by Section 10(b) is action attributable to the government and is subject to constitutional constraints. However, strict scrutiny is not required under the First Amendment, because a more lenient standard of review applies to regulations designed to protect children from indecent materials on television. Even if strict scrutiny were the appropriate standard, Section 10(b) would survive, because the interests in protecting children on which it is based are compelling and the provision is narrowly tailored to advance those interests.

◆ Section 10(b) is the least restrictive means of ensuring that children do not watch indecent programming on leased access channels without their parents' consent. Subscriber-initiated measures alone cannot solve some of the most important problems posed by indecent programming.

◆ The vagueness challenge in this case is speculative. Furthermore, this Court has been offered no alternative definition of indecency that would avoid the supposed vagueness problems of the statute and regulations. The FCC has always erred on the side of determining that material is not legally indecent.

AMICUS CURIAE BRIEFS SUPPORTING THE FCC AND THE UNITED STATES

Morality in Media, Inc.; Time Warner Cable; Family Life Project of The American Center for Law and Justice; National Family Legal Foundation; State of New York.

SUPREME COURT DECISION:

(§ 10(a) 6–3 on judgment, 4–2–3 on rationale)

(§ 10(b) 6–3 on judgment, 4–2–3 on rationale)

(§ 10(c) 5–4 on judgment, 3–2–1–3 on rationale)

BREYER, J.

... [W]e can decide this case ... by closely scrutinizing Section 10(a) to assure that it properly addresses an extremely important problem, without imposing, in light of the relevant interests, an unnecessarily great restriction on speech. The importance of the interest at stake here—protecting children from exposure to patently offensive depictions of sex; the accommodation of the interests of programmers in maintaining access channels and of cable operators in editing the contents of their channels; the similarity of the problem and its solution to those at issue in [*F.C.C.*

v.] *Pacifica* [*Foundation*, 438 U.S. 726 (1978)]; and the flexibility inherent in an approach that permits private cable operators to make editorial decisions, lead us to conclude that Section 10(a) is a sufficiently tailored response to an extraordinarily important problem.

First, the provision before us comes accompanied with an extremely important justification, one that this Court has often found compelling—the need to protect children from exposure to patently offensive sex-related material....

Second, the provision arises in a very particular context—congressional permission for cable operators to regulate programming that, but for a previous Act of Congress, would have had no path of access to cable channels free of an operator's control. The First Amendment interests involved are therefore complex, and involve a balance between those interests served by the access requirements themselves (increasing the availability of avenues of expression to programmers who otherwise would not have them), and the disadvantage to the First Amendment interests of cable operators and other programmers (those to whom the cable operator would have assigned the channels devoted to access)....

Third, the problem Congress addressed here is remarkably similar to the problem addressed by the FCC in *Pacifica*, and the balance Congress struck is commensurate with the balance we approved there. In *Pacifica* this Court considered a governmental ban of a radio broadcast of "indecent" materials[.]...

The Court found this ban constitutionally permissible primarily because "broadcasting is uniquely accessible to children" and children were likely listeners to the program there at issue—an afternoon radio broadcast....

All these factors are present here. Cable television broadcasting, including access channel broadcasting, is as "accessible to children" as over-the-air broadcasting, if not more so....

Fourth, the permissive nature of Section 10(a) means that it likely restricts speech less than, not more than, the ban at issue in *Pacifica*. The provision removes a restriction as to some speakers—namely, cable operators.... Moreover, although the provision does create a risk that a program will not appear, that risk is not the same as the certainty that accompanies a governmental ban. In fact, a glance at the programming that cable operators allow on their own (nonaccess) channels suggests that this distinction is not theoretical, but real.... Finally, the provision's permissive nature brings with it a flexibility that allows cable operators, for example, not to ban broadcasts, but, say, to rearrange broadcast times, better to fit the desires of adult audiences while lessening the risks of harm to children....

The existence of this complex balance of interests persuades us that the permissive nature of the provision, coupled with its viewpoint-neutral application, is a constitutionally permissible way to protect children from the type of sexual material that concerned Congress, while accommodating both the First Amendment interests served by the access requirements and those served in restoring to cable operators a degree of the editorial control that Congress removed in 1984....

Finally, petitioners argue that the definition of the materials subject to the challenged provisions is too vague, thereby granting cable system operators too broad a program-screening authority....

The language, while vague, attempts to identify the category of materials that

Justice Stewart thought could be described only in terms of "I know it when I see it." *Jacobellis v. Ohio*, 378 U.S. 184 (1964)....

[T]he statute's language aims at the kind of programming to which its sponsors referred—pictures of oral sex, bestiality, and rape, ... and not at scientific or educational programs (at least unless done with a highly unusual lack of concern for viewer reaction)....

Further, the statute protects against overly broad application of its standards insofar as it permits cable system operators to screen programs only pursuant to a "written and published policy."...

For the reasons discussed, we conclude that Section 10(a) is consistent with the First Amendment.

The statute's second provision significantly differs from the first, for it does not simply permit, but rather requires, cable system operators to restrict speech—by segregating and blocking "patently offensive" sex-related material appearing on leased channels (but not on other channels).

These requirements have obvious restrictive effects. The several up-to-30-day delays, along with single channel segregation, mean that a subscriber cannot decide to watch a single program without considerable advance planning and without letting the "patently offensive" channel in its entirety invade his household for days, perhaps weeks, at a time. These restrictions will prevent programmers from broadcasting to viewers who select programs day by day (or, through "surfing," minute by minute); to viewers who would like occasionally to watch a few, but not many, of the programs on the "patently offensive" channel; and to viewers who simply tend to judge a program's value through channel reputation, i.e., by

the company it keeps. Moreover, the "written notice" requirement will further restrict viewing by subscribers who fear for their reputations should the operator, advertently or inadvertently, disclose the list of those who wish to watch the "patently offensive" channel.... Further, the added costs and burdens that these requirements impose upon a cable system operator may encourage that operator to ban programming that the operator would otherwise permit to run, even if only late at night....

We agree with the Government that protection of children is a "compelling interest."... But we do not agree that the "segregate and block" requirements properly accommodate the speech restrictions they impose and the legitimate objective they seek to attain.... [N]ot only is [governmental restriction] not a "least restrictive alternative," and is not "narrowly tailored" to meet its legitimate objective, it also seems considerably "more extensive than necessary." That is to say, it fails to satisfy this Court's formulations of the First Amendment's "strictest," as well as its somewhat less "strict," requirements.... The provision before us does not reveal the caution and care that [constitutional] standards ... impose upon laws that seek to reconcile the critically important interest in protecting free speech with very important, or even compelling, interests that sometimes warrant restrictions....

Consequently, we cannot find that the "segregate and block" restrictions on speech are a narrowly, or reasonably, tailored effort to protect children. Rather, they are overly restrictive, "sacrific[ing]" important First Amendment interests for too "speculative a gain." *Columbia Broadcasting Company v. Democratic National Committee*, 412 U.S. [94 (1973).]...

For that reason they are not consistent with the First Amendment....

The statute's third provision, as implemented by FCC regulation, is similar to its first provision, in that it too permits a cable operator to prevent transmission of "patently offensive" programming, in this case on public access channels. 1992 Act, Section 10(c). But there are four important differences.

The first is the historical background.... [C]able operators have traditionally agreed to reserve channel capacity for public, governmental, and educational channels as part of the consideration they give municipalities that award them cable franchises.... [T]he requirement to reserve capacity for public access channels is similar to the reservation of a public easement, or a dedication of land for streets and parks, as part of a municipality's approval of a subdivision of land.... Significantly, these are channels over which cable operators have not historically exercised editorial control. Unlike Section 10(a) therefore, Section 10(c) does not restore to cable operators editorial rights that they once had, and the countervailing First Amendment interest is nonexistent, or at least much diminished....

The second difference is the institutional background that has developed as a result of the historical difference. When a "leased channel" is made available by the operator to a private lessee, the lessee has total control of programming during the leased time slot.... Public access channels, on the other hand, are normally subject to complex supervisory systems of various sorts, often with both public and private elements.... Municipalities generally provide in their cable franchising agreements for an access channel manager, who is most commonly a nonprofit organization, but may also be the municipality, or, in some instances, the cable system owner....

This system of public, private, and mixed nonprofit elements, through its supervising boards and nonprofit or governmental access managers, can set programming policy and approve or disapprove particular programming services. And this system can police that policy by, for example, requiring indemnification by programmers, certification of compliance with local standards, time segregation, adult content advisories, or even by pre-screening individual programs.... Whether these locally accountable bodies pre-screen programming, promulgate rules for the use of public access channels, or are merely available to respond when problems arise, the upshot is the same: there is a locally accountable body capable of addressing the problem, should it arise, of patently offensive programming broadcast to children, making it unlikely that many children will in fact be exposed to programming considered patently offensive in that community....

Third, the existence of a system aimed at encouraging and securing programming that the community considers valuable strongly suggests that a "cable operator's veto" is less likely necessary to achieve the statute's basic objective, protecting children, than a similar veto in the context of leased channels. Of course, the system of access managers and supervising boards can make mistakes, which the operator might in some cases correct with its veto power. Balanced against this potential benefit, however, is the risk that the veto itself may be mistaken; and its use, or threatened use, could prevent the presentation of programming, that, though borderline, is not "patently offensive" to its targeted audience.... And this latter threat must bulk large within a system that already has publicly accountable systems for maintaining responsible programs.

Finally, our examination of the legislative history and the record before us is consistent with what common sense suggests, namely that the public/nonprofit programming control systems now in place would normally avoid, minimize, or eliminate any child-related problems concerning "patently offensive" programming. We have found anecdotal references to what seem isolated instances of potentially indecent programming, some of which may well have occurred on leased, not public access channels....

But these few examples do not necessarily indicate a significant nationwide pattern....

At most, we have found borderline examples as to which people's judgment may differ, perhaps acceptable in some communities but not others, of the type that petitioners fear the law might prohibit....

The upshot, in respect to the public access channels, is a law that could radically change present programming-related relationships among local community and nonprofit supervising boards and access managers, which relationships are established through municipal law, regulation, and contract. In doing so, it would not significantly restore editorial rights of cable operators, but would greatly increase the risk that certain categories of programming (say, borderline offensive programs) will not appear. At the same time, given present supervisory mechanisms, the need for this particular provision, aimed directly at public access channels, is not obvious. Having carefully reviewed the legislative history of the Act, the proceedings before the FCC, the record below, and the submissions of the parties and *amici*

here, we conclude that the Government cannot sustain its burden of showing that Section 10(c) is necessary to protect children or that it is appropriately tailored to secure that end....

For these reasons, the judgment of the Court of Appeals is affirmed insofar as it upheld Section 10(a); the judgment of the Court of Appeals is reversed insofar as it upheld Section 10(b) and Section 10(c).

It is so ordered.

STEVENS, J., CONCURRING

The difference between Section 10(a) and Section 10(c) is the difference between a permit and a prohibition. The former restores the freedom of cable operators to reject indecent programs; the latter requires local franchising authorities to reject such programs....

[T]he public, educational and governmental access channels that are regulated by Section 10(c) are not creations of the Federal Government. They owe their existence to contracts forged between cable operators and local cable franchising authorities....

What is of critical importance to me, however, is that if left to their own devices, those authorities may choose to carry some programming that the Federal Government has decided to restrict. As I read Section 10(c), the federal statute would disable local governments from making that choice. It would inject federally authorized private censors into forums from which they might otherwise be excluded, and it would therefore limit local forums that might otherwise be open to all constitutionally protected speech....

SOUTER, J., CONCURRING

... [I]n charting a course that will permit reasonable regulation in light of the values in competition, we have to accept the likelihood that the media of communication will become less categorical and more protean. Because we cannot be confident that for purposes of judging speech restrictions it will continue to make sense to distinguish cable from other technologies, and because we know that changes in these regulated technologies will enormously alter the structure of regulation itself, we should be shy about saying the final word today about what will be accepted as reasonable tomorrow....

The upshot of appreciating the fluidity of the subject that Congress must regulate is simply to accept the fact that not every nuance of our old standards will necessarily do for the new technology, and that a proper choice among existing doctrinal categories is not obvious....

O'CONNOR, J., CONCURRING IN PART AND DISSENTING IN PART

... The distinctions upon which the Court relies in deciding that Section 10(c) must fall while Section 10(a) survives are not, in my view, constitutionally significant.... I am not persuaded that the difference in the origin of the access channels is sufficient to justify upholding Section 10(a) and striking down Section 10(c). The interest in protecting children remains the same, whether on a leased access channel or a public access channel, and allowing the cable operator the option of prohibiting the transmission of indecent speech seems a constitutionally permissible means of addressing that interest. Nor is the fact that public access programming may be subject to supervisory systems in addition to the cable operator ... sufficient in my mind to render Section 10(c) so ill-tailored to its goal as to be unconstitutional. Given the compelling interest served by Section 10(c), its permissive nature, and fit within our precedent, I

would hold Section 10(c), like Section 10(a), constitutional.

KENNEDY AND GINSBURG, J.J., CONCURRING IN PART, CONCURRING IN THE JUDGMENT IN PART, AND DISSENTING IN PART

... At a minimum, the proper standard for reviewing Sections 10(a) and (c) is strict scrutiny.... I would hold these enactments unconstitutional because they are not narrowly tailored to serve a compelling interest....

Sections 10(a) and (c) present a classic case of discrimination against speech based on its content. There are legitimate reasons why the Government might wish to regulate or even restrict the speech at issue here, but Sections 10(a) and 10(c) are not drawn to address those reasons with the precision the First Amendment requires....

In agreement with the plurality's analysis of Section 10(b) of the Act, insofar as it applies strict scrutiny, I join [that part] of its opinion. Its position there, however, cannot be reconciled with upholding Section 10(a). In the plurality's view, Section 10(b), which standing alone would guarantee an indecent programmer some access to a cable audience, violates the First Amendment, but Section 10(a), which authorizes exclusion of indecent programming from access channels altogether, does not. There is little to commend this logic or result. I dissent from the judgment of the Court insofar as it upholds the constitutionality of Section 10(a).

THOMAS AND SCALIA, J.J., AND REHNQUIST, C.J., CONCURRING IN THE JUDGMENT IN PART AND DISSENTING IN PART

I agree with the plurality's conclusion that Section 10(a) is constitutionally permissible, but I disagree with its conclusion that Sections 10(b) and (c) violate the First Amendment. For many years, we have failed to articulate how and to what extent the First Amendment protects cable operators, programmers, and viewers from state and federal regulation. I think it is time we did so, and I cannot go along with the plurality's assiduous attempts to avoid addressing that issue openly....

Our First Amendment distinctions between media, dubious from their infancy, placed cable in a doctrinal wasteland in which regulators and cable operators alike could not be sure whether cable was entitled to the substantial First Amendment protections afforded the print media or was subject to the more onerous obligations shouldered by the broadcast media.... Over time, however, we have drawn closer to recognizing that cable operators should enjoy the same First Amendment rights as the nonbroadcast media....

[E]ven if the plurality's balancing test were an appropriate standard, it could only be applied to protect speech interests that, under the circumstances, are themselves protected by the First Amendment. But, by shifting the focus to the balancing of "complex" interests, [the plurality] never explains whether (and if so, how) a programmer's ordinarily unprotected interest in affirmative transmission of its programming acquires constitutional significance on leased and public access channels.... It is that question, left unanswered by the plurality, to which I now turn.

It is no doubt true that once programmers have been given, rightly or wrongly, the ability to speak on access channels, the First Amendment continues to protect programmers from certain government intrusions. Certainly, under our current jurisprudence, Congress could not impose a total ban on the transmission of indecent programming.... At the same time, however, the Court has not recognized, as entitled to full constitutional protection, statutorily created speech rights that directly conflict with the constitutionally protected private speech rights of another person or entity. We have not found a First Amendment violation in statutory schemes that substantially expand the speech opportunities of the person or entity challenging the scheme....

In my view, the constitutional presumption properly runs in favor of the operators' editorial discretion, and that discretion may not be burdened without a compelling reason for doing so....

Sections 10(a) and (c) do not burden a programmer's right to seek access for its indecent programming on an operator's system. Rather, they merely restore part of the editorial discretion an operator would have absent government regulation without burdening the programmer's underlying speech rights.

The First Amendment challenge, if one is to be made, must come from the party whose constitutionally protected freedom of speech has been burdened. Viewing the federal access requirements as a whole, it is the cable operator, not the access programmer, whose speech rights have been infringed. Consequently, it is the operator, and not the programmer, whose speech has arguably been infringed by these provisions....

[E]ven were I inclined to view public access channels as public property, which I am not, the numerous additional obligations imposed on the cable operator in managing and operating the public access channels convince me that these channels share few, if any, of the basic characteristics of a public forum.... Public access channels are not public fora, and, therefore, petitioners' attempt to redistribute cable speech rights in their favor must fail. For this reason, and the other reasons articulated earlier, I would sustain both Section 10(a) and Section 10(c).

Unlike Sections 10 (a) and (c), Section 10(b) clearly implicates petitioners' free speech rights. Though Section 10(b) by no means bans indecent speech, it clearly places content-based restrictions on the transmission of private speech by requiring cable operators to block and segregate indecent programming that the operator has agreed to carry. Consequently, Section 10(b) must be subjected to strict scrutiny and can be upheld only if it furthers a compelling governmental interest by the least restrictive means available....

The parties agree that Congress has a "compelling interest in protecting the physical and psychological well-being of minors" and that its interest "extends to shielding minors from the influence of [indecent speech] that is not obscene by adult standards." *Sable* [*Communications of Cal., Inc. v. FCC*, 492 U.S. 115 (1989)].... Because Section 10(b) is narrowly tailored to achieve that well-established compelling interest, I would uphold it. I therefore dissent from the Court's decision to the contrary....

Accordingly, I would affirm the judgment of the Court of Appeals in its entirety. I therefore concur in the judgment upholding Section 10(a) and respectfully dissent from that portion of the judgment striking down Sections 10(b) and (c).

QUESTIONS

1. What were the salient issues in *Denver Area*: (1) whether the term "indecent" in Section 10 of the Cable Television Consumer Protection and Competition Act is vague; (2) whether Sections 10(a) and (c) constitute state action; (3) the extent of Congress's power to protect minors from indecent programming; (4) governmental suppression of constitutionally protected speech in one developing new medium? All of the above?

2. The Court in *Denver Area* was unable to fashion a rule to which a majority of the justices would subscribe. To what extent can this failure be explained by the rapidly changing technology of the cable television industry? Or are the Court's divisions more attributable to disagreements over First Amendment standards?

3. The government argued in its brief that the question in *Denver Area* was "whether *the statute* coerces or otherwise significantly encourages operators to prohibit [certain] programming. If it does not, decisions by cable operators to prohibit indecent programming cannot be attributed to the government...." (Emphasis in original.) Does the Court's opinion in *Denver Area* adequately draw the line between private and state action for First Amendment purposes?

4. To what extent, if any, will the Court's opinion in *Denver Area* curtail sex education, AIDS and abortion education, or other controversial health-related education on cable access channels?

SPEECH AND EMERGING TECHNOLOGIES

Reno v. American Civil Liberties Union
117 S.Ct. 2329 (1997)

SETTING

The Internet traces its origins to experiments by the Department of Defense to link defense-related computer systems so that research and communication could continue even if portions of the network were damaged. Soon, universities, research facilities, and businesses developed computer-based information networks. By the early 1990s, private individuals also had on-line access to information through a global network that came to be known as the Internet. Individuals can obtain access to the Internet in essentially two ways: through use of a personal computer with a modem to connect via telephone to a computer network that is linked to the Internet, or through use of a computer that is directly connected to a network connected to the Internet. Many commercial entities offer modem or direct connection to the Internet, charging subscribers monthly or hourly fees for access. Internet communication is possible to one or several specific individuals or to larger groups through electronic mail (e-mail), list services, and news groups. The range of information available through the Internet is virtually unlimited, including access to sexually explicit material.

In 1996, Congress adopted the Communications Decency Act (CDA) as part of the Telecommunications Act. The reason behind the act, according to Senator Joseph Biden, was that "some of the information traveling over the Internet is tasteless, offensive, and downright spine-tingling." Congress believed that without "some basic rules of the road," the availability and easy accessibility of sexually explicit materials through the Internet would harm children. Consequently, the CDA made it a crime to transmit obscene or indecent materials to minors via online services. The act also contained two defenses to liability—if the defendant made good faith efforts to restrict access by minors to indecent material, or if the defendant restricted access to indecent material by requiring users to gain access only through use of a credit or debit card, an adult access code, or an adult personal identification number.

On the day that President Clinton signed the CDA into law, the American Civil Liberties Union and various other organizations and individuals claiming an interest in on-line speech, filed suit in the U.S. District Court for the Eastern District of Pennsylvania against Attorney General Janet Reno seeking an injunction against enforcement of the CDA. The plaintiffs included public interest organizations such as the Planned Parenthood Federation of America, Human Rights Watch, and Stop Prisoner Rape; several for-profit organizations; and individuals such as Kiyoshi Kuromiya, who runs the Critical Path AIDS site on the World Wide Web. The case was eventually consolidated with a suit filed by the American Library Association and others that included most of the world's largest providers of Internet services. The suit alleged that three sections of the CDA were unconstitutional on their face under the First Amendment and the Due Process Clause of the Fifth Amendment:

Section 223(a)(1)(B), which made it a crime to transmit an indecent communication, knowing that the recipient of the communication is under eighteen years of age.

Section 223(d)(1)(A), which made it a crime to use an "interactive computer service" to "send to a specific person" under eighteen years of age a patently offensive communication.

Section 223(d)(1)(B), which made it a crime to "display" patently offensive material "in a manner available to a person under eighteen years of age."

Following a lengthy fact-finding trial, a three-judge district court panel concluded that, except for communications sent via the World Wide Web, it is impossible for speakers to restrict access to indecent materials to persons over eighteen. As to the World Wide Web, the court concluded that it was "either technologically impossible or economically prohibitive" for most speakers to limit access to indecent materials to persons over the age of eighteen. Consequently, the court concluded that the CDA's ban on making indecent material available to persons under eighteen years of age made it impossible to engage in the constitutionally protected activity of communicating indecent material to adults. The court declared the CDA unconstitutional for that reason and issued a preliminary injunction against enforcement of the challenged provisions. Reno appealed to the Supreme Court of the United States.

HIGHLIGHTS OF SUPREME COURT ARGUMENTS

BRIEF FOR RENO

◆ Through the CDA, Congress has sought to make the Internet a resource that all Americans can use without fear that their children will be exposed to the harmful effects of indecent material. The CDA's indecency restrictions advance the government's interests in protecting children and in ensuring that persons are not deterred from using the Internet and other interactive computer services.

◆ There is no First Amendment right to distribute indecent material to children. Children generally do not possess the same capacity as adults to make informed choices about whether to view indecent material. Such material may have deep and harmful effects on children that cannot readily be undone. Government regulation that prohibits the dissemination of indecent material to children, while not prohibiting dissemination to adults, is fully consistent with the First Amendment.

◆ To comply with the transmission provision, persons need not refrain from communicating indecent material to adults; they need only refrain from disseminating such materials to persons they know to be under the age of eighteen. The "display" provision permits persons to post indecent material on the Internet so long as they condition access on the use of credit cards or other adult identification devices, or otherwise employ "reasonable, effective, and appropriate" measures to ensure that their materials are not available to minors.

◆ The CDA's "display" provision does not operate as a flat ban. It provides numerous opportunities for adult-to-adult communication of indecent material.

◆ Much of the Internet's potential as an educational and informational resource will be lost if substantial numbers of people are unwilling to avail themselves of its benefits because they do not want their children exposed to patently offensive material.

AMICUS CURIAE BRIEFS SUPPORTING RENO

Morality in Media, Inc.; Family Life Project of the American Center for Law and Justice; joint brief of Enough is Enough, the Salvation Army, National Political Congress of Black Women, National Council of Catholic Women, Victims' Assistance Legal Organization, Childhelp USA, Legal Pad Enterprises, Focus on the Family, National Coalition for the Protection of Children and Families, Citizens for Family Friendly Libraries-Georgia, Computer Power Corporation, D/Tex Investigative Consulting, Family Friendly Libraries, Help Us Regain the Children, Jurinet, Inc., Kidz Online, Laura Lederer, Long-On Data Corporation, Mothers Against Sexual Abuse, National Association of Evangelicals, Omaha for Decency, One Voice/American Coalition for Abuse Awareness, Oklahomans for Children and Families, Religious Alliance Against Pornography, Lenore Weitzman, and Wheelgroup Corporation; joint brief of eight U.S. Senators and seventeen members of the House of Representatives.

BRIEF FOR THE AMERICAN LIBRARY ASSOCIATION

◆ The CDA impermissibly criminalizes a broad range of constitutionally protected "indecent" speech. It covers not only commercial purveyors of pornography, but also noncommercial speakers and nonprurient images and texts that have serious value for adults and many minors.

◆ Because of the nature of the Internet, the CDA's prohibition on displaying indecent expression in a manner "available" to minors makes it virtually impossible to communicate an indecent message to adults. Such a ban violates the First Amendment.

◆ The CDA cannot survive the strict scrutiny analysis required of content-based burdens on protected speech. Of all the indecent communications on the Internet, a very large percentage are posted abroad and there is no speaker-based control that government can impose that would prevent those communications from being available to every home that has access to the Internet.

◆ Technology exists to allow parents to prevent access by their children to materials of which they disapprove. Recipient-based controls are a more effective method of restricting access by minors than speaker-based controls.

◆ The CDA is unconstitutionally vague. At trial, the government was unable to explain how speakers could determine what speech the CDA criminalizes. Sponsors of the CDA concede that material with "truly serious value" could be found criminal. A criminal prohibition that turns entirely on whether listeners (or jurors) find the speech in question "patently offensive" comes perilously near to what the First Amendment most emphatically prohibits.

BRIEF FOR AMERICAN CIVIL LIBERTIES UNION

◆ Unless the CDA is stricken down, it will reduce what has been called a "never-ending, worldwide conversation" that links millions of people around the globe to a level deemed suitable for children.

◆ As recently as *Denver Area Educational Television Consortium v. FCC*, this Court has held that the government may not criminalize constitutionally protected speech for adults in the guise of protecting children, yet that is what the CDA does.

◆ The CDA clearly fails strict scrutiny because it is not narrowly tailored. The act will not prevent minors from accessing "indecent" material posted outside the United States and it is significantly more restrictive than readily available user-based blocking software and other alternatives that enable parents to decide what their children will read and see.

◆ The defenses available under the CDA are not available to the majority of speakers on the Internet.

◆ The CDA is both vague and overbroad. Narrowing constructions would contradict the CDA's clear legislative purpose. "Indecency" encompasses a much broader category of speech than the "harmful to minors" standard this Court has articulated in other cases. The act also fails to define the relevant "community" that will set the standard for what is "indecent" on the global Internet.

AMICUS CURIAE BRIEFS SUPPORTING AMERICAN LIBRARY ASSOCIATION AND ACLU

American Association of University Professors; Speech Communication Association; joint brief of Volunteer Lawyers for the Arts, individual artists and art organizations; Playboy Enterprises, Inc.; joint brief of Site Specific, Inc. and Jon Lebkowski; joint brief of Apollomedia Corporation and Bay Area Lawyers for Individual Freedom; joint brief of the Association of National Advertisers, Inc., and the Media Institute; Chamber of Commerce; Feminists for Free Expression; joint brief of Reporters Committee for Freedom of the Press and the Student Press Law Center; joint brief of the National Association of Broadcasters, ABC, CBS, and NBC; James Clancy.

SUPREME COURT DECISION: 7–2

STEVENS, J.

At issue is the constitutionality of two statutory provisions enacted to protect minors from "indecent" and "patently offensive" communications on the Internet.... [W]e agree with the three-judge District Court that the statute abridges "the freedom of speech" protected by the First Amendment....

Regardless of whether the CDA is so vague that it violates the Fifth Amendment, the many ambiguities concerning the scope of its coverage render it problematic for purposes of the First Amendment. For instance, each of the two parts of the CDA uses a different linguistic form. The first uses the word "indecent," while the second speaks of material that "in context, depicts or describes, in terms patently offensive as measured by contemporary community standards, sexual or excretory activities or organs." Given the absence of a definition of either term, this difference in language will provoke uncertainty among speakers about how the two standards relate to each other and just what they mean.... This uncertainty undermines the likelihood that the CDA has been carefully tailored to the congressional goal of protecting minors from potentially harmful materials.

The vagueness of the CDA is a matter of special concern for two reasons. First, the CDA is a content-based regulation of speech. The vagueness of such a regulation raises special First Amendment concerns because of its obvious chilling effect on free speech.... Second, the CDA is a criminal statute. In addition to the opprobrium and stigma of a criminal conviction, the CDA threatens violators with penalties including up to two years in prison for each act of violation. The severity of criminal sanctions may well cause speakers to remain silent rather than communicate even arguably unlawful words, ideas, and images.... As a practical matter, this increased deterrent effect, coupled with the "risk of discriminatory enforcement" of vague regulations, poses greater First Amendment concerns than those implicated by the civil regulation reviewed in *Denver Area Ed. Telecommunications Consortium, Inc. v. FCC* [116 S.Ct. 2374].

The Government argues that the statute is no more vague than the obscenity standard this Court established in *Miller v. California*, 413 U.S. 15 (1973). But that is not so.... Because the CDA's "patently offensive" standard (and, we assume *arguendo*, its synonymous "indecent" standard) is one part of the three-prong *Miller* test, the Government reasons, it cannot be unconstitutionally vague.

The Government's assertion is incorrect as a matter of fact. The second prong of the *Miller* test—the purportedly analogous standard—contains a critical requirement that is omitted from the CDA: that the proscribed material be "specifically defined by the applicable state law." This requirement reduces the vagueness inherent in the open-ended term "patently offensive" as used in the CDA. Moreover, the *Miller* definition is limited to "sexual conduct," whereas the CDA extends also to include (1) "excretory activities" as well as (2) "organs" of both a sexual and excretory nature.

The Government's reasoning is also flawed. Just because a definition including three limitations is not vague, it does not follow that one of those limitations, standing by itself, is not vague. Each of *Miller*'s additional two prongs—(1) that, taken as a whole, the material appeal to the "prurient" interest, and (2) that it "lac[k] serious literary, artistic, political, or scientific value"—critically limits the uncertain sweep of the obscenity definition. The second requirement is particularly important because, unlike the "patently offensive" and "prurient interest" criteria, it is not judged by contemporary community standards.... This "societal value" requirement, absent in the CDA, allows appellate courts to impose some limitations and regularity on the definition by setting, as a matter of law, a national floor for socially redeeming value. The Government's contention that courts will be able to give such legal limitations to the CDA's standards is belied by *Miller*'s own rationale for having juries determine whether material is "patently offensive" according to community standards: that such questions are essentially ones of fact.

In contrast to *Miller* and our other previous cases, the CDA thus presents a greater threat of censoring speech that, in fact, falls outside the statute's scope. Given the vague contours of the coverage of the statute, it unquestionably silences some speakers whose messages would be entitled to constitutional protection. That danger provides further reason for insisting that the statute not be overly broad. The CDA's burden on protected speech cannot be justified if it could be avoided by a more carefully drafted statute.

We are persuaded that the CDA lacks the precision that the First Amendment requires when a statute regulates the content of speech. In order to deny minors access to potentially harmful speech, the CDA effectively suppresses a large amount of speech that adults have a constitutional right to receive and to address to one another. That burden on adult speech is unacceptable if less restrictive alternatives would be at least as effective in achieving the legitimate purpose that the statute was enacted to serve....

It is true that we have repeatedly recognized the governmental interest in protecting children from harmful materials.... But that interest does not justify an unnecessarily broad suppression of speech addressed to adults....

In arguing that the CDA does not so diminish adult communication, the Government relies on the incorrect factual premise that prohibiting a transmission whenever it is known that one of its recipients is a minor would not interfere with adult-to-adult communication.... Given the size of the potential audience for most messages, in the absence of a viable age verification process, the sender must be charged with knowing that one or more minors will likely view it. Knowledge that, for instance, one or more members of a 100-person chat group will be minor—and therefore that it would be a crime to send the group an indecent message—would surely burden communication among adults....

The breadth of the CDA's coverage is wholly unprecedented.... Its open-ended prohibitions embrace all nonprofit entities and individuals posting indecent messages or displaying them on their own computers in the presence of minors. The general, undefined terms "indecent" and "patently offensive" cover large amounts of nonpornographic material with serious educational or other value. Moreover, the "community standards" criterion as applied to the Internet means that any communication available to a nation-wide audience will be judged by the standards of the community most likely to be offended by the message....

The breadth of this content-based restriction of speech imposes an especially heavy burden on the Government to explain why a less restrictive provision would not be as effective as the CDA. It has not done so. The arguments in this Court have referred to possible alternatives such as requiring that indecent material be "tagged" in a way that facilitates parental control of material coming into their homes, making exceptions for messages with artistic or educational value, providing some tolerance for parental choice, and regulating some portions of the Internet—such as commercial web sites—differently than others, such as chat rooms. Particularly in light of the absence of any detailed findings by the Congress, or even hearings addressing the special problems of the CDA, we are persuaded that the CDA is not narrowly tailored if that requirement has any meaning at all.

In an attempt to curtail the CDA's facial overbreadth, the Government advances three additional arguments for sustaining the Act's affirmative prohibitions: (1) that the CDA is constitutional because it leaves open ample "alternative channels" of communication; (2) that the plain meaning of the Act's "knowledge" and "specific person" requirement significantly restricts its permissible applications; and (3) that the Act's prohibitions are "almost always" limited to material lacking redeeming social value....

The Government's [first] position is equivalent to arguing that a statute could ban leaflets on certain subjects as long as individuals are free to publish books....

[The second] argument ignores the fact that most Internet fora—including chat rooms, newsgroups, mail exploders, and the Web—are open to all comers. The Government's assertion that the knowledge requirement somehow protects the communications of adults is therefore untenable....

Finally, we find no textual support for the Government's submission that material having scientific, educational, or other redeeming social value will necessarily fall outside the CDA's "patently offensive" and "indecent" prohibitions....

For the foregoing reasons, the judgment of the district court is affirmed.

It is so ordered.

O'CONNOR, J., WITH WHOM REHNQUIST, C.J., JOINS, CONCURRING IN THE JUDGMENT IN PART AND DISSENTING IN PART

... I view the [CDA] as little more than an attempt by Congress to create "adult zones" on the Internet. Our precedent indicates that the creation of such zones can be constitutionally sound. Despite the soundness of its purpose, however, portions of the CDA are unconstitutional because they stray from the blueprint our prior cases have developed for constructing a "zoning law" that passes constitutional muster....

The creation of "adult zones" is by no means a novel concept. States have long denied minors access to certain establishments frequented by adults. States have also denied minors access to speech deemed to be "harmful to minors." The Court has previously sustained such zoning laws, but only if they respect the First Amendment rights of adults and minors. That is to say, a zoning law is valid if (i) it does not unduly restrict adult access to the material; and (ii) minors have no First Amendment right to read or view the banned material. As applied to the Internet as it exists in 1997, the [CDA] "display" provision and some applications of [its] "indecency transmission" and "specific person" provisions fail to adhere to the first of these limiting principles by restricting adults' access to protected materials in certain circumstances. Unlike the Court, however, I would invalidate the provisions only in those circumstances....

Given the present state of cyberspace, I agree with the Court that the "display" provision cannot pass muster. Until gateway technology is available throughout cyberspace, and it is not in 1997, a speaker cannot be reasonably assured that the speech he displays will reach only adults because it is impossible to confine speech to an "adult zone."...

The "indecency transmission" and "specific person" provisions present a closer issue, for they are not unconstitutional in all of their applications.... [T]he "indecency transmission" provision makes it a crime to transmit knowingly an indecent message to a person the sender knows is under 18 years of age. The "specific person" provision proscribes the same conduct, although it does not as explicitly require the sender to know that the intended recipient of his indecent message is a minor. [Reno] urges the Court to construe the provision to impose such a knowledge requirement, and I would do so....

So construed, both provisions are constitutional as applied to a conversation involving only an adult and one or more minors—*e.g.*, when an adult speaker sends an e-mail knowing the addressee is a minor, or when an adult and minor converse by themselves or with other minors in a chat room....

[H]owever, when more than one adult is a party to the conversation [constitutional problems arise]. If a minor enters a chat room otherwise occupied by adults,

the CDA effectively requires the adults in the room to stop using indecent speech. If they did not, they could be prosecuted under the "indecency transmission" and "specific person" provisions for any indecent statements they make to the group, since they would be transmitting an indecent message to specific persons, one of whom is a minor. The CDA is therefore akin to a law that makes it a crime for a bookstore owner to sell pornographic magazines to anyone once a minor enters his store. Even assuming such a law might be constitutional in the physical world as a reasonable alternative to excluding minors completely from the store, the absence of any means of excluding minors from chat rooms in cyberspace restricts the rights of adults to engage in indecent speech in those rooms. The "indecency transmission" and "specific person" provisions share this defect.

But these two provisions do not infringe on adults' speech in *all* situations.... I do not find that the provisions are overbroad in the sense that they restrict minors' access to a substantial amount of speech that minors have the right to read and view. Accordingly, the CDA can be applied constitutionally in some situations. Normally, this fact would require the Court to reject a direct facial challenge.... I agree with the Court that the provisions are overbroad in that they cover any and all communications between adults and minors, regardless of how many adults might be part of the audience to the communication.

This conclusion does not end the matter, however. Where, as here, "the parties challenging the statute are those who desire to engage in protected speech that the overbroad statute purports to punish ... [t]he statute may forthwith be declared invalid to the extent that it reaches too far, but otherwise left intact." *Brockett v. Spokane Arcades, Inc.*, 472 U.S. 491 (1985).... I would therefore sustain the "indecency transmission" and "specific person" provisions to the extent they apply to the transmission of Internet communications where the party initiating the communication knows that all of the recipients are minors.

Whether the CDA substantially interferes with the First Amendment rights of minors, and thereby runs afoul of the second characteristic of valid zoning laws, presents a closer question....

The Court neither "accept[s] nor reject[s]" the argument that the CDA is facially overbroad because it substantially interferes with the First Amendment rights of minors. I would reject it.

In my view, the universe of speech constitutionally protected as to minors but banned by the CDA—*i.e.*, the universe of material that is "patently offensive," but which nonetheless has some redeeming value for minors or does not appeal to their prurient interest—is a very small one.... Accordingly, in my view, the CDA does not burden a substantial amount of minors' constitutionally protected speech.

Thus, the constitutionality of the CDA as a zoning law hinges on the extent to which it substantially interferes with the First Amendment rights of adults. Because the rights of adults are infringed only by the "display" provision and by the "indecency transmission" and "specific person" provisions as applied to communications involving more than one adult, I would invalidate the CDA only to that extent....

QUESTIONS

1. The constitutional framework in which *Reno* was decided is that sexually explicit communications directed at adults are protected under the First Amendment, but government has a compelling interest in protecting children from sexually explicit materials. Does *Reno* fit within this framework or does it establish a new framework?

2. Apparently, *Reno* stands for the proposition that the Free Speech Clause of the First Amendment is not "one size fits all" when it comes to applying its protection to different communications media. What principled distinctions can be drawn to differentiate various media? Could changes in technology save a statute like the CDA? Could the CDA have been more narrowly tailored to prevent constitutional infirmity?

3. Compare the parties' arguments and the Court's decision in *Reno* with the arguments and decision in *Eichman* (see pp. 235–243). Read together, what insights do the two cases provide into the Court's contemporary approach to free speech questions?

COMMENT

It is difficult to say exactly how large the Internet adult entertainment business is. Dollar for dollar, it is minuscule compared with the estimated eight billion dollars Americans spent offline on adult videos, cable programming, live peep shows, and sex magazines in 1996.

Forrester Research estimated that 1996 online sales of adult merchandise in the United States reached fifty-one-and-a-half million dollars, or about 10 percent of all consumer goods sold over the Internet during 1996. That number does not include revenue from subscriptions or per-minute video phone sex charges, which account for the majority of many online sex companies' sales.

Industry insiders believe revenues will be closer to one hundred fifty million to two hundred million dollars in 1997, but even those are best guesses, as few analysts track the industry and most players are private and do not disclose financial information (Michelle V. Rafter, "Urls! Urls! Urls! The Internet's Burgeoning Sex Industry Helped Spur Passage of Controversial Decency Law," [http://www.latimes.com/], March 17, 1997).

SUGGESTIONS FOR FURTHER READING

Atkin, David, "The Cable Communications Act and the Regulation of Obscene and Indecent Programming: A Constitutional Collision Course," *Free Speech Yearbook* (1990): 58.

de Lourdes, Rocio, "To Air or Not to Err: The Threat of Conditioned Federal Funds for Indecent Programming on Public Broadcasting," 42 *Hasting Law Journal* (1991): 635.

Kleiman, Howard M., "Indecent Programming on Cable Television: Legal and Social Dimensions," *Journal of Broadcasting & Electronic Media* (Summer 1986): 275.

Note, "Indecent Programming on Cable Television and the First Amendment," 51 *Georgetown Law Review* (1983): 254.

Perry, Robert T., and Brian D. Graifman, "*Denver Area* Reveals Struggle over Free Speech in New Media," 216 *New York Law Journal*, August 16, 1996, p. 5.

Utah Legislative Survey, "Cable Television," 1984 *Utah Law Review* (1984): 122.

Wallace, Jonathan, and Mark Mangan, *Sex, Laws and Cyperspace* (New York, NY: M & T Books, 1996).

CHAPTER 4

———⟫●⟨———

FREEDOM OF PRESS AND ASSEMBLY

PRIOR RESTRAINT

Near v. Minnesota
283 U.S. 697 (1931)

SETTING

The language of the First Amendment, ratified in 1791, proclaims "Congress shall make no law ... abridging the freedom ... of the press." This prohibition reflects Americans' general aversion to government censorship. Colonists reacted strongly against the traditional practice in England of requiring publishers to obtain licenses from church and state authorities before making their writing public. From the fifteenth century, when printing presses came into common use, until 1695, when the licensing practice was repealed, English publications had to have prior official approval. Although to this day, in the United States, broadcast licenses are required to operate electronic media and permits are needed to conduct parades and demonstrations, the term "prior restraint" has an odious ring, suggesting that anonymous officials may determine in advance what may be written and published.

The legal roots of the First Amendment trace to the work of Sir William Blackstone. Blackstone's *Commentaries on the Laws of England* (1765–69) summarized the law of Crown libels:

> The *liberty of the press* is indeed essential to the nature of a free state; but this consists in laying no *previous* restraints upon publications. Every free-man has an undoubted right to lay what sentiments he pleases before the public: to forbid this is to destroy the freedom of the press; but if he publishes what is improper, mischievous, or illegal, he must take the consequences of his own temerity.

Blackstone's formulation of freedom of the press coupled the absence of prior restraint, on the one hand, with the possibility of postpublication punishments for writings deemed libelous, on the other. A libel is any printed statement that maliciously attacks a person, causing damage, humiliation, and exposure to public ridicule.

Americans' conception of press freedom evolved from Blackstone's views. Although both prior restraint and prosecution for seditious libel were unpopular, laws like the Sedition Act of 1798 were used to discipline journalists and publishers in the new United States. Jeffersonian resistance to the Adams administration's use of that law to punish its political opponents forged a broadly libertarian understanding of free press that embraced Blackstone's rejection of prior restraint, but rejected his views on subsequent punishment.

The Supreme Court did not address the meaning of press freedom until relatively recently. A judicial agenda crowded, at first, with nation building and, subsequently, with economic issues, left little room for civil liberties. Under the Court's decision in *Barron v. Baltimore*, 7 Peters 243 (1833), that the Bill of Rights applies only to the national government, state restrictions on and prosecutions of publishers created no federal cause of action. It was not until the early twentieth century, when many publishers of writings the government deemed "seditious" faced federal punishment during the First World War, that free press issues reached the Supreme Court. (See the section on "Defining Protected Speech during War and National Emergency" in Chapter 3.) When the Court eventually interpreted the First Amendment, it seemed sympathetic to Blackstone. In *Patterson v. Colorado*, 205 U.S. 454 (1907), for example, Justice Holmes wrote that "[T]he main purpose of [the Free Speech and Press] provisions is to 'prevent all such previous restraints upon publications as had been practiced by other governments,' and they do not prevent the subsequent punishment of such as may be deemed contrary to the public welfare." However, twelve years later, in *Schenck v. United States* (see pp. 167–171), Holmes wrote: "It may well be that the prohibition of laws abridging the freedom of speech is not confined to previous restraints although to prevent them may have been the main purpose.... We admit that in many places and in ordinary times the defendants in saying all that was said in the circular would have been within their constitutional rights." Well after World War I, Minnesota adopted a law that put the issue of prior restraint in peacetime on the Court's agenda.

In 1925, the Minnesota legislature, reacting to the burgeoning yellow journalism of the 1920s, adopted Chapter 285 to allow "an obscene, lewd and lascivious newspaper, magazine or other periodical, or a malicious, scandalous and defamatory newspaper, magazine or other periodical" to be abated as a public nuisance. The act permitted courts to issue injunctions prohibiting persons from publishing such materials. Under the authority of that statute, on November 22, 1927, Hennepin County Attorney Floyd B. Olson brought suit in the District Court of the Fourth Judicial District of Hennepin County against J. M. Near, publisher of a weekly newspaper called the *Saturday Press*. Olson sought an injunction banning publication of the *Saturday Press* as a malicious, scandalous, and defamatory newspaper.

The complaint alleged that on nine dates in September, October, and November, 1927, Near had published and circulated editions of the *Saturday Press* that were "largely devoted to malicious, scandalous, and defamatory articles" about Olson, Minneapolis Mayor George E. Leach, Minneapolis Chief of

Police Frank W. Brunskill, and special law enforcement officer Charles G. Davis, who was working for a civic organization. The articles claimed that Jewish gangster Mose Barnett controlled gambling, bootlegging, and racketeering in Minneapolis and that law enforcement officials were doing nothing to stop him. The following excerpt from an article appearing in the November 19, 1927, edition of the *Saturday Press* conveys the tenor of the writings that Olson found objectionable and whose future publication he sought to enjoin:

Facts Not Theories

"I am a bosom friend of Mr. Olson," snorted a gentleman of Yiddish blood, "and I want to protest against your article," and blah, blah, blah, ad infinitum, ad nauseam.

I am not taking orders from men of Barnett faith, at least right now. There have been too many men in this city and especially those in official life, who HAVE been taking orders and suggestions from JEW GANGSTERS, therefore we HAVE Jew Gangsters, practically ruling Minneapolis....

It was Mose Barnett, a Jew, who boasted that he held the chief of police of Minneapolis in his hand—had bought and paid for him....

Practically every vendor of vile hooch, every owner of a moonshine still, every snake-faced gangster and exbryonic yegg in the Twin Cities is a JEW.

Having these examples before me, I feel that I am justified in my refusal to take orders from a Jew who boasts that he is a "bosom friend" of Mr. Olson....

When I find men of a certain race banding themselves together for the purpose of preying upon Gentile or Jew; gunmen, KILLERS, roaming our streets shooting down men against whom they have no personal grudge (or happen to have); defying OUR laws; corrupting OUR officials; assaulting business men; beating up unarmed citizens; spreading a reign of terror through every walk of life, then I say to you in all sincerity, that I refuse to back up a single step from that "issue"—if they choose to make it so.

If the people of Jewish faith in Minneapolis wish to avoid criticism of these vermin whom I rightfully call "Jews" they can easily do so BY THEMSELVES CLEANING HOUSE....

I am launching no attack against the Jewish people AS A RACE. I am merely calling attention to a FACT. And if the people of that race and faith wish to rid themselves of the odium and stigma THE RODENTS OF THEIR OWN RACE HAVE BROUGHT UPON THEM, they need only to step to the front and help the decent citizens of Minneapolis rid the city of these criminal Jews.

Near demurred to the complaint on the ground that it violated free press rights under both the Minnesota and U.S. constitutions. The district court overruled the demurrer and certified the question of its constitutionality to the Minnesota Supreme Court. That court upheld the statute on state constitutional grounds and remanded the case for trial. After trial, the district court issued a permanent injunction, because it found that the relevant editions of the *Saturday Press* were "chiefly devoted to malicious, scandalous and defamatory articles" concerning the individuals named. It ordered that the *Saturday Press* be abated as a public nuisance.

Near appealed to the Minnesota Supreme Court, raising federal constitutional objections. The supreme court affirmed the district court. Near appealed to the Supreme Court of the United States.

HIGHLIGHTS OF SUPREME COURT ARGUMENTS

BRIEF FOR NEAR

◆ The substantive right of freedom of the press prohibits restraints on publication prior to publication and punishment after publication. However, this case does not involve subsequent restraints because the injunction forbade future publications.

◆ That a previous restraint is unconstitutional is so universally recognized that there is no instance, before this case, where any legislature or Congress has attempted to suppress any newspaper, no matter how disreputable. The only examples similar to this case have been city ordinances, which have been struck down. The general rule is that equity will not under any circumstances enjoin defamation as such, because to do so would violate the constitutional guarantee of a free press and the right to trial by jury.

◆ It must be conceded that the *Saturday Press* did not advocate violent overthrow of government or breach of law. In so far as the newspaper indulged in criminal defamation of individuals, the state may protect itself by indictment for criminal libel. Unless there is incitement to violent overthrow of government or to breach of law, the state has no further rights to vindicate.

BRIEF FOR MINNESOTA

◆ The term "liberty" does not include the free and unrestricted right to publish all matters. Obscene, scandalous or defamatory materials are excluded.

◆ It is within the police power of the state to prohibit engaging in the business of regularly publishing or circulating a malicious, scandalous, and defamatory newspaper. The legislature has general control and supervision over practices that in its judgment are inimical to the public morals and welfare of the state and the exercise of that authority will be sustained unless it appears that the legislation is arbitrary and capricious.

◆ The evil that the Minnesota act seeks to suppress is a nuisance in fact. A newspaper that is regularly devoted to the dissemination of malicious, scandalous, and defamatory matter is subversive of public order and, as such, is a public nuisance.

SUPREME COURT DECISION: 5–4

HUGHES, C.J.

... This statute ... is unusual, if not unique, and raises questions of grave importance transcending the local interests involved in the particular action. It is no longer open to doubt that the liberty of the press and of speech is within the liberty safeguarded by the due process clause of the Fourteenth Amendment from invasion by state action....

It is thus important to note precisely the purpose and effect of the statute as the state court has construed it.

First. The statute is not aimed at the redress of individual or private wrongs.

Remedies for libel remain available and unaffected.... It is aimed at the distribution of scandalous matter as "detrimental to public morals and to the general welfare," tending "to disturb the peace of the community" and "to provoke assaults and the commission of crime." In order to obtain an injunction to suppress the future publication of the newspaper or periodical, it is not necessary to prove the falsity of the charges that have been made in the publication condemned. In the present action there was no allegation that the matter published was not true. It is alleged, and the statute requires the allegation that the publication was "malicious." But, as in prosecutions for libel, there is no requirement of proof by the state of malice in fact as distinguished from malice inferred from the mere publication of the defamatory matter. The judgment in this case proceeded upon the mere proof of publication. The statute permits the defense, not of the truth alone, but only that the truth was published with good motives and for justifiable ends. It is apparent that under the statute the publication is to be regarded as defamatory if it injures reputation, and that it is scandalous if it circulates charges of reprehensible conduct, whether criminal or otherwise, and the publication is thus deemed to invite public reprobation and to constitute a public scandal....

Second. The statute is directed not simply at the circulation of scandalous and defamatory statements with regard to private citizens, but at the continued publication by newspapers and periodical of charges against public officers of corruption, malfeasance in office, or serious neglect of duty. Such charges by their very nature create a public scandal. They are scandalous and defamatory within the meaning of the statute, which has its normal operation in relation to publications dealing prominently and chiefly with the alleged derelictions of public officers.

Third. The object of the statute is not punishment, in the ordinary sense, but suppression of the offending newspaper or periodical.... [A] publisher of a newspaper or periodical, undertaking to conduct a campaign to expose and to censure official derelictions, and devoting his publication principally to that purpose, must face not simply the possibility of a verdict against him in a suit or prosecution for libel, but a determination that his newspaper or periodical is a public nuisance to be abated, and that this abatement and suppression will follow unless he is prepared with legal evidence to prove the truth of the charges and also to satisfy the court that, in addition to being true, the matter was published with good motives and for justifiable ends.

This suppression is accomplished by enjoining publication, and that restraint is the object and effect of the statute.

Fourth. The statute not only operates to suppress the offending newspaper or periodical, but to put the publisher under an effective censorship. When a newspaper or periodical is found to be "malicious, scandalous and defamatory," and is suppressed as such, resumption of publication is punishable as a contempt of court by fine or imprisonment....

If we cut through mere details of procedure, the operation and effect of the statute in substance is that public authorities may bring the owner or publisher of a newspaper or periodical before a judge upon a charge of conducting a business of publishing scandalous and defamatory matter—in particular that the matter consists of charges against public officers of official dereliction—and, unless the owner or publisher is able and disposed to bring competent evidence to satisfy the judge that the charges are true and are published with good motives and for justifiable ends, his newspaper or periodical is suppressed and further publication is made punishable as a contempt. This is of the essence of censorship.

The question is whether a statute authorizing such proceedings in restraint of publication is consistent with the conception of the liberty of the press as historically conceived and guaranteed. In determining the extent of the constitutional protection, it has been generally, if not universally, considered that it is the chief purpose of the guaranty to prevent previous restraints upon publication....

The objection has ... been made that the principle as to immunity from previous restraint is stated too broadly, if every such restraint is deemed to be prohibited. That is undoubtedly true; the protection even as to previous restraint is not absolutely unlimited. But the limitation has been recognized only in exceptional cases.... No one would question but that a government might prevent actual obstruction to its recruiting service or the publication of the sailing dates of transports or the number and location of troops. On similar grounds, the primary requirements of decency may be enforced against obscene publications. The security of the community life may be protected against incitements to acts of violence and the overthrow by force of orderly government.... These limitations are not applicable here. Nor are we now concerned with questions as to the extent of authority to prevent publications in order to protect private rights according to the principles governing the exercise of the jurisdiction of courts of equity.

The exceptional nature of its limita-

tions places in a strong light the general conception that liberty of the press, historically considered and taken up by the Federal Constitution, has meant, principally although not exclusively, immunity from previous restraints or censorship. The conception of the liberty of the press in this country had broadened with the exigencies of the colonial period and with the efforts to secure freedom from oppressive administration. That liberty was especially cherished for the immunity it afforded from previous restraint of the publication of censure of public officers and charges of official misconduct....

The fact that for approximately one hundred and fifty years there has been almost an entire absence of attempts to impose previous restraints upon publications relating to the malfeasance of public officers is significant of the deep-seated conviction that such restraints would violate constitutional right. Public officers, whose character and conduct remain open to debate and free discussion in the press, find their remedies for false accusations in actions under libel laws providing for redress and punishment, and not in proceedings to restrain the publication of newspapers and periodicals....

The fact that the liberty of the press may be abused by miscreant purveyors of scandal does not make any the less necessary the immunity of the press from previous restraint in dealing with official misconduct. Subsequent punishment for such abuses as may exist is the appropriate remedy, consistent with constitutional privilege....

The statute in question cannot be justified by reason of the fact that the publisher is permitted to show, before injunction issues, that the matter published is true and is published with good motives and for justifiable ends. If such a statute, authorizing suppression and injunction on such a basis, is constitutionally valid, it would be equally permissible for the Legislature to provide that at any time the publisher of any newspaper could be brought before a court, or even an administrative officer (as the constitutional protection may not be regarded as resting on mere procedural details), and required to produce proof of the truth of his publication, or of what he intended to publish and of his motives, or stand enjoined. If this can be done, the Legislature may provide machinery for determining in the complete exercise of its discretion what are justifiable ends and restrain publication accordingly. And it would be but a step to a complete system of censorship. The recognition of authority to impose previous restraint upon publication in order to protect the community against the circulation of charges of misconduct, and especially of official misconduct, necessarily would carry with it the admission of the authority of the censor against which the constitutional barrier was erected....

Equally unavailing is the insistence that the statute is designed to prevent the circulation of scandal which tends to disturb the public peace and to provoke assaults and the commission of crime. Charges of reprehensible conduct, and in particular of official malfeasance, unquestionably create a public scandal, but the theory of the constitutional guaranty is that even a more serious public evil would be caused by authority to prevent publication.... There is nothing new in the fact that charges of reprehensible conduct may create resentment and the disposition to resort to violent means of redress, but this well-understood tendency did not alter the determination to protect the press against censorship and restraint upon publication.... The danger

of violent reactions becomes greater with effective organization of defiant groups resenting exposure, and, if this consideration warranted legislative interference with the initial freedom of publication, the constitutional protection would be reduced to a mere form of words....

Judgment reversed.

BUTLER, VAN DEVANTER, MCREYNOLDS, AND SUTHERLAND, J.J., DISSENTING

The decision of the Court in this case declares Minnesota and every other state powerless to restrain by injunction the business of publishing and circulating among the people malicious, scandalous, and defamatory periodicals that in due course of judicial procedure has been adjudged to be a public nuisance. It gives to freedom of the press a meaning and a scope not heretofore recognized, and construes "liberty" in the due process clause of the Fourteenth Amendment to put upon the states a federal restriction that is without precedent....

The [Minnesota] act was passed in the exertion of the state's power of police, and this court is by well-established rule required to assume, until the contrary is clearly made to appear, that there exists in Minnesota a state of affairs that justifies this measure for the preservation of the peace and good order of the state....

The publications themselves disclose the need and propriety of the legislation....

It is of the greatest importance that the states shall be untrammeled and free to employ all just and appropriate measures to prevent abuses of the liberty of the press....

The Minnesota statute does not operate as a previous restraint on publication within the proper meaning of that phrase. It does not authorize administrative control in advance such as was formerly exercised by the licensers and censors, but prescribes a remedy to be enforced by a suit in equity. In this case there was previous publication made in the course of the business of regularly producing malicious, scandalous, and defamatory periodicals. The business and publications unquestionably constitute an abuse of the right of free press. The statute denounces the things done as a nuisance on the ground, as stated by the state Supreme Court, that they threaten morals, peace, and good order. There is no question of the power of the state to denounce such transgressions. The restraint authorized is only in respect of continuing to do what has been duly adjudged to constitute a nuisance.... There is nothing in the statute purporting to prohibit publications that have not been adjudged to constitute a nuisance. It is fanciful to suggest similarity between the granting or enforcement of the decree authorized by this statute to prevent further publication of malicious, scandalous, and defamatory articles and the previous restraint upon the press by licensers as referred to by Blackstone and described in the history of the times to which he alludes....

The judgment should be affirmed.

QUESTIONS

1. State the rule in *Near* and the rule that the dissenters would have adopted. How does the *Near* rule compare with Blackstone's view of freedom of the press?

2. During the period in American constitutional law that *Near* was decided, in cases involving civil liberties, the Court frequently preached the doctrine of judicial restraint and the presumption that laws enacted by state legislatures carried with them a presumption of constitutionality. Is the majority opinion in *Near* an example of judicial restraint? If not, what explains the outcome in *Near*?

3. Near's counsel argued: "If [the Minnesota statute] is constitutional, the Alien and Sedition Laws [of 1798] are back again in a new and aggravated form. Where the Alien and Sedition Laws provided punishment *after trial by jury for past censure* of official acts, the Minnesota statute provides for a trial *without a jury* and for a judgment foreordaining punishments ($1,000 fine or twelve months' imprisonment) *for future censure* of such acts" (emphasis added). Is there any language in the majority opinion that suggests the Court in *Near* was persuaded by this argument? Why is it constitutionally preferable to penalize people after they publish something illegal rather than to prohibit publication beforehand?

4. Law professor Laurence H. Tribe has identified two meanings of the term "prior restraint":

   In some cases the primary concern is that any restraint before dissemination, however temporary, allows the government to destroy the immediacy of the intended speech, overriding the individual's choice of a persuasive moment or an editor's decision of what is newsworthy; dissemination delayed may prove tantamount to dissemination denied. In other cases the primary concern is that any system of censorship insufficiently constrained by the safeguards of the judicial process is apt to overreach; censors uncontrolled by the courts tend to deny publication to material protected by the first amendment. (*American Constitutional Law*, 2nd ed. [Mineola, NY: Foundation Press, 1988], p. 1042)

Which of these concerns is paramount in the *Near* decision? Is one of these concerns more constitutionally defensible than the other?

COMMENT

In the years since *Near*, a variety of press restrictions have been subjected to judicial scrutiny. The decisions summarized below indicate the kinds of regulations evaluated by the Court.

Case: *Grosjean v. American Press Co., Inc.*, 297 U.S. 233 (1936)
Vote: 9–0
Decision: A Louisiana tax statute that requires every newspaper, magazine, or periodical that has a circulation of more than twenty thousand copies per week and that sells advertising for publication, to pay a license tax of 2 percent on its gross receipts, is unconstitutional. Such a tax has a long history of hostile misuse against the freedom of the press. The form in which the tax is imposed is in itself suspicious. It is not measured or limited by the volume of advertisements. It is measured alone by the extent of the circulation of the publication in which the advertisements are carried, with the plain purpose of penalizing the publishers and curtailing the circulation of a selected group of newspapers.

Case: *Joseph Burstyn, Inc. v. Wilson*, 343 U.S. 495 (1952)
Vote: 9–0
Decision: A New York statute authorizing officials to view motion picture films and to issue licenses permitting the films to be shown unless they are "obscene, indecent, immoral, inhuman, sacrilegious, or is of such a character that its exhibition would tend to corrupt morals or incite to crime," is invalid as an unconstitutional abridgment of free speech and free press. The statute does not seek to punish, as a past offense, speech, or writing falling within the permissible scope of subsequent punishment. Instead, it requires that permission to communicate ideas be obtained in advance from state officials who judge the content of the words and pictures sought to be communicated. Such a previous restraint is a form of infringement on freedom of expression to be especially condemned.

Case: *Kingsley Books, Inc. v. Brown*, 354 U.S. 436 (1957)
Vote: 5–4
Decision: A New York statute authorizing municipalities to seek an injunction against the sale and distribution of any written or printed matter of an indecent character, that entitles sellers or distributors to a trial of issues within one day after joinder of issues and a decision within two days of conclusion of the trial, does not amount to prior censorship of literary products and does not violate that freedom of thought and speech protected by the Fourteenth Amendment. The phrase "prior restraint" is not a self-wielding sword, and cannot serve as a talismanic test.

Case: *Times Film Corporation v. Chicago*, 365 U.S. 43 (1961)

Vote: 5–4

Decision: A Chicago ordinance that requires submission of films for examination by city officials as a prerequisite to receiving a permit for their public exhibition, is not void on its face as a prior restraint prohibited by the First and Fourteenth Amendments. There is no complete and absolute freedom to exhibit, even once, any and every kind of motion picture. Not all previous restraints on speech are invalid. The principle forbidding previous restraint "is stated too broadly, if every such restraint is deemed to be prohibited.... (T)he protection even as to previous restraint is not absolutely unlimited. But the limitation has been recognized only in exceptional cases."

Case: *Bantam Books, Inc. v. Sullivan*, 372 U.S. 58 (1963)

Vote: 8–1

Decision: The acts and practices of the Rhode Island Commission to Encourage Morality in Youth amount to a system of informal censorship in violation of the Fourteenth Amendment. With no provision for judicial superintendence before notices to distributors are issued or even for judicial review of the commission's determinations of what constitutes objectionable materials, the commission stops circulation of certain publications in many parts of the state. Publishers or distributors are not entitled to notice and hearing before their publications are listed by the commission as objectionable. The commission's statutory mandate is vague and uninformative, and although the commission's supposed concern is limited to youthful readers, the "cooperation" it seeks from distributors invariably entails complete suppression of listed publications.

Case: *Freedman v. Maryland*, 380 U.S. 51 (1965)

Vote: 9–0

Decision: A procedural scheme in a Maryland motion picture censorship statute fails to provide adequate safeguards against undue inhibition of protected expression because: (1) if the State Board of Censors disapproves a film, the exhibitor is required to assume the burden of instituting judicial proceedings and persuading a court that the censored film is protected expression, (2) once the board has acted against a film, its exhibition is prohibited pending judicial review, however protracted, and (3) the statute provides no assurance of prompt judicial determination.

Case: *Southeastern Promotions, Ltd. v. Conrad*, 420 U.S. 546 (1975)

Vote: 6–3

Decision: Denying permission to use Chattanooga, Tennessee, municipal facilities for the production of the musical *Hair* is a prior restraint that is constitutionally improper because it is imposed without the procedural safeguards necessary to obviate the dangers of a censorship system. Rejection of the application by members of a municipal board charged with managing a city auditorium and a city-leased theater, on the basis of outside reports from which they concluded that the production would not be "in the best interest of the community," is unconstitutional. A system of prior restraint avoids constitutional infirmity only if it takes place under procedural safeguards that are designed to obviate the dangers of a censorship system.

Case: *Nebraska Press Association v. Stuart*, 427 U.S. 539 (1976)

Vote: 9–0

Decision: A state trial judge's order issued in anticipation of a trial for a multiple murder that had attracted widespread news coverage, which restrained the news media from publishing or broadcasting accounts of confessions or admissions made by the defendant to law enforcement officers or third parties, is unconstitutional. While the guarantees of freedom of expression are not an absolute prohibition under all circumstances, the barriers to prior restraint remain high and the presumption against its use continues intact. Although it is unnecessary to establish a priority between First Amendment rights and the Sixth Amendment right to a fair trial under all circumstances, the protection against prior restraint should have particular force in the context of reporting on criminal proceedings.

Case: *Vance v. Universal Amusement Co., Inc.*, 445 U.S. 308 (1980)

Vote: 5–4

Decision: A Texas nuisance statute, authorizing prior restraints of indefinite duration on the exhibition of motion pictures that have not been finally adjudicated to be obscene, is a more onerous prior restraint than the threat of criminal sanctions after a film had been exhibited, since nonobscenity would be a defense to any criminal prosecution. Such a statute cannot be enforced, in the absence of special safeguards governing the entry and review of orders restraining the exhibition of motion pictures, without regard to the context in which they are displayed.

Case: *Minneapolis Star and Tribune Company v. Minnesota Commissioner of Revenue*, 460 U.S. 575 (1983)

Vote: 7–2

Decision: Imposition of a use tax on the cost of paper and ink products consumed in the production of materials for publication violates the First Amendment by imposing a significant burden on freedom of the press. Although there is no legislative history and no indication, apart from the structure of the tax itself, of any impermissible or censorial motive on the part of the Minnesota Legislature in enacting it, the special use tax targets the press for special treatment. When a state so singles out the press, the political constraints that prevent a legislature from imposing crippling taxes of general applicability are weakened, and the threat of burdensome taxes becomes acute. That threat can operate as effectively as a censor to check critical comment by the press. Minnesota has offered no adequate justification for the special treatment of newspapers. Minnesota's ink and paper tax also violates the First Amendment because it targets a small group of newspapers.

PRIOR RESTRAINT

New York Times v. United States
403 U.S. 713 (1971)

SETTING

Publication of politically sensitive information has never been popular with those who wield power. Despite the Court's ruling in *Near v. Minnesota*, government officials have persisted in attempting to impose prior restraints on the publication of information they do not want the public to have. Prior restraint, recall, occurs when a government requires that material be approved before allowing it to be published. Forty years after *Near*, the Court heard a case resulting from one of the most dangerous challenges to the principle of no prior restraint in American history: the attempt by the Nixon administration to enjoin publication of *United States–Vietnam Relations, 1945–1967*, popularly known as the "Pentagon Papers."

The Pentagon Papers is a 47-volume, 7,000-page study commissioned by Secretary of Defense Robert S. McNamara on June 17, 1967, as a top-secret historical analysis of the U.S. role in Indochina. It details American involvement from World War II until May 1968, when President Lyndon B. Johnson capped further military commitments and announced his intention not to run for a second term. Its contents are so candid and sensitive that only fifteen copies of the report were produced. Daniel Ellsberg, one of the authors of the Pentagon Papers, became so alienated from the government's position in support of the Vietnam War that, in the spring of 1971, he decided to release copies of the papers to the press as an act of resistance. The document was still classified "Top Secret-Sensitive" when Ellsberg made available a large portion of it.

The Nixon administration was initially unconcerned about publication of the Pentagon Papers. However, they were "leaked" at a time when the American public's support for the president's conduct of the Vietnam War was eroding. A March 1971 public opinion poll revealed that Nixon's approval rating had fallen to a low of 50 percent, and that support for his conduct of the war had declined to 34 percent. Another survey found that 51 percent of Americans were persuaded that the war was "morally wrong." In April 1971, massive street protests against the war took place, for the first time spearheaded by Vietnam veterans. These circumstances changed the president's view that the Pentagon Papers were embarrassing only to his predecessors. He came to agree with Henry Kissinger, his national security adviser, that the Pentagon Papers undermined not only his own Vietnam policies, but his decision-making style and his credibility. Nixon also worried that subsequent presidents might lose control over classified information.

After examining the Pentagon Papers for several months and debating internally whether to print them, the *New York Times* commenced publication on June 13, 1971, in installment form. The Nixon administration asked the *Times* to cease publishing the papers, but it refused. On June 15, the U.S. Department of Justice requested a temporary restraining order to halt further publication by the *Times*. Three days later, the Justice Department requested a temporary restraining order against the *Washington Post*, which had begun publishing the Pentagon Papers on June 18.

In the *New York Times* case, the U.S. District Court for the Southern District of New York refused the government's request for a temporary restraining order. The government appealed to the Court of Appeals for the Second Circuit, which issued a temporary restraining order and remanded the case to the district court for further hearings. The *New York Times* petitioned the Supreme Court for a writ of certiorari.

In the *Washington Post* case, the District Court for the District of Columbia refused to issue a temporary restraining order. On appeal by the government, the Court of Appeals for the District of Columbia temporarily restrained the *Post* from continuing its series and ordered the district court to hear the government's request for an injunction. On remand, the district court refused the government's request for an injunction, but extended the restraining order to give the government time to appeal. The Court of Appeals for the District of Columbia affirmed. The government petitioned the Supreme Court, asking for a writ of certiorari.

The Supreme Court accepted both cases on June 25, 1971, and stayed further publication of the Pentagon Papers by the *Times* and the *Post*. It heard arguments the next day.

HIGHLIGHTS OF SUPREME COURT ARGUMENTS

BRIEF FOR NEW YORK TIMES

◆ At the core of the First Amendment is an interest in uninhibited, robust, and wide-open debate with respect to public affairs. Any attempt to impose a prior restraint on publication therefore places on the government a heavy burden of rebutting the presumption against prior restraint that is well ingrained in American law.

◆ To the extent that exceptions exist to the rule of no prior restraints, they are in connection with the redress of individual or private wrongs, not debate over an issue of public policy.

◆ The government rests its claim of inherent authority in this case not on extreme emergency, but on ordinary circumstances. The question that looms in the background of this case is whether in extraordinary circumstances of the gravest emergency the president may have inherent authority to act for the public interest, either by proclamation or executive order or by availing himself of judicial process.

◆ If the government's claim to inherent presidential authority cannot stand, its claim must have a statutory basis. No statutory provisions prohibit the dissemination of sensitive government information.

◆ If an exception to the prohibition against prior restraints exists, it would arise only when publication could be held to lead directly and almost unavoidably to a disastrous event. The probabilities must be a near certainty and the chain of causation between the publication and the feared event must be direct.

◆ The Court should define the conditions for applying for an injunction very narrowly so that prior restraint by litigation does not become the government's strategy for restraining or postponing publication of unpopular materials.

AMICUS CURIAE BRIEFS SUPPORTING *NEW YORK TIMES* AND *WASHINGTON POST*

American Civil Liberties Union; National Emergency Civil Liberties Committee; twenty-seven members of the U.S. Congress.

BRIEF FOR THE UNITED STATES

◆ The issue is the narrow question of whether the First Amendment bars a court from prohibiting a newspaper from publishing material the disclosure of which would pose a grave and immediate danger to national security. Whatever the classification of the material (whether "top secret" or "secret"), and however the newspapers may have come into possession of it, the First Amendment does not preclude the issuing of an injunction preventing publication. Courts have authorized prior restraints in many situations, including under cease-and-desist orders and in enforcing statutory copyrights.

◆ A court may enjoin a newspaper from publishing material whose disclosure poses a grave and immediate danger to national security. The authority of the executive department to protect the nation against publication of information whose disclosure would endanger the national security stems from the constitutional power of the president over the conduct of foreign affairs and his authority as commander in chief.

◆ Congress has recognized the authority of the president to protect the secrecy of information relating to foreign affairs and national defense. The first exception to the Freedom of Information Act is for matters that "are specifically required by Executive order to be kept secret in the interest of the national defense or foreign policy."

SUPREME COURT DECISION

(per curiam)

... "Any system of prior restraint of expression comes to this Court bearing a heavy presumption against its constitutional validity." *Bantam Books, Inc. v. Sullivan*, 372 U.S. 58 (1963).... The government "thus carries a heavy burden of showing justification for the imposition of such a restraint." *Organization for a Better Austin v. Keefe*, 402 U.S. 415 (1971). The District Court for the Southern District of New York in the *New York Times* case ... and the District Court for the District of Columbia and the Court of Appeals for the District of Columbia Circuit ... in the *Washington Post* case held that the Government had not met that burden. We agree.

The judgment of the Court of Appeals for the District of Columbia Circuit is therefore affirmed. The order of the Court of Appeals for the Second Circuit is reversed ... and the case is remanded with directions to enter a judgment affirming the judgment of the District Court for the Southern District of New York. The stays entered June 25, 1971, by the Court are vacated. The judgments shall issue forthwith.

So ordered.

BLACK AND DOUGLAS, J.J., CONCURRING

... The Bill of Rights changed the original Constitution into a new charter under which no branch of government could abridge the people's freedoms of press, speech, religion, and assembly. Yet the Solicitor General argues and some members of the Court appear to agree that the general powers of the Government adopted in the original Constitution should be interpreted to limit and restrict the specific and emphatic guarantees of the Bill of Rights adopted later. I can imagine no greater perversion of history....

In the First Amendment the Founding Fathers gave the free press the protection it must have to fulfill its essential role in our democracy.... In my view, far from deserving condemnation for their courageous reporting, the *New York Times*, the *Washington Post*, and other newspapers should be commended for serving the purpose that the Founding Fathers saw so clearly. In revealing the workings of government that led to the Vietnam war, the newspapers nobly did precisely that which the Founders hoped and trusted they would do.

... [W]e are asked to hold that despite the First Amendment's emphatic command, the Executive Branch, the Congress, and the Judiciary can make laws enjoining publication of current news and abridging freedom of the press in the name of "national security." The Government does not even attempt to rely on any act of Congress. Instead it makes the bold and dangerously far-reaching contention that the courts should take it upon themselves to "make" a law abridging freedom of the press in the name of equity, presidential power and national security, even when the representatives of the people in Congress have adhered to the command of the First Amendment and refused to make such a law.... To find that the President has "inherent power" to halt the publication of news by resort to the courts would wipe out the First

Amendment and destroy the fundamental liberty and security of the very people the Government hopes to make "secure."...

DOUGLAS AND BLACK, J.J., CONCURRING [OMITTED]

BRENNAN, J., CONCURRING

... I write separately in these cases only to emphasize what should be apparent: that our judgment in the present cases may not be taken to indicate the propriety, in the future, of issuing temporary stays and restraining orders to block the publication of material sought to be suppressed by the Government.... [E]ven if it be assumed that some of the interim restraints were proper in the two cases before us, that assumption has no bearing upon the propriety of similar judicial action in the future. To begin with, there has now been ample time for reflection and judgment; whatever values there may be in the preservation of novel questions for appellate review may not support any restraints in the future. More important, the First Amendment stands as an absolute bar to the imposition of judicial restraints in circumstances of the kind presented by these cases....

Our cases, it is true, have indicated that there is a single, extremely narrow class of cases in which the First Amendment's ban on prior judicial restraint may be overridden. Our cases have thus far indicated that such cases may arise only when the Nation "is at war." *Schenck v. United States*....

Unless and until the Government has clearly made out its case, the First Amendment commands that no injunction may issue.

STEWART AND WHITE, J.J., CONCURRING

In the governmental structure created by our Constitution, the Executive is endowed with enormous power in the two related areas of national defense and international relations. This power, largely unchecked by the Legislative and Judicial branches, has been pressed to the very hilt since the advent of the nuclear missile age. For better or worse, the simple fact is that a President of the United States possesses vastly greater constitutional independence in these two vital areas of power than does, say, a prime minister of a country with a parliamentary form of government.

In the absence of the governmental checks and balances present in other areas of our national life, the only effective restraint upon executive policy and power in the areas of national defense and international affairs may lie in an enlightened citizenry—in an informed and critical public opinion which alone can here protect the values of democratic government. For this reason, it is perhaps here that a press that is alert, aware, and free most vitally serves the basic purpose of the First Amendment. For without an informed and free press there cannot be an enlightened people.

Yet it is elementary that the successful conduct of international diplomacy and the maintenance of an effective national defense requires both confidentiality and secrecy. Other nations can hardly deal with this Nation in an atmosphere of mutual trust unless they can be assured that their confidences will be kept. And within our own executive departments, the development of considered and intelligent international policies would be impossible if those charged with their formulation could not communicate with each other freely, frankly, and in confidence. In the area of basic national defense the frequent need for absolute secrecy is, of course, self-evident.

I think there can be but one answer to this dilemma, if dilemma it be. The responsibility must be where the power is. If the Constitution gives the Executive a large degree of unshared power in the conduct of foreign affairs and the maintenance of our national defense, then under the Constitution the Executive must have the largely unshared duty to determine and preserve the degree of internal security necessary to exercise that power successfully....

[I]n the cases before us we are asked neither to construe specific regulations nor to apply specific laws. We are asked, instead, to perform a function that the Constitution gave to the Executive, not the Judiciary. We are asked, quite simply, to prevent the publication by two newspapers of material that the Executive Branch insists should not, in the national interest, be published. I am convinced that the Executive is correct with respect to some of the documents involved. But I cannot say that disclosure of any of them will surely result in direct, immediate, and irreparable damage to our Nation or its people. That being so, there can under the First Amendment be but one judicial resolution to the issues before us. I join the judgments of the Court.

WHITE AND STEWART, J.J., CONCURRING

... [A]fter examining the materials the Government characterizes as the most sensitive and destructive [I cannot] deny that revelation of these documents will do substantial damage to public interests. Indeed, I am confident that their disclosure will have that result....

Prior restraints require an unusually heavy justification under the First Amendment; but failure by the Government to justify prior restraints does not measure its constitutional entitlement to a conviction for criminal publication. That the Government mistakenly chose to proceed by injunction does not mean that it could not successfully proceed in another way....

[T]he newspapers are presumably now on full notice of the position of the United States and must face the consequences if they publish. I would have no difficulty in sustaining convictions under [the Espionage Act of 1917 and the U.S. criminal code] on facts that would not justify the intervention of equity and the imposition of a prior restraint....

MARSHALL, J., CONCURRING

... The problem here is whether in these particular cases the Executive Branch has authority to invoke the equity jurisdiction of the courts to protect what it believes to be the national interest....

Even if it is determined that the Government could not in good faith bring prosecutions against the *New York Times* and the *Washington Post*, it is clear that Congress has specifically rejected passing legislation that would have clearly given the President the power he seeks here and made the current activity of the newspapers unlawful. When Congress specifically declines to make conduct unlawful it is not for the Court to redecide those issues—to overrule Congress....

Either the Government has the power under statutory grant to use traditional criminal law to protect the country or, if there is no basis for arguing that Congress has made the activity a crime, it is plain that Congress has specifically refused to grant the authority the Government seeks from this Court. In either case this Court does not have authority to grant the requested relief. It is not for this Court to fling itself into every breach perceived by some

Government official nor is it for this Court to take on itself the burden of enacting law, especially a law that Congress has refused to pass....

BURGER, C.J., DISSENTING [OMITTED]

HARLAN AND BLACKMUN, J.J., AND BURGER, C.J., DISSENTING

... With all respect, I consider that the Court has been almost irresponsibly feverish in dealing with these cases.

... Due regard for the extraordinarily important and difficult questions involved in these litigations should have led the Court to shun such a precipitate timetable. In order to decide the merits of these cases properly, some or all of the following questions should have been faced:

1. Whether the Attorney General is authorized to bring these suits in the name of the United States....

2. Whether the First Amendment permits the federal courts to enjoin publication of stories which would present a serious threat to national security....

3. Whether the threat to publish highly secret documents is of itself a sufficient implication of national security to justify an injunction on the theory that regardless of the contents of the documents harm enough results simply from the demonstration of such a breach of secrecy.

4. Whether the unauthorized disclosure of any of these particular documents would seriously impair the national security.

5. What weight should be given to the opinion of high officers in the Executive Branch of the Government with respect to questions 3 and 4.

6. Whether the newspapers are entitled to retain and use the documents notwith-

standing the seemingly uncontested facts that the documents, or the originals of which they are duplicates, were purloined from the Government's possession and that the newspapers received them with the knowledge that they had been feloniously acquired....

7. Whether the threatened harm to the national security or the Government's possessory interest in the documents justifies the issuance of an injunction against publication in light of—

a. The strong First Amendment policy against prior restraints on publication;

b. The doctrine against enjoining conduct in violation of criminal statutes; and

c. The extent to which the materials at issue have apparently already been otherwise disseminated.

These are difficult questions of fact, of law, and of judgment; the potential consequences of erroneous decision are enormous. The time which has been available to us, to the lower courts, and to the par-

ties has been wholly inadequate for giving these cases the kind of consideration they deserve....

Forced as I am to reach the merits of these cases, I dissent from the opinion and judgments of the Court....

BLACKMUN, J., DISSENTING

... I hope that damage already has not been done [resulting from publication of these papers]. If, however, damage has been done, and if, with the Court's action today, these newspapers proceed to publish the critical documents and there results therefrom "the death of soldiers, the destruction of alliances, the greatly increased difficulty of negotiations with our enemies, the inability of our diplomats to negotiate," to which list I might add the factors of prolongation of the war and of further delay in the freeing of United States prisoners, then the Nation's people will know where the responsibility for these sad consequences rests.

QUESTIONS

1. Assess the constitutional status of press freedom from prior restraint in the aftermath of *New York Times*. Aside from its judgment in the immediate case, how did the justices come down on the issue of government censorship itself? Was it a 7–2 or a 6–3 vote accepting some form of prior restraint?

2. Only fifteen days elapsed between June 15, when the federal government took the *New York Times* to court, and the Supreme Court's decision on June 30, 1971. Is Justice Harlan correct that the Court was "irresponsibly feverish" in *New York Times*? What does Justice Harlan's complaint imply about his view of the appropriate balance between First Amendment interests and national security?

3. In a February 15, 1989, *Washington Post* article entitled, "Secrets Not Worth Keeping," Erwin N. Griswold, who argued on behalf of the government against the *New York Times* and the *Washington Post* when he was solicitor general, said that "the principal concern of the classifiers is not with national security, but rather with governmental embarrassment of one sort or another." What does this statement

suggest about Griswold's assessment of the strength of the government's case in *New York Times*? Griswold is correct that, as a general rule, protecting the government from embarrassment is not a legitimate reason for abridging press freedom. Is there any instance where avoiding official shame might justify limiting publication of information?

4. The Department of Justice obtained criminal indictments against Daniel Ellsberg on generalized charges of espionage, theft, and conspiracy. The "theft" alleged was of information, not of documents, because Ellsberg had photocopied portions of the Pentagon Papers and returned the originals. The Ellsberg prosecution collapsed when it was revealed that former CIA agent E. Howard Hunt, working for a clandestine group popularly known as the "Plumbers" organized at President Nixon's behest, had broken into the home of Ellsberg's psychiatrist in an effort to obtain material with which to discredit Ellsberg. In May 1973, District Judge Byrne dismissed the indictments and granted a mistrial because the "totality of the circumstances" demonstrated government misconduct that "offends 'a sense of justice.'" Two years later, Congress attempted unsuccessfully to pass legislation making it a crime to pass national defense information or any classified information to unauthorized persons.

Should the United States adopt legislation that, among other things, makes it a crime to obtain, convey, receive, or print classified state information? What constitutional provisions, if any, might get in the way?

COMMENTS

1. On June 29, 1971, in the midst of the legal maneuvering over publication of the Pentagon Papers, Alaska Senator Mike Gravel convened the Senate Subcommittee on Public Buildings and Grounds, which he chaired. He proceeded to read aloud summaries of the Pentagon Papers, the publication of which the government was attempting to prevent. When he finished reading, Senator Gravel introduced all forty-seven volumes of the study into the record as an exhibit. He then gave a copy to Beacon Press, a Boston publishing house that had agreed to print the complete text of the Pentagon Papers.

Senator Gravel's actions led to the impaneling of a federal grand jury to investigate the unauthorized release of the Papers to a publisher. The grand jury subpoenaed Leonard Rodberg, one of Gravel's aides, to testify. Rodberg moved to quash the subpoena. The First Circuit Court of Appeals allowed Gravel to intervene on his aide's behalf. The appeals court denied the motion to quash but held that the Speech and Debate Clause (Article I, Section 6, Clause 1) barred inquiry into the senator's actions or motives or those of his aide. It held further that commercial publication of the Pentagon Papers was not a legislative act and thus was unprotected. In *Gravel v. United States*, 408 U.S. 606 (1972), the Supreme Court affirmed, 5–4, but added that Article I, Section 6, Clause 1, does not exempt members of Congress or their aides from liability.

In a second case, the Court enforced the Central Intelligence Agency's (CIA) requirement that its employees sign secrecy agreements promising not to publish information about the agency without the director's prior approval. Former CIA agent Frank Snepp had written *Decent Interval: An Insider's Account of Saigon's Indecent End* (New York, NY: Random House) in 1977, which painted a highly critical picture of the last days of American involvement in Vietnam. His book contained no classified information. Nevertheless, the Court held that Snepp had violated his position of trust and caused the United States irreparable harm. It ordered him to "disgorge the benefits of his faithlessness" by forfeiting all present and future profits from the book to the government and submit all future writings to the CIA for its approval. *Snepp v. United States*, 444 U.S. 507 (1980).

2. In 1983, President Ronald Reagan signed an executive order extending the secrecy and prepublication review requirements approved in *Snepp* to all federal government employees who have access to classified information. Enforceable by the Justice Department, the president's executive order requires review of all information pertaining to intelligence. It encompasses letters to the editor, book reviews, and scholarly papers. Federal agents are authorized to ask government employees to submit to a mandatory polygraph test in the course of investigating information leaks.

PRIOR RESTRAINT

Hazelwood School District v. Kuhlmeier
484 U.S. 260 (1988)

SETTING

Issues of prior restraint continue to be contested in the public school setting, where the debate takes on an additional dimension of disagreement over the extent to which students enjoy the same constitutional rights as adults. A clash between student editors of a Missouri high school newspaper and their principal in 1983 provided a modern example of the problems and the Supreme Court's resolution.

Spectrum was the student newspaper of Hazelwood East High School. Funded by the Board of Education and supplemented by proceeds from selling copies of the newspaper, *Spectrum* was written and edited by the Journalism II class at Hazelwood East. During the 1982–83 school year, more than 4,500 copies of the newspaper were distributed to students, school personnel, and members of the community. During part of that year, the Journalism II class was taught by *Spectrum* advisor Howard Emerson. Among the stories that *Spectrum* student editors had planned, researched, and written for the May 13, 1983, edition was one about the experience of three Hazelwood East students who had been pregnant, and one about the impact of divorce on the lives of Hazelwood East students.

Procedures at Hazelwood East called for the *Spectrum* faculty advisor to submit page proofs of the newspaper for review by the principal before publication. Accordingly, Emerson gave page proofs to Hazelwood East principal Robert E. Reynolds on May 10, three days before the planned publication. Reynolds had concerns about the pregnancy and divorce articles. His three specific objections were that: (1) although the pregnancy story used false names "to keep the identity of these girls a secret," Reynolds worried that the girls' identities nevertheless might be revealed by the information in the story's text; (2) Reynolds believed the pregnancy article's reference to sexual activity and birth control were inappropriate for some of the younger students at Hazelwood East; and (3) Reynolds thought that the divorced parents of a student whose name was used in the divorce article, who had complained about the divorce, should be given an opportunity either to respond to their child's remarks or to consent to their publication. (Reynolds was not aware that Emerson had deleted that student's name from the final version of the divorce article.)

Reynolds believed that there was not enough time to make the changes he thought necessary before the *Spectrum* went to press, so he ordered Emerson to delete the two pages that contained the articles he considered objectionable. Those two pages also contained articles on teenage marriage, runaways and juvenile delinquents, and a general article on teenage pregnancy that Reynolds did not find objectionable. Emerson acquiesced to Reynolds's order and withheld the two pages from publication.

Cathy Kuhlmeier and two other *Spectrum* staff members responded to Reynolds's order by filing suit in the U.S. District Court for the Eastern District of Missouri, seeking an injunction against the order on the ground that it violated their First Amendment rights. The district court denied the injunction, holding that no First Amendment violation had occurred. It held that school officials may impose restraints on students' speech in activities that are "an integral part of the school's educational function—including the publication of a school-sponsored newspaper by a journalism class—so long as their decision has a substantial and reasonable basis, and that principal Reynolds's concerns were "legitimate and reasonable."

The Court of Appeals for the Eighth Circuit reversed. Finding the

Spectrum a public forum as well as part of the school's curriculum, that court concluded that the paper's public forum status precluded school officials from censoring its content except when "necessary to avoid material and substantial interference with school work or discipline ... or the rights of others." The appeals court found "no evidence that the principal could have reasonably forecast that the censored articles or any materials in them would have materially disrupted classwork or given rise to substantial disorder in the school." Accordingly, it concluded that Hazelwood East school officials violated Kuhlmeier's First Amendment rights when they deleted the two pages. The Supreme Court of the United States granted the school district's petition for a writ of certiorari.

HIGHLIGHTS OF SUPREME COURT ARGUMENTS

BRIEF FOR HAZELWOOD SCHOOL DISTRICT

◆ A school-sponsored high school newspaper that is produced by a journalism class, under the supervision of a teacher and subject to the principal's review, is not a public forum. By design and practice, the journalism class was a laboratory situation in which the students worked on a school-sponsored newspaper during class time. There was no intent on the part of school authorities to make the newspaper an open forum.

◆ The journalism students were required to attend class and to work on the newspaper. The teacher assigned the topics and required preparation of the articles that prompted this controversy. Therefore, there was no autonomous expression of opinion by the students that implicates First Amendment values.

◆ The district court correctly found that the principal's excisions were a reasonable effort to protect the privacy of students featured in the articles and their families, to avoid the appearance of official endorsement of sexual norms of the pregnant students, to prevent publication of materials that were inappropriate for high school age readers, and to insure fairness to divorced parents whose actions were characterized in the articles. Deletion of the articles was not motivated by any desire to discriminate against a particular point of view.

AMICUS CURIAE BRIEFS SUPPORTING HAZELWOOD SCHOOL DISTRICT

Joint brief of the National School Boards Association and National Association of Secondary School Principals; Pacific Legal Foundation; School Board of Dade County, Florida.

BRIEF FOR KUHLMEIER

◆ *Spectrum* served as a true conduit for student expression and as such was a limited public forum. Student editors and staff members designed its content around current social topics of relevance to all high school students, including county, state, and national issues. The Curriculum Guide adopted by the school board encouraged the journalism program to adopt professional journalism standards.

◆ *Tinker v. Des Moines Independent Community School District* recognized the free speech rights of school children, subject to restrictions by the state under four circumstances: substantial disruption of school, libel, obscenity, and invasion of the rights of others. None of those circumstances is present in this case.

◆ A claim of "inappropriate content" and the school's interest in fairness do not justify teaching our future citizens that the government can suppress critical discussion of government policies.

◆ If the Court finds a compelling state interest in this case, the First Amendment requires prior written regulations setting out what can be censored, by whom, and for what reasons.

AMICUS CURIAE BRIEFS SUPPORTING KUHLMEIER

Joint brief of American Civil Liberties Union and the American Civil Liberties Union of Eastern Missouri; joint brief of American Society of Newspaper Editors, National Association of Broadcasters, Reporters Committee for Freedom of the Press, and Sigma Delta Chi; People for the American Way; Student Press Law Center; Planned Parenthood Federation of America; NOW Legal Defense and Education Fund.

SUPREME COURT DECISION: 6–3

WHITE, J.

... Students in the public schools do not "shed their constitutional rights to freedom of speech or expression at the schoolhouse gate." *Tinker v. Des Moines*....

We have nonetheless recognized that the First Amendment rights of students in the public schools "are not automatically coextensive with the rights of adults in other settings," *Bethel School District No. 403 v. Fraser*, 478 U.S. 675 (1986), and must be "applied in light of the special characteristics of the school environment." *Tinker*.... A school need not tolerate student speech that is inconsistent with its "basic educational mission," *Fraser*, even though the government could not censor similar speech outside the school.... We thus recognized that "[t]he determination of what manner of speech in the classroom or in school

assembly is inappropriate properly rests with the school board," id., rather than with the federal courts. It is in this context that respondents' First Amendment claims must be considered.

We deal first with the question whether *Spectrum* may appropriately be characterized as a forum for public expression. The public schools do not possess all of the attributes of streets, parks, and other traditional public forums that "time out of mind, have been used for purposes of assembly, communicating thoughts between citizens, and discussing public questions." *Hague v. CIO*, 307 U.S. 496 (1939).... Hence, school facilities may be deemed to be public forums only if school authorities have "by policy or by practice" opened those facilities "for indiscriminate use by the general public,"

Perry Education Assn. v. Perry Local Educators' Assn., 460 U.S. 37 (1983), or by some segment of the public, such as student organizations. *Id.* If the facilities have instead been reserved for other intended purposes, "communicative or otherwise," then no public forum has been created, and school officials may impose reasonable restrictions on the speech of students, teachers, and other members of the school community....

The policy of school officials toward *Spectrum* was reflected in Hazelwood School Board Policy 348.51 and the Hazelwood East Curriculum Guide. Board Policy 348.51 provided that "[s]chool sponsored publications are developed within the adopted curriculum and its educational implications in regular classroom activities." The Hazelwood East Curriculum Guide described the Journalism II course as a "laboratory situation in which the students publish the school newspaper applying skills they have learned in Journalism I."...

School officials did not deviate in practice from their policy that production of *Spectrum* was to be part of the educational curriculum and a "regular classroom activit[y]."...

A decision to teach leadership skills in the context of a classroom activity hardly implies a decision to relinquish school control over that activity.... Accordingly, school officials were entitled to regulate the contents of *Spectrum* in any reasonable manner.... It is this standard, rather than our decision in *Tinker*, that governs this case.

The question whether the First Amendment requires a school to tolerate particular student speech—the question that we addressed in *Tinker*—is different from the question whether the First Amendment requires a school affirma-tively to promote particular student speech. The former question addresses educators' ability to silence a student's personal expression that happens to occur on the school premises. The latter question concerns educators' authority over school-sponsored publications, theatrical productions, and other expressive activities that students, parents, and members of the public might reasonably perceive to bear the imprimatur of the school. These activities may fairly be characterized as part of the school curriculum, whether or not they occur in a traditional classroom setting, so long as they are supervised by faculty members and designed to impart particular knowledge or skills to student participants and audiences.

Educators are entitled to exercise greater control over this second form of student expression to assure that participants learn whatever lessons the activity is designed to teach, that readers or listeners are not exposed to material that may be inappropriate for their level of maturity, and that the views of the individual speaker are not erroneously attributed to the school.... A school must be able to set high standards for the student speech that is disseminated under its auspices—standards that may be higher than those demanded by some newspaper publishers or theatrical producers in the "real" world—and may refuse to disseminate student speech that does not meet those standards. In addition, a school must be able to take into account the emotional maturity of the intended audience in determining whether to disseminate student speech on potentially sensitive topics, which might range from the existence of Santa Claus in an elementary school setting to the particulars of teenage sexual activity in a high school setting. A school must also retain the authority to refuse to sponsor student speech that might reasonably be perceived to advocate drug or alcohol use, irresponsible sex, or conduct otherwise inconsistent with "the shared values of a civilized social order," *Fraser*, or to associate the school with any position other than neutrality on matters of political controversy....

Accordingly, we conclude that the standard articulated in *Tinker* for determining when a school may punish student expression need not also be the standard for determining when a school may refuse to lend its name and resources to the dissemination of student expression. Instead, we hold that educators do not offend the First Amendment by exercising editorial control over the style and content of student speech in school-sponsored expressive activities so long as their actions are reasonably related to legitimate pedagogical concerns....

We also conclude that Principal Reynolds acted reasonably in requiring the deletion from the May 13 issue of *Spectrum* of the pregnancy article, the divorce article, and the remaining articles that were to appear on the same pages of the newspaper....

Reynolds could reasonably have concluded that the students who had written and edited these articles had not sufficiently mastered those portions of the Journalism II curriculum that pertained to the treatment of controversial issues and personal attacks, the need to protect the privacy of individuals whose most intimate concerns are to be revealed in the newspaper, and "the legal, moral, and ethical restrictions imposed upon journalists within [a] school community" that includes adolescent subjects and readers. Finally, we conclude that the principal's decision to delete two pages of *Spectrum*, rather than to delete only the offending articles or to require that they be modified, was reasonable under the circumstances as he understood them. Accordingly, no violation of First Amendment rights occurred.

The judgment of the Court of Appeals for the Eighth Circuit is therefore

Reversed.

BRENNAN, MARSHALL, AND BLACKMUN, J.J. DISSENTING

... If mere incompatibility with the school's pedagogical message were a constitutionally sufficient justification for the suppression of student speech, school officials could censor each of the students or student organizations in the foregoing hypotheticals, converting our public schools into "enclaves of totalitarianism," [*Tinker*], that "strangle the free mind at its source," *West Virginia Board of Education v. Barnette*. The First Amendment permits no such blanket censorship authority. While the "constitutional rights of students in public school are not automatically coextensive with the rights of adults in other settings," *Fraser*, students in the public schools do not "shed their constitutional rights to freedom of speech or expression at the schoolhouse gate," *Tinker*. Just as the public on the street corner must, in the interest of fostering "enlightened opinion," *Cantwell v. Connecticut*, tolerate speech that "tempt[s] [the listener] to throw [the speaker] off the street," id., public educators must accommodate some student expression even if it offends them or offers views or values that contradict those the school wishes to inculcate.

In *Tinker*, this Court struck the balance....

The Court today casts no doubt on *Tinker*'s vitality. Instead it erects a taxonomy of school censorship, concluding that *Tinker* applies to one category and not another. On the one hand is censorship "to silence a student's personal expression that happens to occur on the school premises." On the other hand is censorship of expression that arises in the context of "school-sponsored ... expressive activities that students, parents, and members of the public might reasonably perceive to bear the imprimatur of the school." Ibid.

The Court does not, for it cannot, purport to discern from our precedents the distinction it creates....

Even if we were writing on a clean slate, I would reject the Court's rationale for abandoning *Tinker* in this case. The Court offers no more than an obscure tangle of three excuses to afford educators "greater control" over school-sponsored speech than the *Tinker* test would permit: the public educator's prerogative to control curriculum; the pedagogical interest in shielding the high school audience from objectionable viewpoints and sensitive topics; and the school's need to dissociate itself from student expression. None of the excuses, once disentangled, supports the distinction that the Court draws. *Tinker* fully addresses the first concern; the second is illegitimate; and the third is readily achievable through less oppressive means....

The sole concomitant of school sponsorship that might conceivably justify the distinction that the Court draws between sponsored and nonsponsored student expression is the risk "that the views of the individual speaker [might be] erroneously attributed to the school."... [T]he majority is certainly correct that indicia of school sponsorship increase the likelihood of such attribution, and that state educators may therefore have a legiti-

mate interest in dissociating themselves from student speech.

But "'[e]ven though the governmental purpose be legitimate and substantial, that purpose cannot be pursued by means that broadly stifle fundamental personal liberties when the end can be more narrowly achieved.'" *Keyishian v. Board of Regents*, 385 U.S. [589] (1967). Dissociative means short of censorship are available to the school. It could, for example, require the student activity to publish a disclaimer, such as the "Statement of Policy" that *Spectrum* published each school year announcing that "[a]ll ... editorials appearing in this newspaper reflect the opinions of the *Spectrum* staff, which are not necessarily shared by the administrators or faculty of Hazelwood East," or it could simply issue its own response clarifying the official position on the matter and explaining why the student position is wrong. Yet, without so much as acknowledging the less oppressive alternatives, the Court approves of brutal censorship....

[E]ven if the majority were correct that the principal could constitutionally have censored the objectionable mateial, I would emphatically object to the brutal manner in which he did so.

The Court opens its analysis in this case by purporting to reaffirm *Tinker*'s time-tested proposition that public school students "do not 'shed their constitutional rights to freedom of speech or expression at the schoolhouse gate.'"... That is an ironic introduction to an opinion that denudes high school students of much of the First Amendment protection that *Tinker* itself prescribed.... The young men and women of Hazelwood East expected a civics lesson, but not the one the Court teaches them today.

I dissent.

QUESTIONS

1. What, if anything, does *Hazelwood* add to the doctrine of prior restraint? Is the decision so specific to the public school setting as to have no broad consequences, or does *Hazelwood* mark a shift in the Court's approach?

2. Is *Hazelwood* primarily about free press rights, the rights of public secondary school students, or privacy rights? Or can these issues be separated in the circumstances of this case? If they cannot be separated, what are the consequences for the development of clear judicial doctrine in any of these three areas?

3. To what extent was the Court's decision in *Hazelwood* affected by the facts that *Spectrum* was school sponsored, publicly funded, and published as part of a journalism class? Might the outcome have been different if *Spectrum* were an extra-curricular publication?

SUGGESTIONS FOR FURTHER READING

Anderson, David A., "The Origins of the Press Clause," 30 *University of California Los Angeles Law Review* (1983): 456.

Barnett, Stephen, "The Puzzle of Prior Restraint," 29 *Stanford Law Review* (1977): 539.

Barron, Jerome, *Freedom of the Press for Whom: The Right of Access to Mass Media* (Bloomington, IN: Indiana University Press, 1973).

Blasi, Vincent, "Toward a Theory of Prior Restraint: The Central Linkage," 66 *Minnesota Law Review* (1981): 11.

"Developments in the Law—The National Security Interest and Civil Liberties," 85 *Harvard Law Review* (1972): 1130.

Diamond, David A., "The First Amendment and Public Schools: The Case against Judicial Intervention," 59 *Texas Law Review* (1981): 477.

Emerson, Thomas, "The Doctrine of Prior Restraint," 20 *Law and Contemporary Problems* (1955): 648.

_____, "First Amendment Doctrine and the Burger Court," 68 *California Law Review* (1980): 422.

Friendly, Fred W., *Minnesota Rag: The Dramatic Story of the Landmark Supreme Court Case That Gave Meaning to Freedom of the Press* (New York, NY: Random House, 1981).

Hafen, Bruce, "Developing Student Expression Through Institutional Authority: Public Schools as Mediating Structures," 48 *Ohio State Law Journal* (1987): 42.

_____, "*Hazelwood School District* and the Role of First Amendment Institutions," *Duke Law Journal* (1988): 685.

Henkin, Louis, "The Right to Know and the Duty to Withhold: The Case of the Pentagon Papers," 120 *University of Pennsylvania Law Review* (1971): 271.

Huffman, John L., and Denise M. Trauth, "High School Students' Publication Rights and Prior Restraint," *Journal of Law & Education* (1981): 485.

Hunter, Howard O., "Toward a Better Understanding of the Prior Restraint Doctrine: A Reply to Professor Mayton," 67 *Cornell Law Review* (1982): 283.

Jeffries, John Calvin, Jr., "Rethinking Prior Restraint," 92 *Yale Law Journal* (1983): 409.

Levin, Betsy, "Educating Youth for Citizenship: The Conflict between Authority and Individual Rights in the Public School," 95 *Yale Law Journal* (1986): 1647.

Levy, Leonard W., *Emergence of a Free Press* (New York, NY: Oxford University Press, 1985).

Lofton, John, *The Press as Guardian of the First Amendment* (Columbia, SC: University of South Carolina Press, 1980).

Mayton, William T., "Toward a Theory of First Amendment Process: Injunctions of Speech, Subsequent Punishment, and the Costs of Prior Restraint Doctrine," 67 *Cornell University Law Review* (1982): 245.

McNamara, Robert S., *In Retrospect: The Tragedy and Lessons of Vietnam* (New York, NY: Times Books, 1995).

Powe, L. A., Jr., "H-Bomb Injunction," 61 *University of Colorado Law Review* (1990): 55.

Redish, Martin, "The Proper Role of the Prior Restraint Doctrine in First Amendment Theory," 70 *Virginia Law Review* (1984): 53.

Roe, Richard, "Valuing Student Speech: The Work of the Schools As Conceptual Development," 79 *California Law Review* (1991): 1271.

Rudenstine, David, *The Day the Presses Stopped: A History of the Pentagon Papers* (Berkeley, CA: University of California Press, 1996).

Scordato, Marin, "Distinction without Difference: A Reappraisal of the Doctrine of Prior Restraint," *North Carolina Law Review* (1989): 1.

Shapiro, Martin, *The Pentagon Papers and the Courts* (San Francisco, CA: Chandler Publishing, 1972).

Smith, Jeffrey, *Printers and Press Freedom* (New York, NY: Oxford University Press, 1988).

Soifer, Aviam, "Freedom of the Press in the United States," in *Press Law in Modern Democracies: A Comparative Study*, ed. Pnina Lahav (New York, NY: Longman, 1986).

Sunstein, Cass, "Government Control of Information," *California Law Review* (1986): 889.

"Symposium, *Near v. Minnesota*, 50th Anniversary," 66 *Minnesota Law Review* (1981): 1.

"Symposium: National Security and the First Amendment," 26 *William & Mary Law Review* (1985): 715.

U.S. Department of Defense, *United States Vietnam Relations, 1945–1967* (Washington, D.C.: U.S. Govt. Printing Office, 1971).

Uhlig, Mark A., "From Hazelwood to the High Court," *New York Times Magazine*, September 13, 1987, p. 102.

Ungar, Sanford J., *The Papers and the Papers* (New York, NY: Dutton, 1972).

LIBEL

New York Times v. Sullivan
376 U.S. 254 (1964)

SETTING

Common law has long recognized the tort of libel, defined as injuring a person's reputation by a published writing. The tort of libel has significant implications for the right of free press. When the First Amendment was added to the Constitution, the prevailing American theory of libel came from William Blackstone's *Commentaries on the Laws of England.* As explained in the *Setting* to *Near* (see p. 333), Blackstone stated the standard English view of a free press in his *Commentaries on the Laws of England* when he wrote that liberty of the press consists "in laying no *previous* restraints on publications...." Under English law, however, government was authorized to penalize publishers for material they printed. Consequently, publishers remained liable for civil damages or criminal penalties for printing what was "improper, mischievous, or illegal."

American revolutionary leaders like Thomas Jefferson were concerned about the possibility of press self-censorship that could result from the common-law tradition of awarding damages for injuries to reputation resulting from published material. Taking his cue from one of Blackstone's contemporaries who had criticized Blackstone as "an anti-republican lawyer," Jefferson argued on several occasions that those interested in human liberty would find Blackstone no model. Nevertheless, Blackstone's bifurcated theory of press freedom—no prior restraint but liability for what was printed—continued to influence American judicial interpretations of the Free Press Clause of the First Amendment throughout most of the nineteenth century. If a judge or jury found that published statements reflected adversely on a plaintiff's reputation, the only defense available to defendant publishers was proving the truth of the statement. This requirement led to the result Jefferson feared—self-censorship—because truth, particularly in political matters, is difficult and expensive to prove.

In 1916, Harvard law professor and First Amendment scholar Zechariah Chafee Jr. began an attack on Blackstone's common law approach to press freedom. Chafee argued that the Blackstonian formulation was "... wholly out of accord with a common-sense view of the relations of state and citizen." He contended that a common-sense view would neither bar prior restraint absolutely nor permit publishers to be penalized for exercising freedom of expression.

Several state legislatures took Chafee's cue and enacted laws protecting publishers from libel suits. There was no consistency among the states, however. In 1908, the Kansas Supreme Court adopted an "actual malice" standard for libel cases. Under that rule, a plaintiff claiming defamation had to prove that the publisher printed an untruth deliberately and maliciously, not just carelessly. *Coleman v. MacLennan*, 98 P 281 (1908). Other jurisdictions required a defendant to prove the truth of libelous statements. Doctrinal confusion persisted into the 1960s, when Montgomery, Alabama, city commissioner L. B. Sullivan sued the *New York Times* for libel.

Civil rights leader Dr. Martin Luther King Jr. was arrested in Montgomery in 1960 and charged with perjury in connection with activities associated with the struggle against segregation. A group of sixty-four entertainers, religious activists, public affairs leaders, and trade unionists in New York formed to lend support to civil rights efforts and to raise funds for King's legal defense. In order to solicit contributions throughout the nation, group members agreed to have their names printed as part of a full-page fund-raising advertisement in the *New York Times* on March 29, 1960.

The *New York Times* advertisement (see pp. 364–365) contained endorsements of the appeal for funds by the Reverend Ralph David Abernathy, three other Alabama clergymen who were King's associates in the Southern Christian Leadership Conference (SCLC), and sixteen other persons, all but two of whom were clergy in various southern cities. Their endorsement appeared in the advertisement under a line reading "We in the south warmly endorse this appeal." The advertisement consisted of a ten-paragraph statement entitled, "Heed Their Rising Voices." It charged that King's perjury arrest was part of a campaign to discredit his leadership of the movement to integrate public facilities in the South, and to encourage southern blacks to register and vote. It further alleged that "Southern violators" in Montgomery had expelled students from Alabama State College who had led a demonstration in support of King on the state capitol steps, had surrounded that campus with armed police, had locked students out of the campus dining hall to starve them into submission, had bombed King's home, and had harassed him with seven arrests for speeding, loitering, and other spurious offenses. The advertisement asked for contributions to defend King and other southern Freedom Fighters.

The advertisement contained several errors of fact. The students who had been expelled, for example, had demanded service at an all-white lunch counter; they had not led a capitol demonstration. Police had been deployed near Alabama State College, but they did not ring the campus. The campus dining hall had not been padlocked; only students without meal tickets were denied access to it. Police had arrested King four times, not seven.

L. B. Sullivan, the Montgomery Commissioner of Public Affairs, believed that he was libeled by two paragraphs in the advertisement, even though the ad did not mention him by name. One paragraph referred to "truckloads of police." Another paragraph, mentioning the bombing of King's home and his dubious arrests, charged that "they" (the Montgomery police), had carried out the acts. Sullivan believed that these references to the police reflected derogatorily on him because his duties included supervision of the Montgomery Police Department.

On April 8, 1960, Sullivan made a written demand to the *New York Times*, as well as to Abernathy and his SCLC colleagues, for a printed retraction. The *Times* offered to look into the matter but it did not print a retraction. On April 19, 1960, Sullivan filed a libel suit against the *New York Times* and the ministers who had endorsed the advertisement. The *New York Times* subsequently printed a retraction requested by Alabama Governor John Patterson, indicating that Patterson was not guilty of any improper conduct and apologizing if the March 29 advertisement suggested otherwise.

The case, *Sullivan v. New York Times*, was tried to a jury in a Montgomery circuit court. The trial judge's jury instructions stated that under Alabama law the statements on which Sullivan based his action were "*libelous per se*," meaning that the jury was to presume that publication of the statements slandered Sullivan so he was not required to show any damage, and that falsity and malice also were presumed. The jury returned a verdict of $500,000 for Sullivan. The Supreme Court of Alabama affirmed, finding no fault with the trial judge's instructions or his reliance on the *libel per se* rule. The *New York Times* petitioned the Supreme Court of the United States for review.

HIGHLIGHTS OF SUPREME COURT ARGUMENTS

BRIEF FOR THE *NEW YORK TIMES*

◆ The *libel per se* rule applied by the Alabama courts is an abridgement of the First Amendment freedom of the press. The rule requires publishers to prove the truth of everything they publish, requires no proof of injury by a complaining official, and presumes malice or falsity. The effect is to so restrict the right to protest and criticize the conduct of public officials as to abridge freedom of the press.

◆ The problem with the *libel per se* rule can be seen in this situation by the fact that testimony at trial proved that Sullivan was not injured by the advertisement.

◆ The willingness of newspapers to carry editorial advertisements encourages the widest possible dissemination of information from a wide range of sources. It deserves no lesser treatment than any other mode of publication as to the protection of the First Amendment.

Heed Their Rising Voices

"The growing movement of peaceful mass demonstrations by Negroes is something new in the South, something understandable....

Let Congress heed their rising voices, for they will be heard."

—*New York Times editorial*
Saturday, March 19, 1960

As the whole world knows by now, thousands of Southern Negro students are engaged in wide-spread non-violent demonstrations in positive affirmation of the right to live in human dignity as guaranteed by the U. S. Constitution and the Bill of Rights. In their efforts to uphold these guarantees, they are being met by an unprecedented wave of terror by those who would deny and negate that document which the whole world looks upon as setting the pattern for modern freedom....

In Orangeburg, South Carolina, when 400 students peacefully sought to buy doughnuts and coffee at lunch counters in the business district, they were forcibly ejected, tear-gassed, soaked to the skin in freezing weather with fire hoses, arrested en masse and herded into an open barbed-wire stockade to stand for hours in the bitter cold.

In Montgomery, Alabama, after students sang "My Country, 'Tis of Thee" on the State Capitol steps, their leaders were expelled from school, and truck-loads of police armed with shotguns and tear-gas

protagonists of democracy. Their courage and amazing restraint have inspired millions and given a new dignity to the cause of freedom.

Small wonder that the Southern violators of the Constitution fear this new, non-violent brand of freedom fighter . . . even as they fear the upswelling right-to-vote movement. Small wonder that they are determined to destroy the one man who, more than any other, symbolizes the new spirit now sweeping the South—the Rev. Dr. Martin Luther King, Jr., world-famous leader of the Montgomery Bus Protest. For it is his doctrine of non-violence which has inspired and guided the students in their widening wave of sit-ins; and it this same Dr. King who founded and is president of the Southern Christian Leadership Conference—the organization which is spearheading the surging right-to-vote movement. Under Dr. King's direction the Leadership Conference conducts Student Workshops and Seminars in the philosophy and technique of non-violent resistance.

Again and again the Southern violators have

of others—look for guidance and support, and thereby to intimidate *all* leaders who may rise in the South. Their strategy is to behead this affirmative movement, and thus to demoralize Negro Americans and weaken their will to struggle. The defense of Martin Luther King, spiritual leader of the student sit-in movement, clearly, therefore, is an integral part of the total struggle for freedom in the South.

Decent-minded Americans cannot help but applaud the creative daring of the students and the quiet heroism of Dr. King. But this is one of those moments in the stormy history of Freedom when men and women of good will must do more than applaud the rising-to-glory of others. The America whose good name hangs in the balance before a watchful world, the America whose heritage of Liberty these Southern Upholders of the Constitution are defending, is *our* America as well as theirs . . .

We must heed their rising voices—yes—but we must add our own.

We must extend ourselves above and beyond

ringed the Alabama State College Campus. When the entire student body protested to state authorities by refusing to re-register, their dining hall was padlocked in an attempt to starve them into submission.

In Tallahassee, Atlanta, Nashville, Savannah, Greensboro, Memphis, Richmond, Charlotte, and a host of other cities in the South, young American teenagers, in face of the entire weight of official state apparatus and police power, have boldly stepped forth as

answered Dr. King's peaceful protests with intimidation and violence. They have bombed his home almost killing his wife and child. They have assaulted his person. They have arrested him seven times—for "speeding," "loitering" and similar "offenses." And now they have charged him with "perjury"—a *felony* under which they could imprison him for *ten years.* Obviously, their real purpose is to remove him physically as the leader to whom the students and millions

moral support and render the material help so urgently needed by those who are taking the risks, facing jail, and even death in a glorious re-affirmation of our Constitution and its Bill of Rights.

We urge you to join hands with our fellow Americans in the South by supporting, with your dollars, this Combined Appeal for all three needs—the defense of Martin Luther King,—the support of the embattled students—and the struggle for the right-to-vote.

Your Help Is Urgently Needed . . . NOW !!

Stella Adler
Raymond Pace Alexander
Harry Van Arsdale
Harry Belafonte
Julie Belafonte
Dr. Algernon Black
Marc Blitzstein
William Branch
Marlon Brando
Mrs. Ralph Bunche
Diahann Carroll

Dr. Alan Knight Chalmers
Richard Coe
Nat King Cole
Cheryl Crawford
Dorothy Dandridge
Ossie Davis
Sammy Davis, Jr.
Ruby Dee
Dr. Philip Elliott
Dr. Harry Emerson Fosdick

Anthony Franciosa
Lorraine Hansbury
Rev. Donald Harrington
Nat Hentoff
James Hicks
Mary Hinkson
Van Heflin
Langston Hughes
Morris Iushewitz
Mahalia Jackson
Mordecai Johnson

John Killens
Eartha Kitt
Rabbi Edward Klein
Hope Lange
John Lewis
Viveca Lindfors
Carl Murphy
Don Murray
John Murray
A. J. Muste
Frederick O'Neal

L. Joseph Overton
Clarence Pickett
Shad Polier
Sidney Poitier
A. Philip Randolph
John Raitt
Elmer Rice
Jackie Robinson
Mrs. Eleanor Roosevelt
Bayard Rustin
Robert Ryan

Maureen Stapleton
Frank Silvera
Hope Stevens
George Tabori
Rev. Gardner C. Taylor
Norman Thomas
Kenneth Tynan
Charles White
Shelley Winters
Max Youngstein

We in the south who are struggling daily for dignity and freedom warmly endorse this appeal

Rev. Ralph D. Abernathy
(Montgomery, Ala.)
Rev. Fred L. Shuttlesworth
(Birmingham, Ala.)
Rev. Kelley Miller Smith
(Nashville, Tenn.)
Rev. W. A. Dennis
(Chattanooga, Tenn.)
Rev. C. K. Steele
(Tallahassee, Fla.)

Rev. Matthew D. McCollom
(Orangeburg, S. C.)
Rev. William Holmes Borders
(Atlanta, Ga.)
Rev. Douglas Moore
(Durham, N. C.)
Rev. Wyatt Tee Walker
(Petersburg, Va.)

Rev. Walter L. Hamilton
(Norfolk, Va.)
I. S. Levy
(Columbia, S. C.)
Rev. Martin Luther King, Sr.
(Atlanta, Ga.)
Rev. Henry C. Bunton
(Memphis, Tenn.)
Rev. S. S. Seay, Sr.,
(Montgomery, Ala.)
Rev. Samuel W. Williams
(Atlanta, Ga.)

Rev. A. L. Davis
(New Orleans, La.)
Mrs. Katie E. Whickham
(New Orleans, La.)
Rev. W. H. Hall
(Hattiesburg, Miss.)
Rev. J. E. Lowery
(Mobile, Ala.)
Rev. T. J. Jemison
(Baton Rouge, La.)

COMMITTEE TO DEFEND MARTIN LUTHER KING AND THE STRUGGLE FOR FREEDOM IN THE SOUTH
312 West 125th Street, New York 27, N. Y. UNiversity 6-1700

Chairmen: A. Philip Randolph, Dr. Gardner C. Taylor; *Chairmen of Cultural Division:* Harry Belafonte, Sidney Poitier; *Treasurer:* Nat King Cole; *Executive Director:* Bayard Rustin; *Chairmen of Church Division:* Father George B. Ford, Rev. Harry Emerson Fosdick, Rev. Thomas Kilgore, Jr., Rabbi Edward E. Klein; *Chairman of Labor Division:* Morris Iushewitz

Please mail this coupon TODAY !

┌─────────────────────────────────┐
Committee To Defend Martin Luther King
and
The Struggle For Freedom In The South
312 West 125th Street, New York 27, N. Y.
UNiversity 6-1700

I am enclosing my contribution of $............
for the work of the Committee.

Name ....
(PLEASE PRINT)
Address ....
City .... Zone .... State ....

☐ I want to help   ☐ Please send further information

Please make checks payable to:

Committee To Defend Martin Luther King
└─────────────────────────────────┘

Source: *New York Times v. Sullivan*, 84 S.Ct. 710 (1964).

AMICUS CURIAE BRIEFS SUPPORTING THE *NEW YORK TIMES*

◆ The American Civil Liberties Union; Tribune Company of Chicago; the *Washington Post*.

BRIEF FOR SULLIVAN

◆ The Alabama *libel per se* law is similar to the laws of several states. Under such laws publishers have the defense of proving the truth of statements claimed to be libelous. Alabama law provides untruthful and unprivileged defamers an opportunity to retract and thereby eliminate all but special damages.

◆ According to several Supreme Court opinions, the Constitution confers no absolute immunity on those who defame public officials. If the *Times* succeeds in having the *libel per se* rule declared unconstitutional as applied to public officials, any false statement about any public official will be protected. Such a result would convert the Bill of Rights into a suicide pact.

SUPREME COURT DECISION: 9–0

BRENNAN, J.

… The general proposition that freedom of expression upon public questions is secured by the First Amendment has long been settled by our decisions….

Thus we consider this case against the background of a profound national commitment to the principle that debate on public issues should be uninhibited, robust, and wide-open, and that it may well include vehement, caustic, and sometimes unpleasantly sharp attacks on government and public officials…. The present advertisement, as an expression of grievance and protest on one of the major public issues of our time, would seem clearly to qualify for the constitutional protection. The question is whether it forfeits that protection by the falsity of some of its factual statements and by its alleged defamation of respondent.

Authoritative interpretations of the First Amendment guarantees have consistently refused to recognize an exception for any test of truth—whether administered by judges, juries, or administrative officials—and especially one that puts the burden of proving truth on the speaker. The constitutional protection does not turn upon "the truth, popularity, or social utility of the ideas and beliefs which are offered." As Madison said, "Some degree of abuse is inseparable from the proper use of every thing; and in no instance is this more true than in that of the press."…

If neither factual error nor defamatory content suffices to remove the constitutional shield from criticism of official conduct, the combination of the two elements is no less inadequate. This is the lesson to be drawn from the great controversy over the Sedition Act of 1789, which first crystallized a national awareness of the central meaning of the First Amendment. That statute made it a crime, punishable by a $5,000 fine and five years in prison, "if any person shall write, print, utter or publish … any false, scandalous and malicious writing or writings against the government of the United States, or either house of the Congress ..., or the President ..., with intent to defame ... or to excite against them, or either of them, into contempt or disrepute; or to excite against them ... the hatred of the good people of the United States." The Act allowed the defendant the defense of truth, and provided that the jury were to be judges both of the law and the facts. Despite these qualifications, the Act was vigorously condemned as unconstitutional in an attack joined by Jefferson and Madison....

Although the Sedition Act was never tested in this Court, the attack on its validity has carried the day in the court of history.... [T]he Act, because of the restraint it imposed upon criticism of government and public officials, was inconsistent with the First Amendment....

What a State may not constitutionally bring about by means of a criminal statute is likewise beyond the reach of its civil law of libel. The fear of damage awards under a rule such as that invoked by the Alabama courts here may be markedly more inhibiting than the fear of prosecution under a criminal statute....

The state rule of law is not saved by its allowance of the defense of truth.... A rule compelling the critic of official conduct to guarantee the truth of all his factual assertions—and to do so on pain of libel judgments virtually unlimited in amount—leads to a comparable "self-censorship.".... The rule thus dampens the vigor and limits the variety of public debate. It is inconsistent with the First and Fourteenth Amendments.

The constitutional guarantees require, we think, a federal rule that prohibits a public official from recovering damages for a defamatory falsehood relating to his official conduct unless he proves that the statement was made with "actual malice"—that is, with knowledge that it was false or with reckless disregard of whether it was false or not....

Applying these standards, we consider that the proof presented to show actual malice lacks the convincing clarity which the constitutional standard demands, and hence that it would not constitutionally sustain the judgment for respondent under the proper rule of law....

We think the evidence against the *Times* supports at most a finding of negligence in failing to discover the misstatements, and is constitutionally insufficient to show the recklessness that is required for a finding of actual malice.

We also think the evidence was constitutionally defective in another respect: it was incapable of supporting the jury's finding that the allegedly libelous statements were made "of and concerning" respondent.... There was no reference to respondent in the advertisement, either by name or official position....

Raising as it does the possibility that a good-faith critic of government will be penalized for his criticism, the proposition relied on by the Alabama courts strikes at the very center of the constitutionally protected area of free expression. We hold that such a proposition may not constitutionally be utilized to establish that an otherwise impersonal attack on governmental operations was a libel of an official responsible for those operations....

Reversed and remanded.

BLACK AND DOUGLAS, J.J., CONCURRING

... I base my vote to reverse on the belief that the First and Fourteenth Amendments not merely "delimit" a

State's power to award damages to "public officials against critics of their official conduct" but completely prohibit a State from exercising such a power. The Court goes on to hold that a State can subject such critics to damages if "actual malice" can be proved against them. "Malice," even as defined by the Court, is an elusive, abstract concept, hard to prove and hard to disprove.... [A]nd certainly does not measure up to the sturdy safeguard embodied in the First Amendment. Unlike the Court, therefore, I vote to reverse exclusively on the ground that the *Times* and the individual defendants had an absolute, unconditional constitutional right to publish in the *Times* advertisement their criticisms of the Montgomery agencies and officials....

I regret that the Court has stopped short of this holding indispensable to preserve our free press from destruction.

GOLDBERG AND DOUGLAS, J.J., CONCURRING

... In my view, the First and Fourteenth Amendments to the Constitution afford to the citizen and to the press an absolute, unconditional privilege to criticize official conduct despite the harm which may flow from excesses and abuses. The prized American right "to speak one's mind" about public officials and affairs needs "breathing space to survive." The right should not depend upon a probing by the jury of the motivation of the citizen or press....

It necessarily follows that in a case such as this, where all agree that the allegedly defamatory statements related to official conduct, the judgments for libel cannot constitutionally be sustained.

QUESTIONS

1. Although all nine justices agreed on the result in *Sullivan*, the concurring opinions rejected Justice Brennan's interpretation of the protection the First Amendment affords the press from libel actions. Summarize the three positions. Which, if any, is most constitutionally defensible?

2. Before *Sullivan*, federal courts treated libel as a matter for state courts to determine. On what constitutional theory is libel a state court matter? What are the advantages and disadvantages of returning to such an approach today?

3. In the wake of *Sullivan*, what remedies remain for public officials about whom false statements have been published or broadcast? Has the Court protected "uninhibited, robust, and wide-open" debate in the media at the cost of subjecting public officials to the risk of humiliation? Is the possibility of such humiliation a risk that necessarily accompanies public service?

4. Journalist and legal scholar Anthony Lewis contends that the *Sullivan* "actual malice" rule should immunize the press from all libel claims by public officials. Lewis is concerned that even insubstantial libel claims impose burdens of discovery and trial on the media that are unacceptable under the First Amendment because those burdens

have a chilling effect on press freedom. *"New York Times v. Sullivan Reconsidered: Time to Return to 'The Central Meaning of the First Amendment,'"* 83 *Columbia Law Review* (1983): 603. Is Lewis correct? What are the consequences of his proposal?

COMMENT

Sullivan left two major issues unresolved. First, it did not define "actual malice" or inform future plaintiffs of the exact scope of its application. Second, *Sullivan* did not provide guidelines for distinguishing between "public" and "private" persons. The cases below are examples of how the Supreme Court responded to litigation spawned by *Sullivan* for the ten years until *Gertz v. Robert Welch, Inc.*, 418 U.S. 323 (1974), the libel decision excerpted next.

WHAT IS ACTUAL MALICE?

Case: *Garrison v. Louisiana*, 379 U.S. 64 (1964)

Vote: 9–0

Decision: The criminal defamation conviction of a New Orleans district attorney for comments at a press conference attributing case backlogs to Orleans Parish judges and criticizing their inefficiency, laziness, and excessive vacations, violates the First Amendment. The *Sullivan* actual malice rule limits a state's power to impose criminal sanctions for criticism of the official conduct of public officials. The Louisiana criminal libel statute is unconstitutional because it punishes false statements against public officials if made with ill will, without regard to whether they were made with knowledge of their falsity, or in reckless disregard of whether they are true or false, or if not made in reasonable belief of their truth.

Case: *Linn v. United Plant Guard Workers of America, Local 114*, 383 U.S. 53 (1966)

Vote: 5–4

Decision: The National Labor Relations Act does not preempt a libel action under state law by an employer subject to the act who seeks damages for defamatory statements published during a union organizing campaign by the union and its officers. Although cases involving speech are to be considered "against the background of a profound ... commitment to the principle that debate ... should be uninhibited, robust, and wide-open, and that it may well include vehement, caustic, and sometimes unpleasantly sharp attacks," *New York Times Co. v. Sullivan*, it must be emphasized that malicious libel enjoys no constitutional protection in any context. The malicious utterance of defamatory statements in any form cannot be condoned, and unions should adopt procedures calculated to prevent such abuses.

Case: *Time, Inc. v. Hill*, 385 U.S. 374 (1967)

Vote: 5–4

Decision: A publisher of a newsworthy but inaccurate story is entitled to a jury instruction that a verdict of liability in an action brought under a New York right of privacy statute can be predicated only on finding of knowing or reckless falsity in publication of the article. Under *Sullivan*, factual error, content defamatory of official reputation, or both, are insufficient for an award of damages for false statements unless actual malice—knowledge that the statements are false or in reckless disregard of the truth—is alleged and proved.

PUBLIC OR PRIVATE FIGURE?

Case: *Rosenblatt v. Baer*, 383 U.S. 75 (1966)

Vote: 5–4

Decision: In order to recover damages for libel, a county supervisor must show that alleged imputations, published in a newspaper column, of mismanagement and unlawful taking of government property were made specifically of and concerning the supervisor. The designation of "public official" for purposes of the actual malice rule applies "at the very least to those among the hierarchy of government employees who have, or appear to the public to have, substantial responsibility for control over the conduct of governmental affairs."

Case: *Associated Press v. Walker; Curtis Publishing Company v. Butts*, 388 U.S. 130 (1967)

Vote: 5–4

Decision: The rule limiting libel to malicious falsehoods applies to "public figures" as well as to public officials. Public figures are persons who, because of their public prominence in sports, the media or for other reasons, are well known. Public figures include general Edwin Walker, who participated in racial disorders at the University of Mississippi and Wally Butts, an athletic director accused of "fixing" a college football game.

Case: *Greenbelt Cooperative Publishing Association, Inc. v. Bresler*, 398 U.S. 6 (1970)

Vote: 9–0

Decision: Use of the term "blackmail," in characterizing the negotiating position of a public figure who was seeking zoning variances at the time a city was attempting to acquire a tract of land from him, was not slander when spoken in heated public meetings of city council. Nor was it libel when reported in newspaper articles that fully and accurately reported the public debates. The Constitution permits a public figure to recover money damages for libel only if he can show that the defamatory publication was not only false but was uttered with actual malice.

Case: *Monitor Patriot Co. v. Roy*, 401 U.S. 265 (1971)

Vote: 9–0

Decision: Publications about candidates for public office must be accorded at least as much protection under the First and Fourteenth Amendments as those about occupants of public office under the rule of *New York Times Co. v. Sullivan*. A charge that a senatorial candidate was a "former small time boot-legger," no matter how remote in time or place, can never be irrelevant to an official's or a candidate's fitness.

Case: *Rosenbloom v. Metromedia, Inc.*, 403 U.S. 29 (1971)

Vote: 5–3 (Douglas, J., did not participate.)

Decision: The plurality view is that public-official or public-figure status is not as important in state libel litigation as whether the defamation focuses on "an issue of public or general concern." Rights of free press require special protection and tolerance when the subject matter of the defamation is of public or general concern.

LIBEL

Gertz v. Robert Welch, Inc.
418 U.S. 323 (1974)

SETTING

As the decisions summarized after the excerpt of *New York Times v. Sullivan* illustrate, application of the *Sullivan* rule proved especially problematic for the Court in cases involving individuals who are not directly connected with the government. By 1971, as the summary of *Rosenbloom v. Metromedia*, 403 U.S. 29 (1971) demonstrates, a plurality of three justices—Chief Justice Burger and Justices Brennan and Blackmun—were willing to adopt a new rule, under which libel claims would be analyzed with an eye to whether the alleged defamation involved "an issue of public or general concern." Justice Black adhered to the view that the guarantee of a free press protects publishers against all libel actions. Justice White argued that, in the absence of actual malice, the First Amendment gives the news media a privilege to report and comment on the official actions of public servants, without sparing from public view the reputation or privacy of an individual involved in or affected by any official action. Justices Marshall, Stewart, and Harlan, by contrast, declared that they would not apply the *Sullivan* actual malice test to private individuals. Justice Douglas did not participate.

Rosenbloom was even more controversial than *Sullivan*, because it suggested that the Court might be on the verge of subjecting a private individual to the rigors of the knowing-or-reckless falsity standard of proof in a libel action merely because the alleged defamation was an issue of general public interest. Consequently, when an article in an ultra-conservative publication allegedly libeled a lawyer representing a family in a tort action against a Chicago police officer, Court watchers were eager to learn if the proposed rule in *Rosenbloom* would supplant *Sullivan*.

On June 4, 1968, Chicago policeman Richard Nuccio shot and killed nineteen-year-old Ronald Nelson. Officer Nuccio was subsequently prosecuted and convicted of second-degree murder for the shooting. Nelson's family retained Elmer Gertz to represent them in two civil lawsuits against Nuccio for damages for wrongful death. At the time he was retained by the Nelsons, Gertz had been practicing law in Illinois for approximately forty years. In addition to his practice, Gertz had written several law-related articles and reviews, presented speeches to the public, and was a member and officer of various legal and community organizations. As counsel for the Nelson family, Gertz attended the coroner's investigation into Nelson's death, but he never made any public statements about the civil cases he had filed on behalf of the family.

Robert Welch, Inc., published a monthly magazine entitled *American Opinion* that espoused the doctrines and viewpoints of an arch-conservative, anticommunist organization known as the John Birch Society. In the early 1960s the John Birch Society had begun to warn of a nationwide conspiracy to discredit local law enforcement agencies and to replace those agencies with a nationwide force capable of supporting a communist dictatorship. By the late 1960s, *American Opinion* was distributed through the John Birch Society's 280 bookstores across the country, in addition to being circulated to its 42,000 subscribers.

In late 1968, *American Opinion* editor Scott Stanley Jr. commissioned freelance writer Alan Stang to write an article about the Nuccio trial. Stanley wanted Stang to learn if the "Nuccio murder trial and the publicity around it were part of a continuing Communist effort to blacken the reputation of America's police officers." Stang submitted the article on February 18, 1969. Stanley edited it and it appeared as the lead article in the March 1969 edition of *American Opinion*, entitled "Frame Up, Richard Nuccio and the War on Police." Among other things, the article branded Gertz a "Leninist" and a "Communist-fronter" who had been an officer in the National Lawyers Guild, which was described as a communist organization that "probably did more than any other outfit to plan the Communist attack on the Chicago police during the 1968 Democratic [Party National] Convention." The article also accused Gertz of signing a petition to abolish the House Committee on Un-American Activities, serving as a pallbearer for Jack Ruby, the man who shot President John Kennedy's assassin Lee Harvey Oswald, and being an official of the Marxist League for Industrial Democracy. The article declared:

> Like millions of other Americans, [Gertz] was watching an organized attempt to discredit our local police—organized primarily by the Communist National Lawyers Guild, preeminent in which is the same Elmer Gertz who now appears as the Nelsons' lawyer.

In addition to appearing in *American Opinion*, some 86,000 copies of the article were reprinted and distributed in Chicago and elsewhere. Gertz learned of the article when he received a reprinted copy.

Gertz filed a libel action against Robert Welch, Inc., in U.S. District Court for the Northern District of Illinois, claiming that Stang's article defamed him by inaccurately linking him with communists, which, in addition to other references, was the equivalent of stating that Gertz was a communist, or amounted to an inference that he was a communist. He claimed that the article injured his reputation as a lawyer and as a citizen. Gertz alleged $10,000 in actual damages and requested punitive damages of $500,000. Welch moved to dismiss the suit, apparently on the ground that Gertz's pleading was inadequate. The court denied the motion and held that it is *libel per se* to falsely label a person a communist.

During *voir dire* in the ensuing trial, the court inquired of all prospective jurors whether they had heard anything about Gertz. All indicated that they were not familiar with Gertz, from which the court concluded that he was not a public figure.

At trial, Stanley testified that he had relied solely on Stang's reputation as an author to support the conclusion that Nuccio's trial was part of the communist war on police. Gertz testified that at no time was he contacted by anyone concerning the research for the article or any of its allegations. Gertz also denied all of the specific defamatory statements about him contained in the article. He testified that he believed in the institution of private property, that most of his practice related to property matters, and that he had never been a Leninist, communist, Marxist or anything similar. During closing argument, counsel for Robert Welch, Inc., admitted that the *American Opinion* accusations against Gertz were untrue.

The trial court submitted the case to the jury with the instructions that Gertz was not a public figure and that the article in *American Opinion* about him was *libel per se*. The jury returned a verdict in Gertz's favor in the sum of $50,000. However, the trial court granted judgment notwithstanding the verdict, on the ground that the article "painted the picture of a conspiratorial war being waged by the Communists against the police in general." It stated that the subject matter of the article was protected by the First Amendment and that, under *Rosenbloom*, "by representing the victim's family in litigation brought against the policeman, Gertz thrust himself into the vortex of this important public controversy." Consequently, the court ruled, Gertz was required to show actual malice: that Stanley knew the statements were false when he allowed them to be printed, or that he had allowed them to be printed with reckless disregard of their truth or falsity. Because Gertz failed to prove such malice, the court entered judgment for Welch.

Gertz appealed to the U.S. Court of Appeals for the Seventh Circuit. It affirmed. The Supreme Court of the United States granted Gertz's petition for a writ of certiorari.

HIGHLIGHTS OF SUPREME COURT ARGUMENTS

BRIEF FOR GERTZ

◆ Gertz is not a public official or a public figure. He did nothing to thrust himself voluntarily into the limelight. This situation results in a direct confrontation between the constitutional rights of freedom of speech and privacy.

◆ Judging Robert Welch, Inc., only on its subjective state of mind when it published the article about Gertz robs Gertz of any real opportunity to redress the harm done to him in violation of his constitutional right of privacy.

◆ Even if Gertz is held to the standard of a public official or public figure, there is sufficient evidence in the record to support a finding of actual malice.

◆ Welch's publication had a threefold effect: It tended to destroy Gertz's reputation as a person and as an attorney; it tended to destroy his ability to properly represent his clients; and it tended to destroy his ability to properly represent other clients who had no involvement with this subject matter.

BRIEF FOR ROBERT WELCH, INC.

◆ Gertz is clearly a public figure within the meaning of _Sullivan._ He is also a public figure because he has been appointed to several jobs closely connected with government. He has acted as a _de facto_ public official by appearing on behalf of the Nelson family and questioning witnesses at the coroner's inquest into the death of Ronald Nelson that led to the prosecution of Officer Nuccio.

◆ The subject of Stang's article in _American Opinion_ is clearly a matter of public interest. It is protected by the _Sullivan_ privilege.

◆ Gertz has failed to satisfy the showing of malice required by _Sullivan._ He has not shown that the publisher actually knew the alleged libel was false before publication or that the publisher entertained serious doubts about the truth of the publication before publishing it.

SUPREME COURT OPINION: 5–4

POWELL, J.

This Court has struggled for nearly a decade to define the proper accommodation between the law of defamation and the freedoms of speech and press protected by the First Amendment. With this decision we return to that effort....

The principal issue in this case is whether a newspaper or broadcaster that publishes defamatory falsehoods about an individual who is neither a public official nor a public figure may claim a constitutional privilege against liability for the injury inflicted by those statements....

We begin with the common ground. Under the First Amendment there is no such thing as a false idea. However pernicious an opinion may seem, we depend for its correction not on the conscience of judges and juries but on the competition of other ideas. But there is no constitutional value in false statements of fact. Neither the intentional lie nor the careless error materially advances society's interest in "uninhibited, robust, and wide-open" debate on public issues. They belong to that category of utterances which "are no essential part of any expo-

sition of ideas, and are of such slight social value as a step to truth that any benefit that may be derived from them is clearly outweighed by the social interest in order and morality." _Chaplinsky v. New Hampshire._

Although the erroneous statement of fact is not worthy of constitutional protection, it is nevertheless inevitable in free debate.... And punishment of error runs the risk of inducing a cautious and restrictive exercise of the constitutionally guaranteed freedoms of speech and press. Our decisions recognize that a rule of strict liability that compels a publisher or broadcaster to guarantee the accuracy of his factual assertions may lead to intolerable self-censorship. Allowing the media to avoid liability only by proving the truth of all injurious statements does not accord adequate protection to First Amendment liberties....

The need to avoid self-censorship by the news media is, however, not the only societal value at issue. If it were, this Court would have embraced long ago the view that publishers and broadcasters enjoy an unconditional and indefeasible immunity from liability for defamation....

The legitimate state interest underlying the law of libel is the compensation of individuals for the harm inflicted on them by defamatory falsehood.... Some tension necessarily exists between the need for a vigorous and uninhibited press and the legitimate interest in redressing wrongful injury....

The [*Sullivan*] standard defines the level of constitutional protection appropriate to the context of defamation of a public person. For the reasons stated below, [however], we conclude that the state interest in compensating injury to the reputation of private individuals requires that a different rule should obtain with respect to them.... [Although] it is often true that not all of the considerations which justify adoption of a given rule will obtain in each particular case decided under its authority, ... we have no difficulty in distinguishing among defamation plaintiffs.

The first remedy of any victim of defamation is self-help—using available opportunities to contradict the lie or correct the error and thereby to minimize its adverse impact on reputation. Public officials and public figures usually enjoy significantly greater access to the channels of effective communication and hence have a more realistic opportunity to counteract false statements than private individuals normally enjoy. Private individuals are therefore more vulnerable to injury, and the state interest in protecting them is correspondingly greater....

[T]he communications media are entitled to act on the assumption that public officials and public figures have voluntarily exposed themselves to increased risk of injury from defamatory falsehood concerning them. No such assumption is jus-tified with respect to a private individual.... [P]rivate individuals are not only more vulnerable to injury than public officials and public figures; they are also more deserving of recovery.

For these reasons we conclude that the States should retain substantial latitude in their efforts to enforce a legal remedy for defamatory falsehood injurious to the reputation of a private individual....

We hold that, so long as they do not impose liability without fault, the States may define for themselves the appropriate standard of liability for a publisher or broadcaster of defamatory falsehood injurious to a private individual. This approach provides a more equitable boundary between the competing concerns involved here. It recognizes the strength of the legitimate state interest in compensating private individuals for wrongful injury to reputation, yet shields the press and broadcast media from the rigors of strict liability for defamation....

Our accommodation of the competing values at stake in defamation suits by private individuals allows the States to impose liability on the publisher or broadcaster of defamatory falsehood on a less demanding showing than that required by [*Sullivan*]. This conclusion is not based on a belief that the considerations which prompted the adoption of the [*Sullivan*] privilege for defamation of public officials and its extension to public figures are wholly inapplicable to the context of private individuals. Rather, we endorse this approach in recognition of the strong and legitimate state interest in compensating private individuals for injury to reputation.

But this countervailing state interest extends no further than compensation for actual injury.... [W]e hold that the States may not permit recovery of presumed or punitive damages, at least when liability is not based on a showing of knowledge of falsity or reckless disregard for the truth.... We need not define "actual injury," as trial courts have wide experience in framing appropriate jury instructions in tort actions....

Respondent's characterization of petitioner as a public figure raises a different question. That designation may rest on either of two alternative bases. In some instances an individual may achieve such pervasive fame or notoriety that he becomes a public figure for all purposes and in all contexts. More commonly, an individual voluntarily injects himself or is drawn into a particular public controversy and thereby becomes a public figure for a limited range of issues. In either case such persons assume special prominence in the resolution of public questions....

We would not lightly assume that a citizen's participation in community and professional affairs rendered him a public figure for all purposes. Absent clear evidence of general fame or notoriety in the community, and pervasive involvement in the affairs of society, an individual should not be deemed a public personality for all aspects of his life. It is preferable to reduce the public-figure question to a more meaningful context by looking to the nature and extent of an individual's participation in the particular controversy giving rise to the defamation.

In this context it is plain that petitioner was not a public figure. He played a minimal role at the coroner's inquest, and his participation related solely to his representation of a private client. He took no part in the criminal prosecution of Officer Nuccio. Moreover, he never discussed either the criminal or civil litigation with the press and was never quoted as having

done so. He plainly did not thrust himself into the vortex of this public issue, nor did he engage the public's attention in an attempt to influence its outcome. We are persuaded that the trial court did not err in refusing to characterize petitioner as a public figure for the purpose of this litigation.

We therefore conclude that the [*Sullivan*] standard is inapplicable to this case and that the trial court erred in entering judgment for respondent. Because the jury was allowed to impose liability without fault and was permitted to presume damages without proof of injury, a new trial is necessary. We reverse and remand for further proceedings in accord with this opinion.

It is ordered.

BLACKMUN, J., CONCURRING

... The Court ... seeks today to strike a balance between competing values where necessarily uncertain assumptions about human behavior color the result. Although the Court's opinion in the present case departs from the rationale of the *Rosenbloom* [*v. Metromedia, Inc.*, 403 U.S. 29 (1971)] plurality, in that the Court now conditions a libel action by a private person upon a showing of negligence, as contrasted with a showing of willful or reckless disregard, I am willing to join, and do join, the Court's opinion and its judgment for two reasons:

1. By removing the specters of presumed and punitive damages in the absence of [*Sullivan*] malice, the Court eliminates significant and powerful motives for self-censorship that otherwise are present in the traditional libel action. By so doing, the Court leaves what should prove to be sufficient and adequate breathing space for a vigorous press. What the Court has done, I believe,

will have little, if any, practical effect on the functioning of responsible journalism.

2. The Court was sadly fractionated in *Rosenbloom*. A result of that kind inevitably leads to uncertainty. I feel that it is of profound importance for the Court to come to rest in the defamation area and to have a clearly defined majority position that eliminates the unsureness engendered by *Rosenbloom*'s diversity. If my vote were not needed to create a majority, I would adhere to my prior view. A definitive ruling, however, is paramount....

BURGER, C.J., DISSENTING

... The petitioner here was performing a professional representative role as an advocate in the highest tradition of the law, and under that tradition the advocate is not to be invidiously identified with his client. The important public policy which underlies this tradition—the right to counsel—would be gravely jeopardized if every lawyer who takes an "unpopular" case, civil or criminal, would automatically become fair game for irresponsible reporters and editors who might, for example, describe the lawyer as a "mob mouthpiece" for representing a client with a serious prior criminal record, or as an "ambulance chaser" for representing a claimant in a personal injury action.

I would reverse the judgment of the Court of Appeals and remand for reinstatement of the verdict of the jury and the entry of an appropriate judgment on that verdict.

DOUGLAS, J., DISSENTING

... I have stated before my view that the First Amendment would bar Congress from passing any libel law.... With the First Amendment made applicable to the States through the Fourteenth, I do not see how States have any more ability to "accommodate" freedoms of speech or of the press than does Congress....

There can be no doubt that a State impinges upon free and open discussion when it sanctions the imposition of damages for such discussion through its civil libel laws.... Since in my view the First and Fourteenth Amendments prohibit the imposition of damages upon respondent for this discussion of public affairs, I would affirm the judgment below.

BRENNAN, J., DISSENTING

I agree with the conclusion ... that, at the time of publication of respondent's article, petitioner could not properly have been viewed as either a "public official" or "public figure"; instead, respondent's article, dealing with an alleged conspiracy to discredit local police forces, concerned petitioner's purported involvement in "an event of 'public or general interest.'" *Rosenbloom v. Metromedia, Inc.*, 403 U.S. 29 (1971). I cannot agree, however, that free and robust debate—so essential to the proper functioning of our system of government—is permitted adequate "breathing space," *NAACP v. Button*, 371 U.S. 415 (1963), when, as the Court holds, the States may impose all but strict liability for defamation if the defamed party is a private person and "the substance of the defamatory statement makes substantial danger to reputation apparent." I adhere to my view expressed in *Rosenbloom v. Metromedia, Inc.*, that we strike the proper accommodation between avoidance of media self-censorship and protection of individual reputations only when we require States to apply the *New York Times Co. v. Sullivan* knowing-or-reckless-falsity standard in civil libel actions concerning media reports of the involvement of private individuals in events of public or general interest....

WHITE, J., DISSENTING

... The Court proceeds as though it were writing on *tabula rasa* and suggests that it must mediate between two unacceptable choices—on the one hand, the rigors of the [*Sullivan*] rule which the Court thinks would give insufficient recognition to the interest of the private plaintiff, and, on the other hand, the prospect of imposing "liability without fault" on the press and others who are charged with defamatory utterances. Totally ignoring history and settled First Amendment law, the Court purports to arrive at an "equitable compromise," rejecting both what it considers faultless liability and [*Sullivan*] malice, but insisting on some intermediate degree of fault. Of course, the Court necessarily discards the contrary judgment arrived at in the 50 States that the reputation interest of the private citizen is deserving of considerably more protection.

The Court evinces a deep-seated antipathy to "liability without fault." But this catch-phrase has no talismanic significance and is almost meaningless in this context where the Court appears to be addressing those libels and slanders that are defamatory on their face and where the publisher is no doubt aware from the nature of the material that it would be inherently damaging to reputation. He publishes notwithstanding, knowing that he will inflict injury. With this knowledge, he must intend to inflict that injury, his excuse being that he is privileged to do so—that he has published the truth. But as it turns out, what he has circulated to the public is a very damaging falsehood. Is he nevertheless "faultless"? Perhaps it

can be said that the mistake about his defense was made in good faith, but the fact remains that it is he who launched the publication knowing that it could ruin a reputation....

With a flourish of the pen, the Court also discards the prevailing rule in libel and slander actions that punitive damages may be awarded on the classic grounds of common-law malice, that is, "(a)ctual malice in the sense of ill will or fraud or reckless indifference to consequences."... In its stead, the Court requires defamation plaintiffs to show intentional falsehood or reckless disregard for the truth or falsity of the publication. The Court again complains about substantial verdicts and the possibility of press self-censorship, saying that punitive damages are merely "private fines levied by civil juries to punish reprehensible conduct and to deter its future occurrence." But I see no constitutional difference between publishing with reckless disregard for the truth, where punitive damages will be permitted, and negligent publication where they will not be allowed. It is difficult to understand what is constitutionally wrong with assessing punitive damages to deter a publisher from departing from those standards of care ordinarily followed in the publishing industry, particularly if common-law malice is also shown....

For my part, I would require something more substantial than an undifferentiated fear of unduly burdensome punitive damages awards before retooling the established common-law rule and depriving the States of the opportunity to experiment with different methods for guarding against abuses....

I would reverse the judgment of the Court of Appeals and reinstate the jury's verdict.

QUESTIONS

1. State the rule of *Gertz*. Then review the dissents of Chief Justice Burger, Justice Brennan, and Justice White. Could Justice Powell have framed the *Gertz* rule in a way that would have won the support of any of the dissenters?

2. One of Welch's arguments to the Supreme Court was as follows:

   > Attorneys do not have to take every case that comes their way. Certainly an attorney who takes on a notorious case with political overtones is well aware (especially if like Gertz he has had past famous trials) that he is likely to be associated with the political philosophy (but not necessarily the conduct) of those he represents. Is this not fair comment to be expected, especially if an attorney continues to represent notorious clients of one political persuasion?

   To what extent does Chief Justice Burger respond to this argument in his dissent in *Gertz*?

3. To what extent does *Gertz* modify *Sullivan*? Does *Gertz* make it more or less difficult for plaintiffs in libel actions to prove their case?

4. *Gertz* appears to mark the Court's rejection of the plurality rule in *Rosenbloom v. Metromedia, Inc.*, 403 U.S. 29 (1971). What factors might account for the shift in the Court's perspective in the three years between 1971 and 1974?

5. Law professor Robert C. Post contends: "An important weakness of *Gertz* is that it never explained why the Constitution should preempt common-law defamation doctrine as applied to all cases involving private plaintiffs" (Kermit L. Hall, ed., *The Oxford Companion to the Supreme Court of the United States* [New York, NY: Oxford University Press, 1992], p. 337). Is Post correct?

COMMENT

Litigation continued after *Gertz* to clarify further the meaning of "public figure." The following cases indicate the Court's refinements between *Gertz* and *Hustler Magazine v. Falwell*, 485 U.S. 46 (1988), the libel decision excerpted next.

Case: *Time, Inc. v. Firestone*, 424 U.S. 448 (1976)

Vote: 5–3 (Stevens, J., did not participate.)

Decision: The wife of a member of a wealthy industrial family involved in divorce litigation is not a public figure merely because she has a famous name. Mrs. Firestone does not occupy "[a role] of especial prominence in the affairs of society," and has not been "thrust ... to the forefront of particular public controversies in order to influence the resolution of the issues involved."

Case: *Hutchinson v. Proxmire*, 443 U.S. 111 (1979)

Vote: 8–1

Decision: A research director and professor who received federal funding to conduct animal studies with the goal of objective measurement of aggression is not a public figure so as to make the actual malice standard of proof of *New York Times Co. v. Sullivan* applicable in a lawsuit against a U.S. Senator who presented him with a "Golden Fleece Award." Those charged with alleged defamation cannot, by their conduct, create their own defense by making someone into a public figure when the defamation victim responds in the press.

Case: *Wolston v. Reader's Digest Assn., Inc.*, 443 U.S. 157 (1979)

Vote: 8–1

Decision: A private individual is not automatically transformed into a public figure by becoming involved in or associated with a matter that attracts public attention. The mere fact that a person refuses to appear before a grand jury to testify concerning a matter in which he played only a minor role does not make him a public figure. Neither does his subsequent conviction for contempt.

Case: *Dun & Bradstreet, Inc. v. Greenmoss Builders*, 472 U.S. 749 (1985)

Vote: 5–4

Decision: The "actual malice" rule does not apply in nonmedia defamation actions such as a flawed credit report because such a report involves purely private concerns and hence is entitled to less First Amendment protection than speech involving public concerns. "There is simply no credible argument that this type of credit reporting requires special protection to ensure that 'debate on public issues [will] be uninhibited, robust, and wide-open.'"

Case: *Philadelphia Newspapers, Inc. v. Hepps*, 475 U.S. 767 (1986)

Vote: 5–4

Decision: Where a newspaper publishes speech of public concern, such as organized crime, about a private figure, the private-figure plaintiff cannot recover damages for libel without also showing that the statements are false. To ensure that speech on matters of public concern is not deterred, the common-law presumption that defamatory speech is false cannot stand.

LIBEL

Hustler Magazine v. Falwell
485 U.S. 46 (1988)

SETTING

The Court's reaffirmation in *Gertz* of the "actual malice" standard for public officials and public figures in libel cases did not stem the tide of libel litigation spawned by its 1964 decision in *New York Times v. Sullivan*. As it had in *Rosenbloom v. Metromedia*, 403 U.S. 29 (1971), the Court in *Dun & Bradstreet, Inc. v. Greenmoss Builders*, 472 U.S. 749 (1985) (see above) again suggested that whether alleged defamation affected an area of public interest or public concern would determine a plaintiff's level of proof in libel cases. Three years after *Dun & Bradstreet*, one of the nation's most well-known public and political figures, The Reverend Jerry Falwell, further complicated legal issues involving libel litigation by combining an action for libel with a claim for the tort of intentional infliction of emotional distress. In so doing, Falwell raised the question of whether a public figure may recover damages for intentional infliction of emotional distress without meeting the actual malice standard for libel.

Falwell, who became a "born-again" Christian in 1952 while a student at Lynchburg College, started his career as a religious broadcaster. In 1979, Falwell joined with other prominent conservatives and fellow evangelists to create a political organization known as the Moral Majority. The Moral Majority, Inc., targets what the organization believes to be five major sins: abortion, homosexuality, pornography, humanism, and the fractured family. By 1985, Falwell was unquestionably a public figure, with daily religious broadcasts on over 500 radio stations, 392 television stations, and 10,000 cable television stations.

Larry Flynt's career took a decidedly different path. Flynt once worked on an assembly line at a General Motors plant, but his goal always was to open a string of "Hustler" strip-bars. His Magazine, *Hustler*, began as the in-house newsletter for those enterprises and by 1983 had a monthly publication of over 2.5 million, generating annual revenues of over $20 million. Flynt was paralyzed from the waist down by a would-be assassin in 1978 and ran for president in 1984 as "A Smut Peddler Who Cares." Flynt declared that "I am running as a Republican rather than as a Democrat, because I am wealthy, white, pornographic, and like the nuclear-mad cowboy, Ronnie Reagan, I have been shot for what I believe in."

The November 1983 issue of *Hustler* magazine carried a parody of an advertisement for Campari Liqueur. Campari ads featured celebrities talking about the "first time" they tasted Campari. Jerry Falwell was the featured celebrity in the *Hustler* parody. The parody implied that Falwell's "first time" was during a drunken incestuous rendezvous with his mother in an outhouse. At the bottom of the page was the statement, "AD PARODY—NOT TO BE TAKEN SERIOUSLY."

Falwell did take the ad seriously, however. He filed a diversity action against Flynt in the U.S. District Court for the Western District of Virginia alleging libel, invasion of privacy, and intentional infliction of emotional distress. The district court granted Flynt's motion for a directed verdict on the invasion of privacy claim. The jury found against Falwell on the libel claim, but awarded him $100,000 in compensatory damages and $50,000 in punitive damages on the intentional infliction of emotional distress claim.

The U.S. Court of Appeals for the Fourth Circuit affirmed. It rejected Flynt's argument that the "actual malice" standard of *New York Times v. Sullivan* must be met before Falwell could recover for emotional distress. According to the court of appeals, *Sullivan* emphasized the constitutional importance not of the falsity of the statement or the defendant's disregard for

Hustler magazine publisher Larry Flynt, speaking to reporters at a press conference in 1988, holds a copy of the ad parody that portrayed the Reverend Jerry Falwell as an incestuous drunk. (*Norman Currie/Corbis-Bettmann.*)

the truth, but of the heightened level of culpability embodied in the requirement of "knowing ... or reckless" conduct. It held that the *Sullivan* standard was satisfied by the jury's finding that Flynt had acted intentionally or recklessly. The Supreme Court of the United States granted Flynt's petition for a writ of certiorari.

HIGHLIGHTS OF SUPREME COURT ARGUMENTS

BRIEF FOR *HUSTLER* MAGAZINE AND FLYNT

◆ The First Amendment protects opinion and rhetorical hyperbole. The test that requires that a publication be reasonably understood as describing actual facts about a plaintiff or events which the plaintiff participated applies as a matter of constitutional law to emotional distress claims.

◆ Humor such as that contained in the advertising parody is a typical form of expression of political opinion. Far from being an instrument designed to cause severe emotional harm to a political figure, humor is a means by which political combat is restricted.

◆ The *Sullivan* test is not satisfied by a showing that the publisher intended to cause harm. The test requires knowing or reckless falsity by the publisher. *Sullivan* applies to all claims of injurious falsehood that seek to impose civil liability on critical commentary about public figures. The ad parody was not published with knowing or reckless falsity. Indeed, the ad made no statement of fact whatsoever.

◆ Falwell's evidence of emotional distress was that he was angry and "felt like weeping" when he saw the ad parody. To permit Falwell to recover damages on that evidence is to invite all public figures and public officials to fabricate vague claims of emotional upset in order to recover for unkind language that would not qualify as libelous.

AMICUS CURIAE BRIEFS SUPPORTING *HUSTLER* MAGAZINE

Joint brief of the American Civil Liberties Union Foundation, American Civil Liberties Union of Virginia, CBS, Inc., Capital Cities/ABC, Inc., National Broadcasting Company, Inc., and National Association of Broadcasters; joint brief of Association of American Editorial Cartoonists, Authors League of America, and Mark Russell; Association of American Publishers; Home Box Office, Inc.; Reporters Committee for Freedom of the Press; Richmond Newspapers, Inc.; Volunteer Lawyers for the Arts, Inc.; Law & Humanities Institute.

BRIEF FOR FALWELL

◆ The tort of intentional infliction of emotional distress serves to protect important state interests that are different from the reputational damage protected by libel law. That "actual malice" standard should not be applied to other torts and especially not to those torts for which a false statement of fact is irrelevant.

◆ The policies and interests that underlie the protection against intentional infliction of emotional distress must be balanced against those countervailing considerations of free speech and robust debate. It is the result of the balancing test that will determine the appropriate degree of constitutional protection available in this case.

◆ The state has a substantial interest in preventing intentional infliction of emotional distress. That interest outweighs whatever dubious value Flynt's outrageous publications may possess.

◆ Courts have long recognized that a claim for intentional infliction of emotional distress states a cause of action independent and distinct from both libel and invasion of privacy. Although the two claims do have some overlapping characteristics, they are separate claims. For example, falsity is an essential feature of a libel claim but it is not an element of the claim for intentional infliction of emotional distress.

SUPREME COURT DECISION: 8–0

(Kennedy, J., did not participate.)

REHNQUIST, C.J.

... This case presents us with a novel question involving First Amendment limitations upon a State's authority to protect its citizens from the intentional infliction of emotional distress. We must decide whether a public figure may recover damages for emotional harm caused by the publication of an ad parody offensive to him, and doubtless gross and repugnant in the eyes of most. Respondent would have us find that a State's interest in protecting public figures from emotional distress is sufficient to deny First Amendment protection to speech that is patently offensive and is intended to inflict emotional injury, even when that speech could not reasonably have been interpreted as stating actual facts about the public figure involved. This we decline to do.

At the heart of the First Amendment is the recognition of the fundamental importance of the free flow of ideas and opinions on matters of public interest and concern.... We have therefore been particularly vigilant to ensure that individual expressions of ideas remain free from governmentally imposed sanctions....

The sort of robust political debate encouraged by the First Amendment is bound to produce speech that is critical of those who hold public office or those public figures who are "intimately involved in the resolution of important public questions or, by reason of their fame, shape events in areas of concern to society at large." *Associated Press v. Walker*, decided with *Curtis Publishing Co. v. Butts*, 388 U.S. 130 (1967).... Such criticism, inevitably, will not always be reasoned or moderate; public figures as well as public officials will be subject to "vehement, caustic, and sometimes unpleasantly sharp attacks," *New York Times [v. Sullivan]*....

Of course, this does not mean that any speech about a public figure is immune from sanction in the form of damages. Since *New York Times Co. v. Sullivan*, we have consistently ruled that a public figure may hold a speaker liable for the damage to reputation caused by publication of a defamatory falsehood, but only if the state-

ment was made "with knowledge that it was false or with reckless disregard of whether it was false or not." Id. False statements of fact are particularly valueless; they interfere with the truth-seeking function of the marketplace of ideas, and they cause damage to an individual's reputation that cannot easily be repaired by counter-speech, however persuasive or effective.... But even though falsehoods have little value in and of themselves, they are "nevertheless inevitable in free debate," [*Gertz v. Welch*], and a rule that would impose strict liability on a publisher for false factual assertions would have an undoubted "chilling" effect on speech relating to public figures that does have constitutional value....

Respondent argues, however, that a different standard should apply in this case because here the State seeks to prevent not reputational damage, but the severe emotional distress suffered by the person who is the subject of an offensive publication.... In respondent's view, and in the view of the Court of Appeals, so long as the utterance was intended to inflict emotional distress, was outrageous, and did in fact inflict serious emotional distress, it is of no constitutional import whether the statement was a fact or an opinion, or whether it was true or false. It is the intent to cause injury that is the gravamen of the tort, and the State's interest in preventing emotional harm simply outweighs whatever interest a speaker may have in speech of this type.

Generally speaking the law does not regard the intent to inflict emotional distress as one which should receive much solicitude, and it is quite understandable that most if not all jurisdictions have chosen to make it civilly culpable where the conduct in question is sufficiently "outrageous." But in the world of debate about public affairs, many things done with motives that are less than admirable are protected by the First Amendment....

Respondent contends, however, that the caricature in question here was so "outrageous" as to distinguish it from more traditional political cartoons. There is no doubt that the caricature of respondent and his mother published in *Hustler* is at best a distant cousin of the political cartoons described above, and a rather poor relation at that. If it were possible by laying down a principled standard to separate the one from the other, public discourse would probably suffer little or no harm. But we doubt that there is any such standard, and we are quite sure that the pejorative description "outrageous" does not supply one. "Outrageousness" in the area of political and social discourse has an inherent subjectiveness about it which would allow a jury to impose liability on the basis of the jurors' tastes or views, or perhaps on the basis of their dislike of a particular expression. An "outrageousness" standard thus runs afoul of our longstanding refusal to allow damages to be awarded because the speech in question may have an adverse emotional impact on the audience....

We conclude that public figures and public officials may not recover for the tort of intentional infliction of emotional distress by reason of publications such as the one here at issue without showing in addition that the publication contains a false statement of fact which was made with "actual malice," i.e., with knowledge that the statement was false or with reckless disregard as to whether or not it was true. This is not merely a "blind application" of the *New York Times* standard, ... it reflects our considered judgment that such a standard is necessary to give adequate "breathing space" to the freedoms protected by the First Amendment.

Here it is clear that respondent Falwell is a "public figure" for purposes of First Amendment law. The jury found against respondent on his libel claim when it decided that the *Hustler* ad parody could not "reasonably be understood as describing actual facts about [respondent] or actual events in which [he] participated." The Court of Appeals interpreted the jury's finding to be that the ad parody "was not reasonably believable," and in accordance with our custom we accept this finding. Respondent is thus relegated to his claim for damages awarded by the jury for the intentional infliction of emotional distress by "outrageous" conduct. But for reasons heretofore stated this claim cannot, consistently with the First Amendment, form a basis for the award of damages when the conduct in question is the publication of a caricature such as the ad parody involved here. The judgment of the Court of Appeals is accordingly

Reversed.

WHITE, J., CONCURRING IN THE JUDGMENT

As I see it, the decision in *New York Times Co. v. Sullivan* has little to do with this case, for here the jury found that the ad contained no assertion of fact. But I agree with the Court that the judgment below, which penalized the publication of the parody, cannot be squared with the First Amendment.

QUESTIONS

1. How, if at all, does the Court's opinion in *Hustler Magazine* add to the doctrine of libel developed in previous cases? Does *Hustler* stand for the proposition that a public official or public figure can-

not recover for intentional infliction of emotional distress resulting from a publication unless he or she could also recover for libel?

2. Counsel for Flynt stated in his brief: "It is not only the *Hustler* Magazines of this world which will be threatened if [Jerry Falwell] is allowed to prevail.... The decision below is a dangerous one in a society which values wide-open debate" Why might it have been of tactical importance in this instance to link the rights of *Hustler* magazine with those of other publications? How does parody contribute to wide-open debate?

3. During oral argument, the following exchange took place between Justice Scalia and Alan Isaacman, attorney for *Hustler* Magazine:

> SCALIA. The rule you give us says that, if you stand for public office or become a public figure in any way, you cannot protect yourself, or, indeed, your mother....
>
> ISAACMAN. ... George Washington [is] an example—there's a cartoon in, I think it's in the [C]artoonists' [S]ociety brief—that has George Washington being led on a donkey, and underneath there's a caption that so and so who's leading the donkey is leading this ass, or something to that effect.
>
> SCALIA. I can handle that. I think George could handle that. But it's a far cry from committing incest with your mother in an outhouse. I mean, there's no line between the two? We can't protect that kind of parody and not protect this?

Justice Scalia's questions suggest that he disagreed with Isaacman, yet he joined the majority in *Hustler*. What principles account for the unanimity in *Hustler Magazine*?

4. Reflecting on the muddled state of the constitutional law of libel, a 1988 report from the Annenberg Washington Program advocated that libel lawsuits be prohibited if a complaint resulted in a retraction or an opportunity to reply in print or over the air. If the complainant was not provided the opportunity to respond, the Annenberg Report suggested, either side could ask a court for a declaratory judgment about the truth or falsity of the statement. Is the Annenberg proposal a viable alternative to the "actual malice" and "public figure" tests?

COMMENT

Hustler Magazine did not end the Court's struggle to resolve the constitutional issues involving the law of libel. The following summaries indicate the various doctrinal directions the justices have followed since 1988.

Case: *Harte-Hanks Communications, Inc. v. Connaughton*, 491 U.S. 657 (1989)
Vote: 9–0

Decision: A showing that a publisher engaged in "highly unreasonable conduct constituting an extreme departure from the standards of investigation and reporting ordinarily adhered to by responsible publishers" cannot alone support a verdict in favor of a public figure plaintiff in a libel action. A plaintiff who is a public figure must prove by clear and convincing evidence that the defendant published the false and defamatory material with actual malice, i.e., with knowledge of falsity or with a reckless disregard for the truth.

Case: *Milkovich v. Lorain Journal Co.*, 497 U.S. 1 (1990)

Vote: 7–2

Decision: The First Amendment does not require a separate "opinion" privilege limiting the application of state defamation laws. The breathing space that freedoms of expression require to survive is adequately secured by existing constitutional doctrine. Simply couching a statement—"Jones is a liar"—in terms of opinion—"In my opinion Jones is a liar"—does not dispel the factual implications contained in the statement. An allegation that a former high school wrestling coach perjured himself at an investigatory hearing is sufficiently factual that it is susceptible to being proved true or false and might permit defamation recovery.

Case: *Masson v. New Yorker Magazine, Inc.* 501 U.S. 496 (1991)

Vote: 7–2

Decision: The First Amendment requires that a public figure prove by clear and convincing evidence that the defendant published the defamatory statement with actual malice. However, in place of the term "actual malice," it is better practice that jury instructions refer to publication of a statement with knowledge of falsity or reckless disregard as to truth or falsity. A deliberate alteration of words in six passages does not equate with knowledge of falsity for purposes of *New York Times Co. v. Sullivan* and *Gertz v. Robert Welch, Inc.*, unless it results in a material change in the statement's meaning.

SUGGESTIONS FOR FURTHER READING

Adler, Renata, *Reckless Disregard:* Westmoreland v. CBS, et al.; Sharon v. Time (New York, NY: Vintage Books, 1988).

Anderson, David A., "Libel and Press Self-Censorship," 53 *Texas Law Review* (1975): 422.

Dennis, Everette, and Eli Noam, *The Costs of Libel* (New York, NY: Columbia University Press, 1989).

Dorsen, Harriette K., "Satiric Appropriation and the Law of Libel, Trademark, and Copyright: Remedies without Wrongs," 65 *Buffalo University Law Review* (1985): 923.

Eaton, Joel D., "The American Law of Defamation through *Gertz v. Robert Welch, Inc.* and Beyond: An Analytical Primer," 61 *Virginia Law Review* (1975): 1349.

Epstein, Richard A., "Was *New York Times v. Sullivan* Wrong?" 53 *University of Chicago Law Review* (1986): 782.

Forer, Louis G., *A Chilling Effect: The Mounting Threat of Libel and Invasion of Privacy Action to the First Amendment* (New York, NY: W. W. Norton, 1987).

Franklin, Mark, "Constitutional Libel Law: The Role of Content," 34 *UCLA Law Review* (1987): 1657.

Gertz, Elmer, Gertz v. Robert Welch, Inc.: *The Story of a Landmark Libel Case* (Carbondale, IL: Southern Illinois University Press, 1992).

Gillmour, Donald, *Power, Publicity and the Abuse of Libel Law* (New York, NY: Oxford University Press, 1992).

Givelber, Daniel, "The Right to Minimum Social Decency and the Limits of Evenhandedness: Intentional Infliction of Emotional Distress by Outrageous Conduct," 82 *Columbia Law Review* (1982): 42.

Hentoff, Nat, *Free Speech for Me—But Not for Thee: How the American Left and Right Relentlessly Censor Each Other* (New York, NY: Harper, 1991).

Irons, Peter, *The Courage of Their Convictions: Sixteen Americans Who Fought Their Way to the Supreme Court* (New York, NY: Penguin, 1990), Chapter 14.

Kalven, Harry, "The *New York Times* Case: A Report on 'The Central Meaning of the First Amendment,'" *The Supreme Court Review* (Chicago, IL: University of Chicago Press, 1964).

Kreutzer, Jan Kipp, "Defamation: Problems with Applying Traditional Standards to Non-Traditional Cases—Satire, Fiction and 'Fictionalization,'" 11 *Northern Kentucky Law Review* (1984): 131.

Lewis, Anthony, *Make No Law: The Sullivan Case and the First Amendment* (New York, NY: Random House, 1991).

Lovell, Colin Rhys, "The 'Reception' of Defamation by the Common Law," 15 *Vanderbilt Law Review* (1962): 1051.

Matheson, Scott M., Jr., "Procedure in Public Person Defamation Cases: The Impact of the First Amendment," 66 *Texas Law Review* (1987): 215.

Mead, Terrance C., "Suing Media for Emotional Distress: A Multi-Method Analysis of Tort Law Evolution," 23 *Washburn Law Journal* (1983): 24.

Nelson, Harold L., "Seditious Libel in Colonial America," 3 *American Journal of Legal History* (1959): 160.

Noel, Dix W., "Defamation of Public Officials and Candidates," 49 *Columbia Law Review* (1949): 875.

Note: "First Amendment Limits on Tort Liability for Words Intended to Inflict Severe Emotional Distress," 85 *Columbia Law Review* (1985): 1749.

Pound, Roscoe, "Equitable Relief against Defamation and Injuries to Personality," 29 *Harvard Law Review* (1916): 640.

Prosser, William, "Privacy," 48 *California Law Review* (1960): 383.

Rosenberg, Norman L., *Protecting the Best Men: An Interpretive History of the Law of Libel* (Chapel Hill, NC: University of North Carolina Press, 1986).

Smolla, Rodney A., "Let the Author Beware: The Rejuvenation of the American Law of Libel," 132 *University of Pennsylvania Law Review* (1983): 1.

_____, *Suing the Press: Libel, the Media & Power* (New York, NY: Oxford University Press, 1986).

_____, *Jerry Falwell v. Larry Flynt: The First Amendment on Trial* (Urbana, IL: University of Illinois Press, 1990).

Van Alstyne, William, "First Amendment Limitations on Recovery from the Press," 25 *William & Mary Law Review* (1984): 793.

Veeder, Van Vechter, "The History and Theory of the Law of Defamation," 3 *Columbia Law Review* (1903): 546.

Wade, John W., "Defamation and the Right of Privacy," 15 *Vanderbilt Law Review* (1962): 1093.

OBSCENITY

Roth v. United States
354 U.S. 476 (1957)

SETTING

Obscenity is the term usually applied to acts, writings, utterances, or depictions that offend the sense of morality. Despite the libertarian language of the First Amendment, obscenity has never been regarded as enjoying First Amendment protection and has been subject to control by the states in the exercise of their so-called police powers, which is the inherent power of the state to regulate on behalf of the public health, safety, welfare, and morals.

For hundreds of years, moral consensus about proper human behavior made it unnecessary for the states to regulate obscenity. The first reported obscenity case in the United States did not arise until 1815, and involved a picture of a nude couple. A Pennsylvania court held that it was an offense under common law to exhibit the picture for profit. *Commonwealth v. Sharpless*, 2 Serg. & Rawle 91 (1815).

The reign of Queen Victoria in England, 1837–1901, was a time regarded by some as an era of high moral standards and by others as an era of intolerable prudishness. During Queen Victoria's reign, laws restricting the dissemination of obscene materials became more commonplace in England and in the United States, because American courts frequently looked to their English counterparts for legal guidance. In 1857, for example, Parliament enacted Lord Campbell's Act, which authorized English magistrates to seize "works written for the single purpose of corrupting the morals of youth and of a nature calculated to shock the common feelings of decency in a well regulated mind." In 1868, the first case involving application of Lord Campbell's Act went to trial in England. The case involved a pamphlet that had been published by an anti-Catholic group that was trying to get Protestants elected to Parliament. The pamphlet was entitled "The Confessional Unmasked: Showing the Depravity of the Roman Priesthood, The Iniquity of the Confessional and The Questions Put to Females in Confession." Chief Justice Alexander Cockburn ordered the pamphlet destroyed because it was obscene. Cockburn wrote: "I think the test of obscenity is this, whether the tendency of the matter charged as obscenity is to deprave and corrupt those whose minds are open to such immoral influences, and into whose hands a publication of this sort may fall." *Queen v. Hicklin*, 3 L.R.-Q.B. 360 (1868). The *Hicklin* test embodied Victorian morality.

The quest for moral purity in the United States during the Victorian era was headed by the New York Society for the Suppression of Vice. In the 1860s, that organization began agitating for government censorship of writings that it considered obscene. The Society's charismatic leader was Anthony Comstock, a Civil War veteran who was nominally employed as a clerk in a dry goods store but whose real calling was moral crusader. Comstock single-handedly made obscenity an American political issue. In 1872, he formed an alliance with Morris K. Jesup, president of the Young Men's Christian Association. In December 1872, with Jesup's backing, the twenty-eight-year-old Comstock traveled to Washington, D.C., to lobby Congress to pass a bill drafted by Supreme Court Justice William Strong. The bill became law in 1873. Known popularly as the Comstock Act, the statute provided, in part,

> That no obscene, lewd or lascivious book, pamphlet, picture, paper, print or other publication of an indecent character, or any article or thing designed or intended for the prevention of conception or procuring of abortion ... shall be carried in the mail.

The constitutionality of the Comstock Act was challenged in 1878. In *Ex parte Jackson*, 96 U.S. 727 (1878), the Supreme Court unanimously upheld it. Justice Field's opinion relied on the definition of obscenity that was used in *Queen v. Hicklin*.

Comstock was subsequently appointed a special agent of the Post Office Department. In that capacity, he banned a number of fictional works and sought prosecutions of those who disseminated contraceptive information and nonphysicians, such as midwives, who performed abortions. In contrast to the very few obscenity cases tried in state courts before 1870, there were more than a dozen such prosecutions between 1870 and 1890. Federal prosecutions also proliferated. By the turn of the century, most American courts—state and federal—had adopted the *Hicklin* standard. *Hicklin* is often called an "effects" test because it defines obscenity as material that has the effect of corrupting those in society most susceptible to corruption. The *Hicklin* test was not without its critics, however. Cousins Learned Hand and

Augustus N. Hand, two widely respected federal judges, led the attack on the *Hicklin* test. Learned Hand claimed that *Hicklin* "would forbid all which might corrupt the most corruptible." *United States v. Kennerly*, 209 Fed. 119 (1913). He concluded that adherence to the *Hicklin* test would "reduce our treatment of sex to the standard of a child's library in the supposed interest of a salacious few...."

Augustus Hand rejected the way in which, under *Hicklin*, any isolated passage in a publication could cause the entire work to be declared obscene. In an 1934 opinion, he proposed a different standard:

> ... [T]he proper test of whether a given book is obscene is its dominant effect. In applying this test, relevancy of the objectionable parts to the theme, the established reputation of the work in the estimation of approved critics, if the book is modern, and the verdict of the past, if it is ancient, are persuasive pieces of evidence; for works of art are not likely to sustain a high position with no better warrant for their existence than their obscene content. *United States v. One Book Entitled "Ulysses,"* 72 F. 2d 705.

In 1957, the Supreme Court of the United States dealt the *Hicklin* test a decisive blow. It overturned a loosely drafted Michigan statute that effectively codified the *Hicklin* rule by making it a misdemeanor to sell to the general reading public any book "tending to incite minors to violent or depraved or immoral acts," or "tending to the corruption of the morals of youth." At issue was a paperback copy of John Griffin's *The Devil Rides Outside*. Writing for the majority, Justice Felix Frankfurter condemned the law's "quarantining the general reading public against books not too rugged for grown men and women in order to shield juvenile innocence.... Surely, this is to burn the house to roast the pig." *Butler v. Michigan*, 352 U.S. 380 (1957). *Butler* did not require the Court to define obscenity. Neither did it require the Court to formulate the relevant standard in federal obscenity cases. Only a few weeks later, however, the Court had an opportunity to do both.

The federal obscenity statute, deriving from the original 1873 Comstock Act, prohibited use of the U.S. mails for sending or receiving "obscene, lewd, lascivious or filthy" materials. Violation of the statute was punishable by a fine of up to $5,000, imprisonment for up to five years, or both. Samuel Roth, a sixty-five-year-old poet, publisher, and specialist in "erotica," was indicted in 1955 on twenty-six counts of violating and conspiring to violate the statute by mailing obscene circulars and advertising. Before his 1955 arrest, Roth had been taken into custody eight times and convicted five times for obscenity violations, including a jail sentence for publishing a pirated edition of James Joyce's *Ulysses*.

Roth was tried by a jury in the U.S. District Court for the Southern District of New York. During the proceedings, Roth was permitted to introduce several contemporary novels for comparison purposes, a privilege denied to defendants in several previous obscenity cases. The trial judge instructed the jurors that in order to find Roth guilty they would have to declare that the material that Roth placed in the mail was "calculated to corrupt and debauch the mind and morals of those into whose hands it may fall." According to the judge, the obscenity test the jury was to apply was "the effect of the book, picture or publication considered as a whole, not upon any particular class, but upon all those whom it is likely to reach. In other words, you determine its impact upon the average person in the community."

The jury convicted Roth for violating the statute by mailing circulars that advertised "Photo and Body," "Good Times," and the quarterly magazine *American Aphrodite*. Roth was sentenced to five years in prison and fined $5,000. His conviction was affirmed by the U.S. Court of Appeals for the Second Circuit, which found clear evidence of obscenity. The Supreme Court of the United States granted a limited writ of certiorari to consider the constitutionality of the federal obscenity statute.

Roth was consolidated with a case from California, *Alberts v. California.* Alberts had been convicted in a nonjury trial for advertising such books as *Sword of Desire, She Made It Pay*, and *The Business Side of the Oldest Business*, in violation of California's obscenity statute, which forbade the writing, publishing, or selling of "obscene or indecent" books.

HIGHLIGHTS OF SUPREME COURT ARGUMENTS

BRIEF FOR ROTH

◆ Obscenity laws should exist only at the state level. Maintenance of order and decency is a state police power under the Tenth Amendment. If obscenity is definable at all, it is only with respect to local standards of decency and morality. Those standards cannot be expected to be uniform throughout the nation as a whole.

◆ The absolutist language of the First Amendment prohibits the regulation of speech unrelated to action. The exception provided by the "clear and present danger" test is irrelevant here because there was no reliable evidence put on at trial to show that obscene publications or pictures have any appreciable effect on conduct.

◆ Criminal obscenity statutes violate the Due Process Clause of the Fifth Amendment. Due process requires that an individual know with certainty whether action is criminal before engaging in the conduct. There was no way for Roth or others to know whether material is obscene until after a jury has rendered a verdict reflecting the standards of the particular community from which the jury was drawn.

◆ If there must be statutes dealing with obscenity, civil injunctive relief is the appropriate remedy, not criminal penalties.

BRIEF FOR THE UNITED STATES

◆ The speech and press rights protected by the First Amendment are not absolute. The Founders did not have absolute freedom of speech in mind where public morality is at stake.

◆ Obscenity creates a long-run risk of bad conduct, justifying its prohibition. If Roth is to prevail, the Court will have to recognize a right to be obscene protected by the First Amendment.

◆ The federal obscenity statute does not violate due process because it is aimed narrowly at material that explicitly and purposefully deals with sex conduct in a degraded or perverted way with no compensating artistic aspect whatever.

◆ Common law background and years of judicial construction leave no doubt about the mass of material barred by the statute. The statute gives notice of the proscribed speech at least as definite as other standards, such as reckless driving, that have been approved by courts.

◆ Congress has plenary power to bar the use of the mails for obscene materials unless prevented from doing so by the First Amendment. This is not an area that is appropriate for state regulation.

SUPREME COURT DECISION: 7–2

BRENNAN, J.

... The dispositive question is whether obscenity is utterance within the area of protected speech and press. Although this is the first time the question has been squarely presented to this Court, either under the First Amendment or under the Fourteenth Amendment, expressions found in numerous opinions indicate that this Court has always assumed that obscenity is not protected by the freedoms of speech and press.

The protection given speech and press was fashioned to assure unfettered interchange of ideas for the bringing about of political and social changes desired by the people....

All ideas having even the slightest redeeming social importance—unorthodox ideas, controversial ideas, even ideas hateful to the prevailing climate of opinion—have the full protection of the guaranties, unless excludable because they encroach upon the limited area of more important interests. But implicit in the history of the First Amendment is the rejection of obscenity as utterly without redeeming social importance.... We hold

that obscenity is not within the area of constitutionally protected speech or press....

[S]ex and obscenity are not synonymous. Obscene material is material which deals with sex in a manner appealing to prurient interest. The portrayal of sex, e.g., in art, literature and scientific works, is not itself sufficient reason to deny material the constitutional protection of freedom of speech and press. Sex, a great and mysterious motive force in human life, has indisputably been a subject of absorbing interest to mankind through the ages; it is one of the vital problems of human interest and public concern....

It is ... vital that the standards for judging obscenity safeguard the protection of freedom of speech and press for material which does not treat sex in a manner appealing to prurient interest.

The early leading standard of obscenity allowed material to be judged merely by the effect of an isolated excerpt upon particularly susceptible persons.... Some American courts adopted this standard but later decisions have rejected it and substituted this test: whether to the average person, applying contemporary community standards, the dominant theme of the material taken as a whole appeals to prurient interest. The *Hicklin* test, judging obscenity by the effect of isolated passages upon the most susceptible persons, might well encompass material legitimately treating with sex, and so it must be rejected as unconstitutionally restrictive of the freedoms of speech and press. On the other hand, the substituted standard provides safeguards adequate to withstand the charge of constitutional infirmity.

Both trial courts below sufficiently followed the proper standard. Both courts used the proper definition of obscenity....

The judgments are affirmed.

WARREN, C.J., CONCURRING [OMITTED]

HARLAN, J., CONCURRING IN PART AND DISSENTING IN PART [OMITTED]

DOUGLAS AND BLACK, J.J., DISSENTING

When we sustain these convictions, we make the legality of a publication turn on the purity of thought which a book or tract instills in the mind of the reader. I do not think we can approve the standard and be faithful to the command of the First Amendment, which by its terms is a restraint on Congress and which by the Fourteenth is a restraint on the States....

The test of obscenity the Court endorses today gives the censor free range over a vast domain. To allow the State to step in and punish mere speech or publication that the judge or the jury thinks has an *undesirable* impact on thoughts but that is not shown to be a part of unlawful action is drastically to curtail the First Amendment....

If we were certain that impurity of sexual thoughts impelled to action, we would be on less dangerous ground in punishing the distributors of this sex literature. But it is by no means clear that obscene literature, as so defined, is a significant factor in influencing substantial deviations from the community standards....

The absence of dependable information on the effect of obscene literature on human conduct should make us wary. It should put us on the side of protecting society's interest in literature, except and unless it can be said that the particular publication has an impact on action that the government can control....

I would give the broad sweep of the First Amendment full support. I have the same confidence in the ability of our people to reject noxious literature as I have in their capacity to sort out the true from the false in theology, economics, politics, or any other field.

QUESTIONS

1. What test does Justice Brennan adopt in *Roth* for defining obscenity? On what basis does Justice Douglas dissent?

2. What governmental interests justify regulating obscenity? What First Amendment values justify not regulating obscenity? Does the three-prong *Roth* test provide a practical standard for balancing these competing interests?

3. In its brief, the United States offered the Court the following list as a hierarchical "comparative scale of value" regarding speech meriting First Amendment protection: political speech, religious, economic, sci-

entific, general news and information, social and historical commentary, literature, art, entertainment, music, humor, commercial advertisements, gossip, comic books, epithets, libel, obscenity, profanity, commercial pornography.

Under the First Amendment, is it appropriate to rank different kinds of speech according to its purported social value and, hence, its need for protection? If so, where is the line between protected and unprotected speech?

4. In a subsequent obscenity case, *Jacobellis v. Ohio*, 378 U.S. 198 (1964), Justice Potter Stewart wrote: "I shall not today attempt further to define the kinds of material I understand to be embraced within [the] shorthand description [hard-core pornography]; and perhaps I could never succeed in intelligibly doing so. But I know it when I see it..." ("The Obscenity Cases: Grapes of Roth," in *The Supreme Court Review* [Chicago, IL: University of Chicago Press, 1966]).

   Is Justice Stewart's definition of obscenity any more or less workable than the *Roth* test? Or should the Court recognize that any attempt to define obscene speech necessarily creates what law professor C. Peter McGrath called a "disaster area" and steer clear of such efforts?

5. Should the Court have followed the advice of Roth's counsel and left to the states what Justice Harlan, in *Ginsberg v. New York*, 390 U.S. 629 (1968), called "the intractable obscenity problem"? What are the advantages and disadvantages of trying to articulate a national standard regarding obscenity? Does the First Amendment demand uniformity?

OBSCENITY

Miller v. California
413 U.S. 15 (1973)

SETTING

Roth v. United States was the Supreme Court's first attempt to formulate a national standard for judging obscenity. The decade following *Roth* saw an explosion in the availability of sexually explicit materials and found state and lower federal courts disagreeing about what the *Roth* standards meant or how to apply them. Throughout the 1960s, the Court was unsuccessful in its attempt to forge majority support for criteria by which to determine whether material is obscene. By 1964, the justices had identified three tests for judging obscenity: whether the work appeals to a prurient interest (*Roth*); whether the work is patently offensive (*Manual Enterprises, Inc. v. Day*, 370 U.S. 478 (1962)), and whether the work is utterly without redeeming social value (*Jacobellis v. Ohio*, 378 U.S. 184 (1964)). Two years later, the Court, through Justice Brennan, held: "Each of the three federal constitutional criteria is to be applied independently; the social value of the book can neither be weighed against nor canceled by its prurient appeal or patent offensiveness." *A Book Named* John Cleland's Memoirs of a Woman of Pleasure [Fanny Hill] *v. Attorney General of Massachusetts*, 383 U.S. 413 (1966).

Discord among the justices in the late 1960s made it impossible to find a majority that could agree on ways to clarify the *Roth* test, much less agree on a definition of obscenity. The Court was separated into three groups. One group argued for an "absolutist interpretation" that the First Amendment prohibits any regulation of speech. Another group took a traditional due process approach, contending that unless state regulations of obscenity are irrational or unreasonable, they should be upheld. A third group sought to define obscenity and to apply that definition to specific publications or films on a case-by-case basis.

By 1967, the justices could do no more than declare that a determination of whether a work is obscene would depend on the independent determination of each justice employing his own theory of what constitutes obscenity. *Redrup v. New York*, 386 U.S. 767 (1967). The Court had apparently embraced Justice Stewart's view in *Jacobellis v. Ohio*, 378 U.S. 184 (1964) that although pornography eludes definition, "I know it when I see it...." After *Redrup*, the Court began to issue summary reversal orders if five justices—for whatever reason—decided a work was not obscene. The Court subsequently heard and decided thirty-one cases in this manner. If the *Roth* decision created uncertainty for state and lower federal courts, the *Redrup* approach created virtual chaos.

Despite the Court's inability to define obscenity or to formulate standards for judging it, public concern over various alleged effects of sexually explicit materials did not diminish. In 1968, at the urging of Congress, President Lyndon Johnson appointed a Federal Commission on Obscenity and Pornography. In late September 1970, the commission reported that "empirical research has found no evidence to date that exposure to explicit sexual materials plays a significant role in the causation of delinquent or criminal behavior among youth or adults." By a 12–5 vote it recommended that "federal, state, and local legislation should not seek to interfere with the rights of adults who wish to do so to read, obtain, or view explicit sexual material."

The commission's report was vehemently criticized by the Senate. Several days after the commission issued its report, the Senate, in a 60–5 roll-call vote, adopted a resolution denouncing the report and rejecting its major findings. In mid-October, President Richard Nixon termed the report "morally bankrupt" and pledged to "eliminate smut" while he was president. Three years later, Nixon's appointees to the Supreme Court (Chief Justice Burger and Justices Blackmun, Powell, and Rehnquist) had the opportunity to enunciate new guidelines for resolving obscenity disputes. The case involved the advertising of illustrated "adult" books.

In 1969, bookseller Marvin Miller undertook a mass mailing campaign to advertise the sale of illustrated books entitled *Intercourse, Man-Woman, Sex Orgies Illustrated*, and *An Illustrated History of Pornography*, and a film entitled *Marital Intercourse*. The advertising brochures contained pictures and drawings depicting cunnilingus, sodomy, buggery, and other sexual acts performed in groups of two or more. In June, Miller sent five of the brochures, unsolicited, to a restaurant in Newport Beach, California. The manager of the restaurant and his mother opened the envelope containing the brochures, then complained to the police.

Miller was arrested for violating California's criminal obscenity statute, which made it a misdemeanor to sell or distribute obscene material. According to the statute, "'Obscene' means that to the average person, applying contemporary standards, the predominant appeal of the matter, taken as a whole, is to prurient interest, i.e., a shameful or morbid interest in nudity, sex, or excretion, which goes substantially beyond customary limits of candor in description or representation of such matters and is matter which is utterly without redeeming social importance."

Miller was tried and convicted in the Municipal Court of the Orange County Harbor Judicial District. The Orange County Superior Court affirmed his conviction, denied his petition to certify the case to the California Court of Appeal, Fourth Appellate District, and denied his petition for rehearing. Both California courts held that the "contemporary community standards" component of the obscenity tests from *Roth v. United States* and *Memoirs v. Massachusetts*, 383 U.S. 413 (1966), meant "statewide" standards. Miller appealed to the Supreme Court of the United States. The case was argued in January 1972 and reargued the following November.

HIGHLIGHTS OF SUPREME COURT ARGUMENTS

BRIEF FOR MILLER

◆ The central issue is whether the First Amendment demands an obscenity rule of uniform application irrespective of state lines, or whether states retain the right to determine rules as long as they adhere to the constraints of the Due Process Clause of the Fourteenth Amendment. A national standard of obscenity is required under the *Roth-Memoirs* test. An obscenity standard based on a particular local community would impede the desirable evolutionary tendency in the society toward permitting greater access to and utilization of the most current thoughts and works in the United States or the world.

◆ A national standard is also required under the Commerce Clause. Application of local community standards would impede the free flow of commerce in books, films, magazines, and other materials.

◆ Federal obscenity law has preempted state efforts to regulate obscenity by prohibiting use of the mails. Congress intended to completely occupy the field of action pertaining to obscenity in the context of mailing.

◆ Assuming that a state standard is appropriate, California courts committed reversible error by failing to require proof of community standards. The state offered the testimony of only one witness, a police officer, to establish the community standard on obscenity. The officer based his opinion on an informal survey on an unrepresentative group of people in the state.

◆ The materials Miller distributed were not obscene as a matter of fact.

Even prosecution witnesses testified that the materials had some beneficial use for normal people, and thus were not lacking in redeeming social value.

AMICUS CURIAE BRIEF SUPPORTING MILLER

The American Civil Liberties Union.

BRIEF FOR CALIFORNIA

♦ The Supreme Court has never suggested that the introduction of national experts at a state obscenity trial is required by the First Amendment.

♦ A national obscenity standard is not required by the Commerce Clause because constitutionally the Court's duty to oversee obscenity exists only to safeguard the guarantees of the First Amendment. A conflict under the Commerce Clause could arise only if the federal government had the right to control the morals of citizens under the Commerce Clause.

♦ The prosecution was not required to produce evidence of contemporary community standards in obscenity cases. Such testimony was merely a guide to the jury.

♦ The federal government's authority to regulate obscenity is limited to the transportation of obscene materials through the U.S. mails. States' police powers were unaffected by the limited grant of power to Congress to regulate through the exercise of its postal powers.

♦ The materials Miller distributed were obscene as a matter of law. Justice Stewart stated in *Ginzburg v. United States*, 383 U.S. 463 (1966), that a class of hard-core pornography does exist: "Such materials include photographs, both still and motion picture, with no pretense of artistic value, graphically depicting acts of sexual intercourse, including various acts of sodomy and sadism, and sometimes involving several participants in scenes of orgy-like character." Miller's advertising brochures fall within this definition.

SUPREME COURT DECISION: 5–4

BURGER, C.J.

... This much has been categorically settled by the Court, that obscene material is unprotected by the First Amendment.... We acknowledge, however, the inherent dangers of undertaking to regulate any form of expression. State statutes designed to regulate obscene materials must be carefully limited.... As a result, we now confine the permissible scope of such regulation to words which depict or describe sexual conduct. That conduct must be specifically defined by the applicable state law, as written or authoritatively construed. A state offense must also be limited to words which, taken as a whole, appeal to the prurient interest in sex, which portray sexual conduct in a patently offensive way, and which, taken as a whole, do not have serious literary, artistic, political, or scientific value.

The basic guidelines for the trier of fact must be: (a) whether "the average person, applying contemporary community standards" would find that the work, taken as a whole, appeals to the prurient interest, ... (b) whether the work depicts or describes, in a patently offensive way, sexual conduct specifically defined by the applicable state law, and (c) whether the work, taken as a whole, lacks serious literary, artistic, political, or scientific value. We do not adopt as a constitutional standard the "utterly without redeeming social value" test of Memoirs v. Massachusetts [383 U.S. 413 (1966)] that concept has never commanded the adherence of more than three Justices at one time. If a state law that regulates obscene material is thus limited, as written or construed, the First Amendment values applicable to the States through the Fourteenth Amendment are adequately protected by the ultimate power of appellate courts to conduct an independent review of constitutional claims when necessary....

We emphasize that it is not our function to propose regulatory schemes for the States. That must await their concrete legislative efforts. It is possible, however, to give a few plain examples of what a state statute could define for regulation...

(a) Patently offensive representation or descriptions of ultimate sexual acts, normal or perverted, actual or simulated.

(b) Patently offensive representation or descriptions of masturbation, excretory functions, and lewd exhibition of the genitals.

Sex and nudity may not be exploited without limit by films or pictures exhibited or sold in places of public accommodation any more than live sex and nudity can be exhibited or sold without limit in such public places. At a minimum, prurient, patently offensive depiction or description of sexual conduct must have serious literary, artistic, political, or scientific value to merit First Amendment protection.... In resolving the inevitably sensitive questions of fact and law, we must continue to rely on the jury system, accompanied by the safeguards that judges, rules of evidence, pre-

sumption of innocence and other protective features provide, as we do with rape, murder and a host of other offenses against society and its individual members....

Under the holdings announced today, no one will be subject to prosecution for the sale or exposure of obscene materials unless these materials depict or describe patently offensive "hard core" sexual conduct specifically defined by the regulating state law, as written or construed. We are satisfied that these specific prerequisites will provide fair notice to a dealer in such materials that his public and commercial activities may bring prosecution....

Under a national Constitution, fundamental First Amendment limitations on the powers of the States do not vary from community to community, but this does not mean that there are, or should or can be, fixed, uniform national standards of precisely what appeals to the "prurient interest" or is "patently offensive." These are essentially questions of fact, and our nation is simply too big and too diverse for this Court to reasonably expect that such standards could be articulated for all 50 States in a single formulation, even assuming the prerequisite consensus exists. When triers of fact are asked to decide whether "the average person, applying contemporary community standards" would consider certain matters "prurient," it would be unrealistic to require that the answer be based on some abstract formulation. The adversary system, with lay jurors as the usual ultimate factfinders in criminal prosecutions, has historically permitted triers-of-fact to draw on the standards of their community, guided always by limiting instructions on the law. To require a State to structure obscenity proceedings around evidence of a *national* "community standard" would be an exercise in futility....

In sum we (a) reaffirm the *Roth* holding

that obscene material is not protected by the First Amendment, (b) hold that such material can be regulated by the States, subject to the specific safeguards enunciated above, without a showing that the material is "*utterly* without redeeming social value," and (c) hold that obscenity is to be determined by applying "contemporary community standards," not "national standards." The judgment of the Appellate Department of the Superior Court, Orange County, California, is vacated and the case remanded to that court for further proceedings not inconsistent with the First Amendment standards established by this opinion....

Vacated and remanded for further proceedings....

DOUGLAS, J., DISSENTING

Today we leave open the way for California to send a man to prison for distributing brochures that advertise books and a movie under freshly written standards defining obscenity which until today's decision were never the part of any law.

The Court has worked hard to define obscenity and concededly has failed....

Obscenity cases usually generate tremendous emotional outbursts. They have no business being in the courts. If a constitutional amendment authorized censorship, the censor would probably be an administrative agency. Then criminal prosecutions could follow as if and when publishers defied the censor and sold their literature. Under that regime a publisher would know when he was on dangerous ground. Under the present regime—whether the old standards or the new ones are used—the criminal law becomes a trap. A brand new test would put a publisher behind bars under a new law improvised by the courts after the publication. That was done in *Ginzburg* [*v. United States*, 383 U.S. 463 (1966)] and has all the evils of an *ex post facto* law....

If a specific book, play, paper, or motion picture has in a civil proceeding been condemned as obscene and review of that finding has been completed, and thereafter a person publishes, shows, or displays that particular book or film, then a vague law has been made specific. There would remain the underlying question whether the First Amendment allows an implied exception in the case of obscenity. I do not think it does and my views on the issue have been stated over and again. But at least a criminal prosecution brought at that juncture would not violate the time-honored void-for-vagueness test.

No such protective procedure has been designed by California in this case. Obscenity—which even we cannot define with precision—is a hodge-podge. To send men to jail for violating standards they cannot understand, construe, and apply is a monstrous thing to do in a Nation dedicated to fair trials and due process....

We deal with highly emotional, not rational, questions. To many the Song of Solomon is obscene. I do not think we, the judges, were ever given the constitutional power to make definitions of obscenity. If it is to be defined, let the people debate and decide by a constitutional amendment what they want to ban as obscene and what standards they want the legislatures and the courts to apply. Perhaps the people will decide that the path towards a mature, integrated society requires that all ideas competing for acceptance must have no censor. Perhaps they will decide otherwise. Whatever the choice, the courts will have some guidelines. Now we have none except our own predilections....

BRENNAN, STEWART, AND MARSHALL, J.J., DISSENTING [OMITTED]

QUESTIONS

1. Restate the *Miller* rule. Does *Miller* provide more useful instructions to triers of fact in obscenity cases than *Roth* did? On what basis do Justices Douglas and Brennan dissent? How practical is Justice Douglas's proposed alternative?

2. The offense of mailing pornographic material can be prosecuted either in the jurisdiction where it is mailed or where it is received. Might the "contemporary community standards" portion of the *Miller* test lead to venue shopping by prosecutors seeking forums where they anticipate jury attitudes will be most favorable to conviction? Should the law encourage such a practice?

3. Four other obscenity decisions were announced the same day as *Miller*, and by the same vote. Whereas *Miller* focused on acceptable procedures for judging obscenity, the companion cases addressed the contents of the materials.

   In *Paris Adult Theatre I v. Slaton*, 413 U.S. 49, the Court ruled that states are not precluded from regulating the exhibition of obscene motion pictures in "adult" theaters, as long as the state law as written or authoritatively interpreted by state courts meets the standards for determining obscenity set forth in *Miller*. Obscene, pornographic motion pictures, which are unprotected by the First Amendment, are not constitutionally immune from state regulation simply because they are exhibited only to consenting adults. Neither are states prohibited from concluding that the public interest requires regulation of commercialized obscenity even though there is no conclusive proof of a connection between antisocial behavior and obscene materials.

   In *United States v. 12 200 Foot Reels of Super 8 MM Film*, 413 U.S. 123, the Court held that Congress can exercise its Commerce Clause powers to proscribe the importation of obscene material even if the material is intended for the importer's personal use and possession.

   In *United States v. Orito*, 413 U.S. 139, the majority upheld the power of Congress to forbid the interstate transportation of obscene material by common carrier even though the material is intended for the private use of the transporter or is transported in a manner that involves no risk to children or unconsenting adults.

   Finally, in *Kaplan v. California*, 413 U.S. 115, the Court ruled that a book containing words alone (with no pictures) can be found "obscene" and hence outside of First Amendment protection.

   Miller and the companion cases were decided by 5–4 votes, with all four Nixon appointees joining the majority decisions. What do these four decisions suggest about (a) the Court's commitment to uniformity in the area of obscenity; (b) the principle that legal tests should be proclaimed by judges insulated from public pressure; and (c) federalism?

4. In December 1983, law professor Catharine MacKinnon and author Andrea Dworkin presented an antipornography ordinance to the city council of Minneapolis, Minnesota. Their measure defined pornography as "the sexually explicit subordination of women, graphically or in words," called for it to be treated as discrimination against women, and made it actionable as a personal injury. The city council passed the ordinance, but it was vetoed by the mayor.

A similar ordinance was adopted by the Indianapolis, Indiana, city council but was struck down by the U.S. Court of Appeals for the Seventh Circuit in *American Booksellers Association. Inc. v. Hudnut*, 771 F.2d 323 (1985). The Supreme Court affirmed summarily. *Hudnut v. American Booksellers Association, Inc.*, 475 U.S. 1001 (1986).

What socially relevant differences, if any, exist between obscenity and pornography? Should constitutional protection be extended to one but not the other? Are Dworkin and MacKinnon correct that pornography is equivalent to violence against women, and that the law should treat pornography as an actionable personal injury?

COMMENT

The Court's decision in *Miller* proved no more successful than *Roth* in ending litigation over obscenity. Cases after *Miller* raised, among other things, questions about the meaning of the "community standard" test. The following cases demonstrate the Court's response between *Miller* and *New York v. Ferber*, 458 U.S. 747 (1982), the next excerpted case.

> **Case:** *Jenkins v. Georgia*, 418 U.S. 153 (1974)
> **Vote:** 9–0
> **Decision:** There is no constitutional requirement that juries be instructed in state obscenity cases to apply the standards of a hypothetical statewide community. *Miller* approved, but did not mandate, such an instruction. Jurors may properly be instructed to apply "community standards" without a specification of the "community." Nevertheless, juries do not have unbridled discretion in determining what is "patently offensive" since "no one will be subject to prosecution for the sale or exposure of obscene materials [that do not] depict or describe patently offensive 'hard core' sexual conduct...."
>
> **Case:** *Erznoznik v. City of Jacksonville*, 422 U.S. 205 (1975)
> **Vote:** 6–3
> **Decision:** A municipal ordinance making it a public nuisance and a punishable offense for a drive-in movie theater to exhibit films containing nudity, when the screen is visible from a public street or place, is facially invalid as an infringement on First Amendment rights. By discriminating among movies solely on the basis of content, the ordinance has the effect of deterring drive-in theaters from showing movies containing any nudity, however

innocent or even educational. Such censorship of the content of otherwise protected speech cannot be justified on the basis of the limited privacy interest of persons on the public streets, who if offended by viewing the movies, can readily avert their eyes. Nor can the ordinance be justified as an exercise of the city's police power for the protection of children against viewing the films. Even assuming that such is its purpose, the restriction is broader than permissible because it is not directed against sexually explicit nudity or otherwise limited.

Case: *Young v. American Mini Theaters, Inc.*, 427 U.S. 50 (1976)

Vote: 5–4

Decision: Detroit zoning ordinances that provide that an adult theater may not be located within 1,000 feet of any two other "regulated uses" or within 500 feet of a residential area, are constitutional. That the place where films may be exhibited is regulated does not violate free expression. The city's interest in planning and regulating the use of property for commercial purposes is clearly adequate to support the locational restriction.

Case: *Smith v. United States*, 431 U.S. 291 (1977)

Vote: 5–4

Decision: State law defining "prurient interest" and "patent offensiveness" cannot provide the basis for a jury instruction in a federal prosecution. It is the province of the jury to decide, as a matter of fact, what is obscene in light of the jury's understanding of contemporary community standards. Although state legislatures are not completely foreclosed from setting substantive standards in obscenity cases, they cannot declare what community standards shall be, any more than they may undertake to define "reasonableness."

Case: *Schad v. Borough of Mount Ephraim*, 452 U.S. 61 (1981)

Vote: 7–2

Decision: A local ordinance, as construed to exclude live entertainment including nude dancing throughout the borough, prohibits a wide range of expression that has long been held to be within the protection of the First Amendment. An entertainment program may not be prohibited solely because it displays a nude human figure, and nude dancing is not without First Amendment protection from official regulation.

OBSCENITY

New York v. Ferber
458 U.S. 747 (1982)

SETTING

By the mid-1970s, the production and dissemination of films, magazines, and other materials showing children as young as three years old engaged in virtually every type of sexual activity had become a major industry in the United States. "Kiddy porn" grossed more than $200 million per year. One researcher found no fewer than 264 different magazines showing children engaged in sex. In response to evidence that the children who participate in those activities suffer the same profound physical and psychological injuries suffered by children subjected to other forms of sexual abuse, most state legislatures enacted laws outlawing child pornography.

In 1977, for example, the State of New York launched a major offensive against the exploitation of young people in sexually explicit films. The result was Article 263 of the Penal Law, which prohibited the dissemination of materials depicting sexual conduct of children, regardless of whether the materials were obscene in the legal sense. Section 263.05 prohibited employing, inducing, authorizing, or permitting children under the age of sixteen to engage in sexual conduct during a performance. However, believing that this direct ban would not effectively prevent the abuse of children, the legislature also enacted § 263.15, which prohibited the knowing dissemination of materials, both obscene and nonobscene, that showed children engaged in sexual conduct. Finally, in an effort to obviate a successful constitutional challenge to the ban in § 263.15, the New York legislature enacted § 263.10, which banned only the knowing dissemination of obscene materials showing the sexual conduct of children under the age of sixteen.

Paul I. Ferber was the owner of the Madison Square Book Shop, which specialized in pornography. On March 2, 1978, Ferber sold two films to an undercover police officer. The films depicted young boys masturbating. One film showed a naked boy lying face down on a bed, rubbing against the bed. After a short time, the boy turned over onto his back and masturbated twice to ejaculation. He then lay on his side and placed a dildo between his buttocks as if to insert it into his anus. The other film showed a naked boy masturbating to ejaculation and inserting a dildo into his anus. That film also included scenes of other naked boys—some no older than seven or eight years of age—jumping, sitting, or reclining on a mattress. Those boys were engaged in solo and mutual masturbation and in conduct suggesting oral-genital contact. At the end of the second film, the main child performer got dressed very slowly and picked up what appeared to be U.S. currency that he held toward the camera.

Ferber was arrested and indicted in the New York State Supreme Court on two counts of Promoting an Obscene Sexual Performance by a Child, in violation of § 263.10, and Promoting a Sexual Performance by a Child, in violation of § 263.15. Ferber moved to dismiss the indictment on the ground that § 263.15, Promoting a Sexual Performance by a Child, was unconstitutionally overbroad because it prohibited promotion of nonobscene materials that are protected by the First Amendment as well as prohibiting promotion of obscene materials. His motion to dismiss was denied and he was tried by a jury. Ferber was convicted of Promoting a Sexual Performance by a Child (which did not require proof that the films were obscene) but was acquitted on the indictment of Promoting an Obscene Sexual Performance by a Child.

The Appellate Division of the New York State Supreme Court affirmed. Ferber then appealed to the New York Court of Appeals, again arguing that

§ 263.15 is constitutionally overbroad, because it makes criminal the promotion of material that is not obscene. The New York Court of Appeals agreed, and reversed his conviction. The New York high court reasoned that it was impossible to impose a limiting construction on the law, because there was no doubt that the legislature intended § 263.15 to encompass sexual conduct by children in performances that were not obscene. Two judges dissented. The Supreme Court of the United States granted the State of New York's petition for a writ of certiorari.

HIGHLIGHTS OF SUPREME COURT ARGUMENTS

BRIEF FOR STATE OF NEW YORK

◆ Speech may be regulated to promote a compelling state interest if there is no effective and less restrictive alternative. New York's ban on the dissemination of materials depicting sexual abuse of children was designed to combat the serious threat to the welfare of the state's children by eliminating the economic incentive for the abuse, and thus promotes a compelling state interest.

◆ The New York legislature was entitled to find that making children under the age of sixteen engage in pornography constitutes sexual abuse and is physically, psychologically, and emotionally harmful to the children involved. It is not necessary that such a finding be based on scientific fact; it is sufficient that the harmfulness of using children in pornography has not been scientifically disproved.

◆ This Court has never held that merely because speech does not fit into one of the enumerated categories of unprotected speech, it is absolutely protected under the First Amendment. To the contrary, it has held that the right of free speech is not absolute and may be prohibited if the prohibition furthers a compelling state interest and is the least restrictive alternative to achieving that interest. It is beyond question that protecting children is a compelling state interest.

◆ This Court's test in *Miller v. California* is inadequate, because obscenity convictions are virtually impossible to obtain under its standards.

AMICUS CURIAE BRIEFS SUPPORTING NEW YORK

Covenant House; joint brief of Charles H. Keating Jr., and Citizens for Decency Through Law; Morality in Media, Inc.

BRIEF FOR FERBER

◆ Section 263.15 proscribes nonobscene, clearly protected speech without regard to the context, even where it contains scientific, educational, or other societal value. This overbroad enactment is at war with this Court's longstanding pronouncements that only sexual obscenity falls outside the protections of the First Amendment.

◆ For over twenty-five years, this Court has held that materials of sexual content fall outside the protection of the First Amendment only if they are legally obscene. In *Miller v. California*, this Court emphasized the need for carefully drawn legislation whenever a state seeks to restrict any form of expression and engineered the three-part test that must be satisfied before any work may be deemed obscene. The *Miller* test has thrived because it strikes a reasonable accommodation between the state's interest in controlled obscene material and the public's right to choose what it will read or see. Without the obscenity control factor, § 263.15 is clearly overbroad.

◆ Not only does the statute declare otherwise lawful speech dealing with adolescent sexual conduct to be per se unlawful, it also extends its overbroad reach to conduct that is not considered to be abusive or unlawful in numerous other states from which such materials may emanate. Not every instance of nonobscene but "lewd" exhibition of a child's genitals represents sexual abuse of the child.

◆ This Court has never condoned a wholesale ban on speech because of its content and has always given weight and consideration to the context of the utterance, as well as the responsibility to promote the free exchange of information ranging from the most controversial and distasteful to the most useful and educational.

AMICUS CURIAE BRIEFS SUPPORTING FERBER

Joint brief of American Booksellers Association, Association of American Publishers, Council for Periodical Distributors, Freedom to Read Foundation, International Periodical Distributors Association, National Association of College Stores, American Civil Liberties Union, the Association of American University Presses, New York Civil Liberties Union, and St. Martin's Press.

SUPREME COURT DECISION: 9–0

WHITE, J.

... This case ... constitutes our first examination of a statute directed at and limited to depictions of sexual activity involving children. We believe our inquiry should begin with the question of whether a State has somewhat more freedom in proscribing works which portray sexual acts or lewd exhibitions of genitalia by children....

In *Miller v. California*, a majority of the Court agreed that a "state offense must also be limited to works which, taken as a whole, appeal to the prurient interest in sex, which portray sexual conduct in a patently offensive way, and which, taken as a whole, do not have serious literary, artistic, political, or scientific value." Over the past decade, we have adhered to the guidelines expressed in *Miller*, which subsequently has been followed in the regulatory schemes of most States.

The *Miller* standard, like its predecessors, was an accommodation between the State's interests in protecting the "sensibilities of unwilling recipients" from exposure to pornographic material and the dangers of censorship inherent in unabashedly content-based laws. Like obscenity statutes, laws directed at the dissemination of child pornography run the risk of suppressing protected expression by allowing the hand of the censor to become unduly heavy. For the following reasons, however, we are persuaded that the States are entitled to greater leeway in the regulation of pornographic depictions of children.

First. It is evident beyond the need for elaboration that a State's interest in "safeguarding the physical and psychological well-being of a minor" is "compelling." *Globe Newspaper Co. v. Superior Court*, 457 U.S. 596 (1982).... Accordingly, we have sustained legislation aimed at protecting the physical and emotional well-being of youth even when the laws have operated in the sensitive area of constitutionally protected rights. The prevention of sexual exploitation and abuse of children constitutes a government objective of surpassing importance. The legislative findings accompanying passage of the New York laws reflect this concern.... We shall not second-guess this legislative judgment. That judgment, we think, easily passes muster under the First Amendment.

Second. The distribution of photographs and films depicting sexual activity by juveniles is intrinsically related to the sexual abuse of children in at least two ways. First, the materials produced are a permanent record of the children's participation and the harm to the child is exacerbated by their circulation. Second, the distribution network for child pornography must be closed if the production of material which requires the sexual exploitation of children is to be effectively controlled.... The most expeditious if not the only practical method of law enforcement may be to dry up the market for this material by imposing severe criminal penalties on persons selling, advertising, or otherwise promoting the product....

The *Miller* standard, like all general definitions of what may be banned as obscene, does not reflect the State's particular and more compelling interest in prosecuting those who promote the sexual exploitation of children. Thus, the question under the *Miller* test of whether a work, taken as a whole, appeals to the prurient interest of the average person bears no connection to the issue of whether a child has been physically or psychologically harmed in the production of the work. Similarly, a sexually explicit depiction need not be "patently offensive" in order to have required the sexual exploitation of a child for its production. In addition, a work which, taken on the whole, contains serious literary, artistic, political, or scientific value may nevertheless embody the hardest core of child pornography.... We therefore cannot conclude that the *Miller* standard is a satisfactory solution to the child pornography problem.

Third. The advertising and selling of child pornography provide an economic motive for and are thus an integral part of the production of such materials, an activity illegal throughout the Nation....

Fourth. The value of permitting live performances and photographic reproductions of children engaged in lewd sexual conduct is exceedingly modest, if not *de minimis*. We consider it unlikely that visual depictions of children performing sexual acts or lewdly exhibiting their genitals would often constitute an important and necessary part of a literary performance or scientific or educational work.... Recognizing and classifying child pornography as a category of material outside the protection of the First Amendment is not incompatible with our earlier decisions.... When a definable class of material, such as that covered by Sec. 263.15, bears so heavily and pervasively on the welfare of children engaged in its production, we think the balance of competing interests is clearly struck and that it is permissible to consider these materials as without the protection of the First Amendment.

There are, of course, limits on the category of child pornography which, like obscenity, is unprotected by the First Amendment. As with all legislation in this sensitive area, the conduct to be prohibited must be adequately defined by the applicable state law, as written or authoritatively construed....

The test for child pornography is separate from the obscenity standard enunciated in *Miller*, but may be compared to it for the purpose of clarity. The *Miller* formulation is adjusted in the following respects: A trier of fact need not find that the material appeals to the prurient interest of the average person; it is not required that sexual conduct portrayed be done so in a patently offensive manner; and the material at issue need not be considered as a whole. We note that the distribution of descriptions or other depictions of sexual conduct, not otherwise obscene, which do not involve live performance or photographic or other visual reproduction of live performances, retains First Amendment protection. As with obscenity laws, criminal responsibility may not be imposed without some element of scienter on the part of the defendant.

Section 263.15's prohibition incorporates a definition of sexual conduct that comports with the above-stated principles. The forbidden acts to be depicted are listed with sufficient precision and represent the kind of conduct that, if it

were the theme of a work, could render it legally obscene.... Section 263.15 expressly includes a scienter requirement.

We hold that Sec. 263.15 sufficiently describes a category of material the production and distribution of which is not entitled to First Amendment protection. It is therefore clear that there is nothing unconstitutionally "underinclusive" about a statute that singles out this category of material for proscription. It also follows that the State is not barred by the First Amendment from prohibiting the distribution of unprotected materials produced outside the State.

It remains to address the claim that the New York statute is unconstitutionally overbroad because it would forbid the distribution of material with serious literary, scientific, or educational value or material which does not threaten the harms sought to be combated by the State....

The scope of the First Amendment overbreadth doctrine, like most exceptions to established principles, must be carefully tied to the circumstances in which facial invalidation of a statute is truly warranted. Because of the wide-reaching effects of striking down a statute on its face at the request of one whose own conduct may be punished despite the First Amendment, we have recognized that the overbreadth doctrine is "strong medicine" and have employed it with hesitation, and then "only as a last resort."...

The premise that a law should not be invalidated for overbreadth unless it reaches a substantial number of impermissible applications is hardly novel. On most occasions involving facial invalidation, the Court has stressed the embracing sweep of the statute over protected expression.... This requirement of substantial overbreadth may justifiably be applied to statutory challenges which arise in defense of a criminal prosecution as well as civil enforcement or actions seeking a declaratory judgment....

Applying these principles, we hold that Sec. 263.15 is not substantially overbroad. We consider this the paradigmatic case of a state statute whose legitimate reach dwarfs its arguably impermissible applications....

The judgment of the New York Court of Appeals is reversed, and the case is remanded to that court for further proceedings not inconsistent with this opinion.

So ordered.

BLACKMUN, J., CONCURRING WITHOUT OPINION

O'CONNOR, J., CONCURRING

Although I join the Court's opinion, I write separately to stress that the Court does not hold that New York must except "material with serious literary, scientific, or educational value" from its statute. The Court merely holds that, even if the First Amendment shelters such material, New York's current statute is not sufficiently overbroad to support respondent's facial attack. The compelling interests identified in today's opinion suggest that the Constitution might in fact permit New York to ban knowing distribution of works depicting minors engaged in explicit sexual conduct, regardless of the social value of the depictions....

BRENNAN AND MARSHALL, J.J., CONCURRING

... [T]he State has a special interest in protecting the well-being of its youth. This special and compelling interest, and the particular vulnerability of children, afford the State the leeway to regulate pornographic material, the promotion of which is harmful to children, even though the State does not have such leeway when it seeks only to protect consenting adults from exposure to such material.... But in my view application of Sec. 263.15 or any similar statute to depictions of children that in themselves do have serious literary, artistic, scientific, or medical value, would violate the First Amendment.... The First Amendment value of depictions of children that are in themselves serious contributions to art, literature, or science, is, by definition, simply not "*de minimis.*" At the same time, the State's interest in suppression of such materials is likely to be far less compelling. For the Court's assumption of harm to the child resulting from the "permanent record" and "circulation" of the child's "participation" lacks much of its force where the depiction is a serious contribution to art or science.... [I]t is inconceivable how a depiction of a child that is itself a serious contribution to the world of art or literature or science can be deemed "material outside the protection of the First Amendment."

I, of course, adhere to my view that, in the absence of exposure, or particular harm, to juveniles or unconsenting adults, the State lacks power to suppress sexually oriented materials.

STEVENS, J., CONCURRING

Two propositions seem perfectly clear to me. First, the specific conduct that gave rise to this criminal prosecution is not protected by the Federal Constitution; second, the state statute that respondent violated prohibits some conduct that is protected by the First Amendment. The critical question, then, is whether this respondent, to whom the statute may be applied without violating the Constitution, may challenge the statute on the ground that it conceivably may be applied unconstitutionally to others in situations not before the Court. I agree with the Court's answer to this question but not with its method of analyzing the issue....

A holding that respondent may be punished for selling these two films does not require us to conclude that other users of these very films, or that other motion pictures containing similar scenes, are beyond the pale of constitutional protection. Thus, the exhibition of these films before a legislative committee studying a proposed amendment to a state law, or before a group of research scientists studying human behavior, could not, in my opinion, be made a crime....

I believe a more conservative approach to the [overbreadth] issue would adequately vindicate the State's interest in protecting its children and cause less harm to the federal interest in free expression.... This Court's approach today substitutes broad, unambiguous, state-imposed censorship for the self-censorship that an overbroad statute might produce....

My reasons for avoiding overbreadth analysis in this case are more qualitative than quantitative. When we follow our traditional practice of adjudicating difficult and novel constitutional questions only in concrete factual situations, the adjudications tend to be crafted with greater wisdom. Hypothetical rulings are inherently treacherous and prone to lead us into unforeseen errors; they are qualitatively less reliable than the products of case-by-case adjudication....

QUESTIONS

1. How does *Ferber* modify *Miller?* How does Justice White answer the argument that the New York law is overbroad because it forbids the distribution of material of social value as well as constitutionally unprotected material?

2. In its brief in support of the New York law, Covenant House, a non-profit organization dedicated to the shelter and care of destitute children, argued that the Court's decision in *Hammer v. Dagenhart*, 247 U.S. 251 (1918) (see Volume I, Chapter 5), provided a more appropriate framework than the First Amendment for analyzing the issues in *Ferber*. In *Hammer*, a court, divided 5–4, held the 1916 Keating-Owen Child Labor Act unconstitutional as exceeding congressional authority to regulate commerce. The debate dividing the Court revolved around whether Congress, under Article I, Section 8, Clause 3, or the states, under the Tenth Amendment, had the constitutional authority to combat what was widely recognized as a destructive social practice—child labor.

   Assess the argument that *Hammer* provides a more appropriate framework than the First Amendment for regulating or prohibiting child pornography.

3. Given the Court's problematic attempts to formulate viable standards for regulating various forms of sexual representation, should the Court abandon its quest? Or are there principled distinctions

between obscenity, pornography, and child pornography on which constitutional doctrines could be grounded?

COMMENTS

1. In October 1989, Congress adopted an amendment offered by Senator Jesse Helms to an Interior Department appropriations bill. The amendment provides:

> None of the funds authorized to be appropriated to the National Endowment for the Arts [NEA] ... may be used to promote, disseminate, or produce materials which in the judgment of the National Endowment for the Arts ... may be considered obscene, including but not limited to, depictions of sadomasochism, homoeroticism, the sexual exploitation of children, or individuals engaged in sex acts and which, when taken as a whole, do not have serious literary, artistic, political or scientific value.

The Helms amendment required all applicants for NEA grants to certify that, if funds were awarded, none of the money would be used "to promote, disseminate, or produce materials which in the judgment of the NEA ... may be considered obscene." A federal district court found the certification requirement void for vagueness in violation of the Due Process Clause of the Fifth Amendment. *Bella Lewitsky Dance Foundation v. Frohnmayer*, 754 F.Supp. 774 (C.D. Cal.) (1991).

2. The opinions summarized below indicate the directions in which obscenity doctrine is developing after *Ferber*, as well as demonstrating continuing dissension over these directions.

> **Case:** *Brockett v. Spokane Arcades, Inc.*, 472 U.S. 491 (1985)
>
> **Vote:** 6–2 (Powell, J., did not participate.)
>
> **Decision:** A Washington statute declaring any place a "moral nuisance" if "lewd films are publicly exhibited as a regular course of business" or if "lewd publications constitute a principal part of the stock in trade" is partially invalid on its face. (The statute had never been applied.) The statute provides penalties for persons who deal in "obscene matter," which is defined as appealing to a "prurient interest," which in turn is defined as "that which incites lasciviousness or lust." The statute is invalid insofar as the word "lust" is understood to reach materials that are constitutionally protected because they arouse only a normal, healthy interest in sex.

> **Case:** *City of Renton v. Playtime Theaters, Inc.*, 475 U.S. 41 (1986)
>
> **Vote:** 7–2
>
> **Decision:** A city ordinance that prohibits adult motion picture theaters from locating within 1,000 feet of any residential zone, single- or multiple-family dwelling, church, park, or school is a valid governmental response to the serious problems created by adult theaters and satisfies the dictates of the First Amendment. Since the ordinance does not ban adult theaters altogether, it is properly analyzed as a form of time, place, and manner regulation. "Content-neutral"

time, place, and manner regulations are acceptable if they are designed to serve a substantial governmental interest and do not unreasonably limit alternative avenues of communication.

Case: *Osborne v. Ohio*, 495 U.S. 103 (1990)

Vote: 6–3

Decision: The First Amendment does not prohibit a state from proscribing the private possession and viewing of child pornography. A statute that can be construed to apply only to lewd exhibition or graphic focus on the genitals is not overbroad. States have a compelling interest in protecting the physical and psychological well-being of minors and in destroying the market for the exploitative use of children by penalizing those who possess and view the offending materials. Nevertheless, due process requires that the conviction be reversed and the case be remanded for a new trial because it is unclear whether the conviction was based on a finding that the prosecution had proved each of the elements of the offense.

Case: *Barnes v. Glen Theatre, Inc.*, 501 U.S. 560 (1991)

Vote: 5–4

Decision: A state public indecency law, which requires dancers to wear pasties and G-strings and prohibits total nudity in public places, does not violate the First Amendment. Three justices conclude that the enforcement of Indiana's public indecency law to prevent totally nude dancing does not violate the First Amendment's guarantee of freedom of expression. One justice concludes that the statute—as a general law regulating conduct and not specifically directed at expression, either in practice or on its face—is not subject to First Amendment scrutiny and should be upheld on the ground that moral opposition to nudity supplies a rational basis for its prohibition. One justice, believing that the nude dancing at issue is subject to a degree of First Amendment protection, concludes that the State's interest in preventing the secondary effects of adult entertainment establishments—prostitution, sexual assaults, and other criminal activity—is sufficient to justify the law's enforcement against nude dancing.

SUGGESTIONS FOR FURTHER READING

Bickel, Alexander, "On Pornography," 22 *The Public Interest* (Winter 1971): 25.

Caputi, Mary, *Voluptuous Yearnings: A Feminist Theory of the Obscene* (Lanham, MD: Rowman & Littlefield, 1994).

Chandos, John, ed., *To Deprave and Corrupt* (New York, NY: Association Press, 1962).

Clor, Harry M., *Obscenity and Public Morality: Censorship in a Liberal Society* (Chicago, IL: University of Chicago Press, 1969).

———, "Science, Eros, and the Law: A Critique of the Obscenity Commission Report," 10 *Duquesne Law Review* (1971): 63.

Copp, David, and Susan Wendell, eds., *Pornography and Censorship* (Buffalo, NY: Prometheus Books, 1983).

deGrazia, Edward, *Girls Lean Back Everywhere: The Law of Obscenity and the Assault on Genius* (New York, NY: Random House, 1992).

Dershowitz, Alan, "What is Porn?" 36 *American Bar Association Journal* (November 1, 1986).

Downs, Donald A., *The New Politics of Pornography* (Chicago, IL: University of Chicago Press, 1980).

Dworkin, Andrea, *Pornography: Men Possessing Women* (New York, NY: Perigee Press, 1981).

Gellhorn, Walter, *Individual Freedom and Governmental Restraints* (Baton Rouge, LA: Louisiana State University Press, 1956).

———, "Dirty Books, Disgusting Pictures, and Dreadful Laws," 8 *Georgia Law Review* (1974): 291.

Hawkins, Gordon, and Franklin E. Zimring, *Pornography in a Free Society* (Cambridge, MA: Cambridge University Press, 1988).

Heins, Marjorie, *Sex, Sin, and Blasphemy* (New York, NY: New Press, 1993).

Henken, Louis, "Morals and the Constitution: The Sin of Obscenity," 63 *Columbia Law Review* (1963): 391.

Hixson, Richard F., *Pornography and the Justices: The Supreme Court and the Intractable Obscenity Problem* (Carbondale, IL: Southern Illinois University Press, 1996).

Hunt, Lynn, ed., *The Invention of Pornography* (New York, NY: Zone Books, 1993).

Kalven, Harry, "The Metaphysics of the Law of Obscenity," *The Supreme Court Review* (Chicago, IL: University of Chicago Press, 1960).

———, "A Step Backward," *Chicago Tribune*, August 31, 1974.

Karst, Kenneth, "Boundaries and Reasons: Freedom of Expression and the Subordination of Groups," *University of Illinois Law Review* (1990): 95.

Katz, Stanley, "Privacy and Pornography: *Stanley v. Georgia*," *The Supreme Court Review* (Chicago, IL: University of Chicago Press, 1969).

Kobylka, Joseph F., *The Politics of Obscenity* (Westport, CT: Greenwood Press, 1991).

Krislov, Samuel, "From *Ginzburg* to *Ginsberg*: The Unhurried Children's Hour in Obscenity Litigation," *The Supreme Court Review* (Chicago, IL: University of Chicago Press, 1968).

Lederer, Laura, ed., *Take Back the Night: Women on Pornography* (New York, NY: Morrow, 1980).

Lewis, Anthony, "The First Amendment Under Fire from the Left," *New York Times Magazine*, March 13, 1994, p. 57.

Lockhart, William B., and Robert C. McClure, "Censorship of Obscenity: The Developing Constitutional Standards," 45 *Minnesota Law Review* (1960): 5.

MacKinnon, Catharine A., "Not a Moral Issue," 2 *Yale Law & Policy Review* (1984): 321.

_____, "Pornography, Civil Rights, and Speech," 20 *Harvard Civil Rights-Civil Liberties Review* (1985): 1.

_____, *Feminism Unmodified: Discourses on Life and Law* (Cambridge, MA: Harvard University Press, 1987).

_____, *Only Words* (Cambridge, MA: Harvard University Press, 1993).

Magrath, C. Peter, "The Obscenity Cases: Grapes of *Roth*," *The Supreme Court Review* (Chicago, IL: University of Chicago Press, 1966).

Meyer, Carlin, "Sex, Sin, and Women's Liberation: Against Porn-Suppression," 72 *Texas Law Review* (1994): 1097.

Murphy, Earl Finbar, "The Value of Pornography," 10 *Wayne Law Review* (1964): 655.

Note: "Obscenity and the Right to Be Let Alone: The Balancing of Constitutional Rights," 6 *Indiana Law Review* (1973): 490.

Note: "Community Standards, Class Actions, and Obscenity under *Miller v. California*," 88 *Harvard Law Review* (1975): 1838.

Note: "Anti-Pornography Laws and First Amendment Values," 98 *Harvard Law Review* (1984): 460.

Note: "The Content Distinction in Free Speech After *Renton*," 102 *Harvard Law Review* (1989): 1904.

Posner, Richard, *Sex and Reason* (Cambridge, MA: Harvard University Press, 1992).

Randall, Richard S., *Freedom and Taboo: Pornography and the Politics of a Self Divided* (Berkeley, CA: University of California Press, 1989).

Rembar, Charles, *The End of Obscenity: The Trials of* Lady Chatterly, Tropic of Cancer, *and* Fanny Hill *by the Lawyer Who Defended Them* (New York, NY: Simon and Schuster, 1968).

Report of the Commission on Obscenity and Pornography (Washington, D.C.: U.S. Government Printing Office, 1970).

Report of the Attorney General's Commission on Pornography (Washington, D.C.: U.S. Government Printing Office, 1986).

Richards, David, "Free Speech and Obscenity Law: Toward a Moral Theory of the First Amendment," 123 *University of Pennsylvania Law Review* (1974): 45.

St. John-Stevas, Norman, *Obscenity and the Law* (New York, NY: Macmillan, 1956).

Saunders, Kevin W., *Violence as Obscenity: Limiting the Media's First Amendment Protection* (Durham, NC: Duke University Press, 1996).

Schauer, Frederick F., *The Law of Obscenity* (Washington, D.C.: Bureau of National Affairs, 1976).

_____, "Speech and 'Speech'—Obscenity and 'Obscenity': An Exercise in the Interpretation of Constitutional Language," 67 *Georgia Law Review* (1979): 899.

_____, "Response: Pornography and the First Amendment," 40 *University of Pittsburgh Law Review* (1979): 905.

_____, "Codifying the First Amendment: *New York v. Ferber*," *The Supreme Court Review* (Chicago, IL: University of Chicago Press, 1982).

_____, "Causation Theory and the Causes of Sexual Violence," *American Bar Foundation Research Journal* (1987): 737.

Shapiro, Martin, "Obscenity Law: A Public Policy Analysis," 20 *Journal of Public Law* (1971): 503.

Strossen, Nadine, "The Convergence of Feminist and Civil Liberties Principles in the Pornography Debate," 62 *New York University Law Review* (1987): 201.

Sunderland, Lane, *Obscenity: The Court, the Congress and the President's Commission* (Washington, D.C.: American Enterprise Institute for Public Policy Research, 1975).

Sunstein, Cass, "Pornography and the First Amendment," *Duke Law Journal* (1986): 589.

Symposium: "The Proposed Minneapolis Pornography Ordinance: Pornography Regulation Versus Civil Rights or Pornography Regulation as Civil Rights?" 11 *William Mitchell Law Review* (1985): 35.

West, Robin, "The Feminist-Conservative Anti-Pornography Alliance and the 1986 Attorney General's Commission on Pornography Report," *American Bar Foundation Research Journal* (1987): 686.

ASSOCIATIONAL RIGHTS

National Association for the Advancement of Colored People v. Alabama
357 U.S. 449 (1958)

SETTING

The First Amendment provides in part that Congress shall make no law prohibiting "the right of the people peaceably to assemble." The other guarantees in the First Amendment are stated in unqualified terms, but the right to assemble is limited to "peaceable" assembly, an indication that government may impose regulations on assemblies. Over the years, there has been little doubt about the authority of government to regulative activities like picketing, parades, and rallies. Debate has focused instead on whether those regulations were reasonable.

The First Amendment is silent about the right to associate. However, as Alexis deTocqueville observed during his visit to the United States in the late

1830s, Americans are forever forming associations. He wrote in *Democracy in America*:

> In no country in the world has the principle of association been more successfully used or applied to a greater multitude of objects than in America. Besides the permanent associations which are established by law under the names of townships, cities, and counties, a vast number of others are formed and maintained by the agency of private individuals.... In the United States, associations are established to promote the public safety, commerce, industry, morality, and religion. There is no end which the human will despairs of attaining through the combined power of individuals united into a society.

Americans also band together for political reasons, forming groups that James Madison in *Federalist* No. 10 called "factions." Throughout American history, governments at the state and national levels have outlawed or sought other ways to render harmless political factions that they deemed subversive. States, for example, have enacted criminal syndicalism laws and made illegal membership in organizations like the Communist Party. Although it has long recognized that a limited right of association is integral to the First Amendment, one of the Supreme Court's tasks has been to police the boundary between legitimate laws regulating associations and laws that violate the First Amendment.

In *DeJonge v. Oregon*, 299 U.S. 353 (1937), the Court struck down Oregon's criminal syndicalism law on First Amendment grounds, stating that "peaceable assembly for lawful discussion cannot be made a crime." *DeJonge* reiterated that the right of peaceable assembly is "cognate to those of free speech and free press and is equally fundamental" and cannot be denied "without violating those fundamental principles of liberty and justice which the Fourteenth Amendment embodies in the general terms of its Due Process Clause." During the Cold War era, the Court's decisions on associational freedom were mixed and unpredictable. However, when state governments that were determined to preserve segregation attempted to harass the National Association for the Advancement of Colored People (NAACP) during the civil rights struggles of the 1950s and 1960s, the Court's decisions took a decidedly libertarian turn.

The NAACP was founded in 1909. It is a nonprofit organization committed to combating racial discrimination. The Certificate of Incorporation in New York State states that the NAACP's principal objects are:

> ... voluntarily to promote equality of rights and eradicate caste or race prejudice among the citizens of the United States; to advance the interests of colored citizens; to secure for them impartial suffrage; and to increase their opportunities for securing justice in the courts, education for their children, employment according to their ability, and complete equality before the law.

Early in the organization's history, lawyers employed by the NAACP won significant legal victories in voting discrimination cases, e.g., *Guinn v. United States*, 238 U.S. 347 (1915); successfully challenged racially restrictive housing ordinances, *Buchanan v. Warley*, 254 U.S. 60 (1917); and had overturned criminal convictions based on confessions extracted by torture, *Moore v. Dempsey*, 261 U.S. 86 (1923). Under the leadership of Howard University Law School Dean Charles Hamilton Houston, NAACP Legal Defense Fund (LDF) lawyers, preeminently Thurgood Marshall, were instrumental in winning a series of landmark civil rights decisions that culminated in *Brown v. Board of Education*, 347 U.S. 438 (1954) (see pp. 525–536).

The first NAACP Alabama affiliate was chartered in 1918. The NAACP opened a regional office in Alabama in 1951, where two supervisory and one clerical person were employed. Despite the NAACP's long presence in the state, it was not until 1956—following a successful bus boycott in Montgomery and the Supreme Court's decision in *Brown*—that Alabama Attorney General John Patterson filed suit in Montgomery County Circuit Court to enjoin the organization from conducting further activities in, and to expel it from, Alabama. Patterson relied on a 1940 statute that required corporations chartered in other states ("foreign corporations") to file their corporate charter with the Alabama secretary of state, and designate a place of business and an agent to receive service of legal documents. Patterson's suit alleged that the NAACP had opened a regional office and had organized various affiliates in Alabama; that it had recruited members and solicited contributions within the state; that it had given financial support and furnished legal assistance to Negro students seeking admission to the state university; and that it had supported a Negro boycott of the bus lines in Montgomery to compel the seating of passengers without regard to race. According to Patterson, by continuing to do business in Alabama without complying with the registration statute, the NAACP was "... causing irreparable injury to the property and civil rights of the residents and citizens of the State of Alabama for which criminal prosecution and civil actions afford no adequate relief...."

The circuit court granted Patterson's request for a restraining order against the NAACP. The NAACP moved to dissolve the order. It argued that it was not subject to the state's corporate registration requirements and that, in any event, what Patterson sought to accomplish by the suit would violate the NAACP's rights to freedom of speech and assembly guaranteed under the Fourteenth Amendment to the Constitution. Before the date set for a hearing on the NAACP's motion, the state moved for the production of a large number of the organization's records and papers, including bank statements, leases, deeds, and records containing the names and addresses of all NAACP "members" and "agents." Over the NAACP's objection, the circuit court ordered production of those materials.

In response, the NAACP admitted that its Alabama activities were substantially those alleged in the complaint, and that it had not qualified to do business in the state. It continued to deny that the statute applied to it, but offered to apply for qualification to do business in the state if the ban on doing so were lifted. The organization submitted the requisite forms for registering. However, it did not comply with the court's production order. The organization feared that providing the names and addresses of its members and agents would expose them to economic reprisal, loss of employment, threats, and public hostility. The circuit court held the organization in contempt for failing to comply with the production order and fined the NAACP $10,000. The contempt citation provided that the fine would be subject to reduction or remission if the NAACP complied with the production order within five days. Otherwise, the fine would be increased to $100,000.

At the end of the five-day period, the NAACP produced substantially all the materials specified except its membership lists. NAACP officials explained why they continued to refuse to produce these lists and argued that Alabama could not constitutionally compel disclosure. The NAACP moved to modify or vacate the contempt citation, or stay its execution pending appellate review. That motion was denied. While a similar stay application, which was later denied, was pending before the Supreme Court of Alabama, the circuit court declared the NAACP in continuing contempt and increased the fine to $100,000. Under Alabama law, the effect of the contempt citation was to foreclose the NAACP from having a hearing on the merits of the state's underlying ouster action, or from taking any steps to dissolve the restraining order until it had purged itself of contempt. The Alabama Supreme Court twice dismissed NAACP petitions for certiorari to review the final contempt order. The Supreme Court of the United States granted the NAACP's petition for a writ of certiorari.

HIGHLIGHTS OF SUPREME COURT ARGUMENTS

BRIEF FOR NAACP

◆ This case cannot be properly considered without understanding the background in which it arose. Alabama officials have consistently issued public declarations that the constitutional mandate prohibiting racial discrimination in public education be resisted and segregation strengthened. Those who advocate orderly compliance with *Brown v. Board of Education*, 347 U.S. 483 (1954), have suffered loss of employment and other economic reprisals and have been the targets violence, intimidation, vilification, and physical harm.

◆ The NAACP is a voluntary association whose primary objective is improving the status of people of color in the United States. The organization and its members are entitled to the protection of the Fourteenth Amendment in carrying out speech and associational activities guaranteed by the First Amendment. In these proceedings, Alabama seeks to punish the NAACP and its members for refusing to submit to state interference with its rights of speech and association.

◆ The order requiring the NAACP to disclose its membership list is an unwarranted and arbitrary invasion of an area of personal freedom immune from inquisition by the government. The truth is that in these proceedings Alabama seeks to silence the NAACP and its members, thereby eradicating effective opposition to continued state maintenance of racial segregation.

◆ The right to free discussion of the problems of our society and to engage in lawful activities aimed at their alleviation is one of the unique and indispensable requisites of our system. The fact that government officials in Alabama view the NAACP's goals as ill-advised is of no moment. The right of freedom of association is accorded to dissident and unpopular minorities as well as to those advocating ideas or engaging in activities of which those in power approve.

◆ The NAACP is not engaged in acts of disloyalty or subversion. It merely seeks to eradicate state-imposed racial segregation and discrimination. Since the Constitution forbids such discrimination, justification for restricting the organization's activities, although at war with the policies of the state of Alabama, is totally lacking.

◆ At no point in the proceedings in this case is there evidence that the circuit court sought to strike a fair balance between the interests of the parties. Due process requires rules of procedure that accord with fundamental fairness.

AMICUS CURIAE BRIEF SUPPORTING NAACP

Joint brief of the American Jewish Congress, Commission on Christian Social Progress, American Civil Liberties Union, American Friends Service Committee, American Jewish Committee, American Veterans Committee, Anti-Defamation League of B'nai B'rith, Board of Home Missions of the Congregational and Christian Churches, Council for Christian Social Action of the United Church of Christ, Japanese American Citizens League, Jewish Labor Committee, National Community Relations Advisory Council, United Synagogue of America, Workers Defense League.

BRIEF FOR ALABAMA

◆ This Court is constitutionally barred from reviewing a state court judgment that rests on a nonfederal ground. The sovereignty of state government is fundamental to our constitutional system and requires this Court to confine its review to those cases that inescapably present a federal questions. This case presents no federal question because the NAACP failed to avail itself of the established procedure of petition for a writ of mandamus to review the trial court's order to produce documents.

◆ The procedure used by the state to obtain the records of the NAACP was in keeping with Alabama law. The records were relevant to a determination of the nature and extent of the NAACP's business in Alabama.

◆ A corporation is subject to the restraints of the police power reserved to the states under the Tenth Amendment. A corporation has no right of privacy or privilege against self-incrimination. There is no reason why membership in a corporation devoted to propaganda, promotional activities, and the furthering of the interests of its members should be exempt from registration statutes and penalties for violating them.

◆ Corporations, associations, and similar organized groups have a right to freedom of speech and press. They do not have a right of privacy or secrecy.

SUPREME COURT DECISION: *9–0*

HARLAN, J.

... Effective advocacy of both public and private points of view, particularly controversial ones, is undeniably enhanced by group association, as this Court has more than once recognized by remarking upon the close nexus between the freedoms of speech and assembly.... It is beyond debate that freedom to engage in association for the advancement of beliefs and ideas is an inseparable aspect of the "liberty" assured by the Due Process Clause of the Fourteenth Amendment, which embraces freedom of speech.... Of course, it is immaterial whether the beliefs sought to be advanced by association pertain to political, economic, religious or cultural matters, and state action which may have the effect of curtailing the freedom to associate is subject to the closest scrutiny.

The fact that Alabama, so far as is relevant to the validity of the contempt judgment presently under review, has taken no direct action ... to restrict the right of petitioner's members to associate freely, does not end inquiry into the effect of the production order.... In the domain of these indispensable liberties, whether of speech, press, or association, the decisions of this Court recognize that abridgement of such rights, even though unintended, may inevitably follow from varied forms of governmental action....

It is hardly a novel perception that compelled disclosure of affiliation with groups engaged in advocacy may constitute as effective a restraint on freedom of association[.]... This Court has recognized the vital relationship between freedom to associate and privacy in one's associations.... Compelled disclosure of membership in an organization engaged in advocacy of particular beliefs is of the same order. Inviolability of privacy in group association may in many circumstances be indispensable to preservation of freedom of association, particularly where a group espouses dissident beliefs....

We think that the production order, in the respects here drawn in question, must be regarded as entailing the likelihood of a substantial restraint upon the exercise by petitioner's members of their right to freedom of association. Petitioner has made an uncontroverted showing that on past occasions revelation of the identity of its rank-and-file members has exposed these members to economic reprisal, loss of employment, threat of physical coercion, and other manifestations of public hostility. Under these circumstances, we think it apparent that compelled disclosure of petitioner's Alabama membership is likely to affect adversely the ability of petitioner and its members to pursue their collective effort to foster beliefs which they admittedly have the right to advocate, in that it may induce members to withdraw from the Association and dissuade others from joining it because of fear of exposure of their beliefs shown through their associations and of the consequences of this exposure.

It is not sufficient to answer, as the State does here, that whatever repressive effect compulsory disclosure of names of petitioner's members may have upon participation by Alabama citizens in petitioner's activities follows not from state action but from private community pressures. The crucial factor is the interplay of governmental and private action, for it is only after the initial exertion of state power represented by the production order that private action takes hold.

We turn to the final question whether Alabama has demonstrated an interest in obtaining the disclosures it seeks from petitioner which is sufficient to justify the deterrent effect which we have concluded these disclosures may well have on the free exercise by petitioner's members of their constitutionally protected right of association....

Whether there was "justification" in this instance turns solely on the substantiality of Alabama's interest in obtaining the membership lists. During the course of a hearing before the Alabama Circuit Court on a motion of petitioner to set aside the production order, the State Attorney General presented at length, under examination by petitioner, the State's reason for requesting the membership lists. The exclusive purpose was to determine whether petitioner was conducting intrastate business in violation of the Alabama foreign corporation registration statute, and the membership lists were expected to help resolve this question. The issues in the litigation commenced by Alabama by its bill in equity were whether the character of petitioner and its activities in Alabama had been such as to make petitioner subject to the registration statute, and whether the extent of petitioner's activities without qualifying suggested its permanent ouster from the State. Without intimating the slightest view upon the merits of these issues, we are unable to perceive that the disclosure of the names of petitioner's rank-and-file members has a substantial bearing on either of them. As matters stand in the state court, petitioner (1) has admitted its presence and conduct of activities in Alabama since 1918; (2) has offered to comply in all respects with the state qualification statute, although preserving its contention that the statute does not apply to it; and (3) has apparently complied satisfactorily with the production order, except for the membership lists, by furnishing the Attorney General with varied business records, its charter and statement of purposes, the names of all of its directors and officers, and with the total number of its Alabama members and the amount of their dues. These last items would not on this record appear subject to constitutional challenge and have been furnished, but whatever interest the State may have in obtaining names of ordinary members has not been shown to be sufficient to overcome petitioner's constitutional objections to the production order....

We hold that the immunity from state scrutiny of membership lists which the Association claims on behalf of its members is here so related to the right of the members to pursue their lawful private interests privately and to associate freely with others in so doing as to come within the protection of the Fourteenth Amendment. And we conclude that Alabama has fallen short of showing a controlling justification for the deterrent effect on the free enjoyment of the right to associate which disclosure of membership lists is likely to have. Accordingly, the judgment of civil contempt and the $100,000 fine which resulted from petitioner's refusal to comply with the production order in this respect must fall....

For the reasons stated, the judgment of the Supreme Court of Alabama must be reversed and the case remanded for proceedings not inconsistent with this opinion.

Reversed.

COMMENT

On remand, the Circuit Court of Montgomery County reaffirmed the contempt order that had been issued against the NAACP for failure to comply with the court's membership disclosure order. The circuit court relied on a different portion of its disclosure order that it believed the NAACP had violated. The Alabama Supreme Court affirmed.

In *NAACP v. Alabama*, 360 U.S. 240 (1959), the Supreme Court reversed. It ruled that Alabama courts were foreclosed from reexamining the basis on which the contempt order had originally been imposed. Having finally prevailed on the contempt issue, the NAACP then sought a hearing on the merits regarding the constitutionality of the state's registration law. Unable to obtain a hearing, the organization in 1960 filed suit in the U.S. District Court for the District of Alabama, contending that Alabama was depriving the organization of its constitutional rights by denying it a hearing. The district court dismissed the action, holding that it refused to assume that the judicial officers of Alabama would fail to protect the constitutional rights of all its citizens.

In *NAACP v. Gallion*, 368 U.S. 16 (1961), the Supreme Court vacated the federal district court order and instructed it to conduct a trial on the issue if the Alabama courts did not schedule a hearing by January 2, 1962. In December 1961, the Circuit Court of Montgomery County scheduled a hearing on the merits of the Alabama registration law. Following that hearing, the court upheld the constitutionality of the registration law and permanently enjoined the NAACP from doing "any further business of any description or kind" within the state. The Alabama Supreme Court affirmed.

In *NAACP v. Alabama*, 377 U.S. 288 (1964), the Supreme Court again reversed and remanded for further consideration. The Court held that permanently ousting the NAACP from doing business in Alabama violated the organization's right to associate for the advocacy of ideas. The opinion concluded:

> Should we unhappily be mistaken in our belief that the Supreme Court of Alabama will promptly implement this disposition, leave is given the Association to apply to this Court for further appropriate relief.

QUESTIONS

1. State the rule of *NAACP v. Alabama*. Does the decision stand for the proposition that freedom of association is an integral part of the First Amendment even though there is no reference to associational rights in that amendment? Or is the case better understood in more limited terms, as part of the Supreme Court's ongoing effort to seek enforcement of its decision in *Brown v. Board of Education*, 347 U.S. 483 (1954)?

2. Counsel for the NAACP observed that "Negro Americans' only effective redress lies in ... litigation, in the free exercise of the ballot, and freedom of speech and assembly. Only through joint and concerted

exercise of these rights can a weak and unpopular minority succeed in securing equality before the law." Immediately after making that statement, counsel quoted the following portion of Justice Stone's famous footnote 4 to his opinion in *United States v. Carolene Products Co.*, 304 U.S. 144 (1938) (see Chapter 5, pp. 464–465):

> Nor need we inquire whether similar considerations enter into the review of statutes directed at particular religions, ... or national ... or racial minorities ... whether prejudice against discrete and insular minorities may be a special condition, which tends seriously to curtail the operation of those political processes ordinarily to be relied upon to protect minorities, and which may call for a correspondingly more searching judicial inquiry.

Is the Court's decision in *NAACP* a logical extension of footnote 4 in *Carolene Products*? What theory of judicial power underpins footnote 4 and *NAACP*?

3. In *Bryant v. Zimmerman*, 278 U.S. 63 (1928), the Supreme Court upheld a New York law that required some organizations having oath-bound membership requirements to disclose their membership lists. The Ku Klux Klan argued that the New York statute violated the Due Process Clause of the Fourteenth Amendment. The Court rejected that argument because of the "manifest tendency" of the Klan to engage in conduct "inimical to personal rights and public welfare." What factors distinguish *Bryant* from *NAACP*?

4. In a column titled, "Off the Bench," published in the March 4, 1957, *Montgomery Advertiser*, Judge Walter B. Jones, who had presided over the hearing on Alabama's complaint against the NAACP wrote: "I speak for the White Race, my race[.]... The integrationists and mongrelizers do not deceive any person of common sense with their pious talk of wanting only equal rights and opportunities for other races. Their real and final goal is intermarriage and mongrelization of the American people.... We have all kindly feelings for the world's other races, but we will maintain at any and all sacrifices the purity of our blood strain and race. We shall never submit to the demands of integrationists. The white race shall forever remain white."

Should Judge Jones have recused himself from the case because of his racial views, or were these views irrelevant to the legal issues in *NAACP*?

COMMENT

The cases summarized below suggest the nature of the legal battles that the NAACP continued to fight in the wake of *NAACP v. Alabama*.

Case: *Bates v. City of Little Rock*, 361 U.S. 516 (1960)
Vote: 9–0

Decision: Where a municipal ordinance requires compulsory disclosure of the membership list of the local branch of the NAACP, and such disclosure would work a significant interference with members' freedom of association, the threat of substantial government encroachment on important and traditional aspects of individual freedom was neither speculative nor remote. Public identification of persons in the community as members of the NAACP had been followed by harassment and threats of bodily harm. Fear of community hostility and economic reprisals that would result from public disclosure of the membership list had discouraged new members from joining the organizations and induced former members to withdraw.

Case: *Shelton v. Tucker,* 364 U.S. 479 (1960)

Vote: 5–4

Decision: An Arkansas statute requiring public school teachers to file affidavits listing the names and addresses of all organizations to which they have belonged or contributed within the preceding five years as a prerequisite to employment is unconstitutional. Applied to a teacher who is a member of the NAACP, who was hired on a year-to-year basis, who is not covered by a civil service system, and who has no job security beyond the end of each school year, the filing requirement impairs the right of free association. To compel a teacher to disclose every associational tie impairs that teacher's right of free association, a right closely allied to freedom of speech and a right which, like free speech, lies at the foundation of a free society.

Case: *NAACP v. Button,* 371 U.S. 415 (1963)

Vote: 5–4

Decision: A Virginia statute that prohibits any arrangement by which prospective litigants are advised to seek assistance of particular attorneys, that makes it a crime for a person to advise another that legal rights have been infringed, and that makes it illegal to make referrals to particular attorneys or group of attorneys (such as the legal staff of the Virginia conference of NAACP for assistance), violates the First Amendment. The activities of the NAACP, its affiliates, and legal staff are modes of expression and association that are protected by the First and Fourteenth Amendments, which Virginia may not prohibit, notwithstanding its power to regulate the legal profession and improper solicitation of legal business.

Case: *Gibson v. Florida Legislative Investigation Committee,* 372 U.S. 539 (1963)

Vote: 5–4

Decision: A committee subpoena ordering production of membership records of the Miami Branch of the NAACP, and disclosure of whether specified alleged communists are also members of the NAACP, is not a valid use of the state's legislative investigation function. The First and Fourteenth Amendment rights of free speech and free association are fundamental and are protected not only against heavy-handed frontal attack, but also from being stifled by more subtle governmental interference. Compelled disclosure of affiliation with groups engaged in advocacy may constitute an effective restraint on freedom of association. The legislative committee has not demonstrated a valid governmental interest in obtaining and making public the local association membership information.

Case: *NAACP v. Claiborne Hardware Company,* 458 U.S. 886 (1982)

Vote: 9–0

Decision: The nonviolent activities of members of the NAACP, the Mississippi Action for Progress, and a number of individuals who had participated in a 1966 boycott of white merchants in Claiborne County, Mississippi, are entitled to the protection of the First Amendment against liability in a civil action for damages. Through exercise of their First Amendment rights of speech, assembly, association, and petition, rather than through riot or revolution, petitioners sought to bring about political, social, and economic change. While states have broad power to regulate economic activities, there is no comparable right to prohibit peaceful political activity such as boycotts. Similarly, the First Amendment restricts the ability of the state to impose liability on an individual solely because of his association with another. Civil liability may not be imposed merely because an individual belonged to a group, some members of which committed acts of violence. For liability to be imposed by reason of association alone, it is necessary to establish that the group itself possessed unlawful goals and that the individual held a specific intent to further those illegal aims.

ASSOCIATIONAL RIGHTS

Roberts v. United States Jaycees
468 U.S. 609 (1984)

SETTING

The cases involving the NAACP provide insight into issues involving freedom of association in the context of an organization that is devoted to eradicating racial discrimination in the United States. Increased involvement by women in professions has sparked another kind of controversy, this time the rights of associations that discriminate on the basis of gender.

The United States Jaycees is a national organization founded in 1920, whose by-laws limited full membership to young men aged eighteen to thirty-five. Men over thirty-five and women were eligible only for associate membership. Associate members were not allowed to vote, hold any office, or receive achievement awards. The goal of the Jaycees was to train young men for civic and business leadership and to offer them opportunities for business and community advancement. The organization's primary activity is selling memberships through continuous recruitment of new members.

In 1974 and 1975, the Minneapolis and St. Paul, Minnesota, chapters of the Jaycees began admitting women as regular members of the local chapters. Women soon comprised approximately one-quarter of the membership of the two chapters. The national organization imposed sanctions on both chapters for accepting women as regular members.

At a referendum during its 1975 national convention, the national Jaycees voted 90 percent to 10 percent against allowing women as regular members. A similar referendum at its 1978 convention reaffirmed those results.

On December 15, 1978, the president of the United States Jaycees informed the Minneapolis and St. Paul chapters that a motion would be made at the upcoming national executive board meeting to revoke their charters. Four days later, the presidents of the two chapters filed charges of sex discrimination against the Jaycees with the Minnesota Department of Human Rights. They contended that the Jaycees' policy of excluding women from regular membership violated the Minnesota Human Rights Act. That act prohibits any person from denying "the full and equal enjoyment of the goods, services, facilities, privileges, advantages, and accommodations of a place of public accommodation because of race, color, creed, religion, disability, national origin, or sex."

In 1979, Department of Human Rights hearing examiner George Beck ruled that the Jaycees is a "place of a public accommodation" for purposes of the act, and that its policy of excluding women from regular membership was an "unfair discriminatory practice." He ordered the Jaycees to cease and desist from the practice.

While Beck had the case under advisement, the national Jaycees filed suit in the U.S. District Court of Minnesota against Irene Gomez-Bethke, commissioner of the Department of Human Rights, Minnesota Attorney General Hubert H. Humphrey III, and Beck, claiming that application of the Human Rights Act to the organization would violate the constitutional rights of the male members to speak and associate.

The district court dismissed the suit without prejudice pending the outcome of the Minnesota administrative proceeding. After Beck issued his decision, the national organization filed a renewed complaint in federal district court. That court then certified to the Minnesota Supreme Court the question of whether the Jaycees organization was a place of public accommodation within the meaning of the Human Rights Act. The Minnesota Supreme Court answered in the affirmative. The federal district court then scheduled a trial in the case.

Following trial, the court entered a judgment in favor of officials of the Department of Human Rights. The Jaycees appealed to the Court of Appeals for the Eighth Circuit, which reversed. It held that the Jaycees' right to select its members is protected by the freedom of association guaranteed by the First Amendment, and that the state's interest in prohibiting discrimination was not sufficiently compelling to outweigh interference with that right. Gomez-Bethke, Humphrey, and Beck appealed to the Supreme Court of the United States. The name of Kathryn Roberts, acting commissioner of the Human Rights Department, was substituted for Gomez-Bethke on appeal.

HIGHLIGHTS OF SUPREME COURT ARGUMENTS

BRIEF FOR ROBERTS

◆ Application of the Minnesota Human Rights Act to the Jaycees does not burden the First Amendment rights of the organization to speak, assemble, or petition government for a redress of grievances.

◆ There is no freedom of association independent of an enumerated First Amendment freedom. Freedom of association is a derivative right whose existence the Court sometimes has deemed necessary in order to protect the collective exercise by individuals of enumerated First Amendment rights such as free speech or assembly. Absent a threat to an enumerated freedom, there is no constitutional right of association.

◆ There is no evidence to support the claim that equal membership rights for women will abridge any enumerated First Amendment Right of the Jaycees.

◆ Even if the Court concludes that the Minnesota Human Rights Act does abridge some First Amendment freedom of the Jaycees, the law may still be applied to the organization. The Court has held that even a significant encroachment by the government of a First Amendment freedom is permissible if the regulation furthers a compelling state interest. Equality of access to the marketplace for women is a significant state interest, while granting women full membership privileges will not prevent the Jaycees from carrying on its programs and activities. The declared public policy of the state is to obtain freedom from discrimination for its citizens in public accommodations because of race or sex. Minnesota also demonstrated its commitment to equality for women through ratification of the proposed Equal Rights Amendment.

◆ The claim that there are other avenues of professional development for women is based on the moribund theory of "separate but equal."

◆ An organization that sells goods and privileges in exchange for membership fees and which solicits members from the public at large is a "public accommodation" under the Minnesota Human Rights Act.

AMICUS CURIAE BRIEFS SUPPORTING ROBERTS

American Civil Liberties Union; NAACP Legal Defense and Education Fund.

BRIEF FOR UNITED STATES JAYCEES

◆ Application of Minnesota's public accommodation law to the Jaycees will destroy the Jaycees' ability to achieve its purpose. The core purpose of the organization is to provide *young men* with the benefits of activities directed to civic purposes. The limited service purpose of the Jaycees is precisely like the purpose of hundreds of other organizations. The fact that the Jaycees' central purpose may not, at this period of history, appear as important as the NAACP provides no invitation to state power.

◆ The Supreme Court has acknowledged that the right of association and its necessary corollary—the right of nonassociation—is in itself a fundamental liberty. Rights of association and rights of expression and assembly are inseparable in concept and in practice.

◆ Minnesota has failed to demonstrate a compelling governmental interest for encroaching on the Jaycees' freedom of association.

◆ The Minnesota Human Rights Act is vague in its meaning and overbroad in its application. The definition of a "public accommodation" is vague, which even the state admits. The unexplained exemption of the Kiwanis Club from the reach of the statute makes it impossible to detect what public policy is being served by the statute.

AMICUS CURIAE BRIEFS SUPPORTING UNITED STATES JAYCEES

Rotary International; Boy Scouts of America; Conference of Private Organizations.

SUPREME COURT DECISION: 7–0

(Burger, C.J., and Blackmun, J., did not participate.)

BRENNAN, J.

... The Court has long recognized that, because the Bill of Rights is designed to secure individual liberty, it must afford the formation and preservation of certain kinds of highly personal relationships a substantial measure of sanctuary from unjustified interference by the States. Without precisely identifying every consideration that may underlie this type of constitutional protection, we have noted that certain kinds of personal bonds have played a critical role in the culture and traditions of the Nation by cultivating and transmitting shared ideals and beliefs; they thereby foster diversity and act as critical buffers between the individual and the power of the State. Moreover, the constitutional shelter afforded such relationships reflects the realization that individuals draw much of their emotional enrichment from close ties with others. Protecting these relationships from unwarranted state interference therefore safeguards the ability independently to define one's identity that is central to any concept of liberty.

The personal affiliations that exemplify these considerations, and that therefore suggest some relevant limitations on the relationships that might be entitled to this sort of constitutional protection, are those that attend the creation and sustenance of a family—marriage, childbirth, the raising and education of children, and cohabitation with one's relatives. Family relationships, by their nature, involve deep attachments and commitments to the necessarily few other individuals with whom one shares not only a special community of thoughts, experiences, and beliefs but also distinctively personal aspects of one's life. Among other things, therefore, they are distinguished by such attributes as relative smallness, a high degree of selectivity in decisions to begin and maintain the affiliation, and selectivity in decisions to begin and maintain the affiliation, and seclusion from others in critical aspects of the relationship. As a general matter, only relationships with these sorts of qualities are likely to reflect the considerations that have led to an understanding of freedom of association as an intrinsic element of personal liberty. Conversely, an association lacking these qualities— such as a large business enterprise— seems remote from the concerns giving rise to this constitutional protection. Accordingly, the Constitution undoubtedly imposes constraints on the State's power to control the selection of one's spouse that would not apply to regulations affecting the choice of one's fellow employees.

Between these poles, of course, lies a broad range of human relationships that may make greater or lesser claims to constitutional protection from particular incursions by the State. Determining the limits of state authority over an individual's freedom to enter into a particular association therefore unavoidably entails a careful assessment of where that relationship's objective characteristics locate it on a spectrum from the most intimate to the most attenuated of personal attachments. We need not mark the potentially significant points on this terrain with any precision. We note only that factors that may be relevant include size, purpose, policies, selectivity, congeniality, and other characteristics that in a particular case may be pertinent. In this case, however, several features of the Jaycees clearly place the organization outside the category of relationships worthy of this kind of constitutional protection....

Apart from age and sex, neither the national organization nor the local chapters employ any criteria for judging applicants for membership, and new members are routinely recruited and admitted with no inquiry into their backgrounds. In fact, a local officer testified that he could recall no instance in which an applicant had been denied membership on any basis other than age or sex....

An individual's freedom to speak, to worship, and to petition the government for the redress of grievances could not be vigorously protected from interference by the State unless a correlative freedom to engage in group effort toward those ends were not also guaranteed. According protection to collective effort on behalf of shared goals is especially important in preserving political and cultural diversity and in shielding dissident expression from suppression by the majority. Consequently, we have long understood as implicit in the right to engage in activities protected by the First Amendment a corresponding right to associate with others in pursuit of a wide variety of political, social, economic, educational, religious, and cultural ends....

The right to associate for expressive purposes is not, however, absolute. Infringements on that right may be justified by regulations adopted to serve compelling state interests, unrelated to the suppression of ideas, that cannot be achieved through means significantly less restrictive of associational freedoms. We are persuaded that Minnesota's compelling interest in eradicating discrimination against its female citizens justifies the impact that application of the statute to the Jaycees may have on the male members' associational freedom.

On its face, the Minnesota Act does

not aim at the suppression of speech, does not distinguish between prohibited and permitted activity on the basis of viewpoint, and does not license enforcement authorities to administer the statute on the basis of such constitutionally impermissible criteria. Nor does the Jaycees contend that the Act has been applied in this case for the purpose of hampering the organization's ability to express its views. Instead, ... the Act reflects the State's strong historical commitment to eliminating discrimination and assuring its citizens equal access to publicly available goods and services. That goal, which is unrelated to the suppression of expression, plainly serves compelling state interests of the highest order....

In applying the Act to the Jaycees, the State has advanced those interests through the least restrictive means of achieving its ends. Indeed, the Jaycees has failed to demonstrate that the Act imposes any serious burdens on the male members' freedom of expressive association.... Over the years, the national and local levels of the organization have taken public positions on a number of diverse issues, and members of the Jaycees regularly engage in a variety of civic, charitable, lobbying, fundraising, and other activities worthy of constitutional protection under the First Amendment. There is, however, no basis in the record for concluding that admission of women as full voting members will impede the organization's ability to engage in these protected activities or to disseminate its preferred views. The Act requires no change in the Jaycees' creed of promoting the interests of young men, and it imposes no restrictions on the organization's ability to exclude individuals with ideologies or

philosophies different from those of its existing members....

[E]ven if enforcement of the Act causes some incidental abridgment of the Jaycees' protected speech, that effect is no greater than is necessary to accomplish the State's legitimate purposes....

O'CONNOR, J., CONCURRING

... The Court analyzes Minnesota's attempt to regulate the Jaycees' membership using a test that I find both overprotective of activities undeserving of constitutional shelter and underprotective of important First Amendment concerns....

In my view, an association should be characterized as commercial, and therefore subject to rationally related state regulation of its membership and other associational activities, when, and only when, the association's activities are not predominantly of the type protected by the First Amendment. It is only when the association is predominantly engaged in protected expression that state regulation of its membership will necessarily affect, change, dilute, or silence a collective voice that would otherwise be heard. An association must choose its market. Once it enters the marketplace of commerce in any substantial degree it loses the complete control over its membership that it would otherwise enjoy if it confined its affairs to the marketplace of ideas....

[T]his Court's case law recognizes radically different constitutional protections for expressive and nonexpressive associations. The First Amendment is offended by direct state control of the membership of a private organization engaged exclusively in protected expressive activity, but no First Amendment interest stands in the way of a State's rational regulation of economic transactions by or within a commercial association....

Notwithstanding its protected expressive activities, the Jaycees ... is, first and foremost, an organization that, at both the national and local levels, promotes and practices the art of solicitation and management. The organization claims that the training it offers its members gives them an advantage in business, and business firms do indeed sometimes pay the dues of individual membership for their employees. Jaycees members hone their solicitation and management skills, under the direction and supervision of the organization, primarily through their active recruitment of the members....

Recruitment and selling are commercial activities, even when conducted for training rather than for profit.... The State of Minnesota has a legitimate interest in ensuring nondiscriminatory access to the commercial opportunities presented by membership in the Jaycees.

QUESTIONS

1. Identify the two types of associational freedoms recognized by the Court in *Roberts*. Do the Jaycees fit either catagory? From the perspective of organizations that wish to exclude certain classes of persons, was *Roberts* a "bad" case because of its facts? Do the facts in *Roberts* help to explain the unanimous vote?

2. On what basis did Justice O'Connor concur in *Roberts*? Is her proposed rule more constitutionally defensible than Justice Brennan's majority rule?

3. Several values were in competition in *Roberts*, including issues of federalism, freedom of association, commitments to equality, and cultural pluralism. Does *Roberts* strike an acceptable balance among them? Which, if any, of the values should be sacrificed in order to achieve one or some of the others?

4. Chief Justice Burger and Justice Blackmun recused themselves from participation in *Roberts* because many years before both of them had been members of the Jaycees in Minnesota. Was their recusal appropriate in this case? Under what circumstances should justices recuse themselves from consideration of a case?

5. Law professors Paul Brest and Sanford Levinson ask:

> Can you imagine any circumstances under which a government could require a religious group to adapt its rules of membership to the ostensible requirements of the Constitution? For example, membership by birth in traditional Judaism is by matrilineal descent. This means, among other things, that children of Jewish fathers (but not Jewish mothers) who have been raised as Jews must undergo formal conversion ceremonies before being accepted as members in Jewish congregations; children of

Jewish mothers and non-Jewish fathers need not convert. Could the state constitutionally forbid congregations from applying such clearly discriminatory rules? Or imagine that a legislature attempts to promote the "leadership skills" of female Catholics by making illegal the Roman Catholic Church's refusal to allow women into the priesthood? (*Processes of Constitutional Decisionmaking: Cases and Materials*, 3rd ed. [Boston, MA: Little, Brown, 1992], p. 1456)

What guidelines do the associational rights cases in this section provide for responding to Brest and Levinson's questions?

COMMENT

The Supreme Court revisited the issue of private club members' associational rights in the following cases:

Case: *Board of Directors of Rotary International v. Rotary Club of Duarte*, 481 U.S. 537 (1987)

Vote: 7–0 (Blackmun and O'Connor, J.J., did not participate.)

Decision: Application to local Rotary Clubs of California's Unruh Act—which entitles all persons, regardless of sex, to full and equal accommodations, advantages, facilities, privileges, and services in all business establishments in the State—does not interfere unduly with club members' freedom of private association. In determining whether a particular association is sufficiently intimate or private to warrant constitutional protection, consideration must be given to factors such as size, purpose, selectivity, and whether others are excluded from critical aspects of the relationship. Here, the relationship among Rotary Club members does not warrant protection, in light of the potentially large size of local clubs, the high turnover rate among club members, the inclusive nature of each club's membership, the public purposes behind clubs' service activities, and the fact that the clubs encourage the participation of strangers in, and welcome media coverage of, many of their central activities. Nevertheless, application of the act to California Rotary Clubs does not violate the First Amendment right of expressive association. Although the clubs engage in a variety of commendable service activities that are protected by the First Amendment, the evidence fails to demonstrate that admitting women will affect in any significant way the existing members' ability to carry out those activities.

Case: *New York State Club Association, Inc. v. City of New York*, 487 U.S. 1 (1988)

Vote: 9–0

Decision: A New York City ordinance requiring that certain associations with more than four hundred members comply with that city's Human Rights Law is constitutional. The New York State Club Association's facial First Amendment attack must fail to the extent that it relies on the claim that New York City's Local Law 63 is invalid in all of its applications. As the New York State Club Association concedes, the Human Rights Law's antidiscrimination provisions may be constitutionally applied to at least some of the large covered clubs under *Roberts v. United States Jaycees* and *Board of Directors of Rotary International v. Rotary Club of Duarte*, 481 U.S. 537 (1987). In finding that clubs comparable in size to, or smaller than, clubs covered by the Human Rights Law were not protected private associations, *Roberts* and *Rotary* emphasized the regular participation of strangers at club meetings, a factor that is no more significant to defining a club's nonprivate nature than are Local Law 63's requirements. Similarly, Local Law 63 cannot be said to infringe on every club member's right of expressive association, since, in the absence of specific evidence on the characteristics of any covered club, it must be assumed that many of the large clubs would be able to effectively advance their desired viewpoints without confining their membership to persons having, for example, the same sex or religion.

SUGGESTIONS FOR FURTHER READING

Abernathy, M. Glenn, "Right of Association," 6 *South Carolina Law Quarterly* (1953): 32.

_____, *The Right of Assembly and Association*, rev. ed. (Columbia, SC: University of South Carolina Press, 1981).

Belknap, Michal R., *Federal Law and Southern Order: Racial Violence and Constitutional Conflict in the Post-Brown South* (Athens, GA: University of Georgia Press, 1987).

Bell, Derrick, "Serving Two Masters: Integration Ideals and Client Interests in School Desegregation Litigation," 85 *Yale Law Journal* (1976): 470.

Chafee, Zechariah, Jr., "The Internal Affairs of Associations Not for Profit," 43 *Harvard Law Review* (1930): 993.

_____, "The Problem of the Hostile Audience," 49 *Columbia Law Review* (1949): 1118.

Comment: "State Control over Political Organizations: First Amendment Checks on the Powers of Regulation," 66 *Yale Law Journal* (1957): 545.

"Developments in the Law—Judicial Control of Actions of Private Associations," 76 *Harvard Law Review* (1963): 983.

Emerson, Thomas, "Freedom of Association and Freedom of Expression," 74 *Yale Law Journal* (1964): 1.

Fellman, David, *The Constitutional Right of Association* (Chicago, IL: University of Chicago Press, 1963).

Fiss, Owen, *The Civil Rights Injunction* (Bloomington, IN: Indiana University Press, 1978).

Garet, Ronald R., "Communality and Existence: The Rights of Groups," 56 *Southern California Law Review* (1983): 1001.

Henderson, Lynn N., "Legality and Empathy," 85 *Michigan Law Review* (1987): 1574.

Horn, Robert A., *Groups and the Constitution* (Stanford, CA: Stanford University Press, 1956).

Kalven, Harry, Jr., *The Negro and the First Amendment* (Columbus, OH: Ohio State University Press, 1965).

Karst, Kenneth L., "The Freedom of Intimate Association," 89 *Yale Law Journal* (1980): 624.

———, *Belonging to America: Equal Citizenship and the Constitution* (New Haven, CT: Yale University Press, 1989).

Laski, Harold, "The Personality of Associations," 29 *Harvard Law Review* (1916): 91.

Linder, Douglas O., "Freedom of Association after *Roberts v. Jaycees*," 82 *Michigan Law Review* (1984): 1878.

Lynd, Staughton, "Communal Rights," 62 *Texas Law Review* (1984): 1417.

Murphy, Walter F., "The South Counterattacks: The Anti-NAACP Laws," 12 *Western Political Quarterly* (1959): 371.

Murphy, Walter F., and Robert F. Birkby, "Interest Group Conflict in the Judicial Arena," 42 *Texas Law Review* (1964): 1018.

Note: "Private Attorneys-General: Group Action in the Fight for Civil Liberties," 58 *Yale Law Journal* (1949): 574.

Raggi, Reena, "An Independent Right to Freedom of Association," 12 *Harvard Civil Rights-Civil Liberties Law Review* (1977): 1.

Rice, Charles, *Freedom of Association* (New York, NY: New York University Press, 1962).

Robison, Joseph B., "Protection of Association from Compulsory Disclosure of Membership," 58 *Columbia Law Review* (1958): 614.

Schlesinger, Arthur, "Biography of a Nation of Joiners," 50 *American Historical Review* (1944): 1.

Soifer, Aviam, *Law and the Company We Keep* (Cambridge, MA: Harvard University Press, 1995).

Sturges, Wesley, "Unincorporated Associations as Parties to Action," 33 *Yale Law Journal* (1924): 383.

Sullivan, Kathleen, "Rainbow Republicanism," 97 *Yale Law Journal* (1988): 1713.

Symposium: "Group Legal Services in Perspective," 12 *UCLA Law Review* (1965): 279.

Tushnet, Mark, *The NAACP's Legal Strategy Against Segregated Education* (Chapel Hill, NC: University of North Carolina Press, 1987).

Van Alstyne, William, "The Demise of the Right-Privilege Distinction in Constitutional Law," 81 *Harvard Law Review* (1968): 1439.

Vose, Clement E., *Caucasians Only* (Berkeley, CA: University of California Press, 1959).

Williams, Juan, *Eyes on the Prize: America's Civil Rights Years, 1954–1965* (New York, NY: Penguin, 1988).

CHAPTER 5

---⊃●⊂---

FOURTEENTH AMENDMENT

FOURTEENTH AMENDMENT: INITIAL INTERPRETATION

Slaughter-House Cases
16 Wallace 36 (1873)

SETTING

The Civil War has been called the second American Revolution because of the political and economic changes it wrought in American life. For all practical purposes, the Thirteenth, Fourteenth, and Fifteenth Amendments are the constitution of that revolution. The Thirteenth Amendment, ratified in 1865, marked the first formal change in the Constitution in more than sixty years. It put an official end to slavery and overrode the Three-Fifths Compromise contained in Article I. The abolition of slavery made it possible for southern states to have increased representation in the House of Representatives and the Electoral College. Former slaveholders feared the consequences of black political participation. Some states refused to ratify the Thirteenth Amendment and demanded that the federal government pay former slaveholders for the loss of their property. Many northern entrepreneurs saw former slaves as a source of cheap labor, while northern workers perceived them as a threat to their jobs or wages, and the Republican Party saw them as the source of a powerful political base in the South.

Southern states quickly adopted Black Codes, based on the old slave codes. Among other things, Black Codes prevented blacks from voting, holding certain jobs, serving on juries, owning firearms, traveling and relocating at will, living in certain areas, congregating in groups and intermarrying with whites. Black Codes also imposed more severe criminal punishments on blacks than on whites, subjected blacks to severe curfew restrictions, and locked blacks into disadvantageous agricultural labor systems such as tenancy, sharecropping, and peonage. The goal of the Black Codes was to maintain the social, political, and economic status quo notwithstanding the Thirteenth Amendment. Combined with the terror tactics of the Ku Klux Klan, the Black Codes demonstrated that the states of the former Confederacy were committed to nullifying freemen's liberty.

Six weeks before he was assassinated on April 14, 1865, President Lincoln had created a Freedmen's Bureau to assist former slaves in building new lives and to protect them against the Black Codes and terrorism. When a Congress dominated by "radical Republicans"—who advocated treating the former Confederacy more like conquered provinces than coequal states—attempted to extend authorization for the Freedman's Bureau in 1866, Lincoln's successor, President Andrew Johnson, vetoed the bill. Johnson, a Tennessee native, argued that the Freedman's Bureau gave military courts too much power to resolve issues of racial discrimination or infringements of civil rights.

Although congressional Republicans lacked the votes to override the president's veto, they responded to that veto and to the Black Codes by enacting civil rights legislation. The Civil Rights Act of 1866 nullified the Supreme Court's 1857 decision in *Dred Scott v. Sandford*, 19 Howard 393 (1857) (see Volume I, pp. 150–158), by declaring all persons born or naturalized in the United States to be citizens of the United States. The act set national standards for the protection of freed blacks by declaring that all citizens were to enjoy the equal protection of the laws, and gave federal courts broad enforcement jurisdiction. President Johnson vetoed the Civil Rights Act, declaring that it violated states' rights, but Republicans were able to muster the votes to override that veto.

Despite the veto override, the Civil Rights Act sparked nationwide debates over the enormous powers that the act gave to the national government. Radical Republican leaders in Congress, fearing that the legislation might be weakened, sought to incorporate the major provisions of the act into a new constitutional amendment.

When the Joint Committee on Reconstruction reported the proposed Fourteenth Amendment, it characterized the amendment as "a plan of reconstruction." Over the years, the first section of the amendment, focusing on civil rights, has virtually overshadowed the other four sections. Section 1 begins with the declaration, "All persons born or naturalized in the United States, and subject to the jurisdiction thereof, are citizens of the United States and of the State wherein they reside." That declaration is followed by three clauses, known as the Privileges or Immunities Clause, the Due Process Clause, and the Equal Protection Clause. The Fourteenth Amendment was ratified on July 9, 1868. Like the Thirteenth and Fifteenth Amendments, the fifth section of the Fourteenth Amendment empowers Congress to enforce the provisions of the other sections by "appropriate legislation."

The Privileges or Immunities Clause of the Fourteenth Amendment contains language derived from Article IV, Section 2, of the Constitution, which provides that "The Citizens of each State shall be entitled to all Privileges and Immunities of Citizens of the several States." The meaning of that language has never been clear. However, Ohio Representative John A. Bingham, one of the primary drafters of the Fourteenth Amendment, claimed that the intent of the Privileges or Immunities Clause of the Fourteenth Amendment was to assure that the guarantees of the Bill of Rights would limit the states as well as the national government. In 1871, Bingham declared that he had drafted the Privileges or Immunities Clause in response to the following "suggestion" by Chief Justice Marshall in *Barron v. Baltimore*, 7 Peters 243 (1833) (see Volume I, pp. 649–654):

> Had the framers of [the first eight amendments to the Constitution] intended them to be limitations on the powers of the State governments, they would have imitated the framers of the original constitution and have expressed that intention.

Said Bingham of his efforts in drafting the Privileges or Immunities Clause, "I did imitate the framers of the original Constitution."

Whether Bingham's view of the purpose of the Privileges or Immunities Clause was shared by his congressional colleagues is not clear and there is no language in the amendment that defines the meaning of the privileges or immunities of U.S. citizenship. Consequently, that task fell to the Supreme Court in the *Slaughter-House Cases*. In the course of its opinion, the Court initially addressed the meaning of the Fourteenth Amendment's other two great clauses, due process of law and equal protection of the laws, which are the subject of subsequent sections of this chapter.

The facts of the *Slaughter-House Cases* trace to March 1869, when the Louisiana legislature passed Act 118 entitled, "An act to protect the health of the city of New Orleans, to locate the stock-landings and slaughter-houses, and to incorporate the Crescent City Live Stock Landing and Slaughter-House Company." The new company consisted of seventeen incorporators. Act 118 gave Crescent City a monopoly over slaughterhouses in the city of New Orleans and the parishes of Orleans, Jefferson, and St. Bernard for a period of twenty-five years. Crescent City was authorized to construct one "grand slaughter-house," capable of slaughtering five hundred animals per day, and was given the duty of permitting any person to slaughter animals in its facilities, under penalty of a fine for each refusal. All other stock handling companies and slaughterhouses were ordered closed by June 1, 1869.

New York City, Boston, Milwaukee, and San Francisco had earlier passed statutes similar to Act 118 to protect the public health. The goal of the statutes was to control the dumping of carcasses into municipal water supplies. Although the New Orleans law was presented as a public health act, in fact it was a spoils scheme. The incorporators had distributed cash and stock to New Orleans municipal officials, members of both houses of the Louisiana legislature, and the state governor as bribes to ensure passage of Act 118.

By June 1869, approximately two hundred suits were instituted for and against the Crescent City Live-Stock Company in six district courts in Louisiana. Crescent City sought to enjoin an estimated one thousand other butchers from operating slaughterhouses in violation of the act. Other butchers sued Crescent City and the state of Louisiana in an effort to have the act declared unconstitutional.

By agreement of the parties, all but six cases were dropped. The six cases that proceeded raised all of the legal issues that needed to be resolved and were litigated in the district courts in which they were filed. Under the agreement, they were appealed as a whole to the Louisiana Supreme Court. That court ruled for Crescent City. Opponents of the slaughter-house monopoly petitioned the Supreme Court of the United States for a writ of error.

In March 1871, some of the parties claimed to have reached a settlement and moved for dismissal. Three of the parties objected to having their cases dismissed, claiming they had given no authority to settle their cases. Following argument and decision on the motion to dismiss, three cases were set for argument on the merits. One involved the Butchers' Benevolent Association of New Orleans against the Crescent City Company.

The three cases were argued together in January 1872. Justice Samuel Nelson did not participate. Following argument, the justices split 4–4 on the result. They ordered the case reargued at the next Term. The second argument occurred in February 1873, by which time Justice Ward Hunt had replaced Justice Samuel Nelson.

HIGHLIGHTS OF SUPREME COURT ARGUMENTS

BRIEF FOR THE BUTCHERS' BENEVOLENT ASSOCIATION OF NEW ORLEANS

◆ Act 118 is described as an act of police, adopted by the state to promote salubrity, security, and public order. But laws of police, like other state laws, are valid only if they do not violate the limits of the Constitution.

◆ Act 118 violates the Fourteenth Amendment's Privileges or Immunities Clause. Limiting a man's choice of a trade, depriving him of a business he has pursued, and giving others the exclusive right to practice that trade violates rights of national citizenship declared by the amendment. The purpose of the Fourteenth Amendment was to ensure all men the rights of life, liberty, and property, the right to labor freely, and the enjoyment of the fruits of their own industry.

◆ Act 118 violates the Fourteenth Amendment's Equal Protection Clause. Its purpose was to establish one people through the whole jurisdiction of the United States. The amendment is not confined to any race or class, and contains a universal mandate that all be treated equally. The enrichment of seventeen butchers while depriving nearly one thousand of the same class of a means of earning their daily bread is a denial of equality.

◆ Act 118 violates the Fourteenth Amendment's Due Process Clause. The property of butchers not incorporated by the act was destroyed. The right to move with freedom, to choose one's highway, and to be exempt from impositions are rights that cannot be infringed by legislatures without violating due process.

BRIEF FOR LOUISIANA AND THE CRESCENT CITY COMPANY

◆ Federal law, like Louisiana law, has long recognized the power of the state to grant exclusive franchises and to exercise complete, unqualified, and exclusive power regarding those powers which relate to mere municipal legislation or internal police. The legislature is the sole judge of whether a statute is reasonable and for the benefit of the people.

◆ Even states whose constitutions contain strong statements of individual, inalienable rights—including acquiring, possessing, and protecting property—recognize the authority of the state to enact regulations as part of its police power.

◆ Reliance on the Fourteenth Amendment by the butchers is inappropriate. Had it not been for the status of people of African descent in the United States, the amendment would not have been proposed. The amendment cannot be made to embrace objects other than blacks without sacrificing its spirit.

◆ The Privileges or Immunities Clause is not used for the first time in the Fourteenth Amendment. The original Constitution provided that "the citizens of each state shall be entitled to all privileges and immunities of citizenship in the several states." The privileges and immunities contemplated there are those that are fundamental, such as the right of going into any state for the purpose of residing therein; the right of taking up one's residence therein; becoming a citizen; the right of free entrance and exit and passage through; and the protection of laws affecting personal liberty.

◆ The Privileges or Immunities Clause of the Fourteenth Amendment added no privileges or immunities to the Constitution that citizens of the United States did not enjoy before its adoption. If Act 118 would have been constitutional before adoption of the Fourteenth Amendment, it is constitutional now. If the complaining butchers' argument is accepted, states will lose their ability to impose licenses and license fees, regulate dangerous trades or articles, restrain the manufacture of alcohol and lotteries, enact Sunday closing laws and child labor laws.

SUPREME COURT DECISION: 5–4

MILLER, J.

... The plaintiffs in error ... allege that the statute is a violation of the Constitution of the United States in these several particulars [including]:...

That it abridges the privileges and immunities of citizens of the United States;

That it denies to the plaintiffs equal protection of the laws; and,

That it deprives them of their property without due process of law; contrary to the provisions of the first section of the fourteenth article of amendment.

This court is thus called upon for the first time to give construction to these articles....

The first section of the fourteenth article ... opens with a definition of citizenship—not only citizenship of the United States, but citizenship of the States. No such definition was previously found in the Constitution, nor had any attempt been made to define it by act of Congress....

The first observation we have to make on this clause is, ... it declares that persons may be citizens of the United States without regard to their citizenship of a particular State, and it overturns the *Dred Scott* [*v. Sandford,* 19 Howard 393 (1857)] decision by making *all persons* born within the United States and subject to its jurisdiction citizens of the United States. That its main purpose was to establish the citizenship of the negro can admit of no doubt....

The next observation is more important in view of the arguments of counsel in the present case. It is that the distinction between citizenship of the United States and citizenship of a state is clearly recognized and established. Not only may a man be a citizen of the United States without being a citizen of a state, but an important element is necessary to convert the former into the latter. He must reside within the state to make him a citizen of it, but it is only necessary that he should be born or naturalized in the United States to be a citizen of the Union....

We think this distinction and its explicit recognition in this amendment of great weight in this argument, because the next paragraph of the same section, which is the one mainly relied on by the plaintiffs in error, speaks only of privileges and immunities of citizens of the several States. The argument, however, in favor of the plaintiffs rests wholly on the assumption that citizenship is the same, and the privileges and immunities guaranteed by the clause are the same....

Of the privileges and immunities of the citizen of the United States, and of the privileges and immunities of the citizen of the State, and what they respectively are, we will presently consider; but we wish to state here that it is only the former which are placed by this clause under the protection of the Federal Constitution, and that the latter, whatever they may be, are not intended to have any additional protection by this paragraph of the amendment.

If, then, there is a difference between the privileges and immunities belonging to a citizen of the United States as such, and those belonging to the citizen of the State as such, the latter must rest for their security and protection where they have heretofore rested; for they are not embraced by this paragraph of the amendment....

The first occurrence of the words "privileges and immunities" in our constitutional history is to be found in the fourth of the Articles of the old Confederation....

In the Constitution of the United States ... the corresponding provision is found in section two of the 4th article, in the following words: The citizens of each state shall be entitled to all the privileges and immunities of citizens of the several states....

Fortunately we are not without judicial construction of this clause of the Constitution....

Its sole purpose was to declare to the several States, that whatever those rights, as you grant or establish them to your own citizens, or as you limit or qualify, or impose restrictions on their exercise, the same, neither more nor less, shall be the measure of the rights of citizens of other States within your jurisdiction....

Was it the purpose of the fourteenth amendment ... to transfer the security and protection of all ... civil rights ... from the States to the Federal government? And where it is declared that Congress shall have the power to enforce that article, was it intended to bring within the power of Congress the entire domain of civil rights heretofore belonging exclusively to the States?

All this and more must follow, if the

proposition of the plaintiffs in error be sound....

We are convinced that no such results were intended by the Congress which proposed these amendments, nor by the legislatures of the States which ratified them.

Having shown that the privileges and immunities relied on in the argument are those which belong to citizens of the States as such, and that they are left to the State governments for security and protection, and not by [the Privileges or Immunities Clause] placed under the special care of the Federal government, we may hold ourselves excused from defining the privileges and immunities of citizens of the United States which no State can abridge, until some case involving those privileges may make it necessary to do so.

But lest it should be said that no such privileges and immunities are to be found if those we have been considering are excluded, we venture to suggest some which owe their existence to the Federal government, its National character, its Constitution, or its laws.

One of these is well described in the case of *Crandall v. Nevada* [6 Wallace 35 (1868)]. It is said to be the right of the citizen of this great country, protected by implied guarantees of its Constitution, "to come to the seat of government to assert any claim he may have upon that government, to transact any business he may have with it, to seek its protection, to share its offices, to engage in administering its functions. He has the right of free access to its seaports, through which all operations of foreign commerce are conducted, to the sub-treasuries, land offices, and courts of justice in the several States." And quoting from the language of Chief Justice Taney in another case, it is said "*that for all the great purposes for*

which the Federal government was established, we are one people, with one common country, *we are all citizens of the United States*;" and it is, as such citizens, that their rights are supported in this court in *Crandall v. Nevada*.

Another privilege of a citizen of the United States is to demand the care and protection of the Federal government over his life, liberty, and property when on the high seas or within the jurisdiction of a foreign government. Of this there can be no doubt, nor that the right depends upon his character as a citizen of the United States. The right to peaceably assemble and petition for redress of grievances, the privilege of the writ of *habeas corpus*, are rights of the citizen guaranteed by the Federal Constitution. The right to use the navigable waters of the United States, however they may penetrate the territory of the several States, all rights secured to our citizens by treaties with foreign nations are dependent upon citizenship of the United States, and not citizenship of a State. One of these privileges is conferred by the very article under consideration. It is that a citizen of the United States can, of his own volition, become a citizen of any State of the Union by a *bona fide* residence therein, with the same rights as other citizens of that State. To these may be added the rights secured by the thirteenth and fifteenth articles of amendment, and by the other clause of the fourteenth, next to be considered.

But it is useless to pursue this branch of the inquiry, since we are of opinion that the rights claimed by these plaintiffs in error, if they have any existence, are not privileges and immunities of citizens of the United States within the meaning of the clause of the fourteenth amendment under consideration....

The argument has not been much pressed in these cases that the defendant's charter deprives the plaintiffs of their property without due process of law, or that it denies to them the equal protection of the law....

We are not without judicial interpretation, ... both State and National, of the meaning of [the Due Process C]lause. And it is sufficient to say that under no construction of that provision that we have ever seen, or any that we deem admissible, can the restraint imposed by the State of Louisiana upon the exercise of their trade by the butchers of New Orleans be held to be a deprivation of property within the meaning of that provision....

In the light of the history of these amendments, and the pervading purpose of them, which we have already discussed, it is not difficult to give a meaning to [the equal protection] clause. The existence of laws in the States where the newly emancipated negroes resided, which discriminated with gross injustice and hardship against them as a class, was the evil to be remedied by this clause, and by it such laws are forbidden.

If, however, the States did not conform their laws to its requirements, then by the fifth section of the article of amendment Congress was authorized to enforce it by suitable legislation. We doubt very much whether any action of a State not directed by way of discrimination against the negroes as a class, or on account of their race, will ever be held to come within the purview of this provision. It is so clearly a provision for that race and that emergency, that a strong case would be necessary for its application to any other....

The adoption of the first eleven amendments so soon after the original instrument was accepted shows a prevailing sense of danger at that time from the Federal power and it cannot be denied that such a jealousy continued to exist with many patriotic men until the breaking out of the late Civil War. It was then discovered that the true danger to the perpetuity of the Union was in the capacity of the state organizations to combine and concentrate all the powers of the state, and of contiguous states, for a determined resistance to the general government.

Unquestionably this has given great force to the argument, and added largely to the number of those who believe in the necessity of a strong national government.

But, however pervading this sentiment, and however it may have contributed to the adoption of the Amendments we have been considering, we do not see in those Amendments any purpose to destroy the main features of the general system....

But whatever fluctuations may be seen in this history of public opinion on this subject during the period of our national existence, we think it will be found that this court, so far as its functions required, has always held with a steady and an even hand the balance between State and Federal power, and we trust that such may continue to be the history of its relation to that subject so long as it shall have duties to perform which demand of it a construction of the Constitution, or of any of its parts.

The judgments of the Supreme Court of Louisiana in those cases are affirmed.

FIELD, J., CHASE, C.J., SWAYNE, AND BRADLEY, J.J., DISSENTING

... The privileges and immunities designated in the second section of the fourth article of the Constitution are ... those which of right belong to the citizens of all free governments, and they can be enjoyed under that clause by the citizens of each State in the several States upon the same terms and conditions as they are enjoyed by the citizens of the latter States. No discrimination can be made by one State against the citizens of other States in their enjoyment, nor can any greater imposition be levied than such as is laid upon its own citizens. It is a clause which insures equality in the enjoyment of these rights between citizens of the several States whilst in the same State....

What [the second section of the fourth article of the Constitution] did for the protection of the citizens of one State against hostile and discriminating legislation of other States, the fourteenth amendment does for the protection of every citizen of the United States against hostile and discriminating legislation against him in favor of others, whether they reside in the same or in different States. If under the fourth article of the Constitution equality of privileges and immunities is secured between citizens of different States, under the fourteenth amendment the same equality is secured between citizens of the United States.

It will not be pretended that under the fourth article of the Constitution any State could create a monopoly in any known trade or manufacture in favor of her own citizens, or any portion of them, which would exclude an equal participation in the trade or manufacture monopolized by citizens of other States....

[W]hat the clause in question does for the protection of citizens of one State against the creation of monopolies in favor of citizens of other States, the fourteenth amendment does for the protection of every citizen of the United States against the creation of any monopoly whatever. The privileges and immunities of citizens of the United States, of every one of them, is secured against abridgment in any form by any State. The fourteenth amendment places them under the guardianship of the National authority....

[T]he fourteenth amendment secures the like protection to all citizens [in Louisiana] against any abridgment of their common rights, as in other States. That amendment was intended to give practical effect to the declaration of 1776 of inalienable rights, rights which are the gift of the Creator, which the law does not confer, but only recognizes....

So fundamental has this privilege of every citizen to be free from disparaging and unequal enactments, in the pursuit of the ordinary avocations of life, been regarded, that few instances have arisen where the principle has been so far violated as to call for the interposition of the courts. But whenever this has occurred, with the exception of the present cases from Louisiana, which are the most barefaced and flagrant of all, the enactment interfering with the privilege of the citizen has been pronounced illegal and void....

This equality of right, with exemption from all disparaging and partial enactments, in the lawful pursuits of life, throughout the whole country, is the distinguishing privilege of citizens of the United States. To them, everywhere, all pursuits, all professions, all avocations are open without other restrictions than such as are imposed equally upon all others of the same age, sex, and condition.... The fourteenth amendment, in my judgment, makes it essential to the validity of the legislation of every State that this equality of right should be respected. How widely this equality has been departed from, how entirely rejected and trampled upon by the act of Louisiana, I have already shown. And it is to me a matter of profound regret that its validity is recognized by a majority of this court, for by it the right of free labor, one of the most sacred and imprescriptible rights of man, is violated....

BRADLEY, J., DISSENTING

... [I]n my judgment, the right of any citizen to follow whatever lawful employment he chooses to adopt (submitting himself to all lawful regulations) is one of his most valuable rights, and one which the legislature of a State cannot invade, whether restrained by its own constitution or not.

The right of a State to regulate the conduct of its citizens is undoubtedly a very broad and extensive one, and not to be lightly restricted. But there are certain fundamental rights which this right of regulation cannot infringe. It may prescribe the manner of their exercise, but it cannot subvert the rights themselves.... I speak now of the rights of citizens of any free government....

[E]ven if the Constitution were silent, the fundamental privileges and immunities of citizens, as such, would be no less real and no less inviolable than they now are. It was not necessary to say in words that the citizens of the United States should have and exercise all the privileges of citizens; the privilege of buying, selling, and enjoying property; the privilege of engaging in any lawful employment for a livelihood; the privilege of resorting to the laws for redress of injuries, and the like. Their very citizenship conferred these privileges, if they did not possess them before. And these privileges they would enjoy whether they were citizens of any State or not. Inhabitants of Federal territories and new citizens, made such by annexation of territory or naturalization, though without any status as citizens of a State, could, nevertheless, as citizens of the United States, lay claim to every one of the privileges and immunities which have been enumerated; and among these none is more essential and fundamental than the right to follow such profession or employment as each one may choose, subject only to uniform regulations equally applicable to all....

The granting of monopolies, or exclusive privileges to individuals or corporations, is an invasion of the right of others to choose a lawful calling, and an infringement of personal liberty....

Lastly: Can the Federal courts administer relief to citizens of the United States whose privileges and immunities have been abridged by a State? Of this I entertain no doubt. Prior to the fourteenth amendment this could not be done, except in a few instances, for the want of the requisite authority....

Admitting, therefore, that formerly the States were not prohibited from infringing any of the fundamental privileges and immunities of citizens of the United States, except in a few specified cases, that cannot be said now, since the adoption of the fourteenth amendment. In my judgment, it was the intention of the people of this country in adopting that amendment to provide National security against violation by the States of the fundamental rights of the citizen....

It is futile to argue that none but persons of the African race are intended to be benefited by this amendment. They may have been the primary cause of the amendment, but its language is general, embracing all citizens, and I think it was purposely so expressed....

SWAYNE, J., DISSENTING [OMITTED]

QUESTIONS

1. Summarize Justice Miller's interpretation of the Privileges or Immunities Clause in *Slaughter-House*. Did his reading render the Clause a nullity?

2. Attorneys for the Butchers' Benevolent Association cited the Thirteenth and Fourteenth Amendments in support of their argument against the slaughterhouse monopoly. What principles in those amendments support legal opposition to economic monopoly? Is it surprising that residents of the former Confederacy would deploy a theory premised on federal supervision of state legislation?

3. Historian Charles Warren observed that between 1870 and 1873 the Court "was receding somewhat from the almost unvaried support which it had theretofore given to Congressional power..." (*The Supreme Court in United States History*, 3 vols. [Boston, MA: Little, Brown and Company, 1923], 3: 255). Warren singled out the *Slaughter-House Cases* as indicating when "the change in the attitude of the Court became most marked" (Ibid., p. 257). What elements in *Slaughter-House* are "[s]igns of a reaction in favor of the State powers" (Ibid., pp. 255–256)?

COMMENTS

1. Historian Charles Fairman describes the irony of the *Slaughter-House Cases*:

   > One might have supposed that it would be a case on behalf of Negroes, or the suit of some citizen from the North complaining of treatment in the South, that first raised the Fourteenth Amendment at the bar of the Supreme Court. Instead it was a suit by Southern whites, complaining against Carpetbag legislation; the right they would vindicate was not a political but an economic liberty— namely, to carry on the business of slaughtering cattle, free from a monopoly conferred by the legislature upon a favored group of incorporators. This was all out of accord with what the members of Congress had in mind in their debates. (*History of the Supreme Court of the United States, Volume 6: Reconstruction and Reunion 1864–88, Part One* [New York, NY: Macmillan, 1971], p. 1308)

2. The *Slaughter-House Cases* virtually eliminated the Privileges or Immunities Clause as a source of constitutional protection under the Fourteenth Amendment. The Supreme Court has never overruled the decision. Consequently, civil rights litigation has occurred under the auspices of the Fourteenth Amendment's other two clauses of Section 1: Due Process and Equal Protection of the Laws. However, until 1937 the Court's primary focus was on sorting out the constitutional relationship between government and the economy. The Fourteenth Amendment played an important role in that process, as the first case in the next section—*Lochner v. New York*, 198 U.S. 45 (1905)— demonstrates.

SUGGESTIONS FOR FURTHER READING

Benedict, Michael Les, "Preserving Federalism: Reconstruction and the Waite Court," *The Supreme Court Review* (Chicago, IL: University of Chicago Press, 1978).

Beth, Loren P., "The *Slaughter-House Cases*—Revisited," 23 *Louisiana Law Review* (1963): 587.

Comment, "The Privileges or Immunities Clause of the Fourteenth Amendment: The Original Intent," 79 *Northwestern University Law Review* (1984): 142.

Curtis, Michael Kent, *No State Shall Abridge: The Fourteenth Amendment and the Bill of Rights* (Durham, NC: Duke University Press, 1986).

Farber, Daniel A., and John E. Muench, "The Ideological Origins of the Fourteenth Amendment," 1 *Constitutional Commentary* (1984): 235.

Gerhardt, Michael J., "The Ripple Effects of *Slaughter-House*: A Critique of a Negative Rights View of the Constitution," 43 *Vanderbilt Law Review* (1990): 409.

Gillette, William, *Retreat from Reconstruction, 1869–1879* (Baton Rouge, LA: Louisiana State University Press, 1979).

Hamburger, Philip, "Equality and Diversity: The Eighteenth-Century Debate about Equal Protection and Equal Civil Rights," *The Supreme Court Review* (Chicago, IL: University of Chicago Press, 1992).

Hyman, Harold M., *A More Perfect Union: The Impact of the Civil War and Reconstruction on the Constitution* (New York, NY: Knopf, 1973).

James, Joseph B., *The Framing of the Fourteenth Amendment* (Urbana, IL: University of Illinois, 1956).

Kaczorowski, Robert, *The Politics of Judicial Interpretation: The Federal Courts, Department of Justice and Civil Rights, 1866–1876* (Dobbs Ferry, NY: Oceana, 1985).

———, "Revolutionary Constitutionalism in the Era of the Civil War and Reconstruction," 61 *New York University Law Review* (1986): 863.

Kurland, Philip B., "The Privileges or Immunities Clause: 'Its Hour Come Round at Last?'" 1972 *Washington University Law Quarterly* (1972): 405.

Lucie, Patricia Allan, "White Rights As a Model for Black: Or Who's Afraid of the Privileges or Immunities Clause?" 38 *Syracuse Law Review* (1987): 859.

Murphy, Walter F., "*Slaughter-House*, Civil Rights, and Limits on Constitutional Change," 32 *American Journal of Jurisprudence* (1987): 1.

Nelson, William E., *The Fourteenth Amendment: From Political Principle to Judicial Doctrine* (Cambridge, MA: Harvard University Press, 1988).

Palmer, Robert C., "The Parameters of Constitutional Reconstruction: *Slaughter-House, Cruickshank*, and the Fourteenth Amendment," 1984 *University of Illinois Law Review* (1984): 739.

Polakoff, Keith, *The Politics of Inertia: The Election of 1876 and the End of Reconstruction* (Baton Rouge, LA: Louisiana State University Press, 1973).

Simson, Gary J., "Discrimination against Nonresidents and the Privileges and Immunities Clause," 128 *University of Pennsylvania Law Review* (1979): 379.

Trelease, Allen W., *White Terror: The Ku Klux Klan Conspiracy and Southern Reconstruction* (New York, NY: Harper and Row, 1971).

Varat, Jonathan D., "State 'Citizenship' and Interstate Equality," 48 *University of Chicago Law Review* (1981): 487.

Wilson, Theodore B., *The Black Codes of the South* (Tuscaloosa, AL: University of Alabama Press, 1965).

Woodward, C. Vann, *Reunion and Reaction: The Compromise of 1877 and the End of Reconstruction*, rev. ed. (Garden City, NY: Doubleday, 1956).

DUE PROCESS

Lochner v. New York
198 U.S. 45 (1905)

SETTING

The concept of due process is deeply rooted in Anglo-American jurisprudence. Its origins trace to Chapter 39 of the Magna Charta of 1215—originally the Articles of the Barons—sealed by King John at Runnymede, England. Chapter 39 of the Magna Charta provided:

> No free man shall be seized or imprisoned, or stripped of his rights or possessions, or outlawed or exiled, or deprived of his standing in any other way, nor will we proceed with force against him, or send others to do so, except by the lawful judgment of his equals or by the law of the land.

Two fundamental principles reflected in Chapter 39 and associated with the concept of due process are that the actions of government be conducted according to the rule of law and that government is not above the law. James Madison sought to capture those principles in the Fifth Amendment to the Constitution, which prohibits the national government from depriving any person of life, liberty, or property "without due process of law." The Due Process Clause of the Fourteenth Amendment mirrors the language of the Fifth Amendment and prohibits states from denying any person of life, liberty, or property "without due process of law."

Notwithstanding the deep roots of due process in Anglo-American law and the appearance of the term in the Fifth and Fourteenth Amendments, the meaning and requirements of due process have never been clear. One consistent theory of due process—often referred to as the traditional view—is that governments must follow fair, reasonable, consistent procedures in carrying out their responsibilities. Under this theory, one of the primary functions of judicial review is to assure that lower courts use fair procedures in conducting trials and that the legislative and executive branches adhere to established processes in making and enforcing laws.

Another theory of due process has what commonly is called a substantive component. Under this theory, due process places fundamental substantive limits on laws that governments can make, because there are certain rights and relationships with which government has no authority to interfere. The phrase "economic substantive due process" refers to judge-made legal rules that limit the authority of government to regulate private property and economic relationships between owners of capital and the workers whose labor they purchase for a wage.

The origins of economic substantive due process trace to the middle of the nineteenth century. Many state judges deemed property rights and rights and obligations created by contracts as fixed and absolute. They began to fashion legal rules that would protect property and contractual rights from governmental regulation. Taken together, those rules reflected a variety of views about the relationship between government and the economy. First is the view that there are inherent limitations on the scope of legislative powers and that it is the obligation of judges to declare those limitations in particular cases. By 1875, that view had an adherent on the Supreme Court of the United States. In *Loan Association v. Topeka*, 20 Wallace 655, Justice Samuel Miller, the author of the majority opinion in the *Slaughter-House Cases*, wrote:

> It must be conceded that there are ... rights in every free government beyond the control of the State. A government which recognized no such rights, which held the lives, the liberty, and the property of its citizens subject at all times to the absolute disposition and unlimited control of even the most democratic depository of power, is after all but a despotism.

A second view reflected in the doctrine of economic substantive due process is the idea that judges must look past processes and formalities in evaluating legislation to determine whether a law tramples on fundamental economic rights. By 1877, Justice John M. Harlan had adopted this second view. In *Mugler v. Kansas*, 123 U.S. 623, he wrote, albeit in dictum:

> [Not] every statute enacted ostensibly for the promotion of [public health, safety or morality] is to be accepted as a legitimate exertion of the police powers of the state.... The courts are not bound by mere forms, nor are they to be misled by mere pretenses. They are at liberty, indeed, are under a solemn duty, to look at the substance of things, whenever they enter upon the inquiry whether the legislature has transcended the limits of its authority. If, therefore, a statute purporting to have been enacted to protect the public health, the public morals, or the public safety, has no real or substantial relation to these objects, or is a palpable invasion of rights secured by the fundamental law, it is the duty of the courts to so adjudge, and thereby give effect to the constitution.

The third view reflected in the doctrine of economic substantive due process is that the right of individuals to order their contractual relations privately is among the fundamental liberties that judges are to protect in the name of due process. By 1897, Justice Rufus Peckham was expressing that view on behalf of the Supreme Court of the United States:

> The "liberty" mentioned in [the Fourteenth Amendment] means, not only the right of the citizen to be free from the mere physical restraint of his person, as by incarceration, but the term is deemed to embrace the right of the citizen to be free in the enjoyment of all of his faculties; to be free to use them in all lawful ways; to live and work where he will; to earn his livelihood by any lawful calling; to pursue any livelihood or avocation; and for that purpose to enter into all contracts which may be proper, necessary, and essential to his carrying out to successful conclusion the purposes above mentioned. *Allgeyer v. Louisiana*, 165 U.S. 578 (1897).

A fourth view, which underpinned the development of economic substantive due process, is the notion that any form of regulatory legislation must be "neutral" and serve a "public purpose." Many judges perceived state regulatory legislation—enacted pursuant to the "police power" or inherent power to protect the public health, safety, welfare or morals—as favoring one particular class or social group over others. Those judges were not shy about striking down regulatory statutes that they perceived to be biased in favor of one class or group, typically workers. In 1885, for example, the New York Court of Appeals struck down a state law that outlawed the manufacture of cigars in tenement houses. The law was an attempt to ban the notorious "sweating system" that required employees to perform tedious tasks for long hours under unhealthy conditions at low wages. According to the New York high court, the law interfered with the "profitable and free use" of property by cigar makers and deprived them of property and "some portion of ... personal liberty." Equally important, according to the court, the law was not neutral in its effect:

> What does this act attempt to do? In form, it makes it a crime for a cigar-maker in New York and Brooklyn, the only cities in the State having a population exceeding 500,000, to carry on a perfectly lawful trade in his own home.... [H]e will become a criminal for doing that which is perfectly lawful outside of the two cities named—everywhere else, so far as we are able to learn, in the whole world. *In re Jacobs*, 98 N.Y. 98 (1885).

The doctrine of economic substantive due process had profound consequences for efforts to regulate the industrial economy that emerged after the Civil War. Mechanization and creation of large-scale corporate organizations ushered in the era of factory work in an impersonal urban setting. Skilled craftsmen became assembly line workers doing routinized tasks. Formerly self-employed farmers and small business owners became employees whose relationship to their employers and work were defined by contract. Economic self-sufficiency gave way to labor market vulnerability.

Despite the lobbying efforts of workers, the United States lagged far behind other western industrial nations in adopting statutes regulating wages, hours and working conditions of employees. What little economic regulatory legislation existed in the United States before the 1930s was adopted by state legislatures, but business owners opposed economic regulations as infringements on their rights of property and contract. Workers themselves were deeply divided over issues such as the legitimacy of capitalism, government's role in economic regulation, and the rights of workers who were not White, Anglo-Saxon Protestants. Although states like Massachusetts, New York, Oregon, and Washington were pioneers in enacting legislation designed to protect workers and regulate the economy, their efforts collided with the doctrine of economic substantive due process. The clash was demonstrated in classic form in *Lochner v. New York.*

Throughout the 1880s, New York state bakers had struggled to unionize their industry. At the center of those efforts was a drive to reduce the typical sixteen- to eighteen-hour day that bakers worked to ten hours. Conditions in the bakeries were oppressive. According to one New York baker: "It is nothing unusual for a man to do his night's work and then have to work three or four hours with the day hands. Our trade is the worst paid trade in New York.... This means eight dollars for ninety hours of hard work. Is it any wonder there are so many coffins?"

On April 23, 1887, a mass meeting of bakers adopted a resolution supporting reduced work hours. The bakers' organizing efforts were only partially successful, however. Many bakeries remained nonunion. In order to bring them into line with those bound by collective bargaining agreements, the Baker's Progressive Union lobbied the New York legislature to pass a ten-hour work law for bakers.

The union argued that long hours spent in hot shops damaged bakers' health and jeopardized the production of wholesome bread. An 1892 study, conducted by the New York Commissioner of Labor Statistics with the aid of the organization of Journeymen Bakers, fed agitation for shorter hours. The study found that union bakers in New York City worked an average of ten-and-one-half hours daily, including Sundays, while bakers working in non-union shops averaged twelve-and-one-half hours. The bakers' lobbying campaign was fruitful: New York's 1897 Labor Law provided that no employee could be "required or permitted to work in a biscuit, bread or cake bakery or confectionery establishment more than sixty hours in any one week, or more than ten hours in any one day on the last day of the week." Violation of the law was a misdemeanor.

Compliance with the 1897 statute was poor, as was its enforcement. The Master Bakers' Association, a bakery owners' organization, urged outright noncompliance. In the year it was passed, the ten-hour day provision of the Labor Law was implemented in only 312 of 855 baking establishments inspected by state officials. Among those refusing to comply with the law was Utica bakery owner Joseph Lochner. He was arrested when one of his employees complained to the Factory Inspection Department that Lochner violated the Labor Law by permitting Amam Schmitter, another employee, to work more than 60 hours during the week of April 19–April 26, 1901, at Lochner's nonunion bakery.

Lochner, who had been convicted of a similar offense in 1899 and fined $20, demurred to the charge. His demurrer was overruled. He was tried and convicted in the County Court of Oneida County and fined $50. His conviction was affirmed by a divided Appellate Division and the New York Court of Appeals.

On behalf of Lochner, the Master Bakers' Association petitioned the Supreme Court of the United States for a writ of error.

HIGHLIGHTS OF SUPREME COURT ARGUMENTS

BRIEF FOR LOCHNER

◆ The New York labor law is not a reasonable exercise of the state's police power. The contention that flour dust is unhealthful is disputed by medical authorities. Furthermore, modern baking factories are models of cleanliness and healthfulness. Proper enforcement of the state's health laws will protect bakers working in unsanitary conditions.

◆ The police powers of the state were never intended by the people adopting state and federal constitutions to be so paternal as to take away the treasured freedoms of the individual and his right to pursue life, liberty and happiness. State and federal courts consistently have upheld personal liberties against attempted police power regulations.

◆ The New York law was not intended as a health provision. It is purely a labor law. It reflects the success of almost a decade of lobbying by bakers for ten hour days. It prohibits absolutely the employment of bakers for more than 60 hours per week without regard to loss of property or other emergencies that might arise, the desire of employees to contract for overtime work, or the willingness of employers to pay for extra work in emergencies.

◆ The New York law is distinguishable from other hours limitations laws that had been upheld the by the Court. *Holden v. Hardy*, 169 U.S. 366 (1898), for example, which upheld a Utah law limiting working hours of miners, was justified because working in underground mines has always been recognized as hazardous and unhealthful. The baking trade is not.

BRIEF FOR NEW YORK

◆ The New York law must be recognized as a valid exercise of the state's police power. The police power is necessarily elastic, so as to meet the new and changing conditions of civilization. New York has become a great commercial and manufacturing state. Police power regulations must meet modern conditions, including urban crowding, specialization of labor, and the growth of the factory. Review of the entire statute, of which limitations on hours of labor in bakeries and confectionery establishments is only a small element, eliminates any doubt about its purpose as a public health regulation.

◆ If there are differences of opinion about the wisdom of particular police power enactments, those differences should be resolved by legislatures, not courts.

SUPREME COURT DECISION: 5–4

PECKHAM, J.

... The statute necessarily interferes with the right of contract between the employer and employees, concerning the number of hours in which the latter may labor in the bakery of the employer. The general right to make a contract in relation to his business is part of the liberty of the individual protected by the 14th Amendment of the Federal Constitution. *Allgeyer v. Louisiana*, 165 U.S. 578 [(1897)]. Under that provision no state can deprive any person of life, liberty, or property without due process of law. The right to purchase or to sell labor is part of the liberty protected by this amendment, unless there are circumstances which exclude the right. There are, however, certain powers, existing in the sovereignty of each state in the Union, somewhat vaguely termed police powers, the exact description and limitation of which have not been attempted by the courts. Those powers, broadly stated, and without, at present, any attempt at a more specific limitation, relate to the safety, health, morals, and general welfare of the public. Both property and liberty are held on such reasonable conditions as may be imposed by the governing power of the state in the exercise of those powers, and with such conditions the 14th Amendment was not designed to interfere....

The state, therefore, has power to prevent the individual from making certain kinds of contracts, and in regard to them the Federal Constitution offers no protection. If the contract be one which the state, in the legitimate exercise of its police power, has the right to prohibit, it is not prevented from prohibiting it by the 14th Amendment.... Therefore, when the state, by its legislature, in the assumed exercise of its police powers, has passed an act which seriously limits the right to labor or the right of contract in regard to their means of livelihood between persons who are *sui juris* [possessing full social and civil rights] (both employer and employee), it becomes of great importance to determine which shall prevail,—the right of the individual to labor for such time as he may choose, or the right of the state to prevent the individual from laboring, or from entering into any contract to labor, beyond a certain time prescribed by the state.

This court has recognized the existence and upheld the exercise of the police powers of the states in many cases which might fairly be considered as border ones, and it has, in the course of its determination of questions regarding the asserted invalidity of such statutes, on the ground of their violation of the rights secured by the Federal Constitution, been guided by rules of a very liberal nature, the application of which has resulted, in numerous instances, in upholding the validity of state statutes thus assailed....

It must, of course, be conceded that there is a limit to the valid exercise of the police power by the state.... In every case that comes before this court, therefore, where legislation of this character is concerned, and where the protection of the Federal Constitution is sought, the question necessarily arises: Is this a fair, reasonable, and appropriate exercise of the police power of the state, or is it an unreasonable, unnecessary, and arbitrary interference with the right of the individual to his personal liberty, or to enter into those contracts in relation to labor which may seem to him appropriate or necessary for the support of himself and his family? Of course the liberty of contract relating to labor includes both parties to it. The one has as much right to purchase as the other to sell labor.

This is not a question of substituting the judgment of the court for that of the legislature. If the act be within the power of the state it is valid, although the judgment of the court might be totally opposed to the enactment of such a law. But the question would still remain: Is it within the police power of the state? and that question must be answered by the court.

The question whether this act is valid as a labor law, pure and simple, may be dismissed in a few words. There is no reasonable ground for interfering with the liberty of person or the right of free contract, by determining the hours of labor, in the occupation of a baker. There is no contention that bakers as a class are not equal in intelligence and capacity to men in other trades or manual occupations, or that they are not able to assert their rights and care for themselves without the protecting arm of the state, interfering with their independence of judgment and of action. They are in no sense wards of the state. Viewed in the light of a purely labor law, with no reference whatever to the question of health, we think that a law like the one before us involves neither the safety, the morals, nor the welfare, of the public, and that the interest of the public is not in the slightest degree affected by such an act. The law must be upheld, if at all, as a law pertaining to the health of the individual engaged in the occupation of a baker. It does not affect any other portion of the public than those who are engaged in that occupa-

tion. Clean and wholesome bread does not depend upon whether the baker works but ten hours per day or only sixty hours a week. The limitation of the hours of labor does not come within the police power on that ground.

It is a question of which of two powers or rights shall prevail,—the power of the state to legislate or the right of the individual to liberty of person and freedom of contract. The mere assertion that the subject relates, though but in a remote degree, to the public health, does not necessarily render the enactment valid. The act must have a more direct relation, as a means to an end, and the end itself must be appropriate and legitimate, before an act can be held to be valid which interferes with the general right of an individual to be free in his person and in his power to contract in relation to his own labor....

We think the limit of the police power has been reached and passed in this case. There is, in our judgment, no reasonable foundation for holding this to be necessary or appropriate as a health law to safeguard the public health, or the health of the individuals who are following the trade of a baker. If this statute be valid, and if, therefore, a proper case is made out in which to deny the right of an individual, *sui juris*, as employer or employee, to make contracts for the labor of the latter under the protection of the provisions of the Federal Constitution, there would seem to be no length to which legislation of this nature might not go....

[The] interference on the part of the legislatures of the several states with the ordinary trades and occupations of the people seems to be on the increase....

It is impossible for us to shut our eyes to the fact that many of the laws of this character, while passed under what is claimed to be the police power for the purpose of protecting the public health or welfare, are, in reality, passed from other motives. We are justified in saying so when, from the character of the law and the subject upon which it legislates, it is apparent that the public health or welfare bears but the most remote relation to the law. The purpose of a statute must be determined from the natural and legal effect of the language employed; and whether it is or is not repugnant to the Constitution of the United States must be determined from the natural effect of such statutes when put into operation, and not from their proclaimed purpose....

It is manifest to us that the limitation of the hours of labor as provided for in this section of the statute under which the indictment was found, and the plaintiff in error convicted, has no such direct relation to, and no such substantial effect upon, the health of the employee, as to justify us in regarding the section as really a health law. It seems to us that the real object and purpose were simply to regulate the hours of labor between the master and his employees (all being men, *Sui juris*), in a private business, not dangerous in any degree to morals, or in any real and substantial degree to the health of the employees. Under such circumstances the freedom of master and employee to contract with each other in relation to their employment, and in defining the same, cannot be prohibited or interfered with, without violating the Federal Constitution....

Reversed.

HOLMES, J., DISSENTING

... This case is decided upon an economic theory which a large part of the country does not entertain. If it were a question whether I agreed with that theory, I should desire to study it further and long before making up my mind. But I do not conceive that to be my duty, because I strongly believe that my agreement or disagreement has nothing to do with the right of a majority to embody their opinions in law. It is settled by various decisions of this court that state constitutions and state laws may regulate life in many ways which we as legislators might think as injudicious, or if you like as tyrannical, as this, and which, equally with this, interfere with the liberty to contract.... The 14th Amendment does not enact Mr. Herbert Spencer's *Social Statics [or the Conditions Essential to Human Happiness Specified and the First of Them Developed* (New York: D. Appleton, 1888)].... [A] Constitution is not intended to embody a particular economic theory, whether of paternalism and the organic relation of the citizen to the state or of laissez faire. It is made for people of fundamentally differing views, and the accident of our finding certain opinions natural and familiar, or novel, and even shocking, ought not to conclude our judgment upon the question whether statutes embodying them conflict with the Constitution of the United States.

General propositions do not decide concrete cases. The decision will depend on a judgment or intuition more subtle than any articulate major premise. But I think that the proposition just stated, if it is accepted, will carry us far toward the end. Every opinion tends to become a law. I think that the word "liberty," in the 14th Amendment, is perverted when it is held to prevent the natural outcome of a dominant opinion, unless it can be said that a rational and fair man necessarily would admit that the statute proposed would infringe fundamental principles as they have been understood by the traditions of our people and our law. It does not need research to show that no such sweeping condemnation can be passed upon the statute before us. A reasonable man might think it a proper measure on the score of health. Men whom I certainly could not pronounce unreasonable would uphold it as a first installment of a general regulation of the hours of work. Whether in the latter aspect it would be open to the charge of inequality I think it unnecessary to discuss.

HARLAN, WHITE, AND DAY, J.J., DISSENTING

Granting ... that there is a liberty of contract which cannot be violated even under the sanction of direct legislative enactment, but assuming, as according to settled law we may assume, that such liberty of contract is subject to such regulations as the state may reasonably prescribe for the common good and the well-being of society, what are the conditions under which the judiciary may declare such regulations to be in excess of legislative authority and void? Upon this point there is no room for dispute; for the rule is universal that a legislative enactment, Federal or state, is never to be disregarded or held invalid unless it be, beyond question, plainly and palpably in excess of legislative power.... If there be doubt as to the validity of the statute, that doubt must therefore be resolved in favor of its validity, and the courts must keep their hands off, leaving the legislature to meet the responsibility for unwise legislation. If the end which the legislature seeks to accomplish be one to which its power extends, and if the means employed to that end, although not the wisest or best, are yet not plainly and palpably unauthorized by law, then the court cannot interfere....

Let these principles be applied to the present case....

It is plain that this statute was enacted in order to protect the physical well-being of those who work in bakery and confectionery establishments. It may be that the statute had its origin, in part, in the belief that employers and employees in such establishments were not upon an equal footing, and that the necessities of the latter often compelled them to submit to such exactions as unduly taxed their strength. Be this as it may, the statute must be taken as expressing the belief of the people of New York that, as a general rule, and in the case of the average man, labor in excess of sixty hours during a week in such establishments may endanger the health of those who thus labor. Whether or not this be wise legislation it is not the province of the court to inquire. Under our systems of government the courts are not concerned with the wisdom or policy of legislation. So that, in determining the question of power to interfere with liberty of contract, the court may inquire whether the means devised by the state are germane to an end which may be lawfully accomplished and have a real or substantial relation to the protection of health, as involved in the daily work of the persons, male and female, engaged in bakery and confectionery establishments. But when this inquiry is entered upon I find it impossible, in view of common experience, to say that there is here no real or substantial relation between the means employed by the state and the end sought to be accomplished by its legislation.... Therefore I submit that this court will transcend its functions if it assumes to annul the statute of New York....

QUESTIONS

1. What is the rule of *Lochner v. New York*? What, if any, are its constitutional underpinnings?

2. Is liberty of contract a defensible interpretation of the Fourteenth Amendment Due Process Clause? If so, to what sorts of economic relationships does this interpretation reasonably apply? Business contracts? Working hours? Working conditions? Wages?

3. The legal fiction that employers and employees possess equal rights when entering into labor contracts underlay the majority opinion in *Lochner*. Historically, which social interests benefited from that fiction? Which were disadvantaged?

4. Many critics of *Lochner* argue that the majority cast itself in the role of a "super-legislature," second guessing the judgment of New York's elected representatives that labor statistics documented how prolonged exposure to flour dust was harmful to bakery workers' health, and defeating progressive legislation. Even though the Supreme Court invalidated over two-hundred economic regulations between 1905 and 1935, typically on due process grounds, the Court upheld as many regulations as it rejected. See *The Constitution of the United States: Analysis and Interpretation* (Washington, D.C.: U.S. Government Printing Office, 1987), pp. 1883–2114.

   Under what circumstances, if any, should courts trump legislatures on matters of public policy? Is economic regulation a matter of public policy or tinkering with fundamental rights?

COMMENT

As explored in greater detail in Volume I, Chapter 6, economic substantive due process, as exemplified here by Lochner, assumed that the wage/labor bargain between owners of capital and workers was constitutionally insulated from government regulation. The Court viewed the private market as the proper mechanism for ordering the relationships between employers and employees. In the words of Justice Sutherland, "freedom of contract is ... the general rule and restraint the exception, and the exercise of legislative authority to abridge it can be justified only by the existence of exceptional circumstances...." *Adkins v. Children's Hospital*, 261 U.S. 525 (1923).

The United States and the rest of the world sank into a desperate economic depression beginning in 1929. Between September 3, 1929 and July 8, 1932, the *New York Times* industrial average fell from 452 to 58. Unemployment in the United States soared: By early 1933, almost one-third of the labor force could not find work. Many Americans became homeless, living on the streets or in shanty towns dubbed "Hoovervilles" after Republican

President Herbert Hoover, who generally was opposed to government intervention into and regulation of the economy. Ironically, production outstripped consumption during this period. Workers and farmers who could find work often produced goods that they could not afford to purchase. Oligopolies dominated the key industrial sectors, virtually eliminating economic competition.

As this economic and social calamity unfolded, Franklin D. Roosevelt was elected president. Five days after his inauguration on March 4, 1933, Roosevelt called Congress into special session, halted transactions in gold, and declared a national bank holiday. Over the next months, as part of his New Deal, Roosevelt submitted to Congress legislation including the Agricultural Adjustment Act (AAA) and the National Industrial Recovery Act (NIRA) that contained proposals for extensive governmental regulation and control of the economy. Although passed by large majorities in Congress, the Supreme Court was hostile to Roosevelt's New Deal economic reforms. The Court struck down the AAA and the NIRA, along with other New Deal legislation, often on the ground that the laws violated the rights to make contracts, which the Court viewed as part of the liberty protected by the Due Process Clause of the Fourteenth Amendment.

Critics of the Supreme Court caricatured the Justices as the "Nine Old Men." Following his resounding reelection in 1936, President Roosevelt went to war with the Supreme Court by proposing that the president be authorized to appoint an additional Justice to the Supreme Court for every one who had served ten years and had not retired within six months of his seventieth birthday. Roosevelt's plan, dubbed "Court Packing" by his critics, would have allowed him to appoint six additional justices.

The Senate rejected Roosevelt's proposal. It did so, in part, because of public hostility to the proposal and, in part, because in 1937 the Supreme Court in *West Coast Hotel v. Parrish*, 300 U.S. 379, overruled *Adkins* and upheld a Washington state statute that established minimum wages for women. Chief Justice Hughes's opinion for the 5-vote *Parrish* majority appeared to be the death knell of economic substantive due process, which had dominated Supreme Court jurisprudence for nearly thirty years:

> ... [T]he violation alleged by those attacking minimum wage regulation for women is deprivation of freedom of contract. What is this freedom? The Constitution does not speak of freedom of contract. It speaks of liberty and prohibits the deprivation of liberty without due process of law. In prohibiting that deprivation, the Constitution does not recognize an absolute and uncontrollable liberty. Liberty in each of its phases has its history and connotation. But the liberty safeguarded is liberty in a social organization which requires the protection of law against the evils which menace the health, safety, morals, and welfare of the people. Liberty under the Constitution is thus necessarily subject to the restraints of due process, and regulation which is reasonable in relation to its subject and is adopted in the interests of the community is due process....

DUE PROCESS

Palko v. Connecticut
302 U.S. 319 (1937)

SETTING

Shortly after its abandonment of economic substantive due process, the justices returned to consideration of the requirements of traditional due process. In *Murray v. Hoboken Land & and Improvement Co.*, 18 Howard 272 (1885), the Court explained that judicial review in cases involving traditional due process challenges involves two steps:

> We must examine the constitution itself, to see whether [a particular] process be in conflict with any of its provisions. If not found to be so, we must look to those settled usages and modes of proceeding existing in the common and statute law of England, before the emigration of our ancestors.

Court watchers wondered whether the justices would continue their activist approach to due process of law when questions of economic regulation were not involved. During the 1937 Term, the Court revisited the long-standing question of the relationship between the Bill of Rights and the states.

As explained in the *Setting* to the *Slaughter-House Cases* (1873) (pp. 436–439), Representative John Bingham envisioned that the Fourteenth Amendment Privileges or Immunities Clause would "incorporate" the entire Bill of Rights as a limitation on the states. The Court's decision in the *Slaughter-House Cases* effectively eliminated that prospect. Thereafter, civil rights activists took a new approach. By the 1880s they were arguing that specific guarantees of the Bill of Rights should be held to apply against the states through the Due Process Clause of the Fourteenth Amendment. In *Hurtado v. California*, 110 U.S. 516 (1884), for example, the Court was urged to hold that the Due Process Clause requires that the Fifth Amendment's guarantee of indictment by grand jury be applied against the states. The Court refused to do so. Nonetheless, Justice Matthews wrote:

> According to a recognized canon of interpretation, especially applicable to formal and solemn instruments of constitutional law, we are forbidden to assume, *without clear reason to the contrary*, that any part of this most important amendment [the Fourteenth] is superfluous....
> It follows that any legal proceeding enforced by public authority, whether sanctioned by age and custom, or newly devised in the discretion of the legislative power in furtherance of the general public good, *which regards and preserves [the] principles of liberty and justice*, must be held to be due process of law.... [Emphasis added.]

The Court continued to follow *Hurtado* into the twentieth century, in each instance explaining its view of the requirements of due process with respect to "fairness." In *Maxwell v. Dow*, 176 U.S. 581 (1900), for example, the justices upheld a Utah law that provided for an eight-person jury despite the traditional understanding in federal trials that the Sixth Amendment's right to trial "by an impartial jury" means a jury of twelve. Similarly, in *Twining v. New Jersey*, 211 U.S. 78 (1908), the Court refused to overturn a conviction achieved after a state trial judge had commented on the refusal of the defendants to testify on their own behalf. If a federal judge had made such a comment, it would have run afoul of the Fifth Amendment's protection against self-incrimination.

Despite rejecting the specific claims in *Hurtado, Maxwell*, and *Twining*, it was evident that the justices were committed to the notion that due process of law requires that processes be fair. In 1925, it ruled that some rights and liberties guaranteed by the First Amendment are so "fundamental" that the Fourteenth Amendment's Due Process Clause protects them from impairment by the states. Those rights include speech and press. *Gitlow v. New York*, 268 U.S. 652. By 1932 the Court had ruled that in some circumstances—such as a criminal trial in a racially hostile environment—due process of law requires that the court appoint legal counsel to the defendant. *Powell v. Alabama*, 287 U.S. 45 (1932).

The Court's incremental approach to analyzing the requirements of due process of law as it relates to the Bill of Rights was a virtual invitation to continued litigation. Criminal cases from state courts were likely candidates for litigation because so many provisions of the Bill of Rights relate to the conduct of criminal proceedings. Frank Palko's case provided the court with one of its first opportunities to articulate the meaning of due process of law in the era of post-economic substantive due process.

Palko was indicted by a grand jury for the 1935 premeditated murder of Thomas Kearney in Bridgeport, Connecticut. He was charged with first degree murder but, following a jury trial in Fairfield County Superior Court, was convicted of second degree murder and sentenced to life in prison. A Connecticut statute adopted in 1886 allowed the state, with the permission of the trial judge, to appeal all questions of law arising in the trial of criminal cases.

The state appealed to the Connecticut Supreme Court of Errors, claiming that the trial judge in Palko's case erred by (1) excluding testimony about a confession that Palko allegedly had made; (2) excluding testimony on cross-examination of Palko to impeach his credibility; and (3) imprecisely instructing the jury about the difference between first and second degree murder. These errors, Connecticut contended, led to Palko's conviction for second degree murder rather than first degree murder. The Supreme Court of Errors agreed that the trial judge had committed reversible errors prejudicial to the prosecution and ordered a new trial.

Before the beginning of his second trial, Palko moved to have the indictment dismissed on the ground that trying him a second time after his first trial would subject him to double jeopardy in violation of the Fourteenth Amendment of the Constitution of the United States. His motion was denied. Palko was convicted of first degree murder at his second trial and sentenced to death by electrocution. He appealed his conviction to the Supreme Court of Errors, which affirmed. Palko then appealed to the Supreme Court of the United States.

HIGHLIGHTS OF SUPREME COURT ARGUMENTS

BRIEF FOR PALKO

◆ The verdict in Palko's first trial was an acquittal on the first degree murder charge. Forcing Palko to stand trial a second time on the same charge exposed him to double jeopardy, which is prohibited by the Fifth Amendment.

◆ The right against double jeopardy is such a fundamental and immutable principle of law that it falls within the protection of both the Due Process and Privileges or Immunities Clauses of the Fourteenth Amendment.

◆ The Court should consider the historical analysis in Horace Edgar Flack's book, *The Adoption of the Fourteenth Amendment* (Baltimore, MD: Johns Hopkins University Press, 1908), showing that the drafters of the Fourteenth Amendment intended to make the first eight amendments to the federal constitution applicable to the states.

BRIEF FOR CONNECTICUT

◆ The definition of double jeopardy in a criminal prosecution is a matter of judicial construction by state courts. Little will be left to the powers of the states to administer criminal law if any ruling by state courts becomes a federal question.

◆ The fact that the rule against double jeopardy was established at common law does not mean that the right is a fundamental principle of justice for due process purposes under the Fourteenth Amendment. Other rights recognized at common law, including the right to presentment by a grand jury and right to a jury trial in civil cases, have not been made applicable against the states by the Fourteenth Amendment.

SUPREME COURT DECISION: 8–1

CARDOZO, J.

The argument for appellant is that whatever is forbidden by the Fifth Amendment is forbidden by the Fourteenth also....

His thesis is even broader. Whatever would be a violation of the original bill of rights (Amendments 1 to 8) if done by the federal government is now equally unlawful by force of the Fourteenth Amendment if done by a state. There is no such general rule.

The Fifth Amendment provides, among other things, that no person shall be held to answer for a capital or otherwise infamous crime unless on presentment or indictment of a grand jury. This court has held that, in prosecutions by a state, presentment or indictment by a grand jury may give way to informations at the instance of a public officer.... The Fifth Amendment provides also that no person shall be compelled in any criminal case to be a witness against himself. This court has said that, in prosecutions by a state, the exemption will fail if the state elects to end it.... The Sixth Amendment calls for a jury trial in criminal cases and the Seventh for a jury trial in civil cases at common law where the value in controversy shall exceed $20. This court has ruled that consistently with those amendments trial by jury may be modified by a state or abolished altogether....

On the other hand, the due process clause of the Fourteenth Amendment may make it unlawful for a state to abridge by its statutes the freedom of speech which the First Amendment safeguards against encroachment by the Congress, ... or the like freedom of the press, ... or the free exercise of religion, ... or the right of peaceable assembly, without which speech would be unduly trammeled, ... or the right of one accused of crime to the benefit of counsel.... In these and other situations immunities that are valid as against the federal government by force of the specific pledges of particular amendments have been found to be implicit in the concept of ordered liberty, and thus, through the Fourteenth Amendment, become valid as against the states.

The line of division may seem to be wavering and broken if there is a hasty catalogue of the cases on the one side and the other. Reflection and analysis will induce a different view. There emerges the perception of a rationalizing principle which gives to discrete instances a proper order and coherence. The right to trial by jury and the immunity from prosecution except as the result of an indictment may have value and importance. Even so, they are not of the very essence of a scheme of ordered liberty. To abolish them is not to violate a "principle of jus-

tice so rooted in the traditions and conscience of our people as to be ranked as fundamental." *Snyder v. Massachusetts*, 291 U.S. 97 [1934].... Few would be so narrow or provincial as to maintain that a fair and enlightened system of justice would be impossible without them. What is true of jury trials and indictments is true also, as the cases show, of the immunity from compulsory self-incrimination.... This too might be lost, and justice still be done. Indeed, today as in the past there are students of our penal system who look upon the immunity as a mischief rather than a benefit, and who would limit its scope, or destroy it altogether. No doubt there would remain the need to give protection against torture, physical or mental.... Justice, however, would not perish if the accused were subject to a duty to respond to orderly inquiry. The exclusion of these immunities and privileges from the privileges and immunities protected against the action of the States has not been arbitrary or casual. It has been dictated by a study and appreciation of the meaning, the essential implications, of liberty itself.

We reach a different plane of social and moral values when we pass to the privileges and immunities that have been taken over from the earlier articles of the Federal Bill of Rights and brought within the Fourteenth Amendment by a process of absorption. These in their origin were effective against the federal government alone. If the Fourteenth Amendment has absorbed them, the process of absorption has had its source in the belief that neither liberty nor justice would exist if they were sacrificed.... This is true, for illustration, of freedom of thought and speech. Of that freedom one may say that it is the matrix, the indispensable condition, of nearly every other form of freedom. With rare aberrations a pervasive recognition of that truth can be traced in our history, political and legal. So it has come about that the domain of liberty, withdrawn by the Fourteenth Amendment from encroachment by the states, has been enlarged by latter-day judgments to include liberty of the mind as well as liberty of action....

Is that kind of double jeopardy to which the statute has subjected [the plaintiff] a hardship so acute and shocking that our policy will not endure it? Does it violate those "fundamental principles of liberty and justice which lie at the base of all our civil and political institutions"?... The answer surely must be "no." What the answer would have to be if the state were permitted after a trial free from error to try the accused over again or to bring another case against him, we have no occasion to consider. We deal with the statute before us and no other. The state is not attempting to wear the accused out by a multitude of cases with accumulated trials. It asks no more than this, that the case against him shall go on until there shall be a trial free from the corrosion of substantial legal error.... This is not cruelty at all, nor even vexation in any immoderate degree. If the trial had been infected with error adverse to the accused, there might have been review at his instance, and as often as necessary to purge the vicious taint. A reciprocal privilege, subject at all times to the discretion of the presiding judge, has now been granted to the state. There is here no seismic innovation. The edifice of justice stands, its symmetry, to many, greater than before....

The judgment is affirmed.

BUTLER, J., DISSENTED WITHOUT OPINION

QUESTIONS

1. In *Palko*, Justice Cardozo contended that the right to trial by jury, the immunity from prosecution except as the result of an indictment, and the immunity from compulsory self-incrimination are not essential to "a fair and enlightened system of justice" and, hence, need not be incorporated through the Fourteenth Amendment Due Process Clause as restraints on how states operate their criminal justice systems. Should Justice Butler have provided a written explanation about why he disagreed with that view—if it is that aspect of the majority opinion with which he disagreed? What might such a dissent from Justice Cardozo's opinion say?

2. Justice Cardozo claimed in *Palko* that criminal procedural guarantees are not so essential to "a scheme of ordered liberty" as to be subject to federal court jurisdiction. What criteria should Justices use in deciding which guarantees in the Bill of Rights are "essential" or "nonessential?" Are not all rights in the Bill of Rights equally "essential" or "nonessential"?

3. In his dissent in *Griswold v. Connecticut*, 381 U.S. 479 (1965), Justice Hugo Black wrote: "[O]ne of the most effective ways of diluting or expanding a constitutionally guaranteed right is to substitute for the crucial word or words of a constitutional guarantee another word or

words, more or less flexible and more or less restricted in meaning...." Does Black's criticism of justices substituting their own formulation(s) in lieu of following the text of the Constitution apply to Justice Cardozo's opinion in *Palko*?

COMMENTS

1. In 1938, in a footnote to another case involving economic regulation, the Supreme Court explicitly stated that judicial review of legislation under a substantive due process standard had given way to different judicial concerns. *United States v. Carolene Products Co.*, 304 U.S. 144, involved the Filled Milk Act of 1923. The act prohibited and penalized by fine or imprisonment the shipment of filled milk (defined as any milk to which any fat or oil other than milk fat had been added) in interstate commerce on the grounds that it was "an adulterated article of food, injurious to the public health, and its sale constitutes a fraud upon the public." Carolene Products Company, an Illinois corporation, was indicted in 1935 on two counts of shipping filled milk in interstate commerce.

In the course of his opinion upholding the constitutionality of the Filled Milk Act, Justice Stone wrote: "... regulatory legislation affecting ordinary commercial transactions is not to be pronounced unconstitutional unless in the light of the facts made known or generally assumed it is of such a character as to preclude the assumption that it rests upon some rational basis within the knowledge and experience of the legislators." To this sentence Stone appended footnote 4:

> There may be narrower scope for operation of the presumption of constitutionality when legislation appears on its face to be within a specific prohibition of the Constitution, such as those of the first ten Amendments, which are deemed equally specific when held to be embraced within the Fourteenth. See *Stromberg v. California*, 283 U.S. 359, 369, 370, 51 S.Ct. 532, 535, 536, 75 L.Ed. 1117, 73 A.L.R. 1484; *Lovell v. Griffin*, 303 U.S. 444, 58 S.Ct. 666, 82 L.Ed. 949, decided March 28, 1938.
>
> It is unnecessary to consider now whether legislation which restricts those political processes which can ordinarily be expected to bring about repeal of undesirable legislation, is to be subjected to more exacting judicial scrutiny under the general prohibitions of the Fourteenth Amendment than are most other types of legislation. On restrictions upon the right to vote, see *Nixon v. Herndon*, 273 U.S. 536, 47 S.Ct. 446, 71 L.Ed. 759; *Nixon v. Condon*, 286 U.S. 73, 52 S.Ct. 484, 76 L.Ed. 984, 88 A.L.R. 458; on restraints upon the dissemination of information, see *Near v. Minnesota*, 283 U.S. 697, 713—714, 718—720, 722, 51 S.Ct. 625, 630, 632, 633, 75 L.Ed. 1357; *Grosjean v. American Press Co.*, 297 U.S. 233, 56 S.Ct. 444, 80 L.Ed. 660; *Lovell v. Griffin*, supra; on interferences with political organizations, see *Stromberg v. California*, supra, 283 U.S. 359, 369, 51 S.Ct. 532, 535, 75 L.Ed. 1117, 73 A.L.R. 1484; *Fiske v. Kansas*, 274 U.S. 380, 47 S.Ct. 655,

71 L.Ed. 1108; *Whitney v. California*, 274 U.S. 357, 373—378, 47 S.Ct. 641, 647, 649, 71 L.Ed. 1095; *Herndon v. Lowry*, 301 U.S. 242, 57 S.Ct. 732, 81 L.Ed. 1066; and see Holmes, J., in *Gitlow v. New York*, 268 U.S. 652, 673, 45 S.Ct. 625, 69 L.Ed. 1138; as to prohibition of peaceable assembly, see *De Jonge v. Oregon*, 299 U.S. 353, 365, 57 S.Ct. 255, 260, 81 L.Ed. 278.

Nor need we enquire whether similar considerations enter into the review of statutes directed at particular religious, *Pierce v. Society of Sisters*, 268 U.S. 510, 45 S.Ct. 571, 69 L.Ed. 1070, 39 A.L.R. 468, or national, *Meyer v. Nebraska*, 262 U.S. 390, 43 S.Ct. 625, 67 L.Ed. 1042, 29 A.L.R. 1446; *Bartels v. Iowa*, 262 U.S. 404, 43 S.Ct. 628, 67 L.Ed. 1047; *Farrington v. Tokushige*, 273 U.S. 284, 47 S.Ct. 406, 71 L.Ed. 646, or racial minorities. *Nixon v. Herndon*, supra; *Nixon v. Condon*, supra; whether prejudice against discrete and insular minorities may be a special condition, which tends seriously to curtail the operation of those political processes ordinarily to be relied upon to protect minorities, and which may call for a correspondingly more searching judicial inquiry. Compare *McCulloch v. Maryland*, 4 Wheat 316,428, 4 L.Ed. 579; *South Carolina State Highway Department v. Barnwell Bros.*, 303 U.S. 177, 58 S.Ct. 510, 82 L.Ed. 734, decided February 14, 1938, note 2, and cases cited.

2. Thirty one years after Frank Palko was executed by the state of Connecticut, the Supreme Court held that the Fourteenth Amendment incorporates the right against double jeopardy as a limitation on state actions in the conduct of criminal trials. *Benton v. Maryland*, 395 U.S. 784 (1969).

DUE PROCESS

Adamson v. California
332 U.S. 46 (1947)

SETTING

Palko gave only a partial answer to the question of which provisions of the Bill of Rights are to be included within the phrase "due process of law" for purposes of incorporation against the states. Justice Cardozo's formulation for the Court was that only those guarantees "implicit in the concept of ordered liberty" and those principles of justice "so rooted in the traditions and conscience of our people as to be ranked as fundamental" were limitations on the states. Freedom of speech was such a right. Trial by jury and immunity from double jeopardy were not. *Palko* signaled that the Court would approach questions of incorporation cautiously and incrementally, and that its earlier activist agenda with respect to economic substantive due process would not carry over to traditional due process analysis.

Between 1937 and 1941, the Court's roster was transformed by appointees of President Franklin Roosevelt. Justices Van Devanter, McReynolds, Butler and Sutherland were replaced by Roosevelt appointees Hugo Black, James Byrnes, Frank Murphy and Stanley Reed. Progressive Justices on the Court were succeeded by other progressives or moderates. Felix Frankfurter replaced Cardozo; William O. Douglas replaced Brandeis; and when Stone followed Hughes as Chief Justice, Robert Jackson filled Stone's seat. By 1941, President Franklin Roosevelt had remade the Court more thoroughly than any president in American history. For the most part, Roosevelt appointees wanted to see the liberal policies of the New Deal engrafted into constitutional law. Those justices also appeared to be sympathetic to "modernizing" the Bill of Rights by making more of its provisions applicable against the states. However, it was not clear whether the Roosevelt Court would endorse the *Palko* framework in analyzing due process challenges. One of the early indications of the new Court's approach to due process of law in the criminal arena came in an appeal from the murder conviction of Admiral Dewey Adamson.

Adamson, a poor, black male, was arrested in Los Angeles, California, on August 24, 1944, and charged with the murder of 64-year-old Stella Blauvelt, a white female. Blauvelt's body had been found on the floor of her Los Angeles apartment about a month before Adamson's arrest. Her body was face up, covered with two bloodstained pillows. A lamp cord was wrapped tightly around the neck three times and tied in a knot. Bruises on the hands and face indicated that Blauvelt had been severely beaten before her death. Testing revealed that she had been murdered in broad daylight the day before her body was found.

Adamson was charged by information with first degree murder and burglary. The charging instrument stated that Adamson had been convicted in the 1920s for burglary, larceny and robbery. Adamson admitted to the earlier convictions, which under California law barred the prosecution from mentioning those convictions at his trial for the murder of Blauvelt. However, Article I, Section 13, of the California Constitution provided:

> But in any criminal case, whether the defendant testifies or not, his failure to explain or to deny by his testimony any evidence or facts in the case against him may be commented upon by the court and by counsel and may be considered by the court or by the jury.

Thus, Adamson faced a dilemma: If he took the stand during the murder trial, evidence of his prior convictions could be used to impeach the credibility of his testimony; if he did not take the stand in his own defense, California law allowed the prosecution to comment on his silence.

Adamson was tried in a California Superior Court. At trial, an expert testified that scotch tape that he had removed from a door to the garbage compartment of the kitchen of Blauvelt's apartment contained six latent fingerprints that corresponded with Adamson's fingerprints. The door was found unhinged, leaning against the kitchen sink, and Adamson could have entered the apartment through the garbage compartment. Testimony also revealed that during the investigation of the murder, the tops of three women's stockings were found in and on the dresser in Adamson's room. The stockings were not all the same color, and each was knotted. Blauvelt's body did not have any shoes or stockings on it. However, it appeared that on the day she was murdered, Blauvelt was wearing stockings and the lower part of a silk stocking with the top torn off was laying on the floor under her body. None of the stocking tops found in Adamson's room matched that piece of stocking.

Testimony at trial also revealed that Blauvelt was in the habit of wearing rings with large diamonds and that she was wearing them on the day she died. None of them was found. A witness for the state positively identified Adamson, stating that at some time between August 10 and 14, 1944, she overheard Adamson ask an unidentified person if he was interested in buying a diamond ring. However, no testimony directly linked Adamson to Blauvelt's murder, none of her belongings was found in his possession, and no one saw a black man in her apartment or in her apartment house on the day of the murder.

Although he consistently denied murdering Blauvelt, Adamson did not take the stand to testify at his trial and rested his case without putting on any evidence. During closing argument to the jury, the prosecutor commented at least seven times about Adamson's failure to testify. Among his comments were:

> The defendant has not taken the stand; he has not denied that [he was identified as having offered a diamond ring for sale]; it is uncontradicted in the testimony. There he sits, not getting on the stand, not giving you what his version of the situation is. You have got the right, members of this jury, to consider the fact and consider that four hundred and some odd pages of testimony are uncontradicted from the lips of this defendant.

At the close of his argument, the prosecutor stated:

> In conclusion, I am going to just make this one statement to you: Counsel asks you to find this defendant not guilty. But does the defendant get on the stand and say, under oath, 'I am not guilty'? Not one word from him, and not one word from a single witness.

The judge's jury instructions included the comment that "It is the right of court and counsel to comment on the failure of defendant to explain or deny any evidence against him, and to comment on the evidence, the testimony and credibility of any witness...."

The jury convicted of Adamson of first degree murder and first degree burglary. He was sentenced to death. He moved for a new trial on the ground that Article I, Section 13, of the California Constitution was an unconstitutional infringement on his rights under the Due Process Clause of the Fifth Amendment to the Constitution of the United States and the Privileges or Immunities Clause of the Fourteenth Amendment. That motion was denied. Adamson then appealed to the California Supreme Court, which affirmed his conviction and rejected his federal constitutional challenge to the state constitution. Adamson appealed to the Supreme Court of the United States.

Highlights of Supreme Court Arguments

BRIEF FOR ADAMSON

◆ Article I, Section 13, of the California Constitution violates Due Process under the Constitution of the United States because it amounts to testimonial compulsion and silence in court is tantamount to an admission of guilt. The right not to be compelled to testify against one's self is fundamental.

◆ Article I, Section 13, offends the procedural safeguards guaranteed by the Fourteenth Amendment to fair public trials.

◆ The stockings found in Adamson's apartment were improperly admitted at trial. The prosecution conceded that they were not part of the stocking found under the body and their introduction furnished an additional motive for the crime—a sexual one. The mere suggestion of such a motive was calculated to excite the prejudices of the jury, because Adamson is black and Blauvelt was white.

BRIEF FOR CALIFORNIA

◆ It is true that the Constitution of the United States and most state constitutions guarantee that no person in a criminal trial shall be compelled to testify against himself. However, the right given to prosecutors and judges to comment on a defendant's failure to explain or deny evidence or facts against him does not violate the Fourteenth Amendment and is a right recognized in many states.

◆ California courts have ruled that it was not the intent of Article I, Section 13, to shift the burden of proof in a criminal case. The prosecution still must prove guilt beyond a reasonable doubt.

◆ This Court in *Twining v. New Jersey*, 211 U.S. 78 (1908), rejected the proposition that the privilege against self-incrimination was incorporated against the states by the Fourteenth Amendment. That case is controlling here.

◆ The Due Process Clause does not guarantee that the decisions of state courts shall be free of error or that every ruling during a trial shall be correct. In this case, the highest court of the state concluded that admission of portions of women's stockings found in Adamson's room was not incompetent evidence or that it was introduced to inflame the passions of the jury.

Supreme Court Decision: 5–4

REED, J.

... We shall assume, but without any intention thereby of ruling upon the issue, that state permission by law to the court, counsel and jury to comment upon and consider the failure of defendant "to explain or to deny by his testimony any evidence or facts in the case against him" would infringe defendant's privilege against self-incrimination under the Fifth Amendment if this were a trial in a court of the United States under a similar law. Such an assumption does not determine appellant's rights under the Fourteenth Amendment. It is settled law that the clause of the Fifth Amendment, protecting a person against being compelled to be a witness against himself, is not made effective by the Fourteenth Amendment as a protection against state action on the ground that freedom from testimonial compulsion is a right of national citizenship, or because it is a personal privilege or immunity secured by the Federal Constitution as one of the rights of man that are listed in the Bill of Rights....

After declaring that state and national citizenship co-exist in the same person, the Fourteenth Amendment forbids a state from abridging the privileges and immunities of citizens of the United States. As a matter of words, this leaves a state free to abridge, within the limits of the due process clause, the privileges and immunities flowing from state citizenship. This reading of the Federal Constitution has heretofore found favor with the majority of this Court as a natural and logical interpretation. It accords with the constitutional doctrine of federalism by leaving to the states the responsibility of dealing with the privileges and immunities of their citizens except those inherent in national citizenship. It is the construction placed upon the amendment by justices whose own experience had given them contemporaneous knowledge of the purposes that led to the adoption of the Fourteenth Amendment. This construction has become embedded in our federal system as a functioning element in preserving the balance between national and state power. We reaffirm the conclusion of the *Twining* [*v. New Jersey*, 211 U.S. 78 (1908)] and *Palko* [*v. Connecticut*] cases that protection against self-incrimination is not a privilege or immunity of national citizenship....

For a state to require testimony from an accused is not necessarily a breach of a state's obligation to give a fair trial. Therefore, we must examine the effect of the California law applied in this trial to see whether the comment on failure to testify violates the protection against state action that the due process clause does grant to an accused....

Generally, comment on the failure of an accused to testify is forbidden in American jurisdictions. This arises from state constitutional or statutory provisions similar in character to the federal provisions. California, however, is one of a few states that permit limited comment upon a defendant's failure to testify. That permission is narrow. The California law ... authorizes comment by court and counsel upon the "failure of the defendant to explain or to deny by his testimony any evidence or facts in the case against him." This does not involve any presumption, rebuttable or irrebuttable, either of guilt or of the truth of any fact, that is offered in evidence.... It allows inferences to be drawn from proven facts. Because of this clause, the court can direct the jury's attention to whatever evidence there may be that a defendant could deny and the prosecution can argue as to inferences that may be drawn from the accused's failure to testify.... There is here no lack of power in the trial court to adjudge and no denial of a hearing. California has prescribed a method for advising the jury in the search for truth. However sound may be the legislative conclusion that an accused should not be compelled in any criminal case to be a witness against himself, we see no reason why comment should not be made upon his silence. It seems quite natural that when a defendant has opportunity to deny or explain facts and determines not to do so, the prosecution should bring out the strength of the evidence by commenting upon defendant's failure to explain or deny it. The prosecution evidence may be of facts that may be beyond the knowledge of the accused. If so, his failure to testify would have little if any weight. But the facts may be such as are necessarily in the knowledge of the accused. In that case a failure to explain would point to an inability to explain....

The purpose of due process is not to protect an accused against a proper conviction but against an unfair conviction. When evidence is before a jury that threatens conviction, it does not seem unfair to require him to choose between leaving the adverse evidence unexplained and subjecting himself to impeachment through disclosure of former crimes....

We find no other error that gives ground for our intervention in California's administration of criminal justice.

Affirmed.

FRANKFURTER, J., CONCURRING

... Between the incorporation of the Fourteenth Amendment into the Constitution and the beginning of the present membership of the Court—a period of 70 years—the scope of that Amendment was passed upon by 43 judges. Of all these judges, only one [John Marshall Harlan], who may respectfully be called an eccentric exception, ever indicated the belief that the Fourteenth Amendment was a shorthand summary of the first eight Amendments theretofore limiting only the Federal Government, and that due process incorporated those eight Amendments as restrictions upon the powers of the States. Among these judges were not only those who would have to be included among the greatest in the history of the Court, but—it is especially relevant to note—they included those whose services in the cause of human rights and the spirit of freedom

are the most conspicuous in our history. It is not invidious to single out Miller, Davis, Bradley, Waite, Matthews, Gray, Fuller, Holmes, Brandeis, Stone and Cardozo (to speak only of the dead) as judges who were alert in safeguarding and promoting the interests of liberty and human dignity through law. But they were also judges mindful of the relation of our federal system to a progressively democratic society and therefore duly regardful of the scope of authority that was left to the States even after the Civil War. And so they did not find that the Fourteenth Amendment, concerned as it was with matters fundamental to the pursuit of justice, fastened upon the States procedural arrangements which, in the language of Mr. Justice Cardozo, only those who are "narrow or provincial" would deem essential to "a fair and enlightened system of justice." *Palko v. Connecticut....*

The short answer to the suggestion that the provision of the Fourteenth Amendment, which ordains "nor shall any State deprive any person of life, liberty, or property, without due process of law," was a way of saying that every State must thereafter initiate prosecutions through indictment by a grand jury, must have a trial by a jury of 12 in criminal cases, and must have trial by such a jury in common law suits where the amount in controversy exceeds $20, is that it is a strange way of saying it. It would be extraordinarily strange for a Constitution to convey such specific commands in such a roundabout and inexplicit way....

Indeed, the suggestion that the Fourteenth Amendment incorporates the first eight Amendments as such is not unambiguously urged. Even the boldest innovator would shrink from suggesting to more than half the States that they may no longer initiate prosecutions without indictment by grand jury, or that thereafter all the States of the Union must furnish a jury of 12 for every case involving a claim above $20. There is suggested merely a selective incorporation of the first eight Amendments into the Fourteenth Amendment. Some are in and some are out, but we are left in the dark as to which are in and which are out. Nor are we given the calculus for determining which go in and which stay out. If the basis of selection is merely that those provisions of the first eight Amendments are incorporated which commend themselves to individual justices as indispensable to the dignity and happiness of a free man, we are thrown back to a merely subjective test....

A construction which gives to due process no independent function but turns it into a summary of the specific provisions of the Bill of Rights would, as has been noted, tear up by the roots much of the fabric of law in the several States, and would deprive the States of opportunity for reforms in legal process designed for extending the area of freedom. It would assume that no other abuses would reveal themselves in the course of time than those which had become manifest in 1791. Such a view not only disregards the historic meaning of "due process." It leads inevitably to a warped construction of specific provisions of the Bill of Rights to bring within their scope conduct clearly condemned by due process but not easily fitting into the pigeon-holes of the specific provisions. It seems pretty late in the day to suggest that a phrase so laden with historic meaning should be given an improvised content consisting of some but not all of the provisions of the first eight Amendments, selected on an undefined basis, with improvisation of content for the provisions so selected....

MURPHY AND RUTLEDGE, J.J., DISSENTING

... I agree [with Justice Black] that the specific guarantees of the Bill of Rights should be carried over intact into the first section of the Fourteenth Amendment. But I am not prepared to say that the latter is entirely and necessarily limited by the Bill of Rights. Occasions may arise where a proceeding falls so far short of conforming to fundamental standards of procedure as to warrant constitutional condemnation in terms of a lack of due process despite the absence of a specific provision in the Bill of Rights....

BLACK AND DOUGLAS, J.J., DISSENTING

... My study of the historical events that culminated in the Fourteenth Amendment, and the expressions of those who sponsored and favored, as well as those who opposed its submission and passage, persuades me that one of the chief objects that the provisions of the Amendment's first section, separately, and as a whole, were intended to accomplish was to make the Bill of Rights applicable to the states. With full knowledge of the import of the *Barron* decision, the framers and backers of the Fourteenth Amendment proclaimed its purpose to be to overturn the constitutional rule that case had announced. This historical purpose has never received full consideration or exposition in any opinion of this Court interpreting the Amendment....

[T]he Court ... today declines to appraise the relevant historical evidence of the intended scope of the first section of the Amendment. Instead it [has] relied upon previous cases, none of which had analyzed the evidence showing that one purpose of those who framed, advocated, and adopted the Amendment had been to make the Bill of Rights applicable to the

States. None of the cases relied upon by the Court today made such an analysis.

For this reason, I am attaching to this dissent, an appendix [omitted] which contains a resume, by no means complete, of the Amendment's history.... Whether this Court ever will, or whether it now should, in the light of past decisions, give full effect to what the Amendment was intended to accomplish is not necessarily essential to a decision here. However that may be, our prior decisions, including *Twining*, do not prevent our carrying out that purpose, at least to the extent of making applicable to the states, not a mere part, as the Court has, but the full protection of the Fifth Amendment's provision against compelling evidence from an accused to convict him of crime. And I further contend that the "natural law" formula which the Court uses to reach its conclusion in this case should be abandoned as an incongruous excrescence on our Constitution. I believe that formula to be itself a violation of our Constitution, in that it subtly conveys to courts, at the expense of legislatures, ultimate power over public policies in fields where no specific provision of the Constitution limits legislative power....

At the same time that the *Twining* decision held that the states need not conform to the specific provisions of the Bill of Rights, it consolidated the power that the Court had assumed under the due process clause by laying even broader

foundations for the Court to invalidate state and even federal regulatory legislation. For under the *Twining* formula, which includes nonregard for the first eight amendments, what are "fundamental rights" and in accord with "canons of decency," as the Court said in *Twining*, and today reaffirms, is to be independently "ascertained from time to time by judicial action."... Thus the power of legislatures became what this Court would declare it to be at a particular time independently of the specific guarantees of the Bill of Rights such as the right to freedom of speech, religion and assembly, the right to just compensation for property taken for a public purpose, the right to jury trial or the right to be secure against unreasonable searches and seizures. Neither the contraction of the Bill of Rights safeguards nor the invalidation of regulatory laws by this Court's appraisal of "circumstances" would readily be classified as the most satisfactory contribution of this Court to the nation....

Conceding the possibility that this Court is now wise enough to improve on the Bill of Rights by substituting natural law concepts for the Bill of Rights. I think the possibility is entirely too speculative to agree to take that course. I would therefore hold in this case that the full protection of the Fifth Amendment's proscription against compelled testimony must be afforded by California. This I would do because of reliance upon the original purpose of the Fourteenth Amendment....

COMMENT

After the Supreme Court issued its opinion, Adamson filed a petition for rehearing that emphasized the unfairness of his trial and implored the majority to "join now in the parade toward one more liberty preserved and protected for all peoples under the Constitution." Adamson's petition was denied, and he was executed at San Quentin prison.

QUESTIONS

1. Summarize the positions on incorporation of the Bill of Rights articulated in *Adamson* by Justices Reed, Frankfurter, Murphy, and Black, respectively. What theories of due process and of judicial review underpin each theory?

2. Justice Black excoriated his colleagues for perpetuating "an incongruous excrescence on our Constitution," an approach to constitutional interpretation that "subtly conveys to courts, at the expense of legislatures, ultimate power over public policies" by means of subjective terms such as notions of "civilized standards," "canons of decency," and "fundamental justice." Assume, for the sake of argument, that the Court had adopted Black's "total incorporation" approach to the Bill of Rights. Would total incorporation eliminate the possibility of judicial subjectivity?

3. Justice Black added a 13-page appendix to his dissent in *Adamson* that consisted of an historical review that he believed "conclusively demonstrates that the language of the first section of the Fourteenth Amendment, taken as a whole, was thought by those responsible for its submission to the people, and by those who opposed its submission, sufficiently explicit to guarantee that thereafter no state could deprive its citizens of the privileges and protections of the Bill of Rights." Professor Charles Fairman took issue with Black's conclusion in his article "Does the Fourteenth Amendment Incorporate the Bill of Rights? The Original Understanding," 2 *Stanford Law Review* (1949): 5.

   Does the fact that Black and Fairman, two thoughtful students of the intentions of the drafters of Fourteenth Amendment, come to divergent conclusions suggest that the quest for "original understanding" is chimerical?

DUE PROCESS

Duncan v. Louisiana
391 U.S. 145 (1968)

SETTING

Adamson v. California revealed the existence of two factions dividing the Court over incorporating the Bill of Rights against the states. One—the "*Palko* faction"—was represented by Justice Reed's majority opinion (and Justice Frankfurter's concurrence), which held that the Due Process Clause of the

Fourteenth Amendment selectively incorporates only those parts of the Bill of Rights that, in Justice Cardozo's words in *Palko*, are "of the very essence of a scheme of ordered liberty."

The dissenters in *Adamson*—Black, Douglas, Murphy, and Rutledge—were the second faction. They argued that "the original purpose of the Fourteenth Amendment" was to incorporate the entire Bill of Rights against the states. They contended that, by ignoring that purpose and adhering to the *Palko* selective incorporation approach, the *Adamson* majority adhered to a "'natural law' formula which ... should be abandoned as an incongruous excrescence on our Constitution." They also claimed that the majority's approach "subtly conveys to courts, at the expense of legislatures, ultimate power over public policies in fields where no specific provision of the Constitution limits legislative power."

In 1953, six years after *Adamson* was decided, President Dwight Eisenhower appointed former California Governor Earl Warren Chief Justice of the United States. Under Warren's leadership, the Court for the next fifteen years employed the *Palko* selective incorporation approach to achieve essentially the result that the *Adamson* dissenters sought by applying most—but not all—of the provisions of the Bill of Rights against the states. (See the *Comment* at the end of this section summarizing the Court's incorporation decisions.) *Duncan v. Louisiana* illustrates that, although a majority of the Warren Court agreed on the incorporation outcome, the Justices continued to disagree on the doctrinal basis for incorporation.

In 1966, more than a decade after the Supreme Court declared racially segregated schools unconstitutional in *Brown v. Board of Education*, 347 U.S. 483 (1954), a federal district court ordered that black students be allowed to transfer to the formerly all-white Boothville-Venice School in Plaquemines Parrish, Louisiana. Pursuant to that order, two cousins of Gary Duncan, a 19-year-old black man, transferred to the school in September 1966. One cousin, Bert Grant, was fourteen years of age; the other, Bernard St. Ann, was sixteen.

After they transferred to Boothville-Venice School, Grant and St. Ann were repeatedly assaulted, threatened, and harassed by white students. On October 18, 1966, Duncan was driving past the school and saw four white fourteen-year-old boys confronting his cousins. It was approximately 3:30 in the afternoon and school had just let out. Duncan stopped his car to see what was happening, got out, and approached the group. He exchanged words with his cousins and the white boys, then told his cousins to get into his car. Herman Landry Jr., one of the white boys, muttered to Duncan, "You must think you're tough." At that point, Duncan either touched Landry on the elbow or slapped him on the arm. Duncan then got into his car and he and his cousins drove away.

On December 5, 1996, Duncan was charged in the Twenty-Fifth Judicial District Court of Louisiana (Plaquemines Parrish) with the misdemeanor offense of simple battery against Landry. The Louisiana Revised Statutes defined simple battery as a battery committed without a dangerous weapon.

The offense was punishable by a maximum of two years in prison and a fine of $300. Duncan pleaded "not guilty" and filed a formal demand for a jury trial. His demand was rejected, because Article 779 of the Louisiana Code of Criminal Procedure denied a jury trial on misdemeanor charges, consistent with Louisiana tradition that the right to a trial by jury depends on whether the court could impose a sentence "at hard labor."

Duncan's case was tried by the trial judge without a jury. Duncan and his cousins testified that Duncan had merely touched Landry on the elbow while telling him that it would be best if he went home. The white boys and a white shopkeeper, who was approximately two-hundred and fifty feet away, testified that Duncan had slapped Landry on the arm. The trial judge resolved the factual dispute against Duncan and found him guilty. He sentenced Duncan to sixty days in prison and fined him $150.

Duncan filed for a writ of certiorari in the Louisiana Supreme Court, arguing that Article 779 denied him to the right of trial by jury, contrary to the commands of the Sixth and Fourteenth Amendments. That court declined to issue the writ, stating in a memorandum decision that there was "No error of law in the ruling complained of." Duncan appealed to the Supreme Court of the United States.

HIGHLIGHTS OF SUPREME COURT ARGUMENTS

BRIEF FOR DUNCAN

◆ This Court's decision in *Maxwell v. Dow*, 176 U.S. 581 (1900), holding that the Fourteenth Amendment does not make applicable to the states any of the specific guarantees of the Bill of Rights, is at odds with recent decisions. In recent decisions, apart from the right to trial by jury, this Court has held every guaranty of the Sixth Amendment applicable to state criminal proceedings.

◆ Trial by jury is the only procedural right included in the body of the Constitution and reiterated in the Bill of Rights. The overwhelming majority of states guarantee a jury trial right in criminal cases as broad as that secured in federal courts by the Sixth Amendment.

◆ The decision to apply a particular guarantee of the Bill of Rights to state criminal proceedings has depended on the Court's determination as to whether the right is so fundamental and essential to a fair trial that it is incorporated in the Due Process Clause of the Fourteenth Amendment. Denial of trial by jury lessens the state's burden of persuasion in a criminal proceeding.

BRIEF FOR LOUISIANA

◆ The Sixth Amendment was intended only as an iron-clad restriction to prevent Congress from making changes in jury trials in federal courts. The states reserved to themselves the unrestricted power to change their own constitutional and statutory provisions regarding jury trials. The Fourteenth Amendment did not take this reserved power away from the states.

♦ Even if the Sixth Amendment right to a jury trial applies to the state, Duncan's conviction without a jury is proper because this Court has held that a jury trial is not required in the prosecution of petty offenses.

♦ This Court consistently has held that a jury trial is not essential to due process and that a fair trial may be had without a jury.

♦ If the Sixth Amendment is held to be applicable to the states, many states will be required to change their criminal jury procedures to conform with that of the federal courts. That result was not intended by the Due Process Clause of the Fourteenth Amendment.

AMICUS CURIAE BRIEF SUPPORTING LOUISIANA

State of New York.

SUPREME COURT DECISION

(7–2 on result, 4–3–2 on rule)

WHITE, J.

... The guarantees of jury trial in the Federal and State Constitutions reflect a profound judgment about the way in which law should be enforced and justice administered. A right to jury trial is granted to criminal defendants in order to prevent oppression by the Government. Those who wrote our constitutions knew from history and experience that it was necessary to protect against unfounded criminal charges brought to eliminate enemies and against judges too responsive to the voice of higher authority.... The deep commitment of the Nation to the right of jury trial in serious criminal cases as a defense against arbitrary law enforcement qualifies for protection under the Due Process Clause of the Fourteenth Amendment, and must therefore be respected by the States.

Of course jury trial has "its weaknesses and the potential for misuse," *Singer v. United States*, 380 U.S. 24 (1965). We are aware of the long debate, especially in this century, among those who write about the administration of justice, as to the wisdom of permitting untrained laymen to determine the facts in civil and criminal proceedings. Although the debate has been intense, with powerful voices on either side, most of the controversy has centered on the jury in civil cases....

Our conclusion is that in the American States, as in the federal judicial system, a general grant of jury trial for serious offenses is a fundamental right, essential for preventing miscarriages of justice and for assuring that fair trials are provided for all defendants. We would not assert, however, that every criminal trial—or any particular trial—held before a judge alone is unfair or that a defendant may never be as fairly treated by a judge as he would be by a jury. Thus we hold no constitutional doubts about the practices, common in both federal and state courts, of accepting waivers of jury trial and prosecuting petty crimes without extending a right to jury trial. However, the fact is that in most places more trials for serious crimes are to juries than to a court alone; a great many defendants prefer the judgment of a jury to that of a court. Even where defendants are satisfied with bench trials, the right to a jury trial very likely serves its intended purpose of making judicial or prosecutorial unfairness less likely....

It is doubtless true that there is a category of petty crimes or offenses which is not subject to the Sixth Amendment jury trial provision and should not be subject to the Fourteenth Amendment jury trial requirement here applied to the States. Crimes carrying possible penalties up to six months do not require a jury trial if they otherwise qualify as petty offenses[.]... But the penalty authorized for a particular crime is of major relevance in determining whether it is serious or not and may in itself, if severe enough, subject the trial to the mandates of the Sixth Amendment.... In the case before us the Legislature of Louisiana has made simple battery a criminal offense punishable by imprisonment for up to two years and a fine. The question, then, is whether a crime carrying such a penalty is an offense which Louisiana may insist on trying without a jury.

We think not.... Of course the boundaries of the petty offense category have always been ill-defined, if not ambulatory. In the absence of an explicit constitutional provision, the definitional task necessarily falls on the courts, which must either pass upon the validity of legislative attempts to identify those petty offenses which are exempt from jury trial or, where the legislature has not addressed itself to the problem, themselves face the question in the first instance. In either case it is necessary to draw a line in the spectrum of crime, separating petty from serious infractions. This process, although essential, cannot be wholly satisfactory, for it requires attaching different consequences to events which, when they lie near the line, actually differ very little....

We need not, however, settle in this case the exact location of the line between petty offenses and serious crimes. It is suf-ficient for our purposes to hold that a crime punishable by two years in prison is, based on past and contemporary standards in this country, a serious crime and not a petty offense. Consequently, appellant was entitled to a jury trial and it was error to deny it.

The judgment below is reversed and the case is remanded for proceedings not inconsistent with this opinion.

Reversed and remanded.

BLACK AND DOUGLAS, J.J., CONCURRING

The Court today holds that the right to trial by jury guaranteed defendants in criminal cases in federal courts by Art. III of the United States Constitution and by the Sixth Amendment is also guaranteed by the Fourteenth Amendment to defendants tried in state courts. With this holding I agree for reasons given by the Court. I also agree because of reasons given in my dissent in *Adamson v. People of State of California....*

I want to add that I am not bothered by the argument that applying the Bill of Rights to the States "according to the same standards that protect those personal rights against federal encroachment," interferes with our concept of federalism in that it may prevent States from trying novel social and economic experiments. I have never believed that under the guise of federalism the States should be able to experiment with the protections afforded our citizens through the Bill of Rights....

No one is more concerned than I that the States be allowed to use the full scope of their powers as their citizens see fit. And that is why I have continually fought against the expansion of this Court's authority over the States through the use of a broad, general interpretation of due process that permits judges to strike down state laws they do not like....

FORTAS, J., CONCURRING

... [A]lthough I agree with the decision of the Court, I cannot agree with the implication that the tail must go with the hide: that when we hold, influenced by the Sixth Amendment, that "due process" requires that the States accord the right of jury trial for all but petty offenses, we automatically import all of the ancillary rules which have been or may hereafter be developed incidental to the right to jury trial in the federal courts. I see no reason whatever, for example, to assume that our decision today should require us to impose federal requirements such as unanimous verdicts or a jury of 12 upon the States. We may well conclude that these and other features of federal jury practice are by no means fundamental— that they are not essential to due process of law—and that they are not obligatory on the States....

The draftsmen of the Fourteenth Amendment intended what they said, not more or less: that no State shall deprive any person of life, liberty, or property without due process of law. It is ultimately the duty of this Court to interpret, to ascribe specific meaning to this phrase. There is no reason whatever for us to conclude that, in so doing, we are bound slavishly to follow not only the Sixth Amendment but all of its bag and baggage, however securely or insecurely affixed they may be by law and precedent to federal proceedings....

HARLAN AND STEWART, J.J., DISSENTING

... I believe I am correct in saying that every member of the Court for at least the last 135 years has agreed that our Founders did not consider the requirements of the Bill of Rights so fundamental that they should operate directly against the States. They were wont to believe rather that the security of liberty in America rested primarily upon the dispersion of governmental power across a federal system. The Bill of Rights was considered unnecessary by some but insisted upon by others in order to curb the possibility of abuse of power by the strong central government they were creating....

A few members of the Court have taken the position that the intention of those who drafted the first section of the Fourteenth Amendment was simply, and exclusively, to make the provisions of the first eight Amendments applicable to state action. This view has never been accepted by this Court. In my view, often expressed elsewhere, the first section of the Fourteenth Amendment was meant neither to incorporate, nor to be limited to, the specific guarantees of the first eight Amendments....

Although I therefore fundamentally disagree with the total incorporation view of the Fourteenth Amendment, it seems to me that such a position does at least have the virtue, lacking in the Court's selective incorporation approach, of internal consistency: we look to the Bill of Rights, word for word, clause for clause, precedent for precedent because, it is said, the men who wrote the Amendment wanted it that way. For those who do not accept this "history," a different source of "intermediate premises" must be found. The Bill of Rights is not necessarily irrelevant to the search for guidance in interpreting the Fourteenth Amendment, but the reason for and the nature of its relevance must be articulated.

Apart from the approach taken by the absolute incorporationists, I can see only one method of analysis that has any internal logic. That is to start with the words "liberty" and "due process of law" and attempt to define them in a way that accords with American traditions and our system of government....

[E]ven if I were persuaded that trial by jury is a fundamental right in some criminal cases, I could see nothing fundamental in the rule, not yet formulated by the Court, that places the prosecution of appellant for simple battery within the category of "jury crimes" rather than "petty crimes."...

There is no obvious reason why a jury trial is a requisite of fundamental fairness when the charge is robbery, and not a requisite of fairness when the same defendant, for the same actions, is charged with assault and petty theft. The reason for the historic exception for relatively minor crimes is the obvious one: the burden of jury trial was thought to outweigh its marginal advantages. Exactly why the States should not be allowed to make continuing adjustments, based on the state of their criminal dockets and the difficulty of summoning jurors, simply escapes me....

QUESTIONS

1. In light of *Duncan*, what is the doctrinal status of incorporating the Bill of Rights via the Fourteenth Amendment Due Process Clause? Does a clear conception of due process emerge from the various *Duncan* opinions?

2. Louisiana petitioned the Supreme Court for rehearing following the decision in *Duncan*. It claimed that the plurality opinion, holding that the Sixth Amendment guarantees the right to a jury trial in "serious criminal cases" failed to identify the criteria a state must use to determine what is a serious criminal case as distinguished from a petty offense for which a jury trial is not an entitlement. Louisiana also contended that the plurality left in doubt "whether a twelve-man unanimous jury is necessary for the trial of 'serious criminal cases.'" The Supreme Court denied the petition for rehearing. Why would the plurality have chosen to leave unanswered such important questions in *Duncan*? Was the Court's refusal to confront the question a sign of judicial deference to the states?

3. In 1833, in *Democracy in America*, Alexis de Tocqueville maintained:

   > The institution of the jury ... places the real direction of society in the hands of the governed, or a portion of the governed[.]... He who punishes infractions of the law, is therefore the real master of society. (*Democracy in America*, 2 vols. (New York, NY: Schocken, 1974), I: 333–334)

   What are the constitutional ramifications of Tocqueville's argument in the context of the role of due process in the incorporation debate?

COMMENT

No majority of the Supreme Court has accepted the argument that the Fourteenth Amendment incorporated all of the provisions of the Bill of Rights against the states. Instead, the Court has taken a path of "selective incorporation." Its basic approach has been that some rights are so fundamental that they must apply against the states as well as the national government. The following list of incorporated provisions is adapted from the Congressional Research Service's *The Constitution of the United States: Analysis and Interpretation* (Washington, D.C.: Government Printing Office, 1982), pp. 956–958, n. 12:

FIRST AMENDMENT

Religion

Free Exercise: *Hamilton v. Regents*, 293 U.S. 245 (1934); *Cantwell v. Connecticut*, 310 U.S. 296 (1940).

Establishment: *Everson v. Board of Education*, 330 U.S. 1 (1947); *Illinois ex rel. McCollum v. Board of Education*, 333 U.S. 203 (1948).

Speech

Gitlow v. New York, 268 U.S. 652 (1925); *Fiske v. Kansas*, 274 U.S. 380 (1927); *Stromberg v. California*, 283 U.S. 359 (1931).

Press

Near v. Minnesota, 283 U.S. 697 (1931).

Assembly

Association: *DeJonge v. Oregon*, 299 U.S. 353 (1937); *NAACP v. Alabama*, 357 U.S. 449 (1958).

Petition: *DeJonge v. Oregon*, 299 U.S. 353 (1937); *Hague v. CIO*, 307 U.S. 496 (1939); *Bridges v. California*, 314 U.S. 252 (1941).

FOURTH AMENDMENT

Wolf v. Colorado, 338 U.S. 25 (1949); *Mapp v. Ohio*, 367 U.S. 643 (1961).

FIFTH AMENDMENT

Double Jeopardy: *Benton v. Maryland*, 395 U.S. 784 (1969); *Ashe v. Swenson*, 397 U.S. 436 (1970).

Self-Incrimination: *Malloy v. Hogan*, 378 U.S. 1 (1964); *Griffin v. California*, 380 U.S. 609 (1965).

Just Compensation: *Chicago, B & Q Railroad Co. v. City of Chicago*, 166 U.S. 226 (1897).

SIXTH AMENDMENT

Speedy Trial: *Klopfer v. North Carolina*, 386 U.S. 213 (1967).

Public Trial: *In re Oliver*, 333 U.S. 257 (1948).

Jury Trial: *Duncan v. Louisiana*, 391 U.S. 145 (1968).

Impartial Jury: *Irvin v. Dowd*, 366 U.S. 717 (1961); *Turner v. Louisiana*, 379 U.S. 466 (1965); *Parker v. Gladden*, 385 U.S. 363 (1966).

Notice of Charges: *In re Oliver*, 333 U.S. 257 (1948).

Confrontation: *Pointer v. Texas*, 380 U.S. 400 (1965); *Douglas v. Alabama*, 380 U.S. 415 (1965).

Compulsory Process: *Washington v. Texas*, 388 U.S. 14 (1967).

Counsel: *Powell v. Alabama*, 287 U.S. 45 (1932); *Gideon v. Wainwright*, 372 U.S. 335 (1963); *Argersinger v. Hamlin*, 407 U.S. 25 (1972).

EIGHTH AMENDMENT

Louisiana ex rel Francis v. Resweber, 329 U.S. 459 (1947); *Robinson v. California*, 370 U.S. 660 (1962).

NOT INCORPORATED

Second Amendment, Third Amendment, Grand Jury Indictment Clause of Fifth Amendment, Seventh Amendment.

SUGGESTIONS FOR FURTHER READING

Amar, Akhil Reed, "The Bill of Rights as a Constitution," 100 *Yale Law Journal* (1991): 1131.

_____, "The Bill of Rights and the Fourteenth Amendment," 101 *Yale Law Journal* (1992): 1193.

Baker, Leonard, *Back to Back: The Duel between FDR and the Supreme Court* (New York, NY: Macmillan, 1967).

Benedict, Michael Les, "Laissez-Faire and Liberty: A Re-evaluation of the Meaning and Origins of Laissez-Faire Constitutionalism," 3 *Law and History Review* (1985): 293.

Berman, Edward, "The Supreme Court and the Minimum Wage," 31 *Journal of Political Economy* (1922): 852.

Cortner, Richard C., *The Supreme Court and the Second Bill of Rights: The Fourteenth Amendment and the Nationalization of Civil Rights* (Madison: WI: University of Wisconsin Press, 1981).

Corwin, Edward S., "The Supreme Court and the Fourteenth Amendment," 7 *Michigan Law Review* (1909): 643.

_____, "The Doctrine of Due Process of Law Before the Civil War," 24 *Harvard Law Review* (1911): 460.

_____, *The "Higher Law" Background of American Constitutional Law* (Ithaca, NY: Cornell University Press, 1929).

_____, *Court over Constitution* (Princeton, NJ: Princeton University Press, 1932).

_____, *Liberty against Government: The Rise, Flowering and Decline of a Famous Juridical Concept* (Baton Rouge, LA: Louisiana University Press, 1948).

Curtis, Michael Kent, *No State Shall Abridge: The Fourteenth Amendment and the Bill of Rights* (Durham, NC: Duke University Press, 1986).

Ely, James W., Jr., *The Guardian of Every Other Right: A Constitutional History of Property Rights* (New York, NY: Oxford University Press, 1992).

Fairman, Charles A., "Does the Fourteenth Amendment Incorporate the Bill of Rights? The Original Understanding," 2 *Stanford Law Review* (1949): 5.

Fine, Sidney, *Laissez Faire and the General Welfare State* (Ann Arbor, MI: University of Michigan Press, 1956).

Foster, James C., *The Ideology of Apolitical Politics: Elite Lawyers' Response to the Legitimation Crisis of American Capitalism, 1870–1920* (New York, NY: Garland, 1990).

Frankfurter, Felix, "Hours of Labor and Realism in Constitutional Law," 23 *Harvard Law Review* (1916): 353.

_____, "Mr. Justice Roberts," 104 *University of Pennsylvania Law Review* (1955): 311.

_____, "Memorandum on 'Incorporation' of the Bill of Rights into the Due Process Clause of the Fourteenth Amendment," 78 *Harvard Law Review* (1965): 746.

Funston, Richard, "The Double Standard of Constitutional Protection in the Era of the Welfare State," 90 *Political Science Quarterly* (1975): 261.

Gillman, Howard, *The Constitutional Besieged: The Rise and Demise of Lochner Era Police Powers Jurisprudence* (Durham, NC: Duke University Press, 1993).

Goldstein, Leslie F., "Popular Sovereignty, the Origins of Judicial Review, and the Revival of Unwritten Law," 48 *Journal of Politics* (1986): 51.

Graham, Fred P., *The Due Process Revolution: The Warren Court's Impact on Criminal Law* (New York, NY: Hayden Book Company, 1970).

_____, *The Self-Inflicted Wound* (New York, NY: Macmillan, 1970).

Graham, Howard Jay, "The 'Conspiracy Theory' of the Fourteenth Amendment," 47 *Yale Law Journal* (1938): 371; 48 *Yale Law Journal* (1938): 171; reprinted in *Everyman's Constitution: Historical Essays on the Fourteenth Amendment, the "Conspiracy Theory," and American Constitutionalism* (Madison, WI: State Historical Society of Wisconsin, 1968).

Grey, Thomas, "Do We Have an Unwritten Constitution?" 27 *Stanford Law Review* (1975): 703.

_____, "Origins of the Unwritten Constitution: Fundamental Law in American Revolutionary Thought," 30 *Stanford Law Review* (1978): 843.

Hamilton, Walton H., "The Path of Due Process of Law," in *The Constitution Reconsidered*, ed. Conyers Read (New York, NY: Columbia University Press, 1938).

Hand, Learned, "Due Process of Law and the Eight-Hour Day," 21 *Harvard Law Review* (1908): 495.

_____, *The Spirit of Liberty*, 3rd ed. (New York, NY: Knopf, 1960).

Henkin, Louis, "'Selective Incorporation' in the 14th Amendment," 73 *Yale Law Journal* (1963): 74.

Horwitz, Morton J., *The Transformation of American Law, 1870–1960: The Crisis of Legal Orthodoxy* (New York, NY: Oxford University Press, 1992).

Hovenkamp, Howard, "The Political Economy of Substantive Due Process," 40 *Stanford Law Review* (1988): 443.

_____, *Enterprise and American Law, 1836–1937* (Cambridge, MA: Harvard University Press, 1991).

Howard, A. E. Dick, *The Road from Runnymede: Magna Carta and Constitutionalism in America* (Charlottesville, VA: University Press of Virginia, 1968).

Israel, Jerold, "Selective Incorporation Revisited," 71 *Michigan Law Review* (1982): 253.

Kaczorowski, Robert, *Nationalization of Civil Rights: Constitutional Theory and Practice in a Racist Society, 1866–1883* (New York, NY: Garland, 1987).

Kadish, Sanford, "Methodology and Criteria in Due Process Analysis—Survey and Criticism," 66 *Yale Law Journal* (1957): 319.

Kennedy, Duncan, "Toward an Historical Understanding of Legal Consciousness: The Case of Classical Legal Thought in America, 1850–1940," in *Research in Law and Sociology*, ed. Steven Spitzer, vol. 3 (Greenwich, CT: JAI Press, 1980).

Kans, Paul, *Judicial Power and Reform Politics: The Anatomy of* Lochner v. New York (Lawrence, KS: University of Kansas Press, 1990).

Keynes, Edward, *Liberty, Property, and Privacy: Toward A Jurisprudence of Substantive Due Process* (University Park, PA: University of Pennsylvania Press, 1996).

Leuchtenburg, William E., *The Perils of Prosperity, 1914–1932* (Chicago, IL: University of Chicago Press, 1958).

_____, *Franklin D. Roosevelt and the New Deal* (New York, NY: Harper and Row, 1963).

_____, "The Origins of Franklin D. Roosevelt's 'Court Packing' Plan," *The Supreme Court Review* (Chicago, IL: University of Chicago Press, 1966).

_____, "Franklin D. Roosevelt's Supreme Court 'Packing' Plan," in *Essays on the New Deal*, ed. Harold M. Hollingsworth, et al. (Austin, TX: University of Texas Press, 1969).

_____, "The Case of the Wenatchee Chambermaid," in *Quarrels That Have Shaped the Constitution*, ed. John A. Garraty, rev. ed. (New York, NY: Harper & Row, 1987).

Linde, Hans A., "Without Due Process," 40 *Oregon Law Review* (1970): 125.

_____, "Due Process of Lawmaking," 55 *Nebraska Law Review* (1976): 197.

Lusky, Louis, "Footnote Redux: A *Carolene Products* Reminiscence," 82 *Columbia Law Review* (1982): 1093.

Mason, Alpheus Thomas, *The Supreme Court: Vehicle of Revealed Truth or Power Group, 1930–1937* (Boston, MA: Boston University Press, 1953).

_____, "The Case of the Overworked Laundress," in *Quarrels That Have*

Shaped the Constitution, ed. John A. Garraty, rev. ed. (New York, NY: Harper & Row, 1987).

McCloskey, Robert G., "Economic Due Process and the Supreme Court," *The Supreme Court Review* (Chicago, IL: University of Chicago Press, 1962).

_____, *American Conservatism in the Age of Enterprise, 1865–1910* (New York, NY: Harper & Row, 1964).

Mendelson, Wallace, "A Missing Link in the Evolution of Due Process," 10 *Vanderbilt Law Review* (1956): 125.

_____, *Capitalism, Democracy, and the Supreme Court* (New York, NY: Appleton-Century-Crofts, 1960).

Miller, Geoffrey P., "The True Story of *Carolene Products*," in *The Supreme Court Review* (Chicago, IL: University of Chicago Press, 1987).

Pennock, J. Roland, and John W. Chapman, eds., *Due Process* (New York, NY: New York University Press, 1977).

Phillips, Michael J., "Another Look at Economic Substantive Due Process," *Wisconsin Law Review* (1987): 265.

Porter, Mary Cornelia, "*Lochner* and Company: Revisionism Revisited," in *Liberty, Property, and Government: Constitutional Interpretation Before the New Deal*, ed. Ellen Frankel Paul and Howard Dickman (Albany, NY: State University of New York Press, 1989).

Pound, Roscoe, "Liberty of Contract," 18 *Yale Law Journal* (1909): 454.

Powell, Lewis F., Jr., "*Carolene Products* Revisited," 82 *Columbia Law Review* (1982): 1087.

Powell, Thomas Reed, "The Judiciality of Minimum Wage Legislation," 37 *Harvard Law Review* (1924): 545.

Rutland, Robert A., *Birth of the Bill of Rights, 1776–1791* (Boston, MA: Northeastern University Press, 1991).

Shattuck, Charles E., "The True Meaning of the Term 'Liberty' in Those Clauses in the Federal and State Constitutions Which Protect 'Life, Liberty and Property,'" 4 *Harvard Law Review* (1890): 12.

Sherry, Suzanna, "The Founder's Unwritten Constitution," 54 *University of Chicago Law Review* (1987): 1127.

Siegan, Bernard H., "Rehabilitating *Lochner*," *San Diego Law Review* (1985): 453.

Soifer, Aviam, "The Paradox of Paternalism and Laissez-Faire Constitutionalism: United States Supreme Court 1888–1921," 5 *Law and History Review* (1987): 249.

_____, "Status, Contract, and Promises Unkept," 96 *Yale Law Journal* (1987): 1916.

Tarrow, Sidney, "*Lochner v. New York*: A Political Analysis," 5 *Labor History* (1964): 277.

TenBroek, Jacobus, *Equal Under Law*, new enlarged ed. (New York, NY: Collier 1965).

Warren, Charles, "The New 'Liberty' under the Fourteenth Amendment," 39 *Harvard Law Review* (1926): 431.

Yudof, Mark G., "Equal Protection, Class Legislation, and Sex Discrimination: One Small Cheer for Mr. Herbert Spencer's *Social Statics*," 88 *Michigan Law Review* (1990): 1366.

STATE ACTION DOCTRINE

Civil Rights Cases
109 U.S. 3 (1883)

SETTING

The Fourteenth and Fifteenth Amendments are written in *negative* terms. The Fourteenth Amendment prohibits states from making or enforcing laws that abridge the privileges or immunities of citizens of the United States, or from depriving persons of life, liberty, or property without due process of law, or from denying persons within their jurisdictions of the equal protection of the laws. The Fifteenth Amendment prohibits states from denying or abridging the rights of citizens to vote on account of race, color, or previous condition of servitude. The *positive* grant of power in both amendments is to Congress, which may enforce the amendments with "appropriate legislation."

The former Confederacy did not passively accept these post-Civil War amendments, which were intended to "reconstruct" social relations within the states formerly in rebellion against the United States. In the early 1870s, during the heyday of Reconstruction, white southerners, known as "Redeemers," overthrew hated northern "Carpetbaggers," reasserted control over their state governments and, in the name of white supremacy, tightened the Black Codes adopted after the Civil War. Gradually, Black Codes evolved into statutes known as "Jim Crow" laws that prohibited blacks from using any white public facilities. (Jim Crow is a reference to the song of that name that had been sung before the Civil War by a white actor named Thomas Rice. Rice portrayed a black buffoon in a minstrel show who sang, "Wheel about, turn about, do just so. Every time I wheel about I jump Jim Crow.") Blacks were thereby confined to substandard schools and public accommodations and consigned to a status of social inferiority. Southern constitutions and state laws adopted after the war, which had been imposed by Radical Reconstructionists and their agents and enforced by federal military occupation, were slowly revised to prevent blacks from voting and to subject blacks to strict segregation. Secret organizations such as the Ku Klux Klan, formed after the Civil War, arose to threaten, terrorize, and murder blacks who struggled against the prevailing social order. Congressional responses, such as the Ku Klux Klan Acts that outlawed such activities, were ineffectual and not enforced.

Northern Civil War hero Ulysses S. Grant, who became president in 1868, proved less effective as president than as a Union general. His administration was rocked by scandals. By 1873 the nation was mired in a deep post-War economic depression. It was not until 1875 that Congress was able to complete action on another civil rights bill, proposed by Senator Charles Sumner in 1870. The 1875 Civil Rights Act, grounded in Congress's enforcement powers under Section 5 of the Fourteenth Amendment, guaranteed to all persons within the jurisdiction of the United States full and equal enjoyment of the accommodations of inns, public conveyances, theaters, and other places of public amusement. It imposed stiff civil and criminal penalties on violators. Like the 1866 Civil Rights Act that preceded it, there were serious questions about the constitutionality of the 1875 statute. It was seen by many as beyond the power of Congress and as an incursion into states' rights.

As originally proposed by Senator Sumner, the 1875 Civil Rights Act would also have guaranteed equal access to facilities in public schools, churches, and cemeteries. Those provisions were deleted after Sumner's death, as part of a compromise to rescue the bill from defeat by a coalition of northern and southern members of Congress who opposed school desegregation. The bill became law on March 1, 1875, when signed by President Grant.

Challenges to the Civil Rights Act of 1875 arose almost immediately. Murray Stanley, a Kansas innkeeper, was indicted in U.S. District Court for the District of Kansas for refusing to serve supper to Bird Gee in October 1875, because Gee was black. Stanley demurred to the indictment. The District Court was unable to respond to Stanley's demurrer. It certified two questions to the Supreme Court of the United States. The first was whether the indictment stated an offense punishable by the laws of the United States or cognizable by the federal courts. The second was whether the Civil Rights Act of 1875 was constitutional.

Stanley's case was consolidated with three other criminal cases and one civil case, all brought under the 1875 Civil Rights Act, for refusals to provide services to blacks. The criminal cases involved prosecutions against Samuel Nichols, an innkeeper in Missouri; Michael Ryan, owner of Maguire's theater in San Francisco, California; and Samuel D. Singleton, owner of the Grand Opera House in New York. The civil action was brought by Richard and Sallie Robinson against the Memphis & Charleston Railroad for refusing Mrs. Robinson a first-class railroad ticket in the ladies' car. The cases were known collectively as the *Civil Rights Cases*, and were argued at the 1879 and 1882 Terms of the Court.

HIGHLIGHTS OF SUPREME COURT ARGUMENTS

BRIEF FOR THE UNITED STATES

◆ The 1875 Civil Rights Act addresses public accommodations, guaranteeing equal access to facilities that are part of interstate commerce. Congress had power under the Commerce Clause to pass the act.

◆ The Civil Rights Act is justified by the Fourteenth Amendment. Sponsors of the Fourteenth Amendment were clear that their intent was to give Congress power that had been of questionable constitutionality under the 1866 act.

◆ The 1875 Civil Rights Act is a legitimate exercise of Congress's power under the Thirteenth Amendment. It is appropriate legislation to efface the residuum of slavery.

◆ Inns are instrumentalities of interstate commerce and could be regulated by Congress even before passage of the Civil War Amendments. Innkeepers and theater operators carry on their businesses with licenses from the state. These businesses are quasi-public in nature, giving Congress the right to prohibit any discrimination based on race, color, or previous condition of servitude.

Note: No briefs were submitted on behalf of the defendants in the criminal cases.

BRIEF FOR MEMPHIS & CHARLESTON RAILROAD COMPANY

◆ The conductor denied Mrs. Robinson access to the ladies' car because he thought she was a prostitute and that Mr. Robinson was her paramour. Prostitutes are never allowed to sit in the ladies' car. Color was not a factor in the conductor's decision.

SUPREME COURT DECISION: *8–1*

BRADLEY, J.

... Has Congress constitutional power to make [the 1875 Civil Rights Act]? Of course, no one will contend that the power to pass it was contained in the Constitution before the adoption of the last three [Thirteenth, Fourteenth and Fifteenth] amendments....

The first section of the Fourteenth Amendment,—which is the one relied on,—after declaring who shall be citizens of the United States, and of the several States, is prohibitory in its character, and prohibitory upon the States.... It is State action of a particular character that is prohibited. Individual invasion of individual rights is not the subject-matter of the amendment. It has a deeper and broader scope. It nullifies and makes void all State legislation, and State action of every kind, which impairs the privileges and immunities of citizens of the United States, or which injures them in life, liberty or property without due process of law, or which denies to any of them the equal protection of the laws.... [The first section of the Fourteenth Amendment] does not authorize Congress to create a code of municipal law for the regulation of private rights; but to provide modes of redress against the operation of State laws, and the action of State officers, executive or judicial, when these are subversive of the fundamental rights specified in the amendment. Positive rights and privileges are undoubtedly secured by the Fourteenth Amendment; but they are secured by way of prohibition against State laws and State proceedings affecting those rights and privileges, and by power given to Congress to legislate for the purpose of carrying such prohibition into effect; and such legislation must necessarily be predicated upon such supposed State laws or State proceedings, and be directed to the correction of their operation and effect....

And so in the present case, until some state law has been passed, or some state action through its officers or agents has been taken, adverse to the rights of citizens sought to be protected by the Fourteenth Amendment, no legislation of the United States under said amendment, nor any proceeding under such legislation, can be called into activity, for the prohibitions of the amendment are against state laws and acts done under state authority....

An inspection of the [Civil Rights Act of 1875] shows that it makes no reference whatever to any supposed or apprehended violation of the Fourteenth Amendment on the part of the States. It is not predicated on any such view. It proceeds *ex directo* [immediately] to declare that certain acts committed by individuals shall be deemed offenses, and shall be prosecuted and punished by proceedings in the courts of the United States. It does not profess to be corrective of any constitutional wrong committed by the States; it does not make its operation to depend upon any such wrong committed....

If this legislation is appropriate for enforcing the prohibitions of the amendment, it is difficult to see where it is to stop. Why may not Congress with equal show of authority enact a code of laws for the enforcement and vindication of all rights of life, liberty, and property?... The truth is that the assumption that if the states are forbidden to legislate or act in a particular way on a particular subject, and power is conferred upon Congress to enforce the prohibition, this gives Congress power to legislate generally upon that subject, and not merely power to provide modes of redress against such state legislation or action. The assumption is certainly unsound. It is repugnant to the Tenth Amendment of the constitution....

The law in question, without any reference to adverse State legislation on the subject, declares that all persons shall be entitled to equal accommodations and privileges of inns, public conveyances, and places of public amusement, and imposes a penalty upon any individual who shall deny to any citizen such equal accommodations and privileges. This is not corrective legislation; it is primary and direct; it takes immediate and absolute possession of the subject of the right of admission to inns, public conveyances, and places of amusement. It supersedes and displaces State legislation on the same subject, or only allows it permissive force. It ignores such legislation, and assumes that the matter is one that belongs to the domain of national regulation. Whether it would not have been a more effective protection of the rights of citizens to have clothed Congress with plenary power over the whole subject, is not now the question. What we have to decide is, whether such plenary power has been conferred upon Congress by the Fourteenth Amendment, and, in our judgment, it has not....

But the power of Congress to adopt direct and primary, as distinguished from corrective, legislation on the subject in hand, is sought, in the second place, from the Thirteenth Amendment, which abolishes slavery....

The only question under the present head, therefore, is, whether the refusal to any persons of the accommodations of an inn, or a public conveyance, or a place of public amusement, by an individual, and without any sanction or support from any State law or regulation, does inflict upon such persons any manner of servitude, or form of slavery, as those terms are understood in this country?...

[W]e are forced to the conclusion that such an act of refusal has nothing to do with slavery or involuntary servitude, and that if it is violative of any right of the party, his redress is to be sought under the laws of the State; or, if those laws are adverse to his rights and do not protect him, his remedy will be found in the corrective legislation which Congress has adopted, or may adopt, for counteracting the effect of State laws, or State action, prohibited by the Fourteenth Amendment. It would be running the slavery argument into the ground to make it apply to every act of discrimination which a person may see fit to make as to the guests he will entertain, or as to the people he will take into his coach or cab or car, or admit to his concert or theater, or deal with in other matters of intercourse or business. Innkeepers and public carriers, by the laws of all the States, so far as we are aware, are bound, to the extent of their facilities, to furnish proper accommodation to all unobjectionable persons who in good faith apply for them. If the laws themselves make any unjust discrimination, amenable to the prohibitions of the Fourteenth Amendment, Congress has full power to afford a remedy under that amendment and in accordance with it.

When a man has emerged from slavery, and by the aid of beneficent legislation has shaken off the inseparable concomitants of that state, there must be some stage in the process of his elevation when he takes the rank of a mere citizen, and ceases to be the special favorite of the laws, and when his rights as a citizen, or a man, are to be protected in the ordinary modes by which other men's rights are protected. There were thousands of free colored people in this country before the abolition of slavery, enjoying all the essential rights of life, liberty, and property the same as white citizens; yet no one, at that time, thought that it was any invasion of their personal *status* as freemen because they were not admitted to all the privileges enjoyed by white citizens, or because they were subjected to discriminations in the enjoyment of accommodations in inns, public conveyances, and places of amusement. Mere discriminations on account of race or color were not regarded as badges of slavery....

This conclusion disposes of the cases now under consideration....

HARLAN, J., DISSENTING

... The court adjudges that Congress is without power, under either the Thirteenth or Fourteenth Amendment, to establish [the Civil Rights Act of 1875], and that the first and second sections of the statute are, in all their parts, unconstitutional and void....

The Fourteenth Amendment presents the first instance in our history of the investiture of Congress with affirmative power, by *legislation*, to *enforce* an express prohibition upon the states....

The assumption that this amendment consists wholly of prohibitions upon state laws and state proceedings in hostility to its provisions, is unauthorized by its language....

In view of the circumstances under which the recent amendments were incorporated into the constitution, and especially in view of the peculiar character of the new rights they created and secured, it ought not to be presumed that the general government has abdicated its authority, by national legislation, direct and primary in its character, to guard and protect privileges and immunities secured by that instrument. Such an interpretation of the constitution ought not to be accepted if it be possible to avoid it. Its acceptance would lead to this anomalous result: that whereas, prior to the amendments, Congress, with the sanction of this court, passed the most stringent laws—operating directly and primarily upon the States, and their officers and agents, as well as upon individuals—in vindication of slavery and the right of the master, it may not now, by legislation of a like primary and direct character, guard, protect, and secure the freedom established, and the most essential right of the citizenship granted, by the constitutional amendments. I venture, with all respect for the opinion of others, to insist that the national legislature may, without transcending the limits of the Constitution, do for human liberty and the fundamental rights of American citizenship, what it did, with the sanction of this court, for the protection of slavery and the rights of the masters of fugitive slaves....

It does not seem to me that the fact that, by the second clause of the first section of the Fourteenth Amendment, the states are expressly prohibited from making or enforcing laws abridging the privileges and immunities of citizens of the United States, furnishes any sufficient reason for holding or maintaining that the amendment was intended to deny Congress the power, by general, primary, and direct legislation, of protecting citizens of the United States, being also citizens of their respective States, against discrimination, in respect to their rights as citizens, founded on race, color, or previous condition of servitude. Such an interpretation of the amendment is plainly repugnant to its fifth section, conferring power upon Congress, by appropriate legislation, to enforce, not merely the provisions containing prohibitions upon the states, but all of the provisions of the amendment, including the provisions, express and implied, of the grant of citizenship in the first clause of the first section of the article. This alone is sufficient for holding that Congress is not restricted to the enactment of laws adapted to counteract and redress the operation of state legislation, or the action of state officers of the character prohibited by the amendment. It was perfectly well known that the great danger to the equal enjoyment by citizens of their rights, as citizens, was to be apprehended, not altogether from unfriendly state legislation, but from the hostile action of corporations and individuals in the States. And it is to be presumed that it was intended, by that section, to clothe Congress with power and authority to meet that danger....

[I]f it be ... adjudged that individuals and corporations exercising public functions may, without liability to direct primary legislation on the part of Congress, make the race of citizens the ground for denying them that equality of civil rights which the constitution ordains as a principle of republican citizenship,—then, not only the foundations upon which the national supremacy has always securely rested will be materially disturbed, but we shall enter upon an era of constitutional law when the rights of freedom and American citizenship cannot receive from the nation that efficient protection which heretofore was accorded to slavery and the rights of the master.

My brethren say that when a man has emerged from slavery, and by the aid of beneficent legislation has shaken off the inseparable concomitants of that state, there must be some stage in the process of his elevation when he takes the rank of a mere citizen, and ceases to be the special favorite of the laws.... It is, I submit, scarcely just to say that the colored race has been the special favorite of the laws.... Today it is the colored race which is denied, by corporations and individuals wielding public authority, rights funda-mental in their freedom and citizenship. At some future time it may be some other race that will fall under the ban. If the constitutional amendments be enforced, according to the intent with which, as I conceive, they were adopted, there can-not be, in this republic, any class of human beings in practical subjection to another class, with power in the latter to dole out to the former just such privileges as they may choose to grant....

QUESTIONS

1. Summarize the state action doctrine stated in the *Civil Rights Cases*. Where does private action end and state action begin, according to Justice Bradley? Were Bradley's reasons for holding that Congress exceeded its authority in passing the Civil Rights Act of 1875 consti-tutionally based?

2. What theories of congressional authority under the Fourteenth Amendment underlie the majority and dissenting opinions in the *Civil Rights Cases*? One theory of congressional power is that it is accordion-like and can be expanded or contracted. To what extent was the Court's reluctance in the *Civil Rights Cases* to use the state action doctrine to expand congressional authority over the states related to broader debates over states' rights?

3. Law professors Daniel A. Farber, William N. Eskridge Jr., and Philip P. Frickey ask:

   > Was it much of a solution ... for the Court to remit African Americans, the country's newest citizens, to relief in the state leg-islative process when the common law or statutes of many states required those engaged in "public" callings—e.g., public utilities, common carriers, innkeepers—to serve all *white* persons who rea-sonably sought service? (Daniel A. Farber, William N. Eskridge Jr., Philip P. Frickey, *Constitutional Law: Themes for the Constitution's Third Century* [St. Paul, MN: West, 1993], p. 180)

   What post-Civil War social realities did the Supreme Court choose to overlook in the *Civil Rights Cases*?

4. Justice Bradley wrote for the majority in the *Civil Right Cases*:

   > When a man has emerged from slavery, and by the aid of beneficent legislation has shaken off the inseparable concomitants of that state, there must be some stage in the process of his elevation when he takes the rank of a mere citizen, and ceases to be the special favorite of the laws, and when his rights as a citizen, or a man, are to be protected in the ordinary modes by which other men's rights are protected.

Although penned in 1883, these words have a contemporary ring to them. What views of the role of government, of racial equality, and of constitutional rights inform them?

COMMENT

Historian C. Vann Woodward wrote:

> The court ... was engaged in a bit of reconciliation [in the *Civil Rights Cases*]—reconciliation between federal and state jurisdiction, as well as between North and South, reconciliation also achieved at the Negro's expense.... The *Boston Evening Transcript* of 14 February 1899, admitted that Southern race policy was "now the policy of the Administration of the very party which carried the country into and through a civil war to free the slave." (*The Strange Career of Jim Crow*, 3rd rev. ed. [New York, NY: Oxford University Press, 1974], p. 71)

Justice Joseph Bradley, author of the majority opinion in the *Civil Rights Cases*, was a member of the special commission formed to resolve the contested 1876 Hayes-Tilden presidential election. Bradley cast his vote for Rutherford B. Hayes, the Republican candidate. Hayes had promised to remove federal troops occupying the former Confederate states.

The *New York Times* editorialized approvingly about the decision in the *Civil Rights Cases* as follows:

> The fact is, that, so long as we have State governments, within their field of action we cannot by National authority prevent the consequences of mis-government. The people of the State are dependent on their own civilized ideas and habits for the benefits of a civilized administration of laws. (Quoted in Charles Warren, *The Supreme Court in United States History*, vol. III [Boston, MA: Little, Brown and Company, 1923], pp. 336–337)

The Civil Rights Act of 1875 was the last great Reconstruction statute. Congress did not pass another civil rights act until 1957, eighty-two years later.

STATE ACTION DOCTRINE

Buchanan v. Warley
245 U.S. 60 (1917)

SETTING

The Court's narrow interpretation of the Fourteenth Amendment in the *Civil Rights Cases* helped to usher in an era of strict racial segregation in the South. The decision also seemed to dictate federal government withdrawal from civil rights enforcement. Following the Court's decision, southern and border states adopted even harsher statutes aimed at maintaining separation between the races. In 1910, Baltimore, Maryland, enacted the first municipal segregation ordinance. In May 1914, the city of Louisville, Kentucky, enacted a strict housing segregation ordinance. Violation of that law was punishable by a fine of not more than $50 for each offense.

The avowed rationale for housing segregation ordinances like Louisville's was to prevent conflict and ill-feeling between the races and to preserve the public peace. State courts embraced that rationale, as exemplified by this statement by a Pennsylvania court in 1867:

> The danger to the peace engendered by the feeling of aversion between individuals of different races cannot be denied.... The natural separation of the races is therefore an undeniable fact, and all social organizations which lead to their amalgamation are repugnant to the law of nature. *West Chester Railway Company v. Miles*, 55 Pa.St. 209 (1867).

In November 1914, William Warley, a black, and Charles Buchanan, a Caucasian, agreed to challenge the Louisville ordinance. Warley, a letter carrier who had passed the federal Civil Service exam and wanted to live in a better neighborhood, agreed to buy a lot in a residential neighborhood owned by Buchanan. There were ten residences on the block where Buchanan's lot was located, eight of which were occupied by white residents. The lot was located next to the only two parcels on the block occupied by blacks. The contract between Warley and Buchanan contained the following proviso:

> It is understood that I am purchasing the above property for the purpose of having erected thereon a house which I propose to make my residence, and it is a distinct part of this agreement that I shall not be required to accept a deed to the above property or to pay for said property unless I have the right under the laws of the State of Kentucky and the City of Louisville to occupy said property as a residence.

When Buchanan tendered the deed to Warley, Warley refused to accept it or to pay the purchase price, claiming he would be unable to occupy the house he hoped to build because of the city's segregation ordinance. Buchanan then sued Warley demanding specific performance—carrying out the agreed-upon terms—of the contract, and claiming that the segregation ordinance violated the Fourteenth Amendment.

The Chancery Branch of the Jefferson Circuit Court of Kentucky tried the case on the pleadings. Neither side introduced evidence. The court ruled for Warley, declaring the Louisville ordinance valid and a complete defense to Buchanan's action for specific performance. Buchanan appealed to the Kentucky Court of Appeals, which consolidated the case with *Harris v. City of Louisville*. Harris had been fined for violating the segregation ordinance and sought to have it declared invalid. The court of appeals upheld the ordinance and affirmed the trial courts in both cases. Buchanan petitioned the Supreme Court of the United States for a writ of error.

The case was argued during the 1916 Term before seven justices (Justice Day was ill and the vacancy caused by Justice Lamar's death was not yet filled). It was reargued during the 1917 Term. Between the first and second arguments, Justice Hughes resigned and Justices Brandeis and Clark were appointed.

HIGHLIGHTS OF SUPREME COURT ARGUMENTS

BRIEF FOR BUCHANAN

◆ The Louisville ordinance deprives Buchanan of his property without due process, in violation of the Fourteenth Amendment. If Buchanan cannot sell his lot to a person of color, he cannot sell it at all because it is situated next to the only two residences on the block occupied by black persons and would not be purchased by whites. The ordinance thus took the value out of Buchanan's land, in violation of due process.

◆ The ordinance violates the Equal Protection Clause of the Fourteenth Amendment and abridges Buchanan's privileges and immunities. When owners on one side of the street can sell only to one class of buyers while owners on the other side are not so restricted, the owners do not enjoy the equal protection of the laws. The ordinance also forbids an owner of land in many parts of the city to live on his land if he is black, although he would be free to live on his land if he were white. This is a clear case of racial discrimination, the prevention of which was the goal of the Fourteenth Amendment.

◆ The Louisville ordinance is not a valid exercise of the state's police power because police power regulations are subject to the requirements of the Equal Protection Clause. The Louisville ordinance operates only to protect the rights of a certain class. If this ordinance is upheld, there will be no limits to possible discrimination between citizens.

AMICUS CURIAE BRIEF SUPPORTING BUCHANAN

Baltimore Branch of the National Association for the Advancement of Colored People.

BRIEF FOR WARLEY AND THE CITY OF LOUISVILLE

◆ The decision in this case will settle the constitutionality of similar ordinances in Baltimore, Maryland; Richmond, Virginia; St. Louis, Missouri; and other cities and towns. The Louisville ordinance is fair and equal on its face, enacted by the Louisville city council to accomplish its stated purpose of preventing conflict and ill-feeling between the races and preserving the public peace. The ordinance takes into account the plain fact of human nature.

◆ The ordinance does not violate the Due Process Clause because it does not "take" anyone's property. It merely regulates the occupancy of property. Far from destroying property, the ordinance will protect property from the serious and destructive results of private efforts at segregation.

◆ Legislation segregating the white and colored races has been recognized by the Supreme Court as a valid exercise of the state's police power as long as both races are treated equally. Louisville's ordinance applies equally to blacks and whites. Whether the ordinance is wise, expedient, or necessary is a legislative, not a judicial, judgment.

◆ Buchanan's claims that the Fourteenth Amendment limits a state's ability to abridge the privileges and immunities of a citizen, that equal protection means economically equal privileges, and that equality of privileges means identity of privileges, are not supported by Supreme Court rulings. The Negro is required to work out his own salvation along economic, social, and moral lines.

◆ The Louisville ordinance deals with social and economic imperatives of the most impressive nature. The alternative to this kind of legislation is extra-legal or illegal methods by whites to prevent Negroes from living among them.

AMICUS CURIAE BRIEFS SUPPORTING WARLEY AND LOUISVILLE

Cities of Richmond, Virginia; Baltimore, Maryland; and St. Louis, Missouri.

SUPREME COURT DECISION: 9–0

DAY, J.

... The concrete question here is: May the occupancy, and, necessarily, the purchase and sale of property of which occupancy is an incident, be inhibited by the States, or by one of its municipalities, solely because of the color of the proposed occupant of the premises? That one may dispose of his property, subject only to the control of lawful enactments curtailing that right in the public interest, must be conceded. The question now presented makes it pertinent to enquire into the constitutional right of the white man to sell his property to a colored man, having in view the legal status of the purchaser and occupant....

The statute of 1866, originally passed under sanction of the Thirteenth Amendment, and practically re-enacted after the adoption of the Fourteenth Amendment, expressly provided that all citizens of the United States in any state shall have the same right to purchase property as is enjoyed by white citizens. Colored persons are citizens of the United States and have the right to purchase property and enjoy and use the same without laws discriminating against them solely on account of color. These enact-

ments did not deal with the social rights of men, but with those fundamental rights in property which it was intended to secure upon the same terms to citizens of every race and color....

That there exists a serious and difficult problem arising from a feeling of race hostility which the law is powerless to control, and to which it must give a measure of consideration, may be freely admitted. But its solution cannot be promoted by depriving citizens of their constitutional rights and privileges.

As we have seen, this court has held laws valid which separated the races on the basis of equal accommodations in public conveyances, and courts of high authority have held enactments lawful which provide for separation in the public schools of white and colored pupils where equal privileges are given. But in view of the rights secured by the Fourteenth Amendment to the Federal Constitution such legislation must have its limitations, and cannot be sustained where the exercise of authority exceeds the restraints of the Constitution. We think these limitations are exceeded in laws and ordinances of the character now before us.

It is the purpose of such enactments, and it is frankly avowed it will be their ultimate effect, to require by law, at least in residential districts, the compulsory separation of the races on account of color. Such action is said to be essential to the maintenance of the purity of the races, although it is to be noted in the ordinance under consideration that the employment of colored servants in white families is permitted, and nearby residences of colored persons not coming within the blocks, as defined in the ordinance, are not prohibited.

The case presented does not deal with an attempt to prohibit the amalgamation of the races. The right which the ordinance annulled was the civil right of a white man to dispose of his property if he saw fit to do so to a person of color and of a colored person to make such disposition to a white person.

It is urged that this proposed segregation will promote the public peace by preventing race conflicts. Desirable as this is, and important as is the preservation of the public peace, this aim cannot be accomplished by laws or ordinances which deny rights created or protected by the Federal Constitution.

It is said that such acquisitions by colored persons depreciate property owned in the neighborhood by white persons. But property may be acquired by undesirable white neighbors, or put to disagreeable though lawful uses with like results.

We think this attempt to prevent the alienation of the property in question to a person of color was not a legitimate exercise of the police power of the State, and is in direct violation of the fundamental law enacted in the Fourteenth Amendment of the Constitution preventing state interference with property rights except by due process of law. That being the case the ordinance cannot stand....

[I]t follows that the judgment of the Kentucky Court of Appeals must be reversed.

Questions

1. What distinctions between the federal Civil Rights Act of 1875 (at issue in the *Civil Rights Cases*) and the Louisville, Kentucky, segregated housing ordinance (contested in *Buchanan v. Warley*) account for the different outcomes in the two cases? Is *Buchanan* simply a clear example of the state action doctrine described in the *Civil Rights Cases*? Or does the outcome in *Buchanan* reflect the fact that the Civil Rights Act of 1866, which recognized the rights of all persons to inherit, purchase, lease, sell, and convey property, was effective so long as the rights of whites were involved?

2. Justice Holmes prepared a draft of a dissenting opinion in *Buchanan* that he did not deliver. He argued that Buchanan, the white seller, did not have standing to sue on behalf of a black person's constitutional rights. Should *Buchanan v. Warley* have been dismissed for this reason?

3. *Buchanan* is an example of the Supreme Court employing the Fourteenth Amendment to protect property rights, particularly the rights of white property owners: The Louisville ordinance prevented

white property owners from selling their property to black buyers willing to pay premium prices to move into "better" neighborhoods. Is *Buchanan* nonetheless suggestive of elements of an effective litigation strategy in the field of civil rights?

COMMENT

The Court's declaration that municipal segregation ordinances violate the Constitution did not end housing discrimination based on race. Segregation ordinances were quickly replaced by racially restrictive covenants in private contracts. Restrictive covenants "ran with the land" and prohibited the transfer of real property to, or its occupancy by, blacks. The validity of restrictive covenants was tested in the case of *Corrigan v. Buckley*, 271 U.S. 323 (1926), a case arising in the District of Columbia. A unanimous Supreme Court ruled that such covenants did not violate the Fifth Amendment (nor, by implication, the Fourteenth) because they were wholly private agreements that involved no state action. This judicial analysis of restrictive covenants prevailed until 1948, as described in *Shelley v. Kraemer*, 334 U.S. 1 (1948).

STATE ACTION DOCTRINE

Shelley v. Kraemer
334 U.S. 1 (1948)

SETTING

The northern industrial revolution, the southern poverty and racial oppression that followed the Civil War, and the Great Depression of the 1930s caused huge numbers of blacks to migrate from the South to the North. Population historians refer to this demographic movement as "The Great Migration." Between 1910 and 1920, for example, the black population of Detroit, Michigan, increased 611.3 percent. The black population of Cleveland, Ohio, grew by 307.8 percent, and that of Chicago, Illinois, by 148.2 percent. The percentage of blacks in Gary, Indiana, mushroomed an astonishing 1,283.6 percent. Black migration reached record numbers when the United States began mobilizing for World War II and blacks sought jobs in the defense establishment. In 1941, in response to the threat of a massive protest march on Washington, D.C., by blacks, President Franklin Roosevelt issued an executive order barring racial discrimination in defense industries or government employment. The housing picture, however, was different. Property owners relied on devices like racially restrictive covenants, neighborhood association agreements, and agreements among real estate brokers to restrict the expansion of black residential communities in cities with increasing numbers of black workers.

Employing the state action doctrine, the Supreme Court, in *Buchanan v. Warley*, invalidated racially restrictive municipal housing ordinances. Nevertheless, as noted in the *Comment* following *Buchanan*, racially restrictive covenants between private individuals—contractual agreements limiting the sale of real property to whites only—were held beyond the reach of the Fifth Amendment (and, by implication, the Fourteenth Amendment) in *Corrigan v. Buckley*, 271 U.S. 323 (1926). The use of racially restrictive, private covenants to maintain separation between the races created a rapid increase in social tensions and numerous legal battles in the 1940s.

St. Louis, Missouri, was one of many American cities where whites attempted to contain blacks in clearly defined areas by use of racially restrictive covenants. In 1910, whites in a neighborhood in the northwestern part of the city formed the Marcus Avenue Improvement Association, and drew a "color line" along a number of blocks bordering a predominantly black neighborhood. The following year, the association began putting racial restrictions in deeds to prevent persons of color from purchasing homes on that line or beyond.

In August 1945, J. D. and Ethel Lee Shelley, a black couple, told St. Louis realtor Robert Bishop (also the minister of their evangelical church) that they wished to buy a house. The following month, Bishop purchased a two-apartment house located at 4600 Labadie Avenue, one of the streets on the "color line" identified by the Marcus Avenue Improvement Association. Bishop bought the house in the name of Geraldine Fitzgerald, a white woman. Until Fitzgerald's purchase, all owners of the property had signed restrictive covenants. Bishop then had Fitzgerald sell the property to the Shelleys. When the Shelleys moved into the house in October, the Marcus Avenue Improvement Association filed suit on behalf of Louis and Fern Kraemer, who lived at 3542 Labadie Avenue, to enjoin the Shelleys from occupying the house on the ground that their occupancy would violate the racially restrictive covenant covering the neighborhood. The Kraemers were selected as the plaintiffs because Fern Kraemer's parents had signed the original restrictive covenants in the neighborhood in 1911.

The Circuit Court of the City of St. Louis dismissed the Kraemers' request for an injunction and overruled their motion for a new trial. It ruled that the restrictive covenant was not effective because it had not been signed by all the property owners in the area.

The Kraemers appealed to the St. Louis Court of Appeals, which transferred the case to the Supreme Court of Missouri. That court reversed the trial court on the strength of *Corrigan v. Buckley*, 271 U.S. 323 (1926).

The Shelleys petitioned the Supreme Court of the United States for a writ of certiorari. Their case was consolidated with *McGhee v. Sipes*, which raised the validity of restrictive covenants in the city of Detroit, Michigan.

HIGHLIGHTS OF SUPREME COURT ARGUMENTS

BRIEF FOR THE SHELLEYS

◆ Restrictive covenants based exclusively on race or color violate the 1866 Civil Rights Act, which gives all citizens of the United States the same rights to inherit, purchase, lease, sell, hold, and convey real and personal property. Restrictive covenants, having goals opposite federal and state law, are as unenforceable as any other contract that violates public policy.

◆ If restrictive covenants are legal, judicial enforcement of such covenants constitutes state action in violation of the Fourteenth Amendment. In St. Louis alone, judicial enforcement of restrictive covenants has created a housing crisis affecting over one hundred thousand Negro families, resulting in overcrowding, ill health, death, juvenile delinquency, and crime.

AMICUS CURIAE BRIEFS SUPPORTING THE SHELLEYS

United States; American Association for the United Nations; American Jewish Committee.

BRIEF FOR THE KRAEMERS

◆ This case raises no substantial federal question because no legislative enactment was involved to invoke any provisions of the Fourteenth Amendment. Courts, in adjudicating the contested rights of litigants, do not engage in the kind of state action prohibited by the Fourteenth Amendment.

◆ Private contracts between individuals are not touched by the Fourteenth Amendment or statutes enacted to enforce it.

◆ The Shelleys cannot complain of a due process violation. They had notice of the restrictive covenant when they purchased the home from Geraldine Fitzgerald because it was recorded in the deed.

◆ Claims of equal protection and denial of privileges and immunities are also unavailing because there is no state action involved in restrictive covenants. This case is controlled by *Corrigan v. Buckley*.

◆ If the Shelleys are to prevail, the Court will have to promulgate a doctrine that would, through the Fourteenth Amendment, establish direct federal control of the individual citizens of the United States and destroy State sovereignty.

AMICUS CURIAE BRIEF SUPPORTING THE KRAEMERS

National Association of Real Estate Boards.

SUPREME COURT DECISION: 6–0

(Reed, Jackson, and Rutledge, J.J., did not participate.)

VINSON, C.J.

... It cannot be doubted that among the civil rights intended to be protected from discriminatory state action by the Fourteenth Amendment are the rights to acquire, enjoy, own and dispose of property. Equality in the enjoyment of property rights was regarded by the framers of that Amendment as an essential precondition to the realization of other basic civil rights and liberties which the Amendment was intended to guarantee....

Since the decision of this Court in the *Civil Rights Cases* [of 1883], the principle has become firmly embedded in our constitutional law that the action inhibited by the first section of the Fourteenth Amendment is only such action as may fairly be said to be that of the States. That Amendment erects no shield against merely private conduct, however discriminatory or wrongful.

We conclude, therefore, that the restrictive agreements standing alone cannot be regarded as violative of any rights guaranteed to petitioners by the Fourteenth Amendment. So long as the purposes of those agreements are effectuated by voluntary adherence to their terms, it would appear clear that there has been no action by the State and the provisions of the Amendment have not been violated.

But here there was more. These are cases in which the purposes of the agreements were secured only by judicial enforcement by state courts of the restrictive terms of the agreements....

[F]rom the time of the adoption of the Fourteenth Amendment until the present, it has been the consistent ruling of this Court that the action of the States to which the Amendment has reference includes action of state courts and state judicial officials. Although, in construing the terms of the Fourteenth Amendment, differences have from time to time been expressed as to whether particular types of state action may be said to offend the Amendment's prohibitory provisions, it has never been suggested that state court action is immunized from the operation of those provisions simply because the act is that of the judicial branch of the state government....

We have no doubt that there has been state action in these cases in the full and complete sense of the phrase. The undisputed facts disclose that petitioners were willing purchasers of properties upon which they desired to establish homes. The owners of the properties were willing sellers; and contracts of sale were accordingly consummated. It is clear that but for the active intervention of the state courts, supported by the full panoply of state power, petitioners would have been free to occupy the properties in question without restraint....

We hold that in granting judicial enforcement of the restrictive agreements in these cases, the States have denied petitioners the equal protection of the laws and that, therefore, the action of the state courts cannot stand. We have noted that freedom from discrimination by the States in the enjoyment of property rights was among the basic objectives sought to be effectuated by the framers of the Fourteenth Amendment. That such discrimination has occurred in these cases is clear. Because of the race or color of these petitioners they have been denied rights of ownership or occupancy enjoyed as a matter of course by other citizens of different race or color....

Reversed.

COMMENTS

1. In 1938, the National Association for the Advancement of Colored People (NAACP) incorporated the Legal Defense and Educational Fund (Inc. Fund) to provide full-time staff to pursue civil rights litigation. The Inc. Fund became actively involved in litigating several

issues, including residential segregation in cities, unequal education opportunities, and all-white primaries. Despite the Inc. Fund's interest in restrictive covenant cases, it did not become involved in *Shelley*. According to Richard Kluger, NAACP staff members Thurgood Marshall and Charles Houston thought the petition for certiorari in *Shelley* was premature because of the composition of the Supreme Court and because of attorney George Vaughn's lack of appellate experience. Nonetheless, they helped to file the appeal in *McGhee v. Sipes* (the case consolidated with *Shelley*) after Vaughn filed the petition in *Shelley*. Marshall was lead counsel on appeal in *McGhee*. See Richard Kluger, *Simple Justice* (New York, NY: Vintage Books, 1975), pp. 248–249.

Counsel for the Shelleys relied primarily on legal arguments in attacking the restrictive covenants. Marshall and Houston focused on the negative sociological effects of the covenants, submitting a brief patterned after Louis Brandeis's brief in *Muller v. Oregon*, 208 U.S. 412 (1908). Their brief described the consequences of the ghettos created by restrictive covenants, including crowding, crime, delinquency, and racial tensions that affected the entire community.

2. In companion cases to *Shelley*, also argued by NAACP counsel—*Hurd v. Hodge* and *Urciola v. Hodge*, 334 U.S. 24 (1948)—the Court refused to enforce restrictive covenants in the District of Columbia. Counsel for Hurd and Urciola argued that the covenants violated the Due Process Clause of the Fifth Amendment. The unanimous Supreme Court (Reed, Jackson, and Rutledge not participating) avoided the constitutional question by holding that D.C. courts were prohibited by the Civil Rights Act of 1866 from enforcing the covenants. Justice Frankfurter, in a concurring opinion, argued that sound judicial discretion required denial of relief (i.e., refusal to enforce the covenants) in federal court where the granting of like relief in state courts would violate the Fourteenth Amendment.

3. Justices Reed, Jackson, and Rutledge did not participate in any of the restrictive covenant cases. Considerable speculation surrounded their recusals, ranging from rumors that they themselves owned properties subject to restrictive covenants, to an "alternative rumor" that at least one had spoken out publicly against restrictive covenants.

QUESTIONS

1. Identify the "state action" in *Shelley v. Kraemer* compared to that in *Buchanan v. Warley*. Is such an expansive definition of state action in *Shelley* constitutionally defensible? After *Shelley*, where is the line between state and private action?

2. Rather than devoting its attention primarily to whether there was state action in *Shelley*, should the justices have focused on whether that state action was unconstitutional? What is the difference between these two approaches?

3. Under the rule in *Shelley*, is failure by the state to ban discrimination a form of state action that denies people the equal protection of the laws?

4. The state action doctrine has continued to evolve, as the following cases illustrate. Read the following case summaries, then respond to the questions posed after *Evans v. Abney*, 396 U.S. 435 (1970).

> **Case:** *Williams v. United States*, 341 U.S. 97 (1951)
> **Vote:** 5–4
> **Decision:** A private detective holding a special police officer's card from the City of Miami, Florida, who was accompanied by a regular policeman and who beat robbery suspects to obtain confessions, acted under color of state law in violation of a federal statute. The statute made it an offense for any person, under color of law, to willfully deprive others of any rights, privileges, or immunities secured or protected by the Constitution or laws of the United States.
>
> **Case:** *Barrows v. Jackson*, 346 U.S. 249 (1953)
> **Vote:** 6–1 (Reed and Jackson, J.J., did not participate.)
> **Decision:** A racially restrictive covenant cannot be enforced at law in a suit for damages against a property owner who violated an agreement among neighbors in Los Angeles by selling her property to non-Caucasians without incorporating the racial restrictions. Action by the state court might result in a denial of constitutional rights to non-Caucasians.
>
> **Case:** *Pennsylvania v. Board of Trustees*, 353 U.S. 230 (1957)
> **Vote:** *per curiam*
> **Decision:** The board that operates a "college" created by a will probated in 1831 for "poor white male orphans, between the ages of six and ten years," is an agency of the state of Pennsylvania even though it acts as the trustee of the estate creating the institution. Refusal to admit black boys to the school therefore violates the Fourteenth Amendment.
>
> **Case:** *Burton v. Wilmington Parking Authority*, 365 U.S. 715 (1961)
> **Vote:** 6–3
> **Decision:** A restaurant leased from the state of Delaware, located in a publicly owned and operated parking building, cannot refuse service to Negroes without violating the Equal Protection Clause of the Fourteenth Amendment. When a state leases public property under the circumstances presented in this case, the proscriptions of the Fourteenth Amendment must be complied with by the lessee as though they were binding covenants written into the lease agreement.
>
> **Case:** *Peterson v. City of Greenville*, 373 U.S. 244 (1963)
> **Vote:** 8–1

Decision: When a state segregation law mandates discrimination on the basis of race, and the state's criminal procedures are employed to enforce that discrimination, the fact that a store manager excludes blacks from his store's lunch counter on his own initiative does not remove the element of "state action" from his conduct.

Case: *Lombard v. Louisiana*, 373 U.S. 267 (1963)

Vote: 8–1

Decision: Even in the absence of a local ordinance requiring segregated eating places, convictions of blacks for criminal mischief in connection with sit-in protests at a lunch counter must be reversed because city officials had made statements that they believed segregated facilities should be maintained. Such statements effectively require that public eating facilities be segregated.

Case: *Griffin v. Maryland*, 378 U.S. 130 (1964)

Vote: 6–3

Decision: A Montgomery County deputy sheriff employed as a special policemen by a privately owned amusement park who enforces the park's policy of excluding Negroes engaged in state action in removing Negroes from the park. "If an individual is possessed of state authority and purports to act under that authority, his action is state action. It is irrelevant that he might have taken the same action had he acted in a purely private capacity...."

Case: *Reitman v. Mulkey*, 387 U.S. 369 (1967)

Vote: 5–4

Decision: A 1964 California ballot measure, Proposition 14, which amended the California constitution to prohibit that state from denying any person's right to decline to sell, lease, or rent real property as that person chooses, involves the state in racial discrimination in violation of the Fourteenth Amendment.

Case: *Jones v. Alfred H. Mayer Co.*, 392 U.S. 409 (1968)

Vote: 7–2

Decision: The 1866 Civil Rights Act bars private as well as state-supported racial discrimination in the sale and rental of housing. Congress's authority to enact the legislation stemmed from the Thirteenth Amendment rather than the Equal Protection Clause of the Fourteenth Amendment. The Thirteenth Amendment was adopted to remove the "badges of slavery" and gave Congress power to enforce that removal. The 1866 Civil Rights Act "plainly meant to secure [the right to buy and sell property] against interference from any source whatever, whether governmental or private."

Case: *Evans v. Abney*, 396 U.S. 435 (1970)

Vote: 5–3 (Marshall, J., did not participate.)

Decision: Management by a private trustee of a park bequeathed to the city of Macon, Georgia, on the condition that it serve whites only violates the Fourteenth Amendment because the park retains its public character. However, reversion of the land to the original heirs, since it cannot be operated according to the terms of the will, and its subsequent closure as a park, does not violate the

Fourteenth Amendment because closing the facility deprives blacks and whites equally of its use.

Are there discernable doctrinal trends in the Supreme Court's approach to state action since *Shelley v. Kraemer*? If so, are they consistent? To what extent, if any, are judicial trends in defining the concept of state action related to broader trends in American politics?

STATE ACTION DOCTRINE

Moose Lodge No. 107 v. Irvis
407 U.S. 163 (1972)

SETTING

Drawing on his observations of American life in the 1830s, Frenchman Alexis de Tocqueville wrote in *Democracy in America*:

> Americans of all ages, all conditions, and dispositions constantly form associations. They have not only commercial and manufacturing companies, in which all take part, but associations of a thousand other kinds, religious, moral, serious, futile, general or restricted, enormous or diminutive.

Benjamin Franklin personified the American passion for forming and joining associations that Tocqueville later observed. Franklin founded Junto, a club of Philadelphia artisans and tradesmen. He also organized a subscription library, an academy for educating youth, a volunteer fire department, and a hospital. Franklin was instrumental in establishing the American Philosophical Society, the oldest learned society in the country, and served as a grand master in the Masons. In Franklin's America of the late eighteenth century, voluntary public and private associations flourished. Professional affiliation, occupational groupings, immigrant status, and political causes like temperance and antislavery created shared bonds that spawned various associations.

The nineteenth century witnessed an explosion of voluntary associations that included literacy, social, and humanitarian clubs. Fraternal organizations like the Moose Lodge were among them. The Moose Lodge is a "restricted" association: its members consist only of white males over the age of twenty-one years who are not married to someone other than of the Caucasian or white race, who profess a belief in a supreme being and are of good moral character as well as mentally and physically normal. As amended in 1967, the Constitution of the Supreme Lodge provides:

> The objects and purposes of said fraternal and charitable lodges ... are to unite in the bonds of fraternity, benevolence, and charity all acceptable white persons of good character; to educate and improve their members and the families of their members socially, morally, and intellectually....

Moose Lodge No. 107, located in Harrisburg, Pennsylvania, is a subordinate chartered lodge of the Supreme Lodge of the World, Loyal Order of Moose. Although the lodge receives no public funds, it did receive a license to sell liquor from the Liquor Control Board of the Commonwealth of Pennsylvania.

On December 29, 1968, a white member of Moose Lodge No. 107 brought K. Leroy Irvis, a black, as his guest to the dining room and bar of the local club. When Irvis and his host requested food and beverage service, lodge employees refused because of Irvis's race. Irvis subsequently brought an action in the U.S. District Court for the Middle District of Pennsylvania, naming Moose Lodge and the Pennsylvania Liquor Control Board as parties. He sought an injunction requiring the liquor board to revoke Moose Lodge's liquor license as long as Moose Lodge continued its discriminatory practices. Irvis claimed that because the Pennsylvania Liquor Control Board issued the Moose Lodge a license authorizing the sale of alcoholic beverages on the premises of its private club, the club's refusal to serve him was "state action" for purposes of the Equal Protection Clause of the Fourteenth Amendment. Moose Lodge and the Liquor Control Board moved to dismiss for failure to state a cause of action. The district court denied the motion.

A three-judge panel found that racial discrimination was required by the constitution of Moose Lodge and that discrimination was practiced by Lodge No. 107. The court also found that having a liquor license facilitated Moose Lodge's practice of racial discrimination, because without the ability to serve alcohol, membership would decline. The district court then entered a decree declaring invalid the liquor license issued to Moose Lodge and enjoining the board from reissuing a license "as long as [Moose Lodge] follows a policy of racial discrimination in its membership or operating policies or practices."

Moose Lodge moved to modify the final decree. It asked the court to allow it to continue its racially discriminatory membership policies but to require it to serve the non-Caucasian guests who were invited by members. The district court denied the request. Moose Lodge appealed to the Supreme Court of the United States.

HIGHLIGHTS OF SUPREME COURT ARGUMENTS

BRIEF FOR MOOSE LODGE NO. 107

◆ There is no case or controversy on which the judicial power can operate, because the decree below granted Irvis no personal redress. The decree is punitive, abstract, and essentially legislative in its operation.

◆ The basic constitutional right of privacy and private association extends to membership in a private club. Moose Lodge No. 107 is a private club by every recognized test.

◆ Issuing of a liquor license to a private club does not transform that club's acts into state action under the Fourteenth Amendment.

◆ To revoke any state license held by Moose Lodge No. 107 because its members exercised their constitutional rights of privacy would unjustifiably impinge on those rights.

AMICUS CURIAE BRIEFS SUPPORTING MOOSE LODGE NO. 107

Benevolent and Protective Order of Elks of the United States of America; Washington State Federation of Fraternal, Patriotic, City, and County Clubs.

BRIEF FOR IRVIS

♦ Irvis has maintained a case or controversy within the jurisdiction of a three-judge federal district court and of the Supreme Court of the United States. Irvis sought redress for an injury resulting from being discriminated against by a private club that had called upon the state to support its functioning and, thus, to support its discrimination.

♦ The Pennsylvania Alcoholic Beverage Control System leads to extensive and significant involvement of the state in the affairs of Moose Lodge. Pennsylvania's involvement is so significant that Moose Lodge's racial discrimination constitutes state action in violation of the Fourteenth Amendment.

♦ The presence of state action in Moose Lodge's racial discrimination requires severance of the relationship between the state and Moose Lodge. The district court decree was appropriate and gave effect to the constitutional considerations involved here.

AMICUS CURIAE BRIEFS SUPPORTING IRVIS

Joint brief of the American Jewish Committee, American Jewish Congress, and the Anti-Defamation League of B'nai B'rith; Lawyers' Committee for Civil Rights under Law.

BRIEF FOR THE PENNSYLVANIA LIQUOR CONTROL BOARD

♦ Where the powers exercised or benefits conferred by the state are substantial and direct and go beyond a mere failure to prohibit or refusal to regulate, the conclusion should be that the discriminatory activity in question has risen to the level of state action in violation of the Fourteenth Amendment.

SUPREME COURT DECISION: 6–3

REHNQUIST, J.

... [Moose Lodge] urges ... that we either vacate the judgment below because there is not presently a case or controversy between the parties, or that we reverse on the merits....

Because appellee had no standing to litigate a constitutional claim arising out of Moose Lodge's membership practices, the District Court erred in reaching that issue on the merits. But it did not err in reaching the constitutional claim of appellee that Moose Lodge's guest-service practices under these circumstances violated the Fourteenth Amendment. Nothing in the positions taken by the parties since the entry of the District Court decree has mooted that claim, and we therefore turn to its disposition.

Moose Lodge is a private club in the ordinary meaning of that term....

Moose Lodge's refusal to serve food and beverages to a guest by reason of the fact that he was a Negro does not, under the circumstances here presented, violate the Fourteenth Amendment....

While the principle is easily stated, the question of whether particular discriminatory conduct is private, on the one hand, or amounts to "state action," on the other hand, frequently admits of no easy answer....

Our cases make clear that the impetus for the forbidden discrimination need not originate with the State if it is state action that enforces privately originated discrimination....

The Court has never held, of course, that discrimination by an otherwise private entity would be violative of the Equal Protection Clause if the private entity receives any sort of benefit or service at all from the State, or if it is subject to state regulation in any degree whatever. Since state-furnished services include such necessities of life as electricity, water, and police and fire protection, such a holding would utterly emasculate the distinction between private as distinguished from state conduct set forth in the *Civil Rights Cases* and adhered to in subsequent decisions. Our holdings indicate that where the impetus for the discrimination is private, the State must have "significantly involved itself with invidious discriminations," *Reitman v. Mulkey*, 387 U.S. 369 (1967), in order for the discriminatory action to fall within the ambit of the constitutional prohibition....

There is no suggestion in this record that Pennsylvania law, either as written or as applied, discriminates against minority groups either in their right to apply for club licenses themselves or in their right to purchase and be served liquor in places of public accommodation. The only effect that the state licensing of Moose Lodge to serve liquor can be said to have on the right of any other Pennsylvanian to buy or be served liquor on premises other than those of Moose Lodge is that for some purposes club licenses are counted in the maximum number of licenses that may be issued in a given municipality....

The District Court was at pains to point out in its opinion what it considered to be the "pervasive" nature of the regulation of private clubs by the Pennsylvania Liquor Control Board. As that court noted, an applicant for a club license must make such physical alterations in its premises as the board may require, must file a list of the names and addresses of its members and employees, and must keep extensive financial records. The board is granted the right to inspect the licensed premises at any time when patrons, guests, or members are present.

However detailed this type of regulation may be in some particulars, it cannot be said to in any way foster or encourage racial discrimination. Nor can it be said to make the State in any realistic sense a partner or even a joint venturer in the club's enterprise.... We therefore hold that, with the exception hereafter noted, the operation of the regulatory scheme enforced by the Pennsylvania Liquor Control Board does not sufficiently implicate the State in the discriminatory guest policies of Moose Lodge to make the latter "state action" within the ambit of the Equal Protection Clause of the Fourteenth Amendment.

The District Court found that the regulations of the Liquor Control Board adopted pursuant to statute affirmatively require that "(e)very club licensee shall adhere to all of the provisions of its Constitution and By-Laws." Appellant argues that the purpose of this provision "is purely and simply and plainly the prevention of subterfuge," pointing out that the bona fides of a private club, as opposed to a place of public accommodation masquerading as a private club is a matter with which the State Liquor Control Board may legitimately concern itself.... There can be no doubt that the label "private club" can be and has been used to evade both regulations of state and local liquor authorities, and statutes requiring places of public accommodation to serve all persons without regard to race, color, religion, or national origin....

The effect of this particular regulation on Moose Lodge under the provisions of the constitution placed in the record in the court below would be to place state sanctions behind its discriminatory membership rules, but not behind its guest practices, which were not embodied in the constitution of the lodge. Had there been no change in the relevant circumstances since the making of the record in the District Court, our holding ... that appellee has standing to challenge only the guest practices of Moose Lodge would have a bearing on our disposition of this issue. Appellee stated upon oral argument, though, and Moose Lodge conceded in its brief that the bylaws of the Supreme Lodge have been altered since the lower court decision to make applicable to guests the same sort of racial restrictions as are presently applicable to members.

Even though the Liquor Control Board regulation in question is neutral in its terms, the result of its application in a case where the constitution and bylaws of a club required racial discrimination would be to invoke the sanctions of the State to enforce a concededly discriminatory private rule. State action, for purposes of the Equal Protection Clause, may emanate from rulings of administrative and regulatory agencies as well as from legislative or judicial action.... Although the record before us is not as clear as one would like, appellant has not persuaded us that the District Court should have denied any and all relief.

Appellee was entitled to a decree enjoining the enforcement of §113.09 of the regulations promulgated by the Pennsylvania Liquor Control Board insofar as that regulation requires compliance by Moose Lodge with provisions of its constitution and bylaws containing racially discriminatory provisions. He was entitled to no more. The judgment of the District Court is reversed, and the cause remanded with instructions to enter a decree in conformity with this opinion.

Reversed and remanded.

DOUGLAS AND MARSHALL, J.J., DISSENTING

My view of the First Amendment and the related guarantees of the Bill of Rights is that they create a zone of privacy which precludes government from interfering with private clubs or groups. The associational rights which our system honors permit all white, all black, all brown, and all yellow clubs to be formed. They also permit all Catholic, all Jewish, or all agnostic clubs to be established. Government may not tell a man or woman who his or her associates must be. The individual can be as selective as he desires. So the fact that the Moose Lodge allows only Caucasians to join or come as guests is constitutionally irrelevant, as is the decision of the Black Muslims to admit to their services only members of their race.

The problem is different, however, where the public domain is concerned....

Pennsylvania has a state store system of alcohol distribution. Resale is permitted by hotels, restaurants, and private clubs which all must obtain licenses from the Liquor Control Board. The scheme of regulation is complete and pervasive; and the state courts have sustained many restrictions on the licensees.... Once a license is issued the licensee must comply with many detailed requirements or risk suspension or revocation of the license. Among these requirements is Regulation § 113.09 which says: "Every club licensee shall adhere to all of the provisions of its Constitution and By-laws." This regulation means, as applied to Moose Lodge, that it must adhere to the racially discriminatory provision of the Constitution of its Supreme Lodge that "(t)he membership of lodges shall be composed of male persons of the Caucasian or White race above the age of twenty-one years, and not married to someone of any other than the Caucasian or White race, who are of good moral character, physically and mentally normal, who shall profess a belief in a Supreme Being."...

Were this regulation the only infirmity in Pennsylvania's licensing scheme, I would perhaps agree with the majority that the appropriate relief would be a decree enjoining its enforcement. But there is another flaw in the scheme not so easily cured. Liquor licenses in Pennsylvania, unlike driver's licenses, or marriage licenses, are not freely available to those who meet racially neutral qualifications. There is a complex quota system[.]... [T]he quota for Harrisburg, where Moose Lodge No. 107 is located,

has been full for many years. No more club licenses may be issued in that city.

This state-enforced scarcity of licenses restricts the ability of blacks to obtain liquor, for liquor is commercially available only at private clubs for a significant portion of each week. Access by blacks to places that serve liquor is further limited by the fact that the state quota is filled. A group desiring to form a nondiscriminatory club which would serve blacks must purchase a license held by an existing club, which can exact a monopoly price for the transfer. The availability of such a license is speculative at best, however, for, as Moose Lodge itself concedes, without a liquor license a fraternal organization would be hard pressed to survive.

Thus, the State of Pennsylvania is putting the weight of its liquor license, concededly a valued and important adjunct to a private club, behind racial discrimination....

I would affirm the judgment below.

BRENNAN AND MARSHALL, J.J., DISSENTING

When Moose Lodge obtained its liquor license, the State of Pennsylvania became an active participant in the operation of the Lodge bar. Liquor licensing laws are only incidentally revenue measures; they are primarily pervasive regulatory schemes under which the State dictates and continually supervises virtually every detail of the operation of the licensee's business. Very few, if any, other licensed businesses experience such complete state involvement. Yet the Court holds that such involvement does not constitute "state action" making the Lodge's refusal to serve a guest liquor solely because of his race a violation of the Fourteenth Amendment. The vital flaw in the Court's reasoning is its complete disregard of the fundamental value underlying the "state action" concept. That value is discussed in my separate opinion in *Adickes v. S. H. Kress & Co.*, 398 U.S. 144 (1970):

> The state-action doctrine reflects the profound judgment that denials of equal treatment, and particularly denials on account of race or color, are singularly grave when government has or shares responsibility for them. Government is the social organ to which all in our society look for the promotion of liberty, justice, fair and equal treatment, and the setting of worthy norms and goals for social conduct. Therefore something is uniquely amiss in a society where the government, the authoritative oracle of community values, involves itself in racial discrimination.

Plainly, the State of Pennsylvania's liquor regulations intertwine the State with the operation of the Lodge bar in a "significant way (and) lend (the State's) authority to the sordid business of racial discrimination."...

This is thus a case requiring application of the principle that until today has governed our determinations of the existence of "state action": "Our prior decisions leave no doubt that the mere existence of efforts by the State, through legislation or otherwise, to authorize, encourage, or otherwise support racial discrimination in a particular facet of life constitutes illegal state involvement in those pertinent private acts of discrimination that subsequently occur." *Adickes v. S. H. Kress & Co....*

I therefore dissent and would affirm the final decree entered by the District Court.

QUESTIONS

1. What theory of "state action" informs the majority in *Moose Lodge*? Is the theory consistent with trends in state action doctrine since *Shelley v. Kraemer*? Do the facts in *Moose Lodge* make it a good or a less-than-ideal vehicle for an expansive reading of the state action doctrine?

2. Counsel for Moose Lodge No. 107 asked:

   > If the state must withdraw liquor licenses from admittedly private clubs having racial restrictions (though not from those with religious or ethnic distinctions), then why must not the state (or its municipalities, which are of course simply arms of the state ...) similarly withdraw other licenses covering elements that are a part of and indeed necessary to the very concept of private association, such as shelter, food, and water?

   By contrast, counsel for Irvis opined, "In Pennsylvania's alcoholic beverage control system every licensee has a 'partner,' the State, which participates daily in its affairs." What are the consequences of each argument for the evolution of the state action doctrine?

3. *Amicus* Benevolent and Protective Order of Elks, citing data from the 1970 *Encyclopedia of Organizations*, listed over 36,000 American organizations that have selective membership qualifications or practices based on race, religion, sex, ethnicity, and/or national origin. The *amicus* brief for the Elks' brief also listed over 8,000 Greek-letter fra-

ternities and sororities and youth groups, such as the Girl Scouts, Boy Scouts, and Camp Fire Girls. The combined total membership of these organizations was estimated to be 72,955,000. This figure is over a third of the total American population in 1970. After *Moose Lodge*, what issues involving such organizations are left to litigate regarding the state action doctrine?

COMMENTS

1. After *Moose Lodge*, the Court has handed down important state action decisions in the following cases:

   Case: *Jackson v. Metropolitan Edison Co.*, 419 U.S. 345 (1974)
   Vote: 6–3
   Decision: A privately owned and operated utility corporation, holding a certificate of public convenience issued by the state of Pennsylvania, is not required to provide notice, a hearing, and an opportunity to pay any amounts found due before terminating electric service. Being a heavily regulated private utility with a partial monopoly does not sufficiently connect the state with the challenged termination to make the corporation's conduct "state action" for purposes of the Fourteenth Amendment.

   Case: *Flagg Bros. v. Brooks*, 436 U.S. 149 (1978)
   Vote: 6–3
   Decision: A warehouseman's proposed private sale of goods entrusted to him for storage, as permitted by the self-help provisions of the New York Uniform Commercial Code, is not properly attributable to the State of New York and thus is not state action in violation of the Fourteenth Amendment's Due Process and Equal Protection Clauses.

   Case: *Blum v. Yaretsky*, 457 U.S. 991 (1982)
   Vote: 7–2
   Decision: Privately owned nursing homes providing services that the state would not necessarily provide, even though they are state subsidized and extremely regulated, are not state actors for purposes of the Fourteenth Amendment. Periodically assessing whether Medicaid patients are receiving an appropriate level of care and, if less extensive care is required, transferring such recipients to a less costly facility does not amount to state action.

   Case: *San Francisco Arts & Athletics, Inc. v. United States Olympic Committee*, 483 U.S. 522 (1987)
   Vote: 5–4
   Decision: Federal sponsorship of the U.S. Olympic Committee (USOC) does not make the USOC a governmental actor to whom the Fifth Amendment applies. Consequently, San Francisco Arts & Athletics, Inc. (SFAA) cannot challenge a USOC suit to enjoin SFAA use of the term "Olympics" to describe an athletic competition as an unconstitutional attempt to enforce USOC's rights in a discriminatory manner.

Case: *National Collegiate Athletic Association v. Tarkanian,* 109 S.Ct. 454 (1988)

Vote: 5–4

Decision: The National Collegiate Athletic Association's (NCAA) promulgation and enforcement of rules leading to the University of Nevada at Las Vegas's (UNLV) suspension of its head basketball coach, does not constitute state action. Neither UNLV's role in formulating NCAA rules and policies nor its adoption of those rules transformed NCAA into a state actor.

2. The Supreme Court has recognized that the Due Process Clause of the Fifth Amendment contains an "equal protection component." See *Bolling v. Sharpe,* 347 U.S. 497 (1954). On that theory, the Court has held that the national government is also prohibited from engaging in conduct that denies equal protection of the laws. An example of the Court's approach to state action in the Fifth Amendment context is seen in *Edmonson v. Leesville Concrete Company, Inc.,* 500 U.S. 614 (1991). The Court ruled that a litigant in a civil case in a U.S. district court may not use a peremptory challenge (a device for removing potential jurors from a jury pool without having to provide a reason or "cause" for the removal) to remove prospective jurors on account of their race. Using peremptory challenges to discriminate on the basis of race is government (state) action for constitutional purposes because there is statutory authority for the peremptory challenge.

SUGGESTIONS FOR FURTHER READING

Allen, Francis A., "Remembering *Shelley v. Kraemer,*" 67 *Washington University Law Quarterly* (1989): 709.

Black, Charles, "Foreword: 'State Action,' Equal Protection, and California's Proposition 14," 81 *Harvard Law Review* (1967): 69.

Brest, Paul, "State Action and Liberal Theory," 130 *University of Pennsylvania Law Review* (1982): 1296.

Chemerinsky, Erwin, "Rethinking State Action," 80 *Northwestern University Law Review* (1985).

Choper, Jesse H., "Thoughts on State Action," 57 *Washington University Law Quarterly* (1979): 757.

Frank, John P., and Robert F. Monro, "The Original Understanding of 'Equal Protection of the Laws,'" 50 *Washington University Law Quarterly* (1972): 421.

Glennon, Robert J., Jr., and John E. Nowak, "A Functional Analysis of the Fourteenth Amendment 'State Action' Requirement," *The Supreme Court Review* (Chicago, IL: University of Chicago Press, 1976).

Goldstein, Leslie F., "The Death and Transfiguration of the State Action Doctrine," 4 *Hastings Constitutional Law Quarterly* (1977): 1.

Goodman, Frank I., "Professor Brest on State Action and Liberal Theory, and a Postscript to Professor Stone," 130 *University of Pennsylvania Law Review* (1982): 1331.

Gressman, Eugene, "The Unhappy History of Civil Rights Legislation," 50 *Michigan Law Review* (1952): 1323.

Henkin, Louis, "*Shelley v. Kraemer:* Notes for a Revised Opinion," 110 *University of Pennsylvania Law Review* (1962): 473.

Horowitz, Harold W., "The Misleading Search for 'State Action,'" 30 *Southern California Law Review* (1957): 208.

Hyman, J. D., "Segregation and the Fourteenth Amendment," 4 *Vanderbilt Law Review* (1951): 555.

Irons, Peter, *The Courage of Their Convictions: Sixteen Americans Who Fought Their Way to the Supreme Court* (New York, NY: Penguin, 1990), Chapter 3.

Lewis, Thomas P., "*Burton v. Wilmington Parking Authority*—A Case Without Precedent," 61 *Columbia Law Review* (1961): 1458.

McWilliams, Wilson Carey, *The Idea of Fraternity in America* (Berkeley, CA: University of California Press, 1974).

Note, "Federal Power to Regulate Private Discrimination: The Revival of the Enforcement Clauses of the Reconstruction Era Amendments," 74 *Columbia Law Review* (1974): 449.

Note, "State Court Approaches to the State Action Requirement: Private Rights, Public Values, and Constitutional Choices," 39 *Kansas Law Review* (1991): 495.

Peters, Roger Paul, "Civil Rights and State Non-Action," 34 *Notre Dame Law* (1959): 303.

Schlesinger, Arthur M., "Biography of a Nation of Joiners," in *Paths to the Present*, ed. Arthur M. Schlesinger (New York, NY: Macmillan, 1949).

Schwarzchild, Maimon, "Value Pluralism and the Constitution: In Defense of the State Action Doctrine," *The Supreme Court Review* (Chicago, IL: University of Chicago Press, 1988).

Sunstein, Cass, "*Lochner's* Legacy," 87 *Columbia Law Review* (1987): 873.

Tushnet, Mark, "*Shelley v. Kraemer* and Theories of Equality," 33 *New York University Law School Law Review* (1988): 383.

Vose, Clement E., *Caucasians Only: The Supreme Court, the NAACP, and the Restrictive Covenant Cases* (Berkeley, CA: University of California Press, 1959).

Van Alstyne, William, and Kenneth Karst, "State Action," 14 *Stanford University Law Review* (1961): 3.

Wechsler, Herbert, "Toward Neutral Principles in Constitutional Law," 73 *Harvard Law Review* (1959): 1.

Westin, Alan F., "The Case of the Prejudiced Doorkeeper," in *Quarrels That Have Shaped the Constitution*, ed. John A. Garraty, rev. ed. (New York, NY: Harper and Row, 1987).

EQUAL PROTECTION:
JIM CROW AND SCHOOL DESEGREGATION

Plessy v. Ferguson
163 U.S. 537 (1896)

SETTING

Before the Civil War, slavery in the United States was sanctioned by the Constitution. Slaves were considered chattel. As the property of their owners, they were legally dead. Even free blacks enjoyed few of the rights of citizenship. Through the Thirteenth, Fourteenth, and Fifteenth Amendments, Radical Republicans sought to "reconstruct" the union on a nonslaveholding basis and to arm freedmen with the privileges of citizenship and the right to vote. As explained in the *Setting* to the *Slaughter-House Cases* (see pp. 436–439), however, the former Confederacy moved swiftly after the Civil War to maintain the status quo ante bellum by adopting laws and encouraging practices that, first, disadvantaged blacks, then segregated them. Black Codes replaced the slave codes and mandated strict separation of the races. The political, economic, and social reality for most blacks after the Civil War was little different from their prewar condition. Only the massive federal presence in the South prevented the establishment of total racial apartheid.

Republicans were badly defeated in the congressional elections of 1874, giving Democrats control of Congress for the first time since the Civil War. The presidential election campaign two years later between New York Governor Samuel J. Tilden and Ohio Governor Rutherford B. Hayes was one of the closest and most bitter in American history, as Democrats perceived that they had a chance of winning the White House for the first time since 1860. An electoral commission formed after the disputed election led to a compromise between Hayes and the former Confederacy that assured Hayes the White House in return for his promise to withdraw federal troops from the South. During his first month of office, Hayes withdrew the last of the federal troops, an act that to many symbolized the end of Reconstruction. Reconstruction governments in the states collapsed and state constitutions were rewritten with an eye to preventing black participation in civic affairs. The Civil Rights Act of 1875 was the last serious federal effort to establish civil equality for blacks, and the Supreme Court declared that law unconstitutional in 1883 in the *Civil Rights Cases* (see pp. 485–492). In effect, Justice Bradley's opinion in that case declared that the federal government could not lawfully protect former slaves against the discrimination that private individuals might choose to practice. Within a matter of years, a caste society based on racial apartheid was the unchallenged reality in the South.

Few in the North or in the federal government spoke out against Jim Crow laws or took action to change them. Jim Crow laws touched virtually every facet of life, from hospitals to cemeteries, drinking fountains to rest rooms, schools to transportation facilities and businesses. The facilities available to blacks were invariably inferior to the facilities for whites, to say nothing of the social stigma associated with exclusion from "white only" society. With reconstruction at an end, the only remaining question was whether America's new form of racial apartheid would survive judicial scrutiny under the Fourteenth Amendment.

The Equal Protection Clause of the first section of the Fourteenth Amendment provides that no state may "deny to any person within its jurisdiction the equal protection of the laws." Like privileges or immunities and due process of law, the phrase "equal protection of the laws" is not defined in the Fourteenth Amendment. Senator Jacob Howard, one of the drafters of the Fourteenth Amendment, declared of the Equal Protection Clause:

> ... [it] establishes equality before the law, and it gives, to the humblest, the poorest, the most despised ... the same rights and the same protection before the law as it gives to the most powerful, the most wealthy, or those most haughty.... Without this principle of equal justice to all men and equal protection under the shield of the law, there can be no republican government and none that is really worth maintaining.

In the *Slaughter-House Cases* the Supreme Court acknowledged that the primary purpose of the Fourteenth Amendment was to benefit newly freed blacks. The Court reiterated that understanding in 1880 in *Strauder v. West Virginia*, 100 U.S. 303. *Strauder* involved a black defendant who sought to have his murder trial removed from state court to federal court because West Virginia laws prohibited blacks from serving on trial juries. The Supreme Court ordered the case removed. Justice Strong explained that the purpose of the Fourteenth Amendment was to secure the following:

> to a race recently emancipated, a race that through many generations had been held in slavery, all the civil rights that the superior race enjoy.... [The Fourteenth Amendment] was designed to assure to the colored race the enjoyment of all the civil rights that under the law are enjoyed by white persons, and to give that race the protection of the General Government, in that enjoyment, whenever it should be denied by the States.... The words of the Amendment, it is true, are prohibitory, but they contain a necessary implication of a positive immunity, or right, most valuable to the colored race—the right to exemption from unfriendly legislation against them distinctively as colored; exemption from legal discriminations, implying inferiority in civil society, lessening the security of their enjoyment of the rights which others enjoy and discriminations which are steps towards reducing them to the condition of a subject race.

Six years later, in *Yick Wo v. Hopkins*, 118 U.S. 356 (1886), the Court again indicated that it would look to the Fourteenth Amendment to strike down racially discriminatory laws. *Yick Wo* involved a challenge to an ordinance adopted by the San Francisco, California, Board of Supervisors requiring all laundry businesses to be located in buildings constructed of brick or stone. The effect of the ordinance was to prevent Yick Wo, a native of China, from continuing to operate his laundry business in the wooden building in which it had been located for more than twenty-four years. The Court declared that the ordinance violated the Equal Protection Clause of the Fourteenth Amendment. In his unanimous opinion, Justice Matthews declared:

> Though [a] law itself be fair on its face, and impartial in appearance, yet if it is applied and administered by public authority with an evil eye and an unequal hand, so as practically to make unjust and illegal discrimination between persons in similar circumstances, material to their rights, the denial of equal justice is still within the prohibition of the Constitution.

Thus, although the Equal Protection Clause of the Fourteenth Amendment makes no mention of racial segregation, initial interpretations of that clause suggested that the justices understood the clause as a vehicle for attacking that practice. In 1896, however, the Court in *Plessy v. Ferguson* wrote Jim Crow into the Constitution.

Plessy involved a challenge to Louisiana's Act III, the separate car statute, which was enacted in July 1890. Statutes mandating segregation in transportation had begun appearing on the statute books in the 1880s. Act III required all railway companies carrying passengers to provide "equal but separate accommodations for the white and colored races, by providing two or more passenger coaches for each passenger train, or by dividing the passenger coaches by a partition, so as to secure separate accommodations." Any passenger insisting on going into a coach or compartment to which by race he did not belong was subject to a fine of $25 or imprisonment for twenty days. Train officials who failed to assign passengers to the proper cars or compartments were likewise subject to fine or imprisonment.

Black resistance to Act III developed immediately. Seventeen prominent Louisiana blacks signed a memorial in opposition entitled "American Citizens' Equal Rights Association of Louisiana Against Class Legislation." The memorial declared Act III "unconstitutional, un-American, unjust, dangerous and against sound public policy." In September 1891, blacks in New Orleans formed the Citizens' Committee to Test the Constitutionality of the Separate Car Law to raise money to test the constitutionality of the law. The committee's first effort to bring a test case failed when, on May 25, 1892, the Louisiana Supreme Court held in another case that Act III was unconstitutional as applied to interstate passengers. That ruling caused charges to be dropped against Daniel Desdunes, who had purchased an interstate rail ticket to Mobile, Alabama, and had been indicted for taking a seat in a car reserved for whites. The Committee's second effort involved Homer Adolph Plessy, a thirty-two-year-old friend of Daniel Desdunes's father.

On June 7, 1892, Plessy purchased a first-class railroad ticket on the East Louisiana Railroad for a ride between New Orleans and Covington, Louisiana. Plessy was an "octoroon," a person of seven-eighths Caucasian and one-eighth Negroid blood who frequently "passed" for white. On June 7, however, the conductor had been informed of Plessy's racial mix. After

Plessy boarded a car reserved for whites only, the conductor ordered him to leave that train car and to occupy a seat in a car assigned by the railroad for persons not of the white race. When Plessy refused to move, police were called and he was placed under arrest.

Plessy was taken before Judge John Ferguson of the Criminal District Court of the Parish of New Orleans, where he posted a $500 bond. At his arraignment, he entered a plea that challenged the court's jurisdiction on the ground that Louisiana Act III violated the Constitution of the United States. The Louisiana district attorney demurred to Plessy's plea.

Judge Ferguson overruled Plessy's plea and ordered him to plead to the charge. Plessy applied to the Supreme Court of Louisiana for writs of prohibition and certiorari based on his plea in the trial court. The Louisiana Supreme Court denied his application and also refused a petition for rehearing. Plessy then petitioned the Supreme Court of the United States for a writ of error.

Highlights of Supreme Court Arguments

BRIEF FOR PLESSY

◆ Act III violates the Fourteenth Amendment by abridging the privileges or immunities of Plessy in his character as a citizen of the United States. One such privilege is making use of the accommodations of intrastate common carriers without being amenable to police on account of color. Color is of itself no ground for discipline or for police involvement.

◆ A perpetually recurring injury done by statute on the ground of color alone creates a status of "servitude." It perpetuates the distinction of race and caste among citizens of the United States of both races in violation of the Thirteenth Amendment.

◆ Act III does not extend to all citizens alike the equal protection of the laws. It also provides for the punishment of passengers on railroad trains without due process of law by giving train officials the power to refuse to carry persons who refuse to abide by Act III. The *Civil Rights Cases* strongly support Plessy because this is a clear case of discrimination based on state action.

◆ Color alone provides no basis for the exercise of the state's police power in matters of transportation and education, even though on matters of marriage and family color is relevant to the exercise of that power. The Louisiana separate car statute does not affect the general health or public morals of the whole community, which are the criteria for valid exercise of the police power.

◆ Neither the laws of Louisiana nor Louisiana courts has defined the term "colored race" or "persons of color." Act III impermissibly delegates to conductors on railway trains the right to make such a classification. Race is a question of law which a railroad corporation cannot be authorized to determine.

BRIEF FOR FERGUSON

◆ The separate car statute is based on a similar Mississippi statute. The Mississippi statute was attacked as an interference with interstate commerce, but in *Louisville, N.O. & T.R.R. Co. v. Mississippi*, 133 U.S. 587 (1890), the Court agreed with the Mississippi Supreme Court that the intrastate transportation of passengers is a wholly state matter.

◆ The *Civil Rights Cases* control Plessy's Thirteenth Amendment argument. In that case the Court ruled that denying a person admission to inns, theatres, or public conveyances does not subject that person to any form of servitude or fasten upon him any badge of slavery.

◆ The Fourteenth Amendment does not demand identity of accommodations. It is offended only by states' legislative attempts to establish inequality of treatment. The Louisiana statute was drafted carefully to treat both races alike: A white passenger insisting on going into the coach or compartment set apart for the colored race is guilty of the same offense as a colored passenger insisting on going into the coach or compartment set apart for white passengers.

◆ The *Slaughter-House Cases* made it clear that shared facilities on state railroads is not one of the privileges or immunities protected by the Fourteenth Amendment.

◆ The separate car statute is a valid exercise of the state's police power. The regulation of the civil rights of individuals remains an unquestionably proper subject for the exercise of the state's police power because of the state's responsibility for the comfort of the traveling community. It is also justified on grounds of public policy and expediency.

SUPREME COURT DECISION: 7–1

(Brewer, J., did not participate.)

BROWN, J.

... The constitutionality of [the Louisiana] act is attacked upon the ground that it conflicts with both the Thirteenth Amendment of the Constitution, abolishing slavery, and the Fourteenth Amendment, which prohibits certain restrictive legislation on the part of the States.

That it does not conflict with the thirteenth amendment, which abolished slavery and involuntary servitude, except as a punishment for crime, is too clear for argument. Slavery implies involuntary servitude—a state of bondage; the ownership of mankind as a chattel, or at least the control of the labor and services of one man for the benefit of another, and the absence of a legal right to the disposal of his own person, property, and services....

A statute which implies merely a legal distinction between the white and colored races—a distinction which is founded in the color of the two races, and which must always exist so long as white men are distinguished from the other race by color—has no tendency to destroy the legal equality of the two races, or reestablish a state of involuntary servitude....

The proper construction of [the Fourteenth Amendment] was first called to the attention of this court in the *Slaughter-House Cases*, which involved, however, not a question of race, but one of exclusive privileges. The case did not call for any expression of opinion as to the exact rights it was intended to secure to the colored race, but it was said generally that its main purpose was to establish the citizenship of the negro, to give definitions of citizenship of the United States and of the state, and to protect from the hostile legislation of the states the privileges and immunities of citizens of the United States, as distinguished from those of citizens of the states.

The object of the amendment was undoubtedly to enforce the absolute equality of the two races before the law, but, in the nature of things, it could not have been intended to abolish distinctions based upon color, or to enforce social, as distinguished from political, equality, or a commingling of the two races upon terms unsatisfactory to either. Laws permitting, and even requiring, their separation, in places where they are liable to be brought into contact, do not necessarily imply the inferiority of either race to the other, and have been generally, if not universally, recognized as within the competency of the state legislatures in the exercise of their police power. The most common instance of this is connected with the establishment of separate schools for white and colored children, which have been held to be a valid exercise of the legislative power even by courts of states where the political rights of the colored race have been longest and most earnestly enforced....

Laws forbidding the intermarriage of the two races may be said in a technical sense to interfere with the freedom of contract, and yet have been universally recognized as within the police power of the state....

It is claimed by the plaintiff in error that, in any mixed community, the reputation of belonging to the dominant race, in this instance the white race, is *property*, in the same sense that a right of action, or of inheritance, is property. Conceding this to be so, for the purposes of this case, we are unable to see how this statute deprives him of, or in any way affects his right to, such property. If he be a white man and assigned to a colored coach, he may have his action for damages against the company for being deprived of this so-called property. Upon the other hand, if he be a colored man and be so assigned, he has been deprived of no property, since he is not lawfully entitled to the reputation of being a white man....

So far, then, as a conflict with the Fourteenth Amendment is concerned, the case reduces itself to the question whether the statute of Louisiana is a reasonable regulation, and with respect to this there must necessarily be a large discretion on the part of the legislature. In determining the question of reasonableness it is at liberty to act with reference to the established usages, customs and traditions of the people, and with a view to the promotion of their comfort, and the preservation of the public peace and good order. Gauged by this standard, we cannot say that a law which authorizes or even requires the separation of the two races in public conveyances is unreasonable, or more obnoxious to the Fourteenth Amendment than the acts of Congress requiring separate schools for colored children in the District of Columbia, the constitutionality of which does not seem to have been questioned, or the corresponding acts of state legislatures.

We consider the underlying fallacy of the plaintiff's argument to consist in the assumption that the enforced separation of the two races stamps the colored race with a badge of inferiority. If this be so, it is not by reason of anything found in the act, but solely because the colored race chooses to put that construction upon it. The argument necessarily assumes that if, as has been more than once the case, and is not unlikely to be so again, the colored race should become the dominant power in the state legislature, and should enact a law in precisely similar terms, it would thereby relegate the white race to an inferior position. We imagine that the white race, at least, would not acquiesce in this assumption. The argument also assumes that social prejudices may be overcome by legislation, and that equal rights cannot be secured to the negro except by an enforced commingling of the two races. We cannot accept this proposition. If the two races are to meet upon terms of social equality, it must be the result of natural affinities, a mutual appreciation of each other's merits and a voluntary consent of individuals.... Legislation is powerless to eradicate racial instincts, or to abolish distinctions based upon physical differences, and the attempt to do so can only result in accentuating the difficulties of the present situation. If the civil and political rights of both races be equal, one cannot be inferior to the other civilly or politically. If one race be inferior to the other socially, the constitution of the United States cannot put them upon the same plane....

The judgment of the court below is therefore affirmed.

HARLAN, J., DISSENTING

... In respect of civil rights, common to all citizens, the Constitution of the United States does not, I think, permit any public authority to know the race of those entitled to be protected in the enjoyment of such rights. Every true man has pride of race, and under appropriate circumstances when the rights of others, his equals before the law, are not to be affected, it is his privilege to express such pride and to take such action based upon it as to him seems proper. But I deny that any legislative body or judicial tribunal may have regard to the race of citizens when the civil rights of those citizens are involved. Indeed, such legislation as that here in question, is inconsistent not only with that equality of rights which pertains to citizenship, National and State, but with the personal liberty enjoyed by every one within the United States....

Every one knows that the statute in question had its origin in the purpose, not so much to exclude white persons from railroad cars occupied by blacks, as to exclude colored people from coaches occupied by or assigned to white persons. Railroad corporations of Louisiana did not make discrimination among whites in the matter of accommodation for travelers. The thing to accomplish was, under the guise of giving equal accommodation for whites and blacks, to compel the latter to keep to themselves while traveling in railroad passenger coaches. No one would be so wanting in candor as to assert the contrary. The fundamental objection, therefore, to the statute, is that it interferes with the personal freedom of citizens....

The white race deems itself to be the dominant race in the country. And so it is, in prestige, in achievements, in education, in wealth, and in power. So, I doubt not, it will continue to be for all time, if it remains true to its great heritage, and holds fast to the principles of constitutional liberty. But in view of the constitution, in the eye of the law, there is in this country no superior, dominant, ruling class of citizens. There is no caste here. Our constitution is color-blind, and neither knows nor tolerates classes among citizens. In respect of civil rights, all citizens are equal before the law. The humblest is the peer of the most powerful. The law regards man as man, and takes no account of his surroundings or of his color when his civil rights as guarantied by the supreme law of the land are involved. It is therefore to be regretted that this high tribunal, the final expositor of the fundamental law of the land, has reached the conclusion that it is competent for a state to regulate the enjoyment by citizens of their civil rights solely upon the basis of race.

In my opinion, the judgment this day rendered will, in time, prove to be quite as pernicious as the decision made by this tribunal in the Dred Scott Case [*Scott v. Sandford*, 19 Howard 393 (1857)]....

The present decision, it may well be apprehended, will not only stimulate aggressions, more or less brutal and irritating, upon the admitted rights of colored citizens, but will encourage the belief that it is possible, by means of state enactments, to defeat the beneficent purposes which the people of the United States had in view when they adopted the recent amendments of the constitution, by one of which the blacks of this country were made citizens of the United States and of the states in which they respectively reside, and whose privileges and immunities, as citizens, the states are forbidden to abridge. Sixty millions of whites are in no danger from the presence here of eight millions of blacks. The destinies of the two races, in this country, are indissolubly linked together, and the interests of both require that the common government of all shall not permit the seeds of race hate to be planted under the sanction of law. What can more certainly arouse race hate, what more certainly create and perpetuate a feeling of distrust between these races, than state enactments which, in fact, proceed on the ground that colored citizens are so inferior and degraded that they cannot be allowed to sit in public coaches occupied by white citizens? That, as all will admit, is the real meaning of such legislation as was enacted in Louisiana....

State enactments regulating the enjoyment of civil rights upon the basis of race, and cunningly devised to defeat legitimate results of the [Civil War], under the pretense of recognizing equality of rights, can have no other result than to render permanent peace impossible, and to keep alive a conflict of races, the continuance of which must do harm to all concerned. This question is not met by the suggestion that social equality cannot exist between the white and black races in this country. That argument, if it can be properly regarded as one, is scarcely worthy of consideration; for social equality no more exists between two races when traveling in a passenger coach or a public highway than when members of the same races sit by each other in a street car or in the jury box, or stand or sit with each other in a political assembly, or when they use in common the streets of a city or town, or when they are in the same room for the purpose of having their names placed on the registry of voters, or when they approach the ballot box in order to exercise the high privilege of voting....

QUESTIONS

1. Constitutional historian Charles Lofgren gives this assessment of *Plessy*: "Brown's opinion, for all its sloppiness had a firmer grounding in current law; yet Harlan's was better rooted in republican truths and, at least arguably, in history. The two men had partially failed to join issues, but that is hardly surprising. They spoke to broader audiences—and for larger principles" (*The Plessy Case* [New York, NY: Oxford University Press, 1987], p. 195). Identify the audiences and principles addressed by both opinions.

2. One premise underlying the separate but equal doctrine was that state acts compelling racial separation do not imply racial inequality. Consequently, such laws do not deny equal protection. How might that premise be used to unravel the *Plessy* doctrine?

3. In his *Plessy* dissent, Justice Harlan contended:

   > Our constitution is color-blind, and neither knows nor tolerates classes among citizens. In respect of civil rights, all citizens are equal before the law. The humblest is the peer of the most powerful. The law regards man as man, and takes no account of his surroundings or of his color when his civil rights as guarantied by the supreme law of the land are involved.

   Can constitutional law be color-blind in a race-conscious society?

4. Professor Charles Lofgren also reports that the *Plessy* decision went largely unnoticed at the time and for years afterward. The *New York Times*, for example, gave the decision only passing notice in its regular column on railway news. Charles Warren's *History of the Supreme Court of the United States*, published in 1922, ignored the decision and mentioned it only in a footnote in the 1926 revision. Historians Carl Brent Swisher and Henry Steele Commager also omitted *Plessy* in their constitutional history books. By the mid-twentieth century, by contrast, the decision was notorious, and regarded as the "ultimate blow to the Civil War Amendments and the equality of Negroes" (Charles Lofgren, *The Plessy Case*, pp. 3, 5, 196).

   What insights do the early responses to *Plessy* provide into changing social attitudes about the separation of the races?

COMMENTS

1. Following *Plessy*, the Court was asked to apply the "separate but equal" doctrine in a number of other contexts. Following are summaries of the Court's responses:

Case: *Cumming v. Board of Education*, 175 U.S. 528 (1899)

Vote: 9–0

Decision: The Board of Education of Richmond County, Georgia, is not required to close its high school for white children just because it temporarily suspended for economic reasons the high school for colored children. Under the financial circumstances, the temporary closing of the black high school is not a denial of equal protection of the laws. Education of the people in schools maintained by state taxation is a matter belonging to the states. Federal intervention cannot be justified.

Case: *Berea College v. Kentucky*, 211 U.S. 45 (1908)

Vote: 7–2

Decision: The conviction of Berea College, a private liberal arts college, for permitting white and negro pupils to be educated in the same facilities, is valid because of a Kentucky statute forbidding any person, corporation, or association of persons to maintain a college, school, or institution where persons of white and negro races were both received as pupils for instruction. Even if the statute were unconstitutional as to individuals, it is not unconstitutional as to corporations because it is within the authority of the state to determine the powers conferred upon corporations.

Case: *McCabe v. Atchison, Topeka and Santa Fe Railway Company*, 235 U.S. 151 (1914)

Vote: 9–0

Decision: The Oklahoma Separate Coach Law that permits carriers to provide sleeping, dining, and chair cars to be used exclusively by persons of the white race, violates the Fourteenth Amendment. The legislature erred in assuming the Fourteenth Amendment permits such inequalities in facilities merely because, as luxuries, there would be limited demand for them by the negro race compared to the white race.

Case: *Gong Lum v. Rice*, 275 U.S. 78 (1927)

Vote: 9–0

Decision: A Chinese citizen of the United States is not denied equal protection of the laws when classed among the colored races and assigned to public schools separate from those provided for whites, as long as equal facilities for education are afforded to both classes.

2. The Supreme Court's focus between the end of the nineteenth century and the first several decades of the twentieth century was primarily on the legitimacy of government regulation of the economy and private contractual relationships. Responding to overt racism and racial terrorism was not high on the country's political or legal agendas. World War II, however, thrust the issue of equal protection of the laws in the context of race into the forefront. On December 7, 1941, Japanese naval and air forces attacked the American fleet at the Pearl Harbor naval base in Hawaii, killing 2,335 military person-

nel and 68 civilians. The next day, Congress declared war on Japan. Within a few weeks, anti-Japanese hysteria gripped the West Coast of the United States.

In February 1942, President Franklin Roosevelt issued Executive Order 9066, which authorized the secretary of war to issue orders regulating the activities and movement of over 112,000 persons of Japanese descent living on the Pacific coast, some 70,000 of whom were American citizens. Three months later, Lt. General John L. DeWitt, military commander of the western defense command, issued an order requiring all persons of Japanese ancestry to evacuate an area of California that had been designated a military area and to report to a civil control station in Hayward, California. The order also imposed curfews on persons of Japanese descent.

In *Hirabayashi v. United States*, 320 U.S. 81 (1943), the Supreme Court unanimously upheld the curfew orders despite a claim that they involved racial discrimination in violation of the Fifth Amendment. Although the Fifth Amendment contains no Equal Protection Clause, the Supreme Court has long recognized that the concepts of due process and equal protection are closely related because both stem from principles of fairness. Consequently, the justices have acknowledged that the Fifth Amendment's Due Process Clause contains an "equal protection component." In *Hirabayashi*, the Court concluded that the curfew order, though racially motivated, was valid "as an emergency war measure."

The following year, in *Korematsu v. United States*, 323 U.S. 214 (1944), the Court also upheld the validity of the relocation orders on the ground that they were justified by the country's need to successfully prosecute the war against Japan. However, Justice Black's opinion contained the following statement:

> It should be noted, to begin with, that all legal restrictions which curtail the civil rights of a single racial group are immediately suspect. That is not to say that all such restrictions are unconstitutional. It is to say that courts must subject them to the most rigid scrutiny. Pressing public necessity may sometimes justify the existence of such restrictions; racial antagonism never can....

The rule that classifications based on race are to be subjected to the most rigid judicial scrutiny revolutionized litigation under both the equal protection component of the Fifth Amendment's Due Process Clause and the Equal Protection Clause of the Fourteenth Amendment. The evolution of "strict scrutiny" in the context of race—and debates over its applicability in the context of other classifications that distinguish among groups of people—is a major theme of the cases that follow in this chapter.

EQUAL PROTECTION:
JIM CROW AND SCHOOL DESEGREGATION

Brown v. Board of Education
347 U.S. 483 (1954)

SETTING

In *Plessy v. Ferguson* the Supreme Court put its imprimatur on racial segregation in the United States, notwithstanding the guarantees of the Fourteenth Amendment. As the voting rights cases in Chapter 6 demonstrate, during this same period the Court also sanctioned a variety of devices aimed at frustrating the goals of the Fifteenth Amendment. No frontal assaults were made on the Thirteenth Amendment, but none was needed: Racial apartheid through segregation was the law of the land and there were few prospects for change.

Plessy, of course, rested on a legal fiction: There never were or could be any such thing as "separate but equal" facilities and opportunities for the white and nonwhite races. While most blacks sank under the crushing weight of "separate but equal," a few black intellectuals and white liberals came together to devise a strategy for improving the condition of blacks in the United States. In 1909 they founded the National Association for the Advancement of Colored People (NAACP). During the organization's first twenty-five years it focused on mob violence and lynching, appealing to the conscience of Americans to end those terrorist tactics. Then the organization turned to the law. Its first priority became ending segregation in education, in the belief that improved educational opportunities and the intermingling of the races in educational settings were the long-term solutions to the pervasive patterns of racism in the United States.

In 1935, Howard Law School dean, Charles H. Houston, left his post to become NAACP special counsel. During his six years as dean, Houston transformed Howard Law School from a part-time institution into a full-time school focusing on civil rights law. Houston and one of his former students, Maryland attorney Thurgood Marshall, who had served as chief counsel for the Baltimore branch of the NAACP, believed that the *Plessy* decision contained the seeds of its own demise. Said Marshall in retrospect:

> [T]he best overall strategy seemed to be an attack against the segregation system by lawsuits seeking absolute and complete equalization of curricula, faculty and physical equipment in white and black schools on the theory that the extreme cost of maintaining two "equal" school systems would eventually destroy segregation.

The easiest targets were state universities and professional schools, where costs usually made it impossible for states to maintain equal facilities.

In 1938, in *Missouri ex rel Gaines v. Canada*, 305 U.S. 337, Houston and Marshall's litigation strategy was successful. The state of Missouri operated a law school open to whites only. Lloyd Gaines, a black, qualified for admission on every ground but race. Pursuant to a state statute, university officials offered to pay his tuition at an out-of-state law school that admitted blacks. The Legal Defense Fund, on Gaines's behalf, argued that doing so would violate the "separate but equal" doctrine. The Court agreed. In a 7–2 decision written by Chief Justice Hughes, the Court held that under the Equal Protection Clause of the Fourteenth Amendment, "the State was bound to furnish [Gaines] within its borders facilities for legal education substantially equal to those which the State there afforded for persons of the white race, whether or not other negroes sought the same opportunity." The Court ordered that Gaines be admitted to the University of Missouri law school.

Twelve years later, in 1950, the Court agreed with the NAACP that the law school for blacks in the state of Texas was not equal to the law school operated for whites: The black school had fewer faculty, an inferior library, no full-time librarian, and was not accredited. In a unanimous opinion by Chief Justice Vinson, the Court ruled that Herman Sweatt was entitled to a legal education equivalent to that offered to white law students. *Sweatt v. Painter*, 339 U.S. 629 (1950).

The same day, the NAACP won another unanimous legal victory before the Supreme Court in a challenge to the State of Oklahoma's refusal to admit sixty-eight-year-old George McLaurin to its doctoral program in education. McLaurin had earned his master's degree many years before. The district court ordered McLaurin admitted to the doctoral program, but required him to sit apart from his white peers in the classroom and in the library and to eat his meals in the cafeteria at different hours from his white colleagues. Although McLaurin clearly received instruction in the same facility as other students, the question was whether his separate treatment nonetheless was less than equal. Chief Justice Vinson declared that having been admitted to a state-supported graduate school, McLaurin "must receive the same treatment at the hands of the state as students of other races." *McLaurin v. Oklahoma State Regents for Higher Education*, 339 U.S. 637 (1950).

Despite the NAACP's important victories in *Gaines, Sweatt,* and *McLaurin,* the Court refused the Defense Fund's invitation to overrule *Plessy.* Chief Justice Vinson wrote that "we [need not] reach [the] contention that *Plessy v. Ferguson* should be reexamined in the light of contemporary knowledge respecting the purposes of the Fourteenth Amendment and the effects of racial segregation."

Victories at the university level, however, set the stage for challenges to "separate but equal" in elementary and secondary schools and, ultimately, renewed attacks on the constitutional validity of "separate but equal." Following *McLaurin,* the NAACP began looking for situations in which equality essentially had been achieved among segregated schools in all tangible respects, raising the more difficult question of whether separation itself violated Equal Protection of the Laws.

In 1951, NAACP staff in Topeka, Kansas, were instrumental in persuading Oliver Brown, Mrs. Richard Lawton, and Mrs. Sadie Emmanuel, black parents whose children attended public elementary schools in Topeka, to challenge that state's segregation statutes. A Kansas law enacted in 1949 authorized local school boards in cities with more than fifteen thousand population to "organize and maintain separate schools for the education of white and colored children...." The Board of Education of Topeka divided that city into eighteen geographical divisions, maintaining one elementary school (through grade six) in each division exclusively for attendance by white children, and four schools in each division exclusively for attendance by black children. Students were bused, if necessary, to achieve segregation. Junior high schools and high schools in the district were not segregated.

The Brown, Lawton, and Emmanuel children were required to travel particularly long distances to achieve the school board's goal of segregated schools. Brown's daughter, Linda, for example, was forced to attend Monroe School, about twenty blocks from her home, rather than Sumner School, in her neighborhood. Each morning she had to walk through a dangerous railroad yard to catch a bus that took her to Monroe. The bus usually arrived thirty minutes before the school's doors were unlocked. With assistance from the Legal Defense Fund, Brown, Lawton, and Emmanuel filed suit in the U.S. District Court for the District of Kansas seeking an injunction to restrain the enforcement, operation, and execution of the Kansas statute. They argued that segregated schools deprived their children of equal protection within the meaning of the Fourteenth Amendment.

The case was tried by a three-judge panel. Almost concurrently, similar cases were being tried in South Carolina, Virginia, Delaware, and the District of Columbia. In each, social scientists were called as expert witnesses to testify about the psychological effects of segregation. The Kansas District Court made several findings of fact, including a finding that the black schools in Topeka were equal, or in the process of being equalized, to the white schools. However, finding of Fact No. VIII stated:

> Segregation of white and colored children in public schools has a detrimental effect upon the colored children. The impact is greater when it has the sanction of the law; for the policy of separating the races is usually interpreted as denoting the inferiority of the Negro group. A sense of inferiority affects the motivation of a child to learn. Segregation with the sanction of law, therefore, has a tendency to [retard] the educational and mental development of Negro children and to deprive them of some of the benefits they would receive in a [racially] integrated school system.

Nonetheless, the district court denied injunctive relief, primarily because of *Plessy v. Ferguson.* Brown and his coplaintiffs appealed directly to the Supreme Court of the United States, as allowed by statute following decisions of three-judge federal panels.

The case was first argued during the Court's 1952 Term, Chief Justice Vinson presiding. It was reargued by request of the Court during the 1953 Term, Chief Justice Warren presiding. *Brown* was consolidated with the cases from South Carolina, Virginia, and Delaware.

Highlights of Supreme Court Arguments: *1952 Argument*

BRIEF FOR BROWN

◆ The Kansas statute is an arbitrary and unreasonable exercise of state power in violation of the Fourteenth Amendment. In an unbroken line of decisions beginning in 1940, the Supreme Court has held that a state cannot impose distinctions and restrictions among its citizens based on race or color alone. State efforts to protect citizens against racial discrimination, on the other hand, have been consistently upheld.

◆ The Court's decision in *Sweatt v. Painter*, 339 U.S. 629 (1950), declaring separate but equal law schools unconstitutional, shows the inapplicability of *Plessy*.

◆ Social science research has documented the negative effects of segregation on both minority and majority groups. The results of that research are included in an appendix to the brief. It is nonetheless true that the problems with which this case deals are on the frontiers of scientific knowledge.

AMICUS CURIAE BRIEFS SUPPORTING BROWN

United States; the American Jewish Congress; American Ethical Union; American Civil Liberties Union; American Jewish Committee; American Federation of Teachers; the American Veterans Committee, Inc.; Congress of Industrial Organization.

BRIEF FOR TOPEKA BOARD OF EDUCATION

◆ Matters of public policy are within the exclusive province of the legislature. School boards in Kansas can maintain segregated schools only when explicitly authorized by statute.

◆ The Kansas statute at issue in this case does not violate the Fourteenth Amendment, which protects only personal and individual rights. The district court's Finding of Fact No. VIII, stating the generally detrimental effects of segregation on Negro children, is irrelevant since no showing was made that any of the plaintiffs actually and personally suffered as a result of segregation in the Topeka schools.

◆ *Plessy v. Ferguson* controls this case, because it announced a doctrine applicable to any social situation wherein the two races are brought into contact. *Plessy* was neither weakened nor overruled by *Sweatt v. Painter* because in *Sweatt* the court found unquestionably unequal facilities. In this case the district court found substantially equal facilities.

Highlights of Supreme Court Arguments: *1953 Reargument*

Note: Counsel were instructed to respond to five questions posed by the Court following the 1952 argument. The questions focused on the intent of the Fourteenth Amendment and the extent of the Court's equitable powers should it rule in favor of the plaintiffs.

BRIEF FOR BROWN

◆ The primary purpose of the Fourteenth Amendment was to deprive states of all power to perpetuate a caste system in the United States based on race. Congressional debate demonstrated that the Fourteenth Amendment was to work a revolutionary change in state-federal relations by denying states the power to discriminate on the basis of race. Opponents as well as supporters of the amendment realized that it would prohibit all state action predicated on race or color. Maintenance of separate public school facilities is inconsistent with that goal.

◆ The "separate but equal" doctrine marked an unwarranted departure from mainstream constitutional development. Custom, usage, and tradition rooted in the slave tradition cannot be a constitutional yardstick for measuring state action under the Fourteenth Amendment. The doctrine has been an instrumentality of defiant nullification of the Fourteenth Amendment.

◆ There is convincing evidence that the state legislatures and conventions that ratified the Fourteenth Amendment contemplated and understood that it prohibited state legislation that would require racial segregation in the schools.

◆ There are no compelling reasons for the Court to postpone immediate relief.

AMICUS CURIAE BRIEF SUPPORTING BROWN

United States.

BRIEF FOR TOPEKA BOARD OF EDUCATION

◆ Following argument at the 1952 Term, the board voted to terminate segregation in its elementary schools as rapidly as is practicable. Terminating segregation will be difficult and have far-reaching effects. The public interest requires that Topeka be permitted to accomplish desegregation in a gradual and orderly manner.

BRIEF FOR STATE OF KANSAS

◆ A majority of the Congress that submitted the Fourteenth Amendment did not contemplate that it would abolish segregation in public schools. A majority of the states ratifying the amendment (twenty-four of thirty-seven) must have held the same view because they authorized school segregation at the time. There is no competent evidence that the other thirteen states understood the amendment to preclude racial segregation in public schools.

◆ Abolition of segregation in public schools is not within the judicial power. Under the Constitution and the Fourteenth Amendment, public schools were intended to remain within the control of the states. Should the Court nevertheless find segregation unconstitutional, implementation of desegregation should be supervised by courts of original jurisdiction at the local level.

SUPREME COURT DECISION: 9–0

WARREN, C.J.

... Reargument was largely devoted to the circumstances surrounding the adoption of the Fourteenth Amendment in 1868. It covered exhaustively consideration of the Amendment in Congress, ratification by the states, the existing practices in racial segregation, and the views of proponents and opponents of the Amendment. This discussion and our own investigation convince us that, although these sources cast some light, it is not enough to resolve the problem with which we are faced. At best, they are inconclusive.

In the instant cases, [the question whether *Plessy v. Ferguson* should be held inapplicable to public education] is directly presented. Here, unlike *Sweatt v. Painter* [339 U.S. 629 (1950)] there are findings below that the Negro and white schools involved have been equalized, or are being equalized with respect to buildings, curricula, qualifications and salaries of teachers, and other "tangible" factors. Our decision, therefore, cannot turn on merely a comparison of these tangible factors in the Negro and white schools involved in each of the cases. We must look instead to the effect of segregation itself on public education.

In approaching this problem, we cannot turn the clock back to 1868 when the [Fourteenth] Amendment was adopted, or even to 1896 when *Plessy v. Ferguson* was written. We must consider public education in the light of its full development and its present place in American life throughout the Nation. Only in this way can it be determined if segregation in public schools deprives these plaintiffs of the equal protection of the laws.

Today, education is perhaps the most important function of state and local governments. Compulsory school attendance laws and the great expenditures for education both demonstrate our recognition of the importance of education to our democratic society. It is required in the performance of our most basic public responsibilities, even service in the armed forces. It is the very foundation of good citizenship. Today it is a principal instrument in awakening the child to cultural values, in preparing him for later professional training, and in helping him to adjust normally to his environment. In these days, it is doubtful that any child may reasonably be expected to succeed in life if he is denied the opportunity of an education. Such an opportunity, where the state has undertaken to provide it, is a right which must be made available to all on equal terms.

We come then to the question presented: Does segregation of children in public schools solely on the basis of race, even though the physical facilities and other "tangible" factors may be equal, deprive the children of the minority group of equal educational opportunities? We believe that it does....

To separate [Negro children] from others of similar age and qualifications solely because of their race generates a feeling of inferiority as to their status in the community that may affect their hearts and minds in a way unlikely ever to be undone. The effect of this separation on their educational opportunities was well stated by a finding in the Kansas case by a court which nevertheless felt compelled to rule against the Negro plaintiffs.... Whatever may have been the extent of psychological knowledge at the time of *Plessy v. Ferguson*, [the district court's] finding is amply supported by modern authority.[11] Any language in *Plessy v. Ferguson* contrary to this finding is rejected.

We conclude that in the field of public education the doctrine of "separate but equal" has no place. Separate educational facilities are inherently unequal. Therefore, we hold that the plaintiffs and others similarly situated for whom the actions have been brought are, by reason of the segregation complained of, deprived of the equal protection of the laws guaranteed by the Fourteenth Amendment....

Because these are class actions, because of the wide applicability of this decision, and because of the great variety of local conditions, the formulation of decrees in these cases presents problems of considerable complexity.... We have now announced that such segregation is a denial of the equal protection of the laws. In order that we may have the full assistance of the parties in formulating decrees, the cases will be restored to the docket and the parties are requested to present further argument [on the Court's equitable powers to implement the decision]....

It is so ordered....

[11] K. B. Clark, Effect of Prejudice and Discrimination on Personality Development (Midcentury White House Conference on Children and Youth, 1950); Witmer and Kotinsky, Personality in the Making (1952), c. VI; Deutscher and Chein, The Psychological Effects of Enforced Segregation: A Survey of Social Science Opinion, 26 J. Psychol. 259 (1948); Chein, What are the Psychological Effects of Segregation Under Conditions of Equal Facilities?, 3 Int. J. Opinion and Attitude Res. 229 (1949); Brameld, Educational Costs, in Discrimination and National Welfare (MacIver, ed., 1949), 44–48; Frazier, The Negro in the United States (1949), 674–681. And see generally, Myrdal, An American Dilemma (1944). [In the Court's opinion this footnote contains neither quotation marks nor italics.]

COMMENTS

1. *Bolling v. Sharpe*, 347 U.S. 497 (1954), was argued as a companion case to *Brown*. It involved a challenge to segregation in the public schools in Washington, D.C. Again for a unanimous Court, Chief Justice Warren wrote:

   > The Fifth Amendment, which is applicable in the District of Columbia, does not contain an equal protection clause as does the Fourteenth Amendment, which applies only to the states. But the concepts of equal protection and due process, both stemming from our American ideal of fairness, are not mutually exclusive. The "equal protection of the laws" is a more explicit safeguard of prohibited unfairness than "due process of law," and, therefore, we do not imply that the two are always interchangeable phrases. But, as this Court has recognized, discrimination may be so unjustifiable as to be violative of due process....
   >
   > In view of our decision that the Constitution prohibits the states from maintaining racially segregated schools, it would be unthinkable that the same Constitution would impose a lesser duty on the Federal Government.

   The Court held that racial segregation in the public schools of the District violates the Due Process Clause of the Fifth Amendment.

2. *Brown v. Board of Education* (*Brown II*), 349 U.S. 294 (1955), dealt with

the extent of the Supreme Court's equitable powers to implement the *Brown I* decision. NAACP counsel argued that the Court should order desegregation no later than September 1955, to be completed by the following year, because segregation of the races by government fiat was incompatible with national policy. The states of Kansas and Delaware, and the District of Columbia, claimed to have made considerable progress toward desegregation and asked the Court not to direct implementation decrees toward them. *Amicus curiae* briefs submitted by the States of Florida, North Carolina, Arkansas, Oklahoma, Maryland, and Texas contended that the Court had no role to play in implementation of the 1954 decision. They argued that the Court's only power was to "invite" Congress to resolve the problem of desegregation when Congress deemed it advisable to do so. The United States repeated its position that the Court should let district courts supervise the process of school desegregation, because those courts could be responsive to local conditions that would dictate varying speeds of compliance.

Chief Justice Warren, for a unanimous Court, remanded the cases to the courts that originally heard them, giving them power to fashion decrees according to principles of equity. It directed the courts to take such proceedings and enter such orders and decrees "as are necessary and proper to admit to public schools on a racially nondiscriminatory basis with all deliberate speed the parties to these cases."

QUESTIONS

1. Chief Justice Earl Warren played a crucial leadership role in garnering support for the *Brown I* opinion. In a private memorandum to the justices written during the process of drafting the decision, Chief Justice Warren indicated that he sought to write an opinion in *Brown I* that would be "short, readable by the lay public, non-rhetorical, unemotional, and, above all, non-accusatory" (quoted in Alfred H. Kelly, Wilfred A. Harbison, and Herman Belz, *The American Constitution: Its Origins and Development*, 6th ed. [New York, NY: W. W. Norton, 1983], p. 609).

   Did Warren succeed? What is the legal status of *Plessy v. Ferguson* in light of *Brown*?

2. The decision in the two *Brown* school desegregation cases met with massive resistance throughout the southern United States. It may be easier to understand the vitriolic reaction to the desegregation decisions and comprehend the dimensions of the social problem addressed in *Brown II* by remembering that for 246 years (1619–1865), slavery was a legal institution in America. Eleven difficult years of Reconstruction (1865–1876) followed the Civil War. For the next 87

years (1876–1954), the "Jim Crow" era of segregation was the law of the land.

On March 12, 1956, ninety-six members of Congress expressed their opposition to the *Brown* decisions by signing The Southern Manifesto. The Manifesto contended:

> (1) *Brown II* is an abuse of judicial power; (2) The Fourteenth Amendment does not mention education and did not affect state educational systems; (3) *Plessy* is still good law; (4) Desegregation will cause chaos in the states affected.

The Manifesto called for people of the states to "resist forced integration by any lawful means" and concluded with the pledge "... to use all lawful means to bring about a reversal of this decision which is contrary to the Constitution and to prevent the use of force in its implementation" (*Congressional Record*, 84th Congress 2nd Session, March 12, 1956, pp. 4460–4461, 4515–4516).

The responses to the *Brown* decisions are a reminder of the frailty of judicial review despite its more than one-hundred-fifty-year lineage. Without assistance from the other two branches and public support, are Supreme Court decisions merely statements of legal rules and principles?

3. The Court's phrase, "all deliberate speed," in *Brown II* has been the subject of considerable discussion and not a little criticism. The term is ascribed to Justice Felix Frankfurter by Philip Elman in his article, "The Solicitor General's Office, Justice Frankfurter, and Civil Rights Litigation, 1946–1960: An Oral History" 100 *Harvard Law Review* (1987): 817. In December 1968, Justice Hugo Black said this about the *Brown II* order: "Looking back at it now, it seems to me that it's delayed the process of outlawing segregation. It seems to me ... that it would have been better ... not to have that sentence. To treat that case as an ordinary lawsuit and force the judgment on the counties it affected that minute" (*Congressional Quarterly Weekly Report* 1969, p. 7).

   In retrospect, what would have been a more effective approach to implementation of *Brown I?*

4. Then law professor (now federal district court judge) J. Harvie Wilkinson argued that although *Brown I* may have buoyed the morale of blacks at the time, its undercurrents depressed it:

   > For *Brown* implied first, that black schools, whatever their physical endowments, could not equal white ones; second, that integration was a matter of a white benefactor and a black beneficiary. Events in the aftermath of *Brown* were even more insensitive. Progress was measured in [Department of Health, Education and Welfare] statistics by how many blacks entered the promised land of white classrooms.... The whole gamut of integrationist ideals—from *Brown* to

busing to affirmative action—would incorporate this same conde-scending assumption: that contact with whites was necessary for black students to improve. (*From* Brown *to* Bakke [New York, NY: Oxford University Press, 1979], p.46)

Assess the strength of Wilkinson's argument. In 1954 would that argument have been an apology for maintaining *Plessy*? In the late 1990s, how does this argument figure in ongoing reassessments of previous civil rights strategies centering on litigation to achieve integration—and the goal of integration itself?

5. In 1969, law professor Alexander M. Bickel wrote:

We cannot, said the Court in *Brown v. Board of Education*, "turn back the clock to 1868 when the [Fourteenth] Amendment was adopted, or even to 1896 when *Plessy v. Ferguson* was written. We must consider public education in light of its full development and its present place in American life throughout the Nation." That development, we now know, was not full and not final at the time of *Brown*, and that place is changing. What the *Brown* opinion ultimately envisioned seems for the moment unattainable, and is becoming unwanted. Soon it may be impossible to "turn the clock back" to 1954, when *Brown v. Board of Education* was written. This is not to detract from the nobility of the Warren Court's aspiration in *Brown*, nor from the contribution to American life of the rule that the state may not coerce or enforce the separation of the races. But it is to say the *Brown v. Board of Education*, with emphasis on the education part of the title, may be headed to—dread word—irrelevance. (*The Supreme Court and The Idea of Progress* [New Haven, CT: Yale University Press, 1978], pp. 150–151)

In what way might it be argued that *Brown* is irrelevant at the end of the twentieth century? For what reasons might "[w]hat the *Brown* opinion ultimately envisioned" be "unattainable, and is becoming unwanted"?

6. The school desegregation cases declared unconstitutional the laws of twenty-one states and the District of Columbia. Official responses to these decisions varied. Arizona, Kansas, New Mexico, and Wyoming had permitted racial discrimination under local option. All four complied with the *Brown* decision. Likewise, the District of Columbia and Delaware, Kentucky, Maryland, Missouri, Oklahoma, and West Virginia complied without serious resistance.

As noted above in question 2, ten southern states responded with massive resistance, employing various legal tactics aimed at avoidance, evasion, and delay. North Carolina, Tennessee, and Texas abandoned those tactics by 1957. Alabama, Mississippi, South Carolina, Florida, Georgia, Louisiana, Arkansas, and Virginia continued to wage legal battles against desegregation or to stall its implementation. The following cases are examples of the Supreme Court's responses to state efforts to oppose desegregation between 1963 and 1968 when *Green v. New Kent County School Board*, 391 U.S. 430, the next case excerpted, was decided.

Case: *Goss v. Board of Education*, 373 U.S. 683 (1963)
Vote: 9–0
Decision: Classifications based on race for the purposes of transfers between public schools violate equal protection of the Fourteenth Amendment. A program under which students are allowed to transfer from their zones of residence to another school lends itself to the perpetuation of segregation.

Case: *McNeese v. Board of Education*, 373 U.S. 668 (1963)
Vote: 8–1
Decision: Negro students may challenge in federal court alleged segregation in public schools without first exhausting state administrative remedies.

Case: *Griffin v. School Board*, 377 U.S. 218 (1964)
Vote: 9–0
Decision: Closing public schools, while at the same time giving tuition grants and tax concessions to assist white children in private segregated schools, denies black children equal protection under the Fourteenth Amendment. (Clark and Harlan, J.J., dissented from the holding that federal courts are empowered to order the reopening of public schools.)

Case: *Bradley v. School Board*, 382 U.S. 103 (1965)
Vote: 9–0
Decision: District courts should not approve desegregation plans unless full evidentiary hearings have been held.

Law professor Owen Fiss suggested a distinction between "process-oriented" and "result-oriented" remedies in antidiscrimination cases. "The Fate of an Idea Whose Time Has Come: Antidiscrimination Law in the Second Decade After *Brown v. Board of Education*," 41 *University of Chicago Law Review* (1974): 742. The process orientation "emphasizes the purification of the decisional process," to purge it of racial criteria. The result orientation "emphasizes the achievement of certain results." For example, the process approach would ban race as the basis for pupil assignment. The result approach would insist on racially integrated schools.

To what extent did the four decisions summarized above shift from a process orientation to a result orientation? Does the Constitution mandate results? In practical terms, can one defensibly differentiate among being committed to the principle of (1) desegregated schools, (2) a racially neutral pupil assignment process, and (3) integrated school facilities?

COMMENTS

1. Following *Brown II*, the Supreme Court issued a series of summary *per curiam* decisions upholding lower federal court decisions that invalidated laws segregating state parks, beaches and bath houses, and golf courses. In *Gayle v. Browder*, 352 U.S. 903 (1956), the Court effectively, albeit *sub silentio*, overruled *Plessy v. Ferguson*—a step it had not taken in *Brown I*. *Gayle v. Browder* was a defeat for Montgomery, Alabama, Mayor, W. A. Gayle, and a victory for the Montgomery Improvement Association, the civil rights group that had organized the Montgomery bus boycott after Rosa Parks had refused to yield her seat to a white person on a municipal bus on December 1, 1955.

2. In 1986, *Brown* was reopened when parents of seventeen Topeka, Kansas, children filed suit claiming that the city's schools remained segregated. In reversing the U.S. District Court in Kansas, the U.S. Court of Appeals for the Tenth Circuit found that 58 percent of white students go to schools that are at least 80 percent white and that 36 percent of minorities go to schools that are at least 50 percent minority. The court of appeals found further, "For the most part, the Topeka school district has exercised a form of benign neglect." On June 5, 1989, the Tenth Circuit U.S. Court of Appeals refused to close *Brown v. Board of Education*. Among the parents filing suit in 1986 was Linda Brown Buckner whose father, Oliver Brown, had filed suit on her behalf in *Brown I* in 1951.

EQUAL PROTECTION: JIM CROW AND SCHOOL DESEGREGATION

Green v. School Board of New Kent County, VA
391 U.S. 430 (1968)

SETTING

In *Brown v. Board of Education*, 349 U.S. 294 (1955) (*Brown II*), the Supreme Court ordered federal district courts to oversee school desegregation, to be accomplished with "all deliberate speed." As noted in the materials following the excerpt of *Brown I*, southern defiance of lower court orders implementing the two *Brown* decisions was pervasive. So were violence and threats of violence. In 1956, Federal Bureau of Investigation (FBI) Director J. Edgar Hoover reported to President Dwight D. Eisenhower and the members of his Cabinet that "racial tension has been mounting almost daily since the Supreme Court banned segregation in public schools ... [and] required that integration be established at the earliest practicable date."

Also according to the FBI, the Ku Klux Klan, "pretty much defunct … in the early 1950s," had been resurrected in August 1955 by Eldon Edwards, an Atlanta automobile assembly plant worker. Edwards's organization, the U.S. Klans, Knights of the Ku Klux Klan, Inc., established active branches in Georgia, Alabama, South Carolina, and Florida. Between January 1955, and January 1959, in the eleven former Confederate states, some 210 incidents of racial violence were reported to authorities, ranging from Klan rallies and cross burnings to death threats, the murders of six blacks, twenty-nine assaults with firearms, and forty-four beatings. Between 1955 and 1958, ninety southern homes were damaged by explosives, gun fire, arson, and stoning.

In 1958, the Supreme Court decided *Cooper v. Aaron*, 358 U.S. 1. *Cooper* arose from the stubborn opposition to *Brown I* and *Brown II* by citizens and politicians in Little Rock, Arkansas. The city's school board had moved to desegregate its schools in 1957, in conformity with its understanding of the mandate of *Brown II*. Arkansas Governor Orval Faubus responded by declaring the city's schools off-limits to black children and ordering the National Guard to prevent nine black children from entering Little Rock's public schools. A federal judge enjoined Governor Faubus from resisting public school desegregation and ordered the National Guard removed. The black children's attempts to enter the school were then thwarted by angry white mobs. Mob violence provoked President Dwight Eisenhower, who had been reluctant to intervene in state affairs, to act. Saying that the situation in Arkansas was damaging America's prestige and influence abroad, and was causing our enemies to gloat "over this incident," President Eisenhower ordered the National Guard into federal service on September 24, 1957, and sent about a thousand paratroopers into Little Rock to reopen the schools and enforce order.

One year later, in an extraordinary opinion signed by all nine justices, a unanimous Supreme Court announced:

> We are urged to uphold a suspension of the Little Rock School Board's plan to do away with segregated public schools in Little Rock until state laws and efforts to upset and nullify our holding in *Brown v. Board of Education* have been further challenged and tested in the courts. We reject these contentions.

The *Cooper* Court added:

> Article VI of the Constitution makes the Constitution the "supreme Law of the Land." In 1803, Chief Justice Marshall, speaking for a unanimous Court, referring to the Constitution as "the fundamental and paramount law of the nation," declared in the notable case of *Marbury v. Madison*, that "It is emphatically the province and duty of the judicial department to say what the law is." This decision declared the basic principle that the federal judiciary is supreme in the exposition of the law of the Constitution, and that principle has ever since been respected by this Court and the Country as a permanent and indispensable feature of our constitutional system. It follows that the interpretation of the Fourteenth Amendment enunciated by

this Court in the *Brown* case is the supreme law of the land, and Art. VI of the Constitution makes it of binding effect on the States "any Thing in the Constitution or Laws of any State to the Contrary notwithstanding."

After *Cooper*, states and school districts devised a variety of other means to frustrate the Supreme Court's mandate in *Brown II*. Rather than assigning students to schools according to methods that would achieve desegregation, many districts devised complex procedures that had the effect of perpetuating segregation. One method that came under attack was a freedom-of-choice system initiated by the Virginia legislature in 1964.

New Kent County is located in a rural part of Virginia, east of Richmond. Although there was no residential segregation in the county, its two public schools operated on a segregated basis, as required by the Virginia Constitution of 1902 and statutes enacted pursuant to the constitution. New Kent, a combined elementary and high school, was all white; George W. Watkins, also a combined elementary and high school, was all black. Each school served the entire county. Students were bused to achieve racial segregation.

Under the Supreme Court's decision in *Davis v. County Board of Prince Edward County*, 347 U.S. 483 (1954), decided with *Brown v. Board of Education* (*Brown I*), New Kent's overtly racially discriminatory method of assigning students to schools was unconstitutional. After the Court's two *Brown* decisions, however, New Kent continued to operate a segregated school system, consistent with several statutes enacted by the Virginia legislature as part of its resistance. One of those statutes—the Pupil Placement Act of 1964—divested local school boards of authority to assign children to particular schools and gave that authority to a state Pupil Placement Board. The state board each year reassigned students to the schools they had attended the previous year unless their parents applied to have them assigned to another school. Students who were entering the system for the first time were assigned at the discretion of the board. No racial desegregation occurred.

In March 1965, Charles C. Green and his wife filed a class action suit in the U.S. District Court for the Eastern District of Virginia against the New Kent County school board seeking an injunction against the continued maintenance of segregated schools in the county. The board filed a motion to dismiss for failure to state a claim on which relief could be granted, contending that Green had failed to apply to the state board for a school assignment. The district court denied the motion. The school board then asserted that students in the district were allowed to attend the school of their choice and hence the court lacked jurisdiction to order the relief requested by Green.

While Green's action was pending before the district court, the school board, in August 1965, adopted a freedom-of-choice desegregation plan in an effort to comply with the requirements of the 1964 Civil Rights Act. That plan allowed "permissive transfers" for ten of the twelve grades in the district. Under the plan, each student—except those entering the first and eighth grades—were given the choice whether to attend New Kent or Watkins.

Students who did not make a choice were assigned to the school they had attended the previous year.

The New Kent school board submitted the freedom-of-choice plan to the district court. That court approved the plan, subject to the requirement that teachers and staff be assigned to the schools on a nonracially discriminatory basis, and dismissed Green's suit.

The U.S. Court of Appeals for the Fourth Circuit affirmed, but remanded the case to the district court for entry of a more specific order regarding faculty and staff assignments. Green petitioned the Supreme Court of the United States for a writ of certiorari.

HIGHLIGHTS OF SUPREME COURT ARGUMENTS

BRIEF FOR GREEN

◆ *Brown* condemned compulsory racial assignments of public school children and required a "transition" to a nondiscriminatory system. That goal is not achieved when some schools are maintained or identified as schools for whites and some are maintained or identified as schools for blacks.

◆ Under *Brown*, school districts are required to take affirmative steps to end segregation.

◆ Freedom-of-choice plans typically leave the dual system undisturbed. Although such plans have been adopted in the overwhelming number of districts affected by *Brown*, they have not achieved desegregation.

◆ The evidence is uncontradicted that there are other methods, no more difficult to administer, that would eliminate the dual system of black and white schools. When such alternatives are available, judicial approval of freedom of choice is not constitutionally permissible.

AMICUS CURIAE BRIEFS SUPPORTING GREEN

United States; American Jewish Congress.

BRIEF FOR SCHOOL BOARD OF NEW KENT COUNTY, VA

◆ Under the freedom-of-choice plan, black students have an opportunity they have never before enjoyed—the opportunity to attend the school of their choice. Plaintiffs in this case would have the Court force others to do what they already have the freedom to do. Such an order would restore race as a criterion in the operation of the public schools, contrary to *Brown* and the Fourteenth Amendment.

◆ States have no obligation under the Fourteenth Amendment to enforce compulsory integration of the races throughout a school system.

◆ It is uncontested that some other plan could be implemented to make student assignments to schools. The freedom-of-choice plan, however, is consistent with the experiences of this rural Virginia county. If some other plan is mandated, white children undoubtedly will be withdrawn from the public school system as has occurred in other parts of the country.

SUPREME COURT DECISION: 9–0

BRENNAN, J.

... The pattern of separate "white" and "Negro" schools in the New Kent County school system established under compulsion of state laws is precisely the pattern of segregation to which *Brown I* and *Brown II* were particularly addressed, and which *Brown I* declared unconstitutionally denied Negro school children equal protection of the laws. Racial identification of the system's schools was complete, extending not just to the composition of student bodies at the two schools but to every facet of school operations—faculty, staff, transportation, extracurricular activities, and facilities. [The Court subsequently refers to these as "*Green* factors."] In short, the State, acting through the local school board and school officials, organized and operated a dual system, part "white" and part "Negro."

It was such dual systems that 14 years ago *Brown I* held unconstitutional and a year later *Brown II* held must be abolished; school boards operating such school systems were required by *Brown II* "to effectuate a transition to a racially nondiscriminatory school system." It is of course true that for the time immediately after *Brown II* the concern was with making an initial break in a long-established pattern of excluding Negro children from schools attended by white children. The principal focus was on obtaining for those Negro children courageous enough to break with tradition a place in the "white" schools.... Under *Brown II* that immediate goal was only the first step, however. The transition to a unitary, nonracial system of public education was and is the ultimate end to be brought about; it was because of the 'complexities arising from the transition to a system of public educa-

tion freed of racial discrimination' that we provided for "all deliberate speed" in the implementation of the principles of *Brown I*. Thus we recognized the task would necessarily involve solution of "varied local school problems." In referring to the "personal interest of the plaintiffs in admission to public schools as soon as practicable on a nondiscriminatory basis," we also noted that "(t)o effectuate this interest may call for elimination of a variety of obstacles in making the transition...." Yet we emphasized that the constitutional rights of Negro children required school officials to bear the burden of establishing that additional time to carry out the ruling in an effective manner "is necessary in the public interest and is consistent with good faith compliance at the earliest practicable date."...

It is against this background that 13 years after *Brown II* commanded the abolition of dual systems we must measure the effectiveness of respondent School Board's "freedom-of-choice" plan to achieve that end. The School Board contends that it has fully discharged its obligation by adopting a plan by which every student, regardless of race, may "freely" choose the school he will attend. The Board attempts to cast the issue in its broadest form by arguing that its "freedom-of-choice" plan may be faulted only by reading the Fourteenth Amendment as universally requiring "compulsory integration," a reading it insists the wording of the Amendment will not support. But that argument ignores the thrust of *Brown II*. In the light of the command of that case, what is involved here is the question whether the Board has achieved the "racially nondiscriminatory school system" *Brown II* held must be effectuated in order to remedy the established unconstitutional deficiencies of its segregated system. In the context of the state-imposed segregated pattern of long standing, the fact that in 1965 the Board opened the doors of the former "white" school to Negro children and of the "Negro" school to white children merely begins, not ends, our inquiry whether the Board has taken steps adequate to abolish its dual, segregated system. *Brown II* was a call for the dismantling of well-entrenched dual systems tempered by an awareness that complex and multifaceted problems would arise which would require time and flexibility for a successful resolution. School boards such as the respondent then operating state-compelled dual systems were nevertheless clearly charged with the affirmative duty to take whatever steps might be necessary to convert to a unitary system in which racial discrimination would be eliminated root and branch.... The constitutional rights of Negro school children articulated in *Brown I* permit no less than this; and it was to this end that *Brown II* commanded school boards to bend their efforts.

In determining whether respondent School Board met that command by adopting its "freedom-of-choice" plan, it is relevant that this first step did not come until some 11 years after *Brown I* was decided and 10 years after *Brown II* directed the making of a "prompt and reasonable start." This deliberate perpetuation of the unconstitutional dual system can only have compounded the harm of such a system. Such delays are no longer tolerable, for "the governing constitutional principles no longer bear the imprint of newly enunciated doctrine." *Watson v. City of Memphis*, 373 U.S. 526 (1963).... Moreover, a plan that at this late date fails to provide meaningful assurance of prompt and effective disestablishment of a dual system is also intolerable. "The time for mere 'deliberate speed' has run out," *Griffin v. County School Board of Prince Edward County*, 377 U.S. 218 (1964).... The burden on a school board today is to come forward with a plan that promises realistically to work, and promises realistically to work now....

We do not hold that "freedom of choice" can have no place in such a plan. We do not hold that a "freedom-of-choice" plan might of itself be unconstitutional, although that argument has been urged upon us. Rather, all we decide today is that in desegregating a dual system a plan utilizing "freedom of choice" is not an end in itself....

The Board must be required to formulate a new plan and, in light of other courses which appear open to the Board, such as zoning, fashion steps which promise realistically to convert promptly to a system without a "white" school and a "Negro" school, but just schools....

COMMENT

Justice Brennan added the following footnote (footnote 6) to the first sentence of the Court's decision in *Green* (quoting *Bowman v. County School Board of Charles City County, Va.*, 382 F. 2d 326 (1967)):

> In view of the situation found in New Kent County, where there is no residential segregation, the elimination of the dual school system and the establishment of a "unitary, non-racial system" could be readily achieved with a minimum of administrative difficulty by means of geographic zoning—simply by assigning students living in the eastern half of the county to

the New Kent School and those living in the western half of the county to the Watkins School. Although a geographical formula is not universally appropriate, it is evident that here the Board, by separately *busing* Negro children across the entire county to the "Negro" school, and the white children to the "white" school, is deliberately maintaining a segregated system which would vanish with non-racial geographic zoning. The conditions in this county present a classical case for this expedient. (Emphasis added.)

QUESTIONS

1. Is *Green* better understood as a case about school desegregation or a statement of judicial impatience with persistent resistance to court-ordered school desegregation?

2. Attacking the New Kent County freedom-of-choice plan, counsel for Green argued:

   > All white pupils in New Kent County still attend the schools formerly maintained for their race; the overwhelming majority of Negroes still attend school only with other Negroes at [George W.] Watkins. Here, as in most of the other districts utilizing free choice, one-half of the dual system has been retained intact. Nothing but race can explain the continued existence of this all-Negro school and defer indefinitely its elimination, where all races are scattered throughout the county. Freedom of choice has been in this county, the instrument by which the State has used its resources and authority to maintain the momentum of racial segregation.

   What other factors besides *de jure* segregation might explain the persistence of dual school systems in areas like New Kent County? Is state-mandated desegregation the most effective antidote to state-mandated segregation?

3. A year after its decision in *Green*, and fifteen years after *Brown I*, the Court decided *Alexander v. Holmes County Board of Education*, 396 U.S. 19 (1969), which arose from the state of Mississippi. The Court's unanimous *per curiam* opinion in *Alexander* reads in its entirety:

   > This case comes to the Court on a petition for certiorari to the Court of Appeals for the Fifth Circuit. The petition was granted on October 9, 1969, and the case set down for early argument. The question presented is one of paramount importance, involving as it does the denial of fundamental rights to many thousands of school children, who are presently attending Mississippi schools under segregated conditions contrary to the applicable decisions of this Court. Against this background the Court of Appeals should have denied all motions for additional time because continued operation of segregated schools under a standard of allowing "all deliberate speed" for desegregation is no longer constitutionally permissible. Under explicit holdings of this Court the obligation of every school district is to terminate dual school systems at once and to operate now and hereafter only unitary schools. *Griffin v. County School Board*, 377 U.S. 218 (1964); *Green v. School Board of New Kent County, VA*. Accordingly,
   >   It is hereby adjudged, ordered, and decreed:

1. The Court of Appeals' order of August 28, 1969, is vacated, and the case is remanded to that court to issue its decree and order, effective immediately, declaring that each of the school districts here involved may no longer operate a dual school system based on race or color, and directing that they begin immediately to operate as unitary school systems within which no person is to be effectively excluded from any school because of race or color.

2. The Court of Appeals may in its discretion direct the schools here involved to accept all or any part of the August 11, 1969, recommendations of the Department of Health, Education, and Welfare, with any modifications which that court deems proper insofar as those recommendations insure a totally unitary school system for all eligible pupils without regard to race or color.

The Court of Appeals may make its determination and enter its order without further arguments or submissions.

3. While each of these school systems is being operated as a unitary system under the order of the Court of Appeals, the District Court may hear and consider objections thereto or proposed amendments thereof, provided, however, that the Court of Appeals' order shall be complied with in all respects while the District Court considers such objections or amendments, if any are made. No amendment shall become effective before being passed upon by the Court of Appeals.

4. The Court of Appeals shall retain jurisdiction to insure prompt and faithful compliance with its order, and may modify or amend the same as may be deemed necessary or desirable for the operation of a unitary school system.

5. The order of the Court of Appeals dated August 28, 1969, having been vacated and the case remanded for proceedings in conformity with this order, the judgment shall issue forthwith and the Court of Appeals is requested to give priority to the execution of this judgment as far as possible and necessary.

Alexander clearly reflects the Supreme Court's frustration over the slow pace of school desegregation. What message does *Alexander* send to lower federal courts regarding their enforcement responsibilities under *Brown II?*

EQUAL PROTECTION: JIM CROW AND SCHOOL DESEGREGATION

Swann v. Charlotte-Mecklenburg Board of Education
402 U.S. 1 (1971)

SETTING

The consolidated school district of Charlotte-Mecklenburg, North Carolina, the nation's forty-third largest, was one of the districts that adopted a freedom-of-choice approach in response to the *Brown* decisions. Virtually no desegregation occurred. In 1965, three years before the Court's decision in *Green v. School Board of New Kent County, VA*, Charlotte attorney Julius Chambers, who devoted part of his practice to assisting with cases for the NAACP Legal Defense Fund, persuaded ten black parents to file suit on behalf of their twenty-five children in the U.S. District Court for the Western District of North Carolina against the Charlotte-Mecklenburg school district. The suit asked the court to impose an affirmative duty on the school board to accomplish as much desegregation as possible. The lead plaintiff was James E. Swann, the six-year-old son of Vera and Darius Swann, who had been denied admission to a predominantly white public school near his home.

In response to the suit by the NAACP on behalf of Swann and the other plaintiffs, the federal district court approved a desegregation plan that basically retained freedom of choice, but also closed some of the all-black schools in the district. Three years later, however, approximately fourteen thousand of the school district's twenty-four thousand black students still were attending schools that were 99 percent black.

By 1968, the Supreme Court's patience with devices to prevent desegregation had worn thin. As seen in *Green*, a unanimous Court struck down the freedom-of-choice plan in the school district of New Kent County, Virginia, and instructed local school boards to "come forward with a plan that promises realistically to work … *now* … until it is clear that state-imposed segregation has been completely removed." The *Green* decision gave school boards an affirmative duty to eliminate public school segregation "root and branch."

Relying on *Green*, attorney Chambers took Swann and his coplaintiffs back to the U.S. District Court for the District of North Carolina. That court adopted findings of fact declaring that the school district's freedom-of-choice approach promoted rather than reduced segregation because no white child had chosen to attend any black school, that public school faculties as well as student bodies were segregated, and that the Charlotte-Mecklenburg school board had located and controlled the size and population of schools so as to maintain segregation. The district court ruled that transportation by bus was a legitimate tool for school boards to use to desegregate schools, and ordered the Charlotte-Mecklenburg school board to submit a new desegregation plan.

In 1969, in response to the district court's school busing rule, the North Carolina legislature passed an anti-busing statute. It stated that "No student shall be assigned or compelled to attend any school on account of race, creed, color or national origin, or for the purpose of creating a balance or ratio of race, religion or national origin." Seeking to strike a balance between the district court's order and the anti-busing policy of the legislature, the Charlotte-Mecklenburg school board submitted an interim desegregation plan to the district court. The law called for the busing of black students for the purpose of desegregating all-white schools but retained elements of freedom of choice and rejected the goal of desegregating all-black schools. The district court found the plan unacceptable and ordered the board to submit another plan. In November 1969, the board requested an extension of time, which the district court denied. The board then submitted a partially completed desegregation plan.

Relying on the Supreme Court's 1969 decision in *Alexander v. Holmes County Board of Education*, 396 U.S. 19 (see pp. 542–543), the district court declared the board's plan unsatisfactory. In December 1969, the district court took the controversial step of appointing Dr. John A. Finger Jr., an education professor at Rhode Island College, to draft a desegregation plan. Finger had testified as an expert witness on behalf of the Swann plaintiffs at the original trial. The court also invited the Charlotte-Mecklenburg board to submit yet another plan.

In February 1970, Finger and the Charlotte-Mecklenburg school board submitted separate pupil assignment plans to the district court. The board plan called for closing seven schools, reassigning their pupils, restructuring school attendance zones, substantially reassigning black students at the high school level, creating a single athletic league, eliminating the previously racial basis of the school bus system, creating racially mixed faculties, and modifying the free-transfer system into an optional majority-to-minority transfer system. The Finger plan adopted most of the board plan's proposals for junior high and high school students (although it required more busing at the high school level), but departed from that plan substantially in its proposal for handling the district's seventy-six elementary schools. Instead of relying on geographic zoning, the Finger plan grouped two or three outlying schools with one black inner city school and proposed transporting black students from grades one through four to the outlying white schools and students from grades five and six from the outlying white schools to the inner city black school.

Following review of the two plans, the district court adopted Finger's plan for elementary schools and the board's plan, as modified by Finger, for junior and senior high schools. The school board appealed to the U.S. Court of Appeals for the Fourth Circuit. That court affirmed the district court's order as to faculty desegregation and the junior and senior high school plans, but vacated the order concerning the elementary schools. It expressed fear that the pairing and grouping of elementary schools would place an unreasonable burden on the board and the district's pupils. It remanded the case to the district court for reconsideration and submission of additional plans. Swann petitioned the Supreme Court of the United States for a writ of certiorari. The Supreme Court granted the petition, temporarily reinstated the district court's order, and remanded the case to the district court for further proceedings.

On remand, the district court received two new plans for the elementary schools, one from the U.S. Department of Health, Education, and Welfare, and one from four members of the nine-member Charlotte-Mecklenburg School Board. Following a hearing, the district court found the original Finger plan of February 1970, the board's "minority plan" and a revised Finger plan acceptable. The court directed the school board to adopt one of the three or to come up with a plan of its own. Until then, the original Finger plan would remain in effect. In August 1970, the board "acquiesced" in the Finger plan and the district court ordered it to remain in effect. The Supreme Court then set the case for argument.

HIGHLIGHTS OF SUPREME COURT ARGUMENTS

BRIEF FOR SWANN

◆ The "complete relief" sought by the district court in the face of unlawful segregation in the Charlotte-Mecklenburg district is consistent with prior Supreme Court rulings, particularly *Green*, because it promises to dismantle the district's dual system and provide a unitary system of schools. The court of appeals, by contrast, would allow each court to decide whether the goal of complete desegregation was "reasonable" and whether it could be accomplished by "reasonable" means. The court of appeals' approach would produce less desegregation, at a slower pace, and would invite a variety of delaying tactics in the courts.

◆ The district court's approach is defensible on other grounds as well. It does not seek to impose racial balance in the schools. Under its order, schools in the district would range from 3 percent to 41 percent black. The busing element of the order is feasible in that it would only require busing an additional 5,000 students. The district already transports 23,600 students by bus and another 5,000 by common carrier each day.

AMICUS CURIAE BRIEFS SUPPORTING SWANN

National Education Association; United Negro College Fund; National Urban Coalition; League of Women Voters of the United States; League of Women Voters of North Carolina; League of Women Voters of Charlotte-Mecklenburg; Mississippi Educational Resources Center; Center for Law and Education of Harvard University; Washington Research Center for Studies in Public Policy.

BRIEF FOR CHARLOTTE-MECKLENBURG SCHOOL BOARD

◆ The Fourteenth Amendment does not guarantee children the right to attend schools having prescribed racial mixes. The primary problem with the district court's order is that it assumes such a right to be absolute and not to be diluted by reason of circumstances, costs, disruptions, or educational or administrative considerations.

◆ Prior Supreme Court decisions have guaranteed children the right to attend a school system within which discrimination originating from the old state-imposed duality has been eliminated. In this case, racial imbalance in the schools reflects residential patterns in the district, which have nothing to do with state policy. The desegregation plan submitted by the school board effectively establishes a unitary system.

◆ The busing requirements of the district court's order impinge on the constitutional rights of all children and destroys the concept of the neighborhood school. It is also costly and disruptive of quality educational services.

◆ The district court's order, aimed at achieving racial balance, is a harbinger of massive judicial approval of social theories, the validity of which are questionable. If the district court's school desegregation plan does not achieve its goals, it might be willing to issue orders regarding private residential housing or the issuing of building permits, areas in which judicial intrusion is totally inappropriate.

AMICUS CURIAE BRIEFS SUPPORTING CHARLOTTE-MECKLENBURG SCHOOL BOARD

William C. Cramer, member of Congress; Charles Bennett; Chattanooga, Tennessee, Board of Education; Florida Governor Claude R. Kirk Jr.; Concerned Citizens of Norfolk; Commonwealth of Virginia; State of Florida; School Board of Hillsborough County, Florida; Manatee Co., Florida, School Board; Winston-Salem/Forsyth County Board of Education.

AMICUS CURIAE BRIEF SUPPORTING NEITHER SIDE

Jackson, North Carolina, Chamber of Commerce, and Jackson Urban League.

SUPREME COURT DECISION: 9–0

BURGER, C.J.

... If school authorities fail in their affirmative obligations under [Brown I, Brown II and Green], judicial authority may be invoked. Once a right and a violation have been shown, the scope of a district court's equitable powers to remedy past wrongs is broad, for breadth and flexibility are inherent in equitable remedies....

In seeking to define even in broad and general terms how far this remedial power extends it is important to remember that judicial powers may be exercised only on the basis of a constitutional violation. Remedial judicial authority does not put judges automatically in the shoes of school authorities whose powers are plenary. Judicial authority enters only when local authority defaults....

We turn now to the problem of defining with more particularity the responsibilities of school authorities in desegregating a state-enforced dual school system in light of the Equal Protection Clause....

In ascertaining the existence of legally imposed school segregation, the existence of a pattern of school construction and abandonment is ... a factor of great weight. In devising remedies where legally imposed segregation has been established, it is the responsibility of local authorities and district courts to see to it that future school construction and abandonment are not used and do not serve to perpetuate or re-establish the dual system. When necessary, district courts should retain jurisdiction to assure that these responsibilities are carried out....

The central issue in this case is that of student assignment, and there are essentially four problem areas:...

(1) Racial Balances or Racial Quotas ... In this case, it is urged that the District Court has imposed a racial balance requirement of 71%–29% on individual schools....

The District Judge ... acknowledge[d] that variation "from the norm may be unavoidable." This contains intimations that the "norm" is a fixed mathematical racial balance reflecting the pupil constituency of the system. If we were to read the holding of the District Court to require, as a matter of substantive constitutional right, any particular degree of racial balance or mixing, that approach would be disapproved and we would be obliged to reverse. The constitutional command to desegregate schools does not mean that every school in every community must always reflect the racial composition of the school system as a whole.

As the voluminous record in this case shows, the predicate for the District Court's use of the 71%–29% ratio was twofold: first, its express finding ... that a dual school system had been maintained by the school authorities at least until 1969; second, its finding ... that the school board had totally defaulted in its acknowledged duty to come forward with an acceptable plan of its own, notwithstanding the patient efforts of the District Judge who, on at least three occasions, urged the board to submit plans. As the statement of facts shows, these findings are abundantly supported by the record. It was because of this total failure of the school board that the District Court was obliged to turn to other qualified sources....

We see therefore that the use made of mathematical ratios was no more than a starting point in the process of shaping a remedy, rather than an inflexible requirement....

(2) One-Race Schools The record in this case reveals the familiar phenomenon that in metropolitan areas minority groups are often found concentrated in one part of the city. In some circumstances certain schools may remain all or largely of one race until new schools can be provided or neighborhood patterns change. Schools all or predominantly of one race in a district of mixed population will require close scrutiny to determine that school assignments are not part of state-enforced segregation.

In light of the above, it should be clear that the existence of some small number of one-race, or virtually one-race, schools within a district is not in and of itself the mark of a system that still practices segregation by law.... Where the school authority's proposed plan for conversion from a dual to a unitary system contemplates the continued existence of some schools that are all or predominantly of one race, they have the burden of showing that such school assignments are genuinely nondiscriminatory. The court should scrutinize such schools, and the burden upon the school authorities will be to satisfy the court that their racial composition is not the result of present or past discriminatory action on their part....

(3) Remedial Altering of Attendance Zones The maps submitted in these cases graphically demonstrate that one of the principal tools employed by school planners and by courts to break up the dual school system has been a frank—and sometimes drastic—gerrymandering of school districts and attendance zones. An additional step was pairing, "clustering," or "grouping" of schools with attendance assignments made deliberately to accomplish the transfer of Negro students out of formerly segregated Negro schools and transfer of white students to formerly all-Negro schools. More often than not, these zones are neither compact nor contiguous; indeed they may be on opposite ends of the city. As an interim corrective measure,

this cannot be said to be beyond the broad remedial powers of a court.

We hold that the pairing and grouping of noncontiguous school zones is a permissible tool and such action is to be considered in light of the objectives sought....

(4) Transportation of Students The scope of permissible transportation of students as an implement of a remedial decree has never been defined by this Court and by the very nature of the problem it cannot be defined with precision. No rigid guidelines as to student transportation can be given for application to the infinite variety of problems presented in thousands of situations. Bus transportation has been an integral part of the public education system for years, and was perhaps the single most important factor in the transition from the one-room schoolhouse to the consolidated school....

[T]he remedial techniques used in the District Court's order were within that court's power to provide equitable relief; implementation of the decree is well within the capacity of the school authority....

An objection to transportation of students may have validity when the time or distance of travel is so great as to either risk the health of the children or significantly impinge on the educational process.... It hardly needs stating that the limits on time of travel will vary with many factors, but probably with none more than the age of the students. The reconciliation of competing values in a desegregation case is, of course, a difficult task with many sensitive facets but fundamentally no more so than remedial measures courts of equity have traditionally employed....

On the facts of this case, we are unable to conclude that the order of the District Court is not reasonable, feasible and workable. However, in seeking to define the scope of remedial power or the limits on remedial power of courts in an area as sensitive as we deal with here, words are poor instruments to convey the sense of basic fairness inherent in equity. Substance, not semantics, must govern, and we have sought to suggest the nature of limitations without frustrating the appropriate scope of equity.

At some point, these school authorities and others like them should have achieved full compliance with this Court's decision in *Brown I*. The systems would then be "unitary" in the sense required by our decisions....

Judgment of Court of Appeals affirmed in part; order of District Court affirmed.

QUESTIONS

1. During the 1968 presidential campaign, Richard M. Nixon spoke out against the "liberal activism" of the Warren Court. He promised to appoint what he termed "strict constructionists" to the Court, if elected. Acting on that pledge, President Nixon appointed Warren Burger chief justice in June 1969 and Harry Blackmun associate justice in June 1970. He also instructed his solicitor general, Erwin Griswold, to argue in *Swann* for a "go-slow" approach to desegregation and to oppose the district court's desegregation plan.

   Although the Supreme Court, including its two newest appointees, unanimously upheld busing, racial balance quotas, and gerrymandered school districts in the *Swann* decision, what language in the opinion prevented it from being either a complete victory for the NAACP or a complete defeat for the Nixon administration?

2. Employing busing to achieve racial balance in public school systems has been a volatile, divisive issue in the United States. Ironically, the *Green* Court, in footnote 6 to its opinion, specified busing as one of the means that New Kent County had employed to perpetuate segregated schools. (Recall that segregation laws had the effect of requiring Linda Brown to ride a bus to attend all-black Monroe School in Topeka, Kansas.) In the context of school desegregation, is it possible to disentangle race from attitudes toward busing?

3. *Swann* pertained only to official, *de jure*—legally mandated—segregated public school systems. *De facto*—actually existing—segregation in public schools is more extensive today than when *Swann* was decided in 1971. What policies might remedy racially segregated schools that result from demographic, housing, and/or employment patterns? Do public agencies have a constitutional duty to remedy *de facto* segregation?

4. Public opinion polls in the 1970s and 1980s showed that opposition to desegregation, and to the use of busing to achieve it, were important factors in many parents' decisions to enroll their children in private schools. To what extent, if any, should judges take such matters into account in determining appropriate remedial actions to desegregate public schools?

COMMENTS

1. Attorney Julius Chambers and Federal District Court Judge James B. McMillan paid a high personal price for their involvement in *Swann*. Chambers's law office was firebombed, and his house and car were dynamited. Judge McMillan was picketed, threatened, and hanged in effigy in retaliation for his busing order, and he was reportedly ostracized by the community in which he lived. Bernard Schwartz's case study of *Swann* provides additional insights into the case, particularly the chapter entitled "The Education of a Southern Judge" (*Swann's Way: The School Busing Case and the Supreme Court* [New York, NY: Oxford University Press, 1986]).

2. Since *Swann*, the Court has continued to rule on challenges to school district desegregation plans. Major cases, between 1971 and 1974 when *Milliken v. Bradley*, 418 U.S. 717 (the next case excerpted) was decided, include the following:

> **Case:** *Davis v. Board of School Commissioners of Mobile County*, 402 U.S. 33 (1971)
> **Vote:** 9–0
> **Decision:** Courts are required to consider the possible use of all available techniques to achieve the maximum amount of practicable

desegregation in school districts. A desegregation plan that treats the predominantly black eastern part of the Mobile, Alabama, school district in isolation from the rest of the school system does not adequately consider all alternatives.

Case: *McDaniel v. Barresi*, 402 U.S. 39 (1971)

Vote: 9–0

Decision: Title IV of the Civil Rights Act of 1964 does not prevent state officials from considering race in fixing school attendance lines in compliance with their duty to convert to a unitary school system. The Clarke County, Georgia, Board of Education student assignment plan for desegregating elementary schools properly allows students in heavily concentrated black "pockets" to walk or go by bus to schools in other attendance zones.

Case: *North Carolina State Board of Education v. Swann*, 402 U.S. 43 (1971)

Vote: 9–0

Decision: A North Carolina Anti-Busing Law, forbidding assignment of any student on account of race or for the purpose of creating a racial balance or ratio in the schools, and prohibiting busing, is invalid because it prevents implementation of desegregation plans required by the Fourteenth Amendment.

Case: *Keyes v. School District No. 1, Denver, Colorado*, 413 U.S. 189 (1973)

Vote: 8–1 (White, J., did not participate.)

Decision: When it is proved that a significant portion of a school system is segregated because school authorities have pursued an intentionally segregative policy, the presumption arises that segregation in other portions of the system is similarly the result of official action. The burden is on the district to rebut the presumption that actions regarding other segregated schools in the system are not likewise motivated by the intent to segregate. The district court therefore erred in finding that racial segregation of the Park Hill schools in Denver, Colorado, is attributable to official action but that segregation in central city schools is not the result of official action and that no remedy was required for the central city schools.

EQUAL PROTECTION: JIM CROW AND SCHOOL DESEGREGATION

Milliken v. Bradley
418 U.S. 717 (1974)

SETTING

Public school segregation in the United States has not been limited to the South. After World War II, suburban housing tracts sprang up all over the country. The "white flight" to the suburbs that began in the late 1950s left many cities with inner cities populated primarily by blacks, surrounded by suburban areas populated primarily by whites. The concentration of blacks in the cities resulted in the election of increased numbers of blacks to state and national office, and the election of black mayors in cities like Atlanta, Detroit, and Los Angeles, but did little to end school segregation. Many northern school districts remained segregated in fact (*de facto* segregation), even though not required to be segregated by law (*de jure* segregation). Detroit, Michigan, in the 1960s was an example of *de facto* segregation.

De jure segregation in Michigan was outlawed in 1869. A century later, almost half of the state's population of nine million lived in the tri-county area of Wayne, Oakland, and Macomb Counties. Detroit, the state's largest city, is located in Wayne County. Since 1842, the boundaries of the City of Detroit and the Detroit Board of Education have been coterminous.

In 1940, blacks accounted for 9.2 percent of the population of Detroit; many of them had been drawn to the area to work in the automobile industry. By 1970, blacks made up 43.9 percent of the city's population and black students made up 63.8 percent of the enrollment in the school district. In that year, the district operated 319 schools, of which 30 had no white students in attendance and 11 had no black children in attendance.

In April 1970, the Detroit School Board adopted a plan—known as the April 7 plan—to alter attendance areas for twelve of Detroit's twenty-one high schools in order to increase racial balance over a three-year period. The desegregation plan met with political hostility. Three months later, the Michigan legislature adopted Act 48, mandating freedom of choice and neighborhood school assignments. Section 12 of Act 48 explicitly delayed implementation of the Detroit April 7 plan. The four members of the Detroit School Board who supported the April 7 plan were removed from office in a recall election. The newly constituted school board then rescinded the April 7 plan.

In August 1970, the NAACP, on behalf of two black students in the Detroit School District—Ronald and Richard Bradley—filed a class action suit in the U.S. District Court for the Eastern District of Michigan naming Michigan Governor William G. Milliken and other state and local officials as defendants. The complaint alleged that the Detroit public school system was segregated on the basis of race as a result of the board's and state's actions and sought an injunction to restrain enforcement of Act 48.

The case was initially heard on Bradley's motion to enjoin enforcement of Act 48. The district court denied a preliminary injunction and dismissed Governor Milliken and the Michigan attorney general from the lawsuit. According to the district court, there was no proof that Detroit had a dual school system that was segregated on the basis of race.

On appeal, the U.S. Court of Appeals for the Sixth Circuit held that the district court had erred in dismissing the governor and the attorney general from the case, and that Section 12 of Act 48, which delayed implementation of the April 7 plan, was an unconstitutional interference with the Fourteenth

Amendment. The court of appeals remanded the case to the district court for an expedited trial on the merits.

On remand, Bradley moved for immediate implementation of the April 7 plan. In reply, the Detroit School Board proposed two other plans. The district court ordered implementation of one of those proposals, a so-called "Magnet Plan" designed to "attract children to a school because of its superior curriculum." On appeal from that order, the Sixth Circuit held that the district court had not abused its discretion in refusing to adopt the April 7 plan without an evidentiary hearing, but refused to rule on the merits of the Magnet Plan. Instead, it remanded the case with instructions to proceed immediately to trial on the question of whether the Detroit public school system was racially segregated as a result of unconstitutional practices on the part of the Detroit Board of Education and the state of Michigan.

On September 27, 1971, after a forty-one-day trial, the district court found:

> [g]overnmental actions and inaction at all levels, federal, state and local, have combined, with those of private organizations, such as loaning institutions and real estate associations and brokerage firms, to establish and to maintain the pattern of residential segregation throughout the Detroit metropolitan area.

The district court found that the Detroit Board of Education had created and maintained optional attendance zones that had the "natural, probable, foreseeable and actual effect" of allowing white students to escape attending identifiably black schools. The court also found that the board had drawn school attendance lines in a way that significantly contributed to segregation of the races. Additionally, the court found that in the operation of its school transportation program, which was designed to alleviate overcrowding, the board had bused black students to predominantly black schools, regardless of proximity or availability of space. The effect of such acts, the court concluded, was the creation and perpetuation of school segregation within Detroit.

The district court also made findings regarding the state of Michigan. Until 1971, it found, the Michigan legislature had failed to provide funds for the transportation of students within Detroit to facilitate desegregation, although it had provided many neighboring—mostly white—suburban school districts a full range of state-supported transportation. The district court also found that the state, through Act 48, had acted to "impede, delay and minimize racial integration in Detroit schools" and that the acts of the Detroit Board of Education, as a subordinate entity of the state, were attributable to the state.

Based on those findings, the district court concluded that the Detroit public school system was racially segregated as a result of unconstitutional practices by the Detroit School Board and the state of Michigan. It ordered the board to submit desegregation plans limited to the district and ordered the state to submit desegregation plans encompassing the three-county metropolitan area. The Sixth Circuit Court of Appeals subsequently declared those orders not appealable because they were not final.

On March 24, 1972, after further proceedings on the Detroit and state proposals, the district court declared that "relief of segregation in the public schools of the City of Detroit cannot be accomplished within the corporate geographic limits of the city." The court concluded that it "must look beyond the limits of the Detroit school district for a solution to the problem" because "[s]chool district lines are simply matters of political convenience and may not be used to deny constitutional rights." On June 14, 1972, the district court established tentative boundaries for a metropolitan remedy to Detroit's school segregation and created a nine-member panel to design plans to integrate Detroit's schools and those of fifty-three of the eighty-five suburban schools within those boundaries. On July 11, 1972, in accordance with a recommendation of the panel, the district court ordered the state defendants to purchase "at least" 295 school buses for the purpose of providing transportation under an interim plan to be developed for the 1972–1973 school year.

A divided Sixth Circuit Court of Appeals held that the record supported the district court's findings and conclusions on the constitutional violations committed by the Detroit School Board and by the state of Michigan. The court agreed with the district court that "any less comprehensive a solution than a metropolitan area plan would result in an all black school system immediately surrounded by practically all white suburban school systems, with an overwhelmingly white majority population in the total metropolitan area." Accordingly, the court of appeals concluded, "the only feasible desegregation plan involves the crossing of boundary lines between the Detroit School District and adjacent or nearby school districts for the limited purpose of providing an effective desegregation plan." It held that any suburban school district that might be affected by a metropolitan-wide remedy should be made a party to the case and should be given an opportunity to be heard with respect to the scope and implementation of such a remedy. However, the court of appeals vacated the district court's order directing the acquisition of school buses.

The Supreme Court of the United States granted Milliken's petition for certiorari, which focused primarily on the propriety of the multidistrict remedy to the Detroit segregation problem. The case was consolidated with two related cases from Michigan.

HIGHLIGHTS OF SUPREME COURT ARGUMENTS

BRIEF FOR MILLIKEN AND DETROIT SCHOOL BOARD

◆ The finding that the state committed acts resulting in *de jure* segregation of students, both within the Detroit school district and other school districts in the tri-county area, is not supported by the record. The Detroit school system is not racially imbalanced because of any purposeful act of segregation by the state or the Detroit School Board.

◆ Even if the Detroit school system is a dual system, a Detroit-only remedy would establish the unitary system required by *Green* and *Swann*.

◆ The courts below identified no constitutional violations to serve as a predicate for multidistrict relief. The Constitution does not require racial balance among school districts over a three-county area. The Court should respect the integrity of local political subdivisions.

◆ The lower courts have denied fundamental due process to the school districts other than Detroit that are affected by the desegregation orders.

AMICUS CURIAE BRIEFS SUPPORTING MILLIKEN

United States; State of Indiana.

BRIEF FOR BRADLEY

◆ The record supports the lower courts' findings that for approximately two decades Michigan and Detroit had deliberately segregated black children from white children in Detroit's public schools.

◆ The state, functioning as the common mentor of all systems in the Detroit area, was deeply involved in the segregation practices that affected suburban schools as well as Detroit schools. The only effective remedy is multidistrict in nature.

◆ Suburban school districts have been ordered to do nothing substantial. Their claims of procedural deprivations are prospective only and should be rejected.

AMICUS CURIAE BRIEF SUPPORTING BRADLEY

National Education Association.

SUPREME COURT DECISION: 5–4

BURGER, C.J.

... It is obvious from the scope of the interdistrict remedy ... that absent a complete restructuring of the laws of Michigan relating to school districts the District Court will become first, a de facto "legislative authority" to resolve these complex questions, and then the "school superintendent" for the entire area. This is a task which few, if any, judges are qualified to perform and one which would deprive the people of control of schools through their elected representatives.

Of course, no state law is above the Constitution. School district lines and the present laws with respect to local control, are not sacrosanct and if they conflict with the Fourteenth Amendment federal courts have a duty to prescribe appropriate remedies.... [O]ur prior holdings have been confined to violations and remedies within a single school district. We therefore turn to address, for the first time, the validity of a remedy mandating cross-district or interdistrict consolidation to remedy a condition of segregation found to exist in only one district. The controlling principle consistently expounded in our holdings is that the scope of the remedy is determined by the nature and extent of the constitutional violation. *Swann.* Before the boundaries of separate and autonomous school districts may be set aside by consolidating the separate units for remedial purposes or by imposing a cross-district remedy, it must first be shown that there has been a constitutional violation within one district that produces a significant segregative effect in another district. Specifically, it must be shown that racially discriminatory acts of the state or local school districts, or of a single school district have been a substantial cause of interdistrict segregation. Thus an interdistrict remedy might be in order where the racially discriminatory acts of one or more school districts caused racial segregation in an adjacent district, or where district lines have been deliberately drawn on the basis of race. In such circumstances an interdistrict remedy would be appropriate to eliminate the interdistrict segregation directly caused by the constitutional violation. Conversely, without an interdistrict violation and interdistrict effect, there is no constitutional wrong calling for an interdistrict remedy.

The record before us, voluminous as it is, contains evidence of *de jure* segregated conditions only in the Detroit schools; indeed, that was the theory on which the litigation was initially based and on which the District Court took evidence. With no showing of significant violation by the 53 outlying school districts and no evidence of any interdistrict violation or effect, the court went beyond the original theory of the case as framed by the pleadings and mandated a metropolitan area remedy. To approve the remedy ordered by the court would impose on the outlying districts, not shown to have committed any constitutional violation, a wholly impermissible remedy based on a standard not hinted at in *Brown I* and *II* or any holding of this Court....

[T]here has been no showing that either the State or any of the 85 outlying districts engaged in activity that had a cross-district effect. The boundaries of the Detroit School District, which are coterminous with the boundaries of the city of Detroit, were established over a century ago by neutral legislation when the city was incorporated; there is no evidence in the record, nor is there any suggestion by the respondents, that either the original boundaries of the Detroit School District, or any other school district in Michigan, were established for the purpose of creating, maintaining, or perpetuating segregation of races. There is no claim and there is no evidence hinting that petitioner outlying schools districts and their predecessors, or the 30-odd other school districts in the tricounty area—but outside the District Court's "desegregation area"—have ever maintained or operated anything but unitary school systems. Unitary school systems have been required for more than a century by the Michigan Constitution as implemented by state law. While the schools of only one district have been affected, there is no constitutional power in the courts to decree relief balancing the racial composition of that district's schools with those of the surrounding districts....

We conclude that the relief ordered by the District Court and affirmed by the Court of Appeals was based upon an erroneous standard and was unsupported by record evidence that acts of the outlying districts effected the discrimination found to exist in the schools of Detroit. Accordingly, the judgment of the Court of Appeals is reversed and the case is remanded for further proceedings consistent with this opinion leading to prompt formulation of a decree directed to eliminating the segregation found to exist in

Detroit city schools, a remedy which has been delayed since 1970.

Reversed and remanded.

STEWART, J., CONCURRING

... In reversing the decision of the Court of Appeals this Court is in no way turning its back on the proscription of state-imposed segregation first voiced in *Brown v. Board of Education* or on the delineation of remedial powers and duties most recently expressed in *Swann v. Charlotte-Mecklenburg Board of Education.* In *Swann* the Court addressed itself to the range of equitable remedies available to the courts to effectuate the desegregation mandated by *Brown* and its progeny, noting that the task in choosing appropriate relief is "to correct ... the condition that offends the Constitution," and that "the nature of the violation determines the scope of the remedy...."

By approving a remedy that would reach beyond the limits of the city of Detroit to correct a constitutional violation found to have occurred solely within that city the Court of Appeals thus went beyond the governing equitable principles established in this Court's decisions.

DOUGLAS, J., DISSENTING

... When we rule against the metropolitan area remedy we take a step that will likely put the problems of the blacks and our society back to the period that antedated the "separate but equal" regime of *Plessy v. Ferguson.* The reason is simple.

The inner core of Detroit is now rather solidly black; and the blacks, we know, in many instances are likely to be poorer, just as were the Chicanos in *San Antonio School District v. Rodriguez,* 411 U.S. 1 [(1973)]. By that decision the poorer school districts must pay their own way. It is therefore a foregone conclusion that

we have now given the States a formula whereby the poor must pay their own way.

Today's decision, given *Rodriguez,* means that there is no violation of the Equal Protection Clause though the schools are segregated by race and though the black schools are not only "separate" but "inferior."

WHITE, DOUGLAS, BRENNAN, AND MARSHALL, J.J., DISSENTING

... I am surprised that the Court, sitting at this distance from the State of Michigan, claims better insight than the Court of Appeals and the District Court as to whether an interdistrict remedy for equal protection violations practiced by the State of Michigan would involve undue difficulties for the State in the management of its public schools. In the area of what constitutes an acceptable desegregation plan, "we must of necessity rely to a large extent, as this Court has for more than 16 years, on the informed judgment of the district courts in the first instance and on courts of appeals." *Swann v. Charlotte-Mecklenburg Board of Education.* Obviously, whatever difficulties there might be, they are surmountable; for the Court itself concedes that, had there been sufficient evidence of an interdistrict violation, the District Court could have fashioned a single remedy for the districts implicated rather than a different remedy for each district in which the violation had occurred or had an impact.

I am even more mystified as to how the Court can ignore the legal reality that the constitutional violations, even if occurring locally, were committed by governmental entities for which the State is responsible and that it is the State that must respond to the command of the Fourteenth Amendment. An interdistrict remedy for the infringements that occurred in this case is well within the confines and powers of the State, which is the governmental entity ultimately responsible for desegregating its schools....

Until today, the permissible contours of the equitable authority of the district courts to remedy the unlawful establishment of a dual school system have been extensive, adaptable, and fully responsive to the ultimate goal of achieving "the greatest possible degree of actual desegregation." There are indeed limitations on the equity powers of the federal judiciary, but until now the Court had not accepted the proposition that effective enforcement of the Fourteenth Amendment could be limited by political or administrative boundary lines demarcated by the very State responsible for the constitutional violation and for the disestablishment of the dual system. Until now the Court has instead looked to practical considerations in effectuating a desegregation decree, such as excessive distance, transportation time, and hazards to the safety of the schoolchildren involved in a proposed plan....

MARSHALL, DOUGLAS, BRENNAN, WHITE, J.J., DISSENTING

... [T]he Court today takes a giant step backwards. Notwithstanding a record showing widespread and pervasive racial segregation in the educational system

provided by the State of Michigan for children in Detroit, this Court holds that the District Court was powerless to require the State to remedy its constitutional violation in any meaningful fashion....

We recognized in *Brown II*, and have re-emphasized ever since, that in fashioning relief in desegregation cases, "the courts will be guided by equitable principles. Traditionally, equity has been characterized by a practical flexibility in shaping its remedies and by a facility for adjusting and reconciling public and private needs."...

Desegregation is not and was never expected to be an easy task. Racial attitudes ingrained in our Nation's childhood and adolescence are not quickly thrown aside in its middle years. But just as the inconvenience of some cannot be allowed to stand in the way of the rights of others, so public opposition, no matter how strident, cannot be permitted to divert this Court from the enforcement of the constitutional principles at issue in this case. Today's holding, I fear, is more a reflection of a perceived public mood that we have gone far enough in enforcing the Constitution's guarantee of equal justice than it is the product of neutral principles of law. In the short run, it may seem to be the easier course to allow our great metropolitan areas to be divided up each into two cities—one white, the other black— but it is a course, I predict, our people will ultimately regret. I dissent.

QUESTIONS

1. State the rule of *Milliken v. Bradley*. Is it accurate to characterize the case as holding that when there are no findings of interdistrict violations of the Fourteenth Amendment, no interdistrict remedies are permitted? Does it follow that if segregation does not affect an entire school district a district-wide remedial plan would be inappropriate?

2. *Milliken v. Bradley* marks the first defeat for the NAACP before the

Supreme Court since the beginning of its efforts to desegregate the schools in the 1930s. What factors account for its loss in *Milliken*?

3. In *Milliken*, the policy options were framed as *either* achieving school desegregation *or* protecting local school districts. The former option would have dissolved school district boundary lines. The latter option left public schools in central Detroit predominantly black. What other less dichotomous remedies might have been available? Are courts institutionally suited to fashion such remedies? Are political bodies willing to do so?

COMMENTS

1. In addition to reversing the multidistrict remedy ordered by the lower courts in *Milliken v. Bradley*, the Supreme Court remanded the case to the U.S. District Court for the Eastern District of Michigan to fashion a Detroit-only remedy. In the meantime, the trial judge who had previously presided over the litigation died. On remand, neither the Detroit School Board nor the State of Michigan challenged the factual findings regarding *de jure* segregation in the school district. After extensive hearings, the district court entered an order requiring the board to reassign students to various schools in the district and established guidelines with respect to four educational components—reading, teacher in-service training, testing, and counseling and career guidance. The court ordered the State of Michigan to pay half the cost of implementing the district's remedial programs. In *Milliken v. Bradley* (*Milliken II*), 433 U.S. 267 (1977), the Court, by a unanimous vote, upheld the remedial programs as within a district court's discretion to order as part of a desegregation decree.

2. Between *Milliken I* and *Missouri v. Jenkins*, 495 U.S. 33 (1990), the next case excerpted, the Court continued to grapple with issues of school desegregation and legitimate remedies. The cases summarized below demonstrate the major controversies.

> **Case:** *Pasadena City Board of Education v. Spangler*, 427 U.S. 424 (1976)
>
> **Vote:** 6–2 (Stevens, J., did not participate.)
>
> **Decision:** Once a unitary system has been established, school boards are not required to make annual adjustments in order to maintain a certain racial balance, even though residential patterns and other factors result in changed racial compositions in the schools.

> **Case:** *Columbus Board of Education v. Penick*, 443 U.S. 449 (1979)
>
> **Vote:** 7–2
>
> **Decision:** School board decisions resulting in the purposeful and effective maintenance of a body of separate black schools in a substantial part of a school system are *prima facie* evidence of a dual

system. A system-wide desegregation plan for schools in Columbus, Ohio, is the proper remedy for an enclave of separate, black schools on the near east side of Columbus.

Case: *Washington v. Seattle School District No. 1*, 458 U.S. 457 (1982)

Vote: 5–4

Decision: A Washington state initiative that precludes school boards from requiring students to attend other than neighborhood schools violates the Equal Protection Clause of the Fourteenth Amendment. The initiative uses the racial nature of school busing to define the governmental decisionmaking structure and thereby imposes substantial and unique burdens on racial minorities.

Case: *Crawford v. Los Angeles Board of Education*, 458 U.S. 527 (1982)

Vote: 8–1

Decision: An amendment to the California constitution providing that state courts shall not order mandatory pupil assignment or transportation unless a federal court would be permitted to do so, does not violate the Fourteenth Amendment because it does not embody a racial classification. The Court's decisions do not support the proposition that once a state chooses to do more than is required by the Fourteenth Amendment, it may never do less.

Case: *Board of Education v. Dowell*, 498 U.S. 237 (1991)

Vote: 5–3 (Souter, J., did not participate.)

Decision: Supervision of local school systems was always intended as a temporary measure to remedy past discrimination. Dissolving a desegregation decree after local authorities have operated in compliance with it for a reasonable period of time, despite claims that desegregation has not been achieved, properly recognizes the important values of local control of public school systems. Federal district courts are responsible for determining whether a school board has complied in good faith with a desegregation decree and whether the vestiges of past discrimination have been eliminated to the extent practicable.

EQUAL PROTECTION: JIM CROW AND SCHOOL DESEGREGATION

Missouri v. Jenkins
495 U.S. 33 (1990)

Setting

In *Milliken v. Bradley*, the Court announced a three-part standard for reviewing federal district court remedial orders in desegregation cases. First, the remedy must be related to the condition that is alleged to offend the Constitution. Second, the decree "must indeed be remedial in nature," that is, be designed to restore the victims of discrimination to the position they would have been in if there had been no discrimination. Third, the remedy must take into account the interests of state and local authorities in managing their own affairs. Thirteen years after *Milliken*, the Court added the requirement that appellate courts should be very deferential when reviewing district courts' remedial orders: "[T]he choice of remedies to redress racial discrimination is 'a balancing process left, within appropriate constitutional or statutory limits, to the sound discretion of the trial court.'" *United States v. Paradise*, 480 U.S. 149 (1987). Just how deferential the Supreme Court should be in reviewing remedial orders became a central issue in *Missouri v. Jenkins*.

Before 1954, it is undisputed that the state of Missouri had legally mandated segregated schools for black and white children (*de jure* segregation). In response to *Brown II*, the Kansas City, Missouri School District (KCMSD) adopted a neighborhood school plan that eliminated separate racial zones and drew attendance lines around each school based on the capacity of the building, distances from the building, and factors such as safety, transportation, and terrain. The neighborhood school concept did not substantially change the district's segregated school system. Black schools remained black and white enrollment in the district decreased. Attendance zone changes made by the district throughout the 1960s and early 1970s failed to achieve districtwide integration.

In 1977, the KCMSD and certain students filed suit against the State of Missouri in the U.S. District Court for the Western District of Missouri seeking reassignment of students across district and state lines in order to eliminate interdistrict segregation. The district court realigned the parties, making the KCMSD a defendant. Students, including Kalima Jenkins, then filed an amended complaint that alleged segregation violations within the KCMSD. The KCMSD filed a cross-claim against the state of Missouri, reiterating the claims of interdistrict violations and seeking indemnification against any liability it might face as a defendant.

Following ninety-two days of trial, the district court found that the KCMSD and the state had operated a segregated school system within the KCMSD. However, the court rejected the plaintiffs' request for interdistrict relief. Instead, it ordered the KCMSD and the state to develop a remedial plan to "establish a unitary school system within the KCMSD."

Both the KCMSD and the state submitted remedial proposals. Following a two-week hearing, the district court accepted most of the recommendations of the KCMSD. In June 1985, it issued a remedial order that included the hiring of an additional 125 librarians, specialty teachers, teachers' aides, and counselors; required the KCMSD to acquire additional library materials; required the KCMSD to employ 193 more classroom teachers to lower pupil-teacher ratios; ordered it to provide cash grants to all schools in the district to improve achievement; and ordered the KCMSD to initiate or expand summer school, all-day kindergarten, and before-and-after school programs. The court also ordered the KCMSD to undertake an initial capital improvements program, acknowledging that the condition of the facilities was not due to segregation, but noting that many of the KCMSD's sixty-eight schools were so deteriorated that they presented health and safety hazards and undermined the goal of achieving desegregation.

When it received the district court's order, the KCMSD established a three-year budget of $87.7 million to implement the changes. The court then ordered the State of Missouri to pay all of the costs of several of the programmatic remedial measures and half of the costs of the other measures. The court also ordered the state to pay $27 million toward the $37 million capital improvements program. The court then acknowledged that the KCMSD was unable to finance its share of the remedy ordered. Reasoning that school desegregation requires courts to look beyond legal principles, however, the court ordered a tax increase to finance the desegregation plan.

The effect of the order regarding the tax increase was to enjoin enforcement of a Missouri statute aimed at "rolling back" property tax rates. On appeal, the Eighth Circuit affirmed most of the district court's remedial order, adjusting only the district court's unequal allocation of costs between the state and the KCMSD by ordering the district court to divide the cost of the desegregation order equally between the state and the KCMSD. The Supreme Court denied the state's petition for a writ of certiorari on the question of the allocation of costs between it and the school district.

The district court subsequently issued another remedial order at the request of the KCMSD, ordering it to increase its budget for the second year of the desegregation remedy by $29.4 million. The state was ordered to fund the full cost of the newly-ordered capital improvements and the majority of the increase in program costs. Responsibility for the costs of the other components was divided equally between the district and the state. The court ordered yet a third remedial plan regarding the KCMSD in 1986: a six-year magnet school plan with a price tag of $53 million. The court held the state and the KCMSD jointly and severally liable for the additional $53 million. The court's purpose for doing so was to give the Missouri legislature an incentive to "explore the possibility of enacting legislation that would permit a district involved in a desegregation plan more versatility than it presently has to raise funds with which to support the program."

In 1987, the district court issued yet another remedial order, this one carrying a $37 million price tag and raising the desegregation budget for the 1987–88 school year to $56.8 million. Again, the court held the state and the KCMSD jointly and severally liable, but the state was ordered to contribute 75 percent of the funds and the district 25 percent. The court's rationale for making the state liable for most of the desegregation cost was that "the person who starts the fire has more responsibility for the damages caused than the person who fails to put it out." A few months later, the court ordered an additional $187 million in capital improvements within the district.

Despite its comparatively small financial liability under the 1987 orders, the KCMSD reported a projected budgetary deficit in the millions of dollars.

The district court, declaring that it had "no choice but to exercise its broad equitable powers and enter a judgment that will enable the KCMSD to raise its share of the cost of the plan," and believing that the Supreme Court had previously authorized district courts to impose tax increases to remedy racial discrimination in the schools, ordered the KCMSD to raise property taxes from $2.05 to $4 per $100 of assessed valuation through the 1991–1992 fiscal year. It also ordered the district to issue bonds in the amount of $150 million to meet the capital improvement requirements and ordered local officials to apply a 1.5 percent income-tax surcharge to income generated in the KCMSD. The court specified that the revenues from the new taxes were to be used "not only to eliminate the effects of unlawful segregation but also to insure that there is no diminution in the quality of [the district's] regular academic program."

The Court of Appeals for the Eighth Circuit affirmed both the remedial measures ordered by the district court and the increases in the property tax rates, but it reversed the imposition of the income tax surcharge. With respect to the property tax increases, the appeals court reasoned that federal courts would be reduced to "judicial impotence" if they did not have full powers to implement remedies for violations of constitutional rights. One judge dissented, contending that the State of Missouri should be required to pay for any amount that the KCMSD was unable to pay in order to implement the district court's orders. The Supreme Court of the United States granted the State of Missouri's petition for a writ of certiorari.

HIGHLIGHTS OF SUPREME COURT ARGUMENTS

BRIEF FOR MISSOURI

◆ There is no basis in Article III of the Constitution for declaring that federal courts may order higher state taxes, even to fund a remedy for a constitutional violation. Judicial power encompasses no influence over either the sword or the purse.

◆ Exercise of a judicial taxing power conflicts with powers reserved to the states under the Tenth Amendment. The power to determine appropriate levels of state taxation is an essential element of state sovereignty. The fact that it is remedying a constitutional violation does not give a federal court unbridled power to displace other departments of government, whether state or federal.

◆ It is an astonishing proposition that the powers conferred on the judicial branch under Article III necessarily gave the federal courts a part of the states' sovereign powers over taxation.

AMICUS CURIAE BRIEFS SUPPORTING MISSOURI

Jackson County, Missouri; joint brief of individual and corporate taxpayers who own property in the KCMSD; joint brief of National Governors' Association, National Leagues of Cities, National Conference of State Legislatures, National Association of Counties, Council of State Governments,

U.S. Conference of Mayors, and International City Management Association; State of New Mexico.

BRIEF FOR JENKINS, ET AL.

◆ For decades, Missouri and the KCMSD violated the Constitution through segregation and by failing to eliminate segregation. The only question before this Court is whether constitutional wrongdoers will be compelled to fund the remedies for their misdeeds or whether they will be allowed to shield the consequences of their acts with states' rights theories that are incompatible with principles of federal supremacy.

◆ The national government is obliged to grant appropriate consideration to legitimate state interests and their significant role in the federal structure. Ultimately, however, federal constitutional rights are supreme to the extent that they are incapable of reconciliation with local concerns.

◆ The Tenth Amendment confines no discrete policy areas to the states, absolutely shielding them from national influence under all circumstances at all times.

◆ The problem of school segregation demands a remedy that achieves a constitutional end even if it requires adjusting state interests to accomplish its purpose. Courts are not foreclosed from tailoring remedies that extend into areas otherwise left to the states if necessary to achieve constitutional ends.

AMICUS CURIAE BRIEF SUPPORTING JENKINS, ET AL.

Lawyers' Committee for Civil Rights Under Law.

SUPREME COURT DECISION: 9–0

WHITE, J.

... We granted certiorari to consider the State of Missouri's argument that the District Court lacked the power to raise local property taxes. For the reasons given below, we hold that the District Court abused its discretion in imposing the tax increase. We also hold, however, that the modifications of the District Court's order made by the Court of Appeals do satisfy equitable and constitutional principles governing the District Court's power....

It is accepted by all the parties, as it was by the courts below, that the imposition of a tax increase by a federal court was an extraordinary event. In assuming for itself the fundamental and delicate power of taxation the District Court not only intruded

on local authority but circumvented it altogether. Before taking such a drastic step the District Court was obliged to assure itself that no permissible alternative would have accomplished the required task. We have emphasized that although the "remedial powers of an equity court must be adequate to the task, ... they are not unlimited," *Whitcomb v. Chavis*, 403 U.S. 124 (1971), and one of the most important considerations governing the exercise of equitable power is a proper respect for the integrity and function of local government institutions. Especially is this true where, as here, those institutions are ready, willing, and—but for the operation of state law curtailing their powers—able to remedy the deprivation of constitutional rights themselves.

The District Court believed that it had no alternative to imposing a tax increase. But there was an alternative: ... [I]t could have authorized or required KCMSD to levy property taxes at a rate adequate to fund the desegregation remedy and could have enjoined the operation of state laws that would have prevented KCMSD from exercising this power. The difference between the two approaches is far more than a matter of form. Authorizing and directing local government institutions to devise and implement remedies not only protects the function of those institutions but, to the extent possible, also places the responsibility for solutions to the problems of segregation upon those who have themselves created the problems....

We stand on different ground when we review the modifications to the District Court's order made by the Court of Appeals.... [T]he Court of Appeals held that the District Court in the future should authorize KCMSD to submit a levy to the state tax collection authorities adequate to fund its budget and should enjoin the operation of state laws that would limit or reduce the levy below that amount.... Under the circumstances of this case, we cannot say it was an abuse of discretion for the district Court to rule that KCMSD should be responsible for funding its share of the remedy....

We turn to the constitutional issues. The modifications ordered by the Court of Appeals cannot be assailed as invalid under the Tenth Amendment. "The Tenth Amendment's reservation of nondelegated powers to the States is not implicated by a federal-court judgment enforcing the express prohibitions of unlawful state conduct enacted by the Fourteenth Amendment." *Milliken v. Bradley*....

Finally, the State argues that an order to increase taxes cannot be sustained under the judicial power of Article III. Whatever the merits of this argument when applied to the District Court's own order increasing taxes, a point we have not reached, a court order directing a local government body to levy its own taxes is plainly a judicial act within the power of a federal court. We held as much in *Griffin v. Prince Edward County School Bd.*, 377 U.S. 218 (1964), where we stated that a District Court, faced with a county's attempt to avoid desegregation of the public schools by refusing to operate those schools, could "require the [County] Supervisors to exercise the power that is theirs to levy taxes to raise funds adequate to reopen, operate, and maintain without racial discrimination a public school system...." *Griffin* followed a long and venerable line of cases in which this Court held that federal courts could issue the writ of mandamus to compel local governmental bodies to levy taxes adequate to satisfy their debt obligations.

The State maintains, however, that even under these cases, the federal judicial power can go no further than to require local governments to levy taxes as authorized under state law. In other words, the State argues that federal courts cannot set aside state-imposed limitations on local taxing authority because to do so is to do more than to require the local government "to exercise the power that is theirs." We disagree. This argument was rejected as early as [1867].... It is ... clear that a local government with taxing authority may be ordered to levy taxes in excess of the limit set by state statute where there is reason based in the Constitution for not observing the statutory limitation.... [T]he KCMSD may be ordered to levy taxes despite the statutory limitations on its authority in order to compel the discharge of an obligation imposed on KCMSD by the Fourteenth Amendment. To hold otherwise would fail to take account of the obligations of local governments, under the Supremacy Clause, to fulfill the requirements that the Constitution imposes on them. However wide the discretion of local authorities in fashioning desegregation remedies may be, "if a state-imposed limitation on a school authority's discretion operates to inhibit or obstruct the operation of a unitary school system or impede the disestablishing of a dual school system, it must fall; state policy must give way when it operates to hinder vindication of federal constitutional guarantees." *North Carolina Bd. of Education v. Swann*, 402 U.S. 43 (1971). Even though a particular remedy may not be required in every case to vindicate constitutional guarantees, where (as here) it has been found that a particular remedy is required, the State cannot hinder the process by preventing a local government from implementing that remedy.

Accordingly, the judgment of the Court of Appeals is affirmed insofar as it required the District Court to modify its funding order and reversed insofar as it allowed the tax increase imposed by the District Court to stand. The case is remanded for further proceedings consistent with this opinion.

It is so ordered.

KENNEDY, O'CONNOR, AND SCALIA, J.J., AND REHNQUIST, C.J., CONCURRING IN PART AND CONCURRING IN THE JUDGMENT

... Today's casual embrace of taxation imposed by the unelected, life-tenured Federal Judiciary disregards fundamental precepts for the democratic control of public institutions. I cannot acquiesce in the majority's statements on this point, and should there arise an actual dispute over the collection of taxes as here contemplated in a case that is not, like this one, premature, we should not confirm the outcome of premises adopted with so little constitutional justification. The Court's statements, in my view, cannot be seen as necessary for its judgment, or as precedent for the future....

The judicial taxation approved by the Eighth Circuit is also without parallel.... I agree with the Court that the Eighth Circuit's judgment affirming the District Court's direct levy of a property tax must be reversed. I cannot agree, however, that we "stand on different ground when we review the modifications to the District Court's order made by the Court of Appeals."...

Article III of the Constitution states that "[t]he judicial Power of the United States, shall be vested in one supreme Court, and in such inferior Courts as the Congress may from time to time ordain and establish." The description of the judicial power nowhere includes the word "tax" or anything that resembles it. This reflects the Framers' understanding that taxation was not a proper area for judicial involvement.... Our cases throughout the years leave no doubt that taxation is not a judicial function....

A judicial taxation order is but an attempt to exercise a power that always has been thought legislative in nature....

The confinement of taxation to the legislative branches, both in our Federal and State Governments, was not random. It reflected our ideal that the power of taxation must be under the control of those who are taxed. This truth animated all our colonial and revolutionary history....

At bottom, today's discussion seems

motivated by the fear that failure to endorse judicial taxation power might in some extreme circumstance leave a court unable to remedy a constitutional violation.... I do not think this possibility is in reality a significant one. More important, this possibility is nothing more or less than the necessary consequence of any limit on judicial power. If, however, judicial discretion is to provide the sole limit on judicial remedies, that discretion must counsel restraint. Ill-considered entry into the volatile field of taxation is a step that may place at risk the legitimacy that justifies judicial independence....

This case is a stark illustration of the ever-present question whether ends justify means. Few ends are more important than enforcing the guarantee of equal educational opportunity for our Nation's children. But rules of taxation that override state political strictures not themselves subject to any constitutional infirmity raise serious questions of federal authority, questions compounded by the odd posture of a case in which the Court assumes the validity of a novel conception of desegregation remedies we never before have approved. The historical record of voluntary compliance with the decree of *Brown v. Board of Education* is not a proud chapter in our constitutional history, and the judges of the District Courts and Courts of Appeals have been courageous and skillful in implementing its mandate. But courage and skill must be exercised with due regard for the proper and historic role of the courts....

COMMENT

Before the litigation in *Missouri v. Jenkins*, the voters of the KCMSD had not approved a levy increase since 1969. Between 1970 and 1983, six attempts to increase the rate failed. Although four levies won the approval of a majority of the KCMSD voters, they failed because of the supermajority requirement of the Missouri Constitution. The Court of Appeals for the Eighth Circuit made an important finding of fact: These funding and other state laws seriously hampered the efforts of the KCMSD to raise sufficient funds to pay for the desegregation remedy ordered by the federal district court. All of the initiatives proposed by the KCMSD in response to the district court order failed in 1986 and 1987.

QUESTIONS

1. Explain why the Court's standard of review articulated in *United States v. Paradise*, 480 U.S. 149 (1987), discussed in the *Setting*, compelled Justices Kennedy and three others to concur in *Jenkins* instead of dissent. What would be the consequences of a less deferential standard of review regarding desegregation orders? Would such consequences be salutary?

2. In *Federalist* No. 78, Alexander Hamilton argued that "the judiciary, from the nature of its functions, will always be the least dangerous to the political rights of the Constitution; because it will be least in a capacity to annoy or injure them." From which perspective is the

Court's decision in *Jenkins* not dangerous—from the perspective of Missouri tax payers; state taxation power? From which perspective is its decision very dangerous—from the perspective of judicial power to fashion equitable remedies; Missouri school children?

3. Does the problem of *de jure* segregation that the district court confronted in Missouri in the 1980s suggest that the Court erred in *Brown II* by allowing desegregation to proceed with "all deliberate speed?"

COMMENT

In *Board of Education v. Dowell*, 498 U.S. 237 (1991), the Court by a 5–3 vote (Souter, J., not participating) ruled that the U.S. Court of Appeals for the Tenth Circuit erred in refusing to dissolve a desegregation decree after local authorities had operated in compliance with the decree for five years, even though there was evidence that desegregation had not been achieved in that time. The court of appeals declared that the board would be entitled to such relief only if it could show that not dissolving the decree would result in "a ... grievous wrong evoked by new and unforeseen conditions." According to Chief Justice Rehnquist's majority opinion, federal district court desegregation decrees are not meant to operate in perpetuity: Federal supervision of local school districts has always been intended as a temporary remedy for past discrimination. A finding by a district court that a school system has operated in compliance with the Equal Protection Clause for a reasonable period of time and that it is unlikely that the school board will return to its former ways is sufficient to justify dissolution of a desegregation decree.

EQUAL PROTECTION: JIM CROW AND SCHOOL DESEGREGATION

Freeman v. Pitts
503 U.S. 467 (1992)

SETTING

In the decades after *Brown I* and *Brown II*, federal courts of appeals developed three criteria for measuring whether school districts had achieved unitary status: No discrimination between school children on the basis of race, elimination of all vestiges of a segregated dual system, and operation of a nonsegregated system for a period of several years. Not until 1991, however, did the Supreme Court issue rules to help guide lower courts in determining whether school districts had satisfied these criteria. *Board of Education v. Dowell*, 498 U.S. 237 (1991) (see above), created a two-pronged test to determine whether a school district has achieved sufficient desegregation to be relieved of further responsibility to desegregate: Good faith compliance with a desegregation decree for "a reasonable period of time" and, "as far as practicable," elimination of the vestiges of unlawful discrimination.

By 1991, the personnel on the Supreme Court were dramatically different from the justices who had participated in *Brown I* and initial efforts to implement it. Republican Presidents Nixon, Ford, Reagan, and Bush were responsible for eight of the Court's nine justices. A school desegregation case initiated in DeKalb County, Georgia, in 1968 provided the Republican-dominated Court an opportunity to reflect on *Dowell* and the extent to which federal district courts should continue to supervise public school desegregation.

DeKalb County, Georgia, is a predominantly urban and suburban area outside Atlanta. The DeKalb County School System (DCSS) is the state's largest school district. Despite the 1954 ruling in *Brown I*, until 1966 the DCSS maintained totally segregated public schools in accordance with state law.

In 1966, the DCSS replaced its race-based school attendance zones with a system of geographic attendance zones in which all students, regardless of race, were assigned to a neighborhood school. Every student was also given a freedom-of-choice transfer option that permitted students to transfer to any school in the county. That option led to a number of black students choosing to attend formerly all-white schools but had no significant impact on formerly all-black schools. Freedom-of-choice plans were assailed by civil rights groups because of their failure to achieve desegregation.

In *Green v. County School Board* (see pp. 536–543), the Supreme Court declared that if freedom-of-choice plans failed to eliminate segregation, other means would have to be employed. The *Green* Court established six factors for measuring whether a school district has achieved unitary status: student assignment, transportation, extra-curricular activities, physical facilities, faculty, and staff.

Two months after *Green* was decided, Anna Mae Pitts, mother of DCSS student Willie Eugene Pitts, initiated a class action suit on behalf of all black children in the school district against the DCSS. She filed her suit in the U.S. District Court for the Northern District of Georgia. The lead defendant was Robert Freeman, the DCSS superintendent. Pitts's complaint alleged that the DCSS was operating an illegally segregated school system in violation of the Fourteenth Amendment's guarantee of equal protection of the laws. In response to Pitts's suit, the DCSS volunteered to work with the Department of Health, Education and Welfare (HEW) to develop a plan of desegregation.

On June 12, 1969, with the agreement of the parties, the district court entered three orders that were intended to be a final and terminal plan of desegregation. First, the DCSS was to abandon the freedom-of-choice plan and replace it with a neighborhood school attendance plan designed to prevent white student transfers. Second, the DCSS was to implement the system of neighborhood attendance zones recommended by the Department of Health, Education and Welfare. Finally, the DCSS was to close any remaining all-black schools. The district court retained jurisdiction to ensure that the DCSS complied with its order. The orders were implemented without opposition.

When the district court entered its orders, DeKalb County had a relatively small black student population that was geographically well dispersed throughout the district. In the early 1970s, however, significant demographic changes began to occur. The southern part of the county experienced a large influx of black families while the county as a whole saw a substantial exodus of white families. Half of the black students in the district soon were attending schools with black student populations of over 90 percent.

In 1975, Pitts returned to the district court to challenge changes in school attendance zones brought about by the opening of a new school in the district and the adequacy of the DCSS's efforts to reassign staff in accordance with the 1969 order. The DCSS responded that the attendance zone changes were responses to demographic changes. The district court instituted a majority-to-minority transfer program that allowed students to transfer to schools in which their race was a minority, ordered the DCSS to provide students with free transportation to implement the transfer program, and to reassign faculty and staff according to approximate district-wide racial percentages. The court also created a biracial committee to oversee the student transfer program and proposed attendance zone changes or school site purchases.

Between 1977 and 1979, the DCSS sought judicial approval of several plan modifications. The district court accepted some but rejected others. In 1979, the court denied Pitts's request that it modify the transfer program to respond to "white flight." In 1983, Pitts again returned to the district court, contending that the DCSS improperly limited majority-to-minority transfers to one predominantly white high school and that the district's proposed expansion of another predominantly white high school would perpetuate segregation. The district court ordered the DCSS to accept more black students in the transfer program, but ruled that the district showed no discriminatory intent in its decision to expand the one high school. The court further ruled that, in 1969, the DCSS had achieved unitary status. Pitts appealed that ruling.

The U.S. Court of Appeals for the Eleventh Circuit reversed. It held that the district court erred in declaring the DCSS to be a unitary system without providing Pitts and the other plaintiffs with notice and a hearing on that issue.

In January 1986, the DCSS sought a declaration from the district court that it had achieved unitary status and requested that the case be dismissed. Pitts countered with a request that the court order the DCSS to file a separate plan for high school desegregation. Following a three-week trial to determine whether unitary status had been achieved, the court denied the DCSS's motion for dismissal. It held that the DCSS had made exemplary progress in eliminating segregation and released the DCSS from court supervision regarding four of the six factors outlined in *Green* for measuring unitariness: student assignment, transportation services, extracurricular activities, and physical facilities. However, the court retained jurisdiction over the assignment of teachers and allocation of staff. It held that the DCSS would come into compliance with the requirement for racial equality in the assignment of teachers and principals when all schools in the district possessed minority staffs within 15 percent of the system average. It also ordered the DCSS to distribute equally among its schools its experienced teachers and teachers with advanced degrees and to equalize expenditures among black and white students. Finally, the court denied Pitts's motion requesting an order that the district file a separate high school plan.

The Eleventh Circuit Court of Appeals reversed. It ruled that, as a matter of law, the DCSS retained an affirmative duty to cure racial imbalance in student assignment—regardless of cause—until a condition of "unitariness" was achieved in all of the "*Green* factors." According to the appeals court, "The DCSS may not shirk its constitutional duties by pointing to demographic shifts occurring prior to unitary status." The Eleventh Circuit also declared that the DCSS would not achieve "unitary status" until it simultaneously maintained at least three years of racial equality in the areas of student assignment, faculty, staff, transportation, extracurricular activities, and facilities. Finally, it reaffirmed the power of the district court to order relief relating to any of the six categories until the DCSS achieved unitary status.

The Supreme Court of the United States granted cross-petitions for writs of certiorari.

HIGHLIGHTS OF SUPREME COURT ARGUMENTS

BRIEF FOR FREEMAN

◆ The racial imbalance in the DCSS reflects the shifts in residential housing patterns, not unconstitutional conduct by the district. The district court order is not aimed at the effects of unconstitutional conduct.

◆ Since 1966, the DCSS has participated in the systematic dismantling of its dual school system. There is no evidence that current imbalances in student assignment—or any other aspect of school operations—is a vestige of the former dual school system. Any contemporary racial imbalance in the district is the result of housing preferences of private individuals.

◆ In prior cases the Court has held that despite the importance of eliminating state-imposed segregation in the public schools, remedial efforts cannot go beyond what is necessary to remedy a condition actually caused by a school board's prior unconstitutional conduct. *De facto* segregation caused exclusively by private choices provides no basis for judicial correction because there is no substantive constitutional right to a particular degree of racial balancing or mixing.

◆ Federalism considerations require the courts to recognize that they are ill-equipped to perform the functions of a school board, and that school boards cannot perform their functions when every decision is subject to judicial scrutiny solely on the basis of its effect on racial balance.

◆ The Eleventh Circuit erred in its focus on the achievement of an abstract condition of unitariness rather than on a number of more specific and operational goals. This Court has held that once the condition that created a district court's authority has been eliminated, the court's remedial authority is exhausted. If the Eleventh Circuit's approach is affirmed by this Court, the practical effect will be to extend indefinitely federal court oversight of local school board operations.

AMICUS CURIAE BRIEFS SUPPORTING FREEMAN

United States; Southeastern Legal Foundation, Inc.

BRIEF FOR PITTS

◆ Both the district court and the court of appeals held that the DCSS met neither of the tests in *Dowell*. Its faculty and staff have not been desegregated and its school facilities remain separate and unequal.

◆ The so-called *Green* factors employed by the court of appeals (student assignment, faculty, staff, transportation, extracurricular activities, and facilities) are related to one another and cannot be applied in isolation. If they are applied in isolation, it is certain that the victims of a segregated system will never achieve a fully desegregated system. Federal court supervision of desegregation should not end until a school district has satisfied all the factors.

◆ Even if demographics contributed to the vestiges of current segregation in the school district, the DCSS cannot escape responsibility. This Court has always understood that demographics would change during the process of desegregation and that such change would not excuse a failure to desegregate.

AMICUS CURIAE BRIEFS SUPPORTING PITTS

Lawyers' Committee for Civil Rights Under Law; DeKalb County Branch of the NAACP; American Jewish Committee; Children's Defense Fund; Fund for an Open Society; Mexican American Legal Defense and Educational Fund; Puerto Rican Legal Defense and Education Fund; Southern Christian Leadership Conference.

SUPREME COURT DECISION: 8–0

(Thomas, J., did not participate.)

KENNEDY, J.

... The duty and responsibility of a school district once segregated by law is to take all steps necessary to eliminate the vestiges of the unconstitutional *de jure* system. This is required in order to insure that the principal wrong of the *de jure* system, the injuries and stigma inflicted upon the race disfavored by the violation, is no longer present. This was the ratio-nale and the objective of *Brown I* and *Brown II*....

The objective of *Brown I* was made more specific by our holding in *Green* that the duty of a former *de jure* district is to "take whatever steps might be necessary to convert to a unitary system in which racial discrimination would be eliminated root and branch."...

The concept of unitariness has been a helpful one in defining the scope of the district courts' authority, for it conveys the central idea that a school district that was once a dual system must be examined in all of its facets, both when a remedy is ordered and in the later phases of desegregation when the question is whether the district courts' remedial control ought to be modified, lessened, or withdrawn. But, as we explained last term in *Board of Education of Oklahoma City v. Dowell*, 498 U.S. 237 (1991), the term "unitary" is not a precise concept....

It follows that we must be cautious not to attribute to the term a utility it does not have. The term "unitary" does not confine the discretion and authority of the District Court in a way that departs from traditional equitable principles.

That the term "unitary" does not have fixed meaning or content is not inconsistent with the principles that control the exercise of equitable power. The essence of a court's equity power lies in its inherent capacity to adjust remedies in a feasible and practical way to eliminate the conditions or redress the injuries caused by unlawful action. Equitable remedies must be flexible if these underlying principles are to be enforced with fairness and precision....

We hold that, in the course of supervising desegregation plans, federal courts have the authority to relinquish supervision and control of school districts in incremental stages, before full compliance has been achieved in every area of school operations. While retaining jurisdiction over the case, the court may determine that it will not order further remedies in areas where the school district is in compliance with the degree. That is to say, upon the finding that a school system subject to a court-supervised desegregation plan is in compliance in some but not all areas, the court in appropriate cases may return control to the school system in those areas where compliance has been achieved, limiting further judicial supervision to operations that are not yet in full compliance with the court decree. In particular, the district court may determine that it will not order further remedies in the area of student assignments where racial imbalance is not traceable, in a proximate way, to constitutional violations.

A court's discretion to order the incremental withdrawal of its supervision in a school desegregation case must be exercised in a manner consistent with the purposes and objectives of its equitable power. Among the factors which must inform the sound discretion of the court in ordering partial withdrawal are the following: whether there has been full and satisfactory compliance with the decree in those aspects of the system where supervision is to be withdrawn; whether retention of judicial control is necessary or practicable to achieve compliance with the decree in other facets of the school system; and whether the school district has demonstrated, to the public and to the parents and students of the once disfavored race, its good faith commitment to the whole of the court's decree and to those provisions of the law and the constitution that were the predicate for judicial intervention in the first instance.

In considering these factors, a court should give particular attention to the school system's record of compliance. A school system is better positioned to demonstrate its good-faith commitment to a constitutional course of action when its policies form a consistent pattern of lawful conduct directed to eliminating earlier violations. And with the passage of time the degree to which racial imbalances continue to represent vestiges of a constitutional violation may diminish, and the practicability and efficacy of various remedies can be evaluated with more precision....

The Court of Appeals was mistaken in ruling that our opinion in *Swann* requires "awkward," "inconvenient," and "even bizarre" measures to achieve racial balance in student assignments in the late phases of carrying out a decree, when the imbalance is attributable neither to the prior *de jure* system nor to a later violation by the school district but rather to independent demographic forces....

Where resegregation is a product not of state action but of private choices, it does not have constitutional implications. It is beyond the authority and beyond the practical ability of the federal courts to try to counteract these kinds of continuous and massive demographic shifts. To attempt such results would require ongoing and never-ending supervision by the courts of school districts simply because they were once *de jure* segregated. Residential housing choices, and their attendant effects on the racial composition of schools, present an ever-changing pattern, one difficult to address through judicial remedies....

To say, as did the Court of Appeals, that a school district must meet all six *Green* factors before the trial court can declare the system unitary and relinquish its control over school attendance zones, and to hold further that racial balancing by all necessary means is required in the interim, is simply to vindicate a legal phrase. The law is not so formalistic. A proper rule must be based on the necessity to find a feasible remedy that insures systemwide compliance with the court decree and that is directed to curing the effects of the specific violation....

The judgment is reversed and the case is remanded to the Court of Appeals. It should determine what issues are open for its further consideration in light of the previous briefs and arguments of the parties and in light of the principles set forth in this opinion. Thereupon it should order further proceedings as necessary or order an appropriate remand to the District Court.

It is so ordered.

SCALIA, J., CONCURRING

... Almost a quarter-century ago, in *Green v. School Bd., New Kent County*, this Court held that school systems which had been enforcing *de jure* segregation at the time of *Brown I* had not merely an obligation to assign students and resources on a race-neutral basis but also an "affirmative duty" to "desegregate," that is, to achieve insofar as practicable racial balance in their schools. This holding has become such a part of our legal fabric that there is a tendency, reflected in the Court of Appeals opinion in this case, to speak as though the Constitution requires such racial balancing. Of course it does not: the Equal Protection Clause reaches only those racial imbalances shown to be intentionally caused by the State....

At some time, we must acknowledge that it has become absurd to assume, without any further proof, that violations of the Constitution dating from the days when Lyndon Johnson was President, or earlier, continue to have an appreciable effect upon current operation of schools. We are close to that time. While we must continue to prohibit, without qualification, all racial discrimination in the operation of public schools, and to afford remedies that eliminate not only the discrimination but its identified consequences, we should consider laying aside the extraordinary, and increasingly counterfactual, presumption of *Green*. We must soon revert to the ordinary principles of our law, of our democratic heritage, and of our educational tradition: that plaintiffs alleging Equal Protection violations must prove intent and causation and not merely the existence of racial disparity, that public schooling, even in the South, should be controlled by locally elected authorities acting in conjunction with parents, and that it is "desirable" to permit pupils to attend "schools nearest their homes."

SOUTER, J., CONCURRING

... Before a district court ends its supervision of student assignments ... it should make a finding that there is no immediate threat of unremedied *Green*-type factors causing population or student enrollment changes that in turn may imbalance student composition in [a particular] way. And, because the district court retains jurisdiction over the case, it should of course reassert control over student assignments if it finds that this does happen.

BLACKMUN, STEVENS, AND O'CONNOR, J.J., CONCURRING

... DCSS claims that it need not remedy the segregation in DeKalb County schools because it was caused by demographic changes for which DCSS has no responsibility. It is not enough, however, for DCSS to establish that demographics exacerbated the problem; it must prove that its own policies did not contribute. Such contribution can occur in at least two ways: DCSS may have contributed to the demographic changes themselves, or it may have contributed directly to the racial imbalance in the schools....

The District Court's opinion suggests that it did not examine DCSS' actions in light of the foregoing principles....

[I]n addition to the issues the Court suggests be considered in further proceedings, I would remand for the Court of Appeals to review, under the foregoing principles, the District Court's finding that DCSS has met its burden of proving the racially identifiable schools are in no way the result of past segregation action.

QUESTIONS

1. The *New York Times* editorialized after *Freeman* that "The high court's commitment to finish the work of *Brown v. Board of Education* hangs by a thread" (April 3, 1992, p. A28). Is that assessment accurate, or does *Freeman* reflect a realistic view that the era of legal remedies must give way to other efforts? If the latter, what other efforts should be undertaken to achieve racial balance in public schools? Does the majority in *Freeman* hint at such efforts?

2. The American Civil Liberties Union (ACLU) argued in *Freeman*: "[I]f this Court allows the principle that school districts can desegregate on a piecemeal basis, without careful examination of the interaction of the various facets of the school system's operation, it is difficult to see what would prevent that principle from being extended." Is the ACLU's argument a plea for permanent judicial supervision of public school desegregation? Does such a plea ask courts to perform tasks they are neither capable of, nor responsible for, performing?

3. Chief Justice Earl Warren wrote in *Brown I*, "Today, education is perhaps the most important function of state and local governments.... In these days, it is doubtful that any child may reasonably be expected to succeed in life if he is denied the opportunity of an education. Such an opportunity, where the state has undertaken to provide it, is a right which must be made available to all on equal terms."

Counsel for Robert Freeman argued, "[T]he failure to maintain racial balance [in DCSS] for its own sake is not a remedial failure. If it is a failure at all, it is a social failure. It would serve no valid purpose now to attempt to remedy such a social problem by imposing burdens on school districts that could not have prevented or influenced the housing preferences that created racial imbalance in the schools."

Are these two views contradictory, or are they based on fundamentally differing assumptions about the sources of racial imbalance in American society, the role of schools, and the obligations of state and local governments?

COMMENT

In *United States v. Fordice*, 505 U.S. 717 (1992), the Supreme Court addressed the issue of desegregation in the context of higher education. By an 8–1 vote, the justices identified four aspects of the Mississippi state university system they said rendered it "constitutionally suspect": (1) higher admissions standards in the once all-white universities; (2) the designation of three of the white universities and none of the black ones as "comprehensive universities"; (3) duplication of programs at the white and black universities; and (4) continued operation of eight universities in the state. More fundamentally, Justice White rejected freedom of choice as the correct constitutional standard for courts to use in assessing whether a once-segregated university system had met its obligations under the Equal Protection Clause of the Fourteenth Amendment. He wrote:

> Because the former *de jure* segregated system of public universities in Mississippi impeded the free choice of prospective students, the state in dismantling that system must take the necessary steps to insure that this choice now is truly free. The full range of policies and practices must be examined with this duty in mind.

SUGGESTIONS FOR FURTHER READING

Belknap, Michal R., *Federal Law and Southern Order: Racial Violence and Constitutional Conflict in the Post-Brown South* (Athens, GA: University of Georgia Press, 1987).

Bell, Derrick, "Serving Two Masters: Integration Ideals and Client Interests in School Desegregation Litigation," 85 *Yale Law Journal* (1976): 470.

———, "*Brown v. Board of Education* and the Interest-Convergence Dilemma," 93 *Harvard Law Review* (1980): 518.

_____, *And We Are Not Saved: The Elusive Quest for Racial Justice* (New York, NY: Basic Books, 1987).

Bickel, Alexander M., *The Least Dangerous Branch: The Supreme Court at the Bar of Politics* (Indianapolis, IN: Bobbs-Merrill, 1962).

_____, "A Decade of School Desegregation," 64 *Columbia Law Review* (1964): 193.

_____, *The Supreme Court and the Ideal of Progress* (New Haven, CT: Yale University Press, 1978).

Black, Charles L., Jr., "The Lawfulness of the Segregation Decisions," 69 *Yale Law Journal* (1960): 421.

Blaustein, Albert P., and Clarence Clyde Ferguson Jr., *Desegregation and the Law: The Meaning and Effect of the School Desegregation Cases*, 2nd rev. ed. (New York, NY: Vintage, 1962).

Blaustein, Albert P., and Robert L. Zangrando, eds., *Civil Rights and the Black American: A Documentary History* (New York, NY: Simon & Schuster, 1970).

Brest, Paul, "Foreword: In Defense of the Antidiscrimination Principle," 90 *Harvard Law Review* (1976): 1.

Cook, Anthony E., *The Least of These: Race, Law, and Religion in American Culture* (New York, NY: Routledge, 1997).

Cover, Robert, "The Origins of Judicial Activism in the Protection of Minorities," 91 *Yale Law Journal* (1982): 1287.

Diamond, Paul R., *Beyond Busing: Inside the Challenge to Urban Segregation* (Ann Arbor, MI: University of Michigan Press, 1985).

Dudziak, Mary, "Desegregation as a Cold War Imperative," 41 *Stanford Law Review* (1988): 61.

Fiss, Owen, "School Desegregation: The Uncertain Path of the Law," 4 *Philosophy and Public Affairs* (1974): 3.

_____, "The Fate of an Idea Whose Time Has Come: Antidiscrimination Law in the Second Decade after *Brown v. Board of Education*," 41 *University of Chicago Law Review* (1974): 742.

_____, "The Jurisprudence of Busing," 39 *Law and Contemporary Problems* (1975): 194.

Friedman, Leon, ed., *Southern Justice* (Cleveland, OH: Meridan, 1967).

Garfinkel, Herbert, "Social Science and the School Desegregation Cases," 21 *Journal of Politics* (1959): 37.

Garrow, David J., *Time on the Cross: Martin Luther King, Jr., and the Southern Christian Leadership Conference* (New York, NY: Vintage, 1988).

Graglia, Lino A., *Disaster by Decree: The Supreme Court, Race and the Schools* (Ithaca, NY: Cornell University Press, 1976).

Graham, Hugh Davis, *Civil Rights and the Presidency* (New York, NY: Oxford University Press, 1992).

Greene, Melissa F., *Praying for Sheetrock* (New York, NY: Fawcett Columbine, 1991).

Greenberg, Jack, *Race Relations and American Law* (New York, NY: Columbia University Press, 1959).

_____, *Crusaders in the Courts: How a Dedicated Band of Lawyers Fought for the Civil Rights Revolution* (New York, NY: Basic Books, 1994).

Grodzins, Morton, *Americans Betrayed: Politics and the Japanese Evacuation* (Chicago, IL: University of Chicago Press, 1949).

Gunther, Gerald, "Of Rights and Remedies, Legitimacy and Competence," *Washington University Law Quarterly* (1979): 815.

Handlin, Oscar, "The Goals of Integration," *Daedalus* (Winter 1966): 268.

Haar, Charles M., *Suburbs under Siege: Race, Space, and Audacious Judges* (Princeton, NJ: Princeton University Press, 1996).

Higginbotham, A. Leon, Jr., *In the Matter of Color: The Colonial Period* (New York, NY: Oxford University Press, 1978).

Higham, John, "America's Three Reconstructions," *The New York Review of Books*, November 6, 1997, p. 52.

_____, *Shades of Freedom: Racial Politics and Presumptions of the American Legal Process* (New York, NY: Oxford University Press, 1996).

Hutchinson, Dennis J., "Unanimity and Desegregation," 68 *Georgetown Law Journal* (1979): 1.

Irons, Peter, *The Courage of Their Convictions: Sixteen Americans Who Fought Their Way to the Supreme Court* (New York, NY: Penguin, 1990), Chapter 2.

Jackson, Donald W., *Even the Children of Strangers: Equality under the U.S. Constitution* (Lawrence, KS: University Press of Kansas, 1992).

Kitch, Edmund W., "The Return of Color-Consciousness to the Constitution: *Weber, Dayton* and *Columbus*," *The Supreme Court Review* (Chicago, IL: University of Chicago Press, 1979).

Kluger, Richard, *Simple Justice* (New York, NY: Vintage Books, 1977).

Kull, Andrew, *The Color-Blind Constitution* (Cambridge, MA: Harvard University Press, 1992).

Kurland, Philip B., "'*Brown v. Board of Education* Was the Beginning': The School Desegregation Cases in the United States Supreme Court," *Washington University Law Quarterly* (1979): 309.

Leflar, Robert A., and Wylie H. Davis, "Segregation in the Public Schools— 1953," 67 *Harvard Law Review* (1954): 377.

Lively, Donald E., *The Constitution and Race* (New York, NY: Praeger, 1992).

Loevy, Robert D., ed., *The Civil Rights Act of 1964: The Passage of the Law That Ended Racial Segregation* (Albany, NY: State University of New York Press, 1997).

McCord, John H., *With All Deliberate Speed: Civil Rights Theory and Reality* (Urbana, IL: University of Illinois Press, 1969).

McGee, Henry W., Jr., "Illusion and Contradiction in the Quest for a Desegregated Metropolis," 1976 *University of Illinois Law Forum* (1976): 948.

McKay, Robert B., "With All Deliberate Speed," 31 *New York University Law Review* (1956): 991.

———, "With All Deliberate Speed," 43 *Virginia Law Review* (1957): 1205.

McNeil, Genna Rae, *Charles Hamilton Houston and the Struggle for Civil Rights* (Philadelphia, PA: University of Pennsylvania Press, 1982).

Meador, Daniel J., "The Constitution and the Assignment of Pupils to Public Schools," 45 *Virginia Law Review* (1959): 517.

Miller, Loren, *The Petitioners: The Story of the Supreme Court of the United States and the Negro* (New York, NY: Pantheon, 1966).

Muse, Benjamin, *Virginia's Massive Resistance* (Bloomington, IN: University of Indiana Press, 1961).

Myrdal, Gunnar, *An American Dilemma: The Negro Problem and Modern Democracy*, 2 vols. (New York, NY: Harper and Row, 1944).

Nieman, Donald G., *Promises to Keep: African-Americans and the Constitutional Order, 1776 to the Present* (New York, NY: Oxford University Press, 1991).

Note, "The Courts, HEW and Southern School Desegregation," 77 *Yale Law Journal* (1967): 321.

Note, "The Nixon Busing Bills," 81 *Yale Law Journal* (1972): 1542.

Oberst, Paul, "The Strange Career of *Plessy v. Ferguson*," 15 *Arizona Law Review* (1973): 389.

Olson, Otto, ed., *The Thin Disguise: Turning Point in Negro History* (New York, NY: Humanities Press, 1967).

Orfield, Gary, *Must We Bus? Segregated Schools and National Policy* (Washington, D.C.: Brookings, 1978).

Peltason, Jack W., *Fifty-Eight Lonely Men: Southern Federal Judges and School Desegregation Cases* (New York, NY: Harcourt, Brace & World, 1961).

Pindur, Wolfgang, "Legislative and Judicial Roles in the Detroit School Decentralization Controversy," 50 *Journal of Urban Law* (1972): 53.

Read, Frank T., and Lucy S. McGough, *Let Them Be Judged: The Judicial Integration of the Deep South* (Metuchen, NJ: Scarecrow Press, 1978).

Rodgers, Harrell R., Jr., and Charles S. Bullock, III, *Law and Social Change: Civil Rights Laws and Their Consequences* (New York, NY: McGraw-Hill, 1972).

Rosenberg, Gerald N., *The Hollow Hope: Can Courts Bring About Social Change?* (Chicago, IL: University of Chicago Press, 1991).

Rosengarten, Theodore, *All God's Dangers: The Life of Nate Shaw* (New York, NY: Avon, 1974).

Rostow, Eugene V., "The Japanese American Cases—A Disaster," 54 *Yale Law Journal* (1949): 489.

Sarat, Austin, ed., *Race, Law and Culture: Reflections on* Brown v. Board of Education (New York, NY: Oxford University Press, 1996).

Schwartz, Bernard, *Swann's Way: The School Busing Case and the Supreme Court* (New York, NY: Oxford University Press, 1986).

Shoemaker, Don, ed., *With All Deliberate Speed: Segregation-Desegregation in Southern Schools* (New York, NY: Harper, 1957).

Smith, Robert C., *Racism in the Post-Civil Rights Era: Now You See It, Now You Don't* (Albany, NY: State University of New York Press, 1997).

Stampp, Kenneth M., *The Peculiar Institution: Slavery in the Ante-Bellum South* (New York, NY: Vintage, 1956).

Symposium, "Struggling Toward Opportunity—40 Years Since Little Rock," 30 *PS: Political Science & Politics* (1997):443.

Tushnet, Mark, *The NAACP's Legal Strategy Against Segregated Education, 1925–1950* (Chapel Hill, NC: University of North Carolina Press, 1987).

_____, *Making Civil Rights Law: Thurgood Marshall and the Supreme Court* (New York, NY: Oxford University Press, 1994).

Wade, Wyn Craig, *The Fiery Cross: The Ku Klux Klan in America* (New York, NY: Simon & Schuster, 1987).

Wasby, Stephen L., *Race Relations Litigation in an Age of Complexity* (Charlottesville, VA: University of Virginia Press, 1995).

Wechsler, Herbert, "Toward Neutral Principles of Constitutional Law," 73 *Harvard Law Review* (1959): 1.

Wilkinson, J. Harvie, III, *From* Brown *to* Bakke (New York, NY: Oxford University Press, 1979).

Williams, Juan, *Eyes on the Prize: America's Civil Rights Years, 1954–1965* (New York, NY: Penguin, 1988).

Wolters, Raymond, *The Burden of* Brown*: Thirty Years of School Desegregation* (Knoxville, TN: University of Tennessee Press, 1984).

Woodward, C. Vann, *American Counterpoint: Slavery and Racism in the North-South Dialogue* (Boston, MA: Little, Brown, 1971).

_____, *The Strange Career of Jim Crow*, 3rd rev. ed. (New York, NY: Oxford University Press, 1974).

_____, "The Case of the Louisiana Traveler," in *Quarrels That Have Shaped the Constitution,* ed. John A. Garraty (New York, NY: Harper and Row, 1987).

EQUAL PROTECTION:
SEPARATE SPHERES AND GENDER EQUALITY

Bradwell v. Illinois
16 Wallace 130 (1873)

SETTING

In the view of many women's rights advocates in the nineteenth century, the legal condition of women was basically the same as that of slaves. Women lost both their legal identity and their property when they married. Under the common law doctrine of *coverture*, married women were treated as though they were legally dead. As William Blackstone explained:

> By marriage, the husband and wife are one person in law; the very being or legal existence of the woman is suspended during the marriage, or at least is incorporated and consolidated into that of the husband: under whose wing, protection and cover, she performs everything....

If women did not marry, their social status was negligible. Employment opportunities for women were very limited, the assumption being that women's "natural abilities" suited them mostly for elementary school teaching and nursing. The so-called learned professions—including law—were closed to women because social norms consigned men and women to "separate spheres," casting men as breadwinners in the business world and women as housekeepers in the domestic world.

For well over twenty-five years before the Civil War, a powerful coalition existed in the United States between the antislavery and the women's rights movements. Women's rights advocates argued the cause of abolition and abolitionists argued the cause of women's rights, as both movements sought to eliminate many of the same legal barriers and social prejudices. On July 19, 1848, a group of about three hundred women met at the Wesleyan Chapel in Seneca Falls, New York. They adopted a Declaration of Sentiments. Modeled after the 1776 Declaration of Independence, the Seneca Falls Declaration read, in part:

> The History of mankind is a history of repeated injuries and usurpations on the part of man toward woman, having in direct object the establishment of an absolute tyranny over her. To prove this, let facts be submitted to a candid world....
> He has never permitted her to exercise her inalienable right to the elective franchise....
> Having deprived her of this first right of a citizen, the elective franchise, thereby leaving her without representation in the halls of legislation, he has oppressed her on all sides....

Despite these statements, it was only after Frederick Douglass, editor of the Rochester, New York, abolitionist newspaper, the *North Star*, spoke in favor of a suffrage resolution that the convention resolved: "That it is the duty of women of this country to secure to themselves their sacred right to the elective franchise."

Following the Civil War, the Republican Party had a strong interest in supporting blacks and creating voters to counter the resurgence of the Democratic Party in the South. It had no comparable reason to support women. Over the objections of women's rights advocates, Section 1 of the Fourteenth Amendment extended citizenship to blacks but was silent on the issue of gender. Again over the objections of women's rights advocates, the Fifteenth Amendment prohibited states from abridging the right to vote on the basis of race but included no prohibition against abridging the right to vote on the basis of gender. While blacks sank under the oppression of Black Codes and racial intimidation after the Civil War and adoption of the post-War Amendments, women were left on their own to improve their legal and social status. Women's rights advocates generally targeted two goals: entering professions monopolized by males and winning the right to vote.

Women seeking entrance into the legal profession in the nineteenth century faced several obstacles. One was the widely held opinion that the practice of law is outside the sphere of female capabilities. Another was finding men willing to provide apprenticeships, an important method of obtaining legal education at the time. A third was the legal status of married women. A fourth was the refusal of some states to admit otherwise qualified women lawyers to the bar. Only a few states, like Iowa (which admitted Belle Mansfield to the bar in 1860), interpreted bar entrance requirements broadly enough to admit women. Illinois, the state in which Myra Colby Bradwell resided, was not one of them.

Bradwell studied law in her husband's law office and passed the Illinois bar exam. She also edited a widely respected legal periodical, the *Chicago Legal News*, that published case summaries and Illinois legislative session laws. In September 1869, attorney Robert Hervey submitted a motion to the Superior Court of Chicago requesting that Bradwell be granted a license to practice law in the courts of that state. Hervey's motion contained the usual certificate of qualification and of moral character pursuant to the Illinois statute providing that any "person" of good character having the requisite training was eligible for admission to the bar.

The Superior Court forwarded the motion and application to the Illinois Supreme Court with the recommendation that a license be issued to Bradwell. The Supreme Court denied her application, stating that as a married woman, Bradwell could be bound neither by the express nor implied contracts that the law created between attorneys and clients.

Bradwell filed written argument with the Illinois Supreme Court, which again denied her petition. This time the denial was based on Bradwell's gender rather than her marital status. The court stated that it could not doubt Bradwell's "ample qualifications" but held that it was "certainly warranted in saying that when the legislature gave to this court the power of granting licenses to practice law, it was not with the slightest expectation that this privilege would be extended to women."

Bradwell petitioned the Supreme Court of the United States for a writ of error.

HIGHLIGHTS OF SUPREME COURT ARGUMENTS

BRIEF FOR BRADWELL

♦ The Fourteenth Amendment declares that all persons born or naturalized in the United States are citizens of the United States and of the state in which they reside. It opens to every citizen, male or female, black or white, married or single, the honorable as well as servile employments of life. If the privileges or immunities of a citizen cannot be abridged, the privileges or immunities of all citizens must be the same.

♦ The theory of American government is that all men have certain inalienable rights, including life, liberty, and the pursuit of happiness. In the pursuit of happiness, all avocations, honors, and positions are alike open to everyone. In the protection of these rights, all are equal before the law. If women are allowed to practice law, they might be retained by clients less often as the taste and judgment of the client dictates, but the broad shield of the Constitution is over all, and protects each in whatever measure of success individual merit may secure.

BRIEF FOR ILLINOIS

The State of Illinois made no argument in the case.

SUPREME COURT DECISION: 8–1

MILLER, J.

... We agree ... that there are privileges and immunities belonging to citizens of the United States, in that relation and character, and that it is these and these alone which a State is forbidden to abridge. But the right to admission to practice in the courts of a State is not one of them. This right in no sense depends on citizenship of the United States. It has not, as far as we know, even been made in any State, or in any case, to depend on citizenship at all....

The opinion just delivered [the previous day] in the *Slaughter-House Cases* [see pp. 436–446] renders elaborate argument in the present case unnecessary; for, unless we are wholly and radically mistaken in the principles on which those cases are decided, the right to control and regulate the granting of license to practice law in the courts of a State is one of those powers which are not transferred for its protection to the Federal Government, and its exercise is in no manner governed or controlled by citizenship of the United States in the party seeking such license....

It is unnecessary to repeat the argument on which the judgment in those cases is founded. It is sufficient to say they are conclusive of the present case.

Judgment affirmed.

BRADLEY, FIELD, AND SWAYNE, J.J., CONCURRING

It certainly cannot be affirmed, as an historical fact, that [the practice of law] has ever been established as one of the fundamental privileges and immunities of the sex. On the contrary, the civil law, as well as nature herself, has always recognized a wide difference in the respective spheres and destinies of man and woman. Man is, or should be, woman's protector and defender. The natural and proper timidity and delicacy which belongs to the female sex evidently unfits it for many of the occupations of civil life. The constitution of the family organization, which is founded in the divine ordinance, as well as in the nature of things, indicates the domestic sphere as that which properly belongs to the domain and functions of womanhood. The harmony, not to say identity, of interests and views which belong, or should belong, to the family institution is repugnant to the idea of a woman adopting a distinct and independent career from that of her husband. So firmly fixed was this sentiment in the founders of the common law that it became a maxim of that system of jurisprudence that a woman had no legal existence separate from her husband, who was regarded as her head and representative in the social state; and, notwithstanding some recent modifications of this civil status, many of the special rules of law flowing from and dependent upon this cardinal principle still exist in full force in most States. One of these is, that a married woman is incapable, without her husband's consent, of making contracts which shall be binding on her or him. This very incapacity was one circumstance which the Supreme Court of Illinois deemed important in rendering a married woman incompetent fully to perform the duties and trusts that belong to the office of an attorney and counsellor.

It is true that many women are unmarried and not affected by any of the duties, complications, and incapacities arising out of the married state, but these are exceptions to the general rules. The paramount destiny and mission of woman are to fulfil the noble and benign offices of wife and mother. This is the law of the Creator. And the rules of civil society must be adapted to the general constitution of things, and cannot be based upon exceptional cases....

CHASE, C.J., DISSENTED WITHOUT OPINION

QUESTIONS

1. What was the more damaging aspect of *Bradwell* from the perspective of the women's rights movement—Justice Miller's holding for the Court on the Privileges or Immunities issue, or Justice Bradley's concurring view of women's place in America's "separate spheres"? Does the answer depend upon whether one takes a short- or long-term view of the consequences of *Bradwell*?

2. Political scientist Leslie Friedman Goldstein speculates that part of the reason that the Court rendered its decision in the *Slaughter-House Cases* before its decision in *Bradwell v. Illinois*, even though Bradwell's case was argued first, may be that the Supreme Court received an incomplete record in the *Bradwell* case. The record was incomplete because "Illinois officials apparently considered Myra Bradwell's petition so trivial that they did not even send a lawyer to the Supreme Court to present their side of the case" (*The Constitutional Rights of Women*, rev. ed. [Madison, WI: University of Wisconsin Press, 1988], p. 66).

   There are other indications of contemporary reaction to the *Bradwell* case. For example, the *Boston Daily Advertiser* reported on April 16, 1873: "Judge Bradley's opinion [in *Bradwell*] seemed to cause no little amusement upon the Bench and on the Bar" (quoted in Charles Warren, *The Supreme Court in United States History*, 3 vols. [Boston, MA: Little, Brown and Company, 1923], 3:272, n. 1). Historian Charles Fairman claims that Bradwell's "serious effort to win recognition as a lawyer was commonly treated as somewhat whimsical" by Chicago lawyers (*History of the Supreme Court of the United States, Volume 6: Reconstruction and Reunion 1864–88, Part One* [New York, NY: Macmillan, 1971], p. 1365). *The Nation* observed, "It is a rather ludicrous illustration of the character of the woman [sic] movement that a prominent female agitator should have seized the opportunity to prove the fitness of her sex for professional life, by taking for her first important case one which she must have known the Court would decide against her, unless she supposed that they were likely to be influenced by personal solicitation and clamor, or else they were all gone crazy" (quoted in Charles Warren, *The History of the Supreme Court of the United States*, 3 vols. [Boston, MA: Little, Brown and Company, 1923], 3:272, n. 1).

What explains such dismissive reactions to Bradwell's case?

3. Bradwell was represented before the Supreme Court by Matthew Carpenter, the same lawyer who helped to represent the Crescent City monopoly in the *Slaughter-House Cases*. Unfortunately, there is no record of Carpenter's oral argument in the *Slaughter-House Cases*. We can only assume that he joined with fellow counsel in supporting the theory in the brief for the Crescent City Company that the Fourteenth Amendment was adopted exclusively for the benefit of former slaves and that it could not be made to embrace other objects without sacrificing its spirit. On what basis, then, could Carpenter rely on the Fourteenth Amendment in his argument on behalf of Bradwell?

COMMENTS

1. Political scientist Nancy T. Gilliam reports that under an Illinois law granting freedom of occupational choice to all state citizens, passed in March 1872, Myra Bradwell could have applied for a license to practice despite the Supreme Court's decision in her case. She declined to do so. In March 1890, the Illinois Supreme Court, on its own motion, granted her a license ("A Professional Pioneer: Myra Bradwell's Fight to Practice Law," 5 *Law and History Review* 105, 128, 1987).

2. Section 2 of the Fourteenth Amendment, adopted in 1868, contains the first mention of gender in the Constitution, thrice referring to "male" citizens or inhabitants:

> Representatives shall be apportioned among the several States according to their respective numbers, counting the whole number of persons in each State, excluding Indians not taxed. But when the right to vote at any election for the choice of electors for President and Vice President of the United States, Representatives in Congress, the Executive and Judicial officers of a State, or the mem-

bers of the Legislature thereof, is denied to any of the *male* inhabitants of such State, being twenty-one years of age, and citizens of the United States, or in any way abridged, except for participation in rebellion, or other crime, the basis of representation therein shall be reduced in the proportion which the number of such *male* citizens shall bear to the whole number of *male* citizens twenty-one years of age in such State. (Emphasis added.)

This language resulted from the failure of women's rights advocates to persuade Congress, in the context of increasing social conservatism after the Civil War, to include specific guarantees for women in the Civil War Amendments. Seventy-nine years had elapsed since adoption of the Constitution.

3.   Women were no more successful during this era at employing the Fourteenth Amendment as a means of winning the right to vote. In *Minor v. Happersett*, 21 Wallace 162 (1875), handed down two years after *Bradwell*, the Court rejected the argument that the Fourteenth Amendment conferred suffrage on women as one of the privileges or immunities of national citizenship. Chief Justice Waite wrote:

> There is no doubt that women may be citizens....
>
> In this respect men have never had an advantage over women....
>
> If the right of suffrage is one of the necessary privileges of a citizen of the United States, then the constitution and laws of Missouri confining it to men are in violation of the Constitution of the United States, as amended, and consequently void. The direct question is, therefore, presented whether all citizens are necessarily voters....
>
> Certainly, if the courts can consider any question settled, this is one. For nearly ninety years the people have acted upon the idea that the Constitution, when it conferred citizenship, did not necessarily confer the right of suffrage. If uniform practice long continued can settle the construction of so important an instrument as the Constitution of the United States confessedly is, most certainly it has been done here. Our province is to decide what the law is, not to declare what it should be....
>
> If the law is wrong, it ought to be changed; but the power for that is not with us....

EQUAL PROTECTION: SEPARATE SPHERES AND GENDER EQUALITY

Reed v. Reed
404 U.S. 71 (1971)

SETTING

For over seventy years after *Bradwell* and *Minor v. Happersett*, 21 Wallace 162 (1875), the Supreme Court did not address equal protection in the context of sex-based classifications. To the extent that gender came before the Court, it was in the context of women's liberty to contract, in cases like *Adkins v. Childrens Hospital* and *West Coast Hotel v. Parrish*. (See Volume I, pp. 836–846.) When the question of equality among the sexes returned to the Court in 1948, in *Goesaert v. Clearly*, 335 U.S. 464, it was clear that judicial attitudes toward women had changed only a little since Justice Bradley's *Bradwell* concurrence. In *Goesaert*, a six-vote majority upheld, against an equal protection challenge, a Michigan statute that prohibited women from being licensed as bartenders unless they were the wives or daughters of male owners of licensed liquor establishments. Justice Frankfurter, for the majority, assessed the Michigan law with an eye to whether it had a "rational basis" and hence was subject to the Court's least exacting scrutiny:

> The Constitution in enjoining the equal protection of the laws upon States precludes irrational discrimination as between persons or groups of persons in the incidence of a law. But the Constitution does not require situations "which are different in fact or opinion to be treated in law as though they were the same." *Tigner v. State of Texas*, 310 U.S. 141 [(1940)]. Since bartending by women may, in the allowable legislative judgment, give rise to moral and social problems against which it may devise preventive measures, the legislature need not go to the full length of prohibition if it believes that as to a defined group of females other factors are operating which either eliminate or reduce the moral and social problems otherwise calling for prohibition. Michigan evidently believes that the oversight assured through ownership of a bar by a barmaid's husband or father minimizes hazards that may confront a barmaid without such protecting oversight. This Court is certainly not in a position to gainsay such belief by the Michigan legislature. If it is entertainable, as we think it is, Michigan has not violated its duty to afford equal protection of its laws.

For many years, state laws reflected the traditional view of the appropriate relationship between the sexes in their domestic life: father decides, mother nurtures. For example, some states codified the common law rule that a father is sole guardian of his children. Similarly, a father, but not a mother, could sue for the wrongful death of a legitimate child and a father could make a testamentary guardianship appointment for a child but a mother could do so only if the father was dead or incapable of consent. If parents separated or divorced, many states made the presumption that the mother was presumed to be the preferred custodial parent if the child was of tender years.

In 1864, the first Idaho Territorial Legislature adopted a code designed to facilitate the probate of the estates of deceased persons. Section 15-314 of the Probate Code provided that if several persons demonstrated themselves to be equally capable of serving as the administrator of an estate, "males must be preferred to females, and relatives of the whole to those of the half blood." Section 15-314 was identical to the probate code of California, which in turn was based on the probate code of New York. The code remained in effect and without challenge until it was repealed by the Idaho legislature in 1971. However, § 15-314 was in effect when Richard Lynn Reed, the adopted son of Sally and Cecil Reed, died on March 29, 1967, without a will. His parents, who had separated before Richard died, were his only legal heirs.

Approximately seven months after Richard's death, Sally Reed filed a petition in the Probate Court of Ada County, Idaho, requesting that she be appointed the administrator of her son's estate. Her petition declared that the value of the estate did not exceed $1,000. Before the date set for the hearing on Sally Reed's petition, Cecil Reed filed a competing petition with the court to have himself appointed administrator of his son's estate. The court held a hearing on the two petitions and then entered an order appointing Cecil Reed. The probate court observed that both parents were equally qualified to administer the estate, but that under Idaho Code § 15-314, males were preferred over females.

Sally Reed appealed to the Idaho District Court for the Fourth Judicial District, contending that § 15-314 violated the Idaho Civil Rights Act and the Equal Protection Clause of the Fourteenth Amendment. The district court held that the statute violated the Equal Protection Clause. Cecil Reed appealed that decision to the Idaho Supreme Court, which reversed. That court declared § 15-314 reflected a legitimate state interest and therefore was constitutional. It reasoned, in part, that the statute was "not designed to discriminate but is only designed to alleviate the problem of holding hearings by the court to determine eligibility to administer."

Sally Reed appealed to the Supreme Court of the United States.

Highlights of Supreme Court Arguments

BRIEF FOR SALLY REED

♦ The sex line drawn by § 15-314—mandating subordination of women to men without regard to individual capacity—creates a "suspect classification" that requires close judicial scrutiny. Legislatures may distinguish between individuals on the basis of their need or ability but it may not distinguish on the basis of an unalterable identifying trait over which the individual has no control and for which he or she should not be disadvantaged by the law. Biological differences between the sexes bear no relationship to the duties performed by the administrator of an estate. Section 15-314 takes no account of the respective qualifications of the individuals involved and lacks a fair and substantial relation to a permissible legislative purpose.

♦ Prior decisions of this Court have contributed to the separate and unequal status of women in the United States. The time is ripe for the Court to repudiate the premise that, with minimal justification, the legislature may draw a sharp line between the sexes. At the very least, the Court should reverse the presumption of rationality when sex-based discrimination is implicated.

♦ If the Court retains the "rational basis" standard of review in sex discrimination cases, it should at least require the party defending the statute to prove that it is rational.

AMICUS CURIAE BRIEFS SUPPORTING SALLY REED

Joint brief of the American Veterans Committee, Inc., and the NOW Legal Defense and Education Fund., Inc.; American Civil Liberties Union Foundation; City of New York; National Federation of Business and Professional Women's Clubs, Inc.

BRIEF FOR CECIL REED

◆ Probate preference statutes were enacted to provide a guide in probate practice and have been used by courts in all states to facilitate the probate of estates. Probate statutes that prefer males to females have been deemed rational whenever they have come before the courts.

◆ Although § 15-314 was adopted by an all-male legislature that was elected by an all-male electorate, women have had the right to vote in Idaho since 1896. Section 15-314 was not removed from the books until 1971. Women have therefore joined in the common consent to the statute for many years.

◆ The Fourteenth Amendment was not adopted to prohibit the enactment of laws making a distinction on the basis of sex. *Bradwell v. Illinois* contains a good discussion of what rights were guaranteed by the amendment, made at the time near the enactment of § 15-314.

◆ A recent "equal rights amendment" was defeated after a hearing in the Senate. Chaos would result if that amendment became law and the same chaos would result by adopting Sally Reed's position in this case. The remedy should be with the electorate, not the courts.

SUPREME COURT DECISION: *9–0*

BURGER, C.J.

... The arbitrary preference established in favor of males by § 15-314 of the Idaho Code cannot stand in the face of the Fourteenth Amendment's command that no State deny the equal protection of the laws to any person within its jurisdiction....

Section 15-314 is restricted in its operation to those situations where competing applications for letters of administration have been filed by both male and female members of the same entitlement class[.]... In such situations, § 15-314 provides that different treatment be accorded to the applicants on the basis of their sex; it thus establishes a classification subject to scrutiny under the Equal Protection Clause.

In applying that clause, this Court has consistently recognized that the Fourteenth Amendment does not deny to States the power to treat different classes of persons in different ways.... The Equal Protection Clause of that amendment does, however, deny to States the power to legislate that different treatment be accorded to persons placed by a statute into different classes on the basis of criteria wholly unrelated to the objective of that statute. A classification "must be reasonable, not arbitrary, and must rest upon some ground of difference having a fair and substantial relation to the object of the legislation, so that all persons similarly circumstanced shall be treated alike." *Royster Guano Co. v. Virginia*, 253 U.S. 412 (1920). The question presented by this case, then, is whether a difference in the sex of competing applicants for letters of administration bears a rational relationship to a state objective that is sought to be advanced by the operation of ... § 15-314....

[T]he objective of reducing the workload on probate courts by eliminating one class of contests is not without some legitimacy. The crucial question, however, is whether § 15-314 advances that objective in a manner consistent with the command of the Equal Protection Clause. We hold that it does not. To give a mandatory preference to members of either sex over members of the other,

merely to accomplish the elimination of hearings on the merits, is to make the very kind of arbitrary legislative choice forbidden by the Equal Protection Clause of the Fourteenth Amendment; and whatever may be said as to the positive values of avoiding intrafamily controversy, the choice in this context may not lawfully be mandated solely on the basis of sex....

By providing dissimilar treatment for men and women who are thus similarly situated, the challenged section violates the Equal Protection Clause.

The judgment of the Idaho Supreme Court is reversed and the case remanded for further proceedings not inconsistent with this opinion.

Reversed and remanded.

COMMENT

Ruth Bader Ginsburg of Rutgers Law School was the lead counsel on the brief for Sally Reed in *Reed v. Reed*. In 1993, she became the second woman appointed to the Supreme Court of the United States, joining Justice Sandra Day O'Connor, who was appointed in 1981.

QUESTIONS

1. Although Sally Reed prevailed in the litigation, in what respect might *Reed* be seen as a setback for purposes of Equal Protection analysis? Is there any evidence in the Court's opinion that it considered Sally Reed's argument that classifications based on gender should be subjected to heightened judicial scrutiny?

2. Counsel for Cecil Reed concluded his brief as follows:

   > The briefs of appellant and the *amicus curiae* contain material which is irrelevant [sic] and of more interest to sociologists and legislatures than a court, and more emotional than legal. The gist of appellant's argument is that there "ought to be a law," and if they have briefed the case sufficiently to ascertain the present condition of Idaho Probate Law and the recent indication of the attitude of the Idaho State Legislature as indicated in the 1971 Session Laws they cannot be greatly concerned with this particular case....

   On what reading of the Equal Protection Clause does that argument have merit? To what extent does the Court impermissibly expand on the intentions of the drafters of that amendment when it applies the strictures of the Equal Protection Clause to classifications other than race?

3. Counsel for Sally Reed argued:

> Very recent history has taught us that, where racial discrimination is concerned, this Court's refusal in *Plessy v. Ferguson* to declare the practice unconstitutional, reinforced the institutional and political foundations of racism, made it more difficult eventually to extirpate, and postponed for fifty-eight years the inevitable inauguration of a national commitment to abolish racial discrimination.

Are race and sex comparable classes, defined by physiological characteristics, through which status is fixed by birth? If so, are not classifications based on race and sex equally suspect? What factors might account for the Court's conclusion in *Reed* that a heightened level of judicial scrutiny regarding gender is not constitutionally required?

EQUAL PROTECTION: SEPARATE SPHERES AND GENDER EQUALITY

Craig v. Boren
429 U.S. 190 (1976)

SETTING

In his *Reed* opinion, Chief Justice Burger *seemed* to suggest that laws that discriminate on the basis of sex might be subject to more rigorous judicial review than the sort of review required under a mere "rational basis" test. The next term, the Court revisited the question of the appropriate standard of review in *Frontiero v. Richardson*, 411 U.S. 677 (1973), a Fifth Amendment case challenging a federal legislative classification based on gender. In that case, U.S. Air Force Lieutenant Sharron Frontiero and her husband Joseph challenged two federal statutes that defined spouses of male members of the armed forces as dependents eligible for certain housing, medical, and dental benefits, while spouses of females in the military were not defined as dependents unless they actually were dependent upon their wives for over one-half their support.

Among other things, the Frontieros argued that the Supreme Court should subject the laws to strict judicial scrutiny and require the federal government to prove that its discriminatory approach to fringe benefits was necessary, not merely rationally related to the accomplishment of a permissible governmental purpose.

Although the Supreme Court struck down the discriminatory laws 8–1 (Justice Rehnquist dissented), no majority of the justices could agree on the applicable standard of review. A plurality—Justices Brennan, Douglas, White, and Marshall—declared that classifications based on sex, like classifications based on race, alienage, and national origin, are inherently suspect and must therefore be subjected to close judicial scrutiny. Justice Brennan wrote:

> [T]he [*Reed*] Court implicitly rejected [Idaho's] apparently rational explanation of the statutory scheme, and concluded that, by ignoring the individual qualifications of particular applicants, the challenged statute provided "dissimilar treatment for men and women who are ... similarly situated."... This departure from "traditional" rational-basis analysis with respect to sex-based classifications is clearly justified.

Writing for himself, Justice Blackmun, and Chief Justice Burger, Justice Powell responded:

> It is unnecessary for the Court in this case to characterize sex as a suspect classification, with all of the far-reaching implications of such a holding. *Reed v. Reed*, which abundantly supports our decision today, did not add sex to the narrowly limited group of classifications which are inherently suspect.

Citing *Reed v. Reed*, Justice Stewart merely stated: "The statutes before us work an invidious discrimination in violation of the Constitution." The divided *Frontiero* opinion illustrated the justices' lack of agreement on the appropriate standard of review (or level of judicial scrutiny) to apply to laws that classify on the basis of sex and invited further litigation.

While members of the Supreme Court were sparring over the appropriate level of judicial scrutiny in cases involving classifications based on sex, the Equal Rights Amendment (ERA) was running into trouble politically. First introduced in 1923, versions of the ERA had been promoted in every succeeding session of Congress. In twenty-three words, the proposed Twenty-seventh Amendment declared: "Equality of rights under the law shall not be denied or abridged by the United States or any State on account of sex." Most legal scholars agree that the ERA would have made sex-based classifications inherently suspect. March 22, 1976, was the fourth anniversary of congressional adoption of the ERA. That date saw the ratification process stalled at thirty-four states, four short of the requisite number. No other states voted to ratify that year. On the contrary, Nebraska and Tennessee rescinded their initial ratifications. Although public opinion seemed to support ratification, the ERA was dying.

While the ERA languished and doctrinal confusion prevailed over the standard of review to be applied in cases challenging laws that contained sex-based classifications, the Supreme Court heard arguments in a case brought by a young man challenging a sex-based classification in Oklahoma. An 1890 statute enacted by Oklahoma's first territorial legislature generally established the age of majority for females at eighteen and for males at twenty-one. Subsequent statutes made it unlawful for anyone holding a state license to sell, barter, or give to a minor beer with an alcohol content of 3.2 percent or more. Thus, under Oklahoma law, licensed vendors could sell 3.2

percent beer to females aged eighteen or over but could sell 3.2 percent beer to males only if they were aged twenty-one or older. (The statutes applied only to licensed vendors. Oklahoma law did not prohibit other persons from giving or selling 3.2 percent beer to males over age eighteen.)

In December 1972, Mark Walker, a twenty-year-old student at Oklahoma State University and Carolyn Whitener, a licensed beer vendor at the "Honk and Holler" drive-in convenience store in Stillwater, Oklahoma, filed suit against Oklahoma Governor David Boren and nine other state officials in the U.S. District Court for the Western District of Oklahoma. They sought a declaratory judgment that the Oklahoma statute regarding the sale of 3.2 percent beer violated the Equal Protection and Due Process Clauses of the Fourteenth Amendment.

A district judge for the Western District of Oklahoma dismissed the complaint on the ground that it raised no substantial federal question. Walker and Whitener appealed the dismissal to the Court of Appeals for the Tenth Circuit. That court ruled that the case did raise a substantial federal question, vacated the dismissal, and remanded to the U.S. District Court for the Western District of Oklahoma for trial by a three-judge panel. Following trial, the district court ruled that the classification resulting from the Oklahoma statutes was fairly and substantially related to the objectives of protecting males between the ages of eighteen and twenty-one, and the public generally. Accordingly, the statute did not violate the Fourteenth Amendment. The district court's decision relied heavily on statistical data offered by the state at trial that showed that males in the eighteen to twenty-one age group are more likely to consume beer, that there are greater numbers of vehicle accidents in the younger male group, and that those accidents are related to alcohol use.

During the litigation, Walker passed his twenty-first birthday. He was replaced in the litigation by Curtis Craig, a younger fraternity brother. Craig and Whitener appealed directly to the Supreme Court of the United States, as allowed by federal statute. Craig celebrated his twenty-first birthday before the Supreme Court handed down its decision. Anticipating this possibility, which would deprive Craig of standing to sue, Oklahoma challenged Whitener's standing to sue as well. Her claim was that the Oklahoma statutes arbitrarily imposed financial costs on her business by depriving Walker and Craig of equal protection.

HIGHLIGHTS OF SUPREME COURT ARGUMENTS

BRIEF FOR CRAIG AND WHITENER

◆ This case is controlled by the Court's decision in *Stanton v. Stanton*, 421 U.S. 7 (1975), which held that a Utah statute providing for parental support obligation for sons until age twenty-one but for daughters until age eighteen was irrational. *Stanton* did not require the Court to determine whether some heightened standard of review is required in gender discrimination cases because it found the statute incapable of surviving the lowest standard of review. The Oklahoma statute is as irrational as the Utah statute. If, however, the Court finds the district court's analysis is correct, this case poses the question of the "relevant test" to be applied in gender discrimination cases.

◆ Assuming the proper standard of review to be "rationality," the statistical evidence submitted by the state is stacked and proves nothing more than insignificant differences between male and female sobriety rates in the age group between eighteen and twenty-one.

◆ The state's discrimination is irrational because it bars the soberest and most responsible young males from purchasing beer from a licensed vendor, while allowing access to beer to the drunkest and most irresponsible young females. The irrationality of the statutes is demonstrated by the fact that they accomplish nothing more than requiring a male to purchase beer in a two-step transaction while allowing a female to purchase beer in a one-step transaction.

◆ This is an appropriate case for the Court to acknowledge equality-in-fact in the context of sex. It is impossible to be totally blind to the organic differences between the sexes that has no analogy between the races. Discrimination between the sexes not based on organic differences, however, should be treated as suspect if the discrimination implies inferiority. The discrimination in this case clearly would be void if it were age-racial or age-religious.

AMICUS CURIAE BRIEF SUPPORTING CRAIG AND WHITENER

The American Civil Liberties Union.

BRIEF FOR BOREN

◆ The district court properly applied the test of statutory "rationality" that the Supreme Court declared appropriate in *Reed v. Reed* in cases involving classifications based on gender. The right to purchase beer has never been recognized by any court; therefore, no "heightened" level of judicial scrutiny is required.

◆ The Oklahoma legislature was well within its prerogative in prescribing the regulations it deems most able to protect the people of the state from any harm arising from the sale or use of intoxicants. The Court has consistently upheld states' broad powers in regulating intoxicants following adoption of the Twenty-first Amendment.

◆ The Court's decision in *Goesaert v. Cleary,* 335 U.S. 464 (1948), is additional support for affirming the district court's decision. Under principles of *stare decisis*, that case controls.

◆ The statistical evidence submitted at trial shows different drinking and drinking-influenced behavior patterns between males and females between the ages of eighteen and twenty that support and establish the rationality of the legislative classification.

SUPREME COURT DECISION: 7–2

BRENNAN, J.

[The Court initially concluded that Whitener could rely on the equal protection objections of males 18–20 years of age to establish her claim of unconstitutionality of the age-sex differential.]

... Analysis may appropriately begin with the reminder that *Reed* emphasized that statutory classifications that distinguish between males and females are "subject to scrutiny under the Equal Protection Clause." To withstand constitutional challenge, previous cases establish that classifications by gender must serve important governmental objectives and must be substantially related to achievement of those objectives.... Decisions following *Reed* similarly have rejected administrative ease and convenience as sufficiently important objectives to justify gender-based classifications. And only two Terms ago, *Stanton v. Stanton*, 421 U.S. 7 (1975), expressly stating that *Reed v. Reed* was "controlling," held that Reed required invalidation of a Utah differential age-of-majority statute, notwithstanding the statute's coincidence with and furtherance of the State's purpose of fostering "old notions" of role typing and preparing boys for their expected performance in the economic and political worlds....

In this case, too, "*Reed*, we feel is controlling...." We turn then to the question whether, under *Reed*, the difference between males and females with respect to the purchase of 3.2% beer warrants the differential in age drawn by the Oklahoma statute. We conclude that it does not....

We accept for purposes of discussion the District Court's identification of the objective underlying [the Oklahoma law] as the enhancement of traffic safety.

Clearly, the protection of public health and safety represents an important function of state and local governments. However, appellees' statistics in our view cannot support the conclusion that the gender-based distinction closely serves to achieve that objective and therefore the distinction cannot under *Reed* withstand equal protection challenge....

Even [if appellees'] statistical evidence [were] accepted as accurate, it nevertheless offers only a weak answer to the equal protection question presented here. The most focused and relevant of the statistical surveys, arrests of 18–20-year-olds for alcohol-related driving offenses, exemplifies the ultimate unpersuasiveness of this evidentiary record. Viewed in terms of the correlation between sex and the actual activity that Oklahoma seeks to regulate, driving while under the influence of alcohol, the statistics broadly establish that .18% of females and 2% of males in that age group were arrested for that offense. While such a disparity is not trivial in a statistical sense, it hardly can form the basis for employment of a gender line as a classifying device. Certainly if maleness is to serve as a proxy for drinking and driving, a correlation of 2% must be considered an unduly tenuous "fit." Indeed, prior cases have consistently rejected the use of sex as a decisionmaking factor even though the statutes in question certainly rested on far more predictive empirical relationships than this.

Moreover, the statistics exhibit a variety of other shortcomings that seriously impugn their value to equal protection analysis. Setting aside the obvious methodological problems, the surveys do not adequately justify the salient features of Oklahoma's gender-based traffic-safety law. None purports to measure the use and dangerousness of 3.2% beer as opposed to alcohol generally, a detail that is of particular importance since, in light of its low alcohol level, Oklahoma apparently considers the 3.2% beverage to be "nonintoxicating."... Moreover, many of the studies, while graphically documenting the unfortunate increase in driving while under the influence of alcohol, make no effort to relate their findings to age-sex differentials as involved here. Indeed, the only survey that explicitly centered its attention upon young drivers and their use of beer albeit apparently not of the diluted 3.2% variety reached results that hardly can be viewed as impressive in justifying either a gender or age classification.

There is no reason to belabor this line of analysis. It is unrealistic to expect either members of the judiciary or state officials to be well versed in the rigors of experimental or statistical technique. But this merely illustrates that proving broad sociological propositions by statistics is a dubious business, and one that inevitably is in tension with the normative philosophy that underlies the Equal Protection Clause. Suffice to say that the showing offered by the appellees does not satisfy us that sex represents a legitimate, accurate proxy for the regulation of drinking and driving....

We hold, therefore, that under *Reed*, Oklahoma's 3.2% beer statute invidiously discriminates against males 18–20 years of age....

We conclude that the gender-based differential contained in [the Oklahoma law] constitutes a denial of the equal protection of the laws to males aged 18–20[23] and reverse the judgment of the District Court.

It is so ordered.

BLACKMUN, J., CONCURRING IN PART [OMITTED]

POWELL, J., CONCURRING

... I have reservations as to some of the discussion concerning the appropriate standard for equal protection analysis....

I agree that *Reed v. Reed*, is the most relevant precedent. But I find it unnecessary, in deciding this case, to read that decision as broadly as some of the Court's language may imply. *Reed* and subsequent cases involving gender-based classifications make clear that the Court subjects such classifications to a more critical examination than is normally applied when "fundamental" constitutional rights and "suspect classes" are not present....*

---

[23] Insofar as *Goesaert v. Cleary*, 335 U.S. 464 (1948), may be inconsistent, that decision is disapproved. Undoubtedly reflecting the view that *Goesaert's* Equal Protection analysis no longer obtains, the district court made no reference to that decision in upholding Oklahoma's statute. Similarly, the opinions of the federal and state courts cited earlier in the text invalidating gender lines with respect to alcohol regulation uniformly disparaged the contemporary vitality of *Goesaert*.

* As is evident from our opinions, the Court has had difficulty in agreeing upon a standard of equal protection analysis that can be applied consistently to the wide variety of legislative classifications. There are valid reasons for dissatisfaction with the "two-tier" approach that has been prominent in the Court's decisions in the past decade. Although viewed by many as a result-oriented substitute for more critical analysis, that approach with its narrowly limited "upper-tier" now has substantial precedential support. As has been true of *Reed* and its progeny, our decision today will be viewed by some as a "middle-tier" approach. While I would not endorse that characterization and would not welcome a further subdividing of equal protection analysis, candor compels the recognition that the relatively deferential "rational basis" standard of review normally applied takes on a sharper focus when we address a gender-based classification. So much is clear from our recent cases....

STEVENS, J., CONCURRING

There is only one Equal Protection Clause. It requires every State to govern impartially. It does not direct courts to apply one standard of review in some cases and a different standard in other cases. Whatever criticism may be leveled at a judicial opinion implying that there are at least three such standards applies with the same force to a double standard....

The legislation imposes a restraint on one hundred percent of the males in the class allegedly because about 2 percent of them have probably violated one or more laws relating to the consumption of alcoholic beverages. It is unlikely that this law will have a significant deterrent effect either on that 2 percent or on the law-abiding 98 percent. But even assuming some such slight benefit, it does not seem to me that an insult to all of the young men of the State can be justified by visiting the sins of the 2 percent on the 98 percent.

STEWART, J., CONCURRING

... The disparity created by these Oklahoma statutes amounts to total irrationality. For the statistics upon which the state now relies, whatever their other shortcomings, wholly fail to prove or even suggest that 3.2 beer is somehow more deleterious when it comes into the hands of a male aged 18–20 than of a female of like age. The disparate statutory treatment of the sexes here, without even a colorably valid justification or explanation, thus amounts to invidious discrimination.

BURGER, C.J., DISSENTING

... We have only recently recognized that our duty is not "to create substantive constitutional rights in the name of guaranteeing equal protection of the laws." *San Antonio School Dist. v. Rodriguez*.... Though today's decision does not go so far as to make gender-based classifications "suspect," it makes gender a disfavored classification. Without an independent constitutional basis supporting the right asserted or disfavoring the classification adopted, I can justify no substantive constitutional protection other than the normal ... protection afforded by the Equal Protection Clause.

The means employed by the Oklahoma Legislature to achieve the objectives sought may not be agreeable to some judges, but since eight Members of the Court think the means not irrational, I see no basis for striking down the statute as violative of the Constitution simply because we find it unwise, unneeded, or possibly even a bit foolish....

REHNQUIST, J., DISSENTING

The Court's disposition of this case is objectionable on two grounds. First is its conclusion that *men* challenging a gender-based statute which treats them less favorably than women may invoke a more stringent standard of judicial review than pertains to most other types of classifications. Second is the Court's enunciation of this standard, without citation to any source, as being that "classifications by gender must serve *important* governmental objectives and must be *substantially* related to achievement of those objectives." (Emphasis added.) The only redeeming feature of the Court's opinion, to my mind, is that it apparently signals a retreat by those who joined the plurality opinion in *Frontiero v. Richardson*, 411 U.S. 677

(1973), from their view that sex is a "suspect" classification for purposes of equal protection analysis…. I think the Oklahoma statute challenged here need pass only the "rational basis" equal protection analysis … and I believe it is constitutional under that analysis….

I would have thought that if this Court were to leave anything to decision by the popularly elected branches of the Government, where no constitutional claim other than that of equal protection is invoked, it would be the decision as to what governmental objectives to be achieved by law are "important," and which are not. As for the second part of the Court's new test, the Judicial Branch is probably in no worse position than the Legislative or Executive Branches to determine if there is *any* rational relationship between a classification and the purpose which it might be thought to serve. But the introduction of the adverb "substantially" requires courts to make subjective judgments as to operational effects, for which neither their expertise nor their access to data fits them. And even if we manage to avoid both confusion and the mirroring of our own preferences in the development of this new doctrine, the thousands of judges in other courts who must interpret the Equal Protection Clause may not be so fortunate….

QUESTIONS

1. Does *Craig* have the effect of introducing an intermediate standard of judicial review somewhere between rational basis and strict scrutiny? Despite Justice Powell's denial, in the footnote of his concurrence did he not implicitly endorse a mid-tier level of analysis in sex classification cases? Might not the Court's unanimous *Reed v. Reed* decision provide the best indication of the Court's prevailing approach to sex-based classifications, or do the divergent readings of *Reed* undermine its authority?

2. What standard of review would Justice Rehnquist employ in reviewing sex-based classifications? Is he correct that "the introduction of the adverb 'substantially' requires courts to make subjective judgments as to operational effects, for which neither their expertise nor their access to data fits them"?

3. By the time *Craig* was decided in December 1976, it was becoming evident that the ERA would not be ratified. (Only one additional state ratified the ERA after 1976. Even after Congress extended the ratification deadline by three years and 122 days, until June 30, 1982, supporters' efforts fell short. The final tally was three states short of the required number.)

   Had you been on the Court in 1976, would the status of the ERA ratification process have affected your analysis of the appropriate standard of review in cases challenging sex-based classifications?

COMMENT

The fragmented decision in *Craig* encouraged more litigation on the question of the level of judicial scrutiny in cases involving sex-based classifications. Many cases have been resolved under Title VII of the Civil Rights Act of 1964. Below are examples of cases that the Court resolved on Fourteenth Amendment grounds between *Craig* and *Michael M. v. Superior Court of Sonoma County*, 450 U.S. 464 (1981), the next case excerpted.

Case: *Orr v. Orr*, 440 U.S. 268 (1979)

Vote: 6–3

Decision: An Alabama law providing that husbands, but not wives, may be required to pay alimony following divorce is unconstitutional because the law does not serve important governmental objectives. The sex-based distinction is over-broad and premised on sexual stereotypes insufficiently related to financial need as the basis for awarding alimony.

Case: *Parham v. Hughes*, 441 U.S. 347 (1979)

Vote: 5–3

Decision: A Georgia statute that precludes the father of an illegitimate child who has not legitimated the child from suing for the wrongful death of the child does not violate the Equal Protection Clause because it is a rational method for the state to use in dealing with the problem of proving paternity. Giving the biological father the right to sue for his child's wrongful death only if he has previously acted to identify himself, to undertake his paternal responsibilities, and to legitimate the child, does not reflect any overly broad generalizations about men as a class.

Case: *Caban v. Mohammed*, 441 U.S. 380 (1979)

Vote: 5–3

Decision: A New York statute giving an unwed mother the authority to block the adoption of her child by withholding consent, but not giving the unwed father a similar right, is unconstitutional because it is not substantially related to the state's interest in promoting the adoption of illegitimate children. The sex-based distinction is not required by any universal difference between maternal and paternal relations during a child's development.

Case: *Wengler v. Druggists Mutual Insurance Co.*, 446 U.S. 142 (1980)

Vote: 8–1

Decision: A Missouri worker's compensation statute providing death benefits to widows but not widowers because it is efficient administratively to assume dependence on the part of women but not men, violates the Fourteenth Amendment. Mere administrative convenience is not an important governmental objective justifying discrimination on the basis of sex.

Case: *Kirchberg v. Feenstra*, 450 U.S. 455 (1981)

Vote: 9–0

Decision: A Louisiana law that defines husbands as "head and master" of property owned jointly with their wives, and giving them unilateral control over its disposition, is unconstitutional. The state has failed to show that the statute serves an important governmental interest.

EQUAL PROTECTION:
SEPARATE SPHERES AND GENDER EQUALITY

Michael M. v. Superior Court of Sonoma County
450 U.S. 464 (1981)

SETTING

California's statutory rape law of 1970, Penal Code 261.5, provided that "Unlawful sexual intercourse is an act of sexual intercourse accomplished with a female not the wife of the perpetrator, where the female is under the age of 18 years." Violation of the law was punishable by imprisonment for up to three years.

At about midnight on June 3, 1978, sixteen-year-old Sharon (her last name was not provided because of her juvenile status) and her sister were standing at a bus stop in Rohnert Park, California. The two had been drinking alcohol during the evening. Seventeen-year-old Michael M. (his last name also was not provided because of his juvenile status) and two of his friends approached them. The group walked down to the railroad tracks in the town and talked for a couple of hours while continuing to drink. Sharon and Michael subsequently separated from the group, went into some nearby bushes and started kissing. Sharon eventually told Michael to stop kissing her, but she then accompanied him to a nearby park, where they lay down on a park bench. According to Sharon, Michael told her to take her pants off. She testified:

> I said, "No," and I was trying to get up and he hit me back down on the bench and then I just said to myself, "Forget it," and I let him do what he wanted to do and he took my pants off and he was telling me to put my legs around him and stuff....

According to Sharon, the two then engaged in sexual intercourse.

Michael M. was arrested the next day. The juvenile court found that he was "not a fit subject" for juvenile jurisdiction and on June 27, 1978, he was indicted in the Sonoma County Superior Court for the felony of unlawful sexual intercourse. He moved to dismiss the indictment, claiming that Penal Code § 261.5 violated the Equal Protection Clauses of both the California Constitution and the Constitution of the United States. According to his motion, the statute was invalid because, under it, only females are protected and only males may be prosecuted. His motion was denied.

The California Court of Appeal denied Michael M.'s petition for a writ of prohibition, which would have compelled the superior court to grant his motion to dismiss the indictment. The Supreme Court of California subsequently issued an alternative writ of mandate, ordering the Sonoma County Superior Court to show cause why it should not be compelled to dismiss the indictment. Following receipt of the Superior Court's response, the state supreme court denied Michael M.'s petition for a writ of mandate. It held that, although there was no doubt that § 261.5 discriminated on the basis of sex:

> the obviously discriminatory classification scheme is readily justified by an important state interest.... [T]he immutable physiological fact [is] that it is the female exclusively who can become pregnant. This changeless physical law, coupled with the tragic human costs of illegitimate teenage pregnancies, generates a compelling and demonstrable state interest in minimizing both the number of such pregnancies and their disastrous consequences.

The Supreme Court of the United States granted Michael M.'s petition for a writ of certiorari.

HIGHLIGHTS OF SUPREME COURT ARGUMENTS

BRIEF FOR MICHAEL M.

◆ California's statutory rape law reflects and perpetuates invidious sexual discrimination. The contrast of imprisonment for males for conduct in which females can engage with impunity is perhaps the greatest disparity in the treatment of the sexes ever challenged before this court. Modern statutory rape laws embrace and perpetuate the traditional stereotypical view of the sexes.

◆ The California law arbitrarily holds the male criminally culpable even though the female may be older, more mature, or herself the sexual aggressor.

◆ The California statute does not serve important governmental interests nor is it substantially related to the achievement of any governmental interests. The only governmental interest asserted to justify the gender-based classification of the statute is the prevention of teenage pregnancies. The statute does very little to combat that problem: The statute proscribes male sexual activity irrespective of whether pregnancy can result.

◆ Application of the statute is broader than necessary to prevent pregnancy. The failure of the statute to exclude prepubescent females and couples who use reliable birth control devices evidences an intent to forbid the act of sexual intercourse itself.

AMICUS CURIAE BRIEF SUPPORTING MICHAEL M.

Joint brief of the American Civil Liberties Union and the ACLU of Northern California; Women's Legal Defense Fund.

BRIEF FOR SONOMA COUNTY SUPERIOR COURT

◆ Penal Code § 621.5 serves the important governmental interest of deterring teenage pregnancies by protecting the victim from the act necessary to conception. Because virtually all the significant harmful consequences of teenage pregnancy fall on the young female, the legislature has rationally chosen to provide punishment for the participant who suffers none of the burdens of his conduct.

◆ The statutory classification is not overinclusive because the risk of teenage pregnancy and its frequent occurrence are sufficient to justify the legislation. California is not constitutionally compelled to adopt a gender-neutral statute.

◆ The law challenged in this case is uniquely different from other gender-based classifications considered by this Court previously. They all have involved economic consequences. This statute is based on recognition of the biological distinctions between minor males and females.

◆ The statute is constitutional as applied in this case, because it is being applied in the context of forcible conduct. Michael M. lacks standing to challenge application of the statute in a situation in which the minor female is older than the male and is herself the aggressor.

AMICUS CURIAE **BRIEF SUPPORTING SONOMA COUNTY SUPERIOR COURT**

United States.

SUPREME COURT DECISION: 5–4

REHNQUIST, STEWART, AND POWELL, J.J.,
AND BURGER, C.J.

... As is evident from our opinions, the Court has had some difficulty in agreeing upon the proper approach and analysis in cases involving challenges to gender-based classifications.... Unlike the California Supreme Court, we have not held that gender-based classifications are "inherently suspect" and thus we do not apply so-called "strict scrutiny" to those classifications.... Our cases have held, however, that the traditional minimum rationality test takes on a somewhat "sharper focus" when gender-based classifications are challenged. *Craig v. Boren.* In *Reed v. Reed*, for example, the Court stated that a gender-based classification will be upheld if it bears a "fair and substantial relationship" to legitimate state ends, while in *Craig v. Boren* the Court restated the test to require the classification to bear a "substantial relationship" to "important governmental objectives."

Underlying these decisions is the principle that a legislature may not "make overbroad generalizations based on sex which are entirely unrelated to any differences between men and women or which demean the ability or social status of the affected class." *Parham v. Hughes*, 441 U.S. 347 (1979). But because the Equal Protection Clause does not "demand that a statute necessarily apply equally to all persons" or require "things which are different in fact ... to be treated in law as though they were the same," *Rinaldi v. Yeager*, 384 U.S. 305 (1966), this Court has consistently upheld statutes where the gender classification is not invidious, but rather realistically reflects the fact that the sexes are not similarly situated in certain circumstances....

Applying those principles to this case, the fact that the California Legislature criminalized the act of illicit sexual intercourse with a minor female is a sure indication of its intent or purpose to discourage that conduct. Precisely why the legislature desired that result is of course somewhat less clear.... [T]he individual legislators may have voted for the statute for a variety of reasons. Some legislators may have been concerned about preventing teenage pregnancies, others about protecting young females from physical injury or from the loss of "chastity," and still others about promoting various religious and moral attitudes towards premarital sex.

The justification for the statute offered by the State, and accepted by the Supreme Court of California, is that the legislature sought to prevent illegitimate teenage pregnancies. That finding, of course, is entitled to great deference....

We need not be medical doctors to discern that young men and young women are not similarly situated with respect to the problems and the risks of sexual intercourse. Only women may become pregnant, and they suffer disproportionately the profound physical, emotional and psychological consequences of sexual activity. The statute at issue here protects women from sexual intercourse at an age when those consequences are particularly severe.

The question thus boils down to whether a State may attack the problem of sexual intercourse and teenage pregnancy directly by prohibiting a male from having sexual intercourse with a minor female. We hold that such a statute is sufficiently related to the State's objectives to pass constitutional muster.

Because virtually all of the significant harmful and inescapably identifiable consequences of teenage pregnancy fall on the young female, a legislature acts well within its authority when it elects to punish only the participant who, by nature, suffers few of the consequences of his conduct. It is hardly unreasonable for a legislature acting to protect minor females to exclude them from punishment. Moreover, the risk of pregnancy itself constitutes a substantial deterrence to young females. No similar natural sanctions deter males. A criminal sanction imposed solely on males thus serves to roughly "equalize" the deterrents on the sexes....

We similarly reject petitioner's argument that Sec. 261.5 is impermissibly overbroad because it makes unlawful sexual intercourse with prepubescent females, who are, by definition, incapable of becoming pregnant. Quite apart from the fact that the statute could well be justified on the grounds that very young females are particularly susceptible to physical injury from sexual intercourse ... it is ludicrous to suggest that the Constitution requires the California Legislature to limit the scope of its rape statute to older teenagers and exclude young girls....

Accordingly, the judgment of the California Supreme Court is Affirmed.

STEWART, J., CONCURRING

... [I]t is readily apparent that Sec. 261.5 does not violate the Equal Protection Clause. Young women and men are not similarly situated with respect to the problems and risk associated with intercourse and pregnancy, and the statute is realistically related to the legitimate state purpose of reducing those problems and risks....

[T]he Equal Protection Clause does not mean that the physiological differences between men and women must be disregarded. While those differences must never be permitted to become a pretext for invidious discrimination, no such discrimination is presented by this case. The Constitution surely does not require a State to pretend that demonstrable differences between men and women do not really exist.

BLACKMUN, J., CONCURRING IN THE JUDGMENT

It is gratifying that the plurality recognizes that "[a]t the risk of stating the obvious, teenage pregnancies ... have increased dramatically over the last two decades" and "have significant social, medical, and economic consequences for both the mother and her child, and the State." There have been times when I have wondered whether the Court was capable of this perception, particularly when it has struggled with the different but not unrelated problems that attend abortion issues....

I, however, cannot vote to strike down the California statutory rape law, for I think it is a sufficiently reasoned and constitutional effort to control the problem at its inception. For me, there is an important difference between this state action and a State's adamant and rigid refusal to face, or even to recognize, the "significant ... consequences"—to the woman—of a forced or unwanted conception. I have found it difficult to rule constitutional, for example, state efforts to block, at that later point, a woman's attempt to deal with the enormity of the problem confronting her, just as I have rejected state efforts to prevent women from rationally taking steps to prevent that problem from arising....

BRENNAN, WHITE, MARSHALL, J.J., DISSENTING

... After some uncertainty as to the proper framework for analyzing equal protection challenges to statutes containing gender-based classifications ... this Court settled upon the proposition that a statute containing a gender-based classification cannot withstand constitutional challenge unless the classification is substantially related to the achievement of an important governmental objective.... This analysis applies whether the classification discriminates against males or against females....

[A] State's bare assertion that its gender-based statutory classification substantially furthers an important governmental interest is not enough to meet its burden of proof under *Craig v. Boren.* Rather, the State must produce evidence that will persuade the court that its assertion is true....

The State has not produced such evidence in this case....

Until very recently, no California court or commentator had suggested that the purpose of California's statutory rape law was to protect young women from the risk of pregnancy. Indeed, the historical development of Sec. 261.5 demonstrates that the law was initially enacted on the premise that young women, in contrast to young men, were to be deemed legally incapable of consenting to an act of sexual intercourse. Because their chastity was considered particularly precious, those young women were felt to be uniquely in need of the State's protection. In contrast, young men were assumed to be capable of making such decisions for themselves; the law therefore did not offer them any special protection.

It is perhaps because the gender classification in California's statutory rape law was initially designed to further these outmoded sexual stereotypes, rather than to reduce the incidence of teenage pregnancies, that the State has been unable to demonstrate a substantial relationship between the classification and its newly asserted goal....

STEVENS, J., DISSENTING

... In my opinion, the only acceptable justification for a general rule requiring disparate treatment of the two participants in a joint act must be a legislative judgment that one is more guilty than the other. The risk-creating conduct that this statute is designed to prevent requires the participation of two persons—one male and one female. In many situations it is probably true that one is the aggressor and the other is either an unwilling, or at least a less willing, participant in the joint act. If a statute authorized punishment of only one participant and required the prosecutor to prove that that participant had been the aggressor, I assume that the discrimination would be valid. Although the question is less clear, I also assume, for the purpose of deciding this case, that it would be permissible to punish only the male participant, if one element of the offense were proof that he had been the aggressor, or at least in some respects the more responsible participant in the joint act. The statute at issue in this case, however, requires no such proof....

[E]ven if my logic is faulty and there actually is some speculative basis for treating equally guilty males and females differently, I still believe that any such speculative justification would be outweighed by the paramount interest in evenhanded enforcement of the law. A rule that authorizes punishment of only one of two equally guilty wrongdoers violates the essence of the constitutional requirement that the sovereign must govern impartially.

I respectfully dissent.

QUESTIONS

1. What level of judicial scrutiny did the plurality employ in *Michael M.*? Why? What about the dissenters? Did all of the justices rely on the analytical framework of *Craig v. Boren*? If so, had the Court decided that statutory classifications based on sex are suspect? Subject to what level of judicial scrutiny?

2. Solicitor General Wade H. McCree Jr. argued on behalf of the United States:

   > This case involves one of what we believe is a quite small class of situations in which a legislature may justifiably differentiate between men and women. Undisputed biological facts establish that young men and young women are not similarly situated as to the problems and risks of sexual intercourse. Women alone can become pregnant, and they alone must face the physical and psychological dangers of childbearing or abortion. In addition, sexual intercourse poses serious physical problems for prepubescent females not shared by prepubescent males. Furthermore, because of their physiological differences, women and not men are the victims of forcible heterosexual rape—a problem that statutory rape provisions ameliorate.

   McCree's argument seems to be that because women are different, the state can constitutionally protect them, and not men. Is this line of argument akin to contending that biology is destiny?

3. If Justice Stevens had prevailed in *Michael M.*, and you were legal counsel for the state of California, what changes would you make in § 261.5 to make the law accord with Stevens's opinion? Would Justice

Stevens's approach require eliminating the statutory rape law altogether?

4. California successfully defended its statutory rape law on the ground that it was designed to protect young women from the risk of pregnancy. In fact, the legislative history of the law shows that it was premised on the assumption that young women are legally incapable of consenting to an act of sexual intercourse and therefore are in need of the state's protection. Young men, by contrast, are capable of making such decisions for themselves. What showing must a state make when a statute discriminates on the basis of sex? Could California have successfully defended its statutory rape law if it had acknowledged the law's original purpose?

EQUAL PROTECTION:
SEPARATE SPHERES AND GENDER EQUALITY

Mississippi University for Women v. Hogan
458 U.S. 718 (1982)

SETTING

The Mississippi University for Women (MUW) is a state-supported institution in Columbus, Mississippi, that was established in 1884 as an exclusively female institution. In 1971, MUW opened a college of nursing. At that time, the state supported two other coeducational universities that offered bachelor's degrees in nursing: University of Southern Mississippi in Hattiesburg and University of Mississippi in Jackson. MUW was the only one of Mississippi's public universities that limited its enrollment to females and the state had no university that limited enrollment to males. Although MUW strictly adhered to its all-female enrollment policy for students receiving academic credit, it did permit men to audit courses.

On September 13, 1979, Joe Hogan, a white male resident of Columbus, Mississippi, applied for admission to the nursing program at MUW. Hogan had already earned a nursing certificate and had extensive experience. He wished to earn a Bachelor of Science degree in nursing, which would entitle him to higher pay at his present job at Golden Triangle Regional Medical Center, afford him greater promotional opportunities, and qualify him to be a nurse anesthesiologist.

Hogan applied to MUW because it was close to his home. Attending the Hattiesburg or Jackson campuses—both over 150 miles from Columbus—would require him to uproot his wife and children and to abandon his employment. A week after he submitted his application, Hogan was advised that he had been rejected because MUW restricts enrollment to women. Hogan was otherwise qualified for admission.

Hogan filed suit against MUW in the U.S. District Court for the Northern District of Mississippi, seeking an injunction and declaratory judgment that the single-sex admissions policy violated the Equal Protection Clause of the Fourteenth Amendment. He sought $25,000 in damages, in addition to costs and reasonable attorney fees. The district court denied his claim. It ruled that MUW's gender-based enrollment policy was "not arbitrary" because it bore a "rational relationship to Mississippi's legitimate interest in providing the greatest practical range of educational opportunities for its female student population." Hogan appealed to the U.S. Court of Appeals for the Fifth Circuit. Noting that the district court had erred in using a "rational basis" test and applying the test that gender-based classifications must be substantially related to important governmental objectives in order to withstand constitutional challenge, the Fifth Circuit reversed. The Supreme Court of the United States granted the university's petition for a writ of certiorari.

HIGHLIGHTS OF SUPREME COURT ARGUMENTS

BRIEF FOR MUW

◆ MUW serves a unique purpose: It provides an alternative learning atmosphere for females that is nothing more than educational affirmative action for females. Such a statutory classification denies no rights. Instead, it addresses a national commitment to eliminate—and compensate for—discrimination due to sex.

◆ Analysis of recent scientific studies leads to the conclusion that women's universities and colleges have a unique place in the current scheme of higher education and provide for some female students opportunity for achievement that would be lost by the absorption of male students into the student body.

BRIEF FOR HOGAN

◆ The narrow question is whether MUW has met its burden of demonstrating that its refusal to admit Hogan, solely on account of his sex, is substantially related to achievement of important governmental objectives.

◆ MUW is not operated to promote the goals it now asserts. No woman has ever been president of MUW and its faculty and administration are male-dominated. Its curriculum is heavily weighted in subjects leading to traditionally "female" careers. The institution does not provide students with role models.

AMICUS CURIAE BRIEFS SUPPORTING HOGAN

Joint brief of National League for Women Legal Defense and Education Fund, National Women's Law Center, and Women's Legal Defense Fund.

SUPREME COURT DECISION: 5–4

O'CONNOR, J.

… We begin our analysis aided by several firmly established principles. Because the challenged policy expressly discriminates among applicants on the basis of gender, it is subject to scrutiny under the Equal Protection Clause of the Fourteenth Amendment. That this statutory policy discriminates against males rather than against females does not exempt it from scrutiny or reduce the standard of review. Our decisions also establish that the party seeking to uphold a statute that classifies individuals on the basis of their gender must carry the burden of showing an "exceedingly persuasive justification" for the classification. The burden is met only by showing at least that the classification serves "important governmental objectives and that the discriminatory means employed" are "substantially related to the achievement of those objectives."

Although the test for determining the validity of a gender-based classification is straightforward, it must be applied free of fixed notions concerning the roles and abilities of males and females. Care must be taken in ascertaining whether the statutory objective itself reflects archaic and stereotypic notions. Thus, if the statutory objective is to exclude or "protect" members of one gender because they are presumed to suffer from an inherent handicap or to be innately inferior, the objective itself is illegitimate.

If the State's objective is legitimate and important, we next determine whether the requisite direct, substantial relationship between objective and means is present. The purpose of requiring that close relationship is to assure that the validity of a classification is determined through reasoned analysis rather than through the mechanical application of traditional, often inaccurate, assumptions about the proper roles of men and women. The need for the requirement is amply revealed by reference to the broad range of statutes already invalidated by this Court, statutes that relied upon the simplistic, outdated assumption that gender could be used as a "proxy for other, more germane bases of classification," to establish a link between objective and classification.

Applying this framework, we now analyze the arguments advanced by the State to justify its refusal to allow males to enroll for credit in MUW's School of Nursing. The State's primary justification for maintaining the single-sex admissions policy of MUW's School of Nursing is that it compensates for discrimination against women and, therefore, constitutes educational affirmative action. As applied to the School of Nursing, we find the State's argument unpersuasive.…

It is readily apparent that a State can evoke a compensatory purpose to justify an otherwise discriminatory classification only if members of the gender benefited by the classification actually suffer a disadvantage related to the classification.…

Mississippi has made no showing that women lacked opportunities to obtain training in the field of nursing or to attain positions of leadership in that field when the MUW School of Nursing opened its door or that women currently are deprived of such opportunities.… As one would expect, the labor force reflects [a] predominance of women in nursing.… When MUW's School of Nursing began operation, nearly 98 percent of all employed registered nurses were female.

Rather than compensate for discriminatory barriers faced by women, MUW's policy of excluding males from admission to the School of Nursing tends to perpetuate the stereotyped view of nursing as an exclusively woman's job…. [A]lthough the State recited a "benign, compensatory purpose," it failed to establish that the alleged objective is the actual purpose underlying the discriminatory classification.

The policy is invalid also because it fails the second part of the equal protection test, for the State has made no showing that the gender-based classification is substantially and directly related to its proposed compensatory objective. To the contrary, MUW's policy of permitting men to attend classes as auditors fatally undermines its claim that women, at least those in the School of Nursing, are adversely affected by the presence of men…. In sum, the record in this case is flatly inconsistent with the claim that excluding men from the School of Nursing is necessary to reach any of MUW's educational goals….

Because we conclude that the State's policy of excluding males from MUW's School of Nursing violates the Equal Protection Clause of the Fourteenth Amendment, we affirm the judgment of the Court of Appeals. It is so ordered.

BURGER, C.J., DISSENTING

I agree generally with Justice Powell's dissenting opinion. I write separately, however, to emphasize that the Court's holding today is limited to the context of a professional nursing school. Since the Court's opinion relies heavily on its finding that women have traditionally dominated the nursing profession, it suggests that a State might well be justified in maintaining, for example, the option of an all-women's business school or liberal arts program.

BLACKMUN, J., DISSENTING

… [T]here is inevitable spillover from the Court's ruling today. That ruling, it seems to me, places in constitutional jeopardy any state-supported educational institution that confines its student body in any area to members of one sex, even though the State elsewhere provides an equivalent program to the complaining applicant. The Court's reasoning does not stop with the School of Nursing of the Mississippi University for Women….

POWELL AND REHNQUIST, J.J., DISSENTING

… The issue in this case is whether a State transgresses the Constitution when—within the context of a public system that offers a diverse range of campuses, curricula, and educational alternatives—it seeks to accommodate the legitimate personal preferences of those desiring the advantages of an all-women's college. In my view, the Court errs seriously by assuming—without argument or discussion—that the equal protection standard generally applicable to sex discrimination is appropriate here. That standard was designed to free women from "archaic and overbroad generalizations…" *Schlesinger v. Ballard*, 419 U.S. 498 (1975). In no previous case have we applied it to invalidate state efforts to expand women's choices. Nor are there prior sex discrimination decisions by this Court in which a male plaintiff, as in this case, had the choice of an equal benefit….

By applying heightened equal protection analysis to this case, the Court frustrates the liberating spirit of the Equal Protection Clause. It prohibits the States from providing women with an opportunity to choose the type of university they prefer. And yet it is these women whom the Court regards as the victims of an illegal, stereotyped perception of the role of women in our society....

The Court views this case as presenting a serious equal protection claim of sex discrimination. I do not, and I would sustain Mississippi's right to continue MUW on a rational-basis analysis....

[T]he practice of voluntarily chosen single-sex education is an honored tradition in our country, even if it now rarely exists in state colleges and universities. Mississippi's accommodation of such student choices is legitimate because it is completely consensual and is important because it permits students to decide for themselves the type of college education they think will benefit them most. Finally, Mississippi's policy is substantially related to its long-respected objective....

Questions

1. What level of judicial scrutiny did Justice O'Connor apply in *Hogan*? What about the dissenters? Did Justice Powell suggest that the reasons underlying the particular sex classification would influence his choice about the appropriate level of judicial scrutiny?

2. An *amicus* brief filed on behalf of 18,700 graduates of MUW urged the Court to grant the petition for certiorari and to reverse the Fifth Circuit. Among its arguments was the following:

   The broad spectrum of positive actions to overcome the discriminations and abuses intended to be abolished by the Fourteenth Amendment certainly should include programs to uplift women from their Nineteenth Century status as the suppressed sex. Legions of witnesses could testify to the advantages afforded to achieve that goal by a woman's college or university as opposed to one whose doors are open to both sexes.

   We sincerely believe that the narrow Fourteenth Amendment interpretation of the Fifth Circuit Panel opinion is a regressive and a repressive holding which fails to take into consideration the laudable and progressive purposes of Mississippi's maintenance of its University for Women. The opinion, of course, emasculates the very reason for the existence of the Institution for if it is not Mississippi University for Women, it is by obvious definition a university without *raison d'etre*.

   Is it significant that MUW did not argue at the trial level that its single-sex policy was justified as an affirmative action program for females? If the argument made by MUW graduates were to be made at the appropriate level by graduates of an all-male military school, would it prevail?

3. In light of the way *Hogan* was argued by MUW at the district court level—especially its failure to show that its female-only nursing school was intended to redress historic sex discrimination—what might explain the close Supreme Court vote? What language in the dissenting opinions suggests that the minority justices viewed *Hogan*

as a highly significant opinion in the arena of sex discrimination? Did the justices in dissent suggest that *Hogan* is the beginning of the end of publicly supported single-sex colleges and universities?

4. Ruth Bader Ginsburg was appointed to the Supreme Court in 1993, ten years after *Hogan* was decided. In her first concurring opinion after her confirmation as the second female justice, she observed that the status of sex as a suspect classification "remains an open question." *Harris v. Forklift Systems, Inc.*, 510 U.S. 17 (1993). Was her observation correct?

EQUAL PROTECTION: SEPARATE SPHERES AND GENDER EQUALITY

United States v. Virginia
116 S.Ct. 2264 (1996)

SETTING

Virginia Military Institute (VMI) is a state military college in Lexington, Virginia, founded in 1839. In the early 1990s, VMI's enrollment was approximately 1,250. For its entire history VMI had a policy of admitting only men to its four-year undergraduate degree program. All of Virginia's fourteen other institutions of higher education are coeducational. The VMI curriculum includes liberal arts and science and engineering courses, leading to either a Bachelor of Arts or Bachelor of Science degree.

VMI's mission statement declares that its goal is to produce "citizen-soldiers" who are "educated and honorable men who are suited for leadership in civilian life and who can provide military leadership when necessary." The leadership and character development methods at VMI are "adversative," emphasizing physical rigor, mental stress, absolute equality of treatment, absence of privacy, minute regulation of behavior, and indoctrination of values. The method is implemented through a military-style system that includes the "rat line" (the first seven months during which first-year cadets are treated "like the lowest animal on earth") designed to foster self-confidence by showing cadets that they are capable of doing tasks that surpass their own perceived limits. The "class system" at VMI teaches those who have survived the "rat line" the value system and behaviors that VMI promotes. All VMI cadets live in a military-style environment—they wear uniforms, eat in a mess hall, live in stark barracks, and regularly participate in parades and drills.

In March 1990, responding to a complaint filed with the U.S. attorney general by a female high school student seeking admission to VMI, the United States sued the Commonwealth of Virginia, Virginia Governor George F. Allen, VMI, its superintendent, and others responsible for the operation of VMI. The complaint, filed in the U.S. District Court for the Western District of Virginia, alleged that VMI's men-only admissions policy violated the Equal Protection Clause of the Fourteenth Amendment and sought an order enjoining VMI from excluding women. Two private organizations—the VMI Foundation and the VMI Alumni Association—intervened as defendants. Neither Governor Allen nor the Commonwealth of Virginia participated in the liability phase of the action.

The trial court entered judgment for VMI. It held that the exclusion of women was substantially related to the state interests asserted by VMI—"educating cadets for lives as 'citizen-soldiers'" and fostering "system-wide diversity by providing an opportunity for single-sex education and by providing a distinctive program on military-style education."

The U.S. Court of Appeals for the Fourth Circuit reversed, holding that VMI's admissions policy violated the Equal Protection Clause of the Fourteenth Amendment. Nonetheless, it concluded that admitting women at VMI would result in important institutional changes and remanded the case to the district court "to give the Commonwealth the responsibility to select a course it chooses, so long as the guarantees of the Fourteenth Amendment are satisfied." The Supreme Court of the United States denied VMI's petition for a writ of certiorari.

On remand, VMI proposed maintaining VMI as a male-only institution and creating a women-only Virginia Women's Institute for Leadership (VWIL) as a separate program to be located on the campus of Mary Baldwin College, a private women's liberal arts college founded in 1842 and located approximately thirty-five miles from VMI. Mary Baldwin College is ranked among the best liberal arts colleges in the South and has a Phi Beta Kappa chapter. The VWIL program was to be based on "a cooperative method which reinforces self-esteem rather than the leveling process used at VMI." The task force that was created to design and implement the VWIL program determined that a military model, "especially VMI's adversative method, would be wholly inappropriate for educating and training most women for leadership roles" and rejected VMI's military lifestyle. However, VWIL students would be able to participate in the Mary Baldwin Reserve Officer Training Cadet (ROTC) program for up to four hours per week.

The district court approved VMI's proposed remedial plan. The court acknowledged that the VWIL program "differs substantially from the VMI program," but held that the differences were "justified pedagogically" because of the "developmental and emotional differences between the sexes." The court concluded:

> If VMI marches to the beat of a drum, then Mary Baldwin marches to the melody of a fife and when the march is over, both will have arrived at the same destination.

On appeal, the Court of Appeals for the Fourth Circuit affirmed, based on a three-pronged test that it derived from *Mississippi Univ. for Women v. Hogan*:

1. The governmental objective be "consistent with a legitimate govern-mental role" and "not pernicious"
2. The sex-based classification be "important in serving" that objective
3. The benefits provided to each sex through separate programs be "sub-stantively comparable"

According to the Fourth Circuit:

> If we were to place men and women into the adversative relationship inher-ent in the VMI program, we would destroy, at least for that period of the adversative training, any sense of decency that still permeates the relation-ship between the sexes.

The Supreme Court of the United States granted the U.S. petition for a writ of certiorari. The Commonwealth of Virginia cross-petitioned for certiorari on the ground that the Equal Protection Clause permits a state to offer a peda-gogically beneficial single-sex college program as a complement to its diverse statewide system of public and private higher education. The Supreme Court granted that petition as well.

HIGHLIGHTS OF SUPREME COURT ARGUMENTS

BRIEF FOR UNITED STATES

◆ A state cannot prohibit enrollment in a state institution of higher learn-ing on the basis of sex without an exceedingly persuasive justification. VMI has failed to articulate an important objective that supports the provision of its unique educational opportunity to men only.

◆ The only adequate remedy is for VMI to stop excluding women from its student body because of their sex. The policy of excluding women regardless of their individual abilities and characteristics violates the guarantee of equal protection of the laws.

◆ VMI's admissions policy conveys the message that, while men can sur-mount their limitations and exceed their expectations, for women, biology is destiny.

◆ VMI has failed to show that if women were admitted, the whole pro-gram would collapse.

◆ The VWIL program is not an adequate "parallel" to VMI under the Equal Protection Clause. There are substantial, undisputed differences between the two programs. The differences are deliberate and are unconsti-tutionally premised on explicit and archaic sex-based stereotypes and gener-alizations about the sociological and psychological characteristics of men and women. The VWIL program cannot survive intermediate scrutiny.

AMICUS CURIAE BRIEFS SUPPORTING THE UNITED STATES

Nancy Mellette (South Carolina resident who had applied for admission to the Citadel, the Military College of South Carolina); joint brief of the Employment Law Center, Equal Rights Advocates, Inc., Chinese for

Affirmative Action, National Economic Development and Law Center, Human Rights Advocates, Women's Employment Rights Clinic of Golden Gate College of Law, Professors Maria Blando, Connie de la Vega, Marci Seville, and Stephanie Wildman; joint brief of the American Association of University Professors, Center for Women Policy Studies, Program on Gender, Science and Law, and twenty-five individuals engaged in gender research; joint brief of the National Women's Law Center and American Civil Liberties Union; joint brief of the States of Maryland, Hawaii, Massachusetts, Nevada, and Oregon and the Commonwealth of the Northern Mariana Islands; joint brief of thirteen members of the military and Women Active in Our Nation's Defense, Their Advocates and Supporters; joint brief of twenty-six private women's colleges.

BRIEF FOR VIRGINIA REGARDING SINGLE-SEX COLLEGE PROGRAMS

◆ The liability ruling of the courts below has the effect of precluding government-sponsored single-sex education for students of one gender absent a parallel program for students of the other gender. That standard does not permit states to take into account the pedagogical value of single-sex education for some students and the differing education needs and interests of students.

◆ This Court has recognized that providing diverse educational opportunities is one of the most important objectives of state and local governments.

◆ Requiring the state to offer two single-sex programs in order to justify the continued existence of one program of proven excellence produces only a superficial and formalistic equality while sacrificing the ability of professional educators to respond in the most effective and flexible ways to the challenges of education.

BRIEF FOR VIRGINIA REGARDING LIABILITY

◆ It is an established and unchallenged fact that single-sex education offers substantial pedagogical advantages to many young men and women.

◆ VWIL offers women students the opportunity to obtain a single-sex undergraduate education with military training in an integrated program designed to achieve the same goals as VMI: education, military training, mental and physical discipline, character development, and leadership development.

◆ Expert testimony established that an adversative method of teaching in an all-female school would be inappropriate and would be destructive of women's self-confidence.

◆ The unspoken premise of the United States' brief is that the Constitution should be construed to forbid public single-sex education. Neither precedent nor public policy supports that position. Single-sex education at VMI serves important governmental interests. The proven benefits of single-sex education are a central and important part of the overall experience afforded to VMI's students.

AMICUS CURIAE BRIEFS SUPPORTING VIRGINIA

Joint brief of Wells College, Southern Virginia College, and Saint Mary's College; joint brief of Independent Women's Forum, Women's Economic Project, and four women currently or formerly active in the field of education; joint brief of Center for Military Readiness, Family Research Council, the Minnesota Family Council, Concerned Women for America, Madison Project, Eagle Forum, Free Congress Foundation, and Northstar Legal Center; joint brief of seven scholars and educators with professional interest and expertise in women's education and leadership development; joint brief of Women's Schools Together, Inc., Boys' Schools: An International Coalition, and eighteen individuals concerned with maintaining single-sex education; joint brief of South Carolina and the Citadel; South Carolina Institute of Leadership for Women at Converse College; Mary Baldwin College.

SUPREME COURT DECISION: 7–1

(Thomas, J., did not participate.)

GINSBURG, J.

... Parties who seek to defend gender-based government action must demonstrate an "exceedingly persuasive justification" for that action [*Mississippi Univ. for Women*]....

To summarize the Court's current directions for cases of official classification based on gender: Focusing on the differential treatment or denial of opportunity for which relief is sought, the reviewing court must determine whether the proffered justification is "exceedingly persuasive." The burden of justification is demanding and it rests entirely on the State.... The justification must be genuine, not hypothesized or invented *post hoc* in response to litigation. And it must not rely on overbroad generalizations about the different talents, capacities, or preferences of males and females.

The heightened review standard our precedent establishes does not make sex a proscribed classification....

"Inherent differences" between men and women, we have come to appreciate, remain cause for celebration, but not for denigration of the members of either sex or for artificial constraints on an individual's opportunity. Sex classifications may be used to compensate women "for particular economic disabilities [they have] suffered," *Califano v. Webster*, 430 U.S. 313 (1977), to "promot[e] equal employment opportunity" ... to advance full development of the talent and capacities of our Nation's people. But such classifications may not be used, as they once were, to create or perpetuate the legal, social, and economic inferiority of women. Measuring the record in this case against the review standard just described, we conclude that Virginia has shown no "exceedingly persuasive justification" for excluding all women from the citizen-soldier training afforded by VMI....

Virginia describes the current absence of public single-sex higher education for women as "an historical anomaly." But the historical record indicates action more deliberate than anomalous: First, protection of women against higher education; next, schools for women far from equal in resources and stature to schools for men; finally, conversion of the separate schools to coeducation.

Our 1982 decision in *Mississippi Univ. for Women* prompted VMI to reexamine its male-only admission policy. Virginia relies on that reexamination as a legitimate basis for maintaining VMI's single-sex character. [However], we find no persuasive evidence in this record that VMI's male-only admission policy "is in furtherance of a state policy of 'diversity.'"... A purpose genuinely to advance an array of educational options ... is not served by VMI's historic and constant plan—a plan to "affor[d] a unique educational benefit only to males." However "liberally" this plan serves the State's sons, it makes no provision whatever for her daughters. That is not *equal* protection....

Women's successful entry into the federal military academies, and their participation in the Nation's military forces, indicate that Virginia's fears for the future of VMI may not be solidly grounded. The State's justification for excluding all women from "citizen-soldier" training for which some are qualified, in any event, cannot rank as "exceedingly persuasive," as we have explained and applied that standard....

In the second phase of the litigation, Virginia presented its remedial plan—maintain VMI as a male-only college and create VWIL as a separate program for women....

A remedial decree, this Court has said, must closely fit the constitutional violation; it must be shaped to place persons unconstitutionally denied an opportunity or advantage in "the position they would have occupied in the absence of [discrimination]." See *Milliken v. Bradley*, 433 U.S. 267 (1977). The constitutional

violation in this case is the categorical exclusion of women from an extraordinary educational opportunity afforded men. A proper remedy for an unconstitutional exclusion, we have explained, aims to "eliminate [so far as possible] the discriminatory effects of the past" and to "bar like discrimination in the future." *Louisiana v. United States*, 380 U.S. 145 (1965).

Virginia chose not to eliminate, but to leave untouched, VMI's exclusionary policy. For women only, however, Virginia proposed a separate program, different in kind from VMI and unequal in tangible and intangible facilities....

In myriad respects other than military training, VWIL does not qualify as VMI's equal....

A prime part of the history of our Constitution, historian Richard Morris recounted, is the story of the extension of constitutional rights and protections to people once ignored or excluded. VMI's story continued as our comprehension of "We the People" expanded. There is no reason to believe that the admission of women capable of all the activities required of VMI cadets would destroy the Institute rather than enhance its capacity to serve the "more perfect Union."

For the reasons stated, the initial judgment of the Court of Appeals, is affirmed, the final judgment of the Court of Appeals, is reversed, and the case is remanded for further proceedings consistent with this opinion.

It is so ordered.

REHNQUIST, C.J., CONCURRING IN JUDGMENT

... The Court defines the constitutional violation in this case as "the categorical exclusion of women from an extraordinary educational opportunity afforded to men." By defining the violation in this way, and by emphasizing that a remedy for a constitutional violation must place the victims of discrimination in "'the position they would have occupied in the absence of [discrimination],'" the Court necessarily implies that the only adequate remedy would be the admission of women to the all-male institution.... I would not define the violation in this way; it is not the "exclusion of women" that violates the Equal Protection Clause, but the maintenance of an all-men school without providing any—much less a comparable—institution for women.

Accordingly, the remedy should not necessarily require either the admission of women to VMI, or the creation of a VMI clone for women. An adequate remedy in my opinion might be a demonstration by Virginia that its interest in educating men in a single-sex environment is matched by its interest in educating women in a single-sex institution. To demonstrate such, the State does not need to create two institutions with the same number of faculty Ph D's, similar SAT scores, or comparable athletic fields. Nor would it necessarily require that the women's institution offer the same curriculum as the men's; one could be strong in computer science, the other could be strong in liberal arts. It would be a sufficient remedy, I think, if the two institutions offered the same quality of education and were of the same overall caliber....

In the end, the women's institution Virginia proposes, VWIL, fails as a remedy, because it is distinctly inferior to the existing men's institution and will continue to be for the foreseeable future. VWIL simply is not, in any sense, the institution that VMI is.... I therefore ulti-mately agree with the Court that Virginia has not provided an adequate remedy.

SCALIA, J., DISSENTING

... I have no problem with a system of abstract tests such as rational-basis, intermediate, and strict scrutiny (though I think we can do better than applying strict scrutiny and intermediate scrutiny whenever we feel like it). Such formulas are essential to evaluating whether the new restrictions that a changing society constantly imposes upon private conduct comport with that "equal protection" our society has always accorded in the past. But in my view the function of this Court is to *preserve* our society's values regarding (among other things) equal protection, not to *revise* them; to prevent backsliding from the degree of restriction the Constitution imposed upon democratic government, not to prescribe, on our own authority, progressively higher degrees. For that reason it is my view that, whatever abstract tests we may choose to devise, they cannot supersede—and indeed ought to be crafted so as to reflect—those constant and unbroken national traditions that embody the people's understanding of ambiguous constitutional texts. More specifically, it is my view that "when a practice not expressly prohibited by the text of the Bill of Rights bears the endorsement of a long tradition of open, widespread, and unchallenged use that dates back to the beginning of the Republic, we have no proper basis for striking it down." *Rutan v. Republican Party of Ill.*, 497 U.S. 62 (1990).

Today, however, change is forced upon Virginia, and reversion to single-sex education is prohibited nationwide, not by democratic processes but by order of this Court. Even while bemoaning the sorry, bygone days of "fixed notions" concerning women's education, the Court favors current notions so fixedly that it is willing to write them into the Constitution of the United States by application of custom-built "tests." This is not the interpretation of a Constitution, but the creation of one....

Not content to execute a *de facto* abandonment of the intermediate scrutiny that has been our standard for sex-based classifications for some two decades, the Court purports to reserve the question whether, even in principle, a higher standard (i.e., strict scrutiny) should apply....

[I]t is perfectly clear that, if the question of the applicable standard of review for sex-based classifications were to be regarded as an appropriate subject for reconsideration, the stronger argument would be not for elevating the standard to strict scrutiny, but for reducing it to rational-basis review.... It is hard to consider women a "discrete and insular minorit[y]" unable to employ the "political processes ordinarily to be relied upon," [Footnote 4, *United States v. Carolene Products Co.*, 304 U.S. 144 (1938)], when they constitute a majority of the electorate. And the suggestion that they are incapable of exerting that political power smacks of the same paternalism that the Court so roundly condemns....

As is frequently true, the Court's decision today will have consequences that extend far beyond the parties to the case. What I take to be the Court's unease with these consequences, and its resulting unwillingness to acknowledge them, cannot alter the reality.

Under the constitutional principles announced and applied today, single-sex public education is unconstitutional. By going through the motions of applying a balancing test—asking whether the State has adduced an "exceedingly persuasive justification" for its sex-based classification—the Court creates the illusion that government officials in some future case will have a clear shot at justifying some sort of single-sex public education. Indeed, the Court seeks to create even a greater illusion than that: It purports to have said nothing of relevance to *other* public schools at all....

There are few extant single-sex public educational programs. The potential of today's decision for widespread disruption of existing institutions lies in its application to private single-sex education. Government support is immensely important to private educational institutions....

The only hope for state-assisted single-sex private schools is that the Court will not apply in the future the principles of law it has applied today. That is a substantial hope, I am happy and ashamed to say. After all, did not the Court today abandon the principles of law it has applied in our earlier sex-classification cases? And does not the Court positively invite private colleges to rely upon our ad-hocery by assuring them this case is "unique"? I would not advise the foundation of any new single-sex college (especially an all-male one) with the expectation of being allowed to receive any government support; but it is too soon to abandon in despair those single-sex colleges already in existence. It will certainly be possible for this Court to write a future opinion that ignores the broad principles of law set forth today, and that characterizes as utterly dispositive the opinion's perceptions that VMI was a uniquely prestigious all-male institution, conceived in chauvinism, etc., etc. I will not join that opinion.

QUESTIONS

1. Does Justice Ginsburg's opinion for the Court in *VMI* mark an abandonment of the intermediate scrutiny standard for evaluating sex-based classifications, as Justice Scalia contends in dissent? If so, what is the new standard?

2. On what basis did Chief Justice Rehnquist join the majority in *VMI*? Is there an element of "we tried to warn you" in the chief justice's opinion?

3. Justice Scalia contends in his dissent in *VMI* that "the function of this Court is to *preserve* our society's values regarding (among other things) equal protection, not to *revise* them." (Emphasis in original.) Does Justice Scalia's statement suggest that he would have dissented in a case like *Brown v. Board of Education* on the basis of historical fact and experience?

4. What is the significance, if any, of the following facts in determining whether the majority or dissenting opinions in *VMI* are more sound:

   Almost half of the new male cadets each year at VMI fail the physical fitness test and are offered remedial training.

   VMI has traditionally admitted students who are average in academic performance and, through the character development program, graduates people who have more than average commitment and motivation as well as character.

   Admitting women to VMI would affect the absence-of-privacy rule: Although male cadets would lack privacy from other men and women would lack privacy from other women, members of each sex would enjoy privacy from members of the other sex in some daily life functions.

   At least 15 percent of the females in the VMI applicant pool could successfully undertake all the individual activities required of VMI cadets, including rat line tasks, physical training drills, and the VMI fitness test.

   VMI cadets who participate in National Collegiate Athletic Association sports are excused from "rat training" while practicing their sport.

   A Mission Study Committee in 1983 recommended maintaining VMI as an all-male institution.

   Each of the U.S. military academies admits women; only VMI and the Citadel refuse to do so, making five thousand fewer openings available to women interested in a military career than are available to men.

SUGGESTIONS FOR FURTHER READING

Baer, Judith A., *Equality Under the Constitution: Reclaiming the Fourteenth Amendment* (Ithaca, NY: Cornell University Press, 1983).

_____, *Women in American Law: The Struggle Toward Equality from the New Deal to the Present* (New York, NY: Holmes and Meier, 1996).

Barrett, Edward L., "The Rational Basis Standard for Equal Protection Review of Ordinary Legislative Classifications," 68 *Kentucky Law Journal* (1979–80): 845.

Bartlett, Katharine T., and Rosanne Kennedy, eds., *Feminist Legal Theory: Readings in Law and Gender* (Boulder, CO: Westview, 1991).

Berger, Vivian, "Man's Trial, Woman's Tribulation: Rape Cases in the Courtroom," 77 *Columbia Law Review* (1977): 17.

Blumberg, Grace, "*De Facto* and *De Jure* Sex Discrimination under the Equal Protection Clause: A Reconsideration of the Veteran's Preference in Public Employment," 26 *Buffalo Law Review* (1977): 3.

Brown, Barbara A., Thomas I. Emerson, Gail Falk, and Ann E. Freedman, "The Equal Rights Amendment: A Constitutional Basis for Equal Rights for Women," 80 *Yale Law Journal* (1971): 16.

Chester, Ronald, *Unequal Access: Women Lawyers in a Changing America* (South Hadley, MA: Bergin & Garvey, 1985).

Comment, "Forcible and Statutory Rape: An Exploration of the Operation Objectives of the Consent Standard," 62 *Yale Law Journal* (1952): 55.

Comment, "The Constitutionality of Statutory Rape Laws," 27 *University of California Los Angeles Law Review* (1978): 5.

Crenshaw, Kimberle, "Demarginalizing the Intersection of Race and Sex," *University of Chicago Law Forum* (1989): 139.

Davis, Angela Y., *Women, Race & Class* (New York, NY: Random House, 1983).

Di Gennaro, Judith, "Statutory Rape Law in California: Unequal Protection of the Minor Male," 2 *Criminal Justice Journal* (1979): 239.

Epstein, Cynthia Fuchs, *Women in Law* (Garden City, NY: Doubleday, 1983).

Evans, Sara, *Personal Politics: The Roots of Women's Liberation in the Civil Rights Movement and the New Left* (New York, NY: Vintage Books, 1980).

Flexner, Eleanor, *Century of Struggle*, rev. ed. (Cambridge, MA: Harvard University Press, 1975).

Freedman, Ann E., "Sex Equality, Sex Differences and the Supreme Court," 92 *Yale Law Journal* (1984): 913.

Frug, Mary Jo, "Sexual Equality and Sexual Difference in American Law," 26 *New England Law Review* (1992): 665.

_____, *Postmodern Legal Feminism* (New York, NY: Routledge, 1992).

Getman, Julius G., "The Emerging Constitutional Principle of Sexual Equality," *The Supreme Court Review* (Chicago, IL: University of Chicago Press, 1972).

Ginsburg, Ruth Bader, "Gender and the Constitution," 44 *Cincinnati Law Review* (1975): 1.

_____, "Gender in the Supreme Court: The 1973 and 1974 Terms," *The Supreme Court Review* (Chicago, IL: University of Chicago Press, 1975).

_____, "Some Thoughts on Benign Classifications in the Context of Sex," 10 *Connecticut Law Review* (1978): 813.

_____, "Sex Equality and the Constitution," 52 *Tulane Law Review* (1978): 451.

_____, "Speaking in a Judicial Voice," 67 *New York University Law Review* (1992): 1185.

Goldstein, Leslie Friedman, ed., *Feminist Jurisprudence: The Difference Debate* (Lanham, MD: Rowman & Littlefield, 1992).

Gunther, Gerald, "The Supreme Court 1971 Term, Foreword: In Search of Evolving Doctrine on a Changing Court: A Model for A Newer Equal Protection," 86 *Harvard Law Review* (1972): 1.

Hagan, John, and Fiona Kay, *Gender in Practice: A Study of Lawyers' Lives* (New York, NY: Oxford University Press, 1995).

Hartmann, Susan M., *From Margin to Mainstream: American Women and Politics since 1960* (New York, NY: Knopf, 1989).

Hodes, William W., "Women and the Constitution: Some Legal History and a New Approach to the Nineteenth Amendment," 25 *Rutgers Law Review* (1970): 26.

_____, "A Disgruntled Look at *Reed v. Reed*," 1 *Women's Rights Law Reporter* (1972): 9.

Hoff, Joan, *Law, Gender, and Injustice: A Legal History of U.S. Women* (New York, NY: New York University Press, 1991).

hooks, bell, *Feminist Theory: From Margin to Center* (Boston, MA: South End Press, 1984).

Kanowitz, Leo, "'Benign' Sex Discrimination: Its Troubles and Their Cure," 31 *Hastings Law Quarterly* (1980): 1379.

Kay, Herma Hill, "Models of Equality," *University of Illinois Law Review* (1985): 39.

Kline, Marlee, "Race, Racism, and Feminist Legal Theory," 12 *Harvard Women's Law Journal* (1898): 115.

Law, Silvia A., "Rethinking Sex and the Constitution," 132 *University of Pennsylvania Law Review* (1984): 955.

Lentz, Berhard F., and David N. Laband, *Sex Discrimination in the Legal Profession* (Westport, CT: Quorum Books, 1995).

Littleton, Christine A., "Does It Still Make Sense to Talk about 'Women'?" 1 *UCLA Women's Law Journal* (1991): 15.

MacKinnon, Catharine, *Feminism Unmodified: Discourses on Life and Law* (Cambridge, MA: Harvard University Press, 1987).

Mansbridge, Jane J., *Why We Lost the ERA* (Chicago, IL: University of Chicago Press, 1986).

McGlen, Nancy E., and Karen O'Connor, *Women's Rights: The Struggle for Equality in the 19th and 20th Centuries* (New York, NY: Praeger, 1983).

Minow, Martha, *Making All the Difference: Inclusion, Exclusion, and American Law* (Ithaca, NY: Cornell University Press, 1990).

Morello, Karen Berger, *The Invisible Bar: The Woman Lawyer in America, 1638 to the Present* (New York, NY: Random House, 1986).

Note, "Sex Discrimination and Equal Protection: Do We Need a Constitutional Amendment?" 84 *Harvard Law Review* (1971): 1499.

Olsen, Frances, "Statutory Rape: A Feminist Critique of Rights Analysis," 63 *Texas Law Review* (1984): 387.

_____, "From False Paternalism to False Equality: Judicial Assaults on Feminist Community, Illinois, 1869–1895," 84 *Michigan Law Review* (1986): 1518.

Pierce, Jennifer L., *Gender Trials: Emotional Lives in Contemporary Law Firms* (Berkeley, CA: University of California Press, 1995).

Porter, Mary Cornelia, "Androgny and the Supreme Court," 1 *Women and Politics* (Winter 1980–81): 23.

Posner, Richard A., "An Economic Analysis of Sex Discrimination Laws," 56 *University of Chicago Law Review* (1989): 1311.

_____, *Sex and Reason* (Cambridge, MA: Harvard University Press, 1992).

_____, *Overcoming Law* (Cambridge, MA: Harvard University Press, 1995).

Resnik, Judith, "On the Bias: Feminist Reconsideration of the Aspirations of Our Judges," 61 *California Law Review* (1988): 1877.

Rhode, Deborah L., *Justice and Gender: Sex Discrimination and the Law* (Cambridge, MA: Harvard University Press, 1989).

_____, *Speaking of Sex: The Denial of Gender Inequality* (Cambridge, MA: Harvard University Press, 1997).

Rhode, Deborah L., ed., *Theoretical Perspectives on Difference* (New Haven, CT: Yale University Press, 1990).

Russell, Diana E. H., *The Politics of Rape: The Victim's Perspective* (New York, NY: Stein and Day, 1984).

Scales-Trent, Judith, "Black Women and the Constitution: Finding Our Place, Asserting Our Rights," 24 *Harvard Civil Rights-Civil Liberties Law Review* (1989): 9.

Scott, Joan, "Deconstructing Equality versus Difference," 14 *Feminist Studies* (1988): 33.

Sherry, Suzanna, "Civic Virtue and the Feminine Voice in Constitutional Adjudication," 72 *Virginia Law Review* (1986): 543.

Smith, Patricia, ed., *Feminist Jurisprudence* (New York, NY: Oxford University Press, 1993).

Taub, Nadine, and Elizabeth M. Schneider, "Perspectives on Women's Subordination and the Role of Law," in *The Politics of Law*, ed. David Kairys (New York, NY: Pantheon, 1982).

Symposium, "Feminist Critical Legal Studies and Postmodernism, Part One: A Diversity of Influence," 26 *New England Law Review* (1992): 639.

Symposium, "Feminist Critical Legal Studies and Postmodernism, Part Two: The Politics of Gender Identity," 26 *New England Law Review* (1992): 1173.

Wasserstrom, Richard A., "Racism, Sexism, and Preferential Treatment: An Approach to the Topic," 24 *University of California Los Angeles Law Review* (1977): 581.

Weisberg, D. Kelly, ed., *Feminist Legal Theory: Foundations* (Philadelphia, PA: Temple University Press, 1993).

Wilkinson, J. Harvie, III, "The Supreme Court, the Equal Protection Clause, and the Three Faces of Constitutional Equality," 61 *Virginia Law Review* (1975): 945.

Williams, Joan, "Deconstructing Gender," 87 *Michigan Law Review* (1989): 797.

Williams, Patricia J., *The Alchemy of Race and Rights: Diary of a Law Professor* (Cambridge, MA: Harvard University Press, 1991).

_____, *The Rooster's Egg: On the Persistence of Prejudice* (Cambridge, MA: Harvard University Press, 1995).

Williams, Wendy, "The Equality Crisis: Some Reflections on Culture, Courts, and Feminism," 7 *Women's Rights Law Reporter* (1982): 175.

Wing, Adrien Katherine, ed., *Critical Race Feminism: A Reader* (New York, NY: New York University Press, 1997).

Wriggens, Jennifer, "Rape, Racism, and the Relationship of Racism and Sexism," 6 *Harvard Women's Law Journal* (1983): 6.

EQUAL PROTECTION: AFFIRMATIVE ACTION

Regents of the University of California v. Bakke
438 U.S. 265 (1978)

SETTING

Since the Second World War, efforts to break down social barriers based on factors such as race, gender, and alienage have proceeded on two related fronts. One has been litigation and legislation aimed at removing legal and other formal barriers to equal opportunity. The classic examples of this approach are the school desegregation cases and legislation such as the Civil Rights Act of 1964. The federal government pioneered the second approach by mandating positive—or "affirmative"—action by employers and educational institutions to improve job and schooling opportunities for disadvantaged groups. The rationale of the mandate was that, because of the ways that discrimination skewed the societal playing field, "equality of opportunity" was a hollow promise for many groups of Americans. As President Lyndon Johnson explained to the 1965 Howard University graduating class:

Freedom is not enough. You do not wipe out scars of centuries by saying,

"Now you're free to go where you want and do as you desire." You do not take a person who for years has been hobbled by chains and liberate him, bring him up to the starting line of a race, and then say, "You're free to compete," and justly believe you have been completely fair. Thus it is not enough to open the gates of opportunity. All of our citizens must have the ability to walk through those gates; and this is the next and most profound stage of the battle for civil rights.

Affirmative action policies trace their origins to a series of executive orders, issued over several years by Presidents Roosevelt, Truman, and Eisenhower, that banned employment discrimination. Some of those executive orders were issued in response to protests by civil rights activists, who pointed out the striking incongruity between American ideals and American social conditions in the 1940s and 1950s, and were intended to improve employment opportunities for blacks. Others, such as those issued by President Roosevelt, reflected wartime labor shortages and the need for defense contractors to hire without discriminating against any worker because of race, creed, color, or national origin. In 1961, President Kennedy issued an executive order establishing the President's Committee on Equal Employment Opportunity. That order also required private companies to agree to nondiscriminatory employment policies in order to receive federal contracts. In 1965, President Johnson issued Executive Order 11246, prohibiting employment discrimination by federal contractors on the basis of race, creed, color, and national origin. Three years later Johnson added sex discrimination to the list. When the Office of Federal Contract Compliance was created in 1969, one of its provisions authorized the secretary of labor to ensure nondiscrimination by employers doing business with the government. The regulations developed by the Department of Labor to implement Executive Order 11246 mandated preferential hiring on the ground that preferences were required to remedy the consequences of centuries-old sex- and race-based discrimination.

The national government created other affirmative action programs as well. Public sector programs like the Nixon administration's "Philadelphia Plan," patterned after experimental programs in the building trades in St. Louis, Cleveland, and San Francisco, required contractors to set specific minority hiring goals in order to qualify for federal funding. Such federal regulations and programs spawned adoption of "racially conscious" employment and admissions programs in the private sector as well as in state and local governments.

The medical school at the University of California at Davis (UCD) opened in 1968 with an entering class of fifty students, a number that stabilized at one hundred by 1971. Because of the low number of minority students in the first two classes (no blacks, American Indians or Mexican-Americans), compared with the 25 percent racial and ethnic minority population in California, the faculty implemented a "Task Force" or special admissions program. The goals of the program were to enhance diversity in the student body and the profession, to eliminate historic barriers to medical careers for disadvantaged racial and ethnic minority groups, and to increase aspiration for medical careers on the part of members of those groups.

The UCD Task Force consisted of a separate admissions system operating in coordination with the regular admissions program. Only "disadvantaged" minority applicants qualified for the special program. Factors such as financial means, need to work during undergraduate career, and parents' economic and occupational background were taken into account. Minority applicants with no history of disadvantage were referred to the regular admissions process.

Unlike the regular UCD admissions process, the Task Force did not use an arbitrary grade point average cut-off figure as the basis for determining which applicants were granted admission interviews. The special program also employed an interview process that paralleled the regular program. Final selection of Task Force applicants was made by the full admissions committee. All students admitted under the special program met the requirements for a medical education at Davis.

Allan Bakke, a white student with a Bachelor of Science degree in mechanical engineering from the University of Minnesota, a Master of Science degree in mechanical engineering from Stanford University, and four years' service in the U.S. Marine Corps, applied for admission to the entering classes of 1973 and 1974 under the regular admission program. He was one of 2,464 applicants in 1973 and one of 3,737 applicants in 1974. In 1973, Bakke was granted an interview and received a benchmark score of 468 out of 500. He was rejected because his application was late, and in the general admissions program no applicants who had submitted applications after the deadline with scores lower than 470 were accepted. In 1974, Bakke's application was submitted early. His benchmark score that year was 549 out of 600. Again, he was rejected. In both years, however, sixteen applicants with grade point averages, entrance exam and benchmark scores lower than Bakke's were admitted through the Task Force program.

Following his second rejection, Bakke filed a complaint in the Superior Court of Yolo County, California, seeking injunctive and declaratory relief compelling his admission to Davis Medical School. He claimed that the Task Force program reduced the number of places available to him and thereby denied him equal protection of the laws guaranteed by the Fourteenth Amendment. The university filed a cross-complaint seeking a declaration that the Task Force program was lawful.

The trial court held that the Task Force program discriminated against white applicants on the basis of race and entered judgment against the university on its cross-complaint. It refused to order Bakke's admission, however, because he had not proven that he would have been admitted in the absence of the Task Force program.

The university and Bakke both appealed to the California Court of

Appeal for the Third Appellate District. While the appeals were pending in that court, the California Supreme Court granted the university's petition for a transfer and accepted the case for direct review because of the importance of the issues involved. Relying solely on federal constitutional law, the supreme court held that the Davis Task Force violated the Equal Protection Clause of the Fourteenth Amendment and that the trial court erred by putting the burden on Bakke to prove that he would have been admitted except for the Task Force. However, the court did not prevent the university from formulating a special admission program based on disadvantage. It said, "We do not compel the University to utilize only 'the highest objective academic credentials' as the criterion for admission."

The California Supreme Court subsequently modified its decision and directed that Bakke be admitted to Davis Medical School because of the university's stipulation that it could not prove that Bakke would not have been admitted absent the Task Force program. The university petitioned the Supreme Court of the United States for a writ of certiorari.

HIGHLIGHTS OF SUPREME COURT ARGUMENTS

Note: In their initial briefs, Bakke and the university argued only the relevance of the Equal Protection Clause of the Fourteenth Amendment. The Court requested supplementary briefs on the applicability of Title VI of the Civil Rights Act of 1964, consistent with its policy of resolving controversies on constitutional grounds only if a statutory resolution is not possible. In light of the Court's holding in the opinion that Title VI must be held to proscribe only those racial classifications that would violate the Equal Protection Clause or the equal protection component of the Due Process Clause of the Fifth Amendment, the statutory arguments are not summarized here.

BRIEF FOR THE BOARD OF REGENTS

◆ The outcome in this case will decide for future decades whether blacks, Chicanos, and other insular minorities are to have meaningful access to higher education and real opportunities to enter the learned professions, or whether they will be penalized indefinitely by the disadvantages flowing from previous pervasive discrimination.

◆ Evidence is compelling that use of racially blind admissions criteria has resulted in near total exclusion of historically disfavored minorities from the medical profession. In 1970, for example, only 2.1 percent of physicians in the United States were black. As competition for admission to medical schools intensifies, failure to implement race-conscious admissions policies will prolong indefinitely essentially all-white student bodies and the extreme scarcity and isolation of minority physicians.

◆ Unlike law schools, which rely on numerical indicators, medical schools have traditionally placed more emphasis on noncognitive factors in the admission process. The Davis Task Force program is another step in the process of broadening admissions criteria.

◆ Use of racial criteria in any context is cause for concern. Use of racial criteria for purposes of achieving racial diversity in schools and countering the effects of a legacy of discrimination, however, have been judicially approved. The use of race as a criterion in medical school admissions is justified in light of the long history of discrimination against racial and other insular minorities.

◆ It is inappropriate to characterize the Task Force program as setting racial "quotas" for each class because there is no floor beneath which minority presence is permitted to fall. Every student admitted to Davis is fully qualified. If fewer than sixteen minority applicants are qualified, the goal is not met.

◆ "Strict scrutiny" is not the appropriate standard of judicial review in this case. That standard is appropriate only to racial classifications aimed at harming groups historically alienated and denied a voice in political affairs. Applying the strict scrutiny standard to measures intended to aid such groups would stand the Equal Protection Clause on its head and result in unwarranted judicial intervention in matters of educational policy properly reserved to the states and to educators.

◆ Even if the Court does apply a strict scrutiny standard of review, the Davis Task Force program is valid because the goals of the program are as compelling as any imaginable in the country. Attempts to achieve those goals through other means—such as aggressive recruitment and attempting to build more medical schools—have failed. Only if the Court finds the goals of the program illegal can the California Supreme Court's decision be affirmed.

AMICUS CURIAE BRIEFS SUPPORTING THE BOARD OF REGENTS

United States; thirty-four organizations including the American Bar Association, the American Civil Liberties Union, the National Council of Churches, and the American Association of University Professors, several colleges and universities, and public institutions such as the California Fair Employment Practices Commission also urged upholding of the Davis program.

BRIEF FOR BAKKE

◆ Bakke was barred from attending Davis Medical School because of its racial quota admission policy. The Equal Protection Clause prohibits states from discriminating against "any person" on the basis of race. The Court's consistent modern view of the clause is that discrimination on the basis of race is unlawful unless strictly necessary to promote a compelling state interest. An important social objective, which is all California has shown, does not amount to a compelling state interest.

◆ Davis cannot defend its admission program as the only way for it to achieve its objective of greater racial diversity in the student body and in the medical profession because it has never tried any other approach.

♦ Several intractable problems will arise if the Davis quota is given judicial sanction, including: the acceptable size of a quota, which of numerous groups should be included, whether an applicant has to be a "full-blooded" member of the group to qualify, whether quotas should extend beyond national, ethnic, and racial groups to religious groups, and how long quotas should remain in effect. Supervising quotas would also require substantial judicial intervention.

♦ The Davis Task Force program must be distinguished from affirmative action programs. The latter are designed to enable persons to advance in society on the basis of individual merit. They do not vest a "group right" to racial proportionality as does the Davis program. Administration of the Davis program transcends any fair interpretation of "affirmative action" and enters a realm that is constitutionally forbidden because it seeks out persons, regardless of their lower qualifications, who satisfy the school's racial preference.

♦ The standard of judicial review in racial discrimination cases does not vary depending on the asserted purpose of the discrimination. State-imposed discrimination affecting a fundamental right or based on a suspect classification must meet the test of strict judicial scrutiny. Since the decision in *Sweatt v. Painter*, 339 U.S. 629 (1950), the Court's teaching has been the same: Discrimination on the basis of race is illegal, immoral, unconstitutional, inherently wrong, and destructive of a democratic society.

♦ An affirmative action program that allocates a scarce resource in favor of one race to the detriment of others is not permissible. Preferential treatment under the guise of affirmative action is the imposition of one form of racial discrimination in place of another.

♦ The issues involved in this case are complicated and require a sensitive response. The Supreme Court of the United States, like the California Supreme Court, can give the university broad discretion to search for alternative measures to deal with the problem of low minority representation in medical school and the medical profession that do not violate constitutional rights.

AMICUS CURIAE BRIEFS SUPPORTING BAKKE

Fifteen organizations including the U.S. Chamber of Commerce, the American Federation of Teachers, Young Americans for Freedom, the Anti-Defamation League of B'Nai B'rith, the Fraternal Order of Police, and the American Subcontractors Association, and several individuals who had been or believed they would be affected by affirmative action programs.

AMICUS CURIAE BRIEFS SUPPORTING NEITHER SIDE

National Urban League; the National Organization for Women; the United Auto Workers, and fourteen other organizations; twenty-two physicians; the Equal Employment Council.

SUPREME COURT DECISION

(5–4 invalidating Davis's special admissions program, 5–4 allowing race to be considered in the admissions process)

POWELL, J.

... Although many of the Framers of the Fourteenth Amendment conceived of its primary function as bridging the vast distance between members of the Negro race and the white "majority," *Slaughter-House Cases*, the Amendment itself was framed in universal terms, without reference to color, ethnic origin, or condition of prior servitude.... Indeed, it is not unlikely that among the Framers were many who would have applauded a reading of the Equal Protection Clause that states a principle of universal application and is responsive to the racial, ethnic, and cultural diversity of the Nation....

Petitioner urges us to adopt for the first time a more restrictive view of the Equal Protection Clause and hold that discrimination against members of the white "majority" cannot be suspect if its purpose can be characterized as "benign." The clock of our liberties, however, cannot be turned back to 1868.... It is far too late to argue that the guarantee of equal protection to *all* persons permits the recognition of special wards entitled to a degree of protection greater than that accorded others....

Moreover, there are serious problems of justice connected with the idea of preference itself. First, it may not always be clear that a so-called preference is in fact benign. Courts may be asked to validate burdens imposed upon individual members of a particular group in order to advance the group's general interest.... Nothing in the Constitution supports the notion that individuals may be asked to suffer otherwise impermissible burdens in order to enhance the societal standing of their ethnic groups. Second, preferential programs may only reinforce common stereotypes holding that certain groups are unable to achieve success without special protection based on a factor having no relationship to individual worth.... Third, there is a measure of inequity in forcing innocent persons in respondent's position to bear the burdens of redressing grievances not of their making....

If it is the individual who is entitled to judicial protection against classifications based upon his racial or ethnic background because such distinctions impinge upon personal rights, rather than the individual only because of his membership in a particular group, then constitutional standards may be applied consistently. Political judgments regarding the necessity for the particular classification may be weighed in the constitutional balance, *Korematsu v. United States*, 323 U.S. 214 (1944), but the standard of justification will remain constant. This is as it should be, since those political judgments are the product of rough compromise struck by contending groups within the democratic process. When they touch upon an individual's race or ethnic background, he is entitled to a judicial determination that the burden he is asked to bear on that basis is precisely tailored to serve a compelling governmental interest. The Constitution guarantees that right to every person regardless of his background....

[T]he purpose of helping certain groups whom the faculty of the Davis Medical School perceived as victims of "societal discrimination" does not justify a classification that imposes disadvantages upon persons like respondent, who bear no responsibility for whatever harm the beneficiaries of the special admissions program are thought to have suffered. To hold otherwise would be to convert a remedy heretofore reserved for violations of legal rights into a privilege that all institutions throughout the Nation could grant at their pleasure to whatever groups are perceived as victims of societal discrimination. That is a step we have never approved....

Petitioner simply has not carried its burden of demonstrating that it must prefer members of particular ethnic groups over all other individuals in order to promote better health-care delivery to deprived citizens. Indeed, petitioner has not shown that its preferential classification is likely to have any significant effect on the problem....

Ethnic diversity ... is only one element in a range of factors a university properly may consider in attaining the goal of a heterogeneous student body. Although a university must have wide discretion in making the sensitive judgments as to who should be admitted, constitutional limitations protecting individual rights may not be disregarded. The question remains whether the program's racial classification is necessary to promote this interest....

The diversity that furthers a compelling state interest encompasses a far broader array of qualifications and characteristics of which racial or ethnic origin is but a single though important element. Petitioner's special admissions program, focused *solely* on ethnic diversity, would hinder rather than further attainment of genuine diversity....

The experience of other university admissions programs, which take race into account in achieving the educational diversity valued by the First Amendment, demonstrates that the assignment of a fixed number of places to a minority group is not a necessary means toward that end....

It has been suggested that an admissions program which considers race only as one factor is simply a subtle and more sophisticated—but no less effective—means of according racial preference than the Davis program. A facial intent to discriminate, however, is evident in petitioner's preference program and not denied in this case. No such facial infirmity exists in an admissions program where race or ethnic background is simply one element—to be weighed fairly against other elements—in the selection process.... In short, good faith would be presumed in the absence of a showing to the contrary[.]...

[I]t is evident that the Davis special admissions program involves the use of an explicit racial classification never before countenanced by this Court. It tells applicants who are not Negro, Asian, or Chicano that they are totally excluded from a specific percentage of the seats in an entering class. No matter how strong their qualifications, quantitative and extracurricular, including their own potential for contribution to educational diversity, they are never afforded the chance to compete with applicants from the preferred groups for the special admissions seats. At the same time, the preferred applicants have the opportunity to compete for every seat in the class.

The fatal flaw in petitioner's preferential program is disregard of individual rights as guaranteed by the Fourteenth Amendment.... Such rights are not absolute. But when a State's distribution of benefits or imposition of burdens hinges on ancestry or the color of a person's skin, that individual is entitled to a demonstration that the challenged classification is necessary to promote a substantial state interest. Petitioner has failed to carry this burden. For this reason, that portion of the California court's judgment holding petitioner's special admissions program invalid under the Fourteenth Amendment must be affirmed.

In enjoining petitioner from ever considering the race of any applicant, however, the courts below failed to recognize that the State has a substantial interest that legitimately may be served by a properly devised admissions program involving the competitive consideration of race and ethnic origin. For this reason, so much of the California court's judgment as enjoins petitioner from any consideration of the race of any applicant must be reversed.

With respect to respondent's entitlement to an injunction directing his admission to the Medical School, petitioner has conceded that it could not carry its burden of proving that, but for the existence of its unlawful special admissions program, respondent still would not have been admitted. Hence, respondent is entitled to the injunction, and that portion of the judgment must be affirmed....

BRENNAN, WHITE, MARSHALL, AND BLACKMUN, J.J., CONCURRING IN PART AND DISSENTING IN PART

... [O]n the basis of the undisputed factual submissions before this Court, Davis had a sound basis for believing that the problem of underrepresentation of minorities was substantial and chronic and that the problem was attributable to handicaps imposed on minority applicants by past and present racial discrimi-

nation. Until at least 1973, the practice of medicine in this country was, in fact, if not in law, largely the prerogative of whites. In 1950, for example, while Negroes constituted 10% of the total population, Negro physicians constituted only 2.2% of the total number of physicians. The overwhelming majority of these, moreover, were educated in two predominantly Negro medical schools, Howard and Meharry. By 1970, the gap between the proportion in the population had widened: The number of Negroes employed in medicine remained frozen at 2.2% while the Negro population had increased to 11%. The number of Negro admittees to predominantly white medical schools, moreover, had declined in absolute numbers during the years 1955 to 1964....

Unlike discrimination against racial minorities, the use of racial preferences for remedial purposes does not inflict a pervasive injury upon individual whites in the sense that wherever they go or whatever they do there is a significant likelihood that they will be treated as second-class citizens because of their color. This distinction does not mean that the exclusion of a white resulting from the preferential use of race is not sufficiently serious to require justification; but it does mean that the injury inflicted by such a policy is not distinguishable from disadvantages caused by a wide range of government actions, none of which has ever been thought impermissible for that reason alone.

In addition, there is simply no evidence that the Davis program discriminates intentionally or unintentionally against any minority group which it purports to benefit. The program does not establish a quota in the invidious sense of a ceiling on the number of minority applicants to be admitted. Nor can the program reasonably be regarded as stigmatizing the program's beneficiaries or their race as inferior. The Davis program does not simply advance less qualified applicants; rather, it compensates applicants, who it is uncontested are fully qualified to study medicine, for educational disadvantages which it was reasonable to conclude were a product of state-fostered discrimination. Once admitted, these students must satisfy the same degree requirements as regularly admitted students; they are taught by the same faculty in the same classes; and their performance is evaluated by the same standards by which regularly admitted students are judged. Under these circumstances, their performance and degrees must be regarded equally with the regularly admitted students with whom they compete for standing. Since minority graduates cannot justifiably be regarded as less well qualified than nonminority graduates by virtue of the special admissions program, there is no reasonable basis to conclude that minority graduates at schools using such programs would be stigmatized as inferior by the existence of such programs.

Accordingly, we would reverse the judgment of the Supreme Court of California holding the Medical School's special admissions program unconstitutional and directing respondent's admission, as well as that portion of the judgment enjoining the Medical School from according any consideration to race in the admissions process....

SEPARATE OPINION OF WHITE, J. [OMITTED]

MARSHALL, J., CONCURRING IN PART AND DISSENTING PART

... I do not agree that petitioner's admissions program violates the Constitution. For it must be remembered that, during most of the past 200 years, the Constitution as interpreted by this Court did not prohibit the most ingenious and pervasive forms of discrimination against the Negro. Now, when a State acts to remedy the effects of that legacy of discrimination, I cannot believe that this same Constitution stands as a barrier....

The position of the Negro today in America is the tragic but inevitable consequence of centuries of unequal treatment. Measured by any benchmark of comfort or achievement, meaningful equality remains a distant dream for the Negro....

In light of the sorry history of discrimination and its devastating impact on the lives of Negroes, bringing the Negro into the mainstream of American life should be a state interest of the highest order. To fail to do so is to ensure that America will forever remain a divided society.

I do not believe that the Fourteenth Amendment requires us to accept that fate. Neither its history nor our past cases lend any support to the conclusion that a university may not remedy the cumulative effects of society's discrimination by giving consideration to race in an effort to increase the number and percentage of Negro doctors....

While I applaud the judgment of the Court that a university may consider race in its admissions process, it is more than a little ironic that, after several hundred years of class-based discrimination against Negroes, the Court is unwilling to hold that a class-based remedy for that discrimination is permissible.... The dream of America as the great melting pot has not been realized for the Negro; because of his skin color he never even made it into the pot.

These differences in the experience of the Negro make it difficult for me to accept that Negroes cannot be afforded greater protection under the Fourteenth Amendment where it is necessary to remedy the effects of past discrimination. In the *Civil Rights Cases*, the Court wrote that the Negro emerging from slavery must cease "to be the special favorite of the laws." We cannot in light of the history of the last century yield to that view....

BLACKMUN, J., CONCURRING IN PART AND DISSENTING IN PART [OMITTED]

STEVENS, STEWART, REHNQUIST, J.J., AND BURGER, C.J., CONCURRING IN PART AND DISSENTING IN PART

... Both petitioner and respondent have asked us to determine the legality of the University's special admissions program by reference to the Constitution. Our settled practice, however, is to avoid the decision of a constitutional issue if a case can be fairly decided on a statutory ground.... The more important the issue, the more force there is to this doctrine. In this case, we are presented with a constitutional question of undoubted and unusual importance. Since, however, a dispositive statutory claim was raised at the very inception of this case, and squarely decided in the portion of the trial court judgment affirmed by the California Supreme Court, it is our plain duty to confront it. Only if petitioner should prevail on the statutory issue would it be necessary to decide whether the University's admissions program violated the Equal Protection Clause of the Fourteenth Amendment....

I concur in the Court's judgment insofar as it affirms the judgment of the Supreme Court of California. To the extent that it purports to do anything else, I respectfully dissent.

QUESTIONS

1. *Bakke* raised three specific questions: (1) whether Bakke should be admitted to the University of California, Davis Medical School; (2) whether that school unconstitutionally had applied a racial "quota" in choosing among applicants for admission; and (3) whether the race of an applicant may ever be taken into consideration in professional school admissions decisions. The justices wrote six separate opinions. Identify how a majority of the justices answered each of the specific questions raised.

2. Can the Court's decision in *Bakke* be reconciled with its decision in *Brown v. Board of Education* (see pp. 525–536)?

3. In order to maintain his status as an injured party, Allan Bakke was forced to stay out of medical school until the litigation in his case was over. Bakke's medical career was postponed for several years as a consequence. Is it sound judicial policy to require such sacrifices on the part of litigants who challenge social policies?

COMMENT

Sometimes the Court has avoided reaching constitutional issues in affirmative action cases by basing its decision on provisions of the Civil Rights Act of 1964, which outlaws discrimination on the basis of race, sex, color, religion, and national origin. At other times, the Court has interpreted the Equal Protection Clause, or the equal protection component of the Due Process Clause of the Fifth Amendment, as ground for its decision. The cases summarized below indicate the Court's approaches to legal problems raised by affirmative action programs between *Bakke* and *City of Richmond v. J.A. Croson Co.*, 488 U.S. 469 (1989), the next case excerpted.

Case: *United Steelworkers of America v. Weber*, 443 U.S. 193 (1979)

Vote: 5–2 (Powell and Stevens, J.J., did not participate.)

Decision: A corporation's voluntary affirmative action plan, arrived at as part of a collective bargaining agreement, that grants preference to black employees over more senior white employees in admission to in-plant craft training programs, does not violate the Civil Rights Act of 1964. Federal statutes do not prohibit all private, voluntary race-conscious affirmative action plans.

Case: *Fullilove v. Klutznick*, 448 U.S. 448 (1980)

Vote: 6–3

Decision: The minority business enterprise provision of the Public Works Employment Act of 1977, requiring that 10 percent of the federal funds granted for local public works projects be used by state and local grantees to procure services or supplies from businesses owned and controlled by minority group members, does not violate the equal protection component of the Due Process Clause of the Fifth Amendment. (No majority of justices could agree on the reasoning for the decision.)

Case: *Firefighters Local Union No. 1784 v. Stotts*, 467 U.S. 561 (1984)

Vote: 6–3

Decision: A city's modification of its seniority system in order to remedy past general patterns of discrimination violates the Civil Rights Act of 1964. Cities may not modify a staff reduction plan to avoid laying off on a last-hired-first-fired basis even when the effects of such layoffs may have a disparate impact on minorities.

Case: *Wygant v. Jackson Board of Education*, 476 U.S. 267 (1986)

Vote: 5–4

Decision: A collective bargaining agreement between a school district and a teachers' union providing that, if layoffs became necessary, there would be no greater a percentage of minority teachers laid off than the percentage of minority personnel employed at the time, violates the Equal Protection Clause. (No majority of justices could agree on the reasoning for the decision.)

Case: *Local 28, Sheet Metal Workers v. Equal Employment Opportunity Commission*, 478 U.S. 421 (1986)

Vote: 5–4

Decision: A district court order imposing a 29 percent nonwhite membership goal on Local 28 of the Sheet Metal Workers International Association because of a pattern and practice of discrimination against blacks and Hispanics, and establishing a fund to be used to remedy such discrimination, does not violate the equal protection component of the Due Process Clause of the Fifth Amendment.

Case: *Local No. 93, International Association of Firefighters v. Cleveland*, 478 U.S. 501 (1986)

Vote: 6–3

Decision: A federal district court consent decree between an independent organization and a city, imposing the use of racial quotas and goals for nine years to remedy the effects of past discrimination in hiring, assigning, and promoting does not violate the Civil Rights Act of 1964.

Case: *United States v. Paradise,* 480 U.S. 149 (1987)

Vote: 5–4

Decision: A federal district court order requiring that, in order to remedy four decades of discriminatory conduct, 50 percent of all promotions to the rank of corporal in the Alabama State Patrol are to go to blacks until either approximately 25 percent of rank was composed of black troopers, or a promotion plan for rank conforming with prior court orders and decrees and other legal requirements was developed and implemented, does not violate the Equal Protection Clause. (No majority of justices could agree on the reasoning for the decision.)

Case: *Johnson v. Transportation Agency, Santa Clara County, California,* 480 U.S. 616 (1987)

Vote: 6–3

Decision: A voluntary affirmative action plan for hiring and promoting minorities and women allowing a county agency to consider the sex of a qualified candidate as one factor in making promotions within a traditionally segregated job classification where women are significantly underrepresented does not violate the Civil Rights Act of 1964.

EQUAL PROTECTION: AFFIRMATIVE ACTION

City of Richmond v. J.A. Croson Co.
488 U.S. 469 (1989)

SETTING

During the 1970s and early 1980s, while the Supreme Court by narrow majorities generally upheld the validity of affirmative action programs, a groundswell of public opposition developed against efforts to remedy the effects of past discrimination. Attacks on the theoretical, policy, and practical aspects of affirmative action came from all sides. One of the most effective arguments made by opponents was that affirmative action is a class-conscious remedy that violates the American principle of equality of opportunity. By the end of the 1980s, those criticisms, coupled with resolute opposition to affirmative action by three conservative presidential administrations, took their toll. As constitutional scholar Jesse H. Choper observed, "The extent to which the equal protection clause of the fourteenth amendment ... permits government to use racial classification to remedy prior racial discrimination is one of the most significant and controversial issues of our time."

Personnel changes on the Supreme Court called into doubt that institution's continued support for affirmative action. Chief Justice Warren Burger and Justice Lewis Powell, cautious supporters of affirmative action programs, and Justice Potter Stewart, an opponent, retired in the 1980s. President Ronald Reagan, an outspoken critic of affirmative action, appointed Justices Sandra Day O'Connor, Antonin Scalia, and Anthony Kennedy, and elevated William H. Rehnquist to chief justice. In 1989, the Court and its new members had an opportunity to rethink the constitutionality of affirmative action in the context of minority business enterprise (MBE) set-asides.

In April 1983, the Richmond, Virginia, city council adopted by ordinance a five-year Minority Business Utilization Plan that required prime contractors who were awarded city construction contracts to subcontract at least 30 percent of the dollar amount of each contract to one or more MBEs. The plan defined an MBE as any company in the United States at least 51 percent of which was owned and controlled by black, Spanish-speaking, Oriental, Indian, Eskimo, or Aleut citizens. The plan was declared "remedial" in nature, but was adopted after a public hearing at which no direct evidence was presented that the city or its prime contractors had discriminated against minority subcontractors. However, relying on the Supreme Court's decision in *Fullilove v. Klutznick*, 448 U.S. 448 (1980) (see p. 634) the city council believed that it had sufficient evidence of widespread racial discrimination in the construction industries to justify the plan. For example, statistics showed that while the population of Richmond was 50 percent black, only 0.67 percent of the city's prime contracts had been awarded to minority businesses between 1978 and 1983.

Paragraph D of administrative rules adopted pursuant to the plan required a prime contractor to set aside 30 percent of the contract for MBE subcontractors unless the contractor could justify waiving the requirement by showing that it could not be met. Purchasing procedures contained in the administrative rules required contractors who bid on city projects to submit a commitment form naming the MBEs they would use on the contract and the percentage of the total contact price awarded to MBEs.

In September 1983, the City of Richmond issued an invitation to contractors to bid on the installation of plumbing fixtures at the city jail. The city specified that the plumbing fixtures would have to be manufactured by one of two companies—Acorn Engineering or Bradley Manufacturing.

The J.A. Croson Co. was a contractor that wished to bid on the city's project. Croson had considerable difficulty locating an MBE interested in supplying the fixtures. When it did locate an interested MBE, Continental Metal Hose, that company was unable to quote Croson a price for the fixtures because it was having difficulty obtaining credit from its supplier.

When bids on the city jail project were opened in October, Croson was the only company to have submitted a bid. Approximately a week after receiving the contract, it applied for a waiver of the 30 percent set-aside on the ground that Continental Metal Hose was "unqualified" because Continental still had not provided a price for the plumbing fixtures and no other MBEs had expressed an interest in the project.

When Continental learned that Croson had applied for a waiver, it submitted a bid to Croson for plumbing fixtures that was some $6,000 higher than the price for fixtures that Croson had included in its bid to the city and approximately 7 percent over the market price of the fixtures. Continental also informed the city that it was a qualified MBE that could supply the plumbing fixtures for the city jail project. The city subsequently denied Croson's request for a waiver and Croson's request that the overall contract price be increased because of the unexpectedly high bid from Continental for the plumbing fixtures.

Shortly thereafter, Croson filed suit in the U.S. District Court for the Eastern District of Virginia against the City of Richmond, seeking a declaration that the Minority Business Utilization Plan violated the Equal Protection Clause of the Fourteenth Amendment, an injunction against its enforcement, and monetary damages. The district court held for Richmond. The U.S. Court of Appeals for the Fourth Circuit affirmed, relying on the Supreme Court's decisions in *Bakke* and *Fullilove.*

The Supreme Court granted Croson's petition for a writ of certiorari and vacated the Fourth Circuit's opinion in light of its intervening decision in *Wygant v. Jackson Board of Education*, 476 U.S. 267 (1986). In *Wygant*, a deeply divided Court struck down a collective bargaining agreement that had been entered into by a Michigan school district providing that, if layoffs became necessary, there would be no greater percentage of minority personnel laid off than the percentage of minority personnel employed by the district at that time. A plurality held that the existence of societal discrimination, without more, is an insufficient basis for imposing racially discriminatory legal remedies that work against innocent people. However, five members of the *Wygant* Court agreed that the Equal Protection Clause of the Fourteenth Amendment does not require a public employer's affirmative action plan to be preceded by a formal finding that the employer had committed discriminatory acts in the past.

On remand, and in light of *Wygant*, a divided Fourth Circuit struck down Richmond's Minority Business Utilization Plan. The Court emphasized that when the city adopted the plan it relied only on statistical evidence of discrimination rather than on actual evidence of past discrimination by the city. Hence, the plan was not supported by a compelling governmental interest in remedying past discrimination. Even if the city did have a compelling interest, the Fourth Circuit held that the 30 percent set-aside requirement was not narrowly tailored to accomplish a remedial purpose. The Supreme Court granted the City of Richmond's petition for a writ of certiorari.

HIGHLIGHTS OF SUPREME COURT ARGUMENTS

BRIEF FOR THE CITY OF RICHMOND

◆ *Wygant v. Jackson Board of Education*, 476 U.S. 267 (1986) does not control this case because in that case there was no probative evidence of any sort of discrimination. The statistical evidence presented to the city council in this case documents the long history of racial discrimination throughout the nation's construction industry.

◆ State and local governments have a legitimate and substantial interest in ameliorating or eliminating the disabling effects of identified discrimination in public works programs. If Richmond had not acted to remedy the problem, there would be no remedy.

◆ Even without evidence of its own discrimination, Richmond's plan is justified by the existence of pernicious industry discrimination and the effects of that discrimination on public contracting. Racial discrimination in the local construction industry has substantially foreclosed minority access to city contracting opportunities.

◆ The intermediate level of judicial scrutiny that has been endorsed by several members of the Supreme Court is the appropriate standard of review in this case because racial classifications are not inherently suspect when they are used as part of a remedy for the effects of identified racial discrimination.

AMICUS CURIAE BRIEFS SUPPORTING THE CITY OF RICHMOND

Joint brief of the American Civil Liberties Union and the American Civil Liberties Union of Northern California; joint brief of the Lawyers' Committee for Civil Rights Under Law, Mexican-American Legal Defense and Educational Fund, NOW Legal Defense and Educational Fund, the National Association for the Advancement of Colored People, and the Women's Legal Defense Fund; Maryland Legislative Black Caucus; the National Association for the Advancement of Colored People Legal Defense and Educational Fund; joint brief of the National League of Cities, U.S. Conference of Mayors, National Association of Counties, and International City Management Association; State of Maryland; joint brief of the States of New York, California, Connecticut, Illinois, Massachusetts, Minnesota, New Jersey, Ohio, Oregon, Rhode Island, South Carolina, Washington, West Virginia, Wisconsin, Wyoming, and the District of Columbia.

BRIEF FOR J.A. CROSON

◆ *Wygant v. Jackson Board of Education*, 476 U.S. 267 (1986), requires that before an asserted governmental interest in adopting a racial preference can be accepted as "compelling," there must be findings of prior discrimination by the governmental unit involved. If this finding is to be drawn from mere statistical evidence, the evidence must focus on the population that is relative for comparative purposes, such as the availability of qualified minorities in the relevant construction businesses.

◆ The Minority Business Utilization Plan was adopted on a belief that .67 percent of the $124 million of certain of the city's contracts were being awarded to minority prime contractors. There is no information in the record about that figure being related to societal discrimination. Furthermore, the .67 percent figure fails to compare relevant populations.

◆ This Court has never approved a race-conscious legal remedy absent discrimination that can be traced to the government's own actions.

◆ In *Fullilove v. Klutznick*, 448 U.S. 448 (1980), this Court acknowledged that race-conscious remedies must be as narrowly tailored as possible to achieve their remedial purposes. The City of Richmond's plan is overbroad in its definition of the minorities to be included and places an unduly harsh competitive burden on nonminority contractors. Neither the waiver provision nor the five-year duration of the plan is closely related to the plan's objectives.

AMICUS CURIAE BRIEFS SUPPORTING J.A. CROSON

United States; Anti-Defamation League of B'nai B'rith; Pacific Legal Foundation; joint brief of the Washington Legal Foundation and the Lincoln Institute for Research and Education.

SUPREME COURT DECISION: 6–3

O'CONNOR AND WHITE, J.J., AND REHNQUIST, C.J.

... The Richmond Plan denies certain citizens the opportunity to compete for a fixed percentage of public contracts based solely upon their race. To whatever racial group these citizens belong, their "personal rights" to be treated with equal dignity and respect are implicated by a rigid rule erecting race as the sole criterion in an aspect of public decisionmaking.

Absent searching judicial inquiry into the justification for such race-based measures, there is simply no way of determining what classifications are "benign" or "remedial" and what classifications are in fact motivated by illegitimate notions of racial inferiority or simple racial politics. Indeed, the purpose of strict scrutiny is to "smoke out" illegitimate uses of race by assuring that the legislative body is pursuing a goal important enough to warrant use of a highly suspect tool. The test also ensures that the means chosen "fit" this compelling goal so closely that there is little or no possibility that the motive for the classification was illegitimate racial prejudice or stereotype....

While there is no doubt that the sorry history of both private and public discrimination in this country has contributed to a lack of opportunities for black entrepreneurs, this observation, standing alone, cannot justify a rigid racial quota in the awarding of public contracts in Richmond, Virginia. Like the claim that discrimination in primary and secondary schooling justifies a rigid racial preference in medical school admissions, an amorphous claim that there has been past discrimination in a particular industry cannot justify the use of an unyielding racial quota.

It is sheer speculation how many minority firms there would be in Richmond absent past societal discrimination, just as it was sheer speculation how many minority medical students would have been admitted to the medical school at Davis absent past discrimination in educational opportunities. Defining these sorts of injuries as "identified discrimination" would give local governments license to create a patchwork of racial preferences based on statistical generalizations about any particular field of endeavor....

The District Court accorded great weight to the fact that the city council designated the Plan as "remedial." But the mere recitation of a "benign" or legitimate purpose for a racial classification is entitled to little or no weight.... Racial classifications are suspect, and that means that simple legislative assurances of good intention cannot suffice.

The District Court also relied on the highly conclusionary statement of a proponent of the Plan that there was racial discrimination in the construction industry "in this area, and the State, and around the nation." It also noted that the city manager had related his view that racial discrimination still plagued the construction industry in his home city of Pittsburgh. These statements are of little probative value in establishing identified discrimination in the Richmond construction industry. The factfinding process of legislative bodies is generally entitled to a presumption of regularity and deferential review by the judiciary.... But when a legislative body chooses to employ a suspect classification, it cannot rest upon a generalized assertion as to the classification's relevance to its goals.... A governmental actor cannot render race a legitimate proxy for a particular condition merely by declaring that the condition exists.... The history of racial classifications in this country suggests that blind judicial deference to legislative or executive pronouncements of necessity has no place in equal protection analysis....

The city and the District Court also relied on evidence that MBE membership in local contractors' associations was extremely low. Again, standing alone this evidence is not probative of any discrimination in the local construction industry. There are numerous explanations for this dearth of minority participation, including past societal discrimination in education and economic opportunities as well as both black and white career and entrepreneurial choices. Blacks may be disproportionately attracted to industries other than construction.... The mere fact that black membership in these trade organizations is low, standing alone, cannot establish a *prima facie* case of discrimination.

For low minority membership in these associations to be relevant, the city would have to link it to the number of local MBEs eligible for membership. If the statistical disparity between eligible MBEs and MBE membership were great enough, an inference of discriminatory exclusion could arise. In such a case, the city would have a compelling interest in preventing its tax dollars from assisting these organizations in maintaining a racially segregated construction market....

In sum, none of the evidence presented by the city points to any identified discrimination in the Richmond construction industry. We, therefore, hold that the city has failed to demonstrate a compelling interest in apportioning public contracting opportunities on the basis of race. To accept Richmond's claim that past societal discrimination alone can serve as the basis for rigid racial preferences would be to open the door to competing claims for "remedial relief" for every disadvantaged group. The dream of a Nation of equal citizens in a society where race is irrelevant to personal opportunity and achievement would be lost in a mosaic of shifting preferences based on inherently unmeasurable claims of past wrongs.... We think such a result would be contrary to both the letter and spirit of a constitutional provision whose central command is equality....

As noted by the court below, it is almost impossible to assess whether the Richmond Plan is narrowly tailored to remedy prior discrimination since it is not linked to identified discrimination in any way. We limit ourselves to two observations in this regard.

First, there does not appear to have been any consideration of the use of race-neutral means to increase minority business participation in city contracting.... Many of the barriers to minority participation in the construction industry relied upon by the city to justify a racial classification appear to be race neutral. If MBEs disproportionately lack capital or cannot meet bonding requirements, a race-neutral program of city financing for small firms would, a fortiori, lead to greater minority participation. The principal opinion in *Fullilove* found that Congress had carefully examined and rejected race-neutral alternatives before enacting the MBE set-aside.... There is no evidence in this record that the Richmond City Council has considered any alternatives to a race-based quota.

Second, the 30% quota cannot be said to be narrowly tailored to any goal, except perhaps outright racial balancing....

... [T]he city's only interest in maintaining a quota system rather than investigating the need for remedial action in particular cases would seem to be simple administrative convenience. But the interest in avoiding the bureaucratic effort necessary to tailor remedial relief to those who truly have suffered the effects of prior discrimination cannot justify a rigid line drawn on the basis of a suspect classification....

Because the city of Richmond has failed to identify the need for remedial action in the awarding of its public construction contracts, its treatment of its citizens on a racial basis violates the dictates of the Equal Protection Clause. Accordingly, the judgment of the Court of Appeals for the Fourth Circuit is

Affirmed.

STEVENS, J., CONCURRING IN PART AND CONCURRING IN THE JUDGMENT

... I ... do not agree with the premise that seems to underlie today's decision, as well as the decision in *Wygant v. Jackson Board of Education*, 476 U.S. 267 (1986), that a governmental decision that rests on a racial classification is never permissible except as a remedy for a past wrong.... I do, however, agree with the Court's explanation of why the Richmond ordinance cannot be justified as a remedy for past discrimination[.]...

[I]nstead of carefully identifying the characteristics of the two classes of contractors that are respectively favored and disfavored by its ordinance, the Richmond City Council has merely engaged in the type of stereotypical analysis that is a hallmark of violations of the Equal Protection Clause. Whether we look at the class of persons benefited by the ordinance or at the disadvantaged class, the same conclusion emerges....

KENNEDY, J., CONCURRING IN PART AND CONCURRING IN THE JUDGMENT

... For purposes of the ordinance challenged here, it suffices to say that the State has the power to eradicate racial discrimination and its effects in both the public and private sectors, and the absolute duty to do so where those wrongs were caused intentionally by the State itself. The Fourteenth Amendment ought not to be interpreted to reduce a State's authority in this regard, unless, of course, there is a conflict with federal law or a state remedy is itself a violation of equal protection. The latter is the case presented here....

[G]iven that a rule of automatic invalidity for racial preferences in almost every case would be a significant break with our precedents that require a case-by-case test, I am not convinced we need adopt it at this point....

SCALIA, J., CONCURRING IN THE JUDGMENT

I agree with much of the Court's opinion, and, in particular, with Justice O'Connor's conclusion that strict scrutiny must be applied to all governmental classification by race, whether or not its asserted purpose is "remedial" or "benign." I do not agree, however, with Justice O'Connor's dictum suggesting that, despite the Fourteenth Amendment, state and local governments may in some circumstances discriminate on the basis of race in order (in a broad sense) "to ameliorate the effects of past discrimination."...

In my view there is only one circumstance in which the States may act by race to "undo the effects of past discrimination": where that is necessary to eliminate their own maintenance of a system of unlawful racial classification. If, for example, a state agency has a discriminatory pay scale compensating black employees in all positions at 20% less than their nonblack counterparts, it may assuredly promulgate an order raising the salaries of "all black employees" to eliminate the differential....

It is plainly true that in our society blacks have suffered discrimination immeasurably greater than any directed at other racial groups. But those who believe that racial preferences can help to "even the score" display, and reinforce, a manner of thinking by race that was the source of the injustice and that will, if it endures within our society, be the source of more injustice still....

MARSHALL, BRENNAN, AND BLACKMUN, J.J., DISSENTING

... The essence of the majority's position is that Richmond has failed to catalog adequate findings to prove that past discrimination has impeded minorities from joining or participating fully in Richmond's construction contracting industry. I find deep irony in second-guessing Richmond's judgment on this point. As much as any municipality in the United States, Richmond knows what racial discrimination is; a century of decisions by this and other federal courts has richly documented the city's disgraceful history of public and private racial discrimination....

More fundamentally, today's decision marks a deliberate and giant step backward in this Court's affirmative-action jurisprudence. Cynical of one municipality's attempt to redress the effects of past racial discrimination in a particular industry, the majority launches a grapeshot attack on race-conscious remedies in general. The majority's unnecessary pronouncements will inevitably discourage or prevent governmental entities, particularly States and localities, from acting to rectify the scourge of past discrimination. This is the harsh reality of the majority's decision, but it is not the Constitution's command....

The remaining question with respect to the "governmental interest" prong of equal protection analysis is whether Richmond has proffered satisfactory proof of past racial discrimination to support its twin interests in remediation and in governmental nonperpetuation....

The varied body of evidence on which Richmond relied provides a "strong," "firm," and "unquestionably legitimate" basis upon which the city council could determine that the effects of past racial discrimination warranted a remedial and prophylactic governmental response.... Richmond acted against a backdrop of congressional and Executive Branch studies which demonstrated with such force the nationwide pervasiveness of prior discrimination that Congress presumed that "'present economic inequities'" in construction contracting resulted from "'past discriminatory systems.'"...

In my judgment, Richmond's set-aside plan also comports with the second prong of the equal protection inquiry, for it is substantially related to the interests it seeks to serve in remedying past discrimination and in ensuring that municipal contract procurement does not perpetuate that discrimination....

Today, for the first time, a majority of this Court has adopted strict scrutiny as its standard of Equal Protection Clause review of race-conscious remedial measures. This is an unwelcome development. A profound difference separates governmental actions that themselves are racist, and governmental actions that seek to remedy the effects of prior racism or to prevent neutral governmental activity from perpetuating the effects of such racism....

In concluding that remedial classifications warrant no different standard of review under the Constitution than the most brutal and repugnant forms of state-sponsored racism, a majority of this Court signals that it regards racial discrimination as largely a phenomenon of the past, and that government bodies need no longer preoccupy themselves with rectifying racial injustice. I, however, do not believe this Nation is anywhere close to eradicating racial discrimination or its vestiges. In constitutionalizing its wishful thinking, the majority today does

a grave disservice not only to those victims of past and present racial discrimination in this Nation whom government has sought to assist, but also to this Court's long tradition of approaching issues of race with the utmost sensitivity....

Today's decision, finally, is particularly noteworthy for the daunting standard it imposes upon States and localities contemplating the use of race-conscious measures to eradicate the present effects of prior discrimination and prevent its perpetuation....

Nothing in the Constitution or in the prior decisions of this Court supports limiting state authority to confront the effects of past discrimination to those situations in which a *prima facie* case of a constitutional or statutory violation can be made out....

In adopting its *prima facie* standard for States and localities, the majority closes its eyes to ... constitutional history and social reality....

The majority today sounds a full-scale retreat from the Court's longstanding solicitude to race-conscious remedial efforts "directed toward deliverance of the century-old promise of equality of economic opportunity." *Fullilove [v. Klutznick*, 448 U.S. 448 (1980)]. The new and restrictive tests it applies scuttle one city's effort to surmount its discriminatory past, and imperil those of dozens more localities. I, however, profoundly disagree with the cramped vision of the Equal Protection Clause which the majority offers today and with its application of that vision to Richmond, Virginia's, laudable set-aside plan. The battle against pernicious racial discrimination or its effects is nowhere near won. I must dissent.

BLACKMUN AND BRENNAN, J.J., DISSENTING [OMITTED]

QUESTIONS

1. What standard of review did the *Croson* Court employ in reviewing challenges to affirmative action problems under the Equal Protection Clause of the Fourteenth Amendment? How is that standard different from *Bakke* and *Fullilove v. Klutznick*, 448 U.S. 448 (1980)?

2. Should the Equal Protection Clause permit cities to exercise the power delegated to them by states to enact minority set-aside plans as remedies for past discrimination without a threshold showing of the city's own participation in that discrimination? Consider this argument made by fifteen states and the District of Columbia in their joint *amicus* brief in *Croson*:

   > Localities ... will clearly be discouraged from adopting voluntary remedial measures such as affirmative action plans and set-aside programs if those measures must be preceded by factfinding demonstrating that they have engaged in illegal discrimination.... In developing this record, localities might not only fuel existing racial tensions, but would expose themselves to potential liability for prior discrimination.

COMMENTS

1. *Croson* demonstrates the Court's recent response to a challenge to an affirmative action program brought under the Equal Protection Clause of the Fourteenth Amendment. In the 1990s, the Court decided two other important cases involving affirmative action programs attacked under the equal protection component of the Fifth Amendment. *Metro Broadcasting, Inc. v. Federal Communications Commission*, 497 U.S. 547 (1990), involved a challenge to the Federal Communications Commission (FCC) policy of awarding enhancement credit for ownership and participation by members of minority groups (Black, Hispanic surnamed, American Eskimo, Aleut, American Indian, and Asiatic American extraction) when reviewing applications for new radio or television broadcast station licenses. In a 5–4 opinion reflecting the views of Justices Brennan, White, Marshall, Blackmun, and Stevens, the Court upheld the FCC policy. The majority adopted an "intermediate" level of scrutiny as the appropriate standard of review of federal affirmative action programs because they had been mandated by Congress. The majority held that the FCC policy reflected important governmental objectives identified by Congress and was substantially related to those objectives. Republican appointees O'Connor, Rehnquist, Scalia, and Kennedy dissented: two of them faulted the majority for not applying a strict scrutiny level of review required under the Equal Protection Clause of the Fourteenth Amendment.

Five years later, in *Adarand Constructors, Inc. v. Pena*, 515 U.S. 200 (1995), the Court ruled that the appropriate standard of review in *all* cases involving racial classifications imposed by the government—federal, state or local—is strict scrutiny. Justices O'Connor, Kennedy, Thomas, Scalia, and Chief Justice Rehnquist were in the majority. *Adarand* overruled *Metro Broadcasting* to the extent that *Metro Broadcasting* had applied a different standard of review.

2. On March 18, 1996, the Fifth Circuit Court of Appeals decided *Hopwood v. Texas*, 861 F.Supp. 551, 84 F.3d 720, holding that the University of Texas, Austin, Law School may not use race as a factor in admission decisions. The Court offered this summary of affirmative action doctrine from *Bakke* through *Adarand*:

> Justice Powell's argument in *Bakke* garnered only his own vote and has never represented the view of a majority of the Court in *Bakke* or any other case. Moreover, subsequent Supreme Court decisions regarding education state that non-remedial state interests will never justify racial classifications. Finally, the classification of persons on the basis of race for the purpose of diversity frustrates, rather than facilitates, the goals of equal protection....
>
> As the *Adarand* Court states, the *Bakke* Court did not express a majority view and is questionable as binding precedent....
>
> Since *Bakke*, the Court has accepted the diversity rationale only once in its cases dealing with race. Significantly, however, in that case, *Metro Broadcasting, Inc. v. Federal Communications Comm'n*, the five-Justice majority relied upon an intermediate scrutiny standard of review to uphold the federal program seeking diversity in the ownership of broadcasting facilities. In *Adarand*, the Court squarely rejected intermediate scrutiny as the standard of review for racial classifications, and *Metro Broadcasting* is now specifically overruled to the extent that it was in conflict with this holding. No case since *Bakke* has accepted diversity as a compelling state interest under a strict scrutiny analysis.

New York Times columnist Anthony Lewis characterized *Hopwood* as "draconian." *Hopwood*'s premise, argues Lewis, "is that universities should admit students only on 'merit,' meaning test scores. But no good university does that. Each considers what the applicant is and may be: the obstacles she has overcome, her potential for growth, her skill at sports and music and other things" (Anthony Lewis. "Whiter Than White." [http://www.nytimes.com/]. May 23, 1997).

The Supreme Court of the United States denied the State of Texas's petition for a writ of certiorari in *Texas v. Hopwood*, 116 S.Ct. 2581 (1996). Justices Ginsburg and Souter wrote:

> Whether it is constitutional for a public college or graduate school to use race or national origin as a factor in its admissions process is an issue of great national importance. The petition before us, however, does not challenge the lower courts' judgments that the

particular admissions procedure used by the University of Texas Law School in 1992 was unconstitutional. Acknowledging that the 1992 admissions program "has long since been discontinued and will not be reinstated," ... the petitioners do not defend that program in this Court[.]... Instead, petitioners challenge the rationale relied on by the Court of Appeals. "[T]his Court," however, "reviews judgments, not opinions." *Chevron U.S.A. Inc. v. Natural Resources Defense Council, Inc.*, 467 U.S. 837, 842 (1984). Accordingly, we must await a final judgment on a program genuinely in controversy before addressing the important question raised in this petition.

3. In 1996, nearly 55 percent of California voters adopted Proposition 209. The initiative eliminated affirmative action programs run by state or local governments in the areas of public employment, contracting, and education that gave "preferential treatment" on the basis of race, sex, color, ethnicity, or national origin. President Clinton responded to Proposition 209:

As you know, my position on affirmative action is that a lot of the things we had been doing should be changed. But my formulation of "mend it, don't end it," I still think, is the best thing for America. If states are prohibited from taking "appropriate steps" to help the disadvantaged we'll all have to regroup and find new ways to achieve the same objective.

The constitutionality of Proposition 209 was immediately challenged and the U.S. District Court for the Northern District of California granted a preliminary injunction enjoining the state from implementing the act. The U.S. Court of Appeals for the Ninth Circuit vacated the injunction and remanded. *Coalition for Economic Equity v. Wilson*, 110 F.3d 1431 (1997). That court then denied a motion to stay its decision pending petition for a writ of certiorari to the Supreme Court of the United States. 122 F.3d 718 (1997). In November 1997, the Supreme Court of the United States denied the petition for a writ of certiorari, 66 USLW 3177, ending efforts to block implementation of Proposition 209.

4. After California banned affirmative action, the percentage of blacks admitted to the University of California Berkeley Law School (Boalt Hall) dropped 81 percent, while at U.C.L.A. it dropped 80 percent. The State of Texas also abolished affirmative action, resulting in a drop in black admittees at its law school by over 84 percent.

Patrick Woolley, one of two black professors at the University of Texas Law School, responded to the numbers saying "I'm concerned we're moving toward the resegregation of the law school. Certainly even with affirmative action, no law school class has ever been brimming over with African Americans or Hispanics" (Karen W. Arenson. "Rate of Minority College Enrollment Is Slowing." [http://www.nytimes.com/]. May 19, 1997; Rene Sanchez and Sue

Anne Pressley, "Minority Admissions Fall With Preferences Ban: Steep Declines at Two States' Flagship Universities Raise Alarm on Campuses Nationwide," *Washington Post*, May 19, 1997, p. A01).

SUGGESTIONS FOR FURTHER READING

Bakke Symposium: "Civil Rights Perspectives," *Harvard Civil Rights-Civil Liberties Law Review* (1979): 1.

Bergmann, Barbara R., *In Defense of Affirmative Action* (New York, NY: Basic Books, 1996).

Blasi, Vincent, "*Bakke* as Precedent: Does Mr. Justice Powell Have a Theory?" 67 *California Law Review* (1979): 21.

Brest, Paul, and Miranda Oshige, "Affirmative Action for Whom?" 47 *Stanford Law Review* (1995): 855.

Choper, Jesse H., "Continued Uncertainty As to the Constitutionality of Remedial Racial Classifications: Identifying the Pieces of the Puzzle," 72 *Iowa Law Review* (1987): 255.

Comment, "The Constitutionality of Affirmative Action in Public Employment: Judicial Deference to Certain Politically Responsible Bodies," 67 *Virginia Law Review* (1981): 1235.

Comment, "Minority Construction Contracts," 12 *Harvard Civil Rights-Civil Liberties Law Review* (1977): 693.

Comment, "Reverse Discrimination: The Supreme Court Defines a Significant Limitation of the Permissible Use of Race in Affirmative Action," 26 *Washburn Law Journal* (1987): 618.

Cox, Archibald, "The Supreme Court, 1965 Term—Forward: Constitutional Adjudication and the Promotion of Human Rights," 80 *Harvard Law Review* (1966): 91.

Days, Drew S., III, "*Fullilove*," 96 *Yale Law Journal* (1987): 453.

Dreyfuss, Joel, and Charles Lawrence III, *The Bakke Case: The Politics of Inequality* (New York, NY: Harcourt Brace Jovanovich, 1979).

Dworkin, Ronald, *Taking Rights Seriously* (Cambridge, MA: Harvard University Press, 1977).

Eastland, Terry, *Ending Affirmative Action: The Case for Colorblind Justice* (New York, NY: Basic Books, 1996).

Ely, John Hart, "The Constitutionality of Reverse Racial Discrimination," 41 *University of Chicago Law Review* (1974): 723.

Fletcher, William A., "The Discretionary Constitution: Institutional Remedies and Judicial Legitimacy," 91 *Yale Law Journal* (1982): 635.

Foster, James C., and Mary C. Segers, et al., *Elusive Equality: Liberalism, Affirmative Action, and Social Change in America* (Port Washington, NY: Associated Faculty Press, 1983).

Glazer, Nathan, *Affirmative Discrimination* (New York, NY: Basic Books, 1976).

Glover, Robert W., *Minority Enterprise in Construction* (New York, NY: Praeger, 1977).

Kaplan, John, "Equal Justice in an Unequal World: Equality for the Negro—the Problem of Special Treatment," 61 *Northwestern University Law Review* (1966): 363.

Karst, Kenneth L., and Harold W. Horowitz, "Affirmative Action and Equal Protection," 60 *Virginia Law Review* (1974): 955.

———, "The *Bakke* Opinions and Equal Protection Doctrine," *Harvard Civil Rights-Civil Liberties Law Review* (1979): 7.

Larson, E. Richard, "Race Consciousness in Employment after *Bakke*," 14 *Harvard Civil Rights-Civil Liberties Law Review* (1979): 215.

Levinson, Daniel R., "A Study of Preferential Treatment: The Evolution of Minority Business Enterprise Assistance Programs," 49 *George Washington Law Review* (1980): 61.

Lewis, Anthony, "*Bakke* May Change a Lot While Changing No Law," *New York Times*, July 2, 1978, sec. 4, p. 4.

Livingston, John C., *Fair Game? Inequality and Affirmative Action* (San Francisco, CA: W. H. Freeman, 1979).

Moreno, Paul D., *From Direct Action to Affirmative Action: Fair Employment Law and Policy in America, 1933–1972* (Baton Rouge, LA: Louisiana State University Press, 1977).

Note, "A Madisonian Interpretation of the Equal Protection Doctrine," 91 *Yale Law Journal* (1982): 1403.

Note, "Principles of Competence: The Ability of Public Institutions to Adapt Remedial Affirmative Action Plans," 53 *University of Chicago Law Review* (1986): 581.

O'Neill, Timothy, "The Language of Equality in a Constitutional Order," 75 *American Political Science Review* (1981): 626.

———, Bakke *and the Politics of Equality: Friends and Foes in the Classroom of Litigation* (Middletown, CT: Wesleyan University Press, 1985).

O'Neill, Robert M., "Preferential Admissions," 80 *Yale Law Journal* (1971): 699.

———, *Discriminating Against Discrimination* (Bloomington, IN: Indiana University Press, 1975).

Roche, George C., III, *The Balancing Act: Quota Hiring in Higher Education* (La Salle, IL: Open Court, 1974).

Rossum, Ralph A., *Reverse Discrimination: The Constitutional Debate* (New York, NY: Marcel Dekker, 1980).

Sedler, Robert Allen, "Beyond *Bakke*: The Constitution and Redressing the Social History of Racism," 14 *Harvard Civil Rights-Civil Liberties Law Review* (1979): 133.

Schnapper, Eric, "Affirmative Action and the Legislative History of the Fourteenth Amendment," 71 *Virginia Law Review* (1985): 753.

Sindler, Allan P., Bakke, Defunis, *and Minority Admissions* (New York, NY: Longman, 1978).

Sowell, Thomas, *Black Education, Myths and Tragedies* (New York, NY: McKay, 1972).

_____, *Affirmative Action Reconsidered: Was It Necessary in Academia?* (Washington, D.C.: American Enterprise Institute, 1975).

Sullivan, Kathleen M., "Sins of Discrimination: Last Term's Affirmative Action Cases," 100 *Harvard Law Review* (1986): 78.

tenBroek, Jacobus, *Equal under Law*, new enlarged ed. (New York, NY: Collier Books, 1965).

Van Alstyne, William, "Rites of Passage: Race, the Supreme Court, and the Constitution," 46 *University of Chicago Law Review* (1979): 775.

Welch, Susan, and John Gruhl, "The Impact of the *Bakke* Decision on Black and Hispanic Enrollment in Medical and Law Schools," 71 *Social Science Quarterly* (1990): 548.

Wilkinson, J. Harvie, III, *From* Brown *to* Bakke (New York, NY: Oxford University Press, 1979).

Wright, J. Skelly, "Color-Blind Theories and Color-Conscious Remedies," 47 *University of Chicago Law Review* (1980): 213.

OTHER PROTECTED CATEGORIES? ECONOMIC CLASS

Edwards v. California
314 U.S. 160 (1941)

SETTING

Poverty has always been a fact of American life. While the public has traditionally been somewhat generous to those who are clearly blameless for their indigence—such as the sick, aged, mentally ill, and physically handicapped—it has typically treated the poor as possessing character and personality flaws. When the Constitution was adopted, the common law and many state statutes assumed that paupers were "immoral" and subjected them to arrest and imprisonment. Some states forced poor people to display the letter "P" prominently on their clothing. Other states put paupers in the same category as slaves, even subjecting them to sale at public auction. The Protestant work ethic and belief in the virtues and consequences of market competition provided powerful ideological support for treating the poor as pariahs throughout the nineteenth century.

Until the Great Depression of the 1930s, "poor relief" was assumed to be the responsibility of state and local governments. For the most part, the Supreme Court was sympathetic to the attempts of states to solve their own social problems, even allowing them to exclude "undesirables" from their borders. In *New York v. Miln*, 11 Peters 102 (1837), for example (see Volume I, Chapter 3), the Court by a vote of 6–1 upheld a local ordinance aimed at preventing certain aliens from entering the port of New York, even though the ordinance seemed squarely at odds with the Court's 1824 decision in *Gibbons v. Ogden*, 9 Wheaton 1, that gave Congress broad powers to regulate interstate commerce (also in Volume I, Chapter 3).

In 1901, as part of its effort to control its welfare budget, the California legislature enacted legislation that prevented the migration of paupers into the state. When the 1901 statute was passed, California confronted no acute pauper immigration problem. During the Great Depression, however, tenant farmers, sharecroppers, and small-scale farmers flocked to California. In the decade between 1930 and 1940, more than 1.2 million new residents moved to California, increasing the state's total population by more than 25 percent. In the San Joaquin and Sacramento Valleys, population increased by as much as 40 to 50 percent every five years. Employment opportunities did not keep pace with the population growth. Most of the indigent immigrants were receiving federal relief when they arrived, but after one year they became dependent on California's state and county welfare programs. For the most part, indigent immigrants who came to California during this period lived in camps in the open countryside, where the sanitary and living conditions were appalling. Disease and crime were commonplace.

The westward migration of paupers during the 1930s had dramatic consequences for state welfare and pension budgets and strained other state resources as well. Between 1936 and 1937, for example, California expended over $82 million in public assistance. Between 1940 and 1941, that figure rose to over $138 million. The California legislature responded to the crisis of indigent immigrants in 1937 by reenacting its 1901 antipauper legislation in the form of § 2615 of the Welfare and Institutions Code. It provided:

> Every person, firm or corporation, or officer or agent thereof that brings or assists in bringing into the State any indigent person who is not a resident of the State, knowing him to be an indigent person, is guilty of a misdemeanor.

California was one of twenty-eight states to enact such an antimigratory statute during this period.

Fred F. Edwards challenged § 2615 of California's Welfare and Institutions Code under the following facts, stipulated to by the parties:

> The Appellant, Fred F. Edwards, a citizen of the United States and a resident of the State of California, left Marysville, California, on December 21, 1939, for Spur, Texas. The object of this trip was to bring his wife's brother, Frank Duncan, a citizen of the United States and Texas, back to Marysville. Appellant arrived at Spur, Texas, on December 24, 1939, and learned that Duncan then had no job and had last been employed by the

[Works Project Administration.] Appellant at that time learned that Duncan was an indigent person and at all times mentioned herein, appellant knew Duncan to be indigent. It was agreed between Duncan and appellant that appellant would drive Duncan from Spur, Texas, to Marysville, California, in appellant's car. Appellant and Duncan left Spur, Texas, on January 1, 1940, entered California from Yuma, Arizona, on January 3, 1940, and arrived in Marysville on January 5, 1940. At the time Duncan arrived in Marysville he was without funds and lived at appellant's home until he was given assistance by the Farm Security Administration about ten days after his arrival in Marysville. Duncan had no employment after his arrival in California, until after he was given assistance by the Farm Security Administration. Duncan had about twenty dollars ($20.00) when he left Spur, Texas; this money was all spent before his arrival at Marysville.

Edwards was charged with violating § 2615. He demurred to the complaint but his demurrer was overruled. Edwards was tried and convicted in Justice's Court of Marysville Township, Yuba County, and received a suspended sentence of six months imprisonment. He appealed to the Yuba County Superior Court, which affirmed his conviction on the ground that § 2615 was a valid exercise of the state's police power. Under California law in effect at the time, no appeal or review was available in state court for a decision of the Superior Court reviewing a decision of the Justice's Court. Edwards therefore appealed directly to the Supreme Court of the United States. Following the first argument, the Court ordered the case reargued at its next Term.

HIGHLIGHTS OF SUPREME COURT ARGUMENTS

BRIEF FOR EDWARDS

◆ Section 2615 violates the Commerce Clause of Article I, Section 8, Clause 3. There is no question that the passage of persons from state to state constitutes commerce. The protection of freedom of passage is readily found in the Commerce Clause, whether people are carried by common carrier or otherwise and whether their passage is paid for by themselves or someone else. The natural and reasonable effect of the statute is to defer, impede, and bar the movement of people through commerce.

◆ Poverty is not a "moral pestilence." Poor migrants are not improper subjects of the protection of commerce. This country is an economic unit with a predominantly national market.

◆ Section 2615 is void on its face and operates to deprive Edwards of liberty without due process of law and to deny him the equal protection of the laws. Freedom of movement and of residence must be a fundamental right in a democratic state.

AMICUS CURIAE BRIEF SUPPORTING EDWARDS

John H. Tolan, for the Select Committee of the House of Representatives.

BRIEF FOR CALIFORNIA

♦ The police power reserved to the states under the Constitution consists of the power to regulate the relative rights and duties of all within the state's jurisdiction so as to guard the public morals, the public safety, the public health, and the common good—or what is more usually referred to as the general welfare of the people.

♦ The Court as early as *New York v. Miln*, 11 Peters 102 (1837), recognized the right of a state to exclude paupers from its boundaries under the police power.

♦ A state statute that happens to affect interstate commerce is not necessarily void. The Commerce Clause is subject to a valid exercise of a state's police power even though interstate commerce may be incidentally affected.

♦ The State of California does not wish to shirk or evade the responsibilities of taking care of its own indigents, but does not desire and is not in a position to shoulder the burden of caring for the indigents from a great many of her sister states, especially from the regions of the Great Plains and the South.

SUPREME COURT DECISION: 9–0

BYRNES, J.

... The issue presented in this case ... is whether the prohibition embodied in Section 2615 against the "bringing" or transportation of indigent persons into California is within the police power of that State. We think that it is not, and hold that it is an unconstitutional barrier to interstate commerce.

The grave and perplexing social and economic dislocation which this statute reflects is a matter of common knowledge and concern. We are not unmindful of it. We appreciate that the spectacle of large segments of our population constantly on the move has given rise to urgent demands upon the ingenuity of government....

But this does not mean that there are no boundaries to the permissible area of State legislative activity. There are. And none is more certain than the prohibition against attempts on the part of any single State to isolate itself from difficulties common to all of them by restraining the transportation of persons and property across its borders....

The burden upon interstate commerce is intended and immediate; it is the plain and sole function of the statute. Moreover, the indigent non-residents who are the real victims of the statute are deprived of the opportunity to exert political pressure upon the California legislature in order to obtain a change in policy.... We think this statute must fail under any known test of the validity of State interference with interstate commerce.

It is urged, however, that the concept which underlies Section 2615 enjoys a firm basis in English and American history. This is the notion that each community should care for its own indigent, that relief is solely the responsibility of local government. Of this it must first be said that we are not now called upon to determine anything other than the propriety of an attempt by a State to prohibit the transportation of indigent non-residents into its territory. The nature and extent of its obligation to afford relief to newcomers is not here involved. We do, however, suggest that the theory of the Elizabethan poor laws no longer fits the facts. Recent years, and particularly the past decade, have been marked by a growing recognition that in an industrial society the task of providing assistance to the needy has ceased to be local in character. The duty to share the burden, if not wholly to assume it, has been recognized not only by State governments, but by the Federal government as well....

What has been said with respect to financing relief is not without its bearing upon the regulation of the transportation of indigent persons. For the social phenomenon of large-scale interstate migration is as certainly a matter of national concern as the provision of assistance to those who have found a permanent or temporary abode. Moreover, and unlike the relief problem, this phenomenon does not admit of diverse treatment by the several States. The prohibition against transporting indigent non-residents into one State is an open invitation to retaliatory measures, and the burdens upon the transportation of such persons become cumulative. Moreover, it would be a virtual impossibility for migrants and those who transport them to acquaint themselves with the peculiar rules of admission of many states....

Whether an able-bodied but unemployed person like Duncan is a "pauper" within the historical meaning of the term is open to considerable doubt.... But assuming that the term is applicable to him and to persons similarly situated, we do not consider ourselves bound by the language referred to. *City of New York v. Miln* [11 Peters 102 (1837)] was decided in 183[7]. Whatever may have been the notion then prevailing, we do not think that it will now be seriously contended that because a person is without employment and without funds he constitutes a "moral pestilence." Poverty and immorality are not synonymous....

Reversed.

DOUGLAS, BLACK, AND MURPHY, J.J., CONCURRING

... I am of the opinion that the right of persons to move freely from State to State occupies a more protected position in our constitutional system than does the movement of cattle, fruit, steel and coal across state lines. While the opinion of the Court expresses no view on that issue, the right involved is so fundamental that I deem it appropriate to indicate the reach of the constitutional question which is present.

The right to move freely from State to State is an incident of national citizenship protected by the privileges and immunities clause of the Fourteenth Amendment against state interference.... Now it is apparent that this right is not specifically granted by the Constitution. Yet before the Fourteenth Amendment it was recognized as a right fundamental to the national character of our Federal government. It was so decided in 1868 by *Crandall v. Nevada*, 6 Wall[ace] 35....

So, when the Fourteenth Amendment was adopted in 1868 it had been squarely and authoritatively settled that the right to move freely from State to State was a right of national citizenship. As such it was protected by the privilege and immunities clause of the Fourteenth Amendment against state interference....

In the face of this history I cannot accede to the suggestion ... that the commerce clause is the appropriate explanation of *Crandall v. Nevada*[.]...

The conclusion that the right of free movement is a right of national citizenship stands on firm historical ground. If a state tax on that movement, as in the *Crandall* case, is invalid, *a fortiori* a state statute which obstructs or in substance prevents that movement must fall. That result necessarily follows unless perchance a State can curtail the right of free movement of those who are poor or destitute. But to allow such an exception to be engrafted on the rights of national citizenship would be to contravene every conception of national unity. It would also introduce a caste system utterly incompatible with the spirit of our system of government.... Since the state statute here challenged involves such consequences, it runs afoul of the privileges and immunities clause of the Fourteenth Amendment.

JACKSON, J., CONCURRING

... This Court should ... hold squarely that it is a privilege of citizenship of the United States, protected from state abridgment, to enter any state of the Union, either for temporary sojourn or for the establishment of permanent residence therein and for gaining resultant citizenship thereof. If national citizenship means less than this, it means nothing....

It is here that we meet the real crux of this case. Does "indigence" as defined by the application of the California statute constitute a basis for restricting the freedom of a citizen, as crime or contagion warrants its restriction? We should say now, and in no uncertain terms, that a man's mere property status, without more, cannot be used by a state to test, qualify, or limit his rights as a citizen of the United States. "Indigence" in itself is neither a source of rights nor a basis for denying them. The mere state of being without funds is a neutral fact—constitutionally an irrelevance, like race, creed, or color. I agree with what I understand to be the holding of the Court that cases which may indicate the contrary are overruled....

QUESTIONS

1. *Edwards* came to the Supreme Court in the following legal environment: Courts in Connecticut, New York, Vermont, Michigan, New Hampshire, and Ohio had either upheld convictions for violating statutes like § 2615 or reversed on grounds other than constitutionality. In New York, Illinois, and Colorado, courts had upheld convictions under statutes similar to § 2615 for transporting paupers from one county to another within the state. Courts in Minnesota, Illinois, Connecticut, and Pennsylvania had upheld statutes providing for the removal of poor or indigent persons from one county to another and a North Dakota court had ruled against removal to a point outside the state on the ground that that state's statute provided only for removal within the state. The State of California was able to identify "no case in which a statute similar to § 2615 has been held to be unconstitutional." In the context of this legal and political "climate of opinion," what might explain the Court's decision in *Edwards*?

2. The *amicus* brief by John Tolan on behalf of Edwards added another constitutional theory: Section 2615 "is in violation of the privileges

and immunities clauses of the Constitution of the United States....
Regarding that theory, Tolan argued:

> [A]s there are no cases or even language to the effect that a person
> without funds or resources in search for employment in another
> State can be precluded from coming into that State, and since this
> is the first case where the issues are so clearly drawn, we feel that
> there is sufficient authority in the very strong language quoted
> from the decisions interpreting the meaning and intent of the "priv-
> ileges and immunities" clauses to warrant a decision that the State
> of California cannot deny migration into the State the classes of
> persons which Mr. Duncan represents. To hold otherwise, would
> be a violation of the fundamental right to pass freely and "to reside
> and work within the bounds of the United States wherever he may
> choose, ... a privilege and attribute of State and Federal citizenship
> definitely guaranteed by the Constitution of the United States.

Is Tolan's theory a more sound constitutional basis for the decision
in *Edwards* than the Commerce Clause theory that the Court
adopted? Why would the majority opt to endorse the Commerce
Clause theory rather than the Privileges or Immunities theory in
resolving *Edwards*? Reread Justice Miller's opinion in the *Slaughter-
House Cases* (see pp. 436–446) as a frame of reference for thinking
about this question.

3. Could *Edwards* have been decided on Equal Protection grounds? If
the Court had done so, would it have had to declare that legislative
classifications based on indigency are subject to strict judicial
scrutiny? What are the strengths and weaknesses of that
approach?

OTHER PROTECTED CATEGORIES? ECONOMIC CLASS

Shapiro v. Thompson
394 U.S. 618 (1969)

SETTING

The Supreme Court's abandonment of economic substantive due process in
1937 coincided with its suggestion in footnote 4 to *United States v. Carolene
Products* (pp. 464–465) that the justices were adopting a new approach to interpretation of the Equal Protection Clause of the Fourteenth Amendment. The
"new equal protection" involved subjecting two categories of statutes to
heightened judicial scrutiny. The first category was statutes that infringed on
fundamental rights of a personal or civil nature. In *Skinner v. Oklahoma*, 316
U.S. 535 (1942), the Court provided an example of how it would review such

statutes. The State of Oklahoma, like most states at the time, allowed sexual sterilization of the mentally handicapped and habitual criminals who had been convicted three or more times for felonies involving "moral turpitude." Jack Skinner had been convicted once for stealing chickens and twice for armed robbery, and was ordered to submit to a vasectomy under the Oklahoma Criminal Sterilization Act. The Supreme Court unanimously ruled that the statute violated one of "the basic civil rights of man," because marriage and procreation "are fundamental to the very existence and survival of the race."

The second category of state statute subjected to heightened judicial scrutiny under the "new equal protection" approach are statutes that create classifications of persons and then treat those classifications differently. Beginning with *Korematsu v. United States*, 323 U.S. 214 (1944) (pp. 523–524), the Court declared classifications based on race to be "inherently suspect" and subject to strict judicial scrutiny. Cases in the section on *Separate Spheres and Gender Equality* demonstrate that the Court remains uncertain about the appropriate level of judicial scrutiny in cases that challenge legal classifications based on sex.

The Court's "new equal protection" analysis was a virtual invitation to litigants to challenge statutes for the purpose of having the Supreme Court define which rights are fundamental and which legislative classifications are inherently suspect. Along with challenges to state statutes based on the Privileges or Immunities Clause, Fourteenth Amendment litigation swelled the Court's docket, particularly during the Warren Court era. As it had in the 1930s, poverty in America provided fertile soil for such litigation.

In 1962, sociologist Michael Harrington called the nation's poor *The Other America* (New York, NY: Macmillan, 1962). They included unskilled workers, migrants, the elderly, minorities, and millions of others who lived in what Harrington called the "economic underworld of American life." One of the goals of President John Kennedy's New Frontier was ending poverty in America. President Lyndon Johnson's Great Society included a "war" on poverty, waged by programs such as a billion-dollar Economic Opportunity Act; community action programs to assist local areas in addressing their particular problems; job training programs; incentives to small businesses to hire the unemployed; and a domestic program called Volunteers in Service to America (VISTA), through which people could help the poor become self-sufficient.

The Johnson administration never won the war on poverty, but the number of public assistance recipients exploded during the 1960s. Between December 1960 and February 1969, for example, some 800,000 families were added to the rolls of those receiving Aid to Families with Dependent Children (AFDC), a federally funded program that was administered differently in each state. That 107 percent increase in just over eight years contrasted with a 17 percent expansion during the 1950s. The greatest percentage increase occurred in the northeast region of the United States.

Differences in levels of welfare benefits among the states combined with

Americans' legendary mobility to create policy dilemmas for states with relatively generous welfare programs: how to prevent indigents from coming to their jurisdictions to take advantage of the higher benefits. Vivian Thompson, a pregnant nineteen-year-old unwed mother of one, provided the Supreme Court an opportunity to rule on the issue.

Thompson was a resident of Boston, Massachusetts, where she received AFDC benefits. In 1966, she moved to Hartford, Connecticut, to be closer to her mother. When Thompson applied for AFDC benefits in Connecticut, she was told that she was qualified except for the fact that she had not resided in Connecticut for one year, as required by § 17-2d of the Connecticut General Statutes. Section 17-2d imposed a one-year residency requirement on persons who came to the state "without visible means of support for the immediate future."

Thompson filed suit in the U.S. District Court for the District of Connecticut against Bernard Shapiro, Connecticut commissioner of welfare, seeking a declaration that § 17-2d was unconstitutional, an injunction against its enforcement, and money damages. She claimed that the one-year residency requirement discriminated against her on the basis of poverty, in violation of the Privileges or Immunities Clause of the Fourteenth Amendment.

Relying on *Edwards v. California*, a three-judge panel entered judgment for Thompson. It also held that California's durational residency requirement infringed on the right to travel freely from state to state. Shapiro appealed to the Supreme Court of the United States, as allowed by statute for review of three-judge federal district court opinions. The case was argued twice before the Supreme Court, once in May 1968 and again in October 1968. On reargument, it was combined with similar cases from the District of Columbia and Pennsylvania.

HIGHLIGHTS OF SUPREME COURT ARGUMENTS

BRIEF FOR SHAPIRO

◆ The discrimination against potential applicants for state welfare benefits contained in § 17-2d is reasonable and not racially motivated. The Connecticut legislature established the residency requirement because of the high cost of welfare and the fact that some people move to the state simply to take advantage of the state's high welfare payments.

◆ There is no constitutionally imposed or common law duty on states to provide public assistance. It would be an exercise in judicial arrogance to hold § 17-2d unconstitutional.

◆ The district court erred in its reliance on *Edwards v. California*, because California's was a criminal statute while the Connecticut statute is civil.

◆ Historically, pauper relief has been a state and local function. As the Court has recognized in previous cases, the Fourteenth Amendment was not intended to strip states of their power to meet problems previously left to their solution. Connecticut should remain free to give priority in the distribution of its welfare monies to people who have contributed to the economy or who have demonstrated a willingness to do so.

AMICUS CURIAE BRIEFS SUPPORTING SHAPIRO

Ohio; Texas; California; Iowa; Delaware.

BRIEF FOR THOMPSON

◆ Connecticut's durational residency requirement infringes on the right of indigent persons to travel guaranteed by the Privileges or Immunities Clause of the Fourteenth Amendment. The Court declared the right to travel "basic" in *United States v. Guest*, 383 U.S. 745 (1966). The residency requirement also interferes with the right to reside in a state, declared by Justice Johnson in a circuit court decision in *Corfield v. Coryell*, 6 Fed. Cas. 546 (C.C.E.D. Pa. 1823).

◆ Connecticut's residency requirement violates the Equal Protection Clause of the Fourteenth Amendment by discriminating against people on the basis of wealth. Only those without visible means of support are denied welfare benefits. The state of being without funds is a neutral fact and should be as constitutionally irrelevant as race, creed, or color.

◆ The Connecticut residency requirement is not reasonably related to the statutory purpose of the state's welfare statute, which is to assist all families with dependent children. Since 1896, the Court has required that classifications bear a reasonable and just relation to an act and not be made arbitrarily.

AMICUS CURIAE BRIEFS SUPPORTING THOMPSON

The American Civil Liberties Union; American Jewish Congress; the Center on Social Welfare Policy and Law; City of New York.

SUPREME COURT DECISION: **6–3**

BRENNAN, J.

... We do not doubt that the one-year waiting period device is well suited to discourage the influx of poor families in need of assistance. An indigent who desires to migrate, resettle, find a new job, and start a new life will doubtless hesitate if he knows that he must risk making the move without the possibility of falling back on state welfare assistance during his first year of residence, when his need may be most acute. But the purpose of inhibiting migration by needy persons into the State is constitutionally impermissible.

This Court long ago recognized that the nature of our Federal Union and our constitutional concepts of personal liberty unite to require that all citizens be free to travel throughout the length and breadth of our land uninhibited by statutes, rules, or regulations which unreasonably burden or restrict this movement....

More fundamentally, a State may no more try to fence out those indigents who seek higher welfare benefits than it may try to fence out indigents generally.

Implicit in any such distinction is the notion that indigents who enter a State with the hope of securing higher welfare benefits are somehow less deserving than indigents who do not take this consideration into account. But we do not perceive why a mother who is seeking to make a new life for herself and her children should be regarded as less deserving because she considers, among other factors, the level of a State's public assistance. Surely such a mother is no less deserving than a mother who moves into a particular State in order to take advantage of its better educational facilities....

We recognize that a State has a valid interest in preserving the fiscal integrity of its programs. It may legitimately attempt to limit its expenditures, whether for public assistance, public education, or any other program. But a State may not accomplish such a purpose by invidious distinctions between classes of its citizens. It could not, for example, reduce expenditures for education by barring indigent children from its schools. Similarly, in the cases before us, appellants must do more than show that denying welfare benefits to new residents saves money. The saving of welfare costs cannot justify an otherwise invidious classification.

In sum, neither deterrence of indigents from migrating to the State nor limitation of welfare benefits to those regarded as contributing to the State is a constitutionally permissible state objective....

[W]e reject appellants' argument that a mere showing of a rational relationship between the waiting period and these four admittedly permissible state objectives will suffice to justify the classification....

The argument that the waiting-period requirement facilitates budget predictability is wholly unfounded. The records in all three cases are utterly devoid of evidence that either State or the District of Columbia in fact uses the one-year requirement as a means to predict the number of people who will require assistance in the budget year....

Similarly, there is no need for a State to use the one-year waiting period as a safeguard against fraudulent receipt of benefits; for less drastic means are available, and are employed, to minimize that hazard....

We conclude therefore that appellants in these cases do not use and have no need to use the one-year requirement for the governmental purposes suggested. Thus, even under traditional equal protection tests a classification of welfare applicants according to whether they have lived in the State for one year would seem irrational and unconstitutional. But, of course, the traditional criteria do not apply in these cases. Since the classification here touches on the fundamental right of interstate movement, its constitutionality must be judged by the stricter standard of whether it promotes a *compelling* state interest. Under this standard, the waiting-period requirement clearly violates the Equal Protection Clause....

Accordingly, the judgments ... are affirmed.

STEWART, J., CONCURRING [OMITTED]

WARREN, C.J., AND BLACK, J., DISSENTING

... I believe that the dispositive issue is whether under its commerce power Congress can impose residence requirements....

I am convinced that Congress does have power to enact residence requirements of reasonable duration or to authorize the States to do so and that it has exercised this power.

The Court's decision reveals only the top of the iceberg. Lurking beneath are the multitude of situations in which States have imposed residence requirements including eligibility to vote, to engage in certain professions or occupations or to attend a state-supported university. Although the Court takes pains to avoid acknowledging the ramifications of its decision, its implications cannot be ignored. I dissent.

HARLAN, J., DISSENTING

... In upholding the equal protection argument, the Court has applied an equal protection doctrine of relatively recent vintage: the rule that statutory classifications which either are based upon certain "suspect" criteria or affect "fundamental rights" will be held to deny equal protection unless justified by a "compelling" governmental interest....

I think that ... the "compelling interest" doctrine is sound when applied to racial classifications, for historically the Equal Protection Clause was largely a product of the desire to eradicate legal distinctions founded upon race. However, I believe that the more recent extensions have been unwise....

When the right affected is one assured by the Federal Constitution, any infringement can be dealt with under the Due Process Clause. But when a statute affects only matters not mentioned in the Federal Constitution and is not arbitrary or irrational, I must reiterate that I know of nothing which entitles this Court to pick out particular human activities, characterize them as "fundamental," and give them added protection under an unusually stringent equal protection test....

QUESTIONS

1. Some of the language in Justice Brennan's opinion suggests that the Court decided *Shapiro* on the basis of indigence as a suspect classification instead of on the fundamental right to travel. What difference would it make, legally and politically, if the Supreme Court had decided *Shapiro* on the basis that classifications based on income are "suspect" and therefore are subject to strict judicial scrutiny?

2. What doctrinal relationship, if any, exists between *Edwards v. California* and *Shapiro v. Thompson*? Is one decision more constitutionally sound than the other?

3. Law professor Kenneth L. Karst writes:

   The right to travel is a doctrinal orphan grown to vigorous adulthood. As the Articles of Confederation (1781) recognized expressly, the freedom of interstate movement follows logically from the recognition of our nationhood. The Constitution contains no similarly explicit guarantee, but the logic of nationhood remains, reinforced by two centuries of nationalizing experience. The modern right to travel may still be searching for its doctrinal sources, but its historical base is secure. (*Encyclopedia of the American Constitution*, 4 vols. [New York, NY: Macmillan, 1986], 3: 1593)

Can the right to travel be defended as among the privileges or immunities of national citizenship? If so, does its historical base provide an avenue for reviving the Privileges or Immunities Clause of the Fourteenth Amendment, essentially moribund since the *Slaughter-House Cases*?

4. What theory of federalism is reflected in Justice Brennan's opinion in *Shapiro*? How does it differ from that underlying Chief Justice Warren's dissent? Can Chief Justice Warren's dissent in *Shapiro* be reconciled with his decisions imposing federal constitutional rights on the states via the Fourteenth Amendment? Might his service as attorney general of California when *Edwards v. California* was argued help explain Warren's discomfort with *Shapiro v. Thompson*?

COMMENTS

1. The Court's tentative move toward treating indigency as a suspect classification went no further after *Shapiro*. In *Dandridge v. Williams*, 397 U.S. 471 (1970), the Court upheld, 6–3, a Maryland Department of Public Welfare regulation that placed an absolute limit of $250 per month on the amount of a grant under AFDC, regardless of size of family and its need. Justice Potter Stewart wrote for the Court:

   > In the area of economics and social welfare, a State does not violate the Equal Protection Clause merely because the classifications made by its laws are imperfect. If the classification has some "reasonable basis," it does not offend the Constitution simply because the classification "is not made with mathematical nicety or because in practice it results in some inequality."

2. Although, following *Shapiro*, the Court has neither expanded on the fundamental right to travel nor formally elevated poverty to the status of a suspect class, litigation on the durational residency requirement issue addressed in *Shapiro* has continued, as the decisions below indicate.

   Case: *Dunn v. Blumstein*, 405 U.S. 330 (1972)
   Vote: 6–1 (Powell and Rehnquist, J.J., did not participate.)
   Decision: A one-year state, and a three-month county residency requirement as prerequisites to voting do not further a compelling state interest and are overbroad.

Case: *Vlandis v. Klein*, 412 U.S. 441 (1973)

Vote: 6–3

Decision: An irrebuttable presumption, for tuition purposes, that out-of-state students who come to Connecticut to attend a state college continue to hold nonresident status for the entire duration of their attendance denies due process where a reasonable and much less restrictive alternative exists to determine residency.

Case: *Memorial Hospital v. Maricopa County*, 415 U.S. 250 (1974)

Vote: 8–1

Decision: States may not require a year's residence in a county as a condition for an indigent to receive nonemergency hospitalization or medical care at the county's expense. Arizona's requirement violates the Equal Protection Clause of the Fourteenth Amendment.

Case: *Sosna v. Iowa*, 419 U.S. 393 (1975)

Vote: 6–3

Decision: A one-year residency requirement as prerequisite to initiating divorce proceedings does not deny equal protection in light of weighty issues possibly at stake and the interests in minimizing the risk of having Iowa divorces subject to collateral attack.

Case: *Zoble v. Williams*, 457 U.S. 55 (1982)

Vote: 8–1

Decision: A legislative scheme, enacted to distribute part of Alaska's mineral income fund, whereby each resident would receive one dividend unit for each year of residency since 1959, violates the Equal Protection Clause. Neither Alaska's asserted interests in creating a financial incentive for individuals to remain in the state nor prudent management of the fund is related to the distinction between individuals who were residents before 1959 and those who became residents after.

Case: *Supreme Court of New Hampshire v. Piper*, 470 U.S. 274 (1985)

Vote: 8–1

Decision: A state supreme court ruling limiting admission to the New Hampshire bar to state residents is unconstitutional under the Privileges and Immunities Clause of Article I, Section 2. A state may discriminate against nonresidents only where the reasons for doing so are substantial and where differential treatment between residents and nonresidents bears a close and substantial relationship to such reasons. Neither circumstance exists here.

Case: *Supreme Court of Virginia v. Friedman*, 487 U.S. 59 (1988)

Vote: 7–2

Decision: A state supreme court rule requiring out-of-state lawyers admitted to practice law in another state to become permanent residents of Virginia in order to be admitted to the bar without taking the Virginia bar examination is unconstitutional. This discrimination against nonresidents does not bear a close relationship to substantial state objectives.

OTHER PROTECTED CATEGORIES? ECONOMIC CLASS

San Antonio Independent School District v. Rodriguez
411 U.S. 1 (1973)

SETTING

Education has long been assumed to be one of the best ways for individuals to break out of poverty. Public education, like public welfare, has traditionally been regarded as a state function. States, in turn, have historically relied on the property tax as the primary method of funding public schools. Under such a system, children of poor parents inevitably attend schools with low tax bases while children of affluent parents attend schools with high tax bases.

In 1949, Texas adopted a complex system for financing public education. The heart of the program, known as the Minimum Foundation Program, called for state and local contributions to a fund earmarked for teacher salaries and operating and transportation costs. The state financed an average of 80 percent of the Minimum Foundation Program with school districts, as a unit, providing the other 20 percent. Each district's share of the 20 percent, however, was determined by an economic index reflecting its taxpaying ability. Districts with greater ability to pay the local contribution, therefore, received less than 80 percent, while districts that lacked the ability to raise substantial local funds received more than 80 percent. Significantly, each district had the option to supplement the statewide minimum program with additional funds raised by local *ad valorem* (according to value) property taxes.

In July 1968, Demetrio Rodriguez, an organizer of the Edgewood District Concerned Parents Association, and other Mexican-American parents and children residing in the Edgewood Independent School District in San Antonio (Bexar County), Texas, filed a class action suit in U.S. District Court for the Western District of Texas. They sought to enjoin continued use of the Texas school financing system. The San Antonio Independent School District, six other school districts in the San Antonio metropolitan area, the state board of education, the commissioner of education, and the attorney general of Texas, were named as defendants.

Rodriguez and the other plaintiffs claimed that the Texas school financing system violated the Equal Protection Clause of the Fourteenth Amendment by making educational expenditures a function of the wealth of a school district: It allowed districts with high property values to raise more dollars for education than districts with low property values and failed to compensate for the inequalities in fiscal capacity among school districts. The result of this financing plan, they argued, was to assure that poor and minority group children received an inferior education.

For purposes of illustrating their argument, the plaintiffs contrasted the level of public funding in their Edgewood neighborhood schools, the poorest of the district's seven school systems, with the funding level for its richest, Alamo Heights. The 1970 total property value in Edgewood divided by the number of students in that district averaged $5,429 per student. For Alamo Heights the comparable figure was $45,095. Although Edgewood parents taxed themselves at San Antonio's highest rate, property taxes there generated only $26 per pupil. State and federal funds added $330 to this figure for an annual total $356 per pupil expenditure. The Alamo Heights residents taxed themselves at the district's lowest rate and still generated $333 per pupil. Adding the state and federal contributions of $251 brought the annual per pupil expenditure to $584, almost twice the Edgewood figure.

The defendants moved to dismiss the complaint on the ground that it failed to state a cause of action. A three-judge panel of the federal district court denied the motion to dismiss, but dismissed the school districts as defendants. The case continued to carry the San Antonio Independent School District's name, however. (That district subsequently joined with Rodriguez and the others in challenging the state's school finance system.) The district court also dismissed the claim of discrimination against Mexican-Americans.

Following trial, the district court held that education is a fundamental interest and that the Equal Protection Clause of the Fourteenth Amendment embodies a standard of "fiscal neutrality." It enjoined enforcement of Texas school finance laws "insofar as they discriminate against plaintiffs and others on the basis of wealth other than the wealth of the state as a whole." The district court stayed its mandate for two years to give the defendants and the Texas legislature an opportunity to implement a financing system compatible with the Fourteenth Amendment.

The Texas Board of Education appealed to the Supreme Court of the United States.

HIGHLIGHTS OF SUPREME COURT ARGUMENTS

BRIEF FOR SAN ANTONIO SCHOOL DISTRICT

◆ The constitutional standard of "fiscal neutrality" discovered by the district court was advocated by John E. Coons, William H. Cline, and Stephen D. Sugarman, in *Private Wealth and Public Education* (Cambridge, MA: Harvard University Press, 1970). While the book is a splendid, scholarly achievement, dangerous consequences would follow if it were read into the Constitution. The "fiscal neutrality" theory is based on at least two unwarranted assumptions. First is that there is a relationship between quality of education and the amount of money spent on education. It is reasonable to assume that there is some minimum sum of dollars beneath which a sound education could not be had, but beyond that minimum there is no evidence that more dollars mean better education.

◆ The second flawed assumption in the "fiscal neutrality" theory is that the market value of taxable property per pupil is an adequate measure of wealth. Scholarly research on this subject indicates that it is very difficult to specify the degree to which personal and school district wealth coincide.

♦ The district court erred in concluding that because education is very significant to the individual, it is "fundamental" in the sense of subjecting the state's school finance system to strict scrutiny. Declaring education a fundamental interest would require reversal of several Supreme Court decisions, including cases holding that welfare and housing are not fundamental despite their significance to individuals.

♦ The appropriate standard of judicial review of the Texas school financing system is whether it has a rational basis. It would be doctrinaire in the extreme to hold that there is no rational basis for a system that has been in effect for so long.

♦ The Court should consider the practical consequences of the district court's decision. The state cannot afford to subsidize "poor" districts so they can spend as much as "wealthy" districts on education. Taking money away from some districts and giving it to others is also impractical. It would threaten the jobs of tenured teachers in some districts and cause chaos in the bond system districts used to finance construction.

AMICUS CURIAE BRIEFS SUPPORTING SAN ANTONIO SCHOOL DISTRICT

California school officials and tax collectors; attorney general of New Jersey; joint brief of thirty state and local governments.

BRIEF FOR RODRIGUEZ

♦ The evidence is clear that the quality of education a school is able to provide relates to the amount of funds it has available. Wealthier schools in Bexar County are able to provide three to four times more counselors, better libraries, smaller classes, a more stable teacher pool, more sophisticated teaching aids, better maintained facilities, and more square footage of space per student. The Texas system of school finance favors the affluent and discriminates against those whose need is greatest. It does so through state action: The state draws school district boundaries making some districts poorer than others and allows districts to rely on property tax revenues.

♦ Although the Supreme Court has never declared that education is a fundamental right, the conclusion was implicit in such cases as *Brown v. Board of Education*. The effect of the Texas financing system, which provides poor students with an inferior education, is to deprive those students of an equal ability to communicate and to diminish their influence in the political and social process.

♦ Classifications that unequally burden the poor with respect to enjoyment of a fundamental interest are constitutionally suspect. The poor, like racial and ethnic minorities, have long been viewed as among the "discrete and insular minorities" recognized in *United States v. Carolene Products*, 304 U.S. 144 (1938), as deserving special judicial solicitude.

◆ Even if the Court rejects "strict scrutiny" as the appropriate level of judicial review of the Texas school finance system, the state cannot establish a reasonable basis for denying an equal educational opportunity to children living in poor districts. Appeals to longevity and local control do not suffice because the system serves no purpose except to make wealth the basis for determining the allocation of educational dollars. Poor districts in Texas often have less than one-tenth the taxable wealth of rich districts. In order for the Edgewood District to offer its students the same level of education afforded to Alamo Heights District students, for example, it would have to set its tax rate at more than eight times the rate of Alamo Heights.

◆ No child is responsible for poverty. Yet poor children are denied a reasonable opportunity to succeed in life because of their economic status, a characteristic over which they have no control. The Court has often shown concern for the interests of children. Education is the one service provided by the state designed to lift children from poverty and to permit them, through their own efforts, to achieve socioeconomic success.

AMICUS CURIAE BRIEFS SUPPORTING RODRIGUEZ

The San Antonio Independent School District; the superintendent of public instruction of California and the California comptroller general; joint brief of the National Education Association and four other educational organizations; joint brief of fourteen organizations including the City of Baltimore, four New Jersey cities, the AFL-CIO, the League of Women Voters, and the National Urban League; NAACP Legal Defense and Education Fund; joint brief of governors of Minnesota, Maine, South Dakota, Wisconsin, and Michigan; John Serrano Jr., and his son, Anthony.

AMICUS CURIAE BRIEFS SUPPORTING NEITHER SIDE

Commonwealth of Pennsylvania; joint brief of several Texas banks, and the Securities Industry Association; Bond Counsel.

SUPREME COURT DECISION: 5–4

POWELL, J.

... We must decide, first, whether the Texas system of financing public education operates to the disadvantage of some suspect class or impinges upon a fundamental right explicitly or implicitly protected by the Constitution, thereby requiring strict judicial scrutiny....

The wealth discrimination discovered by the District Court in this case, and by several other courts that have recently struck down school-financing laws in other States, is quite unlike any of the forms of wealth discrimination heretofore reviewed by this Court. Rather than focusing on the unique features of the alleged discrimination, the courts in these cases have virtually assumed their findings of a suspect classification through a simplistic process of analysis: since, under the traditional systems of financing public schools, some poorer people receive less expensive educations than other more affluent people, these systems discriminate on the basis of wealth. This approach largely ignores the hard threshold questions, including whether it makes a difference for purposes of consideration under the Constitution that the class of disadvantaged "poor" cannot be identified or defined in customary equal protection terms, and whether the relative—rather than absolute—nature of the asserted deprivation is of significant consequence. Before a State's laws and the justifications for the classifications they create are subjected to strict judicial scrutiny, we think these threshold considerations must be analyzed more closely than they were in the court below....

[I]t is clear that appellees' suit asks this Court to extend its most exacting scrutiny to review a system that allegedly discriminates against a large, diverse, and amorphous class, unified only by the common factor of residence in districts that happen to have less taxable wealth than other districts. The system of alleged discrimination and the class it defines have none of the traditional indicia of suspectness: the class is not saddled with such disabilities, or subjected to such a history of purposeful unequal treatment, or relegated to such a position of political powerlessness as to command extraordinary protection from the majoritarian political process.

We thus conclude that the Texas system does not operate to the peculiar disadvantage of any suspect class.... [A]ppellees ... also assert that the State's system impermissibly interferes with the exercise of a "fundamental" right and that accordingly the prior deci-

sions of this Court require the application of the strict standard of judicial review....

It is not the province of this Court to create substantive constitutional rights in the name of guaranteeing equal protection of the laws. Thus, the key to discovering whether education is "fundamental" is not to be found in comparisons of the relative societal significance of education as opposed to subsistence or housing. Nor is it to be found by weighing whether education is as important as the right to travel. Rather, the answer lies in assessing whether there is a right to education explicitly or implicitly guaranteed by the Constitution....

Education, of course, is not among the rights afforded explicit protection under our Federal Constitution. Nor do we find any basis for saying it is implicitly so protected. As we have said, the undisputed importance of education will not alone cause this Court to depart from the usual standard for reviewing a State's social and economic legislation. It is appellees' contention, however, that education is distinguishable from other services and benefits provided by the State because it bears a peculiarly close relationship to other rights and liberties accorded protection under the Constitution. Specifically, they insist that education is itself a fundamental personal right because it is essential to the effective exercise of First Amendment freedoms and to intelligent utilization of the right to vote. In asserting a nexus between speech and education, appellees urge that the right to speak is meaningless unless the speaker is capable of articulating his thoughts intelligently and persuasively. The "marketplace of ideas" is an empty forum for those lacking basic communicative tools....

We need not dispute any of these propositions. The Court has long afforded zealous protection against unjustifiable governmental interference with the individual's rights to speak and to vote. Yet we have never presumed to possess either the ability or the authority to guarantee to the citizenry the most *effective* speech or the most *informed* electoral choice. That these may be desirable goals of a system of freedom of expression and of a representative form of government is not to be doubted. These are indeed goals to be pursued by a people whose thoughts and beliefs are freed from governmental interference. But they are not values to be implemented by judicial intrusion into otherwise legitimate state activities....

It should be clear, for the reasons stated above and in accord with the prior decisions of this Court, that this is not a case in which the challenged state action must be subjected to the searching judicial scrutiny reserved for laws that create suspect classifications or impinge upon constitutionally protected rights.

We need not rest our decision, however, solely on the inappropriateness of the strict-scrutiny test. A century of Supreme Court adjudication under the Equal Protection Clause affirmatively supports the application of the traditional standard of review, which requires only that the State's system be shown to bear some rational relationship to legitimate state purposes. This case represents far more than a challenge to the manner in which Texas provides for the education of its children. We have here nothing less than a direct attack on the way in which Texas has chosen to raise and disburse state and local tax revenues. We are asked to condemn the State's judgment in conferring on political subdivisions the power to tax local property to supply revenues for local interests. In so doing, appellees would have the Court intrude in an area in which it has traditionally deferred to state legislatures. This Court has often admonished against such interferences with the State's fiscal policies under the Equal Protection Clause....

It must be remembered, also, that every claim arising under the Equal Protection Clause has implications for the relationship between national and state power under our federal system. Questions of federalism are always inherent in the process of determining whether a State's laws are to be accorded the traditional presumption of constitutionality, or are to be subjected instead to rigorous judicial scrutiny.... [I]t would be difficult to imagine a case having a greater potential impact on our federal system than the one now before us, in which we are urged to abrogate systems of financing public education presently in existence in virtually every State.

The foregoing considerations buttress our conclusion that Texas' system of public school finance is an inappropriate candidate for strict judicial scrutiny....

We hardly need add that this Court's action today is not to be viewed as placing its judicial imprimatur on the status quo.... But the ultimate solutions must come from the lawmakers and from the democratic pressures of those who elect them.

Reversed....

STEWART, J., CONCURRING

I join the opinion and judgment of the Court because I am convinced that any other course would mark an extraordinary departure from principled adjudication under the Equal Protection Clause of the Fourteenth Amendment....

Unlike other provisions of the Constitution, the Equal Protection clause confers no substantive rights and creates no substantive liberties. The function of the Equal Protection Clause, rather, is simply to measure the validity of *classifications* created by state laws....

BRENNAN, J., DISSENTING

... [T]here can be no doubt that education is inextricably linked to the right to participate in the electoral process and to the rights of free speech and association guaranteed by the First Amendment.... This being so, any classification affecting education must be subjected to strict judicial scrutiny, and since even the State concedes that the statutory scheme now before us cannot pass constitutional muster under this stricter standard of review, I can only conclude that the Texas school financing scheme is constitutionally invalid.

MARSHALL AND DOUGLAS, J.J., DISSENTING

... In my judgment, the right of every American to an equal start in life, so far as the provision of a state service as important as education is concerned, is far too vital to permit state discrimination on grounds as tenuous as those presented by this record....

Texas has chosen to provide free public education for all its citizens, and it has embodied that decision in its constitution. Yet, having established public education for its citizens, the State, as a direct consequence of the variations in local property wealth endemic to Texas' financing scheme, has provided some

Texas schoolchildren with substantially less resources for their education than others. Thus, while on its face the Texas scheme may merely discriminate between local districts, the impact of that discrimination falls directly upon the children whose educational opportunity is dependent upon where they happen to live. Consequently, the District Court correctly concluded that the Texas financing scheme discriminates, from a constitutional perspective, between schoolchildren on the basis of the amount of taxable property located within their local districts....

This Court has repeatedly held that state discrimination which either adversely affects a "fundamental interest" or is based on a distinction of a suspect character must be carefully scrutinized to ensure that the scheme is necessary to promote a substantial, legitimate state interest.... The majority today concludes, however, that the Texas scheme is not subject to such a strict standard of review under the Equal Protection Clause. Instead, in its view, the Texas scheme must be tested by nothing more than that lenient standard of rationality which we have traditionally applied to discriminatory state action in the context of economic and commercial matters.... By so doing, the Court avoids the telling task of searching for a substantial state interest which the Texas financing scheme, with its variations in taxable district property wealth, is necessary to further. I cannot accept such an emasculation of the Equal Protection Clause in the context of this case....

WHITE, DOUGLAS, AND BRENNAN, J.J., DISSENTING [OMITTED]

QUESTIONS

1. What is the constitutional question in *Rodriguez*—whether poverty is a suspect classification or education is a fundamental right? What is the significance of the answer for purposes of constitutional analysis?

2. How compelling are the federalism concerns raised by Justice Powell (a former president of the Richmond, Virginia, school board) in *Rodriguez*? Are not issues pertinent to the relationship between state and federal power inherent in every Equal Protection claim?

3. *Rodriguez* was decided at a time when schools were still coping with Court-ordered desegregation. Might the political furor unleashed by the desegregation decisions have been a factor in the Court's decision-making process in *Rodriguez*? Should it?

4. What factors account for ongoing controversies in school funding? To what extent does public school funding reflect issues regarding wealth and its proper distribution?

COMMENTS

1. In *Kadrmas v. Dickinson Public Schools*, 487 U.S. 450 (1988), the Court by a 5–4 vote reiterated its view that education is not a fundamental right. It held that a 1979 North Dakota statute that permits some school districts to charge a user fee for bus transportation does not violate the Equal Protection Clause. According to the Court, statutes that have different effects on the wealthy and the poor are not, on that account alone, subject to strict scrutiny under the Equal Protection Clause. By contrast, the supreme courts of the States of California, Connecticut, Wyoming, and Vermont have ruled that under their respective state constitutions, disparities in public school funding are illegal.

2. The controversy over the funding of Texas public schools has not abated in the years since *Rodriguez*. In his 1997 State of the State address, Texas Governor George W. Bush proposed a sweeping restructuring of that state's tax system, calling for a $3 billion-a-year cut in local property taxes and a vastly expanded role for the state in public school financing. Bush proposed to pay for the property tax cut by a one-half-cent increase in the state sales tax and by imposing new taxes on businesses, including a first-ever tax on lawyers, accountants, doctors, and others who belong to professional partnerships (Sam Howe Verhovek, "George W. Bush Unveils Tax Plan for Texas." [http://www.nytimes.com/]. January 30, 1997).

SUGGESTIONS FOR FURTHER READING

Areen, Judith, and Leonard Ross, "The *Rodriguez* Case," *The Supreme Court Review* (Chicago, IL: University of Chicago Press, 1976).

Bennett, Robert W., "The Burger Court and the Poor," in *The Burger Court: The Counter-Revolution That Wasn't*, ed. Vincent Blasi (New Haven, CT: Yale University Press, 1983).

Binion, Gayle, "The Disadvantaged Before the Burger Court: The Newest Unequal Protection," 4 *Law & Policy Quarterly* (1982): 37.

Black, Charles L., Jr., "Further Reflections on the Constitutional Justice of Livelihood," 86 *Columbia Law Review* (1986): 1103.

Bork, Robert H., "The Impossibility of Finding Welfare Rights in the Constitution," 1979 *Washington University Law Quarterly* (1979): 695.

Brigham, John, "Property and the Supreme Court: Do the Justices Make Sense?" 16 *Polity* (Winter 1983): 242.

Brudno, Barbara, "Wealth Discrimination in the Supreme Court: Equal Protection for the Poor from *Griffin* to *Maher*," in *Constitutional Government in America*, ed. Ron Collins (Durham, NC: Carolina Academic Press, 1980).

Bussiere, Elizabeth, *(Dis)Entitling the Poor: The Warren Court, Welfare Rights, and the American Political Tradition* (University Park, PA: University of Pennsylvania Press, 1997).

Clune, William H., III, "The Supreme Court's Treatment of Wealth Discrimination under the Fourteenth Amendment," *The Supreme Court Review* (Chicago, IL: University of Chicago Press, 1975).

Cox, Archibald, "Foreword: Constitutional Adjudication and the Promotion of Human Rights," 80 *Harvard Law Review* (1966): 80.

Gambitta, Richard A. L., "Litigation, Judicial Deference, and Policy Change," in *Governing Through Courts*, ed. Richard A. L. Gambitta, Marlynn L. May, and James C. Foster (Beverley Hills, CA: Sage, 1981).

Graham, Robert L., and Jason H. Kravitt, "The Evolution of Equal Protection—Education, Municipal Services, and Wealth," 7 *Harvard Civil Rights-Civil Liberties Law Review* (1972): 105.

Grey, Thomas, "The Disintegration of Property," in *Nomos XXII: Property*, ed. J. Roland Pennock and John W. Chapman (New York, NY: New York University Press, 1980).

Harrington, Michael, *The Other America: Poverty in the United States* (Baltimore, MD: Penguin, 1963).

_____, *The New American Poverty* (New York, NY: Holt, Reinhart and Winston, 1984).

Pendleton, Howard, "The Privileges and Immunities of Federal Citizenship and *Colgate v. Harvey*," 87 *University of Pennsylvania Law Review* (1939): 262.

Karst, Kenneth, "Invidious Discrimination: Justice Douglas and the Return of the 'Natural-Law-Due-Process Formula,'" 16 *University of California Los Angeles Law Review* (1969): 716.

Karst, Kenneth, and Harold Horowitz, "*Reitman v. Mulkey*: A Telophase of Substantive Equal Protection," *The Supreme Court Review* (Chicago, IL: University of Chicago Press, 1967).

Krislov, Samuel, "The OEO Lawyers Fail to Constitutionalize a Right to Welfare," 58 *Minnesota Law Review* (1973): 211.

MacPherson, C. B., "Human Rights as Property Rights," *Dissent* (Winter 1977): 76.

_____, *Property: Mainstream and Critical Positions* (Toronto, ONT: University of Toronto Press, 1978).

McCann, Michael W., "Resurrection and Reform: Perspectives on Property in the American Constitutional Tradition," 13 *Politics & Society* (1984): 143.

Michelman, Frank I., "Foreword: On Protecting the Poor Through the Fourteenth Amendment," 83 *Harvard Law Review* (1969): 7.

_____, "Welfare Rights in a Constitutional Democracy," 1979 *Washington University Law Quarterly* (1979): 659.

_____, "Property as a Constitutional Right," 38 *Washington and Lee Law Review* (1982): 1101.

Note, "Depression Migrants and the States," 53 *Harvard Law Review* (1940): 1031.

Note, "Educational Financing, Equal Protection of the Laws, and the Supreme Court," 70 *Michigan Law Review* (1972): 1324.

O'Neill, Timothy, "The Language of Equality in a Constitutional Order," 75 *American Political Science Review* (1981): 626.

Perry, Michael J., "Modern Equal Protection: A Conceptualization and Appraisal," 79 *Columbia Law Review* (1979): 1023.

Piven, Frances Fox, and Richard A. Cloward, *Regulating the Poor: The Function of Public Welfare* (New York, NY: Vintage Books, 1972).

_____, *Poor People's Movements: Why They Succceed, How They Fail* (New York, NY: Vintage Books, 1979).

Reich, Charles, "The New Property," 73 *Yale Law Journal* (1964): 771.

Reinstein, Robert, "The Welfare Cases: Fundamental Rights, the Poor, and the Burden of Proof in Constitutional Litigation," 44 *Temple Law Quarterly* (1970): 1.

Richards, David A. J., "Equal Opportunity and School Financing," 41 *University of Chicago Law Review* (1973): 32.

_____, *Conscience and the Constitution* (Princeton, NJ: Princeton University Press, 1993).

Shapiro, Martin, "The Constitution and Economic Rights," in *Essays in the Constitution of the U.S.*, ed. M. Judd Harmon (Port Washington, NY: Kennikat Press, 1978).

Simon, Peter, "Liberty and Property in the Supreme Court: A Defense of *Roth* and *Perry*," 7 *California Law Review* (1983): 146.

Stewart, Richard, "The Reformation of American Administrative Law," 88 *Harvard Law Review* (1975): 712.

Tushnet, Mark, "The Newer Property: Suggestions for the Revival of Substantive Due Process," *The Supreme Court Review* (Chicago, IL: University of Chicago Press, 1975).

Van Alstyne, William, "Cracks in the 'New Property': Adjudicative Due Process in the Administrative State," 62 *Cornell Law Review* (1977): 445.

_____, "The Recrudescence of Property Rights as the Foremost Principle of Civil Liberties: The First Decade of the Burger Court," 43 *Law and Contemporary Problems* (Summer 1980): 66.

Veseth, Michael, "The Economics of Property Rights and Human Rights," 41 *American Journal of Economics* (1982): 169.

Winter, Ralph K., Jr., "Poverty, Economic Inequality, and the Equal Protection Clause," *The Supreme Court Review* (Chicago, IL: University of Chicago Press, 1972).

OTHER PROTECTED CATEGORIES? NATIONAL ORIGIN

Plyler v. Doe
457 U.S. 202 (1982)

SETTING

The United States has been called a "permanently unfinished" society, a reference to its being a nation of immigrants. For many years the United States invited immigrants, because laborers were needed to develop land, build roads, canals, turnpikes, and railroads, and to work in the country's emerging and growing industries. Between the time of the American Revolution and the Civil War, Europeans had strong incentives to come to the United States, including political revolutions in France, Spain, Germany, Greece, Italy, and Belgium, floods in Germany, and a potato famine in Ireland. In the 1830s and 1840s, it is estimated that 2.5 million men, women, and children came to the United States. An additional 2.7 million arrived in the 1850s. Most were from England, Ireland, and Germany and most had little money because they were fleeing bad conditions at home. Many had little choice but to accept low-paying jobs or to homestead on western lands.

In the 1880s, southern and eastern Europe and Asia sent another wave of immigrants to the United States. Many of these new arrivals settled in the big cities and became sources of cheap labor for the industrial revolution. Some, spurred by the discovery of gold in California and the availability of cheap land, went west. By 1882, Congress had become so fearful of the numbers of Asians coming to the United States that it passed the Chinese Exclusion Act.

According to the census of 1890, the United States no longer had a wilderness frontier. Historian Frederick Jackson Turner conjectured that the closing of the frontier helped to explain many of the country's problems, including urban crowding, poverty, crime, and disease. Immigrants quickly came to be associated with those problems. Before 1890, immigrants were needed and largely welcomed, and there was always a place for them to go. By the end of the 1890s, however, anti-immigrant sentiment was widespread. The Immigration Restriction League lobbied Congress to pass laws to keep out "undesirable" immigrants, which usually meant those from non-Anglo-Saxon countries. Literacy tests were established to assure that persons who wanted to come to the United States could read and write English. Congress established quotas for immigrants from various parts of the world, limiting immigration by some groups and encouraging it from others. So-called "Red Scares" during World Wars I and II fueled anti-European immigrant sentiment in the United States for a period of time.

During World War II, agricultural labor shortages prompted the federal government to initiate the Bracero Program with Mexico, under which the United States could import workers temporarily from Mexico to work as farm laborers. The efforts of social activists who opposed the living conditions of braceros in migrant farm camps and the opposition of organized labor that feared cheap labor put an end to the Bracero Program in 1964. Mexican laborers continued to come into the country, however, settling primarily in California, Arizona, New Mexico, Colorado, and Texas. By the late 1970s, it is estimated that there were between six and twelve million illegal aliens in the United States, with between 675,000 and one million in the state of Texas alone. Most engaged in migrant farm labor; many had been recruited to come to the United States. The overwhelming number of illegal aliens in the state of Texas were from Mexico.

In an attempt to respond to the large numbers of illegal aliens within its borders—and in part in reaction to its belief that the U.S. Immigration and Naturalization Service was not doing its job in patrolling the two-thousand-mile border between the United States and Mexico—the Texas legislature in 1975 amended § 21.031 of that state's Education Code. The amendment provided that only citizens and legally admitted aliens were entitled to free public elementary and secondary education in Texas. Under the revisions, local school districts were authorized to apply for state reimbursement only for citizens or legally admitted aliens. Legal opposition to the statute developed immediately. One case arose out of Smith County, Texas, where the Tyler Independent School District (TISD) is located.

The Tyler school board realized that if it were to charge admission to illegal aliens to attend TISD schools, that would be tantamount to exclusion. Consequently, it absorbed the cost of educating all children until the

1977–1978 school year. Then it announced that it would have to charge tuition in the amount of $1,000 annually.

In September 1977, parents of illegal alien children, using the assumed names J. and R. Doe, filed a class action lawsuit in the U.S. District Court for the Eastern District of Texas on behalf of all school-age children of Mexican origin residing in Smith County, Texas, who could not establish that they had been legally admitted into the United States. The parents had resided in Tyler for a number of years and all of the children had attended Tyler schools in the past. The suit sought a declaration that § 21.031 violated the Equal Protection Clause and an injunction against its enforcement. The Does named TISD Superintendent James Plyler and the TISD board as defendants. The state of Texas subsequently intervened as a defendant.

The district court issued a preliminary injunction against enforcement of § 21.031. It subsequently ruled that illegal aliens are entitled to the protection of the Equal Protection Clause of the Fourteenth Amendment and that § 21.031 violated the guarantee of equal protection of the laws. The court reasoned that "the state's exclusion of undocumented children from its public schools ... may well be the type of invidiously motivated state action for which the suspect classification doctrine was designed." According to the district court, however, § 21.031 could not survive even a "rational basis" level of review.

The U.S.Court of Appeals for the Fifth Circuit affirmed. That court agreed with the district court that under any standard of judicial review, § 21.031 could not pass constitutional muster. Plyler and the state of Texas appealed to the Supreme Court of the United States. The Court consolidated the case with *Texas v. Certain Named and Unnamed Undocumented Alien Children.*

HIGHLIGHTS OF SUPREME COURT ARGUMENTS

BRIEF FOR PLYLER

◆ Although the Due Process Clause has been interpreted to apply to illegal aliens, *Shaughnessey v. United States*, 345 U.S. 206 (1953), there is no basis for holding that the Equal Protection Clause is applicable to illegal aliens. Extending the Equal Protection Clause in this context would subvert any orderly solution to the pressing political problems caused by illegal aliens and would cause an unwarranted intrusion into areas reserved to the political branches of the government. The judiciary is not the proper branch of government to decide what resources should be dedicated to illegal aliens.

◆ Illegal aliens, by definition, lack legal rights. Consequently, legislation that refers to illegal aliens as a class cannot be subjected to strict judicial scrutiny.

◆ Even if the Equal Protection Clause is applicable, § 21.031 is not unconstitutional because education is not a fundamental right. Preservation of the state's resources for the education of its lawful residents and elimination of an inducement for illegal immigration are sufficient basis for upholding the constitutionality of the statute.

◆ The State of Texas should not be compelled to educate the indeterminate number of alien children who are brought to this country in order to secure an American education. Forcing the state to do so will only promote permanent, unlawful immigration.

AMICUS CURIAE BRIEF SUPPORTING PLYLER

Pacific Legal Foundation.

BRIEF FOR THE DOES

◆ The Equal Protection Clause prohibits a state from denying the equal protection of the laws to any *person* within its jurisdiction. Hence, the children in this case are entitled to the protection of that clause regardless of their legal status in the United States.

◆ Regardless of the standard of judicial review employed in this case, § 21.031 is constitutionally infirm on Equal Protection grounds.

◆ The facts of this case distinguish it from *San Antonio School District v. Rodriguez*. In that case, the issue was relative inequalities among districts and in that context the Court was not willing to apply a heightened level of judicial scrutiny. This case involves the absolute denial of schooling, which must be deemed a fundamental right. Education, like freedom of speech and equality of access to the ballot, is preservative of the rights and liberties that are the nation's bedrock.

◆ Heightened judicial scrutiny is always appropriate when a state chooses to punish individuals for the wrongs committed by others. If a wrong has been committed in this situation, it is the attempt of financially desperate parents seeking to make a living and to preserve their family's unity.

◆ Heightened judicial scrutiny is also appropriate because the harm contained in § 21.031 is being visited upon children whose parents are unable to protect their interests through the political process.

AMICUS CURIAE BRIEFS SUPPORTING DOE

American Jewish Committee; Asian American Legal Defense and Education Fund; Edgewood Independent School District; joint brief of the National Education Association, and the League of United Latin American Citizens.

Note: The United States also submitted an *amicus curiae* brief, addressing only Supremacy Clause issues.

SUPREME COURT DECISION: 5–4

BRENNAN, J.

... The Fourteenth Amendment provides that "[n]o State shall ... deprive any person of life, liberty, or property, without due process of law; nor deny to any person *within its jurisdiction* the equal protec-

tion of the laws." (Emphasis added.) ... Aliens, even aliens whose presence in this country is unlawful, have long been recognized as "persons" guaranteed due process of law by the Fifth and Fourteenth

Amendments.... Indeed, we have clearly held that the Fifth Amendment protects aliens whose presence in this country is unlawful from invidious discrimination by the Federal Government....

The Equal Protection Clause was intended to work nothing less than the abolition of all caste-based and invidious class-based legislation. That objective is fundamentally at odds with the power the State asserts here to classify persons subject to its laws as nonetheless excepted from its protection....

Our conclusion that the illegal aliens who are plaintiffs in these cases may claim the benefit of the Fourteenth Amendment's guarantee of equal protection only begins the inquiry. The more difficult question is whether the Equal Protection Clause has been violated by the refusal of the State of Texas to reimburse local school boards for the education of children who cannot demonstrate that their presence within the United States is lawful, or by the imposition by those school boards of the burden of tuition on those children....

Sheer incapability or lax enforcement of the laws barring entry into this country, coupled with the failure to establish an effective bar to the employment of undocumented aliens, has resulted in the creation of a substantial "shadow population" of illegal migrants—numbering in the millions—within our borders. This situation raises the specter of a permanent caste of undocumented resident aliens, encouraged by some to remain here as a source of cheap labor, but nevertheless denied the benefits that our society makes available to citizens and lawful residents. The existence of such an underclass presents most difficult problems for a Nation that prides itself on adherence to principles of equality under law.

The children who are plaintiffs in these cases are special members of this underclass. Persuasive arguments support the view that a State may withhold its beneficence from those whose very presence within the United States is the product of their own unlawful conduct. These arguments do not apply with the same force to classifications imposing disabilities on the minor children of such illegal entrants....

Of course, undocumented status is not irrelevant to any proper legislative goal. Nor is undocumented status an absolutely immutable characteristic since it is the product of conscious, indeed unlawful, action. But Sec. 21.031 is directed against children, and imposes its discriminatory burden on the basis of a legal characteristic over which children can have little control. It is thus difficult to conceive of a rational justification for penalizing these children for their presence within the United States. Yet that appears to be precisely the effect of Sec. 21.031.

Public education is not a "right" granted to individuals by the Constitution. *San Antonio Independent School Dist. v. Rodriguez.* But neither is it merely some governmental "benefit" indistinguishable from other forms of social welfare legislation. Both the importance of education in maintaining our basic institutions, and the lasting impact of its deprivation on the life of the child, mark the distinction.... In addition, education provides the basic tools by which individuals might lead economically productive lives to the benefit of us all. In sum, education has a fundamental role in maintaining the fabric of our society. We cannot ignore the significant social costs borne by our Nation when select groups are denied the means to absorb the values and skills upon which our social order rests.

In addition to the pivotal role of education in sustaining our political and cultural heritage, denial of education to some isolated group of children poses an affront to one of the goals of the Equal Protection Clause: the abolition of governmental barriers presenting unreasonable obstacles to advancement on the basis of individual merit. Paradoxically, by depriving the children of any disfavored group of an education, we foreclose the means by which that group might raise the level of esteem in which it is held by the majority.... Illiteracy is an enduring disability. The inability to read and write will handicap the individual deprived of a basic education each and every day of his life. The inestimable toll of that deprivation on the social, economic, intellectual, and psychological well-being of the individual, and the obstacle it poses to individual achievement, make it most difficult to reconcile the cost or the principle of a status-based denial of basic education with the framework of equality embodied in the Equal Protection Clause....

These well-settled principles allow us to determine the proper level of deference to be afforded Sec. 21.031. Undocumented aliens cannot be treated as a suspect class because their presence in this country in violation of federal law is not a "constitutional irrelevancy." Nor is education a fundamental right; a State need not justify by compelling necessity every variation in the manner in which education is provided to its population.... But more is involved in these cases than the abstract question whether Sec. 21.031 discriminates against a suspect class, or whether education is a fundamental right. Section 21.031 imposes a lifetime hard-

ship on a discrete class of children not accountable for their disabling status. The stigma of illiteracy will mark them for the rest of their lives. By denying these children a basic education, we deny them the ability to live within the structure of our civic institutions, and foreclose any realistic possibility that they will contribute in even the smallest way to the progress of our Nation. In determining the rationality of Sec. 21.031, we may appropriately take into account its costs to the Nation and to the innocent children who are its victims. In light of these countervailing costs, the discrimination contained in Sec. 21.031 can hardly be considered rational unless it furthers some substantial goal of the State....

Appellants argue that the classification at issue furthers an interest in the "preservation of the state's limited resources for the education of its lawful residents." Of course, a concern for the preservation of resources standing alone can hardly justify the classification used in allocating those resources. The State must do more than justify its classification with a concise expression of an intention to discriminate. Apart from the asserted state prerogative to act against undocumented children solely on the basis of their undocumented status—an asserted prerogative that carries only minimal force in the circumstances of these cases—we discern three colorable state interests that might support Sec. 21.031.

First, appellants appear to suggest that the State may seek to protect itself from an influx of illegal immigrants. While a State might have an interest in mitigating the potentially harsh economic effects of sudden shifts in population, Sec. 21.031 hardly offers an effective method of dealing with an urgent demographic or economic problem. There is no evidence in the record suggesting that illegal entrants impose any significant burden on the State's economy. To the contrary, the available evidence suggests that illegal aliens underutilize public services, while contributing their labor to the local economy and tax money to the state fisc....

Second, while it is apparent that a State may "not ... reduce expenditures for education by barring [some arbitrarily chosen class of] children from its schools," *Shapiro v. Thompson*, appellants suggest that undocumented children are appropriately singled out for exclusion because of the special burdens they impose on the State's ability to provide high-quality public education. But the record in no way supports the claim that exclusion of undocumented children is likely to improve the overall quality of education in the State.... Of course, even if improvement in the quality of education were a likely result of barring some number of children from the schools of the State, the State must support its selection of this group as the appropriate target for exclusion. In terms of educational cost and need, however, undocumented children are "basically indistinguishable" from legally resident alien children.

Finally, appellants suggest that undocumented children are appropriately singled out because their unlawful presence within the United States renders them less likely than other children to remain within the boundaries of the State, and to put their education to productive social or political use within the State. Even assuming that such an interest is legitimate, it is an interest that is most difficult to quantify. The State has no assurance that any child, citizen or not, will employ the education provided by the State within the confines of the State's borders....

If the State is to deny a discrete group of innocent children the free public education that it offers to other children residing within its borders, that denial must be justified by a showing that it furthers some substantial state interest. No such showing was made here. Accordingly, the judgment of the Court of Appeals in each of these cases is

Affirmed.

MARSHALL, J., CONCURRING

While I join the Court's opinion, I do so without in any way retreating from my [dissenting] opinion in *San Antonio Independent School District v. Rodriguez.* I continue to believe that an individual's interest in education is fundamental[.]... Furthermore, I believe that the facts of these cases demonstrate the wisdom of rejecting a rigidified approach to equal protection analysis, and of employing an approach that allows for varying levels of scrutiny depending upon "the constitutional and societal importance of the interest adversely affected and the recognized invidiousness of the basis upon which the particular classification is drawn." Id.... It continues to be my view that a class-based denial of public education is utterly incompatible with the Equal Protection Clause of the Fourteenth Amendment.

BLACKMUN, J., CONCURRING

... In my view, when the State provides an education to some and denies it to others, it immediately and inevitably creates class distinctions of a type fundamentally inconsistent with those purposes ... of the Equal Protection Clause. Children denied an education are placed at a permanent and insurmountable competitive disadvantage, for an uneducated child is denied even the opportunity to achieve.

And when those children are members of an identifiable group, that group—through the State's action—will have been converted into a discrete underclass. Other benefits provided by the State, such as housing and public assistance, are of course important; to an individual in immediate need, they may be more desirable than the right to be educated. But classifications involving the complete denial of education are in a sense unique, for they strike at the heart of equal protection values by involving the State in the creation of permanent class distinctions....

Because I believe that the Court's carefully worded analysis recognizes the importance of the equal protection and preemption interests I consider crucial, I join its opinion as well as its judgment.

POWELL, J., CONCURRING

... In these cases, the State of Texas effectively denies to the school-age children of illegal aliens the opportunity to attend the free public schools that the State makes available to all residents. They are excluded only because of a status resulting from the violation by parents or guardians of our immigration laws and the fact that they remain in our country unlawfully. The appellee children are innocent in this respect....

In reaching this conclusion, I am not unmindful of what must be the exasperation of responsible citizens and government authorities in Texas and other States similarly situated. Their responsibility, if any, for the influx of aliens is slight compared to that imposed by the Constitution on the Federal Government. So long as the ease of entry remains inviting, and the power to deport is exercised infrequently by the Federal Government, the additional expense of admitting these children to public schools might fairly be shared by the Federal and State Governments. But it hardly can be argued rationally that anyone benefits from the creation within our borders of a subclass of illiterate persons many of whom will remain in the State, adding to the problems and costs of both State and National Governments attendant upon unemployment, welfare, and crime.

BURGER, C.J., AND WHITE, REHNQUIST, AND O'CONNOR, J.J., DISSENTING

... The dispositive issue in these cases, simply put, is whether, for purposes of allocating its finite resources, a state has a legitimate reason to differentiate between persons who are lawfully within the state and those who are unlawfully there. The distinction the State of Texas has drawn—based not only upon its own legitimate interests but on classifications established by the Federal Government in its immigration laws and policies—is not unconstitutional....

The Equal Protection Clause guarantees similar treatment of similarly situated persons, but it does not mandate a constitutional hierarchy of governmental services. Justice Powell, speaking for the Court in *San Antonio Independent School Dist.*, put it well in stating that to the extent this Court raises or lowers the degree of "judicial scrutiny" in equal protection cases according to a transient Court majority's view of the societal importance of the interest affected, we "assum[e] a legislative role and one for which the Court lacks both authority and competence." Yet that is precisely what the Court does today.

Without laboring what will undoubtedly seem obvious to many, it simply is not "irrational" for a state to conclude that it does not have the same responsibility to provide benefits for persons whose very presence in the state and this country is illegal as it does to provide for persons lawfully present. By definition, illegal aliens have no right whatever to be here, and the state may reasonably, and constitutionally, elect not to provide them with governmental services at the expense of those who are lawfully in the state....

Denying a free education to illegal alien children is not a choice I would make were I a legislator. Apart from compassionate considerations, the long-range costs of excluding any children from the public schools may well outweigh the costs of educating them. But that is not the issue; the fact that there are sound policy arguments against the Texas Legislature's choice does not render that choice an unconstitutional one.

The Constitution does not provide a cure for every social ill, nor does it vest judges with a mandate to try to remedy every social problem.... Moreover, when this Court rushes in to remedy what it perceives to be the failings of the political processes, it deprives those processes of an opportunity to function. When the political institutions are not forced to exercise constitutionally allocated powers and responsibilities, those powers, like muscles not used, tend to atrophy. Today's cases, I regret to say, present yet another example of unwarranted judicial action which in the long run tends to contribute to the weakening of our political processes....

QUESTIONS

1. What standard of review does the majority employ in *Plyler*? What does the majority hold with respect to the question of whether education is a fundamental right? Is its holding consistent with *Rodriguez*?

2. The *Plyler* majority appeared to conclude that preserving a state's scarce educational resources and discouraging illegal immigration are not sufficient interests to justify a statute such as § 21.031 under the Equal Protection Clause. If those are not rational (or compelling) considerations, what might be? Must *Plyler* be read as holding that federal immigration policy and practice preempts state and local concerns?

3. Was Chief Justice Burger correct that *Plyler* is an example of judicial policy making rather than judicial review?

4. Justice Robert Jackson wrote in *Johnson v. Eisentrager*, 339 U.S. 763 (1950):

> The alien, to whom the United States has been traditionally hospitable, has been accorded a generous and ascending scale of rights as he increases his identity with our society. Mere lawful presence in the country creates an implied assurance of safe conduct and gives him certain rights; they become more extensive and secure when he makes preliminary declaration of intention to become a citizen, and they expand to those of full citizenship upon naturalization. During his probationary residence, this Court has steadily enlarged his right against Executive deportation except upon full and fair hearing.... And, at least since 1886, we have extended to the

person and property of resident aliens important constitutional guaranties—such as the due process of law of the Fourteenth Amendment. *Yick Wo v. Hopkins*, 118 U.S. 356.

Is *Plyler* an example of the continuation of that legal tradition? If so, is there evidence that the tradition is eroding?

COMMENT

In November 1994, California voters adopted Proposition 187. Among other things, it requires state personnel—including school teachers, health care workers, and social workers—to identify, question, investigate, and report to the Immigration and Naturalization Service persons suspected of being in the country illegally. Proposition 187 also requires that persons who cannot prove citizenship or legal residency be denied access to free public education, health care, and police assistance.

The U.S. District Court for the Central District of California issued a preliminary injunction blocking enforcement of Proposition 187. The U.S. Court of Appeals for the Ninth Circuit denied the state's motion to vacate the injunction. *Gregorio T. v. Wilson*, 597 F.3d 1002 (1995). On November 14, 1997, the district court issued a memorandum of law declaring that the Federal Welfare Reform Act of 1996 superceded Proposition 187. Litigation is continuing.

SUGGESTIONS FOR FURTHER READING

Acuna, Rudolfo, *Occupied America: A History of Chicanos* (New York, NY: Harper and Row, 1988).

Baer, Judith A., *Equality under the Fourteenth Amendment* (Ithaca, NY: Cornell University Press, 1983).

Bickel, Alexander M., "The Original Understanding and the Segregation Decision," 69 *Harvard Law Review* (1955): 1.

Carlinger, David, *The Rights of Aliens*, 2nd ed. (Carbondale, IL: Southern Illinois University Press, 1990).

Chuman, Frank F., *The Bamboo People: The Law and Japanese-Americans* (Del Mar, CA: Publishers, Inc., 1976).

Cornelius, Wayne A., *The Future of Mexican Immigrants in California: A New Perspective for Public Policy* (San Diego, CA: University of California Center for U.S.-Mexican Studies, 1981).

_____, *America in the Era of Limits: Migrants, Nativists, and the Future of U.S.-Mexican Relations* (San Diego, CA: University of California Center for U.S.-Mexican Studies, 1982).

_____, *Mexican Migration to the United States: Origins, Consequences, and Policy Options* (San Diego, CA: University of California Center for U.S.-Mexican Studies, 1989).

Crockcroft, James D., *Outlaws in the Promised Land: Mexican Immigrant Workers and America's Future* (New York, NY: Grove Press, 1986).

Davis, Marilyn P., *Mexican Voices American Dreams: An Oral History of Mexican Immigration to the United States* (New York, NY: Henry Holt, 1990.)

Ferguson, Edwin E., "The California Alien Land Law and the Fourteenth Amendment," 35 *California Law Review* (1947): 61.

Gordon, Charles, "The Racial Barrier to American Citizenship," 93 *University of Pennsylvania Law Review* (1945): 237.

Greenfield, Gary A., and Don B. Kates Jr., "Mexican Americans, Racial Discrimination and the Civil Rights Act of 1866," 63 *California Law Review* (1975): 662.

Hutchinson, Dennis J., "More Substantive Equal Protection? A Note on *Plyler v. Doe,*" *The Supreme Court Review* (Chicago, IL: University of Chicago Press, 1982).

Karst, Kenneth L., "Foreword: Equal Citizenship under the Fourteenth Amendment," 91 *Harvard Law Review* (1977): 1.

_____, *Belonging to America: Equal Citizenship and the Constitution* (New Haven, CT: Yale University Press, 1989).

López, Gerald P., "Undocumented Mexican Migration: In Search of a Just Immigration Law and Policy," 28 *University of California Los Angeles Law Review* (1981): 615.

Lusky, Louis, "Footnote Redux: A '*Carolene Products*' Reminiscence," 82 *Columbia Law Review* (1982): 1093.

McGovney, Dudley O., "The Anti-Japanese Alien Land Laws of California and Ten Other States," 35 *California Law Review* (1947): 7.

Note, "The Equal Treatment of Aliens: Preemption or Equal Protection?" 31 *Stanford Law Review* (1979): 1069.

Note, "State Burdens on Resident Aliens: A New Preemption Analysis," 89 *Yale Law Journal* (1980): 940.

Note, "Developments in the Law—Immigration and the Rights of Aliens," 96 *Harvard Law Review* (1983): 1286.

Ortega, Joe C., "The Plight of the Mexican Wetback," 58 *American Bar Association Journal* (1972): 251.

Portes, Alejandro, and Rubén G. Rumbaut, *Immigrant America: A Portrait* (Berkeley, CA: University of California Press, 1990).

Project Report, "*De Jure* Segregation of Chicanos in Texas Schools," 7 *Harvard Civil Rights-Civil Liberties Law Review* (1972): 307.

Rosberg, Gerald M., "The Protection of Aliens from Discriminatory Treatment by the National Government," *The Supreme Court Review* (Chicago, IL: University of Chicago Press, 1977).

Sandmeyer, Elmer C., *The Anti-Chinese Movement in California* (Urbana, IL: University of Illinois Press, 1939).

Tushnet, Mark, "The Optimist's Tale," 132 *University of Pennsylvania Law Review* (1984): 1257.

Wollenberg, Charles, *All Deliberate Speed, Segregation and Exclusion in California Schools, 1885–1975* (Berkeley, CA: University of California Press, 1978).

OTHER PROTECTED CATEGORIES? DISABILITY

City of Cleburne, Texas v. Cleburne Living Center
473 U.S. 432 (1985)

SETTING

One mark of a society is the way it treats its most disadvantaged—the young, the poor, and the mentally retarded. In the early decades of American history, families were responsible for the care of their mentally retarded relatives. Some were kept at home. Others went homeless and depended on churches and other charities for handouts. Still others wound up in jails or almshouses (also known as poorhouses). Those who were homeless or were sent to jails or almshouses usually suffered greatly and died quickly. In the first decades of the nineteenth century, most states responded to the growing numbers of mentally retarded persons by establishing asylums that separated them from criminals and from the rest of society. Asylums were at best human warehouses where living conditions were typically appalling and treatment was unavailable.

The worst period of legal discrimination against the mentally retarded began in the late nineteenth century and lasted well into the 1930s. The eugenics movement that began in the 1890s had particularly pernicious consequences. Eugenicists believed that the human species could be improved—if not perfected—through genetic engineering. Organizations like the American Breeders Association examined the relationship between heredity and mental retardation. The mentally retarded were regarded as the defective products of flawed heredity, threats to society, and dangers to the survival of the human species. They were blamed for most of the criminality and immorality in the society. In response to the influence of the eugenics movement, many states adopted laws that prevented the "feeble minded" from marrying and voting. Between 1907 and 1931, twenty-nine states enacted laws that allowed the sexual sterilization of the mentally retarded and some states even debated the execution of retarded people to prevent them from harming society. Mentally retarded children were systematically excluded from public schools and several states had laws providing that parents who placed their children in state institutions could not obtain their discharge. In 1917, Congress put a ban on the foreign immigration of retarded persons.

In the 1930s and 1940s, photojournalists exposed the wretched conditions in which institutionalized mentally retarded persons were forced to live. In response, various reforms were proposed, including parole programs, outpatient clinics, and special classes to assist the mentally retarded to live in the community. By the 1950s, the goal had become "habilitation": elevating the mentally handicapped to their highest level of personal accomplishment.

In the 1960s and 1970s, a variety of forces combined to alter public policy regarding the care and treatment of the mentally retarded. President John F. Kennedy, whose sister, Rosemary, was mentally retarded, created a President's Panel on Mental Retardation. In 1962, that panel recommended that the mentally handicapped be treated through what it called a "continuum of care." Federal monies were used to rehabilitate dilapidated institutions and to build new ones. By the end of the decade, President Richard Nixon's "New Federalism," which promised to return power to the states and their communities, gave more responsibilities to states and localities to pay for the maintenance and upkeep of the facilities that had been built with federal monies. Renewed exposés by social reformers and lawsuits brought by parents and relatives of mentally retarded inmates of state institutions demonstrated that the conditions in many institutions were deplorable. Those examples, combined with pressures to reduce state budgets, resulted in programs such as "deinstitutionalizing," "mainstreaming," "normalizing," and "community placement" for the mentally retarded.

In 1965 the state of Texas, like most other states, began major revisions in its public policy regarding the mentally retarded. Within a few years, that policy included a preference for community-based living alternatives for the mentally retarded, made available through state, local, and private providers. Between 1971 and 1982, the number of state institutions for retarded persons decreased from 279 to 182 and the number of institutionalized residents dropped from 189,546 to 119,335. Group homes for the mentally retarded, such as the Cleburne Living Center (CLC), a private corporation, grew proportionately.

In July 1980, Jan Hannah purchased a house at 210 Featherston Street in Cleburne, Texas, with the intention of leasing it to the CLC as a supervised group home for thirteen mentally retarded adults. Hannah was vice president of CLC. She paid $59,000 for the house and intended to rent it to CLC for $1,300 per month. The house had four bedrooms and two baths, and Hannah planned to add another half-bath. It was located on a large corner lot near downtown, close to a two-story apartment house, a dentist's office, and a public junior high school. A public park and recreation facility, the public library, and the central business district were within walking distance of the house. According to the CLC, the residents would work at ordinary jobs in the community or in workshops and would increase their skills in independent living. Staff members would be present around the clock. CLC planned to charge residents $48.10 per day to live there, which was the state per diem rate.

State authorities inspected the house and approved it for the intended use. However, the City of Cleburne informed Hannah and the CLC that they would need to obtain a "special use permit" from the city before they could operate the group home because Section 16, subdivision 9, of the city's zoning ordinance required such permits for facilities that were to be used as "hospitals for the insane or feeble-minded, or alcoholic [sic] or drug addicts, or penal or correctional institutions." The city had determined that the CLC proposed use should be classified as a "hospital for the feebleminded."

In August 1980, the Cleburne Planning and Zoning Commission recommended against granting the special use permit, on the ground that the people who would occupy the house were mentally retarded. In October, the city council, by a 3–1 vote, agreed with the planning commission.

The following month, the CLC (by then named Community Living Concepts) joined Hannah and the Johnson County Association for Retarded Citizens in a lawsuit in the U.S. District Court for the Northern District of Texas against the city and a number of its officials for lost profits associated with the purchase and intended lease of the house. They sought a declaration that the zoning ordinance that required a special use permit for the establishment of CLC's business was unconstitutional because it discriminated against retarded persons. The district court found that "[i]f the potential residents of the Featherston Street home were not mentally retarded, but the home was the same in all other respects, its use would be permitted under the city's zoning ordinance" and that the city council's decision "was motivated primarily by the fact that the residents of the home would be persons who are mentally retarded." The court applied a "rational basis test" and concluded that the ordinance was rationally related to the city's legitimate purposes, including responding to the safety and fears of residents in the adjoining neighborhood, and was neither arbitrary nor capricious.

The U.S. Court of Appeals for the Fifth Circuit reversed. It ruled that mentally retarded persons are a "quasi-suspect class" for purposes of analysis under the Equal Protection Clause of the Fourteenth Amendment, which requires that a statutory classification serve important governmental interests and be substantially related to the achievement of those objectives. In light of the "unfair and often grotesque mistreatment" of the mentally retarded, and their lack of political power, the appeals court concluded that the Cleburne zoning ordinance failed to pass constitutional muster.

The Supreme Court of the United States granted the City of Cleburne's petition for a writ of certiorari.

HIGHLIGHTS OF SUPREME COURT ARGUMENTS

BRIEF FOR CITY OF CLEBURNE

◆ The mentally retarded are not a "quasi-suspect" class for purposes of Equal Protection analysis because they do not meet the indicia of "suspectness" that is necessary to accord that status to a group. They are not a "discrete and insular minority" because their disability, while immutable, has not subjected them to purposeful unequal treatment and they have not been relegated to a position of political powerlessness.

◆ Mild retardation, which is what affects almost ninety percent of all mentally retarded persons, is hardly discernible in formal contact, unlike race or gender.

◆ Mental retardation is a legitimate classification for legislative purposes because the term refers to deficits in intellectual development and social adaptation. Because the mentally retarded are less able to care for themselves, they are appropriately classified as such in legislation.

◆ Attitudes toward the mentally retarded have changed since the 1950s. Public understanding of mental retardation has improved and they are the recipients of the benefits of considerable legislation. Neither are the mentally retarded politically powerless, as evidenced by the passage of such legislation.

◆ A rational basis standard of review should be used in reviewing legislation affecting the mentally retarded. It is without question that the city has a legitimate interest in the location and appropriateness of structures to house the mentally retarded.

AMICUS CURIAE BRIEF SUPPORTING THE CITY OF CLEBURNE

United States.

BRIEF FOR CLEBURNE LIVING CENTER

◆ The crux of this case is whether the possession of the trait of mental retardation makes a citizen less entitled to live meaningfully in an American community. Under whatever analytical standard the Court chooses to employ, the city's blatantly exclusionary actions are prohibited. The Cleburne ordinance cannot pass even the most minimal test.

◆ The record demonstrates that the Cleburne ordinance protects only one interest: the illegitimate one of not wanting to live next to a group of retarded people. Denial of the special permit was motivated by the fact that the proposed residents of the house are mentally retarded. The denial was not tied to any legitimate governmental objectives.

◆ Recent, sporadic public policy successes on behalf of the mentally retarded do not mean that deep-rooted, false stereotypes have been eliminated and that heightened judicial scrutiny is not needed.

◆ A determination that mental retardation is a quasi-suspect classification will not place the Court in a constitutional straitjacket. Laws that classify on the basis of mental retardation will not be automatically invalidated, as has been demonstrated in other areas (such as gender and legitimacy) where heightened judicial scrutiny is employed.

AMICUS CURIAE BRIEFS SUPPORTING CLEBURNE LIVING CENTER

Joint brief of the American Association of Mental Deficiency, the Association for Persons with Severe Handicaps, the American Psychological Association, the American Psychiatric Association, the American Orthopsychiatric

Association, the American Association of University Affiliated Programs for the Developmentally Disabled, and the Council for Exceptional Children; joint brief of the American Civil Liberties Union Foundation, the New York Civil Liberties Union, the American Civil Liberties Union Foundation of California, and the American Civil Liberties Foundation of Texas; joint brief of Connecticut, Arkansas, California, Colorado, Illinois, Louisiana, North Dakota, Rhode Island, Tennessee, and West Virginia; State of Texas; State of Maryland; joint brief of the National Association for Rights Protection and Advocacy, the Normalization Safeguards Project, the Foundation for Dignity, the Brums Foundation, and plaintiffs in twelve pending cases involving community homes; joint brief of Pennsylvania, Iowa, Michigan, Minnesota, New Hampshire, New Jersey, Ohio, and Wisconsin.

SUPREME COURT DECISION: 6–3

WHITE, J.

... [W]here individuals in the group affected by a law have distinguishing characteristics relevant to interests the State has the authority to implement, the courts have been very reluctant, as they should be in our federal system and with our respect for the separation of powers, to closely scrutinize legislative choices as to whether, how, and to what extent those interests should be pursued. In such cases, the Equal Protection Clause requires only a rational means to serve a legitimate end.

Against this background, we conclude for several reasons that the Court of Appeals erred in holding mental retardation a quasi-suspect classification calling for a more exacting standard of judicial review than is normally accorded economic and social legislation. First, it is undeniable, and it is not argued otherwise here, that those who are mentally retarded have a reduced ability to cope with and function in the everyday world. Nor are they all cut from the same pattern: as the testimony in this record indicates, they range from those whose disability is not immediately evident to those who must be constantly cared for. They are thus different, immutably so, in relevant respects, and the States' interest in dealing with and providing for them is plainly a legitimate one. How this large and diversified group is to be treated under the law is a difficult and often a technical matter, very much a task for legislators guided by qualified professionals and not by the perhaps ill-informed opinions of the judiciary. Heightened scrutiny inevitably involves substantive judgments about legislative decisions, and we doubt that the predicate for such judicial oversight is present where the classification deals with mental retardation.

Second, the distinctive legislative response, both national and state, to the plight of those who are mentally retarded demonstrates not only that they have unique problems, but also that the lawmakers have been addressing their difficulties in a manner that belies a continuing antipathy or prejudice and a corresponding need for more intrusive oversight by the judiciary....

Such legislation ... singling out the

retarded for special treatment reflects the real and undeniable differences between the retarded and others. That a civilized and decent society expects and approves such legislation indicates that governmental consideration of those differences in the vast majority of situations is not only legitimate but also desirable. It may be, as CLC contends, that legislation designed to benefit, rather than disadvantage, the retarded would generally withstand examination under a test of heightened scrutiny.... The relevant inquiry, however, is whether heightened scrutiny is constitutionally mandated in the first instance. Even assuming that many of these laws could be shown to be substantially related to an important governmental purpose, merely requiring the legislature to justify its efforts in these terms may lead it to refrain from acting at all. Much recent legislation intended to benefit the retarded also assumes the need for measures that might be perceived to disadvantage them.... Especially given the wide variation in the abilities and needs of the retarded themselves, governmental bodies must have a certain amount of flexibility and freedom from judicial oversight in shaping and limiting their remedial efforts.

Third, the legislative response, which could hardly have occurred and survived without public support, negates any claim that the mentally retarded are politically powerless in the sense that they have no ability to attract the attention of the lawmakers. Any minority can be said to be powerless to assert direct control over the legislature, but if that were a criterion for higher level scrutiny by the courts, much economic and social legislation would now be suspect.

Fourth, if the large and amorphous class of the mentally retarded were deemed quasi-suspect for the reasons given by the Court of Appeals, it would be difficult to find a principled way to distinguish a variety of other groups who have perhaps immutable disabilities setting them off from others, who cannot themselves mandate the desired legislative responses, and who can claim some degree of prejudice from at least part of the public at large. One need mention in this respect only the aging, the disabled, the mentally ill, and the infirm. We are reluctant to set out on that course, and we decline to do so....

Our refusal to recognize the retarded as a quasi-suspect class does not leave them entirely unprotected from invidious discrimination. To withstand equal protection review, legislation that distinguishes between the mentally retarded and others must be rationally related to a legitimate governmental purpose. This standard, we believe, affords government the latitude necessary both to pursue policies designed to assist the retarded in realizing their full potential, and to freely and efficiently engage in activities that burden the retarded in what is essentially an incidental manner. The State may not rely on a classification whose relationship to an asserted goal is so attenuated as to render the distinction arbitrary or irrational.... Beyond that, the mentally retarded, like others, have and retain their substantive constitutional rights in addition to the right to be treated equally by the law.

We turn to the issue of the validity of the zoning ordinance insofar as it requires a special use permit for homes for the mentally retarded....

The short of it is that requiring the permit in this case appears to us to rest on an irrational prejudice against the mentally retarded, including those who would occupy the Featherston facility and who would live under the closely supervised and highly regulated conditions expressly provided for by state and federal law.

The judgment of the Court of Appeals is affirmed insofar as it invalidates the zoning ordinance as applied to the Featherston home. The judgment is otherwise vacated, and the case is remanded.

It is so ordered.

STEVENS, J., AND BURGER, C.J., CONCURRING

... In every equal protection case, we have to ask certain basic questions. What class is harmed by the legislation, and has it been subjected to a "tradition of disfavor" by our laws? What is the public purpose that is being served by the law? What is the characteristic of the disadvantaged class that justifies the disparate treatment? In most cases the answer to these questions will tell us whether the statute has a "rational basis." The answers will result in the virtually automatic invalidation of racial classifications and in the validation of most economic classifications, but they will provide differing results in cases involving classifications based on alienage, gender, or illegitimacy. But that is not because we apply an "intermediate standard of review" in these cases; rather it is because the characteristics of these groups are sometimes relevant and sometimes irrelevant to a valid public purpose, or, more specifically, to the purpose that the challenged laws purportedly intended to serve.

The record convinces me that this permit was required because of the irrational fears of neighboring property owners, rather than for the protection of the mentally retarded persons who would reside in respondent's home....

Accordingly, I join the opinion of the Court.

MARSHALL, BRENNAN, AND BLACKMUN, J.J., CONCURRING IN PART AND DISSENTING IN PART

... The refusal to acknowledge that something more than minimum rationality review is at work here is, in my view, unfortunate in at least two respects. The suggestion that the traditional rational-basis test allows this sort of searching inquiry creates precedent for this Court and lower courts to subject economic and commercial classifications to similar and searching "ordinary" rational-basis review—a small and regrettable step back toward the days of *Lochner v. New York*. Moreover, by failing to articulate the factors that justify today's "second order" rational-basis review, the Court provides no principled foundation for determining when more searching inquiry is to be invoked. Lower courts are thus left in the dark on this important question, and this Court remains unaccountable for its decisions employing, or refusing to employ, particularly searching scrutiny. Candor requires me to acknowledge the particular factors that justify invalidating Cleburne's zoning ordinance under the careful scrutiny it today receives.

I have long believed the level of scrutiny employed in an equal protection case should vary with "the constitutional and societal importance of the interest adversely affected and the recognized invidiousness of the basis upon which the particular classification is drawn." *San Antonio Independent School District v. Rodriguez....* When a zoning ordinance works to exclude the retarded from all residential districts in a community, these two considerations require that the ordinance be convincingly justified as substantially furthering legitimate and important purposes....

The fact that retardation may be deemed a constitutional irrelevancy in some circumstances is enough, given the history of discrimination the retarded have suffered, to require careful judicial review of classifications singling out the retarded for special burdens.... Whenever evolving principles of equality, rooted in the Equal Protection Clause, require that certain classifications be viewed as potentially discriminatory, and when history reveals systemic unequal treatment, more searching judicial inquiry than minimum rationality becomes relevant....

As the history of discrimination against the retarded and its continuing legacy amply attest, the mentally retarded have been, and in some areas may still be, the targets of action the Equal Protection Clause condemns. With respect to a liberty so valued as the right to establish a home in the community, and so likely to be denied on the basis of irrational fears and outright hostility, heightened scrutiny is surely appropriate....

To my knowledge, the Court has never before treated an equal protection challenge to a statute on an as-applied basis. When statutes rest on impermissibly overbroad generalizations, our cases have invalidated the presumption on its face. We do not instead leave to the courts the task of redrafting the statute through an ongoing and cumbersome process of "as applied" constitutional rulings....

In my view, the Court's remedial approach is both unprecedented in the equal protection area and unwise. This doctrinal change of course was not sought by the parties, suggested by the various *amici*, or discussed at oral argument. Moreover, the Court does not persuasively reason its way to its novel remedial holding nor reconsider our prior cases directly on point. Instead, the Court simply asserts that "this is the preferred course of adjudication." Given that this assertion emerges only from today's decision, one can only hope it will not become entrenched in the law without fuller consideration....

Questions

1. On what basis did the *Cleburne* majority reject "intermediate scrutiny" as the appropriate level of judicial review in cases involving laws that classify based on mental retardation? Why did the Court nonetheless invalidate the Cleburne city ordinance?

2. Did the Court adopt a middle-tier level of scrutiny in *Cleburne* without acknowledging it—in effect accepting what law professor Laurence H. Tribe terms "covertly heightened scrutiny" (*American Constitutional Law*, 2nd ed. [Mineola, NY: Foundation Press, 1988], p. 1443)? Does Justice Marshall agree with Tribe's analysis?

3. Does the majority in *Cleburne* mean that the Court rejected the argument that "[m]entally retarded people are a quintessential, discrete, and insular minority"? If so, on what grounds?

4. Are there any similarities between the Equal Protection analysis employed in *Cleburne* and that which the Court used in the *Reed-Frontiero-Craig* line of cases? (See pp. 586–599.)

5. In footnote 24 of his opinion in *Cleburne*, Justice Marshall wrote: "No single talisman can define those groups likely to be the target of classifications offensive to the Fourteenth Amendment and therefore warranting heightened or strict scrutiny; experience, not abstract logic, must be the primary guide." If the Court adopted Marshall's view, what groups of people would arguably be entitled to heightened judicial scrutiny of state laws that contain classifications?

COMMENT

Table 5.1 summarizes the Supreme Court's analysis of state law classifications and fundamental rights under the Fourteenth Amendment.

TABLE 5.1   SUMMARY OF FOURTEENTH AMENDMENT ANALYSIS: CLASSIFICATIONS AND FUNDAMENTAL RIGHTS

BASIS FOR CLASSIFICATION	FUNDAMENTAL RIGHT	JUDICIAL PRESUMPTION	STANDARD OF REVIEW	GOVERNMENT'S BURDEN
Race, alienage	Travel, vote, marriage, reproduction	Inherently suspect	Strictest scrutiny	Compelling state interest
Illegitimacy, gender, illegal aliens	—	Maybe, maybe not constitutional	Intermediate scrutiny	Classification related to a substantial governmental interest
Economic classes, mentally retarded, age	—	Constitutional	Rational basis	Statute enacted according to established procedures

SUGGESTIONS FOR FURTHER READING

Baer, Judith A., *Equality under the Fourteenth Amendment* (Ithaca, NY: Cornell University Press, 1983).

Burgdorf, Marcia Pearce, and Robert L. Burgdorf Jr., "A History of Unequal Treatment: The Qualifications of Handicapped Persons As a 'Suspect Class' under the Equal Protection Clause," 15 *Santa Clara Lawyer* (1975): 855.

_____, "The Wicked Witch Is Almost Dead: *Buck v. Bell* and the Sterilization of Handicapped Persons," 50 *Temple Law Quarterly* (1977): 995.

Burt, Robert A., "Pennhurst: A Parable," in *In the Interest of Children*, ed. Robert Mnookin (New York, NY: W. H. Freeman, 1985).

Chamberlin, J. P., "Current Legislation—Eugenics and Limitations of Marriage," 9 *American Bar Association Journal* (1923): 429.

Comment, "Mental Illness: A Suspect Classification?" 83 *Yale Law Journal* (1974): 1237.

Gunther, Gerald, "Foreword: In Search of Evolving Doctrine on a Changing Court: A Model for a Newer Equal Protection," 86 *Harvard Law Review* (1972): 1.

Johnson, Michael A., "Zoning and Community Group Homes for the Mentally Retarded—Boon or Bust?" 7 *Ohio Northern Law Review* (1980): 64.

Karst, Kenneth, "Foreword: Equal Citizenship under the Fourteenth Amendment," 91 *Harvard Law Review* (1977): 1.

Kevles, Daniel J., *In the Name of Eugenics: Genetics and the Uses of Human Heredity* (Berkeley, CA: University of California Press, 1985).

Kressel, Laurence, "The Community Residence Movement: Land Use Conflicts and Planning Imperatives," 5 *New York University Review of Law & Social Change* (1975): 137.

Linde, Hans, "Due Process of Lawmaking," 55 *Nebraska Law Review* (1976): 197.

Linn, Brian J., and Lesly J. Bowers, "The Historical Fallacies Behind Legal Prohibitions of Marriages Involving Mentally Retarded Persons—The Eternal Child Grows Up," 13 *Gonzaga Law Review* (1978): 625.

Lusky, Louis, "Footnote Redux: A *'Carolene Products'* Reminiscence," 82 *Columbia Law Review* (1982): 1093.

Murdock, Charles W., "Sterilization of the Retarded: A Problem or a Solution?" 62 *California Law Review* (1974): 917.

Note, "Legislative Purpose, Rationality, and Equal Protection," 82 *Yale Law Journal* (1972): 123.

Note, "Mental Illness: A Suspect Classification?" 83 *Yale Law Journal* (1974): 1237.

Note, "Quasi-Suspect Classes and Proof of Discriminatory Intent: A New Model," 90 *Yale Law Journal* (1981): 912.

Note, "The Suspect Context: A New Suspect Classification Doctrine for the Mentally Handicapped," 26 *Arizona Law Review* (1984): 205.

Perry, Michael J., "Modern Equal Protection: A Conceptualization and Appraisal," 79 *Columbia Law Review* (1979): 1023.

Powell, Lewis F., Jr., "*Carolene Products* Revisited," 82 *Columbia Law Review* (1982): 1087.

Reiner, Jane E., "A Review of the Conflict between Community-Based Group Homes for the Mentally Retarded and Restrictive Zoning," 82 *West Virginia Law Review* (1980): 669.

Roberto, Elizabeth, "Can the Mentally Retarded Enjoy 'Yards That Are Wide'?" 28 *Wayne Law Review* (1982): 1349.

Scull, Andrew, *Decarceration: Community Treatment and the Deviant: A Radical View* (Englewood Cliffs, NJ: Prentice Hall, 1977).

Trent, James W., *Inventing the Feeble Mind: A History of Mental Retardation in the United States* (Berkeley, CA: University of California Press, 1994).

Tyor, Peter L., and Leland V. Bell, *Caring for the Retarded in America: A History* (Westport, CT: Greenwood Press, 1984).

Williams, Paul, and Bonnie Shoultz, *We Can Speak for Ourselves: Self Advocacy for Mentally Handicapped People* (Bloomington, IN: Indiana University Press, 1984).